Why Do You Need This New Edition?

If you're wondering why you should buy this new edition of *Abnormal Child and Adolescent Psychology*, here are nine good reasons.

1. DSM-5. This revised edition incorporates the most recent *Diagnostic and Statistical Manual of Mental Disorders* (DSM-5).

2. Current Research. This new edition incorporates the most current research in the field throughout, exploring new findings and issues, while confirming or extending previous findings in various ways.

3. New Learning Objectives, entitled Looking Forward, appear at the beginning of each chapter. The Learning Objectives alert you to the most important concepts from the chapter, so you can better organize and understand the material. In addition, at each chapter's end an Overview/Looking Back section provides a review of this material.

4. New coverage of the dimensional approach to classifying and diagnosing psychological disorder. This edition captures the heightened interest in how best to classify and diagnose a psychological problem, whether with a categorical approach, or a dimensional approach that describes a range or continuum of severity.

5. Progress in understanding causes of psychopathology. Across the chapters of the book, the authors explore the substantial progress made in understanding the causes of psychopathology. Special attention is given to etiological models of problem behavior.

6. Advances in understanding of genetic processes. The authors explore advances in the field that implicate gene effects and their interaction with the environment.

7. Notable progress in the prevention of disorders is reflected in the authors' discussion of new findings in the field.

8. Special consideration is given to issues of high social interest, such as terrorism and war, poverty, child maltreatment, substance use, and bullying and victimization.

9. MySearchLab with eText provides engaging experiences that personalize learning. eText—Just as with the printed text, you can highlight and add notes to the eText or download it to your iPad. Assessment—chapter quizzes and flashcards offer immediate feedback. Writing and Research—A wide range of writing, grammar and research tools and access to a variety of academic journals, census data, Associated Press newsfeeds, and discipline-specific readings help you hone your writing and research skills.

Eighth Edition

ABNORMAL CHILD AND ADOLESCENT PSYCHOLOGY WITH DSM-V UPDATES

Rita Wicks-Nelson
West Virginia University Institute of Technology,
Professor Emeritus

Allen C. Israel
University at Albany, State University of New York

PEARSON

Boston   Columbus   Indianapolis   New York   San Francisco   Upper Saddle River
Amsterdam   Cape Town   Dubai   London   Madrid   Milan   Munich   Paris   Montréal   Toronto
Delhi   Mexico City   São Paulo   Sydney   Hong Kong   Seoul   Singapore   Taipei   Tokyo

Editor in Chief: Ashley Dodge
Acquisitions Editor: Susan Hartman
Editorial Assistant: Lori Cinar
Director of Marketing: Brandy Dawson
Executive Marketing Manager: Kelly May
Marketing Coordinator: Jessica Warren, Theresa Graziano, or Courtney Stewart
Managing Editor: Denise Forlow
Program Manager: Reena Dalal
Senior Operations Supervisor: Mary Fischer
Operations Specialist: Diane M. Peirano
Art Director: Jayne Conte

Cover Designer: Karen Salzbach
Cover Image: Shutterstock/Zurijeta
Director of Digital Media: Brian Hyland
Digital Media Project Management: Learning Mate Solutions, Ltd.
Digital Media Project Manager: Tina Gagliostro
Full-Service Project Management and Composition: Integra Software Services Pvt. Ltd./Allan A. Rayer
Printer/Binder: Courier Kendallville
Cover Printer: Lehigh-Phoenix Color
Text Font: 10/12, Minion

Credits and acknowledgments borrowed from other sources and reproduced, with permission, in this textbook appear on appropriate page within text (or on page 511).

Many of the designations by manufacturers and seller to distinguish their products are claimed as trademarks. Where those designations appear in this book, and the publisher was aware of a trademark claim, the designations have been printed in initial caps or all caps.

Library of Congress Cataloging-in-Publication Data

Wicks-Nelson, Rita.
  Abnormal child and adolescent psychology, with DSM-5 updates / Rita Wicks-Nelson, West Virginia University Institute of Technology, professor emeritus, Allen C. Israel, University at Albany, State University of New York. —[Revised] eighth edition.
     pages cm
  Revision of 8th ed., 2013.
  Includes bibliographical references and indexes.
  ISBN-13: 978-0-13-376698-1 (alk. paper)
  ISBN-10: 0-13-376698-5 (alk. paper)
  1. Behavior disorders in children.   2. Diagnostic and statistical manual of mental disorders.
  5th ed.   I. Israel, Allen C.   II. Title.   III. Title: Abnormal child and adolescent psychology, with Diagnostic and statistical manual of mental disorders, 5th edition, updates.
  RJ506.B44W534 2015
  618.92'89—dc23

                                                                            2013044772

2 3 4 5 6 7 8 9 10 V092 16 15 14

ISBN 10:   0-133-76698-5
ISBN 13: 978-0-133-76698-1

BRIEF CONTENTS

CONTENTS

PREFACE

In roughly one hundred years, the study of young people has moved from relative ignorance to considerable knowledge about human development in general and disordered behavior more specifically. The last few decades arguably have witnessed unprecedented progress in understanding the problems of children and adolescents and how they and their families might be assisted. Of course, there is much yet to be learned and the needs of youth are considerable, so the study of young people is an especially worthwhile enterprise. We hope that this text makes clear the challenge and excitement of the endeavor.

Now in its updated eighth edition, *Abnormal Child and Adolescent Psychology* has enjoyed enormous success. It has been gratifying for us to know that it continues to make a substantial contribution to the field. At the inception of this text (initially entitled "Behavior Disorders of Children"), relatively few comprehensive books were available in the field. Just as important was the need for a text that emphasized certain themes that we considered critical to the study of problems of youth. These themes have stood the test of time, have evolved, and have become more widely and subtly recognized as essential. Indeed, their early incorporation into the text undoubtedly accounts in part for its ongoing success.

THEME 1: DEVELOPMENTAL PSYCHOPATHOLOGY

At the heart of the text is the partnership of the developmental psychopathology perspective and the more traditional (usual) clinical/disorder approach. The latter underscores description of the symptoms, causes, and treatments of disorders of young people. The developmental psychopathology perspective assumes that problems of youth must be viewed within a developmental context. The developmental psychopathology perspective is articulated in early chapters of the book and guides discussion of specific disorders in subsequent chapters.

A primary assumption of developmental psychopathology is the belief that normal and disturbed behavior are related and are best viewed as occurring along a dynamic pathway of growth and experience, with connections to the past and to the future. This proposition is reflected in the text in several ways. Consideration is given to the timing and processes of normal development and how these may go awry in psychopathology. We also take seriously the assumption that behavioral development cannot be readily parsed by age, and thus we employ a broad time frame for discussing psychological problems in childhood and adolescence. Understanding these problems is enhanced by anchoring them in the early years of life and linking them to outcomes in adulthood.

THEME 2: MULTIPLE TRANSACTIONAL INFLUENCES

A second theme woven throughout the text is the view that behavioral problems result from transactions among variables. With few—if any—exceptions, behavior stems from multiple influences and their continuous interactions. Biological structure and function, genetic transmission, cognition, emotion, social interaction, and numerous aspects of the immediate and broader environment play complex roles in generating and maintaining psychological and behavioral functioning. Developmental psychopathologists are committed to the difficult task of understanding and integrating these multiple influences—efforts that are addressed throughout the text.

THEME 3: THE INDIVIDUAL IN CONTEXT

Following from this, a third theme emphasizes that the problems of the young are intricately tied to the social and cultural contexts in which they experience life. Children and adolescents are embedded in a circle of social and environmental influences involving family, peer, school, neighborhood, societal, and cultural circumstances. At any one time, youths bring their personal attributes to these circumstances, are affected by them, and in turn, influence other people and situations. Meaningful analysis of psychological problems thus requires that the individual be considered in developmental context. Such aspects as family interactions, friendships, gender, educational opportunity, poverty, ethnicity and race, and cultural values all come into play.

THEME 4: THE EMPIRICAL APPROACH

A fourth major theme is a bias toward the empirical approach. Prudent and insightful thinking is required in both figuring out the puzzles of behavioral problems and applying acquired knowledge. We believe that empirical approaches and the theoretical frameworks that rely on scientific method provide the best avenue for understanding the complexity of human behavior. Research findings thus are a central component of the book and inform our understanding of the problems experienced by youth and how the lives of young people might be improved.

THEME 5: THE PERSON AT THE CENTER

Concern for the optimal development of the child or adolescent is given important emphasis throughout this text. While there is no doubt that empirical studies further our understanding of development, it is helpful to examine problems from a more personal viewpoint. Thus, by also viewing problems through the lens of the experience of troubled youths and their families, students better come to understand how psychopathology is manifested, what needs a youth may have, how intervention can help a child, and a plethora of other factors. The many case descriptions in the text are vital in bringing forth the personal. So also are the several other individual accounts, quotations, and photographs. Real-life is singularly captured by the hyperactive child who realizes that he is considered a "bad boy," the sister who believes she has become a better person through caring for her intellectually challenged brother, and the parents who report being "jolted" by a TV description of a youth whose problems were similar to those of their undiagnosed child.

ORGANIZATION OF THE TEXT

As a relatively comprehensive introduction to the field, *Abnormal Child and Adolescent Psychology* includes theoretical and methodological foundations of the field and devotes most discussion to specific problems of youth—that is, to the characteristics, epidemiology, developmental course, etiology, assessment, treatment, and prevention of psychopathology. Although we have not formally divided the chapters into broader sections, they are conceptualized as three units.

UNIT I, consisting of Chapters 1 through 5, presents the foundation for subsequent discussion. A broad overview of the field is presented, including basic concepts, historical context, developmental influences, theoretical perspectives, research methodology, classification and diagnosis, assessment, prevention, and treatment approaches. These chapters draw heavily on the psychological literature and also recognize the multidisciplinary nature of the study and treatment of youth. We assume that readers have some background in psychology, but we have made an effort to serve those with relatively limited background or experience.

UNIT II, consisting of Chapters 6 through 14, addresses major disorders. There is considerable organizational consistency across these chapters. For most disorders, classification, clinical description, epidemiology, developmental course, etiology, assessment, and prevention/treatment are discussed in that order. At the same time, flexible organization is a guiding principle so that the complexity inherent in specific chapter topics is not sacrificed.

- Chapter 6 (anxiety and related disorders) and Chapter 7 (mood disorders) focus on internalizing disorders.
- Chapter 8 (conduct problems) and Chapter 9 (attention-deficit hyperactivity disorder) discuss externalizing disorders.
- Specific and pervasive developmental problems are presented in Chapter 10 (language and learning disorders), Chapter 11 (intellectual disability), and Chapter 12 (autism spectrum disorder and schizophrenia).
- Chapter 13 (basic physical functions) and Chapter 14 (medical conditions) focus on health- and medical-related problems.

UNIT III consists of Chapter 15, which rounds out and extends what has gone before. The chapter examines evolving concerns regarding the development of youth. The focus is on selected critical family issues, mental health services, and briefly on youth living in countries other than the United States.

CONTENT: HIGHLIGHTS AND UPDATES

It almost goes without saying that the study of the psychopathology of youth, as it catapults ahead, must include judicious consideration of recent research and issues. Such consideration is reflected by the provision of new information throughout the text. The updated content not only points to new findings and issues but, importantly, it also confirms or extends previous findings in various ways. Moreover, in reviewing new information we have been especially sensitive to topics that are currently of high interest and concern. The following are notable instances of highlighted and updated topics.

- This edition of the text captures the heightened interest in how best to classify and diagnose psychological problems. It includes diagnostic criteria and information from the most recent version of the DSM (DSM-5) and gives appreciable attention to how the dimensional approach has informed and is likely to continue to inform developments in the classification of psychopathology of youth.
- The substantial progress in understanding the causes of psychopathology is exemplified across chapters. Special attention is given to etiological models of problem behavior.
- Similarly, increased and updated consideration is given to neurological findings, particularly those from brain imaging studies.
- Consonant with advances in the field, genetic processes and new findings that implicate gene effects and their interaction with the environment receive greater attention.
- Receiving particular attention are the complex roles of the family and peers within the transaction of multiple influences on the development of problems in children and adolescents.
- The developmental course and outcome of major disorders continues to have high priority.
- Attention is given to the role of sex/gender in psychopathology—both to differences in prevalence, symptoms, and outcome as well as to factors that may underlie them.
- Continued and increased attention is given to the various roles of culture, ethnicity, and race in psychopathology. An example is how cultural considerations may influence assessment and treatment.
- Notable progress being made in the prevention of disorder is reflected in new findings and extended discussion. Early intervention efforts—such as for reading disability and autism—can be viewed as merging prevention and treatment.
- Examples of specific individual and family treatments are generously interwoven throughout the chapters, with an emphasis on evidence-based intervention. To take an example, the latest findings from the most comprehensive multimodal treatment of ADHD are examined.
- Increased attention is also given to efforts to improve accessibility of evidence-based treatments, to how such treatments can be disseminated from research to "real-world" settings, and to the role that technology may play in these efforts.
- We continue to give particular consideration to problems that recently have been reported to have increased in prevalence—such as bipolar disorder, autism, and obesity. Discussion includes potential reasons for rising prevalence and, for some disorders, whether the apparent increase actually exists.
- Similar consideration is given to specific problems that remain or have become of high societal interest—such as terrorism and war, poverty, child maltreatment, substance use, and bullying/victimization.
- Also updated and/or expanded is discussion of issues that have been or still are particularly controversial. These include debates over inappropriate or excessive use of medication in children, discredited claims of a link between vaccines and autism, and the effects of attendance of children with intellectual disability in regular rather than special education classrooms.

FEATURES: SOME OLD, SOME NEW

As will be obvious to users of the previous edition, we have retained the basic organization of the chapters, which appears to work well. Similarly, specific features of the book continue to emphasize for students a person-oriented, applied perspective. The text is rich in case descriptions and in accounts of assessment and treatment. An additional feature, the Accents, allows for detailed discussion of particular topics of interest, for example, fetal alcohol syndrome, infant mental health, ADHD in African American boys, and stigma linked to the term "mental retardation." Further, the text continues to be rich in illustrations—graphs, tables, photos, drawings—without an excessiveness that can be confusing to readers.

Other features of the text are especially aimed at facilitating student learning. Included in this edition is Looking Forward, which focuses students' attention at the beginning of each chapter on the central issues to be addressed. Looking Forward roughly follows the organization of the chapter and sets the stage for the overview at the chapter's end, referred to as Overview/Looking Back. In addition, important or new terms in each chapter appear in bold in the text and also are listed as Key Terms at the conclusion of the chapter. Finally, several supplementary teaching and learning materials, described in the following section, add to the value of *Abnormal Child and Adolescent Psychology* for both students and instructors.

SUPPLEMENTARY TEACHING AND LEARNING MATERIALS

For access to all instructor resources, go to www.pearsonhighered.com/irc

Instructor's Resource Manual

(0205999484) is designed to make your lectures more effective and save preparation time. This extensive resource gathers the most effective activities and strategies for teaching.

Test Item File

(0205999603) contains multiple choice, true/false, and essay questions. Each question has been accuracy checked to ensure that the correct answer was marked and the page reference was accurate. **MyTest Test Bank** (0205036473) is a powerful assessment-generation program that helps instructors easily create and print quizzes and exams. For more information, go to www.PearsonMyTest.com.

PowerPoint Slides

(0205994210) provide an active format for presenting concepts from each chapter and feature relevant figures and tables from the text.

MySearchLab with eText

(0205036740) can be packaged with this text. MySearchLab provides engaging experiences that personalize learning. **eText**—as with the printed text, you can highlight and add notes to the eText or download it to your iPad. **Assessment**—chapter quizzes and flashcards offer immediate feedback and report directly to the gradebook. **Writing and Research**—A wide range of writing, grammar and research tools and access to a variety of academic journals, census data, Associated Press newsfeeds, and discipline-specific readings help you hone your writing and research skills.

Speaking Out Videos

(0131933329, 0136003036, 0132308916) help students understand how the DSM criteria apply to actual people with psychological disorders. Interviews with real patients, along with their friends and family, enable students to see symptoms of various conditions as well as understand the impact of these symptoms on the individual's daily functioning. Contact your Pearson representative: http://www.pearsonhighered.com/educator/replocator/

ACKNOWLEDGMENTS

The reviewers of the seventh edition of the book were indispensable for the many comments and suggestions for improvement they provided. We would like to thank:

    Paul Conditt, University of Northern Iowa

    Rebecca Francis, West Virginia State University

    Janet Garske, Hocking College

    Lisa Green, Baldwin Wallace College

    Steven Landau, Illinois State University

    Stephanie Little, Wittenberg University

    Suzanne Morin, Shippensburg University

    Robert J. Resnick, Randolph-Macon College

    Lee Rosen, Colorado State University

    Timothy Stickle, University of Vermont

    Gaston Weisz, Adelphi University

In addition, our sincere thanks are extended to Jennifer Malatras for her assistance in multiple aspects of the preparation of the manuscript. Also, we wish to acknowledge our genuine appreciation of the efforts of Celia Tam, Melissa Lehrbach, Stephanie Rohrig, Joseph Galligan, and Melanie Lavides in locating and checking material for this edition.

Also thanks to the Pearson team: Susan Hartman, Executive Editor; Lori Cinar, Editorial Assistant; Denise Forlow, Managing Editor; and Reena Dalal, Program Manager.

Finally, we note that the order of authorship was originally decided by a flip of the coin to reflect our equal contribution. Our continuing collaboration has been one of equality and friendship.

Rita Wicks-Nelson

Allen C. Israel

CHAPTER 1

Introduction

LOOKING FORWARD

After reading this chapter, you should be able to discuss:

- How psychological disorders are defined and identified
- Prevalence of psychological disorders
- The relationship between developmental level and psychological disorders
- The relationship between gender and psychological disorders
- Historical influences on understanding psychological disorders
- Current study and practice of abnormal child and adolescent psychology

*To be young is to bounce balls as high
as the heavens, gobble up fairytales, walk
tightropes without falling, love friends with glee, and
peer at the wondrous future.*

*To be young is to feel ignorant and useless, to
be alone and unlovable, to ride the waves of ups
and downs and unending insecurities.*

The early years of life have long been described in extremes of emotions, behaviors, and encounters. In fact, most individuals who look back on their own youth admit not only to some of the extremes—but also to a sizable portion of more moderate experiences. And they frequently view their youth as a special time of growth and opportunity. It is against this backdrop that we embark on the study of the psychological problems of childhood and adolescence.

This book is written for those who ask questions about and have concerns regarding less-than-optimal development of youth. It addresses definitions, characteristics, origins, development, diagnosis, prevention, and amelioration of maladaptive functioning. We anticipate, and hope, that you will find this field of study as satisfying as we do. It is an area of study that encompasses both humanitarian concerns for young people and scientific intrigue.

The last decades have been a particularly promising time to study behavioral and psychological disturbance. The current need for increased understanding, prevention, and treatment is substantial, and is recognized in many parts of the world. At the same time, research into the development of youth continues to grow by leaps and bounds, with contributions from many disciplines. As is usually true in science, increased knowledge and improved methods have led to new questions and paradoxes. This combination of new understandings, new questions, and new avenues of inquiry gives both promise and enthusiasm to the study of the problems of young people.

DEFINING AND IDENTIFYING ABNORMALITY

Behavioral repertoires come in endless varieties, and many kinds of disorders are discussed in this text (see Accent: "Some Faces of Problem Behavior"). Various labels have been applied to such problems: abnormal behavior, behavioral disturbance, emotional disorder, psychological deficit, mental illness, psychopathology, maladaptive behavior, developmental disorder, and so forth. Moreover, systems have been constructed to categorize problems and to offer guidelines to professionals for identifying abnormality. Underlying this effort are complex issues in defining and distinguishing psychopathology.

The criteria for abnormality are primarily based on how a person is acting or what a person is saying and only rarely include a specific known marker for disorder. Of course, most of us would agree that problems are evident when individuals do not acquire speech, are unable to feed themselves, or see and hear things that others do not. But less dramatic instances are harder to judge and a fine line can exist between what is considered disordered and what is normal. Young people of specific ages display behaviors that may or may not be considered signs of disturbance, such as noncompliance with parental rules, social withdrawal, high activity level, fearfulness, sadness, and delayed reading skills. Thus, we must ask, "When do we consider behaviors abnormal?" and "How can we distinguish everyday problems from more serious indications of psychopathology?" There are no simple answers to these questions, but it is informative to consider several factors that enter into judgments about psychological or behavioral disturbances.

ACCENT
Some Faces of Problem Behavior

Four-year-old **Joey** had been kicked out of preschool, where he had sat on the floor and stared, refused to talk, and hit any child who touched him. If the teacher insisted that he participate in activities, he screamed, cried, and banged his arms and legs on the floor. Similar behaviors occurred at home. Joey rarely talked or showed emotion, and he slept fitfully, banged his head against the wall, and rocked back and forth. (Adapted from Morgan, 1999, pp. 3–4)

Lakeshia had always been considered a slow learner but these difficulties had sometimes been beneath the "radar screen" of her teachers, perhaps in part because she was quiet and well-behaved. She repeated second grade and had a tutor, but by the time she was in fifth grade, Lakeshia was failing all her subjects. An evaluation indicated low-average to borderline overall intelligence and ratings of attention and learning problems in the clinically borderline range. (Adapted from Hathaway, Dooling-Litfin, & Edwards, 2006, pp. 402–405)

Nine-year-old **Juan** was referred by his teacher due to classroom behavior problems. He was fidgety, did not pay attention, usually did not answer questions, and bothered classmates when they were working. Juan, who spoke mostly Spanish at home, exhibited above-average cognitive ability and average academic skills. His mother reported that he was easily distracted and had difficulty completing homework, but she felt that Juan's behavior was consistent with that of children whom she observed growing up in Mexico. (Adapted from DuPaul et al., 2010, p. 555)

Anne had begun to worship Satan and noted that praying to Satan brought her relief from distress. Anne had dyed her hair black, dusted her face with white powder, and looked like a character in a vampire story rather than a 14-year-old. Anne reported that she had difficulty falling asleep because she worried about her grades and her parents' divorce, for which she believed she was partly responsible. She found it hard to concentrate in school, was irritable, and had lost weight. She had no energy, no longer enjoyed activities with friends, and spent most of her time in her room. Anne denied any intent or plan for suicide, involvement with cults, or drug use. (Adapted from Morgan, 1999, pp. 35–37)

Atypical and Harmful Behavior

Psychological problems frequently are viewed as atypical, odd, or abnormal—all of which imply that they deviate from the average. Indeed, "ab" means "away" or "from," whereas "normal" refers to the average or standard. However, being atypical in itself hardly defines psychopathology. People who display exceptionally high intelligence and social competence are generally considered fortunate, and their "oddness" is looked upon with favor. The deviations we are considering are assumed to be harmful in some way to the individual. The American Psychiatric Association (2013), for example, defines disorder as a syndrome of clinically significant behavioral, cognitive, or emotional disturbances that reflect dysfunction in underlying mental processes, and that is associated with distress or disability in important areas of functioning.

Abnormality or psychopathology is viewed as interfering with adaptation, that is, with individuals fitting the circumstances of their lives. Psychopathology hinders or prevents the young person from negotiating developmental tasks, whether acquiring language skills, emotional control, or satisfactory social relationships. Disorder may be viewed as residing *within* the individual. Alternatively, it can be regarded as the individual's reactions to circumstances—with the interface of the person with other people or environmental conditions. The latter, more appropriate, perspective emphasizes that behavior is inextricably linked with the larger world in which it is embedded.

Developmental Standards

Age, as an index of developmental level, is always important in judging behavior, but it is especially important for children and adolescents because they change so rapidly. Judgments about behavior rely on **developmental norms,** which describe the typical rates of growth, sequences of growth, and forms of physical skills, language, cognition, emotion, and social behavior. These serve as developmental standards from which to evaluate the possibility that "something is wrong."

Behavior can be judged as anomalous relative to these norms in a number of ways, as indicated in Table 1.1. Delayed development, or failure to keep up with typical developmental change, indicates that something is awry. Children sometimes may achieve developmental norms and then regress, or return, to behavior typically seen in younger individuals.

Several other signs are noteworthy. These include atypical frequency, intensity, or duration of behavior, as well as the display of behavior in inappropriate situations. It is not unusual for a child to display fear, for example, but fearfulness may be a problem if it occurs excessively, is

TABLE 1.1	Behavioral Indicators of Disorder

Developmental delay

Developmental regression or deterioration

Extremely high or low frequency of behavior

Extremely high or low intensity of behavior

Behavioral difficulty persisting over time

Behavior inappropriate to the situation

Abrupt changes in behavior

Several problem behaviors

Behavior qualitatively different from normal

extremely intense, does not weaken over time, or is shown in harmless situations. Concern might also be expressed for the youth whose behavior abruptly changes, as when an outgoing adolescent turns solitary, or when a child displays several questionable behaviors. All of these indications of disturbance are quantitative differences from developmental norms.

Yet another manifestation that may signal the need for help is behavior that appears qualitatively different from the norm. That is, the behavior—or the sequence in which it develops—is not seen in normal growth. For instance, most children are socially responsive to their caretakers soon after birth, but children diagnosed as autistic display atypical unresponsive behaviors, such as lack of normal eye contact. Qualitatively different behaviors frequently indicate a pervasive problem in development.

Culture and Ethnicity

The term **culture** encompasses the idea that groups of people are organized in specific ways, live in specific environmental niches, and share specific attitudes, beliefs, values, practices, and behavioral standards. Culture is a way of life that is transmitted from generation to generation. It is unsurprising, then, that although many disorders are found across cultures—that is, they are universal—there are some cross-cultural differences. Rates of disorders have been found to vary and disorders may be expressed in subtly different ways (Canino & Alegria, 2008; Rutter, 2011). An example of the latter is anxiety disorder; it appears to be universal but is expressed more through bodily symptoms in Asian and Latino groups than in European Americans (Serafica & Vargas, 2006). Whether any disorder is specific to a single culture and not found otherwise is less clear.

Cultural analyses describe the many ways in which cultures shape normal and abnormal development and also conceptualize, explain, and treat psychopathology. **Cultural norms** have broad influence on expectations,

The behavior that is expected of or considered appropriate for a child varies across cultures.

judgments, and beliefs about the behavior of youth. Children in the United States, for example, are expected to show less self-control and less deference to adults than children in some other parts of the world (Weisz et al., 1995). Weisz and his colleagues found that teachers in Thailand reported more conduct problems among their students than teachers in the United States, but trained observers reported just the opposite for the two student groups. The researchers suggested that Thai teachers may hold students to a more demanding behavioral standard—and thus see more problems and more readily label them.

The different ways in which problem behaviors may be explained and treated were shown in an investigation in which mothers of North African and Middle Eastern background living in Israel were interviewed about their children who were developmentally delayed (Stahl, 1991). Almost half of the mothers gave magic-religious causes for the condition. They believed in demons entering the body, an Evil Eye, and punishment from God. These mothers accordingly relied on magic-religious treatments such as burning a piece of cloth belonging to the person who cast the Evil Eye, praying, or getting help from a rabbi. Their behaviors were in keeping with the cultural beliefs of their native countries.

The above findings suggest the need to consider ethnicity or race when assessing various aspects of abnormality. **Ethnicity** denotes common customs, values, language, or traits that are associated with national origin or geographic area. **Race,** a distinction based on physical characteristics, can also be associated with shared customs,

values, and the like. Ethnic or racial groups embedded within a heterogeneous society may show different rates of psychopathology, express psychopathology somewhat differently, and hold beliefs and standards different from those of the dominant cultural group (Anderson & Mayes, 2010). Even when parenting behaviors are similar in dominant and ethnic groups, the effects on offspring may be dissimilar due to the different values held by these groups (Eichelsheim et al., 2010).

An example of ethnic difference in the United States is provided by comparisons between European American and Asian American parents concerning the achievement behavior of their children (Ly, 2008). In general, compared to European American parents, Asian American parents assign greater importance to the child's effort—for example, in academic success—than to the child's ability. However, there are relatively few cultural comparisons of families with children with disability. As part of one such study, parents were asked to rate the success of their intellectually disabled children's performance on a task and also rate the degree to which performance was due to ability and effort. The Asian American parents viewed their children as less successful (real differences did not exist), held lower expectations for future success, and attributed performance to lower ability and lower effort (Figure 1.1). They also reported different emotional reactions to their children's performance. Although this study had limitations (e.g., families were volunteers), it demonstrates the need for sensitivity to possible ethnic/racial differences in the study of psychopathology of young people.

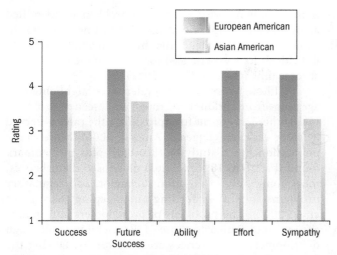

FIGURE 1.1   Parent ratings of their child's task performance. *Adapted from Ly, 2008.*

Other Standards: Gender and Situations

Expectations based on gender also contribute to defining problem behavior. **Gender norms** significantly influence development; they affect emotions, behaviors, opportunities, and choices. In most societies, males are expected to be relatively more aggressive, dominant, active, and adventurous, while females are expected to be more passive, dependent, quiet, sensitive, and emotional. These gender stereotypes play a role in judgments about normality. We would probably be less inclined to worry about the hypersensitive, shy girl and the excessively dominant boy than about their opposite-sex counterparts.

Judgments of deviance or normality of behavior also take into account **situational norms**—what is expected in specific settings or social situations. Energetic running may be quite acceptable on a playground but not allowed in a library. Norms for social interaction can be quite subtle; for example, how a statement is voiced can either compliment or insult another person. Individuals in all cultures are expected to learn what is acceptable and to act in certain ways in certain situations, given their age and gender. When they do not, their competence or societal adjustment may be questioned.

The Role of Others

Youth, especially young children, hardly ever refer themselves for clinical evaluation, thereby declaring a problem. The identification and labeling of a problem is more likely to occur when others become concerned—for example, when parents worry about their child's social isolation or when a teacher is troubled about a child's inability to learn.

Referral of youth to mental health professionals thus may have as much or more to do with the characteristics of parents, teachers, or family physicians as with the young people themselves (Costello & Angold, 1995; Verhulst & van der Ende, 1997). Indeed, disagreement often exists among adults as to whether a child or adolescent "has a problem." This may in part be due to different adults being exposed to different child behaviors but adult attitudes, sensitivity, tolerance, and ability to cope all play a role in identifying disorders.

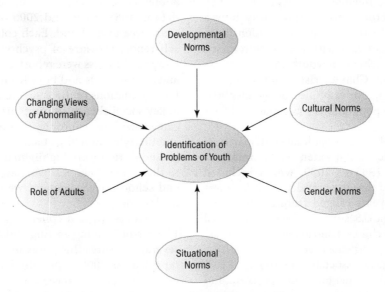

FIGURE 1.2   Several factors enter into judgments about normality and abnormality.

Changing Views of Abnormality

Finally, judgments about abnormality are not set in stone. Examples abound. In the 1800s, masturbation was considered a sign of disturbance or a behavior that could cause insanity (Rie, 1971). Nail biting was once seen as a sign of degeneration (Anthony, 1970). Excessive intellectual activity in young women was believed by some to lead to mental problems (Silk et al., 2000). Today these views are not given credence.

Many factors undoubtedly contribute to change in judgments about abnormality. Enhanced knowledge and theoretical modifications have played a role. So has transition in cultural beliefs and values. For example, eating disorders, once found almost exclusively in Western societies, have increased worldwide in the past decades, perhaps due to wider adoption of the modern Western preference for slender body size (Harkness & Super, 2000).

In summary, psychopathology cannot simply be defined as an entity carried around within a person. It is most appropriately viewed as a judgment that a person's behavior, emotion, or thinking is atypical, dysfunctional, and harmful in some way—a judgment involving knowledge about development, cultural and ethnic influences, social norms, and the people making the judgment.

HOW COMMON ARE PSYCHOLOGICAL PROBLEMS?

The prevalence of behavioral or psychological disorder suggests the extent to which prevention, treatment, and research are needed. However, frequency depends on several factors, most importantly how a disorder is defined and the criteria set for identification. Rates of disorder can vary with the measures used and whether parents, teachers, or youth themselves are the source of information. Characteristics of the population examined—regarding, for example, age, gender, and clinic versus community populations—can make a difference in prevalence.

Given such complexity, considerable disparity is found in rates of problems. An extensive summary of studies reported from 1985 to 2000, which included several countries, showed that the prevalence of disorders in youths ages 4 to 18 years ranged from 5.4 to 35.5% (Fombonne, 2002). Recent U.S. surveys of major emotional and conduct disorders in children and adolescents indicate rates of about 13 to 22% (Merikangas et al., 2010a; 2010b). The American Psychological Association (2007) cited 10% of youth as having a serious mental health problem and another 10% as having mild to moderate problems. Many of the youths reported as having a problem are identified as displaying symptoms of more than one disorder. In addition, there is evidence that by young adulthood, most individuals have experienced some type of mental problem at some time (Copeland et al., 2011).

Although research of prevalence has highlighted the age range from childhood through adolescence, problems in preschoolers appear to approximate the rates observed in older children (Egger & Angold, 2006). Moreover, a population-based study of 18-month-olds in Denmark found that 16 to 18% exhibited diagnosed disturbances, most commonly of emotion, behavior, and regulatory problems such as in feeding and sleeping (Skovgaard et al., 2007). The problems of preschoolers and infants appear quite similar to those of older children, although developmental differences are noteworthy. During the last few decades, the field of infant mental health has emerged as a multidimensional effort to better understand and enhance the development of very young children (Zeanah & Zeanah, 2009). (See Accent: "Infant Mental Health.")

Concern has been expressed that societal change during the last several decades has resulted in an increased risk of disorders for the young. Some change and its cause are obvious; for example, medical advances have increased the survival of infants born prematurely or with physical problems, and these infants have relatively high rates of behavioral and learning difficulties. However, due to variations across studies and methodological issues, it has been difficult to draw overall conclusions about such historical or so-called **secular trends.**

As examples of this work, we look at two studies of adolescents. Sweeting, Young, & West (2009) collected data in 1987, 1999, and 2006 on 15-year-olds from the same area in Scotland. Each cohort completed the same self-report measure of psychological stress. Substantial increases in stress were reported by girls from 1987 to 1999 and by both girls and boys from 1999 to 2006. Searching for explanations of the data, the investigators then looked at key social changes during this time period, which were categorized as economic, family, education, and values and lifestyle (Sweeting et al., 2010). The role of the family and education were highlighted as plausible contributors to the secular changes. Worries, arguments with parents, and school disengagement were especially cited by the adolescents.

Collishaw and colleagues (2010) compared 16- to 17-year-olds living in England in 1986 and in 2006 on several measures. Increases in emotional problems were reported for 2006, especially for girls. For boys, parent-rated difficulties showed a rise whereas boys themselves reported little change except for an elevation of frequent

ACCENT
Infant Mental Health

Despite long interest in very early occurring problems, the idea that infants could have mental health problems had been puzzling to and even resisted by some individuals. Perhaps the notion of innocent infancy seemed mismatched to maladjustment, stigma, and mental illness. Or perhaps infant mental health problems were thought impossible as long as infants were viewed as having limited emotional and cognitive capacity (Tronick & Beeghly, 2011).

Increased understanding of the very early years of life has notably contributed to interest in and acceptance of the idea of infant mental health. The age range considered by those studying infant mental health has expanded in recent years (Egger & Emde, 2011; Zeanah & Zeanah, 2009). In pediatrics—the medical specialty focusing on children— "infant" typically refers to the first year of life. In the mental health field, birth to 3 years was initially taken as the span of interest; this age range has been extended to age 5 or so. In many respects, we can expect continuities between the mental health of very young and older children, but some aspects of infant mental health, if not unique, are sufficiently different to merit special comment. Here, we note four of these.

First, concern for infants historically has emphasized the importance of the infant–child relationship and how the development of very young children strongly depends on the caregiving context (Zeanah & Zeanah, 2009). Early descriptions of infant mental health appeared in case reports of infant symptoms originating from emotional deprivation in orphanages, disturbances in infant–child attachment, and rearing by parents with psychological

disorder (Egger & Emde, 2011). The child's relationship with caregivers remains important in the field.

Second, of particular concern is the need for reliable and valid criteria for identifying and categorizing mental health problems for very young children (Egger & Emde, 2011). Methods and systems used with older children are largely viewed as insufficiently sensitive to developmental differences, and those currently used for infants as requiring improvement.

Third, the role of primary health care practitioners is noteworthy. Most all infants/toddlers are seen by general physicians, pediatricians, or various other health care providers as part of "well-child" visits (Zeanah & Gleason, 2009). These practitioners frequently are the first professionals to hear about feeding and sleep problems, delayed motor or language milestones, and behavioral difficulties. It is thus imperative that they have general knowledge of infant mental health principles and practices, including screenings for symptoms, and a good working relationship with families and mental health professionals.

Fourth, prevention of disorder is inherent in infant mental health. The relief of symptoms is critical, of course, but because infants change so rapidly, high priority must be given to their future development. In addition, research shows that early prevention is especially effective. Thus, treatment goes hand in hand with prevention of future difficulties, and there is a call for efforts to support policies and programs that promote the well-being of infants and very young children (Nelson & Mann, 2010).

---

depression/anxiety (Figure 1.3). The largest changes were reported for symptoms of worry, irritability, fatigue, sleep problems, panic, and feeling worn out. The investigators

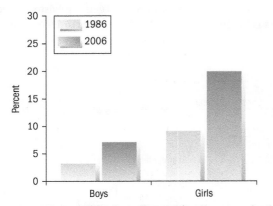

FIGURE 1.3 Percentage of youth reporting frequent feelings of anxiety or depression, 1986 and 2006. *From Collishaw et al., 2010.*

surmised that the 2006 findings were not due to greater willingness of adolescents to report mental health problems nor to increased parental divorce. Further investigation determined that maternal emotional problems had increased during the time span and likely contributed to, but not completely explained, the findings (Schepman et al., 2011).

Overall, research findings are mixed regarding secular trends in young people, with some studies but not all showing increases and some indicating decreases (Collishaw et al., 2004; Costello, Erkanli, & Angold, 2006; Tick, van der Ende, & Verhulst, 2008; Twenge et al., 2010). Moreover, the research results often are complex with regard to types of problems, gender, social class, family, and the like. Continued concern is certainly appropriate, as understanding trends in frequency of problems and what might contribute to change can be valuable in prevention and intervention.

Whether or not problems are increasing, there is little doubt that young people have substantial needs. Yet their mental health problems too often go unrecognized in schools, primary health facilities, and other settings (Hoagwood, 2005a). In addition, it is estimated that two-thirds to three-quarters of needy youth with diagnosable disorders do not receive adequate treatment (Federal Interagency Forum on Child and Family Statistics, 2011; Merikangas et al., 2011). Mental health services are insufficient, are less available in the most needy communities, and lack effective coordination.

There are several reasons for concern about this situation. Surely, no one wants to see young people suffer the pain or lowered quality of life associated with psychopathology. Moreover, early disturbances can interfere with subsequent developmental processes, leading to an accumulation of problems. Half of all adults with mental illness reported having symptoms by age 14, so that the study of psychopathology of youth has implications across the lifespan (From Discovery to Cure, 2010). Furthermore, mental health problems in young people adversely influence families and the broader society, as reflected in health care expenditures and other indices. Indeed, according to the World Health Organization, many of the disorders that carry the heaviest burden of adult death and disability in the developed areas of the world are related to mental health and are often first observed in youth (Merikangas, Nakamura, & Kessler, 2009).

HOW ARE DEVELOPMENTAL LEVEL AND DISORDER RELATED?

Of concern to professionals and parents alike is whether and how psychological difficulties are related to developmental level. Some relationship does exist between specific problems and the age at which they usually first appear or are identified. Figure 1.4 depicts the age association for several disturbances. The reason for the link is sometimes obvious. Chronological age is correlated with developmental level that, in turn, makes some disorders more likely

than others. For instance, developmental speech problems appear when children are first acquiring language skills. But other aspects of onset may be less obvious. Actual onset can occur gradually, with symptoms and social impairment escalating over time. For some disorders, time of onset varies according to gender. Moreover, the time at which a disorder is said to occur may depend on extraneous circumstances. For example, although more severe cases of intellectual disability are identified early in life, most are recognized during the school years when classroom demands call attention to children's abilities to learn.

Taking these distinctions into account, information about developmental level and disorder is helpful in several ways. Knowing the usual age of onset can point to etiology. Very early occurrence suggests genetic and/or prenatal etiology, whereas later onset directs attention to additional developmental influences. Knowing the typical age of onset also serves as a guide to judging the severity or outcome of a disorder: cases that occur especially early are likely to be more severe. For example, typical onset of drug abuse is in adolescence; if it occurs earlier, it is especially associated with severe drug dependency and mental problems later in life (Wills & Dishion, 2004). In addition, parents, teachers, and other adults who are aware of the usual timing of disorder may be more sensitive to the signs of specific problems in youth. In turn, this can lead to preventing the disorder or facilitating early treatment, an outcome thought to aid in reducing the severity or the persistence of disorder and the secondary problems that often are associated with psychological problems (McGorry et al., 2010).

HOW ARE GENDER AND DISORDER RELATED?

For decades, the role of gender in psychopathology in the young was neglected (Crick & Zahn-Waxler, 2003). Several fascinating findings have now emerged. Consistent over the years is the finding of gender differences in the overall rates

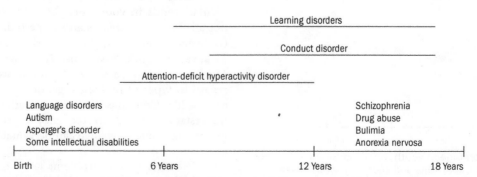

FIGURE 1.4 The age ranges during which some specific disorders typically first occur, are identified, or are most likely to be observed.

TABLE 1.2	Gender Prevalence for Some Disorders of Youth	
HIGHER FOR MALES		
Autism spectrum disorder		Attention-deficit hyperactivity disorder
Oppositional disorder		Conduct disorder
Drug abuse		Language disorder
Intellectual disability		Reading disability
HIGHER FOR FEMALES		
Anxieties and fears	Depression	Eating disorder

of many disturbances, with males being more frequently affected than females (Rutter & Sroufe, 2000). Gender differences have been found across time and in many different countries (Seedat et al., 2009). Table 1.2 shows the findings for several specific disorders. But the picture actually is much more complex.

Some gender differences are related to age. Males are particularly vulnerable to neurodevelopmental disorders that occur early in life, whereas females are more vulnerable to emotional problems and eating disorders that more commonly are seen at adolescence (Rutter, Caspi, & Moffitt, 2003). As shown in Figure 1.5, gender differences may exist not only in the rates of disorder but also in developmental change for externalizing problems (aggression, delinquency) and internalizing problems (anxiety, depression, withdrawal, bodily complaints). In addition, problems may be expressed differently according to gender. For example, males tend to display overt physical aggression while females are more likely to exhibit relational aggression by harmful gossip or rumor spreading (Zalecki & Hinshaw, 2004). The severity, causes, and

consequences of some disorders may also vary with gender. There is still much to learn about gender differences (e.g., Dekker et al., 2007), and methodological issues must be considered.

Methodological Issues, True Differences

To some extent, reported gender differences may result from methodological practices. In the past, a bias existed for studying males, and an emphasis on one gender over the other can result in mistaken inferences about gender differences. Misleading reports of gender differences also can result from females or males being more willing to report certain problems, for example, girls being more willing to speak of emotional difficulties.

Gender-specific prevalence of disorders also can be an artifact of referral bias when clinical samples are studied. Clinical samples are biased toward boys, partly because help is sought for the disruptive behavior exhibited more often by boys than by girls. Thus, boys with reading problems may be referred over girls with reading problems due

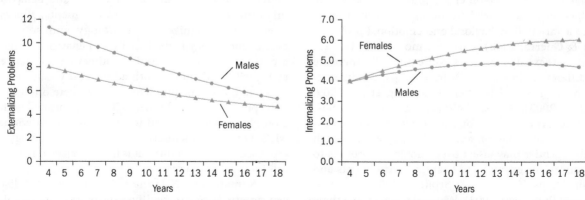

FIGURE 1.5 The presence and developmental change for externalizing and internalizing problems in youth age 4 to 18 years. Externalizing problems drop with age for both genders, while internalizing problems rise for females. *From Bongers, Koot, van der Ende, & Verhulst, 2003.*

to boys' higher rates of disruptive behaviors (Shaywitz, Fletcher, & Shaywitz, 1996). Although boys probably do have more reading problems, referral bias can give misleadingly high rates of disorder.

The bias in clinic samples may affect gender rates in another, more indirect, way (Hartung & Widiger, 1998). When more boys are seen in mental health facilities, they become the subject of more research. In turn, the disorders are described in the way boys express the symptoms, which may not be identical to the symptom picture in girls. When these descriptions (criteria) are used for identifying the disorder, fewer girls will fit the symptom picture and be identified. For example, this possibility is thought to be relevant to attention-deficit hyperactivity disorder in girls (Waschbusch & King, 2006).

Although methodological issues caution us to examine research carefully, the weight of the evidence does point to some real gender differences. To what might they be attributed? Both biological and psychosocial influences, observed prenatally onward, might reasonably underlie gender-specific psychopathology (Rutter et al., 2003; Zahn-Waxler et al., 2006). Differential biological vulnerabilities and strengths may exist. Biological differences between the sexes—in sex chromosomes, sex hormones, and brain structure and function—play a fundamental role in gender development and differences. Biological maturity occurs later in boys, and the X and Y chromosomes are likely related to specific disorders in complicated ways. In addition, biological sex differences may exist in response to stress and in emotion, which we would expect to be relevant to psychological disturbances.

At the same time, boys and girls are differentially exposed to risk and to protective experiences associated with psychopathology. Consider the following examples. From infancy onward, boys suffer a higher rate of traumatic brain injury, which increases their risk of intellectual impairments (Anderson et al., 2001). Boys are more often physically victimized by peers, an event that is related to a variety of behavioral and emotional problems (Hanish & Guerra, 2002). Girls are more likely to have inappropriate sexual encounters. More generally, there are gender differences in sociability, friendships, and interaction with parents and teachers (Auyeung et al., 2009; Rutter et al., 2003). Boys and girls also experience different sex-role expectations for how they should express emotion, control behavior, and the like. It is also worth noting that gender may affect psychological responses to circumstances, for example, to chaotic environments and family problems (Cicchetti & Sroufe, 2000; Leinonen, Solantaus, & Punamäki, 2003). We might expect that these gender-differentiated experiences would result in gender differences in psychopathology.

Further investigation of gender effects has the potential to inform us about the causes, prevention, and treatment of abnormal behavior. More generally, we have seen that what may appear to be simple issues regarding the psychopathology of children and adolescents often is multifaceted. Despite the complexities, progress is being made in understanding the needs of the young. This relatively recent circumstance is illuminated in the next section.

HISTORICAL INFLUENCES

Humans have long speculated on behavioral dysfunction, but early interest focused primarily on adulthood. Some analyses suggest that this was partly because children were not considered very different from adults and because they had high death rates that hindered parental attachment and interest (Ariès, 1962). However, at least by the seventeenth century, children were viewed as having physical, psychological, and educational needs that required nourishment, nurturance, and instruction (Pollock, 2001). By the early eighteenth century, they were variously seen as either stained with original sin, as innately innocent and needy of protection, or as blank slates upon which experience would write. By the end of the nineteenth century adolescence was conceived as a distinct period of transition between childhood and adulthood that entailed specific change, challenge, and opportunity (Demos & Demos, 1972). Differing and often conflicting views of childhood and adolescence continue to this day, undoubtedly influencing perspectives on problem behaviors and how abnormality should be treated.

Progress in the Nineteenth Century

The nineteenth century brought efforts to record the growth and abilities of the young, as well as progress in understanding disturbed development and behavior. By this time, two explanations of adult mental illness had long been recognized: demonology and somatogenesis. **Demonology** is the belief that behavior results from a person's being possessed or otherwise influenced by evil spirits or demons. Both adults and youths acting in unusual, bizarre, or problematic ways were often thought to be possessed by evil spirits. Closely associated with religion, demonology tended to cast suffering individuals as wicked or evil in themselves. Although demonology is still espoused in some cultures, it is largely rejected in scientifically advanced societies.

Somatogenesis is the belief that mental disorder can be attributed to bodily malfunction or imbalance. This perspective was advocated by Hippocrates, considered the father of medicine, when little was known about the workings of the human body. Although the influence of somatogenesis has waxed and waned, it has remained a hardy hypothesis. By the late nineteenth century, a dominant assumption regarding psychopathology was that inheritance, and degeneration that began in childhood, led to irreversible disease, which could be transmitted to the next generation (Costello & Angold, 2001). Today, due to advances in the biological sciences, somatogenesis is a dominant view that garners much enthusiasm.

Efforts to identify and classify mental illness progressed by the late nineteenth century. Emil Kraepelin, in 1883, published a classification system in which he tried to establish a biological basis for mental disorder. Kraepelin recognized that particular symptoms tended to group together—to occur in **syndromes**—and therefore he thought they might have a common physical cause. He viewed each disorder as distinct from others in origin, symptoms, course, and outcome (Widiger & Clark, 2000). Eventually his work would be the basis of modern classification systems for mental disorders.

Although the study of youth generally lagged behind the study of adults, the first records of childhood disorders appeared early in the nineteenth century (Rie, 1971). By the end of the century, a few efforts had been made to classify

children's disturbances, and causes had been proposed. Aggression, psychoses, hyperactivity, and "masturbatory insanity" in youth were all noted, with mental retardation receiving by far the most attention (Bernstein, 1996). An optimistic remedial approach to mental retardation began in Europe and spread to the United States—only to give way later to custodial institutionalization that would not be rectified for many decades.

Meanwhile, around the beginning of the twentieth century, several developments began to fundamentally alter how children and adolescents were viewed, ideas about how their development might go awry, and how they might be treated (Table 1.3). Professional and scientific activities were interwoven with progressive efforts regarding young people, females, and weak and ill members of society (Silk et al., 2000).

Sigmund Freud and Psychoanalytic Theory

One of these developments was the rise of **psychoanalytic theory** and its associated treatment, psychoanalysis. Sigmund Freud's theory was the first modern systematic attempt to understand mental disorders in psychological terms. Indeed, it was critical to **psychogenesis,** the belief

TABLE 1.3	Some Early Historical Landmarks
1896	The first child clinic in the United States was established at the University of Pennsylvania by Lightner Witmer.
1905	Alfred Binet and Theophil Simon developed the first intelligence tests to identify children who could benefit from special educational efforts.
1905	Sigmund Freud's *Three Essays on the Theory of Sexuality* described a startlingly different view of childhood development.
1908	In *A Mind That Found Itself*, Clifford Beers recounted his mental breakdown and advocated an enlightened view of mental disorders, initiating the mental hygiene and child guidance movements.
1909	G. Stanley Hall invited Sigmund Freud to lecture on psychoanalysis at Clark University in Worcester, Massachusetts.
1909	William Healy and Grace Fernald established the Juvenile Psychopathic Institute in Chicago, which would become the model for the child guidance clinics.
1911	The Yale Clinic of Child Development was established for child development research under the guidance of Arnold Gesell.
1913	John B. Watson introduced behaviorism in his essay "Psychology as a Behaviorist Views It."
1917	William Healy and Augusta Bronner established the Judge Baker Guidance Center in Boston.
1922	The National Committee on Mental Hygiene and the Commonwealth Fund initiated a demonstration program of child guidance clinics.
1924	The American Orthopsychiatric Association was established.
1928–1929	Longitudinal studies of child development began at Berkeley and Fels Research Institute.
1935	Leo Kanner authored *Child Psychiatry*, the first child psychiatry text published in the United States.

that mental problems are caused by psychological variables. As a young neurologist, Freud became convinced, based on his study of adults, that unconscious childhood conflicts and crises were the keys to understanding behavior.

Freud proposed three structures of the mind whose goals and tasks made conflict inevitable: the id, ego, and superego. Moreover, anxiety could be generated as a danger signal to the ego—the problem-solving part of the mind—that id impulses unacceptable to the superego were seeking to gain consciousness. Freud proposed that to protect itself from awareness of unacceptable impulses, the ego creates defense mechanisms that distort or deny the impulses. Although defense mechanisms can be adaptive, they may also generate psychological symptoms.

The psychoanalytic perspective rests on a psycho-sexual stage theory of development. As the child develops, the focus of psychological energy passes from one bodily zone to the next, leading the child through five fixed stages—oral, anal, phallic, latency, and genital. The first three stages involve particular crises that are crucial for later development. During the oral stage, the child must be weaned; during the anal stage, the child must be toilet trained; during the phallic stage, the child must resolve the crisis brought on by the desire to possess the opposite-sex parent (the Oedipal conflict for the boy, the Electra conflict for the girl). For Freud, the basic personality was laid down during these first three stages—by age 6 or 7—and healthy development was hindered by failure to resolve the crisis during each stage. (See Accent: "Little Hans: A Classic Psychoanalytic Case.")

In *Three Essays on the Theory of Sexuality*, published in 1905, and in his 1909 lectures at Clark University in Worcester, Massachusetts, Freud introduced his radical ideas about the importance of childhood to adult development (Evans & Koelsch, 1985; Rie, 1971). His views were controversial from the start and are criticized on several grounds. For example, they rested primarily on impressions from case studies, involved large inferences from what he observed to what he interpreted as existing, and were difficult to test. Freud's ideas nevertheless had enormous influence (Eisenberg, 2001).

Classical psychoanalytic theory has been modified by a number of workers. Some minimized sexual forces and emphasized social influences, among them Erik Erikson, who proposed an influential theory of psychosocial development. Freud's daughter, Anna, elaborated his ideas and applied them to children (Fonagy & Target, 2003). By the 1930s, Freud's ideas provided a framework for conceptualizing child, adolescent, and adult behavior. They helped to establish psychiatry as a major discipline in the study and treatment of childhood disorders. In 1935, Leo Kanner authored the first child psychiatry text published in the United States.

Modification of traditional psychoanalysis has occurred over the decades (Fonagy & Target, 2003; Gabbard, 2000). Some basic concepts have been altered, newer forms of therapy have evolved, and research on infant and child development has been considered. Current psychoanalytic psychotherapy emphasizes affect, interpersonal relations, past experiences, and recurring themes in the client's

ACCENT
Little Hans: A Classic Psychoanalytic Case

Freud's well-known case of "Little Hans" illustrates both the concept of symptoms arising from defense mechanisms and the phallic stage of development. Although the analysis is widely rejected today, the case served as a model for the psychoanalytic interpretation of childhood phobias (Freud, 1953/1909).

Hans was very affectionate toward his mother and enjoyed "cuddling" with her. When Hans was almost 5, he returned from a daily walk with his nursemaid frightened, crying, and wanting to cuddle with his mother. The next day, when the mother herself took him for a walk, Hans expressed a fear of being bitten by a horse, and that evening he insisted on cuddling with his mother. He cried about having to go out the next day and expressed considerable fear concerning horses.

These worsening symptoms were interpreted by Freud as reflecting the child's conflict over the sexual impulses he had toward his mother and fear of castration by his father.

Hans's ego employed three defense mechanisms to keep the unacceptable impulses unconscious or distorted. First, Hans's wish to attack his father, the rival for his mother's affection, was *repressed* in memory. The next step was *projection* of the unacceptable impulses onto the father: Hans believed that his father wished to attack him, rather than the other way around. The final step was *displacement*, wherein the perceived dangerousness of the father was displaced onto a horse. According to Freud, the choice of the horse as a symbol of the father was due to numerous associations of horses with Hans's father. For example, the black muzzles and blinders of horses were viewed as symbolic of the father's mustache and eyeglasses. The fear Hans displaced onto horses permitted the child's ambivalent feelings toward his father to be resolved. He could now love his father. In addition, perceiving horses as the source of anxiety allowed Hans to avoid anxiety by simply avoiding horses (Kessler, 1966).

Both Sigmund Freud and his daughter, Anna Freud, were influential in the development of the psychodynamic conceptualizations of childhood disorders.

functioning, with the goal of fostering psychological capacities and resources (Shedler, 2010). Although the overall influence of psychoanalytic theory has waned, among its many contributions are an emphasis on psychological causation, mental processes, unconscious motivation, anxiety and other emotions, infant and childhood experiences, and the child–parent relationship.

Behaviorism and Social Learning Theory

In 1913, John B. Watson's essay "Psychology as a Behaviorist Views It" introduced **behaviorism** in the United States. Unlike Freud, Watson placed little value on describing developmental stages and on early psychological conflicts. Instead, he drew on theories of learning to emphasize that most behavior, adaptive or maladaptive, could be explained by learning experiences. Widely quoted is the following statement, which reflected his belief in the power of experience to shape children's development:

> Give me a dozen healthy infants, well-formed, and my own specified world to bring them up in and I'll guarantee to take any one at random and train him to become any type of specialist I might select—doctor, lawyer, merchant, chief and yes, even beggar-man and thief, regardless of his talents, penchants, tendencies, abilities, vocations, and race of his ancestors. (Watson, 1930, p. 104)

Among the models that Watson drew on was classical conditioning, described earlier by Pavlov, whose animal studies demonstrated learning that occurred through the pairing of new with old stimuli. In addition to placing a strong emphasis on learning and environment, Watson was committed to testing ideas by experimental methods, as were other behaviorists (Horowitz, 1992).

E. L. Thorndike (1905) made an early contribution to behaviorism by formulating the Law of Effect. Simply put, this law states that behavior is shaped by its consequences.

John B. Watson was a highly influential figure in the application of the behavioral perspective.

If the consequence is satisfying, the behavior will be strengthened in the future; if the consequence is unpleasant, the behavior will be weakened. Thorndike considered the Law of Effect a fundamental principle of learning and teaching; later researchers substantiated his idea. Of special note is B. F. Skinner, who is widely known for his work on operant learning—that is, for investigating and writing on the application of behavioral consequences to the shaping of behavior (Skinner, 1948; 1953; 1968). Skinner can be viewed as Watson's descendant in his emphasis on learning, the environment, and experimental methods (Horowitz, 1992).

Behaviorism, like psychoanalytic theory, thrived in the United States during the first half of the twentieth century. Its impact on behavioral disorders came gradually as learning principles were applied to behavior. Albert Bandura (1977) expanded the learning approach through his study of how humans learn from others. His work on observational learning, which highlighted the social context and cognition, became a major influence (Grusec, 1992).

Learning is, of course, fundamental to human functioning, and its application to many facets of problem behavior is widespread (Jacob & Pelham, 2000). Learning approaches can improve the lives of youngsters experiencing emotional, cognitive, and social disorders. The explicit application of learning principles to the assessment and treatment of behavioral problems is referred to as behavior modification or behavior therapy. Approaches that emphasize the combination of learning principles and the social context and/or cognition are referred to as **social learning** or **cognitive–behavioral perspectives.**

Mental Hygiene and Child Guidance Movements

The twentieth century saw another important thread being woven in different settings. Despite early interest in adult psychopathology, much remained to be done, and treatment often consisted of custodial care. The **mental hygiene movement** aimed to increase understanding, improve treatment, and prevent disorder from occurring at all.

In 1908, Clifford Beers wrote an account, *A Mind That Found Itself*, of the insensitive and ineffective treatment he had received as a mental patient. Beers proposed reform, and he obtained support from renowned professionals, including Adolf Meyer. Offering a "commonsense" approach to studying the patient's environment and to counseling, Meyer viewed the individual as integrated across thought, emotion, and biological functioning (Cicchetti, 2006). He also advocated a new professional role—the psychiatric social worker (Achenbach, 1982).

Beers's efforts led to the establishment of the National Committee for Mental Hygiene to study mental dysfunction, support treatment, and encourage prevention. In part because childhood experiences were viewed as influencing adult mental health, children became the focus of attention in the **child guidance movement** (Rie, 1971).

In 1896, at the University of Pennsylvania, Lightner Witmer had set up the first child psychology clinic in the United States (McReynolds, 1987; Ross, 1972). This clinic primarily assessed and treated children who had learning difficulties. Witmer also founded the journal *Psychological Clinic* and began a hospital school for long-term observation of children. He related psychology to education, sociology, and other disciplines.

An interdisciplinary approach was taken by psychiatrist William Healy and psychologist Grace Fernald in Chicago in 1909, when they founded the Juvenile Psychopathic Institute. The approach of this institution, which focused on delinquent children, became the model for child guidance (Santostefano, 1978). Freudian theory was integrated with educational, medical, and religious approaches in child guidance clinics (Costello & Angold, 2001). Healy and his wife, psychologist Augusta Bronner, opened the Judge Baker Guidance Center in Boston in 1917, and several other child clinics subsequently followed. The clinics began to treat cases of personality and emotional problems, and flourished in the 1920s and 1930s. Some of these clinics are still providing services to youth. In 1924, the child guidance movement became formally represented in the newly formed American Orthopsychiatric Association, which today includes a variety of professionals concerned about children and adolescents.

Scientific Study of Youth

It was also during the early twentieth century that systematic study of youth became widespread. In 1918, barely a handful of psychologists and psychiatrists were full-time scholars of childhood; by 1930 more than 600 such professionals could be counted (Smuts, 2006). Perhaps the most influential figure in this endeavor was G. Stanley Hall (Cravens, 1992). Among other things, he collected data on the problems of youth in order to understand mental disorder, crime, social disorder, and the like (White, 1992). Hall wrote extensively on youth, trained students who later became leaders in the field, and as president of Clark University invited Freud to lecture in 1909. He also helped establish the American Psychological Association, of which he was the first president.

At about the same time, an important event occurred in Europe: Alfred Binet and Theophil Simon were asked to design a test to identify children who were in need of

G. Stanley Hall contributed to the early scientific study of youth and served as the first president of the American Psychological Association.

special education (Siegler, 1992). Their 1905 Binet–Simon test became the basis for the development of intelligence tests, and it encouraged efforts to measure other psychological attributes.

Another outstanding figure was Arnold Gesell, who meticulously recorded the physical, motor, and social behavior of young children in his laboratory at Yale University (Thelen & Adolph, 1992). He charted developmental norms, created an extensive film archive of child behavior, and was a strong advocate for optimal rearing conditions for youth.

Around 1920, child study began to benefit from several longitudinal research projects that evaluated youth as they developed over many years. Research centers existed at the universities of California, Colorado, Michigan, Minnesota, Ohio, and Washington; other research centers were at Fels Research Institute, Columbia Teachers College, Johns Hopkins University, and the Iowa Child Welfare Station. Knowledge about normal development began to accumulate that eventually was applied to the study of child and adolescent disorders. (See Accent: "Mrs. Hillis: Improving Corn, Hogs, and Children in Iowa.") Some of these institutes still operate, albeit in different forms, while others closed their doors after several decades; all had tremendous influence on scientific study of the young (Smuts, 2006).

CURRENT STUDY AND PRACTICE

Today, the study and practice of abnormal child and adolescent psychology reflect the diverse historical theories, movements, and events that were set into motion in the early decades of the twentieth century. Some of the early approaches and occurrences are presently more significant than others and many new influences have come into play. Thus, both older and more recent assumptions, concepts,

ACCENT
Mrs. Hillis: Improving Corn, Hogs, and Children in Iowa

The establishment of the Iowa Child Welfare Research Station was sparked by Mrs. Cora Bussey Hillis, who demonstrated how advocacy for children can go hand in hand with advocacy for science (Cravens, 1993; Sears, 1975). Mrs. Hillis, a clubwoman married to an attorney, had considerable social and political influence. Life's tragedies, particularly the loss of three of her five children, directed and reinforced her passionate interest in child welfare.

Mrs. Hillis was aware of the respected agricultural station of the college in Ames, Iowa. In her mind's eye, she saw a comparable child welfare station that would be devoted to research, teaching, and dissemination of knowledge. The center would focus on problems in children's development and health. Researchers and professionals would be trained to work directly with children and parents. A body of knowledge would be constructed and disseminated to

the public as rapidly as possible. Mrs. Hillis had faith that if research could "improve corn and hogs it could also improve children" (Sears, 1975, p. 17).

Working closely with Mrs. Hillis on the project was Carl Emil Seashore, a psychologist and admirer of G. Stanley Hall, who was dean of the graduate school at the State University of Iowa, in Iowa City. These two dominant, stubborn individuals did not always agree on the goals for the station, and they faced many obstacles, including difficulty in obtaining Iowa legislative support (Cravens, 1993). In 1917—after years of advocacy with women's clubs, education groups, and politicians—Mrs. Hillis achieved her dream when the Station opened at the Iowa City campus. It was a site of prolific and leading research on children's physical, mental, and social development for almost 60 years.

and knowledge give shape to a dynamic and multidisciplinary field.

The primary goals of the field are to identify, describe, and classify psychological disorder; to reveal the causes of disturbance; and to treat and prevent disorder. Highly valuable in meeting these aims is the developmental psychopathology perspective, which is discussed in chapter 2 of this text. Here, we briefly note some premises that we view as central to the field, as well as issues relevant to working with young people and their families.

- With few, if any, exceptions, psychological problems stem from multiple causes that must be reckoned with if we are truly to understand, prevent, and ameliorate such problems.
- Normal and abnormal behavior go hand in hand, and we must study one in order to understand the other.
- The complexity of human behavior calls for systematic conceptualization, observation, data collection, and hypothesis testing.
- Continued efforts are needed to construct and verify treatment and prevention programs.
- Whether they are in treatment, prevention, or research settings, young people have a right to high-quality care that is sensitive to their developmental level, family role, and societal status.
- Advocacy for the well-being of youth is appropriate, particularly because of their relative lack of maturity and social influence.

Working with Youth and Their Families

Professionals interact with children, adolescents, and their families in many settings—research-based, medical, educational, and legal, to name a few. The focus of the present discussion is the clinical setting.

INTERDISCIPLINARY EFFORTS   More than one professional is often involved in clinical activities with a young person. Among these are psychologists, psychiatrists, social workers, and special education teachers.

The majority of psychologists working with child and adolescent problems have specialized in clinical psychology; others may have specialized in school, developmental, or educational psychology. They usually hold a doctoral degree (Ph.D. or Psy.D.). Psychology has sturdy roots in the laboratory and an interest in both normal and abnormal behavior. Psychologists thus receive training in research, and have direct contact in assessing and treating individuals. Psychiatrists, on the other hand, hold a doctorate in medicine (M.D.); they are physicians who have specialized in the treatment of mental disturbance. Although psychiatrists function in ways similar to those of psychologists, they are more likely to view psychopathology as a medical dysfunction and to employ medical treatments, especially pharmacological treatments.

Social workers generally hold a master's degree (M.A.) in social work. Like psychologists and psychiatrists, they may counsel and conduct therapy, but their special focus is more broadly working with the family and other social systems in which young people are enmeshed.

Special education teachers, who usually have obtained a master's degree, emphasize the importance of providing optimal educational experiences. They are able to plan and implement individualized educational programs, thus contributing to interventions for many disorders.

Youngsters with problems also come to the attention of nurses, physicians, teachers in regular classrooms, and workers in the legal system. Indeed, these professionals may be the first to hear about a problem. Substantial coordination among professionals and agencies is thus often necessary and valuable.

THE ROLE OF PARENTS   Professional contact with youth typically involves some, often crucial, communication with families, usually with one or more parents. Families differ in their needs, including needs for support, basic education about psychopathology, and information about the availability of services. Depending on the situation, parents may play various roles in actual intervention (Kendall, 2006). As consultants, they have unique information about their child and can offer a valuable perspective of the situation. They may serve as collaborators with mental health professionals in carrying out treatment for their offspring—in effect, serving as cotherapists. When they are more directly involved in the difficulties, parents may participate as coclients with their child or adolescent. A recent meta-analysis showed moderate benefits from parent–child therapy compared to individual child treatments (Dowell & Ogles, 2010).

Unsurprisingly, parents vary in the knowledge they have about mental health and in their motivation and ability to participate. They may seek consultation for many reasons: concern for their sons and daughters, the relief of their own worries, or fulfillment of school or court referrals. Some may have inappropriate goals or believe that the outcome of treatment depends only on the mental health worker. Despite these and other issues, however, many parents form a cooperative and constructive alliance with the mental health worker, which may positively affect the outcome of intervention (Kazdin, Whitley, & Marciano, 2006; Weisz & Kazdin, 2010).

Whatever the situation and setting, parental involvement is usually recommended, although the type of services to families depends on whether needs are best met by education, support, skills training, cotherapy, and the like (Hoagwood, 2005a). The optimal degree of parental involvement in child-centered therapy also must be evaluated. For example, relatively little parental participation may be suitable for anxious youth whose parents are overprotective (Kendall, 2006).

WORKING WITH YOUNG CLIENTS   The relative immaturity, inexperience, and vulnerability of children and adolescents require special considerations. Knowledge about and attitudes toward mental health may be quite variable among children. Gender differences also may exist. In a Scottish adolescent sample, Williams and Pow (2007) found negative attitudes were more common in boys, who reported less knowledge of, and less desire for, information about mental health.

Young children may lack the ability to identify problems, and they most frequently enter treatment at the suggestion or coercion of adults. Adolescents often have more input into the decision to seek clinical services, but many are sensitive about autonomy, and this issue requires special attention (Cicchetti & Rogosch, 2002). Efforts by the mental health worker to create a **therapeutic alliance** with the client—that is, to forge a trusting personal bond and collaboration on treatment—may increase the chance of a successful outcome (Green, 2006; Weisz & Kazdin, 2010).

In working with youth, knowledge and mindfulness of normal development and developmental issues are essential for evaluating problems and planning intervention. We have seen that developmental norms serve as a guide to judging whether behaviors should be of concern. Moreover, optimal growth requires that youngsters master developmental tasks (e.g., school achievement, forming friendships), progress that often is hindered by psychological disturbance. For example, an anxious child with good cognitive skills can develop academic deficits stemming from fears of and withdrawal from classroom activities. Treatment planning may thus need to address not only the anxiety but also the academic problems. In addition, choice of treatment techniques must be developmentally sensitive (Holmbeck, Devine, & Bruno, 2010). For young children, play or modeling techniques may be more appropriate than cognitive methods. On the other hand, the development of more complex thinking during adolescence makes the success of cognitive approaches more likely.

Finally, youth have basic rights that must be recognized and protected. Ethical standards set by the American Psychological Association (2002) address issues regarding both clinical and research activities. The guidelines concerning intervention include the rights to informed consent to treatment, to participate in deciding the goals of treatment, and to receive confidential care. With young clients, developmental level enters into determining the exact ways in which these considerations play out. For example, the principle of **informed consent** requires that the client consent to participate with full understanding of how treatment will proceed (Hoagwood & Cavaleri, 2010). However, children cannot legally give consent and parental or guardian consent is required. This requirement can sometimes be waived, for instance, to allow a minor living apart from parents to consent to receive treatment.

When they treat young people, mental health workers often face a unique mix of ethical and legal issues. Consider the following situation.

AARON

Clinical, Legal, and Ethical Considerations

Mrs. Schulz, recently divorced, is seeking therapy for her 6-year-old son, Aaron. The father has shared custody and is responsible for treatment costs. He insists that Aaron is fine and does not need therapy. Mr. Schulz suggests that the problem lies with his ex-wife. The therapist, believing that Aaron requires treatment, is in a bind. Apart from legal issues of consent needed to see a child, she recognizes that proceeding without the father's consent might well lead to his undermining treatment. She must decide what is in the best interests of the child in the long run. She wishes that she had involved the father from the beginning.

Adapted from Schetky, 2000, p. 2944.

In some situations, mental health workers may be called on for legal testimony, raising the ethical issues of confidentiality and potential harm to the client (Schetky, 2000). Other situations—for example, the possibility that the client may harm others or him- or herself—can demand a break in confidentiality or additional action (Oltmanns & Emery, 2007). Confidentiality is also an issue when child abuse is suspected. Mental health professionals must report this circumstance, whether or not it threatens the therapeutic relationship. In such instances, professionals must understand and meet legal requirements and must inform families of the kinds of things that must be reported. Ethical and legal dilemmas regarding psychological disorders are not uncommon in working with clients, but they are of special concern when they involve young people who are limited in speaking for themselves.

Overview/Looking Back

DEFINING AND IDENTIFYING ABNORMALITY

- Behaviors are judged as abnormal on the basis of their being atypical, harmful, and inappropriate. Standards for behavior depend on developmental, cultural, gender, and situational norms.
- Adult attitudes, sensitivities, and tolerance play a role in identifying disturbances in young people, and what is considered as abnormal may change over time.

HOW COMMON ARE PSYCHOLOGICAL PROBLEMS?

- The rates of psychopathology vary depending on several factors. Estimates are generally in the 13 to 22% range for U.S. children and adolescents. Prevalence in preschoolers appears similar, and interest in infant mental health has increased.
- There is some evidence that rates of disorders among youth are increasing.
- Two-thirds to three-quarters of needy youth may not be receiving adequate treatment.

HOW ARE DEVELOPMENTAL LEVEL AND DISORDER RELATED?

- Some association exists between the onset or identification of specific disorders and age/developmental level, due in part to the timing of the child's emerging abilities and environmental demands placed on the child. Onset may occur gradually, however.

HOW ARE GENDER AND DISORDER RELATED?

- Gender differences occur in the rates of disorder, with boys exhibiting higher rates for many disorders. Other important gender differences exist, for example, in the timing, developmental change, and expression of problems.

- Although methodological factors, including biased clinical samples, probably account in part for reported gender differences, numerous biological and psychosocial factors underlie true gender differences.

HISTORICAL INFLUENCES

- Early interest in psychopathology focused on adults, with problems attributed to demonology or somatogenesis.
- The nineteenth century saw progress in identifying and classifying mental illness. Several childhood disorders were identified, and biological causation held sway.
- The early decades of the twentieth century brought new knowledge and understanding through psychoanalytic theory, behaviorism and social learning theory, the mental hygiene and child guidance movements, and increased scientific study of youth.

CURRENT STUDY AND PRACTICE

- The current study and practice of the psychopathology of youth is shaped both by past and more recent efforts. Emphasis is given to multiple causation, the relation between normal and abnormal behavior, scientific approaches, effective treatment and prevention, and advocacy.
- Working with youth often involves multidisciplinary approaches. Parents, who may play various roles in intervention, are important to its success. Regarding young clients, consideration must be given to attitudes, developmental abilities and needs, and ethical and legal requirements.

Key Terms

developmental norms *3*
culture, cultural norms *3*
ethnicity *4*
race *4*
gender norms *5*
situational norms *5*
secular trends *6*

demonology *10*
somatogenesis *10*
syndromes *11*
psychoanalytic theory *11*
psychogenesis *11*
behaviorism *13*
social learning perspective *14*

cognitive–behavioral perspective *14*
mental hygiene and child guidance
 movements *14*
therapeutic alliance *17*
informed consent *17*

CHAPTER 2

The Developmental Psychopathology Perspective

LOOKING FORWARD

After reading this chapter, you should be able to discuss:

- Paradigms, theories, and models in the study of psychopathology
- The developmental psychopathology perspective
- The concept of development
- How causation is variously conceptualized
- Pathways of development
- Aspects of risk, vulnerability, and resilience
- Continuity and change in psychological disorders
- Examples of how normal and abnormal development go hand in hand

Hardly a day passes without each of us wondering about many aspects of development and behavior. We want to know how our father manages to be consistently helpful, why our friends' personalities differ so much, what led a classmate to suddenly drop out of school, and whether a talented actor will be able to stop abusing drugs. Generally, the more usual the behavior or situation, the fewer questions we have, and the more easily answered they seem. It is the unexpected that is more likely to confound us—especially when a behavior appears to be problematic or harmful in some way.

The ability to explain abnormality is of critical interest to those who investigate psychopathology and those who primarily treat it. Although it is possible to treat and prevent disturbances without fully understanding them, increased knowledge significantly aids these efforts. Behavioral scientists also are committed to more generally exploring an array of fundamental questions about human functioning. In this chapter, we present a framework for conceptualizing aspects of psychological disturbances of young people.

ELIZABETH

No Obvious Explanation

Elizabeth Fellows was referred to a therapist by her physician, who outlined concerns about a possible eating disorder. Elizabeth's mother, who had taken her to the physician, was worried. Not only had she heard Elizabeth vomiting in the bathroom on three occasions, but Elizabeth also had dropped all of her friends and stayed home in her bedroom. Mrs. Fellows reported that until approximately 6 months ago, Elizabeth had seemed fairly normal to her. Since then, Elizabeth had spent more and more time by herself, dropping even Katie, with whom she had been friends since kindergarten. Elizabeth had been a straight A student; now she was earning Bs and Cs. Mrs. Fellows acknowledged that 10th grade had been a difficult one, but she felt that Elizabeth's personality was changing. Mrs. Fellows was unable to remember any single event that had occurred in the past 6 months that might explain her daughter's behavior.

Adapted from Morgan, 1999, p. 46.

PERSPECTIVES, THEORIES, MODELS

Much of today's understanding of both normal and abnormal behavior comes from applying the assumptions and methods of science. The writings of Thomas Kuhn (1962) and others have made us aware that science is not a completely objective endeavor. Like all of us, scientists must think about and deal with a complex world. To study and understand phenomena, scientists adopt a perspective— a view, an approach, or cognitive set. When a perspective is shared by investigators, it may be termed a **paradigm**. Paradigms typically include assumptions and concepts, as well as ways to evaluate these.

There are several benefits to adopting a particular view. A perspective helps make sense of the puzzling and complex universe. It guides the kinds of questions we ask, what we select for investigation, what we decide to observe and how we observe it, and how we interpret and make sense of the information we collect. A perspective influences how a problem is approached, investigated, and interpreted.

There are also disadvantages in taking a perspective—mostly related to the fact that acting on a certain view sets some limitations. When we ask certain questions, we may preclude others. When we observe some things, we do not examine others. When we choose particular methods and instruments to detect certain phenomena, we undoubtedly miss other phenomena. We limit the ways in which we might interpret and think about new information. Taking a perspective is a trade-off—albeit one that, on balance, is more beneficial than detrimental.

Theories

Closely related to the process of taking a perspective—and sharing its benefits and limitations—is the process of theory construction. Simply put, a **theory** is a formal, integrated set of principles or propositions that explains phenomena. Although the term "theories" may be used casually to mean a hunch or educated guess, scientific theories are supported by accepted evidence that often has accumulated gradually. Moreover, theories provide formal propositions that can be tested, thereby advancing knowledge. Because they provide concepts and formal propositions that can be tested, theories are highly valued by researchers and clinicians.

As we saw in chapter 1, biological, psychoanalytic, and behavior/social learning explanations of psychopathology were rooted in concepts developed in the early twentieth century. Currently, numerous theories that vary in scope offer explanations of child and adolescent problems. They focus on emotion, self-regulation, brain functioning, higher level cognition, family interaction, and many other facets of functioning.

Models

In addition to having a theory to guide the study of psychopathology, it is often helpful to employ a model—a representation or description—of the phenomenon of study. Of particular current interest are models that encourage us to simultaneously consider the numerous factors potentially involved in psychopathology.

At the heart of **interactional models** is the assumption that variables interrelate to produce an outcome. One such approach, the **vulnerability–stress model**, conceptualizes the multiple causes of psychopathology as the working together of a vulnerability factor(s) and a stress factor(s). In this model, both vulnerability (also referred to as diathesis) and stress are necessary. They may be biological, psychological, or social factors—although vulnerability often has been considered as biological and stress as environmental. For example, a child's presumed biological susceptibility for anxiety may interact with the stress of parental divorce, resulting in child problems. Interactional models have contributed much to our understanding of psychopathology, although transactional models have become particularly dominant (Price & Zwolinski, 2010).

individual environment past experience

Transactional models are widely employed in the study of both normal and abnormal development. The basic assumption is that development is the result of ongoing, reciprocal transactions between the individual and the environmental context. The individual is viewed as an active agent who brings a history of past experience that has shaped her or his current functioning. The environmental context is viewed as variables that are close to (proximal) or farther from (distal) the person.

Transactional models fall into the domain of **systems models** in that they incorporate several levels, or systems, of functioning in which development is viewed as occurring over time as the systems interact or enter into ongoing transactions with each other. For example, a biopsychosocial model may integrate brain and genetic functioning, behavior, and several aspects of the social environment. In such a model, change at one level of functioning is assumed to influence other levels. Another example of a systems model is the ecological model, which places the individual within a network of environmental influences and assumes transactions between the person and these influences, as well as among the several levels of the environment. Throughout this text, we have opportunity to see how various models facilitate the study of problem behavior.

THE DEVELOPMENTAL PSYCHOPATHOLOGY PERSPECTIVE: AN OVERVIEW

Since the 1970s, the **developmental psychopathology perspective** that we call upon in this text has rapidly become influential in the study of psychological disorders of youth. This perspective integrates the understanding and study of normal developmental processes with those of child and adolescent psychopathology (Hinshaw, 2008). It is interested in the origins and developmental course of disordered behavior, as well as individual adaptation and competence. Central to the approach was the coming together of developmental psychology and clinical child/adolescent psychology and psychiatry (Cicchetti, 1984; 1989). Developmental psychology has traditionally taken normal development as its subject matter; it is especially focused on understanding universal principles of how people grow and change during their lifetime. The primary interest of clinical psychology and psychiatry is in identifying the symptoms of psychological disorders, understanding the causes of disorders, and alleviating the difficulties. In addition to these disciplines, contributions to developmental psychopathology come from a variety of other areas, including the biological sciences, sociology, and philosophy (Cicchetti, 2010a; Hinshaw, 2008).

Developmental psychopathology is a systems framework for understanding disordered behavior in relation to normal development. Rather than imposing specific theoretical explanations, it is a way of combining various theories or approaches around a core of developmental knowledge, issues, and questions (Achenbach, 1990). Individuals working within a developmental psychopathology framework may be informed by cognitive, behavioral, psychodynamic, family, genetic, or other theories. In any case, however, several assumptions are central to the developmental psychopathology perspective. We turn to these after first examining the concept of development.

CONCEPT OF DEVELOPMENT

The concept of **development** can seem deceptively simple. Most people would probably offer growth as a synonym, with growth meaning not only bigger but also better. And many would recognize that development requires time. However, any definition that stops here would fall far short of a full description of development.

Although many different depictions and explanations have been proposed, there is some consensus among theorists on the essence of development (e.g., Cicchetti & Toth, 2009; Cummings, Davies, & Campbell, 2000; Sroufe, 2009).

- Development refers to change over the lifespan that results from ongoing transactions of an individual with biological, psychological, and sociocultural variables, which themselves are changing.
- Although quantitative change in development is noteworthy—for example, an increase in the number of a child's social interactions—qualitative change is more salient—for example, a change in the features or qualities of social interactions.
- Early development of the biological, motor, physical, cognitive, emotional, and social systems follows a general course. Within each system, structures and functions become more finely differentiated and also integrated. Integration occurs across systems as well, enhancing organization and complexity.
- Development proceeds in a coherent pattern, so that for each person, current functioning is connected both to past and future functioning. Development thus can be thought of as proceeding along pathways or trajectories of more or less complexity. In youth, developmental pathways are relatively open and flexible, but there is some narrowing of possibilities over time.
- Over the lifespan, developmental change may produce higher modes of functioning and the

attainment of goals, but change is not inevitably positive. Physical aging in adulthood brings decrements in functioning, and maladaptive behavior can develop at any time during the lifespan.

With the concept of development serving as a backdrop, we now turn to four overlapping issues that are central to the developmental psychopathology approach: the search for causal factors and processes, pathways of development, risk and resilience, and continuity of problems over time.

SEARCHING FOR CAUSAL FACTORS AND PROCESSES

There is a long history of trying to explain the causes, or etiology, of abnormal development in relatively simple ways. An example is the basic **medical model**. This model considers disorders to be discrete entities—things, if you will—that result from specific and limited biological causes within the individual. This explanatory approach was reinforced in the early 1900s by the realization that the microorganism that caused syphilis sometimes affected the brain, thereby causing mental disturbance. Now we realize that a single cause seldom, if ever, accounts for most psychological or behavioral outcomes. (In fact, this is also true for many physical illnesses; for example, biological, psychological, and social factors appear to contribute to cardiac disease.) Thus, as is commonly acknowledged, the understanding of outcome rests on identifying multiply variables concerning both the developing person and contextual factors.

A full account of causation requires, however, more than identification of contributory factors. Developmental psychopathologists seek to understand how causal factors work together and what the underlying processes or mechanisms might be.

In conceptualizing causation, it is useful to distinguish between direct and indirect causes. When a **direct effect** operates, variable X leads straight to the outcome. An **indirect effect** is operating when variable X influences one or more other variables that, in turn, lead to the outcome. Establishing indirect effects is usually more difficult as the path of influences may be complex. Consider, for example, the reported association between parental alcohol use and children's adjustment problems. Might one or more variables underlie this link? Keller, Cummings, and Davies (2005) were interested in the possible role of marital conflict and ineffective parenting. The results of their study suggested that problem drinking led to marital conflict that, through parenting difficulties, led to child problems. The findings supported the hypothesis that, given parental

alcohol problems, marital conflict and ineffective parenting are mediators of child difficulties. The term **mediator** refers to a factor or variable that explains or brings about an outcome, more specifically, by indirect means. The identification of mediators is crucial to understanding causal processes.

So also is the identification of moderators. A **moderator** is a variable that influences the direction or the strength of the relationship between an independent (or predictor) variable and a dependent (or criterion) variable. For example, suppose that boys and girls are exposed to the same treatment but that the outcome is more positive for boys than for girls. Here, it appears that gender moderates the relationship between treatment and outcome. Or to take another example, if cultural context moderates the influence of an experience, outcome may differ in some way for children of different cultural backgrounds. (See Accent: "A Possible Moderating Influence of Culture.")

In examining causation, it is also useful to make a distinction among necessary, sufficient, and contributing causes. A **necessary cause** must be present in order for the disorder to occur. A **sufficient cause** can, in and of itself, be responsible for the disorder. In Down syndrome, which is characterized by intellectual disability, known genetic anomalies are both necessary (they must be present) and sufficient (other factors are not required). By contrast, in the debilitating disorder of schizophrenia, brain dysfunction is thought to be necessary but perhaps not sufficient. Brain abnormality is implicated in schizophrenia, but other factors must be present in order for the condition to arise. It is also important to recognize that **contributing causes** can be operating; these are not necessary or sufficient. In some disorders, several factors may contribute by adding or multiplying their effects to reach a threshold to produce the problem.

The search for causation, as we will see in chapter 4, may employ various research strategies and designs. No matter what the approach, however, a strength of the developmental psychopathology perspective is its focus on understanding the mix of causal processes. We now further examine concepts and assumptions that contribute to this quest.

PATHWAYS OF DEVELOPMENT

The developmental psychopathology perspective assumes that abnormal behavior does not appear out of the blue. Rather, it emerges gradually as the child and environmental influences transact (Cummings, Davies, & Campbell, 2000). Development is characterized as involving progressive adaptations or maladaptations to changing circumstances. It can be viewed as a pathway over time that

ACCENT
A Possible Moderating Influence of Culture

Parents in many countries report or endorse the use of mild physical discipline—such as spanking, slapping, grabbing, or restraining—in certain situations, although differences exist in the degree to which they use or accept such practices (Deater-Deckard, Dodge, & Sorbring, 2005; Lansford et al., 2004; 2005). In general, such punishment is correlated with aggression or acting out in childhood and adolescence. Evidence exists, however, that the link between physical punishment and acting out may be moderated by the cultural context.

Lansford and her colleagues (2005) hypothesized that acting-out behavior would be reduced in cultures in which physical discipline was viewed as more normative. They assessed cultural normativeness by parent and child perceptions of physical discipline. Their hypothesis was supported in the study of six different countries (Thailand, China, Philippines, India, Kenya, and Italy). Consonant with this finding, some research in the United States indicates that physical punishment is more normative in African American than European American families, and also that the link between physical discipline and child aggression/acting-out may be weaker in African American families.

These moderating effects can be variously interpreted. For example, if parental behavior is viewed as normative, the punished child may be less likely to feel rejected, an outcome generally related to child adjustment. Or the child may be more likely to perceive physical punishment as a reflection of parental concern for their offspring. Indeed, there is evidence that firm parenting is seen as less intrusive in African American families (Anderson & Mayes, 2010). Whatever underlies the moderating affect, Lansford and colleagues warn that their findings should not be taken as encouraging physical punishment, which was generally associated with child aggression and also with other maladjustment. The results do suggest, however, the value of examining the possible moderating role of cultural context.

is forged by cascades of changing circumstances and reactions. Thus, development is not cast in stone; rather, it is open or probabilistic. New situations, or new reactions to ongoing circumstances, can bring about redirection.

One way to better understand psychopathology is to describe and understand pathways of adaptation and maladaptation. For example, we can examine research efforts that focused on general developmental trajectories

OMG! I JUST GOT BORN

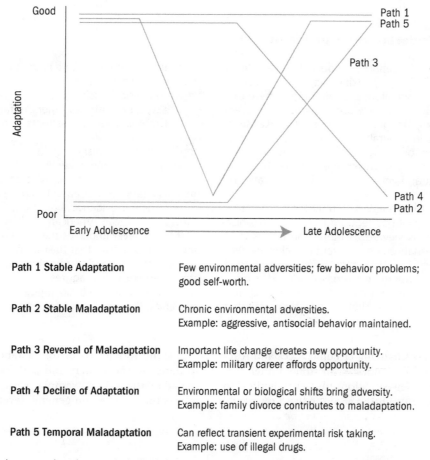

Path 1 Stable Adaptation   Few environmental adversities; few behavior problems; good self-worth.

Path 2 Stable Maladaptation   Chronic environmental adversities.
Example: aggressive, antisocial behavior maintained.

Path 3 Reversal of Maladaptation Important life change creates new opportunity.
Example: military career affords opportunity.

Path 4 Decline of Adaptation Environmental or biological shifts bring adversity.
Example: family divorce contributes to maladaptation.

Path 5 Temporal Maladaptation Can reflect transient experimental risk taking.
Example: use of illegal drugs.

FIGURE 2.1   Five developmental pathways during adolescence.   *Adapted from Compas, Hinden, & Gerhardt, 1995.*

across the adolescent years (Compas, Hinden, & Gerhardt, 1995). Figure 2.1 presents the five trajectories and briefly describes each one. Path 1 is characterized by stable good adaptation. This pathway is associated with relatively low exposure to negative circumstances, and the adolescents show positive self-worth and few problems. Path 2 indicates stable maladaptation, whereby youths who already are having problems experience adversities and inadequate resources to relieve them. The remaining paths involve significant change in developmental direction during adolescence. Path 3 shows maladaptation that turns into positive outcome, due at least in some cases to environmental opportunity. Path 4 indicates an initial adaptation that, due to adversities, ends with decline. Path 5 depicts a temporary decline and a bouncing back to adaptive behavior, as might occur, for example, in experimental short-term drug use. An obvious aspect of these trajectories is that adaptation level at any given time does not necessarily predict later functioning.

Substantial progress is being made in mapping developmental trajectories with regard to specific problems or disorders, as we will see in later chapters. Both stable and changing pathways are commonly observed, even for a single problem. For example, childhood aggression appears stable into adulthood for some individuals but ceases with the transition into adolescence for others (Hinshaw, 2008).

Equifinality and Multifinality

The transactional and probabilistic nature of development is recognized in the principles of equifinality and multifinality. **Equifinality** refers to the fact that diverse factors can be associated with the same outcome. In other words, children can have different experiences, or follow different pathways, and yet develop the same problems (Figure 2.2). Equifinality is observed in a number of child and adolescent disorders. A well-documented example is the finding that different pathways exist to antisocial behavior.

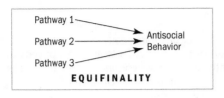

FIGURE 2.2 Examples of how both equifinality and multifinality operate in development.

The second principle, **multifinality**, refers to the fact that an experience may function differently depending on a host of other influences that may lead to different outcomes. Simply put, children can have many of the same kinds of experiences and yet end up with different problems or no difficulties at all. A well-recognized example concerns child maltreatment. Children who are abused by adults are at risk for later behavioral disturbance, but different children display different kinds of problems.

The principles of equifinality and multifinality are a reflection of a common theme in the development of behavior: Enormous complexity usually must be addressed in terms of what is likely to happen along life's pathways. In this regard, the concepts of risk and resilience contribute further to understanding the development of psychological problems.

RISK, VULNERABILITY, AND RESILIENCE

Risk and Vulnerability

Risks are variables that precede and increase the chance of psychological impairments. Substantial investigation points to several important aspects of risk (e.g., Kopp, 1994; Liaw & Brooks-Gunn, 1994; Pungello et al., 2010; Sameroff, 2006; Shanahan et al., 2008).

- Although a single risk certainly can have an impact, multiple risks are particularly harmful.
- Risks tend to cluster; for instance, children at risk due to low parental education are more likely to reside in disadvantaged communities.
- The intensity, duration, and timing of a risk can make a difference. (See Accent: "The Timing of Risky Experiences.")
- The effects of many risk factors appear nonspecific, a finding reflected in the principle of multifinality. This is not always the case, however, and further research is needed.
- Risk factors may be different for the onset of a disorder than for the persistence of the disorder.
- A risk may increase the likelihood of future risks by increasing the child's susceptibility for problems or adversely affecting the environmental context.

ACCENT
The Timing of Risky Experiences

An important theoretical and practical concern in developmental psychopathology is to better understand when and how experiences have different effects depending on the age or developmental level of the individual.

The timing of an event can make a difference for several reasons (Rutter, 1989; 2006). Among these, the effects of experience on the nervous system may be different depending on the developmental level of the nervous and other biological systems. Similarly, the effect of experience can vary with age-related psychological functioning, for example, the child's ability to think adaptively about an adverse event. Whether an experience is normative or nonnormative may also matter. Normative events happen to most people at more or less predictable time (e.g., puberty between ages 11 and 14) whereas nonnormative events occur only to certain persons at atypical times (e.g., very early or late onset of puberty). Nonnormative events may be

problematic because they put the individual "out of sync" with, for example, social expectations and supports.

Historically, there has been a strong interest in the proposition that early influences may be especially powerful. O'Connor and Parfitt (2009) describe three developmental models that illustrate how early adverse experience has been conceptualized. The *sensitive period* model predicts that exposure to risk during a specific window of time may have permanent effects, whereas the same exposure at a different time has little or no influence. Research has shown that sensitive periods operate in normal development in animals, but the application of this model to human development may be limited. The *developmental programming* model proposes that some features of the individual can be set, or programmed, by early environmental occurrences, and that these features persist into the future. For example, early trauma may program a child's biological reactivity to

(continued)

(*continued*)

stressful events, which is preserved over time. The *life-course model* proposes that early experience can have long-term consequences but only when the experience is maintained, reinforced, or accentuated in some way. A major idea here is that early risk can lead to poor adaptation, which increases the probability of subsequent maladaptation.

Despite the interest in the timing of experiences, the timing effect is difficult to demonstrate (O'Connor & Parfitt, 2009). For one thing, early influences are hard to isolate because exposure to risks of interest—say, poverty or parental psychopathology—often continues over time. It is similarly difficult to isolate the effects of adversity occurring at later times. Especially notable is adolescence, a transitional time characterized by remarkable physical, hormonal, psychological, and social role changes that may involve heightened strengths and vulnerabilities (Graber et al., 2004; Steinberg, 2009).

A central aim of risk research is to understand how risk is translated into psychopathology (Price & Zwolinski, 2010). Initially, it is necessary to identify risk factors, and numerous risks have been recognized as operating across cultures. They are associated with biological, cognitive, psychosocial, and other domains (Table 2.1). Some of these factors appear to reside in the youth's tendency to respond maladaptively to life circumstances, and the term **vulnerability** often is applied to this subset of risk factors. Vulnerability may be inborn (e.g., genetic conditions) or acquired (e.g., learned ways of thinking), and although somewhat enduring can be modified.

Given the complexities of development, it is appropriate to view risk within a transactional model that includes both environmental circumstances and the individual. An example of this approach is shown in Figure 2.3. This conceptual model relates risky life experiences (stressors) to psychopathology (Grant et al., 2003). The risky experiences are major or minor events that can be acute, occurring suddenly and perhaps disastrously (e.g., a damaging accident), or they can be chronic, persisting over time (e.g., poverty). The model proposes that these experiences produce a variety of processes in the individual—biological, psychological, and social—that mediate, or lead to, psychopathology. In addition, the relationship between stressors and child mediators can be moderated by attributes of the child or the environment. For example, the child's age, gender, or sensitivity to the environment can influence the strength of this relationship. Finally, this model recognizes two-way influences between the components, thereby reflecting the dynamic processes of development.

TABLE 2.1	Examples of Developmental Risk Factors

Hereditary influence; gene abnormalities

Prenatal or birth complications

Below average intelligence or learning difficulty

Psychological/social: difficult temperament, poor regulation of emotion and behavior, social incompetence, peer rejection

Poor parenting and family abuse, neglect, disorganization, conflict, psychopathology, stress

Poverty

Disorganized neighborhood

Racial, ethnic, or gender injustice

Nonnormative stressful events such as early death of a parent, natural catastrophes, armed conflict, or war

Based in part on Coie et al., 1993.

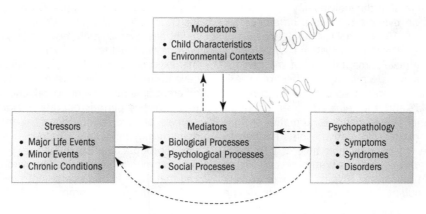

FIGURE 2.3   A model of the relation between adversities (stressors) and psychopathology.   *Adapted from Grant et al., 2003.*

Resilience

Resilience is defined by relatively positive outcome in the face of significantly adverse or traumatic experiences (Luthar, 2006). Resilience speaks to individual differences in response to risk, in the ability to resist or overcome life's adversities (Ingram & Price, 2010; Rutter, 2006).

Resilience is often defined as the absence of psychopathology, a low level of symptoms, or adaptation beyond what would be expected in situations that overcome many individuals (Luthar 2006; Masten, 2001). It also can be defined in terms of competence regarding the **developmental tasks**, or cultural age-expectations, applied to young people. In this case, resilience is demonstrated when an individual meets major developmental tasks despite unfavorable life circumstances. Table 2.2 provides some of these widely agreed-on developmental tasks.

As with research on risk, investigation of resilience has evolved over time (Cicchetti, 2010b; Sapienza & Masten, 2011). The initial interest in resilience led to descriptions of why some individual succumb to adversities while others rise above threat. An early groundbreaking study was conducted with children born in 1955 on the Hawaiian island of Kauai (Werner & Smith, 1982; 2001). A high-risk group was identified on the basis of early exposure to at least four risk factors. In late adolescence, most of the high-risk children had developed behavioral and/or learning problems, but one-third of the youth were successfully negotiating life. The resilience of these youths originated from three broad categories: personal attributes, family characteristics, and support from outside the family. This trio of categories has been found in many investigations, and can be thought of as sources of protective factors—that is, factors that counter risk factors operating in the situation. The sources of resilience are well-recognized factors that are beneficial to most children, a finding that Masten (2001) referred to as the "ordinary magic" of resilience.

Currently, there is wide agreement on several correlates of resilience or protective factors. As indicated in

TABLE 2.2	Examples of Developmental Tasks
Age Period	**Task**
Infancy to preschool	Attachment to caregivers
	Language
	Differentiation of self from environment
	Self-control and compliance
Middle childhood	School adjustment
	Academic achievement
	Getting along with peers
	Rule-governed conduct
Adolescence	Successful transition to secondary schooling
	Academic achievement
	Involvement in extracurricular activities
	Forming close friendships within and across gender
	Forming a cohesive sense of self-identity

From Masten & Coatsworth, 1998.

ANN AND AMY

The "Ordinary Magic" of Resilience

Ann and Amy were from different family circumstances, and at 6 years of age their functioning was dissimilar. Ann was from an affluent family background, with parents who had an intact marriage and optimally managed both child-rearing and emotional relations with Ann. Amy, on the other hand, was from more difficult circumstances, with a single-parent father who had experienced an acrimonious divorce. During assessment at age 6, Ann was well adjusted, whereas Amy evidenced problems in the clinical range.... However, over the next several years, Amy was able to take advantage of her social and athletic skills to develop good social relations with classmates, and her parents (ex-spouses) learned ways to interact much more amicably as they faced custody-related decisions and problems. For example, Amy's noncustodial mother gradually came to contribute faithfully to child support, even though she had remarried and had another child. An assessment conducted when both Ann and Amy were 10 years of age indicated that Ann, whose family circumstances had continued to be stable, supportive, and positive, still scored as well-adjusted, but Amy now also scored as well-adjusted and above average in social competence.

Adapted from Cummings et al., 2000, p. 40.

TABLE 2.3	Correlates of Resilience in Young People
Problem solving skills	
Skills in self-regulation	
Positive views of self	
Achievement motivation	
Perceived self-efficacy and control	
Active coping strategies	
Close, caring family relationships	
Supportive relationships with adults in the community	
Friends or romantic partners	
Spirituality, finding meaning in life	

Adapted from Cicchetti, 2010, and Sapienza & Masten, 2011.

Table 2.3, some of these are attributes of the individual— for example, skills in problem solving and self-regulation. In this sense, resilience is viewed as residing within the individual and can be regarded as the opposite of vulnerability (Ingram & Price, 2010). Figure 2.4 depicts resilience and vulnerability at opposite ends of a continuum of vulnerability interacting with varying levels of (environmental) stress. At the resilience end of the continuum, more stress is required for disorder to occur. With vulnerability, even low stress can result in mild disorder, and severity of disorder increases as stress level rises.

Research on resilience has gone beyond identifying correlates or protective factors to searching for underlying processes. Much attention is currently being given to biological processes. Central to this work is the study of coping with stress (Feder, Nestler, & Charney, 2009). Individual genetic composition plays a role in a person's response to stress, and the interaction of genes and exposure to stress helps shape brain circuits that are thought to be relevant to resilience.

Resilience is an ongoing, complex process. Whether any single variable protects an at-risk child may depend on the situation. Or resilience may occur in some risk situations (e.g., family conflict) and not others (e.g., peer pressure). Further, an at-risk youth may show positive outcome in some domains of functioning (e.g., emotional) and not others (e.g., academic achievement) (Luthar, 2006). In addition, for any individual, resilience may be modified over time with changing circumstances that alter strengths and vulnerabilities. Indeed, increased interest exists in how positive functioning is maintained over time, cascades from one functional domain to another (e.g., from early academic competence to later social competence), or spreads from one level to another (e.g., from the biological to psychosocial or vice verse) (Sapienza & Masten, 2011). Advances in the understanding of resilience are immensely important to the prevention of psychopathology and to optimizing the development of youth.

CONTINUITY OF DISORDER

Inherent in the developmental psychopathology perspective is an interest in understanding continuity and change over time. Development is defined in terms of change,

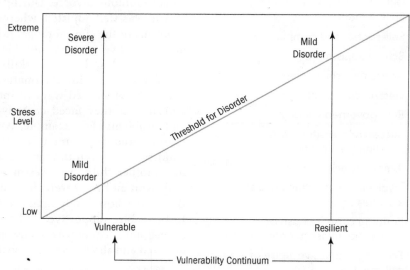

FIGURE 2.4 The relationship of vulnerability and resilience along a continuum. Resilience implies resistance to disorder. *Adapted from Ingram & Price, 2010.*

and humans certainly are malleable. But there are limits to malleability and we can expect to see both change and continuity in an individual. When a young handsome man reaches old age, he may still be attractive compared to his peers, but his face will be both different from and similar to its earlier appearance. We can generally expect the same for psychological functioning.

When the issue of continuity or change is applied to the study of psychological disorders, a basic question is, "Does a disorder at an earlier time in life carry over to later life?" This question is important for understanding the development of problems, and it has implications for treatment and prevention. Treatment is desirable for any disturbance that causes discomfort and maladaptation, but problems that persist warrant increased concern. Moreover, knowing that early problems predict later disturbance puts high priority on efforts to intervene early in the process.

What is known about the continuity of problems or disorders? Given the transactional quality of development, it is unsurprising that the answer is not simple and is still being investigated. Considering the wide array of problems, both continuity and discontinuity have been observed and we cannot assume that the young merely grow out of psychopathology. Some disorders, such as the sleep and eating problems of very young children, are likely to cease. Among those that tend to persist are intellectual deficiencies related to genetic abnormalities, autism, and schizophrenia. The picture is especially complex for still other problems. Antisocial behavior often carries over; for example, children who rank high in aggression compared to their peers maintain this high ranking in adolescence (Hinshaw, 2008). But this does not hold for all individuals, and some may no longer display aggression. It is thus essential to distinguish subgroups within a disorder that might show different trajectories.

In considering whether or not a disorder continues over time, investigators have recognized that the expression of a problem may change in form with development; that is, **heterotypic continuity** may occur. Hyperactivity in an 8-year-old that is manifest by restless, fidgety movement may present itself by inability to relax during the teen years and adulthood. As well, we would expect that depression in childhood would be expressed somewhat differently from depression in adolescence or adulthood. **Homotypic continuity** also may be observed, however; that is, how a problem is expressed may be relatively stable over time.

In general, continuity of problems can be anticipated to vary with the length of time being examined, the kinds of psychopathology or symptoms, and other variables. A host of questions can be asked about which variables predict continuity of problems. Do symptoms that are severe rather than mild forecast continuity? Is continuity more likely when a child simultaneously displays more than one disorder? Is gender related to continuity and, if so, with regard to all or only some disorders? Many of these questions are being addressed by researchers, which will be discussed later in this text.

Also under investigation are the processes responsible for carrying psychopathology forward in time. Several have been demonstrated or proposed, as summarized in Figure 2.5 (Rutter, 2006; Sroufe, Coffino, & Carlson, 2010). Continuity may be sustained by environmental constancy—as when poor parental care or poor schooling persists and continues to negatively affect development. Genetic predisposition may be involved, and early problems or experiences can affect the development of the brain and other biological systems in ways that make continuity likely. Another process concerns the construction of mental representations or views of the social environment. Based on their experiences people set up expectations and the like and tend to act in accordance with such representations, thus bringing continuity to their behavior. In addition, continuity can result from a chain of negative circumstances or interactional behavior patterns. For example, continuity may stem from children's being

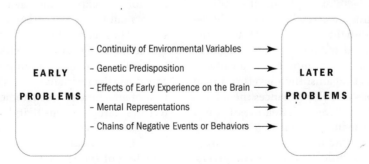

FIGURE 2.5   Factors carrying problems forward in time.

channeled into environments that perpetuate a maladaptive style—as when an ill-tempered boy limits opportunity by dropping out of school, thereby creating frustrating situations, to which he responds with more irritability, lack of control, and the like (Caspi, Elder, & Bem, 1987).

We should note that our present discussion of continuity and change focuses on whether a disorder, or symptoms of a disorder, in youth is observed at a later time in the person's life. A related question is whether early disorder predicts other kinds of problems later in life (Copeland et al., 2009). This important issue is addressed in subsequent chapters that examine specific disorders.

NORMAL DEVELOPMENT, PROBLEMATIC OUTCOMES

So far in this chapter, we have discussed core aspects of the developmental psychopathology perspective. We now briefly examine select areas of development in order to illustrate how normal developmental processes and less-than-optimal outcomes go hand in hand. These areas are attachment, temperament, emotion, and social cognitive processing. These examples also describe development as involving the overlap and interdependence of the biological, social, emotional, and cognitive domains of functioning.

Attachment

From infancy onward, virtually all children and their caregivers seem biologically prepared to interact in ways that foster their relationship. Most parents are remarkably sensitive in understanding and responding to their babies' signals and needs. Infants, in turn, are sensitive to parental emotional–social signals. Such synchronous interactions are the basis for the special social–emotional bond called early **attachment**, which develops gradually and becomes evident when the child is 7 to 9 months of age.

Recognizing that Freudian theory gave importance to the mother–child relationship, Bowlby (1969) emphasized that behaviors that facilitate attachment—smiling, crying, eye contact, proximity to caretakers, and the like— were biologically "wired" into the human species to ensure that infants would be nurtured and protected by caregivers. These behaviors are regarded as a component of an attachment system, which protects against high levels of threat or fear in stressful situations and also enhances the infant's exploration of novel and challenging situations (Kobak et al., 2006; Lyons-Ruth, Zeanah, & Benoit, 2003).

Bowlby viewed attachment as part of the ongoing transactions between a child and major caregivers,

Infants and their caregivers are predisposed to interact in ways that foster attachment.

which help shape developmental pathways to adaptive or less adaptive outcomes. He and subsequent workers proposed that the child's attachment experiences result in internal representations, or expectations, about the caregiver's availability and responsiveness. Expectations regarding the trustworthiness of caregivers affect the child's ability to regulate emotion and cope with stress and are tied to the acquisition of confidence and self-worth—all of which are carried into future relationships and behavior.

Attachment has been examined across the lifespan but especially in early development. In infancy, attachment is studied with Ainsworth's procedure, the Strange Situation. Here, a caregiver (usually the mother), the infant, and a stranger interact in a comfortable room. The caregiver leaves and returns several times, while the child's behavior is observed in this potentially threatening situation. Initial research indicated that many infants could be categorized as displaying **secure attachment** or one of two types of **insecure attachment** (Kobak et al., 2006). Securely attached infants, when distressed by caregiver separation, seek contact with her upon her return, react positively, and use the caregiver as a secure base from which they venture forth to explore the environment. Insecurely attached infants fail to use the caregiver as a resource to cope with stress. They tend either to give fewer signals of distress and ignore the caregiver (the avoidant type) or display distress and make ineffective attempts to seek contact with the caregiver (the resistant type). The development of one pattern of attachment over another depends on child characteristics, caregiver sensitivity to the infant's needs, and the broader social context (Meins et al., 2001).

Later research revealed a pattern of **disorganized attachment** (Green & Goldwyn, 2002; Lyons-Ruth et al.,

2003). This pattern reflects the lack of a consistent strategy to organize behavior under stressful situations. Infants seem apprehensive and they display contradictory behaviors that may be misdirected and atypical (Table 2.4). The pattern is associated with child maltreatment and poor parenting (Shumaker, Deutsch, & Brenninkmeyer, 2009), and found at much greater frequency in high-risk than low-risk families (Juffer, Bakermans-Kranenburg, & van IJzendoorn, 2005). It is hypothesized that the child may experience the parent as frightening, unavailable, or threatening—and the child's behavior may become disorganized in the face of this circumstance.

In later childhood and adolescence, the attachment system includes peer and romantic relationships, and measurement shifts to self-reports and interviews about the child–parent relationship (Schumaker et al., 2009). Early attachment experiences are thought to carry over to later relationship, and parents still play a critical role. The concepts of secure and insecure attachment are still relevant, although consensus is lacking regarding the categories that best represent later attachment.

The relationship of attachment patterns to other behaviors has been extensively investigated. Secure attachment has been associated with adaptive behavior in childhood and adolescence, such as competence and positive peer interactions (Kobak et al., 2006). In contrast, insecure attachment and especially disorganized attachment are linked to several maladaptive behaviors—aggression, anxiety, substance use, delinquency, academic deficits, low self-esteem, poor peer interaction, unusual or bizarre classroom behavior, and dissociative behaviors (Brumariu & Kerns, 2010; Kobak et al., 2006; Lyons-Ruth et al., 2003; Zeanah & Smyke, 2009).

TABLE 2.4	Some Indications of Disorganized/ Disoriented Attachment

Infant displays contradictory behaviors, such as seeking contact with the caregiver and also avoiding the caregiver.

Movements and expressions are undirected, misdirected, incomplete, or interrupted.

Movements and expressions are frozen or appear as in "slow motion."

Infant appears apprehensive regarding the caregiver.

Disorganization or disorientation is obvious in disoriented wandering, confused or dazed expression, or multiple rapid changes of affect.

Adapted from Lyons-Ruth, Zeanah, & Benoit, 2003.

The association of attachment categories and later behavior is modest in strength and is not always found. Indeed, attachment itself can change from secure to insecure and vice versa, and modifications in family circumstances likely play a role (Thompson, 2000). However, attachment theory is a dominant approach to understanding the influence of early close relationships on current or later psychological functioning (Rutter, Kreppner, & Sonuga-Barke, 2009; Sroufe et al., 2010). In this regard, attachment can serve as a risk or protective factor (Kochanska, Philibert, & Barry, 2009).

Temperament

The word "**temperament**" generally refers to basic disposition or makeup. The concept of temperament is an old one, going back to the classical Greek era. Current interest can be traced to Chess and Thomas's study of New York City children (1972; 1977). These investigators recognized environmental influences on the development of behavior, but they were struck by individual differences in how infants behaved from the first days of life. On the basis of parental interviews and actual observations, Chess and Thomas were able to demonstrate that young babies had distinct individual differences in temperament that were somewhat stable over time.

Chess and Thomas defined temperament in terms of nine dimensions of behavioral style that included reactivity to stimuli, regulation of bodily function, mood, and adaptability to change. They also identified three basic temperamental categories or styles: easy, slow-to-warm, and difficult. The latter temperament—characterized in part by intense reactivity and negative mood—has especially been associated with social and psychological disturbance (Rothbart & Posner, 2006; Nigg, 2006b).

Chess and Thomas avoided simplistic notions about temperament and development. They suggested that early biologically based temperamental differences occur in the presence of parents who themselves differ in how they react to and manage their children. Parental responding, in turn, influences child reactions, which affects parental reactions, and so on—all of which occurs within the broader context of a changing environment. The investigators proposed that temperament is malleable and that final outcome depends on **goodness-of-fit,** that is, how the child's behavioral tendencies fit with parental characteristics and other environmental circumstances. Their case description of Carl demonstrates that a good match can facilitate adaptation.

Chess and Thomas's basic insight into temperament has stood the test of time. Temperament is viewed as

CARL

A Case of Goodness-of-Fit

"[Early] in life Carl had been one of our most extreme 'difficult child' temperamental types, with intense, negative reactions to new situations and slow adaptability only after many exposures. This was true whether it was the first bath or first solid foods in infancy, the beginning of nursery school and elementary school, first birthday parties, or the first shopping trip. Each experience evoked stormy responses, with loud crying and struggling to get away. However, his parents learned to anticipate Carl's reactions, knew that if they were patient, presented only one or a few new situations at a time, and gave Carl the opportunity for repeated exposure to the new, he would finally adapt positively.... His parents recognized that the difficulties in raising Carl were due to his temperament and not to their being 'bad parents.' The father even looked on his son's shrieking and turmoil as a sign of 'lustiness.' As a result of this positive parent–child interaction Carl never became a behavior problem even though the 'difficult' child as a group is significantly at higher risk for disturbed development."

Chess & Thomas, 1977, pp. 220–221.

individual differences in behavioral style that are thought to develop into later personality through environmental interaction (van den Akker et al., 2010). Early temperament is moderately stable over time and can predict later temperament and adult personality. The role of biology in temperamental difference is illustrated in measures such as heart rate and subtle brain structure (Schwartz et al., 2010). Parenting practices have been associated with changes in temperament, demonstrating the role of environmental processes.

As research on temperament has proceeded, different dimensions or categories of temperament have been presented. Most accounts include aspects of positive/negative emotion, approach/avoidance behaviors, activity level, sociability, attention, or self-regulation (e.g., Rothbart & Posner, 2006). In discussing the relationship of temperament to childhood or later adjustment, Sanson and colleagues (2009) suggested that 3 dimensions of temperament are widely recognized, albeit the labels may vary across studies (Table 2.5). In general, *negative reactivity* has

been associated with many types of problems; *inhibition* (approach-avoidance) with worry and anxiety; and *self-regulation* with low levels of acting-out behaviors, good social competence, and academic adjustment. The picture is complex, however. For example, outcome can vary as the result of interactions between dimensions of temperament. Also noteworthy is that the research on temperament requires careful consideration because various dimensions or categories have been presented and different labels employed.

Nigg (2006b) suggested two perspectives of temperament and psychopathology. One considers problem behavior as an extreme of normal temperament. For example, attention-deficit hyperactivity disorder may reflect the extreme of temperamental tendencies for impulsivity and inattention. The second perspective views temperament as a risk or protective factor, depending on the specific temperamental tendency and circumstance.

It is noteworthy that temperament has been included in a broader consideration of children's susceptibility and malleability to environmental circumstances. Specifically, it has been proposed that difficult temperament is associated with an increased sensitivity to the environment regardless of the quality of the environment. (See Accent: "Sensitivity to Context: For Better or Worse.")

TABLE 2.5	Three Widely Recognized Dimensions of Temperament
Negative Reactivity	Refers to emotional volatility and irritability. Sometimes called negative emotionality, anger, or distress proneness. A basic component of most definitions of temperament and an aspect of difficult temperament in most research.
Inhibition	Describes the child's response to new persons or situations. Also referred to as approach withdrawal, social withdrawal, or sociability.
Self-regulation	Refers to processes that facilitate or hinder reactivity. Includes effortful control of attention (e.g., task persistence), emotion (e.g., self-soothing), and behavior (e.g., delay of gratification).

Adapted from Sanson, Letcher, Smart et al., 2009.

ACCENT
Sensitivity to Context: For Better or Worse

As already noted, children with difficult temperament have been reported as having especially negative outcomes to environmental adversities. These youth are considered to be highly reactive and are regarded as a high-risk group. However, some investigators have argued for a more nuanced perspective. They propose that reactivity is linked to a more general sensitivity to environmental context, for better or worse. In other words, highly reactive youths are more malleable to a variety of experiences (Ellis et al., 2011; Pluess & Belsky, 2011). An obvious implication of this proposal—sometime referred to as the **differential susceptibility hypothesis**—is that reactive children should not only be more affected than other youth by adversities but *also* by advantageous environments.

In a test of the hypothesis, Bradley and Corwyn (2008) looked at the interaction of child temperament and measures of parenting as related to externalizing problems in young children. Based on infant assessment, the children were categorized as exhibiting easy, average, or difficult temperament. Parenting behavior was measured by observation of the mother interacting with the child on several occasions. Assessment of problem behavior was based on teacher ratings of the children when they were in first grade. Overall, the hypothesis was supported. Figure 2.6 indicates the findings with regard to three child temperaments and mother's sensitivity. The children with difficult temperament had the highest problem scores with low-sensitivity mothers (poor parenting) but the lowest problem scores with high-sensitivity mothers (good parenting). The same pattern occurred with two other measures of parenting. Thus, children with difficult temperament appeared more susceptible than other youth to the kind of parenting they received, for better or worse.

Several additional investigations, using various measures, provide support for the hypothesis of differential susceptibility to the environment (Belsky & Pluess, 2009; Ellis et al., 2011; Essex et al., 2011; Obradović et al, 2010). The

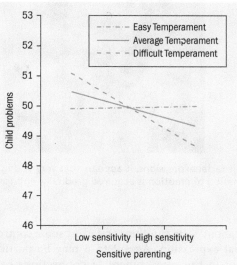

FIGURE 2.6   The interaction of child temperament and parenting. The findings suggest that children with difficult temperament were more affected by both low sensitivity and high sensitivity parenting.   *Adapted from Bradley & Corwyn, 2008.*

genetic studies are quite striking: individuals possessing the gene of interest are more negatively affected by adversity and more positively affected by a supportive situation than other persons. The genetic findings suggest that differential susceptibility has a biological basis, but other findings suggest that the environment also plays a role.

Further testing of the differential susceptibility hypothesis has implication for child development (Belsky & Pluess, 2009). For example, if children with difficult temperament are more susceptible not only to low-quality parenting/child care but also to high-quality parenting/child care, supportive environments may be especially beneficial for them.

Emotion and Its Regulation

Emotional reactivity and regulation are elements of temperament, but emotion is not identical to temperament and is deserving of further discussion. Three elements of **emotion** are widely recognized: (1) private "feelings" of sadness, joy, anger, disgust, and the like; (2) autonomic nervous system arousal and bodily reactions such as rapid heartbeat; and (3) overt behavioral expressions such as smiles, scowls, and drooping shoulders. The emotions may be viewed as relatively brief or as more general mood states that vary in intensity and that are experienced as positive or negative.

Human emotion is evident early in life and is rapidly entwined with social development. Early on, infants express basic emotions such as joy, sadness, disgust, and fear; in the second year of life, more complex emotions become obvious, such as shame and guilt (Rosenblum, Dayton, & Muzik, 2009). Appropriate emotional responses to others also appear early; for example, the social smile is evident by 2 months. By 12–18 months, infants display social referencing by using the expressions of others' to guide their own responses; for instance, in approaching or avoiding an object. Two- and 3-year-olds are able to name

From their facial expressions, it appears that very young children experience basic emotions such as happiness and unhappiness. The regulation of emotion is acquired gradually, and for some children much more easily than for others.

and talk about basic emotions and exert some control over emotional expression. Ages 2 to 5 may be particularly important in the development of connections between emotion and cognition (Izard et al., 2002). During childhood, further progress is made in understanding and regulating the emotions. Emotion has a biological basis that interacts with environmental influence, and is shaped by family socialization and the broader cultural context (Izard et al., 2006). There is evidence that family quality of care, open discussion of emotion, and modeling of emotional behavior all have influence (Eisenberg, 2006).

Emotions enter into virtually all human experience and serve several general functions (Izard et al., 2006; Lemerise & Arsenio, 2000). They play a role in communication, are involved in the development of empathy, and motivate and guide individual cognition and behavior. Emotions play a critical role in psychological difficulty or maladjustment. Sadness and anger are components of depression and aggression. Undue fear and anxiety—particularly when they endure over time—can require professional assistance. Even positive emotions can interfere with adaptive functioning; for example, the expression of joy may be excessive or inappropriate to the situation.

UNDERSTANDING AND REGULATION   The understanding of emotion is important to child competence and adjustment (Eisenberg, Spinard, & Eggum, 2010). In one study, for example, emotion knowledge and social problems in 5- to 7-year-olds were examined (Schultz et al., 2001). Emotion knowledge was defined in terms of the children's ability to identify (1) emotional expressions on others' faces and (2) the emotion that would be experienced by a person in particular circumstances. As predicted, children who showed low levels of emotion knowledge tended

to have social problems and withdrawal 2 years later. Other research demonstrates a link between difficulty in understanding emotion and later academic or psychological problems (Fine et al., 2003; Izard et al., 2002).

Similarly, the complex task of emotion regulation enters into both positive and negative adjustment. All children must acquire the ability to regulate the emotions. This task includes learning to initiate, maintain, and modulate the feelings, biological responses, and expressions of emotion (Eisenberg, 2006). As with other aspects of emotion, parenting plays a critical role in facilitating the development of regulation. For example, the mother's sensitivity to infant cues can be important in helping the infant to cope with stress (Albers et al., 2008).

Emotion regulation can be viewed as an aspect of the effortful control considered to be crucial to adaptive and competent development (Moffitt et al., 2011). The importance of self-regulation was demonstrated in a study that found high levels of negative emotions combined with poor regulatory skills to be associated with both low social competence and behavioral problems. Children with good regulatory skills did not have these outcomes—regardless of whether they were high or low in emotionality (Eisenberg et al., 1997).

Social Cognitive Processing

In contrast to feeling states that motivate and guide behavior, the cognitive domain of functioning has to do with knowing or understanding through higher order thinking processes. The role of cognition in various disorders of young people is being vigorously pursued. Here, we only consider one aspect of cognition: **social cognitive processing**.

Social cognitive processing has to do with thinking about the social world. It focuses on how individuals take in, understand, and interpret social situations—and how behavior is then affected (Lemerise & Arsenio, 2000). Of immediate concern to our discussion is the role that interpretation of the social situation can play in maladaptive behavior. To take an example, numerous studies indicate that children and adolescents who display more than average aggression or who have been rejected by their peers tend to interpret the behaviors of others as hostile (Horsley, de Castro, & Van der Schoot, 2010). That is, they appear to have a bias to attribute hostility to others, especially when provoked.

It is noteworthy that although social information processing emphasizes cognition, emotion is viewed as playing an integral role (Arsenio & Lemerise, 2004; Dodge & Rabiner, 2004). Cognition and emotion may interact in various ways (cf. Lemerise & Arsenio, 2000). Poor understanding of emotion likely plays a role in a child's misperceptions of social cues (Denham et al., 2002). Also, a youth who is already emotionally aroused may be highly prone to misperceptions. For example, the arousal of negative emotions in highly aggressive boys can increase their attribution of hostile intent to others (de Castro et al., 2003). Alternatively, the perception of hostility in others can arouse feelings of negative emotions. As these examples demonstrate, research on social cognitive processing contributes to our understanding of how thinking and emotions are united in the interchange between individuals and their environments (Rutter & Sroufe, 2000).

Cognitive processing of the social context influences much human functioning. For an everyday example, consider that children's perception of their parents' interaction with them or with each other is related to parental influence on the children (Gomez et al., 2001). Regarding psychological problems, specific beliefs and attributions about the world and the self appear to operate in depression, anxiety, and negative peer relationships, among other difficulties.

Inherent in the topics we have just examined—attachment, temperament, emotion, and social cognition processing—is the assumption that development is rooted in both biological and experiential factors and their transactions with the child or adolescent. Influences on the development of psychopathology are further explored in chapter 3.

Overview/Looking Back

PERSPECTIVES, THEORIES, MODELS

- Perspectives (paradigms), theories, and models are critical to the scientific study of human development.
- Theories, which consist of formal propositions to explain phenomena, are highly valued because they permit the testing of hypotheses.
- Interactional and transactional models presume that several factors, working together, underlie psychopathology.

DEVELOPMENTAL PSYCHOPATHOLOGY PERSPECTIVE: AN OVERVIEW

- The developmental psychopathology perspective explores psychological disturbances with respect to several core developmental issues. A systems framework for organizing other perspectives or theories of psychopathology, it integrates normal and maladaptive development.

CONCEPT OF DEVELOPMENT

- Development refers to change over time resulting from transactions of an individual with biological, psychological, and sociocultural factors. Early development follows a general course and proceeds in a coherent pattern.

SEARCHING FOR CAUSAL FACTORS AND PROCESSES

- A major goal of developmental psychopathology is to uncover the multiple causes of psychological disorders and underlying processes.
- It is important to differentiate direct and indirect influences; mediating and moderating influences; and necessary, sufficient, and contributing causes.

PATHWAYS OF DEVELOPMENT

- Development proceeds along complex probabilistic pathways, as reflected in the principles of equifinality and multifinality.

RISK, VULNERABILITY, AND RESILIENCE

- Risk factors increase the chance of psychopathology; many kinds have been identified. Risk is best conceptualized within a transactional model.
- Among important aspects of risk are the number; general or specific effects; and intensity, duration, and timing of risks. Early risk may be particularly influential.

- Vulnerability refers to individual attributes that may act as risk factors.
- Resilience refers to relatively positive outcome in the face of adversity or risk. Protective factors that confer resilience include individual, family, and extra-familial variables.
- When viewed as attributes of the individual, resilience can be considered as the opposite of vulnerability.

CONTINUITY OF DISORDER

- Continuity of disorder over time varies, but it cannot be assumed that most children outgrow psychopathology. Both homotypic and heterotypic continuity are observed. Among the processes that underlie continuity are environmental stability, biological mechanisms, and psychological functioning.

NORMAL DEVELOPMENT, PROBLEMATIC OUTCOMES

- Patterns of early socioemotional attachment between children and their caregivers have been described. Secure attachment is associated with later positive outcome; insecure and disorganized/disoriented patterns are associated with unfavorable outcome.
- Temperament refers to biologically based, modestly stable individual styles of behaving that enter into the transactions of development. Temperament can be viewed as a risk or protective factor.
- Emotion is evident early in infancy and develops rapidly in childhood. Emotional reactivity, knowledge, and regulation are central in adaptive and maladaptive development.
- Cognitive processing of the social world is implicated in several forms of psychological problems. For example, highly aggressive children have a cognitive bias to view the world as hostile.

Key Terms

paradigm *20*
theory *20*
interactional models *20*
vulnerability–stress model *20*
transactional models *21*
systems models *21*
developmental psychopathology perspective *21*
development *21*
medical model *22*
direct effect, indirect effect *22*
mediator *22*

moderator *22*
necessary, sufficient, contributing causes *22*
equifinality *24*
multifinality *25*
risk factors *25*
vulnerability *26*
resilience *27*
developmental tasks *27*
heterotypic continuity, homotypic continuity *29*
attachment *30*

secure, insecure, disorganized attachment *30*
temperament *31*
goodness-of-fit *31*
differential susceptibility hypothesis *33*
emotion *33*
social cognitive processing *34*

CHAPTER 3

Biological and Environmental Contexts of Psychopathology

LOOKING FORWARD

After reading this chapter, you should be able to discuss:

- Brain and nervous system development, structure, and function
- Pre-, peri-, and postnatal risks to the nervous system
- The genetic context of development, including genetic research
- Basic learning/cognitive processes and their role in development
- An ecological model of sociocultural influences on development
- The family context of development, including maltreatment and divorce
- Influences of peers on development
- Community and societal contexts of development

The aim of this chapter is to consider the major biological and environmental contexts of the development of psychological problems. We discuss the nervous system and brain, genetics, learning and cognition, and the social/cultural contexts of development. Basic information is provided and emphasis is placed on influences on behavioral and psychological disorders.

BRAIN AND NERVOUS SYSTEM

Brain Development: Biology and Experience

The development of the brain and nervous system is arguably among the most fascinating of all developmental processes. Much early growth is biologically guided but the influence of experience is critical.

The nervous system begins to develop shortly after conception when a group of cells called the neural plate thickens, folds inward, and forms the neural tube. The rapidly developing cells migrate to fixed locations. The brain contains millions of multifunctioning cells, the glial cells, and **neurons** that are specialized to chemically transmit impulses within the nervous system and to and from other body parts. These cells continue to become more interconnected and functional, and nerve fibers become sheathed in **myelin**, a white substance that increases the efficiency of communication in the brain. Both before and after birth, an excess of neurons and connections are produced, apparently setting the brain up to ensure flexibility (Rapoport & Gogtay, 2008). Different brain areas develop more rapidly than others. For example, the enormous growth of connections among neurons that are related to vision and hearing peaks a few months after birth, but occurs much more slowly in the frontal part of the brain involved in complex, flexible thinking (Thompson-Schill, Ramscar, & Chrysikou, 2009).

Adolescence is a time of notable brain maturation (Steinberg, 2009). Change occurs in brain chemistry; connections between brain regions proliferate; the amount of gray matter (cell bodies) decreases in the front part of the brain whereas white matter increases, reflecting continuing myelination. As with earlier brain development, these changes have implications for psychological and behavioral functioning.

The development of the brain results from both intrinsic biological programming and experience, that is, activity-dependent processes. Both before and after birth the shaping of the brain involves the mechanism of **pruning**, whereby unneeded cells and connections are eliminated. For example, brain regions important in the visual system of animals rely in part on pruning, a process that requires experience with patterned visual input (Grossman et al., 2003). In humans, pruning is thought to underlie the decrease in gray matter that occurs in adolescence. Enormous progress has been made in understanding developmental change in the structures and functioning of the human brain, including both biological and environmental influences (Steinberg, 2009).

Structure

The brain and spinal cord together form the **central nervous system**. The nerves outside the central nervous system that transmit messages to and from it compose the **peripheral nervous system**, which has two subsystems. One of these, the somatic system, involves the sensory organs and muscles and is engaged in sensing and voluntary movement. The other, the autonomic system, helps involuntary regulation of arousal and the emotions. The branches of the autonomic system either increase arousal (sympathetic system) or work to slow arousal and maintain bodily functioning (parasympathetic system). The entire nervous system communicates within itself, and is in close communication with the **endocrine system**, a collection of glands intricately involved in bodily functions through the release of hormones.

"Young man, go to your room and stay there until your cerebral cortex matures."

The brain—a wrinkled mass atop the spinal cord—has three major interconnected divisions. The **hindbrain** includes the pons, medulla, and cerebellum. Among other functions, the pons relays information and the medulla helps regulate heart function and breathing. The cerebellum is involved in movement and cognitive processing. A small area called the **midbrain** contains fibers that connect the hindbrain and upper brain regions. It also shares with the hindbrain netlike connections, the reticular activating system, which influences arousal states such as waking and sleeping. Sometimes the midbrain and hindbrain are called the brain stem (Figure 3.1).

The third major division, the **forebrain**, consists chiefly of two cerebral hemispheres, the outer surface of which is referred to as the cortex. The hemispheres are connected to each other by the corpus callosum, and each hemisphere has four lobes. The cerebral hemispheres are involved in a wide range of activities, such as sensory processing, motor control, and higher mental functioning that includes information processing, learning, and memory.

Situated below the cerebral hemispheres and deep in the brain are several subcortical structures. The thalamus is involved in processing and relaying information between the cerebral hemispheres and other parts of the central nervous system. The hypothalamus regulates basic urges such as hunger, thirst, and sexual activity. The multistructured limbic system, which includes the hippocampus and amygdala, plays a central role in memory and emotion.

Neurotransmission

Although neurons vary in size, shape, and chemistry, they all have three major parts: a multifunctional **cell body**, **dendrites**, and an **axon**. Communication between neurons occurs across a **synapse**, the small gap between the cells (the synaptic gap, or cleft). The dendrites of a neuron receive chemical messages from other neurons that result in an electric impulse being sent down the axon. When the impulse reaches the end of the axon, packets of chemicals—the **neurotransmitters**—are released. They cross the synaptic gap and are taken up by the receptor sites on the dendrites of the receiving neuron. The receiving neuron, in turn, generates new electrical impulses (Figure 3.2). Among the major neurotransmitters are dopamine, serotonin, norepinephrine, glutamate, and GABA, whose role in brain functioning is being intensely investigated.

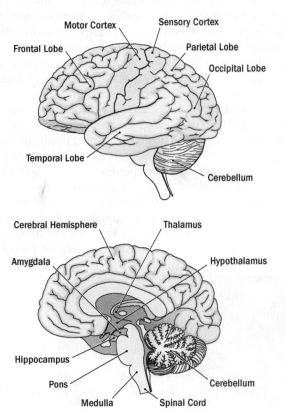

FIGURE 3.1 The outer view (top) and cross-sectional view (bottom) of the human brain.

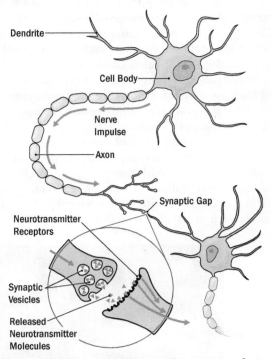

FIGURE 3.2 Messages are transmitted in a neuron from dendrites, to the cell body, to the axon, and then, through the release of neurotransmitters, across the synaptic gap to other neurons.

The complexity of communication is hard even to imagine. Neurons may make thousands of connections to other neurons, and neurotransmitters may travel multiple pathways to receptor sites. Neurotransmitters can act to excite or inhibit neurons, that is, make them more or less likely to fire an impulse. Communication is far from helter-skelter, however. Brain regions work together, forming pathways, or circuits, that are associated with different neurotransmitters and functions.

NERVOUS SYSTEM AND RISK FOR DISORDERED FUNCTIONING

The nervous system is a major aspect of the constitutional factors that influence psychological functioning and behavior. Impaired functioning can result from inheritance or from early-occurring abnormalities of the genetic processes that guide nervous system development. Thus, dysfunction can be "wired in" from the beginning. However, harm can also be attributed to events that occur during pregnancy (prenatal), at about the time of birth (perinatal), or during later development (postnatal).

Prenatal Influences

Numerous prenatal influences can put the developing child at risk. Among these are poor maternal diet and health. Research also shows that maternal stress can alter the fetal biological system, including the brain, in ways that can affect susceptibility to later psychological problems (Cicchetti, 2010; Talge, Neal, & Glover, 2007).

At one time, it was believed that the fetus was protected from most harmful substances, or **teratogens**, that might enter the mother's bloodstream. We now know that a variety of agents can be detrimental. Potentially harmful drugs include alcohol, tobacco, and thalidomide. Radiation, environmental contaminants—such as lead, mercury, and polychlorinated biphenyls (PCBs)—and many maternal diseases—such as rubella, syphilis, gonorrhea, and AIDS—also can be harmful. Teratogens are associated with malformation, low birthweight, fetal death, and functional and behavioral impairment (Hogan, 1998; Perera et al., 2011; Singer et al., 1997; Taylor & Rogers, 2005).

Teratogens are thought to interfere with brain cell formation and migration, as well as other developmental processes (Koger, Schettler, & Weiss, 2005; Lebel, Roussotte, & Sowell, 2011). Perhaps unsurprising, the amount of exposure to a teratogen makes a difference in outcome. So does the timing of exposure during gestation. In general, specific structures and systems are most sensitive to harm when they are rapidly developing (Talge et al., 2007). It is thought that the genetic endowment of the developing organism can act as a risk or protective factor regarding the effects of teratogens or maternal stress.

The adverse consequence of prenatal exposure is exemplified by **Fetal Alcohol Syndrome (FAS)**, which lies at the most severe end of a spectrum of alcohol related disorders. Suspected for many years before it was documented, FAS is characterized by abnormal brain development, retarded growth, birth defects, and neurological signs such as impaired motor skills and unusual gait (American Academy of Pediatrics, 2000; Fetal Alcohol Syndrome, 2003; Fryer et al., 2007). Specific facial abnormalities also are observed. These include small eyes, a thin upper lip, and a smooth philtrum (flattening or absence of the usual indentation under the nose) (Astley et al., 2009). MRI imagining has revealed effects on multiple regions of the brain, with the most common findings being reduced brain volume and malformations of the corpus callosum (Lebel et al., 2011). Psychological difficulties include lower intelligence, specific cognitive impairments, learning disabilities, hyperactivity, and conduct disorder. The effects of maternal alcohol use vary with several factors, including the amount of alcohol exposure, timing of exposure, mother's age and health, and fetal susceptibility. FAS symptoms can be pervasive and persistent, and many children without the full-blown syndrome are impaired with lesser alcohol-related symptoms (Chasnoff et al., 2010). Whereas educational programs and family support can be of help, the tragedy is that FAS and related conditions are completely preventable by maternal abstinence from alcohol. Extensive

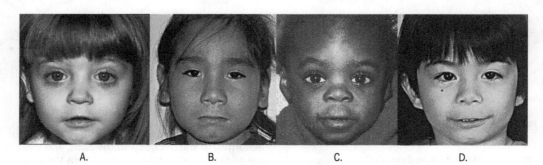

Examples of the FAS facial phenotype (small eyes, smooth philtrum, and thin upper lip) across four races: (A) Caucasian. (B) Native American. (C) African American, (D) Asian American. Copyright 2012, Susan Astley PhD, University of Washington.

work is being conducted on FAS. Notable are the efforts of the FAS Diagnostics and Prevention Network in the state of Washington that encompass diagnosis, intervention, training, education, and research.

While recognizing the adverse effects of prenatal alcohol and other teratogens, we must regard research results cautiously. It is, of course, unacceptable to conduct controlled experiments in which pregnant women are exposed to harmful agents, and the feasible research strategies make it challenging to establish causality. Because teratogens tend to cluster, it is difficult to distinguish the impact of one teratogen from another. For example, prenatal use of illicit substances is often associated with alcohol and cigarette use (Lester, Andreozzi, & Appiah, 2006). Further, prenatal substance abuse is associated with poverty, which can influence children's development both prenatally *and* during the child's subsequent development, making it difficult to establish the timing of influence (Brown et al., 2004).

These difficulties require carefully designed research. Lavigne and colleagues (2010), for example, studied the effects of maternal tobacco smoking, which has been shown to carry risk. Knowing that women who smoke are different from nonsmokers in several ways, including in parenting behaviors and psychopathology, the researchers controlled for possible effects of several variables. Smoking was then no longer associated with child behavior problems. In addition to carefully designed human studies, research on prenatal influences has benefited from work with animals, which allows intentional exposure to teratogens and the testing of causal hypotheses.

Perinatal and Postnatal Influences

Developmental risks are associated with birth. Excessive medication given to the mother, unusual delivery, and anoxia (lack of oxygen) can result in neurological problems in the newborn.

Preterm delivery (birth less than 37 weeks into gestation) and low birthweight (less than 5½ pounds) are associated with death and a variety of developmental problems, including behavioral and academic difficulties (Aarnoudse-Moens et al., 2009; Johnson et al., 2011). In the United States, the overall rate of prematurity is about 12%, with considerable variation across race/ethnic groups (MMWR, 2011). The earlier an infant is born and the lower the birthweight, the greater the risk. A relationship between low birthweight and structural brain abnormalities has been shown from infancy through adolescence (Milgrom et al., 2010; Nagy, Lagercrantz, & Hutton, 2011). Developmental outcome depends on the interplay of biological and psychosocial factors.

Postnatal effects on the nervous system can result from malnutrition, accident, illness, or exposure to chemicals. For example, air pollution may affect cognition (Suglia et al., 2008), and exposure of children to lead, even at low levels, appears to have a negative impact on brain processes involved in attention, cognition, and behavior (e.g., Marcus, Fulton, & Clarke, 2010).

When brain damage occurs in youth, a major concern is the degree to which the resulting problems can be remediated. At issue is the **plasticity**, or flexibility, of the brain to recover. There is evidence that the young, immature nervous system is relatively adept at restoring itself or at transferring functions to undamaged brain areas. Plasticity has been shown especially in vision, audition, motor, and language functioning (Rapoport & Gogtay, 2008). For example, brain damage to the language areas of the brain results in less impairment in childhood than in adulthood. On the other hand, damage to the immature brain may set up a cascade of negative effects on future brain development, and deficits may become apparent over time (Limond & Leeke, 2005). The timing, extent, severity, and region of damage, as well as the kind and amount of environmental support and therapy provided, are among the factors that influence recuperation.

GENETIC CONTEXT

Genetic contributions to behavioral development operate in complex ways. The basic genetic material is contained in all body cells. It consists of **chromosomes** containing **DNA** (deoxyribonucleic acid), functional segments of which are called **genes**. At conception, billions of chromosome combinations are possible for any one individual, and other genetic mechanisms result in even greater variability. Chromosomes may exchange genes, break and reattach to each other, and change by mutation, which is spontaneous alteration of the DNA molecule.

In some cases, early genetic processes result in structural defects in the chromosomes or a lack or excess of the 23 pairs of chromosomes found in most human cells. These "errors" may be inherited but many are new occurrences. In either case, the consequence can be dire, and can result in the death of the early-developing organism. Less severe outcomes include a variety of medical syndromes involving physical, intellectual, and psychological abnormalities. These instances are certainly of interest to mental health workers, although most individual differences relevant to psychopathology involve more subtle genetic processes, many of which implicate inheritance.

The study of genetic influences on individual differences in behavior is known as **behavior genetics**. Behavior genetics seeks to establish the extent of genetic influence on attributes, discover the genes involved, understand how the genes operate, and reveal the paths from genes to characteristics (Plomin & Davis, 2009). Evidence for genetic

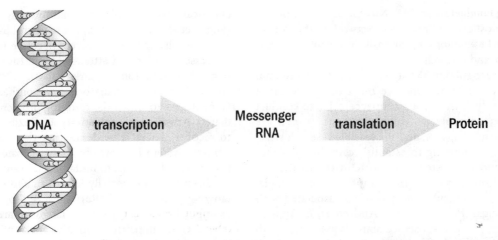

DNA   transcription   Messenger RNA   translation   Protein

FIGURE 3.3   The sequence of nucleotides (T, A, C, G) in DNA in the cell nucleus is transcribed to messenger RNA and then the information is translated for the production of proteins.

influence has been established for many attributes and psychological disorders, and progress is gradually being made in the discovery of the underlying genetic processes.

In the following discussion, we introduce some of the major methods and findings of behavior genetics with a focus on psychopathology. Keep in mind that even today, genetic influence is often misunderstood. Genes act indirectly and in complex ways to guide the biochemistry of cells (Rutter, Moffitt, & Caspi, 2006). Any single gene may affect many bodily processes and, as well, interact with other genes and environmental factors. As applied to an individual, the term *genetic code* refers to the order in which four nucleotides (adenine, thymine, guanine, and cytosine) appear in particular regions of a gene. This sequence is the basis for the **transcription**, or synthesis, of messenger

RNA, a molecule that carries the information to other parts of the cell, where it plays a role in the **translation** of the code into the manufacture of proteins (Figure 3.3).

The genetic code is critical in determining protein manufacture, and so are processes that regulate coding (Plomin & Davis, 2009). Regulation is a complex process. Indeed, only a part of each gene (the exon) codes for proteins and a larger part is engaged in regulatory mechanisms. Moreover, about half of the RNA that is transcribed is not messenger RNA but is instead involved in the activation or suppression of the protein-coding DNA. There is increasing evidence for the influence of both the internal and external environments on the processes of transcription, translation, and gene expression. (See Accent: "Epigenetics and Gene Expression".) As even this brief description makes clear, the

ACCENT
Epigenetics and Gene Expression

The term **epigenetics,** once applied to embryonic development, now usually refers to reversible modifications of the genome that help regulate gene function without changing the actual genetic code. Several epigenetic processes are being investigated. Widely studied are specific chemical changes in the DNA molecule (methylation) and in the histone proteins that are wrapped with DNA in the cell nucleus. These modifications can be passed on during usual cell duplication (mitosis) and also during the formation of the ova and sperm (meiosis), which means they can be inherited. They make it more or less likely that a gene will be expressed or suppressed.

In recent years, it has become increasingly recognized that epigenetic change can occur in response to the environment. Correlational research with humans and controlled

studies with animals indicate that exposure to food shortages, high fat diet, environmental toxins, and other experiences can result in epigenetic change, which in some cases is transmitted to subsequent generations never exposed to the conditions (Anway & Skinner, 2006; Roth & Sweatt, 2011).

Epigenetic processes hold enormous promise of helping to elucidate gene–environment interaction, developmental phenomena, and mental disorder. For example, the effects of early experience on humans may operate through epigenetic mechanisms. Indeed, it has been demonstrated in animal studies that the quality of early maternal care can induce methylation of DNA. Among the disorders being explored for epigenetic mechanisms are fetal alcohol syndrome, autism, schizophrenia, and intellectual disability (Ramsey, 2010; Rutten & Mill, 2009).

path from individual genetic endowment—the **genotype**—to the observable characteristics of the person—the **phenotype**—is indirect and incredibly intricate.

Single-Gene Inheritance

Gregor Mendel, a monk who experimented with plants in a monastery garden in Moravia in the mid-nineteenth century, is credited with discoveries crucial to modern genetics. Among Mendel's contributions are descriptions of the inheritance of certain characteristics that are influenced by a single gene. He correctly hypothesized that each parent carries two hereditary factors (later called genes), but passes on only one to the offspring. A gene can be **dominant**—its transmission by either parent leads to the display of traits associated with it—or **recessive**—only its transmission by both parents result in associated traits. Dominant and recessive patterns of inheritance, as well as the sex-linked pattern, described later in this text, are involved in the inheritance of many human attributes and disorders.

In general, the effects of single genes are quite predictable, and often result in individuals either having or not having the relevant phenotype. One way to establish single-gene influence on a specific disorder is to identify a person with the disorder—the **index case** or the **proband**—and determine whether a known pattern of single-gene inheritance runs in the family.

Multiple-Gene Inheritance: Quantitative Methods

As important as single-gene effects are, multiple genes are more often implicated in complex human characteristics, such as intelligence, and in psychological disorders. Referred to as **quantitative trait loci (QTL)**, these genes are inherited in the usual patterns, but each has relatively small influence—which combines to create a larger effect (Plomin, 2005; Plomin & Crabbe, 2000). The genes may vary in the size of their influence, interact with each other, and be interchangeable in some instances. Any one gene thus may not be sufficient or necessary for a disorder, and indeed may be carried by a person without the disorder. Multiple genes working together result in a range of phenotypes, varying from lesser to greater display of the characteristic. Multigenic influence is less predictable, or more probabilistic, than single-gene inheritance.

Research into multiple-gene influence relies on a combination of evidence from a variety of **quantitative genetic methods**. Family, twin, and adoption studies are important in establishing genetic influence on an attribute (Table 3.1). Quantitative genetic methods allow the assessment of **heritability**, the degree to which genetic influence accounts for variance in behavior among individuals in the population studied. Overall results suggest that heritability for psychological disorders or dimensions rarely exceeds 50% (Plomin & Davis, 2009). This means that substantial variation in attributes has a basis in other biological factors, the environment, or some interplay of genes with these other influences.

Quantitative genetic research also provides information on the contribution of environmental influences and how genes work together. Both shared and nonshared environmental influences are recognized. **Shared environmental influences** refer to influences that contribute to family members developing in similar ways. Examples might be exposure to intellectual stimulation, environmental toxins, or divorce, which similarly affect siblings. **Nonshared environmental influences** refer to influences that are different for children growing up in the same family and result in siblings being different from each other. Examples might be the effects of differential treatment

TABLE 3.1	Behavior Genetic Methods: Family, Twin, and Adoption Studies
Family Studies	These evaluate the likelihood of family members displaying the same or similar attributes as the index case. If genetic influence is operating, family members who are genetically closer to the index case should be more likely than those less close to display the attribute. However, this pattern is also consistent with family psychosocial influence.
Twin Studies	Comparison is made between monozygotic twins, who share 100% of their genes, and dizygotic twins, who share on average 50% of their genes. Genetic influence is suggested when monozygotic twins are more concordant (similar to each other) than dizygotic twins.
Adoption Studies	Adopted and nonadopted individuals and their families are compared in various ways. For adopted children with a disorder, the rate of a disorder can be examined in their biological families and adoptive families. Higher rate in the former indicates genetic influence.
	Another strategy starts with biological parents with a disorder and examines the rate of the disorder in their offspring who were adopted by nonrelated families. This rate can be compared to the rate in the biological children of the adoptive parents. A higher rate in the adopted children indicates genetic effects.

of siblings by the parents or of siblings having different friends or teachers. Nonshared environmental effects generally have been credited with having greater influence on psychological and behavioral outcomes, but recent research suggests that shared influences may contribute to many forms of child and adolescent problems as well (Burt, 2009; Burt et al., 2011).

Although quantitative research methods can examine a single attribute, multivariate designs focus on two or more attributes. These designs make it possible to estimate the degree to which genetic and environmental factors that influence one attribute also influence another (Plomin, Kovacs, & Haworth, 2007). For example, twin studies have shown genetic overlap in language and reading disability (Plomin & Davis, 2009). In these instances, the disorders share so-called "generalist" genes. However, nonshared genes and/or environmental influences make the disorders different from each other (Lahey et al., 2011). Overall, multivariate studies and other sophisticated quantitative analyses permit the evaluation of models of genetic transmission and of the interaction of genetic and environmental influences (e.g., Harlaar et al., 2005; Rutter et al., 2006).

Searching For Genes and Their Effects: Molecular Methods

Molecular genetics is a rapidly expanding field that seeks to discover the genes associated with a disorder, the biochemicals coded by the genes, and how these biochemicals are involved in behavior. Research with animals is critical in these endeavors; for example, gene functioning can be "knocked out" and the effects can be studied. In research with humans, the methods of linkage analysis and association analysis are central (Eley & Rijsdijk, 2005; Plomin & McGuffin, 2003).

The aim of **linkage analysis** is to reveal the location of a defective gene, that is, the specific chromosome and the place on the chromosome. This strategy takes advantage of the fact that genes on the same chromosome, especially when located close to each other, are generally transmitted together to the offspring. The strategy also takes advantage of genetic markers—segments of DNA with a known chromosome location, whose inheritance can be followed. Linkage analysis determines whether a specific disorder appears among family members in the same pattern as a genetic marker. If it does, it can be presumed that a gene that influences the disorder is located on the same chromosome as the marker and is close to the marker. Thus, the approximate genetic address for the disorder is revealed.

Association analysis searches for genes in a different way (Plomin & McGuffin, 2003). This method tests whether a particular form of a gene is associated with a trait or disorder in the population. A comparison is made between the genetic material of persons with a specific disorder and that from a matched control group. The focus may be a particular gene—called a candidate gene—that is suspect, based on theory or past research. As an example, the candidate genes DRD4 and the DAT1 have been found to be associated with attention-deficit hyperactivity disorder. Association analysis is more suitable than linkage analysis to identify multiple genes that have relatively small influence on a disorder or trait (Plomin & Davis, 2009). For some disturbances, a very large number of genes appear to be involved, indicating a sizable task for genetic investigators.

Advanced genetic technology has improved the search for genes. **Genome-wide linkage** and **genome-wide association analyses** enable researchers to scan across the genomes of individuals or large portions of the genome. These analyses, which require large samples, are able to examine millions of DNA sequences. Of critical interest are small variations in the nucleotides of the DNA molecule. In addition, these methods can examine variations in the number of duplications and deletions of segments of DNA (copy number variations). Variations in nucleotides or in copy number that appear more often in individuals with a disorder suggest a possible causal role.

Gene–Environment Interplay

Although we have already noted that genetic and environmental influences work together, it is important to examine this interplay in greater detail. Of substantial importance are gene–environment interactions and gene–environment correlations. These occurrences have been increasingly recognized in developmental processes.

Gene–environment interaction (GxE) refers to differential sensitivity to experience due to differences in genotype (Plomin & Crabbe, 2000). An example is children whose genotype carries two recessive genes for the condition called PKU (phenylketonuria). These children, but not those who carry only one of these recessive genes, develop intellectual disability when they digest certain foods. Another example is the interaction of variations in the 5-HTT gene and reactions to stressful life events (Caspi et al., 2003). That is, individuals carrying a particular form of the gene, but not another form, are more likely to react to aversive life events so that they suffer symptoms of depression in later life. Such compelling instances call attention to the influence of gene–environment interaction, and there is much current interest in this process.

Gene–environment correlation (GE) refers to genetic differences in exposure to environments. Three kinds of gene–environment correlations have been described: passive, reactive, and active (Table 3.2). *Passive* GE correlations stem from parents transmitting both their genes and gene-related rearing environments to their

TABLE 3.2	Types of Gene–Environment Correlations Demonstrating How Genetic Predisposition and Aspects of the Environment Are Linked

PASSIVE

A family's environment is influenced by the genetic predisposition of the parents. The child experiences this environment and *also* shares the genetic predisposition of the parents. This mechanism occurs at birth and is "passive" in the sense that the child has relatively little active input.
Example: *The child who has a genetic propensity for a high activity level also experiences a high-activity family environment.*

REACTIVE

A child evokes reactions from other people on the basis of her or his genetic predisposition, so that the child's genetic propensities are linked to environmental experiences.
Example: *Others react to the child's gene-based high activity level.*

ACTIVE

A child, particularly as he or she grows older, selects or creates environments on the basis of his or her genetic predisposition.
Example: *The child with a genetic propensity for high activity level engages in activities requiring high activity rather than restrained, quiet activities such as reading.*

Adapted from Plomin, 1994b.

offspring. *Reactive* GE correlations reflect both the child's genetic endowment and reactions from others to the child's gene-related characteristics. *Active* GE correlations are based on both the child's genetic endowment and the child's active selection of gene-related experiences. As children move through life, the impact of passive GE correlations may give way to the influences of reactive and active GE correlations. The importance of gene–environment correlations is that they inform us that a person's experiences are not independent of genetic influences. In fact, there is considerable evidence that genetic influences play a role in determining the experiences a person will have—and thus the risks and protections that will be encountered (Rutter & Silberg, 2002).

LEARNING AND COGNITION

Learning and cognition are inextricably intertwined with development. The abilities to learn and think not only become more advanced over time, but also facilitate other kinds of development as the child transacts with the environment. Our present discussion of this topic is introductory, and the vital role that learning and cognition play in psychopathology is woven throughout the text.

Classical Conditioning

Pavlov focused attention on the process of **classical conditioning** by demonstrations that hungry dogs, which normally salivate when food is present, could learn to salivate to neutral stimuli presented just prior to the presentation of food. In classical conditioning, the individual learns to respond to a stimulus that previously did not elicit the response. Many aspects of this kind of learning have been described. For example, once a new response (the conditioned response) is acquired, it can generalize to similar situations and can have far-reaching effects on emotion and behavior.

Historically, two early studies based on classical conditioning had a notable impact on the application of learning to problem behavior. (See Accent: "Albert and Peter: Two Historic Cases.") The now-famous case of little Albert was an early illustration of the conditioning of fear, whereas the case of Peter demonstrated that fearful responses could be eliminated by the application of classical conditioning principles.

Operant Learning

A second basic type of learning is **operant learning**, which was set forth in Thorndike's Law of Effect recognizing that a positive consequence of a behavior will strengthen the behavior while a negative consequence will weaken it. The work of B. F. Skinner was especially influential. Operant, or instrumental, conditioning emphasizes the consequences of behavior. Behavior is acquired, strengthened, weakened, maintained, eliminated, or emitted in some circumstances but not in others through reinforcement, punishment, and other learning processes (Table 3.3). Operant learning is ubiquitous; through it, knowledge is acquired and adaptive and maladaptive behaviors are shaped.

ACCENT
Albert and Peter: Two Historic Cases

As reported by Watson and Rayner (1920), Albert, an 11-month-old child, initially showed no fear reactions to a variety of objects, including a white rat. He did, however, exhibit fear when a loud sound was produced by the striking of a steel bar. Watson and Rayner attempted to condition fear of the white rat by producing the loud clanging sound each time Albert reached for the animal. After several of these pairings, Albert reacted with crying and avoidance when the rat was presented without the noise. It was later shown that the infant's fear generalized to other furry objects. Thus, it appeared that fear could be learned through classical conditioning. Interestingly, upon the completion of the study, Albert's whereabouts became a mystery until Beck, Levinson, and Irons (2009), after a lengthy effort, presented evidence to show that Albert probably lived for a short period of time on the grounds of Johns Hopkins University, the site of the study and where his mother was employed. He lived only to age 6, however; his life was cut short by illness, probably meningitis. Albert's legacy is the role he played in a demonstration that helped shape the

early development of the discipline of psychology, including raising ethical questions about conditioning fear in children.

The landmark study by Mary Cover Jones (1924) described the treatment of Peter, a boy nearing 3 years of age, who exhibited fear of furry objects. Jones first attempted to treat Peter by placing him in the presence of a rabbit, along with children who liked the rabbit and petted it. The treatment appeared to be working but was interrupted when Peter became ill for nearly 2 months. Just prior to his return to treatment, he was also frightened by a large dog. With Peter's fear back at its original level, Jones decided to treat Peter with a counterconditioning procedure, which involved allowing Peter to eat some of his favorite foods while the animal was moved progressively closer. In this way, the feared stimulus was associated with pleasantness. The procedure was apparently successful in reducing the boy's fears, and he was ultimately able to hold the animal by himself. Although this study has methodological weaknesses, it stimulated the development of treatments for psychological disturbance based on the principles of classical conditioning.

TABLE 3.3   Some Fundamental Operant Conditioning Processes

Term	Definition	Example
Positive reinforcement	A stimulus is presented following a response (*contingent* upon the response), increasing the frequency of that response.	Praise following good behavior increases the likelihood of good behavior.
Negative reinforcement	A stimulus is withdrawn contingent on a response, increasing the frequency of that response.	Removal of a mother's demands following a child's tantrum increases the likelihood of tantrums.
Extinction	A weakening of a learned response is produced when the reinforcement that followed it no longer occurs.	Parents ignore bad behavior, and it decreases.
Punishment	A response is followed by either an unpleasant stimulus or the removal of a pleasant stimulus, thereby decreasing the frequency of the response.	A parent scolds a child for hitting, and the child stops hitting; food is removed from the table after a child spits, and the spitting stops.
Generalization	A response is made to a new stimulus that is different from, but similar to, the stimulus present during learning.	A child has a stern uncle with a mustache and develops fear of all men with mustaches.
Discrimination	A stimulus comes to signal that a certain response is likely to be followed by a particular consequence.	An adult's smile indicates that a child's request is likely to be granted.
Shaping	A desired behavior that is not in the child's repertoire is taught by rewarding responses that are increasingly similar to (*successive approximations* of) the desired response.	A mute child is taught to talk by initially reinforcing any sound, then a sound somewhat like a word, and so on.

The principles of operant conditioning have been applied to a broad range of behavioral problems with regard to their etiology, maintenance, and especially treatment. The specific applications of these procedures, discussed in succeeding chapters of this book, all share the assumption that problem behavior can be changed through a learning process and that the focus of treatment should be on the consequences of behavior.

Observational Learning

Observational learning is another fundamental way through which individuals change due to experience. A wide range of behaviors can be acquired by observing others perform them—from jumping rope, to cooperation or aggression, to social skills. As with other forms of learning, observational learning can lead to both the acquisition and the removal of problem behaviors. Early work by Bandura (1997) and his colleagues, as well as subsequent research, demonstrated how problem behaviors may be acquired through the observation of a model.

Although observational learning may seem simple, it is actually quite complex. Children can learn new responses by watching a model. However, they are more likely to display the responses if they observe the model being reinforced for the behavior and are less likely to display them if they observe the model being punished. As with other kinds of basic learning processes, observational learning can generalize. A child who observes another child being scolded for shouting may become quiet in other ways (inhibition). The observation of shooting and fighting on television may lead a child to exhibit other forms of aggression, such as verbal abuse and physical roughness (disinhibition). In neither case is the exact behavior of the model imitated; rather, a class of behaviors becomes either less likely or more likely to occur because of observation of the model.

Whether imitation is specific or generalized, complex cognitive processes are required for observational learning to occur (Bandura, 1977). The child must attend to salient features of the model's behavior, organize and encode this information, and store the information in memory. The child's imitation of the model in the near or far future depends on several factors, including recall of the information and expectation that the behavior will garner desired consequences. Observational learning is central in the social learning perspective, which recognizes that what children observe influences their understanding of the world and their behavior.

Cognitive Processes

Various approaches to cognition focus on how individuals mentally process information and think about the world. Briefly put, individuals perceive their experiences, construct concepts or schemas that represent experience, store information in memory, and employ their understanding to think about and act in the world. Among the many higher order mental operations involved are perception, attention, memory, and mental manipulation of information. Different facets of cognition are implicated in many different kinds of problems—intellectual disabilities, specific learning disabilities, aggression, anxiety, and attention deficits, to name a few. The present discussion examines one cognitive viewpoint, the cognitive-behavioral perspective, which has contributed substantially to both understanding and treating problems of youth.

COGNITIVE-BEHAVIORAL PERSPECTIVE The **cognitive-behavioral perspective** incorporates cognition, emotion, behavior, and social factors (Kendall, 2006; Kendall et al., 1997b). It is assumed that behaviors are learned and maintained by the interaction of internal cognitions and emotions with external environmental events. Cognitive factors influence whether the individual pays attention to environmental events, how the person perceives events, and whether these events affect future behavior. A basic hypothesis is that maladaptive cognitions are related to maladaptive behavior. As an example of support for this assumption, maladaptive thoughts and beliefs have been found among phobic and anxious children. For instance, in test situations, children with test anxiety frequently report more off-task thoughts, more negative self-evaluations, and fewer positive self-evaluations (Ollendick & King, 1998).

Kendall and colleagues suggest one way to distinguish the complex cognitive functions that contribute to the development, maintenance, and treatment of psychopathology (Kendall, 2006; Kendall et al., 1997b). *Cognitive structures* are schema for representing information stored in memory. Constructed over time from experience, they screen new experiences and can trigger other cognitive operations. *Cognitive content* refers to the actual content of the cognitive structures stored in memory. *Cognitive processes* refer to how people perceive and interpret experience. The combination of cognitive structures, content, and processes—interacting with actual events—results in *cognitive products*. (See Accent: "Thinking About Missteps.")

Kendall (2006) also recognizes the important difference between cognitive deficiencies and cognitive distortions. *Cognitive deficiencies* refer to an absence of

ACCENT
Thinking About Missteps

Kendall (2006) offers an interesting—albeit less than pleasant—example of the workings of cognition. Consider, he suggests, the experience of what you would say to yourself if you stepped on something a dog had deposited on a lawn. For many people, a cognitive *structure* representing this event might automatically trigger a self-statement of dismay: "Oh sh--!" This statement reflects *cognitive content*. Individuals who respond thusly might then proceed to cognitively *process* the event in quite different ways, which is significant to the outcome. Some might think about social embarrassment (Did anyone see me?); others might have self-denigrating thoughts (I can't even walk!); still others might give little attention to the experience and nonchalantly walk on. Subsequent to processing the event, individuals would draw conclusions about the event; for example, they might make causal attributions. These are cognitive *products*. Some individuals might attribute the problem to themselves (I can't do anything right!); others might blame whoever allowed the dog access to the lawn (I bet the guy knew someone would step in it!). As noted by Kendall, all of these processes are involved in a person making sense of experience. It is not so much an event itself but cognitions surrounding the event that influence the emotional and behavioral consequences for the person.

thinking. The lack of forethought and planning exhibited by an impulsive child is an example of cognitive deficiency. *Cognitive distortions* are inaccurate thought processes that are dysfunctional. Depressed children viewing themselves as less capable than their peers even though others do not hold this view is an example of cognitive distortion.

Cognitive-behavioral therapy aims, through behavior-based procedures and structured sessions, to modify maladaptive cognitive structures, deficiencies, and distortions. The particular ways in which the approach both conceptualizes and treats specific disorders of youth are presented throughout this text.

SOCIOCULTURAL CONTEXT: AN OVERVIEW

Development, whether adaptive or maladaptive, occurs within and is influenced by an elaborate sociocultural context. Although there are various ways to conceptualize this context, ecological models have grown in importance during the last few decades. (Ecology refers to the interrelationship of organisms and their environments.)

Figure 3.4 presents one way in which young people are perceived to be embedded within, and interacting with, numerous domains of overlapping, transactional environmental influences or systems. The youth is surrounded by three contexts—family, community, and society/culture—each of which consists of structures, institutions, values, rules, relationships, and other aspects that influence development. The arrows in the figure emphasize the potential interactions among the systems. For example, a child both is influenced by and influences peers, who may influence and be influenced by the child's parents and the school. In general, we would expect proximal contexts—the inner

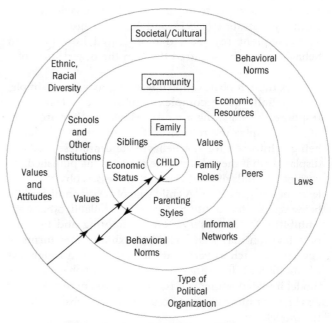

FIGURE 3.4 Youth are embedded in, and interact with, a number of contexts that are influenced by each other. *Based in part on Belsky (1980); Bronfenbrenner (1977); and Lynch & Cicchetti (1998).*

circles—to have relatively more direct impact on the child than more distal contexts. It would also be anticipated that the nature and importance of any one domain would vary with the developmental level of the individual, an obvious example being an increase in peer influence from infancy into adolescence. This model serves as a backdrop for further discussion of select aspects of sociocultural influences on development.

FAMILY CONTEXT, MALTREATMENT, AND DIVORCE

For many reasons, the family has been considered a critical force in development of the young (Masten & Shaffer, 2006). Family relationships and experiences are dominant from the first days of life and endure in some way over the lifespan of most individuals. The family plays a major role in socializing the child to behave in culturally acceptable ways and in transmitting cultural values and traditions. Families are also the conduit of food, shelter, neighborhood residence, education, and other opportunities to experience the world. The family may function as a mediator or moderator in development, and provide either risk or protection.

Although many kinds of family relationships are considered influential, including sibling and grandparent interactions, the parent–child relationship is considered dominant for most youth. It is worth noting that the family is most appropriately viewed as a complex, interacting system. Not only do parents affect children and each other, but children also influence parents in subtle and not-so-subtle ways.

Parent Roles, Styles, Psychopathology

PARENT ROLES   Historically, the influence of mothers has received much more attention than the influence of fathers by theorists and researchers, in part due to parenting roles. Mothers have been considered primary in day-to-day care, nurturance, management, and other aspects of child development—and have been more implicated in, and sometimes blamed for, the disturbances of their offspring. Nevertheless, recent decades have witnessed increased attention to fathers, including the roles fathers play in the family (Waller, 2010). In the United States, the view of fathers as breadwinners harks back to the industrial revolution (Lamb, 2010). Around the time of the Great Depression (1930), emphasis was given to the father as a model of masculinity important to sex-role development of their sons. By the 1970s, greater emphasis was given to fathers as providers of custodial care and emotional involvement. It is recognized today that fathers assume several roles—breadwinners, role models, companions, protectors, teachers, and the like—although the importance of these roles may vary across fathers and social/cultural groups (Waller, 2010). It appears, however, that fathers' emotional involvement and guidance are highly valued today.

Due perhaps in part to their different roles, fathers and mothers may interact somewhat differently with their children, but sensitive fathering predicts positive child development just as sensitive mothering does. Paternal influence on the child may be direct or may operate

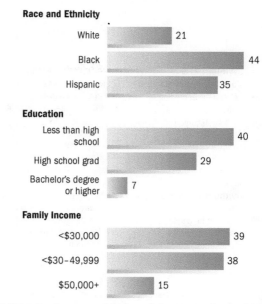

FIGURE 3.5   Percent of fathers living apart from at least one of their children 18 years or younger.   *From Livingston & Parker, Pew Research Center, 2011.*

indirectly, for instance, through interaction of the father with the mother. In any event, current understanding of parental roles and influences must consider that although today's fathers appear more involved with their children than in past times, many live apart from their children due to family divorce and other circumstances (Livingston & Parker, 2011). A recent report showed that in 1960, 11% of fathers lived apart and in 2010 this figure had risen to 27%. Race/ethnicity and social class indices are associated with the percent of fathers living apart from their children (Figure 3.5). Absent fathers largely miss sharing daily activities, but 40% in a recent survey said they are in touch with their children several times a week. On the other hand, nearly one-third reported that they talk or exchange e-mail less than once a month, and 27% said they had not seen their children at all in the previous year.

PARENTING STYLES   The quality of the relationship between parents and their offspring, beginning with early attachment, is believed to be crucial to development and adjustment. One area of influence concerns the relatively characteristic ways in which parents deal with and manage their offspring (Maccoby, 1992; Wood et al., 2003). Such **parenting styles** can be viewed as sets of attitudes, goals, and patterns of parenting practices that affect outcomes for children and adolescents.

Two major dimensions historically have been central in parent–child relationships. One dimension is degree of control, or discipline, and the other is degree of warmth,

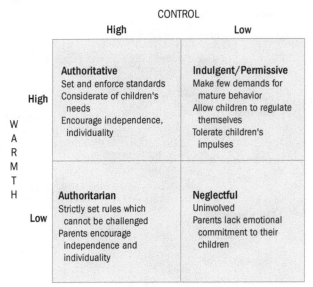

FIGURE 3.6   Patterns of parental behavior.   *Based in part on Maccoby & Martin, 1983.*

or acceptance. Figure 3.6 presents the four parenting styles according to these dimensions. Authoritative parenting generally is associated with the most favorable child attributes. Authoritative parents assume control; set rules and expect their children to abide by the rules; follow through with consequences; and are simultaneously warm, accepting, and considerate of the needs of their offspring. Their children, in turn, tend to be independent, socially responsible, prosocial, and self-confident. In contrast, children of authoritarian, indulgent/permissive, and neglectful parents are thought to be at greater risk for less-than-optimal behaviors, including aggression, withdrawal, dependence, low self-esteem, irresponsibility, antisocial behaviors, anxiety, and school problems (e.g., Steinberg et al., 1994; Wood et al., 2003).

The dimensions of control and warmth continue to be important in the study of parenting practices, and much has also been learned about the effects of parent sensitivity, parent harshness, and parent monitoring (Warren et al., 2010). In considering parental practices, it is worthwhile to bear in mind the following issues (Eisenberg et al., 2010; Eiser et al., 2005; O'Connor et al., 2006). *First,* effective parenting involves consideration of each youth's needs, as well as developmental level. Appropriate control for a 7-year-old child would not be expected to apply to a 15-year-old. *Second,* parenting practices may in part be a response to the child's characteristics as well as other relationships and circumstances in the family. *Third,* the extent to which the analysis of parenting practices holds across cultures and situations is noteworthy. For example,

authoritative parenting may be less appropriate when local cultural values differ from those of mainstream culture in the United States. And in the United States authoritarian parenting may protect children who are reared in disadvantaged environments.

PARENT PSYCHOPATHOLOGY   The relationship between parent psychopathology and child adjustment has received considerable attention. Perhaps unsurprising, parent disturbance is a risk factor. Maternal depression, anxiety, and substance abuse are among several disorders linked to problems in offspring (Boris, 2009; Tompson et al., 2010). Although research on the association of father and child psychopathology lagged until more recently, it is clear that paternal problems also carry risk for children and adolescents (Flouri, 2010). Paternal antisocial behavior, substance abuse, ADHD, and depression are among the disorders implicated in child adjustment.

In general, both genetic transmission and environmental factors underlie the association of parent and offspring psychopathology. Children may inherit a genetic predisposition that increases risk and/or be affected by a risky family environment. As we have seen in our previous discussion of gene–environment correlation, genetic influence transmitted from parent to child may go hand in hand with the kind of family environment set up by the parent. But even when the child does not inherit vulnerability genes, parent psychopathology may negatively influence parenting, cause family stress, and otherwise create a less-than-optimal rearing environment.

Maltreatment

Maltreatment of youth is an extreme failure to provide adequate parenting. It can also be viewed as a failure of the larger social system to provide conditions that foster adequate parenting. Such undue failure to protect the child and/or provide positive aspects of parenting might be expected to adversely affect a wide array of developmental processes and increase the risk for a variety of problematic outcomes.

Although child maltreatment has probably existed since the beginning of civilization, recent concern is usually dated to the early 1960s (Cicchetti & Olsen, 1990). Especially influential was an article by pediatrician C. Henry Kempe and his colleagues, in which the term *battered child syndrome* was coined (Kempe et al., 1962). Their efforts were stimulated by alarm at the large number of children at pediatric clinics with nonaccidental injuries. By 1970, all 50 states had mandated the reporting of child abuse. In 1974 the U.S. Congress passed the Child Abuse Prevention and Treatment Act (Public Law 93–247) to give national focus to the problem and to prescribe actions that

TABLE 3.4   Definitions of the Major Forms of Maltreatment

1. **Physical abuse:** An act of commission by a caregiver that results or is likely to result in physical harm, including death of a child. Examples include kicking, biting, shaking, stabbing, or punching a child. Spanking is usually considered a disciplinary action but can be classified as abusive if the child is bruised or injured.
2. **Sexual abuse:** An act of commission, including intrusion or penetration, molestation with genital contact, or other forms of sexual acts in which children are used to provide sexual gratification for the perpetrator. This type of abuse also includes acts such as sexual exploitation and child pornography.
3. **Neglect:** An act of omission by a parent or caregiver that involves a refusal to provide, or a delay in providing, health care; failure to provide basic needs such as food, clothing, shelter, affection, and attention; inadequate supervision; or abandonment. This failure to act holds true for both physical and emotional neglect.
4. **Emotional abuse:** An act of commission or omission that includes rejecting, isolating, terrorizing, ignoring, or corrupting a child. Examples of emotional abuse are confinement; verbal abuse; withholding sleep, food, or shelter; exposing a child to domestic violence; allowing a child to engage in substance abuse or criminal activity; refusing to provide psychological care; and other inattention that results in harm or potential harm to a child. The abuse must be sustained and repetitive.

From English, 1998.

the states should take. Since the late 1970s, the problem has become both a major public concern and the focus of increased research and professional attention (Cicchetti & Manly, 2001).

Unfortunately, the magnitude of the problem is significant. According to a report issued by the U.S. Department of Health and Human Services (DHSS) (2011), in 2009 there were over 700,000 children who were victims of abuse and neglect. In addition, in that year an estimated 1,770 children died due to abuse or neglect.

DEFINING MALTREATMENT   When most people hear the widely used term **child abuse**, they assume that it refers to physical assault and serious injury. However, the general legal definition of child abuse or maltreatment that has evolved over several decades includes both the commission of injuries and acts of omission, that is, failure to

care for and protect (National Institute of Mental Health, 1977). The Keeping Children and Families Safe Act of 2003 defines child abuse and neglect as at a minimum:

> any recent act or failure to act on the part of a parent or caretaker which results in death, serious physical or emotional harm, sexual abuse or exploitation, or an act or failure to act which presents an imminent risk of serious harm (DHHS, 2010).

The term **maltreatment** thus refers to both abuse and neglect. Four major types of maltreatment are typically described in the literature: physical abuse, sexual abuse, neglect, and emotional abuse (psychological maltreatment). The definitions of these are presented in Table 3.4. Figure 3.7 shows the percentage of types of maltreatment in the United States in 2009 (DHHS, 2010).

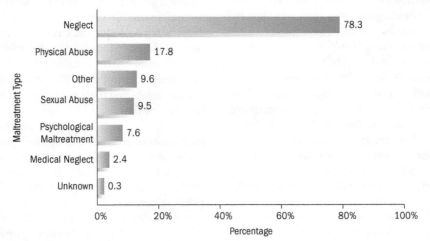

FIGURE 3.7   Child maltreatment cases 2009 by type. Note more than one type of maltreatment may be substantiated per child. Therefore percentages total more than 100%. *From U.S. Department of Health & Human Services, Child Maltreatment 2009 (Washington, DC, 2010).*

The 9.6% of "other" types of maltreatment indicated in Figure 3.7 includes events such as abandonment, threats of harm, and congenital drug addiction.

It is probably easier to detect physical abuse than other forms of maltreatment. However, the nature and severity of injuries can vary considerably. In some cases, injuries may be intentionally inflicted, but more often they result from extreme forms of discipline and physical punishment. Moreover, whereas we can define physical abuse as a separate category from other forms of maltreatment, children likely experience it in conjunction with emotional abuse and/or neglect.

In general, sexual abuse refers to sexual experiences that occur between youth and older persons or to the sexual exploitation of the young, such as in pornographic film. Sexual abuse of girls is more common than that of boys, and cases of sexual abuse can vary with factors such as age of onset of abuse, the identity of the primary perpetrator, the number of perpetrators, the severity of the abuse, and whether the abuse was accompanied by physical violence or threats (Finkelhor, 1994; Wolfe, 2006).

Neglect, the most common form of maltreatment, refers to failure to provide for a child's basic needs. Defining a parent–child relationship as neglectful, especially in less extreme instances, clearly requires sensitivity to family and cultural values and to considerations of economic and social conditions. Neglect can involve a failure to meet physical needs—such as the need for health care or physical shelter—or it can involve abandonment or inadequate supervision. Neglect may also take the form of not meeting the youngster's educational needs by allowing repeated truancy or not attending to special education needs. The child's emotional needs may also be neglected. Emotional neglect is difficult to define, however. It may include failure to ensure adequate psychological care or failure to protect the youngster from witnessing harmful situations involving violence or substance use.

The definition of emotional (or psychological) maltreatment is probably the most difficult to agree on and the most controversial. Different standards for appropriate parenting practices and for desired outcomes are particularly at issue when psychological maltreatment is considered (Azar, Ferraro, & Breton, 1998; McGee & Wolfe, 1991). Emotional maltreatment is defined as persistent and extreme actions or neglect that thwart the child's basic emotional needs and that are damaging to the behavioral, cognitive, affective, or physical functioning of the child (Brassard, Hart, & Hardy, 2000; Cicchetti & Lynch, 1995). Emotional maltreatment can be seen both as a distinct entity and as part of all abuse and neglect (Binggeli, Hart, & Brassard, 2001).

FACTORS CONTRIBUTING TO MALTREATMENT

Conceptualizations of maltreatment recognize the complex, multiple, and interrelated determinants of the problem (Azar & Wolfe, 2006; Belsky, 1993; Cicchetti, Toth, & Maughan, 2000; Margolin et al., 2009). The following general factors are recognized as contributing to maltreatment:

- Characteristics of the abuser
- Characteristics of the child
- Parenting practices
- Parent–child interactional processes
- Social/cultural influences

The latter category includes both the immediate social environment (e.g., family, employment, extended family, social networks) and the larger social/cultural context (e.g., poverty, societal tolerance for violence). It is recognized that maltreatment most often occurs in the context of family, social, and community deprivation and exposure to multiple sources of violence. Many influences have been examined for their contribution to maltreatment. Here we highlight only some of the findings.

Parents are the perpetrators of abuse in approximately 80% of cases (DHHS, 2010). Parents who began their families at a younger age, many in their teens, are often the perpetrators (Connelly & Straus, 1992; Dixon, Hamilton-Giachritsis, & Browne, 2005). This finding may be understood, at least in part, within the context of parenting skills. Abusive parents exhibit a variety of deficits in parenting (Azar & Wolfe, 2006). They tend to engage in fewer positive interactions with their child and less interaction overall, to use more coercive and negative discipline techniques, and to use fewer explanations when disciplining their child. These parents also may exhibit negative attitudes toward parenting, limited child-rearing knowledge, inappropriate expectations regarding developmentally suitable behavior, lower tolerance for common demanding behavior such as infant crying, and misattributions of the child's motivation for misbehaving.

Several other characteristics of abusive parents have been noted, including difficulty in managing stress, difficulty in inhibiting their own impulsive behavior, social isolation from family and friends, more emotional symptoms and mood changes, and more physical health problems. High rates of substance abuse and partner violence in the home have also been reported (Wekerle et al., 2007).

It has been found that abusive parents are more likely to have experienced abuse (Kaufman & Zigler, 1987). However, it is generally agreed that the majority of maltreated children do not become abusive parents. What, then, is the link between generations? This pathway is clearly the result of a complex interaction of risk and protective factors that include characteristics of the individual, family, and social environment. For example, Dixon and colleagues (Dixon et al., 2005) found that intergenerational continuity of maltreatment was increased by the presence of poor parenting styles, parent age under 21 years, parent history of psychopathology, and residence with a violent adult. Other information also supports the increased risk of maltreatment associated with residing in a home where there is domestic violence (DHHS, 2010).

In addition to looking at characteristics of abusing parents, professionals have asked whether certain attributes of children increase the likelihood of their being the target of maltreatment. Youngest children are the most vulnerable. From birth to 1 year of age appears to be a period of high risk for maltreatment and about one-third of victims are younger than 4 years of age (DHHS, 2010). In addition, research suggests that children and adolescents with disabilities (e.g. physical disability, visual or hearing impairment, intellectual disability, learning disability) are at high risk. Also those youth who display behavioral or emotional problems or interpersonal styles that adversely interact with caregiver characteristics and stress are at high risk (Bonner et al., 1992; DHHS, 2010; Wolfe, 2006). For example, a child's early feeding problems and irritability may place increased strain on a highly stressed parent who has limited parenting abilities. This may lead the caregiver to withdraw and become neglectful. Caregiver neglect may, in turn, lead to increases in dependent behavior and demands by the child (Wekerle & Wolfe, 2003).

Maltreatment also is influenced by the larger social context. A relationship between socioeconomic disadvantage and abuse, and particularly neglect, has been described (English, 1998). It is important to recognize, however, that the majority of families who experience disadvantage do not maltreat their offspring. Although it is hard to isolate the specific causal factors, reduced resources, stress, and other problems associated with socioeconomic disadvantage put the family and child at increased risk. The relationship of poverty and maltreatment may be due to other factors as well (Azar & Bober, 1999). For example, poor interpersonal and problem-solving skills in parents may lead both to economic disadvantage and to problematic parenting, including maltreatment. Cultural factors, too, may play a role. Korbin and colleagues (1998), for instance, found that impoverishment had a lesser impact on maltreatment in African American neighborhoods than in European American neighborhoods. This difference seemed to be mediated by the perceived quality of social connectedness found in the two kinds of neighborhoods. A sense of community, resources, and extended family may serve as protective factors against maltreatment.

CONSEQUENCES OF MALTREATMENT Basic developmental processes are disrupted by maltreatment. The social and emotional support necessary for children's successful adaptations is diminished, interfering with many areas of development. Furthermore, these youngsters may have fewer opportunities for positive experiences that may reduce the risk associated with maltreatment (Azar & Wolfe, 2006; Haskett et al., 2006; Salzinger et al., 2001; Toth et al., 2011).

Some evidence suggests that early maltreatment may be associated with neurobiological outcomes, such as dysregulation of the stress regulating system (the limbic-hypothalamic-pituitary-adrenocortical system), alteration of neurotransmitter systems, and alteration of structural and functional regions of the brain (Bremner, 2006; Gordis et al., 2010; Gunnar & Vazquez, 2006; Margolin & Gordis, 2000). The degree to which these neurobiological outcomes occur seems to be related to a number of factors (De Bellis, 2001; McCrory, De Brito, & Viding, 2010), including individual genetic makeup, age of onset of abuse, duration of abuse, and the presence of trauma-related psychological symptoms. There may also be gender differences in adverse brain development outcomes, with both boys and girls being affected but males being more vulnerable.

The effects of maltreatment are a telling example of how adverse environments may alter basic biological functioning. The neurobiological outcomes may, in turn, contribute to cognitive and psychosocial difficulties. De Bellis's (2001) developmental traumatology model describes how neurobiological outcomes may underlie the variety of negative outcomes associated with abuse and neglect. In this model, maltreatment and its effects are viewed within a broad ecological-transactional model that recognizes the effects of many other variables (Figure 3.8). For instance, the neurobiological changes resulting from the stress of maltreatment may be positively modified by subsequent supportive caregiving environments.

Given the neurobiological outcomes and the failure of parenting involved, it is unsurprising that maltreatment can result in a variety of undesirable outcomes. Children can manifest health-related difficulties (e.g., physical injury, sexually transmitted diseases) and appreciable impairments in all early developmental domains and various areas of later adjustment. Indeed, problems may be serious enough to meet the diagnostic criteria for a variety of psychological disorders (Azar & Wolfe, 2006; English, 1998; Kearney et al., 2010; Wolfe, Rawana, & Chiodo, 2006; Yates, 2004). The impact may also be evident at different developmental stages from infancy through adolescence and into adulthood (Shaffer, Yates, & Egeland, 2009; Springer et al., 2007;

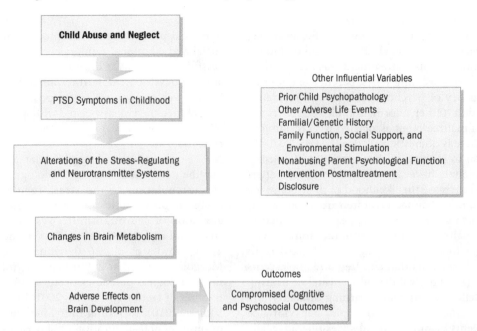

FIGURE 3.8   A developmental traumatology model of biological stress systems and brain maturation in maltreated children. In this model compromised neurocognitive and psychosocial outcomes are understood to be a result of adverse brain development. PTSD = posttraumatic stress disorder.   *Adapted from De Bellis, 2001.*

Wolfe, 2006). Although this is certainly a disheartening picture, it should be acknowledged that some maltreated children develop as competent individuals and that youths can be resilient even in the face of maltreatment (Cicchetti, 2010; Haskett et al., 2006).

In general, then, the impact of maltreatment is best viewed as undermining normal developmental processes affecting areas such as attachment, cognitive functioning, self-concept, social relationships, and emotional regulation (Azar & Bober, 1999; Haskett et al., 2006; Wekerle & Wolfe, 2003). Outcomes of maltreatment are likely to be affected by many factors including the type and severity of maltreatment, developmental timing, characteristics of the youngster's family, peer relationships, and neighborhood (Finkelhor, Ormrod, & Turner, 2007; Haskett et al., 2006; Jaffee et al., 2007; Manly et al., 2001). For example, research suggests that physical abuse places children at particular risk for the development of externalizing and antisocial behavior problems (Jaffee et al., 2004; Lau & Weisz, 2003). Given the combination of factors that causes maltreatment, effective prevention and intervention need to address many contexts—individual, familial, community, cultural, and societal—and thus include multiple components (Azar & Wolfe, 2006; Trickett et al., 1998; Wolfe, 2006). As we gain more precise understanding of maltreatment, we are better able to shape interventions that are most effective and that fit specific needs (DHHS, 2010).

Changes in Family Structure: Divorce

In research about the family, it has often been assumed that families consist of parents and children together in the home. In fact, families have always been more varied. Even so, by most standards, dramatic changes have occurred in family structure during the last few decades in the United States and similar countries. Children are living in a variety of family types (e.g., nuclear/two-parent, single-parent, adoptive, blended, extended). Notably, the percentage of single-parent families has increased markedly during the last several decades (Figure 3.9). Single-parent families make up approximately 30% of all families with children, about one-sixth of these being headed by fathers (U.S. Census Bureau, 2010). Most youths living in nontraditional homes do well, but as a group they are at risk for a variety of difficulties.

That many marriages end in divorce is well documented. The divorce rate in the United States increased dramatically in the 1960s and 1970s, reaching a peak about 1980. This trend has leveled off and perhaps declined in recent years (National Center for Health Statistics, 2011). Yet, it is estimated that about half of first marriages and about 60% of second marriages end in divorce (Amato & Irving, 2006; Sutton, 2003). Over one million youngsters a year may experience parental divorce. However compelling, this statistic does not fully capture the problem. Many children experience considerable

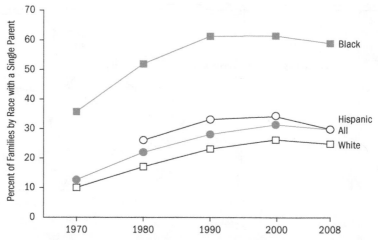

FIGURE 3.9 Percentage of families with a single parent by race and Hispanic origin from 1970 to 2008. *Adapted from U.S. Census Bureau,* **Statistical Abstract of the United States: 1998, 2003** *(118th and 123rd eds. and Current Population Reports, 2008), Washington, DC: 1996, 2003, 2010.*

stress prior to the divorce. Some go through periodic separation and discord in families in which divorce petitions are filed and withdrawn. Others experience more than one divorce. Moreover, divorce and subsequent reconstitution of the family are not static events, but rather are a series of family transitions that modify the lives of children (Barber & Demo, 2006; Hetherington & Stanley-Hagan, 1999; Wallerstein, 1991).

HEIGHTENED RISK   Children and adolescents from divorced and remarried families are at increased risk for developing adjustment problems (Barber & Demo, 2006; Grych & Fincham, 1999; Hetherington & Kelly, 2002; Potter, 2010; Reifman et al., 2001). Those who experience multiple divorces are at greater risk. Difficulties occur in many areas of functioning: academic, social, emotional, and behavioral.

There is, nonetheless, considerable variability in outcome (Fine & Harvey, 2006). Indeed, the vast majority of children from divorced or remarried families function in the normal range, and some youths experience positive outcomes (Barber & Demo, 2006). Through divorce, some move out of highly conflicted and violent situations. A portion, particularly girls, may move into less stressful and more supportive circumstances. They may actually experience opportunities for the development of exceptional competencies (Amato & Keith, 1991; Fine & Harvey, 2006; Hetherington & Kelly, 2002; Hetherington & Stanley-Hagan, 1999). However, these findings should not lead us to ignore the clinical significance of the adjustment problems experienced by some young people. An important question then is what accounts for increased risk for youths

who develop adjustment difficulties and for the resilience of those who do not.

PREDICTORS OF ADJUSTMENT   When considering the influence of family divorce, it is important to note that any deviation from traditional family structure has often been viewed as problematic. This perspective is, in general, not well supported. Of course, two parental figures in a good partnership generally have much to offer the child. However, the effects of family composition/parent absence are not simple and are likely modified by factors such as parent adjustment, quality of family relationships, the child's age and gender, and the availability of both parents to the child (Barber & Demo, 2006; Braver, Ellman, & Fabricius, 2003; Jaffee et al., 2003). Furthermore, there are cultural and ethnic differences in how family is defined. The presence of extended family in the household, for example, is more likely among African American families than among European American families, as is an informal network of kin and friends available to function in parental roles (Emery & Kitzmann, 1995).

Hetherington and her colleagues (Hetherington, Bridges, & Insabella, 1998) suggest a model, based on a set of interrelated risks, to explain the links between divorce/ remarriage and a child's adjustment. As Figure 3.10 shows, adjustment to marital transitions encompasses complex interactions among a large number of influences. To add to the complexity, while the process of family transitions is occurring, children and the developmental tasks they face are also changing (O'Connor, 2003). In addition, ethnic and cultural influences are salient in this process. With such complexities in mind, we turn to an examination of

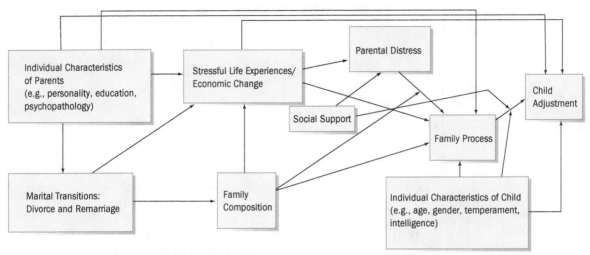

FIGURE 3.10 A transactional model of the predictors of children's adjustment following divorce and remarriage. *From Hetherington, Bridges, & Insabella, 1998.*

some of the influences likely to affect the adjustment of children and adolescents to marital transitions.

A central aspect of the divorce process is the interaction among family members, particularly the ongoing relationship between the two parents. Indeed, the degree of marital discord prior to the divorce is considered to be a primary influence on the adjustment of children in the family. High levels of marital conflict—particularly marital violence—are problematic (Barber & Demo, 2006; Cummings et al., 2009; Jaffee, Poisson, & Cunningham, 2001; Kelly, 2000). Following divorce, the ongoing relationship between the parents, between each parent or stepparent and the child, and between each parent and potential stepparents or significant others contributes to complicated family transitions that affect the child (Hakvoort et al., 2011; Hetherington et al., 1998).

Preexisting individual characteristics also contribute to a child's adjustment. Individual attributes of adults (e.g., antisocial behavior, depression) place some parents at risk for marital discord and multiple marital transitions. These and similar attributes also impact the adult's ability to parent effectively. Individual characteristics of the youth may also contribute to adjustment. Children with an easy temperament may be better able to cope with the disruptions associated with marital transitions. Those with a difficult temperament may be more likely to elicit negative responses from their stressed parents and to have greater difficulty adapting to parental negativity and marital transitions. They may be less capable of eliciting the support of other people around them (Hetherington et al., 1998). Also, a child's prior level of behavioral problems is likely to play a role in adjustment. Indeed, when prior level of

adjustment is taken into account, differences between children due to marital transitions are greatly reduced.

The relationship between parental characteristics, child characteristics, and the ongoing divorce process is, however, complex. For example, the child's prior level of adjustment may have resulted in part from the marital friction that contributed to the divorce. In turn, the challenges of parenting a difficult child may have contributed to the marital difficulty and divorce. Furthermore, the parental characteristics that played a role in the divorce, as well as child behavior problems, may be influenced by common genetic contributions (Jockin, McGue, & Lykken, 1996; McGue & Lykken, 1992). Shared genes may contribute, for example, to the likelihood of parent antisocial behavior (a risk for divorce) and acting-out problems in children and adolescents.

Gender also may affect adjustment to marital transitions. Earlier reports suggested that boys were more affected by divorce and girls by remarriage. More recent studies report less pronounced and less consistent gender differences. Improvements in research methodology may in part be responsible for this finding. So may changes in custody and visitation arrangements, which have possibly increased father involvement. The effect of gender is probably complex, depending on the aspect of adjustment studied, gender differences in patterns of development, pubertal timing, and other such factors (Ellis, 2004; Hetherington & Stanley-Hagan, 1999). Clearly, the role that individual characteristics play in adjustment to divorce is complicated.

Another factor that may be involved in children's adjustment is ethnic differences. For example, African American youth may benefit more from living in stepfamilies and from greater authoritarian parenting than white adolescents. It has been suggested that improved income, supervision, and role models provided by some stepfathers may be more advantageous to African American children because they are more likely to live in risky neighborhoods with fewer resources and greater crime and violence (Anderson & Mayes, 2010; Barber & Demo, 2006; McLanahan & Sandefur, 1994).

Finally, the divorce process may include changes in family circumstances that, although peripheral to the reasons for the marital dissolution, affect how well the family does (Amato, 2000). For example, custodial mothers and their children often experience economic decline after divorce, with many living below the poverty level. A lower standard of living and economic instability are associated with conditions that increase risk for youth, such as living in more dangerous neighborhoods

and attending less adequate schools. Divorce may result in other stressful family life changes, such as more frequent moves and changes in schools. Much of the impact of these divorce-related circumstances on child functioning may be mediated by their effect on family processes in general and on the stability of the family environment in particular (Sun & Li, 2011; Them, Israel, Ivanova, & Chalmers, 2003). (See Accent: "Family Stability.") Economic stress and other changes can contribute to dysfunctional family relations (e.g., conflict) and interfere with effective parenting (Hetherington et al., 1998). Within this context, however, it is important to remember that positive experiences such as a stable family environment, good parent–child communication, and supportive relationships with another adult may serve as protective factors for youngsters experiencing divorce-related events (Doyle et al., 2003; Menning, 2002; Velez et al., 2011).

ACCENT
Family Stability

Family stability is an aspect of the family environment that often emerges in the discussion of children's development and adjustment, with higher levels of stability associated with better outcomes. What is meant by "family stability"? Often, it is conceptualized in terms of the stability of family structure—for example, maintaining a household with a nuclear family structure as compared to separation or divorce. While this view is reasonable, it is also possible to consider a broader notion of family stability.

In an attempt to offer a broader conceptualization, Israel and colleagues (Israel, Roderick, & Ivanova, 2002; Ivanova & Israel, 2006; Sheppard, Malatras, & Israel, 2010) have suggested a model of family stability that encompasses two components. The first component, *global family stability*, addresses changes in family structure, such as those that may be associated with divorce, as well as family life changes described as accompanying events such as divorce or parental death (Hetherington & Stanley-Hagan, 1999; Tremblay & Israel, 1998). Family life changes may include, for example, changes in residence, schools, and household composition (who lives in the child's home). The term *global* is used to describe these structural and family life changes as they are deemed more distal from the youth's daily experiences and are less easily controlled by the child or parent.

The second component, *molecular family stability*, refers to the predictability and consistency of family activities and routines. These may include daily routines such as those that occur at bed or mealtimes; activities that children engage

in with the family on a regular basis, such as weekend activities or religious observances; or activities that do not involve family members but are arranged and supported by the family, such as extracurricular activities or time with friends. It is expected that differences exist in how families achieve stability—one family may have regular mealtime routines while another regularly participates in joint outings and activities—and also that families may create stability in different ways over time, perhaps adjusting to the developmental level of the child. Moreover, molecular family stability is conceptualized as a parenting skill and as a component of stability that is more proximal to the youth's daily experiences and more accessible to intervention. Thus, professionals may be able to work with families to develop predictable and regular family activities and routines that may help create a sense of stability within the context of a family environment that may be otherwise disrupted. Molecular family stability has, indeed, been demonstrated to be associated with adjustment (Israel et al., 2002; Ivanova & Israel, 2006; Sokolowski & Israel, 2008).

The creation of a stable family environment is likely to be important to all children and families and may be particularly so for those undergoing multiple transitions. Such transitions occur frequently for families experiencing separation, divorce, and remarriage, for example. Other life circumstances also may present challenges. One example suggested by recent circumstances is the transitions and challenges faced by U.S. military families experiencing deployment of a parent. The model of family stability offered by Israel and

(continued)

(continued)

colleagues may be one way of helping to understand the potential impact of military deployment on families and children (Sheppard, Malatras, & Israel, 2010). Military deployment may, for example, be associated with the family life changes that are part of the concept of global family stability (e.g., changes of residence or household residents). On the other hand, aspects of military life for some families may protect against such instability (e.g. military housing on a base with other military families).

The military deployment process can be viewed as having several transitions for families—preparing for deployment, deployment, sustaining the family while the parent is away, preparation for redeployment home, and the period following the return home. These transitions may be repeated if the service member has multiple deployments away from home. The multiple phases of the deployment cycle may present challenges with regard to maintaining typical family activities and routines (molecular family stability). This may be the case during actual deployment and also with regard to the challenges that the service member/parent and family may face after the service member returns home. The ability of the parents to create stability in the family environment may be one factor influencing the adjustment of children in families facing the challenges associated with military deployment.

PEER INFLUENCES

From infancy onward, individuals relate socially to each other and peer relations are likely to grow in influence. The peer group provides a unique developmental context that influences immediate and long-term social and cognitive growth (Dunn, 1996; Parker et al., 2006). Areas in which peer interactions may play a unique and/or essential role include the development of sociability, empathy, cooperation, and morality; negotiation of conflict and competition; control of aggression; and socialization of sexuality and gender roles. Peer relations may ensure the development of social competence in the face of adversity, thereby preventing or reducing the likelihood of disorder (Cicchetti, Toth, & Bush, 1988; Sroufe et al., 2000). They may also be associated with the presence of disorder.

Individual child characteristics—emotional, cognitive, and social—enter into the development of peer relationships (Hay, Payne, & Chadwick, 2004). So also do other social relationships. Early attachment experiences in the family are thought to be related to peer relationships and social competence (Rudolph & Asher, 2000). Parental hostility, coercion, lack of involvement, and authoritarian/restrictive styles are associated with child aggression and peer rejection (Dekovic & Janssens, 1992; Dishion, 1990). Teachers also can play a role in shaping peers' attitudes toward one another (White & Kistner, 1992), and neighborhood characteristics can influence the likelihood that a youngster will affiliate with deviant peers (Brody et al., 2001).

The multifaceted nature of peer relationships has been increasingly appreciated (Bukowski & Adams, 2005). Early research primarily focused on overall peer status, that is, on whether the peer group accepted, rejected, or neglected the target child. Additional interest has been directed at particular relationships, such as that between bullies and their victims (Perren & Alsaker, 2006). The nature and role of friendship also has received attention (Mikami, 2010). A close friendship is viewed as a mutual relationship that, among other positive aspects, can serve as protection against risk factors, including the risk of being excluded, rejected, or neglected by classmates (Bukowski, Laursen, & Hoza, 2010; Criss et al., 2002). Unsurprisingly, children tend to select friends who have similar interests or are similarly adjusted. Whereas this can strengthen positive attitudes and behaviors, it also can magnify and encourage psychological difficulties and deviant behavior (Mikami, 2010; Parker et al., 2006).

An extreme instance of such negative outcome was described in the analyses of the relationship of two students who engaged in a murderous rampage at Columbine High School (Cullen, 2009; Larkin, 2007). Although complex circumstances undoubtedly led to the event, it was suggested that the adolescent boys desperately needed each other, reinforced each other, and could not have carried out the attack alone.

Peer interactions provide a unique and essential opportunity to develop certain skills.

One of the most commonly cited reasons for interest in peer relationships is their association with later adjustment. Children who experience peer rejection, who are withdrawn and socially isolated, or who associate with deviant peers are at risk for later difficulties (Bukowski et al., 2010; Laird et al., 2001; Rubin et al., 2003; van Lier & Koot, 2010). Indeed, difficult peer relationships often underlie children's referrals to mental health centers and are reported among children with a variety of disorders (Parker et al., 2006). There is a bidirectional association of peer difficulties with adjustment problems. Not only do peer difficulties contribute to the development of behavioral disorders, but the presence of disorder also adversely affects peer relationships (Achenbach & Rescorla, 2001).

How is the association of early peer problems with later psychological disturbances to be understood? It is possible that in some instances the relationship is not causal, that some unidentified general tendency independently causes both peer and other difficulties (Parker et al., 2006). When a causal link is suspect, one hypothesis is that a child's initial tendencies and social experiences enter into a negative transaction with peers that leads the child to behave in ways that perpetuate peer rejection and other difficulties.

COMMUNITY AND SOCIETAL CONTEXTS

School Influences

The school is one of the most central contexts in children's lives. Although a primary function of the school is to teach intellectual skills and knowledge, schools are expected to guide additional aspects of development (Pianta, 2006). Schools help socialize youth to societal norms and values, shape motivation to achieve, and contribute to socioemotional growth and mental health. School influences operate through distal factors such as district resources and educational policy and proximal influences such as classroom climate, instruction, and social relationships.

The structure and organization of schools can be more or less conducive to healthy development. Consider, for example, that today's educational system often requires children to move into middle schools in early adolescence. Thus, at a time of notable biological and other social change, children must also adapt to new school demands. These frequently include more unsupervised time, less parent–teacher communication, and exposure to a wider assortment of peers (Stormshak et al., 2011). The transition to middle school can be a risky time.

Social relationships are a crucial component of school life. Schools are the locale for important peer interactions—for supportive friendships, rejection and bullying, and social cliques. Among the many factors that might affect these interactions is variations in school settings (Pianta, 2006). For example, school size, division of students into educational tracts, and opportunity for informal social contact all might have influence.

Student–teacher relationships are often critical to young people, many of whom remember in adulthood their most favored or "hated" teachers. Such relationships may play a role in positive normative development, operate as a risk factor, or serve as protection against risk (O'Connor, Dearing, & Collins, 2011). Perhaps unsurprising, high-quality relationships are associated with positive child outcomes, whereas conflicted relationships are linked with unfavorable behavioral and academic outcomes (Crosnoe et al., 2010; Ray, 2007). Relationship stress and student perception of teacher behavior are important factors. For example, in a study that followed students from sixth through eighth grade, student perception of increasing teacher support appeared causally related to student increases in self-esteem and decreases in depression (Reddy, Rhodes, & Mulhall, 2003).

Successful completion of school is widely viewed as contributing to positive development, but success is not realized by many youths. Low socioeconomic status, academic failure, behavioral problems, and lack of family support are among the factors associated with dropping out of school or repeating a grade level (Mattison, 2000). Unfortunately, large inequities often exist between schools attended by students from upper class backgrounds and schools attended by children of lower social class and minority backgrounds. Of course, schools do not have control over all the determinants of student success, but there is consensus that schools have some responsibility to both children's cognitive development and their social and emotional growth (Durlak et al., 2011). Some schools have incorporated social and emotional learning programs aimed at preventing problems such as academic failure and substance abuse, enhancing social competence, and providing students the opportunity to contribute to their social environments.

Socioeconomic Status and Poverty

Socioeconomic status (SES), or social class, is indexed by factors such as income, educational achievement, and occupational level, which correlate with one another. Virtually all societies are stratified according to social class, and social class is marked by differences in many facets of life—environmental conditions, social interactions, values, attitudes, expectations, and opportunities.

Although good adjustment and psychological problems occur in all social classes, the relatively higher risk associated with lower social class has led to an emphasis on the effects of poverty. Young people who live in families of low SES experience increased risk for

TABLE 3.5	Percentage of Youth Under 18 Living in Poverty, 2010
All Youth	22.0
White, Non-Hispanic	12.4
Asian	13.6
Hispanic	35.0
Black	38.2

U.S. Bureau of the Census, *Income, Poverty, and Health Insurance Coverage in the United States: 2010.* Report P60, n. 238, Table B-2, pp. 68–73.

negative outcomes such as developmental delay, learning disabilities, school failure, and behavioral and psychological problems (van Oort et al., 2011). Unfortunately, a long-observed pattern in the United States is higher poverty rates in young people than in other age groups. In 2010, 22 percent of youths under age 18 lived in families below the poverty line (U.S. Bureau of the Census, 2010). Rates varied considerably by race and Hispanic origin (Table 3.5). In addition, living in poverty was disproportionately high in single female-headed households (32%) compared to married-couple households (6.2%).

In discussing the impact of family income on children's achievements and verbal ability, Duncan and Brooks-Gunn (2000) pointed to the probable importance of poverty's *persistence, depth,* and *timing.* Poverty that persists over time, is severe, and occurs early in the child's life has the most negative effects.

In addition, exposure to multiple risks that accumulate over time is related to developmental outcome (Evans, 2004). Figure 3.11 shows a striking difference in the number of cumulative risks experienced by poor and middle-class children in the third to fifth grade. Poor children are more likely to have exposure to unsafe levels of lead, pesticides, and air pollution; inadequate water supplies; and poor sanitation. They are more likely to live in crowded homes with structural defects, rodent infestation, and other safety hazards.

Family processes undoubtedly play a crucial role in mediating the influence of poverty. Although family genetics may be implicated, additional influences are involved (Evans, 2004; Pungello et al., 2010). Children growing up in poor homes often lack learning resources such as books, appropriate toys, and computers. Parenting in low SES homes tends to be harsher and less sensitive and responsive (Burchinal et al., 2006; Evans, 2004) compared with that in middle-class homes, where parents give relatively more time, effort, and verbal attention to their young children. In addition, the stress of being poor may increase the likelihood of parent–child conflict, and it is likely that family separation and lower marital quality are also linked to poverty (Evans, 2004).

The many-faceted effects of poverty influence development through varied pathways. In a recent study, Hanson and colleagues (2011) focused on how environmental variations might shape brain development in humans. They reasoned that living in poverty often involves heightened stress and reduced environmental stimulation—both of which have been shown to affect neural functioning.

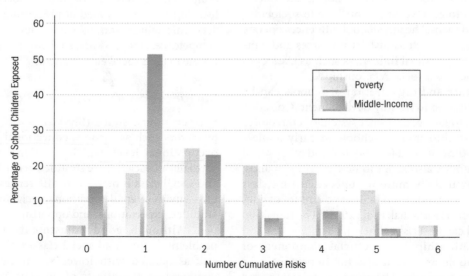

FIGURE 3.11 Percentage of poor and nonpoor school children exposed to cumulative physical and psychosocial environmental risks. *From Evans, 2004.*

Drawing on a database of youth 4 to 18 years of age, the investigators showed a direct association between poverty and the volume of gray matter of the hippocampus, a brain area affected by stress that is linked to cognition and behavioral regulation. Although the study does not definitely establish a causal pathway—and many other aspects of poverty may affect the brain—it suggests one mechanism through which the environment may put poor youth at risk for numerous negative outcomes.

Neighborhoods

All neighborhood/community contexts influence children and adolescents, but investigations have focused on poor urban neighborhoods. Current interest in neighborhood influences arose, in part, because poor families became increasingly clustered in urban areas during the 1970s and 1980s (Leventhal & Brooks-Gunn, 2000). Many of these communities are characterized by public housing and by a disproportionate number of families from minority ethnic/racial background. Although it would be a mistake to assume that such neighborhoods are identical, all too often they provide a developmental context that is far from optimal.

Separating neighborhood effects from family and other influences is difficult, but some evidence exists for the independent influence of neighborhoods. Leventhal and Brooks-Gunn (2000) reviewed findings regarding child and adolescent outcomes for academic skills, mental health, and sexuality. The most consistent finding was that living in an affluent neighborhood provided substantial benefits to youth with regard to school readiness and achievement, especially for European American youngsters. The best evidence for effects on mental health was for an association between low-SES neighborhoods and acting-out/aggressive behavior. In general, the strength of community influence was in the small to moderate range.

Drawing on research findings and theoretical explanations, Leventhal and Brooks-Gunn discussed a conceptualization of the mechanisms or pathways of community influences (Figure 3.12).

- One pathway is *community resources*, which includes opportunities for learning offered in schools, libraries, and museums; quality day care; medical services; and employment.
- The second pathway focuses on *relationships*, especially within the family. It includes parents' personal characteristics; parenting styles and supervision; support networks for parents; and physical and organizational features of the home such as cleanliness, safety, and regular schedules and routines.

Very poor neighborhoods generally provide a context that is less than optimal for the development of youth.

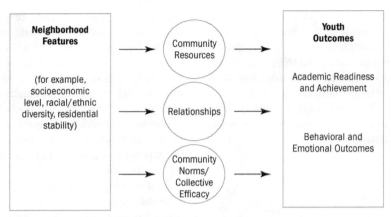

FIGURE 3.12 Three proposed mechanisms or pathways linking community characteristics to outcomes for youth. *Based on Leventhal & Brooks-Gunn, 2000.*

- The third, *community norms/collective efficacy*, refers to the extent to which communities are organized to maintain behavioral norms and order. To varying degrees formal institutions or informal networks monitor or supervise the behavior of individuals and watch for physical risks that might exist. The neighborhood scrutinizes child and adolescent behavior, the availability of illegal substances, and violence, crime, and similar activities.

Of these pathways, influence was clearest for norms/collective efficacy and relationships. Regarding the latter, family functioning interfaces with characteristics of the community and can act as a risk or protective influence. For example, neighborhood disadvantage is linked to children's affiliations with deviant peers, and harsh or inconsistent parenting appears to encourage this association whereas nurturant or involved parenting discourages it (Brody et al., 2001). Or to take another example, parents who reside in more dangerous neighborhoods tend to be more restrictive. They may cope with adverse conditions by withdrawing from them and intensely monitoring their children. Indeed, parental monitoring can provide a protective shield (Buckner, Mezzacappa, & Beardslee, 2003; Luthar & Goldstein, 2004).

Assuming that even small effects of neighborhood characteristics impact many youths, numerous ameliorative efforts have been aimed at communities. A comprehensive approach was the federally sponsored Moving to Opportunity for Fair Housing Demonstration (MTO). Volunteer families were randomly selected to receive the opportunity to move from very poor to higher SES neighborhoods and then were compared with families that were left behind. Although there were some positive effects of this intervention, many questions were raised (Popkin, Leventhal, & Weismann, 2008). Indeed, the results of this intervention and similar programs directed to the psychological well-being of youth are complex, and some researchers are more optimistic than others regarding community approaches to improve the lives of children (Ludwig & Mayer, 2006; Tolani & Brooks-Gunn, 2005).

Culture, Ethnicity, and Minority Status

All of the contexts we have already discussed operate within a still larger cultural context consisting of a society's beliefs and values, social structures, social roles and norms, and ways of "doing business."

Influences stemming from cultural factors may have broad positive or negative effects. For example, certain practices in the United States may inadvertently foster conduct problems in youth. A case in point concerns the exposure of youth to high levels of aggressive and violent content in media. Decades of research indicate that observing such television, film, and video games can contribute to aggressive behavior, desensitization to violence, and decreased prosocial behavior in children (American Academy of Pediatrics, 2009; Anderson et al., 2010).

Risk stemming from the cultural context may be particularly high for individuals whose ethnic/racial background is other than mainstream. Indigenous groups deal with unique historical issues and matters of **acculturation**, that is, modifications in culture resulting from cultures coming into contact with each other. In many countries, indigenous groups have higher rates of poverty, psychopathology, health problems, educational disadvantages, and the like. In the United States, the poverty rate for Native Americans is high (DeNavas-Walt et al., 2006), and this population has high rates of birth, unemployment, suicide, alcoholism, and death relative to the general population and in some cases to other minority groups (Spicer & Sarche, 2006; Stiffman et al., 2007). Adolescents of American Indian background have high rates of substance abuse, disruptive behavior, and incarceration in the juvenile justice system (Hawkins, Cummins, & Marlatt, 2004; Novins et al., 1999; Novins, Beals, & Mitchell, 2001; Storck et al., 2009).

In the United States, ethnic/racial diversity has grown enormously in the last few decades, and Hispanic children made up 23% of the child population in 2010 (Federal Interagency Forum on Child and Family Statistics, 2011). Children of immigrants—whether foreign or U.S. born—require special consideration. In 2008, almost 25% of youth age 17 and under lived with an immigrant parent (Tienda & Haskins, 2011). Parents may lack proficiency in the English language and be economically limited. Moreover, they may be undocumented, a situation that threatens cultural integration and opportunity. Although the national background of these families varies greatly, immigrant children generally are at risk for poverty, low educational attainment, and behavior problems.

Immigrant and minority groups also commonly face prejudice and discrimination, and devaluation by others may be perceived relatively early in life. Prejudice and discrimination not only reduces opportunity but also has other influences. For example, negative prejudgment and stereotyping of African American students may adversely affect their academic performance (Cohen et al., 2009; Steele, 1997; Winerman, 2011). Discrimination and perceived racism have been associated with aggression, antisocial acts, and depression in African American children and adolescents (Nyborg & Curry, 2003). Perhaps

unsurprising, among the variables that may protect these youths from some negative outcomes is the degree to which they identify with their ethnic/racial group and are reared to be proud of their heritage (Anderson & Mayes, 2010; Caughty et al., 2002; DuBois et al., 2002).

Some investigators emphasize the need to consider the effects of the unique experiences of youth of minority ethnic and racial background on development (Anderson & Mayes, 2010; Garcia-Coll et al., 1996; Spencer et al., 2006). It is suggested that developmental models for nonmainstream youth include the possible influences of prejudice, discrimination, acculturation, racial socialization and identity, and cultural values. (We would add to this the need for similar consideration of other youth who, due to handicapping conditions or sexual orientation, experience more than a usual share of devaluation and prejudice.)

Finally, we should note the disadvantages often experienced by minority groups in seeking and receiving mental and other health services (e.g., Spicer & Sarche, 2006; Sue, 2003). In addition to inaccessible or inadequate services in needy communities, professionals in multicultural settings may lack the awareness of cultural differences and the skills and openness to others required for productive work (Fowers & Davidow, 2006; Pedersen & Pope, 2010). To facilitate cultural competence, the American Psychological Association (2003) has published guidelines for training, practice, and other aspects of serving multicultural communities. There is little doubt that the need is substantial.

Overview/Looking Back

BRAIN AND NERVOUS SYSTEM

- Early brain development depends on the interaction of biological programming and experience.
- The various parts of the nervous system and brain function as a whole, with specific areas playing primary roles in specific functions. Communication occurs through complex neurotransmission among neurons.

NERVOUS SYSTEM AND RISK FOR DISORDERED FUNCTIONING

- Damage to the brain can result from genetic, prenatal, perinatal, and postnatal events. Numerous prenatal risks have been identified, and their effects depend on several variables.
- The capacity of young people to recover from brain damage is not easy to predict.

GENETIC CONTEXT

- The basic genetic material consists of chromosomal DNA residing in all body cells. Transcription and translation of the genetic code is affected by the internal and external environment. Epigenetic modifications of DNA play a role in gene expression.
- Genetic influences on development occur through single-gene and multiple-gene processes. Such influences are studied through a variety of quantitative (family, twin, and adoption studies) and molecular (linkage and association) analyses.
- Hereditary influences, as well as shared and non-shared environmental effects, have been demonstrated for many disorders. Less is known about the specific genes involved and how they operate.
- The collaboration of genetic and environmental influences is shown in gene–environment interactions and gene–environment correlations.

LEARNING AND COGNITION

- Learning and cognition are critical to development. Classical conditioning, operant learning, observational learning, and higher order cognitive processes play major roles in the origins and treatment of psychological disorders.

SOCIOCULTURAL CONTEXT: AN OVERVIEW

- The sociocultural context of development consists of overlapping, transactional domains of influences that include family, peers, community, societal, and cultural influences.

FAMILY CONTEXT, MALTREATMENT, AND DIVORCE

- Family interaction is complex, with fathers and mothers performing overlapping but not identical roles. Studies of parenting styles suggest that an authoritative, warm style generally fosters favorable development. Parent psychopathology is a developmental risk factor.
- Today's analyses of family life include the maltreatment of children and adolescents, the many factors that contribute to it, and its varied effects.
- Divorce is best conceptualized as a complex process of family transition that heightens developmental risk. Its effects depend on multiple variables.

PEER INFLUENCES

- Peers influence each other in many, perhaps unique, ways through friendship and other relationships. Poor peer relationships in childhood are associated with problematic behavior in childhood and later life.

COMMUNITY AND SOCIETAL CONTEXTS

- School resources, culture, and relationships are a central context for the development of youth. Schools teach intellectual skills and knowledge as well as many aspects of social development.
- Low socioeconomic status and the poverty associated with it disadvantage children in many areas of development. Poor children are exposed to multiple physical and psychosocial risks. The effects of poverty are mediated in part by family factors.
- Young people are influenced by the neighborhoods in which they reside. Neighborhood influences operate through community resources, family relationships, and community norms/efficacy.
- The broad cultural context influences development through family and community variables. Indigenous, minority, and immigrant groups often experience the risks of poverty, prejudice, and discrimination, as well as inadequate mental health care.

Key Terms

neurons *37*
myelin *38*
pruning *38*
central nervous system *38*
peripheral nervous system *38*
endocrine system *38*
hindbrain, midbrain, forebrain *39*
cell body, dendrites, axons *39*
synapse *39*
neurotransmitters *39*
teratogens *40*
Fetal Alcohol Syndrome (FAS) *40*
brain plasticity *41*
chromosomes *41*

DNA *41*
genes *41*
behavior genetics *41*
transcription *42*
translation *42*
epigenetics *42*
genotype, phenotype *43*
dominant genes, recessive genes *43*
index case, proband *43*
quantitative trait loci (QTL) *43*
quantitative genetic methods *43*
heritability *43*
shared and nonshared environmental
    influences *43*

linkage analysis *44*
association analysis *44*
genome-wide linkage and association
    analyses *44*
gene–environment interaction *44*
gene–environment correlation *44*
classical conditioning *45*
operant learning *45*
observational learning *47*
cognitive-behavioral perspective *47*
parenting styles *49*
child abuse *51*
child maltreatment *51*
acculturation *62*

Research: Its Role and Methods

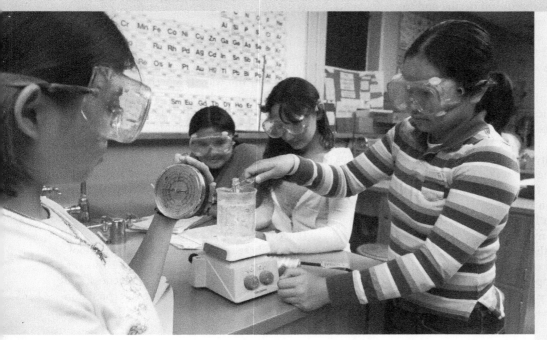

As a discipline, psychology is committed to the view that science can provide the most complete and valid information about human functioning, behavior, and development. Although common sense tells us much about behavior, science aims to go beyond common sense to systematic, reliable, and accurate knowledge. The general purpose of science is to describe and explain phenomena.

The word *science* comes from the Latin word for "knowledge," or "to know," but refers to knowledge gained by particular methods of inquiry. We might know the world from reading literature or listening to music, but we would not consider knowledge gained in this way to be scientific knowledge. Scientific understanding derives from systematic formulation of a problem, observation and collection of data, and interpretation of findings by what is considered acceptable procedures. Despite some misgivings—and even warnings of danger—about the scientific study of humans, we have come to value what science can tell us about ourselves.

FUNDAMENTALS OF RESEARCH

The numerous major questions relevant to developmental psychopathology are progressively being addressed by scientific investigations (Figure 4.1). Of course, these general questions are transformed into countless more specific queries. To answer them, it is sometimes necessary only to describe phenomena. We can count the number of cases of particular disorders and can describe the symptoms of disorders. At other times, it is necessary to determine the conditions under which a phenomenon occurs and to discover its relationship to other variables. Frequently, the quest is to determine cause-and-effect relationships.

We previously have noted that researchers rarely, if ever, simply pose and try to answer questions in an intellectual vacuum. They are guided by already established information, concepts, perspectives, or theories, and by their own inclinations. Theoretical concepts and assumptions guide research goals, choice of variables, procedures, analyses, and conclusions. But there is always at least a touch of subjectivity and creativity in the posing of research questions and in deciding how best to seek answers.

It is common to try to test specific hypotheses derived from theoretical notions. **Hypothesis testing** is valuable because it tends to build knowledge systematically rather than haphazardly. Any one investigation rarely proves that a hypothesis is either correct or incorrect; instead, it provides evidence for or against the hypothesis. In turn, a hypothesis that is supported serves as evidence for the accuracy and explanatory power of the underlying theory. An unsupported hypothesis, in contrast, serves to disprove, limit, or redirect the theory. Together, observations and theory advance scientific understanding.

Just as researchers ask a variety of questions and pose hypotheses, they work in a variety of settings, ranging from the natural environments of the home or community to controlled laboratory settings. Different strategies and designs are used, depending on the purposes of the research—and on ethics and practicality, too. In all cases, however, careful consideration must be given to selection of participants, observation and measurement, reliability, and validity.

Selection of Participants

For good reason, research reports require the description of the participants and the way they were selected. This information is important in judging the adequacy of investigations and interpretations of the findings.

Investigations of development and abnormal psychology are typically interested in drawing general conclusions about a population of interest. Because it is rarely possible to study an entire population, the next best choice is to examine a representative sample. Representativeness is best achieved by **random selection** of participants from the population, that is, by choosing each participant by chance. Even this goal may not be feasible; for example, it is impossible to randomly select a sample from *all* preschoolers or *all* children with intellectual disability. However, efforts can be made to approximate representativeness, and the extent to which it is achieved affects the interpretation of the research findings.

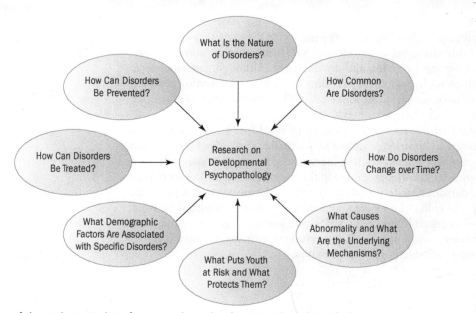

FIGURE 4.1   Some of the major questions for research on developmental psychopathology.

In the study of psychological disorders, research participants are often drawn from clinics, hospitals, and other facilities serving youths with problems. Such clinic populations are unlikely to represent the entire population of young people with disorders. They may exclude children whose families cannot afford treatment or for whom help was not sought due to denial, shame, fear, or high levels of adult tolerance. Clinic populations can also *over*represent youths who experience more serious symptoms or who act out or otherwise disturb people. Such **selection bias** has important implications. We have seen, for instance, how working with clinic populations rather than general populations, or boys rather than girls, might affect how disorders are defined. The characteristics of research participants and the way that participants are chosen are critical in planning and drawing conclusions from research investigations.

Observation and Measurement

At the heart of scientific endeavors are observation and measurement, both of which can be challenging to behavioral scientists. Whereas it is relatively simple to observe and measure overt action, thought and emotion are more

Direct observation allows the researcher systematically to measure behavior as it is occurring.

elusive. In any case, the scientist must provide an **operational definition** of the behavior or concept being studied. That is, some observable and measurable operation must be selected to define the behavior or concept. Aggression might be operationalized as the frequency with which children actually shove or threaten their playmates; depression might be operationalized by a score on a scale that measures adolescent reports of feelings of sadness and hopelessness.

In the attempt to tap all sources of information, behavioral scientists make many kinds of observations and measurements. They directly observe overt behavior in naturalistic or laboratory settings; employ standardized tests; record physiological functioning of the brain, sensory organs, or heart; ask people to report or rate their own behavior, feelings, and thoughts; and collect the reports of others about the subject of investigation. Increasingly, highly technical genetic methods to study chromosomes and neuroscience procedures to image the brain have become additional sources of information.

Whatever the measure, it should be valid, that is, be an accurate indicator of the attribute of interest. There are several kinds of **validity** (Table 4.1). For instance, construct validity exists if a questionnaire about anxiety gets at what is accepted as the underlying concept or meaning of anxiety. The observations also must be **reliable**, that is, the data would be similar, or consistent, if measurements were taken again under similar circumstances. Numerous considerations and practices are required to ensure objective, accurate, and dependable observation and measurement.

Consider, for example, a study that used naturalistic observation to investigate childhood depression (Dadds et al., 1992). **Naturalistic observation** consists of directly observing individuals in their "real world," at times simply to describe naturally occurring behavior and at other times to answer specific questions or to test hypotheses. In this study, a comparison was made of parent–child interaction in families that had a child who was referred to a clinic for either depression, conduct disorder, or depression/conduct disorder. The families, and a group of nonclinic families, were videotaped during a typical evening meal. The videotaped behavior was then independently coded by observers who were trained to use a carefully constructed observation system, the Family Observation Schedule. This instrument provided 20 categories for parent and child behaviors—among them smiling, frowning, praising, and complaining. The reliability of measurement was then examined to determine whether the taped behaviors were coded in a consistent way by the independent coders. Such **interobserver reliability** is known to be generally higher when the observation schedule is optimally specific and clear. In this study, interobserver reliability was checked by an additional observer, who coded one-third of the tapes. The

TABLE 4.1	Some Types of Validity Pertaining to Measurement
Content Validity	Refers to whether the content of a measure corresponds to the content of the attribute of interest
Construct Validity	Refers to whether a measure corresponds to the construct (concept) underlying the attribute of interest
Face Validity	Refers to whether a measure, on its surface, seems appropriate to the attribute of interest
Concurrent Validity	Refers to whether the scores on a measure correlate with scores on another acceptable measure of the attribute of interest
Predictive Validity	Refers to whether the scores on a measure predict later scores on another acceptable measure of the attribute of interest or other outcomes of interest

investigation also benefited from the observers' having no knowledge of each family's clinical status, that is, the problems displayed by the children. Nor did the observers know the hypotheses being tested. Such **observer "blindness"** decreased the chance that the observers would be biased by such information. All of these features—a well-constructed observational measure, observer training, a check on the reliability of the coding, and blind observation—addressed important standards for measurement in research.

Reliability of Research Results

The concepts of reliability and validity apply to the results of research as well. The findings of a research study are assumed to report a "truth" about the world. The scientific method assumes that truth repeats itself, given identical or similar conditions; consequently, it can be observed again by others. Replication of findings is thus an important component of scientific work. If the same truth is not reported under similar conditions, the original finding is considered unreliable or inconsistent, and it remains questionable. The need for reliability, or repeatability, of results places a burden on researchers to be clear and concise as they conceptualize and conduct their study, and to communicate their findings so that others may replicate and judge their work.

Validity of Research Results

Whereas reliability refers to the consistency or repeatability of results, validity refers to the correctness, soundness, or appropriateness of scientific findings. The validity of research findings is a complex matter; in general, validity must be judged in terms of the purpose of the research and the way the results are used. Of major concern are internal and external validity.

The purpose of much research is to offer an explanation for phenomena. **Internal validity** refers to the extent to which the explanation is judged to be correct or sound. Many factors pose a threat to internal validity,

depending on the methods and research designs employed (Shadish, Cook, & Campbell, 2002). Given the purpose of the research, as well as practical and ethical considerations, investigators do well to select methods and conduct research so as to maximize internal validity. In general, the extent to which alternative explanations can be ruled out determines the certainty that the offered explanation is valid.

External validity addresses generalizability, the extent to which the results of an investigation apply to other populations and situations. Although researchers are virtually always interested in generalizability, it cannot be assumed. Findings based on European American children in the United States may or may not hold for children of Mexican American ancestry; findings from research with animals may or may not apply to humans; findings from highly controlled studies conducted in controlled settings may or may not hold in real world settings. The question of generalizability is rarely, if ever, completely answered but evidence for external validity increases as various populations, settings, and methods are used.

BASIC METHODS OF RESEARCH

There are many ways to approach and conduct research. Investigations may focus on a single person or on one or more groups of individuals. Researchers may exert comparatively more or less control over the procedures and settings. The time frame of the study may be relatively brief, or it may last several years. Nevertheless, all research methods have strengths and weaknesses, and the choice of one over another reasonably depends on the purpose and other aspects of the investigation. Moreover, conclusions are impressive when they are based on a convergence of findings from investigations that employ different methods.

There is no single way to conceptualize or categorize research methods. One useful distinction is between **descriptive**, or **nonexperimental**, and **experimental**

**"Miss Rogers, Sally Green. Is it true my son's research project is
'the effect of too much television on a typical ten-year-old?'"**

methods. The general purpose of descriptive methods is to portray a phenomenon of interest. Observations are made and analyzed in a variety of ways. The attributes and life of a single child may be described; the behaviors of groups of adolescents who vary in some way may be compared. Frequently the relationship of two or more variables of interest is described. Nonexperimental methods are widely employed, and they may involve sophisticated correlational and multivariate statistical analysis to study complex relationships.

Experimental studies can be viewed as randomized or quasi-experimental (Shadish et al., 2002). **Randomized experiments** are highly esteemed because they come closest to establishing cause-and-effect relationships. They require that a manipulation (A) be made, followed by an examination of the effects (B). A causal relationship exists when variation in A is related to variation in B and alternative explanations of this relationship are unlikely. Crucial to ruling out alternative explanations are random assignment of participants to the manipulation, as well as experimenter control of the procedures and extraneous factors.

Quasi-experimental studies are similar to randomized experiments in that they include a manipulation and various controls. However, participants are not randomly assigned to the manipulation. This difference reduces the confidence with which causal explanations can be made. Take, for example, a hypothetical study in which families of diagnosed children volunteer for parent training and subsequently are compared to similar families who do not receive the treatment. If the training group performed better, can it be concluded that the training is effective? Perhaps the volunteer parents had better skills to begin with or were more motivated than the no-treatment parents to perform well. In fact, we cannot rule out the possibility that something besides treatment caused the effect. There are ways, however, to strengthen the argument for causation. Had each group been measured before and then after the manipulation, and had the training group made greater pre-post gains than the no-treatment group, we would have evidence for the effectiveness of the training.

With the distinctions in mind between descriptive and experimental methods, we next examine four basic research methods common in the study of developmental psychopathology.

Case Studies

The **case study** is a descriptive, nonexperimental method commonly used in investigations of psychological disorders. It focuses on an individual—describing the background, present and past life circumstances, functioning, and characteristics of the person. Case studies can tell us something about the nature, course, correlates, outcomes, and possible etiology of psychological problems. In addition, they can bridge the gap that all too often exists between clinical practice and research endeavors (Kazdin, 1998).

The following is an abridged version of a case report of a boy who was considered at-risk for a serious and quite rare disorder, childhood schizophrenia.

MAX

Risk for Childhood Schizophrenia

Max was a 7-year-old boy when he was first referred for psychiatric evaluation by his school principal.... Long-standing problems such as severe rage outbursts, loss of control, aggressive behavior, and paranoid ideation had reached crisis proportions.

Max was the product of an uncomplicated pregnancy and delivery, the only child of a professional couple. There was a history of "mental illness" in the paternal grandmother and two great-aunts. Max's early development was characterized by "passivity."...He used a bottle until age three. Verbal development was good; he spoke full sentences at 1 year. Toilet training was reportedly difficult....

Max was clumsy and had difficulty manipulating toys, his tricycle, and his shoelaces. When he began nursery school, he was constantly in trouble with other children....Max "developed a passion for animals."...At age five Max acquired an imaginary companion, "Casper—the man in the wall" who was ever present. Max insisted that he could see him, although no one else could. Casper's voice, he said, often told him he was a bad boy.

Max's behavior was so unmanageable during the first and second grade he was rarely able to remain in the classroom....Max described animals fighting and killing people....The psychologists noted a schizoid quality because of the numerous references to people from outer space, ghosts, and martians, as well as the total absence of human subjects....Despite his high intelligence (IQ 130), Max was experiencing the world as hostile and dangerous. The psychologist considered Max to be at great risk for schizophrenia, paranoid type.

Cantor & Kestenbaum, 1986, pp. 627–628.

The case study continues, telling of Max's enrollment in special schools and his psychotherapy. Parental involvement, rewards for appropriate behavior, and medication were all employed. Despite some quite disturbed behaviors, improvement occurred, and Max eventually was able to attend a university engineering program.

The primary goal of this case report was to illustrate an approach to treating children with severe disturbances and to emphasize that treatment must be tailored to each child's needs. Case studies can meet such a goal, for one of their strengths is the power to illustrate (Kazdin, 2011). They can richly describe phenomena, even phenomena so rare that they would be difficult to study in other ways. They can provide hypotheses to be tested by other methods as well as demonstrations that run counter to acceptable ideas. The weaknesses of the case study concern reliability and validity. The descriptions of life events often go back in time, raising questions about their reliability and accuracy. When case studies go beyond description to interpretations, there are few guidelines to judge the validity of the interpretations. Moreover, since only one person is examined, the findings cannot be generalized confidently to others. Despite weaknesses, however, the descriptive case study has a long history in the study of psychopathology and continues to make contributions.

Correlational Studies

Correlational studies are nonexperimental investigations that describe the relations between two or more factors without exposing the participants to a manipulation. They may be conducted in the natural environment or in the laboratory in a variety of ways, and can involve many variables in complex research designs. Statistical procedures are employed to determine the strength and nature of the relationship.

Here we only examine the basic aspects of the method. In its simplest form, the question asked is, Are factors X and Y related, and, if so, in what direction are they related, and how strongly? After the researchers select an appropriate sample, they obtain a measure of variable X and of variable Y from each participant. Statistical analysis of these two sets of scores is then performed. In this case, the Pearson product–moment coefficient, r, could be computed.

The value of Pearson r, which always ranges between +1.00 and −1.00, indicates the direction and the strength of the relationship.[1] Direction is indicated by the sign of the coefficient. A positive sign (+) means that high scores on the X variable tend to be associated with high scores on the Y variable, and that low scores on X tend to be related to low scores on Y. This relationship is referred to as a **positive correlation** (or direct correlation). A negative

[1]p................lcu-
lat................eral
pr................tion
co................

sign (−) indicates that high scores on X tend to be related to low scores on Y, and that low scores on X tend to be related to high scores on Y. This is a **negative correlation** (also called an indirect, or inverse, correlation).

The strength or magnitude of a correlation is reflected in the absolute value of the coefficient. The strongest relationship is expressed by an r of +1.00 or −1.00. As the absolute value of the coefficient value decreases, the relationship becomes weaker. A coefficient of .00 indicates no relationship at all and the scores on one variable tell us nothing about the scores on the other variable.

Suppose that an investigator explored the association of secure attachment in infancy with childhood adjustment. For each participant, the researcher obtained a measure of secure attachment in infancy and a measure of adjustment in childhood. The hypothetical data appear in Table 4.2. Pearson r for the data was calculated, and its value is +0.82. How would this finding be interpreted? The positive sign indicates that children who scored higher on secure attachment tended to score higher on later adjustment. The magnitude of the coefficient indicates that the relationship is strong (since 1.00 is a perfect positive relationship).

When a correlation exists, knowing a person's score on one variable allows us to predict the person's performance on the other variable. It does not, however, permit us automatically to draw a cause-and-effect conclusion. One problem is that of directionality. If a positive correlation were found between parenting behaviors and child adjustment, it is possible that parenting caused child maladjustment or, alternatively, that child maladjustment caused parents to behave in a certain way. The direction of causation is unclear. The problem can sometimes be solved by examining the nature of the variables. For example, if a correlation between insecure early attachment and later childhood problems exists, it is impossible for later adjustment to cause early insecure attachment.

However, even when directionality is not a problem, a correlation may be caused by one or more unknown variables. Perhaps children's social competence is responsible for both the quality of their early attachment and their later social adjustment. To evaluate this possibility, social competence could be measured and a statistical technique could be applied to partial out, or hold constant, its effects. To the extent that the correlation remains, it is not explained by social competence. As helpful as partialing techniques are in ruling out the effects of other possible causal factors, however, an investigator can never be sure that all possible causative variables have been evaluated.

Despite the aforementioned weaknesses, research designs that employ correlational analysis are of considerable value in abnormal psychology. They are useful when an investigator wants to determine whether any relationships exist among variables before advancing specific hypotheses. They can be invaluable when the variable of interest cannot be manipulated—due to ethical or other considerations—such as maltreatment, social class, drug use, or genetic differences.

In addition, techniques such as structural modeling, too complicated to discuss here, permit researchers to explore complex relationships and to have more confidence in their hypotheses about cause and effect. The researcher hypothesizes specific patterns of relationships among the variables being studied. Statistical techniques are then employed to determine how well the collected data fit the model that the researcher specified. Examples of the use of this and other methods based on correlations to address questions about psychological disturbance appear throughout this text. (See Accent: "Experiments of Nature.")

TABLE 4.2	Data from a Hypothetical Study of Infant Secure Attachment and Childhood Adjustment. The Pearson r Value is +0.82, Which Indicates a Strong Positive Relationship between the Variables	
Child	Variable X Attachment Score	Variable Y Childhood Adjustment Score
Daniel	2	5
Nicky	3	4
Sara	4	12
Beth	7	16
Jessica	9	10
Alia	11	22
Brent	13	18

ACCENT
Experiments of Nature

Despite their name, **experiments of nature** are not experiments in the usual sense of this word and do not involve a manipulation. The condition of interest may not even be manipulable by researchers. These studies examine naturally occurring events and contrast a condition of interest with a condition in a comparison group (Shadish et al., 2002). Correlational and other statistical analyses may be used to evaluate the relationships of interest.

A noteworthy example is the investigation of the effects of institutionalization on children's development. There is a lengthy history of comparing children who reside in orphanages with children who had been adopted from orphanages or had never been institutionalized. These studies indicate an adverse effect of institutionalization on intellectual development, physical health, and an array of

behaviors (MacLean, 2003; Merz & McCall, 2011). Lengthy institutionalization and poor quality of orphanages are associated with worse outcomes (Rutter, 2005; Smyke et al., 2007).

Like all research methods, experiments of nature have weaknesses and strengths (O'Connor, 2003). Regarding the effects of institutionalization, a major weakness is the potential selection bias inherent in the groups. For example, children who are adopted from orphanages may have had fewer difficulties even prior to leaving than children who remained behind. Such a selection bias complicates the interpretation of the findings. Despite weaknesses, however, natural experiments have enriched our understanding of life circumstances that cannot readily be manipulated by researchers.

Randomized Experiments

The randomized experiment is sometimes referred to as the "true" experiment in that it is the strongest method for inferring causal links between variables. A controlled manipulation (the **independent variable**) is presented to participants who are randomly assigned to different conditions. The outcome of the manipulation is measured (the **dependent variable**), and differences among the conditions are then evaluated. With the exception of the independent variable, the groups are treated as similarly as possible so that group differences can be attributed to the independent variable. In addition, random assignment of participants to groups makes it likely that any differences are not caused by initial group disparity but by the manipulation itself.

To illustrate the experiment, we draw on an early report of the Abecedarian Project, a research project of historic interest because it was among the first efforts to ask whether at-risk children could benefit from a child-centered, intellectually stimulating environment provided as part of a day care service (Campbell et al., 2001; Ramey & Campbell, 1984). Potential participants were identified through prenatal clinics and the local social service department. Families were identified as at-risk on the basis of a survey, and selected before or soon after the birth of the participant child. The investigators then paired the families according to similarity on the High Risk Index, and the children from each pair were randomly assigned to one of two conditions, either the treatment or the control group (Ramey & Campbell, 1984).

The independent variable was the provision of the educational program. Children in the treatment group began day care by 3 months of age, and their development was tracked

until they reached 54 months. The educational program included language, motor, social, and cognitive components, varying somewhat with the child's age. Control-group children did not attend the day care center and were not exposed to the educational program. Efforts were made to otherwise equate their experiences with those of the treatment group: They were given similar nutritional supplements, pediatric care, and supportive social services. The dependent variable was standardized developmental or intelligence tests administered to all the children twice annually.

The test results revealed that beginning at 18 months, children in the treatment group scored higher than children in the control group, and this difference was **statistically significant**.[2] Figure 4.2 shows one way of examining the findings. It indicates that at 24, 36, and 48 months, the educationally treated children were much less likely to obtain intelligence scores at or below 85 than were the control children. The researchers concluded that the educational program resulted in intellectual benefits for the treated at-risk youngsters.

Is this conclusion justified; that is, does the study have internal validity? The method by which the subjects were selected and assigned makes it unlikely that the results simply reflect group differences that existed prior to the study. Moreover, efforts were made to treat the experimental and control groups similarly except for the independent variable. To the degree that this was accomplished, it can be

---

[2]Statistical significance concerns the probability that a finding is not due to mere chance. A common convention is that a statistically significant finding would occur by chance only 5 or less times were the study repeated 100 times. Statistical significance tests can be applied to many kinds of research methods.

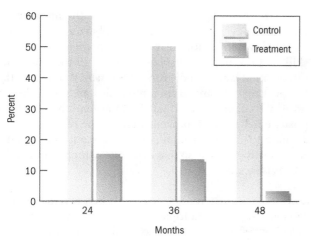

FIGURE 4.2 Percentage of Stanford-Binet IQ scores at or below 85 at three ages for treatment and control subjects. *From Ramey & Campbell, 1984.*

argued that the study is internally valid and that the results are due to the treatment. With regard to this issue, caution is appropriate, however. When research is conducted in the laboratory, it is relatively easy to control the experiences of the groups. In an experiment such as Ramey and Campbell's, the degree of control and thus internal validity are less clear.

An additional issue concerns the actual collection of data. It appears that those who gave the standardized tests might have known the group to which each child had been assigned, raising the question of bias in data collection. At the same time, the individual testers had been randomly assigned to testing sessions, a procedure that could offset possible bias.

What about external validity, or generalizability, of the findings? External validity is enhanced by the intervention actually being conducted in a day care center, the setting in which the program likely would be used. However, the positive effects of treatments may not accrue when they are employed in circumstances other than those in which they were initially demonstrated. (See Accent: "Translational Research: From Lab to Real-World Settings.")

The purpose of our discussion of the Abecedarian Project is to illustrate the randomized experiment, but it is noteworthy that the project is a landmark investigation of early educational intervention (Pungello et al., 2010). The participants in the study were followed into young adulthood, and long-terms benefits were demonstrated (Campbell & Ramey, 1994; Campbell et al., 2001). The project also was depicted in the television documentary *My Brilliant Brain* (The Carolina Abecedarian Project-FPG Child Development, 2008).

ACCENT
Translational Research: From Lab to Real-World Settings

The issue of generalizability of treatment is part of a more general concern about the gap between research and the application of knowledge. This concern has been addressed by various professional and government groups. The National Institutes of Health (NIH) has been especially influential in guiding efforts to link basic research to applications in the real world, with the goal of improving human health (Guerra, Graham, & Tolan, 2011). The NIH call for **translational research** has been conceptualized as a two-step model or as two types of research.

As applied to mental health, Type 1 research—often referred to as "bench to bedside"—focuses on basic research to identify problems, etiology, and the design and testing of interventions to improve well-being. Much progress has been made in recent years in such efforts. This includes research demonstrations of beneficial effects on youth of a range of interventions and preventions (Kazan et al., 2010). However, numerous investigations show that these benefits may not accrue in clinical practice. Perhaps real-world clinical cases may be more complex, or the application of empirically tested interventions may differ substantially, for example, by being less organized or structured (Hibbs & Jensen, 2005; Kamon, Tolan, & Gorman-Smith, 2006). To remedy the situation, it is suggested that researchers build the characteristics of real-world settings into the designs and evaluations of interventions.

In addition, given the prevalence of disorder in youth and the lack of access to care, there is much need to successfully move evidence-based mental health care to a broader scale, that is, from "bedside to community." Type 2 translational research focuses on the broad scale adoption, implementation, and sustainability of evidence-based interventions by community systems that deliver care (Guerra et al., 2011). Researchers have begun to develop a science of implementation. Although still in relatively early stages, crucial components of implementation are being studied (Fixsen et al., 2010; McHugh & Barlow, 2010). These components include the decision by a service agency to adopt an evidence-based program; the training and evaluation of practitioners; the organizational change usually required, such as commitment to the program and "unfreezing" of current practices; and the evaluation and maintenance of the new program in the community. Substantial government and private resources, as well as professional efforts, are being invested in system-level implementation.

Single-Case Experimental Designs

Single-case experimental designs involve a manipulation with a single (or a few) participant(s). They are sometimes referred to as time-series designs because measures of the dependent variable are repeated across time periods. The designs are frequently used to evaluate the effects of clinical interventions. External validity is not strong, because generalization from a single participant cannot be confidently made. It can be enhanced, however, by repeating the study with different subjects or in different settings. The issue of internal validity can be approached with the use of specific design features that control for the possibility of alternative explanations.

REVERSAL DESIGNS   In the ABA reversal design, a problem behavior is carefully defined and measured across time periods, during which the subject is exposed to different conditions. During the first period (A), measures are taken of the behavior prior to intervention. This baseline measure serves as a standard against which change can be evaluated. In the next period (B), the intervention is carried out while the behavior is measured in the identical way. The intervention is then removed; that is, there is a return to the same condition as during baseline (A).

Figure 4.3 gives a hypothetical example of the ABA design. Appropriate play behavior occurs at low frequency during the baseline, increases during the treatment phase B, and decreases when the intervention is removed in the second A phase. In studies in which behavior improves during intervention, particularly if clinical treatment is the aim, a fourth period, during which the successful intervention is reintroduced, must be added. Typically the relevant behaviors show improvement again.

The ABA design is limited in that the intervention may make reversal of the targeted behavior unlikely. For example, when treatment results in increased academic skill, a child may not display decreases in the skill when intervention is removed. From a treatment standpoint, this is a positive outcome; from a research standpoint, there is no way to demonstrate that the intervention caused the positive behavior. In other instances, the researcher may hesitate to remove a manipulation once it is associated with positive change, so that a definite demonstration of its effects is lacking.

MULTIPLE BASELINE DESIGNS   When reversal designs are inappropriate, multiple baseline designs may be suitable. Multiple baselines are recorded, which may represent different behaviors of a participant, the same behavior of a participant in different settings, the same behavior of a few different participants, and so on. Intervention is then presented to observe the effects on one of the baselines but not the others. If effects are found, they likely are due to intervention rather than extraneous factors. In this way, multiple baseline designs provide some basis for internal validity.

Consider, for example, the multiple baseline design in which two behaviors by a single child are recorded across time. After baselines are established for both behaviors, the intervention is made for only one behavior. During the next phase, the intervention is applied to the other behavior as well. A clinician may hypothesize, say, that a child's temper tantrums and throwing of objects are maintained by adult attention to these behaviors. Withdrawal of attention would thus be expected to reduce the behaviors. Support for the hypothesis can be seen in Figure 4.4,

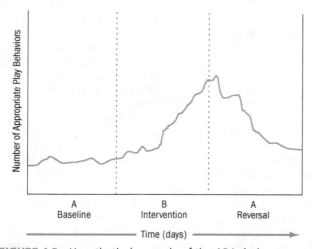

FIGURE 4.3   Hypothetical example of the ABA design.

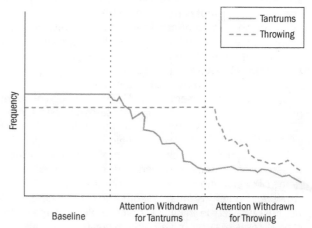

FIGURE 4.4   Frequency of tantrums and throwing across the phases of a hypothetical multiple baseline, single-subject experiment.

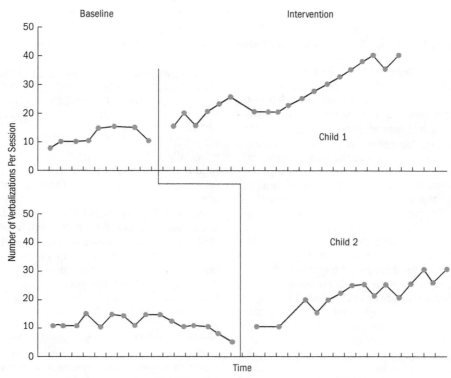

FIGURE 4.5 Number of verbalizations of two children across the phases of a hypothetical multiple baseline experiment.

a hypothetical graph of the frequency of both behaviors across time periods. Because behavior change follows the pattern of the treatment procedure, it is likely that withdrawal of attention and not some other variable caused the change.

In another commonly used multiple baseline design, baselines are recorded for multiple participants, and intervention follows different timelines (Gliner, Morgan, & Harmon, 2000). Figure 4.5 demonstrates a hypothetical study in which intervention is provided to increase the verbalization of nonverbal developmentally delayed children. Here, baselines are recorded for two children and Child 1 is then provided the treatment, successively followed by treatment for Child 2. Similar patterns of change for both children upon introduction of the intervention increases confidence that the treatment actually caused improvement.

There are numerous other single-case experimental designs (Kazdin, 2011). They all permit the researcher-clinician to test hypotheses while working with a single or a few participants and, in the case of treatment, to focus on the youth of immediate concern. Moreover, although control of extraneous factors is more easily effected in the laboratory, single-case research is relatively easy to conduct in natural environments (Morgan & Morgan, 2001). The method thus has the potential to capture actual clinic practice.

To summarize, the research methods we have discussed in this section vary in several ways, and each has weaknesses and strengths. Nonexperimental methods are appropriate for describing phenomena and are especially useful when a manipulation is not feasible. Experimental methods best meet the standards of internal validity and best permit causal inferences to be drawn. The choice of research method depends on the purpose of the investigation, as well as practical and ethical considerations. Scientific endeavors are enriched by the availability of various methods, which are employed in numerous approaches to understanding psychopathology. (See Accent: "Epidemiological Research: More Than Counting Noses.")

ACCENT
Epidemiological Research: More than Counting Noses

Epidemiology can be defined as the quantitative study of the distribution and causes of disorder in human populations (Regier & Burke, 2000). The approach has a basis in medicine and public health, and initially focused on investigating infectious diseases. Cases of disorder are identified in large populations, or representative samples of the populations, and several kinds of data about the disorders may be collected and analyzed.

One goal of epidemiology is to monitor the frequency of disorders in populations, including how frequency may change over time. Frequency may be measured in several ways. Incidence refers to the number of new cases that appear in a particular time period, often in 1 year. Prevalence refers to the presence of a disorder in a population at a particular time; for example, the number of cases or proportion of the population can be determined. Lifetime prevalence refers to the number or proportion of people in a population who have had the disorder at any time during their life. The focus on general populations rather than on clinical samples is especially valuable in that it reduces the likelihood of selection bias inherent in clinical samples. "Counting noses" is valuable in that it informs us about the need for treatment, whether a disorder is increasing or decreasing, and the like. But epidemiology does more than simply count noses (Costello, Egger, & Angold, 2005a).

By associating the frequency of disorder with specific characteristics of populations—that is, determining how cases of disorder are distributed in a population—epidemiology provides information pertinent to risk and causation. For example, the revelation that prevalence of eating disorder in populations increases at adolescence, especially in females, puts emphasis on causal questions regarding timing and gender. That is, what is there about adolescence and about being female that puts individuals at risk?

Epidemiology seeks to understand what groups of people are at high risk for a disorder, what factors or other dysfunctions are correlated with the disorder, what the causes and modes of transmission are, and how the disorder can be prevented or reduced. Epidemiologists interested in young people are applying the developmental perspective, for example, by studying disorders longitudinally from the time of risk to onset of disorder to outcome (Costello & Angold, 2000; 2006). The epidemiological approach is important in furthering the understanding of genetic effects and gene–environment causation, an area of research requiring large to very large representative samples (Lahey, D'Onofrio, & Waldman, 2009). The approach thus broadly contributes to understanding, preventing, and treating psychological problems of youth.

TIME FRAMES IN RESEARCH

In addition to the distinctions among research methods described above, investigations differ with regard to time.

Cross-Sectional Research

In this approach, participants are observed at one point in time, as if a snapshot were being taken. Group comparisons are frequently made between groups that differ in age or developmental status. For instance, aggression displayed by 6-, 10-, and 14-year-olds might be compared. **Cross-sectional research** is relatively inexpensive and efficient, and has contributed significantly to understanding development and psychological problems.

Nevertheless, tracing developmental change with cross-sectional research is problematic and can be misleading. If older youth display more aggression, it might be concluded that aggression "naturally" increases with development. But this conclusion may not be warranted. What we are seeing is an *age difference*, which is not necessarily *developmental change*. Perhaps specific experiences of the age groups are responsible for the findings. The

14-year-olds might have received more reinforcement for displaying aggression during a time period characterized by greater violence and aggression.

Retrospective Longitudinal Research

Consistent with the meaning of the word *retrospective*, **retrospective longitudinal research** goes back in time. Youths may be identified on some variable of interest—such as a specific disorder—and information about their earlier characteristics and life experiences is then collected. One type of study that is frequently retrospective is the **case-control study**, in which a group that has been diagnosed with a disorder is compared with a group without the disorder. The purpose of this follow-back method is to seek hypotheses about the predictors or causes of the observed disturbance. In retrospective studies, caution is warranted by possible unreliability of the data because old records and memories of the past may be sketchy, biased, or mistaken. Nevertheless, the discovery of a relationship of earlier-occurring variables with the disorder can suggest risk or causal factors.

Prospective Longitudinal Research

In **prospective longitudinal research**, individuals are observed and then evaluated with repeated observations as time passes. In "seeing" development as it occurs, the method can uniquely answer questions about the nature and course of development. For instance, children with language disabilities can be tested at specific time intervals to discern how the deficits change as the children develop. Comparison with a group showing no language problems would be valuable. Prospective longitudinal research can be informative with regard to numerous questions. Youth who experience birth complications, an early traumatic event, or risks associated with poverty can be assessed over periods of time to determine factors related to their development. Girls and boys diagnosed with ADHD can be followed into adulthood to ascertain possible gender difference in outcome and the variables implicated.

This method is highly valued, but there are several drawbacks. The studies are expensive and require investigators to commit to a project for many years. Retaining participants over long periods of time may be difficult, and the loss of participants can bias the sample when dropouts are more transient, less psychologically oriented, or less healthy than those who continue. Another problem is that repeated testing of participants may make them test-wise, but attempting to control for this by changing test instruments makes it difficult to compare earlier and later findings. In addition, in planning long-term studies, researchers must take educated guesses about which variables to observe along the way, and they may miss relevant factors. For example, in discussing their 30-year longitudinal project, Sroufe and colleagues (2005) noted that in hindsight they would have included measures of neurophysiological functioning that might have provided valuable information.

Finally, in interpreting longitudinal results, it is important to consider possible societal changes. If individuals were followed from birth in 1980 through 2000, their development might be different, due to historical factors, from that of persons followed from birth in 2000 through 2020. The groups would likely have different experiences, for example, in the social environment or educational opportunity. These possible generational, or cohort, effects must be considered in interpreting longitudinal studies.

Accelerated Longitudinal Research

To overcome some of the weaknesses of the cross-sectional and prospective longitudinal methods, researchers interested in developmental change can conduct **accelerated longitudinal research**, which combines the two approaches in a variety of designs. Take, for example, a

Age Group	Time		
	I (2011)	II (2014)	III (2017)
A	3	6	9
B	6	9	12
C	9	12	15

FIGURE 4.6 Schema of an accelerated longitudinal research design in which children of different ages are examined cross-sectionally and longitudinally.

hypothetical study in which groups of children of different ages are studied over a relatively short time span. At Time I, children ages 3, 6, and 9 years are examined in a cross-sectional study. Similar examination of the same children occurs again 3 years later at Time II, and again another 3 years later at Time III. Figure 4.6 depicts the study. From reading down the columns of the figure, cross-sectional comparisons can be made at three different times. In addition, as is apparent by reading from left to right across the figure, the children (A, B, and C) are studied longitudinally over a 6-year period (2011–2017). The age range in the investigation is thus 12 years (from 3 to 15 years), although the study is completed in 6 years.

Various comparisons can provide a wealth of information from such a design. To consider a possibility, if anxiety were found to increase with age at Times I, II, and III (cross-sectional analyses) and also across time for each group of children (the longitudinal analyses), evidence would be strong for developmental change over the entire age range. Moreover, by comparing anxiety at age 6, or 9, or 12 (as shaded in the figure), the impact of societal conditions could also be evaluated. It might be found, for example, that anxiety at age 9 increased from the year 2011 to 2014 to 2017. Since only one age is involved, this increase is not developmental and likely indicates a change in societal conditions during the years under investigation. Thus, accelerated longitudinal designs can be a powerful way to separate age differences and developmental changes, while taking generational effects into consideration.

QUALITATIVE RESEARCH

Most of the research on psychopathology of youth is quantitative. That is, the various methods collect and analyze numerical data that represent the world in some way (Yoshikawa et al., 2008). Quantitative research is essential to the empirical or positivistic paradigm that underlies much of the scientific progress made in modern times (Eisner, 2003). This perspective favors theory-guided objective measurement done by objective investigators in controlled situations.

In contrast, **qualitative research** collects and analyzes non-numerical information and favors methods such as in-depth interviews, intensive case studies, and life histories rather than controlled laboratory and experimental manipulations. Naturalistic observation is also important, with observations often recorded in narrative forms rather than with a restrictive coding of categories. Participant observation, in which the observer engages in and becomes part of the setting, is valued as a way to collect credible data and to optimize understanding. All these methods are consistent with the assumptions and values of qualitative research, which emphasize real-world contexts and the belief that human behavior and development can best be understood from a personal frame of reference when individuals have the opportunity to speak about their beliefs, attitudes, and experience (Higgins et al., 2002; Simonton, 2003).

It is not unusual to collect large amounts of written data in qualitative research. Once collected, the narrative data are conceptualized, analyzed, and interpreted. This process may entail coding or categorizing statements or written observations. The categories are often viewed as arising naturally from the data rather than being based on predetermined expectations or constructed coding systems. What gets coded, how the coding is accomplished, and how data are interpreted vary with the approach and aims of the study. Quantification of data is minimal and statistical analysis may have little, if any, role.

Like other strategies, qualitative methods have weaknesses and strengths. Sample size is often small, huge amounts of data can be difficult and costly to analyze, and questions are raised about reliability and validity. At the same time, with its focus on the individual in context, qualitative research can increase basic knowledge, suggest hypotheses for further testing, and illustrate and enrich quantitative findings.

Examples of Qualitative Studies

Some of the topics that have been examined with qualitative methods are life experiences of individuals diagnosed in childhood as learning disabled, parents' and siblings' adjustment to having a handicapped family member, parents' experiences regarding their child's life-threatening illness, disadvantaged parents' attitudes about family ties, and adolescent attitudes toward their society (Fiese & Bickman, 1998; Flaton, 2006; Krahn, Hohn, & Kime, 1995; McNulty, 2003; Torney-Purta, 2009; Waller, 2010).

As an example of the strategy, consider a study of parents' experiences as participants in a support program called Parent to Parent (Ainbinder et al., 1998). The specific purpose of the program was to provide support for parents who had a child with disabilities, such as intellectual disability or chronic illness. Each parent was matched with a trained supporting parent who had a child with a similar disability and who provided information and emotional support, usually by telephone. One of the ways in which the program was evaluated was through a qualitative, semistructured interview with participating parents, which explored the impact and meaning of being matched with a supportive parent. The transcribed telephone interviews were coded and categorized according to themes that emerged from the telephone conversations. Among the themes were the way the program was helpful, reasons for program failure, skills and information learned by the parents, and personal growth of the parents. The following from the parent interviews exemplifies learning by the parent:

> I wanted some reassurance that [our daughter] is likely to have most of the same things everybody else has, as far as you know, going to school and having friends, going out and doing things. And [our supporting Parent's] daughter's involved in a lot of things. She's got a good life. And that gave me a great deal of hope about the future of our daughter, that she can have a good life, too. (p. 104)

Overall, the data indicated that talking, sharing, comparing, and learning with others who are perceived as similar can enhance coping and adaptability. The qualitative analysis of Parent to Parent provided understanding of the strengths and weaknesses of the program in a way that other data, collected from quantitative surveys, had not provided.

Combining Qualitative and Quantitative Methods

Qualitative and quantitative strategies have often been viewed as adversarial (Rogers, 2000), and yet they are not necessarily at odds with each other and are often employed together. The combination of the approaches can be valuable in addressing many questions and issues (Yoshikawa et al., 2008). For example, research on culture and child rearing requires observation of behaviors and activities relevant to child rearing, as well as understanding the goals and beliefs underlying these activities. Quantitative methods can be suitable to determine the prevalence of certain child rearing practices, and qualitative methods may be particularly fitting to reveal the goals of child rearing held by the culture. To take another example, a study of friendship drew on quantitative data to show that in late adolescence girls and boys reported equal support from friends; however, qualitative findings indicated that the meaning and function of friend support was different for girls and boys. In general, quantitative procedures provide more traditional data collection and hypothesis testing whereas qualitative procedures provide flexible, broad-scope investigation.

ETHICAL ISSUES

Scientific research is enormously beneficial, but it brings concerns about the welfare and rights of participants. Underlying such concerns is sensitivity to individual rights—both ethical and legal—and to past documented abuse of research participants. One well-known instance in which the problem of abuse was raised involved research into the natural course of hepatitis. From the 1950s to the 1970s, children with mental retardation who resided in the Willowbrook school in the state of New York were deliberately infected with hepatitis in order to study the disease (Glantz, 1996). Although specific instances like this of past abuse in biomedical research appear especially egregious, ethical issues in all areas require continuous attention.

For many years, government agencies and professional organizations have published ethical guidelines for research. Philosophical underpinnings were presented in the *Belmont Report: Ethical Principles and Guidelines for the Protection of Human Subjects of Research*, which led to the Code of Federal Regulations pertaining to human research participants (National Commission, 1979). The American Psychological Association's *Ethical Principles of Psychologists and Code of Conduct* addresses the multiple professional roles of psychologists, including that of the researcher (American Psychological Association, 2002). The guidelines of the Society for Research in Child Development specifically address research with youth. Table 4.3 shows an abridged version of these standards (two additional Principles concern scientific and personal misconduct of the researcher). There is considerable overlap in the guidelines adopted by different agencies and disciplines.

Depending on funding and the setting, research proposals may be reviewed by federally mandated **Institutional Review Boards (IRBs)**, or by local review boards. IRBs consider such issues as the scientific soundness of the proposed research, voluntary consent of the participants, and potential harm and benefits to the participants (U.S. Department of Health and Human Services, 2005). Particular consideration is given to vulnerable persons, including youth, the mentally disabled, and the economically disadvantaged. Whether or not an official review is required, adhering to ethical standards is a mandate for all researchers. Although doing as mandated may seem quite simple, ethical concerns are often complex. The following discussion covers a few major issues.

Voluntary Informed Consent

Fundamental to most ethical guidelines is the voluntary consent of individuals to participate, given that they understand the investigation. The requirement of voluntary **informed consent**, which is viewed as a component of respect due all participants, often calls for written consent. Among other things, participants should know the purpose of the research, procedures, risks and benefits, and their option to refuse participation or to withdraw at any time (Hoagwood & Cavaleri, 2010). They should have the competence to understand the information and to judge risk and benefits. It is presumed that immaturity hinders children's ability to fully understand these issues and make informed decisions. Thus, until children have reached the legal age of consent, usually age 18, consent on their behalf is required from their parents or guardians. For adolescents, consent generally involves consent from the youth and the parent.

Like some other standards, the American Psychological Association's standard allows some exceptions to this guideline, such as for research on educational curricula that would likely create no stress or harm. In addition, it recommends that persons not of legal age should nevertheless be asked to assent, or agree, to participate. Descriptions of the research need to be tailored to the developmental level of the person. For example, Miller (1998) suggests that the following information might appropriately be conveyed to the young child: a general idea of what will happen ("play a game"), where it will occur ("in Mr. Smith's office"), how many people will be involved ("just you and me"), how long it will take ("about 20 minutes"), whether others will do the same thing ("lots of kids from the class will be doing this"), whether a reward will be offered ("get a little prize at the end"), and the opportunity to assent ("Would you like to come?"). Obviously, with infants and toddlers, informed consent is an unreasonable expectation, and parental or guardian consent is usually sufficient.

Confidentiality

Research involves the participants giving personal information of some sort, whether they complete surveys or tests, describe their feelings, or allow others to observe their behavior. The principle of **confidentiality** assumes that participants have the right to control the degree to which personal information can be disclosed to others. It is often necessary for the researcher to know the

TABLE 4.3	Ethical Standards for Research with Children
Principle 1	**Nonharmful Procedures.** No research operation that may physically or psychologically harm the child should be used. The least stressful operation should be used. Doubts about harmfulness should be discussed with consultants.
Principle 2	**Informed Consent.** The child's consent or assent should be obtained. The child should be informed of features of the research that may affect his or her willingness to participate. When research participants are infants, their parents should be informed. If consent would make the research impossible, it may be ethically conducted under certain circumstances; judgments should be made with Institutional Review Boards.
Principle 3	**Parental Consent.** Informed consent of parents, guardians, and those acting in loci parentis (e.g., school superintendents) similarly should be obtained, preferably in writing.
Principle 4	**Additional Consent.** Informed consent should be obtained of persons, such as teachers, whose interaction with the child is the subject of the research.
Principle 5	**Incentives.** Incentives to participate in the research must be fair and not unduly exceed incentives the child normally experiences.
Principle 6	**Deception.** If deception or withholding information is considered essential, colleagues must agree with this judgment. Participants should be told later of the reason for the deception. Efforts should be made to employ deception methods that have no known negative effects.
Principle 7	**Anonymity.** Permission should be gained for access to institutional records, and anonymity of information should be preserved.
Principle 8	**Mutual Responsibilities.** There should be clear agreement as to the responsibilities of all parties in the research. The investigator must honor all promises and commitments.
Principle 9	**Jeopardy.** When, in the research, information comes to the investigator's attention about circumstances that may jeopardize the child's welfare, the information must be discussed with parents or guardians and experts who can arrange for assistance to the child.
Principle 10	**Unforeseen Consequences.** When research procedures result in unforeseen, undesirable consequences for the participant, the consequences should be corrected and the procedures redesigned.
Principle 11	**Confidentiality.** The identity of participants and information about them should be kept confidential. When confidentiality might be threatened, this possibility and methods to prevent it should be explained as part of the procedures of obtaining informed consent.
Principle 12	**Informing Participants.** Immediately after data collection, any misconceptions that might have arisen should be clarified. General findings should be given to the participants, appropriate to their understanding. When scientific or humane reasons justify withholding information, efforts should be made to ensure that withholding has no damaging consequences.
Principle 13	**Reporting Results.** Investigators' words may carry unintended weight; thus, caution should be used in reporting results, giving advice, and making evaluative statements.
Principle 14	**Implications of Findings.** Investigators should be mindful of the social, political, and human implications of the research, and especially careful in the presentations of findings.

Summarized from the Society for Research in Child Development, 2007. http://www.srcd.org/ethicalstandards.html.

identity of the participants who provide specific information. However, information can be kept confidential by numbering or otherwise coding individual reports, securing storage of data, and limiting access to data (Hoagwood & Cavaleri, 2010).

Several issues arise when the participants are children or adolescents (Richards, 2003). Parents, schools, and other agencies involved may be interested in the course and outcome of the research. The researcher can limit the information given to parents, as in cases in which disclosure can put the child at risk. On the other hand, in some instances, the sharing of information might potentially benefit the young person, for example, in research on adolescent use of illicit drugs. Investigators may reveal information when participants appear in danger of harming themselves or others. Participating youth, parents, and relevant agencies should understand the limits of confidentially prior to the investigation.

Balancing It All: Harm and Good

A critical ethical principle is that no serious harm—physical, psychological, legal, or economic—should be done to participants. Research that, for instance, engages children in aggressive acts or exposes them to aggressive models raises questions of possible harm. Children also participate in research on the effects of medications, which can entail complex ethical dilemmas. Clearly, it is necessary to guard against the potential for harm, a principle that is referred to as **nonmaleficence**.

Moreover, the ethical principle of **beneficence**, based on respect for each individual, requires that benefits be maximized. It is not always possible for individuals to benefit personally from the research that they participate in, but a risk–benefit ratio should be considered (Hoagwood & Cavaleri, 2010). In general, when greater benefit to the participant is likely, greater risk of harm is more acceptable. Obviously this guideline has limits in that risk of serious harm is virtually never acceptable.

In the final analysis, judgments about what is ethical often involve balancing several factors. Indeed, IRBs were instituted to aid in finding a balance between society's

When a youth participates in research, informed consent by a parent or guardian, and possibly by the youth, should usually be obtained. What constitutes informed consent by a child is a complex issue.

need for knowledge and participants' need for protection in research (Hayes, 2003). The individual's competence to understand and voluntarily consent, the risk of harm, and the possibility of benefit all play a crucial role in guiding ethical standards. Like other ethical concerns, the ethics of research can never be a completely settled matter, and ongoing discussion and tension are appropriate. Reasonable balance must be maintained, however, if beneficial research is to go forward.

Overview/Looking Back

FUNDAMENTALS OF RESEARCH

- The aim of science is to describe phenomena and offer explanations for them.
- Scientific knowledge is based on systematic formulation, observation, and interpretation of findings. Hypothesis testing builds knowledge systematically and is tied to the advancement of theory.
- The selection of research participants is critical. Random selection best ensures that a sample represents the population from which it is drawn.
- Observation and measurement are accomplished in various ways in various settings. The behavior or concept being studied must be operationalized. Efforts should be made to achieve reliable and valid measurements.

- Reliability (consistency) of research results is important, as is validity (correctness) of findings. Internal validity is the degree to which alternative explanations for results can be confidently ruled out. External validity refers to generalizability of findings to other populations and settings.

BASIC METHODS OF RESEARCH

- Numerous research methods are employed, each suited to particular purposes and each having weaknesses and strengths. Research methods can be categorized as descriptive (nonexperimental) or experimental, the latter of which can be viewed as randomized or quasi-experimental.

- Case studies can provide compelling descriptions; correlational methods provide information about the relationships among variables.
- Randomized experiments and single-subject experiments best meet the standards for establishing causality.

TIME FRAMES IN RESEARCH

- The cross-sectional strategy examines groups of people at a particular point in time; it is not a strong tool for evaluating developmental change.
- Retrospective longitudinal research goes back in time; it can generate hypotheses. The prospective longitudinal strategy, which makes repeated observations forward over time, is valued for tracing development.
- Accelerated longitudinal designs combine the cross-sectional and prospective longitudinal approaches to permit examination of developmental change, age differences, and the influence of generational effects.

QUALITATIVE RESEARCH

- Qualitative research places high value on individuals' perception of their experiences in their natural environments. Data are collected through in-depth interviews, life histories, and the like. This strategy and the quantitative strategy—which values control, manipulation, and quantitative measures—are often seen as adversarial but can be complementary.

ETHICAL ISSUES

- Ethical issues in the conduct of research are addressed by several government agencies and professional organizations. Youth and those with mental disabilities require special protection.
- Central to ethical guidelines are voluntary informed consent, confidentiality, and assessment of risks and benefits to the participant.

Key Terms

hypothesis testing *66*
random selection *66*
selection bias *67*
operational definition *67*
validity of measurement *67*
reliability of measurement *67*
naturalistic observation *67*
interobserver reliability *67*
observer blindness *68*
internal validity *68*
external validity *68*
descriptive (nonexperimental) methods *68*
experimental methods *68*

randomized experiments *69*
quasi-experimental studies *69*
case study *69*
correlational studies *70*
positive correlation *70*
negative correlation *71*
experiments of nature *72*
independent variable *72*
dependent variable *72*
statistical significance *72*
translational research *73*
single-case experimental designs *74*
epidemiology *76*
cross-sectional research *76*

retrospective longitudinal research *76*
case-control study *76*
prospective longitudinal research *77*
accelerated longitudinal research *77*
qualitative research *78*
Institutional Review Boards (IRBs) *79*
informed consent *79*
confidentiality *79*
nonmaleficence *81*
beneficence *81*

CHAPTER 5

Classification, Assessment, and Intervention

LOOKING FORWARD

After reading this chapter, you should be able to discuss:

- Processes of classification and diagnosis

- DSM and empirical approaches to classifying psychological problems of youth

- How assessment is conducted and various approaches to assessment

- Various approaches to prevention of problems of youth

- Various modes and strategies of treatment for problems of youth

H ow are behavioral disorders of childhood and adolescence defined, grouped, evaluated, and treated? In this chapter we will introduce the processes of classification, assessment, and intervention.

The terms *classification, taxonomy,* and *diagnosis* are used to refer to the process of description and grouping. **Classification** and **taxonomy** are the delineation of major categories or dimensions of behavioral disorders, done for either clinical or scientific purposes. **Diagnosis** usually refers to assigning a category of a classification system to an individual. **Assessment** refers to evaluating youngsters, in part to assist the processes of classification and diagnosis and in part to direct intervention. All of these entwined processes are intricately related to the clinical and scientific aspects of child and adolescent disorders.

CLASSIFICATION AND DIAGNOSIS

Classification systems are employed to systematically describe a phenomenon. Biologists have classification systems for living organisms, and physicians classify physical dysfunction. Similarly, systems exist to classify psychological dysfunction. These systems describe categories or dimensions of problem behaviors, emotions, and/or cognitions. A **category** is a discrete grouping, for example, anxiety disorder, into which an individual's symptoms are judged to fit or not fit. In contrast, the term **dimension** implies that an attribute is continuous and can occur to various degrees. Thus, for example, a child may exhibit high, moderate, or low levels of anxiety.

Any classification system must have clearly defined categories or dimensions. In other words, the criteria for defining a category or dimension must be explicitly stated. Clear and explicit definitions allow for good communication among professionals. Also, one must be able to clearly discriminate diagnostic groupings from one another. It must be demonstrated, too, that a category or dimension actually exists. That is, the features used to describe a category or dimension must occur together regularly, in one or more situations or as measured by one or more methods.

Classification systems must be reliable and valid. These terms were applied to research methods in chapter 4. When applied to classification or diagnosis, the terms retain the general meanings of consistency and correctness but are used in somewhat different ways.

Interrater reliability refers to whether different diagnosticians use the same category to describe a person's behavior. For example, it addresses the question, Is Maria's behavior called separation anxiety by two or more professionals who observe it? **Test–retest reliability** asks whether the use of a category is stable over some reasonable period of time. For example, is Sean's difficulty, originally diagnosed as oppositional–defiant disorder, diagnosed as the same disorder when he returns for a second evaluation?

There are also questions about the **validity** of diagnostic systems. To be valid, a diagnosis should provide us with more information than we had when we originally defined the category. Thus diagnoses should give us information about the etiology of a disorder, the course of development that the disorder is expected to take, response to treatment, or some additional clinical features of the problem. Does the diagnosis of conduct disorder, for example, tell us something about this disorder that is different from other disorders? Does the diagnosis tell us something about what causes this problem? Does it tell us what is likely to happen to youngsters who have this disorder and what treatments are likely to help? Does it tell us additional things about these young people or their backgrounds? The question of validity is thus largely one of whether we know anything we did not already know when we defined the category. Another important aspect of validity is whether our description of a disorder is accurate. Is the way we have described and classified this disorder the way it actually exists? Answering this question is often not an easy matter.

Finally, the **clinical utility** of a classification system is judged by how complete and useful it is. A diagnostic system that describes all the disorders that come to the attention of clinicians in a manner that is useful to them is more likely to be employed.

The DSM Approach

The most widely used classification system in the United States is the American Psychiatric Association's ***Diagnostic and Statistical Manual of Mental Disorders (DSM)***. The Tenth Revision of the ***International Classification of Diseases (ICD)*** developed by the World Health Organization (1992) is an alternative system that is widely employed. There has been some concern that the DSM coverage of disorders has not given sufficient attention to younger children (Egger & Emde, 2011). The **Diagnostic Classification of Mental Health and Developmental Disorders of Infancy and Early Childhood, Revised (DC: 0–3)**, one response to this concern, is a system developed to classify mental disorders of very young children (Zero to Three, 2005). We will focus our discussion on the DSM because it is the dominant system in the United States.

The DSM is often referred to as a **clinically derived classification** system. Clinically derived classification systems are based on the consensus of clinicians that certain characteristics occur together. These have been described as "top down" approaches (Achenbach, 2000). Committees of experts propose concepts of disorders and then choose diagnostic criteria for defining disorders. It is from these criteria that the development of assessments and evaluations proceed.

The DSM is also a **categorical approach** to classification; a person either does or does not meet the criteria for a diagnosis. In a categorical approach the difference between normal and pathological is one of *kind* rather than one of *degree*. This approach also suggests that distinctions can be made between *qualitatively* different types of disorders.

The DSM is an outgrowth of the original psychiatric taxonomy developed by Kraepelin in 1883. There have been a number of revisions of the DSM system. The most recent revision is the DSM-5. The DSM-5 provides information regarding a large number of disorders. These disorders are organized into groups of related disorders (chapters). A description and diagnostic criteria are provided for each disorder. In addition, there is accompanying text material that provides information about features that may be associated with a disorder (e.g., low self-esteem) and information regarding cultural, age, and gender features; probable course of the disorder; prevalence; familial patterns; and so on (American Psychiatric Association [APA], 2013).

Historically, the classification of abnormal behavior focused primarily on adult disorders and there was no extensive classification scheme for child and adolescent disorders (Silk et al., 2000). By the 1960s, it had become obvious that a more extensive system was needed. In response, the DSM-II, III, III-R, and IV expanded appreciably the number of categories specific to children and adolescents and a section of disorders "usually first diagnosed in infancy, childhood, or adolescence" was introduced. In addition, some "adult" diagnoses (e.g., anxiety disorders, mood disorders, schizophrenia, sleep disorders) could be used for children and adolescents. The DSM-5 no longer has a separate grouping of "disorders usually first diagnosed in infancy, childhood, or adolescence." Attention is still given to disorders experienced by children and adolescents; however, the disorders previously included in this section, like all other disorders, are placed within chapters of related disorders. For example, separation anxiety disorder is described in the chapter on anxiety disorders and attention-deficit hyperactivity disorder (ADHD) is described in the chapter on neurodevelopmental disorders.

Various changes in the organization and structure of categories have been characteristic of the development of the DSM system (APA, 1968; 1980; 1987; 1994; 2013). In DSM-5 the organization reflects groupings (chapters) of related disorders. Disorders within a grouping or, indeed, disorders in adjacent chapters are thought to be similar with regard to symptoms or with regard to factors such as genetic, neural, or environmental risks; cognitive or emotional processes; or response to treatment.

Thus, the DSM approach provides criteria for the diagnosis of and information related to specific disorders. From this a clinician working with a particular youth could derive a diagnosis thought to capture the youth's problems (e.g., Conduct Disorder, Separation Anxiety Disorder). In addition to providing a diagnosis, it is suggested that the clinician may wish to indicate other information that may be relevant in working with this youth. This can include other difficulties that may be the focus of clinical attention (e.g., academic problems) or any current medical condition (e.g., arthritis or diabetes) that may be relevant to understanding or treating the youth. In addition, psychosocial or environmental problems that might affect diagnosis, treatment, or prognosis (e.g., death of a family member or housing problems) might be noted. In certain circumstances, the clinician might also be called upon to provide a judgment of the young person's overall level of functioning or disability. Including such information can help provide a fuller view of the problems of a particular young person. This is illustrated by the application of such an approach to a young boy, Kevin.

KEVIN

Seeking a Diagnosis

Kevin is a 9-year-old third-grader. He was brought to the clinic after his teacher repeatedly called home about his worsening behavior in school. The teacher described Kevin as likeable and friendly, but also said that, among other things, he repeatedly disrupted the class with his antics, hummed and made noises, blurted out answers, and had to be constantly reminded to stay in his seat. He was full of energy on the playground, but seemed to have few playmates and was often last to be chosen for teams. When playing games such as softball, he might be in the outfield concentrating on things in the sky or interesting pebbles on the ground. Although he seemed very bright, Kevin seldom completed his assignments in class. Despite his mother's report of considerable time and effort being spent on getting Kevin to concentrate on and complete his homework, papers sent home were seldom returned and homework was forgotten or left crumpled in his book bag.

At home Kevin is always on the go, his play is noisy and he leaves a trail of toys in his wake. Chores are left uncompleted or not done at all. Kevin's mother describes him as "the sweetest boy imaginable," but also as a "real handful." A physical examination indicates that Kevin is healthy, well nourished, and in good physical condition except for several scrapes, bruises, and healed lacerations. The only significant medical history is a broken wrist at age 3 that resulted from a fall from a high wall that Kevin had managed to climb. Kevin's birth and early development were normal, and he reached developmental milestones at a normal or early time.

To illustrate how one might make a DSM diagnosis and provide other information, here is a diagnosis and some additional information relevant to Kevin's case that might be provided by his clinician.

Diagnosis: Attention-Deficit Hyperactivity Disorder, Combined Type
Other Difficulties: Academic Problem
Related Medical Conditions: None
Psychosocial or Environmental Problems: Impending school expulsion
Overall Adjustment: Serious impairment in schoolwork, moderate impairment in social relationships

Adapted from Frances & Ross, 2001, pp. 8–11.

CONSIDERING THE DSM APPROACH The development of the DSM approach to classification continues to be an ongoing process (APA, 2013; Regier et al., 2009). A number of concerns have been central to that process. One important aspect of the discussion of the DSM approach to classification is what has been termed **comorbidity.** This term is used to describe the situation in which youths meet the criteria for more than one disorder. The use of the term is controversial and some prefer the term **co-occurrence** (Lilienfeld, Waldman, & Israel, 1994; Widiger & Clark, 2000). Comorbidity typically implies the simultaneous existence of two or more distinct disorders in the same individual. Such co-occurrence is frequently reported (see Accent: "Co-Occurrence: A Common Circumstance") and has led some to question the DSM approach to classification. Do these youths have multiple distinct disorders, or are there other ways of understanding the many difficulties that they are experiencing?

There are multiple ways to interpret a situation in which a child or an adolescent meets the diagnostic criteria for more than one disorder (Angold, Costello, & Erkanli, 1999; Carson & Rutter, 1991; Hudziak et al., 2007; Youngstrom, 2010). It may be that many disorders have mixed patterns of symptoms. For example, mood disorders may be characterized by a mixture of depression and anxiety. Another alternative is that there are shared risk factors: Some of the same risk factors lead to the problems used to define both disorders. Or perhaps the presence of one disorder creates an increased risk for developing the other disorder. A related idea is that the second problem is a later stage in a developmental progression in which earlier problems may or may not be retained, even as additional difficulties develop. For example, for some children and adolescents, a diagnosis of oppositional defiant disorder is followed by a diagnosis of conduct disorder. It has been suggested, by some, that for these young people the diagnoses may represent a developmental pattern of a single common condition.

These are only some of the possible ways to explain "comorbidity." The issues involved in understanding co-occurrence of disorders are complex, and at present the solution to this issue remains unclear. However, the frequency of co-occurrence and the conceptual issues it raises are at the heart of how best to conceptualize child and adolescent psychopathology and discussions of the current DSM approach (Craske, 2012; Knapp & Jensen, 2006; Lilienfeld, 2003; Rutter, 2011; Youngstrom, 2010).

Over time efforts have been made to improve the DSM system. These include the more comprehensive coverage of child and adolescent disorders, the increased use of structured diagnostic rules, and attempts to draw on empirical data in a more consistent fashion (Widiger et al., 1991). However, clinical, scientific, conceptual, and political issues have also been raised (Angold & Costello, 2009; Carrey & Ungar, 2007; Egger & Emde, 2011; Follette & Houts, 1996; Jensen & Mrazek, 2006; Rutter, 2011). Because the DSM is currently the dominant approach to classification, it is important to mention some of the other concerns that have been raised regarding this system.

For example, while greater attention to the disorders of children and adolescents can be seen as a positive development, there is at the same time concern about the proliferation of categories and the very comprehensiveness of the DSM system (Houts, 2002; Rutter, 2011). This raises the fundamental question (Follette & Houts, 1996; Silk et al., 2000) that perhaps we have overdefined pathological behavior—in other words, too broadly defined children's behavior as deviant (cf. Richters & Cicchetti, 1993). Designating common misbehaviors or various problems in academic skill areas such as reading and mathematics as mental disorders are examples of this concern.

A major consideration that has guided the development of the DSM is reliability. In earlier versions, disagreements between diagnosticians (interrater reliability) resulted from inadequate criteria for making a diagnosis. Thus efforts were made starting with the DSM-III to improve interrater reliability by replacing general descriptions of disorders with clearer and more delineated diagnostic criteria based on a listing of symptoms. This approach, of more structured diagnostic rules, has improved communication among clinicians and researchers and has increased inter-clinician agreement in diagnosis. As would be expected, however, reliability still varies and may depend on the specific disorder and the nature and source of information (Leyfer & Brown, 2011). Characteristics of the youths such as gender or ethnicity, or characteristics of the clinician also may affect reliability. Furthermore, evidence of higher levels of reliability has typically been obtained under research conditions in which diagnosticians are given special training and employ procedures different from those likely to be used in typical clinical practice (APA Working Group on Psychoactive Medications for Children and Adolescents, 2006; Nathan & Langenbucher, 1999; Pottick et al., 2007; Valo & Tannock, 2010).

It has been argued as well that diagnostic research has focused too heavily on reliability and clarity of communication. Although these issues are clearly important, it is also crucial for the DSM to provide an accurate representation of the nature of disorders. Whether a system is useful or helpful for clinicians, a question of utility, is different from whether it is a good description of the true nature of clinically significant differences in psychological functioning—a question of validity (Knapp & Jensen, 2006; Sonuga-Barke, 1998).

ACCENT
Co-Occurrence: A Common Circumstance

Children and adolescents who are evaluated by professionals in clinic or school settings often present with several different problems. These problems frequently fit the criteria for a number of different disorders, and thus clinicians often give these children or adolescents more than one diagnosis. How best to conceptualize these instances of co-occurrence or comorbidity is an ongoing concern. The description of Samuel that follows illustrates this common circumstance.

SAMUEL

A Case of Co-Occurring Disorders

Samuel, an 11-year-old child, was referred to a clinic for attempted suicide after he had consumed a mixture of medicines, prescribed to his mother, in an attempt to kill himself. Samuel had slept at home for almost 2 days, when he was finally awakened by his mother and brought to the hospital.

Samuel lived in an inner-city neighborhood and since second grade had been in repeated

Adapted from Rapoport & Ismond, 1996.

trouble for stealing and breaking into empty homes. He had academic difficulties, was assigned to a special reading class, and was truant from school on a number of occasions. His mother may have experienced several major depressive episodes, sometimes drank heavily, and may have relied on prostitution for income. Samuel's father had not been in contact with the mother since Samuel was born.

At his interview, Samuel appeared sad and cried at one point. He reported having severe "blue periods," the most recent of which had been continuous for the past month. During these periods he thought that he might be better off dead. Samuel also reported that he had recently started to wake up in the middle of the night and had been avoiding his usual neighborhood "gang."

Samuel was given a diagnosis of Major Depressive Disorder, and a diagnosis of Persistent Depressive Disorder/Dysthymia (a more chronic form of depression) was also considered. In addition he received a diagnosis of Conduct Disorder, Childhood Onset Type, and a diagnosis of Specific Learning Disorder with impairment in reading.

Indeed, many of the questions raised to guide the future development of classification are questions of the validity of the current system. For example, validity would be indicated if research discovered treatments or etiologies that were *specific to particular disorders*. However, many medications have been reported as being effective in treating several DSM disorders (Brown et al., 2009; Kupfer, First, & Regier, 2002). Similarly, with regard to etiology, research studies have challenged the assumption that separate disorders have entirely different underlying genetic and neurobiological basis. For example, it has been found that anxiety and depression may share genetic and neurobiological factors (Franić et al., 2010; Vaidyanathan, Patrick, & Cuthbert, 2009; Williamson et al., 2005).

An additional concern is that the DSM promotes a disease/medical model that overly emphasizes biological etiology and treatment, and that conceptualizes disorder as being within the child rather than resulting from multiple causes and from the interaction of the child and the environment (Carrey & Ungar, 2007; Cicchetti, 2010; Silk et al., 2000; Sroufe, 1997).

Concern has also been expressed regarding the degree of attention to issues of age/developmental level, cultural context, and gender in the DSM (Achenbach, 2000; Hudziak et al., 2007; Nathan & Langenbucher, 1999; Silk et al., 2000). In DSM-5 differences in age-, gender-, and culture-related expressions of symptoms have been added for some diagnoses. The DSM-5 also does include, in the text that accompanies each set of diagnostic criteria and elsewhere, sections that address developmental, cultural, and gender-related features. This textual material may alert clinicians to variations associated with developmental level, culture, and gender. Nevertheless, diagnostic criteria are largely the same for both sexes and for all ages and cultures.

This approach may have important consequences. For example, it has been pointed out that if one applies a set of fixed cutpoints (number of symptoms needed for diagnosis) to diagnostic criteria, disorders may appear to have prevalence rates that vary with age and gender (Achenbach, 2000; Hudziak et al., 2007). The same applies to cultural differences. We could ask, however, whether these are real differences in rates of disorders.

For example, the DSM indicates that ADHD occurs more frequently in males. This sex difference in diagnosis led the literature on ADHD to be based largely on males. However, even non-deviant boys exhibit higher rates of behaviors characteristic of ADHD than do girls. Thus, the sex difference in ADHD might be an artifact of higher base rates of these behaviors in boys. If these sex differences in base rates in the population were considered in setting diagnostic cutpoints (e.g., slightly decreasing the number of required criteria for girls), would gender differences in prevalence of ADHD still emerge? Hudziak and colleagues (2005) not only employed a measure that contained DSM ADHD items (the Conners' Rating Scales—CRS) but also provided sex norms. These researchers used the CRS to measure ADHD and used the sex-specific norms to determine which children were statistically deviant on ADHD scales. This approach resulted in as many girls as boys meeting the criteria for ADHD— nearly equal prevalence for boys and girls. By contrast, if DSM criteria (where diagnostic thresholds do not differ by sex) were used, many girls who were impaired failed to meet diagnostic criteria. In a similar way, reported declines in the rates of ADHD diagnoses with age may also be an artifact of the age-related decline in base rates of ADHD behaviors.

In addition to affecting estimates of prevalence, the issue of whether to have fixed or variable cutoffs or criteria based on sex, age-related, or cultural considerations has implications for who will be identified as needing services. In some cases "fixed" cutoffs may, as illustrated above, result in failing to identify individuals who may benefit from services. Under other circumstances individuals whose behavior may not be deviant might be designated as having a disorder.

Furthermore, as we try to understand the development of psychopathology, research suggests that the potentially complex interactions of culture, context, and behavior deserve attention. By way of some examples, Gil and colleagues (2000) found that among U.S.-born Latino adolescent males, a greater predisposition toward alcohol involvement emerges over time as traditional values of family, cohesion, and social control deteriorate. Also, McLaughlin, Hilt, & Nolen-Hoeksema (2007) found that being a Latina American girl was associated with more comorbid disorders compared to being European American or African American. From these examples and other information, it seems clear that future diagnostic and classification systems will need to pay increasing attention to issues of cultural and developmental context (Alarcon et al., 2002; Lewis-Fernandez et al., 2010; Pine et al., 2011; Rescorla et al., 2007; 2011).

Finally, a frequently expressed concern regarding the validity of the current DSM is a basic concern with its categorical approach (see Accent: Dimensionality and the DSM). For example, research has supported the validity of three subtypes of Attention-Deficit Hyperactivity Disorder. However, Hudziak and his colleagues (1998) conducted structured diagnostic assessments of a large community sample of adolescent female twins. Their findings again supported the existence of the subtypes but suggested that the subtypes were best conceptualized as three dimensions (continuously distributed between clinical and nonclinical levels) rather than three distinct categories. This and other research (Craske, 2012; Shaw et al., 2011) suggest the importance of considering a dimensional conceptualization of ADHD and other disorders.

Researchers point out that the practice of dichotomizing continuous symptoms to form a disorder category and a nondisorder category results in reduced statistical power and may lead to misleading research outcomes. An illustration of this is provided by an example of the use of diagnosis in treatment research. Individuals with eating disorders were randomly assigned to either a treatment or self-help control condition. The presence or absence of a diagnosis of bulimia nervosa at the end of treatment was used as the outcome measure. The researchers did not find significant outcome differences between the two treatment groups using this categorical approach to assess outcome. However, when a dimensional approach—the frequency of binges and purges—was used to determine outcome, a significant group difference did emerge (APA, 2011).

A central issue in the continuing evolution of the DSM will be how to integrate dimensional concepts of psychopathology into this classification system (APA, 2013). An approach to classification which considers problems of children and adolescents dimensionally does already exist. We turn now to an examination of this empirically based approach to classification.

Empirical Approaches to Classification

The **empirical approach to classification** of behavioral problems is an alternative to the clinical approach to taxonomy. It is based on the use of statistical techniques to identify patterns of behavior that are interrelated. The general procedure is for a parent or some other respondent to indicate the presence or absence of specific behaviors by the youth. The information from these responses is quantified in some way. For example, the respondent marks a "0" if the youth does not exhibit a certain characteristic, a "1" if the youth displays a moderate degree

ACCENT
Dimensionality and the DSM

Attempts to develop a system of classification and diagnosis are, and should be, an ongoing process that is driven by scientific advances. The current DSM is a categorical approach to classification/diagnosis. A disorder is present or is not. One disorder is separate and distinct from another. Information based on research in several areas has prompted some to consider whether a categorical approach is appropriate or adequate for use in clinical diagnosis or research classification. The question that then follows is whether more continuous conceptualizations and dimensional considerations need to be incorporated into the diagnostic system (Hudziak et al., 2007; Rutter, 2011). Indeed, the issue of "dimensionality" was part of the ongoing process of developing the new edition of the DSM (APA, 2013). Here we briefly review some of the findings and thinking that have led to consideration of a dimensional strategy. Additional information that speaks to this issue is presented throughout the book.

What do we mean by the term *dimensionality* and how might we incorporate it into the DSM? Both the terms *spectrum* and *dimension* are often heard in such discussions.

The term **spectrum** has come to be employed to describe groups of disorders that are thought to share certain psychological or biological qualities. For example, in chapter 12 we will see that the term *autism spectrum disorders* has come to be used to describe difficulties that were once separately diagnosed as autism, Asperger's syndrome, and other pervasive developmental disorders. Thus, a number of related disorders may not be considered as separate, but rather as part of a larger spectrum of disorders.

The term **dimension** refers to a quantitative rather than qualitative approach to thinking about disorders. In a separate section of the text, the DSM suggests that the idea of dimensionality might be incorporated into the DSM in a number of ways. For example, dimensional assessment of the number, frequency, or intensity of symptoms might supplement a "yes" or "no" decision as to whether a youth meets the criteria for a diagnosis. For example, one might indicate the number of inattentive and hyperactive-impulsive symptoms rather than only indicating whether a child meets the criteria for a diagnosis of attention-deficit hyperactivity disorder. Indeed, research findings suggest that specifying the number of symptoms facilitates research and the ability to predict the likely course of a disorder, and can guide clinical interventions (Lahey & Wilcutt, 2010).

What has been termed cross-cutting assessment is another way that the DSM approach has attempted to address the issue of dimensionality (APA, 2013). The term *cross-cutting* is used because it involves measures that cut across boundaries of any single disorder. This assessment addresses areas of clinical importance that are not necessarily part of the diagnostic criteria for a youth's specific disorder. They may, however, be important with regard to considerations such as prognosis, treatment planning, and treatment outcome. Thus, for example, measurement of the degree of depressed mood, anxiety, sleep problems, or substance use might be completed for all youth being seen at a clinic.

These are some of the ways that the DSM approach has begun to address dimensionality. However, many consider these as only modest alterations and the current DSM still clearly retains a categorical rather than a continuous or dimensional conceptualization of disorder. Accumulating research, however, suggests that dimensionality will become an important part of future diagnostic systems. For example, the National Institute of Mental Health (NIMH) has launched a project to develop new research-based diagnostic criteria that adopt a dimensional approach.

---

of the characteristic, and a "2" if the characteristic is clearly present. Such information is obtained for a large number of young people. Statistical techniques such as factor analysis are then employed, and groups of items that tend to occur together are thus identified (Achenbach, 1998). These groups are referred to as factors or clusters. The term **syndrome** is also often employed to describe behaviors that tend to occur together, whether they are identified by empirical or clinical judgment procedures. Thus, rather than relying on clinicians' views about which behaviors tend to occur together, researchers can employ empirical and statistical procedures as the basis for developing a classification scheme.

Substantial evidence exists for two **broadband syndromes**, or general clusters of behaviors or characteristics.

One of these clusters has been given the various labels of **internalizing**, overcontrolled, or anxiety-withdrawal. Descriptions such as anxious, shy, withdrawn, and depressed are some of the characteristics associated with this grouping. The second grouping has been variously labeled **externalizing**, undercontrolled, or conduct disorder. Fighting, temper tantrums, disobedience, and destructiveness are frequently associated with this pattern.

The Achenbach instruments are among the measures used to derive the two broadband clusters just described. The Child Behavior Checklist (CBCL) is completed by the parents of youths 6 to 18 years of age (Achenbach & Rescorla, 2001). The Teacher Report Form (TRF) is a parallel instrument completed by teachers of youths 6 to 18 years old, and the Youth Self-Report (YSR) is completed by youths who are 11 to 18 years of age. Parallel measures for younger children, the CBCL for Ages 1½ –5 and the C-TRF (Caregiver–Teacher Report Form) are also available (Achenbach & Rescorla, 2000).

In addition to the two broadband syndromes labeled *Internalizing* and *Externalizing*, research with these instruments has identified empirically defined, less general, or **narrowband syndromes**. These syndromes for the school-age scales are described in Table 5.1. Every child who is evaluated receives a score on each of the syndromes, resulting in a profile of syndrome scores for a particular child (see Figure 5.1; p. 95). This approach to classification evaluates each youngster on several dimensions.

Thus, this approach to classification differs from the clinical approach of the DSM in several ways. One important difference between the two approaches is how groupings are defined and formed (empirically versus clinical consensus). A second important difference is that the empirical approach to classification views problems as dimensional rather than categorical. It suggests that differences between individuals are quantitative rather than qualitative and that the difference between normal and pathological is one of degree rather than one of kind (Achenbach, 2000).

Empirically based classifications also employ data from **normative samples** as a frame of reference for judging the problems of an individual youth. For the CBCL, TRF, and YSR, for example, there are two sets of norms against which

to compare an individual child's or adolescent's scores. A youth's scores can be compared with norms for nonreferred youths or with norms for other young people referred for mental health services. There are separate norms for each sex in particular age ranges, as rated by each type of informant. Thus, there are separate parent informant CBCL norms for boys 6 to 11, boys 12 to 18, girls 6 to 11, and girls 12 to 18, and separate similar norms for teacher and for youth informants (Achenbach & Rescorla, 2001). A youth's scores can also be evaluated with respect to norms from multiple cultures (Achenbach & Rescorla, 2007).

To evaluate the behavior problems of an 11-year-old boy named Jason, for example, one could compare Jason's scores on the empirically based syndromes derived from his parents' reports with two sets of norms: norms of parent reports for nonreferred 11-year-old boys and norms of parent reports for clinic-referred 11-year-old boys. Scores based on Jason's teacher's TRF could be compared with two similar sets of norms of teachers' reports for 11-year-old boys. And scores based on Jason's own YSR could be compared with norms of responses of nonreferred and clinic-referred boys of his age.

It is worth noting that, in addition to the dimensions/syndromes described above and outlined in Table 5.1, the Achenbach instruments can be scored to yield scales that correspond to some DSM categories (Achenbach, Dumenci, & Rescorla, 2003; Achenbach & Rescorla, 2007).

TABLE 5.1	Eight Narrowband Syndromes Common to the CBCL, TRF, and YSR with Sample Items	
INTERNALIZING SYNDROMES		
Anxious/Depressed	**Withdrawn/Depressed**	**Somatic Complaints**
Cries a lot	Rather be alone	Overtired
Fearful, anxious	Shy, timid	Aches, pains
Feels worthless	Withdrawn	Stomachaches
MIXED SYNDROMES		
Social Problems	**Thought Problems**	**Attention Problems**
Lonely	Hears things	Can't concentrate
Gets teased	Sees things	Can't sit still
Not liked	Strange ideas	Impulsive
EXTERNALIZING SYNDROMES		
Rule-Breaking Behavior	**Aggressive Behavior**	
Lacks guilt	Mean to others	
Bad friends	Destroys others' things	
Steals at home	Gets in fights	

Adapted from Achenbach & Rescorla, 2001.

These DSM-oriented scales are one way that the two approaches might be compared.

RELIABILITY   Reliability studies of empirically derived systems generally indicate that problem scores are quite reliable. The pattern of reliability is both interesting and informative (Achenbach & Rescorla, 2001).

Test–retest reliability correlations from two ratings by the same informant are often in the 0.80 and 0.90 ranges. So, for example, correlation for the Total Problems score on the CBCL is 0.94. Interrater reliability between different informants observing the child in the same situation is also quite good, although lower than for two evaluations by the same person. The mean agreement of mothers and fathers on the CBCL problem scales is 0.76.

Level of interrater agreement, however, is notably lower between raters who observe youth in distinctly different situations. The average correlation between parents' and teachers' Total Problem Scores, for example, is 0.35. Youths' Total Problem Scores are significantly, but modestly, related to parents' (0.54) and teachers' (0.21) ratings. These lower correlations may reveal something more than just the reliability of a particular approach to classification. This lower interrater agreement may suggest something about the classification process in general and about the youth's behavior in particular (Achenbach, 2011). A young person's behavior may have aspects that are consistent across time and situations, but it may also vary considerably with different individuals and in different situations. In addition, certain attributes may be more or less evident to different individuals or to other persons compared with the youths themselves (e.g., aggression versus feelings of loneliness). Thus, such findings also alert us to the possible limitations and bias of any one rater's perspective, whether this perspective is obtained by responses to a particular instrument or by clinical interview (Achenbach, McConaughy, & Howell, 1987; De Los Reyes & Kazdin, 2005; Hay et al., 1999).

VALIDITY   The validity of empirically derived classification systems is indicated by a variety of studies. The same broadband syndromes have emerged in a variety of studies employing different instruments, different types of informants, and different samples, suggesting that the categories reflect valid distinctions (Achenbach & Rescorla, 2001). The findings show that the syndromes are valid ones because they emerge under a variety of conditions. Cross-cultural studies that find similar syndromes add further support; however, they also point to possible cultural differences in how youngsters' problems are manifested (Achenbach, Rescorla, & Ivanova, 2005; Ivanova et al., 2007a, b; 2010; Weisz et al., 2006).

Validity is also supported when differences in scores relate to other criteria. Indeed, a comparison of young people referred for outpatient mental health services with a sample of nonreferred young people matched for SES, age, and gender indicated that the clinical sample differed significantly from the nonreferred sample on all scores (Achenbach & Rescorla, 2001).

Also, differences between youths with high scores on different syndromes can address the validity of empirically identified syndromes. For example, comparison of young children with internalizing problems and those with externalizing problems has shown that they may differ with respect to the type of negative emotion they express and the style of emotion regulation and control that they exhibit (Eisenberg et al., 2001). Similarly, evidence suggests different correlates for the two syndromes *within* the externalizing domain (see Table 5.1). For example, research suggests that the aggressive syndrome is associated with stronger biochemical correlates and heredity, and greater developmental stability, than is the rule-breaking syndrome (Achenbach, 1998; Eley, 1997). Finally, scores on empirically derived syndromes have also been shown to predict outcomes such as future problems, use of mental health services, and police contacts (Achenbach et al., 1995; Stanger et al., 1996). Such findings support the validity of the empirical and dimensional approach to classification.

Stigmatization and the Impact of Labels

As we have already noted, classification and diagnosis are intended to facilitate understanding and treatment of psychological problems. Although classification is intended as a scientific and clinical enterprise, it can be seen as a social process. The **diagnostic label** places the youngster in a subgroup of individuals and this has implications for how the young person may be viewed and treated by others. If this impact is negative, this may be due, in part, to the stigma associated with mental illness. **Stigmatization** refers to stereotyping, prejudice, discrimination, and self-degradation that may be associated with membership in a socially devalued group. (See Accent: The Impact of Stigmatization.)

Any negative impact of a diagnostic label may actually detract from the original purpose of categorizing—that of helping young people (Hinshaw, 2005). When attempting to define a mental disorder (APA, 2013) it is important to remember that formal classification is intended to categorize disorders, not people (Cantwell, 1980). Thus it is correct to say, for example, "Billy Greene has autism." However, it is incorrect to say "Billy Greene the autistic child."

It is important to be aware of the potential negative effects of the labeling process. Labels can contribute to a variety of unintended consequences. Overgeneralization is one concern. It may incorrectly be assumed that all youngsters labeled with attention-deficit hyperactivity disorder, for example, are more alike than they actually are. Such an assumption readily leads to neglect of the individual child or adolescent. Labels also may produce negative perceptions of youngsters. For example, Walker and colleagues (2008) presented vignettes of a child labeled as having either ADHD, depression, or asthma to a large sample of youths ages 8–18. Other than the disorder designation, the description of the child was the same. Children with ADHD or depression were viewed as more likely to engage in antisocial behavior and violence than the children described as having asthma.

Also, expectations regarding a youth may be biased by the presence of a label. Others may act in a manner that is guided by such expectations, influencing the youth to behave in a manner consistent with such expectations. The negative expectation that may be transmitted by labels is suggested by the findings of a study by Briggs and colleagues (1994). Adults read vignettes of a 6-year-old child engaged in aggressive behavior on a school playground. The stories varied regarding the family history of the child (normal, mother dying of cancer, sexually abused). After reading the vignette, the adults completed a questionnaire about their expectations regarding the behavior of the child. Results indicated that the adults had different expectations regarding the sexually abused child; for example, they believed that the sexually abused child would have more behavior problems and lesser achievement than either of the other two children.

Labels may not always produce negative expectations, however. Some suggest that labels provide an "explanation" for the child's problematic behavior. When an adult understands why the child is behaving in this manner, the adult may be less likely to have negative reactions and may have more appropriate expectations for the child. That labels do not always lead to negative expectations is illustrated in a study by Wood and Valdez-Menchaca (1996). Adults interacted with four children, one of whom had previously been diagnosed with a language disorder (LD). The adults were randomly assigned to one of two conditions: The first was a nonlabel condition in which the child with LD was not identified, and the second was a label condition in which the child with LD was identified. Adults in the nonlabel group ranked the child with LD as significantly less likable, less productive, and less academically competent

ACCENT
The Impact of Stigmatization

The stigma associated with mental illness is increasingly realized to be a central issue by those concerned for the well-being of children, adolescents, and their families (Hinshaw, 2010; Mukolo, Heflinger, & Wallston, 2010; Penn et al., 2005). Stigmatization may affect youths in multiple ways. It may affect both youths with a disorder and youths whose parents have a mental disorder.

Stigmatization is often thought of as involving three dimensions: negative stereotypes, devaluation, and discrimination. Stereotyping means that a young person with a disorder may be viewed in terms of negative traits or attributes such as being dangerous or incompetent. Devaluing may lead to separation from others and loss of status. Discrimination refers to actions that limit the young person's rights and power. In addition, the youth may internalize negative evaluations and develop a negative view of his or her abilities and even him- or herself. Research suggests a number of other ways that stigmatization affects youths. For example, a young person with a disorder may experience a variety of negative social experiences, be denigrated, and be rejected by peers. The young person may also experience a similar impact of stigmatization in interactions with adults and even professionals. Also, the youth's parents may be blamed for their child's difficulties. This, along with the stigma associated with the young person's disorder, may reduce the likelihood that the family will seek help (Pescosolido et al., 2008).

We also know that parental psychopathology is a risk factor for future child psychopathology. The stigma associated with mental disorders may prevent parents with a disorder from seeking help and thereby increase their children's risk. Also, the stigma associated with the parent's disorder may inhibit open family discussion and thereby further increase risk, limiting support for the children and perhaps leading them to blame themselves for their parents' or family's difficulties. There also may be increased risk if the parent and family feel the need to conceal the parent's difficulties, thereby reducing access to social support.

Understanding stigmatization and its impact is clearly a complex and difficult issue. Education regarding child psychopathology and the issue of stigmatization is clearly part of the solution. However, a broader effort is needed to overcome stigmatization. As Hinshaw (2005) has stated,

For children and adolescents, stigma processes occur in families, schools, and communities; the notion of 'fit' between child and setting is crucial for the diagnosis of the child as mentally disturbed. Hence, community tolerance and acceptance of developmental disorders—and community facilitation of accommodation for youth with special educational needs—are essential components of fostering academic, social, and life competence (p. 726).

than the other children. Adults in the label group did not. They had observed the same inappropriate behaviors as the adults in the nonlabel group but they appeared to be more accepting of such behavior.

Finally, concern has been voiced that diagnostic labeling minimizes attention to the interpersonal and social context in which the child's behavior exists (Silk et al., 2000; Sroufe, 1997). Traditional diagnostic categories ignore the fact that a youngster's problems "belong" to at least one other person—the one who is identifying or reporting the problems (Algozzine, 1977; Lilly, 1979). As we shall see throughout this book, there is much evidence that the way a youth is described and viewed may reflect as much on the individual doing the describing as it does on the behavior of the child or adolescent.

Many experts involved in the study and treatment of young people are concerned about potential negative consequences of diagnostic labels, and these experts advocate for various ways to reduce the possible harmful effects. Categorization, however, is embedded in our thinking and contributes to the advancement of our knowledge. Completely discarding categorization is neither desirable nor possible. Thus it is important to improve classification systems and at the same time to be sensitive to social factors inherent in the use of categories, the social status imparted by a label, and the impact of labels on the young person and the family (Adelman, 1996; Hinshaw, 2010).

ASSESSMENT

Evaluating child and adolescent problems is a complex process. By the time a young person comes to the attention of a clinician, the presenting problem is usually, if not always, multifaceted. But because assessment is the first part of any contact, the professional's knowledge of the problem is limited. Both of these factors, as well as common sense and caution, argue that the best interests of the young person are most likely served by a comprehensive assessment of multiple facets of the young person and his or her environment.

ALICIA

An Initial Assessment

The parents of 6-year-old Alicia were seeking assistance in understanding her problems and ways to help their daughter improve her adjustment at home and school and with her peers. The parents described Alicia as impulsive, moody, and having difficulty in school. The initial information provided by the parents indicated that several male relatives on the mother's side of the family were mentally retarded and that one of these relatives had recently been diagnosed with a fragile X syndrome chromosomal disorder. The clinician hypothesized that Alicia might be a fragile X carrier because females are carriers for the defective gene associated with the syndrome. Based on initial information the clinician also hypothesized that Alicia might have ADHD and a learning disability.

Information about Alicia was gathered from several sources: the parents (interview, rating scales, daily behavioral logs, observation of parent–child interactions), the teacher (rating scales, academic performance and test scores), and Alicia herself (interview, direct observation, psychoeducational testing). Information obtained during the assessment revealed that Alicia had many characteristics of females who carry the fragile X chromosome. This was discussed with the parents

and referral for a genetic evaluation revealed that this was indeed the case. The assessment also indicated that Alicia met the diagnostic criteria for ADHD and that she had a learning problem.

In addition, evaluation revealed that Alicia's parents provided a structured yet stimulating environment for her. Alicia had friends, successfully engaged in age-appropriate activities, and felt loved by her parents. She also realized that her impulsive behavior created problems for herself and her family. Positive aspects of the case were Alicia's desire to please and her good social skills, warm and loving parents, and supportive home and school environments.

The assessment led to intervention strategies that included a change in Alicia's class placement and resource support, support for the family, referral to a support group for parents of children with fragile X syndrome, behavior management techniques for the parents, and brief individual work with Alicia to help her recognize her strengths and cope with her difficulties. The clinician indicated that Alicia would likely adapt and continue to develop successfully, but further assessment and intervention might be needed as new challenges were encountered.

Adapted from Schroeder & Gordon, 2002, pp. 49–50.

Conducting a Comprehensive Assessment

As we shall see throughout our discussion, behavioral disorders in youth are complex, often encompassing a variety of components rather than a single problem behavior. Furthermore, these problems typically arise from, and are maintained by, multiple influences. Such influences include biological factors; aspects of the youngster's behavioral, cognitive, and social functioning; and influences of the family and other social systems such as peers and school. Thus an assessment must be comprehensive in evaluating a variety of potential presenting problems, measuring a variety of aspects of youth themselves, and assessing multiple contexts and other individuals.

Information must be obtained from a number of sources (e.g., the youth, parents, teachers) to assess problems that may vary by context or that may be displayed differently in the presence of different individuals. A child may behave differently at home, in school, and in playing with his or her peers. Also, observers may view the same or similar behaviors differently. A mother who is depressed and experiencing life stresses may be less able to tolerate minor deviations from expected behavior. Such differences in perception may be important both in understanding the presenting problems and in planning interventions. Assessment thus requires the use of multiple and varied methods as well as familiarity with assessment instruments for individuals of many different ages. The process requires considerable skill and sensitivity.

Assessment may be best accomplished by a team of clinicians carefully trained in the administration and interpretation of specific procedures and instruments. It is desirable for clinicians to employ **evidence-based assessment**—procedures that rely on empirical evidence and theory to guide their selection and support their validity (Hunsley & Mash, 2011; Kazdin, 2005). As we will see later in this chapter when we discuss empirically supported treatments, such evidence-based or empirically supported practice is an ongoing goal for researchers and clinicians.

Because assessment is usually conducted immediately on contact with the young person or family, it demands special sensitivity to anxiety, fear, shyness, manipulativeness, and the like. If treatment ensues, assessment should be a continuous process, so that new information can be gleaned and the ongoing effects of treatment can be ascertained. In this way, the clinician remains open to nuances and can avoid rigid judgments about a multifaceted and complex phenomenon.

The Interview

THE GENERAL CLINICAL INTERVIEW   The **general clinical interview** is clearly the most common method of assessment (Watkins et al., 1995). Information on all areas of functioning is obtained by interviewing the child or adolescent and various other people in the social environment.

Whether the young person will be interviewed alone will probably vary with age. An older child or adolescent generally is more capable and is more likely to provide valuable information. Nevertheless, clinicians often elect to interview even a very young child in order to obtain their own impressions. Preschool and grade school children can provide valuable information if appropriate developmental considerations are used to tailor the interview to the individual child (Bierman & Schwartz, 1986; Kamphaus & Frick, 1996). For example, an adultlike face-to-face interview may be intimidating for a young child, so a more successful technique may be to model the interview after a familiar play or school task.

Most clinicians seek information concerning the nature of the problem, past and recent history, present conditions, feelings and perceptions, attempts to solve the problem, and expectations concerning treatment. The general clinical interview is used not only to determine the nature of the presenting problem and perhaps to help formulate a diagnosis but also to gather information that allows the clinician to conceptualize the case and to plan an appropriate therapeutic intervention.

STRUCTURED DIAGNOSTIC INTERVIEWS   The general clinical interview is usually described as open-ended or unstructured. Because such interviews are most often conducted in the context of a therapeutic interaction and are employed along with a variety of other assessment instruments, it has been difficult to evaluate reliability and validity. **Structured diagnostic interviews** have arisen in part to create interviews that are likely to be more reliable. They also have been developed for the more limited purpose of deriving a diagnosis based on a particular classification scheme, such as the DSM; for use in research; or in order to screen large populations for the prevalence of disorders. These interviews can be conducted with the youth and/or parent(s). The Anxiety Disorders Interview for Children Schedule (ADIS; Silverman & Albano, 1996), the Diagnostic Interview for Children and Adolescents (DICA; Reich, 2000), and the Schedule for Affective Disorders and Schizophrenia for School-Age Children (K-SADS; Ambrosini, 2000) are examples of these diagnostic interviews.

In the unstructured general clinical interview, there are no particular questions that the clinician must ask, no designated format, and no stipulated method to record information. That is not to say that there are no guidelines or agreed-on procedures for conducting an effective interview. Indeed, there is an extensive literature on effective interviewing (McConaughy, 2005; Sattler, 1998). However, unstructured interviews are intended to give the clinician great latitude. In contrast, structured diagnostic interviews consist of a set of questions that the interviewer asks the youngster. There are rules for how the interview is to be conducted, and explicit guidelines for recording and scoring the youngster's responses (McClellan & Werry, 2000).

Problem Checklists and Self-Report Instruments

Problem checklists and rating scales were described in our discussion of classification (pp. 90–91). There is a wide variety of such instruments. Some are for general use—such as the Child Behavior Checklist (Achenbach & Rescorla, 2001), the Personality Inventory for Children (Lachar & Gruber, 2001), and the Behavior Assessment System for Children (Reynolds & Kamphaus, 2004). Others are used with particular populations. The Conners Rating Scales (Conners, 2008), for instance, can be used when attention-deficit hyperactivity disorder needs to be assessed.

A considerable empirical literature suggests that these instruments may be valuable tools for clinicians and researchers (Frick & Kamphaus, 2001). In one study, the parent-reported problems and competencies of youth assessed at intake into mental health services were compared with those of demographically matched nonreferred youngsters (Achenbach & Rescorla, 2001). Checklist scores clearly discriminated between the clinic and nonreferred children regarding both behavior problems and social competencies.

A general rating scale may thus help a clinician judge the child's adjustment relative to norms for referred and nonreferred populations. This procedure can help to evaluate the appropriateness of the referral. Once a particular presenting problem is identified, the clinician might use a more specific rating scale.

Furthermore, rating scales completed by different informants may help the clinician gain a fuller appreciation of the clinical picture and of potential situational aspects of the child's problem. For example, Figure 5.1 illustrates the differences in responses of a young girl's mother and father. Differing perceptions of two informants may provide important information to a clinician. For example, the CBCL, TRF, and YSR in the Achenbach instruments make it possible to compare multiple informants' reports

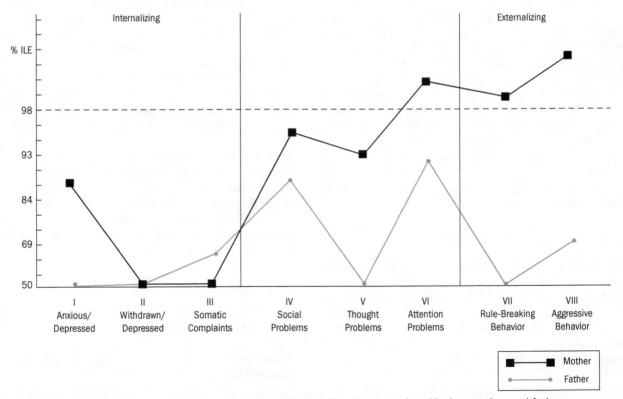

FIGURE 5.1 Profiles of an 11-year-old girl based on Child Behavior Checklists completed by her mother and father.

about the child with respect to a common set of problem items and dimensions. When two or more respondents use these instruments to describe a child or adolescent, a statistic can be computed indicating the degree of agreement. This degree of agreement for a particular youth can then be compared with the degree of agreement between comparable informants for a large representative sample. Thus it is possible to know whether the degree of agreement between Tommy's mother and his teacher is less than, similar to, or greater than the average mother–teacher agreement about boys in Tommy's age range.

In addition, the clinician or researcher may also draw on an array of **self-report measures**. Here, too, there are general measures and there are also self-report measures to assess specific problems such as anxiety and depression (Kovacs, 1992; 2003; March et al., 1997). Instruments also are available to assess constructs related to adjustment such as self-control and self-concept (Connell, 1985; Harter, 1985). Many of these measures will be described in later chapters that focus on particular child and adolescent problems.

Parents and other adults may also be asked to complete self-report instruments about themselves. These instruments may assess specific problems, for example, a parent's own anxiety or depression. Or they may evaluate a wide array of aspects of adult functioning. For instance, the feelings, attitudes, and beliefs of adults, particularly with respect to the child or adolescent, may be assessed (e.g., the Stability of Activities in the Family Environment—Israel, Roderick, & Ivanova, 2002; the Parenting Stress Index—Abidin, 1995), or aspects of the family environment may be measured (e.g., the Family Environment Scale—Moos & Moos, 1994; and the Parent–Adolescent Relationship Questionnaire—Robin, Koepke, & Moye, 1990). Such assessment can provide important information about the social environment and factors that may influence problem behavior. The use of such measures acknowledges that the presenting problem is complex and exists in a social context.

Observational Assessment

Early attempts to observe children's behavior used diaries or continuous observations and narrations that were deliberately nonselective (Wright, 1960). From this tradition evolved observations of a more focused, pinpointed set of behaviors that could be reliably coded by observers (Bijou et al., 1969). Such structured observations continue to be a potentially important aspect of the assessment process (Le Couteur & Gardner, 2008). They involve watching and systematically observing the behavior of a youth or parent, or some other aspect of the young person's environment as it occurs.

Behavioral observations are frequently made in the child's natural environment, although situations are sometimes created in clinic or laboratory settings to approximate naturally occurring interactions. Observations can include reports of single, relatively simple, and discrete behaviors of the child; interactions of the child and peers; and complex systems of interactions among family members (Israel, Pravder, & Knights, 1980; Kolko, 1987; Reid, 1978). Clearly, ongoing interactions are more difficult to observe and code than are the behaviors of a single individual; however, they are likely to be theoretically and clinically relevant.

The first step in any behavioral observation system involves explicitly pinpointing and defining behaviors. Observers are trained to use the system and note whether a particular behavior or sequence of behaviors occurs. Research indicates that a number of factors affect reliability as well as validity and clinical utility of observational systems (Hops, Davis, & Longoria, 1995). For example, the complexity of the observational system and changes over time in the observers' use of the system (observer drift) are two such factors. Reactivity (a change in an individual's behavior when the individual knows that he or she is being observed) is often cited as the greatest impediment to the utility of direct observation. Careful training, periodic monitoring of observers' use of the system, and use of observers already in the situation (e.g., teachers) are some recommended ways to reduce distortions in the information obtained from direct observation.

Behavioral observations are the most direct method of assessment and require the least inference. The difficulty and expense involved in training and maintaining reliable observers is probably the primary obstacle to their common use in nonresearch contexts. Since direct observation has long been considered the hallmark of assessment from a behavioral perspective, attempts have been made to create systems that are more amenable to widespread use. Direct observation is, however, just one aspect of a multimethod approach to behavioral assessment that can include self-monitoring of behavior, interviews, ratings and checklists, and self-report instruments.

Projective Tests

At one time the most common form of psychological test employed to assess children was the projective test. These tests are less commonly used today, in large part because of debates regarding lack of empirical norms, reliability, and validity (Anastasi & Urbina, 1997; Erickson, Lilienfeld, & Vitacco, 2007; Lilienfeld, Wood, & Garb, 2000; Kleiger, 2001; Knoff, 1998).

Projective tests were derived from the psychoanalytic notion of projection as a defense mechanism: One way the ego deals with unacceptable impulses is to project them onto some external object. It is assumed that the impulses cannot be expressed directly. Therefore, many projective tests present an ambiguous stimulus, allowing the individual to project "unacceptable" thoughts and impulses, as well as other defense mechanisms onto the stimulus. Projective tests are also used by some clinicians in a manner that involves less psychodynamic inference (Chandler, 2003). For example, the young person may see an ambiguous stimulus in terms of past experiences and present desires and thus be prompted to report these. Analyses that examine formal aspects of a test response—for example, the distance between human figures that the child draws—may also be used. Interpretations are then made on the basis of this response style rather than on the content of the response.

Projective tests may ask a child to interpret an image or to create his or her own picture. In the Rorschach test, the youth is asked what he or she sees in each of 10 ink blots. The most commonly used methods for scoring and interpretation are based on characteristics of the response, such as the portion of the blot responded to (location), factors such as color and shading (determinants), and the nature of what is seen in the blot (content) (Exner & Weiner, 1995). The Human Figure Drawing, or Draw-a-Person test (Koppitz, 1984; Machover, 1949;

Mitchell, Trent, & McArthur, 1993) requires the child to draw a picture of a person and then a second person of the opposite sex. The House-Tree-Person technique (Buck, 1992) asks the child to draw a house, a tree, and a person. In the Kinetic Family Drawing technique (Burns, 1987), the child is asked to draw a picture of everyone in the family, including himself or herself, "doing something." Typically the clinician then asks questions about the drawings. Murray's (1943) Thematic Apperception Test (TAT), the Children's Apperception Test (CAT) (Bellak & Abrams, 1997; Bellak & Bellak, 1982), and the Roberts Apperception Test for Children (Roberts, 2005) provide the young person with pictures for which he or she is asked to make up a story. Figure 5.2 presents pictures similar to those used in the CAT.

Intellectual–Educational Assessment

The evaluation of intellectual and academic functioning is an important part of almost all clinical assessments. Intellectual functioning is a central defining feature for disorders such as intellectual disability and learning disabilities, but it may also contribute to and be affected by a wide array of behavioral problems. Compared with most other assessment instruments, tests of intellectual functioning tend to have better normative data, reliability, and validity. Although our present discussion of these instruments is brief, we will consider additional information in later chapters.

FIGURE 5.2 Drawings similar to those employed in the CAT.

INTELLIGENCE TESTS   By far the most commonly employed assessment devices for evaluating intellectual functioning are tests of general intelligence. The Stanford–Binet (Roid & Barram, 2004); the Wechsler tests—the Wechsler Preschool and Primary Scale of Intelligence (Wechsler, 2002) and the Wechsler Intelligence Scale for Children (Wechsler, 2003); and the Kaufman Assessment Battery for Children (Kaufman & Kaufman, 2004) are some of the intelligence tests widely used in clinical settings. All are individually administered and yield an **intelligence (IQ) score**. The average score is 100, and an individual score reflects how far above or below the average person of his or her age an individual has scored.

Intelligence tests have long been the subject of heated controversy. Critics have argued that the use of IQ scores has caused intelligence to be viewed as a real thing, a rigid and fixed attribute, rather than as a concept that is complex and subtle. Critics also claim that intelligence tests are culturally biased and have led to social injustice (cf. Kamin, 1974; Kaplan, 1985). Although intelligence tests are popular and useful in predicting a variety of outcomes, continued concern with legal, ethical, and practical issues demand that they be used cautiously, that efforts be made to improve intelligence tests, and that their usage be monitored for appropriateness (Kamphaus, 1993; Perlman & Kaufman, 1990).

DEVELOPMENTAL SCALES   Assessment of intellectual functioning in very young children, and particularly in infants, requires a special kind of assessment instrument. A popular measure is the Bayley Scales of Infant and Toddler Development (Bayley, 2005). The Bayley can be used to assess children from 1 to 42 months of age and includes scales that assess multiple aspects of development. Performance on developmental tests yields a **developmental index** rather than an intelligence score. Unlike intelligence tests, which place considerable emphasis on emphasize language and abstract reasoning abilities, developmental scales place considerable emphasis on sensorimotor skills and simple social skills. For example, the Bayley examines the ability to sit, walk, place objects, attend to visual and auditory stimuli, smile, and imitate adults. Perhaps because they tap somewhat different abilities, there is only a low correlation between developmental scales, particularly when they are administered early, and measures of intellectual functioning later in childhood. Early developmental test scores may, however, be predictive of later intellectual functioning for children with serious developmental disabilities (Sattler, 1992).

ABILITY AND ACHIEVEMENT TESTS   In addition to assessing a youth's general intellectual functioning, it is often necessary or helpful to assess a child or adolescents's functioning in a particular area. **Ability and achievement tests** have been developed for this purpose (Katz & Slomka, 1990; Stetson & Stetson, 2001). The Wide Range Achievement Test (Wilkinson & Robertson, 2006) and the Woodcock Reading Mastery Tests (Woodcock, 2011), for example, are two measures of academic achievement that are administered to an individual youth. Tests such as the Iowa Test of Basic Skills (Hoover, Dunbar, & Frisbie, 2001) and the Stanford Achievement Test (Harcourt Assessment, 2003) are group-administered achievement tests employed in many school settings. Specific ability and achievement tests may be particularly important to professionals working with children who have learning and school-related problems.

Assessment of Physical Functioning

GENERAL PHYSICAL ASSESSMENT   Assessment of physical functioning can provide several kinds of information valuable to understanding disordered behavior. Family and child histories and physical examinations may reveal genetic problems that are treatable by environmental manipulation. For example, phenylketonuria (PKU) is a recessive gene condition that is affected by dietary treatment. Avoidance of phenylalanine in the child's diet prevents most of the cognitive problems usually associated with the condition. In addition, diseases and defects may be diagnosed that affect important areas of functioning either directly (e.g., a urinary tract infection causing problems in toilet training) or indirectly (e.g., a sickly child being overprotected by parents). Also, signs of atypical or lagging physical development may be an early indication of developmental disorders that eventually influence many aspects of behavior.

PSYCHOPHYSIOLOGICAL ASSESSMENT   Changes in physiological systems are associated with both externalizing and internalizing problems (Pliszka, 2011; Swearer et al., 2011; Weyandt et al., 2011). Thus, **psychophysiological assessments** are often conducted in circumstances where a child or adolescent's arousal level is of concern. Because of the equipment that is necessary, such assessments are more common in research settings than in general clinical practice. Evaluation of heart rate, muscle tension, and respiration rate are examples of these assessments. Measures of electrical activity in the autonomic nervous system, such as skin conductance, or in the central nervous system, such as the electroencephalogram (EEG), are also often aspects of psychophysiological assessments.

ASSESSMENT OF NERVOUS SYSTEM FUNCTIONING

The assessment of the nervous system is particularly important to understanding a wide array of disorders (Goldstein & Reynolds, 2011). These assessment techniques potentially provide information regarding the etiology of disorder and also benefit treatment research by providing information regarding the mechanisms through which treatments, particularly medications, have their effects (Fleck et al., 2010; Pliszka, 2011). Assessment of the nervous system is also an important aspect of evaluating outcomes for youngsters who experience brain injury (Yeates et al., 2007). The assessment of nervous system–behavior relationships requires the coordinated efforts of neurologists, psychologists, and other professional workers.

Neurological Assessment   **Neurological assessment** can be achieved by a number of procedures that directly assess the integrity of the nervous system. To record an electroencephalograph (EEG) or an event-related potential (ERP), electrodes are placed on the child or adolescent's scalp that record activity of the brain cortex in general or during a time when the youth is engaged in information-processing tasks. EEG/ERP activation patterns have contributed to the understanding of brain functioning in a number of populations, including young people at risk for anxiety and mood disorders and youth with learning and language disorders, attention-deficit hyperactivity disorder, and autism (Banaschewski & Brandeis, 2007; Pliszka, 2011; Rothenberger, 2009; Swearer et al., 2011).

Newer technologies such as **brain imaging** techniques have vastly improved our ability to assess brain structure and function (Fleck et al., 2010; Gerber & Peterson, 2008; Kesler et al., 2011; Pennington, 2009). For example, **magnetic resonance imaging (MRI)** methods are noninvasive procedures that also produce images of brain structure. A set of methods often referred to as structural or volumetric MRI makes use of magnet and radiowaves to create a 3D computer image of brain regions. A variety of other MRI procedures also assess the structure and integrity of the brain. For example, diffusion tensor imaging utilizes measurements of water diffusion to examine the integrity of the brain's white matter. Magnetic resonance spectroscopy provides information on concentrations of neurochemicals in localized brain regions.

Functional magnetic resonance imaging (fMRI) uses the same technology as structural MRI and produces images by tracking subtle changes in oxygen in different parts of the brain. When particular parts of the brain are called on to perform some task, these regions receive increased blood flow and thus increased oxygen. The MRI scanner detects these changes and produces pictures of the brain that indicate areas of activity.

Other techniques help reveal brain activity. **Positron emission tomography (PET) scans**, for example, determine the rate of activity of different parts of the brain by assessing the use of oxygen and glucose, which fuel brain activity. The more active a particular part of the brain is,

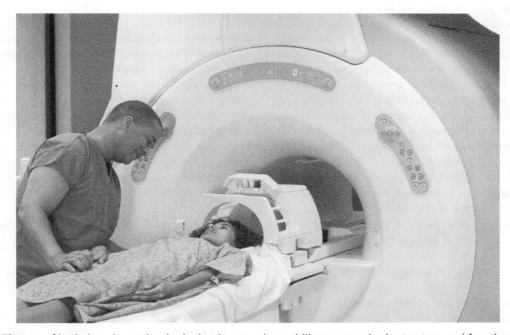

The use of brain imaging technologies has improved our ability to assess brain structure and function.

the more oxygen and glucose it uses. After a small amount of radioactive substance has been injected into the bloodstream, amounts of radiation appearing in different areas of the brain are measured while the person engages in a particular task. Many images are taken of the brain, to create a color-coded picture that indicates different levels of activity in different parts of the brain.

Neuropsychological Evaluations   **Neuropsychological evaluation** is a way of thinking about behavior that makes use of tests that assess attributes such as general intellectual abilities, attention, memory, learning, sensorimotor skills, and verbal skills. Inferences are made about brain functioning on the basis of the individual's performance on these assessment tasks.

Neuropsychological evaluations have a number of uses (McCaffrey, Lynch, & Westervelt, 2011; Reynolds & Mayfield, 2011). For example, they may be used to describe changes in psychological functioning that may arise out of alterations in the central nervous system or other disorders or conditions. They also may be used to assess changes over time and to develop a prognosis; for example, evaluating recovery from head injury. Neuropsychological evaluations also may provide guidelines for treatment planning.

The current interest in neuropsychological evaluation is attributable, at least in part, to increased sensitivity to the needs and legal requirements of providing services to children with handicapping conditions—some of whom exhibit problems presumed to have a neurological etiology. Also, due to advances in medicine, increasing numbers of children survive known or suspected neurological trauma. The increase in survival rates of infants born prematurely is one example. Children with cancer who receive treatment that includes the injection of substances into the spinal column and radiation to the head are another example.

Neuropsychological evaluation appreciates the need for broadly based assessment. Two widely used collections of instruments are the Halstead–Reitan Neuropsychological Test Battery for Children (Reitan & Wolfson, 1993) and the Nebraska Neuropsychological Children's Battery (Golden, 1997). As the term *battery* implies, these instruments consist of several subtests or scales, each intended to assess one or more abilities. The use of a broad spectrum of tests is the usual strategy employed in neuropsychological approaches to assessment (Reynolds & Mayfield, 2011). The spectrum may be fixed batteries like the examples just mentioned, or flexible batteries based on combinations of existing tests. Table 5.2 lists some of the domains that are assessed by these various tests. The importance of these various domains of functioning will become apparent as we discuss specific disorders.

TABLE 5.2	Some Domains Evaluated in Neuropsychological Assessment
Attention
Memory
New learning
Language comprehension and expression
Executive functions (e.g., planning, inhibition, abstract reasoning)
Visual-spatial function
Motor and visual-motor function
General intelligence
Academic achievement

Neuropsychological evaluation of children (pediatric neuropsychology) is still a relatively young field. Part of this ongoing effort is the development of instruments that derive from evolving research on cognitive development, neurological development, and brain–behavior relationships and that include reference to normative child development data (Pavuluri & Sweeney, 2008; Reynolds & Mayfield, 2011; Yeates et al., 2007). Research is also being directed toward developing strategies that more clearly specify impairment and guide rehabilitation.

INTERVENTION: PREVENTION AND TREATMENT

Intervention is an umbrella term applied to both systematic prevention and treatment of psychological difficulty. **Prevention** refers to interventions targeting individuals who are not yet experiencing a clinical disorder, that is, those in the general population or those at risk for disorder. For example, an eating disorder prevention program may be offered to all middle school students or for those at particular risk based on some early signs of unusual eating habits or weight concerns. On the other hand, **treatment** traditionally describes interventions for individuals already experiencing clinical levels of some problem (or symptoms that approach diagnostic levels). For example, youngsters who are diagnosed with Obsessive-Compulsive Disorder may receive a combination of medication and behavioral strategies to treat their problems.

Figure 5.3 illustrates one way of conceptualizing the variety of intervention strategies employed to assist youth and their families. In this model, formulated by Weisz, Sandler, Durlak, & Anton (2005), the upper semicircle contains various intervention strategies. The interventions are

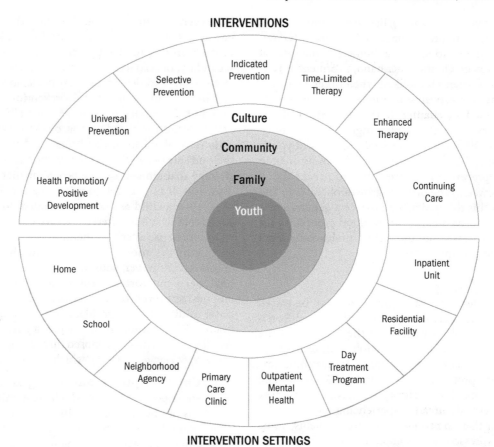

FIGURE 5.3 A model of interventions and intervention settings. *Adapted from Weisz, Sandler, Durlak, & Anton, 2005.*

Note: Primary strengths reside in youth, families, communities, and cultures (center), supported and protected by effective interventions (examples in upper semicircle), delivered within an array of life settings (examples in lower semicircle).

arrayed from the most universally applicable at the left to the most narrowly focused at the right and with prevention strategies to the left and treatment strategies to the right. The lower semicircle presents a sample of the range of potential settings in which interventions may be offered. The intervention settings are arrayed from the least restrictive on the left to the most restrictive on the right.

The concentric circles in the middle of the figure are meant to indicate that individual youths' strengths are supported by family and community connections influenced by cultural and ethnic differences (Weisz et al. 2005). The various intervention strategies shown in the figure are viewed as complementary to one another and in combination may be used to assist a particular youth or population at different points in time. Multiple interventions may be delivered in the same setting, or interventions may be delivered in multiple settings.

Both prevention and treatment programs may be delivered in the home, the school, or a neighborhood agency.

Treatment also may be delivered in specialized settings such as an outpatient mental health clinic. It is sometimes necessary to remove youths from their family home and provide treatment in residential settings (e.g., group homes, therapeutic camping programs, facilities that are part of the juvenile justice system) or inpatient hospital units. These settings are usually considered only for severe behavior problems. The problems may be so difficult to treat that if the youths continue to reside at home, there is not enough contact or control for a successful outcome. Concern may also exist that youths may harm themselves or others and, therefore, that closer supervision is necessary. Children or adolescents may also be removed from the home because circumstances there are highly problematic, suggesting that successful interventions could not be achieved at home. Unfortunately, the lack of availability of alternative placements or appropriate funding can result in young people being placed in institutional settings when interventions in the home, with additional support provided to the family, or in less restrictive environments, like foster homes, might be successful. Typically, professionals strive to use interventions that allow youths to remain at home and that permit families to stay intact. On the other hand, treatment in residential settings is often undertaken when other modes of intervention have not proven successful.

As discussed in chapter 1, the beginning of the twentieth century brought notable progress to the United States regarding the mental and social problems of young people. Currently, there is enthusiasm and commitment to promoting the prevention and treatment of psychological dysfunction, as well as the positive growth of children and adolescents. In this discussion we provide a general sense of what may be involved in the intervention process. In the chapters that follow, we examine various multi-component interventions for specific disorders.

Prevention

In the United States, interest in prevention can be traced to the early twentieth-century writings of Clifford Beers, the mental hygiene movement, and the creation of the child guidance clinics (Coie, Miller-Johnson, & Bagwell, 2000; Heller, 1996). However, progress did not come easily. Mental health professionals were trained for treatment, not prevention, and high priority was given to funding the care of individuals already experiencing mental health problems rather than to preventing future problems. Some professionals expressed doubts about the basis for prevention, since the etiology of psychological disorders is often multifactorial and difficult to establish. Moreover, specific prevention efforts—such as sex education and drug programs—were sometimes resisted by the general public because they were thought to intrude on parental prerogatives or values (Enzer & Heard, 2000).

Several arguments may be made for increasing prevention efforts. From a humanitarian viewpoint, prevention is clearly desirable because it averts discomfort and suffering. Practical considerations also argue for prevention. There are not enough (and may never be enough) professionals to treat mental disorders (Coie et al., 2000), intervention is unlikely to be available to certain groups of people, and treatment is exceedingly costly. In addition, increased understanding of risk and protective factors in psychopathology provides a firmer basis for prevention efforts. Importantly, evidence for the beneficial effects of prevention programs has been accumulating (Durlak & Wells, 1997; Evans et al., 2005d; Weisz et al., 2005).

CONCEPTUALIZING PREVENTION   Caplan is usually credited with being a catalyst for the preventive approach in mental health (Lorion, 2000). Based on the public health assumption that major diseases have been controlled only

by preventive efforts, Caplan's (1964) three-prong model has served as a general framework for thinking about prevention. In this model, prevention is viewed as primary, secondary, or tertiary. *Primary prevention*, which attempts to stave off disorders in the first place, involves both general health enhancement and prevention of specific dysfunction. *Secondary prevention* is usually defined as the effort to shorten the duration of existing cases through early referral, diagnosis, and treatment. It is a "nipping in the bud" strategy. *Tertiary prevention* is an after-the-fact strategy that aims to reduce problems that are residual to disorders. It might seek to minimize the negative impact of labeling a child as learning disabled, to rehabilitate an adolescent who has suffered a severe mental disorder, or to ward off relapse after treatment.

Caplan's model and the terms he used are still employed. However, somewhat different approaches also have been put forth. Many conceptualizations tend to emphasize preventive efforts occurring prior to the full onset of disorders or problems (rather than tertiary programs). The Institute of Medicine, a part of the National Academy of Sciences, proposed three components (Munoz, Mrazek, & Haggerty, 1996), which are evident in Figure 5.3.

1. **Universal prevention strategies** are targeted to entire populations for which greater than average risk has not been identified in individuals. Hypothetical examples are encouraging parents to read to their children to avoid learning problems, and promoting exercise and proper diet to avoid obesity.
2. **Selective prevention strategies** (also called **high-risk prevention strategies**) are targeted to individuals who are at higher than average risk for disorder. Intervention might be directed toward individuals or subgroups with biological risks, high stress, family dysfunction, or poverty.
3. **Indicated prevention strategies** are targeted to high-risk individuals who show minimal symptoms or signs forecasting a disorder, or who have biological markers for a disorder but do not meet the criteria for the disorder.

It is noteworthy that the Institute of Medicine's influential model did not include efforts designed to foster wellness, that is, health promotion and positive development (Munoz et al., 1996). As exemplified in Figure 5.3, other workers include health promotion and wellness in prevention and recommend fostering individual competence and self-esteem, social connections to others, security, and optimism as protection from disorder and disease (Albee, 1986; 1996; Cowen, 1991; 1994; Weissberg, Kumpfer, & Seligman, 2003). In this regard, Albee noted that many mental disorders are linked to poverty, sexism, and racism and that such social ills must be confronted. The American Psychological Association's Task Force on Prevention: Promoting Strength, Resilience, and Health in Young People endorsed the broader wellness approach (Weissberg et al., 2003).

DIVERSITY OF PREVENTION PROGRAMS Given the several components of prevention, it is unsurprising that interventions vary tremendously in aims, focus, and setting. Programs to enhance positive development require input from fields such as human development, mental health, community planning, social policy, and the like; a developmental psychopathology approach is valuable in pointing to factors that facilitate optimal growth and resilience (Cicchetti & Rogosch, 2002). Other prevention programs for children have emphasized the modification of either the environment or children's learning or behavior and have involved mental health professionals, teachers, parents, and college students as agents of change (Durlak & Wells, 1997). In practice, however, many prevention interventions target at-risk populations, for example, children with developmental delays or single-parent families.

A distinction can be made between programs that focus on preventing a potential array of negative outcomes and programs that focus on specific symptoms of disorders. The former include, for example, interventions with economically disadvantaged children to prevent the varied cognitive, social, and emotional adversities associated with poverty (e.g., Peters, Petrunka, & Arnold, 2003). Programs focusing more on specific psychopathology include, for example, interventions for deterring the development of depression or conduct-disordered behaviors (Clarke & DeBar, 2010; Hinshaw, 2002a; Reid, Webster-Stratton, & Baydar, 2004).

Treatment

Clinicians are likely to be called on to treat children and adolescents whose problems are multifaceted. For example, a youth may simultaneously have problems involving anxiety and depression, social problems with peers, and academic difficulties. Indeed, it is likely that a young person will have multiple presenting problems. Furthermore, problems may vary with situations and may be more broadly defined to include other individuals. Thus clinical attention often will be directed not only to the child or adolescent but also to family members and perhaps school personnel and peers. Treatment is therefore likely to contain multiple elements that address different aspects of the clinical problem.

There are a number of ways to conceptualize treatment approaches. For example, a clinician's theoretical conceptualization of the presenting problem and of the process by which change occurs will influence how treatment is provided. Thus, a psychologist whose conceptualization of the disorder emphasizes environmental influences and contingencies is likely to consider treatments that include both the youth and significant others and that focus on modifying environmental stimuli and the consequences of behavior. Meanwhile, a psychologist whose conceptualization emphasizes cognitive processes is likely to consider interventions aimed at modifying particular cognitions, and a psychologist whose conceptualization emphasizes interpersonal processes or family dynamics is likely to consider treatments that focus on these aspects of a problem. Nevertheless, many professionals realize that psychological problems are subject to multiple influences and that treatment may involve multiple components.

As seen in Figure 5.3, treatment can also be conceptualized in terms of the length of treatment required and the number of strategies employed. Treatment may involve a limited number of sessions (e.g., 20) and a standard treatment protocol, it may be enhanced by booster sessions and supplemental strategies, or it may require a variety of strategies used in an ongoing way over an extended period.

PSYCHOLOGICAL TREATMENT MODES The mode in which treatment is delivered is another aspect of treatment efforts. Treatment may be delivered in a variety of modes (e.g., individual therapy, family therapy). Indeed, one or more modes of treatment can be employed to assist a particular child or adolescent.

Individual and Group Psychotherapy Therapists may see the young client in individual one-to-one sessions. A therapist working with a child or adolescent with an anxiety disorder may, for example, help the young person to understand the problem and teach the youth active ways of confronting and coping with the anxiety. These sessions may resemble the verbal interchanges and activities of adult sessions or, particularly with young children, may employ play as the primary mode of interaction between the therapist and the child. Alternatively, various forms of individually focused treatment may be delivered in a group rather than in an individual format. The same assumptions and methods that guide individual therapies may be used. The group format may be selected in order to serve larger numbers of children and adolescents (Johnson, Rasbury, & Siegel, 1997). Another advantage of this choice is that groups offer the opportunity for socialization experiences not present in the individual mode. Group treatment also may be more appealing to young people because it is less threatening; demonstrates that peers, too, have difficulties; and often includes opportunities for activities not likely to occur in a one-to-one relationship with an adult therapist.

The use of play as a mode of therapy is common with younger children. Play allows for the establishment of rapport, but it also provides a means of communication more age-appropriate than verbal forms of therapy.

Play Therapy The need to alter treatment procedures to fit the young child's level of cognitive and emotional development is one factor that has produced nonverbal modes of working with children. The use of play as a therapeutic vehicle is a common mode of treatment with young children. This is consistent with the importance of play in their development (Rubin, Bukowski, & Parker, 2006). Rather than relying exclusively on abstract verbal interactions, the therapist uses play to facilitate communication. Play may also be a more familiar way for the child to interact with an adult and may help make the child feel at ease. A therapist may use puppets and dolls, have the child draw or paint, employ specially created board games, or use children's books that tell the story of children with similar difficulties. In this manner, most practitioners use play as a part of therapy. Another option is to use play itself as a therapeutic vehicle and **play**

therapy as a more structured and distinct approach to treatment (Ablon, 1996; Russ, 1995). The two most well-known perspectives on play therapy are derived from the psychodynamic and the client-centered perspectives.

Early psychoanalytic therapists agreed that child patients required a different mode of treatment than the highly verbal, free association mode used in adult psychoanalysis. Melanie Klein (1932) gave the child's play a prominent role in the therapeutic process and used it as the basis for psychoanalytic interpretation. In contrast, Anna Freud viewed play as only one potential mode of expression and placed less emphasis on symbolic interpretation of play. For example, she disagreed with Klein that a child opening a woman's handbag was symbolically expressing curiosity regarding the contents of the mother's womb. She suggested that, rather, the child might be responding to a previous experience in which someone brought a gift in a similar receptacle (Freud, 1946). Anna Freud's position on play tended to become the dominant view (Johnson et al., 1997).

Another major influence on the evolution of play therapy was the work of Virginia Axline, who developed her approach from the client-centered perspective associated with Carl Rogers. The basic principles outlined by Axline (1947) remain the guidelines for contemporary client-centered play therapy (Johnson et al., 1997). The therapist adjusts his or her communication style to create the appropriate accepting, permissive, and nondirective therapeutic environment. The use of play with young children helps to create such an environment.

Family Therapy and Parent Training Clinicians may also work with the young person's parents or family. We will see that working with the family can take many forms. Here we highlight a few examples.

Including members of the family as part of the therapeutic process is consistent with the understanding that a clinical problem exists in a social context and that the family is a very important part of that context. Clinicians who treat adolescents with eating disorders, for example, frequently work with the entire family to change maladaptive family interaction patterns that may contribute to the development and maintenance of eating disorders (le Grange & Lock, 2010; Robin & le Grange, 2010). Similarly, clinicians working with youngsters who have significant conduct problems, such as juvenile offending and substance abuse, may seek to develop critical competencies and establish adaptive relationships by involving the family as well as other social systems in the treatment process (Henggeler & Schaeffer, 2010; Waldron & Brody, 2010).

Parent training is a common therapeutic tool. Many professionals have taken the position that change in the child or adolescent's behavior may best be achieved by

Treatment may involve the youth, parent(s), and other family members.

producing changes in the way that the parents manage the young person. This viewpoint is consistent with the observation that the parent's perception, as well as the child's actual behavior, results in the child being referred for treatment. Siblings of the referred youth may have similar problems (Fagan & Najman, 2003); this is another reason that it may be helpful to work with the entire family or provide parents with a general set of parenting skills.

Parent training procedures have been applied to a wide array of child and adolescent problems. A number of approaches have emerged, and popular books presenting these approaches appear on the shelves of bookstores everywhere. However, in terms of systematic applications and research, most work has come from the social learning/behavioral approach.

Behavioral parent training has received a great deal of clinical and research attention, and has inspired many reviews and discussions (Kazdin, 1997; McMahon, Wells, & Kotler, 2006; Webster-Stratton & Hancock, 1998). Efforts have focused on teaching parents to identify and monitor behaviors and to manage the consequences, or contingencies, that they apply to their children's behavior. Parent training approaches also include skills such as verbal communication and expression of emotion. In addition, parent training programs attempt to consider the impact of stressors such as socioeconomic disadvantage, single-parent status, social isolation, and parental depression on the effectiveness of treatment. Parent training is frequently employed as part of a multifaceted approach to treatment, and specific cultural adaptations may be implemented (Martinez & Eddy, 2005). Other components may include additional therapeutic work with the parent, direct

work with the child, or work with the teacher and the school (Kazdin, 2010; Webster-Stratton & Reid, 2010).

TREATMENT STRATEGIES A therapist employing one of the modes of treatment described above also is likely to make use of a number of treatment strategies as a way of delivering that mode of treatment to the young person and her or his family. The most commonly used strategy to deliver services probably remains the tradition of weekly office visits with a therapist. However, as illustrated in Table 5.3, a variety of

TABLE 5.3	Examples of Alternative Strategies for Providing Treatment Content to Youth and Families
Embedding illustrations of core principles and skills in video vignettes for parents	
Embedding concepts and lessons in stories or videos for youths	
Therapists as coaches for parents as they interact with their children in real time	
Building intervention into summer camp programs	
Employing traveling therapists who functions in the youths' environment	
Teaching skills to foster care providers	
Teaching skills to parents through easily readable books with accompanying DVDs	
Computer-based programs along with varying degrees of therapist involvement	

Adapted, in part, from Weisz & Kazdin, 2010.

strategies have begun to be developed to provide treatment content to youth and their families. The array of available treatment strategies is likely to continue to evolve as professionals consider effective use of technology in their efforts to assist youth and their families (Dimeff et al., 2011; Kendall et al., 2011).

PHARMACOLOGICAL TREATMENT Pharmacological treatments (medications) are another mode of the intervention that is employed for a variety of childhood and adolescent disorders (APA, 2006; Gleason, 2009; Vitiello, 2006). Medications that affect mood, thought processes, or overt behavior are known as **psychotropic** or **psychoactive**, and treatment that uses medication is called **psychopharmacological treatment**.

The decision whether to use psychopharmacological treatment is, in part, determined by the nature of the presenting problem. However, other considerations such as possible side effects and a family's comfort with using medication need to be considered and discussed. Racial/ethnic and income differences contribute to the rates of psychotropic medication use in young people. For example, Leslie and colleagues (2003) reported that among a large sample of families receiving publicly funded services, caregivers of African American and Latino children were less likely to report use of such medication than caregivers of white children. Higher income and private insurance also were associated with a greater likelihood of psychotropic medication use.

Psychotropic drugs produce therapeutic effects by influencing the process of neurotransmission. These medications can affect neurotransmission by

- altering neurotransmitter production
- interfering with neurotransmitter storage
- altering the release of a neurotransmitter
- interfering with the inactivation of a neurotransmitter
- interfering with the reuptake of a neurotransmitter and
- interacting with receptors for a neurotransmitter.

For some psychoactive drugs, there is a specific and clearly hypothesized mechanism for action, whereas for others the specific reasons for effectiveness are unknown.

Children and adolescents have been increasingly treated with psychotropic medications and, while the use of psychotropic medications can be a helpful component of treatment, concern is frequently expressed regarding this trend. There often are particular considerations involved and concerns expressed regarding the treatment of preschool-age children with psychotropic medications (Gleason, 2009; Greenhill et al., 2003a; Zito et al., 2000). Research regarding the efficacy and safety of many of these medications for children and adolescents often lags behind their use. Thus, ethical and practical concerns remain as

research continues to address issues of safety and effectiveness (APA, 2006; Correll, 2008; Gleason, 2009; Koelch, Schnoor, & Fegert, 2008; Liu et al., 2011; McKinney & Renk, 2011; Vitiello, 2006). Such research is needed to guide the appropriate use of psychotropic medications as part of intervention plans, particularly for young people with serious difficulties.

Evidence-Based Interventions

In subsequent chapters in this text, as part of our discussion of various disorders of youth, we examine interventions for specific disorders. Interventions for which there is empirical support are emphasized—that is, prevention programs and treatments that have been deemed worthy through scientific evaluation. This approach follows from one of the themes of this text, an orientation toward empirical approaches and the methods of science.

This same emphasis, along with an increasing demand that professionals be held accountable for the effectiveness of the services they offer, was among the considerations that led professional organizations to identify such interventions. As part of this evolving effort (Chorpita & Daleiden, 2010; Weisz & Kazdin, 2010) several different terms, including **evidence-based interventions** and **empirically supported interventions** have been used to describe treatments for which such evidence exists. Also, criteria have been proposed to designate interventions that are evidence based or empirically supported (Chambless & Hollon, 1998; Flay et al., 2005; Ollendick, King, & Chorpita, 2006).

A number of professional organizations, including the Society of Clinical Psychology (a division of American Psychological Association), have proposed such criteria (Chambless & Hollon, 1998) and these criteria have many features in common (Kazdin, 2011). In order for a treatment to be considered evidence-based, it is commonly suggested that there must be well-controlled research indicating that the treatment is effective in producing change in comparison with another intervention or no treatment. Furthermore, these findings must be replicated and it is often considered preferable that the findings are replicated by two independent research groups. A growing number of evidence-based interventions have been identified and throughout the remaining chapters our discussion is sensitive to the need for interventions for which empirical evidence is strongest. As noted in chapter 4, a continuing concern, however, revolves around the question of the applicability and transportability of interventions from the research setting to implementation in typical service settings (Chorpita & Daleiden, 2010; Fixsen et al., 2010). This has sometimes been called the "science-to-service gap" or translational research and is clearly an important focus of our evolving efforts to help children and adolescents (Weisz & Kazdin, 2010) (see p. 73).

Overview/Looking Back

- Classification, assessment, and intervention are interrelated processes and are intricately related to the clinical and scientific aspects of child and adolescent disorders.

CLASSIFICATION AND DIAGNOSIS

- Classification systems must have clearly defined categories or dimensions that can be discriminated from each other. Classification systems must be reliable and valid. Diagnostic systems are also judged by their clinical utility.
- The DSM, the system most commonly employed in the United States, is a clinically derived system and a categorical approach to classification. Clinically derived classification relies on consensus among clinicians regarding disorders and their definition.
- The current version of the DSM organizes disorders into groups (chapters) of related disorders. The disorders within a group are thought to be similar with respect to considerations such as risk factors, cognitive and emotional processes, or response to treatment.
- The problem of comorbidity—youngsters' meeting the criteria for more than one disorder—presents particular challenges.
- Over time efforts have been made to improve the DSM system. The current version features greater coverage of child and adolescent disorders, more highly structured rules for diagnosis, and attempts to draw on research in a more consistent fashion.
- Although reliability of the DSM has been improved by more structured diagnostic rules, there is still variation across categories, and reliability may be affected by the conditions under which information is obtained and diagnoses are made. The question of validity has received considerable attention, and the validity of various aspects of the DSM system is an ongoing concern.
- The development of the DSM approach continues to address criticisms regarding issues of age/developmental level, gender, and cultural context as well as concerns based on other clinical and scientific grounds.
- The ongoing development of the DSM system has involved consideration of how to introduce "dimensionality" into an essentially categorical system.
- Empirical approaches to classification rely on behavior checklists and statistical analyses, and tend to be associated with dimensional rather than categorical approaches to classification.
- The Achenbach instruments, including the Child Behavior Checklist, Teacher Report Form, and Youth Self-Report, are examples of checklists employed in the empirical approach. There is good support for the existence of two broad syndromes—externalizing and internalizing—and support for narrower syndromes within each general syndrome.
- Information from multiple informants can reveal the possible influence of situational differences on behavior and differences due to the respondent's perspective.
- Critics of diagnostic systems remind us of the possible dangers of labeling children and adolescents and of the potential impact of stigmatization.

ASSESSMENT

- Conducting a comprehensive assessment is necessary, not only for classification and diagnosis but also for planning and executing appropriate interventions. The complex process of assessment requires a multifaceted approach.
- The general clinical interview is the most common form of assessment. Structured interviews are often organized to provide information for a DSM diagnosis.
- Problem checklists can sample a wide range of behavior problems or focus on those problems particular to a specific disorder. These checklists may enable the clinician to compare a young person's behavior with appropriate norms and to examine issues such as situational aspects of a youth's behavior and the perceptions of various informants.
- Self-report measures are available for both the young person and the relevant adults in the child or adolescent's life. These instruments can be used to assess constructs directly related to the presenting problem (e.g., anxiety, depression) or related constructs of potential interest (e.g., self-concept, self-control, parenting stress, family environment).
- Observation of behavior is central to a behavioral/cognitive-behavioral approach and is a direct method of assessment. The impracticality of implementing current observation systems in general clinical practice is an impediment to their widespread use.
- Projective tests are probably less commonly used than they once were, as a result of questions concerning their reliability and validity.
- Intellectual–educational assessments are conducted for a wide range of presenting problems. These assessments evaluate general intelligence and developmental levels, as well as specific abilities and achievement. Although intelligence tests are popular,

they are in many ways controversial and they should be used and interpreted with caution.

- Assessment of physical functioning, especially of the nervous system, is important for many behavior problems. Methods include case histories, medical examinations, the EEG, and several newer techniques, such as the MRI, PET scan, and fMRI. Much attention has also been given to neuropsychological testing as a means of indirectly assessing known or suspected problems in central nervous system functioning.

INTERVENTION: PREVENTION AND TREATMENT

- Intervention strategies can range from the most universally applicable to the most narrowly focused. Interventions may be implemented in a range of settings.
- The Institute of Medicine model of prevention describes three types of prevention strategies: universal, selective/high-risk, and indicated strategies. Other models not only include those strategies, but also add broad health promotion and wellness approaches.

- Treatment of children and adolescents usually includes several elements, because young people are likely to have multiple problems. Treatments are likely to include family members and may need to incorporate school personnel and peers as well.
- Various modes and settings for treatment of youngsters and their families are available. Psychotherapy may be conducted with a single child or adolescent or in groups. Play can be an important aspect of therapy, especially with younger clients. Treatments often include family members, focus on the family as a unit, or incorporate parent training in child management skills. Psychotropic medications have increasingly been employed in the treatment of child and adolescent disorders. Treatment may take place in a variety of settings including the clinician's office, schools, and various residential facilities.
- Demand for professionals to be accountable for the effectiveness of their services along with an increasing emphasis on empiricism has led professional organizations to develop evidence-based interventions.

Key Terms

classification 83
taxonomy 83
diagnosis 83
assessment 83
category 84
dimension 84, 89
interrater reliability 84
test–retest reliability 84
validity 84
clinical utility 84
Diagnostic and Statistical Manual of Mental Disorders (DSM) 84
International Classification of Diseases (ICD) 84
Diagnostic Classification: 0–3 84
clinically derived classification 84
categorical approach 84
comorbidity 86
co-occurrence 86
empirical approach to classification 88
spectrum 89
syndrome 89

broadband syndrome 89
internalizing syndrome/behaviors 89
externalizing syndrome/behaviors 89
narrowband syndrome 90
normative sample 90
diagnostic label 91
stigmatization 91, 92
evidence-based assessment 94
general clinical interview 94
structured diagnostic interview 94
problem checklist 95
self-report measure 96
behavioral observation 96
intelligence (IQ) score 98
developmental index 98
ability/achievement test 98
psychophysiological assessment 98
neurological assessment 99
brain imaging 99

magnetic resonance imaging (MRI) 99
functional magnetic resonance imaging (fMRI) 99
positron emission tomography (PET) scan 99
neuropsychological evaluation 100
intervention 100
prevention 100
treatment 100
universal prevention strategies 102
selective/high-risk prevention strategies 102
indicated prevention strategies 102
play therapy 104
parent training 104
psychotropic/psychoactive 106
psychopharmacological treatment 106
evidence-based/empirically supported intervention 106

CHAPTER 6

Anxiety and Related Disorders

LOOKING FORWARD

**After reading this chapter,
you should be able to discuss:**

- Internalizing disorders
- How anxiety, fears, and
  worries are defined and
  experienced and how anxiety
  and related disorders are
  classified
- Features of each of
  different disorders
- The epidemiology and
  developmental course of the
  different disorders
- Biological and psychosocial
  influences related to the
  development of anxiety and
  related disorders
- Assessment strategies
  for a youth presenting
  with anxiety and related
  difficulties
- Psychological and
  pharmacological treatments
  and prevention of anxiety
  and related disorders

This chapter begins our examination of specific problems and disorders. The children and adolescents discussed in this and the next chapter are variously described as anxious, fearful, withdrawn, timid, depressed, and the like. They seem to be very unhappy and to lack self-confidence. These youngsters are often said to have emotional difficulties that they take out on themselves; thus, their problems are often termed **internalizing disorders**.

AN INTRODUCTION TO INTERNALIZING DISORDERS

Empirical efforts to classify child and adolescent behavior disorders have clearly found support for a broad syndrome composed of internalizing problems (see chapter 5). Some suggest that this general grouping of emotional/internalizing disorders best describes the clinical picture (Watson,

O'Hara, & Stuart, 2008). Alternatively, many of the problems included in clinically defined classifications would be thought of as internalizing disorders. Specific terms such as phobias, obsessions and compulsions, anxiety disorders, depression, and mood disorders are likely to be used within clinical classification systems such as the Diagnostic and Statistical Manual of Mental Disorders (DSM).

However, the relationship among, or the ability to distinguish between, the more specific clinical diagnostic categories is often discussed. Thus, for example, there is the question of whether, in children and adolescents, the various anxiety diagnoses described in the DSM represent clearly distinct disorders. Why is this the case? While this is a complex issue, there are a number of key related concerns. For example, risk factors have been found to contribute to a variety of disorders. That is, a particular risk factor may not be associated with one particular disorder, but may contribute to the development of several different disorders (Shanahan et al., 2008).

Another, related, concern is the high rate of co-occurrence of internalizing disorders. Considerable evidence indicates that a given child or adolescent often meets the criteria for more than one of the different disorders (American Academy of Child and Adolescent Psychiatry [AACAP], 2007; Angold, Costello, & Erkanli, 1999; Bernstein et al., 2008; Kessler et al., 2009). The phenomenon of an individual's meeting the criteria for more than one disorder, which is often termed comorbidity, was discussed in chapter 5. The dilemma is an appreciable one.

It has also been suggested that what are sometimes viewed as separate disorders may be different expressions of one or more general dispositions toward the development of internalizing difficulties (Vaidyanathan, Patrick, & Cuthbert, 2009). Particular environments or experiences shape this general disposition into a particular pattern of symptoms, or disorder (Williamson et al., 2005). Cultural differences may be one influence that operates in this manner. For example, it is not clear that there are differences among cultural groups in the overall prevalence of anxiety disorders. However, cultural differences in the prevalence of specific anxiety disorders and types of symptoms are reported (Anderson & Mayes, 2010; Austin & Chorpita, 2004; Pina & Silverman, 2004; Trosper et al., 2012). For example, higher rates of separation anxiety disorder and of somatic/physiological symptoms in Hispanic than in European American children have been cited (Ginsburg & Silverman, 1996; Varela et al., 2004). The strong value that Hispanic cultures place on familial interdependence (collectivism) and on empathizing with others and remaining agreeable (simpatia) may contribute to shaping a general anxious disposition to this particular expression of anxiety.

With these considerations in mind, let us turn to an examination of internalizing disorders. In this chapter, we examine anxiety and related disorders, and in chapter 7, we discuss mood disorders.

DEFINING AND CLASSIFYING ANXIETY DISORDERS

What do we mean when we say that someone is anxious? Barlow (2002) suggests that

> **anxiety** seems best characterized as a future-oriented emotion, characterized by perceptions of uncontrollability and unpredictability over potentially aversive events and a rapid shift in attention to the focus of potentially dangerous events or one's own affective response to these events. (p. 104)

Fear and anxiety have much in common, and the terms are at times used interchangeably. However, a distinction is often made between **fear** as a reaction to an immediate/present threat characterized by an alarm reaction, and anxiety as a future-oriented emotion characterized by an elevated level of apprehension and lack of control. In general, anxiety and fear are viewed as a complex pattern of three types of reactions to a perceived threat (Barrios & O'Dell, 1998; Lang, 1984). This tripartite model describes overt behavioral responses (e.g., running away, trembling voice, eyes closing), cognitive responses (e.g., thoughts of being scared, self-deprecatory thoughts, images of bodily harm), and physiological responses (e.g., changes in heart rate and respiration, muscle tension, stomach upset).

In contrast to the complex combination of three components that define fear and anxiety, **worry**—thoughts about possible negative outcomes that are intrusive and difficult to control—is viewed as a cognitive component of anxiety (Barlow, 2002; Vasey & Daleiden, 1994).

One of the challenges facing clinicians is to decide whether the anxiety exhibited by a child or adolescent is normal and perhaps transitory, or atypical and persistent (Albano, Chorpita, & Barlow, 2003; Bosquet & Egeland, 2006). Anxiety is a basic human emotion. It can serve an adaptive function by alerting the youngster to novel or threatening situations. Anxiety is thus part of normal developmental processes by which the young person learns, for example, to identify and cope with arousal, develop competencies, and become more autonomous. Thus, young children learn to cope with the dark and separation, while adolescents deal with the anxieties of beginning high school and dating. What then do we know about typical fear, worry, and anxiety?

Fears and anxieties are quite common in children. It is only when these are persistent, are intense, interfere with functioning, or are developmentally inappropriate, they may require clinical attention.

Normal Fears, Worries, and Anxieties

GENERAL PREVALENCE   Several classic studies of general populations indicate that children exhibit a surprisingly large number of fears, worries, and anxieties (Jersild & Holmes, 1935; Lapouse & Monk, 1959; MacFarlane, Allen, & Honzik, 1954). Parents may underestimate the prevalence of fears in their children, particularly older children who are increasingly able to mask their emotions (Gullone, 2000).

GENDER, AGE, AND CULTURAL DIFFERENCES   Most research suggests that girls exhibit a greater number of fears than boys. This difference is clearer in older children and less clear in preschool and elementary school children. Studies generally suggest greater fear intensity in girls as well (Gullone, 2000). Findings of sex differences probably should be interpreted with caution because gender-role expectations may, in part, be responsible for differences between boys and girls in displaying and admitting to fears (Ginsburg & Silverman, 2000).

It is commonly reported that both the number and the intensity of fears experienced by children decline with age (Gullone, 2000). Worry becomes prominent in children at about 7 years of age and becomes more complex and varied as children develop.

Certain fears appear to be more common at particular ages: for example, fear of strangers at 6 to 9 months, fear of imaginary creatures during the second year, fear of the dark among 4-year olds, and social fears and fear of failure in older children and adolescents (Gullone, 2000; Miller, Barrett, & Hampe, 1974). Similarly, preschoolers

may worry about imaginary threats, young children about their physical safety, and older children and adolescents about social situations and their competence. Thus, threats to youngsters' well-being are a prominent worry across age (Silverman, La Greca, & Wasserstein, 1995). Changes in the content of fears and worries likely reflect ongoing cognitive, social, and emotional development.

Cross-cultural examinations of common fears suggest similarities across cultures. The Fear Survey Schedule for Children (FSSC-R; Ollendick, 1983) is an inventory of fear stimuli and situations. The FSSC-R has been translated into a number of different languages. The most common fears were similar across different countries and cultures and girls were found to score higher than boys (Fonesca, Yule, & Erol, 1994).

Classification of Anxiety Disorders

Most authorities would not usually view age-appropriate anxieties as requiring clinical attention unless they were quite intense or continued longer than expected. However, if the fear or anxiety, even though short-lived, creates sufficient discomfort or interferes with functioning, intervention may be justified. Furthermore, anxiety disorders, if left untreated, may follow a chronic course and be associated with additional difficulties (Kendall et al., 2004; Pliska, 2011). How do we then define and classify disorders of childhood and adolescence in which anxiety is an important feature?

THE DSM APPROACH   The DSM describes a number of anxiety and related disorders. The DSM Anxiety Disorders chapter includes Separation Anxiety Disorder, Specific Phobia, Social Anxiety Disorder (Social Phobia), Selective Mutism, Panic Disorder, Agoraphobia, and Generalized Anxiety Disorder. In addition, separate, but related, chapters include related disorders such as Obsessive-Compulsive Disorder, Posttraumatic Stress Disorder, Acute Stress Disorder, Reactive Attachment Disorder, and Disinhibited Social Engagement Disorder. A child or adolescent can be diagnosed with one or more of the anxiety and related disorders included in the DSM. We will define and discuss each of these disorders in our examination of specific disorders. The definitions of most of these anxiety and related disorders involve similar processes such as apprehension of objects or situations, and avoidant/anxiety-reducing behaviors.

THE EMPIRICAL APPROACH   Empirical systems that are based on statistical procedures have yielded subcategories of internalizing disorders that include anxiety-related problems. Within the broad category of internalizing

TABLE 6-1	Behavior Problems Included in the Anxious/Depressed Syndrome	
Cries a lot	Feels too guilty	
Fears	Self-conscious	
Fears school	Feels hurt when criticized	
Fears doing bad		
Must be perfect	Talks or thinks of suicide	
Feels unloved		
Feels worthless	Anxious to please	
Nervous, tense	Fears mistakes	
Fearful, anxious	Worries	

From Achenbach & Rescorla, 2001.

disorders, for example, Achenbach (Achenbach & Rescorla, 2001) describes an anxious/depressed syndrome (see Table 6-1). There is not, however, a separate anxiety syndrome or other narrower syndromes that correspond to the specific anxiety and related disorders of the DSM. This suggests that in youths, various anxiety and depression symptoms tend to occur together. Other internalizing syndromes, such as "somatic complaints" (e.g., feeling dizzy, having stomachaches) and "withdrawn/depressed" (e.g., refusing to talk, feeling withdrawn), also contain symptoms that are likely to be part of anxiety and related difficulties.

EPIDEMIOLOGY OF ANXIETY DISORDERS

Anxiety disorders are among the most common disorders experienced by children and adolescents. Estimates of prevalence may vary considerably. Prevalence rates of 2.5 to 5% are often cited (Rapee, Schniering, & Hudson, 2009). However, rates as high as 12 to 25% are sometimes cited (American Psychiatric Association [APA], 2006; Kessler et al., 2009).Young people are likely to meet the criteria for more than one anxiety disorder. Also, evidence suggests that an appreciable portion of anxious youth is likely to continue to meet the criteria for one or more anxiety disorders from childhood to adolescence, and through young adulthood. These youth are also likely to develop other problems (Rapee, Schniering, & Hudson, 2009).

Research suggest that girls are slightly more likely than boys to have an anxiety disorder (Collishaw et al., 2010; Costello, Egger, & Angold, 2005b). There is limited methodologically sound information regarding ethnic differences. It is unclear as to whether there are overall differences in the prevalence of anxiety and related disorders in different

ACCENT
Culture, Ethnicity, and Disorder

Culture and ethnicity affect child and adolescent psychopathology in many ways. For example, certain disorders (e.g., social anxiety) may be more prevalent in certain cultures or ethnic groups. What then do prevalence findings tell us about the development of anxiety and related disorders?

Whether or not there are differences in prevalence, there may be cultural/ethnic differences in anxiety presentation. For example, certain symptoms (e.g., somatic symptoms) may be more common in certain cultures or ethnic groups. Also, the way in which symptoms are expressed should be considered. For example, the content of anxious cognitions may vary.

How does consideration of culture and ethnicity help us understand the development of anxiety and related disorders? For example, are certain risk factors more prevalent in certain groups or in the communities in which they reside? Are there cultural differences in parenting that increase the risk for, or serve as, protective factors against the development of these disorders? Also, discrimination and/or the process of acculturation may be stresses that can contribute to anxiety or challenge developing coping skills.

Appreciation of the necessity for culturally sensitive assessment has increased. Instruments that were developed in one cultural context may not accurately assess anxiety in a different cultural context or ethnic group. Also, symptoms may not group into different factors in the same way for all cultural or ethnic groups. This may be due in part, as suggested above, to the differences in the ways in which anxiety presents. But this may also be due to differences in how anxiety is thought about and understood by members of different cultural groups. Language may also be an important consideration in conducting an assessment. Differences may emerge in assessment findings depending on the language employed in interviews or assessment instruments.

There has also been an increasing sensitivity to treatment issues. Adapting effective treatment programs to better fit particular cultures suggests that such adaptations may increase the effectiveness of these treatments and make them more acceptable to members of different cultural groups. It is also important to appreciate that there may be important ethnic/cultural differences in the likelihood of youngsters and their families seeking treatment. Increasing the use of and access to effective interventions serves the larger goal of helping children, adolescents, and their families. Clearly, these considerations apply not only to anxiety disorders, but also to many, if not all, of the disorders considered in future chapters.

ethnic groups. However, there may be differences with regard to the prevalence of specific disorders (e.g., separation anxiety, social anxiety) across ethnic groups (Anderson & Mayes, 2010; Austin & Chorpita, 2004; Roberts, Ramsay, Roberts, & Xing, 2006).

SPECIFIC PHOBIAS

Phobias, as contrasted with developmentally appropriate fears, are of concern because they are excessive, cannot be reasoned away, are beyond voluntary control, lead to avoidance, and interfere with functioning (Miller et al., 1974).

Diagnostic Criteria

The essential feature of the diagnosis of **Specific Phobia** is a marked fear of, or anxiety regarding, a specific object or situation (e.g., animals, heights). In addition, the diagnosis requires the following:

1. An immediate anxiety response occurs almost every time the person is exposed to the phobic stimulus.
2. The person must either avoid the anxiety situation(s) or endure any exposure with anxiety or distress.
3. The fear or anxiety is out of proportion to the actual risk.
4. The fear or anxiety is persistent (six or more months).

In addition to these main features, the fear must produce considerable distress or must interfere significantly with the young person's normal routine, academic functioning, or social relationships. The DSM acknowledges developmental differences by noting that in children anxiety may be expressed by crying, tantrums, freezing, or clinging.

Description

Behaviorally, youths with specific phobias try to avoid the situation or object that they fear. For example, children who have an extreme fear of dogs may refuse to go outside. When confronted with a large dog, they may "freeze" or run to their parents for protection. In addition, the youngster may describe feelings of tension, panic, or disgust regarding the phobic object. Often a young person's reactions include thoughts of catastrophic events that may occur upon exposure to the phobic situation. Physical reactions such as nausea, rapid heart rate, and difficulty in breathing may also occur. Any or all of these reactions may occur even when contact with the feared situation is merely anticipated. Thus, the young person's phobia not only restricts his or her own activities, but also is likely to change the lifestyle and activities of the family as a whole.

"I'm not a scaredy-cat—I'm phobic."

CARLOS

A Specific Phobia

Carlos, a 9-year-old Hispanic American boy, presented at a child anxiety clinic with an avoidance of buttons. The problem began in kindergarten when Carlos was 5 years old. Carlos was working on an art project that involved buttons and ran out of buttons. He described being asked to come to the front of the classroom to get additional buttons from a large bowl on the teacher's desk. In reaching for the buttons, his hand slipped and all the buttons in the bowl fell on him. Carlos reported being distressed at that moment and both he and his mother report an increasing avoidance of buttons since that time. As time progressed it became more difficult for Carlos to handle buttons. Carlos also reported that he viewed buttons contacting his body as disgusting (e.g., "buttons are gross"). This led to interference in several aspects of Carlos's and his family's life such as not being able to dress himself and difficulty concentrating in school as a result of preoccupation with not touching his school uniform buttons or anything touched by his buttoned shirt.

Adapted from Silverman & Moreno, 2005, pp. 834–835.

Epidemiology

Specific phobias are among the most commonly diagnosed anxiety disorders in children and adolescents (Costello, Egger, & Angold, 2005a). Although estimates vary somewhat, prevalence is generally reported as between 3 and 4% in community samples (Albano et al., 2003; Foa & Commission on Adolescent Anxiety Disorders, 2005a). Specific phobias are often more prevalent in girls than in boys (Silverman & Moreno, 2005). Information regarding ethnic differences is limited, but comparisons between European American, African American, and Hispanic youngsters suggest more similarities than differences (Last & Perrin, 1993; Roberts et al., 2006; Silverman & Ginsburg, 1998).

Youths with specific phobias usually have more than one phobia and are likely to meet the criteria for other disorders. Additional diagnoses include other anxiety disorders, depression and mood disorders, and externalizing disorders such as oppositional defiant disorder. In a community sample of adolescents, Essau and colleagues (2000) report that nearly half of the youngsters with a specific phobia met the criteria for another anxiety disorder, and depressive and

somatoform disorders (physical symptoms in the absence of a known physical pathology) were also common. In addition, Verduin and Kendall (2003) report that nearly half of a clinical sample of youth whose primary diagnosis was another anxiety disorder also met the criteria for a specific phobia.

Developmental Course

A large proportion of specific phobias are thought to begin in early to middle childhood. These phobias are commonly believed to be relatively benign, and improvement is expected over time with or without treatment. However, there is reason to question this perception and to think in terms of continuity over time (Silverman & Moreno, 2005; Sterba, Prinstein, & Cox, 2007). Findings from Essau and colleagues' (2000) sample of German adolescents, for example, suggest that, for some youngsters, phobic symptoms persist over time and are associated with impaired functioning. This finding is consistent with reports of phobic adults that suggest that specific phobias are likely to begin in childhood and may for some individuals persist into adulthood (Kendler et al., 1992b; Öst, 1987). A reasonable suggestion, therefore, is that specific phobias are likely to begin during childhood and, that for at least some individuals, they may persist over time.

SOCIAL ANXIETY DISORDER (SOCIAL PHOBIA)

Diagnostic Criteria

The criteria for diagnosing a social anxiety disorder (social phobia) are parallel to those employed in diagnosing a specific phobia. However, here the concern is with anxiety related to social or evaluative situations rather than with a specific object or non-social situation. Thus, the essential feature of **social anxiety disorder (social phobia)** is a marked or persistent fear of acting in an embarrassing or humiliating way in social or performance situations.

As was the case with specific phobias, the criteria acknowledge developmental differences by noting that children may express anxiety differently than adults. Furthermore, to distinguish social anxiety disorder from other aspects of social development, children receiving the diagnosis would experience social anxiety with peers and not just with adults.

In addition to these main features, the social anxiety must interfere significantly with the young person's normal routine, academic functioning, or social relationships or must produce marked distress. Also, the anxiety/phobia must have duration of at least 6 months.

Description

Youths with social anxiety fear social activities and situations such as speaking, reading, writing or performing in public, initiating or maintaining conversations, speaking to authority figures, and interacting in informal social situations (Beidel, Turner, & Morris, 1999).

The behavioral component of this social anxiety is most frequently manifested by the avoidance of situations that involve social interactions or evaluation. Young people may avoid even everyday and seemingly mundane activities, such as eating in public. Albano, Chorpita, and Barlow (2003) describe a teenage girl who spent every lunch period in a bathroom stall in order to avoid the school cafeteria. In the cognitive realm, concerns about being embarrassed or negatively evaluated are common for these young people. They are likely to focus their thoughts on negative attributes that they perceive in themselves, to negatively evaluate their performance, and to interpret others' responses as critical or disapproving even when this is not the case. Somatic symptoms such as restlessness, blushing, and sweating and complaints of illness and stomachaches are common physiological symptoms reported in youths with social anxiety disorder (Ginsburg, Riddle, & Davies, 2006).

Because these young people try to avoid social situations, they may miss school and may be unlikely to participate in recreational activities. For example, younger children may not attend birthday parties or participate in Scout meetings, whereas adolescents are unlikely to attend school events, such as club meetings or dances, or to date. At least some of these young people may therefore feel lonely and have few, or low-quality, friendships (Parker et al., 2006).

Youths with social anxiety disorder often report feelings of lesser self-worth, as well as of sadness and loneliness. Over time they may also experience lesser educational achievement (Ginsburg, LaGreca, & Silverman, 1998; Velting & Albano, 2001). The potential consequences for a young person are thus quite broad.

Selective Mutism and Social Anxiety

A young kindergarten girl, Amy, does not speak in school or with her peers. She has been this way since beginning preschool. Amy and others like her (see Bruce: Selective Mutism) might be given a diagnosis of Selective Mutism (SM).

Young people with **selective mutism** do not talk in specific social situations. These situations, such as the classroom or play activities, are ones in which their peers typically do talk or in which talking is important to development. Mutism occurs despite the fact that the youths speak in other situations. For example, they

LOUIS

Social Anxiety Disorder and Its Consequences

Louis, a 12-year-old white male, was referred by his school counselor because of periodic episodes of school refusal, social withdrawal, and excessive need for reassurance. On an almost daily basis Louis would claim he could not remain in the classroom. He would generally be sent to the nurse or counselor's office until his mother came and took him home early. Louis had few friends and rarely participated in social activities that involved other children. Louis found parties, eating in public, and using public restrooms particularly difficult. Spanish class was also particularly difficult because of regular assignments to read aloud or to carry on conversations with classmates. Louis's mother described him as always having been excessively fearful, timid, scared of everything, and needing constant reassurance. The mother herself had a history of anxiety problems, was fearful of meeting new people, and had little social contact, saying "it's basically just Louis and me." Louis received the diagnoses of Social Anxiety Disorder and Generalized Anxiety Disorder.

Adapted from Silverman & Ginsburg, 1998, pp. 260–261.

may speak easily with family members if no one else is present. The reported average age of onset is between about 2.5 and 4 years of age, but may go unrecognized until the child enters school at about age 5 (Viana, Beidel, & Rabian, 2009). These youths are typically described as shy, withdrawn, fearful, and clingy (APA, 2013). Some also display language problems and stubborn, disobedient, and oppositional behavior (Cohan et al., 2008; Ford et al., 1998).

SM is thought to develop as a function of a complex interplay of environmental and genetic influences (Viana et al., 2009). Some evidence suggests that SM might be conceptualized as an extreme form of social anxiety (Chavira et al., 2007; Standart & Le Couteur, 2003). For example, a majority, and perhaps as high as 90 to 100%, of children with SM also meet diagnostic criteria for social anxiety disorder (Black & Uhde, 1995; Manassis et al., 2003). There is also some support for the idea that children with SM are more socially anxious than children with social anxiety disorder who are not selectively mute. The relationship between selective mutism and social anxiety disorder remains unclear (Viana et al., 2009; Yeganeh et al., 2003). However, clinicians who work with young people with SM

BRUCE

Selective Mutism

Bruce, an 8-year-old boy from a two-parent household with several siblings, was referred for treatment. His mother reported that he spoke only to his immediate family members and not to extended family, teachers, or peers. Bruce had been prescribed Prozac by his psychiatrist and was stabilized on the medication for 3 months. It is particularly challenging to conduct an assessment and get the child to serve as the primary informant in cases such as Bruce's. By gathering information from multiple informants, observations, and getting Bruce to participate nonverbally in some assessment tasks, an assessment was completed and Bruce met criteria for selective mutism and social anxiety disorder. Bruce's mother reported that he had spoken in school on only one occasion—shortly after he began taking Prozac he said one short phrase in class when he was frustrated. She also reported that he was not teased by peers, but reported instead that classmates spoke for him if they noticed he needed something. In other settings his immediate family spoke for him, and Bruce would not speak, even to his immediate family, in public places. At the clinic, during the assessment, he spoke with his family, but only behind closed doors and without the therapist present.

A 21-session cognitive-behavioral treatment program was provided for Bruce and family members. By the end of treatment Bruce's symptoms were greatly improved and he no longer met the criteria for selective mutism. Treatment gains were maintained at a 6-month follow-up.

Adapted from Reuther, Davis, Moree, & Matson, 2011.

may need to consider their clients' potentially severe levels of social anxiety and possible oppositional behavior and language problems in planning treatments.

Epidemiology

Social anxiety disorder is estimated to be present in approximately 1 to 2% of children, and about 3 to 4% of adolescents, with estimates of about 9% lifetime prevalence for adolescents (Costello et al., 2005a; Hirshfeld-Becker, 2010; Kessler et al., 2009). It is also a common diagnosis in clinic populations. Last and colleagues (1992) report that 14.9% of youths, assessed at an anxiety disorders clinic, were given a primary diagnosis of social anxiety disorder, and 32.4% had a lifetime

history of the disorder. On the basis of reports of youngsters seen in clinics and retrospective reports, middle to late adolescence is the typical age of onset (Chavira & Stein, 2005; Strauss & Last, 1993). This finding is consistent with the developmental considerations discussed below. Although social anxiety disorder is most frequently diagnosed in adolescents, it can occur earlier (Bernstein et al., 2008; Costello et al., 2005b). Prevalence probably increases with age, and the disorder may be under-recognized, particularly in adolescents (Chavira & Stein, 2005). One reason that the problem may be underrecognized is that youngsters with social anxiety disorder may minimize their problems in order to present themselves in a desirable way (DiBartolo et al., 1998). This tendency would be consistent with a concern about negative evaluation. Slightly higher rates are reported for girls, but it is not clear whether there are sex differences in the prevalence of social anxiety disorder (Chavira & Stein, 2005; Ford et al., 2003).

Most young people with social anxiety disorder also meet the criteria for one or more other disorders (Bernstein et al., 2008; Chavira & Stein, 2005). As with Louis, another anxiety disorder is the most common additional diagnosis. For example, in a sample of children, 7–10 years of age, diagnosed with social anxiety disorders, 84% met criteria for at least one other anxiety disorder. On average, children met the criteria for about two co-occurring disorders (Bernstein et al., 2008). Table 6-2 illustrates the

TABLE 6-2	Comorbid Diagnoses of Children with Social Anxiety Disorder
Comorbid Diagnosis	**Percentage**
Generalized anxiety disorder	73
Separation anxiety disorder	51
Specific phobia	36
Attention-deficit/ hyperactivity disorder	9
Conduct disorder	4
Dysthymia	4
Major depressive disorder	2
Obsessive-compulsive disorder	2
Oppositional defiant disorder	2
Posttraumatic stress disorder	2

Adapted from Bernstein et al. 2008.

percentages of the various co-occurring disorders in this sample. Adolescents, in particular, may meet the criteria for a major depressive disorder.

Developmental Course

Social anxiety disorder can be viewed within the context of developmental factors (Hayward et al., 2008; Velting & Albano, 2001). In young children between the ages of 6 months and 3 years, stranger anxiety and separation anxiety are common. The self-consciousness that is an essential part of what we mean by social anxiety disorder, however, does not develop until later. The abilities to see oneself as a social object and to feel embarrassment may emerge at about 4 or 5 years of age. Envisioning the perspective of other people and then experiencing concern over their possible negative evaluation probably do not emerge until about 8 years of age. By late childhood or early adolescence, these cognitive developmental prerequisites and the awareness that one's appearance and behavior can be the basis for others' evaluations are in place. So, for example, Westenberg and colleagues (2004) assessed fears among a sample of children and adolescents (8 to 18 years of age) from the Netherlands. Fears of social and achievement evaluation increased with age, and these age-related changes in fears were associated with level of social-cognitive maturity.

By late childhood or early adolescence, youths are regularly required to perform tasks that have a social-evaluative component. They are, for example, expected to speak in class, engage in group activities, and perform in athletic or musical events. Responsibility for initiating and arranging social activities is also shifting. Parents are no longer likely to be highly involved in arranging social interactions. Young adolescents also may be expected to engage in different social activities such as attending school dances and dating. The combination of these social demands and the development of self-awareness can set the stage for the emergence of social anxiety. Social anxiety disorder may be thought to evolve from anxiety that is typical in this developmental period but that is magnified for some youngsters by individual differences and social demands (Gazelle, 2010; Neal & Edelmann, 2003; Parker et al., 2006).

Because adolescence is a period during which social anxieties are quite common, it may be particularly difficult to distinguish between normal and abnormal social anxiety. Interpretation of severity, defined in the DSM diagnostic criteria by phrases such as "almost invariably," "marked distress," "intense anxiety," and "interferes significantly," becomes particularly important in this age group (Clark et al., 1994). The view that some level of social anxiety is common during adolescence is supported by research data (Velting & Albano, 2001). For example, Essau, Conradt, and Peterman (1999) found that approximately 51% of a community sample of youths between the ages of 12 and 17 reported at least one specific social fear. However, only some smaller proportion of youths develops more general and clinical level problems (Chavira & Stein, 2005).

SEPARATION ANXIETY

We have chosen to describe separation anxiety followed by a discussion of school refusal because much of what has been written about the problem of school refusal and its etiology has derived from a separation anxiety perspective. In addition, given that compulsory education laws require all children to attend school, it seems likely that many children with separation anxiety would also have problems with school attendance.

Diagnosis and Classification

The DSM category of **Separation Anxiety Disorder** (SAD) is intended to describe anxiety regarding separation from a major attachment figure and/or home. The anxiety experienced by the young person exceeds what might be expected given a youth's developmental level. Diagnostic criteria include eight symptoms describing various concerns about separation from, being alone without, or worry of harm befalling, major attachment figures. One of the eight symptoms specifically addresses reluctance or refusal to go to school. These separation concerns are accompanied by persistent and excessive worry or distress and related sleep and physical problems (e.g., headaches, abdominal complaints, nausea, vomiting).

For a child to receive the diagnosis of Separation Anxiety Disorder, the DSM requires the presence of three or more symptoms for at least 4 weeks and the problems

Adolescence is a period during which involvement in a variety of social activities is expected. Some young people find these social demands particularly difficult.

must cause significant distress or impairment in social, school, or other areas of functioning.

Description

Young children experiencing separation anxiety may be clingy and follow their parents around. They may express general fear or apprehension, experience nightmares, or complain of somatic symptoms (e.g., headaches, stomachaches, nausea, palpitations). Older children may complain about not feeling well, think about illness or tragedy that might befall them or their caregivers, become apathetic and depressed, and be reluctant to leave home or to participate in activities with their peers. Some young people may threaten to harm themselves. This threat is usually viewed as a means of escaping or avoiding separation, and serious suicidal behavior is rare.

Epidemiology

Estimates of the prevalence of separation anxiety disorder in community samples typically range from about 3 to 12% of young people. Among youths referred to clinics, approximately 12% to one-third receive a primary diagnosis of Separation Anxiety Disorder (Canino et al., 2004; Silverman & Dick-Niederhauser, 2004; Suveg, Aschenbrand, & Kendall, 2005). Prevalence is higher in children than in adolescents, and the disorder is uncommon in older adolescents. Children and adolescents with separation anxiety disorder often also meet diagnostic criteria for other disorders. Generalized Anxiety Disorder seems to be the most common other diagnosis received (Last, Strauss, & Francis, 1987; Verduin & Kendall, 2003). The status of sex and of ethnic differences in prevalence remains unclear (Ford et al., 2003; Suveg et al., 2005). Some studies report a greater prevalence of SAD among girls than among boys, but others report no sex differences. Clinical samples suggest no ethnic differences in rates, but there is some suggestion of greater rates in community samples of African American youths.

Developmental Course

Anxiety concerning separation from a primary caregiver is part of the normal developmental process in infants. From the first year of life through the preschool years, children typically exhibit periodic distress and worry when they are separated from their parents or other individuals to whom they have an attachment. Indeed, the absence of any separation distress may indicate an insecure attachment. Even in older children, it is not uncommon for expectations, beliefs, and prior separation experiences to lead to feelings of homesickness when the children are separated from their parents (Thurber & Sigman, 1998). Such distress is

KENNY

Separation Anxiety

Kenny, a 10-year-old boy, lived with his parents and his two half-siblings from his mother's previous marriage. He was brought to an anxiety disorders clinic by his parents because he was extremely fearful and had refused to go to school during the past several months. Kenny was also unable to be in other situations in which he was separated from his parents—such as when playing in the backyard, at Little League practice, [and] staying with a sitter. When separated from his parents, Kenny cried, had tantrums, or threatened to hurt himself (e.g., jump from the school window). Kenny also exhibited high levels of anxiety, a number of specific fears, significant depressive symptomatology (e.g., sad mood, guilt about his problems, occasional wishes to be dead, and periodic early awakening). Kenny's separation problems appeared to have begun about a year earlier when his father was having drinking problems and was away from home for prolonged periods of time. Kenny's separation problems gradually worsened over the year.

Adapted from Last, 1988, pp. 12–13.

viewed as problematic only when distress about separation persists beyond the expected age or is excessive.

For children with separation anxiety, symptoms often progress from milder to more severe. For example, a child's complaints of nightmares may lead to the parents allowing the child to sleep in their bed on an intermittent basis. This often rapidly progresses to the child sleeping with one or both parents on a regular basis (Albano et al., 2003). Most children appear to recover from separation anxiety disorder (Kearney et al., 2003); however, in some, the symptoms may persist and they may develop a later disorder, with depression being particularly common (Last et al., 1996). In adolescents, separation anxiety, if present, may be the precursor of more serious problems (Blagg & Yule, 1994; Tonge, 1994).

SCHOOL REFUSAL

Definition

Some children and adolescents exhibit excessive anxiety regarding school attendance. When these young people do not attend school, their condition is typically termed **school refusal**. School refusal is not a DSM diagnosis;

however, reluctance or refusal to go to school is one of the eight symptoms listed for the DSM diagnosis of SAD, and some youths who exhibit school refusal do receive this diagnosis. However since a young person need present with only three of the eight listed symptoms to receive the diagnosis of SAD, not all young people with separation anxiety disorder exhibit school refusal. In addition, not all school refusers show separation anxiety (Kearney, Eisen, & Silverman, 1995; Last & Strauss, 1990). Although the most common conceptualization of school refusal attributes the problem to separation anxiety, some young people may fear a particular aspect of the school experience, in which case they might be diagnosed under the specific phobia or social anxiety disorder categories. For example, a youth may fear going to school because of anxiety regarding academic performance, evaluation, speaking in public, conflict with peers, or meeting new people.

Thus, it is best not to view all cases of school refusal as being similar or as having a single cause. Indeed, school refusal should probably be considered heterogeneous and multicausal (Suveg, Aschenbrand, & Kendell, 2005). One suggestion is that it might be more useful to classify school refusal by the function that the behavior serves—by a **functional analysis**—rather than by symptoms (Kearney, 2008). Some youths may refuse to go to or stay in school due to avoidance of school-related stimuli (e.g., riding the school bus) that provoke negative affect, such as anxiety and depression. Also, occasions that require social interactions and activities that involve evaluation are likely to occur during the school day. Another function of school refusal might be to escape from these situations. Alternatively, children and adolescents who refuse to attend school may receive attention from others. For these young people school refusal behaviors (e.g., complaints of illness) may elicit attention from parents. Finally, youths who refuse to go to school may receive positive reinforcement for such behavior in the form of tangible reinforcers such as being able to watch television or play video games, or they may be served special treats. Using a functional analysis approach, treatment programs can be designed that address one or more functions that school refusal behavior serves for a particular young person.

Description

A certain degree of anxiety and fear about school is common for children and adolescents, but some exhibit excessive anxiety regarding school attendance. The behaviors, thoughts, and somatic complaints characteristic of separation anxiety are often part of the picture of school refusal. Young people, particularly adolescents, may also show signs of depression. They are often absent from school on a regular basis, may fall behind in the academic work, and sometimes have to repeat a grade. In addition, because they miss opportunities for social experiences, they are likely to experience difficulties with their peers as well. School refusal can be a serious problem that causes considerable distress for both the youth and his or her caregivers and that may also interfere with the young person's development. Clinical reports suggest that onset of these problems often follows some life stress, such as a death, an illness, a change of school, or a move to a new neighborhood.

School refusal is often differentiated from **truancy**. Truants are usually described as unlikely to be excessively anxious or fearful about attending school. They typically are absent on an intermittent basis, often without parental knowledge. The school refuser, in contrast, is usually absent for continuous extended periods, during which time the parents are aware that the youth is at home. Truants are often described as poor students who exhibit other conduct problems, such as stealing and lying. There is considerable disagreement as to whether truancy or school attendance problems associated with conduct problems and antisocial behaviors should be included in the concept of school refusal (King & Bernstein, 2001).

Refusing to go to school and/or to be separated from parents is a common reason for referral for psychological services.

Epidemiology and Developmental Course

School refusal is usually estimated to occur in 1 to 2% of the general population and in about 5% of all clinic-referred cases; it is equally common in boys and girls (Suveg et al., 2005). School refusal can be found in youths of all ages. Like separation anxiety disorder, however, it seems more likely to occur at major transition points. There is the suggestion that, in younger children, the problem is likely to be related to separation anxiety, but children in middle-age groups or early adolescence are likely to have complex and mixed presentations of anxiety and depressive disorders. Prognosis seems best for children under the age of 10 years, and treatment seems to be particularly difficult for older youths and those who are also depressed (Bernstein et al., 2001; Blagg & Yule, 1994). If problems are left untreated, serious long-term consequences may result (Suveg et al., 2005).

In working with school refusers, the majority of clinicians of all orientations stress the importance of getting the young person back to school (Blagg & Yule, 1994; King, Ollendick, & Gullone, 1990). Successful strategies take an active approach to the problem, finding a way of getting the young person back to school even if this is difficult or requires the threat of legal intervention. Applying cognitive-behavioral interventions that include exposure to fearful situations, teaching the youth coping skills, and incorporating training and advice for parents and teachers have shown promise in achieving both regular school attendance and overall improvement in functioning (King et al., 2000; Suveg et al., 2005).

GENERALIZED ANXIETY DISORDER

Phobias, social anxiety, separation anxiety, and school refusal represent relatively focused anxiety difficulties. However, anxiety is sometimes experienced in a less focused manner.

Diagnostic Criteria

Generalized Anxiety Disorder (GAD) is characterized by excessive anxiety and worry about a number of events or activities. The child or adolescent finds these anxieties or worries difficult to control. Thus, a youth with generalized anxiety will experience excessive anxiety and worry that is not confined to a specific type of situation. Unlike the youth with social anxiety, where the focus may be on social and performance situations, or the youth with separation anxiety, where the focus may be on separation from home or familiar people, the distress the youth with generalized anxiety feels is not limited to a specific type of situation.

The DSM diagnostic criteria require that this generalized anxiety and worry are associated with one or more of six symptoms:

1. restlessness, feeling keyed up or on edge
2. being easily fatigued
3. difficulty concentrating
4. irritability
5. muscle tension
6. disturbed sleep.

Some of these symptoms must be present most days for the past 6 months, and the symptoms must cause significant distress or impairment in important areas of the young person's functioning. The DSM acknowledges some developmental difference in that a child need only display one or more (contrasted with three for adults) of the six symptoms listed above. Although GAD is the way that generalized anxiety is defined by the DSM, various questions remain about how to understand and define generalized anxiety in children and adolescents (Ellis & Hudson, 2010), and how similar these symptoms are to those used to diagnose depression (Costello et al., 2005b; Kendall, Hedtke, & Aschenbrand, 2006).

Description

Clinicians frequently describe children and adolescents who worry excessively and exhibit extensive fearful behavior. They are often described as "little worriers." These intense worries are not due to some specific recent stress and are not focused on any particular object or situation, but rather occur in regard to a number of general life circumstances and are not due to a specific recent stress. These youths also seem excessively concerned with their competence and performance in a number of areas (e.g., academics, peer relations, sports) to the point of being perfectionistic and setting unreasonably high standards for themselves. They may also worry about things like family finances and natural disasters. They repeatedly seek approval and reassurance, and exhibit nervous habits (e.g., nail biting) and sleep disturbances. Physical complaints such as headaches and stomachaches are common (Albano et al., 2003; APA, 2013). The following description of John captures the clinical picture of generalized anxiety disorder.

Epidemiology

Epidemiological studies of nonclinic samples suggest that generalized anxiety disorder is a relatively common problem. Estimates, among youth of all ages, vary from about 2 to 14% (Anderson et al., 1987; Canino et al., 2004; Cohen et al., 1993b; Costello, 1989; Lavigne et al., 2009). Generalized

JOHN

Generalized Anxiety Disorder

Like his mother, John had a very low opinion of himself and his abilities.... and found it difficult to cope with the "scary things" inside himself. His main problem had to do with the numerous fears that he had and the panic attacks that overtook him from time to time. He was afraid of the dark, of ghosts, of monsters, of being abandoned, of being alone, of strangers, of war, of guns, of knives, of loud noises, and of snakes.... Like his mother again, he had many psychosomatic complaints involving his bladder, his bowels, his kidneys, his intestines, and his blood.... He also suffered from insomnia and would not or could not go to sleep until his mother did.... He was also afraid to sleep alone or to sleep without a light, and regularly wet and soiled himself. He was often afraid but could not say why and was also fearful of contact with others.

Anthony, 1981, pp. 163–164.

anxiety disorder is probably the most common anxiety disorder among adolescents (Clark et al., 1994). Estimates of rates in the general population of adolescents range from 3.7 to 7.3% (Kashani & Orvaschel, 1990; McGee et al., 1990; Whitaker et al., 1990).

The disorder is common among youths seen in clinical settings. Keller and colleagues (1992), for example, report that 85% of the youths with an anxiety disorder were diagnosed with the disorder, although other estimates are not quite this high.

The disorder is sometimes reported to be more common in girls, but there are also reports of no sex differences in prevalence. The median age of onset is estimated to be about 10 years of age. The number and intensity of symptoms seem to increase with age (Ford et al., 2003; Keller et al., 1992; Kendall et al., 2006).

Children and adolescents who meet the diagnostic criteria for GAD are likely to meet the diagnostic criteria for additional disorders (Masi et al., 2004), and rates of such co-occurrence seem higher for youths with GAD than for those with other diagnoses (Silverman & Ginsburg, 1998). Depression, separation anxiety, and phobias are common co-occurring disorders (Masi et al., 2004; Verduin & Kendall, 2003).

GAD may be overdiagnosed in children (APA, 2013), and some have questioned whether it is a distinct disorder. What is now considered the separate disorder of GAD might instead be an indication of a dimension of general constitutional vulnerability toward anxiety or emotional reactivity (Flannery-Schroeder, 2004). It may be that professional help is sought when youths with high levels of this dimension of general vulnerability exhibit other anxiety or internalizing disorders (Beidel, Silverman, & Hammond-Laurence, 1996).

Developmental Course

GAD does not seem transitory (Keller et al., 1992). Symptoms may persist for several years (Cohen, Cohen, & Brook, 1993a). Persistence may be particularly likely for those with more severe symptoms. A greater number of severe overanxious symptoms, increased impairment, and an increased risk of alcohol use have been reported among adolescents with this disorder (Clark et al., 1994; Kendall et al., 2006; Strauss, 1994).

An examination of developmental differences in co-occurring disorders provides some interesting information (Masi et al., 2004; Strauss et al., 1988). For example, although rates of co-occurrence are high for youngsters of all ages, young children seem more likely to receive a concurrent diagnosis of separation anxiety disorder, and adolescents a concurrent diagnosis of depression or social anxiety disorder. These findings may suggest a developmental difference in how generalized anxiety is experienced. Alternatively, since separation anxiety is generally more common in young children and depression and social anxiety are more common in adolescents, these findings may also be viewed as consistent with questions, raised above, about whether GAD is a distinct disorder or an indication of a dimension of heightened general vulnerability.

PANIC ATTACKS AND PANIC DISORDER

Intense, discrete experiences of extreme anxiety, like Frank's, that seem to arise quickly and often, are known as panic attacks, and are another way that adolescents and children experience anxiety.

Diagnostic Criteria

A distinction is made between panic attacks and panic disorder.

PANIC ATTACKS   A **panic attack** is a discrete period of intense fear or terror that has a sudden onset and reaches a peak quickly—within a few minutes. The DSM describes the 13 physical and cognitive symptoms listed below. Four or more of these symptoms must be present during an episode.

1. cardiac reactions (e.g., rapid heart rate)
2. sweating

3. shaking or trembling
4. feeling short of breath or smothering
5. feeling as if choking
6. feeling chest discomfort or pain
7. feelings of abdominal distress or nausea
8. feeling faint or lightheaded
9. feeling chill or flushed
10. feeling numbness or tingling (parathesias)
11. feelings of unreality (derealization) or of being detached from oneself (depersonalization)
12. fear of "going crazy" or of losing control
13. fear of dying

Panic attacks are typically differentiated by the presence or absence of triggers. Unexpected (uncued) panic attacks occur spontaneously or "out of the blue" with no apparent situational trigger. In contrast, expected (cued) panic attacks have an obvious trigger or cue. Expected panic attacks may occur, for example, when the person is exposed to or anticipates a feared object or situation (e.g., a dog) or when the person encounters situations in which panic attacks previously occurred. Panic attacks are not themselves a disorder within the DSM system, but they may occur in the context of a variety of anxiety or other disorders. For example, panic attacks may occur with **agoraphobia** (anxiety about being in a situation in which escape may be difficult or embarrassing). In severe cases of agoraphobia, a youth may remain at home or become terrified of leaving home. This agoraphobia is an attempt to avoid certain circumstances in which an uncontrollable or embarrassing anxiety or panic attacks may occur. The youth with agoraphobia may fear that in such situations escape may be difficult or help may not be available.

PANIC DISORDER   While panic attacks may occur in the context of a variety of disorders, these attacks are a central component of **panic disorder**. Panic disorder involves recurrent unexpected panic attacks. To receive a DSM diagnosis of panic disorder, a month or more of one or both of the following must follow at least one of these attacks:

- persistent concern about having other panic attacks or worry about the implications of the attack ("going crazy," having a heart attack)
- a significant maladaptive change in behavior related to attacks (e.g., avoidance of situations).

Although there is an established literature regarding adults, it is only relatively recently that the occurrence of panic in children and adolescents has received attention. This discrepancy was, in part, due to controversy regarding the existence of panic attacks and panic disorder in youths

FRANK

Panic Attacks

While falling asleep, Frank often experienced discrete episodes of his heart beating quickly, shortness of breath, tingling in his hands, and extreme fearfulness. These episodes lasted only 15 to 20 minutes, but Frank could not fall asleep in his bedroom and began sleeping on the living room couch. His father brought him back to his bed once he was asleep, but Frank was tired during the day, and his schoolwork began to deteriorate.

Adapted from Rapoport & Ismond, 1996, pp. 240–241.

(Kearney & Silverman, 1992; Kearney et al., 1997; Klein et al., 1992; Suveg et al., 2005). Much of the controversy revolved around two issues.

One issue is whether young people experience both the physiological and cognitive symptoms of panic. Adults who experience panic attacks report fear of losing control, going "crazy," or dying during the attack. They also worry about future attacks. Such cognitive symptoms may not occur in children or young adolescents.

The second issue arises based on the requirement that panic attacks be unexpected (uncued) in order to diagnose panic disorder. It may be difficult to determine whether panic experienced by young person is truly uncued. Youths may think attacks are "out of the blue" because they may not be sufficiently aware of, or as likely to monitor, cues in their environment. Careful and detailed questioning may be needed to reveal precipitating cues. This problem is particularly acute in younger children.

Epidemiology

Although the diagnosis of panic may be difficult, it is suggested that panic attacks and panic disorder occur in adolescents and, to a lesser degree, in prepubertal children (Ollendick, Birmaher, & Mattis, 2004a; Suveg et al., 2005). For example, many adults who experience panic attacks or panic disorder report that onset occurred during adolescence or earlier.

Also, both community samples and clinic-based studies suggest that panic attacks may not be uncommon in adolescents. For example, 16% of young people between the ages of 12 and 17 in a community sample of Australian youths reported at least one full-blown panic attack in their lifetimes (King et al., 1997) and similar rates were reported in a sample of German adolescents (Essau, Conradt, &

Petermann, 1999). Regarding panic disorder, the condition is rarely diagnosed prior to mid or late adolescence (Suveg et al., 2005). For example, Ford and colleagues (2003) found that while panic disorder was rarely diagnosed in younger British children, about 0.5% of youths between the ages of 13 and 15 met the criteria for panic disorder. Similar or slightly higher rates have been reported in a community sample of Puerto Rican, German, and U.S. youths (Canino et al., 2004; Essau et al., 1999; Kessler et al., 2009). In clinical samples of adolescents, reported prevalence is higher—about 10 to 15% (e.g., Biederman et al., 1997; Last & Strauss, 1989). Panic attacks occur equally in boys and girls; however, panic disorder is typically reported more frequently in girls. Little information is available regarding ethnic differences (Suveg et al., 2005).

Description and Developmental Pattern

Adolescents who experience panic attacks experience considerable distress and impairment. Few, however, seem to seek treatment (Ollendick et al., 2004a). Studies of adolescents seen in clinics indicate that these youths evidence both the physiological and cognitive symptoms of panic. For example, Kearney and colleagues (1997) found that physiological symptoms of panic attacks were the most commonly reported symptoms, but the cognitive symptoms of fear of "going crazy" and fear of dying were also reported by 50% of youngsters.

Whether panic attacks are cued or spontaneous is less clear. Psychosocial stressors (e.g., family conflict, peer problems) were reported as possible precipitants by 26 of the 28 adolescents in this study. Some studies, however, report that for some youths, panic attacks are judged to be spontaneous. As we have mentioned, though, there is a problem in judging the spontaneous nature of panic attacks in young people.

Less is known regarding panic in younger children. Although both panic attacks and panic disorder are reported in clinical samples of children, their expression may differ somewhat from their presentation in adolescents and adults. Young children may report a general fear of becoming sick rather than describing specific physiological symptoms such as palpitations or breathlessness, or verbalizing fears of dying, going crazy, or losing control (Albano et al., 2003).

Youths with panic attacks or panic disorder who present at clinics are likely to have a family history of panic attacks or other severe anxiety symptoms. They are also likely to present with a variety of other symptoms, and the majority meet the criteria for additional diagnoses, particularly other anxiety disorders and depression (Kearney et al., 1997; Masi et al., 2000). Many of the youths with panic disorder seen in clinical settings also exhibit agoraphobia (Suveg et al., 2005). The high proportion of youth who report a history of separation anxiety led to the suggestion that separation anxiety disorder is a precursor to panic disorder. There are findings of neurophysiological signs of greater arousal among infants of mothers with panic disorder than among controls. This is consistent with the idea of an early vulnerability (Warren et al., 2003). However, it seems likely that separation anxiety disorder would be only one of many possible paths to the development of panic disorder (Hayward et al., 2004; Ollendick et al., 2004a).

REACTIONS TO TRAUMATIC EVENTS

How do young people react to experiencing natural disasters such as hurricanes, other disasters such as fires or ships sinking, kidnapping, or the violence of a terrorist attack or war?

Trauma is usually defined as an event outside everyday experience that would be distressing to almost anyone. Early descriptions of children's exposure to trauma suggested that reactions would be relatively mild and transient, and thus these experiences were not given a great deal of attention. However, reports began to emerge of more severe and long-lasting reactions.

The investigation of 26 children kidnapped from their Chowchilla, California, school bus in 1976 is one study that influenced the understanding of children's posttraumatic responses. The children and their bus driver were held for 27 hours. At first they were driven around in darkened vans; then they were moved to a buried tractor trailer, where they remained until some of the victims dug themselves out. The child victims and at least one parent of each child were interviewed within 5 to 13 months of the kidnapping. All of the children were found to be symptomatic, with 73% showing moderately severe or severe reactions. Assessments 2 to 5 years after the kidnapping revealed that many symptoms had persisted (Terr, 1979; 1983).

Diagnostic Criteria

Systematic study of youths' reactions to trauma was also stimulated by the introduction, in the third version of the DSM, of a specific diagnosis—**Posttraumatic Stress Disorder** (PTSD). In DSM III, IV, and IVTR PTSD was included among the anxiety disorders. In DSM-5, PTSD (as well as **Acute Stress Disorder**—ASD) is part of a separate grouping of Trauma- and Stressor-Related Disorders. However, these disorders continue to be viewed as related to the anxiety disorders.

In addition to PTSD and ASD, the DSM-5 grouping of Trauma- and Stressor-Related Disorders also includes

Reactive Attachment Disorder and **Disinhibited Social Engagement Disorder**. Both of these disorders are viewed as reactions to the trauma or stressor of social neglect (see Accent: The Absence of Adequate Caregiving). Also included in this chapter is what are termed **Adjustment Disorders**. These disorders describe marked emotional or behavioral symptoms of distress that a person develops in response to an identifiable stressor and which interfere with important areas of functioning. In an adjustment disorder, the disturbance of adjustment occurs within three months of the onset of the stressor and lasts no longer than 6 months after the stressor or its consequences have ended. Adjustment disorder may be displayed with depressed mood, anxiety, disturbances of conduct, or with a combination of these types of symptoms. We will concentrate our discussion on reactions to traumatic events and PTSD.

The current DSM describes a set of PTSD criteria that apply to adults, adolescents, and children older than 6 years of age. Separate criteria also are described for children 6 and younger.

The diagnosis of PTSD is defined by the development of a characteristic set of symptoms following exposure to one or more traumatic events. Thus, to receive a diagnosis of PTSD the young person must experience exposure to a serious traumatic event(s). The child or adolescent is considered to have experienced exposure if she or he has directly experienced the traumatic event, or has witnessed a traumatic event occurring to others, or has learned that a traumatic event occurred to a close relative or friend. In addition, repeated or extreme exposure to aversive information about a traumatic event(s) may also be considered traumatic exposure, but not if such exposure is only through modes such as electronic media or television. The diagnosis of PTSD also requires that following exposure to the traumatic event(s) the person must experience symptoms from each of four different clusters:

- Reexperiencing
- Avoidance
- Negative alterations in cognitions and mood
- Arousal and reactivity

The reexperiencing cluster describes intrusive symptoms that begin after the traumatic event. This cluster of symptom includes disturbing memories of the traumatic event, recurrent distressing trauma-related dreams, prolonged or intense psychological distress or physiological reactions in response to cues that are reminders of the event, or dissociative reactions. **Dissociation** refers to alterations in self-awareness. Dissociative reactions my include depersonalization (feeling cut off from one's feelings or environment) and derealization (a marked sense of unreality). Thus, the person experiencing a dissociative reaction

may act or feel as if the traumatic event were recurring (e.g., flashbacks).

Avoidance symptoms may include persistent efforts to avoid trauma-related thoughts or feelings. This reaction may also include avoidance of external stimuli (e.g., people or situations) associated with the trauma.

Negative alterations in cognitions and mood may include cognitive symptoms such as difficulty in remembering important aspects of the traumatic event, distorted thoughts about the causes or consequences of the traumatic event, or exaggerated negative beliefs or expectations. Alterations in mood may include persistent negative emotional states (e.g., fear, anger, shame), persistent inability to experience positive emotions, diminished interest in significant activities, or feelings of detachment from others.

The fourth cluster of symptoms involves marked alteration in the young person's arousal or reactivity that begins or worsens after the occurrence of the traumatic event(s). These symptoms may include irritable behavior and angry outbursts, reckless behavior, heightened vigilance, exaggerated startle responses, concentration difficulties, or sleep disturbances.

The DSM acknowledges potential developmental differences in the expression of PTSD. For example, the description of reexperiencing symptoms indicates that children, rather than reporting memories, may engage in repetitive trauma-related play or that children who have experienced a trauma may have frightening dreams without recognizable trauma-related content. These developmental considerations were included in earlier versions of the DSM; however, there were still concerns that young children were underdiagnosed using existing criteria and that it was necessary to pay greater attention to developmental considerations in defining posttraumatic stress disorder in children. Indeed, some suggested that existing criteria were not appropriate for infants or very young children and alternative criteria were proposed (De Young, Kenardy, & Cobham, 2011; Salmon & Bryant, 2002; Scheeringa, 2009). In response to such concerns DSM-5 has included a separate parallel set of criteria for children 6 years of age and younger. This corresponding set of criteria reduces the number of symptoms required for diagnosis and provides examples of how the various symptoms of PTSD might present in this age group.

The diagnostic criteria for Acute Stress Disorder (ASD) are similar to those for PTSD. The principal distinction is that ASD symptoms last for at least 3 days, but less than 4 weeks, whereas PTSD lasts for at least 1 month following the trauma or has a delayed onset. A young person with significant immediate reaction to a trauma may be given the diagnosis of ASD. This diagnosis may help alert adults to a youth's needs; however, it is unclear how well ASD predicts later PTSD (De Bellis & Van Dillen, 2005).

ACCENT
The Absence of Adequate Caregiving

In the section on Trauma- and Stressor-Related Disorders, the DSM describes two disorders, **Reactive Attachment Disorder** and **Disinhibited Social Engagement Disorder** that are, in part, defined by the absence of adequate caregiving during childhood. For both of these disorders it must be established that the child has experienced extremes of insufficient care. This level of social neglect is evidenced by one or more of the following:

A persistent lack of having caregivers provide for basic needs such as affection, comfort, and stimulation

Repeated changes of primary caregivers—thus limiting opportunities to form stable attachments

Rearing in unusual situations (e.g., institutions with poor child–staff ratios) that severely limit opportunities to form attachments.

The two disorders are, thus, thought to share a common etiology, inadequate caregiving, but differ in how the child's difficulties are expressed.

The diagnosis of reactive attachment disorder describes children who display extremely underdeveloped attachments to their adult caregivers. A socially neglected child receiving this diagnosis displays persistent inhibited and withdrawn behavior toward adult caregivers. The child, when distressed, rarely seeks comfort and when comfort is offered the child rarely responds. In addition, the child displays a persistent social/emotional disturbance that is characterized by symptoms such as minimal social and emotional responsiveness, limited positive affect, and unexplained fearfulness, irritability, or sadness.

In contrast, a socially neglected child receiving a diagnosis of disinhibited social engagement disorder displays socially disinhibited behaviors. A child receiving this diagnosis displays a pattern of culturally inappropriate, overly familiar behavior toward strangers. This child might show little or no reticence in approaching or interacting with unfamiliar adults, be overly familiar (verbally or physically) with unfamiliar adults, fail to check back with an adult caregiver when venturing away or when in unfamiliar settings, and/or be willing to go off with an unfamiliar adult with little or no hesitation.

Both these diagnosis are intended to apply only to children who should be developmentally ready and able to form appropriate selective attachments. Thus, for both diagnoses, the child must have a developmental age of at least 9 months.

Description

The reactions of young people to traumatic events may vary considerably. Many exhibit symptoms without meeting the criteria for a diagnosis of PTSD, but they still experience considerable distress and interference with functioning.

Most youths become upset at reminders of the trauma, and they experience repetitive, intrusive thoughts about the event. Even children who experience mild levels of exposure to life-threatening disasters may have such thoughts. Preschool and school-age children frequently reenact aspects of the disaster in drawings, stories, and play. Initially such behavior may be part of reexperiencing symptoms, but it may become a useful part of the recovery process as well. Saylor, Powell, and Swenson (1992), for example, report that after Hurricane Hugo occurred in South Carolina, children's play progressed from blowing houses down to acting out the role of roofers during rebuilding.

Young people may also exhibit increased frequency and intensity of specific fears directly related to or associated with the traumatic experience. Thus adolescent British girls on a school trip who experienced the sinking of their cruise ship developed fears of swimming, of the dark, or of boats and other forms of transportation. These girls, however, did not show elevated levels of unrelated fears as compared to those of schoolmates who did not go on the trip or with girls from a comparable school (Yule, Udwin, & Murdoch, 1990).

Separation difficulties and clingy, dependent behaviors are also common. These behaviors may be exhibited as reluctance to go to school or as a desire to sleep with parents. Other sleep problems, such as difficulty in getting to sleep, nightmares, and repeated dreams related to the traumatic event, are also common. A sense of vulnerability and loss of faith in the future have also been reported. In adolescents, this loss may interfere with planning for future education and careers; moreover, school performance is reported to suffer. Other commonly noted symptoms include depressed mood, loss of interest in previously enjoyed activities, irritability, and angry or aggressive outbursts. Guilt about surviving when others have died can also occur. It is also common for young people to meet the criteria for additional and multiple diagnoses (Pfefferbaum, 1997).

PTSD and Child Abuse

Child maltreatment is one form of trauma that has been viewed within the framework of PTSD. Indeed, many youngsters who experience abuse exhibit meaningful symptoms or meet the diagnostic criteria for PTSD (De Bellis & Van Dillen, 2005). In chapter 3 (pp. 53–54) we saw

A number of factors influence children's reactions to a traumatic event, including aspects of the experience and the reactions of their parents and other adults.

that a developmental traumatology model of child maltreatment suggests that trauma-induced changes in neurobiology underlie the development of psychopathology in maltreated children (De Bellis, 2001). In this model, PTSD symptoms are considered to be the key mediator linking maltreatment and subsequent psychopathology. Accordingly, PTSD symptoms are the initial problems that then contribute to the potential development of a wide range of behavioral and emotional problems at different times of life.

Epidemiology

Natural disasters, terrorism, and accidents are catastrophic events that are unpredictable in nature, making it difficult to determine the number of children and adolescents who will be exposed to traumatic events each year (Fletcher, 2003). However, we do know that young people are frequently exposed to maltreatment and are frequent victims of violent crime. Some may be at particular risk. For example, infants and younger children are at greater risk for maltreatment (Wekerle & Wolfe, 2003) and homeless adolescents are at increased risk for victimization (Stewart et al., 2004). It seems likely that an appreciable number of young people experience

a traumatic event. Indeed, a survey of children and adolescents indicated that about one-quarter had experienced a serious traumatic event by the age of 16 (Costello et al., 2002).

Fletcher (2003) indicates that about one-third of youths exposed to traumatic events are diagnosed with PTSD—a rate slightly higher than for traumatized adults—and some findings suggest that half or more of exposed youths experience PTSD (De Bellis & Van Dillen, 2005). Most studies find a higher incidence of PTSD among girls. As indicated earlier, developmental differences may exist in how PTSD is expressed, particularly in very young children. Research also suggests that children, adolescents, and adults may differ with regard to some basic neurobiological responses to trauma (De Bellis, 2001; Lipschitz et al., 2003). For example, there may be differences in the response of the hypothalamic-pituitary-adrenal (HPA) axis, a critical neurohormonal regulatory system, that, under conditions of extreme stress, causes the release of neurohormones, including cortisol. The response of this system is one of the mechanisms that is thought to underlie the development of PTSD and other difficulties.

On average, the incidence of particular PTSD symptoms appears to be above 20%. The PTSD cluster of symptoms (reexperiencing, avoidance, alterations in cognition/mood, and arousal) has been reported in youths from a variety of different cultures (Perrin, Smith, & Yule, 2000). The most frequently occurring category of symptom is probably reexperiencing (De Bellis & Van Dillen, 2005).

Not all children and adolescents experience the same pattern or intensity of symptoms, and not all youths who experience traumas meet the criteria for PTSD. The amount of time that symptoms persist may vary, and problems may fluctuate over time. A number of factors seem to influence youths' initial reactions and the duration and severity of symptoms (La Greca, Silverman, & Wasserstein, 1998; Trickey et al., 2012; Udwin et al., 2000).

The nature of the traumatic event may influence reactions. For example, one can group stressors into two categories: (1) acute, nonabusive stressors—nonabusive traumatic events that occur only once, like floods or accidents, and (2) chronic or abusive stressors—ongoing stressors like war or physical or sexual abuse (Fletcher, 2003). Some symptoms of PTSD appear likely to occur regardless of the type of traumatic event (e.g., trauma-related fears, difficulty sleeping). However, other symptoms vary depending on the type of trauma experienced. Also, while young people experiencing either kind of trauma appear equally likely to receive the diagnosis of PTSD, other diagnoses that they are likely to receive may vary. These differences are illustrated in Table 6-3. It may seem surprising that some symptoms or problems occur more often among young people exposed to acute, nonabusive trauma than

TABLE 6-3 Rates of PTSD Symptoms and Associated Symptoms/Diagnoses in Response to Acute, Nonabusive Stressors and Chronic or Abusive Stressors

	TYPE OF STRESSOR	
	Acute-Nonabusive	Chronic or Abusive
DSM Symptom Cluster		
Reexperiencing	92%	86%
Avoidance/cognitive mood alterations	30%	54%
Overarousal	55%	71%
Associated Symptoms/Diagnoses		
PTSD	36%	36%
Generalized anxiety	55%	26%
Separation anxiety	45%	35%
Panic	35%	6%
Depression	10%	28%
ADHD	22%	11%

Adapted from Fletcher, 2003.

among those exposed to chronic or abusive trauma. One possible explanation may be that children or adolescents exposed to chronic stressors come to some kind of accommodation over time with their traumas (Fletcher, 2003).

The degree of exposure to the traumatic event also appears to be an important influence. Pynoos and his colleagues (1987) studied 159 California schoolchildren who were exposed to a sniper attack on their school in which one child and a passerby were killed and 13 other children were injured. Children who were trapped on the playground showed much greater effects than those who had left the immediate vicinity of the shooting or who were not in school that day. At a 14-month follow-up among the most severely exposed children, 74% still reported moderate to severe PTSD symptoms, whereas 81% of the nonexposed children reported no PTSD (Nader et al., 1991). Although level of exposure to this life-threatening trauma was an important factor, reactions did occur among children who did not experience a high degree of exposure. Less exposed children who had a subjective experience of threat and greater knowledge of the schoolmate who was killed were more likely to have PTSD symptoms.

Individual differences that existed prior to a traumatic event (e.g., anxiety level, ethnicity) are also likely to influence the youth's reaction (La Greca et al., 1998). So, for example, a child or adolescent's prior level of general anxiety may influence her or his reaction to the traumatic event.

Developmental Course and Prognosis

In general, symptoms of PTSD decline over time, but substantial numbers of children and adolescents continue to report difficulties. For example, La Greca and her colleagues (1996) examined third- through fifth-grade children during the school year after Hurricane Andrew occurred in Florida. Symptoms of avoidance and alterations of cognition/mood were present in about 49% of the children at 3 months but only about 24% of the children at 10 months. Similarly, the number of children with symptoms of arousal decreased from 67 to about 49% in the same time period. However, substantial numbers of children continued to report reexperiencing symptoms—approximately 90% at 3 months and 78% at 10 months.

Children's initial attempts at coping may also affect the course of their reactions. Children who tend to use negative coping strategies (e.g., blaming others, screaming) may be more likely to experience persistent symptoms (La Greca et al., 1996). The reactions of children and adolescents to traumatic events are also related to the reactions of their parents and others in their environment. If the parents themselves suffer severe posttraumatic stress or for some other reason are unable to provide an atmosphere of support and communication, their children's reactions are likely to be more severe.

ACCENT
Reactions to Mass Violence

On September 11, 2001, terrorists attacked New York City and Washington DC. Many people suffered the loss of a loved one in the attack or in rescue efforts. Nearly 3,000 persons were known to be or presumed dead. Survivors, relatives, and many more were left with vivid images of planes crashing into buildings, buildings burning and falling, loss of human life, and terror and sadness on the faces of those involved. What is the impact of such events on children and adolescents?

In reaction to an earlier event, the 1995 Oklahoma City bombing, young people who lost loved ones, friends, or acquaintances, or who simply lived nearby, experienced both immediate and continuing symptoms of posttraumatic stress (PTS; Gurwitch, Kees, & Becker, 2002; Pfefferbaum et al., 1999a; Pfefferbaum, Seale, & McDonald, 2000). Symptoms included trembling, nervousness, fear, shock, and fear that a family member or friend might be hurt. Two years following the attack, many youths still reported posttraumatic stress symptoms and impaired functioning at home or school. The symptoms were greatest for those who had lost an immediate family member, but many of those who had lost a more distant relative, friend, or acquaintance remained affected as well. Television exposure was a significant predictor of PTSD symptoms (Pfefferbaum et al., 1999b; 2001).

Similar reactions occurred following the September 11 attacks. The impact on families was appreciable. In New York City, many children and adolescents knew someone who was killed, knew a teacher or coach who lost someone, or had a parent who was among the responders to the attacks. Often many hours passed between the attacks and the reunion of parent and child (Hoven et al., 2009; Stuber et al., 2002). In the Washington DC area, service use increased over the same period for the previous year (Hoge & Pavlin, 2002).

Most youths learned about the attacks indirectly. They may have watched the events on television in their classrooms, been informed by others or through subsequent media coverage. Indeed, widespread and frequent media coverage brought the trauma into many homes around the country (Noppe, Noppe, & Bartell, 2006; Saylor et al., 2003). Many youths, even children physically distant from the attacks, may have experienced stress-related symptoms and worry about safety (Hoven et al., 2009; Schuster et al., 2001; Whalen et al., 2004).

Evidence suggests that for most, there was a modest effect of the attacks in terms of psychological symptoms. However, some youths experienced significant sympotmatolgy, especially those who suffered a loss or who had a family member who was directly exposed but survived (Eisenberg & Silver, 2011).

Parents' own reactions to the events and their parenting behaviors interact with characteristics of the child (e.g., temperament), and her or his environment (e.g., school) to affect the risk of PTS symptoms (Mijanovich & Weitzman, 2010; Wilson et al., 2010). Also, time watching TV significantly correlated with the number of reported stress symptoms (Otto et al., 2007; Schuster et al., 2001). Interestingly, viewing positive images (e.g., heroics and rescues) did not help—again greater viewing was associated with more child PTS symptoms (Saylor et al., 2003).

Reactions to mass violence seem similar in many ways to reactions to other traumatic events, but there may be unique aspects (Fremont, 2004). Terrorism presents an unpredictable threat and there is extensive media coverage. There is also a profound effect on the adults and communities that typically provide support for young people. There may, for example, be considerable impact on development (e.g., emotion regulation, coping, and social and political attitudes) as well as on longer-term post-disaster life disruptions (e.g., lost jobs, restricted travel) and economic hardship (Comer et al., 2010; Eisenberg & Silver, 2011).

In the wake of the events of September 11, attention continues to be focused on investigating and understanding the effects of such trauma and on developing successful interventions (Eisenberg & Silver, 2011; Hoven et al., 2009). After the attacks, an extensive screening (CATS Consortium, 2007) in New York City indicated that as many as 75,000 young people experienced PTSD symptoms, and many reported other symptoms (e.g., depression, other anxiety disorder symptoms). However, fewer than one-third of these youths sought help (Hoagwood et al., 2007).

OBSESSIVE-COMPULSIVE DISORDER

Diagnostic Criteria

Obsessive-compulsive disorder (OCD) was included among the anxiety disorders in earlier versions of the DSM. In DSM-5 OCD is part of a separate grouping of Obsessive-Compulsive and Related Disorders. OCD and these disorders, however, continue to be viewed as related to the anxiety disorders. In addition to OCD, this DSM chapter describes several other disorders including hoarding disorder, trichotillomania (hair-pulling disorder), excoriation (skin-picking) disorder, and body dysmorphic disorder (preoccupation with perceived flaws in one's physical appearance that are not observable or perceived as

STANLEY

The Martian Rituals

...at age seven Stanley saw a television program in which friendly Martians contacted human beings by putting odd thoughts into their heads. On the basis of that program Stanley decided his compulsion to do everything in a sequence of four was a sign that the Martians had picked him as their "contact man" on earth. After two years of sterile counting rituals, no contact had been made and Stanley gave up this explanation. He did not, however, give up counting.

Rapoport, 1989, p. 84.

only slight to other individuals). We will concentrate our discussion on obsessive-compulsive disorder.

Obsessions are unwanted, repetitive, intrusive thoughts that are not simply excessive real-life concerns and that, in most individuals, cause considerable distress or anxiety. **Compulsions** involve repetitive, stereotyped behaviors that the youth feels compelled to perform and that are meant to reduce anxiety or to prevent a dreaded event. **Obsessive-Compulsive Disorder** (OCD) involves either obsessions or compulsions, or in a majority of young people, both (March & Mulle, 1998). The DSM criteria for OCD also indicate that young children may not be able to articulate why they engage in these compulsions. However, even among very young children, odd repetitive acts may be seen as strange. Children, as we see in the case of Stanley, may even initially have their own explanations. The child may, over time, come to recognize that the ideas

or behaviors involved are unreasonable yet still feel the need to repeat them.

Another criteria for the diagnosis of OCD is that the obsessions or compulsions are highly time consuming and that they interfere considerably with normal routines, academic functioning, and social relationships (Piacentini et al., 2003). The impact on Sergei's life illustrates the nature and consequences of the disorder.

Description

Judith Rapoport and her colleagues at the National Institute for Mental Health (NIMH) conducted a series of studies that increased the attention given to obsessive-compulsive behavior in young people. Table 6-4 indicates common obsessions and compulsions among children and adolescents reported by this group and others (Henin & Kendall, 1997; Leonard et al., 2005; Rapoport, 1989).

Compulsive rituals are reported more frequently than obsessions; this finding is different from reports concerning adults, in which obsessions and compulsions are reported at fairly equivalent rates. There appear to be two broad themes to the excessive concerns and rituals: The first theme is a preoccupation with cleanliness, grooming, and averting danger, and the second theme is a pervasive doubting—not knowing when one is "right."

Childhood obsessive-compulsive disorder is often recognized only when symptoms are very severe. If a youth reaches out for help, it is frequently only after years of suffering. Young people often admit having kept their problems a secret. Among those who do seek help, many indicate that their parents were unaware of their problem. For example, diagnostic interviews conducted with a community-based sample of youths ages 9 through 17 and their mothers found that of the 35 cases of OCD identified, 4

TABLE 6-4	Some Common Obsessions and Compulsions

Obsessions

Contamination concerns (e.g., dirt, germs, environmental toxins)

Harm to self or others (e.g., death, illness, kidnapping)

Symmetry, order, exactness

Doing the right thing (scrupulosity, religious obsessions)

Compulsions

Washing, grooming

Repeating (e.g., going in and out of a door)

Checking (e.g., doors, homework)

Ordering or arranging

SERGEI

Impairment in Functioning

Sergei is a 17-year-old former high school student. Only a year or so ago Sergei seemed to be a normal adolescent with many talents and interests. Then, almost overnight he was transformed into a lonely outsider, excluded from social life by his psychological disabilities. Specifically, he was unable to stop washing. Haunted by the notion that he was dirty—in spite of the contrary evidence of his senses—he began to spend more and more of his time cleansing himself of imaginary dirt. At first his ritual ablutions were confined to weekends and evenings and he was able to stay in school while keeping them up, but soon they began to consume all his time, forcing him to drop out of school, a victim of his inability to feel clean enough.

Rapoport, 1989, p. 83.

Keeping things in certain specific locations and order is common. It is only when these kinds of behaviors interfere with a young person's normal functioning that they should cause concern for clinicians and other adults.

youths were diagnosed as having OCD on the basis of the parent's report, and 32 as the result of the youth's report, but in only 1 case did the youth and parent concur (Rapoport et al., 2000).

Epidemiology

Epidemiological studies of nonreferred adolescents suggest a prevalence rate of about 1% and a lifetime prevalence rate for OCD of about 1.9% in the general adolescent population (Flament et al., 1988; Rapoport et al., 2000). Most estimates also suggest that at younger ages, boys outnumber girls, but that by adolescence, the genders are equally represented (March et al., 2004; Rapoport et al., 2000). Among a sample of 70 consecutive child and adolescent cases seen at NIMH, 7 had an onset prior to the age of 7 years, and the mean age of onset was 10 years of age. The onset of obsessive-compulsive symptoms in boys tended to be prepubertal (mean age 9), whereas in girls, the average onset was around puberty (mean age 11) (Swedo et al., 1989c). Similar age differences in onset of OCD symptoms have also been reported among community samples (Rapoport et al., 2000).

Most children and adolescents diagnosed with obsessive-compulsive disorder meet the criteria for at least one other disorder (Geller et al., 2003a; Rapoport & Inhoff-Germain, 2000). Multiple anxiety disorders,

attention-deficit hyperactivity disorder, conduct and oppositional disorders, substance abuse, and depression are commonly reported (Leonard et al., 2005; Rapoport & Inhoff-Germain, 2000). Obsessive-compulsive disorder also often occurs with **Tourette syndrome** (a chronic disorder with a genetic and neuroanatomical basis characterized by motor and vocal tics and related urges) or other tic disorders (Scharf et al., 2012; Swain et al., 2007). **Tics** are sudden, rapid, recurrent, stereotyped motor movements or vocalizations. Although it remains unclear, there is some thought that children and adolescents with tics represent a distinct subtype of OCD with regard to symptomatology, developmental course, family patterns, and response to treatment (APA, 2013; Storch et al., 2008; Swain et al., 2007).

Developmental Course and Prognosis

Behavior with obsessive-compulsive qualities occurs in various stages of normal development (Evans & Leckman, 2006). For example, very young children may have bedtime and eating rituals or may require things to be "just so." Disruption of these routines often leads to distress. Also, young children are often observed to engage in repetitive play and to show a distinct preference for sameness. In his widely read book for parents, Benjamin Spock noted that mild compulsions—such as stepping over cracks in the sidewalk or touching every third picket in a fence—are quite common in 8-, 9-, and 10-year olds (Spock & Rothenberg, 1992). Many readers of this text likely recall engaging in such behaviors. Behaviors that are common to the youth's peer group are probably best viewed as games. Only when they dominate the young person's life and interfere with normal functioning is there cause for concern. In addition, the specific content of OCD rituals generally does not resemble common developmental rituals and OCD rituals have a later stage of onset. It is not clear whether developmental rituals represent early manifestations of obsessive-compulsive disorder in some children (Evans & Leckman, 2006).

There is heterogeneity regarding the course of OCD. The disorder follows a course in which symptoms emerge and fade over time. Multiple obsessions and compulsions are usually present at any one time, and usually the symptoms change in content and intensity over time (Leonard et al., 2005; Rettew et al., 1992). Research also suggests that the disorder is likely to be chronic. Although about three-quarters of youths receiving treatment may show substantial improvement, problems persist. However, persistence may be lower than once thought (Leonard et al., 2005).

ETIOLOGY OF ANXIETY AND RELATED DISORDERS

The development of anxiety and related disorders is influenced by multiple risk factors that interact with one another in complex ways (Barlow, 2002; Bosquet & Egeland, 2006; Pliska, 2011). Our understanding of risk factors and causal mechanisms continues to evolve and be informed by ongoing research.

Biological Influences

There is evidence for a genetic contribution to anxiety and related disorders (Smoller, Gardner-Schuster, & Misiaszek, 2008). Aggregation of anxiety disorders in families is consistent with a genetic contribution. For example, family studies indicate that children whose parents have an anxiety disorder are at risk for developing an anxiety disorder (Beidel & Turner, 1997; Merikangas, 2005), and parents whose children have anxiety disorders are themselves likely to have anxiety disorders (Last et al., 1991). In addition, more specific examinations of the influence of inheritance (e.g., twin studies, genome-wide association studies) indicate a genetic component that, along with environmental influences, contributes to the development of anxiety and related disorders (Franić et al., 2010).

Estimates of the degree of heritability for anxiety disorders vary but moderate heritability is suggested. In the Virginia Twin Study of Adolescent Behavioral Development (Eaves et al., 1997), heritability estimates for anxiety tended to be lower than for other disorders; however, other findings suggest higher heritability estimates (Bolton et al., 2006). Heritability may depend on the nature of the anxiety presentation and is perhaps greatest for generalized anxiety and OCD (Eley et al.,2003). Also, some research suggests that heritability may be greatest for younger children. As children grow up, the relative contribution of genetic influences may decrease and the influence of shared family environment may increase (Boomsma, van Beijsterveldt, & Hudziak, 2005).

In sum, findings suggest that genetic factors may play a role in the development of anxiety and related disorders. There may be different patterns of inheritance for different anxiety disorders. Alternatively, what may be inherited, rather than a specific anxiety disorder, is a general tendency, such as emotional and behavioral reactivity to stimuli. Furthermore, this general tendency may be a risk factor for depression as well as anxiety. These findings also indicate a substantial contribution of environment to anxiety disorders. Thus, there may be a general genetic risk and unique experiences may contribute to specific expressions of this vulnerability (Boomsma, van Beijsterveldt, & Hudziak, 2005; Gregory & Eley, 2007; Lichenstein & Annas, 2000; Muris, 2006; Smoller et al., 2008; Williamson et al., 2005).

Genetic influences may be expressed through differences in specific brain circuits and neurotransmitter systems (Pliska, 2011). For example, neurotransmitters such as serotonin are thought to play a role in the development of anxiety and panic. The neurotransmitter gamma aminobutyric acid (GABA) also has received attention. GABA is known to inhibit anxiety. Anxious individuals have low levels of GABA in particular areas of the brain. Attention also has focused on corticotrophin-releasing hormone (CRH). CRH, when released in reaction to stress or a perceived threat, has effects on other hormones and areas of the brain implicated in anxiety.

The limbic system—and the amygdala, in particular—is the portion of the brain that is most often thought to be associated with anxiety. Neuroscience research has examined processes such as attention, fear conditioning, and other emotional learning and has made use of neuroimaging techniques such as the fMRI. Findings suggest that the amygdala and portions of the prefrontal cortex play a role in anxiety. For example, anxious and non-anxious youth shown threatening stimuli have been found to exhibit different reactions in these regions of the brain (Pine, Guyer, & Leibenluft, 2008).

BIOLOGICAL INFLUENCES FOR OCD Many professionals have come to believe in a biological basis for obsessive-compulsive disorder (Evans & Leckman, 2006; Leonard et al., 2005; McMaster, O'Neill, & Rosenberg, 2008). Twin and family studies also suggest considerable heritability for OCD (Eley et al., 2003; Matthews & Grados, 2011). For example, the disorder has been found to be more prevalent among youths with a first-degree relative with obsessive-compulsive behavior than among the general population, and many parents of youths with the disorder meet diagnostic criteria for OCD or exhibit obsessive-compulsive symptoms. In addition, a number of studies have reported that both OCD and Tourette syndrome (or less severe tic disorders) occur in the same individuals at higher-than-expected rates, and these studies have found a familial association between the two disorders (Spessot & Peterson, 2006; Swain et al., 2007). It seems likely that OCD and Tourette's syndrome have some shared genetic basis (Matthews & Grados, 2011). Research is ongoing to identify the network of genes involved in the development of OCD (Grados, 2010).

Neuroimaging studies have suggested that obsessive-compulsive disorder is linked to neurobiological abnormalities of the basal ganglia, a group of brain structures lying under the cerebral cortex and several areas of the prefrontal cortex (Evans & Leckman, 2006; Leonard et al., 2005; Rauch & Britton, 2010). A subset of cases of obsessive-compulsive disorder, known as **PANDAS** (pediatric autoimmune neuropsychiatric disorders associated with streptococcal infections), has been noted. This subset of OCD involves a sudden onset or exacerbation of OCD symptoms following infection and the youth also exhibits tics. Although a clear picture regarding this potential subgroup of OCD remains to be established, they are believed to result from an autoimmune reaction produced when antibodies formed by the body against the streptococcal cells react with and cause inflammation in cells of the basal ganglia (Leckman et al., 2011).

TEMPERAMENT   The general vulnerability to anxiety discussed earlier may be associated with aspects of the child's temperament—biologically based, possibly inherited, individual differences in emotionality, attention, behavioral style, and the like (Bosquet & Egeland, 2006; Fox, 2010; Pérez-Edgar & Fox, 2005; Rapee & Coplan, 2010).

An important contribution to an understanding of the relationship of temperament and anxiety disorders has been described by Jerome Kagan and his colleagues (Kagan, 1997). Their findings are based on longitudinal research regarding the temperament quality known as **behavioral inhibition** (BI). Behaviorally inhibited children are identified as hypervigilant of their environment, particularly in novel or unfamiliar situations, and extremely likely to withdraw from unfamiliar people or events. It is suggested that about 15–20% of children would display heightened behavioral inhibition and that about half of these children will continue to display these characteristics across childhood (Degnan & Fox, 2007; Fox et al., 2005). Particular autonomic and brain activity patterns, including greater autonomic system reactivity, elevated morning cortisol levels, and heightened

activation in the amygdala to novel or threatening stimuli have been reported (Degnan, Almas, & Fox, 2010; Fox & Pine, 2012; Perez-Edgar et al., 2007).

Of particular interest is the development of internalizing problems in these inhibited children. At 5.5 years of age, children who were originally classified as inhibited had developed more fears than had uninhibited children. Furthermore, whereas fears in uninhibited children could usually be related to a prior trauma, this was not true for the inhibited children (Kagan, Reznick, & Snidman, 1990). Other research also suggests that inhibited children are at risk for developing anxiety disorders such as social anxiety, separation anxiety, and agoraphobia. Inhibited children, compared with noninhibited children, also seem more likely to meet the criteria for multiple anxiety disorders. While there are conceptual and methodological issues with regard to the temperament–anxiety relationship, this and other evidence suggests that BI and similar temperamental differences may, in the context of certain environmental influences such as parenting styles or peer relationships, be a vulnerability pathway toward the development of anxiety disorders during later childhood, adolescence, and young adulthood (Biederman et al, 1993; Chronis-Tuscano et al., 2009; Degnan et al., 2010; Hirshfeld-Becker et al., 2007; Nigg, 2006b).

Gray (1987) has described a functional brain system (described further in chapter 8), part of which is a behavioral inhibition system (BIS), involving multiple areas of the brain. The BIS system is related to the emotions of fear and anxiety, and tends to inhibit action in novel or fearful situations or under conditions of punishment or nonreward. Gray's model of inhibition has also informed thinking about the contribution of temperament to the development of anxiety disorders (Chorpita, 2001; Lonigan et al., 2004).

Another approach to the contribution of temperament to anxiety disorders derives from Clark and Watson's (1991) model of emotion and the concept of **negative affectivity** (NA). NA is a temperamental dimension characterized by a general and persistent negative (e.g., nervous, sad, angry) mood. Research supports the hypothesis that the development of both anxiety and depression may be characterized by high levels of NA and that this may, in part, be responsible for high rates of co-occurrence of these disorders. Depression, but not anxiety, is thought to be characterized by low levels of the separate temperamental dimension of positive affectivity—pleasurable mood (Chorpita, 2002; Gaylord-Harden et al., 2011; Lonigan et al., 2004).

Negative affectivity may also combine with low levels of the temperamental factor of **effortful control** (EC), the ability to employ self-regulative processes (Lonigan et al., 2004). Children and adolescents with anxiety may show a bias toward attending to threatening stimuli. Anxious youths with high NA thus may attend to more negative stimuli and react more strongly to them. They would, therefore, have a need for greater EC. Thus, the combination of the temperamental qualities of low EC and high NA may contribute to the development and maintenance of anxiety and anxiety disorders.

Psychosocial Influences

Psychosocial influences are clearly a part of the complex interplay of risk factors that can lead to the development of anxiety and related disorders. Children and adolescents with a general vulnerability to anxiety may be exposed to a variety of experiences that alter their risk for anxiety disorders.

One way of conceptualizing psychosocial influences is Rachman's three pathway theory. Rachman (1977; 1991) suggested three main ways in which fears and phobias might be learned: through the classical conditioning of fear, through modeling—observing another's fearful reaction to a situation, and through transmission of verbal threat information. There is research support for each of these pathways toward the development of fear (Askew & Field, 2008; Field, 2006; Mineka & Zinbarg, 2006; Muris & Field, 2010).

The first pathway, through classical conditioning, is illustrated by Watson & Rayner's case of Little Albert (see page 46) and there is support for this model as one potential route to the development of fears. The child's development of fear or anxiety, thus, may begin with exposure to some traumatic or threatening event and subsequent avoidance is reinforced by reducing anxiety.

The second pathway, in which the child vicariously learns to fear some object or situation by observing another's fearful reactions, suggests that children may learn to be anxious from their parents who prompt, model, and reinforce anxious behavior. Parents, who are themselves anxious, in particular, express and model fearful behavior (Degnan et al., 2010). That children can learn from observing their parents' reactions is illustrated in a study of toddlers who were presented with a rubber snake or rubber spider (Gerull & Rapee, 2002). The toddlers' approach to or avoidance of these toys was measured. Toddlers whose mothers' expressions were negative toward a toy in an earlier trial were less likely to approach and more likely to show negative emotional reactions to the toy. Similarly, infants of anxious mothers exhibited fearful behaviors and avoidance of a female stranger who had previously interacted with their mothers. The infants' avoidance was related to the anxiety they saw expressed by their mothers and the mothers' low level of encouragement (Murray et al., 2008).

Rachman's third pathway suggests that fear may be acquired through the transmission of information. Thus, in addition to modeling anxious behaviors, parents may transmit information that a situation is threatening. A study by Field and Schorah (2007) illustrates the transmission of information pathway. Children 6 to 9 years of age were given information (threatening, positive, or no information) regarding unknown animals. The children were asked to approach and put their hand into a box that contained the novel animal. The children's heart rates were significantly higher when they approached the box that supposedly contained the animal for which they had received threatening information.

In addition to modeling anxious behavior or relating information of fearful and traumatic experiences, parents may influence the development of anxiety through other parenting styles or practices (Degnan et al., 2010). For example, Dadds and his colleagues (1996) demonstrated that anxious children and their parents are more likely to perceive threat and therefore choose avoidant solutions to ambiguous social problems. Videotaped discussions between children 7 to 14 years old and their families revealed that parents of anxious children listened less to their children, pointed out fewer positive consequences of adaptive behavior, and were more likely to respond to a child's solutions that were avoidant. In contrast, parents of nonclinic children were more likely to listen to their children and agree with their children's plans that were not avoidant. Following the family discussion, children from both groups were asked for their plan for the situation. Anxious children offered more avoidant solutions. Parenting practices may thus contribute to the development of certain cognitive styles, for example, to the perception of situations as threatening (Field & Lester, 2010).

The impact of parenting to the development of anxiety disorders may begin early in the caregiving process (Main, 1996). The quality of early caregiving can contribute to the development of anxious behavior, particularly among children with a fearful temperament (Fox, Hane, & Pine, 2007). For example, Hane and Fox (2006) investigated the impact of maternal care behaviors, defined by constructs such as sensitivity and intrusiveness. They found that infants receiving low-quality maternal care behaviors exhibited EEG and behavioral differences, including more fearful behavior, compared with infants who received high-quality maternal care behaviors.

It has been suggested that the psychosocial influences on the development of anxiety is related to the child's perception of control and the child's development of an avoidant coping style (Chorpita, 2001; Chorpita & Barlow, 1998; Rapee et al., 2009). From birth, caregiving that is sensitive to the infant's needs helps to reduce/control arousal before it becomes overwhelming. It is thought that through such caregiving processes children learn to regulate their emotions. As children develop, what constitutes sensitive parenting changes with changes in the children's needs and in a way that fosters their developing abilities to self-regulate.

Parents of anxious children have often been described as overprotective or intrusive. Such **overprotective/intrusive parenting** is defined by parent–child interactions that anticipate threats, overly regulate and limit children's activities, and instruct children in how to think and feel (Rapee et al., 2009; Wood et al., 2003). Such parenting behavior may affect children's sense of control/effectiveness, and their development of adaptive problem-solving and coping styles. Mothers of anxious children have been observed to be more intrusive and more critical with their children than mothers of non-anxious children (Hudson & Rapee, 2002; Hudson, Comer, & Rapee, 2008). However, influences are likely bidirectional (van der Bruggen, Stams, & Bögels, 2008). An anxious child may evoke an overprotective and intrusive parental response (Hudson, Doyle, & Gar, 2009).

Insecure mother–child attachments have also been shown to be a risk factor for the development of anxiety disorders (Bögels & Brechman-Toussaint, 2006; Brumariu & Kerns, 2010; Colonnesi et al., 2011). As described earlier (pp. 30–31), the attachment relationship is thought to contribute to the child's development in a number of important ways including emotion regulation and the nature of social relationships. It is not surprising, then, that an insecure attachment may be one of the factors that contributes to the development of anxiety disorders.

We have been discussing how families may contribute to the development of anxiety problems in children. We should also remember that families can protect children from developing these problems. Family support, for example, has been found to protect children who are exposed to traumatic circumstances (Donovan & Spence, 2000). And families may foster children's abilities to cope with potentially anxiety-provoking circumstances.

Peer relationships are another aspect of socialization that can affect the development of anxiety in children and adolescents (Degnan et al., 2010). There may be several ways in which peer relationships influence the development of anxiety. Withdrawn/inhibited youth may be rated as less popular by their peers and peer exclusion may occur because children's withdrawn and inhibited behavior is contrary to childhood peer interaction norms (Rubin, Bukowski, & Parker, 2006). Being withdrawn and rejected or excluded by one's peers has been found to be associated with internalizing difficulties including high levels of anxiety (Klima & Repetti, 2008). Similarly, withdrawn children may be viewed as easy targets for bullying and victimization by peers and this, also, has been found to be related to high levels of anxiety. In contrast to the risk associated with being socially withdrawn, being part of a peer group may be a protective factor with regard to the development of anxiety even if one's "crowd" is not an "in group" (La Greca & Harrison, 2005). Similarly, having a close friend may protect a youth from the negative effects of rejection by the larger peer group. But the close friendships of withdrawn youth may also serve as risk factors. These close friends may themselves be withdrawn and less socially capable and these friendships may be of lower quality in terms of aspects such as communication and guidance. This then may serve to maintain the inhibited youths' behavior and make social relationships less satisfying. In these ways such friendships may contribute to the development of problematic levels of anxiety and to social anxiety in particular (La Greca & Harrison, 2005; Shanahan et al., 2008).

ASSESSMENT OF ANXIETY DISORDERS

A comprehensive assessment of a child or adolescent presenting with anxiety will likely involve a variety of assessment needs. Assessment strategies must be developmentally sensitive. They must address ongoing developmental changes and appreciate differences in comprehension and expressive abilities (Silverman & Ollendick, 2005). The assessment process should be guided by how anxiety and anxiety disorders are conceptualized and differentiated from developmentally typical fears and worries (Kendall et al., 2000; March & Albano, 1998; Southam-Gerow & Chorpita, 2007).

Assessment also needs to be sensitive to the needs of culturally, ethnically diverse populations (Anderson & Mayes, 2010; Cooley & Boyce, 2004). For example, Wren and colleagues (2007) examined the properties of a widely used rating scale for anxiety disorders in a multi-ethnic population. They found ethnic differences in the factor structure—that is, items that comprised the different anxiety factors (e.g., somatic/panic, generalized) of the scale varied by ethnicity. The variation was greatest for Hispanic children and their parents. Ethnicity also may influence the reporting of particular anxiety symptoms. For example, Pina and Silverman (2004) found that ethnicity and language choice (Spanish or English) influenced the reporting of somatic symptoms. Thus, initial and ongoing assessment presents a considerable challenge.

The child or adolescent's anxiety is not the only thing that needs to be addressed. The young person's environment will need to be assessed as well. For example, it may be desirable to assess the specific environmental events that are associated with heightened anxiety, to evaluate patterns of family interactions and communication, to assess the reactions of adults or peers to the young person's behavior, and to assess the existence of problems in other family members. The assessment of multiple aspects of the problem and the use of multiple informants, including the child or adolescent, are likely to yield valuable information.

Assessment of anxiety disorders is often guided by the tripartite model of anxiety. Thus assessment methods address one or more of the three response systems (behavioral, cognitive, physiological). Various methods of assessment exist (Greco & Morris, 2004; Silverman & Ollendick, 2005; Southam-Gerow & Chorpita, 2007).

Interviews and Self-Report Instruments

As is usually the case, a general clinical interview is likely to yield information that is valuable to the clinician in formulating an understanding of the case and in planning an intervention. The youth and at least one parent will typically be interviewed. Structured diagnostic interviews are available and may be employed to derive a clinical diagnosis (Silverman & Ollendick, 2005). For example, the Anxiety Disorders Interview Schedule for Children (ADIS) is a semistructured interview for the child and parent (Silverman & Albano, 1996) designed to determine the DSM diagnoses.

The most widely used method for assessing child and adolescent anxiety is self-report instruments. These measures provide reports of the behavioral, cognitive, and physiological aspects of anxiety. It is clearly important to assess symptoms from the child's or adolescent's viewpoint because it may be difficult for adults reliably to identify the existence of such discomfort. However, particularly younger children may have difficulty in labeling and communicating their subjective feelings, creating a considerable assessment challenge. Parallel measures that allow parents, teachers, and clinicians to describe the youth's anxiety also are available.

There are a number of different types of self-report measures. Some instruments allow children and adolescents to report how anxious they are in a specific situation. There are also self-report instruments that assess overall (across situations) subjective anxiety, such as the State-Trait Anxiety Inventory for Children (Spielberger, 1973) and the Revised Children's Manifest Anxiety Scale (Reynolds & Richmond, 2008), which contains items such as "I have trouble making up my mind" and "I am afraid of a lot of things." Also, the Multidimensional Anxiety Scale for Children (MASC), developed by March and his colleagues (1997), is a self-report measure that addresses the multidimensional nature of anxiety.

In addition, there are self-report instruments specifically designed to address the cognitive component of anxiety. The Negative Affect Self-Statement Questionnaire (Ronan, Kendall, & Rowe, 1994) is used to assess the cognitive content associated with negative affect. A subscale for assessing anxious self-talk (e.g., "I am going to make a fool of myself") can discriminate between anxious and nonanxious children. The Coping Questionnaire-Child Version (Kendall et al., 1997a) assesses the child's ability to cope with anxiety in challenging situations. The Children's Automatic Thoughts Scale (Schniering & Rapee, 2002) assesses automatic thoughts about threats, failure, and hostility.

Some self-report instruments also exist to assess specific anxiety disorders; for example, the Revised Fear Survey Schedule for Children (Ollendick, 1983) to assess specific fears, the Social Anxiety Scales for Children and Adolescents (La Greca, 1999), and the Social Phobia and Anxiety Inventory for Children (Beidel, Turner, & Morris, 1995). The Screen for Child Anxiety Related Emotional Disorders (SCARED; Birmaher et al., 1997; 1999) assesses for the symptoms of several anxiety disorders.

Given that children and adolescents with anxiety disorders often present with a variety of other problems as well, the assessment process should include a broader exploration of problem areas. Instruments, such as the Achenbach behavior checklists, can help in describing a range of behavior problems. These instruments also provide an examination of various perspectives (the youngster, parents, teacher) on problems.

Direct Observations

Direct observation procedures are primarily employed for assessing the overt behavioral aspects of fears and anxieties, but may also be used to assess environmental influences that may be controlling anxiety (Dadds, Rapee, & Barrett, 1994; Silverman & Ollendick, 2005). Behavioral avoidance tests require the child or adolescent to perform a series of tasks involving the feared object or situation. Thus the young person might be asked to move closer and closer to a feared dog and then increasingly to interact with the dog.

Observations can also be made by observers in the natural environment where the fear or anxiety occurs. Alternatively, self-monitoring procedures require the youth to observe and to systematically record his or her own behavior. A daily diary of such observations may be part of an initial assessment and is also often part of treatment efforts.

Physiological Recordings

As noted earlier, the physiological aspects of anxiety are included in self-report instruments. However, this component of anxiety can be more directly assessed by measuring parameters such as heart rate, blood pressure, skin conductance, and cortisol levels. Practical difficulties often inhibit clinicians from obtaining these measures. However, should methods become more accessible, these assessments might be conducted more frequently and be of appreciable value.

INTERVENTIONS FOR ANXIETY AND RELATED DISORDERS

Psychological Treatments

Much of the research on treatments for children and adolescents with anxiety disorders has supported the use of behavioral or cognitive-behavioral interventions (AACAP, 2007; APA, 2006; Silverman, Pina, & Viswesvaran, 2008). Several behavioral techniques for treating phobias, and cognitive-behavioral procedures for treating anxiety disorders (separation anxiety, social anxiety, generalized anxiety disorders) are considered either "well established" or "probably efficacious."

    Exposure to anxiety-provoking situations is a central element of successful fear-reduction and anxiety treatment programs (Chorpita & Southam-Gerow, 2006; Ollendick, Davis, & Muris, 2004; Silverman & Kurtines, 2005). Thus many of the behavioral treatments for phobias and components of cognitive-behavioral treatments for other anxiety disorders can be conceptualized as various ways of facilitating the youth's exposure to the relevant anxiety object or situation.

RELAXATION AND DESENSITIZATION **Relaxation training** teaches individuals to be aware of their physiological and muscular reactions to anxiety and provides them with skills to control these reactions. By tensing and relaxing various muscle groups, the person comes to sense early signs of bodily tension and to use these sensations as signals to relax. With practice the person is able to relax muscle groups in real-life situations when initial signs of tension are detected. Cue-controlled relaxation can also be taught. During muscle relaxation training, the individual is taught to subvocalize a cue word such as "calm." The cue word can be used in actual situations when anxiety is anticipated or experienced to help induce a relaxed state. Relaxation procedures are often accompanied by the incorporation of imagery—the therapist encourages the client to create vivid positive mental images designed to produce relaxation.

    When relaxation training is combined with exposure to feared situations, the procedure is known as **desensitization** or **systematic desensitization**. In imaginal desensitization, a hierarchy of fear-provoking situations is constructed, and the person is asked to visualize scenes, progressing from the least to the most fear producing. These visualizations are presented as the person is engaged in relaxation. This process is repeated until the most anxiety-provoking scene can be comfortably visualized. In in vivo desensitization, the actual feared object or situation is employed rather than using visualizations.

MODELING A commonly employed behavioral procedure is **modeling**. The early work of Bandura and his colleagues (e.g., Bandura & Menlove, 1968) was the impetus for subsequent research. In all modeling therapies, the youth observes another person interacting adaptively with the feared situation. The model can be live or symbolic (e.g., on film). Participant modeling, in which observation is followed by the fearful child joining the model in making gradual approaches to the feared object, is one of the most potent treatments (Ollendick et al., 2004b).

CONTINGENCY MANAGEMENT Modeling and systematic desensitization and its variants are treatments that were developed as ways of reducing a young person's fear or anxiety. **Contingency management** procedures are based on operant principles and, instead, address the child or adolescent's avoidant/anxious behavior directly by altering the contingencies for such behavior—ensuring that positive consequences follow exposure to but not avoidance of the feared stimulus and that the young person is rewarded for improvement. These procedures are also sometimes described as reinforced practice. Contingency management or reinforced practice has been shown to be effective in treating fears and phobias and as part of the treatment for other anxiety disorders (Kendall & Suveg, 2006; Ollendick et al., 2004b). Contingency management is often combined with modeling, relaxation, or desensitization procedures.

COGNITIVE-BEHAVIORAL TREATMENTS There is considerable support for the efficacy of cognitive-behavioral treatment programs for anxiety disorders in children and adolescents (APA, 2006; Roblek & Piacentini, 2005; Silverman et al., 2008). These treatment programs integrate a number of behavioral and cognitive-behavioral strategies. The overall goals of these interventions are to teach the young person to:

- recognize the signs of anxious arousal,
- identify the cognitive processes associated with anxious arousal, and
- employ strategies and skills for managing anxiety.

TABLE 6-5	Treatment Strategies Included in Cognitive-Behavioral Treatments for Anxiety Disorders in Children and Adolescents

Education about anxiety and emotions

Teaching awareness of bodily reactions and physical symptoms

Relaxation procedures

Recognition and modification of anxious self-talk and anxious cognitions

Role playing and contingent reward procedures

Teaching problem-solving models

Use of coping models

Exposure to anxiety-provoking situations

Practice in using newly acquired skills in increasingly anxiety-provoking situations

Homework assignments

Develop ways to generalize gains and prevent relapse

Adapted from Kendall & Suveg, 2006; Kendall et al., 2010.

Cognitive-behavioral treatment (CBT) programs employ a variety of therapeutic strategies to achieve these goals, as shown in Table 6–5.

CBT for children with anxiety disorders is illustrated by the work of Kendall and his colleagues (Kendall, Furr, & Podell, 2010). They describe a 16-week program, which makes use of a variety of behavioral and cognitive behavioral procedures (see Table 6-5), and is divided into two segments. The first eight sessions are devoted to introducing basic concepts and a progressive building of skills. During the second eight sessions, these skills are practiced in situations that expose the child to increasing levels of anxiety. The behavioral strategies include modeling, in vivo exposure, role play, relaxation training, and contingency management. The cognitive strategies include recognizing the physiological symptoms of anxiety, challenging and modifying anxious talk, developing a plan to cope with the situation, evaluating the success of coping efforts, and utilizing self-reinforcement. Throughout treatment the therapist serves as a coping model, demonstrating each of the new skills in each new situation. The following preparation of a youngster for an in vivo exposure—a visit to a mall—illustrates an exchange that might occur between a therapist and a child during Kendall's cognitive-behavioral treatment program.

THERAPIST: So are you feeling nervous now?

CHILD: I don't know. Not really.

THERAPIST: How would you know you were starting to get nervous?

CHILD: My heart would start beating faster.

THERAPIST: (recalling a common somatic complaint for this child) What about your breathing?

CHILD: I might start breathing faster.

THERAPIST: And what would you be thinking to yourself?

CHILD: I might get lost or I don't know where I am.

THERAPIST: And what are some things you could do if you start getting nervous?

CHILD: I could take deep breaths and say everything is going to be okay.

THERAPIST: That's good, but what if you were unsure where you were or got lost?

CHILD: I could ask somebody.

THERAPIST: Yes, you could ask somebody. Would it be a good idea to ask one of the guards or policemen? How are you feeling? Do you think you are ready to give it a try?

(Kendall & Suveg, 2006, p. 273)

The program, for children 7–13, makes use of the *Coping Cat Workbook* (Kendall, 1992; Kendall & Hedtke, 2006) and the acronym "FEAR" to highlight the four skills that the child learns in the program (Kendall et al., 2010).

F—Feeling frightened? (recognizing bodily symptoms of anxiety)

E—Expecting bad things to happen? (recognizing anxious cognition—See Figure 6-1)

A—Attitudes and actions that may help (developing a repertoire of coping strategies)

R—Results and rewards (contingency management)

Research supports the efficacy of this approach (Kendall & Suveg, 2006; Kendall et al., 2010). For example, children diagnosed with anxiety disorders randomly assigned to a treatment condition fared better by the end of treatment than control children on a number of anxiety measures. Treated children returned, on average, to the normal range on these measures. In addition, 64% of the children who were treated no longer met diagnostic criteria for an anxiety disorder, compared with 5% (1 case) of the control children. Follow-up assessments, over 7 years, of young people enrolled in this program indicated that these treatment gains were maintained (Kendall et al., 2004). Research also suggests the efficacy of delivering cognitive-behavior therapy in a group rather than in an individual format (Liber et al., 2008; Pahl & Barrett, 2010; Silverman et al., 2008). Kendall's program is a child-focused program, but the contextual influences on anxiety are appreciated. Thus, parents are involved as consultants and collaborators. They attend two sessions and actively participate in a supportive role.

A teen program also is available (Kendall et al., 2002). In addition, a computer-assisted version of the child program has been developed (Kendall et al., 2011). The first half of the program is completed independently by the child and the second half, primarily exposure sessions, is completed with the assistance of a therapist/coach.

An Australian adaptation of Kendall's program, referred to as the FRIENDS program, extended the role of family involvement (Barrett, Dadds, & Rapee, 1996; Pahl & Barrett, 2010). The program has a child-focused component using the *Coping Koala Group Workbook*, an adaptation of Kendall's *Coping Cat Workbook* and program. In addition, in the family component, the child and parents are treated in small family groups. Thus, in addition to treating the child with cognitive-behavioral procedures, the program trains parents in, and allows them to and practice, child management, anxiety management, and communication and problem-solving skills to build a supportive family environment.

Research evaluations of the program indicate that the vast majority of youths, in both a child-only or child-plus-family treatment, no longer meet criteria for an anxiety disorder by the end of treatment, nor at follow-up several years later. Greater involvement of parents may be the treatment of choice for some young people. Findings from this and other research suggest the value of parent participation and indicate that this may particularly be the case for younger children and cases in which the parents themselves

FIGURE 6-1 A therapist can use illustrations such as this to help elicit a child's anxiety-related cognitions or self-talk.

are highly anxious (Kendall et al., 2008; Pahl & Barrett, 2010; Wood et al., 2006).

Pharmacological Treatments

Several psychotropic medications are frequently suggested for treating youngsters with anxiety and related disorders. The evidence for efficacy is strongest for selective serotonin reuptake inhibitors (SSRIs; e.g., fluvoxamine, fluoxetine, sertraline) in treating generalized anxiety, separation anxiety, and social anxiety disorders. These disorders have clinical features in common, exhibit similar familial relationships with adult disorders, and frequently co-occur in young people (AACAP, 2007; APA, 2006). SSRIs may reduce anxious arousal but may not address the anxiety coping skills that are also addressed by CBT (Scharfstein et al., 2011). While side effects of SSRIs are typically described as mild and transitory, the FDA has issued a warning to carefully monitor youngsters on SSRIs for worsening depression or suicidality. Also, the benefit and risks of long-term use require continued investigation (AACAP, 2007; Rynn et al., 2011). Thus, the use of pharmacological treatment for anxiety in youth may not be the treatment of first choice; it may be used when the young person's symptoms are severe. Investigations of when the combination of CBT and SSRIs may be appropriate are needed (Gleason et al., 2007; Rynn et al., 2011; Walkup et al., 2008).

Treating Obsessive-Compulsive Disorder

Obsessive-compulsive disorder differs in a number of ways from the other anxiety disorders we have reviewed (e.g., known and suspected etiological factors, patterns of co-occurrence). Indeed, there is some consideration as to whether OCD should be grouped with the anxiety disorders (APA, 2011; Stein et al., 2010). We will therefore provide a brief separate discussion of treatment for this disorder.

Two kinds of intervention, alone or in combination, seem to be the current treatments of choice for obsessive-compulsive disorder (AACAP, 2012; Barrett et al., 2008; Franklin, Freeman, & March, 2010; Pediatric OCD Treatment Study [POTS] Team, 2004; Watson & Rees, 2008). Cognitive-behavioral interventions are the first-line treatment of choice. Medication is the other treatment option. Various selective serotonin reuptake inhibitors (SSRIs; e.g., fluoxetine, sertraline, paroxetine, and fluvoxamine) and the serotonin reuptake inhibitor clomipramine have been demonstrated as effective pharmacological treatments, with SSRIs preferred because of their more tolerable side effects. However, the efficacy of medications is modest, with many treated young people experiencing clinically significant continuing symptoms (Freeman et al., 2009). Also, scrutiny regarding the safety of SSRIs suggests caution in their use (Koelch, Schnoor, & Fegert, 2008; Leonard et al., 2005; Pliska, 2011; Waslick, 2006). Whether and under what circumstances to combine CBT with medication remains a topic of ongoing investigation (APA, 2006; Abramowitz et al., 2005; Franklin et al., 2010; POTS, 2004).

CBT treatment typically involves education about OCD, training in modifying cognitions to resist obsessions and compulsions and to enhance change, and contingency management and self-reinforcement. The central aspect of cognitive-behavioral approaches, however, is **exposure** with **response prevention** (Franklin, Freeman, & March, 2010). The child or adolescent is gradually exposed to the situation that causes anxiety and the compulsive ritual is prevented by helping the youngster resist the urge to perform the ritual.

In imaginal exposure, the child is presented with a detailed and an embellished description of the feared situation for several minutes so as to create anxiety. At the same time, the child is not permitted to engage in any thoughts or behaviors to avoid the anxiety. The several-minute exposure is repeated until the anxiety is reduced to a predetermined level. The following is an example of imaginal exposure to anxiety-provoking germs.

> You walk up to the school door and have to open the door with your hands. You forgot your gloves, so there is nothing to protect you from the germs. As you touch the handle, you feel some sticky and slimy wet stuff on your hand and your skin begins to tingle. Oh no! You've touched germs that were left there by someone and they're oozing into your skin and contaminating you with some sickness. You start to feel weak, and can feel the germs moving under your skin. You try to wipe your hands on your clothes, but it's too late. Already the germs are into your blood and moving all through your body. You feel weak and dizzy, and you can't even hold the door open. You start to feel like you're going to vomit, and you can taste some vomit coming up to your throat...
>
> (ALBANO & DiBARTOLO, 1997)

In addition to, or as an alternative to, imaginal exposure, the child may be exposed to the actual anxiety-provoking situations. Training to enhance generalization and prevent relapse is also included. The involvement of the family, especially with younger children, may be an important component of treatment (Franklin et al., 2010; Freeman et al., 2009).

Prevention of Anxiety Disorders

There are multiple reasons to think in terms of preventing anxiety disorders (Weissberg, Kumpfer, & Seligman, 2003). Anxiety disorders are common in childhood and adolescence. Furthermore, anxiety disorders may increase the risk for other disorders and the impact of these conditions may extend throughout the child and adolescent period and into adulthood. The development of formal and manualized prevention programs has only relatively recently begun (Foa & Commission on Adolescent Anxiety Disorder, 2005b; Miller et al., 2011).

The content of prevention programs for anxiety is highly similar to that described in the discussion of cognitive-behavioral treatments for anxiety disorders (Pahl & Barrett, 2010). Indicated prevention programs target individuals who already display some symptoms but do not meet diagnostic criteria or have a mild form of the targeted problem. For example, an intervention based on the FRIENDS program, described earlier, was offered to youths between the ages of 7 and 14 years of age and their parents. Youths ranged from those who did not have a disorder but showed mild anxious features to those who met the criteria for an anxiety disorder but were in the less severe range (Dadds et al., 1999). A two-year follow-up that compared these youths with a control group that did not receive the intervention suggested that the program was useful in preventing youths with mild to moderate anxiety problems from developing more serious anxiety disorders.

A selected prevention program targets youths who may be at risk for a later anxiety disorder. Rapee and colleagues (2005) provided a brief (six 90-minute sessions) parent education program to parents of preschool children with high levels of withdrawn/inhibited behaviors—a risk factor for later anxiety disorders. The group sessions provided information on the nature and development of anxiety, parent management techniques (especially the role of overprotection in maintaining anxiety), principles of gradual exposure to anxiety provoking situations, and cognitive restructuring of the parents' own worries. At a 12-month follow-up, children whose parents participated in the program exhibited lower levels of anxiety diagnoses than those whose parents received no intervention.

Barrett and colleagues (2006) have described a school-based universal prevention program provided to Grade 6 (ages 10 to 11 years) and Grade 9 (ages 13 to 14 years) youth in several schools. Again, the intervention was the FRIENDS program. At the end of the intervention, and at a 36-month follow-up, participants reported significantly lower anxiety scores and were less likely to be classified as high risk than those in the control condition who did not receive the intervention. Youths in Grade 6 appeared to benefit more than students in Grade 9, suggesting the value of earlier intervention.

Overview/Looking Back

AN INTRODUCTION TO INTERNALIZING DISORDERS

- There is appreciable evidence of a broad category of child and adolescent internalizing problems. Conclusions regarding more specific disorders are less certain. One issue of particular concern is the high rate of co-occurrence of multiple internalizing disorders.

DEFINING AND CLASSIFYING ANXIETY DISORDERS

- Anxiety or fear is generally viewed as a complex pattern of three response systems: overt behavioral, cognitive, and physiological responses. Anxiety is part of normal developmental processes.
- Fears are quite common in children. There seem to be age- and gender-related variations in numbers and content of fears. The most common fears seem to be similar across cultures.
- The DSM-5 describes a number of anxiety and related disorders including Separation Anxiety Disorder, Specific Phobia, Social Anxiety Disorder, Panic Disorder, Generalized Anxiety Disorder, Obsessive-Compulsive Disorder, Posttraumatic Stress Disorder, Acute Stress Disorder, Reactive Attachment Disorder, and Disinhibited Engagement Disorder.
- The empirical approach to classification describes subcategories of internalizing disorders. These subcategories do not, however, suggest separate anxiety disorders and suggest that anxiety and depression tend to co-occur.
- Anxiety disorders are among the most common disorders experienced by children and adolescents.

SPECIFIC PHOBIAS

- Phobias, as distinguished from normal fears, are excessive, persistent, or nonadaptive. Specific phobias are among the most commonly diagnosed anxiety disorders in children and adolescents. They are likely to begin in childhood and may persist over time. Young people with this diagnosis, as with other anxiety disorders, frequently have co-occurring disorders.

SOCIAL ANXIETY DISORDER

- Children and adolescents with social anxiety are likely to be concerned about being embarrassed or negatively evaluated.
- Young people with selective mutism do not talk in selected social situations. Selective mutism may be an extreme form of social anxiety.
- Prevalence of social anxiety probably increases with age. Social anxieties are quite common during adolescence, making the interpretations of prevalence and degree of disturbance difficult.
- Young people with social anxiety disorder are also likely to meet the criteria for one or more other disorders and depression is a common co-occurring problem among adolescents.

SEPARATION ANXIETY AND SCHOOL REFUSAL

- Separation anxiety is excessive anxiety regarding separation from a major attachment figure and/or home. It is a common problem among children but becomes less common by adolescence.
- School refusal is anxiety that keeps a child or adolescent from attending school. This term accommodates cases of both separation anxiety and phobias or anxieties related to aspects of the school situation. School refusal in adolescence is likely to be complex.
- Treatment of school refusal is most successful if it is begun early, and it probably needs to be tailored to the specific kinds of school refusal exhibited.

GENERALIZED ANXIETY DISORDER

- Children and adolescents diagnosed with generalized anxiety disorder (GAD) exhibit excessive worry and anxiety that is not focused on any particular object or situation. GAD is probably the most common anxiety disorder among adolescents. GAD is common among youths seen in clinical settings, and the disorder may persist. The issue of overlap with other diagnoses is of concern with regard to how GAD is conceptualized.

PANIC ATTACKS AND PANIC DISORDER

- Panic attacks may be expected (cued) or unexpected (uncued), and they may occur in the context of several anxiety disorders. Panic disorder is associated with recurrent unexpected panic attacks. The presence of panic in adolescents seems likely, but the existence, particularly of unexpected panic, in younger children is less clear. Family histories of panic and severe anxiety are commonly reported.

REACTIONS TO TRAUMATIC EVENTS

- The diagnosis of posttraumatic stress disorder requires reexperiencing of a traumatic event, avoidance of stimuli associated with the trauma, problematic alterations in cognitions and mood, and symptoms of increased arousal.
- There may be age-related differences in reactions to trauma and reactions may differ based on the nature of the traumatic event.
- The diagnosis of acute stress disorder may be given during the first month following the trauma. In general, symptoms decline over time, but substantial numbers of youths continue to report symptoms a long time after the trauma.
- The diagnoses of reactive attachment disorder and disinhibited social engagement disorder describe two types of reactions to social neglect.
- Adjustment disorders describe time-limited reactions to stressors.
- Degree of exposure to the trauma, preexisting youth characteristics and coping abilities, and reactions of parents are among the influences that may determine a young person's reaction to a trauma.

OBSESSIVE-COMPULSIVE DISORDER

- Obsessive-compulsive disorder (OCD) is characterized by repetitive and intrusive thoughts and/or behaviors. OCD is more common than once thought and often appears to follow a chronic course.

ETIOLOGY OF ANXIETY AND RELATED DISORDERS

- The development and maintenance of anxiety and related disorders are influenced by multiple factors that interact in complex ways.
- There is a familial aggregation for anxiety disorders. Genetic factors may play a role, but for many disorders, what may be inherited is a general tendency toward emotional reactivity. Evidence for a genetic and biological basis seems strongest for obsessive-compulsive disorder and generalized anxiety disorder.
- A general vulnerability to anxiety may be associated with the child's temperament. The temperament characteristic of behavioral inhibition appears to be a risk factor for the development of anxiety disorders.
- Psychosocial influences play a considerable role in the development of anxiety and related disorders. Direct exposure, imitation, information transmission, parenting practices, and peer relationships are some of the mechanisms of influence.

ASSESSMENT OF ANXIETY DISORDERS

- Assessments of anxiety should consider developmental issues and various perspectives on the young person's problem, information about a full range of problems, and information about the child or adolescent's environment should be obtained.
- Assessment of anxiety is typically guided by the three response systems: behaviors, cognitions, and physiological responses.
- Self-report instruments provide subjective reports of the various aspects of anxiety. Direct observation and behavioral approach tests assess overt behavioral aspects. Physiological recordings of anxiety are conducted less frequently.

INTERVENTIONS FOR ANXIETY AND RELATED DISORDERS

- Appreciable support exists for the effectiveness of psychological treatments for youths' anxiety and related problems. Many treatments are, at least in part, based on exposure to the feared stimulus.
- Procedures such as modeling, desensitization, and contingency management contribute to successful treatment. Cognitive-behavioral treatments that include a number of therapeutic strategies have proven effective in treating anxiety disorders. Pharmacotherapy, if employed, is usually an adjunct to psychological treatments.

- Cognitive-behavioral treatments involving exposure and response prevention and pharmacological treatment employing selective serotonin reuptake inhibitors have been shown to be effective in treating obsessive-compulsive disorder.

- Investigations of prevention programs, drawing on cognitive-behavioral procedures, suggest that they may be effective in preventing the development of anxiety disorders.

Key Terms

internalizing disorders *109*
anxiety *110*
fear *110*
worry *110*
phobia *113*
Specific Phobia *113*
Social Anxiety Disorder (Social Phobia) *114*
Selective Mutism *115*
Separation Anxiety Disorder *117*
school refusal *118*
functional analysis *119*
truancy *119*
Generalized Anxiety Disorder *120*
panic attack *121*

agoraphobia *122*
panic disorder *122*
trauma *123*
Posttraumatic Stress Disorder *123*
Acute Stress Disorder *123*
Reactive Attachment Disorder *124*
Disinhibited Social Engagement Disorder *124*
Adjustment Disorders *124*
dissociation *124*
obsessions *129*
compulsions *129*
Obsessive-Compulsive Disorder *129*
Tourette syndrome *130*
tics *130*

PANDAS *132*
behavioral inhibition *132*
negative affectivity *132*
effortful control *132*
overprotective/instrusive parenting *134*
exposure *136, 139*
relaxation training *136*
desensitization (systematic desensitization) *136*
modeling *136*
contingency management *136*
response prevention *139*

Mood Disorders

Problems of mood or affect are the other major aspect of internalizing disorders. Children and adolescents can experience moods that are, on the one hand, unusually sad, or on the other hand, unusually elated. When these moods are particularly extreme or persistent or when they interfere with the individual's functioning, they may be labeled as "depression" and "mania," respectively.

For a long time mood disorders in children and adolescents did not receive much attention. The increase in interest in affective problems can be traced to a number of influences. Promising developments in the identification and treatment of mood disorders in adults played a role. Also, the emergence of a number of assessment measures allowed researchers to examine the phenomenon in clinical and normal populations of youngsters. In addition, improvements in diagnostic practices have facilitated the study of mood disorders in children and adolescents. However, finding that we can apply adult diagnostic criteria to youths should not lead us to prematurely conclude that these phenomena are the same in youths and adults.

When we attempt to place mood disorders in separate categories, we confront many of the same problems that we found in examining anxiety disorders. For example, children and adolescents who meet the criteria for a diagnosis of depression are often also given other diagnoses. Should we think of these problems as distinct entities or, for example, as part of a larger internalizing construct (Trosper et al., 2012)? Nonetheless, examining depression and mania makes sense in terms of how the research and treatment literature is organized.

A HISTORICAL PERSPECTIVE

A brief look at history can aid our understanding of current views of childhood depression. The dominant view in child clinical work for many years was the orthodox psychoanalytic perspective. From this perspective, depression was viewed as a phenomenon of superego and mature ego functioning (Kessler, 1988). It was argued, for example, that in depression, the superego acts as a punisher of the ego. Because a child's superego is not sufficiently developed to play this role, it was believed to be impossible for a depressive disorder to occur in children. It is not surprising, therefore, that depression in children received little attention.

A second major perspective added to the controversy regarding the existence of a distinct disorder of childhood depression. The concept of **masked depression** held that there was indeed a disorder of childhood depression, but that the sad mood and other features usually considered essential to the diagnosis of depression frequently were not present. It was believed that an underlying depressive disorder did exist but that it was "masked" by other problems (depressive equivalents), such as hyperactivity or delinquency. The "underlying" depression itself was not directly displayed but could be inferred by the clinician. Some professionals, indeed, suggested that masked depression was quite common and that because it was masked, childhood depression was underdiagnosed (Cytryn & McKnew, 1974; Malmquist, 1977).

The notion of masked depression was clearly problematic. There was no operational way to decide whether a particular symptom was or was not a sign of depression. Were, for example, a child's angry outbursts a part of an aggressive style or a sign of depression? Indeed, the symptoms that were suggested as masking depression included virtually the full gamut of problem behaviors in youths. The concept of masked depression was, therefore, quite controversial.

This concept was important, however. It clearly recognized depression as an important and a prevalent childhood problem. And the central notions of masked depression—that depression in children does exist and may be displayed in a variety of age-related forms different from adult depression—are still widely held. The concept that depression is manifested differently in children and adults contributed, in part, to the evolution of a developmental psychopathology perspective.

Early in the evolution of this perspective, it was suggested that behaviors that led to the diagnosis of depression (e.g., insufficient appetite, excessive reserve) might be only transitory developmental phenomena that were common among children in certain age groups (Lefkowitz & Burton, 1978). This early position drew attention to the need to differentiate transient episodes of sadness and negative affect, which may be common reactions among children, from more long-lasting expressions of such emotions. Also, the distinction between depression as a *symptom* and depression as a *syndrome* is important to consider here. One or two depressive behaviors may be viewed as typical of that developmental stage. However, it is different to suggest that a cluster of such behaviors accompanied by other problems and impaired functioning is likely to occur in a large number of children (Kovacs, 1997). The developmental perspective has become an important aspect of the study of mood disorders (Cicchetti, 2010; Luby, 2009; Rudolph, Hammen, & Daley, 2006).

THE DSM APPROACH TO THE CLASSIFICATION OF MOOD DISORDERS

Mood disorders are sometimes described as **unipolar** (one mood is experienced, typically depression) or **bipolar** (both moods are experienced, depression and mania). The DSM includes descriptions of both unipolar and bipolar mood disorders. In the DSM, depression and mania are described in two chapters titled "Depressive Disorders" and "Bipolar and Related Disorders." However, despite these kinds of distinctions, the relatedness of these two groups of mood disorders is acknowledged in several ways. This includes providing a "specifier" for both depressive and bipolar disorders that allows the diagnostician to indicate the potential presence of mixed depressive and manic symptoms for both types of disorders.

We begin our examination of mood disorders with the problem of depression, then consider mania/bipolar disorder, and conclude with a discussion of suicide.

DEFINITION AND CLASSIFICATION OF DEPRESSION

Defining Depression

Understanding depression in children and adolescents is a complex task. The phenomenon itself involves a complex interplay of influences and a complex clinical presentation. In addition, there have been a variety of perspectives on depression in young people and a variety of ways in which depression has been defined.

Research findings indicate that different groups of youths may or may not be designated as depressed, depending on how depression is defined and assessed (Carlson & Cantwell, 1980; Hammen & Rudolph, 2003; Kaslow & Racusin, 1990). Such variations can lead to different conclusions regarding the causes and correlates of depression.

How the source of information and the method employed can affect how depression is viewed is illustrated in a study by Kazdin (1989). DSM diagnoses of 231 consecutive child admissions to an inpatient psychiatric facility were made on the basis of direct interviews with the children and their parents. This method of diagnosing depression was compared with diagnosis based on exceeding a cutoff score on the Children's Depression Inventory (CDI). Both the children and their parents completed the CDI. In addition, children and/or their parents completed other measures to assess attributes reported to be associated with depression. Different groups of children appeared to be designated as depressed depending on the method employed. For example, near but below one-third of the cases met the criteria for depression using two of the three definitions (DSM, child CDI, parent CDI) and 4.8% of the children met all three criteria for depression. In addition, characteristics associated with depression varied depending on the method used. Some of these results are illustrated in Table 7–1. When depression was defined as a high child-reported score on the CDI, depressed children differed from nondepressed children on the characteristics associated with depression. They were more hopeless; had lower self-esteem; made more internal (as opposed to external) attributions regarding negative events; and, on the basis of a locus of control scale, were more likely to believe that control was due to external factors rather than to themselves. Depressed and nondepressed children defined by the other two criteria (parent CDI and DSM) did not differ from each other on these "depression-related" characteristics. When depression was defined by the parent CDI score, children with high depression scores exhibited more problems across a wide range of symptoms (as measured by the Child Behavior Checklist—CBCL) than those with very low depression scores. Depression as designated by the other two criteria did not appear to be associated with this wide range of problems. Thus conclusions regarding correlates of depression may be affected by the informant and method employed to designate youths as depressed.

It is not possible at this point to make definitive statements about the "correct" definition of depression. It is probably fair, however, to state that the dominant view is that child/adolescent depression is a syndrome, or disorder, and that the most often employed definition is that offered by the DSM.

TABLE 7.1   **Mean Characteristic Scores of Depressed and Nondepressed Children as Designated by Different Criteria for Depression**

	Criteria					
	Children's Depression Inventory (By Child)		Children's Depression Inventory (By Parent)		DSM Diagnosis	
Measures	High	Low	High	Low	Depressed	Nondepressed
Hopelessness	7.3	3.3	5.3	5.0	5.4	4.8
Self-esteem	22.7	38.9	28.2	30.8	29.2	30.9
Attributions	5.4	6.5	5.8	5.8	6.0	6.0
Locus of control	9.8	6.8	8.2	8.7	7.9	8.4
Total behavior problems (CBCL)	75.8	75.3	81.6	69.0	76.5	75.0

Adapted from Kazdin, 1989.

Depressive Disorders: The DSM Approach

The DSM describes several types of depressive disorders. These disorders all have in common symptoms of sad, empty, or irritable mood accompanied by related somatic and cognitive changes.

Major Depressive Disorder (MDD) is the primary DSM category for defining depression. This disorder is described by the presence of one or more major depressive episodes. The symptoms required for the presence of a major depressive episode are listed below and are the same for children, adolescents, and adults (with one exception). The one exception is that in children or adolescents, irritable mood can be substituted for depressed mood. Indeed, some reports suggest that a majority of depressed youths (over 80%) exhibit irritable mood (Goodyer & Cooper, 1993; Ryan et al., 1987).

1. Depressed or irritable mood
2. Loss of interest or pleasure
3. Change in weight or appetite
4. Sleep problems
5. Motor agitation or retardation
6. Fatigue or loss of energy
7. Feelings of worthlessness or guilt
8. Difficulty thinking, concentrating, or making decisions
9. Thoughts of death or suicidal thoughts/behavior

To diagnose a major depressive disorder, the DSM requires that five or more of the above symptoms listed above must be present. One of these symptoms must be either depressed (or irritable) mood or loss of interest or pleasure. In addition, the symptoms must be present for two weeks and the symptoms must cause clinically significant distress or impairment in important areas of the youth's functioning (e.g., social, school).

Major depressive disorder is characterized by one or more depressive episodes (with remission of symptoms between episodes). In contrast, **Persistent Depressive Disorder (Dysthymia)** describes a more chronic form of depression. The term persistent depressive disorder was introduced in DSM-5 as a substitute for the earlier diagnosis of dysthymic disorder. Persistent depressive disorder (dysthymia) is essentially a disorder in which many of the symptoms of a major depressive episode are present, perhaps in less severe form, but are more chronic—that is, they persist for a longer period of time. Depressed mood (or in children and adolescents, irritable mood) is present for at least one year (two years in adults) along with two or more of the other symptoms listed below.

1. Depressed or irritable mood
2. Poor appetite of overeating
3. Sleep disturbance
4. Low energy or fatigue
5. Loss of self-esteem
6. Concentration or decision-making problems
7. Feelings of hopelessness

Again, the symptoms must cause clinically significant distress or impairment. The term **double depression** has sometimes employed to describe instances in which both chronic and less severe depression (dysthymia) and major depressive episodes are present. Dysthymia is typically described as developing prior to the occurrence of a major depressive episode.

A new diagnosis, **Disruptive Mood Dysregulation Disorder**, is also included in the chapter on depressive disorders. This diagnosis was added in DSM-5 in an attempt to address a problem we will turn to later in this chapter—potential confusion concerning, and overdiagnosis of, bipolar disorder in children. Disruptive mood dysregulation disorder is described as symptoms of persistent irritability and frequent outbursts (e.g., extreme temper outbursts, physical aggression). The young person's angry or irritable mood is described as present even between the temper outbursts and as present most of the day and nearly every day. Age of onset for these symptoms is before 10 years of age and the diagnosis is not intended to be given before age 6 or after age 18. While this pattern of symptom presentation might be confused with a bipolar presentation, children with the disruptive mood dysregulation disorder symptom pattern are thought to be more likely to later develop unipolar depressive disorders or anxiety disorders rather than a bipolar disorder (American Psychiatric Association [APA], 2013).

Depression: Empirical Approaches

Syndromes that involve depressive symptoms have also been identified by empirical approaches to taxonomy. This finding is illustrated by the syndromes of the Achenbach instruments (p. 90). The syndromes that include depressive symptoms that regularly occur together also include symptoms characteristic of anxiety and withdrawn behavior. Thus this research does not find a syndrome that includes symptoms of depression alone. A mixed presentation of depression and anxiety features has emerged consistently in research with children and adolescents.

How best to define and classify depression in children and adolescents remains a focus of ongoing research. One issue is determining developmentally sensitive criteria, as youths may experience depression differently at various points in development. A second issue is that depression in young people may best be conceptualized as dimensional rather than categorical (Hankin et al., 2005). Many professionals have chosen to concern themselves with children and adolescents who exhibit constellations of depressive symptoms whether or not they meet the DSM criteria for a mood disorder. This approach makes sense in that it is not clear that the cutoff set by the diagnostic criteria is the critical one. Many youths who fall short of meeting diagnostic criteria may still exhibit impairment in everyday functioning and be at risk for future difficulties (Georgiades et al., 2006; Graber & Sontag, 2009; Lewinsohn et al., 2000).

Description of Depression

In everyday usage, the term *depression* refers to the experience of a pervasive unhappy mood. This subjective experience of sadness, or dysphoria, is also a central feature of the clinical definition of depression. Descriptions of children and adolescents viewed as depressed suggest that they experience a number of other problems as well. Concern may be expressed about a youth's irritability and temper tantrums—sudden outbursts, tears, yelling, throwing things. Adults who know the child may describe loss of the experience of pleasure, social withdrawal, lowered self-esteem, inability to concentrate, and poor schoolwork as changes in the young person. Alterations of biological functions (sleeping, eating, elimination) and somatic complaints are often noted as well. The young person may also express thoughts of wishing to die.

These children and adolescents frequently experience other psychological disorders. Anxiety disorders, such as separation anxiety disorder, are probably the most commonly noted. Conduct disorder and oppositional

Sad affect, or dysphoria, is the central characteristic of most definitions of depression.

defiant disorder also occur among depressed youth. Among depressed adolescents, alcohol and substance abuse are also common additional problems.

The case of a 15-year-old boy, Nick, illustrates many of these features as well as some of the factors that contribute to the development and course of depression.

EPIDEMIOLOGY OF DEPRESSION

Major depressive disorder is the most frequently diagnosed mood disorder among children and adolescents (Graber & Sontag, 2009; Kessler et al., 2009; Lewinsohn, Rohde, & Seeley, 1998). Among youth with unipolar disorders, about 80% experience MDD, 10% dysthymia without MDD, and

10% "double depression." In community surveys, overall prevalence rates for major depressive disorder are estimated to be about 12%, with rates in children ranging between 0.4 and 2.5%, and in adolescents between 0.4 and 8.3%. Lifetime prevalence rates for MDD are reported to range from 4 to 25%, with rates of about 15 to 20% among adolescents and 1.5 to 2.5% among children (Costello, Egger, & Angold, 2005a; Graber & Sontag, 2009; Kessler et al., 2009; Lavigne et al., 2009). The epidemiology of dysthymia is less well studied. Prevalence rates between 0.5 and 1.5% for children and between about 1.5 and 8.0% among adolescents have been reported (Birmaher et al., 1996; Kessler et al., 2009; Lavigne et al., 2009).

Reported prevalence rates probably underestimate the scope of the problem. For example, lifetime prevalence rates, rather than prevalence rates at any one point in time, indicate that episodes of clinical depression may be quite common, particularly among adolescents. In the Oregon Adolescent Depression Project (OADP), a large prospective epidemiological study of a representative community sample of adolescents ages 14 to 18, Lewinsohn and his colleagues (1998) estimated that by age 19, approximately 28% of adolescents will have experienced an episode of major depressive disorder (35% of the females and 19% of the males). Other information suggests lifetime prevalence rates of diagnosable depressive disorders among the general population as high as 20 to 30% (Compas, Ey, & Grant, 1993; Lewinsohn et al., 1993a). This finding means that about 1 out of 4 young people in the general population experiences a depressive disorder sometime during childhood or adolescence. Even higher estimates emerge when other definitions of clinical levels of depression are employed. For example, 40 to 50% of the OADP youths scored above the criteria for depression "caseness" on a standard self-report depression questionnaire. As a comparison, 16 to 20% of adults meet "caseness" criteria.

Finally, the extent of the problem is even clearer when one includes young people who exhibit depressive symptoms but who do not meet diagnostic criteria. These youths are not included in the prevalence estimates just cited. However, such youths often exhibit impairments in their academic, social, and cognitive functioning and also are at greater risk for future disorders than are youths not exhibiting depressive symptoms (Graber & Sontag, 2009; Lewinsohn et al., 1998).

Age and Sex

Age and sex are clearly relevant to estimates of the prevalence of depression in young people (Cyranowski et al., 2000; Graber & Sontag, 2009; Zahn-Waxler, Shirtcliff, & Marceau, 2008). Depression is less prevalent in younger children than in adolescents (Ford, Goodman, & Meltzer, 2003; Lavigne et al., 2009). Usually no gender differences are reported for children less than 12 years of age (Angold & Rutter, 1992; Fleming, Offord, & Boyle, 1989; Lavigne et al., 2009). When differences are reported, depression is more prevalent in boys than in girls during this age period (Anderson et al., 1987). Yet among adolescents, depression is more common among girls and begins to approach the 2:1 female-to-male ratio usually reported for adults (Graber & Sontag, 2009; Lewinsohn et al., 1994). This age–gender pattern is illustrated in Figure 7.1. It is worth noting that for adolescents of *both* sexes, depression is more prevalent than in younger

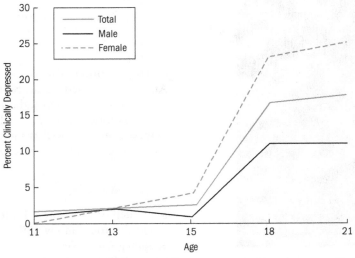

FIGURE 7.1 The development of clinical depression by age and sex. *From Hankin, Abramson, Moffitt, Silva, McGee, & Angell, 1998.*

children (Angold & Rutter, 1992; Cohen et al., 1993b; Lewinsohn et al., 1993a; Whitaker et al., 1990).

The OADP findings and other information (Graber & Sontag, 2009; Nolen-Hoeksema & Girgus, 1994; Wade, Cairney, & Pevalin, 2002) suggest that the sex difference in major depressive disorder prevalence probably emerges between the ages of 12 and 14. Consistent with this picture are findings from the Dunedin Multidisciplinary Health and Development Study, a large epidemiological study conducted in New Zealand (Hankin et al., 1998). Rates of clinical depression (major depressive episode or dysthymia) in these youths were assessed at a number of points between the ages of 11 and 21. At age 11, males showed a tendency to have higher rates of depression than females; at 13, there were no gender differences; and at ages 15, 18, and 21, females had higher rates of depression. Sex differences were greatest between 15 and 18, and rates of depression began to level off after age 18. Findings of other investigators suggest that sex differences in depression may be more pronounced among youngsters referred for mental health services than in nonreferred samples (Compas et al., 1997).

Socioeconomic, Ethnic, and Cultural Considerations

Lower socioeconomic status (SES) is reported to be associated with higher rates of depression. The link is probably through influences such as income, limited parental education, chronic stress, family disruption, environmental adversities, and racial/ethnic discrimination (Anderson & Mayes, 2010; Hammen & Rudolph, 2003; Wight, Sepúlveda, & Aneshensel, 2004). Although such SES differences may have a disproportionate impact on certain ethnic groups, there is not adequate information regarding racial and ethnic differences in the prevalence of depression. Comparable rates are typically reported in various ethnic groups (Canino et al., 2004; Gibbs, 2003; Hammen & Rudolph, 2003), except for a suggestion of higher rates among Latina American girls (Anderson & Mayes, 2010; Organista, 2003). Although comparable rates are typically reported for African American (AA) and European American (EA) youngsters, a comparison of youngsters in grades 3 to 5, followed over a school year, suggests an interesting ethnicity by sex interaction (Kistner et al., 2007). These findings are illustrated in Figure 7.2. AA boys reported more depressive symptoms than AA girls and EA boys and girls. Also, AA boys' depressive symptoms increased during the school year, whereas depression in the other groups decreased or remained stable. For the full sample, as well as for the AA boys, academic achievement deficits predicted increases in depressive symptoms over time.

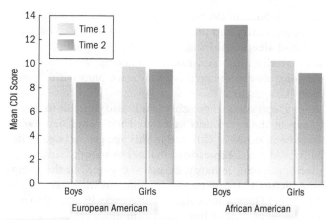

FIGURE 7.2 Mean depressive symptom scores for third- through fifth-grade European American and African American boys and girls. *Note: CDI: Children's Depression Inventory. Adapted from Kistner, David-Ferdon, Lopez, & Dunkel, 2007.*

Co-occurring Difficulties

Finally, children and adolescents who are depressed typically experience other problems as well (Birmaher et al., 1996; Garber, 2010; Lewinsohn et al., 1998; Rawana et al., 2010; Treatment for Adolescents with Depression Study [TADS], 2005). Indeed, reports suggest that about 40 to 70% of youths diagnosed with MDD also meet the criteria for another disorder, and 20 to 50% have two or more additional disorders. Common additional nonmood disorders are anxiety disorders, disruptive behavior disorders, eating disorders, and substance abuse disorders.

DEPRESSION AND DEVELOPMENT

It is interesting to examine how depression is manifested and how its prevalence changes at different developmental periods. Although the diagnostic criteria in the DSM are largely the same for children, adolescents, and adults, depression may be manifested differently in these groups.

Schwartz, Gladstone, and Kaslow (1998) describe the phenomenology of depression at different developmental stages. Infants and toddlers lack the cognitive and verbal abilities necessary to self-reflect and report depressive thoughts and problems. It is difficult, therefore, to know what the equivalent to adult depressive symptoms may be in this age group. Given these differences in cognitive and language abilities, and other developmental differences, it is likely that depressive behavior in this age group may be quite different than in adults. Interestingly, the description of infants separated from their primary caregivers in many ways seems similar to that of depression (Bowlby, 1960; Spitz, 1946). These and other distressed infants, as well as infants of depressed mothers, have been observed to be less active and more withdrawn and to exhibit feeding and sleep problems, irritability, less positive affect, sad facial expression, excessive crying, and decreased responsiveness—behaviors often associated with depression (Luby, 2009).

Depression in preschoolers is also difficult to assess. Many of the symptoms associated with later depression have been noted in children in this age group (e.g., irritability, sad facial expression, changes of mood, feeding and sleep problems, lethargy, excessive crying) but the symptom picture may also present in different ways (see Amy—Preschool Depression). Again, differences in cognition and language, as well as limited information, make it a challenge to understand how these behaviors may be related to the experience of depression in older individuals and whether or not these represent stable patterns.

For the period of middle childhood (6 to 12 years), there is more evidence that a prolonged pattern of depressive symptoms may emerge. Younger children in this age group typically do not verbalize the hopelessness and self-deprecation associated with depression. However, 9- to 12-year olds who exhibit other symptoms of depression may verbalize feelings of hopelessness and low self-esteem. Still, in youngsters in this age group, depressive symptoms may not be a distinctive syndrome but may occur with a variety of symptoms usually associated with other disorders. So, for example, as mentioned before, mixed depressed/anxious syndromes rather than separate depressed syndromes emerge in empirical taxonomies (Achenbach & Rescorla, 2001).

During the early adolescent period, the manifestation of depression is in many ways similar to the way it appears in the childhood period. Over time, however, probably in relation to shifts in biological, social, and cognitive development, depression in older adolescents starts to resemble more closely the symptoms of adult depression (Cyranowski et al., 2000). In their community sample of adolescents, Lewinsohn and his colleagues (1998) report a median age of onset for major depressive disorder at 15.5 years.

As part of their longitudinal research and their effort to examine the relationship of age of onset and familial contributions to depression, Harrington and his colleagues (1997) compared a group of prepubertal-onset depressed youngsters to a group whose onset of depression was postpubertal. Rates of depression in relatives of youths in the two groups did not differ. There were, however, other differences in the families of the two groups. Manic disorders tended to be more common among relatives of the postpubertal-onset group, whereas there were higher rates of criminality and family discord among relatives of

AMY

Preschool Depression

Amy, 3 years, 6 months of age, presented to her pediatrician with stomachaches, associated with periodic vomiting, and regression in toilet training that had begun after the birth of a sibling. A medical work-up for gastrointestinal symptoms was negative and Amy and her family were referred to a mental health clinic. Amy's parents reported that she displayed a decreased interest in food and some sleep disturbance. In addition, they reported that Amy had become socially withdrawn at school and, at home, periods of extended sadness and episodes of irritability and social withdrawal occurred when her needs were not immediately met. The parents indicated that Amy was interested in her infant sibling and interacted with the baby in a positive way, but had displayed considerable anticipatory anxiety prior to the sibling's birth. They also reported that Amy had always been shy and slow to warm and that she was extremely fussy and difficult-to-sooth as an infant. An extensive family history of depression was reported that included maternal depression during the pregnancy with Amy.

During her visit to the clinic Amy was slow to warm, displayed muted affect, and appeared shy. She did not appear to be persistently sad. Amy did, in fact, brighten at times during observational play and displayed age-appropriate play with her mother, who appeared positive, but fatigued and lacking in enthusiasm. During a brief separation from her mother, Amy became immediately withdrawn, stopped playing, appeared sad, and made no attempt to find her mother. Also, Amy became tearful and said she felt hurt and "left out" when the toys were put away while she was briefly out of the playroom.

Adapted from Luby, 2009, pp. 417–418.

the prepubertal depressed youngsters. This evidence supports the view of prepubertal-onset depressive disorders as distinct from postpubertal-onset depression. In addition, continuity to major depression in adulthood was lower among prepubertal-onset youngsters than among those with postpubertal onset of depression. This finding is also consistent with viewing adolescent-onset depression as more similar to adult forms of the disorder and different from earlier onset depression.

Adolescence thus appears to be a period when depressive syndromes similar to adult depression have their onset. As noted before, there is a significant increase in the prevalence of depression in adolescence, and prevalence may reach adult levels in late adolescence (Graber & Sontag, 2009; Wight et al., 2004). What, then, is the clinical course of depression during adolescence and into adulthood? How long does an episode of major depression last? Are there future episodes?

Episodes of depression in adolescents may last for an appreciable period of time and for some individuals may present a recurring problem (Swearer et al., 2011). In the OADP community sample (Klein et al., 2001; Lewinsohn et al., 1998), the median duration of an episode of major depressive disorder was 8 weeks, with a range from 2 to 520 weeks. Earlier onset of depression (at or before the age of 15) was associated with longer episodes. The recurrent nature of depression is illustrated by the finding that among these adolescents, 26% had a history of recurrent major depressive episodes. Kovacs (1996), in her review of studies of clinically referred youths, found a median duration of major depressive disorder episodes of 7–9 months. It was found that about 70% of these clinically referred youths had recurrences of major depressive disorder episodes when followed for 5 or more years. Thus the duration of episodes in clinical samples may be more than three times the duration in community samples, and recurrence of a major depressive episode more than twice as likely.

A sample of participants in the OADP project was interviewed after their 24th birthday. Those who prior to age 19 had met criteria for major depressive disorder or adjustment disorder with depressed mood were more likely to meet criteria for major depressive disorder during young adulthood than their peers with a nonaffective disorder or no disorder prior to age 19 (Lewinsohn et al., 1999). In addition, follow-up studies suggest that some adolescents with major depressive disorder develop bipolar disorder within 5 years after the onset of depression, but which individuals and what percentage do so is not clear (Birmaher et al., 1996; Diler, Birmaher, & Miklowitz, 2010; Kovacs, 1996; Lewinsohn et al., 1999).

ETIOLOGY OF DEPRESSION

Most contemporary views of depression suggest a model that integrates multiple determinants, including biological, social-psychological, family, and peer influences.

Biological Influences

Biological views of depression have focused on genetic and biochemical dysfunction. In addition, areas such as sleep patterns and structural and functional brain differences have received attention. Although there are some similarities regarding biological correlates of depression in adults and youths, developmental differences have also been noted (Garber, 2010).

GENETIC INFLUENCES   Genetic influences are generally thought to play a role in depression in children and adolescents (Franić et al., 2010; Rice, Harold, & Thapar, 2002; Zalsman, Brent, & Weersing, 2006). Support for the role of genetics in depression derives from a number of findings. For example, the data based on twin, family, and adoption studies in adults suggest a heritability component (Kendler et al., 1992a; Weissman, Kidd, & Prusoff, 1982; Wender et al., 1986). Findings from twin and family designs with child and adolescent samples also suggest a genetic component for depressive symptomatology (Garber, 2010; Glowinski et al., 2003; Weissman et al., 2005). The genetic contribution may be greater for adolescent depression than for depression in prepubertal children (Scourfield et al., 2003).

Research that suggests heritability in depression also indicates the importance of environmental influences and the likely complex interaction of genes and environment (Garber, 2010; Klein, Torpey, & Bufferd, 2008). For example, Eaves, Silberg & Erkanli (2003) suggest that the same genes that affect early anxiety later increase exposure to environmental influences that contribute to depression. Also Glowinski and colleagues (2003), in their study of a large sample of female adolescent twins, found evidence for genetic influences and also evidence for a large contribution of nonshared environment.

There is also the issue of what is inherited. In a family genetic study by Rende and colleagues (1993), significant genetic influence was found when the depressive symptomatology of the full sample was examined. However, surprisingly, a significant genetic influence on depression was not found if only youngsters with high levels of depression were considered. These authors and others suggest that genetic influence operates through factors such as temperament, cognitive style, and stress reactivity to affect the full range of depressive symptomatology (Compas, Connor-Smith, & Jaser, 2004; Garber, 2010). It might then be that extreme depressive symptomatology may result, against this background of moderate genetic influence, under conditions of stressful life experiences.

BRAIN FUNCTIONING AND NEUROCHEMISTRY   The role of brain structure and function and the dysregulation of the neurochemical and neuroendocrine systems in the etiology of depression have received considerable attention. The study of these processes in depression is complex and difficult. Research on several fronts that is increasingly sensitive to developmental considerations is ongoing (Garber, 2010; Zalsman et al., 2006b).

The role of neurotransmitters, such as serotonin, norepinephrine, and acetylcholine, has been a central aspect of the study of the biochemistry of depression (Thase, 2009). The impetus to study these neurotransmitters came from findings that the effectiveness of certain antidepressant medications with adults was related to the individuals' levels of these neurotransmitters or receptivity to them. For example, low neurotransmitter levels may occur when too much neurotransmitter is reabsorbed by the neuron, or when enzymes break down the neurotransmitter too efficiently. This process is thought to result in too low a level of neurotransmitter at the synapse to fire the next neuron. Research continues to explore the role of neurotransmitters; however, the mechanisms of action are likely to be quite complicated, rather than simply the amount of neurotransmitters available.

Studies of the neuroendocrine systems (connections between the brain, hormones, and various organs) add to this etiological picture. Dysregulation of the neuroendocrine systems involving the hypothalamus, pituitary gland, and the adrenal and thyroid glands is considered a hallmark of adult depression. Investigations of the dysregulation of the stress hormone cortisol and of growth hormones produced by the pituitary gland are examples of neuroendocrine factors that have been examined with regard to depression in children and adolescents. These neuroendocrine systems are also regulated by neurotransmitters. Thus the picture regarding depression is likely to be a complex one and the rapid biological changes during childhood and adolescence create a particular challenge.

Our understanding of the neurobiology of child and adolescent depression remains relatively limited. Research, however, suggests that during the earlier developmental periods of childhood and adolescence, the neuroregulatory system is not equivalent to that in adulthood. Later in development (in older adolescents), among those who are more severely depressed, or those at high risk for depression, biological indicators may be more similar to those for depressed adults (Garber, 2010; Kaufman, Blumberg, & Young, 2004; Yang et al., 2010; Zalsman et al., 2006). Thus, although many researchers still find evidence for a biological dysfunction in childhood depression, a simple translation of the adult findings is not sufficient.

For example, disturbances of sleep are associated with clinical levels of depression (Emslie et al., 2001). Research has indicated that EEG patterns during sleep are strong biological markers of major depressive disorders in adults (Kupfer & Reynolds, 1992; Thase, Jindal, & Howland, 2002). Many of the sleep findings reported in adults have not been reliably observed in children diagnosed with depressive disorders, but some of these patterns are reported in older adolescents (Brooks-Gunn et al., 2001; Garber, 2010; Zalsman et al., 2006b). For example, depressed adults have more time in and different characteristics of the rapid eye movement (REM) stage of sleep. These sleep differences are not characteristic of depressed children, but some abnormalities related to REM sleep may be present in depressed adolescents.

A second example is the role of **cortisol**, a stress hormone produced in the adrenal glands. Adults with major depression exhibit dysregulation of the stress response including higher basal levels of cortisol and production of excessive levels of cortisol in response to stress. Similar patterns have not been observed consistently in investigations of cortisol functioning in young people. However, increased cortisol response levels similar to those for depressed adults may occur among older and more severely depressed adolescents and those at higher risk (Brooks-Gunn et al., 2001; Garber, 2010; Zalsman et al., 2006b).

Neuroimaging studies, employing structural and functional MRI, have found evidence of anatomical and functional abnormalities in the prefrontal cortex, amygdala, and other areas of the brain in depressed adults. Fewer studies have been conducted with children and adolescents, but there is some evidence that suggests structural and functional abnormalities of areas such as the amygdala and the prefrontal cortex of depressed adolescents and among offspring of depressed mothers (Garber, 2010; Yang et al., 2010; Zalsman et al., 2006b).

How can we understand these various findings? In general, differences in biological markers of depression might suggest that the child, adolescent, and adult disorders are different. Alternatively, such differences in biological markers may represent developmental differences in the same disorder.

Temperament

Temperament is typically viewed as having a genetic or biological basis, but environmental influences are also thought to affect its development. Links between the development of depression and aspects of temperament have been suggested. Two aspects of temperament have received particular attention and various terms have been employed to describe these constructs. **Negative affectivity** (NA) is thought of in terms of qualities such as a tendency to experience negative emotions, be sensitive to negative stimuli, and be wary and vigilant. **Positive affectivity** (PA) is thought to be characterized by qualities such as approach, energy, sociability, and sensitivity to reward cues. Clark and Watson's (1991) tripartite model suggests that high levels of NA are associated with both anxiety and depression but that low levels of PA are uniquely associated with depression. There is research to support the role of NA and PA in the development of depression in children and adolescents. However, the clear distinctions between anxiety disorders and depression suggested by the tripartite model may be less clear (Anderson & Hope, 2008). It seems clear, however, that the contribution of these temperament qualities to the development of depression occurs in interaction with environmental influences. The link between temperament and depression may, for example, be greater for children whose parents employ harsh and inconsistent discipline than for those who experience parental warmth. And positive temperamental qualities may serve as a buffer against the contribution of parental rejection to depression. Thus, with regard to the development of depression, the relation between child temperament and parenting (as well as other environmental influences such as peer rejection and recent live events) is likely bidirectional (Garber, 2010).

Social-Psychological Influences

The influences mentioned as interacting with temperament are illustrations of environmental influences thought to impact the development of depression. We will consider several of the social-psychological influences that have been examined with regard to depression in children and adolescents.

SEPARATION AND LOSS   A common psychological explanation of depression is that it results from separation, loss, or rejection (Garber, 2010). For example, as mentioned earlier (pp. 149–150), infants separated from their primary caregivers may exhibit behavioral and biological patterns similar to those seen in depression. Psychoanalytic explanations of depression, following from Freud, emphasize the notion of object loss. The loss may be real (parental death, divorce) or symbolic. Identification with and ambivalent feelings toward the lost love object are thought to result in the person's directing hostile feelings concerning the love object toward the self. Some psychodynamic writers emphasize loss of self-esteem and feelings of helplessness that result from object loss, and they minimize the importance of aggression turned inward toward the self (Kessler, 1988).

Some behaviorally oriented explanations also involve the ideas of separation and loss by emphasizing the role of inadequate positive reinforcement in the development of depression (Ferster, 1974; Lewinsohn, 1974). Loss of or separation from a loved one is likely to result in a decrease in the child's sources of positive reinforcement. However, it is recognized that inadequate reinforcement may also result from factors such as not having adequate skills to obtain desired rewards.

Support for the theory that separation may play a role in the genesis of depression came from several different sources. For example, a fairly typical sequence of reactions of young children to prolonged separation from their parents was described by investigators (e.g., Bowlby, 1960; Spitz, 1946). In this so-called anaclitic depression, the child initially goes through a period of "protest" characterized by crying, asking for the parents, and restlessness. This is followed shortly by a period of depression and withdrawal. Most children begin to recover after several weeks.

The theme of separation-loss is a central concept in many theories of depression. The loss may be real or imagined.

The connection between loss and depression also has been examined in adult depression. For a long time, the widely held view was that early loss puts one at high risk for later depression—especially women. More recent examinations of this issue question this view, in part because most studies were plagued with methodological problems (Finkelstein, 1988; Tennant, 1988). The current view is that early loss is not in and of itself pathogenic. The link between such loss and later depression is not direct. Rather, it is hypothesized that loss, as well as other circumstances, can set in motion a chain of adverse circumstances such as lack of care, changes in family structure, and socioeconomic difficulties that put the individual at risk for later disorder (Bifulco, Harris, & Brown, 1992; Saler & Skolnick, 1992).

Much of the research on the association between loss and depression has relied on the retrospective reports of adults. However, investigation of the impact of loss on children has received some attention (Dowdney, 2000; Tremblay & Israel, 1998). For example, Sandler and his colleagues found support for a model consistent with the indirect effects of loss (West et al., 1991). In a sample of 92 families who had lost a parent within the previous 2 years, depression in children (ages 8 to 15) was not directly linked to the loss. Rather, the level of demoralization of the surviving parent, family warmth, and stable positive events following the loss mediated the effects of parental death on depression in these young people. Indeed, children who experience the positive aspects of these family variables are likely to be resilient following the loss of a parent (Lin et al., 2004). Also, children who participated in a Family Bereavement Treatment that targeted these family and child risk variables exhibited less grief in general and fewer problematic grief reactions over a 6-year period (Sandler et al., 2010).

COGNITIVE-BEHAVIORAL/INTERPERSONAL PERSPECTIVES Behavioral, cognitive, and cognitive-behavioral perspectives encompass many related and overlapping concepts. Influences such as interpersonal skills, cognitive distortions, views of self, control beliefs, self-regulation, and stress are the focus of these perspectives. The ways in which depressed individuals relate to others and are viewed by others, and the ways that these individuals view themselves and think, are believed to contribute to how depression develops and is maintained (Garber, 2010; Hammen, 1992; Kaslow, Adamson, & Collins, 2000).

Writers such as Ferster (1974) and Lewinsohn (1974) suggested that a combination of lowered activity level and inadequate interpersonal skills plays a role in the development and maintenance of depression.

Interpersonal theories of depression emphasize a transactional relationship. Depressed youths both contribute and react to problematic relationships. It is suggested that depressed individuals do not elicit positive interpersonal responses from others. Indeed, there is evidence that depressed youths may display deficits in social functioning, have negative interpersonal expectations and perceptions, and are viewed less positively by others (Klein et al., 2008; Parker et al., 2006; Vujeva & Furman, 2011).

A variety of cognitions may be related to depression. A **learned helplessness** explanation of depression (Seligman & Peterson, 1986) suggests that some individuals, as a result of their learning histories, come to perceive themselves as having little control of their environment. This learned helplessness is in turn associated with the mood and behaviors characteristic of depression. Separation may be a special case of learned helplessness: The child's fruitless attempts to bring the parent back may result in the child's thinking that personal action and positive outcome are independent of each other.

Helplessness conceptualizations emphasize how the person thinks about activity and outcome—a person's **attributional** or **explanatory style**. Depressed individuals may have an explanatory style in which they blame themselves (internal) for negative events and view the causes of events as being stable over time (stable) and applicable across situations (global). The opposite style, external-unstable-specific attributions for positive events, may also be part of this depressed style. In revisions of this perspective, the interaction of stressful life events with cognitive style is given greater emphasis (Abramson, Metalsky, & Alloy, 1989). This revision is referred to as the **hopelessness** theory of depression. Attributional style (a vulnerability or diathesis) acts as a moderator between negative life events that the person sees as important (a stress) and hopelessness. Hopelessness, in turn, leads to depression. Figure 7.3 illustrates how the hopelessness theory of depression views the development of depression. The theory predicts that a young person with a diathesis of a negative attributional style who is also exposed to the stress of high levels of negative life events is more likely to develop depression. A number of studies have reported maladaptive attributional styles and hopelessness in depressed youths (Kaslow et al., 2000; Schwartz et al., 2000), and the vulnerability-stress notions of hopelessness theory have received support (Conley et al., 2001; Joiner, 2000). However, there is ongoing attention to inconsistencies in findings, developmental patterns, potential gender differences, and a clearer articulation of the relationship of attributional style and life

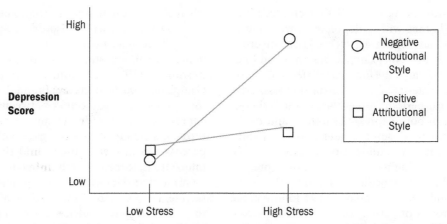

FIGURE 7.3   A schematic depiction of the interaction of attributional style and stress in the development of depression.

events (Abela & Hankin, 2008; Garber, 2010; Kaslow et al., 2000; Rueger & Malecki, 2011).

The role of cognitive factors in depression is also the major emphasis of other theorists. Beck (1967; 1976), for example, assumes that depression results from negative views of the self, others, and the future. Depressed individuals, Beck hypothesizes, have developed certain errors in thinking that result in their distorting even mildly annoying events into opportunities for self-blame and failure. Although findings are mixed, some research studies have found evidence in depressed youths of **cognitive distortions** such as those suggested by Beck's theory (Gencöz et al., 2001; Stark, Schmidt, & Joiner, 1996). Depressed youths exhibit a tendency to catastrophize, overgeneralize, personalize, and selectively attend to negative events.

The nature of the link between cognitive influences such as attributional style, hopelessness, or cognitive distortion and depression requires further clarification (Graber & Sontag, 2009; Hammen & Rudolph, 2003; Kaslow et al., 2000; Rudolph et al., 2006). It is unclear whether these cognitions play a causal role in depression as an underlying vulnerability or are associated with depression in some other way—perhaps co-occurring with depression, being a consequence of depression, or being part of an ongoing reciprocal interplay with depression. Nonetheless, challenging and changing problematic cognitions has become a central component of cognitive-behavioral treatments for depression. These procedures are typically referred to as **cognitive restructuring**.

The dimension of control, part of the helplessness perspective discussed before, has also been the focus of additional consideration. Weisz and colleagues, for example, have found that low levels of perceived competence (the ability to perform relevant behavior) and perceived noncontingency (outcomes are not contingent on behavior) are both related to depression in children (Weisz et al., 1993). Similarly, researchers have examined style of coping with stress as a component of the development of depression. For example, lower levels of active coping (e.g., problem solving) and greater levels of rumination (repeatedly going over something in one's mind) and disengagement coping (e.g., avoidance) have been associated with young people's depression. Evolving models of stress and coping are likely to contribute to a greater understanding of the development of depression (Abela et al., 2012; Compas et al., 2004; Garber, 2010; Graber & Sontag, 2009). Given the suggestion of these difficulties in depressed youths, it may be worthwhile to examine the type of coping and self-regulatory behavior evoked or encouraged by parents of depressed youths (Goodman & Brand, 2009; Kaslow et al., 2000). With this observation in mind, we turn to the influences of parental depression on children and adolescents.

Impact of Parental Depression

A major area of research on childhood depression has been an examination of children of depressed parents. There are several reasons for the proliferation of such research. Because family aggregation of mood disorders in adults was known to exist, it was presumed that examining children of parents with mood disorders would reveal a population likely to experience childhood depression. Such a high-risk research strategy could be a more efficient means of investigating the problem than a random sampling of the population would be. In addition, such research might provide information on the continuity among child, adolescent, and adult mood disorders.

Numerous studies have found that children and adolescents from homes with a depressed parent are at increased risk for developing a psychological disorder (Goodman et al., 2011). For example, Hammen and her colleagues (1990) compared the long-term effects of maternal depression and maternal chronic medical illness. Over the course of a 3-year period, with evaluations at 6-month intervals, children of both depressed mothers and medically ill mothers exhibited elevated rates of psychological disorder as compared with children of healthy mothers. Rates of disorder were higher for children of depressed mothers than for those with medically ill mothers.

Weissman and her colleagues (1997) followed the children of two groups of parents over a 10-year period. At the time of the follow-up, the offspring were in late adolescence or were adults. Parents and youths were assessed with a structured diagnostic interview. Youths for whom neither parent had a psychological disorder (low risk) were compared with those for whom one or both parents had a diagnosis of major depressive disorder (high risk). The youths with depressed parents had increased rates of MDD, particularly before puberty. The high-risk group also had increased rates of other disorders, including phobias and alcohol dependence. In addition, children of depressed parents experienced more serious depression than children of nondepressed parents. However, the depressed offspring of depressed parents were less likely to receive treatment than those of nondepressed parents; in fact, more than 30% never received any treatment.

Beardslee and his colleagues examined the impact of parental depression in a nonclinically referred population (Beardslee, Versage, & Gladstone, 1998; Beardslee et al., 1996). Families were recruited from a large health maintenance organization. Assessments, including a structured diagnostic interview, were conducted initially and 4 years later. Families were divided into three categories: parents with no diagnosis, parents with a nono-mood disorder, and one or both parents with a mood disorder. Parental non-mood disorder, parental MDD, and the number of diagnosed disorders that the child experienced prior to the first assessment predicted whether the youth experienced a serious mood disorder during the time between assessments.

The findings presented here suggest that the risk associated with parental depressions may not be specific. Children with a depressed parent appear to be at risk for a variety of problems, not just depression. And children of parents with other diagnoses or with chronic medical conditions may also be at risk for depression. Perhaps various disorders that youngsters experience share common risk factors, whereas some risk factors are specific to depression. It is also possible that some disruptions to effective parenting are common to parents with various disorders, whereas other disruptions are more likely to occur among parents with a particular disorder such as depression.

There may be a variety of mechanisms whereby depressive mood states in parents are associated with dysfunction in their children (Cummings, Davies, & Campbell, 2000; Goodman & Brand, 2009). Shared heredity may play a role in the link between parental and child depression. Parental depression may also have an impact through a variety of nonbiological pathways. For example, parents can influence their child through parent–child interactions, through coaching and teaching practices, and by arranging their child's social environment. Before we turn to a discussion of these mechanisms, it is important to remember that influences between parent and child are likely to be bidirectional (Elgar et al., 2004). A depressed youth may, for example, generate additional stress that lessens the adult's ability to parent effectively.

MECHANISMS OF PARENTAL INFLUENCE As we indicated before, both depression in adults and depression in young people are associated with certain characteristic ways of thinking and cognitive styles. Depressed parents may transmit these styles to their children. Garber and Flynn (2001), for example, assessed mothers and their children annually over 3 years, starting when the children were in sixth grade. A maternal history of depression was associated with lower perceived self-worth, a negative attributional style, and hopelessness among the children. Maladaptive ways of thinking may be modeled by parents and parents' maladaptive cognitions may also affect the manner in which depressed adults parent their offspring (Callender et al., 2012).

For example, the behavior of depressed parents may be accompanied by negative affect such as anger or hostility. Also, the depressed parents' absorption in their own difficulties may lead them to be withdrawn, less emotionally available, and to be perceived as less rewarding by their offspring. Depression may also make parents inattentive to their children and unaware of their children's behavior. Monitoring of a child's behavior is a key element in effective parenting. In addition, to being inattentive, depressed parents may also perceive behaviors to be problematic that other parents do not. This difference in perception is important, because being able to ignore or tolerate low levels of problematic behavior is likely to lead to less family disruption. Observation of families with a depressed parent or child reveal these relationship difficulties and indicate that interactional patterns in these families may serve to maintain the depression in the parent or child (Dadds et al., 1992; Garber, 2010; Ge et al., 1995; Hops et al., 1987). Depressed behavior by one family member may be maintained because it serves to avoid or reduce the high levels of aggression and discord that may be present in such families.

MARY

Family Interactions and Depression

Mary is an adolescent with considerable problems with anxiety and depression. Mary's mother was diagnosed with major depression. Her parents fought often and frequently the topic was money or problems and stresses related to her father's job. Mary's mother dealt with these difficulties by self-medicating with alcohol and developed a serious drinking problem. The conflicts, alcohol abuse, and other stresses seemed to have contributed to the development of symptoms of depression in Mary's mother. For the good of all the family members and because of her concern for her mother, Mary felt that she had to serve as a mediator for her parents' disputes and that she was responsible for alleviating her mother's sadness. Over time these family conflicts and problems contributed to Mary developing psychological difficulties of her own.

Adapted from Cummings, Davies, & Campbell, 2000, pp. 305–306.

In addition to marital discord, families with a depressed parent may exist in adverse contexts (e.g., social disadvantage/low standard of living) and may experience high levels of stressful life events (e.g., health and financial difficulties). These circumstances in turn are likely to exacerbate a parent's depressive episodes and contribute to disruptions in parenting. For example, high levels of parental stress may restrict the parent's ability to involve the child in activities outside the home and may limit the family's social networks. Thus the child may have limited opportunity to interact with other adults outside the family or to have access to other sources of social support.

Finally, the link between parent and child depression has been viewed in the context of attachment (Cicchetti & Toth, 1998; Elgar et al., 2004). The emotional unavailability and insensitivity that may be associated with parental depression have been shown to be strong and reliable predictors of insecure parent–child attachments. Attachment theory holds that children's internal working models or representations of the self and the social world are strongly influenced by early attachments. It is through these early relationships that the child also first experiences and learns to regulate intense emotions and arousal. In other words, working models that guide future experiences are thought to be first developed in these early attachment

relationships. In children with insecure parent–child attachments, the cognitive and emotional contents of these working models have been described as remarkably similar to the cognitive and emotional patterns characteristic of depression (Cummings et al., 2000). Insecure attachments may interfere with the child's developing capacity to regulate affect and arousal and may be associated with poorer self-concept and less trust in the availability and responsiveness of the social world.

The effects of parental depression on offspring probably vary with the age and gender of the child (Goodman et al., 2011; Lovejoy et al., 2000). Furthermore, although children of depressed parents are at increased risk for a number of difficulties, not all these children experience adverse outcomes (see the descriptions of Joe and Frank). Many form secure attachments, experience good parenting, and do not develop disorders (Beardslee et al., 1998; Brennan, Le Brocque, & Hammen, 2003).

Indeed, there may be multiple ways in which family influences serve as protective factors against the potential adverse impact of parental depression. For example, Ivanova and Israel (2006) examined the influence of family stability (defined as the predictability and consistency of family activities and routines) on adjustment in a clinical sample of children. Children's reports of family stability as measured by the Stability of Activities in the Family Environment (SAFE; Israel, Roderick, & Ivanova, 2002) significantly attenuated the impact of parental depression on child internalizing, externalizing, and total problems. That is, parental depression was associated with problems in child adjustment when family stability was low, but not when family stability was high. Figure 7.4 illustrates this protective effect of family stability on parent-reported ineternalizing problems.

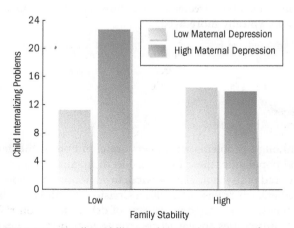

FIGURE 7.4 Family stability moderates the impact of parental depression on children's internalizing problems. *Adapted from Ivanova & Israel, 2006.*

Different Outcomes

Joe's father was diagnosed with major depression and his paternal grandfather also experienced episodes of depression... but both his parents were attentive and responsive to him. Even when Joe's father's depressive symptoms were severe, he remained attentive and emotionally warm. Joe's mother was very supportive of his father and they had a secure marriage.... Joe also had a close and supportive relationship with his two sisters. Joe did well in school and was popular, although he tended to be shy in large groups. He attended an excellent university, studied medicine, and became a pediatrician. Joe married, and he and his wife were happy and were attentive and responsive parents. Joe experienced periods of anxiety and occasional mild to moderate symptoms of depression. The symptoms were rarely more than subclinical and Joe never felt the need to seek therapy.

Frank's mother was diagnosed with major depressive disorder and her mother has also been depressed. His mother and father were divorced when Frank was 10. This followed many years of intense marital conflict.... Both parents had also been generally emotionally unresponsive toward the children,... and they involved Frank and his sister in their marital conflicts.... Frank and his sister fought with each other and were never close to each other. In preschool Frank was highly aggressive and difficult.... By adolescence, Frank was habitually delinquent, and he dropped out of high school. As an adult, Frank was diagnosed with a depressive disorder and his interpersonal relationships were tumultuous and typically short-lived.

Adapted from Cummings, Davies, & Campbell, 2000, pp. 299–300.

Peer Relations and Depression

Although problems with peers are common in the general population, these problems do distinguish youngsters referred to psychological services from nonreferred youths (Achenbach & Rescorla, 2001). Consistent with views that emphasize interpersonal aspects of depression, peer relation difficulties appear to contribute to the development and maintenance of depression (Garber, 2010; McCauley, Pavlidis, & Kendall, 2001).

Peer status, for example, has been found to be associated with adjustment difficulties, including depression. A study by Kupersmidt and Patterson (1991) illustrates the relationship between peer status and adjustment. The sociometric status of a sample of second, third, and fourth graders was assessed by asking the children to nominate their most liked and least liked peers. A peer status grouping was determined for each child. Two years later when the children were in the fourth through the sixth grade, several assessment instruments were completed, including a modified version of the Achenbach Youth Self-Report (YSR). As an index of a negative outcome, the authors examined whether a child had scores in the clinical range in one or more specific problem areas (the narrowband syndromes of the YSR). Rejected boys and girls exhibited higher than expected rates of clinical-range difficulties. Girls with neglected peer status had even higher levels of clinical-range difficulties.

The authors also examined the relationship between peer status and each of the more specific problem areas

A withdrawn or socially isolated child may need assistance in developing appropriate social skills and in increasing peer interactions.

defined by the various narrowband behavior problem scores. There was no relationship between peer status and any specific behavior problem for boys. However, a finding of particular interest emerged for girls. Rejected girls were more than twice as likely to report high levels of depression than average, popular, and controversial girls. Furthermore, neglected girls were more than twice as likely as rejected girls and more than five times as likely as the other groups of girls to report depression problems.

Peer relation difficulties may both contribute to the development and be a consequence of depression. Pederson and colleagues (2007) illustrate one possible way in which peer relations may contribute to the development of depression. Their findings support a mediational model in which early disruptive behavior leads to subsequent peer relational difficulties during middle childhood, which, in turn, is associated with early adolescent depressive symptoms. However, depression may also contribute to peer relational difficulties. Indeed, depression in young people has been found to be associated with a number of interpersonal characteristics important to peer relations and friendships. For example, depressed youngsters may perceive themselves as less interpersonally competent, have negative views of peers, have problematic social problem-solving styles, and exhibit distortions in processing of social information (Garber, 2010; Parker et al., 2006). Many of the problems in social relationships that accompany depression in young people may arise, in part, from the depressed youth's perceptions, including that others are rejecting and critical. This perception may then lead to behaviors by the depressed youngster that annoy peers, limit friendships, and result in isolation. Thus, as elsewhere, a reciprocal and transactional model of influences probably characterizes the contribution of peer and other social relationships to the development of depression.

ASSESSMENT OF DEPRESSION

The assessment of depression is likely to involve a number of strategies, to sample a broad spectrum of attributes, and to include information from a variety of sources (Klein, Dougherty & Olino, 2005; Rudolph & Lambert, 2007). Structured interviews may be employed to yield a DSM diagnosis, although they are more likely to be employed in research than in typical clinical settings. As we have seen, depression may manifest itself in a number of ways throughout development, and children and adolescents who experience depression are likely to exhibit other difficulties. A general clinical interview and the use of a broad assessment instrument like the Child Behavior Checklist are common. Because a variety of influences may contribute to the development of depression, it is helpful to assess

the parents, family, and social environments as well as the child or adolescent.

A variety of measures that focus on depression and related constructs have been developed (Reynolds, 1994; Rudolph & Lambert, 2007). Of these, self-report instruments are among the most commonly employed. They are particularly important, given that many of the key problems that characterize depression, such as sadness and feelings of worthlessness, are subjective. The Children's Depression Inventory (CDI) (Kovacs, 1992; 2003) is probably the most frequently used measure of this type. It is an offshoot of the Beck Depression Inventory that is commonly used for adults. The CDI asks youths to choose which of three alternatives best characterizes them during the past 2 weeks. Twenty-seven items sample affective, behavioral, and cognitive aspects of depression. Research on gender and age differences, reliability, validity, and clinically meaningful cut-off scores has been conducted for the CDI (Reynolds, 1994). The Reynolds Child Depression Scale (Reynolds, 1989) and Reynolds Adolescent Depression Scale (Reynolds, 1987; 2002) also have been reported to have good psychometric properties (Reynolds, 1994). Despite the widespread use of self-report measures, some research suggests caution in assuming equivalent measurement of depression across various racial–ethnic groups (Crockett et al., 2005).

Many self-report measures are also rephrased so that they can be completed by significant others such as the child's parents (Clarizio, 1994; Rudolph & Lambert, 2007). Measures completed by both the child and the parent often show only low levels of correlation, and agreement may vary with the age of the youngster (Kazdin, 1994; Renouf & Kovacs, 1994). These results suggest that information provided by different sources may tap different aspects of the child's difficulties. Assessment measures can also be completed by teachers, clinicians, or other adults (Clarizio, 1994; Rudolph & Lambert, 2007). Ratings by peers can likewise provide a unique perspective.

Measures of constructs related to depression have also been developed. For example, attributes such as self-esteem (e.g., Harter, 1985) and perceived control over events (e.g., Connell, 1985) are likely candidates for evaluation. In addition, assessing various cognitive processes such as hopelessness (Kazdin, Rodgers, & Colbus, 1986), attributional style (Seligman & Peterson, 1986), and cognitive distortions (e.g., Leitenberg, Yost, & Carroll-Wilson, 1986) have been and are likely to be helpful for both clinical and research purposes.

A number of observational measures can aid the assessment of depression in children and adolescents (Garber & Kaminski, 2000; Rudolph & Lambert, 2007). Systematic observations of depressed youth interacting with others in controlled settings can potentially provide

TABLE 7.2	Categories and Examples of Depression-Related Behaviors that Can Be Observed in Social Interaction Tasks

Emotions: smiling, frowning, crying, happiness, sadness, anger, fear

Affect Regulation: control or expression of affect

Problem Solving: identifying problems, proposing solutions

Nonverbal Behaviors: eye contact, posture

Conflict: noncompliance, ignoring, demanding, negotiating

Cognitive Content: criticism, praise, self-derogation

Speech: rate, volume, tone of voice, initiation

Engaged or Disengaged: enthusiasm, involvement, persistence

On or Off Task Behavior

Physical Contact: threatening, striking, affection

Symptoms: depression, irritability, psychomotor agitation or retardation, fatigue, concentration

Adapted from Garber & Kaminski, 2000.

an opportunity to observe the social behavior of these youngsters with significant others. Table 7.2 lists some of the categories of behaviors that can be observed using existing systems for coding social interactions relevant to depression. A clinician also may wish to assess, through observation, certain aspects of functioning such as parent–child communication as part of evaluating treatment goals. Observational measures may not be used as frequently as other assessment measures because they require considerable training and coding itself is very labor intensive. There is also concern regarding the ecological validity of these observations, that is, the extent to which a brief laboratory interaction reflects real-world social interactions.

TREATMENT OF DEPRESSION

Making effective treatment of depression available to young people is challenging. Often young people and their families do not seek treatment and effective psychological treatments are not available in many communities. Our discussion of treatment emphasizes pharmacological, cognitive-behavioral, and interpersonal treatments, because these interventions, alone and in combination, have received the most research attention (David-Ferdon & Kaslow, 2008; Garber, 2010; TADS Team, 2005).

Pharmacological Treatments

The practice of prescribing antidepressant medication for children and adolescents is widespread (Vitiello, Zuvekas, & Norquist, 2006). However, such treatment is controversial, because the effectiveness and safety of pharmacotherapy with depressed youngsters remains unclear (APA, 2006; Moreno, Roche, & Greenhill, 2006; Swearer et al., 2011). Tricyclic antidepressants (TCAs) such as imipramine, amitriptyline, nortriptyline, and desipramine were once widely used to treat depression in young people. But TCAs have not been demonstrated to be effective in treating depressed youth and they have many side effects. **Selective serotonin reuptake inhibitors** (SSRIs) such as fluoxetine and paroxetine and other second-generation antidepressants such as bupropion and venlafaxine also have been employed with depressed children and adolescents. SSRIs prevent the reabsorption of serotonin and, thus, more serotonin is available to the brain. SSRIs have fewer side effects than TCAs and are more likely to be recommended when medication is prescribed.

However, the use of such medications is based on limited research that does not clearly support the effectiveness of these antidepressant medications in either prepubertal children or adolescents (Gleason et al., 2007; Reyes et al., 2011; Swearer et al., 2011). Also, little is known regarding long-term effectiveness.

Medications may ultimately prove to be effective, alone or in combination with other treatments for certain youths. However, because antidepressant medications are developed and marketed principally for adults, there are less well-established guidelines for their administration and less systematic data on their safety. Issues of safety and side effects are of concern because little is known regarding the long-term impact of these medications on development, particularly in young children (APA, 2006; Emslie et al., 2006; Moreno et al., 2006). Particular concern has been expressed about the possible association between SSRIs and increases in suicidal behavior (Hammad et al., 2006; Vitiello & Swedo, 2004). As mentioned in our discussion of SSRIs in the treatment of anxiety disorders, such concerns led the FDA to issue a warning about their use with children and adolescents.

Since depression is itself associated with suicide, the issue of risk and benefit from the use of SSRIs is an important one. Families and clinicians may ask: Is the risk of not employing SSRIs to treat depression in certain youth who may be at risk for suicide greater than the suicide risk associated with the use of these medications? If antidepressants are employed in treatment, the FDA recommends that the youths return to the clinician's office for more frequent visits, particularly in the early stages of treatment or at times of dosage changes, and recommends that caregivers and clinicians be vigilant about unusual changes in behavior (U.S. Food and Drug Administration, 2007).

COMBINED TREATMENTS   The Treatment of Adolescent Depressions Study (TADS Team, 2004; 2007; 2009) examined the combined use of fluoxetine (an SSRI) and a form of cognitive-behavior therapy (CBT). Adolescents (ages 12 to 17) with moderate to severe major depression were randomly assigned to treatment with fluoxetine alone, CBT alone, CBT combined with fluoxetine, or placebo (pill). The TADS Team has reported that at the end of treatment, the combined treatment produced the greatest improvement in symptoms of MDD and was superior to either treatment alone. However, by the end of an 18-week follow-up period (week 36) there were no differences between the three treatment conditions. Overall, treatment gains were maintained at a one-year follow-up (TADS Team, 2009). While the results of this study are important, aspects of the methodology and interpretation of results have been questioned. Also, rates of **remission** (no longer meeting diagnostic criteria or cutoff scores) were low, many youths continued to have significant symptoms, and some youths who had improved experienced a worsening of depression during the follow-up period (Brent, 2006; Kennard et al., 2006, TADS Team, 2009).

However, an additional potential benefit of the combined treatment is germane to concerns about SSRIs and suicide risk. During the treatment period, suicide-related events were greatest among youths treated with fluoxetine alone (9.2%)—nearly twice as many as in the other conditions (Emslie et al., 2006). This suggests that, for youths treated with SSRIs, the combination of fluoxetine with CBT may offer some protection against suicidal events. Such events may be particularly likely for youths with severe depressive symptoms and following interpersonal stressors such as conflicts with family members (Vitiello et al., 2009).

The Treatment of Resistant Depression in Adolescents (TORDIA) study (Weersing & Brent, 2010) was based on an earlier demonstration of the effectiveness of a cognitive-behavioral treatment with adolescents who met criteria for MDD (Brent et al., 1997). The adolescents in the TORDIA study had been depressed an average of two years, had a diagnosis of MDD, and evidenced significant suicidality and comorbidity. The participants also had a previously failed trial of an SSRI. They were randomly assigned to either a medication (a switch to a medication different from their previous SSRI) alone or a medication plus CBT condition. The CBT offered was an individual treatment protocol and also involved the family in a CBT-based approach to family problem solving. After

12 weeks of the program 55% of the CBT-plus-medication participants, as compared to 41% of the medication-switch-alone participants, showed a substantial clinical improvement. In this sample of seriously depressed youths, the results supported the value of the combination of CBT and medication switch. In addition, the superiority of the combined treatment approach was more evident among youths with a greater number of co-occurring diagnoses (Asarnow et al., 2009).

Psychosocial Treatments

In developing psychosocial interventions for depressed children and adolescents it is reasonable to draw on successful interventions employed with adults. Although this is reasonable there are cautions that should be observed with such an approach. For example, the lives of depressed youths differ from those of adults. Children and adolescents have ongoing daily contact with parents that may contribute to the problem of depression. Also, youths are exposed on a daily basis to the potential negative consequences of social skill difficulties and the impact of peer relation difficulties. Adults, on the other hand, may arrange their lives to avoid familial and social contacts. The development of treatments that address relevant developmental experiences of depressed children and adolescents are likely to be the most effective.

Most psychological interventions for depression in children and adolescents derive from a cognitive-behavioral perspective. Cognitive-behavioral treatments confront and modify the young person's maladaptive cognitions (e.g., problematic attributions, excessively high standards, negative self-monitoring), focus on goals such as increasing pleasurable experiences; increasing social skills; and improving communication, conflict resolution, social problem-solving, and coping skills. Two programs are described here to illustrate interventions derived from a cognitive-behavioral perspective.

Stark, Reynolds, and Kaslow (1987) compared self-control, behavioral problem solving, and a waiting list (no treatment) control in treating depressed 9- to 12-year olds. The school-based self-control treatment focused on teaching children self-management skills such as self-monitoring, self-evaluation, and self-reinforcement. Behavioral problem solving emphasized education, self-monitoring of pleasant events, and group problem solving directed toward improving social behavior. Both treatments resulted in improvements and were superior to the control group. The two treatments did not differ from each other, however. On the basis of these results and subsequent findings Stark and his colleagues (1991) developed an expanded cognitive-behavioral treatment program that combined the self-control component with behavioral problem-solving elements, with other cognitive strategies, and with parent training and family involvement. This expanded intervention was compared to a traditional counseling control condition that was offered to 4th–7th graders with high levels of depressive symptoms. Monthly family meetings were included in both conditions. At the end of treatment, youth in the CBT treatment reported fewer depressive symptoms than control youth.

Drawing on this earlier work (2010) have more recently developed a school-based group CBT program for 9–13-year-old girls named the ACTION Treatment Program. A brief description of the content of the 20-session program, that also illustrates components characteristic of many CBT interventions for depression, is provided in Table 7.3. The authors suggest that the main goals and themes of the ACTION program are captured by three messages on a card given to the girls (Stark et al., 2010, p. 94).

1. If you feel bad and you don't know why, use coping skills.
2. If you feel bad and you can change the situation, use problem solving.
3. If you feel bad and it is due to the negative thoughts, change the thoughts.

The session contents address these three core skills and a subgoal throughout is to target **behavioral activation**— activities that encourage the participants to be active and do pleasant things. A parent training (PT) component sought to help parents model and reinforce the use of therapeutic skills, to change the affective tone and communication style of the family, and to create a supportive environment that sends the girls a positive message.

Participants were randomly assigned to a CBT, CBT+PT, or a minimal contact control condition. At posttreatment girls in the two active treatment conditions reported significantly lower levels of depressive symptoms than girls in the control condition. Also, 80% of the treatment girls as compared to 45% of control girls no longer met criteria for a depressive disorder. While there were some differences, the two treatment conditions did not differ from each other on these central measures. Improvements in the treated girls were maintained at one-year posttreatment.

A cognitive-behavioral intervention known as the Adolescent Coping with Depression program, a skills-training, multi-component group intervention, has been developed by Lewinsohn, Clarke, and colleagues (Clarke & DeBar, 2010; Rohde et al., 2005). In an initial study (Lewinsohn et al., 1990), adolescents ages 14 to 18 who met diagnostic criteria for depression were randomly assigned to one of three conditions: adolescent-only, adolescent-and-parent, and wait-list control. Adolescents attended sixteen 2-hour sessions, twice a week, in a group or class-like setting, that focused on monitoring of mood and, increasing pleasant events, identifying and controlling irrational and negative thoughts, teaching methods of relaxation, increasing social skills, and teaching conflict

TABLE 7.3	Primary Child Components of the ACTION Treatment Program for Girls
Meeting Number	**Primary Treatment Component**
1	Introductions and discussion of basic aspects of program
2	Affective education and introduction to coping
Individual session 1	Review concepts and develop treatment goals
3	Affective education and coping skills
4	Extend group cohesion; review goals, application of coping skills
5	Extend coping skills, introduction to problem solving
6	Cognition and emotion, introduction to idea of cognitive restructuring
7–9	Apply problem solving
Individual session 2	Review concepts and individualize therapeutic activities
10	Prepare for and practice cognitive restructuring in session
11	Continue illustrating cognitive restructuring
12–19	Cognitive restructuring practice and self-maps (identifying individual strengths)
20	Bring it all together and termination activity

Adapted from Stark et al., 2010.

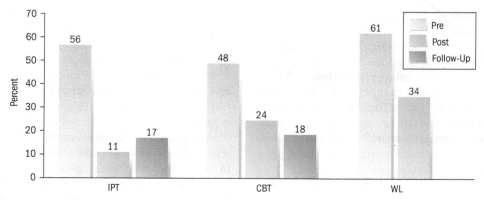

FIGURE 7.5 Percentage of severely depressed adolescents at pretreatment, posttreatment, and follow-up for each condition. IPT, interpersonal psychotherapy treatment; CBT, cognitive-behavioral treatment; WL, wait-list control; Pre, pretreatment; Post, posttreatment. *From Rosselló & Bernal, 1999.*

resolution (communication and problem-solving) skills. In the parent-involvement condition, parents met for 9 weekly sessions. They were provided with information on the skills being taught to their teenagers and were taught problem-solving and conflict resolution skills.

Relative to the youths in the control group, individuals in the treatment groups improved on depression measures. For example, at the end of treatment, the recovery rate for treated adolescents was 46% whereas only 5% of the control group no longer met diagnostic criteria. The teenagers in the treatment conditions were followed for two years after the end of treatment, and their treatment gains were maintained. Control participants were not available for follow-up, because they were offered treatment at the end of the treatment period. A second similar study (Clarke et al., 1999) yielded comparable findings. In both studies there were few or no significant advantages for parent involvement. This may have been due, in part, to relatively low rates of parental participation (Clarke & DeBar, 2010).

The effectiveness of interpersonal psychotherapy for adolescents (IPT-A), modified from interpersonal psychotherapy for depressed adults, has also been examined (Jacobson & Mufson, 2010). IPT-A is based on the premise that whatever the causes, depression is intertwined with the individual's interpersonal relationships. The therapist, through a variety of active strategies, helps the adolescent understand current interpersonal issues such as separation from parents, role transitions, romantic relationships, interpersonal deficits, peer pressure, grief, and single-parent family status. Mufson and colleagues (1999) found that adolescents diagnosed with major depressive disorder who received IPT-A showed improvement in depressive symptoms, social functioning, and problem-solving skills compared with control youths whose clinical condition was monitored. A second study by Mufson and colleagues, in a

school setting, also reported a greater reduction in depressive symptoms for IPT-A compared with a treatment control condition (Mufson et al., 2004). Rosselló and Bernal (1999) compared IPT-A with cognitive-behavioral therapy and a wait-list control in a sample of clinically depressed adolescents in Puerto Rico. Both treatment groups showed significant improvements in depressive symptoms (see Figure 7.5) and self-esteem compared with those in the control condition.

It is interesting to note that the studies by Mufson and colleagues included a large proportion of Latino youths and that Rosselló and Bernal made efforts to incorporate interpersonal aspects of Latino culture into their treatment: *personalismo*—the preference for interpersonal contacts, and *familismo*—a strong identification with and attachment to family. This was accomplished through a variety of adaptations to the treatment, such as selection of examples, sayings, and images from the adolescents' culture and context; emphasis on the interpersonal nature of the therapeutic approach; and discussion of family dependence and independence (Rosselló & Bernal, 1999; 2005). Although adolescents in both treatment groups in the Rosselló and Bernal study had comparable improvements in depression, improvement for some other outcome measures was better in the IPT-A group. The authors suggest that this may be because of the consonance of IPT-A with Puerto Rican cultural values. In a similar vein, McClure and colleagues (2005) have developed a family treatment for depressed African American adolescent girls—the Adolescent Depression Empowerment Psychosocial Treatment (ADEPT)—that includes elements of CBT, IPT-A, and family treatments that are delivered in a culturally sensitive manner. These efforts highlight the importance of evaluating the efficacy of treatments for different cultural groups (APA, 2006).

Treatments that are derived from a cognitive-behavioral perspective and treatments that address interpersonal and family aspects of depression in children and adolescents are promising. But findings are modest, particularly with regard to severely depressed youth, those with co-occurring disorders, and younger children, and with regard to long-term effectiveness (APA, 2006; Weisz, McCarty, & Valeri, 2006). Efforts to identify key elements, refine treatment, determine optimal treatment length, and generally improve the effectiveness for both psychological and pharmacological treatments are ongoing.

PREVENTION OF DEPRESSION

A number of universal depression prevention programs have been implemented and evaluated (Spence & Shortt, 2007). Most of these programs have been school-based and have emphasized cognitive-behavioral procedures; a few have included components drawn from an interpersonal psychotherapy perspective. These programs are offered to all youths in a particular grade(s) at one or more schools.

For example, Spence and colleagues (Spence, Sheffield, & Donovan, 2003; 2005) evaluated a teacher-implemented, classroom-based universal intervention that taught Australian eighth graders a range of problem-solving and cognitive coping skills to deal with challenging life circumstances. Sixteen schools were randomly assigned to the intervention or a control condition. Over the time of the program, students in the intervention condition did better than those in the control condition. The positive impact of the intervention (an increase in problem-solving skills and a decrease in depression symptoms) was most evident for those students with initial high levels of depressive symptoms. However, at 1, 2, 3, and 4 year follow-ups there were no differences in depressive symptoms (or for problem-solving skills) for the students in the two conditions. A separate large-scale evaluation for ninth graders (Sheffield et al., 2006) failed to find any differences between intervention and control conditions even at the end of the program.

In general, the findings for universal prevention programs for child and adolescent depression have been modest, at best, and at long-term follow-ups effects have not been maintained. However, there is probably enough success to suggest that efforts should continue. As Spence and Shortt (2007) suggest, interventions may need to be longer and more intensive and, in keeping with ecological models of the etiology of depression, preventive approaches may need to place a greater emphasis on decreasing risk factors and increasing protective factors in the youth's environment.

Several of the universal programs reported greater impact for those youngsters with moderate to high initial levels of depressive symptoms. This may suggest the value of indicated prevention approaches. A number of such programs have been attempted, and, again, many of these programs are derived from a cognitive-behavioral approach (David-Ferdon & Kaslow, 2008; Evans et al., 2005b). The Adolescent Coping With Stress course (CWS-A) is an extension of the Adolescent Coping with Depression treatment program (pp. 162–163) that emphasizes the cognitive restructuring component of the intervention (Clarke & DeBar, 2010; Rohde et al., 2005). It is intended to prevent future depression in at-risk adolescents. Adolescents in the ninth grade at three high schools who had high scores on the Center for Epidemiologic Studies Depression Scale, but who were not currently depressed based on a structured diagnostic interview, were assigned to either a 15-session, after-school, cognitive-behavioral group intervention or a usual-care control condition (Clarke & DeBar, 2010). At one-year follow-up there were significantly fewer cases of either MDD or dysthymia among adolescents receiving the CWS-A intervention (14% versus 26%). Clarke and colleagues (2001) conducted a similar evaluation of the CWS-A intervention offered by a health maintenance organization (HMO). In this case the course was offered to youths with subsyndromal levels of depression whose parents were receiving treatment for depression at the HMO. At a 15-month follow-up there were fewer new episodes of affective disorder in the CWS-A group (9%) than in the treatment-as-usual control group (29%). These and other indicated prevention programs suggest that this approach to intervention is promising and worth continued attention.

BIPOLAR DISORDERS

Does a 7-year-old child who demonstrates significant "rages," has clear evidence of ADHD and a family history positive for depression on the maternal side and bipolar disorder on the paternal side represent a safe candidate for stimulant treatment for his ADHD? What if he also has episodic day-long periods of being excessively giggly, needing little sleep, and appearing more active and talkative than usual? Does this represent a natural variant of childhood or is this a child who is showing early signs of a pediatric bipolar spectrum disorder ... and who will be at risk for future substance use, legal problems, incarceration, and suicide attempts? (Danner et al., 2009, p. 271)

The description by Danner and colleagues of clinical and conceptual issues in many ways captures the challenges faced in considering the development of bipolar disorder and its presentation in children and adolescents. How might a youth with bipolar disorder present? Is there a pediatric bipolar disorder that is similar to the disorder seen in adults? How might the presentation be distinguished from other disorders? How might this be different from more typical developmental patterns? What is the likely developmental course? These and other questions have become part of the substantial increase in attention to bipolar disorder in youth.

DSM Classification of Bipolar Disorders

The DSM category of **Bipolar and Related Disorders** describes disorders that involve the presence of mania as well as depressive symptoms. **Mania** is typically described as a period of abnormally, persistently elevated or irritable mood and increased energy or activity that is also persistent. The elevated mood that is experienced during mania is often described as **euphoric mood** and is characterized by features such as inflated self-esteem; high rates of activity, speech, and thinking; distractibility; and exaggerated feelings of physical and mental well-being. Children may exhibit happiness or "goofiness" that is excessive or inappropriate to the situation or the child's developmental level. Inflated self-esteem and grandiosity, in children, may take the form of overestimating one's abilities ("I'm the smartest person in the school.") or attempting feats that are dangerous. These displays of euphoric mood represent changes that are clearly different from the child's typical behavior.

To meet the criteria for a manic episode, mania (lasting a week or more) and at least three (or four if the mood is only irritable) of the following additional symptoms must be present:

1. Inflated self-esteem
2. Decreased need for sleep
3. More talkative than usual
4. Racing thoughts
5. Distractibility
6. Increased goal-directed activity or motor agitation
7. Excessive activity that can lead to negative outcomes (e.g., excessive spending, sexual indiscretions)

Also, to receive a bipolar disorder diagnosis, the manic episode must result in a distinct impairment in social or academic functioning or require hospitalization to prevent youths from harming themselves or others.

The DSM includes a number of bipolar diagnoses that might be given to children and adolescents. The diagnosis of Bipolar I Disorder requires the presence of one or more manic episodes and typically also involves a history of major depression. Bipolar II Disorder includes a history of major depression and hypomania. **Hypomania** is defined as a euphoric mood that is of shorter duration (four consecutive days) and less severe than a manic episode. Cyclothymic Disorder involves chronic, but mild, fluctuations between distinct periods of hypomanic and depressive symptoms that do not meet the diagnostic criteria for major depressive or hypomanic episodes. In earlier versions of the DSM there was also a category of Bipolar Disorder Not Otherwise Specified (NOS). This diagnosis was used for cases with symptoms characteristic of bipolar disorders but that did not meet full criteria for the other bipolar diagnoses. A large number of youth with bipolar symptoms received this NOS diagnosis (Birmaher & Axelson, 2005). The DSM-5 has, here and elsewhere, replaced the NOS terminology, but the general purpose of this designation remains the same. For bipolar presentations, the term NOS has been replaced with the diagnoses of Other Specified Bipolar and Related Disorder and Unspecified Bipolar and Related Disorder that, similar to NOS, are meant to be employed when symptoms of bipolar disorders are displayed, but the full criteria for other bipolar disorders are not met. In the first diagnosis, the clinician chooses to indicate the reasons that full criteria for another bipolar disorder are not met. In the "unspecified" diagnosis the clinician elects not to specify the reasons why the full criteria for another bipolar diagnosis are not met.

A major issue in the discussion of the diagnosis of bipolar disorders in youths is the question of the degree to which child-onset and adult-onset "versions" of bipolar disorders should be considered as the same or different disorders. Historically, the DSM criteria have been primarily the same for adults, children, and adolescents. In the DSM-5 this largely continues to be the case; however, sensitivity to potential developmental issues has begun to be addressed. For example, in the text accompanying the diagnostic criteria, examples are provided of how symptoms such as euphoric mood and grandiosity might present in children. Also, earlier in the chapter (see p. 146), the introduction, in DSM-5, of a diagnosis of disruptive mood dysregulation disorder as a type of depressive disorder was described. This diagnosis was introduced because of concerns regarding overdiagnosis of bipolar disorders in children.

A number of considerations have contributed to the ongoing concern with employing the same criteria to diagnose bipolar disorders in youths and adults. For example, there appear to be differences as well as similarities in the neurobiology of cases of child- and adult-onset of bipolar disorders (Fleck et al., 2010).

In addition, juvenile mania is often characterized by symptom presentations and patterns that may differ from the typical descriptions of bipolar disorders in adults. Important developmental differences in presentation challenge clinicians to apply the existing criteria while being sensitive to developmental differences in expression AACAP, 2007; Danner et al., 2009; Luby, Belden, &

Tandon, 2010; Meyer & Carlson, 2010). For example, in adults a typical clinical picture is of a cyclical disorder with acute onset of distinct episodes of mania or depression with periods of relatively good functioning between episodes. In contrast, some youths may not exhibit these distinct episodes. Instead, they may exhibit a chronic pattern (e.g., most days) of mood dysregulation without intervening periods of good functioning. Furthermore, young people are likely to exhibit very short mood episodes, very frequent mood shifts, and patterns of mixed moods rather than separate periods of depressed or manic mood.

This makes the usual "adult" distinctions a considerable challenge—defining what constitutes a manic or mood episode and describing how episodes cycle (Geller, Tillman, & Bolhofner, 2007). Should children who do not show episodic mood changes or who exhibit elevated symptoms of mania without meeting diagnostic criteria be considered a subtype of a group of juvenile bipolar disorders, or should they be classified in some other way (Brotman et al., 2006; Danner et al., 2009; Leibenluft & Rich, 2008)? For example, are children with a pattern of severe mood dysregulation (chronic irritability and hyperarousal)—a pattern that is persistent rather than occurring in distinct episodes—better classified as having a bipolar disorder, or as having disruptive mood dysregulation—a depressive disorder? (See Scott: Mixed Moods and Aggression)

Also, euphoric mood is often considered the hallmark of adult mania/bipolar disorder. There are, however, a number of challenges to defining a comparable mood in youth. For one, in youth, irritable mood is commonly associated with bipolar disorder. Thus, there is the question of what is the predominant mood. Also, mania, particularly in prepubertal youth, if present, may look very different than in adult samples.

In diagnosing bipolar disorder in children there is also the additional challenge of distinguishing symptoms of mania from typical behaviors. This can be a challenging task. One approach by Kowatch and colleagues (2005) describes the strategy of FIND (frequency, intensity, number, and duration of symptoms), and thresholds for each index. This is meant to assist clinicians in judging whether behavior is a symptom of bipolar disorder rather than a manifestation of developmentally more typical behavior. Similarly, Geller and her colleagues (2003) have attempted to describe how various mania criteria may present in children. Table 7.4 provides examples of what may be viewed as symptoms of mania in children and contrasting examples of typical child behavior. In making a diagnosis, clinicians must judge the child's behavior based on a number of considerations. For example, is the behavior appropriate for the child's age and developmental level? Are the behaviors, which might be appropriate in one context, displayed in contexts where they

---

SCOTT

Mixed Moods and Aggression

Scott, a 4-year-old boy was referred because of concerns about periods of extreme irritability associated with aggression that were interrupted by periods of sadness, guilt, and remorse. Scott's mother was unable to manage his intense tantrums that occurred multiple times daily and seemed to arise with little or no apparent provocation. But the greatest concern was aggression toward his younger sibling. Scott was hospitalized after pushing his younger sister down a flight of stairs and subsequently becoming inconsolably sad and crying for several hours.

Adapted from Luby, Belden, & Tandon, 2010, p. 116.

---

are clearly inappropriate or unexpected? What is the degree of impairment or interference with expected functioning?

Young people with bipolar disorder also are likely to present with high rates of co-occurring problems and disorders. For example, reported rates of comorbidity with ADHD are often quite high (e.g., 86%; Geller et al., 2000). Also, these patterns of co-occurrence may be different from those seen in adults. For example, manic episodes and bipolar disorders in older adolescents may in some ways be similar to adult presentations. However, manic episodes in adolescents are more likely to be associated with antisocial behaviors, school truancy, academic failure, or substance use. Manic episodes in adolescents are also likely to include psychotic features. Also, bipolar disorder may initially present as depression with alterations of mood occurring only after some period of time.

Thus, diagnosing bipolar disorder in youth may be difficult because of confusion regarding definition, the symptom presentation, and overlap with co-occurring disorders. For a number of reasons, whether or how one should apply current DSM bipolar criteria to youth is part of ongoing debate and these concerns are likely to impact future diagnostic approaches (American Academy of Child and Adolescent Psychiatry [AACAP], 2007; Leibenluft & Rich, 2008; Meyer & Carlson, 2010; Pavuluri, Birmaher & Naylor, 2005). Part of this debate considers whether bipolar presentations may be better conceptualized as a collection of dimensional symptoms or as a spectrum of presentations rather than as distinct categorical disorders. It is suggested that this alternative dimensional approach may prove fruitful for understanding the presentations of both

TABLE 7.4 **Examples of Manifestations of Mania Symptoms in Children and Typical Child Behavior**

Symptom	Child Mania	Typical Child
Elated mood	A 9-year-old girl continually danced around the house saying "I'm high, over the mountain high." A 7-year-old boy was repeatedly taken to the principal for clowning and giggling in class (when no one else was).	A child was very excited when the family went to Disneyland on Christmas morning.
Grandiose behaviors	An 8-year-old girl set up a paper flower store in her classroom and was annoyed and refused to do class work when asked to by the teacher. A 7-year-old boy stole a go-cart. He knew it was wrong to steal, but did not believe it was wrong for him. He thought that the police were arriving to play with him.	A 7-year-old boy pretended he was a fireman, directing others and rescuing victims. In his play, he did not call the firehouse. His play was age-appropriate and not impairing.
Hypersexual behavior	An 8-year-old boy imitated a rock star— gyrating his hips and rubbing his crotch during an interview. A 9-year-old boy drew pictures of naked ladies in public and said that they were his future wife.	A 7-year-old played doctor with a same-age friend.

Adapted from Geller et al., 2003.

youths and adults and may help in conceptualizing these problems across the full developmental spectrum (Alloy et al., 2010; Cicchetti, 2010; Danner et al., 2009; Meyer & Carlson, 2010; Youngstrom, 2010).

Description of Bipolar Disorders

With the challenge of how to define and diagnose bipolar disorder in mind, descriptions of young people with bipolar disorder often describe a variety of features. Kowatch & DelBello (2006) describe manic symptoms that may be displayed by children and adolescents with bipolar disorder. These are presented in Table 7.5 and we draw on their report for our description. Children with mania may irritate those around them by being extremely happy or silly when there seems to be no reason for this euphoric mood. Adolescents may also be extremely silly or unrealistically optimistic. Irritable mood also is common. A child may have many intense outbursts of anger. An adolescent may be extremely oppositional, curt, or hostile. Parents often report multiple intense mood swings daily (labile mood). Young people also report needing less sleep than usual and report having more energy than usual. Children and adolescents, when manic, may appear very restless or driven. They also may offer grandiose views of their ability. Youths may do many things over a short period of time and, initially, be fairly productive. They may, however, become increasingly disorganized and unproductive as their mania progresses. Young people may be loud, intrusive, and difficult to interrupt. Their speech may be rapid, pressured,

unintelligible, or difficult to follow, and they may report that their thoughts are racing—they can't get their ideas out fast enough. The child or adolescent may also exhibit what is often termed "flight of ideas"—changing topics rapidly in a way that is confusing to others. Even adults who are

TABLE 7.5 **Manic Symptoms that May Be Displayed by Youths with Bipolar Disorders**

Euphoric mood

Irritable mood

Mood swings

Decreased need for sleep

Unusual energy

Hyperactivity

Increased goal-directed activity

Grandiosity

Accelerated, pressured, or increased amount of speech

Racing thoughts

Flight of ideas

Distractibility

Poor judgment

Hallucinations

Delusions

Adapted from Kowatch & DelBello, 2006.

familiar with them cannot easily follow their words. When manic, youths are easily distracted. Children and adolescents with mania also may show poor judgment, becoming involved in impulsive or high-risk pleasurable behaviors (e.g., frequent fighting, alcohol or drug use, reckless driving). Some youths with bipolar disorder also may experience hallucinations and delusions (see pp. 330–331).

Epidemiology of Bipolar Disorders

Definitional and methodological issues make accurate estimates of prevalence of manic symptoms and bipolar disorders difficult. Bipolar disorder is thought to be relatively rare in childhood and adolescence, but it seems that the diagnosis has become more common (AACAP, 2007; Danner et al., 2009). Moreno and colleagues (2007) report on a national representative survey of visits to a physician's office by youths (ages 0–19 years). If one examines office visits in which the youths received a mental disorder diagnosis, one sees that the percentage of visits with a diagnosis of bipolar disorder increased from 0.42% in 1994–1995 to 6.67% in 2002–2003. This increase was larger than that among adults. Similarly, Blader and Carlson (2007) report an increase of bipolar disorder diagnoses among hospitalized youth. Between 1996 and 2004, the diagnosis rate increased from 1.4 to 7.3 per 10,000 for children and from 5.1 to 20.4 per 10,000 for adolescents.

Estimates of the prevalence of bipolar disorders among children and adolescents vary between 0 and 6% in community samples and 17 and 30% in clinical samples (Danner et al., 2009; Kessler et al., 2009). It is generally reported that females and males are equally represented and that bipolar disorder is much less prevalent in prepubertal youths than after puberty.

Similar to what we noted in our discussion of depression, in community samples of adolescents, manic-like symptoms of elevated, expansive, or irritable mood are present in adolescents who do not meet the criteria for a bipolar disorder. The youths with these **subsyndromal** symptoms do experience substantial impairment in functioning (Diler et al., 2010; Kessler, Avenevoli, & Merikangas, 2001). Indeed, as we have indicated, some evidence suggests a bipolar spectrum, that is, a continuum extending from normal emotion regulation difficulties to subsyndromal symptoms to mild and severe forms of the disorder rather than a categorical distinction (Alloy et al., 2010; Diler et al., 2010; Lewinsohn, Seeley, & Klein, 2003; Papolos, 2003; Youngstrom, 2010).

A number of other conditions commonly co-occur in youths diagnosed with bipolar disorder. Attention-deficit hyperactivity disorder, conduct disorder, oppositional defiant disorder, and substance abuse or dependence are among the problems commonly reported (Diler et al., 2010; Evans et al., 2005a; Kowatch & DelBello, 2006; Papolos, 2003). These youths also experience significant impairment in cognitive, school, social, and family functioning (Alloy et al., 2010; Lewinsohn, Klein, & Seeley, 1995a; Lewinsohn et al., 2003; McClure-Tone, 2010; Pavuluri et al., 2009). Their families face a considerable challenge and require assistance and support that is sensitive to the child's difficulties and the family's needs (Fristad & Goldberg-Arnold, 2003; Miklowitz & Goldstein, 2010). The feelings of one mother who received support through an online support group illustrate this need.

BIPOLAR DISORDERS

Families Need Support

One of the biggest stressors is the total isolation and lack of support. I *never* have a moment to myself. I have no friends, I have no life. I spend almost every day with a feeling of mortal terror that we will return to the horror before diagnosis and stabilization. No parent or child should ever have to experience what we and the many other parents I've met at CABF (Child and Adolescent Bipolar Foundation) have had to go through. I am tired of this life. I grieve for the loss of what I thought motherhood would be.... If I did not have the lifeline, I don't know what I would do some nights. I can log on after a bad day and get the support and strength to start the new day with a smile so that I can be there for my boys.

Adapted from Hellander, Sisson, & Fristad, 2003, p. 314.

Developmental Course and Prognosis

Youth with bipolar disorders may experience relatively early onset of affective difficulties. They also may experience such difficulties for appreciable periods of time and follow a fluctuating course of high rates of recovery and recurrence (Diler et al., 2010).

Lewinsohn, Klein, and Seeley (1995a) examined the course of bipolar disorder in a large community sample of adolescents (ages 14 to 18). The median duration of the most recent manic episode for these youngsters was 10.8 months. Among the participants in the study, youths diagnosed with bipolar disorder had experienced their first affective episode earlier (mean age = 11.75 years old) than had adolescents with a history of major depression with no periods of mania (mean age = 14.95 years old). The total amount of time spent with an affective disorder was longer for the youths with bipolar disorder as well. The estimated mean duration of affective disorder for these youths with bipolar disorder was 80.2 months compared with a mean duration of 15.7 months for youths in the OADP sample with major depressive disorder. This finding and others suggest that in some young people, a depressive disorder may be an early stage of bipolar disorder. The transition from MDD to bipolar disorder may be more likely to occur in youngsters with an earlier onset of depression. As early as the preschool years, there may be a subgroup of depressed children, with a family history of bipolar disorder, that are at heightened risk for exhibiting mania later in their development (Luby et al., 2010).

Some of the adolescents in the OADP sample who met the criteria for bipolar disorder experienced a chronic/recurrent course. Twelve percent had not remitted by age

JOSEPH

Early Bipolar Symptoms

Based on information gathered at his first hospital admission, Joseph suffered from childhood illnesses more than his eight siblings. By the time he started school at age 6 his parents described him as already having periods of being tired. Although Joseph was usually considered a "jolly boy who enjoyed himself," there were episodes of crying, irritability, and depressed moods. At school he was sometimes "extra good" and at others he "lost all interest."

By the time he was 13, the family said, "they could see it coming." Joseph began having alternating periods of "quietness and irritability." He would be at the playground ordering others around and being overly bossy at one moment and at the next he would be withdrawn, sitting quietly reading the Bible. For periods of a week or so, Joseph would sit around, tired, not talking and sometimes crying. During these times he seemed "scared."

There were rapid and extreme changes when Joseph would destroy whatever his siblings were playing with. During these times Joseph was overactive, restless, overtalkative, bold, loud, demanding, and exhibited hostile behavior and angry outbursts. The brief spells of being "quiet versus irritable" persisted through ages 13 and 14. Joseph's symptoms and the cycling worsened dramatically at age 15, when he was first admitted to the hospital meeting the criteria for a bipolar disorder.

Adapted from Egeland, Hostetter, Pauls, & Sussex, 2000, p. 1249.

24 (that is, they continued to meet diagnostic criteria) and of those in remission at age 18, about one-quarter had another episode between the ages of 19 and 24 (Lewinsohn et al., 2003). Individuals with bipolar disorder during adolescence were far more likely to meet criteria for bipolar disorder during young adulthood than adolescents with subsyndromal bipolar disorder. Adolescents with subsyndromal bipolar disorder, however, did experience high rates of major depressive disorder during young adulthood.

Geller and colleagues (2003) studied a group of prepubertal children and early adolescents with bipolar disorder. These youths were assessed in a research setting, but received care from their own community practitioners. During a 2-year period about two-thirds of these young people experienced recovery (defined as at least 8 consecutive weeks not meeting DSM criteria for mania or hypomania). A little over half of them relapsed after recovery and many continued to meet the criteria for another disorder during their recovery.

Prospective data are limited. However, the retrospective and prospective information that is available suggests that youngsters with bipolar disorders or symptoms might continue to display symptoms of affective and other disorders and experience considerable social and academic impairment, at least into the early adult period (Birmaher & Axelson, 2005; Danner et al., 2009).

Risk Factors and Etiology

Discussions of the etiology of bipolar disorder have tended to emphasize biological influences and, indeed, genetic and neurobiological factors appear to be central to understanding the disorder. However, there also is growing consensus that bipolar disorder is a condition in which there is a genetic diathesis and for which, from the very beginnings of life, environmental experiences make a major contribution to the complex and dynamic interplay of influences that shape the expression of such mood difficulties at each developmental level (Cicchetti, 2010; Meyer & Carlson, 2010; Youngstrom, 2010).

A family history of bipolar disorders is clearly a risk factor (Willcutt & McQueen, 2010). Biological siblings and parents of youth diagnosed with bipolar disorder have appreciably higher-than-expected rates of bipolar disorder. Also, children of adult bipolar patients have an increased risk for bipolar disorder and mood disorders, in general. However, it is important to note that the majority of children of bipolar adults do not have a diagnosable bipolar disorder or other mood disorder (Evans et al., 2005a).

Other research suggests a significant genetic influence (Meyer & Carlson, 2010; Willcutt & McQueen, 2010). Adult twin and adoption studies are consistent in showing a strong genetic component for bipolar disorders and indirect evidence from twin studies with children suggests significant heritability for bipolar disorder in children and adolescents. Heritability estimates of about 60–90% are reported in adult studies. Research employing candidate gene and linkage and association analysis is attempting to identify specific genes that may be involved. These molecular genetic studies, in combination with neuroimaging techniques, suggest that multiple genes, affecting activation of areas of the brain such as the amygdala, are involved in the development of bipolar disorder and that no single gene is either a necessary or sufficient cause (Arnold, Hanna, & Rosenberg, 2010; Liu et al., 2010).

Twin studies and other research also suggest that environmental influences play a role in the development of bipolar disorder (Alloy et al., 2010; McClure-Tone, 2010; Meyer & Carlson, 2010; Willcutt & McQueen, 2010). Stressful life events, family relationships, and parenting styles have received considerable attention. Social difficulties with peers and poor social support are also noted as potential environmental influences that may interact with biological vulnerabilities over the course of development to impact the expression of bipolar symptoms and related difficulties. Additional research is needed to elucidate the timing and role of these and other environmental influences on the initial development, maintenance, and life-course of bipolar presentations.

Assessment of Bipolar Disorders

In the assessment of bipolar disorder in children and adolescents a broad spectrum of information is, again, the assessment goal (Danner et al., 2009; Youngstrom, 2010). Structured diagnostic interviews such as versions of the K-SADS have been employed to make diagnostic decisions and to obtain additional information (Axelson et al., 2003; Danner et al., 2009; Geller et al., 2001). However, the length of such interviews makes them less useful in most clinical situations. A number of mania rating scales have been adapted from adult scales and developed for use with clinicians, parents, and youths themselves. The Young Mania Rating Scale (YMRS; Young et al., 1978) has been adapted for use with children and adolescents (PYMRS; Youngstrom, Findling, & Feeny, 2004). The General Behavior Inventory, designed to assess symptoms of depression, hypomania, mania, and mixed mood states has been adapted for use with children and adolescents and as a parent-report measure (Danielson et al., 2003; Youngstrom et al., 2001). Collecting information using these rating scales on large representative samples of children and adolescents is needed in order to provide comparison to information on normative development

and to be sensitive to the possible range of mania/bipolar presentations (Youngstrom, 2010).

Treatment of Bipolar Disorders

The treatment of bipolar disorder requires a multimodal approach to the disorder itself as well as attention to likely co-occurring difficulties and the considerable involvement of the family (AACAP, 2007; Mendenhall & Fristad, 2010; Miklowitz & Goldstein, 2010). The young patient with mania may need to be admitted to a child or adolescent hospital unit so as to ensure the youth's safety and to provide an adequately controlled environment. The choice to use an inpatient setting would be guided by the level of disturbance displayed, the risk of harm or suicide, the level of support that the family is able to provide, and the need for medical supervision of medication.

The most common treatment for bipolar disorder is pharmacotherapy, and this is often considered the first-line treatment for the disorder (AACAP, 2007). Pharmacotherapy for mania typically consists of mood stabilizers such as lithium and valproate, and atypical antipsychotics (e.g., aripiprazole, olanzapine, quetiapine, risperidone) alone or in combination (AACAP, 2007; Kowatch, Strawn, & DelBello, 2010). However, there are questions regarding methodological adequacy of some key research. Also, methodologically adequate research regarding treatment of youths remains relatively limited, in particular regarding younger children, and there remains concern with regard to significant adverse and long-term effects (Kowatch et al., 2010; Liu et al., 2011; Tsai et al., 2011). Treatment of the depressive aspects of the disorder may include the use of medications such as SSRIs. However, caution is suggested because antidepressants have been reported to destabilize the patient's mood or to incite a manic episode (AACAP, 2007; Kowatch et al., 2010).

Although pharmacological treatment is typically employed in treating bipolar youth, the need to include other treatment components and the importance of incorporating family members (see Table 7.6) is also recognized. **Psychoeducation**, which seeks to educate the patient and family about the disorder, its likely course, and the nature of treatment, is an important component of interventions. In addition to a psychoeducational component, individual and family therapy is often recommended. Programs designed for youths and their families have been developed and are undergoing evaluation (Mendenhall & Fristad, 2010; Miklowitz & Goldstein, 2010). These treatment programs include education of the youth and family about the disorder and its treatment plus many of the cognitive-behavioral elements described in the psychosocial treatment of depression. Also, some programs include dialectical

TABLE 7.6 Why Include the Family in Treatment?

- Children and adolescents diagnosed with bipolar disorder usually reside with their families.
- The family is likely to be instrumental in seeking and facilitating the treatment of their child.
- The disorder has significant impact on the family and family relationships and family members are often affected by its societal stigma.
- The affective climate of the family environment can affect the course of the disorder and the success of medication treatments.
- Multiple members of the family are often affected by bipolar disorder.

Adapted from Miklowitz & Goldstein, 2010.

behavior therapy (DBT; originally developed for adults with borderline personality disorder), which focuses on emotional dysregulation and which also contains psychoeducation, and cognitive behavioral strategies. DBT also includes mindfulness techniques to help family members focus awareness and gain an increased sense of control over thoughts and emotions. Support groups and other forms of assistance for families, such as the website of the Child and Adolescent Bipolar Foundation (CABF) are likely to be needed as well (Hellander et al., 2003; Kowatch & DelBello, 2006).

SUICIDE

Suicide is often mentioned in discussions of mood disorders. This association probably occurs because depression, in particular, is an important risk factor for suicide, and the two problems share etiological and epidemiological patterns. However, although the two problems overlap, they are also distinct. The majority of depressed youngsters do not attempt or commit suicide, and not every suicidal youth is depressed. Discussion of suicide includes not only concern with completed suicides, but also with attempted suicides and suicidal thoughts. There is reason to attend to this full range of suicidal behavior (Bridge, Goldstein, & Brent, 2006; Hawton & Fortune, 2008).

Prevalence of Completed Suicides

The rate of completed suicide is relatively low among young people compared with adults and lower for prepubertal children than for adolescents. Completed suicide by young people is nevertheless of concern. From the mid-1950s to the early 1990s the suicide rate among adolescents and young adults rose markedly. Since the mid-1990s there has been a steady decline. However,

overall rates remain about twice what they were when the marked rise began and suicide is the third leading cause of death among youth (National Center for Health Statistics, 2011). The 1980 suicide rate among 15- to 19-year olds was 8.5 per 100,000 and the 2007 rate was 6.9 per 100,000—a decrease. In contrast, suicides among younger children are occurring at a higher rate. In 1980, the suicide rate among young people between the ages of 5 and 14 was 0.4 per 100,000. Although suicides remained a relatively rare event in this age group, the 2007 rate was 0.5 youths per 100,000—an increase of 25%. Rates per 100,000 in 2007 of male deaths from suicides exceed those for females in both the 5- to 14-year-old (0.6 and 0.3) and 15- to 19-year-old (11.1 and 2.5) age groups. Rates are higher for White (non-Hispanic or Latino) youth than for other ethnic groups, with the exception of Native American youth.

Suicidal Ideation and Attempts

If one considers the entire range of suicidal behavior, prevalence appears quite high, particularly among adolescents. Clearly, it is difficult to accurately assess the prevalence of suicidal behavior. Many attempts may go undetected and unreported, because not all cases seek medical or some therapeutic care. Also, methodological and definitional issues may limit interpretation of self-reports of suicidal ideation and attempts. Even some completed suicides may be mistakenly viewed as accidents.

Based on the national Youth Risk Behavior Survey (Centers for Disease Control and Prevention, 2010) the percentage of youths in grades 9 to 12 in the United States who seriously considered suicide significantly decreased between 1991 and 2009. However, despite this decrease, during the same period, there was a significant increase in the number of young people who made an injurious suicide attempt. The information in Table 7.7 illustrates these trends. Rates of injurious suicide attempts (needing medical attention) seem particularly high among Hispanic/Latino youths. Although more young males die by suicide, females report more suicidal ideation and attempts.

A prospective longitudinal study of approximately 1,500 adolescents between 14 and 18 years of age by Lewinsohn and his colleagues (1996) also provides information about the prevalence of adolescent suicidal behavior. A total of 19.4% of these adolescents had a history of suicidal ideation. Such ideation was more prevalent in females (23.7%) than in males (14.8%). And although more frequent suicidal ideation predicted future suicide attempts, even mild and relatively infrequent suicidal thoughts increased the risk for an attempt.

| TABLE 7.7 | Suicidal Behaviors among Youths in Grades 9–12 | | | |

| | Percent Who Seriously Considered Suicide | | | |
| | 1991 | | 2009 | |
	Male	Female	Male	Female
White (Not Hispanic or Latino)	21.7	38.6	10.5	16.1
Black or African American	13.3	29.4	7.8	18.1
Hispanic or Latino	18.0	34.6	10.7	22.0

| | Percent Youths with Injurious Suicide Attempt | | | |
| | 1991 | | 2009 | |
	Male	Female	Male	Female
White (Not Hispanic or Latino)	1.0	2.3	3.8	6.5
Black or African American	0.4	2.9	5.4	10.4
Hispanic or Latino	0.5	2.7	5.1	11.1

National Center for Health Statistics, 2010.

Suicide attempts had occurred in 7.1% of this community sample. Females (10.1%) were more likely than males (3.8%) to attempt suicide. Suicide attempts before puberty were uncommon. The majority of attempts made by females consisted of either ingestion of harmful substances (55%) or cutting themselves (31%). Males employed a wider variety of methods—ingestion (20%), cutting (25%), gun use (15%), hanging (11%), and other methods, such as shooting air into their veins or running into traffic (22%). Some adolescents attempted suicide more than once. The first 3 months after an attempt were a period of particularly high risk for a repeated attempt. Reattempts were made by approximately 27% of the boys and 21% of the girls during this time. The likelihood of a suicidal attempt by these youngsters remained above the rates expected in the general population for at least 2 years. At 24 months, 39% of the boys and 33% of the girls had reattempted.

Young people are often thought to be vulnerable to suicide because their problem-solving and self-regulatory skills and their abilities to cope with stressful circumstances may be limited. Some young people may be faced with circumstances that cause considerable stress that they view as beyond their control. These youths may also have limited understanding that undesirable situations can and often do change.

Suicide and Psychopathology

Suicide is often thought of as a symptom of disorders such as depression. Indeed, depression is related to suicide among children and adolescents, and constructs such as hopelessness that are associated with depression have been found to predict suicidal behavior (Flisher, 1999; Hawton & Fortune, 2008). For example, in a longitudinal study, Kovacs, Goldston, and Gatsonis (1993) found that a significantly greater proportion of youths with depressive disorders attempted suicide than did those with other disorders. However, suicidal behavior can be associated with a variety of disorders, and suicide risk increases with the number of diagnoses. There is a significant association between bipolar disorder and risk for suicide. Also, conduct disorder and substance abuse diagnoses are common among completed suicides. Indeed, some research suggests considerable diagnostic heterogeneity among young suicide completers. Therefore, although depression is an important risk factor, the presence of a depressive disorder is neither necessary nor sufficient for the occurrence of suicidal behavior. It is probably important to be aware that some professionals indicate that the presence of problems (e.g., aggression and impulsivity in combination with or independent of depression) at levels below criteria for a diagnosis of disorder also increase the risk of suicidal behavior (Hendin et al., 2005a; King et al., 1992).

Risk Factors

There is no typical suicidal youth, and multiple factors likely contribute to risk for suicide (De Wilde, Kienhorst, & Diekstra, 2001; Gould et al., 2003; Hendin et al., 2005a). A history of prior suicide attempts is a strong predictor of completed suicide. However, multiple

PATTY

A Suicide Attempt

Patty, a pretty 8-year old, took an overdose of two of her mother's imipramine tablets just before going to sleep. Nobody knew about this until the next morning when Patty's mother had to wake her when she did not get up in time for school. Patty complained of a headache, dizziness, and tiredness. She was tearful and irritable and argued that her mother should "Leave me alone. I want to die." Alarmed, Patty's mother brought her to the pediatrician, who recommended that Patty be hospitalized for evaluation of suicidal behavior.... He believed that Patty would not be safe at home. Patty insisted that the "best thing would be for me to die."

Patty's mother told the pediatrician that the last 2 months had been very stressful for the family. She and her husband had separated and were planning to divorce. The mother described feeling very depressed and anxious over the last year. Her husband often came home drunk and would be very hostile to her and threaten her....

Patty is a fine student and has many friends.... Patty's teacher had spoken to her mother about Patty's behavior over the previous 2 months. Patty was fidgety in class and unable to concentrate; she often day-dreamed. Her homework assignments were often not completed and her grades had dropped. Unlike her earlier behavior, Patty, in the last month, had preferred to be alone and had not joined her peers in after-school activities. She also had several arguments with her best friend.

Adapted from Pfeffer, 2000, p. 238.

characteristics of the youths' social environment and of the youths themselves appear to be risk factors of suicidal behavior.

A family history of suicidal behavior increases risk. Family factors (such as abuse, low parental monitoring, and poor communication) and family disruption are also frequently cited as risk factors. Although improved research is needed, it would appear that youngsters who attempt suicide are likely to grow up in families characterized by high levels of turmoil (De Wilde et al., 2001; Wagner, Silverman, & Martin, 2003). However, high levels of involvement and support from family, as well as from schools or other institutions, may serve a protective function (Gould et al., 2003; Hendin et al., 2005a).

Other factors such as bullying, high levels of stress in school, social relations, and sociocultural influences—including the ready availability of firearms—are also thought to contribute to increased risk. Considerable concern also exists regarding **contagion** ("imitation" or increased suicidal behavior) following media reports or presentations of stories of youth suicide (Gould et al., 2003; Hendin et al., 2005a).

As suggested above, psychological disorders that are characterized by attributes such as depression, hopelessness, impulsivity, and aggression contribute to suicide risk. In addition, research suggests that biological factors such as abnormalities in serotonin function and genetic influences may possibly affect suicide risk (Bridge et al., 2006; Hawton & Fortune, 2008). Other individual risk factors include poor interpersonal problem-solving ability and physical illness. Minority sexual orientation may be a risk factor of particular concern (Silenzio et al., 2007).

It is frequently suggested that suicide is more common among gay and lesbian youth than among the general adolescent population. There does not appear to be evidence for a higher rate of completed suicide in these groups (AACAP, 2001; Catalan, 2000). However, the view that these young people are at increased risk for suicidal ideation and attempted suicide is widely held. Several studies of sizeable community samples suggest a two- to sevenfold increase in risk, and these youngsters also may be more likely to make suicide attempts that require medical attention (AACAP, 2001; Silenzio et al., 2007). Why might this be the case?

Research suggests that gay, lesbian, and bisexual youth are likely to report experiences that are known to be important risk factors. For example, they are more likely to be bullied and victimized at school. Many clinicians believe that the difficulties of dealing with the stigma of homosexuality and the interpersonal difficulties that this may bring might lead to depression, and there are reports of high levels of depression in such youth.

Data from the National Study of Adolescent Health (Add Health Study), a nationally representative study of U.S. adolescents, support the view that sexual orientation is a risk factor for suicidal ideation and suicide attempts, and suggest that this risk is, in part, due to known adolescent risk factors (Russell & Joyner, 2001). About 12,000 adolescents completed the survey in their homes, and information regarding the issues of sexuality and suicide was collected in a manner to minimize issues of privacy and confidentiality. Youths with a same-sex orientation (having a same-sex romantic attraction or relationship) were more likely to report suicidal thoughts and were more than twice as likely to attempt suicide as their same-sex peers. It is

ACCENT
Non-Suicidal Self-Injury

When clinicians and researchers discuss serious self-inflicted injury such behavior typically includes both unsuccessful suicide attempts and repeated self-injury without a suicidal intent. This latter category is often referred to as "non-suicidal self-injury" (NSSI) and includes behaviors such as cutting, burning, hitting, and biting oneself that are likely to cause pain, bleeding, or bruising.

The distinction is not necessarily an easy one (Crowell, Beauchaine, & Lenzenweger, 2008; Goldston & Compton, 2007). Distinguishing non-suicidal self-injury from suicide attempts requires a discrimination of intent. One might carefully ask the young person whether "any part of them" wanted to die when engaging in the self-mutilating behavior. Often the distinction, however, is made based on the presumed lethality of the behavior (e.g., cutting or burning versus hanging or use of a gun).

NSSI is relatively rare early but increases during adolescence. Estimates of prevalence suggest that between about 5 and 25% of adolescents engage in non-suicidal self-injury behaviors. Such behavior is more commonly observed in females than in males (Heilborn & Prinstein, 2010; Shaffer & Jacobson, 2009).

Since it is presumed that there is no suicidal intent, what might motivate the behavior? The self-injurious behavior is typically viewed as being impulsive rather than well planned. Several different reasons why youth may engage in NSSI have been suggested. All involve some form of psychological distress. Thus, for example, engaging in self-injury might be a way of coping with difficult feelings (depression, anxiety), relieving unbearable tension, expressing anger or frustration, distracting oneself through physical pain from other highly negative feelings, or as a way to stop feeling "numb" or "empty" (Goldston & Compton, 2007). In regards to etiology, NSSI is often hypothesized to develop in youths who have a biological vulnerability to intense emotionality and who experience family and peer relationships that are high in conflict. These social environments fail to support the youth's attempts to manage emotions and emotion dysregulation may place the adolescent at risk for NSSI (Adrian et al., 2011; Crowell, Beauchaine, & Linehan, 2009).

In adults non-suicidal self-mutilating behavior is part of the criteria for a diagnosis of Borderline Personality Disorder. Research suggests that among adolescents NSSI co-occurs with a variety of disorders including major depressive disorder, anxiety disorders, externalizing disorders, and substance abuse (Jacobson et al., 2008; Nock et al., 2006). Some researchers and clinicians have suggested that NSSI should be considered as a separate disorder in future classification systems so as to facilitate identification and treatment of adolescents who engage in cutting and other self-injurious behaviors (APA, 2013; Shaffer & Jacobson, 2009).

important to note, however, that the vast majority of youth with a same-sex sexual orientation reported no suicidal thoughts or attempts (about 85% of boys and 72% of girls). Youngsters with a same-sex orientation also scored higher on several important adolescent suicide risk factors: more alcohol abuse and depression, higher rates of suicide attempts by family members and friends, and victimization experiences. These and other findings suggest that sexual orientation, per se, is not a risk factor for suicide attempts, but rather same-sex orientation interacts with known risk factors common to all adolescents (Savin-Williams & Ream, 2003). Awareness of risk factors for suicidal ideation and attempts that may be of relatively greater importance to lesbian, gay, and bisexual youth may deserve particular attention (Silenzio et al., 2007).

Suicide Prevention

The review by the Commission on Adolescent Suicide Prevention (Hendin et al., 2005a) suggests that attempts to prevent youth suicide are widespread. The most common programs have taken a universal prevention approach—targeting all youth in a specific setting, such as schools, regardless of individual risk. There are two types of universal prevention programs (Hendin et al., 2005c). Suicide awareness and education programs aim to increase students' awareness of, and knowledge about, suicidal behavior and to encourage them to seek help. These programs also seek to improve awareness by school staff and other adults in the community. Most awareness and education programs involve a limited number of brief sessions and are frequently part of a larger curriculum targeting high-risk behaviors. While these programs are widely applied, if and how they are effective remains unclear. For example, while many programs report increased student knowledge regarding suicide, the impact of this on suicidal behavior is unknown (Hendin et al., 2005c).

Screening programs seek to identify youth who are at risk and refer them to treatment. The assumption of such programs is that the suicidal behaviors and the psychopathology associated with suicide (e.g., depression, substance abuse) often go unnoticed and untreated. It is also assumed that identification of at-risk youth will increase the number receiving treatment and that treatment will decrease suicides. The success of such approaches relies on the availability of screening measures that are both sensitive (able to detect youth at risk for suicide) and selective (able to avoid identifying many more as at risk who are not). Timing of the screening (e.g., at the beginning of high school, before exams) may also affect the likelihood of accurate identification. It is not clear whether screening programs are cost-effective or result in high rates of follow-through by those identified as at-risk. Getting identified at-risk youth to follow through with treatment recommendations is clearly a complex issue—involving, for example, appropriate encouragement of youth, parental support, and availability of quality treatment services. There is no clear evidence that screening programs reduce suicide risk factors or suicidal behavior (Hendin et al., 2005c).

Selective or targeted suicide prevention programs are directed at youth who may have not yet exhibited suicidal behavior, but who are thought to be particularly vulnerable to suicide (Hendin et al., 2005b). For example, such a program might target youngsters who have recently been exposed to the suicide of a family member or peer. The assumption of such programs is that exposed youth are at increased risk for depression, posttraumatic stress, and suicidal behavior. These programs, sometimes referred to as "postvention," are often implemented through schools and seek to support grieving youth, to identify those at risk, and to assist the community in returning to its normal functioning. In general, scientifically valid evaluations have lagged behind the development and implementation of prevention programs. Much remains to be learned about youth suicide and effective intervention.

Overview/Looking Back

- Children and adolescents may experience moods that are unusually sad (depression) or unusually elated (mania).

A HISTORICAL PERSPECTIVE

- The classical psychoanalytic theory of depression suggested that the problem did not exist in children.
- The concept of masked depression, although problematic, brought greater attention to the problem and highlighted developmental issues. A developmental perspective to understanding depression has continued to evolve.

THE DSM APPROACH TO THE CLASSIFICATION OF MOOD DISORDERS

- In the DSM depression and mania are described in the category of Mood Disorders.
- The DSM describes four types of mood episodes that serve as the building blocks for the diagnosis of mood disorders.

DEFINITION AND CLASSIFICATION OF DEPRESSION

- The definition of depression is affected by how depression is measured and who provides information.
- Major Depressive Disorder, Persistent Depressive Disorder (Dysthymia), and Disruptive Mood Dysregulation Disorder are among the DSM diagnoses related to depression.

- Empirical approaches to classification suggest that children and adolescents experience syndromes that include a mixed presentation of depression and anxiety features.
- Developmental differences in presentation of depression challenge the use of the same diagnostic criteria in all age groups. Whether it is best to conceptualize depression as dimensional rather than categorical is an ongoing consideration.
- The subjective experience of sadness is a central feature of the clinical definition of depression. Descriptions of children and adolescents viewed as depressed suggest that they experience a number of other problems as well.

EPIDEMIOLOGY OF DEPRESSION

- Major depressive disorder is the most frequently diagnosed mood disorder among children and adolescents.
- Episodes of clinical depression are quite common among adolescents. Depression is more prevalent among adolescents than children and among girls during adolescence.
- Higher rates of depression are reported among low SES groups. Although comparable rates of depression are typically reported for different ethnic groups, research suggests attention to possible differences.
- Youths who are depressed are likely to experience a number of other difficulties and to meet the diagnostic criteria for a variety of other disorders.

DEPRESSION AND DEVELOPMENT

- How depression is manifested varies by developmental period.
- Episodes of depression may last for an appreciable period of time and for some youngsters may present a recurring problem.

ETIOLOGY OF DEPRESSION

- Most contemporary views of depression in children and adolescents suggest a model that integrates multiple determinants.
- Research suggests a genetic component to depression and also considerable environmental influence.
- Research on the biochemistry of depression emphasizes the role of neurotransmitters and the neuroendocrine system. Findings suggest that during childhood and early adolescence, the biological aspects of depression likely differ from adult cases. Anatomical and functional abnormalities in particular areas of the brain and differences in temperament have also received attention with regard to the etiology of depression.
- Separation/loss has been a major theme in many theories of depression. Cognitive and behavioral theories suggest additional contributions to the development of depression, including interpersonal and cognitive aspects of functioning.
- A learned helplessness perspective suggests that a learned perception of lack of control leads to a cognitive style and behaviors characteristic of depression. Hopelessness theory emphasizes the interaction of stressful life events and cognitive style.
- Cognitive theories, such as Beck's, and self-control models of depression have also received attention.
- Parental depression appears to be related to childhood dysfunctions, but this relationship does not seem to be either specific to childhood depression or inevitable. Various mechanisms may link parental depression and child dysfunction.
- Interpersonal relationships with peers contribute to the development of depression, and a youth's depression affects peers' relationships with the depressed youth.

ASSESSMENT OF DEPRESSION

- Assessment of depression is likely to sample a broad spectrum of attributes and to involve a number of strategies. It is important to obtain information from a variety of informants and through a variety of measures.
- A variety of assessment strategies are available. Self-report measures completed by the youth are among the most commonly employed and may be particularly important.
- Instruments available to assess attributes associated with depression (e.g., hopelessness) and observational measures add to our ability to conduct a thorough assessment.

TREATMENT OF DEPRESSION

- The prescription of antidepressant medications to treat children and adolescents with depression is widespread and may be an important component of treatment for some youths. However, the use of medications continues to be controversial, because there are concerns about efficacy and safety. Selective serotonin reuptake inhibitors are most commonly employed.
- Treatments derived from behavioral and cognitive-behavioral perspectives and treatments that address interpersonal and family aspects of depression in youngsters are promising. However, continued development of treatments that are sensitive to multiple aspects of psychological, social, and family influences and to cultural differences are a goal.

PREVENTION OF DEPRESSION

- A number of universal depression prevention programs have been implemented. Most have employed cognitive-behavioral procedures and some have included interpersonal components. In general, the effectiveness of universal prevention programs has been modest and not maintained over the long term.
- Indicated prevention programs, derived from a cognitive-behavioral approach, have also been implemented and appear to be effective in preventing depression in at-risk youth.

BIPOLAR DISORDERS

- Bipolar disorders involve the presence of mania as well as depressive symptoms.
- The DSM describes a number of bipolar disorders including Bipolar I Disorder, Bipolar II Disorder, Cyclothymic Disorder, and Other Specified (or Unspecified) Bipolar and Related Disorders.
- There are a number of challenges in using "adult" bipolar disorder criteria to diagnose children and adolescents, and behavior may vary with development.
- Definitional issues make estimates of prevalence difficult. Bipolar disorders are thought to be rare, particularly in pre-pubertal youngsters. However, the

diagnosis of bipolar disorders in youths has become more common.

- Youths with bipolar disorders are likely to experience co-occurring disorders and to exhibit considerable impairment in functioning.
- Young people who meet the criteria for bipolar disorders may experience a chronic and recurrent course of difficulties.
- A family history of bipolar disorders is probably the primary risk factor. A strong genetic influence is suggested and environmental influences likely interact with this genetic diathesis to shape mood and related difficulties.
- Development of assessment approaches for bipolar disorders that are specific to children and adolescents is ongoing.
- Treatment of bipolar disorders requires a multimodal approach. The primary treatment involves the use of pharmacological agents, particularly mood stabilizers. Psychoeducation, incorporating family members into treatment, and the use of CBT and DBT strategies are likely to be components of treatment as well. Research regarding all aspects of treatment for bipolar disorders in youth is needed.

SUICIDE

- Completed suicide is a serious concern. The range of suicidal behavior that includes suicidal thoughts and attempted suicide is more prevalent than actual, completed suicide.
- Suicidal behavior is related to depression but to other problems as well.
- Multiple complex factors contribute to suicidal behavior.
- Attempts to prevent youth suicide are widespread; however, the impact or success of such programs is unclear.

Key Terms

masked depression *144*
unipolar mood disorder *144*
bipolar mood disorder *144*
Major Depressive Disorder *146*
Persistent Depressive Disorder
  (Dysthymia) *146*
double depression *146*
Disruptive Mood Dysregulation
  Disorder *146*
cortisol *152*
negative affectivity *152*

positive affectivity *152*
learned helplessness *154*
attributional (explanatory)
  style *154*
hopelessness *154*
cognitive distortions *155*
cognitive restructuring *155*
selective serotonin reuptake
  inhibitors *160*
remission *161*
behavioral activation *162*

Bipolar and Related Disorders *165*
mania *165*
euphoric mood *165*
hypomania *165*
subsyndromal *168*
psychoeducation *170*
contagion *173*

Conduct Problems

In this chapter and the next, we discuss problems often described as *externalizing*. This term denotes problems that tend to place young people in conflict with others. These behaviors are in contrast to the seemingly more inner-directed problems discussed in the two previous chapters. Various other terms also are employed to describe these types of problems—disruptive, impulsive, undercontrolled, oppositional, antisocial, conduct-disordered, and delinquent. Although there is a general understanding of this broad category, attempting to understand, define, and subcategorize such behavior is ongoing.

Among disruptive behavior problems, a distinction has often been made between inattention, hyperactivity, and impulsivity on the one hand, and aggression, oppositional behaviors, and more serious conduct problems on the other. The behaviors in the first grouping are discussed in greater detail in the next chapter, which is devoted to attention-deficit hyperactivity disorder (ADHD). The oppositional and conduct problem behaviors of the second grouping are considered in this chapter. Young people with these problems have high rates of referral for mental health and other social and legal services, and some portion of these youths have contributed to broad societal concern with levels of violence and crime. Conduct problems are thus the focus of considerable societal and scientific concern.

A number of constructs exist to describe such youth. We use the term *conduct problems* to refer to this general group of disruptive/antisocial behavior problems. The terms *conduct disorder* and *disruptive behavior disorder* are used to refer to the particular diagnostic grouping that addresses these kinds of difficulties. The term **delinquency** is primarily a legal term used in the criminal justice system to describe youth who exhibit conduct problem/antisocial behavior. As a legal term, it refers to a juvenile (usually under age 18) who has committed an index crime or a status offense. An index crime is an act that would be illegal for adults as well as for juveniles (e.g., theft, aggravated assault, rape, or murder). A status offense is an act that is illegal only for juveniles (e.g., truancy, association with "immoral" persons, violation of curfews, or incorrigibility).

CLASSIFICATION AND DESCRIPTION

Disruptive behaviors are common at various stages of development. Clinicians commonly hear complaints of noncompliant, aggressive, and antisocial behavior. Parents and teachers often describe young children and adolescents who do not follow directions, do not comply with requests, or seem irritable or angry. Preschool age children often hit, kick, or bite other children. From early school years through middle school children may engage in various forms of aggression and bullying. Many adolescents engage in dangerous behaviors and use illegal substances. The fact that these problems are common and disruptive makes them a topic of concern for parents and for those who work with youths. They may cause considerable distress for parents and teachers, create discord among family members, or interfere with classroom functioning. Extreme and persistent forms of these behaviors cause a degree of disturbance and destruction well beyond the common experience. Thus they are of particular concern not only for the family but also for institutions such as the school and for society at large. The seeming persistence of these behaviors over time for some individuals—perhaps from early childhood through adult life—also contributes to their importance. Table 8.1 provides an overview of types of conduct-problem behaviors that adults often describe as problematic and aversive and the DSM disorders associated with them.

DSM Approach: Overview

The diagnoses of Oppositional Defiant Disorder and Conduct Disorder, which are discussed in the present chapter, fall within the larger DSM category of Disruptive, Impulse-Control, and Conduct Disorders. This DSM chapter, in addition to oppositional defiant disorder and conduct disorder, includes disorders such as intermittent explosive disorder, antisocial personality disorder, pyromania (fire setting), kleptomania (stealing), and the diagnoses of other specified and unspecified disruptive, impulse-control, and conduct disorders.

Intermittent Explosive Disorder is characterized by recurring and frequent behavioral outbursts. The aggressive outbursts may be verbal (e.g., temper tantrums, tirades) and/or physical (e.g., physical aggression toward property or persons or animals). These outbursts are seen as representing the individual's failure to control impulsive aggressive behavior. Thus the outbursts are generally impulsive or angry and not premeditated or committed so as to achieve a tangible objective. Outbursts are often rapid and brief and the response is grossly out of proportion to the perceived provocation. The diagnosis is not intended for children younger than 6 years of age or for youths whose aggressive behavior might better be explained by another disorder (e.g., bipolar disorder, disruptive mood dysregulation disorder, adjustment disorder).

TABLE 8.1	Types of Conduct Problem Behaviors Viewed as Problematic From Early Childhood Through Adolescence and Related Disorders	
Developmental Period	**Problem Behaviors**	**Related Disorders**
Early childhood	Noncompliance oppositional temper tantrums	Oppositional defiant disorder
Middle childhood	Overt/covert antisocial behavior relational aggression	Oppositional defiant disorder conduct disorder
Adolescence	Delinquency substance use high-risk sexual behavior	Conduct disorder

Adapted from Dishion and Patterson, 2006.

HENRY

Preschool Oppositional Behavior

Mrs. Sweet reported that her 3.5-year-old son, Henry, was causing problems. She viewed Henry as a normal, active, bright boy. However, she felt the need to talk with a professional because her friends and family had made some comments about Henry's escalating disruptive behavior.

Henry was the older of two children and had a 9-month-old sister. Mrs. Sweet's responses to initial questionnaires indicated that she perceived Henry as engaging in a significant amount of disruptive behavior but the behavior was not problematic to her. The mother's log of the past week contained descriptions of inappropriate behaviors such as: "Henry hit his grandfather on the shin with a baseball bat" and "Henry scraped a knife across the kitchen wall."

Mr. Sweet did not attend the initial interview because he saw the difficulty as primarily "my wife's problem." Mrs. Sweet indicated that Henry's developmental milestones were within normal limits but that from birth Henry had been a "difficult" child. Henry spent three mornings a week at a preschool and these were problem-free. The teachers initially reported, however, that they had to be rather "firm" in their expectations. When Henry was invited to spend time with friends in their homes things went well. Difficulties were reported when friends visited him—his behavior was described as very active, getting into things that were forbidden, and in general creating chaos. Henry's father often took Henry on full-day outings and thoroughly enjoyed this time. Mr. Sweet felt that his wife should be firmer with Henry. Mrs. Sweet described the major problems as "not listening," "refusing to do as requested," and "talking back." All of these occurred primarily with her, but were beginning to occur with other people in the family.

According to Mrs. Sweet, on a typical day Henry managed routine events such as eating and bathing easily. However, when any demands were placed on him, he would refuse to comply. To avoid confrontations, Mrs. Sweet spent much of her time rearranging her schedule, but this was becoming increasingly difficult as her 9-month-old demanded more of her attention.

Henry came to a clinic-observation session wearing an army camouflage outfit, cowboy hat, and boots, and carrying two six-shooters and a toy machine gun. He greeted the clinician with "I'm going to shoot your eyes out." The clinician responded with a firm "We don't talk like that in my office." Henry quickly responded in a contrite voice, "Oh, I'm sorry." Observation of parent–child interaction indicated that Mrs. Sweet gave Henry a high rate of noncontingent positive reinforcement, placed many demands on him, and tried to get compliance through reasoning. Henry placed many demands on his mother and rarely complied with her requests. Henry and his mother seemed to enjoy playing together. Henry refused to comply with his mother's requests to pick up the toys; however, he readily complied with the clinician's requests to clean up the toys.

A recommendation was made that both parents attend classes on child development and management. Both parents and Henry were also involved in treatment sessions to increase positive parent–child interactions, to set age-appropriate limits, to increase Henry's compliance, and to determine a consistent method of discipline. This parent training program was carried out over a 6-week period with two follow-up appointments. After treatment, Henry was still described as "headstrong"; however, both parents felt that his behavior was acceptable and for the most part easily managed.

Adapted from Schroeder & Gordon, 2002, pp. 374–376.

The diagnosis of **Antisocial Personality Disorder (APD)** is included in this grouping of disorders, and also is included among the Personality Disorders. The diagnosis of APD may be applied to individuals who display a persistent pattern of aggressive and antisocial behavior after the age of 18. APD is characterized by "a pattern of disregard for, and violation of, the rights of others" (American Psychiatric Association [APA], 2000).

This pattern is often accompanied by multiple illegal and aggressive behaviors. The diagnosis of APD requires that the pattern be present since the age of 15 with evidence that the individual did meet, or would have met, the criteria for Conduct Disorder with an onset before 15 years of age.

We will concentrate our discussion on oppositional defiant disorder and conduct disorder.

DSM Approach: Oppositional Defiant Disorder

Children and adolescents are often stubborn, do not comply with requests or directions, and in a variety of ways exhibit oppositional behavior. The case of Henry illustrates that not all such behavior is indicative or predictive of clinical problems. Indeed, perhaps particularly for older children and adolescents, appropriate and skilled assertions of autonomy may be desirable and may facilitate development (Johnston & Ohan, 1999). It is the less skilled and excessive oppositional and defiant behavior that may indicate present or future problems.

Oppositional Defiant Disorder (ODD) is described by a pattern of symptoms that the DSM groups into three clusters: angry/irritable mood, argumentative/defiant behavior, and vindictiveness. In order to receive a diagnosis of ODD a young person must *frequently* (beyond what is normative for the youth's age, gender, and culture) display at least four of the symptoms listed below.

1. loses temper
2. easily annoyed/touchy
3. angry and resentful
4. argues with adults/authority figures
5. refuses to comply with or defies adult's requests or does not follow rules
6. deliberately annoys others
7. blames others for own mistakes or bad behavior
8. spiteful or vindictive

The symptoms must be present for a period of at least 6 months and the frequency of mood or behavioral symptom occurrence required for a diagnosis varies by developmental level. For children younger than 5 years of age these symptoms must occur on most days, whereas for youths 5 years or older the symptoms must occur at least once a week. A lesser frequency is required for the spiteful or vindictive behavior criteria—at least twice within the 6-month period. Diagnosticians are also asked to specify the severity of ODD symptoms as mild (occur in only one setting—most frequently the home), moderate (some symptoms present in two settings), or severe (some symptoms present in three or more settings) (APA, 2013).

By grouping the symptoms of ODD, the DSM highlights that the criteria for ODD contain both emotional/mood (e.g., angry) and behavioral (e.g., argues) indicators. It is suggested that youths often display the behavioral features of ODD without the problems of negative mood. However, youths diagnosed with ODD who do display the negative mood features typically exhibit the behavioral symptoms as well. There is some suggestion that both the emotional and behavioral symptoms of ODD contribute to the prediction of later disruptive/externalizing disorders. However, the emotional symptoms of ODD may also contribute uniquely to the prediction of later internalizing disorders (Stringaris & Goodman, 2009).

In considering a diagnosis of Oppositional Defiant Disorder it is important to distinguish problem level behaviors and emotional reactions from expected levels of opposition and assertiveness. Thus, a behavior or emotional reaction must be judged to occur more frequently than is typical for a young person of comparable age. Furthermore, in order to make a diagnosis of ODD the oppositional defiant behaviors and emotional reactions must cause distress for the youth or others or result in meaningful impairment in the young person's social, academic, or other important area of functioning.

Oppositional and noncompliant mood and behavior is clearly a common problem, particularly during preschool age and again during adolescence (Coie & Dodge, 1998; Loeber et al., 2000). Although similar mood and behavior is prevalent among non-clinic children as early as preschool, clinical level oppositional-defiant mood and behavior should be distinguished from normative problem behaviors. Diagnosis should therefore require high levels of such problems. Noncompliance represents a practical problem for parents, teachers, and clinicians. Also, high levels of noncompliant, stubborn, and oppositional behavior may represent for some youngsters the earliest steps on a developmental path of persistent antisocial behavior and other difficulties (Loeber, Burke, & Pardini, 2009b). The appropriateness of the ODD diagnosis thus rests on a balance between "overdiagnosing" common problems of children and adolescents as disorders versus ignoring potential serious problems that also may be early precursors of persistent antisocial behaviors or other problems.

DSM Approach: Conduct Disorder

The diagnosis of **Conduct Disorder** represents more seriously aggressive and antisocial behaviors. Indeed, the violence and property destruction characteristic of many of these behaviors may considerably impact individuals, families, and communities. Nonaggressive conduct-disordered behaviors (e.g., truancy, theft) also can result in considerable harm.

The essential feature of the diagnosis of conduct disorder is a repetitive and persistent pattern of behavior that violates both the basic rights of others and major age-appropriate societal norms. The 15 criteria used by the DSM to define the disorder are organized into the following four categories:

• Aggression to people and animals
• Destruction of property

- Deceitfulness or theft
- Serious violations of rules

The aggression category includes behaviors such as bullying, physical fights, use of a weapon, physical cruelty to people or animals, stealing while confronting a victim, and forced sexual activity. In the non-aggressive property destruction category a differentiation is made between destruction of property by fire setting versus some other means. The deceitfulness or theft grouping includes breaking into someone else's house, building, or car; lying to avoid obligations or obtain good or favors; and stealing without confronting the victim. The serious violation of rules grouping includes staying our at night despite parental prohibitions (beginning before age 13), running away from home, and school truancy (beginning before age 13). The diagnosis of Conduct Disorder requires that three or more of these behaviors be present during the past 12 months, with at least one of them present in the past 6 months. Also the behavior must cause clinically meaningful impairment in social or academic functioning (American Psychiatric Association [APA], 2013).

Subtypes of conduct disorder are described based on the age of onset. A diagnosis of Childhood-Onset or Adolescent-Onset is made based on whether one or more of the criterion behaviors had an onset prior to age 10. If there is insufficient information regarding age of onset, an "Unspecified Onset" may be indicated. The diagnostician may also specify the severity as mild, moderate, or severe based on the number of conduct problems and the degree of harm that they cause to others. In addition, the diagnostician may specify if the youth being diagnosed with a conduct disorder has what is termed limited prosocial emotions—lack of guilt, lack of empathy, lack of concern about poor school or other performance, shallow or deficient feelings or emotions (American Psychiatric Association [APA], 2013). These qualities, which have also been described as "callous unemotional traits," are described further in our discussion of the developmental course of conduct problems (see Accent: Callous-Unemotional Traits, p.192).

The symptoms included in the DSM criteria for Conduct Disorder include diverse behaviors. Because only three symptoms are required for a diagnosis, the diagnosis of Conduct Disorder may represent a heterogeneous group of youths with different subtypes of conduct disorder. Such heterogeneity may be of particular concern for research investigations.

There are a number of concerns regarding the conduct disorder diagnosis (Moffitt et al., 2008). (See Accent: "Are Conduct Problems a Mental Disorder") For example, most research regarding conduct disorder has focused on school-age children and adolescents. The DSM indicates that the onset of conduct disorders typically occurs during middle childhood and adolescence. Thus, current criteria may not be applicable to younger children. Yet research also suggests that such problem behavior begins early and persistent problems might be prevented with early intervention. Some have suggested modification of the DSM criteria so that they become more applicable to preschool children (Wakschlag & Danis, 2009). One of the challenges in undertaking such an effort would be to be able to discriminate between conduct problem behaviors that are very common in this age group and more serious behaviors that might be predictive of longer-term and more persistent difficulties.

In a similar fashion, concerns have been raised as to whether current conduct disorder criteria are equally applicable to both sexes. As we will see conduct disorder is diagnosed more frequently in boys (a ration of 3:1 or 4:1). Some have questioned whether this represents a true sex difference in prevalence or is due to bias in the diagnostic criteria. Indeed, the DSM does not contain sex-specific criteria. The forms of aggression included in the DSM criteria may be more characteristic of boys, and girls may be more likely to display relational aggression (see p. 184) than physical aggression. Findings that girls with subclinical levels of conduct disorder symptoms go on to develop clinically significant problems also raises concerns about the adequacy with which criteria capture conduct disorder in females. Continuing to include girls in research on conduct disorder will help inform decisions regarding the development of diagnostic criteria.

Empirically Derived Syndromes

The DSM diagnoses represent a categorical approach to externalizing problems. As with other problems, there is considerable evidence suggesting the benefit of conceptualizing externalizing problems in a dimensional rather than categorical manner (Walton, Ormel, & Krueger, 2011). An alternative dimensional approach to disruptive behavior problems does exist. As we saw in chapter 5, an empirically derived syndrome involving aggressive, oppositional, destructive, and antisocial behavior has been identified in numerous studies. This syndrome is frequently referred to as **externalizing**. It is robust in that it emerges employing a variety of measures, reporting agents, and settings. There have been efforts to distinguish narrower groupings within this broad externalizing syndrome.

Achenbach and Rescorla (2001), for example, have described two syndromes, **aggressive behavior** (e.g., argues a lot, destroys things, is disobedient, fights) and **rule-breaking behavior** (e.g., breaks rules, lies, steals, is

ACCENT
Are Conduct Problems a Mental Disorder?

The diagnosis of Conduct Disorder is frequently part of the controversy over what constitutes psychopathology or mental disorder (Hinshaw & Lee, 2003; Richters & Cicchetti, 1993). Richters and Cicchetti addressed this question in part by asking if Mark Twain's characters of Tom Sawyer and Huckleberry Finn suffered from a mental disorder. As these authors point out, the two boys engaged in a sustained pattern of antisocial behavior that would warrant a diagnosis of conduct disorder—lying, stealing, aggression, truancy, running away, cruelty to animals. The boys were judged by the townspeople in social–moral terms and opinions were mixed as to whether, at heart, they were good or bad boys.

The question of what constitutes a conduct disorder is complex. One issue is whether it is appropriate to place the locus of the deviant behavior entirely within the individual and ignore the social/cultural context. As can be seen from the following excerpt the DSM acknowledges this issue:

> Conduct Disorder diagnosis may at times be potentially misapplied to individuals in settings where patterns of disruptive behavior are viewed as near-normative (e.g., in very threatening, high-crime areas or war zones). Therefore, the context in which the undesirable behavior occurred should be considered (APA, 2013, p. 474).

How to determine whether a youth's behavior is a reaction to a specific cultural environment or an indication of individual psychopathology is a considerable challenge. Clinicians and researchers must be sensitive and aware of both typical development and the real impact of poverty, stress, and violent communities on the development of antisocial behavior.

truant), within the broader externalizing syndrome. The behaviors that are characteristic of these two syndromes are listed in Table 8.2. Youths may exhibit one or both types of problems. The validity of this distinction is supported by a variety of research findings (Achenbach & Rescorla, 2001). For example, research suggests a higher degree of heritability for the aggressive than for the rule-breaking syndrome (Edelbrock et al., 1995). Developmental differences also exist between the two syndromes. In a longitudinal analysis, Stanger, Achenbach, and Verhulst (1997) found that the average scores of the two syndromes declined between ages 4 and 10. After age 10, however, the scores on the aggressive syndrome continued to decline, whereas scores on the rule-breaking syndrome (previously called delinquent) increased. These findings are illustrated in Figure 8.1. These same authors also found that the stability (the similarity of a particular individual's behavior at two points in time) was higher for the aggressive than for the rule-breaking (delinquent) syndrome. These and other findings suggest that it is important to distinguish between types of externalizing/conduct disorder problems.

Empirical approaches to classifying conduct disorders also suggest other ways of grouping problem behaviors within this broad category. These approaches are not mutually exclusive and indeed do overlap with the aggressive/rule-breaking distinction and with each other. Some approaches suggest a distinction based on *age of onset*: a later-onset or adolescent-onset category consisting principally of nonaggressive and rule-breaking behaviors, and an early-onset category that includes these behaviors as well as aggressive behaviors. The *salient symptom* approach is based on the primary behavior problem being displayed. Distinguishing antisocial children whose primary problem is aggression from those whose primary problem is stealing is an example. It may be particularly important to single out aggressive behavior in this way. There is support for distinguishing aggression from other conduct-disordered behavior on the basis of its social impact, correlates, gender differences, and developmental course (Loeber & Stouthamer-Loeber, 1998).

Expansion of the salient symptom distinction suggests a broader distinction (Dishion & Patterson, 2006; Loeber & Schmaling, 1985) between **overt**, confrontational antisocial behaviors (e.g., fighting, temper tantrums), and **covert**, or concealed, antisocial behaviors (e.g., fire setting, stealing, truancy). A further expansion suggests that in addition to the overt–covert distinction, one might also consider a distinction between destructive and nondestructive conduct behavior problems (Frick, 1998). Examples of antisocial behaviors that are overt and destructive include aggression, cruelty to animals, fighting, assault, and bullying. Some overt antisocial behaviors may be nondestructive, for example, stubborn, oppositional, or defiant behavior, temper tantrums, and arguing are overt, but nondestructive. Examples of antisocial behaviors that are covert and destructive include lying and property damaging behaviors such as stealing, fire setting, and vandalism. And, finally, status offenses such as running away from home and truancy and substance use

TABLE 8.2	Behaviors from the Aggressive and Rule-Breaking Syndromes

Aggressive Behavior	Rule-Breaking Behavior
Argues a lot	Drinks alcohol
Defiant	Lacks guilt
Mean to others	Breaks rules
Demands attention	Bad friends
Destroys own things	Lies, cheats
Destroys others' things	Prefers older kids
Disobedient at home	Runs away
Disobedient at school	Sets fires
Gets in fights	Sex problems
Attacks people	Steals at home
Screams a lot	Swearing
Explosive	Thinks of sex too much
Easily frustrated	Tardy
Stubborn, sullen	Uses tobacco
Mood changes	Truant
Sulks	Uses drugs
Suspicious	Vandalism
Teases a lot	
Temper	
Threatens others	
Loud	

Items listed are summaries of the actual content (wording) of items on the instruments. Most items are included in the Child Behavior Checklist (CBCL), Teacher Report Form (TRF), and Youth Self Report (YSR) versions of these syndromes, whereas others are specific to one or two of these instruments. Adapted from Achenbach & Rescorla, 2001.

are examples of antisocial behaviors that are covert and nondestructive. The various ways of distinguishing among conduct-disordered behaviors continue to be explored in the context of an empirical and a developmental approach to understanding conduct problems.

Gender Differences: Relational Aggression

Gender differences exist in prevalence, developmental course, and the influences that contribute to the development of conduct problems (Crick & Zahn-Waxler, 2003; van Lier et al., 2007b). Perhaps the most basic aspect of gender differences is the way that conduct problems are expressed in boys and girls. Much of the research on conduct disorders has been based on male samples. We saw earlier (p. 88) how focusing on one gender can influence estimates of prevalence of a disorder and how a disorder is defined.

It is frequently reported that boys exhibit significantly higher levels of aggression than do girls. Is this because girls are less aggressive? Crick and colleagues (Crick & Grotpeter, 1995; Crick & Zahn-Waxler, 2003) started with a general definition of aggression as intent to hurt or harm others. They noted that during early and middle childhood peer interactions tended to be segregated by gender. This suggested that children's aggression would focus on social issues most salient in same-gender peer groups. In studying externalizing behaviors, aggression has generally been defined in terms of overt physical or verbal behaviors intended to hurt or harm others (e.g., hitting or pushing, threatening to beat up others). It was reasoned that this is consistent with the characteristics of instrumentality and physical dominance typical of boys during childhood. Girls, in contrast, are focused on developing close, dyadic relationships. It was thus hypothesized that girls' attempts to harm others may focus on relational issues—behaviors intended to damage another individual's feelings or friendships. Examples of such **relational aggression** include the following:

- purposefully leaving a child out of some play or other activity
- getting mad at another person and excluding the person from a peer group
- telling a person you will not like him or her unless he or she does what you say
- saying mean things or lying about someone so that others will not like the person (Crick & Grotpeter, 1996)

Relational aggression may fit within the realm of covert antisocial behavior (Dishion & Patterson, 2006) and is found from preschool age through adolescence (Crick, Casas, & Ku, 1999; Prinstein, Boergers, & Vernberg, 2001). Moreover, relational aggression is associated with peer rejection, depression, anxiety, and feelings of loneliness and isolation (Crick, Casas, & Mosher, 1997; Crick & Grotpeter, 1995; Crick & Nelson, 2002).

Thus, it appears important to broadly define aggression. For one thing, a sole focus on physical aggression might fail to identify aggressive girls. Crick and Grotpeter (1995) found that over 80% of aggressive girls would not have been identified by a definition limited to physical aggression. The concept of relational aggression challenges the view that girls are nonaggressive and suggests caution

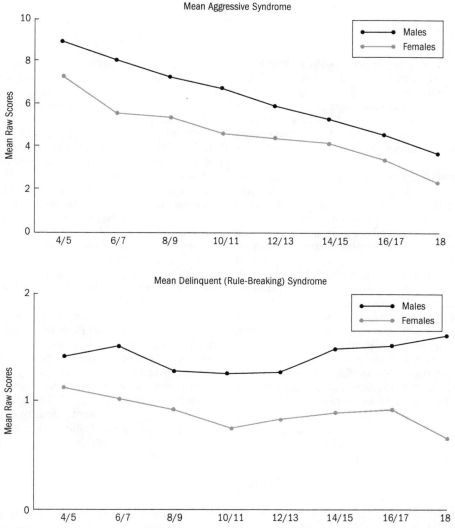

FIGURE 8.1 Mean aggressive and delinquent (rule-breaking) syndrome scores by age for males and females. *Adapted from Stanger, Achenbach, & Verhulst, 1997.*

in making non-gender-specific interpretations of findings (Javdani, Sadeh, & Verona, 2011).

Violence

The problem of youth and violence is a major concern (Margolin & Gordis, 2000; Reppucci, Woolard, & Fried, 1999). **Violence** is typically defined as an extreme form of physical aggression. Violence might be defined as aggressive acts that cause serious harm to others, such as aggravated assault, rape, robbery, and homicide, whereas aggression might be defined as acts that inflict less serious harm (Loeber & Stouthamer-Loeber, 1998).

Thus much of what we discuss throughout this chapter regarding aggressive and conduct-problem behavior applies to violence as well. However, additional factors may influence the development of violence, and there may be different needs for the prevention and treatment of violent behavior.

When one speaks about youth violence, there are at least two concerns. First, there is the concern regarding youth as perpetrators of violent acts. Although rates of violent offenses by juveniles have dropped considerably since the late 1990s, an appreciable number of youths are involved in violent behavior. For example, nearly 15% of arrests for violent crimes in the United States involve a

ACCENT
Fire Setting

Youth under age 15 account for about 44% of arrests for arson in the United States (U.S. Department of Justice, 2010) and for similar or higher percentages in other countries (Lambie & Randell, 2011). Fire setting produces serious damage in terms of loss of life, injury, posttraumatic symptoms, and property damage. It is associated with serious difficulties for the youth, family, and community (Kolko, 2005).

Child and adolescent fire setters are a heterogeneous group of youths. Therefore, there are attempts to subtype juvenile fire setters (Kolko, 2002; Lambie & Randell, 2011). For example, youths might be viewed as differing in their motivation for fire setting. Some young fire setters may have an unusual interest and involvement with fire, perhaps in the context of inadequate supervision. It is suggested that for other youth fire setting is motivated by attention seeking—a "cry for help." For others, fire setting may be part of a larger picture of more general psychopathology. Fire setters might also be subtyped based on the severity and persistence of fire setting behavior, and whether such behavior is associated with high levels of family dysfunction and broader youth psychopathology.

It seems clear, however, that for a large proportion of juvenile fire setters, this behavior is associated with the presence of other antisocial behavior. Fire setting represents a behavior that would be described as covert. Thus, fire setting may be seen as part of a cluster of covert antisocial behaviors that include destruction of property, stealing, lying, and truancy. In fact, among both community and clinically referred youths, level of covert antisocial behavior predicted later fire setting (Kolko et al., 2001).

Although only a relatively small proportion of youths with conduct problems engage in fire setting, these youngsters are likely to display more severe conduct problems (MacKay et al., 2006). Indeed, even among those youth with serious antisocial behavior, antisocial fire setters display more extreme antisocial behavior. Fire setters are at increased risk for later juvenile court referral and arrest for a violent crime beyond what would be predicted by the presence of conduct disorder (Becker et al., 2004).

The factors that may contribute to the development of fire setting in such youth appear similar to those that contribute to the development of conduct-disordered behavior in general. These factors include aspects of the youth (e.g., aggression, impulsivity), parents (e.g., lack of involvement, poor monitoring of the child), and family (e.g., conflict, stressful life events). Fire setters may be exposed to a greater number and a more extreme form of the risk factors that have been described for conduct disorders in general (McCarty, McMahon, & Conduct Problems Prevention Research Group, 2005). For example, child fire setters were more likely to come from homes with marital violence and to have fathers who drank and abused pets (Becker et al., 2004). Also, Kazdin and Kolko (1986) found poorer marital adjustment and higher levels of psychological difficulties—depression in particular—among mothers of fire setters compared with mothers of non-fire setters.

---

juvenile offender. Specifically, juveniles accounted for approximately 10% of arrests for murder, 15% for rape, 25% for robbery, and 12% for aggravated assault (U.S. Department of Justice, 2010).

The second concern is that young people are frequent victims of violence. Young people exposed to violence also are at significant risk. Part of this exposure is contact with violent peers, but youth also are exposed to violence by adults and in a number of other ways, including watching television, seeing movies, and playing video games. If one also includes in this number youths who are physically abused, who witness domestic violence, and who reside in neighborhoods with high rates of violence, the picture is even more troubling.

Youths chronically exposed to violence may suffer abnormal neurological development and dysregulation in the biological systems that are involved in arousal and managing stress (Gordis et al., 2006). These changes can have far-reaching psychological and physical consequences

(Margolin & Gordis, 2000). Young people exposed to violence, either as victims or as witnesses, are at increased risk for developing aggressive, antisocial, and other externalizing problems. But they are also at risk for developing internalizing difficulties such as anxiety, depression, and somatic symptoms (Gordis, Margolin, & John, 2001; Schwab-Stone et al., 1999).

Schools are one arena given considerable attention with regard to violence. Concern exists about students bringing dangerous weapons to school and about the high rate of violence in schools (Snyder & Sickmund, 2006). In the wake of several highly publicized incidents, schools and communities felt pressure to reduce the risk of violence and to protect their schoolchildren. Changes in school procedures were implemented to increase security, educational efforts were initiated to increase student awareness and to emphasize nonviolent social problem-solving strategies, and pressure was exerted to provide additional services to students at risk for committing violent acts.

Although the intense media attention on dramatic school incidents increased community awareness and efforts, it probably also contributed to other actions that may be somewhat more controversial. These include the installation of metal detectors in schools, instructions by some school administrators for students to report any strange behavior by their peers, and a variety of similar policies. Although there is reason for concern about school violence, it is unclear whether there has been a drastic increase in rates of violence in schools, and some of the actions that have been taken have had negative effects on young people. It also has been noted that only a small percentage of youth violence takes place on school grounds and that the rate of violent crimes committed by youth remains low during the school day but spikes at the close of the school day (Snyder & Sickmund, 2006). School violence should therefore probably be considered and addressed with an appreciation of violence in the larger community and society. Also, programs to reduce violence in schools should do so in a manner that creates a school atmosphere that facilitates the overall development of young people while ensuring their safety.

Bullying

Many people are familiar with the problem of bullying either through personal experience or through literature, television, or movies. Interest in this topic was generated by the work of Olweus (1993; 1994) in Scandinavia and by media attention following incidents of school violence in which bullying was implicated.

Bullying is characterized by an imbalance of power and involves intentionally and repeatedly causing fear, distress, or harm to someone who has difficulty defending him- or herself. Estimates of the incidence of bullying depend, in part, on definitions employed. Bullying begins to emerge in the preschool years and is common among elementary school children (Hay, Payne, & Chadwick, 2004; Schwartz et al., 1997). Research findings across many countries suggest that between about 9 and 54% of children are involved in bullying (Craig et al., 2009; Nansel et al., 2004). Data from a sample of over 15,000 youths throughout the United States suggest the scope of the problem during middle school and beyond (Nansel et al., 2001). Students in grades 6 through 10 reported involvement in bullying. About 30% reported moderate or frequent involvement (about 13% as a bully, 11% as a victim, and 6% as both). Frequency of bullying was higher for 6th graders through 8th graders than among students in the 9th and 10th grades. These rates are consistent with other findings (Ball et al., 2008). In general, there is a decrease with age in the percentage of youths who report being bullied (Craig et al., 2009; Kumpulainen, Räsänen, & Henttonen, 1999; Wolke et al., 2000). Reports of increasing

Bullying among boys is often characterized by physical aggression and intimidation.

use of the Internet to bully, intimidate, and embarrass victims suggest that these figures may underestimate the prevalence of bullying (David-Ferdon & Hertz, 2007). A youth's genetic endowments, as well as environmental influences, contribute to which children become bullies, victims, or both bully and victim (Ball et al., 2008; Shakoor et al., 2011).

Males were more likely than females to be involved as both perpetrators and victims. Boys are exposed to more direct open attacks than are girls. Indirect bullying can occur in the form of spreading of rumors, manipulation of friendship relationships, and social isolation. This form of bullying may be harder to detect. Girls are exposed more to this subtle form of bullying than to open attacks. Boys, however, may be exposed to this indirect bullying at rates comparable to that of girls.

The typical bully is described by Olweus (1994) as being highly aggressive to both peers and adults; having a more positive attitude toward violence than students in general; being impulsive; having a strong need to dominate others; having little empathy toward victims; and, if a boy, being physically stronger than average. Not all highly aggressive youths are bullies. Differences between bullies and other aggressive young people and the processes that underlie bullying remain to be clarified.

The typical victim is more anxious and insecure than other students, and is cautious, sensitive, quiet, nonaggressive, and suffering from low self-esteem. If victims are boys, they are likely to be physically weaker. This so-called submissive, nonassertive style often seems to precede being selected as a victim (Schwartz, Dodge, & Coie, 1993). Also, victims often do not have a single good friend in their class. The protective importance of having a friend, especially a popular one, was illustrated in an interview with Eric Crouch, the 2001 Heisman Trophy winner as the outstanding college football player:

"What'll it be, Tyler—your lunch money or heaps of verbal abuse?"

HENRY

A Victim of Bullying

Henry was a quiet and sensitive 13-year old. For several years he had been harassed and attacked occasionally by some of his classmates.... During the past couple of months, the attacks had become more frequent and severe.

Henry's daily life was filled with unpleasant and humiliating events. His books were pushed from his desk, his tormentors broke his pencils and threw things at him, they laughed loudly and scornfully when he occasionally responded to the teacher's questions. Even in class, he was often called by his nickname, the "Worm."

As a rule, Henry did not respond; he just sat there expressionless at his desk, passively waiting for the next attack. The teacher usually looked in another direction when the harassment went on. Several of Henry's classmates felt sorry for him but none of them made a serious attempt to defend him.

A month earlier, Henry had been coerced, with his clothes on, into a shower. His two tormentors had also threatened him several times to give them money and steal cigarettes for them. One afternoon, after having been forced to lie down in the drain of the school urinal, Henry quietly went home, found a box of sleeping pills, and swallowed a handful. Henry's parents found him unconscious but alive on the sofa in the living room. A note on his desk told them that he couldn't stand the bullying any more, he felt completely worthless, and believed the world would be a better place without him.

Adapted from Olweus, 1993, pp. 49–50.

It was a source of pride to his mother...that as a popular grade school kid, Eric often befriended students whom others teased. "I talk to them, become friends with them," he would tell his mother, "and they didn't get teased anymore." (Murphy, 2001, p. 64)

In addition to warding off victimization, support from a close friend may buffer the effects of victimization (Prinstein et al., 2001).

It is clearly important to address the bully–victim problem. Bullying may be part of a more general antisocial, conduct-disordered developmental pattern, and thus bullies are at risk for continuing behavior problems. Indeed, Olweus (1994) reports that 60% of boys classified as bullies in grades six through nine were convicted of at least one officially registered crime by age 24 and that 35 to 40% of former bullies had three or more convictions by this age, compared with only 10% of control boys.

The consequences for the victims of bullying also suggest the importance of intervening early. Repeated victimization is likely to be highly stressful and have appreciable negative consequences for some youth. For example, Sugden et al. (2010) found that some children may be particularly predisposed to experience the consequences of bullying. A particular variant of the serotonin transporter (5-HTT) gene is associated with greater risk of emotional disturbance after exposure to stressful events. Children who are bullied frequently and who had this particular variation of the 5-HTT genotype were more likely to exhibit emotional problems at age 12 than were frequently bullied children with other genotypes, even when controlling for pre-victimization emotional problems and other risk factors. Victims of bullying experience a variety of negative outcomes, particularly depression and loneliness (Hawker & Boulton, 2000).

The victims of bullying form a large group of youths whom, to a great extent, may be ignored by school personnel, and whose parents may be relatively unaware of the problem (Shakoor et al., 2011). One can imagine the effects of going through years of school in a state of fear, anxiety, and insecurity. Some of these young people may, indeed, be at increased risk for suicide (Winsper et al., 2012). A case described by Olweus (Henry) illustrates the pain that youngsters may suffer.

EPIDEMIOLOGY

Conduct problems are one of the most frequently occurring child and adolescent difficulties. Exact prevalence is difficult to establish, due to a number of methodological and definitional factors (Essau, 2003; Loeber et al., 2000). Investigations employing DSM criteria suggest rates for ODD between about 1 and 15% with an average of 3.3%, and rates for CD between about 2 and 10% with a median of 4% (American Psychiatric Association [APA], 2013; Canino et al., 2004; Fleitlich-Bilyk & Goodman, 2004; Ford, Goodman, & Meltzer, 2003; Kessler et al., 2009; Lavigne et al., 2009). A retrospective report of a large nationally representative sample of U.S. adults suggests a lifetime prevalence of ODD during childhood and adolescence of 10.2% (Nock et al., 2007).

Gender, Age, and Context

Conduct disorders are more commonly diagnosed in boys than in girls; a ratio of about 3:1 or 4:1 is typically cited. The DSM definition of conduct disorder, however, may emphasize "male" expressions of aggression (e.g., physical aggression). Thus conduct disorder may be underestimated in girls. Higher rates of ODD are also reported in boys. However, the degree of sex difference for ODD remains unclear and the applicability of the DSM criteria to girls has been questioned (Loeber et al., 2000; Maughan et al., 2004; Waschbusch & King, 2006). Sex and age differences in the prevalence of ODD and CD, based on a nationally representative sample in Great Britain (Maughan et al., 2004), are illustrated in Figure 8.2.

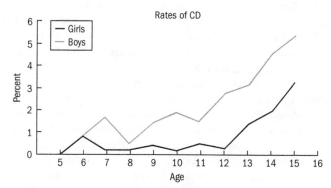

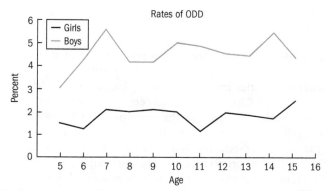

FIGURE 8.2 Rates of conduct disorder (CD) and oppositional defiant disorder (ODD) by age and sex. *Adapted from Maughan et al., 2004.*

An increasing prevalence of conduct disorder with age is often reported for both boys and girls and there is some suggestion that, due to particular risk for girls in the period around puberty, the gender ratio narrows temporarily in the mid-teens (Maughan et al., 2004; Moffitt et al., 2001). Some reports suggest a decline in oppositional defiant disorder with age, but findings are inconsistent and may be affected by existing diagnostic practices (Maughan et al., 2004; Weyandt, Verdi, & Swentosky, 2011).

Ethnic and socioeconomic differences are often reported. However, Roberts and colleagues (2006) examined the presence of a disruptive disorder or ADHD in African American, European American, and Mexican American youth, ages 11–17 years, and found no differences in prevalence for the combined problem category. Contextual factors such as poverty and the stress of high-crime neighborhoods are thought to increase the risk for conduct-disordered behavior. Greater prevalence is reported in urban than in rural environments (Canino et al., 2004; Fleitlich-Bilyk & Goodman, 2004). Also, official records often indicate greater delinquency among lower class and minority youths and in neighborhoods characterized by high crime rates. Such differences may be due to selection of certain groups for prosecution, suggesting that definitions other than official records should be considered. However, estimates based on alternative methods, such as self-report, present other methodological difficulties. Although further documentation is needed, real associations between conduct-disordered behavior/delinquency and social class and neighborhoods probably do exist; however, they are probably more moderate than was once contended. The influence of these variables on child and adolescent conduct problem behavior is probably mediated by their impact on factors such as the ability of adults to parent effectively (Capaldi et al., 2002).

Patterns of Co-occurrence

Children and adolescents who receive one of the disruptive disorder diagnoses also frequently experience other difficulties and receive other diagnoses (American Academy of Child and Adolescent Psychiatry, 2007b). Most youths who receive the diagnosis of CD do meet the criteria for ODD. In the Developmental Trends Study of clinic-referred boys 7 to 12 years old, 96% of those who met criteria for CD also met criteria for ODD. The reported average age of onset was about 6 years for ODD and about 9 years for CD, suggesting that among boys with conduct disorder, this disorder is preceded by behaviors characteristic of oppositional defiant disorder and that these behaviors are "retained" as additional antisocial behaviors emerge. On the other hand, ODD does not always result in CD. Of the boys with ODD (but no CD) at the initial assessment, 75% had not progressed to CD 2 years later. About half of the boys with ODD at Year 1 continued to meet the criteria for ODD at Year 3, and about one quarter no longer met the criteria for ODD. Thus, although most cases of conduct disorder meet the criteria for oppositional defiant disorder, most youngsters with oppositional defiant behaviors do not progress to a conduct disorder.

There is also considerable co-occurrence of oppositional defiant disorder and conduct disorder with attention-deficit hyperactivity disorder (Waschbusch, 2002). Among children diagnosed with ADHD, it is estimated that between 35 and 70% develop ODD, and between 30 and 50% develop CD (Johnston & Ohan, 1999). When these disorders co-occur, ADHD seems to precede the development of the other disorders. It might be speculated that the impulsivity, inattention, and overactivity of ADHD present a particular parenting challenge. When parents' skills are limited, a pattern of noncompliant and aversive parent–child interactions may be set in motion (Patterson, DeGarmo, & Knutson, 2000). The challenges of parenting an ADHD child may thus play a role in the early onset of ODD behaviors and may continue over the course of development to maintain and exacerbate ODD/CD behaviors. Parent–child relationships are only one of the potential mechanisms whereby the presence of ADHD may increase the risk for ODD/CD. However, findings from a twin study suggest that although ADHD, ODD, and CD are each influenced by genetic and environmental factors, the covariation of the three disorders may be appreciably influenced by shared environmental factors (Burt et al., 2001). Such a finding is consistent with the potential contribution of parenting. Whatever factors contribute to the co-occurrence of these disorders, the co-occurrence of disruptive behavior disorders and ADHD may be one possible path toward more persistent and more severe conduct problems (Beauchaine & Neuhaus, 2008; Lahey, 2008).

In addition, youths with disruptive behavior disorders commonly experience a variety of other difficulties including substance use problems. Also, young aggressive children are frequently rejected by their peers (Parker et al., 2006). Youths with persistent conduct problems are also frequently described as having certain neurocognitive impairments and lower school achievement (Lahey, 2008; Maguin & Loeber, 1996). Verbal and language deficits, in particular, have been reported among community and clinical samples, as well as deficits in **executive functions** (higher order cognitive functions that play a role in information processing and problem solving) (Gilmour et al., 2004; Moffitt et al., 2001). How such difficulties and conduct disorders relate to each other is a complex issue that suggests a number of questions. In what ways do cognitive and language difficulties contribute to the development of conduct disorders? What is the relationship among these deficits, conduct disorder, and poor academic performance? To what extent are some of these deficiencies related to ADHD—are they characteristic of only the subset of youths with conduct disorder who also have ADHD?

Internalizing disorders also occur at higher than expected rates among youths with disruptive disorders (Loeber & Keenan, 1994; Loeber et al., 2000). Indeed, there is some suggestion that early co-occurrence of conduct and internalizing problems is associated with particularly high risk for negative long-term outcomes (Sourander et al., 2007). Estimates of the rate of co-occurrence of conduct problems and anxiety disorders vary widely. Also, the literature on the nature of the association between anxiety and conduct problems is unclear and often contradictory (Ford et al., 2003; Hinshaw & Lee, 2003; Lahey, 2008). A central question is whether anxiety increases or decreases the risk for conduct disordered behavior. In any event, the co-occurrence of anxiety and conduct problems is likely to be due to multiple influences (Gregory, Eley, & Plomin, 2004).

The co-occurrence of depression and conduct disorder is also clearly appreciable. Among a community sample of older adolescents, Lewinsohn, Rohde, and Seeley (1995b) found that a major depressive disorder co-occurred in 38% of youngsters with a disruptive behavior disorder (CD, ODD, or ADHD). In clinical samples, approximately 33% of children and adolescents have a co-occurrence of conduct and depressive disorders (Dishion, French, & Patterson, 1995). In community and clinic populations, boys show greater co-occurrence than girls (Dishion et al., 1995; Lewinsohn et al., 1995b). Numerous factors may help account for the frequent co-occurrence of conduct problems and depression. It may be that one disorder creates a risk for the other. For example, frequent failures and conflict experiences may contribute to depression in youth with conduct problems, the negative affect associated with oppositional behavior may predict later depression, or in some youth depression may be expressed as irritable, angry, antisocial behavior. Alternatively, the disorders may co-occur because of shared etiology including genetic and environmental influences.

DEVELOPMENTAL COURSE

Stability of Conduct Problems

An important aspect of conduct problems is their reported stability over time for at least some individuals (Lahey, 2008; Loeber, Burke, & Pardini, 2009a). Considerable evidence exists that the presence of early conduct-disordered behavior is related to the development of later aggressive and antisocial behavior and to a range of adverse psychological and social-emotional outcomes (Burke et al., 2005; Fergusson, Horwood, & Ridder, 2005a; 2008; Hiatt & Dishion, 2008).

However, the question of the stability or continuity of antisocial/conduct-disordered behavior is a complex one. It appears that some but not all youngsters continue to exhibit aggressive and antisocial behavior (Loeber et al., 2009a; NICHD Early Child Care Research Network, 2004) (see Accent: Callous-Unemotional Traits). The challenges are to describe patterns of both continuity and discontinuity, characterize shifts in the form that antisocial behaviors may take, and identify variables that influence the trajectory of antisocial behavior over time. Various ways of viewing developmental trajectories of conduct/antisocial problems have been proposed (Loeber et al., 2009a; Weyandt et al., 2011). We will examine two of these to illustrate thinking about developmental trajectories.

Age of Onset

Many studies have found that early age of onset is related to more serious and persistent antisocial behavior (Babinski, Hartsough, & Lambert, 1999; Fergusson & Woodward, 2000; Loeber & Farrington, 2000; Tolan & Thomas, 1995). A number of authors have proposed two distinct developmental patterns leading toward antisocial behavior, one with a childhood onset and the other with a late/adolescent onset (Hinshaw et al., 1993; Moffitt, 1993; 2006).

CHILDHOOD ONSET The **childhood-onset developmental pattern** fits with the notion of the stability of conduct-disordered behavior. Indeed, Moffitt (1993; 2006) terms this pattern "life-course persistent antisocial behavior." The child and adolescent literature and retrospective studies of antisocial adults are consistent with this picture of stable conduct-disordered behavior among particular groups of children and adolescents. It must be remembered, however, that a substantial number of children with an early onset of antisocial behavior do not persist on this pathway. The early-onset pathway is less common than the adolescent-onset

ACCENT
Callous-Unemotional Traits

We have seen that there have been efforts to identify subgroups of youth who display conduct disordered/antisocial behavior. Of particular interest are efforts to identify those youth who display an early start and life-course persistent pattern of extreme antisocial and aggressive behavior. Investigators have explored the notion of callous-unemotional traits as one way of potentially identifying such a subgroup of youth (Kahn et al., 2012) and DSM-5 has included "limited prosocial emotions" as a potential specification to the diagnosis of conduct disorder (see pg. 182).

Psychopathy is a characteristic associated with antisocial personality disorder and is described as a pattern of traits such as a lack of empathy; a deceitful, arrogant, manipulative interpersonal style; and an impulsive and irresponsible behavioral style. Psychopathy has been associated with a particularly severe and violent group of antisocial adults (Porter & Woodworth, 2006). Interest and debate regarding psychopathy in children and adolescents has also developed (Salekin, 2006). Much of this interest has centered on the notion of callous-unemotional traits.

What is meant by **callous-unemotional traits**? A dimension of problematic affective experiences has been consistently identified to be part of the description of the notion of psychopathy in adults. This dimension has been labeled as "callous-unemotional traits" (CU) and consists of attributes such as a lack of guilt, lack of empathy, and callous use of others for one's own gain. This concept has been extended to youth and measures have been developed to assess such traits in children and adolescents. Research suggests that the behaviors that define CU are sufficiently stable to warrant considering the idea of an individual "trait" that is stable across development and predictive of adult psychopathy (Byrd, Loeber, & Pardini, 2012; Frick & White, 2008). It should be noted, however, that while CU traits are relatively stable, the level of these traits does decrease in some portion of youth who initially score high on these attributes.

Research studies of children and adolescents have demonstrated that CU traits are associated with conduct problems, aggression, and delinquency. Of particular interest are findings that indicate that within samples of antisocial youth, CU traits are important in designating a group of such youth who are more aggressive, exhibit a more stable pattern of problem behavior, are more likely to have an early onset of delinquency, and are at increased risk for later antisocial and delinquent behavior. In addition, there is research consistent with the notion of different risk factors and different developmental processes than those described for other conduct-problem/antisocial youth (Frick & White, 2008; Pardini et al., 2012).

The idea of youth with stable CU traits being a distinct group of antisocial youth, for example, is supported by research indicating a substantial genetic influence on CU traits. Viding and colleagues (2005; 2008), for example, used participants from a large twin study to investigate the heritability of early-onset antisocial behavior in children at 7 and then again at 9 years of age. They found substantially greater heritability of early-onset antisocial behavior, at both points in time, among children high on CU than among those antisocial children low on CU traits.

Other research also has supported the idea that CU traits are associated with distinct characteristics that are distinguishable from general measures of conduct problems and antisocial behavior (Frick & White, 2008). These distinct characteristics include deficits in how negative emotional stimuli are processed; cognitive characteristics such as less sensitivity to punishment cues and more positive outcome expectancies in aggressive situations with peers; and personality attributes of fearlessness, thrill-seeking, and low levels of trait anxiety/neuroticism. Thus, such research suggests that there may be a subgroup of antisocial youth, described as having callous-unemotional traits, who have a particular temperamental style that leads to the development of distinct personality traits and the development of more persistent and severe aggressive and antisocial behaviors. It is important to remember, however, that influences are likely bidirectional. Thus, for example, the CU traits of a youth may affect how he or she is parented, but parenting likely also affects the developmental course of how CU traits are expressed (Hawes et al., 2011).

pattern (Hinshaw et al., 1993; Moffitt, 1993). Youths following this early-onset pattern are also more likely from preschool on to exhibit other problems, such as attention-deficit hyperactivity disorder, neurobiological, and neurocognitive deficits, and academic difficulties (Raine et al., 2005; van Goozen et al., 2007). These early difficulties may be the starting point for one

developmental pathway characterized by early onset and by persistent disruptive and antisocial behavior during childhood and adolescence. For some this pathway may lead to Antisocial Personality Disorder and other negative outcomes in adulthood (Fergusson, Horwood, & Ridder, 2005b; Maughan & Rutter, 1998; Moffitt et al., 2002).

Even though there is stability of problematic behavior for some youngsters with an early onset, antisocial behaviors exhibit qualitative change in the course of development. Hinshaw and colleagues (1993) describe the features of this heterotypic continuity of antisocial behavior:

> The preschooler who throws temper tantrums and stubbornly refuses to follow adult instructions becomes the child who also initiates fights with other children and lies to the teacher. Later, the same youth begins to vandalize the school, torture animals, break into homes, steal costly items, and abuse alcohol. As a young adult, he or she forces sex on acquaintances, writes bad checks, and has a chaotic employment and marital history. (p. 36)

Some individuals with a difficult temperament may have an even earlier onset: during infancy. However, better specification of the features of disruptive behavior among very young children and additional research are needed (Frick & Morris, 2004; Moffitt, 2006; Wakschlag & Danis, 2009).

ADOLESCENT ONSET   An **adolescent-onset developmental pattern** is illustrated in the Dunedin Multidisciplinary Health and Development Study (McGee et al., 1992). Prospective examination of a birth cohort of New Zealand youths revealed a large increase in the prevalence of nonaggressive conduct problems but no increase in aggressive behavior at age 15 compared with age 11. These young people were clearly exhibiting problem behavior; for example, they were as likely to be arrested for delinquent offenses as were childhood-onset delinquents. However, their offenses were less aggressive than those of childhood-onset delinquents. The majority of females were adolescent-onset cases, while males composed most of the conduct disorder cases at age 11. This rather common emergence during adolescence of nonaggressive antisocial behavior is contrasted to early-onset antisocial behavior.

The adolescent-onset pattern is the more common developmental pathway. Individuals who exhibit this pattern show little oppositional or antisocial behavior during childhood. During adolescence, they begin to engage in illegal activities, and although most exhibit only isolated antisocial acts, some engage in enough antisocial behavior to qualify for a diagnosis of conduct disorder. However, the antisocial behaviors are less likely to persist beyond adolescence and thus are sometimes termed *adolescent-limited* (Moffitt, 1993; 2006). Some of the youths do continue to have difficulties later in life. Experiences such as incarceration or disruption in education may contribute to more negative outcomes. However, these difficulties may not be as severe as the outcomes for the life-course-persistent individuals (Moffitt et al., 2002). It is important to determine which individuals discontinue and which persist or escalate their antisocial behavior as they enter adulthood, and to identify what accounts for these differences over time (Moffitt, 2006; White, Bates, & Buyske, 2001).

Developmental Paths

In addition to groupings of individuals by age of onset, much attention also has been given to the conceptualization of developmental progressions of conduct problems (e.g., Dodge, 2000; Farrington, 1986; Loeber et al., 1993; Patterson, DeBaryshe, & Ramsey, 1989). Loeber (1988) proposed a model that illustrates some of the attributes that might characterize the developmental course of conduct disorders within individuals. The model suggests that at each level, less serious behaviors precede more serious ones but that only some individuals progress to the next step. Progression on a developmental path is characterized by increasing diversification of antisocial behaviors. Children and adolescents who progress show new antisocial behaviors and may retain their previous behaviors rather than replacing them. Individuals may differ in their rate of progression.

LOEBER'S THREE-PATHWAY MODEL   Loeber and colleagues (1993; 2009a) have suggested a model that conceptualized antisocial behavior along multiple pathways. On the basis of a longitudinal study of inner-city youths, and following from distinctions between conduct problem behaviors described earlier, Loeber proposed a triple-pathway model (see Figure 8.3):

- an overt pathway starting with minor aggression, followed by physical fighting, followed by violence;
- a covert pathway starting with minor covert behaviors, followed by property damage, and then moderate to serious delinquency; and
- an authority conflict pathway prior to age 12, consisting of a sequence of stubborn behavior, defiance, and authority avoidance.

Individuals may progress along one or more of these pathways. As illustrated in Figure 8.5, entry into the authority conflict pathway typically begins earlier than entry into the other two pathways, and not all individuals who exhibit early behaviors on a particular pathway progress through the subsequent stages. The percentage

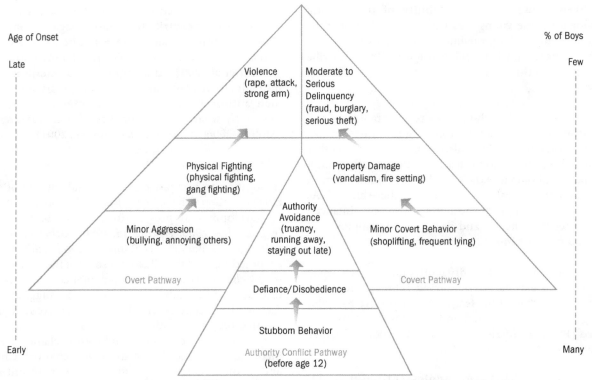

Age of Onset

Late

Violence
(rape, attack,
strong arm)

Moderate to
Serious
Delinquency
(fraud, burglary,
serious theft)

Physical Fighting
(physical fighting,
gang fighting)

Property Damage
(vandalism, fire setting)

Authority
Avoidance
(truancy,
running away,
staying out late)

Minor Aggression
(bullying, annoying others)

Minor Covert Behavior
(shoplifting, frequent lying)

Overt Pathway

Covert Pathway

Defiance/Disobedience

Stubborn Behavior

Early

Authority Conflict Pathway
(before age 12)

% of Boys

Few

Many

FIGURE 8.3 Three pathways to boys' problem behavior and delinquency. *Adapted from Loeber & Hay, 1994.*

of youngsters exhibiting behaviors characteristic of later stages of a pathway is less than those exhibiting earlier behaviors.

Investigators continue their efforts to describe the developmental pathways of antisocial, conduct-disordered behavior. At the same time, they also seek to identify the influences that first put youngsters on those pathways and that determine whether the antisocial behavior will continue or desist.

ETIOLOGY

The development of conduct problems is likely to involve the complex interplay of a variety of influences (Dishion & Patterson, 2006; Tremblay, 2010; Weyandt, Verdi, & Swentosky, 2011). Table 8.3, adapted from Loeber and Farrington (2000), provides a list of categories and examples of empirically validated risk factors for childhood aggression and later delinquency. Although such listings are informative, how the various influences come together in the development of conduct problems is quite complex. In our description we present influences in separate sections, but it is important to remember that causal explanations typically involve

transactional influences and multiple variations in the association of influences (Burke, Pardini, & Loeber, 2008; Lahey et al., 2008; Lee, 2011). While our emphasis will be on individual, relationship, and biological influences, the larger contexts in which these occur should not be ignored (Dishion & Patterson, 2006).

The Socioeconomic Context

Multiple findings suggest the importance of the larger social context. For example, the impact of poverty on oppositional and conduct problems has been demonstrated among several ethnic groups (Costello et al., 2003; Macmillan, McMorris, & Kruttschnitt, 2004) (see Accent: Moving Out of Poverty). Other influences that are associated with poverty, such as neighborhood context, also have received attention. Ingoldsby & Shaw (2002) consider the risk associated with residing in a disadvantaged community. Such neighborhoods are defined by a lack of economic and other resources, social disorganization, and racial division and tension. These factors are likely to increase the risk of exposure to neighborhood violence and involvement with neighborhood-based deviant peer groups, and thus lead to increased risk for early-onset antisocial

TABLE 8.3	Examples of Risk Factors for Child Aggression and Later Serious and Violent Juvenile Offending

Child Factors

Impulsive behavior

Hyperactivity (when co-occurring with disruptive behavior)

Early aggression

Early-onset disruptive behavior

Family Factors

Parental antisocial behavior

Parents' poor child-rearing practices

Parental neglect and abuse

Maternal depression

Low socioeconomic status

School Factors

Association with deviant siblings and peers

Rejection by peers

Neighborhood and Societal Factors

Neighborhood disadvantage and poverty

Disorganized neighborhood

Availability of weapons

Media portrayal of violence

Adapted from Loeber & Farrington, 2000.

behavior. Perceived discrimination has also been found to amplify the effect of contextual risks for African American youth (Brody et al., 2006). Socioeconomic and other disadvantages likely reflect a process in which adverse individual, family, school, and peer factors combine to increase a young person's chance of developing conduct problems (Chung & Steinberg, 2006; Fergusson, Swain-Campbell, & Horwood, 2004). It is also likely that positive family, peer and school influences can be protective and moderate the effects of disadvantage (Brody et al., 2006).

Aggression as a Learned Behavior

Aggression is a central part of the definition of conduct-disordered behavior and a common difficulty among nonreferred children. Children clearly may learn to be aggressive by being rewarded for such behavior (Patterson, 1976). Also, children may learn through imitation of aggressive models. They vicariously learn new and novel aggressive responses. Exposure to aggressive models also makes aggressive responses already in the child's repertoire more likely to occur—that is, disinhibition of aggression may occur. In addition, beyond learning-specific aggressive behaviors, young people may acquire general "scripts" for aggressive/hostile interpersonal behavior.

Children and adolescents certainly have ample opportunity to observe aggressive models. Parents who engage in physical aggression toward their spouses or

ACCENT
Moving Out of Poverty

Costello and colleagues (2003) report on what might be described as a natural experiment (see p. 72) that addresses the impact of poverty on conduct problems. The Great Smoky Mountains Study investigated the development of mental disorder and the need for mental health services for youth in North Carolina. Over several years data were collected from a sample of children, 25% of whom were American Indian. In the middle of the 8-year study, a casino opened on the Indian reservation that equally raised the income of all the American Indian families. This allowed a comparison of children whose families moved out of poverty, remained poor, or were never poor. Youngsters whose families moved out of poverty showed a significant decrease in symptoms, whereas no change occurred for the other children. The ex-poor children now exhibited nearly the same low rate of disorder as the never-poor, which was lower than that of the persistently poor. The effect was quite specific to oppositional and conduct problems rather than anxiety and depression. Further analysis suggested that the lessening of problems could be attributed to the family's having increased time to adequately supervise their offspring. An important aspect of this study is that the move out of poverty was not caused by characteristics of the families or the child—and so the findings could more clearly be attributed to the move from poverty itself.

who physically punish their children serve as models for aggressive behavior. In fact, children exhibiting excessive aggressive or antisocial behaviors are likely to have siblings, parents, and even grandparents with histories of conduct problems and records of aggressive and criminal behavior (Farrington, 1995; Huesmann et al., 1984; Waschbusch, 2002) and to have observed especially high rates of aggressive behavior in their homes (Kashani et al., 1992; Margolin, 1998; Patterson, DeBaryshe, & Ramsey, 1989). Aggression is also ubiquitous in television programs and in other media (Anderson et al., 2003; Bushman & Anderson, 2001).

Family Influences

The family environment can play an important role in the development of conduct-disordered behaviors. As indicated before, a high incidence of deviant or criminal behavior has been reported in families of youths with conduct problems. Longitudinal studies, in fact, suggest that such behavior is stable across generations (D'Onofrio et al., 2007; Glueck & Glueck, 1968; Huesmann et al., 1984). It seems, then, that conduct-disordered children may be part of a deviant family system. Numerous family variables have been implicated, including low family socioeconomic status, large family size, marital disruption, poor-quality parenting, parental abuse and neglect, and parental psychopathology (Dishion & Patterson, 2006; Patterson, Reid, & Dishion, 1992; Waschbusch, 2002). We highlight a few of these influences.

PARENT–CHILD INTERACTIONS AND NONCOMPLIANCE
The manner in which parents interact with their children contributes to the development of conduct-disordered behavior. Defiant, stubborn, and noncompliant behaviors are often among the first problems to develop in children. Given that these occur in both clinic and nonclinic families, what factors might account for the greater rates in some families? One possible factor is suggested by evidence that parents differ in both the number and the types of commands that they give. Parents of clinic-referred children issue more commands, questions, and criticisms. Also, prohibitions and commands that are presented in an unclear, angry, humiliating, or nagging manner are less likely to result in child compliance (Dumas & Lechowicz, 1989; Forehand et al., 1975; Kuczynski & Kochanska, 1995). Consequences that parents deliver also affect the child's noncompliant behavior (Brinkmeyer & Eyberg, 2003; Forehand & McMahon, 1981). A combination of negative consequences (time-out) for noncompliant behavior and rewards and attention for appropriate behavior seems to be related to increased levels of compliance.

THE WORK OF PATTERSON AND HIS COLLEAGUES
Gerald Patterson and his colleagues have created the Oregon Model—a developmental intervention model for families with aggressive antisocial children—based on a social interaction learning perspective (Forgatch & Patterson, 2010; Patterson et al., 1975; 1992; Reid, Patterson, & Snyder, 2002). Although this approach recognizes that characteristics of the child may play a role, the emphasis is on the social context.

> If we are to change aggressive childhood behavior, we must change the environment in which the child lives. If we are to understand and predict future aggression, our primary measures will be of the social environment that is teaching and maintaining these deviant behaviors. The problem lies in the social environment. If you wish to change the child, you must systematically alter the environment in which he or she lives. (Patterson, Reid, & Eddy, 2002, p. 21)

Patterson developed what he refers to as coercion theory to explain how a problematic pattern of behavior develops. Observations of referred families suggested that

A child may engage in aversive behaviors in order to get something that he or she wants. If the parent repeatedly gives in, this capitulation may contribute to coercive patterns of interaction in the family.

acts of physical aggression were not isolated behaviors. On the contrary, such acts tended to occur along with a wide range of noxious behaviors that were used to control family members in a process labeled as **coercion**. How and why does this process of coercion develop?

One factor is parents who lack adequate family management skills. According to Patterson (1976; Patterson et al., 1992), parental deficits in child management lead to increasingly coercive interactions within the family and to overt antisocial behavior. Central to this process are the notions of **negative reinforcement** and the **reinforcement trap**. Here is an example:

- A mother gives in to her child's tantrums in the supermarket and buys him a candy bar.
- The short-term consequence is that things are more pleasant for both parties:
  - The child has used an aversive event (tantrum) to achieve the desired goal (candy bar).
  - The mother's giving in has terminated an aversive event (tantrum and embarrassment) for her.
- Parents pay for short-term gains, however, with long-term consequences:
  - Although the mother received some immediate relief, she has increased the probability that her child will employ tantrums in the future.
  - The mothers, too, has received negative reinforcement that increases the likelihood that she will give in to future tantrums.

In addition to this negative reinforcement trap, coercive behavior may also be increased by direct positive reinforcement. Aggressive behavior may meet with social approval.

The concept of reciprocity, in combination with the notion of reinforcement, adds to our understanding of how aggression and coercion may be learned and sustained. Children as young as nursery school age can learn in a short time that attacking another person in response to some intrusion can terminate that intrusion. In addition, the victim of the attack may learn from the experience and may become more likely to initiate attacks in the future. But the eventual victim of escalating coercion also provides a negative reinforcer by giving in, thereby increasing the likelihood that the "winner" will start future coercions at higher levels of intensity and thus will get the victim to give in more quickly. In clinic families the coercive interactions are stable over time and across settings.

The description of a coercive process and ineffective parenting has served as the basis for Patterson's intervention project and for his evolving developmental model (Forgatch & Patterson, 2010; Patterson et al., 1992; 2002). In addition

to describing the "training" of antisocial behavior in the home, the model describes a relationship between antisocial behavior and poor peer relationships and other adverse outcomes (Dishion & Patterson, 2006; Snyder, 2002). It is suggested that ineffective parenting produces the coercive, noncompliant core of antisocial behavior, which in turn leads to these other disruptions. Furthermore, it is hypothesized that each of these outcomes serves as a precursor to subsequent drift into deviant peer groups.

Later in the process covert antisocial behaviors develop and are "added to" the overt/aggressive behaviors. Covert problem behaviors may develop as a way of avoiding harsh parenting practices and also may be reinforced by peers (Forgatch & Patterson, 2010).

The perspective of Patterson and his coworkers has expanded to include a wide array of variables (e.g., poverty, stress, high-crime neighborhoods) that affect the family process and, thus, the problems known to be associated with antisocial behavior (Dishion & Patterson, 2006; Forgatch & Patterson, 2010). At the core of this complex theoretical model is the Parent Management Training—Oregon Model. Parenting training in this model seeks to both reduce coercive parenting practices and improve positive parenting practices.

To illustrate these parenting practices, consider parental discipline and parental monitoring both of which contribute to, and are influenced by, the child's antisocial behavior. **Parental discipline** is defined by an interrelated set of skills: accurately tracking and classifying problem behaviors, ignoring trivial coercive events, and using effective consequences when necessary to back up demands and requests. Compared with other parents, parents of problem children have been found to be overinclusive in the behaviors that they classify as deviant. Thus these parents differ in how they track and classify problem behavior. These parents also "natter" (nag, scold irritably) in response to low levels of coercive behavior or to behavior that other parents see as neutral and are able to ignore. Parents of antisocial children fail to back up their commands when the child does not comply, and they also fail to reward compliance when it does occur.

Parental monitoring of child behavior is also important to prevent the development and persistence over time of antisocial behavior. The amount of time a child spends unsupervised by parents increases with age. The amount of unsupervised time also is positively correlated with antisocial behavior. Patterson described treatment families as having little information about their children's whereabouts, whom the children were with, what they were doing, or when they would be home. This situation probably arises from a variety of considerations, including the repeated failures that these parents experienced in controlling their children even when difficulties occurred right in front of them. Also, requesting information would likely lead to a series of confrontations that the parents preferred to avoid. These parents did not expect to receive positive responses to their involvement either from their own children or from social agencies such as schools (Patterson et al., 1992).

It should be remembered that, within this model, parent and child behaviors are reciprocal in their influence. Thus, the parents' behaviors and parenting practices are also shaped by the child's behavior.

EXTRAFAMILIAL INFLUENCES AND PARENTAL PSYCHOPATHOLOGY   The question of why some families and not others exhibit inept management practices has received some attention. Patterson (Patterson et al., 1992) posits that any number of variables may account for changes over time in family management skills. The handing down of faulty parenting practices from one generation to the next, in part, explains the problematic parenting-characteristics of antisocial families. Also, Patterson's own findings and those of other investigators support the relationship between extrafamilial stressors (e.g., daily hassles, negative life events, financial problems, family health problems) and parenting practices (Capaldi et al., 2002; Dishion & Patterson, 2006; Wahler & Dumas, 1989). Social disadvantage and living in neighborhoods that require a very high level of parenting skills also place some families at risk. Finally, various forms of parental psychopathology are associated with poor parenting practices. Parents who themselves have antisocial difficulties may be particularly likely to have parenting practices (e.g., inconsistent

discipline, low parental involvement) associated with the development of conduct-disordered behavior (Capaldi et al., 2002). Also, heavy drinking by parents may lower their threshold for reacting adversely to their child's behavior and also may be associated with inept monitoring of the child and less parental involvement (El-Sheikh & Flanagan, 2001; Lahey et al., 1999; West & Prinz, 1987). Figure 8.4 illustrates a model of how a variety of influences may disrupt effective parenting and lead to child antisocial behavior.

MARITAL DISCORD   Parental conflict and divorce are common in homes of children and adolescents with conduct problems (Cummings, Davies, & Campbell, 2000; O'Leary & Emery, 1985). The conflict leading to and surrounding the divorce are principal influences in this relationship, and divorces characterized by less conflict and greater cooperation are associated with fewer problems in children (Amato & Keith, 1991; Hetherington, Bridges, & Insabella, 1998). If aggression between the parents is also present, childhood disorder seems even more likely than would be expected on the basis of marital discord alone (Cummings, Goeke-Morey, & Papp, 2004; Jaffee, Poisson, & Cunningham, 2001; Jouriles, Murphy, & O'Leary, 1989). The relationship between marital conflict and conduct disorders can be explained in a number of ways. Parents who engage in a great deal of marital conflict or aggression may serve as models for their children. The stress of marital discord may also interfere with parenting practices such as the ability to monitor the child's behavior. Hostility and anger may also affect the child's emotion regulation development and thereby contribute to conduct problems. The relationship between discord and conduct problems may also

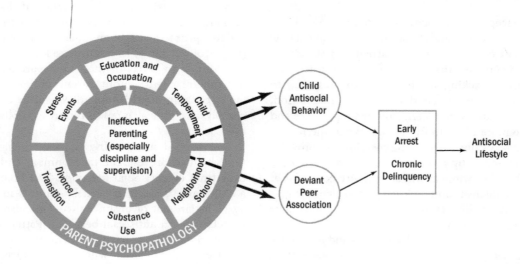

FIGURE 8.4   A mediational model for the association of family context and antisocial behavior. *Adapted from Capaldi et al., 2002.*

Marital discord and aggression between parents can contribute to the development of conduct-disordered behavior in children.

operate in the opposite causal direction; that is, the child's disruptive behavior may contribute to marital discord.

Also, both child conduct problems and marital discord may be related to a "third variable," such as parental antisocial disorder. Indeed, there are high rates of antisocial personality disorder (APD) among parents of conduct-disordered youths, and APD is associated with high rates of marital instability and discord (Farrington, Ullrich, & Salekin, 2010).

The relationship between marital conflict and child adjustment is likely to be complex and change over time. It is important to remember that these problems exist in a larger context (Davies & Cummings, 2006). It may be that a high level of environmental risk (related to family and community/neighborhood factors such as socioeconomic difficulties and high-crime neighborhoods) directly affects the youth and is also experienced by the parents, contributing to both marital and parent–child difficulties (Farrington et al., 2010; Klahr et al., 2011; Richards et al., 2004; Wahler & Dumas, 1989).

MALTREATMENT AND CONDUCT PROBLEMS   Early maltreatment, particularly physical abuse, is a risk factor for aggression and serious conduct problems (Cullerton-Sen et al., 2008; Lansford et al., 2002). Physically maltreated youngsters often display high levels of hostility and aggression and have frequent angry outbursts. These youngsters have higher than expected rates of conduct and oppositional defiant disorders.

Various mechanisms probably account for the association between maltreatment and conduct problems. As might be expected, persistent maltreatment may be particularly detrimental. For example, Bolger and Patterson (2001) found that chronically maltreated children were more likely to be aggressive and rejected by peers. A suggested mechanism for this maltreatment-aggression-peer rejection pattern is the coercive interactional style the child has learned in the family of origin.

Physical maltreatment may also contribute to learning of problematic cognitive/social information-processing patterns. Indeed, the relationship between early maltreatment and later aggressive behavior is, in part, mediated by biased social information-processing patterns such as interpreting ambiguous social cues as threatening and responding to them with aggression (Cullerton-Sen et al., 2008; Dodge, 2003). Thus, physical maltreatment may, in part, contribute to conduct problems through the development of problematic peer relationship and cognitive processes.

However, not all youths who are maltreated exhibit aggression and conduct problems. There may be a variety of factors that influence the relationship between maltretment and outcomes (Margolin & Gordis, 2004). Individual differences, for example, may moderate outcomes.

Gordis and colleagues (2010) examined individual differences in sympathetic nervous system (SNS) and parasympathetic nervous system (PNS) activity as moderators of the link between childhood maltreatment and adolescent aggression. Both SNS and PNS functioning have been linked to aggression (see pp. 203–204) and various mechanisms for the association between SNS and PNS activity and aggression have been offered (Beauchaine, 2001; Raine, 2005). Level of aggression

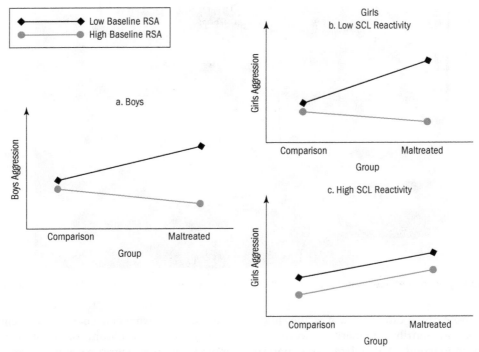

FIGURE 8.5 How autonomic nervous system functioning may be protective against the effects of maltreatment on the development of aggressive behaviors in boys and girls. *Adapted from Gordis et al., 2010.*

was examined in adolescents who had experienced prior maltreatment and in a non-maltreated comparison group. Overall, levels of aggression were higher for the maltreated youths. However, individual differences moderated this relationship. As illustrated in Figure 8.5a, boys with a high baseline level of a measure of heart rate across the respiratory cycle (RSA—respiratory sinus arrhythmia)—an indicator of PNS functioning—exhibited levels of aggression comparable to comparison boys. In contrast, maltreated boys with low baseline RSA exhibited higher levels of aggression. This protective effect of high baseline RSA also was observed for maltreated girls, but with one further qualification. The protective effect was found, but only for those girls who, in addition to high RSA levels, also exhibited low levels of skin conductance (SCL) reactivity—an indicator of SNS functioning (see Figures 8.5 b and c). This suggests that for girls the moderating effect of PNS differences was further moderated by SNS differences.

Peer Relations

Peer relations are part of the complex interplay of influences that contribute to the development of conduct problems (Hay et al., 2004; Lahey, 2008). Parents are often

concerned that their children are being influenced by peers whose behavior they view as "bad" or "dangerous." Such concern may be reasonable. Early exposure to aggressive peers may be one factor in the early initiation of aggressive and antisocial behavior, and later association with deviant peers can contribute to the maintenance and escalation of such behavior (Fergusson & Horwood, 1998; Laird et al., 2001; Snyder, 2002).

Difficulties in interpersonal relations have repeatedly been found among youngsters with conduct problems (Lochman, Whidby, & FitzGerald, 2000; Parker et al., 2006). Peers often reject children who display disruptive and aggressive behavior (Bierman, 2004; Coie, Belding, & Underwood, 1988). Rejected aggressive children suffer immediate social consequences and are at risk for negative long-term outcomes such as delinquency, adult criminality, educational failure, and adult psychological maladjustment (Farrington et al., 2010; Laird et al., 2001; Parker et al., 2006).

Not all aggressive youths are rejected, however, and those who are may not be without friends. Beginning in childhood and accelerating in adolescence, conduct-disordered and delinquent youngsters may have friends who also engage in aggressive and antisocial behaviors. Research shows that the interactions and influences that characterize these deviant peer associations play a role in the initiation, maintenance, and acceleration of antisocial behavior (Dishion & Patterson, 2006). For example, Fergusson and Horwood (1998) reported on the linkages between early conduct problems and outcomes at age 18 in a group of New Zealand children studied longitudinally since birth. They found that conduct problems at age 8 were associated with poorer outcomes, such as leaving school by age 18 without appropriate educational qualifications and a period of 3 months or more of unemployment. One of the factors that mediated the relationship between early aggression and later poor outcomes was peer affiliations. Adolescents, who between the ages of 14 and 16 reported having friends who were delinquent, or who used illegal substances, were at greater risk for later negative outcomes.

Peer influences are not independent of other contextual factors (Dishion & Patterson, 2006). For example, in their longitudinal study of New Zealand youngsters, Fergusson and Horwood (1999) found that family variables such as parental conflict, parental history of drug abuse and criminal behavior, and problematic early mother–child interactions were predictive of affiliation with deviant peers at age 15. Cultural and community influences come into play as well. Brody and colleagues (2001) found, in a sample of African American children, that difficulty with deviant peers was less likely if parents were nurturing and involved, but more likely if parenting was harsh and inconsistent. Furthermore, affiliation with deviant peers was less likely in neighborhoods with collective socialization practices (e.g., adults who were willing to monitor and supervise youths from their own and other families). Community economic disadvantage also was associated with greater likelihood of deviant peer affiliation, and the benefits of nurturant/involved parenting and collective socialization were most pronounced for youngsters from the most disadvantaged neighborhoods.

There may be individual differences regarding the effect of deviant peer affiliation on youth. For example, Lee (2011) investigated the influence of genetic influences on the impact of deviant peers. The monoamine oxidase-A gene (MAOA) has been suggested to play a role in antisocial behavior since the enzyme associated with this gene plays a role in the efficient processing of relevant neurotransmitters. A large sample of adolescents was designated as belonging to either a high (greater efficiency) or low-activity (lower efficiency) genotype group based on the number of repeats in a specific region of the MAOA gene. Greater affiliation with deviant peers was found to be associated with higher levels of both overt and covert antisocial behavior (ASB) across a 6-year period. However, a gene–environment interaction was found for

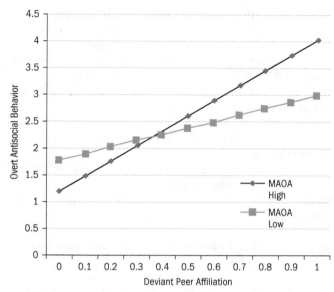

FIGURE 8.6 Overt antisocial behavior is influenced by the interaction of monoamine oxidase-A (MAOA) genotype and affiliation with deviant peers. *Adapted from Lee, 2011.*

overt antisocial behavior. The influence of deviant peer affiliation was significantly stronger for youth with the high-activity MAOA genotype (see Figure 8.6). However, the MAOA genotype did not seem to play a similar role with regard to covert antisocial behavior. There was not a similar gene–environment interaction for covert antisocial behavior. These findings illustrate, once again, the complex interaction of influences on the development of behavior.

Cognitive–Emotional Influences

Consider the adolescent boy who is walking down the street and is approached by a group of peers who begin to call him names, laugh, and tease him. Some boys respond to this situation by getting angry, escalating the conflict, and perhaps reacting violently, whereas other boys are able to deflect attention to another topic, ignore it, laugh, make light of the teasing, or firmly ask that the teasing stop. The cognitive and emotional processes that occur during this situation constitute proximal mechanisms for aggressive behavior. (Dodge, 2000, p. 448)

Examining how children and adolescents think and feel about social situations is part of understanding conduct problems. For example, they may attribute hostility to another child's actions or may fail to take another person's perspective, fail to use social problem-solving skills, fail to think before they act, or, in general, fail to use self-regulation skills to control their emotions and behavior. These social-cognitive-emotional processes are part of the development and persistence of aggressive and antisocial behavior (Dodge, 2000; Lochman et al., 2000). Specific social information-processing patterns such as a focus on the positive aspects of aggression and a lack of responsiveness to emotional stimuli may be characteristic of youngsters with the callous/unemotional traits described earlier (White & Frick, 2010).

The model articulated by Dodge and his colleagues illustrates how one might address social–emotional cognitions (Crick & Dodge, 1994; Dodge, 2003). The model suggests that cognitive processing begins with encoding (looking for and attending to) and then interpreting social and emotional cues. The next steps involve how to respond and include searching for possible alternative responses, selecting a specific response, and finally enacting the selected response. Investigations reveal that youths with conduct problems have poorer social problem-solving skills and display cognitive deficits and distortions in various parts of this process (Fontaine, Burks, & Dodge, 2002). For example, during the earlier stages of the process, aggressive youths may use fewer social cues and misattribute hostile intent to their peers' neutral actions. Furthermore, they may be more likely to perceive and label the arousal they experience in conflict situations as anger rather than other emotions. These reactions to internal arousal may contribute to further distortion and restricted problem solving (Lochman et al., 2000). Thus, later in the process they may also generate fewer responses and ones that are less likely to be effectively assertive and are more likely to be aggressive solutions. They may also expect that aggressive responses will lead to positive outcomes. Problematic social-cognitive-emotional processes may start quite early in life and be part of the stability of early-onset conduct-disordered behavior (Coy et al., 2001).

Dodge and his colleagues (Dodge, 1991; Schwartz, Dodge et al., 1998) distinguish between two types of aggressive behavior: reactive aggression and proactive aggression. **Reactive aggression** is an angry ("hot-blooded") retaliatory response to a perceived provocation or frustration. **Proactive aggression**, in contrast, is generally not associated with anger and is characterized by deliberate aversive behaviors (starting fights, bullying, teasing) that are oriented to specific goals or supported by positive environmental outcomes. Different social-cognitive deficiencies may be associated with these different types of aggression (Schippell et al., 2003). Reactively aggressive youths appear to display deficiencies in early stages of the social-cognitive process; for example, they

underutilize social cues and attribute hostile intent to others. Proactively aggressive youths display deficiencies in later stages of the process; for example, they are likely to positively evaluate aggressive solutions and to expect that they will lead to positive outcomes. It is suggested that the two types of aggression also seem to be related to different outcomes.

A study by Brendgen and colleagues (2001), for example, illustrates different outcomes associated with the reactive–proactive distinction. This study also reminds us, once again, of the interrelatedness of influences. A sample of Caucasian, French-speaking boys from low socioeconomic neighborhoods in Montreal, Canada, were categorized at 13 years of age as either nonaggressive, proactive–aggressive, reactive–aggressive, or both proactive- and reactive–aggressive. The boys, at 16–17 years of age, were asked to report on their delinquency-related physical violence (e.g., beat up other boys, used a weapon in a fight) and on their physical violence against a dating partner. In general, proactive aggression was associated with greater delinquency-related violence, and reactive aggression with greater dating violence. However, the relationship between proactive aggression and delinquency-related violence was moderated by level of parental supervision. The relationship was strong for boys who had experienced low levels of parental supervision during their early adolescent years, but the relationship was weak for boys who had experienced higher levels of parental supervision during this period. Similarly, the relationship between reactive aggression and dating violence was mediated by level of maternal warmth and caregiving. The relationship was strong for boys who had experienced low levels of maternal warmth and caregiving during their development, but this relationship was weak among boys who had experienced higher levels of maternal warmth and caregiving. Thus, although development of proactive and reactive aggression may be influenced by social–cognitive style, the developmental course of such behavior seems to be affected by styles of parenting.

Biological Influences

Contemporary discussions of the role of biological influences emphasize transactions among multiple biological and nonbiological influences (Tremblay, 2010; Viding & Larsson, 2010).

GENETICS That aggressive, antisocial, and other conduct-related behaviors run in families, within and across generations, is consistent with both environmental and genetic explanations of the development of such behavior. Despite considerable variation in estimates, that appears related to how conduct problem/antisocial behavior is measured and the source of information, there appears to be moderate genetic influence on such behavior (Farrington et al., 2001; Weyandt et al., 2011). However, there may be greater heritability for problems in childhood than in adolescence (Young et al., 2009) and there is also the suggestion of a lesser genetic component for adolescent delinquency than for adult criminal behavior. How might this difference be explained? The childhood-onset versus adolescent-limited distinction discussed earlier may be germane. Conduct-disordered behavior and delinquent behavior are quite common during adolescence, and in many cases, they do not persist into adulthood. It might, therefore, be reasonable to hypothesize an increased genetic component for antisocial behavior that persists from childhood into adult life (Eley, Lichtenstein, & Moffitt, 2003; Moffitt, 2006).

Although genetic influences may play some role, they are likely to be indirect and interact in complex ways with environmental influences, such as social conditions, family variables, and certain social learning experiences in determining etiology (Rhee & Waldman, 2003; Weyandt et al., 2011). Earlier we described a finding by Lee (2011), regarding overt antisocial behavior, of an interaction between an MAOA genotype and affiliation with deviant peers. Similarly, a gene–environment interaction is suggested in the work of van Lier and colleagues (2007a). Their research, on a sample of 6-year-old twins, examined the contribution of affiliation with aggressive friends to level of aggression. Affiliation with aggressive peers was a risk factor for aggression. However, the contribution of having an aggressive friend was greatest for those children who were already at high genetic risk for aggression.

In a similar vein, in a sample of 5-year-old twins and their families a gene–environment interaction was suggested regarding the contribution of maltreatment to the presence of conduct disorder (Jaffee et al., 2005). The presence of maltreatment increased the probability of a CD diagnosis by 2% among children at low genetic risk for CD and 24% among children at high genetic risk.

NEUROBIOLOGICAL INFLUENCES Psychophysiological variables have been frequently hypothesized to be related to antisocial behavior. Support for this notion comes from studies that find differences between delinquent or conduct-disordered youths and control youths on measures of autonomic arousal such as heart rate, electrodermal response (skin conductance), and cortisol levels (Beauchaine et al., 2008; Cappadocia et al., 2009; Weyandt et al., 2011). Thus, a link between both the sympathetic and parasympathetic aspects of the autonomic nervous system functioning and conduct-problem behavior has been suggested.

Quay (1993) hypothesized a biological foundation for aggressive, life-course persistent conduct disorders. This hypothesis is based on Gray's (1987) theory of brain systems: a **behavioral inhibition system** (BIS) and a **behavioral activation (or approach) system** (BAS) that have distinct neuroanatomical and neurotransmitter systems. The BIS is related to the emotions of fear and anxiety, and tends to inhibit action in novel or fearful situations or under conditions of punishment or nonreward. The BAS tends to activate behavior in the presence of reinforcement; it is associated with reward seeking and pleasurable emotions. An imbalance between the two systems is hypothesized to create a predisposition that in combination with adverse environmental circumstances produces behavior problems. Quay (1993) suggested that an underactive behavioral inhibition system (BIS) combined with an overactive reward system (BAS) may be implicated in the genesis of persistent aggressive conduct disorders.

There is an alternative model of how the two systems may operate. In this view, conduct-disordered, aggressive behavior results from an underactive BAS system in combination with an underactive BIS system (Beauchaine et al., 2001). Conduct-disordered and aggressive behavior represents a form of sensation seeking in response to chronic underarousal created by an underactive BAS system. Youths characterized as conduct-disordered also have low levels of inhibition (underactive BIS system) and engage in aggressive and other antisocial behaviors to achieve satisfactory reward states and positive arousal.

A third system described by Gray (1987) might also be involved in conduct disorders. The **fight/flight system** (F/F) also involves distinct brain and autonomic nervous system functioning. It is proposed to mediate defensive reactions under conditions of frustration, punishment, or pain. Thus, stimuli that are viewed as threatening would activate the F/F system. Certain youths, such as those with conduct-disordered behavior, may have a reduced threshold for F/F responding, whereas youths with higher thresholds may possess characteristics such as social competence and empathy toward others in distress. In general, the BIS and BAS are viewed as motivational, whereas the F/F system is viewed as an emotion regulation system (Beauchaine et al., 2001).

Structural and functional brain deficits have also been hypothesized to be associated with antisocial and disruptive behaviors. The frontal lobes, in particular, may play a role, through deficits in verbal and executive functions (e.g., inhibitory control, sustaining attention, abstract reasoning, goal formation, planning, emotion regulation) (Cappadocia et al., 2009; Rubia et al., 2008; Weyandt et al., 2011). Thus, neuroimaging studies have noted impaired patterns of frontal cortex functioning among youth with antisocial and aggressive behavior problems. Patterns of frontal cortex activity associated with lack of inhibitory control, problems in self-monitoring of task performance, and other cognitive abilities have been observed. However, findings are not always consistent across studies. Also, questions remain regarding sex differences and the specificity of findings to conduct disorder. Frontal cortex activity functioning and related executive functioning deficits are not unique to conduct disorder; they have been found in youth with a variety of disorders. Thus, one goal is to clarify the unique roles of such deficits in CD/ODD versus co-occurring disorders such as ADHD (Weyandt et al., 2011). Furthermore, neurobiological conceptualizations of conduct disorder development such as these may not apply to all conduct-disordered youngsters, but only to certain subgroups such as those youths with co-occurring ADHD or to those with callous-unemotional traits.

Before turning to our discussion of assessment and intervention for conduct problems, we examine the problem of substance use.

SUBSTANCE USE

Adolescent substance use is an important clinical and public health problem. The use of alcohol and other drugs is common among adolescents and preadolescents (Johnston et al., 2011; National Institute on Drug Abuse, 2006). Substance use and conduct disorder are often considered as part of a larger externalizing behavior construct and there are probably both common (shared) and specific aspects of the two problems (Castellanos-Ryan & Conrod, 2011). The use of alcohol and other drugs can, thus, be part of the constellation of antisocial and rule-breaking behaviors exhibited by conduct-disordered youths. Indeed, the disruptive behavior disorders (CD and ODD) are the most likely disorders to be associated with youth substance use (Fergusson et al., 2007). Some youths engage in substance use, but do not display antisocial behavior.

There is widespread concern regarding illegal (**illicit**) **drugs** such as marijuana, cocaine, ecstasy, hallucinogens (e.g., LSD), and heroin. There also is concern regarding use of **licit drugs** (drugs that are legal for adults or by prescription) and other substances. Alcohol, nicotine, psychoactive medications (e.g., stimulants, sedatives), over-the-counter medications (e.g., sleep aids and weight reduction aids), steroids, and inhalants (e.g., glue, paint thinner) are readily accessible and potentially harmful. They may play a role in starting some young people on a course of long-term and increased substance use (Flory et al., 2004; Georgiades & Boyle, 2007; Mayes & Suchman, 2006).

Classification and Description

Many adolescents experiment with substance use. One definition of a substance use problem views any use of alcohol or other substance by a minor as abuse since such use is illegal. However, those working with young people typically try to distinguish between time-limited patterns of experimentation or lesser use that are developmentally normative and patterns that may have serious short- and long-term consequences (Chassin et al., 2010).

The DSM substance-related and addictive disorders category describes pathological uses of ten classes of substances (e.g., alcohol, cannabis, hallucinogens, stimulants) and also includes gambling disorder. The excessive use of these classes of drugs and gambling are presumed to have in common the direct activation of brain reward systems. The substance-related disorders are divided into two groups: substance use disorders and substance-induced disorders. **Substance Use Disorders** involve a pattern of behavioral, cognitive, and physiological symptoms that indicate that the individual continues to use the substance despite appreciable substance-related problems. The diagnostic criteria used to describe this pattern of symptoms cluster into four groups:

- impaired control over substance use
- social impairment (e.g., interpersonal, school)
- risky use
- pharmacological criteria (tolerance, withdrawal).

Diagnosticians can also indicate the severity (mild, moderate, severe) based on the number of symptom criteria that are met. **Substance-Induced Disorders** include conditions of intoxication, withdrawal, and other mental disorders (e.g., depressive disorders, anxiety disorders, bipolar, and related disorders) that are due to the recent use of a particular substance (American Psychiatric Association [APA], 2013).

The DSM criteria for substance-related and addictive disorders are the same for youths and adults. However, the developmental appropriateness of these criteria for adolescents has been questioned (Chassin et al., 2010). Adolescents, for example, often display symptoms that are just below diagnostic thresholds. Also, tolerance may be overestimated as youths "learn to use" substances. Withdrawal also may be overestimated based on short-term physiological reactions to "binge" pattern uses that are more common among adolescents. These developmental/diagnostic issues may explain why adolescents with lower levels of use are more likely than adults to be diagnosed with substance use disorders. The possibility that characteristics of typical neurobiological development may make youths more susceptible to substance use during the adolescent period of development, however, should not be ignored.

Epidemiology

According to the Monitoring the Future (MTF) study (Johnston et al., 2011)—a long-term study of American adolescents that annually surveys large samples of 8th, 10th, and 12th graders—there has been a decline in substance use among young people since the peak years in the late 1990s. For example, illicit drug use has declined about 20% since these peak years However, approximately 21% of 8th graders, 37% of 10th graders, and 48% of 12th graders have used an illicit substance. Marijuana is the most widely used illicit drug and reports of daily use of marijuana have increased in all three grades.

The use of legal drugs is also reason for concern. Nicotine, for example, remains a problem in this age group. Also, alcohol, which is the most used substance among all age groups, including young people, remains in widespread use, according to the MTF study. While juvenile alcohol use seems to have stabilized or declined, there is still concern, For example, 27% of 12th graders, 15% of 10th graders, and 5% of 8th graders report having been drunk at least once in the previous month (Johnston et al., 2011). There is also concern with the misuse of prescription drugs such as amphetamines and tranquilizers.

In addition, as reports of use of some substances declines there is concern about the increased popularity of other drugs. It is suggested that increases and decreases in the use of particular drugs are due to shifts in the perceived benefits and perceived risks that young people come to associate with each drug. The concern is that rumor of the supposed benefits spreads faster than information about adverse consequences.

Findings regarding sex, SES, and ethnic differences in substance use are not consistent. Issues of how substance use is defined, how epidemiological information is obtained, and which substances are studied probably contribute to different conclusions. Most findings suggest greater illicit drug use among males. With regard to SES, research suggests higher rates of substance use among youth from both higher and lower SES backgrounds (Chassin et al., 2010). It is often assumed that substance use problems are more prevalent among certain ethnic groups such as American Indians, African Americans, and Latino/Hispanic youngsters than they are among European American youths. Indeed, lifetime substance use appears highest among American Indians; however, African American youth are often reported to have lower rates of substance use than European American and other ethnic groups (Chassin et al., 2010; Mayes & Suchman, 2006; Roberts, Ramsey, Roberts, & Xing, 2006). One limitation of information regarding SES and ethnicity may be that many findings are derived from school-based studies. The differential school

RODNEY

Alcohol and Nicotine Use

"It was so hard to start, I had no idea it would be harder to stop." Rodney, age 17, didn't recall much about the motorcycle accident that had put him in the hospital. It involved quite a few brandy Alexanders and too little about hanging onto the passenger bar of the motorcycle. He was clear-headed enough to realize that he badly needed a cigarette.

By the time Rodney was 12, he was already attending high school classes, had won several statewide scholastic contests, and had appeared twice on a popular TV quiz show. When he was 14, his parents reluctantly let him accept a scholarship to a small but prestigious liberal arts college. "Of course I was the smallest one there…I'm sure I started smoking and drinking to compensate for my size."

Six months into college, Rodney was smoking a pack and a half a day. When studying for exams (he often felt he wasn't "measuring up"), he found himself lighting one cigarette from another, going through several packs in a day this way—far more than he meant to. The following year, he read the Surgeon General's report on smoking and saw a video about lung cancer ("in living—no dying—color"). He swore he would never smoke again, but he noticed that he became restless, depressed, and "so irritable my roommate begged me to light up again." Over the next year he had tried twice more to quit.

Rodney's parents were hardworking churchgoers who had never touched a drop of alcohol. Both had been appalled at what alcohol had done to their own fathers. Several times in the last few months, when he was so badly hung over he couldn't attend classes, Rodney had vaguely wondered whether he was about to follow in his grandfathers' unsteady footsteps.

When Rodney first awakened after the accident he had pins through his femur and a terrific hangover. Now, 2 days later, his vital signs were stable and normal except for a pulse of only 56. "I don't suppose you could smuggle in some nicotine gum?" Rodney asked.

Adapted from Morrison & Anders, 1999, pp. 286–287.

drop-out rates among SES and ethnic groups may make it difficult to obtain an accurate picture regarding prevalence.

Adolescents with substance use problems typically display a number of other difficulties (Armstrong

& Costello, 2002; Georgiades & Boyle, 2007; Roberts, Roberts, & Xing, 2007). Many use multiple drugs. Academic and family difficulties are common, as are delinquent behaviors. As indicated earlier, substance use is often conceptualized as a later-occurring part of a constellation of conduct problem behaviors. It is not surprising, therefore, that young people who use drugs often meet the criteria for externalizing/disruptive behavior disorders (ODD, CD) in particular. Mood and anxiety disorders also are frequently associated with substance use problems.

Etiology and Developmental Course

Researchers and clinicians agree that multiple risk factors and multiple etiological pathways influence whether young people begin, increase, and maintain substance use (Chassin, Hussong, & Beltran, 2009; Mayes & Suchman, 2006; Meyers & Dick, 2010). Cavell, Ennett, and Meehan (2001) have described various risk and protective factors thought to be involved in substance use developmental pathways. These factors overlap considerably with the factors that influence the development of conduct problems in general. Here we draw on Cavell and colleagues' (2001) conceptualization to provide examples of risk and protective factors.

Individual differences, such as temperament, self-regulation, and problem-solving are often implicated in the onset and escalation of substance use. Cognitive-affective components—attitudes, expectations, intentions, and beliefs about control—are particularly prominent in conceptualizations of adolescent substance use. For instance, the anticipation of positive or negative consequences for drinking is an important proximal influence on alcohol use. The importance of expectancy regarding the effects of alcohol is illustrated in a study of the development of drinking behavior (Smith & Goldman, 1994; Smith et al., 1995). Over a 2-year period during which many of the youngsters first began to drink, expectations that drinking would facilitate social interactions predicted initiation into drinking. Those who expected social facilitation also drank more over the 2-year period, and future expectations regarding the effects of drinking became more positive.

Families are an important influence on adolescent substance use patterns. Aspects of parent–child relationships such as less secure attachment, high level of family conflict, and ineffectiveness of parenting skills have been linked to adolescent substance use. Also, social learning theory explanations have drawn attention to the role of modeling of behavior and attitudes. Because parents and older siblings are potential models for such behavior, the child of a parent who uses or misuses alcohol or some other substance may be at particular risk. Research by Hops and his colleagues (Hops et al., 2000), for example, indicates that when parents or older siblings use tobacco, alcohol, or marijuana, adolescents are more likely to initiate use of these substances. More than the specific drug-use behavior observed is affected by modeling. The adolescent may also initiate the use of other substances that serve a similar function (e.g., escape, perceived facilitation of social interactions). Furthermore, the attitude displayed by the parent can affect the young person's behavior. Adolescents are more likely to use substances, for example, when they perceive less parental disapproval for use (Chassin et al., 1998).

Peer factors are considered among the strongest influences on adolescent substance use (Dishion & Owen, 2002; Dishion & Patterson, 2006). Perceived peer substance use and perceived peer approval have been shown to be important factors. Social learning theory explanations also suggest that adolescents who interact with substance-using peer models and who expect positive consequences from substance use will initiate and continue substance use. However, it is difficult to establish direct peer influence. To begin with, adolescent substance users tend to choose friends who use drugs. Also, research findings are based on adolescents' perceptions of their peers' behavior, and such perceptions may be affected by the bias to see one's own choices as common (Cavell et al., 2001).

School, neighborhood, community, and societal influences are likely to contribute to adolescent substance use. Poor academic performance and low involvement in school activities, for example, have been linked to substance use. In contrast, schools that foster a sense of commitment and community have lower rates of use. Although some information suggests that low-income and high-risk neighborhoods are associated with greater adolescent substance use, findings are mixed. Some studies suggest higher rates of initial experimentation in more affluent and suburban neighborhoods. Apart from difference in rate of use, the risks associated with substance experimentation may be greater for youths who reside in poorer neighborhoods, particularly if other members of their families also use or abuse substances (Chassin et al., 2010). Larger social and cultural influences, such as availability of drugs and social norms regarding drug use, also contribute to the likelihood and degree of youths' substance use. Clearly, continuing research on these influences is needed.

A variety of theories and conceptualizations that are not necessarily mutually exclusive have been suggested as ways of explaining how risk and protective factors operate in the development of substance use. Social learning theory, as we have seen, emphasizes processes such as imitation, expectancy, and consequences. We will briefly examine a selection of other theoretical and conceptual models.

Association with a peer group that supports the use of alcohol and other drugs may be a contributing influence to the development of substance use and abuse.

One particular model views adolescence as a period of increasing freedom and exploration, and of a transition that is marked by attempts to engage in certain behaviors deemed appropriate for adults but not for adolescents (Bachman et al., 2002; Jessor & Jessor, 1977). Use of alcohol is an example of such a behavior. Individual differences and environmental variables are assumed to affect the rate at which an individual makes the transition to adulthood and thereby the age of onset of these behaviors. There also may be developmental changes in neurocircuitry during adolescence that make this a period of greater vulnerability for experimentation with substances and substance use disorders (Chambers, Taylor, & Potenza, 2003).

Adolescent substance use has also been viewed as developing within a negative affect, stress, and coping pathway (Colder et al., 2009). From this perspective, young people who are prone to experience high negative affect or who are facing greater negative life events and perceived stress, and/or those with elevated physiological responses to stress, may be more likely to use alcohol and other substances. Substance use may serve a coping function for the adolescent, or at least it is perceived to do so. Whereas some young people employ a variety of adaptive-active coping mechanisms (e.g., seeking information, considering alternatives, taking direct action), others may rely more heavily on the use of avoidant coping mechanisms (e.g., distraction, social withdrawal, wishful thinking) and use alcohol and other substances to deal with negative emotions and stress.

As we noted, young people frequently use more than one substance. One way of explaining this trend, as we

have seen, is imitation of substance-using models. Another explanation posits a developmental sequence. The so-called gateway theory suggests that legal drugs such as alcohol and tobacco are entry-level drugs that precede the use of illicit drugs. It is highly unusual for a nonuser to go directly to the use of illegal drugs. This theory suggests that participation in one stage increases the likelihood of participation in the next stage; however, only a subgroup at each stage progresses to the next level. The earlier the young person begins one stage, the greater is the likelihood that he or she will progress to other drug use (Mayes & Suchman, 2006). Also, heavier use at any stage seems to be associated with "progress" to the next stage. Findings that alcohol and drug use are beginning early are particularly disturbing in the context of this or any developmental stage model.

Neurobiological influences and adolescent brain development also are given frequent consideration (Rutherford, Mayes, & Potenza, 2010). Research has highlighted important developmental changes in brain systems regarding motivation/reward sensitivity on the one hand, and cognitive control on the other (Chassin et al., 2010). For example, changes occurring early in adolescence regarding dopaminergic systems, involving limbic and associated areas of the brain, are thought to produce changes in sensation seeking and increases in the salience of reward and, perhaps, adolescents' positive reactions to substances. In contrast, the changes in prefrontal regions and increases in white matter associated with development of cognitive control (executive function) systems are thought to develop more slowly and continue into the mid-20s. This developmental gap may place adolescents at increased risk for risky behaviors and substance use, in particular (Steinberg 2007: 2009).

There is support for genetic influences on substance use. This is particularly the case for clinical levels of use and less so for the substance initiation that may be most characteristic of adolescence. For more typical adolescent use, genetics may play a lesser role and environmental influences may be particularly important. Explanations of particular genetic mechanisms influencing substance use have suggested various genes that are associated with the various hypothesized pathways to substance use (e.g., reactivity to stress and disinhibition/undercontrol) that have been described (Chassin et al., 2010).

Clearly, no single factor or theory can easily explain which youths start or persist in problematic substance use (Mayes & Suchman, 2006; Meyers & Dick, 2010; Zucker, 2006). Explanations must include an array of variables—biological, psychological, and social—that interactively affect development over time. It seems clear, however, that conduct problems are associated with adolescent substance use patterns (Fergusson, Horwood, & Ridder, 2007; Hussong, Bauer, & Chassin, 2008). We return now to our examination of the broader conduct problem domain.

ASSESSMENT

As is the case for most child and adolescent problems, assessment of conduct problems is likely to be a complex and multifaceted process. In the following sections we describe the primary procedures likely to be used by clinicians working to assess these children and adolescents. It should be recognized that the assessment process will likely need to address a variety of problems and is also likely to include evaluation of the problems of others in the youth's environment, and their attitudes and skills (e.g., parenting), as well as ongoing life stresses (Lochman et al., 2000; McMahon & Frick, 2007).

Interviews

A general clinical interview with the parents and older children and adolescents themselves is typically part of the assessment process. An interview with younger children may not be as easily conducted or may not be a reliable source of information; however, the opportunity to interact with the young child may be helpful to the clinician. An interview with the entire family and with the teacher or school personnel may also provide valuable information. Structured interviews can help provide a comprehensive understanding of problems and their context, and can also help determine a diagnosis.

Behavior Rating Scales

Among general rating scales useful for assessing conduct problems are the Achenbach instruments (Achenbach & Rescorla, 2001) and the Behavior Assessment System for Children (BASC; Reynolds & Kamphaus, 2004). They allow evaluation of a broad array of problems through the reports of multiple informants. Also useful are behavior rating scales that focus specifically on conduct problems and disruptive behavior. The Conners' Parent and Teacher Rating Scales (Conners, 2008), the Eyberg Child Behavior Inventory (ECBI), and the Sutter-Eyberg Student Behavior Inventory (SESBI) are examples (Eyberg & Pincus, 1999).

The Self-Report Delinquency Scale (SRD; Elliott, Huizinga, & Ageton, 1985) is a widely used youth self-report measure of conduct problems. Consisting of items derived from the Uniform Crime Reports and including index offenses (e.g., theft, aggravated assault), other delinquent behaviors, and drug use, it is intended for use with youngsters 11 to 19 years old. Self-report measures are less commonly used with younger children because these children may not be capable of reporting conduct problems accurately.

Behavioral Observations

There are a large number of behavioral observation systems designed for use in clinic, home, and school settings (McMahon & Frick, 2007; Foster & Robin, 1997). Behavioral observations are a desirable part of the assessment process because they avoid the potential bias of reports based on interviews and questionnaires and may measure aspects of conduct problem behaviors not captured by these other approaches (Weyandt et al., 2011).

The Behavioral Coding System (Forehand & McMahon, 1981) and the Dyadic Parent–Child Interaction Coding System II (Eyberg et al., 2005) are two similar observational systems for assessing parent–child interactions in the clinic. Both observe the parent and the child in situations that vary from free-play and child-directed activities to adult-directed activities, and both focus on parental commands (antecedents) and consequences for child compliance or noncompliance. The Interpersonal Process Code (Rusby, Estes, & Dishion, 1991) is another observational system that is an outgrowth of observational systems developed by Patterson and his colleagues.

The observational systems just described have also been used in home settings, and these and other systems have been employed in schools (e.g., The Fast Track School Observation Program; Conduct Problems Prevention Research Group, 1992). Practicing clinicians seldom use these systems because they are complex and require extensive periods of training and trained observers. The observations themselves are lengthy, and it is challenging to coordinate with the times when relevant behaviors are occurring in homes or schools. An alternative to using trained observers in the home or other natural environments is to train adults in the child's environment to record and observe certain behaviors. An advantage of this approach is the opportunity to observe and record behaviors that occur at low rates (e.g., stealing or fire setting) and that would likely be missed by trained observers making occasional visits.

INTERVENTION

Because of the challenges posed by children and adolescents with conduct problems and the impact they have on others, many different interventions have been attempted. Only a portion of these has received a careful empirical evaluation of their effectiveness. Here we will briefly describe some of the interventions that are often employed and that research suggests are supported or promising.

Parent Training

Parent training is among the most successful approaches to reducing aggressive, noncompliant, and antisocial behaviors in youth (Brestan & Eyberg, 1998; Hagen, Ogden, & Bjornebekk, 2011; Kazdin, 1997; Maughan et al., 2005). **Parent training** programs have a number of features in common (see Table 8.4).

Some parent training programs have focused on reducing oppositional and defiant behavior. However, compliance is not always a positive behavior, and the child's ability to say "no" to certain requests may be desirable either to train or to retain (Dix et al., 2007). In this regard, it is important to assure that parents do not expect perfect compliance, which is neither the norm nor highly desirable in our society. A perfectly quiet, docile child should not be the treatment goal.

The program developed by Forehand and his colleagues illustrates successful parent training that focuses on noncompliant behavior (Forehand & McMahon, 1981; McMahon & Forehand, 2003). Parents of noncompliant children (ages 4–7 years) were taught to give direct, concise commands, allow the child sufficient time to comply, reward compliance with contingent attention, and apply negative consequences for noncompliance. Successful treatment of noncompliance also seems to reduce other problem behaviors, such as tantrums, aggression, and crying (Wells, Forehand, & Griest, 1980). Furthermore, at follow-up, treated children were not different from non-clinic community children across multiple areas such as academic performance, relationships with parents, and adjustment (Long et al., 1994). An additional benefit appeared to be that untreated siblings increased their compliance, and it seems likely that this outcome was due, at least in part, to the mother's use of her improved skills with the untreated child (Humphreys et al., 1978).

Attention to the effective use of parent commands to increase compliance and decrease inappropriate behavior is also part of the parent–child interaction therapy (PCIT) program developed by Eyberg and her colleagues (Querido & Eyberg, 2005; Zisser & Eyberg, 2010). This program

---

TABLE 8.4 Common Features of Parent Training Programs

- Treatments are conducted primarily with the parents.
  - The therapist teaches the parents to alter interactions with their child so as to increase prosocial behavior and to decrease deviant behavior.
  - Young children may be brought into sessions to train both the parents and the child in how to interact. Older youths may participate in negotiating and developing behavior change programs.
- New ways of identifying, defining, and observing behavior problems are taught.
- Social learning principles and procedures that follow from them are taught (e.g., social reinforcement, points for prosocial behavior, time out from reinforcement, loss of privileges).
- Treatment sessions are an opportunity to see how techniques are implemented and to practice using techniques. Behavior change programs implemented in the home are reviewed.
- The child's functioning in school is usually incorporated into treatment.
  - Parent-managed reinforcement programs for school and school-related behavior are often part of the behavior-change program.
  - If possible, the teacher plays a role in monitoring behavior and providing consequences.

Adapted from Kazdin, 1997.

seeks to enhance parent–child attachment and to improve the poor behavior management skills of the parent. Here we highlight the portion of the program that teaches parents to use effective commands (Querido, Bearss, & Eyberg, 2002). The rules for effective use of commands that parents are taught (along with examples) are presented in Table 8.5.

As we have seen, Patterson's conceptualization of the development of antisocial behavior evolved in the context of treating conduct problem children and their families. The importance of parenting skills in Patterson's formulation led to the development of an evolving treatment program that focused on improving parenting skills (Forgatch & Patterson, 2010; Patterson et al., 1975; 1992; Reid et al., 2002). The program teaches parents to pinpoint problems, to observe and record behavior, to more effectively use social and nonsocial reinforcers for appropriate or prosocial behavior, and to more effectively withdraw reinforcers for undesirable behavior. Each family attends clinic and home sessions and has regular phone contact with a therapist, who helps develop interventions for particular targeted behaviors and who models desired parenting skills. Problematic behaviors in the school and other community settings are also targeted, and interventions involve both the parents and relevant personnel.

Webster-Stratton and her colleagues (2005; Webster-Stratton & Reid, 2010) have developed a multifaceted treatment program for young children (ages 2–8 years) with conduct problems, including oppositional defiant and conduct disorder, known as the Incredible Years Training Series. One component of the program is a standard package of videotaped programs of modeled parenting skills. These videos, which contain a large number of vignettes of about 2 minutes each, include examples of parents interacting with their children in both appropriate and inappropriate ways. The videos are shown to groups of parents, and following each vignette, there is a therapist-led discussion of the relevant interactions. Parents are also given homework assignments that allow them to practice parenting skills at home with their children.

The treatment program has been evaluated in a number of studies in which it has been compared with various control conditions (Webster-Stratton & Reid, 2010). Parents completing the program have rated their children as having fewer problems than have control parents and rated themselves as having better attitudes and more confidence regarding their parenting role. Observations in the home have also shown these parents to have better parenting skills and their children to have greater reductions in problem behavior. These improvements were maintained at one- and three-year follow-up evaluations. Webster-Stratton (Webster-Stratton & Reid, 2010) has also expanded the program to include additional components that enhance parents' interpersonal skills

TABLE 8.5	Rules for Effective Commands from the PCIT Program
Rule	**Example**
Be *direct* rather than indirect.	Draw a circle. *Instead of* Will you draw a circle?
State command *positively*.	Come sit beside me. *Instead of* Stop running around!
Give commands *one at a time*.	Put your shoes in the closet. *Instead of* Clean your room.
Be *specific* rather than vague.	Get down off the table. *Instead of* Be careful.
Be *age appropriate*.	Draw a square. *Instead of* Draw a cube.
Be *polite and respectful*.	Please give me the block. *Instead of* Stop banging and give me the block now!
Explain commands *before* they are given or *after* they are obeyed.	Please wash your hands. *After the child obeys* Thank you. Clean hands keep germs away from your food so you won't get sick.
Use commands only when necessary or appropriate.	(As child is running around) Please sit in this chair. (Good time) *But not* Please give me a tissue. (Not good time and consider if command is necessary.)

Adapted from Zisser & Eyberg, 2010.

and the social support that the family receives (ADVANCE), improve the child's social problem-solving skills (Dinosaur Curriculum), promote parental involvement in school and academic activities (School), and train teachers in effective classroom management strategies (Teacher).

Cognitive Problem-Solving Skills Training

Parent training approaches focus on family aspects of conduct-disordered behavior. Other treatments focus more specifically on aspects of the youth's functioning. Among these are ones that derive from the interpersonal and social-cognitive aspects of conduct-disordered behavior. These interventions address social-cognitive deficiencies and distortions as part of the intervention. The Anger Coping Program of Lochman and colleagues illustrates the types of problem-solving skills trained in these types of interventions (see Table 8.6).

Webster-Stratton and colleagues' cognitive-behavioral, social skills, problem-solving, and anger management training program (Dinosaur Curriculum part of the Incredible Years series) is another example of interventions that address such deficits and skills (Webster-Stratton, 2005; Webster-Stratton & Reid, 2010). Children ages 3–8 years with early-onset conduct problems receive the treatment in small groups. The program addresses interpersonal difficulties typically encountered by young children who have conduct problems. With therapist guidance, the children are taught to cope with such situations through a variety of techniques. Videotaped vignettes of children in stressful situations are viewed and discussed, and acceptable solutions and coping skills are practiced. The intervention is made developmentally appropriate and includes the use of materials such as child-size puppets, coloring books, cartoons, stickers, and prizes to enhance learning. Strategies to ensure generalization to other settings are included in the children's sessions. Also, parents and teachers, who are involved through receiving regular letters, are asked to reinforce the targeted skills whenever they notice the child using them at home or at school and to complete weekly good-behavior charts. As compared with a waiting-list group of children, at posttreatment those in the treatment program exhibited significantly fewer aggressive, noncompliant, and other externalizing problems at home and school, more prosocial behavior with peers, and more positive conflict management strategies. Most of the posttreatment changes were maintained at a one-year follow-up. Combining this child-focused intervention with interventions targeting training of parents and/or teachers resulted in greater improvement (Webster-Stratton & Reid, 2010).

COMBINED TREATMENTS Kazdin and his colleagues (Kazdin, 2005; 2010) also have demonstrated the potential benefit of combining parent training and cognitive problem-solving skills training in treating children with conduct problems. A combination of cognitive problem-solving skills training (PSST) and parent management training (PMT), similar to the procedures described before, proved superior to either treatment alone for children 7 years of age and older. (PMT alone is offered for children up to 6 years of age.) Treatment led to significant improvements in the youths' functioning at home, at school, and in the community, immediately after treatment and at a one-year follow-up, as well as to improvements in parental stress and functioning. In addition, the combined treatments resulted in a greater proportion of the youths falling within normative levels of functioning. Also, adding a treatment component that addresses parent sources of stress improved outcomes for the child. These findings, along with the multi-component Webster-Stratton program described earlier, suggest the value of interventions that address the multiple influences operating in conduct-disordered youth and their families. Treatment components may be combined depending on the nature and pervasiveness of the youth and family's problems.

Community-Based Programs

The kinds of interventions described as successful with younger conduct-disordered children, such as parent training, may be less successful with adolescents and chronic juvenile delinquents. Placing severely conduct-disordered or delinquent youth in institutions that are a part of the criminal justice system is a frequently considered alternative. Concerns exist regarding the effectiveness of such interventions and the

Session	Content/Focus
	TABLE 8.6 Anger Control Program Sessions
1	Introduction and group rules
2	Understanding and writing goals
3	Anger management: puppet self-control task
4	Using self-instruction
5	Perspective taking
6	Looking at anger
7	What does anger feel like?
8	Choices and consequences
9	Steps for problem solving
10	Problem solving in action
11	Student video productions – situations that illustrate lack of anger control and aggression – review situations using learned concepts and skills

Adapted from Lochman et al., 2010.

impact of placement in such institutions that exposes young people to a subculture in which deviant behaviors may be learned and reinforced. These concerns and the success of some community-based programs have led to the search for effective alternatives to institutionalization.

The Teaching Family Model (TFM) developed at Achievement Place is an oft-cited example of a community-based program for delinquent youth and an example of behaviorally based (largely operant) interventions (Fixsen, Wolf, & Phillips, 1973; Phillips, 1968). Adolescents who were declared delinquent or dependent neglect cases lived in a house with two trained teaching parents. The youths attended school during the day and also had regular work responsibilities. The academic problems, aggression, and other norm-violating behaviors exhibited by these adolescents were viewed as an expression of failures of past environments to teach appropriate behaviors. Accordingly, these deficits were corrected through modeling, practice, instruction, and feedback. The program centered on a **token economy** in which points and praise were gained for appropriate behaviors and were lost for inappropriate behaviors. Points could be used to purchase a variety of privileges that were otherwise unavailable. If a resident met a certain level of performance, the right to go on a merit system and thus avoid the point system could be purchased. This process was seen as providing a transition to usual sources of natural reinforcement and feedback, such as praise, status, and satisfaction. The goal was gradually to transfer a youth who was able to perform adequately on merit to his or her natural home. The teaching parents helped the natural parents or guardians to structure a program to maintain gains made at Achievement Place.

Both the program's developers and independent investigators evaluated the effectiveness of TFM (Kirigin, 1996; Weinrott, Jones, & Howard, 1982). These evaluations suggested that the TFM approach was more effective than comparison programs while the adolescents were involved in the group home setting. However, once they left this setting, differences disappeared.

Difficulties in transitions back to the youths' own families and failure to achieve long-term effectiveness are common in all interventions with delinquent populations. Given this consideration, the developers of TFM suggested a "long-term supportive family model" in which specially trained foster parents would provide care for a single adolescent into early adulthood (Wolf, Braukmann, & Ramp, 1987). Multidimensional treatment foster care (MTFC) interventions have been developed (Chamberlain & Smith, 2003). Like the TFM approach, many of these programs are based on behavioral-social learning theory: the youth remains in the community, the youth is placed in family-like settings, and interventions occur in natural settings. However, one or perhaps two young people, rather than a group of youths, are placed in a specialized foster care home. This decision is consistent with literature suggesting possible negative effects of interventions that permit these youths to associate with peers with similar antisocial histories (Dishion & Dodge, 2005). Foster parents are trained in behavior management skills and are provided with supervision and support by program staff. Explicit behavioral goals are set, and a systematic program including a point system is employed. The youth's school is also involved. Individual weekly sessions with a therapist that emphasize building skills are also provided for the youth. During the MTFC stay, staff work with the youth's parents or other aftercare personnel to prepare them (and the young person) for reunification. Research indicates that participants in the MTFC program were less likely to engage in delinquent activities, showed larger decreases in official criminal referrals, were less likely to run away, and had fewer arrests (Smith & Chamberlain, 2010). Effective MTFC programs have been developed for both severely delinquent boys and girls and have been found to be cost-effective (Aos, Miller, & Drake, 2006; Smith & Chamberlain, 2010).

Multisystemic Therapy

Interventions with antisocial youth are likely to require the cooperation of multiple human service agencies. Often it is difficult to coordinate services, and individualizing such efforts to fit the needs of youngsters and their families is even more challenging.

Multisystemic Therapy (MST; Henggeler & Schaeffer, 2010) is a family- and community-based approach. Based on Bronfenbrenner's (1977) social ecological model (see p. 48), the young person is considered to exist within a number of systems, including family, peers, school, neighborhood, and community. MST focuses on enhancing the family's strengths and uses empirically supported treatments derived from family systems therapy, parent training, and cognitive-behavioral therapy to treat adolescents and their families. The approach seeks to preserve the family and to maintain the youths in their homes. MST addresses not only the family system but also skills of the youth and extra-familial influences, such as peers, school, and neighborhood. Clinicians are available to the family 24/7. Family sessions are conducted in the home and community settings at times convenient for families and are flexible and individualized for each family. The basic principles of MST are summarized in Table 8.7.

The effectiveness of MST in treating serious antisocial behavior in adolescents has received considerable empirical support (Henggeler & Schaeffer, 2010). A report on a comparison of MST to the usual services offered to serious

MAGGIE

The Need for Multiple Services

Maggie is a 13-year-old white seventh-grader who lives with her unemployed, crack-addicted mother, mother's live-in boyfriend, two sisters (ages 10 and 8), and a daughter of one of her mother's crack-addicted friends. Maggie was referred because she was physically violent at home (e.g., she was arrested several times for assaulting family members), at school (e.g., she beat a classmate with a stick and threatened to kill a teacher), and in the neighborhood (e.g., she was arrested twice for assaulting residents of her housing development). Many of Maggie's aggressive actions followed all-night binges by her mother. Maggie, who primarily associates with delinquent peers, was placed in a special class, and was recommended for expulsion from school. The family resides in a high-crime neighborhood, and the only source of income is welfare benefits.

Adapted from Henggeler et al., 1998, p. 23.

TABLE 8.7	Principles of Multisystemic Therapy

- The presenting **problem is assessed and defined from multiple perspectives** (e.g., youth, family members, teachers, juvenile justice personnel) **and in multiple domains** (e.g., youth, family, peers, school).
- Interventions are developed that **address problems in multiple domains** and do so in a **highly integrated manner**.
- Interventions are designed to be **intensive** (i.e., daily or weekly effort by family members).
- Interventions are **developmentally appropriate**.
- Interventions are **present-focused and action oriented**.
- Interventions are designed to **encourage responsible behavior** by all parties.
- Interventions are designed to, from the beginning, **promote generalization and maintenance** of therapeutic gains.
- Interventions make use of **strengths** in various ecological contexts as levers for change and an **optimistic perspective** is communicated.
- Intervention effectiveness is **evaluated continuously** from multiple perspectives, fed back into the system, and **needed modifications made** to the intervention.

Adapted from Henggeler & Schaeffer, 2010.

---

juvenile offenders and their families illustrates this approach (Henggeler, Melton, & Smith, 1992). These youths were at imminent risk for out-of-home placement. They averaged 3.5 previous arrests, 54% had at least one arrest for a violent crime, and 71% had been incarcerated previously for at least 3 weeks. The findings of this study indicate that MST was significantly more effective than the usual services. In addition, families receiving the MST intervention reported increased family cohesion, whereas reported cohesion decreased in the other families. Also, aggression with peers decreased for MST youths but remained the same for the youths receiving usual services. Multiple other reports indicate the usefulness of MST with a variety of populations, including violent and chronic juvenile offenders, adolescent sexual offenders, substance abusing and dependent youths, and youth presenting for psychiatric emergencies. These findings suggest the long-term effectiveness and cost-effectiveness of this approach (Aos et al., 2006; Curtis, Ronan, & Borduin, 2004; Henggeler & Schaffer, 2010).

Pharmacological Intervention

Various types of psychoactive medications have been employed in the treatment of aggression and ODD and CD. These include mood stabilizers such as lithium and atypical antipsychotics such as risperidone. Research support for the use of such medications in treating disruptive behavior disorders is limited, however (APA, 2006; McKinney & Renk, 2011). It is important to remember that many youngsters with these disorders show symptoms of, or meet the diagnostic criteria for, attention-deficit hyperactivity disorder. There is considerable support for pharmacological interventions for ADHD (American Academy of Child and Adolescent Psychiatry [AACAP], 2007a). Thus children and adolescents who also present with this co-occurrence may benefit from the use of medications such as stimulants. However, from a research perspective, evaluations of pharmacological treatments for ODD or CD would need to ensure that the medication's effectiveness was not due to the presence of ADHD symptoms in the population studied. Much of the available research can be critiqued for failing to control adequately for such considerations.

Given lack of approval of medications for treating CD or ODD, and a broad uneasiness regarding increased use of psychoactive medications with children, there is concern regarding the use of such medications to treat disruptive behavior problems (Gleason et al., 2007; McKinney & Renk, 2011). When psychoactive medication is employed in the treatment of aggressive conduct-disordered youngsters, it should be part of a multimodal treatment approach that includes parent training and other psychological interventions (AACAP, 2007b).

Prevention

The difficulties in treating adolescents with serious and persistent conduct disorders, the multidetermined nature of antisocial behavior, and the potential stability of conduct-disordered behavior certainly suggest that efforts should be directed at early, multifaceted, flexible, and ongoing interventions for some youngsters. Here we offer some examples of efforts at early intervention.

Interventions that provide treatment to families of young children with oppositional defiant behavior or early signs of aggression or similar programs also might be considered as prevention strategies. Successful treatment can reduce early aspects of the development of conduct-disordered behavior. Also, improvement of parenting skills and family interactions, for example, can reduce risk factors and provide protective influences associated with the developmental progression of conduct problems. Thus, interventions that target preschool and early elementary-age children and their families can be considered treatment for existing conduct problems and prevention of later conduct disorders.

Beyond this conceptual overlap, some of the treatment programs described earlier have been employed as prevention programs. For example, Webster-Stratton (2005) and her colleagues evaluated The Incredible Years program as a prevention program. The BASIC parent program was provided to Head Start families in some randomly selected centers in addition to the regular Head Start program. Compared with control families at centers that received regular Head Start offerings, participating mothers improved their parenting skills. Their children exhibited significantly less misbehavior and more positive affect compared to control children whose behavior remained unchanged. In addition, teachers reported increased involvement by program parents, whereas reports indicated that control parents' involvement remained the same. One year later, in kindergarten, improvements in parenting behavior and in child behavior and affect were maintained. Webster-Stratton has reported that the program is effective with socioeconomically disadvantaged Head Start families of multiple ethnicities as well as with families referred for child abuse and neglect. Other independent investigators also have successfully employed the program as a preventive intervention (Gardner, Burton, & Klimes, 2006; Gross et al., 2003; Hutchings et al., 2007; Posthumus et al., 2012).

There are also selective prevention trials focused on conduct problems that provide comprehensive intervention over a long period of time. For example, the Fast Track project (Conduct Problems Prevention Research Group, 1992; 2002b) is a multisite collaborative project that is following a large high-risk sample of children identified as displaying high rates of conduct problems during kindergarten as well as a representative sample of children from the same schools. Half of the children in the high-risk sample participated in an intensive and long-term intervention. This is consistent with the need to provide multiple interventions over an extended period of development for some early-onset conduct-problem youngsters. The program targets the behaviors, skills, and other risk factors involved in the development of the early-onset pathway of conduct problems. Intervention components include parent training, social-cognitive skills training, attention to peer affiliation, academic tutoring, home visits, and teacher-based classroom intervention. Evaluations of the effects of the intervention have been encouraging and have provided information regarding the variables that mediate change in conduct problems (Conduct Problems Prevention Research Group, 1999; 2002a; 2004; Erath et al., 2006; Milan et al., 2006).

The Oregon group has adapted their clinical model to several prevention efforts. These interventions recognize that there is a need for programs that offer differing "levels" of intervention based upon the needs of the youth and family and that appreciate that youths' problems are embedded in multiple environments (Dishion & Stormshak, 2007). For example, the Adolescents Transition Program (ATP; Dishion & Kavanagh, 2002) is a family-based intervention that is embedded in the school setting and that has the goal of reducing adolescent problem behavior. It offers three levels of service to families. A Family Resource Center in the school facilitates parent–school collaboration and provides information and education to parents. This is a universal intervention. The Family Check-Up is a selected intervention offered to families identified as having an at-risk youth. This brief intervention provides an assessment, attempts to maintain current positive parenting, and seeks to enhance motivation to change problematic parenting practices. An indicated level of intervention is available to families of youth with ongoing conduct problems. A number of professional interventions, similar to those described in the discussion of treatment programs, are offered to these families. ATP has been shown to be helpful in addressing conduct problems (Dishion & Stormshak, 2007). For example, adolescents whose families engaged in the Family Check-Up during grade 6 exhibited less substance use and other problem behavior between the ages of 11 and 17 and also had lower arrest records by age 18 relative to matched controls (Connell et al., 2007). The Family Check-Up was initially developed, and shown to be efficacious, for adolescents. It also has been successfully adapted for use with 2-year-olds (Gill et al., 2008).

Overview/Looking Back

CLASSIFICATION AND DESCRIPTION

- Aggression, oppositional behavior, and other antisocial behaviors are among the most common problems of referred youths, as well as of young people in the general population.
- The DSM contains a group of disorders that includes Oppositional Defiant Disorder (ODD) and Conduct Disorder (CD), along with Intermittent Explosive Disorder, Antisocial Personality Disorder, and other disruptive, impulse-control, and conduct disorders.
- ODD is described as a pattern of negativistic, hostile, and defiant behavior. CD is described as a repetitive and persistent pattern of behavior that violates both the basic rights of others and societal norms. Two subtypes, childhood-onset and adolescent-onset, are indicated.
- Empirical approaches have consistently identified a syndrome of aggressive, oppositional, antisocial behaviors. Two narrow syndromes within this broad externalizing syndrome have been designated as aggressive behavior and rule-breaking behavior.
- Other ways of distinguishing among groupings of conduct problems, such as age of onset, an overt versus covert distinction, and a further destructive–nondestructive distinction, have also been suggested.
- There are gender differences in prevalence, developmental course, and etiological influences of conduct problems. In part, such differences may be related to how aggression is expressed. The concept of relational aggression has contributed to understanding gender differences.
- Fire setting is a covert behavior that may occur among youths with severe conduct problems.
- The high rates of violent behavior among young people have led to action on multiple fronts, particularly in schools.
- It is important to address bullying since bullying may be part of a more general antisocial developmental pattern. The victims of bullying also are at considerable risk.

EPIDEMIOLOGY

- Conduct problems are one of the most frequently occurring child and adolescent difficulties.
- Conduct disorder and oppositional defiant disorder are more commonly diagnosed in boys.
- An increasing prevalence of conduct disorder with age is often reported. The pattern for oppositional defiant disorder is less clear.

- Contextual factors such as poverty and the stress of high-crime neighborhoods are thought to increase the risk for conduct problems.
- An important question is whether oppositional defiant disorder is a precursor of conduct disorder.
- Youths who receive the diagnoses ODD or CD are likely to experience other difficulties. In particular, there is a high rate of co-occurrence of ODD and CD with ADHD. ADHD appears to be a risk factor for the other two disorders.

DEVELOPMENTAL COURSE

- An important aspect of conduct problems is their reported stability over time for at least some individuals. The issue of stability is, however, a complex one.
- Callous-unemotional traits have been suggested as an attribute that may be characteristic of a subgroup of youths who display stable aggressive and antisocial behavior.
- Age of onset is an important aspect of the development of conduct problems. A childhood-onset or life-course persistent pathway is of great concern. An adolescent-onset path is more common, and antisocial behavior among such youths may be less likely to persist beyond adolescence.
- Conduct-disordered behavior has been conceptualized in terms of developmental progressions or paths. Pathways characterized by overt, covert, and authority conflict behaviors have been described.

ETIOLOGY

- Conduct problems likely develop through a complex interaction of influences.
- Influences from the socioeconomic context, such as poverty, neighborhood disadvantage, and related stress, affect the development of conduct-disordered behavior.
- Parents, other family members, and media portrayals may serve as models for aggression and other conduct-disordered behavior.
- Family variables also are an important influence on the development of conduct-disordered behavior. Important mechanisms through which family influence occurs are parental involvement and parenting practices. The work of Patterson and his colleagues has contributed to our knowledge in this area.

- Stresses on the family, the parents' own psychological difficulties, marital discord, and child maltreatment affect both the likelihood of a child developing conduct problems and the course of the behavior.
- Peer relations both contribute to and are affected by conduct problems. Aggressive youths are often rejected by their peers, with both immediate and long-term consequences. However, these youths may not be without friends and the influence of bad companions is a concern.
- Cognitive-emotional characteristics of the youths, such as social information-processing skills and interpersonal problem-solving skills, also contribute to the development and persistence of conduct-disordered behavior.
- Biological influences, such as genetic and neurobiological influences, likely also play a role.

SUBSTANCE USE

- The use of alcohol and drugs may be a part of a pattern of antisocial and rule-breaking behavior. Substance use and substance-induced disorders are described in a group of DSM substance-related and addictive diagnoses. The high rate of substance use by young people is a widespread concern. A variety of theories, models, and risk factors have been suggested to explain substance use.

ASSESSMENT

- Assessment of conduct problems is likely to be complex and multifaceted. Interviews, behavior rating scales, and behavioral observations are employed.

INTERVENTION

- Parent training is among the most successful approaches. Parent training is central to efforts to improve parent management skills and, thereby, reduce noncompliant and other conduct problem behavior and increase appropriate and prosocial behaviors.
- Interventions employing cognitive problem-solving skills training focus on aspects of the youth's functioning. Research findings suggest the value of treatment programs that combine parent training and cognitive problem solving approaches and address multiple influences.
- Community-based programs include the Teaching Family Model and Multidimensional Treatment Foster Care. Multisystemic Therapy is a systems-based intervention that attempts to keep the youths in their homes. It addresses the youths' functioning within various systems such as family, peers, school, neighborhood, and community.
- Various types of psychoactive medications have been employed in the treatment of conduct-disordered and antisocial behavior. Research support for the use of such medications is, however, limited.
- Interventions that provide treatment to families of young children with oppositional defiant behavior or early signs of aggression might be considered prevention strategies. Indeed, some treatment programs for young children have been adapted as prevention programs.
- Other selected prevention programs provide comprehensive interventions over long periods of time for at-risk youths. There are also programs that offer different "levels" of intervention based on the needs of the youth and family.

Key Terms

delinquency *179*
Intermittent Explosive Disorder *179*
Antisocial Personality Disorder *180*
Oppositional Defiant Disorder *181*
Conduct Disorder *181*
externalizing problems *182*
aggressive behavior syndrome *182*
rule-breaking behavior syndrome *182*
overt conduct problems *183*
covert conduct problems *183*
relational aggression *184*
violence *185*

bullying *187*
executive functions *191*
psychopathy *192*
callous/unemotional traits *192*
childhood-onset developmental
 pattern *191*
adolescent-onset developmental
 pattern *193*
coercion *197*
negative reinforcement *197*
reinforcement trap *197*
parental discipline *197*

parental monitoring *197*
reactive aggression *202*
proactive aggression *202*
behavioral inhibition system *203*
behavioral activation system *203*
fight/flight system *203*
illicit drugs *204*
licit drugs *204*
substance use disorders *204*
substance-induced disorders *204*
parent training *209*
token economy *212*

Attention-Deficit Hyperactivity Disorder

Elliot was extremely active as an infant and toddler. His mother discovered him at 12 months repeatedly climbing out of his crib onto a nearby dresser and jumping from the dresser to the crib. He was enrolled in preschool at age three because his mother was exhausted keeping up with him. Subsequently his teachers noted an inability to sit still and listen respectfully; "disruptive," "silly," and "loud and fast-moving" behavior; and eventually problems with social interactions. (McGrath & Peterson, 2009a, pp. 169–170)

Joan was referred for an evaluation in the eighth grade due to poor school performance. Concerns about academic progress started in early elementary school. By third grade she needed help in reading, and academic problems increased by fifth grade. Now an eighth-grader, Joan has difficulties in focusing and attending, organizing, keeping track of assignments, completing work on time, and reading and writing. (McGrath & Peterson, 2009, p. 174)

The heterogeneous manifestations of attention-deficit hyperactivity disorder (ADHD), some of which are noted in the above case descriptions, are recognized in both dimensional and categorical classifications.

Only a few disturbances of youth have garnered as much public interest and have been so surrounded by debate as ADHD. Controversy has focused on both the nature of ADHD and the pharmacological treatment that was widely introduced in the late 1960s.

EVOLVING IDEAS ABOUT ADHD

What we now refer to as ADHD is a neurodevelopmental disturbance that has lifelong implications. ADHD has traveled a winding path of definitions (Barkley, 2003; Milich, Balentine, & Lynam, 2001). One early account of the disorder was given by the English physician George Still, who described a group of boys with a "defect in moral control" as inattentive, impulsive, overactive, lawless, and aggressive, among other things. In the United States, epidemics of encephalitis in 1917–1918 aroused interest in patients who suffered this brain infection and who were left with some of these attributes. A comparable clinical picture also was noted in children who had suffered head injury, birth trauma, and exposure to infections and toxins.

By the late 1950s, emphasis was given to overactivity or motor restlessness in these children, and the terms *hyperkinesis*, *hyperkinetic syndrome*, and *hyperactive child syndrome* were variously applied. In time, hyperactivity was downgraded in importance, and attention deficits took center stage. The shift was reflected in the DSM-III (1980), which recognized attention deficit disorder (ADD) either *with* hyperactivity or *without* hyperactivity.

More change was yet to come. In the DSM-III-R (1987), the disorder was relabeled "Attention Deficit Hyperactivity Disorder." Children received the diagnosis if they showed 8 or more of 14 items, which could be different mixes of inattention, hyperactivity, and impulsivity. That is, the disorder was viewed as unidimensional, so that any mix of symptoms met the criteria. Nevertheless, the relationship of these three primary features of ADHD was unsettled. Were they part of a single dimension? Or co-occurring but independent of each other? Were two of them alike but different from the third? In time, the unidimensional view fell by the wayside when factor analytic research designed to better understand the nature of ADHD suggested that the disorder consisted of two dimensions or factors: (1) inattention and (2) hyperactivity-impulsivity. There is now substantial cross-cultural agreement on the validly of these two factors (Bauermeister et al., 2010). Further, their association appears to be attributable to shared genetic influence, although each factor also has unique genetic influences (Greven, Asherson et al., 2011).

Critical issues remain concerning the nature and treatment of ADHD, and the last decade or so has brought considerable change to the field. With increased recognition that ADHD did not disappear after childhood, adolescents and adults were given more consideration. In addition, advances in genetics and brain science have continued to create new challenges.

DSM CLASSIFICATION AND DIAGNOSIS

The current DSM recognizes the two factors of inattention and hyperactivity-impulsivity, and uses the label "Attention-Deficit/Hyperactivity" (American Psychiatry Association, 2013). Examples of symptoms of inattention are:

- makes careless mistakes in school or at work
- seems to not listen when spoken to
- fails to follow through on instructions, chores, etc.
- has difficulty in organizing activities
- is distracted by extraneous stimuli

Hyperactivity and impulsivity are exemplified by:

- fidgets with hands or feet or squirms in seat
- runs about inappropriately
- talks excessively
- has difficulty in waiting one's turn
- interrupts or intrudes on others

Depending on the symptom presentation a child is diagnosed into one of three subtypes: **Predominately Inattentive** (ADHD-I), **Predominately Hyperactive/Impulsive** (ADHD-HI), and **Combined** (ADHD-C) that shows both factors.

Diagnosis of ADHD demands the presence of several symptoms before age 12, and display of symptoms for at least 6 months. Because all the criterion behaviors are observed to some degree in normal children and may vary with developmental level, diagnosis is given only when symptoms are at odds with developmental level. The symptoms must be pervasive; that is, they must occur in at least two settings (e.g., home and school). There also must be evidence that the symptoms interfere with, or reduce the quality of, social, academic, or occupational functioning. In addition, the symptoms cannot be explained by other mental disorder.

Our discussion now turns to further description of the primary, or core, features of ADHD and to difficulties that are secondarily associated with the disorder. The general label "attention-deficit hyperactivity disorder" (ADHD) is used to refer to youth diagnosed with the disorder.

DESCRIPTION: PRIMARY FEATURES

Inattention

Adults who come into contact with children with ADHD report various signs of inattention. These children do not listen to what is said to them, are easily distracted, do not stick to a task but jump rapidly from one activity to another, are disorganized, lose things, and daydream. One seemingly baffling aspect of the disorder is that the children appear unable to focus and concentrate at some times, but at other times they are able to sit for hours drawing or building with blocks. In fact, attention is situational; it can appear normal when the child is interested or otherwise motivated but problematic when the task is boring, repetitive, or effortful (Goldstein, 2011).

Although the reports of adults provide good global descriptions of ADHD, formal observation and controlled research have been conducted to validate and elucidate attention deficits. Children and adolescents with ADHD do pay less attention to their work than children with learning disabilities or normal controls (Barkley, 2006f; Kofler, Rapport, & Alderson, 2008). In the laboratory, children with ADHD do less well than control children on many tasks that demand attention, and specific deficits have been identified.

Among these is a deficit in *selective attention* (Brodeur & Pond, 2001; Huang-Pollock, Nigg, & Carr, 2005; Lorch et al., 2000). Selective attention is the ability to focus on relevant stimuli and not be distracted by irrelevant stimuli. For children with ADHD, distraction appears more likely when tasks are boring or difficult or when irrelevant stimuli are novel or salient. Impairment also has been found in *attentional alerting*, that is, the ability to immediately focus on something of importance (Nigg & Nikolas, 2008). In addition, children with ADHD have difficulty in *sustained attention*—in continuing to focus on a task or stimulus over a period of time.

It is noteworthy that attention has many components and is conceptualized in different ways (Nigg, Hinshaw, & Huang-Pollock, 2006; Rothbart & Posner, 2006). Different components, or abilities, develop over different periods and are linked to different brain structures or systems. There is much interest in the role that attention might play in the higher-order regulation of behavior and emotion. It is hypothesized that an executive attention network, involving anterior structures of the brain, modulates the activation of other brain networks (Rothbart & Posner, 2006). Executive attention is thought to be important in tasks requiring the individual, for example, to monitor conflicting stimuli or to suppress a response. As such, executive attention is critical in ADHD because the regulation of behavior is considered central in the disorder.

Hyperactivity and Impulsivity

HYPERACTIVITY   Children with ADHD are described as always on the run, driven by a motor, restless, fidgety, and unable to sit still (Barkley, 2006f). They may display gross bodily movements and talk excessively to themselves or others. In the classroom, they are out of their

seats, moving their arms and legs, and engaging in things irrelevant to the task at hand.

Although much of the information about activity problems comes from parent and teacher reports, objective assessment can be made with direct observations and with actigraphs. The latter are small devices worn by the child to measure movement. Objective measures indicate the excessive movement of children with ADHD, as well as variation across youngsters and situations. In one study, actigraph recording showed no differences in the morning between children with or without ADHD, but in the afternoon non-ADHD youngsters became less active and ADHD youngsters became more active (Figure 9.1). Another study that recorded movement continuously for 1 week showed that boys with hyperactivity were more active than controls during school reading and mathematics but not physical education and lunch/recess (Porrino et al., 1983). In general, motor excess and restlessness are more likely to occur in highly structured situations that demand children to sit still and regulate their behavior in the face of little reinforcement.

IMPULSIVITY   The essence of impulsivity is a deficiency in inhibiting behavior, holding back, or controlling behavior, which appears as "acting without thinking." The child may interrupt others, cut in line in front of others, or heedlessly engage in dangerous behaviors. Activities that require patience or restraint are not well accomplished. Impulsivity often leads others to judge the youth as careless, irresponsible, immature, lazy, or rude (Barkley, 1998).

In the laboratory, impulsivity has been assessed in different ways. Variations of the stop-signal task are widely used (Nigg, 2001). For example, stimuli—such as the letter X and the letter O—are presented on a screen, and the child is told to press one of two keys depending on which stimulus is presented. Key presses are to be withheld on a minority of trials when a special signal (a tone) comes on, so that the child must sometimes rapidly inhibit (stop) the

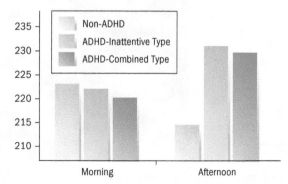

FIGURE 9.1   Mean activity level for morning and afternoon sessions. *Adapted from Dane, Schachar, & Tannock, 2000.*

response. Deficits on the stop-signal task have been shown in several studies with ADHD children (Oosterlaan, Logan, & Sergeant, 1998). This finding, in conjunction with other research, makes clear that problems with inhibition of motor responses are an important aspect of attention deficit-hyperactivity disorder.

DESCRIPTION: SECONDARY FEATURES

In addition to the core problems of ADHD, youths with the disorder experience more than their share of difficulties in diverse areas of functioning. We note, however, that the findings are disproportionately based on school-age children displaying the combined subtype of ADHD, so that caution must be taken in applying them to other youths with ADHD.

Motor Skills

Motor incoordination may affect about half of children with ADHD, a figure that exceeds that for typically developing children (Barkley, 2006a). The difficulties are shown in clumsiness, delay in motor milestones, poor performance in sports, and the like. The child may show neurological soft signs, and various tests indicate deficits in fine motor coordination and timing. A gender difference in motor control appears to favor girls with ADHD, perhaps due to earlier brain maturation (Cole et al., 2008). Children with ADHD appear especially affected when the task involves complex movement and sequencing, which suggests that higher order control processes such as organization and regulation of behavior are affected (Kalff et al., 2003).

Intelligence, Academic Achievement

As a group, children with ADHD perform somewhat lower on intelligence tests than normal control groups, but the association seems modest (Barkley, 2006a). A range of general intelligence is demonstrated, including into the gifted range (Antshel et al., 2007). Many children have specific learning disabilities in reading, mathematics, and other academic areas, which are not due to lowered intelligence (a topic discussed later in the chapter).

Reduced academic achievement is prominent among youth with ADHD (Frazier et al., 2007; Galéra et al., 2009). Academic failure is indicated by low achievement test scores, low school grades, being held back in grade, placement in special education classes, and failure to graduate from secondary school. As many as 56% of children need academic tutoring, 30% may repeat a grade, and 30 to 40% may experience at least one special education placement (Barkley, 2006a). Moreover, from 10 to 35% may fail to graduate high school. A study by Kent and colleagues (2011) found that adolescents with ADHD dropped out of school about 8 times as often as those without ADHD. Teachers noted incomplete homework assignments, excessive absences from school, and failure to work up to potential.

Executive Functions

A subset of children with ADHD exhibit deficits on numerous experimental and neuropsychological tasks that are interpreted as difficulties in **executive functions** (Corbett et al., 2009; Nigg et al., 2006). Executive functions refer to several cognitive processes that are central in the regulation

Although roughhouse play is part of typical childhood activities, the child with ADHD often displays excessively energetic and undercontrolled behavior.

of goal-directed behavior. Executive functions are involved in planning and organizing actions; they include working memory, verbal self-regulation, inhibition of behavior, and motor control. Central in these abilities is the brain's prefrontal cortex and its connections to other brain areas (Miller & Hinshaw, 2010). For children with ADHD, as well as typically developing youths, childhood executive functions have implications for concurrent functioning and they predict academic and social functioning in adolescence.

Adaptive Behavior

Relative to their level of general intelligence, children with ADHD have been shown to have deficiencies in many domains of everyday adaptive behavior. The discrepancy appears larger than for typically developing children and for select other disorders (Barkley, 2006a). Deficits in self-care and independence are sometimes at the level that would be expected with much greater intellectual impairment (Hinshaw, 1998). Many of the children engage in behavior more immature than what their abilities seem to warrant, and require greater monitoring by adults than what might be anticipated. Although failure to learn everyday skills may occur, failure to *perform* known skills might well be more crucial (Barkley et al., 2002). Indeed, because ADHD involves

deficits in sustained attention and in executive functions, which aid in implementing goal-directed behavior, ADHD is frequently viewed as a disorder of performance rather than a deficit in knowing what to do (Goldstein, 2011).

Social Behavior and Relationships

Social difficulties are reported in a high proportion of cases of ADHD, and are an important reason for adults to seek professional help for youths with ADHD. Impairments in social behavior displayed by these children often are associated with two behavioral elements (Nijmeijer et al., 2008). One element concerns restless and intrusive behaviors shown by excessive activity, inappropriate talkativeness, and interrupting others. The other element is an aggressive, negative style of social interaction, exemplified by physical and verbal aggression toward others, rule breaking, and hostile controlling behavior. This negative style likely reflects oppositional defiant disorder (ODD) or conduct disorder (CD) that frequently co-occurs with ADHD. Less recognized, the inattention shown in ADHD also may be linked to social difficulties because it is correlated with not listening, being distracted, having a slow behavioral style, and showing a tendency toward anxiety, shyness, and withdrawal.

"Can't you just relax and enjoy my childhood?"

Not all children with ADHD have social problems, however, which raises the question, What underlies social difficulties? Various explanations have been offered. The youngsters may only inadequately process social-emotional cues (Cadesky, Mota, & Schachar, 2000). Or they may know what is appropriate but be unable to enact the proper behavior, especially when excited or irritated (Melnick & Hinshaw, 1996). Deficits in regulating the emotions, planning and organizing, and working memory, all observed in ADHD, may mediate the relationship between the disorder and poor peer functioning (Mikami, 2010). Moreover, some children with ADHD-C have a relatively stable **positive self-bias** regarding their social competence, behavioral conduct, and academic competence (Hoza et al., 2010; Owens et al., 2007). They are unaware of their negative impact on others, rate their relationships as excessively positive, and overestimate the degree to which they are liked and accepted. It would be mistaken, however, not to recognize that some youngsters with the disorder are aware of, and feel bad about, their social difficulties.

PEER AND TEACHER RELATIONS   Given all this, it is not surprising that children with ADHD are frequently disliked and rejected by peers. After only a few social exchanges, peers may view the child with ADHD as disruptive and unpredictable and react with rejection and withdrawal (de Boo & Prins, 2007). An estimated 50% or more of school-age children with ADHD are peer rejected, compared to 10 to 15% of comparison youths (Mikami, 2010). Whereas negative reactions apply more strongly to children who are impulsive and hyperactive, youths with only attention problems tend to be neglected or ignored (Hinshaw, 1998; 2002b).

In addition to being rejected or neglected, children with ADHD have trouble making and keeping friends, which requires specific skills such as the ability to emotionally connect and express caring (Mikami, 2010). Among other things, the lack of friends means less opportunity to acquire social competence and empathy, and to be protected from bullying. And as we have seen (p. 59), peer problems predict psychological and academic difficulties.

Unfortunately, the child–teacher relationship is also affected. Distractible, disruptive school behaviors can be exhibited very early (Campbell, 2002). In one study, preschool teachers rated young children with ADHD as having more problem behavior and less social skill than typical children (DuPaul et al., 2001). In another study, teachers of young children associated all subtypes of ADHD with less cooperation and other positive behaviors, and they associated hyperactivity-impulsivity with disruptive and less self-controlled behavior (Lahey et al., 1998). Teachers tend to be directive and controlling when interacting with children with ADHD.

FAMILY RELATIONS   ADHD clearly takes a toll on family interaction. Negative exchanges may occur as early as the child's preschool years. In general, parents are less rewarding and more negative and directive (Barkley, 2006d). Mother–child relations appear more difficult than father–child interactions, although the latter are affected. Evidence exists that mothers give more commands and rewards to sons than daughters, and that interactions are more emotional and rancorous. Negative interactions appear to stem from the child's behavior, and conflicts are strongly associated with the child's being oppositional. Families with adolescents who have both ADHD and oppositional disorder appear to have more than the usual number of arguments, negative communications, and hostility (Edwards et al., 2001).

Broader family characteristics associated with ADHD (e.g., marital conflict, stress) play a role in child–parent relationships, and may affect the child's relationship with peers (Mikami et al., 2010). Parents of youths with ADHD are themselves at genetic risk for a variety of problems, including the symptoms of ADHD. A negative family profile is especially associated with the child's being oppositional or displaying conduct problems.

CORY

Being a "Bad Boy"

[Cory's] mother, Mrs. Conner, called the therapist's office in tears....[Cory's] teacher, Ms. Hall, had recommended that [he] be immediately placed on Ritalin, as his hyperactivity was disturbing the class....Mrs. Conner reported that [Cory] was an active child who was always running around the house and crashing into the furniture. She stated that he had walked early, at ten months, and had been keeping her running ever since....

Mr. Conner...believed that [Cory] was being allowed to disrupt class and the teachers just didn't punish him....He went on to report that if he had acted the way [Cory] was acting in school he would have "gotten a beating."...

[Cory] reported that he knew his parents and his teacher were mad at him for being "so bad."

From Morgan, 1999, pp. 6–8.

Health, Sleep, Accidents

There are many reports of general or specific health problems associated with ADHD, including allergies and asthma, but the data are inconsistent and do not allow clear conclusions (Barkley, 2006a).

It is not unusual for parents to report sleep difficulties in children with ADHD. The problems involve inability to fall asleep, night awakening, fewer hours of sleep, and involuntary movements during sleep (e.g., teeth grinding, leg restlessness). However, objective laboratory studies of overnight sleep are inconsistent regarding physiological differences in sleep (e.g., Barkley, 2006a; Kirov et al., 2007). Moreover, it is suggested that sleep difficulties may be due to co-occurring symptoms, such as anxiety and depression. Treatment with stimulant medication may also interfere with sleep.

Relatively well documented is that children with ADHD suffer more accidental injury than those without ADHD (CDC, 2010). A comprehensive review cited 57% of the children as "accident prone," and noted that 15% had at least four or more serious injuries such as broken bones, head lacerations, bruises, lost teeth, and poisonings (Barkley, 2006a). What accounts for these risks? Inattention and impulsivity have been related to unintentional injury (Rowe, Simonoff, & Silberg, 2007). According to parents, children with ADHD are inattentive in risky situations and unmindful of the consequences of their actions. Also noteworthy are motor incoordination, defiant and aggressive behavior associated with ADHD, and inadequate parental monitoring. Some of these factors are involved in the difficulties displayed by adolescents with ADHD regarding automobile-related behaviors. (See Accent: "Autos, Adolescence, and ADHD.")

DSM SUBTYPES

As already noted, the DSM-5 recognizes three subtypes of ADHD: Predominantly Inattentive (ADHD-I), Predominantly Hyperactive/Impulsive (ADHD-HI), and the combination of these symptoms (ADHD-C). This conceptualization was based on research demonstrating the clustering of symptoms and other group differences. Many investigations, including studies in different countries, have provided evidence to validate the subtypes (Gadow et al., 2000; Gomez et al., 1999; Graetz et al., 2001; Hudziak et al., 1998; Lahey et al., 1994). Nonetheless, the data are mixed and issues have arisen regarding subtypes.

One of these issues concerns the diagnosis of ADHD-HI, which requires six symptoms of hyperactivity-impulsivity and fewer than six of inattention. The diagnosis is given to relatively few children, research on ADHD-HI is scant, and the subtype is minimally discussed in this chapter. It has been suggested that ADHD-HI is an early developmental stage of ADHD-C rather than a unique subtype (Barkley, 2006f). In some cases, what seems to be ADHD-HI in preschoolers might better be considered as oppositional defiant behaviors, which may or may not fade.

It is the combined subtype that is most prevalent in clinic samples and has most often been described and investigated. Diagnosis requires that the individual manifest at least six symptoms of hyperactivity-impulsivity and of inattention. The case description of Jimmy illustrates ADHD-C exhibited in a child of almost 7 years of age. The presence of inattention, hyperactivity, and impulsivity are obvious.

The symptoms of ADHD-C can be compared to those of the ADHD, predominantly inattentive subtype. ADHD-I appears to be the most prevalent subtype in

ACCENT
Autos, Adolescence, and ADHD

Most adolescents in the United States look forward to the time they can drive an automobile, whereas parents greet the advent with mixed emotions and worry. Parents appear to have good reason for concern (Barkley, 2006a; CDC, 2010). Several studies give evidence, through self-report and official records, that young people with ADHD are at heightened risk for:

- repeated traffic citations, especially for speeding,
- repeated and more severe vehicular crashes,
- suspension of driving licenses, and
- illegal driving prior to obtaining a license.

In young drivers with ADHD, there is some evidence of inattention, distractibility, and problems in inhibition

(Barkley, 2006a). In a study of young adults who had scored high on ADHD symptoms during adolescence, inattention was linked to serious motor accidents after other influential factors, such as conduct problems and relatively little driving experience, were accounted for (Woodward, Fergusson, & Horwood, 2000). A limited number of investigations have found differences in ratings of actual driving habits, that is, in safely maneuvering and otherwise managing the vehicle. Both adolescents and young adult drivers with ADHD rated themselves as using poorer driving behaviors, and they were similarly rated by others who knew them well (Barkley, 2006a).

Combined Subtype of ADHD

Jimmy was not seen as a "bad" child by his parents; he was not oppositional, aggressive, stubborn, or ill-tempered. But he was in constant motion, and often wandered off, sometimes getting into dangerous situations such as running into the road without looking. Jimmy seemed eager to please his parents, but frequently did not follow through on their requests. It seemed that Jimmy was sidetracked by other things he found more interesting. His parents adopted an active style of dealing with him—monitoring him, reminding him, using immediate reinforcement and punishment.

When Jimmy was enrolled in preschool, his inattentive, overactive, and impulsive behaviors led his parents to withdraw him from one program and his being asked to leave a second program. Among the difficulties were talking during quiet times, lack of interest in group activities, distracting others, and engaging in too much imaginative play. Similar kinds of behaviors were reported in kindergarten, where he had problems focusing attention, being too active, and being unable to work independently. An evaluation at that time showed Jimmy to have high average intelligence but achieving at somewhat lower levels.

By first grade, Jimmy's impulsivity began to interfere with his social relationships. He was described as immature and silly. His peers complained of his bothering them, grabbing them, and pulling them, and although Jimmy was friendly he was unable to maintain friendships. His behavior, more acceptable at early ages, was no longer accepted by peers. The coach noted an inability to participate in organized sports and off-task and silly behaviors. Teachers too had complaints: Jimmy did not follow directions or complete academic tasks on time, and he was disruptive due to excessive activity and noise making. He had fallen behind academically.

From Hathaway, Dooling-Litfin, & Edwards, 2006, pp. 390–391.

population-based samples of children, and interest in an inattentive subtype has existed for many years. Recall, if you will, that the DSM had once recognized a category of attention deficit disorder without hyperactivity. ADHD-I resembles this older category but the DSM-5 diagnosis, along with the requirement of at least six symptoms of inattention, permits up to five symptoms of hyperactivity-impulsivity. Thus, some cases of ADHD-I do not look like "pure" inattention. It is also noteworthy that research with inattentive children has sometimes found a factor referred to as **sluggish cognitive tempo** (Garner et al., 2010). Children displaying a sluggish cognitive tempo tend to be lethargic, prone to daydreams, confused, and more socially withdrawn (Hartman et al., 2004; Milich et al., 2001). These behaviors do not appear on the DSM list of symptoms for ADHD. The portrayal of Tim (p. 225) shows sluggish cognitive tempo and attention deficits in childhood into adolescence. Tim's profile is notably different from the restless, on-the-go, and disruptive behaviors of a child with hyperactive and impulsive behaviors.

For subtypes of a disorder to be valid, they must be different not only in symptoms but also in other important features. Children with ADHD-I are thought to be distinct from those with ADHD-C in several ways (Bauermeister et al., 2005; Faraone et al., 1998; Milich et al., 2001). Age of onset appears to be later, and girls with ADHD appear more likely to be diagnosed with the inattentive subtype than other subtypes (Zalecki & Hinshaw, 2004). ADHD-I children appear more passive and shy; they engage in less fighting and aggression. ADHD-I also is less associated with externalizing disorders and perhaps more strongly linked with internalizing symptoms (Lahey & Willcutt, 2010). Unsurprising then, inattentive children are less rejected by their peers, although they may be isolated. Evidence also exists for differences in educational history, genetics, and biological brain functioning between the inattentive and combined subtypes (Schmitz, Ludwig, & Rohde, 2010).

Although these differences are viewed as supporting ADHD-I as a valid subtype of ADHD, the matter is not settled. Differences between ADHD-I and ADHD-C often have not been found on neuropsychological testing and laboratory studies of inattention and impulsivity (Hinshaw, 2001; Lahey, 2001; Nigg et al., 2002; Pelham, 2001). And prenatal maternal smoking is associated with ADHD regardless of subtype (Schmitz et al., 2010). Such findings suggest to some that the subtypes are not distinct and that ADHD-I may instead be a milder version of ADHD-C.

With an eye toward this issue, Nigg (2006a) and colleagues studied the families of children with ADHD subtypes. Compared with controls, children with ADHD-I did not have elevated family rates of ADHD-C. But children with ADHD-C had elevated family rates of ADHD-I. It was suggested that youths with ADHD-I actually include both (1) children who compose a distinct subtype and (2) children who have a milder version of the ADHD-C subtype.

In addition, some researchers have proposed that inattentive children fall into either a group described by the

TIM

Predominantly Inattentive Subtype of ADHD

Tim was a quiet, somewhat introverted child who was not noticeable in a crowd. His early development was unremarkable, and he was not a behavior problem.

In elementary school, Tim's behavior and academic performance were adequate. But he did not volunteer information, often appeared in a daze, and often did not catch what teachers said when they called upon him. He had no problem in reading words but had difficulty staying with a train of thought, which created comprehension problems. Approaching third grade, with new demands for independent schoolwork, Tim began to have increased difficulties, including completing his work on time. The school determined that he was not eligible for special services, but school personnel commented on his attention lapses, poor focusing, being "spacey," and getting lost in daydreams. His grades in middle school became less consistent, ranging from Bs to Ds, and productivity declined further in seventh and eighth grades. Tim's attention problems and poor study habits took a larger toll in high school, and he was transferred to a vocational high school in eleventh grade.

Despite academic problems, Tim made and kept friends, although he was reserved and indifferent to organized recreational activities. His academic performance was a source of conflict with his mother, who reported that Tim was often irritable, talked back, and blamed others for his mistakes. He was, however, cooperative in other ways, for example, in completing home chores. Based on assessment when he was almost 18 years of age, Tim was described as presumably of average intelligence, with a chronic history of inattentiveness, distractibility, and underachievement.

From Hathaway, Dooling-Litfin, & Edwards, 2006, pp. 410–411.

DSM-5 inattention symptoms *or* a group characterized by dreamy, sluggish cognitive tempo. The latter group might represent a unique subtype of ADHD, or perhaps even a distinct disorder (Barkley, 2006d; Milich et al., 2001; Todd et al., 2005). It has been suggested that sluggish cognitive tempo may involve deficits in selective attention and slow cognitive processing.

Still other investigators, noting that the DSM category of ADHD-I permits up to five symptoms of hyperactivity-impulsiveness, defined inattention subgroups more strictly—that is, by *only* inattention or inattention plus *only a few* HI symptoms. The aim of the strategy was to determine whether stricter criteria would result in differentiating an inattention subtype from other subgroups or typically developing children. The strategy sometimes succeeded and sometimes failed (Carr, Henderson, & Nigg, 2010; Schmitz et al., 2010). It is thus unclear whether stricter criteria for the diagnosis of an inattentive group could prove useful.

A more general concern about DSM subtyping has to do with instability of diagnosis. Children diagnosed into a particular subtype at one point in time often are assigned to a different subtype at another time. Whereas true change could occur, methodological factors appear to play a role. Valo and Tannock (2010) found that as many as 50% of cases in a clinic sample of children were reclassified depending on the assessment instruments used, whether parents or teachers were the informants, and how the information from different sources was combined to reach a diagnosis. Such diagnostic instability challenges the usefulness of the subtypes for clinical and research purposes.

Overall, then, although the two dimensions of attention and hyperactivity-impulsiveness are supported, there is considerable concern and dissatisfaction over the DSM's current conceptualization of these dimensions into three subtypes.

CO-OCCURRING DISORDERS

A remarkable fact about ADHD, especially ADHD-C, is the degree to which it coexists with other disorders or symptoms, including learning disabilities, externalizing and internalizing disorders, and autistic symptoms (Sinzig, Walter, & Doepfner, 2009). As with other psychopathologies, rates of co-occurrence depend on the samples, measures, the specific disorders, and the like. Comorbidity is higher in clinic than in community samples, with more of the referred youngsters likely than not to have another disorder (Costin et al., 2002) and a sizable number exhibiting two or more disorders. Indeed, "pure" ADHD seems to be the exception rather than the rule (Jarrett & Ollendick, 2008). Comorbidity generally is related to greater impairment and developmental risk.

Learning Disabilities

Reports of the rates of learning disability (LD) in youth with ADHD vary enormously, with an overall range of 15 to 40% suggested (Rucklidge & Tannock, 2002;

Schachar & Tannock, 2002). A recent study reported the cumulative incidence of reading disorder by age 19 in those with ADHD to be around 50% for both males and females, much higher than for those without ADHD (Yoshimasu et al., 2010). Unsurprisingly, children with ADHD and LD are at greater risk for academic impairment than children with only ADHD (Smith & Adams, 2006).

Although the relationship between ADHD and learning problems is not completely understood, evidence exists that ADHD leads to reading disability rather than the other way around. Moreover, inattention is more crucially involved than hyperactivity/impulsivity (Greven, Rijsdijk et al., 2011; Paloyelis et al., 2010). Comorbid ADHD and reading problems also appear to reflect the combination of cognitive deficits found in each of the separate disorders—for example, the executive dysfunctions of ADHD and the phonological (language sound) deficits of reading disability (Gooch, Snowling, & Hulme, 2011). The co-occurrence of symptoms of ADHD with reading problems appears to be largely due to shared genetic influence that can persist over time.

Externalizing Disorders

Researchers once wondered whether ADHD and conduct disorders (ODD and CD) were actually only one common disorder. Epidemiological and clinic studies made it clear, however, that these disorders have distinct symptom clusters and other distinct features (Hinshaw & Lee, 2003; Nadder et al., 2001; Waschbusch, 2002). For example, ADHD is more strongly associated with neurocognitive impairment than ODD (Luman et al., 2009), differences in brain abnormalities between ADHD and CD are reported (Rubia et al., 2009), and ODD and CD are more strongly related than ADHD to adverse family factors and psychosocial disadvantage (Waschbusch, 2002).

However, ADHD can lead to ODD that in turn can lead to CD, and the symptoms of ODD and CD frequently co-occur. Indeed substantial percentages of children and adolescents with ADHD develop ODD alone or with CD (Barkley, 2006d). The co-occurrence of the symptoms of these disorders in clinic and nonreferred groups has been extensively investigated. Compared with children with only ADHD, those with the combination often appear more disturbed and impaired, both in ADHD symptoms and conduct problems (Barkley, 1998; Jensen, Martin, & Cantwell, 1997; Waschbusch, 2002). This finding holds for preschoolers as well (Gadow & Nolan, 2002). Importantly, behavioral difficulties appear earlier in children with the combined profile, problems are likely to persist, and outcome is more negative. Other differences are noteworthy. ADHD with co-occurring conduct problems is generally more strongly associated with coercive parent–child interactions, parental psychiatric symptoms and substance abuse, and disadvantaged social class (e.g., Hinshaw & Lee, 2003; Waschbusch, 2002).

Internalizing Disorders

The estimated comorbidity rate of ADHD and anxiety is 25 to 35%, either in clinic or community samples (Barkley, 2006d; Jarrett & Ollendick, 2008). Some, but not all, data suggest that children with both disturbances are less hyperactive and impulsive than those with ADHD who do not have anxiety disorders, and they may display fewer conduct problems and higher levels of inattention. The presence of anxiety with ADHD also may be associated with some differences in performance on cognitive tasks, and differential response to interventions has inconsistently been shown (Hechtman, 2005; Manassis, Tannock, & Barbosa, 2000). Limited research suggests that the comorbid condition is associated with maternal anxiety and overprotective families that discourage autonomy (Jarrett & Ollendick, 2008).

The co-occurrence of ADHD with mild depressive symptoms and major depression is found at varying rates in children and adolescents and in clinic and community samples (Barkley, 2003; Biederman et al., 1996). Perhaps 25 to 30% of ADHD cases on average have major depression. ADHD plus depression frequently results in poorer outcome than either disorder alone (Barkley, 2006d). The association of ADHD with depression is probably complex. For example, one study of clinic youths suggested that ADHD led to ODD and then to various paths to depression (Burke et al., 2005) (Figure 9.2). The co-occurrence of ADHD with depression in youths has been associated with greater family stress and pathology, as well as with an increased risk of family members having both disorders (Barkley, 2006d). Interestingly, the positive illusory bias exhibited by some children with ADHD may serve as short-term protection against depression (Mikami, Calhoun, & Abikoff, 2010).

The co-occurrence of ADHD and bipolar disorder has been reported in the range of 10 to 20% (Barkley, 2003), but there is controversy about this finding (Barkley, 2006d; Hechtman, 2005). The controversy stems in part from the similarity of the symptoms of ADHD and the mania of bipolar disorder; for example, high rates of activity and talkativeness are observed in both ADHD and mania. There is still much to learn about this and other co-occurring conditions.

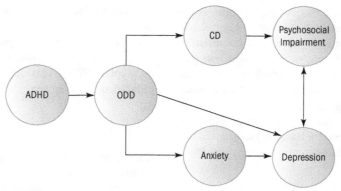

FIGURE 9.2 A developmental model suggested by a study of boys from age 7–12 to age 18. The relationship of ADHD to depression was complex. *Adapted from Burke et al., 2005.*

EPIDEMIOLOGY

The prevalence of ADHD in U.S. school-age children has been estimated as 3 to 7% (American Psychiatric Association, 2000), and recent data suggest the higher figure or perhaps somewhat greater prevalence. A review of multiple approaches to data collection concluded that 6 to 7% prevalence was quite consistently found in the United States (Nigg & Nikolas, 2008). Based on U.S. national surveys of parents, the percentage of youths 5 to 17 years of age who had ever been diagnosed increased from 6.9 to 9% from the years 1998–2000 through 2007–2009 (Akinbami et al., 2011). However, it is unclear whether increased rates indicated a true change or factors such as parental recall or greater identification and diagnosis of ADHD.

In considering prevalence, the distinction must be made between clinically diagnosed ADHD and designations based on parent or teacher ratings of symptoms. Rates are typically higher in the latter kind of reports, and can reach over 20% (e.g., Nolan, Gadow, & Sprafkin, 2001). In fact, higher rates might be expected because the method usually does not include criteria employed for clinical diagnosis such as age of onset, pervasiveness of symptoms, and functional impairment.

In general, less is known about prevalence during the preschool and adolescent years than during childhood. Nevertheless, follow-up studies of children diagnosed with ADHD show declines into adolescence. This finding may be confounded by the fact that diagnostic items for ADHD are suitable for children but have less adequately described how the disorder may be manifested in adolescence (Barkley, 2010; Nigg et al., 2006). Thus, adolescent ADHD has perhaps been underdiagnosed, although it appears that rates may be escalating (MMWR, 2010; Swanson & Volkow, 2009).

Gender

Although gender differences vary across studies, boys consistently outnumber girls. In the general population, the ratio of boys to girls is about 2:1 (American Psychiatric Association, 2013). In community samples, this ratio has been reported as 3.4 boys to 1 girl and as higher in clinic samples (Barkley, 2006f).

Gender differences in clinic samples probably reflect a referral bias due to boys' greater aggressive and antisocial behavior. In addition, the diagnostic criteria are biased toward behaviors observed more in males—such as running, climbing, and leaving one's seat in the classroom. Moreover, when girls are identified it appears to be more on the basis of inattentive and disorganized behaviors, which, it can be argued, are less noticeable than hyperactivity and impulsiveness. These factors may help account for the finding that some girls display the symptoms of ADHD but at levels that do not meet the DSM criteria (Waschbusch & King, 2006). Concern is expressed that girls are underdiagnosed, thereby missing out on preventive or ameliorative interventions.

In order to understand better the impairments of girls with ADHD, Hinshaw and colleagues compared a community sample of girls, ages 6 to 12, with a matched sample of girls without ADHD (Hinshaw 2002b; Hinshaw et al., 2002). Among the findings for those with ADHD were executive function deficits, academic problems, negative peer evaluations, and high rates of anxiety, mood disorder, and conduct problems. Similar results were obtained with girls ascertained from pediatric and psychiatric referrals (Biederman et al., 1999). These studies indicate the need to address the impairments of girls with ADHD.

The question of gender differences has been studied more directly by comparing girls with boys. An early meta-analysis of the research showed that girls were less hyperactive, displayed fewer externalizing symptoms, and had lower intelligence (Gaub & Carlson, 1997). No gender differences were found for a number of other behaviors and correlates. Subsequent reviews were both consistent and inconsistent with these findings and with one another. Later research has provided a clearer picture. It does seem that, in clinic samples, girls display more inattention and less hyperactivity-impulsivity, lower language skills and IQ, and higher rates of internalizing symptoms (Rucklidge & Tannock, 2002; Sowell et al., 2003). Nevertheless, the picture that has emerged also suggests similarities across gender.

Social Class, Race/Ethnicity, and Culture

ADHD appears in all social classes, with higher rates sometimes associated with lower SES (Barkley, 2006f). In the United States, prevalence appears low but increasing among Hispanic youths relative to non-Hispanic youths, and higher in Caucasian children compared to African American youths (MMWR, 2010). Such group differences are probably due to several factors. (See Accent: "ADHD and African American Youth.")

The symptoms of ADHD are reported worldwide with a clinical picture similar to that reported in the United States. That is, the disorder occurs more in boys than girls,

tends to decline in adolescence, and shows many of the same associated characteristics and comorbidities (Canino & Alegría, 2008). Worldwide prevalence has been estimated at slightly over 5%, but it is quite variable across cultures (Nigg & Nikolas, 2008). This may be due to differences in sampling, diagnostic systems, informants, and cultural values.

DEVELOPMENTAL COURSE

It is especially important to study attention-deficit hyperactivity disorder across developmental levels. Because ADHD emerges early for many children, examination of the first years of life can be critical to understanding the origin of the disorder. At the same time, children do not necessarily "outgrow" ADHD, as was once believed, so the developmental course of ADHD can be understood only by observing the persistence of symptoms into adolescence and adulthood.

Infancy and the Preschool Years

At least some cases of ADHD might begin in infancy, but how would ADHD manifest itself so early in life? Behaviors symptomatic of attention-deficit hyperactivity disorder are commonly reported by preschool age, but relatively

ACCENT
ADHD and African American Youth

There is relatively little research on ADHD and children from minority ethnic/racial families, but the lack of information pertaining to African American children is being remedied. Miller, Nigg, & Miller (2009) reviewed research published from 1990 to 2007 that compared these youths, ages 3 to 18, to Caucasian youths. Two major findings emerged.

First, as rated by their parents and teachers, African American youths had more ADHD symptoms than Caucasian youths. SES appeared not to account for this finding, nor did bias on the part of teachers to overrate ADHD behaviors in African American students. Acknowledging that the research base is still small, the reviewers suggested that if African American youths truly exhibit more symptoms, one reason is their disproportionately high exposure to risk factors. For example, these youths tend to have high rates of low birthweight, exposure to lead, and other early developmental insults.

The second major finding of the meta-analysis was that African American youths were diagnosed with ADHD at two-thirds the rate of Caucasian youths. The reviewers asked: What explains this seemingly contradictory result? Based on the review, they suggested the following factors:

- Access to treatment appears to differ by race, with African Americans less likely to receive care and thus diagnosis.
- Barriers to seeking treatment may include families not knowing where to go for help and having negative expectations regarding treatment. Distrust may also exist regarding the educational system that is often vital to identification and care.
- African American parents may be less informed about the disorder; for example, holding inaccurate beliefs about causation (e.g., that excess dietary sugar is causal).
- African American parents may be more likely to hold perceptions about ADHD that discourage help-seeking; for example, that a child's condition reflects an inherent characteristic of the child or bad parenting.

All of the above factors could lead to lack of care for African American children and increased symptoms. Continued research is needed, though, to confirm or extend some of the findings. Miller, Nigg, and Miller suggest that future investigation should explore etiological risk factors for these youths and, in addition, how aspects of African American experiences and culture affect perceptions of ADHD and its treatment.

little is known about this age group (McGrath & Peterson, 2009a). Sanson and colleagues (1993) reported that a group of children who were hyperactive and aggressive at age 8 had displayed early difficult temperament, and by age 3 to 4 had been more active and less cooperative and manageable than typical children. ADHD may result from temperamental tendencies involving poor self-regulation and strong approach behaviors (Nigg, 2006b; Sanson et al., 2009).

Campbell's (2002) study of hard-to-manage preschoolers indicates that problems often lessened, but that for some children symptoms persisted and could meet the criteria for ADHD in childhood. Investigation is ongoing to distinguish early behaviors that might predict later ADHD or conduct problems from the "normal misbehaviors" of young children (Wakschlag & Danis, 2009).

Shaw, Lacourse, and Nagin (2005) have contributed to our understanding of the early course of ADHD symptoms by following a community sample of boys from urban, low-income families from age 1.5 to 10 years. Based on multiple assessments of the core symptoms of ADHD, four developmental paths were suggested. Figure 9.3 shows these trajectories and the percentage of children associated with each of them. Twenty percent of the children displayed a chronically high level of symptoms from age 2 into childhood, and 47% exhibited a relatively stable moderate level of symptoms. Although generalization from this study cannot be made readily, the general findings parallel a study with older children.

Childhood

Most cases of ADHD are referred between the ages of 6 and 12—probably in part due to school demands that children pay attention, follow rules, get along with others, and otherwise regulate their own behavior (Campbell, 2000; Hechtman, 2005). These are the years that have been well described and documented, and during which deficits in inattention may become more obvious. Self-regulation and self-organization are problematic, social relationships can be far from satisfactory, and poor academic achievement is observed. Clinical-level oppositional behaviors, conduct problems, and internalizing symptoms also can become apparent in some children.

Adolescence and Adulthood

In adolescence, the primary symptoms of ADHD—especially hyperactive/impulsive behaviors—decrease in a substantial number of cases, so that the diagnosis of ADHD may no longer apply. Still, the disorder often persists, with estimates ranging from about 40 to 80% of affected youth (Hansen, Weiss, & Last, 1999; Smith, Barkley, & Shapiro, 2006; Willoughby, 2003). Two aspects of symptom manifestation are noteworthy. *First*, heterotypic continuity of symptoms is likely. That is, the core symptoms may carry over in somewhat different forms; for example, overactive running about in childhood may later become manifest as inability to relax. *Second*, many adolescents who no longer meet diagnostic criteria nevertheless display high symptom levels compared to their non-ADHD peers (Barkley, 2010).

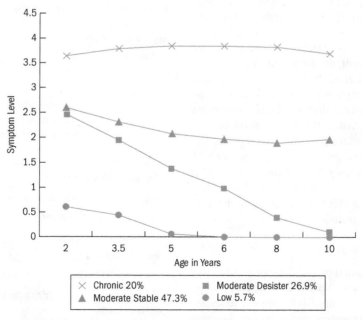

FIGURE 9.3 Trajectories of hyperactivity/attention problems. *Adapted from Shaw, Lacourse, & Nagin, 2005.*

Several longitudinal studies of ADHD leave no doubt that the disorder puts these children at risk for a variety of problems in adolescence. These include poor school achievement, reading problems, internalizing problems, conduct disorder, antisocial behavior, drug use or abuse, social problems, accidents, symptoms of eating disorder, and teenage pregnancy (Fischer et al., 1993; Hinshaw et al., 2006; McGee et al., 2002; Slomkowski, Klein, & Mannuzza, 1995; Smith et al., 2006). Issues that often challenge family relationships in adolescence—noncompliance to rules and conflicts over curfews and schoolwork—may be particularly prominent (Robin, 2006). Although earlier work disproportionately focused on boys, more recent data confirmed that ADHD is similarly hazardous to girls (Biederman et al., 2010; Hinshaw et al., 2006). In a study that assessed adjustment in adolescent girls who had been identified in childhood either with or without ADHD, only 16% compared to 86%, respectively, were positively adjusted in several domains (Owens et al., 2009).

Based on studies that followed ADHD into the adult years, perhaps 40 to 60% of cases still display some core deficits and other problems (Hechtman, 2011). Problems included impaired social relationships, depression, low self-concept, antisocial behavior and personality, drug use, and educational and occupational disadvantage (Biederman et al., 2006; Mannuzza et al., 1993; 1998; Smith et al., 2006; Weiss & Hechtman, 1986). A recent follow-up of girls with ADHD found that, in adulthood, 62% had some ADHD symptoms and significantly greater lifetime risks for mood, anxiety, and antisocial disorders relative to comparison girls. When these now-grown-up girls (mean age of 22 years) were compared to young men of the same age who had similarly been diagnosed with ADHD and similarly followed, risk for later problems was clear in both groups (Biederman et al., 2010). However, the profile of specific disorders was different, as illustrated in Figure 9.4.

Interest has increased in adults who for the first time are identified with the symptoms of ADHD and retrospectively report a history of childhood ADHD symptoms (Faraone & Antshel, 2008). Although the question of reliability must be raised regarding retrospective reports, the prevalence of adult ADHD in the United States appears to be about 4%, with perhaps only 25% of the cases having been diagnosed in childhood or adolescence. These cases of adult ADHD support the view of ADHD as a chronic, lifelong condition for many individuals.

Variation and Prediction of Outcome

In examining the developmental progression of ADHD, it is important to consider the overall picture. *First*, core symptoms, especially hyperactivity-impulsivity, appear to lessen over time. *Second*, many secondary problems develop and can exist into later years. *Third*, the course and outcome

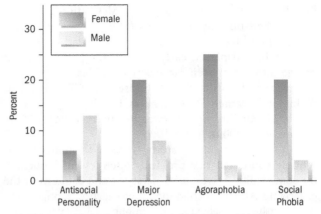

FIGURE 9.4 Percent of young adult females and males exhibiting specific disorders 11 years after being identified with ADHD in childhood/adolescence. *From Biederman et al., 2010.*

of ADHD vary. Some children overcome disorder; others continue to show different kinds and degrees of problems. This fact prompts the question, What variables predict outcome? Many predictors of adolescent and adult problems have been identified (Table 9.1). Genetic factors may have considerable influence on continuity, but the picture is complex. For example, risks may be different for different areas of functioning (Campbell, 1995; Fergusson, Lynskey, & Horwood, 1997; Lahey & Willcutt, 2010; Lambert, 1988; McGee et al., 2002). Poor educational outcome appears especially associated with early deficits in attention, intelligence, and academic skill, as well as with internalizing symptoms and some child-rearing practices. In contrast, the continuance of antisocial behavior is especially associated with family disturbance and the child's aggression and conduct problems.

TABLE 9.1	Some Variables That May Predict Adolescent and Adult Outcomes of Childhood ADHD

Age of onset

Severity of symptoms

Aggression; conduct problems

Academic performance

General intelligence

Family adversities

Parents' ADHD and psychiatric disorder

Parents' child-rearing practice; parent–child interaction

Genetic factors

NEUROPSYCHOLOGICAL THEORIES OF ADHD

Neuropsychological dysfunction in youths with ADHD has led to hypotheses to help account for the disorder. If one imagines a path leading from abnormal genes to ADHD, impaired neuropsychological functions are viewed as laying somewhere along the path. (As such, they are called endophenotypes.) Several accounts of ADHD implicating such functions have been offered; they emphasize executive functions, inhibition, attention, arousal, response to reward, time perception, working memory, or self-regulation (Aguiar, Eubig, & Schantz, 2010; Nigg et al., 2006). These accounts, which tend to be conceptually related, vary in how comprehensive they are, and frequently reference brain functioning. Our discussion highlights executive functions, reward sensitivity, and temporal processing.

Executive Functions and Inhibition

As we have already seen, children with ADHD exhibit deficits in executive functions, the higher order skills required for planning, organizing, and implementing goal-directed behavior (Corbett et al., 2009). One component of executive functions is the ability to inhibit responses. Impairments in executive functions and inhibition, which are well documented in ADHD, hold a central place in various explanations of the disorder.

As an example, we consider Barkley's (1998; 2006b) multifaceted model, which gives a central role to **response inhibition** in the hyperactivity-impulsivity of ADHD. Behavioral inhibition is viewed as critical to the performance of four other executive functions that influence the motor control of behavior (Figure 9.5).

Behavioral inhibition is viewed as consisting of three abilities. *First* is the ability to inhibit prepotent responses, that is, responses that are likely to be reinforced or have a history of reinforcement. *Second* is the ability to

interrupt responses that are already underway and proving ineffective. The *third* ability then comes into play, which is the ability to inhibit competing stimuli—to protect the operation of the executive functions from interference. It can be thought of as freedom from distraction. By preventing prepotent responses, stopping ineffective responses, and hindering distraction, behavioral inhibition sets the occasion for self-regulation, which involves other executive functions. These are briefly described below.

- Nonverbal working memory is part of the memory system that allows the person to hold information in mind, or "on-line," that will be used to control a subsequent response. It involves memory of sensory-motor action.
- Internalization of speech can be thought of as verbal working memory. It allows the person to mentally reflect on rules and instructions that have been internalized to guide behavior.
- Self-regulation of affect, motivation, and arousal involves processes that allow the person to adapt emotion and motivation. It might involve, for example, a lessening of anger, which can affect motivation and arousal.
- Reconstitution allows the person to analyze and synthesize, that is, to break down and recombine nonverbal and verbal units. It allows the construction of novel, creative behaviors or sequences of behaviors.

These four executive functions provide the means for the individual to self-regulate his or her behavior. A child is able to engage in task-relevant, goal-directed, flexible behavior. In contrast, when inhibition is disordered, these executive functions—and thus self-regulation and adaptability—are adversely affected.

Sensitivity to Reward

Unusual **sensitivity to reward** has been noted in children with ADHD (Luman et al., 2009; Nigg & Nikolas, 2008). This has been described as a motivational problem that is displayed as excessive reward-seeking behavior and decreased sensitivity to punishment. Children with ADHD have been shown to do poorly under partial schedules of reinforcement and otherwise low incentives (e.g., Slusarek et al., 2001). Particularly notable is an atypically high preference for immediate reward over delayed reward, even when the immediate reward is smaller. One study suggested that children with ADHD may have abnormal cardiac responses to reward and punishment (Luman et al., 2007). These findings can be interpreted as abnormality in the brain's reward system, which may lead to differences in responding to the usual contingencies involved in paying attention, staying on task, following rules, and the like.

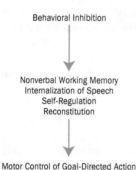

FIGURE 9.5 A schema of Barkley's model of attention-deficit hyperactivity disorder, combined type. *Adapted from Barkley, 1997.*

Temporal Processing and Aversion to Delay

The ability to process time is a multidimensional, fundamental skill that involves perceiving and organizing sequences of events and anticipating the occurrence of future events (Aguiar et al., 2010). Children with ADHD have a deficit in **temporal processing** that is exhibited in a variety of tasks; for example, they underestimate the passage of time. The processing of time is thought to be important in controlling and adapting behavior, and perhaps related to difficulties in waiting and planning (Luman et al., 2009).

Sonuga-Barke and colleagues have proposed that one path to ADHD involves an aversion to the delay of time. In general, **delay aversion** would be manifested by attempts to avoid or escape delay (Sonuga-Barke et al., 2004). From this perspective, the preference that children with ADHD show for immediate over delayed reward may have more to do with avoiding delay than with the reward itself (Sonuga-Barke, 1994). It is argued that in situations where delay cannot be escaped or avoided, children will attend to aspects of the environment that help "speed up" the perception of time. Antrop and colleagues (2000) evaluated this idea by observing children with and without ADHD when they had to wait in a room with little available stimulation. On some measures, the children with ADHD engaged in more activity, presumably to lessen a subjective sense of delay. In another study, Sonuga-Barke and colleagues (2004) found support for the prediction that children with ADHD would be more sensitive to environmental cues for delay because delay has particular emotional or motivational significance for them.

Multiple Pathways?

Because many impairments in ADHD have been found, the early belief that a single neuropsychological or cognitive deficit would explain ADHD has given way to the hypothesis that multiple impairments more likely explain the disorder (McGrath & Peterson, 2009a). It is possible that a single deficit is central for some children while a different deficit defines others, and that subtypes based on neuropsychological impairments might exist. Perhaps ADHD is best viewed as a large umbrella that subsumes groups of individuals who exhibit different deficits and different etiological pathways (Taylor & Sonuga-Barke, 2008).

Although research on this issue is not extensive, a dual-pathway model has been offered. It proposed independent pathways in the development of the disorder, encompassing two alternative explanations (Sonuga-Barke, Dalen, & Remington, 2003). According, one pathway is mediated by executive function deficits and the other by delay aversion. Somewhat different brain circuitry is thought to underlie these pathways. There is some evidence for the dual-pathway model (Martell, Nikolas, & Nigg, 2007; Thorell, 2007).

More recently, Sonuga-Barke, Bitsakou, and Thompson (2010) explored the possibility that temporal processing might constitute a third pathway. Children with ADHD and non-ADHD control children were given tasks that evaluated either inhibition, or delay aversion, or temporal processing. For those with ADHD, the co-occurrence of deficits on these three kinds of tasks was no greater than expected by chance. Moreover, deficits on only one type of task was observed in many children. The findings supported a triple pathway model and subtypes of neuropsychological impairment. Such heterogeneity in ADHD requires further research.

NEUROBIOLOGICAL ABNORMALITIES

Brain damage or injury was once considered primary in ADHD. When it became evident that brain damage could not be identified in most children with the disorder, it was assumed that some undetectable "minimal brain dysfunction" existed. By the late 1950s and early 1960s, the need for better empirical evidence was recognized. Today, substantial evidence implicates brain dysfunction.

Numerous brain structures are implicated in ADHD, including the frontal lobe and underlying striatal regions, parietal lobe, temporal lobe, thalamus, corpus callosum, and cerebellum. Reduced brain volume has been revealed for several brain structures, with reductions in total volume estimated at 3 to 5% (Taylor, 2009). There tends to be an association between small brain volume and severity of ADHD symptoms (Aguiar et al., 2010). Research has also found an absence of the asymmetry observed in the frontal lobes in typical development in which the right lobe is usually larger than the left (McGrath & Peterson, 2009a).

Interest has focused particularly on the prefrontal lobes and connections to the striatal region that lies deeper in the brain and to the cerebellum (Figure 9.6). The research findings are compelling. Smaller-than-average size of the prefrontal area and parts of the striatum and cerebellum has been associated with ADHD (Aguiar et al., 2010; Barkley, 2006e, Yeo et al., 2003). And volume of the frontal, striatal, and temporal lobe region has been found to be directly related to inhibition (McAlonan et al., 2009). The prefrontal lobe and striatal area have been associated with the core symptoms of ADHD, as well as many of the neuropsychological deficits identified in ADHD—such as inhibition, working memory, and other executive functions—as well as reward and motivation (Casey et al., 1997; Semrud-Clikeman et al., 2000; Volkow et al., 2009). In addition, various brain scans and electrophysiological measures indicate that youths with ADHD have decreased

Dopamine System

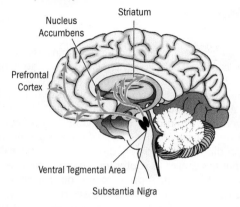

Norepinephrine System

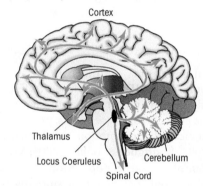

FIGURE 9.6   The frontal cortex, striatum, and cerebellum and their connections play an important role in ADHD. Dopamine and norepinephrine circuits are implicated in the disorder. *Adapted from Aquiar, Eubig, & Schantz, 2010.*

blood flow, decreased glucose utilization, and slow brain waves—all signs of underactivity—in the frontal areas and pathways connected to the striatal areas and the cerebellum (Dickstein et al., 2006; McGrath & Peterson, 2009a).

Another focus of neurobiological research is the biochemistry of the brain. The best evidence implicates deficiencies in dopamine and norepinephrine (see Figure 9.6). These neurotransmitter circuits have branches in the areas involving executive functions, reward, and motivation—all implicated in ADHD (Taylor & Sonuga-Barke, 2008; Volkow et al., 2009). Consistent with these findings, medications used to treat ADHD increase dopamine and norepinephrine by facilitating their release into the synapses or by blocking their reuptake by the presynaptic neurons (Aguiar et al., 2010). Nevertheless, it is likely that the interaction of several neurotransmitters is involved in ADHD, including serotonin and acetylcholine.

Several conclusions can be drawn from investigations of the brain. *First*, abnormalities in the frontal, striatal,

and cerebellar structures and their networks appear to play an important role. *Second*, underarousal of the brain is implicated. *Third*, dopamine and norepinephrine deficiency are implicated. *Fourth*, other brain regions have been implicated. ADHD is undoubtedly a heterogeneous disorder with disturbances in various brain regions or networks involved. Progress has been made in understanding brain functioning but much is still to be learned.

A key issue regarding brain abnormalities in ADHD is whether they represent a deviation from typical development or a delay in maturation. The hypothesis of delayed brain maturation has received some support. In typical development, the cortex of the brain thickens (increases in volume) throughout childhood, reaches a peak in late childhood, and thins out in adolescence. This progression occurs in primary sensory areas before higher order association areas. A study by Shaw and colleagues (2007) has shown the same pattern in youths with ADHD, but with notable delay. In the typically developing comparison group, 50% of the cortical points reached peak thickness at the median age of 7.5 years; in the ADHD group this figure was 10.5 years. Delayed maturation was greatest in the prefrontal region. Interestingly, recent research on the developmental thinning of the cortex in ADHD has addressed another crucial issue concerning ADHD: whether it is best viewed as categorical or dimensional. (See Accent: "ADHD: Category or Dimension?")

ETIOLOGY

Genetic Influences

Strong support for substantial genetic effects on ADHD comes from both quantitative and molecular genetic research. The families of children with ADHD have higher rates of psychopathology than would be expected, and between 10 to 35% of first-degree family members are likely to have ADHD (Barkley, 2006e; Tannock, 1998). Children of parents with ADHD are also at high risk for the disorder. Family aggregation studies also suggest genetic influence on the co-occurrence of ADHD with some other disorders. Further, limited research shows reduced brain size in the unaffected siblings of children with ADHD (Durston et al., 2004), and lower frontal area activity in parents who themselves had displayed symptoms of hyperactivity (Hechtman, 1991; Taylor, 1994; Zametkin & Rapoport, 1986).

Twin studies provide clear evidence of genetic influence. Estimates of heritability are as high as .90, with average heritability across studies at about .80 (Elia et al., 2010; Smith et al., 2006). Heritability has been documented with a variety of measures, informants, and populations.

ACCENT
ADHD: Category or Dimension?

Shaw and colleagues (2011) noted the considerable debate over whether ADHD should be viewed as a category with distinct boundaries or as represented dimensionally. In fact, much research suggests that the symptoms of ADHD, as well as the neuropsychological impairments associated with it, lie on a continuum of severity. Those diagnosed with the disorder are seen as situated at the extreme of the continuum. The investigators were interested in incorporating the biological underpinnings of ADHD into the debate.

They contrasted MRI brain images of youths, 8 years or older, diagnosed with ADHD with images from typically developing youths. All participants were evaluated for hyperactivity/impulsivity behaviors. The investigators then examined the rate of cortical thinning relative to the severity of these behaviors, or symptoms. The estimated rate of thinning was slowest for the youths with ADHD, as would be expected from previous research. Tellingly, across all the participants, rate of thinning depended on the severity of symptoms, with greater severity associated with progressively slower rates of thinning. The finding that non-diagnosed, typically developing youths exhibited brain changes similar to youths with the syndrome of ADHD lends neurobiological support to the dimensional view of ADHD. Although this study addresses only one aspect of the neurobiology of ADHD, it presents important findings (Klein, 2011; Shaw et al., 2011).

Individuals defined categorically with the diagnosis of ADHD or its subtypes have been studied, as well as individuals defined dimensionally (Goldstein, 2011).

Molecular studies have increased our understanding of the etiology of ADHD. The DRD4 and the DAT1 genes—both involved with dopamine transmission—were the first to be associated with the disorder and other genes, including genes involving norepinephrine and serotonin, have been implicated (Taylor, 2009). Genome-wide association studies are being conducted and suggest that the genes identified each have only very small effects (Neale et al., 2010).

Recent genome-wide scans have begun to compare copy number variations (CNVs) in ADHD samples and healthy controls. One investigation showed a higher rate of rare missing or duplicated segments of DNA in children with the disorder, particularly those with lower IQ, (Williams et al., 2010). (A CNV is considered rare when its population rate is less than 1%.) Another study did not find increased rates, but the rare inherited CNVs that were identified involved genes important in CNS development, synaptic transmission, learning, and behavior (Elia et al., 2010). Such structural variations, and the candidate genes they suggest, will undoubtedly be further investigated.

Overall, it appears that the genetics of ADHD is far from simple. Perhaps there are no genes with large effects (Goldstein, 2011). Moreover, genetic heterogeneity is likely—that is, different genes or variations in a single gene, or different genetic mechanisms might contribute to the disorder. Genes may interact with each other and with other influences. In this regard, it is important to note that heritability estimates include the effects of gene–environment interaction (Taylor & Sonuga-Barke, 2008). The need for increased research on gene–environment interaction is warranted.

Prenatal Influences and Birth Complications

Prenatal conditions are inconsistently associated with symptoms of ADHD or diagnosed ADHD. The discrepant findings may in part be due to methodological issues (Lavigne et al., 2010). Nonetheless, prenatal tobacco smoking and alcohol consumption may be hazardous (Linnet et al., 2003; Rodriguez & Bohlin, 2005; Vuijk et al., 2006). For example, a large population study conducted in Finland showed that maternal smoking was associated with hyperactivity after adjustment for several other variables (Kotimaa et al., 2003). In an extensive U.S. study that followed women from pregnancy to the time their offspring were 14 years old, prenatal alcohol use was linked to activity level, attention deficits, and difficulties in organizing tasks (Streissguth et al., 1995). Interestingly, gene–environment interactions have been reported between DRD4 or DAT1 genes and prenatal smoking or alcohol exposure (McGrath & Peterson, 2009a). For example, a variation of the DAT1 gene was found to moderate the risk of prenatal alcohol exposure (Brookes et al., 2006). In addition, animal studies showing adverse effects of prenatal alcohol and nicotine exposure on the brains of offspring are consistent with the reduced size of brain networks reported for ADHD (Mick et al., 2002).

Some studies indicate a higher risk for ADHD among children who suffered injury at birth or were born preterm or with low birthweight (Smith et al., 2006). A recent study of a national cohort of children born in Sweden between 1987 and 2000 found that both moderate and especially extreme prematurity increased the risk of ADHD at school age (Lindström, Lindblad, & Hjern, 2011). The findings were not accounted for by genetic, perinatal, or socioeconomic variables, but low maternal education raised the effect of moderate prematurity. Low birthweight also is associated with risk of attention problems or ADHD (Aarnoudse-Moens et al., 2009; Heinonen et al., 2010). In addition, small body size and head circumference at birth were implicated in a study in which the effects appeared not accounted for by several other factors (Lahti et al., 2006).

Diet and Lead

The possible etiological role of diet has been of interest for many years. One controversial idea was that foods containing artificial dyes, preservatives, and naturally occurring salicylates (e.g., in tomatoes and cucumbers) were related to hyperactivity. Subsequent research largely did not support the claim (Harley & Matthews, 1980; Spring, Chiodo, & Bowen, 1987). Similarly, meta-analysis of research showed that neither the behavior nor cognitive functioning of children with ADHD was affected by sugar intake (Wolraich, Wilson, & White, 1995). It is generally accepted that food does not play a strong, if any, role in causing ADHD. Nevertheless, there is some renewed interest in the hypothesis that hypersensitivity to select foods or additives may affect a subset of children with ADHD (Nigg et al., 2012; Pelsser et al., 2011).

That lead should be suspected of causing ADHD is not unreasonable because lead exposure has been linked to deficits in biological functioning, cognition, and behavior. Recent research showed an association of lead exposure with diagnosed ADHD, as well as with deficits in several executive functions known to be impaired in children with ADHD (Eubig, Aguiar, & Schantz, 2010; Nigg et al., 2008). The overall influence of lead exposure on ADHD may be quite small (Barkley, 2006a), but this does not imply that caution should be thrown to the wind, nor that lead does not have other negative effects on children. Prudence demands the continued protection of children from lead based paints, toys, automobile emissions, leaded crystal and ceramic dishes, and solder on old copper pipes.

Psychosocial Influences

Few researchers and clinicians believe that psychosocial factors are a primary cause of ADHD. For one thing, genetic risk appears to account for a substantial portion of the variance of ADHD symptoms in the general population and in diagnosed ADHD (Burt, 2009; Wood et al., 2010). There is some evidence, however, that psychosocial factors are likely to affect the severity, continuity, and nature of the symptoms, as well as associated and co-occurring disturbances.

Family factors are among the psychosocial variables thought to be especially influential. Numerous family correlates of children's ADHD have been described, including economic disadvantage, stress, conflict and separation, and poor mental health and coping (Barkley, 2006d; Goodman & Stevenson, 1989; McGee et al., 2002). Nigg and Hinshaw (1998) observed that boys who had ADHD with or without antisocial behavior were more likely to have mothers with a history of depression and/or anxiety and fathers with a childhood history of ADHD. Tully and colleagues (2004) examined ADHD symptoms displayed by 5-year-old twins who had been born with low birthweight; they found that maternal warmth had a moderating effect on ratings of symptoms.

Overall, there is evidence that ADHD in children can affect parent behavior and that parent behavior can influence the nature and perhaps development of ADHD (Johnston & Mash, 2001). Family influence nevertheless should be regarded cautiously, as findings have been inconsistent. And more needs to be learned about the possible interaction of genetic and psychosocial influences, and other ways in which these influences may be correlated. For example, a child and parent may share a genotype that readily leads to impulsive, disorganized behavior (Nigg, 2006a). The parent's behavior may affect the child's development of self-regulation, and the child's behavior may elicit ineffective parenting. Thus, inheritance is a factor and gene–environment correlation comes into play.

Children's school behavior is important in the identification and diagnosis of ADHD. How teachers manage the behavior of their students might play a role in shaping classroom attentiveness and impulsivity (Leflot et al., 2010). In addition, classroom organization and how activities are structured can influence a child's behavior and academic achievement, perhaps especially a child predisposed to ADHD (Pfiffner, Barkley, & DuPaul, 2006). This does not imply that teacher behavior causes ADHD but that it may affect its manifestation and outcome.

A SCHEMA OF THE DEVELOPMENT OF ADHD

Overall, the research on ADHD has led to better understanding of genetic influences on ADHD, how brain functioning is related to the symptoms of the disorder, and how environmental influences may play some etiological role or shape and maintain the problem behaviors. Figure 9.7 presents a simple schematic representation of the development of ADHD, which draws on the work of Taylor and Sonuga-Barke (2008). It indicates that various risk genes, possibly interacting with prenatal or perinatal influences, give rise to brain abnormalities and correlated neuropsychological impairments. As we have seen, different brain anomalies have been found in ADHD, as well as in

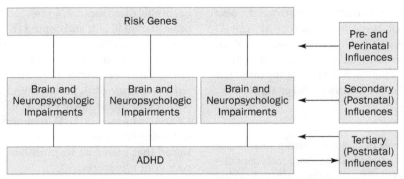

FIGURE 9.7 A complex of interacting genetic and environmental influences result in different pathways in the development of ADHD. *Based on Taylor & Sonuga-Barke, 2008.*

different neuropsychological impairments. Thus, different pathways may lead to the diagnosis of ADHD. (The schema shows three hypothetical pathways.) Postnatal environmental influences play important roles in these pathways. Some secondary factors may directly affect brain processes (e.g., diet, toxins). Other, tertiary, influences may mediate or moderate outcome by way of social interaction (e.g., negative parenting). This complex of influences can lead not only to ADHD but also to the various disorders that commonly co-occur with ADHD.

This schema, does not, of course, include everything about the developmental course of ADHD. For example, it says nothing about the relative importance of genetic and environmental influences, nor is it very informative regarding some social, academic, and other functional problems that often characterize the disorder. Nevertheless, Figure 9.7 provides a basic framework for thinking about the development of ADHD.

ASSESSMENT

Whether the purpose of assessment is identification of ADHD, planning for treatment, or both, several aspects of the disorder serve as useful guidelines (Barkley, 1990; 1997; Hinshaw & Erhardt, 1993; Pliszka et al., 2007).

- Because ADHD is best conceptualized as a biopsychosocial disorder, assessment must be broad-based.
- Because ADHD is a developmental disorder, a developmental history is important and assessment will vary somewhat with developmental level.
- Because ADHD is pervasive and may manifest itself differently in different settings, information specific to the settings should be obtained.
- Because ADHD has high rates of co-occurrence with other psychological disorders, assessment requires careful distinction from other disorders.

The following discussion emphasizes the psychological and social factors most pertinent to assessment, and draws heavily on Barkley and Edwards (2006) and Pliszka and colleagues (2007).

Interviews

ADHD is most often assessed early in life, so parents are critical in the interview process. Information needs to be obtained about the child's specific problems and impairments, strengths, developmental and medical history, academic achievement, and peer relationships. Questions about family stress and relationships are recommended because these are central in the child's social environment and have implications for treatment. A semistructured interview combined with a standardized structured interview (e.g., The Diagnostic Interview for Children and Adolescents) offers a reliable and efficient way to collect a wealth of information (Barkley & Edwards, 2006).

It is also important to assess specific parent–child interactions, not only for diagnosis but also for treatment planning. It is useful to pose specific questions, directing attention to specific situations relevant to the child's problems and how they are managed. Questions may be asked about what the child does, how the parents respond, and how often problems occur in specific situations such as mealtimes, or when the child is asked to complete chores.

The youth being assessed should also be interviewed. With younger children, the interview may simply be a time for getting acquainted, establishing rapport, and observing the child's appearance, language, interpersonal skills, and the like (Barkley & Edwards, 2006). Observations must be interpreted cautiously, however, because children with ADHD may act more appropriately during office visits than they do in other settings. Discussion with older children and adolescents can include their views on their problems, school performance, peer relationships, the way they see their family functioning, what they think would make life better, and the like. Although the report of youths with ADHD may reflect a positive bias toward their symptoms, a private interview permits the reporting of problems or issues they may not want to discuss in the presence of parents (Pliszka et al., 2007). Interviews need to be adapted to the child's developmental status, of course, and with children it is beneficial to approach issues as they might see them (Table 9.2).

Teacher interviews can be invaluable to address difficulties in the school setting that may not be validly assessed by parents (Mitsis et al., 2000). A direct interview is preferable, with a focus on learning, academic problems, and peer interaction. In addition, information can be obtained about parent–school interaction and cooperation, as well as school services. Some youth with ADHD have rights to special evaluation and educational services. Indeed, many of these children receive special education services under the Individuals with Disabilities Education Act, often under the categories of learning disabilities or behavior/emotional disturbance. (See p. 271 for relevant discussion.)

Rating Scales

Parent and teacher rating scales and checklists, which are popular tools for assessing ADHD, can provide a great deal of information with relatively little time and effort. Many of the scales are reliable and valid, are consistent with the DSM conceptualization of ADHD, and can contribute to clinic and research efforts (Collett, Ohan, & Myers, 2003). Some of these tools are broad in scope and identify not only ADHD but also its co-occurrence with other disorders. Scales with a narrower focus are useful in assessing specific aspects of ADHD.

An example of a widely employed instrument is the Conners rating scales. Based on elements of previous Conners scales, the Conners Third Edition offers parent, teacher, and self-report scales in long and abbreviated forms (Conners, 2008). The scales address both ADHD symptoms and associated disorders for ages 8 to 18 for the self-report version and 6 to 18 for the other two versions (Table 9.3). The ADHD Index is designed to rapidly identify those at risk for ADHD, and can be used to monitor the effectiveness of treatment. The Global Index, also sensitive to treatment effects, assesses general psychopathology.

Direct Observation

Direct observation in natural settings can be extremely useful because the behavioral manifestations of ADHD are situational. Home and school observations can be well worth the time they require, and observations to target behaviors for intervention can be critical to successful treatment (Jacob & Pelham, 2000). Signs of the primary features of ADHD are of utmost importance, of course, but so also are indications of noncompliance, aggression, attention-seeking, and other characteristics of social interactions and relationships. Several observational coding systems for ADHD are available.

TABLE 9.2 It Is Beneficial to Pose Interview Questions That Consider the Child's Perspective. These Examples Target the Child's School Experience

- "Do you ever find that you've been sitting in class, and all of a sudden you realize your teacher has been talking and you have no idea what she's [or he's] talking about?"
- "Does it ever seem to take you longer to get your work done compared to other kids?"
- "Do you think your work is messier than other kids' work?"
- "Do you have trouble keeping track of things you need for school?"
- "Do you have trouble finishing your homework?"
- "Does your teacher ever have to speak to you because you're talking when you're not supposed to be talking, or fooling around when you're supposed to be working?"

From *Barkley & Edwards, 2006.*

TABLE 9.3 Conners Third Edition Scales and Forms

Hyperactivity/impulsivity

Inattention

Learning problems

Executive functions

Aggression

Peer relations

Family relations

Oppositional defiant disorder

Conduct disorder

ADHD symptoms

ADHD Index

Global Index

From *Conners, 2008.*

Other Procedures

Additional assessment methods are often useful and/or necessary. Standardized tests of intelligence, academic achievement, and adaptive behavior can be helpful, particularly in clarifying issues pertaining to academic functioning.

Various kinds of procedures to specifically evaluate inattention and impulsivity have been developed (Gordon, Barkley, & Lovett, 2006). For example, the Conners' Continuous Performance Test II requires the client to press a computer key or click a mouse when any letter except X appears on a screen. Designed for children 6 years and over, the CPT II can be used in screening or diagnosing ADHD and monitoring treatment. The Connors' Kiddie Continuous Performance Test is an adaptation for 4- and 5-year-olds.

When medical factors are suspect, medical evaluation can provide information potentially useful in treatment or in understanding ADHD. Such assessment reasonably includes a neurological examination, but neurological tests such as the EEG and brain scans are not generally recommended for children because they do not validly distinguish ADHD and may present safety issues (Pliszka et al., 2007).

INTERVENTION

Prevention

It is reasonable to assume that prenatal care, avoidance of environmental toxins, and optimal family life might help prevent or minimize ADHD. Nevertheless, the most effective efforts are likely to be directed at both early treatment of symptoms and reduction of secondary problems that interfere with healthy development. As we have seen, the core symptoms of ADHD not only have immediate impact, but may also set into motion an array of functional problems that continue even after core symptoms lessen. It is important that these functional impairments be considered (Pelham et al., 2010).

For example, academic tutoring may avert the school problems many children with ADHD experience. Another example is training parents to manage their child with disruptive behaviors in order to prevent further development of noncompliant or oppositional child behaviors, which could put the child at risk for ODD and CD (Anastopoulos, Rhoads, & Farley, 2006). Efforts to facilitate appropriate social interaction might also be important because the negative social behaviors often observed in ADHD can be long lasting and affect other areas of functioning. In addition, monitoring the child's behavior for drug use/abuse and interventions aimed at interfering with this developmental path are important (Charach et al., 2011; Wilens, 2011).

Pharmacological Treatment

Many treatment approaches exist for ADHD—for example, cognitive-behavioral training, social skills training, and individual counseling (Toplak et al., 2008). Nevertheless, by far the most widely employed interventions—judged as evidence-based, short-term treatments—are stimulant medications, behaviorally oriented approaches, and a combination of these (American Psychological Association, 2006). Our discussion begins with pharmacological treatment.

A report by Bradley in 1937 is usually cited as the first treatment of childhood behavioral disorders with **stimulant medication** (Swanson & Volkow, 2009). Many pharmacological agents have been used since then, but stimulants are the most frequently prescribed psychotropic medications for children, primarily for ADHD. The stimulants increase dopamine and norepinephrine in the brain's neural networks. Among the most commonly used are methylphenidate and amphetamine (Table 9.4). The slow release, long-acting versions of these medications require only a daily dose and are more often used than the immediate release, short-acting versions that must be taken several times a day.

Although much controversy surrounds the use of stimulants, in the view of most professionals these medications help alleviate the primary deficits of ADHD. Seventy to 75% of medicated children show increased attention and reduced impulsivity and activity level (Connor, 2006;

TABLE 9.4	Some Commonly Used Medications to Treat ADHD

Stimulants (s)short acting, (l)long acting
  Methlyphenidate
    Ritalin (s)
    Concerta (l)
    Daytru (Patch)

  Amphetamines
    Dexedrine (s)
    Adderal (s)
    Adderal XR (l)

Norephinephrine Reuptake Inhibitor
  Atomoxetine (Strattera)

Other Medications
  Antidepressants
    Bupropion
    Tricyclics (Imipramine, Desipramine)
  Antihypertensives
    Clondine
    Guanfacine

Van der Oord et al., 2008). In addition, stimulants can reduce co-occurring aggressive, noncompliant, oppositional behaviors, and to a lesser extent, social problems. Perhaps not surprising, parents and teachers interact more positively with children who are benefiting from medication (Chronis et al., 2003). Some research also indicates benefits for academic performance, although the effects may be small and further investigation is needed (Marcus & Durkin, 2011; Scheffler et al., 2009).

Most research on stimulants has been conducted with school-age children, but some recent studies have included preschoolers and adolescents. Due largely to increased medication use with preschoolers (Zito et al., 2000), the National Institutes of Mental Health funded a multisite, randomized study of 3 to 5.5-year olds. Significant decreases were found for ADHD symptoms, although the effects were smaller than for school-age children and there was concern about side effects (Greenhill et al., 2006). Stimulants also benefit adolescents, although the response rate may be somewhat less than for children (Connor, 2006). Overall, an impressive amount of data support the claim for the effectiveness of stimulants across settings, measures, and ages. Nevertheless, stimulants do not work well for all youths and families, a fact that often goes unacknowledged. (See Accent: "Medication Does Not Always Work.") In addition, several concerns are expressed regarding pharmacological treatment of ADHD.

CONCERNS An often-expressed concern is adverse biological side effects, which may affect preschoolers more than older children (Wigal et al., 2006). Sleep problems, decreased appetite, stomach pain, headaches, irritability, and jitteriness have all been reported. The effects are often mild to moderate and may diminish in a few weeks, but can lead to discontinuance of treatment. Also reported is a small suppression of growth in height and weight (Faraone et al., 2008), which may weaken over time and become normal when treatment ceases. Aware of the issue of growth suppression, Shaw and colleagues (2009) examined cortical brain growth in adolescents and found no association with stimulant treatment. An initiation or worsening of motor and vocal tics has been reported but the finding has been challenged (Gadow et al., 2007; Pliszka et al., 2007).

There is also continuing concern that stimulant use in childhood is a risk factor for later substance use/abuse. Several recent investigations have confirmed that children with ADHD are at significant risk for developing use/abuse for nicotine, alcohol, marijuana, cocaine, and other drugs (Charach et al., 2011; Lee et al., 2011). However, it is not clear that early use of stimulants *causes* later drug abuse. Numerous factors may be involved. For example, shared genetic influence may underlie risk for both ADHD symptoms and substance abuse, and the comorbidity of ADHD and externalizing disorders may play a role (Brook et al., 2010; Wilens, 2011). Nonetheless, a related issue that warrants a watchful eye is the abuse of the stimulants themselves. In this regard, it is recommended that stimulants not be prescribed if there is any known or suspected drug use (Connor, 2006).

Despite the legitimate concerns about medication treatment, when stimulants are prescribed and used appropriately, they are considered relatively safe for most young people. This does not mean, of course, that the need for monitoring should be taken lightly. Individuals vary in their responses to different medications and to different dosages. Indeed, warnings exist, for example,

ACCENT
Medication Does Not Always Work

For a variety of reasons, medication is not a preferred or effective treatment for some youths and families, as the following indicate.

- For a small number of children, biological side effects are not tolerated.
- Research shows that the primary symptoms of ADHD are not alleviated in 10 to 20% of children (Anastopoulos et al., 2006) and perhaps a larger percentage of preschoolers.
- Even when symptoms are alleviated, in only about 50% of cases is behavior improved so as to be comparable to that of typical children.

- Improvement dissipates when these drugs are no longer taken, and long-term effects have not been well documented (Molina et al., 2009; Pfiffner et al., 2006).
- An estimated 25 to 45% of children do not adhere to treatment regimes; more than half of patients with ADHD discontinue treatment regardless of its efficacy (Pappadopulos et al., 2009). Parents may not always be aware of their child's non-adherence.
- Medication is simply rejected by some families (Vitiello et al., 2001). Limited data show that African American families especially may be unenthusiastic about pharmacological treatment (Miller et al., 2009).

about the use of Adderall XR in youths with underlying heart defects. Nonstimulant medications may be options for some children, but these also have side effects (Lewis, 2010). Monitoring is always essential and reasonable caution always appropriate.

Even so, critics have argued that medication is too readily prescribed. This argument is supported by a rise in prescriptions from the 1980s through the 2000s, with a fourfold increase among children from 1987 to 1996 (Zuvekas, Vitiello, & Norquist, 2006). Medication use leveled off between 2000 and 2007 among children 0–14 years of age, but increased in adolescents and young adults (Swanson & Volkow, 2009). Some critics argue that medication serves as a "quick fix" for some schools and parents. In this regard, it is interesting that some research shows differences in medication use across countries and greater use of stimulants in the United States (Zito et al., 2008). Several related factors are likely to explain such differences: cultural beliefs about behavioral disturbances and pharmacological intervention, government policies, advertising by pharmaceutical companies, and the like.

The issue of medication treatment is complex. For example, research suggests that combining even low-intensity behavioral treatment with stimulants may allow for lower dosage of medication—and thus fewer side effects (Fabiano et al., 2007). More general is the issue of inappropriate prescription practices. Reich and colleagues (2006) found that 59% of boys and 46% of girls who met the criteria for ADHD received medication, whereas 35% receiving stimulant medication did not meet the diagnostic criteria, although they had symptoms of ADHD. Yet another investigation, which showed increased use of anti-psychotic medications in 2-to-5-year-olds, found that almost one-fourth of the cases were of ADHD, and that most of the children had not received an assessment, a psychotherapy visit, or a visit with a psychiatrist during the year examined (Olfson et al., 2010).

Concern about the use and misuse of medication for ADHD has at times led to heated controversy, fed by media coverage in major magazines and on television. Media attention that serves to educate is beneficial, of course. Unfortunately, concerns about medications have sometimes been expressed in emotionally charged, exaggerated—and perhaps harmful—ways by parents, professionals, and organized groups (Barkley, 1998; Swanson et al., 1995). At the same time, professionals who recognize the benefits of stimulants also point to their limitations and warn against their misuse or overuse. An additional consideration in the overall picture is the potential conflict of interest inherent in the participation of large pharmaceutical companies in clinical trials evaluating the effectiveness of medications, as well as the considerable marketing and advertising of medications (Swanson & Volkow, 2009).

Behaviorally Oriented Treatment

The substantial benefits of behaviorally oriented interventions for children and adolescents with ADHD have been shown in a variety of research designs (Fabiano et al., 2009; Van der Oord et al., 2008). The usual behavioral strategies are employed to target the primary symptoms of ADHD and to improve functional domains such as social relationships. Most interventions are conducted in the home or school, with parents or teachers working directly with the child. In addition, parent training programs are offered to optimize parents' management of their child with ADHD.

PARENT TRAINING (PT)   In general, parent involvement in treatment for youth disorders is beneficial (Dowell & Ogles, 2010). Parent training is an important aspect in treating ADHD. The disorder takes a toll on the parent–child relationship, parents tend to become overly directive, and some may view themselves as lacking the normal skills of parenting (Anastopoulos, Smith, & Wien, 1998). These facts coupled with the obvious influence that parents have on their offsprings' behavior make families a natural focus of intervention. Still, PT may not always be appropriate (Anastopoulos et al., 2006). It is most suitable for children ages 4 to 12, and for families in which ADHD appears as a basis of family difficulty. PT may not be suitable when parents are experiencing excessively high levels of stress due to marital conflicts or other circumstances.

Although parent training programs vary somewhat, they share the goal of teaching child management techniques (Anastopoulos & Farley, 2003). As an example, we briefly examine an intervention that emphasizes the management of the core symptoms of ADHD and noncompliance and defiance in children between 4 and 12 years of age. This focus is consistent with the view that ADHD involves a deficit in behavioral inhibition and risk for conduct disturbances. Appropriate parental management of child behavior is viewed as bringing the child's behavior under increased parental control, facilitating the child's awareness of behavioral consequences, preventing the development of comorbid conditions, and alleviating parental stress.

The treatment program consists of 10 components that are covered in 8 to 12 sessions with an individual family or groups of families. As Table 9.5 indicates, in addition

TABLE 9.5	Steps in the Parent Training Intervention Described by Anastopoulos, Rhoads, and Farley

1. Program overview and overview of ADHD
2. Discussing parent–child relationships, principles of behavioral management
3. Improving parent skills in using positive attention ("catching the child being good")
4. Extending positive attention; teaching how to give commands
5. Establishing a home token/point system
6. Adding response cost to child management
7. Teaching the use of time-out for more serious child misbehavior
8. Managing behavior in public places, such as grocery stores and church
9. Handling school issues (e.g., daily report card); preparing for termination of PT
10. Booster session to review child status and troubleshoot problems

Adapted from *Anastopoulos, Rhoads, & Farley, 2006.*

TABLE 9.6	Hypothetical Child–Teacher Contingency Contract

I agree to do the following:
1. Take my seat by 8:10 every morning.
2. Remain in my seat unless Ms. Duffin gives permission to me or the class to leave seats.
3. Not interrupt other students when they are speaking.
4. Complete morning written work as assigned before lunch break.
5. Complete afternoon written work as assigned before gym or recess In the afternoon.

I agree that when I do the above, I will:
…earn extra time In the computer corner
…earn extra time to do artwork
…earn extra checkmarks that I can trade for art supplies.

I agree that if I do not do 1–5 above each day, I will:
…not be able to participate in recess activities.

Based on *DuPaul, Guevrement, & Barkley, 1991.*

to training in behavioral management, the sessions include information to increase understanding of ADHD, discussion of special and future problems, consideration of the child's school situation, and a booster session for review and troubleshooting.

In families in which the child's behavior is oppositional and disruptive, PT can improve parenting skills and child behavior and, to a lesser extent, reduce ADHD symptoms (American Psychological Association, 2006). More is known about the effects on school-age children, but similar changes have been found in preschoolers and adolescents. PT appears to be one of the most validated treatments for children with ADHD who display oppositional, defiant behavior.

CLASSROOM MANAGEMENT Teachers' behavioral management is an important aspect of student deportment, including off-task, disruptive behavior (Leflot et al., 2010). School-based behavioral intervention is effective in addressing inattention, disruptive behavior, and academic performance in children with ADHD. Most commonly the teacher administers contingency management intervention, and typically receives training and consultation from a mental health specialist (Jacob & Pelham, 2000). Procedures usually include token reinforcement, time out, and response cost. Contingency contracting, in which the child and the teacher sign a written agreement specifying how the child will behave and the contingencies that will accrue, can be helpful (Table 9.6). Often essential is

a daily report card sent to parents that reflects the child's performance regarding targeted behaviors. The report card serves as feedback to the child, informs parents so that they can reward the child for progress, and promotes communication between the teacher and the parents. (See Accent: "The Summer Treatment Program" for an intervention using many of these behavioral techniques to strengthen functional outcomes.)

There is some evidence that children with different subtypes of ADHD might profit from different kinds of teacher strategies (Pfiffner et al., 2006). For example, those with ADHD-I might especially benefit from interventions that accommodate a slow work style. However, the targeting of behaviors on an individual basis is a key to success. Effective targeting should include the following considerations:

- Skills and behaviors that replace specific problems should be emphasized. A child with organizational problems needs to be taught how to manage desk and locker space, while a child with social deficits needs to learn appropriate interaction.
- Although on-task performance is important, broader academic performance goals need to be targeted. Amount of work completed is an important element for achievement. Young children need to strengthen basic skills (reading, writing, arithmetic) so they will not fall behind, while older students need help in additional academic areas.

The well-being of children with ADHD is undoubtedly influenced by teachers' skills in organizing and managing classroom activities and behavior.

- Behaviors occurring in situations that commonly cause difficulties need to be targeted—for example, behaviors required during recess and transitions between classes or activities.

Although behavioral interventions have typically focused on managing behavior through contingency-based principles, the structure and organization of both the classroom and learning tasks may be important to children with ADHD (Pfiffner et al., 2006). Classrooms that are well organized and predictable may be especially helpful for children with ADHD. Placing the child's desk away from other children and near the teacher can reduce peer reinforcement of inappropriate behavior and also facilitate teacher monitoring and feedback. Regarding learning tasks, there are several useful strategies. Among these are increasing stimulation within the task—for example, by the use of color, shape, or tape recordings—keeping the length of the task within the child's attention span, and varying the format and materials. There is evidence that allowing the child some task-related choice facilitates work productivity, and that computer-assisted instruction (which often includes clear rules, segmented tasks, and swift feedback) increases attention and work productivity. While many of these strategies are generally advantageous, they may be of critical help to students with ADHD. There is, however, a need for further research in this area.

Teachers are crucial, of course, in influencing the learning environment of the classroom and in implementing behavioral programs. A considerable amount of teachers' time and energy is required to effectively manage children with disabilities, as well as to collaborate with parents, administrators, and other professionals. Teachers generally appear to favor positive over negative contingencies, behavioral plus medication over medication-only approaches, and time-efficient (e.g., daily report cards) over time-consuming (e.g., response cost) techniques (Pfiffner et al., 2006; Pisecco, Huzinec, & Curtis, 2001). In general, teacher knowledge, beliefs, attitudes, flexibility, tolerance for the disruptions common in ADHD, and interactional style may be important variables regarding the success of classroom-based programs (Greene, 1995).

Multimodal Treatment

As we have seen, the limitation and criticism of medication treatment has continued to raise questions about its use for ADHD. At the same time, behavioral methods often require much effort, time, and expense. This situation has resulted in the implementation and evaluation of multimodal treatments that combine the two approaches (Abikoff et al., 2004a, 2004b; Van der Oord et al., 2008).

THE MTA STUDY The **Multimodal Treatment Assessment Study (MTA)** is the largest long-term evaluation of treatment options. This six-center investigation was initiated by the National Institutes of Mental Health. Close to 600 children with ADHD-C, ages 7 to 9 years, were randomly assigned to one of four treatment conditions

ACCENT
The Summer Treatment Program (STP)

Many professionals now view ADHD as a chronic disorder that usually requires comprehensive treatment over long periods of time. This view underlies the Summer Treatment Program developed by Pelham and colleagues (2005; 2010). The program is an intensive social learning intervention that targets the functional impairments of ADHD rather than its primary symptoms. The reason for this focus is that functional behaviors are related to the outcome of attention-deficit hyperactivity disorder. Available for youths ages 5 to 15, the program operates in a camp-like setting, typically for 7 to 8 weeks on weekdays. The goals are to improve (1) peer relationships (social skills, problem solving), (2 adult relationships (compliance), (3) academic performance, and (4) self-efficacy.

The participants are placed in small age-matched groups overseen by college student interns. The group serves as a natural backdrop for intensive work on peer and adult relationships. Social skills training is provided in brief daily sessions that include modeling and role playing, and there is opportunity for group problem solving. Appropriate social skills are continually prompted and reinforced with a point reward system.

Each day, the groups spend about 3 hours in classroom sessions conducted by teachers and aides. It is recognized not only that children with ADHD have academic problems but also that summer months without academic learning puts even typically developing youths at risk for losing academic ground. About 2 hours of classroom time are devoted to individualized assignments in academic areas, cooperative reading with another student, and individualized computer-based skill building. The third hour is devoted to individual and group art projects. The latter provides the opportunity for cooperative peer interaction and the less structured activities can build skills for the transfer to regular school settings in which ADHD students often have difficulties.

The remainder of each day is given to leisure activities in group play and sports. Children with ADHD frequently have poor motor skills and fail to follow game rules, which can contribute to peer rejection and low self-esteem. The STP children receive intensive skill training and coaching. Although the skills are valued in themselves, sport competence also is valued because it is thought to enhance self-efficacy and behavior change.

The STP emphasizes behavioral approaches, and staff members are highly trained to record a child's behavior and respond appropriately. Parents have daily contact with staff members, participate in a daily report card component, and attend weekly training sessions designed to implement at home the behavioral techniques employed in the program. Opportunity also exists for evaluating the need and use of medication. When children return to school in the autumn, monthly parent training is offered, and teachers are aided in establishing a report card system.

Research on the nature and treatment of ADHD is an important component of the STP. The program has been manualized and adopted at many community and university sites. Evaluations at multiple sites document low dropout rates, high parent satisfaction, and improved participant behavior, primarily functional behavior. The STP has been recognized as a model and innovative intervention by the American Psychological Association and other organizations.

Children in the STP receive skill training and coaching to enhance development.

lasting for 14 months (MTA Cooperative Group, 1999a). The treatments were as follows:

- *Medication Treatment.* Children received medication, mostly methylphenidate, with dosage carefully assigned, monitored, and adjusted at monthly sessions with the child and parents. Teacher input was available for these sessions, and medication was given for the entire time period.
- *Behavioral Treatment.* The intensive program consisted of parent training sessions, school-based intervention, and a child-focused summer camp experience. Training gradually leveled off and by the end of the treatment period parents were seen monthly or not at all.
- *Combined Treatment.* The medication and behavioral treatments were integrated.
- *Community Care Treatment.* Children in this comparison group received various routine treatments in their communities. As it turned out, 67% were on medication, with dosage levels lower than for the medication treatment group. The children were seen only once or twice by a physician, and there was no teacher contact for feedback.

Initial evaluations of the MTA study were conducted before, during, and at the end of treatment. Numerous measures were taken of core ADHD symptoms, associated problems, and family factors. Core ADHD symptoms were reduced in all groups over the 14-month treatment, but the amount of improvement varied with the type of treatment (MTA Cooperative Group, 1999a; 1999b). Overall, the medication and combined treatments were superior to behavioral and community care treatments, and did not differ from each other. However, the findings were numerous and complex. For example, for several measures the combined treatment had the greatest effect, including parent ratings of externalizing and internalizing symptoms and measures of reading achievement (MTA Cooperative Group, 1999a). In addition, for children with comorbid ADHD and anxiety, behavioral treatment was as effective as the medication or the combined treatment (Rieppi et al., 2002). Moreover, social class moderated some of the outcomes. Families with more education benefited the most from the combined treatment, but this was not so for families with less education.

Posttreatment Follow-Ups Several posttreatment evaluations have examined the persistence of effects of the four treatments on select measures. At 24 months after the initiation of intervention

children who had been in the medication or combined treatments still showed improvement compared with the other children regarding ADHD and oppositional defiant symptoms, but not some other problems (MTA Cooperative Group, 2004a; 2004b). But the positive effects were about 50% weaker than they had been at the end of treatment.

Subsequent follow-ups (at 36, 72, and 96 months) indicated no significant group differences on several ADHD symptom and functional scores (Jensen et al., 2007; Molina et al., 2009). Figure 9.8 shows the results for parent ratings of three symptom domains from the beginning of treatment. Included are ratings for a later-added comparison group of children. As can be seen, all of the MTA groups showed some improvement over time. Nevertheless, at the 96-month evaluation, 30% were diagnosed with ADHD, most commonly with ADHD-I. And the MTA participants performed relatively poorly compared to the comparison group on numerous measures. For example, they were doing less well in school, had relatively high rates of arrest and delinquency, and a greater number met the DSM criteria for ODD or CD (Molina et al., 2009).

It is perhaps unsurprising that the early benefits of medication and combined treatments were not maintained for a longer period of time. Children and families were treated for a relatively short period, and at the termination of treatment had been on their own to make decisions about various intervention options. The effects of medication are not sustained when medication is discontinued, and previous research had suggested only short-term effects of behavioral and combined treatments. The MTA study clearly confirms that intervention for ADHD must be sustained over time.

It is probably fair to say that at the present time, practitioners take various stances with regard to intervention. Medication is widely employed but is not given first preference by every professional and every family (Leslie et al., 2007). Many mental health professionals believe that a combination of medication and behaviorally oriented treatments is the best approach for a disorder that is as multidimensional as ADHD and carries considerable risk for comorbid disorders. Overall, progress has been made in treating ADHD. An increased number of medications provides options for the child or adolescent, behavioral intervention has been improved, and research results offer some guidance for treatment. At the same time, there is room for considerable improvement regarding medication prescription, follow-up visits, discontinuance of treatment, and poor outcome (Zima et al., 2010).

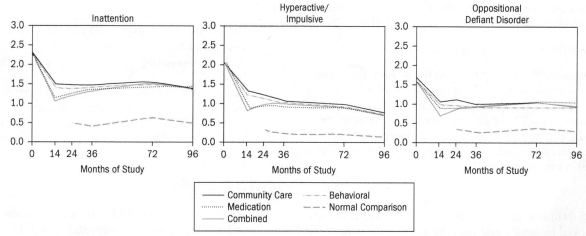

FIGURE 9.8 Mean scores (parent ratings) on three symptom domains across months, the MTA study. *From Molina et al., 2009.*

Overview/Looking Back

EVOLVING IDEAS ABOUT ADHD

- Accounts of ADHD have shifted over time regarding symptoms and their conceptualization. Two dimensions are now recognized as valid: inattention and hyperactivity-impulsivity.

DSM CLASSIFICATION AND DIAGNOSIS

- The DSM recognizes three subtypes of ADHD: Predominately Inattentive, Predominately Hyperactive/Impulsive, and Combined.
- Diagnosis demands the presence of symptoms for at least 6 months by age 12 and impairment in at least two settings.

DESCRIPTION: PRIMARY FEATURES

- The core problems of inattention, hyperactivity, and impulsivity are described by parents and teachers and demonstrated with various laboratory instruments.

DESCRIPTION: SECONDARY FEATURES

- As a group, youths with ADHD display several secondary difficulties, among which are motor problems, somewhat lowered intelligence, academic failure, adaptive behavior deficits, social and conduct problems, and accident risk.

DSM SUBTYPES

- Many differences and similarities exist between ADHD-I and ADHD-C, and less is known about ADHD-HI. Several dissatisfactions are voiced about the subtypes.

CO-OCCURRING DISORDERS

- ADHD co-occurs at high rates with learning disabilities, externalizing disorders, and internalizing disorders.

EPIDEMIOLOGY

- About 3 to 7% of school-age children are estimated to have ADHD, with rates at the higher end more likely. Boys are diagnosed more frequently than girls, who display more inattention and less hyperactivity/impulsivity. Rates appear somewhat higher in children of lower social class, and ethnic/racial differences exist.

DEVELOPMENTAL COURSE

- Hyperactivity and impulsivity are observed in preschoolers and a minority of these children continues to have problems into childhood.
- For some children, the primary features of childhood ADHD continue into adolescence and to a lesser degree into adulthood. Core features appear to weaken over time, but secondary difficulties are apparent. Continuity of problems is linked to several variables.

NEUROPSYCHOLOGICAL THEORIES OF ADHD

- Neuropsychological theories of ADHD emphasize various abnormalities, such as executive dysfunctions, unusual sensitivity to reinforcement, temporal processing deficits, and aversion to delay.
- Barkley's model, which applies to ADHD-C, proposes that deficits in behavioral inhibition interfere with other executive functions to produce

impairment in the regulation of behavior. There is evidence for multiple pathways to ADHD.

NEUROBIOLOGICAL ABNORMALITIES

- Evidence exists for structural and functional abnormalities of the brain. Several regions are implicated, especially frontal-striatal-cerebellar networks. There is evidence for underactivity of the brain, and dopamine and norepinephrine are implicated. Delayed maturation of the brain may also underlie ADHD.

ETIOLOGY

- Substantial genetic transmission of ADHD is indicated by family and twin studies. Several genes have been identified. Genetic influence appears complex, probably involving many genes with small effects and genetic heterogeneity.
- There is some evidence for adverse effects of prenatal alcohol and tobacco use and low birthweight. Diet is unlikely to be an important causal factor. Exposure to lead is a small, but significant, factor in some cases.
- The psychosocial environment plays a role in shaping and maintaining ADHD behaviors. Both family factors and teacher behavior are important considerations.

A SCHEMA OF THE DEVELOPMENT OF ADHD

- The development of ADHD can be depicted as following different pathways consisting of genetic risk, perhaps interacting with pre- or perinatal influences to produce brain and neuropsychological impairments that are influenced by additional postnatal factors.

ASSESSMENT

- The identification of ADHD requires broad-based assessment that takes into account developmental level, various settings, and co-occurrence with other disorders.
- A comprehensive assessment includes interviews with the youth, parents, and teachers; the administration of standardized rating scales; direct observation; intelligence and achievement testing; and consideration of medical and social factors.

INTERVENTION

- Primary prevention of ADHD includes prenatal care and avoidance of environmental toxins. Important in prevention are early efforts to minimize core and secondary functional problems.
- There is substantial evidence that stimulant medication can relieve core and perhaps some secondary symptoms of ADHD for many youths. However, there are numerous concerns and limitation regarding medication use.
- Behaviorally oriented interventions, including parent training and school-based interventions, are evidence-based treatments for ADHD.
- The MTA study, the largest multimodal, long-term comparison of treatments, revealed initial but waning benefits for medication and medication plus behavioral treatments.
- Many researchers and professionals believe that multimodal treatment of the various aspects of ADHD is most appropriate.

Key Terms

Language and Learning Disabilities

S pecific problems that arise in the development of language and learning are discussed in this chapter. These disabilities can vary from subtle to severe, interfere with the innumerable daily needs and pleasures of communication, cast a shadow of failure and frustration over the school years, and adversely affect adult occupational life. Indeed, it can be argued that language and learning disorders have had increasing impact on individual lives because of escalating demands for certain kinds of skills and learning in our industrial and technologically sophisticated world.

Child and adolescent difficulties in language and learning are associated with many known medical, genetic, and behavioral syndromes. Such conditions are not, however, the focus of this chapter. Rather, our primary interest is in youths who display specific impairments that are out of keeping with other aspects of their development. It is assumed that disturbance occurs relatively early and is not readily explained by social factors.

Professionals from diverse disciplines have been interested in language and learning problems—notably educators, psychologists, physicians, and language specialists. Approaching their work from different perspectives, they have generated diverse, albeit often overlapping, terminology, definitions, emphases, causal theories, and treatments. This rich history is reflected throughout the present chapter.

A BIT OF HISTORY: UNEXPECTED DISABILITIES, UNMET NEEDS

Specific language and learning problems have been recognized for a long time. Two major themes have left a strong mark on the field (Lyon, Fletcher, & Barnes, 2003; Lyon et al., 2006). One is scientific and clinical interest in understanding individuals who display specific deficits that appear discrepant with their intelligence or other abilities. The other, more applied, theme is an emphasis on the need to improve services to young people exhibiting such deficits.

Curiosity about discrepant, or unexpected, lack of abilities within individuals can be traced to work in Europe in the 1800s. Consider as an early example the description of the 10-year-old boy, Thomas.

Despite the boy's successes, it was reported that he was unable to learn to read. Many similarly puzzling cases were presented by physicians, and the field developed an early medical orientation that linked specific impairments with brain abnormalities. For example, in the latter 1880s, Broca described the inability of his adult patients to express themselves verbally while maintaining the capacity to comprehend what others said. Soon after, Wernicke documented brain lesions in patients who had problems in understanding language but otherwise did not exhibit language and cognitive impairment. Each of these men traced the specific disability to an area in the brain that now carries his name. Over many years, brain damage in adults was linked to behavioral symptoms such as specific

THOMAS

So Many Abilities

He was apparently a bright and in every respect an intelligent boy. He had been learning music for a year and had made good progress in it.... In all departments of his studies where the instruction was oral he had made good progress, showing that his auditory memory was good.... He performs simple sums quite correctly, and his progress in arithmetic has been regarded as quite satisfactory. He has no difficulty in learning to write. His visual acuity is good.

Hinshelwood, 1917, pp. 46–47.

speech problems, learning difficulties, and inattention (Hammill, 1993). Such developmental problems in youth were similarly hypothesized to be caused by brain injury or brain dysfunction of some sort, perhaps too subtle to be identified.

As Table 10.1 indicates, behavioral scientists in the United States, building on the European work, began to contribute a psychological orientation to the study of learning problems (Hallahan & Mock, 2003). Although brain dysfunction was often assumed, etiology was downplayed in favor of understanding the characteristics of learners and the educational remediation of learning deficits (Lyon et al., 2003). By the mid-1900s, several kinds of interventions were recommended. Nevertheless, concern

TABLE 10.1 Historical Overview of the Field of Learning Disabilities	
European Foundation Period (c. 1800–1920)	European physicians and researchers explore links between brain injury and disabilities (e.g., in language and reading)
U.S. Foundation Period (c. 1920–1960)	Building on European work, psychologists, educators, and others focus on identification of disabilities and remediation in educational settings via language, perceptual, and motor approaches
Emergent Period (c. 1960–1975)	Emergence of the concept of learning disabilities (LD) Various groups offer definitions of LD Advocacy by parents and professionals for effective educational services
Solidification Period (c. 1975–1985)	Solidification of federal definition and regulations for LD Focus on empirically validated research (e.g., on memory)
Turbulent Period (c. 1985–2000)	Efforts to reach consensus on definition Dramatic growth in number of LD students Continued research; progress on etiology, intervention Continued vexing questions (e.g., about definition, special education)

Based on Hallahan & Mock, 2003.

was growing that a group of children had educational needs that were not being met by the schools.

In 1963, representatives from several organizations met at a symposium sponsored by the Fund for Perceptually Handicapped Children. In his address to the participants, Samuel Kirk, a well-respected psychologist, noted that the children of their concern exhibited a variety of deficiencies that were presumed to be related to neurological dysfunction—especially learning difficulties, perceptual problems, and hyperactivity. Kirk suggested and defined "learning disabilities" as a suitable term that he believed could encourage and guide the assessment and educational intervention so needed by these children. That evening the conferees organized into what is today called the Learning Disabilities Association of America (Hammill, 1993).

Kirk's presentation is recognized as a milestone in the emergence of the concept of learning disabilities (Lipka & Siegel, 2006; Lyon et al., 2006). Parents and educators henceforth played an important role in an area previously dominated by physicians and psychologists (Hallahan & Kauffman, 1978; Taylor, 1988). Parents were given hope that their children's problems were limited and treatable; teachers were relieved of the suspicion that they were to blame for student failure; concerned professionals were provided a term that could make children eligible for special services. It was recognized that youth labeled as "learning disabled" constituted a heterogeneous group.

By the late twentieth century, efforts were made to reach consensus on the definitions of learning disabilities, provide special education services, and conduct research into these disabilities. The last few decades have seen progress, and the number of youth categorized as learning disabled has dramatically increased. Nonetheless, challenges remain regarding the definition and conceptualization of specific language and learning disabilities, as well as related issues.

DEFINITIONAL CONCERNS

To understand the problems of definition we turn to the **Education for All Handicapped Children Act of 1975** (Public Law 94-142), which has had enormous influence on the field of language and learning disorders or disabilities. A sweeping educational mandate, it has been amended several times over the years and retitled the **Individuals with Disabilities Education Act (IDEA)**. Its definition of learning disability has had an impact on the educational system, children and families, clinicians and researchers.

Specific learning disability means a disorder in one or more of the basic psychological processes involved in understanding or in using language, spoken or written, in which the disorder may manifest itself in an imperfect ability to listen, think, speak, read, write, spell, or to do mathematical calculations. The term includes such conditions as perceptual handicaps, brain injury, minimal brain dysfunction, dyslexia, and developmental aphasia. The term does not include children who have learning problems which are primarily the result of visual, hearing, or motor handicaps, or mental retardation, or emotional disturbance, or of environmental, cultural, or economic disadvantage. (U.S. Office of Education, 1977, p. 65083)

This is a general definition that refers to disorder in basic psychological processes, but does not identify them. Although the definition points to several conditions, there are no specific criteria for identifying disabilities. In addition, the definition excludes children whose disabilities are due to several factors that could be expected to cause learning problems. The exclusionary criteria have been questioned, partly because it may be difficult to differentiate learning problems due to emotional disturbance, lack of motivation, or cultural or economic disadvantage. The presence of exclusionary criteria, in combination with the lack of specific criteria to define learning disabilities, has led to the statement that learning disabilities are defined more by what they are *not* than by what they are.

Definitional concerns have resulted in different, albeit overlapping, definitions and ways to identify disabilities (Dean & Burns, 2002; Lyon et al., 2006). Definitional problems have led to different prevalence rates, incomparability of groups chosen for research purposes, and varying standards to determine whether children will receive special education services. Here, we provide a snapshot of the definitional problem by considering how learning disabilities have often been identified and a newer approach that is both criticized and gaining acceptance.

Identifying Specific Disabilities

A lack of agreed-upon criteria to identify learning disabilities has been a continuing problem. What criteria and methods are to be used to decide that a child's language or learning skills are below expectations? In fact, different guidelines have been offered and several methods generated.

IQ-ACHIEVEMENT DISCREPANCY   A common way to identify disabilities has been by a discrepancy between the individual's intellectual ability and specific achievement level. It is assumed that if a specific disability exists, performance on measures of *general* ability (typically IQ tests) will exceed performance on achievement tests of the hypothesized *specific* impairment. Guidelines often call for the discrepancy to be severe or significant, but this has been defined somewhat differently. A discrepancy of two or more standard deviations between intelligence test scores and achievement test scores often is employed, but smaller differences have been acceptable.

BELOW AVERAGE ACHIEVEMENT: GRADE OR AGE

Another approach identifies disabilities by determining that the youth is performing below expected grade level in at least one academic area. Variations occur in the specific criterion, however. Thus, a sixth grader, for example, might be labeled with a learning disability when his or her achievement is on a fourth- *or* fifth-grade level. A general problem with this method of identification is that a large

discrepancy is more serious for a younger than an older child: being 2 years behind is more serious for a third grader than for a sixth grader.

Poor achievement can also be identified by comparing the child's performance with those of peers of the same age on standardized tests of language, reading, writing, and arithmetic. The degree to which performance must fall below that of peers varies with school districts and researchers. The criterion is usually set in the range of one to two standard deviations below the mean on standardized tests.

The poor achievement and especially the IQ-achievement discrepancy approaches have been challenged in numerous ways (Dyck et al., 2004; Hollenbeck, 2007).

ACCENT
Response to Intervention

RTI is a framework to identify and address student learning. Key components of the approach include school-wide instruction/intervention, monitoring of student progress, and identification of disability (Drummond, Gandhi, & Elledge, 2011). Although RTI may be viewed by some as replacing the identification of learning disabilities by IQ-achievement discrepancy, it is best considered as only one component of a broader evaluation.

The RTI approach moves children through a series of interventions of increasing intensity (Hollenbeck, 2007). A group of children—say, kindergartners—is first exposed to a specific intervention—for example, a research-based reading program—and each child's reading skills are monitored. Children with deficits next receive special, more intensive intervention, perhaps in small groups, followed by another evaluation. At this point, or perhaps after an even more intensive additional intervention, the child who has not positively responded is recognized as having a disability and is eligible for special education services. Figure 10.1 represents this multilevel system of intervention/identification. It is noteworthy that Level III of this representation is the most variable across programs and is sometimes special education services.

Overall, there is considerable variation in how states and schools implement RTI. Implementation requires many decisions, including decisions about the selection of evidence-based intervention, criteria for determining deficits, and how RTI is conducted in classrooms. These issues are being worked out primarily for younger students and for reading, whereas there is considerable need to address advanced reading skills, other content areas, and older students (Drummond et al., 2011).

Moreover, there are broader unresolved issues. Not all professionals are in favor of moving from traditional methods of identification to an approach with unanswered questions. There also is concern that including all students in the process shifts the conceptualization of learning

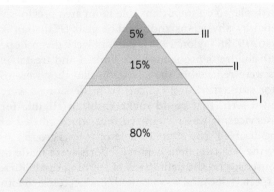

Level I: Instruction and screening is provided to all students as general curriculum.

Level II: More intensive instruction is provided in small groups to targeted students.

Level III: Instruction is individualized to targeted students' needs and is more intensive in terms of number and duration of sessions.

FIGURE 10.1   Three levels of RTI's increasingly intensive instruction (intervention) and identification. Level I generally addresses the learning needs of about 80% of students, Level II about 15%, and Level III about 5%. *Adapted from* Drummond et al., 2011.

disability as a *specific* disability to a more general disability of low achievement, perhaps resulting in some students not receiving needed special attention. In contrast, a group of professionals view RTI positively—as wider educational reform to strengthen early intervention and prevention of learning problems (Fuchs, Fuchs, & Stecker, 2010). They have small faith in the benefits of special education and favor all students receiving services in the general education classroom. Thus, there are basic differences in beliefs about the purpose and nature of RTI.

For example, it has been argued that intelligence tests rely strongly on language abilities, so that overall intelligence may be underestimated in children with language or learning disabilities—making a discrepancy less probable. Others have pointed out that when a discrepancy from a high IQ is identified, the "disability" might be quite different from that of a discrepancy from a much lower IQ. Still another criticism is that there is no way to discriminate between deficits of the child and of poor instruction. Serious questions also have been raised about the exclusion of children considered to be "slow learners," that is, for whom a discrepancy is not found (Stanovich, 1989; Vellutino et al., 2004). There is growing recognition that in several ways specific disabilities do not differ much from general learning problems that do not meet discrepancy formulations (Hulme & Snowling, 2009; Scruggs & Mastropieri, 2002). Overall, these arguments have weakened the IQ-achievement discrepancy approach. Nonetheless, intelligence often is considered by requiring that the child with low achievement also exhibit average intelligence or at least an IQ higher than the score that typically defines mental retardation (about 70). By this practice, children who exhibit both low achievement and relatively low intelligence are not considered as learning disabled.

RESPONSE TO INTERVENTION (RTI) A relatively recent innovative approach to defining learning disabilities depends on exposing children to intervention prior to diagnosing them with a disability. The approach was given impetus in the latest 2004 reauthorization of IDEA, which suggested that educational agencies might consider the child's response to research-based intervention (Hollenbeck, 2007). The rationale is that children whose response to valid intervention is poorer than that of their peers can be identified as having a learning disability (Fuchs, Fuchs, & Hollenbeck, 2007). Although implementation of RTI has gained momentum in the schools, professionals hold differing views and attitudes regarding the approach, and there are many unresolved issues. (See Accent: "Response to Intervention.")

Despite the problems of definitional confusion, substantial progress has been made in understanding language and learning disabilities. We begin the following discussion with language disorders because they are likely to be identified earlier and because they are often implicated in other disabilities.

LANGUAGE DISABILITIES

The study and treatment of language impairments has been both independent of and integrated with the study and treatment of "learning disabilities," which typically refer to reading, writing, and arithmetic. Language disabilities have historically been known as *aphasia*, a term that means loss of language due to brain damage or dysfunction. When the matter at hand is developmental disorder in youth—as it is in our discussion—aphasia is not an accurate fit, and the terms *developmental aphasia* and *developmental dysphasia* were once employed. These terms have largely given way to *language impairment (LI)*, *specific language impairment (SLI)*, or *language disorder (LD)*.

Normal Language Development

An overview of normal language development serves as a framework for understanding disabilities. Language, as we usually know it, is a system of communication based on sounds that are combined into words and sentences to represent experience and carry meaning. Table 10.2 defines the basic components of language that must be mastered by all users of oral and written language.

Phonology has to do with the basic sounds of a language. English has 42 basic sounds, or **phonemes**. As a written language, it has 26 alphabet letters, which singly or in combinations are called **graphemes**. There is a correspondence between phonemes and graphemes. Alphabet letters are, of course, combined to form words, which carry meaning. **Morphology** has to do with the formation of words, and **syntax** refers to the organization of words into phrases and sentences. Morphology and syntax are parts of **grammar**, the system of rules that organize a language. Thus, English speakers who follow the rules say "He dances well," not "He well dance." The rules of language help facilitate meaning in communication, which is referred to as **semantics**. Finally, **pragmatics** is the use of language in context; in social situations it includes such aspects as taking turns when speaking with another person or judging when to initiate conversation.

Superimposed on the basic components of language are reception and expression. **Receptive language** has to do with the comprehension of messages sent by others.

TABLE 10.2	Basic Components of Language
Phonology	Sounds of a language and rules for combining them
Morphology	Formation of words, including the use of prefixes and suffixes (e.g., un, ed, s) to give meaning
Syntax	Organization of words into phrases and sentences
Semantics	Meanings in language
Pragmatics	Use of language in specific contexts

Expressive language concerns the production of language, that is, sending messages. Reception is developmentally acquired earlier than expression—as anyone who tries to learn a second language quickly discovers.

Infants come into the world geared for language; their amazing capacity progresses rapidly and in sequential milestones during the first few years of life (Table 10.3). During the first year, infants can distinguish and produce sounds that are not part of the native language that surrounds them, and then this ability contracts to the sounds of their language. Thus, it appears that an innate ability to process language sounds is shaped through experience. By their first birthdays, most infants are saying a few words. Some speech sounds are more difficult than others, and individual differences in pronunciation, or articulation, become obvious. Even before this time, infants have begun to understand the communications of others.

By 2 years of age, most children have gone from saying single words, to two-word utterances, to longer strings of words set in meaningful phrases or sentences. Vocabulary increases dramatically, different parts of speech are acquired, and the ability to arrange words improves. Comprehension also grows, and parents of 3-year-olds perceive that they are talking with someone who is no longer an "infant." Indeed, infancy—a term derived from a Latin word that means "incapable of speech"—is often said to be over at age 2. Progress continues at a rapid rate and includes pragmatics. By age 7, many of the basics of language are acquired, although language development continues into adolescence and even into adulthood.

DSM Classification and Diagnosis

From even a brief review of language development, it is obvious that a variety of impairments might occur. Problems can exist in phonology, morphology, syntax, semantics, and so forth. It is possible, then, to classify disabilities in several ways. However, attempts to subgroup language disabilities according to such language components have not been very successful. Rather, the distinction is often made between difficulties in expressive language and difficulties in receptive language (Peterson

---

TABLE 10.3 **Early Acquisition of Language and Communication**

	Reception	Expression
Birth to 6 months	Reacts to sudden noise. Is quieted by a voice. Locates sound. Recognizes name and words like "bye-bye."	Cries. Babbles, laughs. Initiates vocal play. Vocalizes to self. Experiments with voice.
6 to 12 months	Stops activity to "no." Raises arms to "come up." Obeys simple instructions. Understands simple statements.	Makes sounds that exist in the culture's language. Combines vowel sounds. Imitates adult sounds. Says first words.
12 to 18 months	Carries out two consecutive commands. Understands new words. Listens to nursery rhymes.	Uses ten words. Requests objects by name. Connects sounds so that they flow like a sentence.
18 to 24 months	Recognizes many sounds. Understands action words like "show me."	Uses short sentences. Uses pronouns. Echoes last words of a rhyme.
24 to 36 months	Follows commands using "in," "on," "under." Follows three verbal commands given in one utterance.	Uses possessive, noun–verb combinations. Ninety percent of communications are understandable by primary caregiver.
36 to 48 months	Increases understanding of others' messages and social context of communication.	Uses increasingly complex language forms, such as conjunctions and auxiliary verbs.

Based on Bryant, 1977; Whitehurst, 1982.

& McGrath, 2009b). Differences are also drawn between speech sound impairments and language impairments (Newbury & Monaco, 2010).

The DSM-5 considers these distinctions under the broad category of Communication Disorders (American Psychiatric Association, 2013). (The DSM-5 also includes stuttering and social communication disorder, which are not discussed here.) In both Speech Sound Disorder and Language Disorder, symptom onset must occur during early development, abilities must be below those expected for age, and limitations must interfere with communication, social participation, and academic or occupational achievement. The following discussion describes these difficulties as they are presented in the clinical and research literature.

Description

SPEECH SOUND DISORDER (SSD)   To be diagnosed with this disorder, a child must fail to display developmentally appropriate and dialect-appropriate speech sounds. The difficulties are not due to physical, neurological, or hearing problems (American Psychiatric Association, 2013).

Children with SSD exhibit impairments in articulating speech sounds, a skill that follows a typical pattern. For example, the sounds *l, r, s, z, th, ch, dzh,* and *zh* are usually acquired relatively late. In SSD the course of speech production is generally similar to that of typical development, but it is delayed and proceeds more slowly (Johnson & Beitchman, 2005c). Children with impaired speech make incorrect

RAMON

Speech Sound Problems

Ramon was a talkative boy whose speech was virtually unintelligible despite his normal hearing and language comprehension. The rhythm and melody of his speech suggested that he was trying to produce multiword communications typical for his age. He produced only a few vowels and some early-developing consonants. Many of his spoken words were thus indistinguishable. He said "bahbah" for bottle, baby, and bubble, and used "nee" for knee, need, and Anita (his sister). Ramon also omitted consonant sounds at the end of words. On occasion, he reacted with frustration and tantrums to the difficulties in making his needs understood.

Adapted from Johnson & Beitchman, 2005c, p. 3151.

speech sounds, substitute easily made sounds for more difficult ones, or omit sounds. Since most children display some misarticulation as they acquire the linguistic and motor skills necessary for speech, developmental norms are crucial in diagnosis. Only 50% of speech may be intelligible in typically developing 2-year-olds, whereas most speech is understandable at age 4 (American Psychiatric Association, 2013). The case of Ramon describes severe speech sound problems of a 3-year-old boy.

The production of speech sound requires motor control of the lips, tongue, and jaws in coordination with breathing and vocalizing. But SSD may also involve difficulties in understanding the sound structure of the language, that is, in phonology. Thus, for example, a child may have difficulty in knowing which word rhymes with another or whether "soup" or "coat" starts with the same sound as "Sam" (Bishop, 2002). Bishop and Norbury (2008) illustrate the difference between problems in simple articulation and phonology with this example: native speakers of English often have difficulty in learning to produce the French words "rue" and "roux." This is not due to articulation per se but due to failure to acquire the speech sounds of French. Speakers of French handle the vowels in a way different from what English speakers do. Phonological problems involving the understanding of the sound structure of a language can have serious developmental implications.

LANGUAGE DISORDER   The DSM cites the primary diagnostic features of language disorder as difficulties in acquiring or using language due to impairments in comprehending or producing vocabulary, sentences, and discourse (American Psychiatric Association, 2013). Deficits are not due to sensory or motor problems, other medical or neurological conditions, nor to intellectual disability or global developmental delay. Diagnosis depends on the combination of the child's history, clinical observation, and performance on standardized tests of language ability. Both expression and reception of language are implicated.

Expressive problems involve the production of language with regard to vocabulary, grammar, and other aspects of language output. Youngsters with expressive problems may have a limited amount of speech and may speak in extremely short, simple sentences. Vocabulary may be small; critical parts of sentences may be missing; unusual word order may be displayed. Especially problematic, children may exhibit undue errors in marking word forms such as plurals or verb tense. In addition, phonological problems may be observed. However, children with expressive problems understand speech and age-level concepts, and thus they can appropriately respond to others' communications. Some of these characteristics are seen in the description of Amy, a sociable, active 5-year-old (Johnson & Beitchman, 2005a).

Problems in Language Expression

One day while Amy was playing with her friend Lisa, each girl told the story of Little Red Riding Hood to her doll. Lisa's story began: "Little Red Riding Hood was taking a basket of food to her grandmother who was sick. A bad wolf stopped Riding Hood in the forest. He tried to get the basket from her but she wouldn't give it to him."

By contrast, Amy's story demonstrated marked difficulties in verbal expression: "Riding Hood going to grandma house. Her taking food. Bad wolf in a bed. Riding Hood say, what big ears, grandma? Hear you, dear. What big eyes, grandma? See you, dear. What big mouth, grandma? Eat you all up!"

Many features of Amy's story are characteristic of expressive difficulties of children of Amy's age: short, incomplete sentences; simple sentence structure; omission of grammatical function words (e.g., is, the) and endings (e.g., possessives); problems in question formation; and incorrect use of pronouns (e.g., "her" for "she"). Nonetheless, when tested by methods that did not require verbal responding, it was clear that Amy understood the details and plot of the Riding Hood tale as well as her friend did. Amy also demonstrated adequate comprehensive skills in her kindergarten classroom, where she ably followed the teacher's verbal instructions.

Adapted from Johnson & Beitchman, 2005a, p. 3138.

Problems in Language Reception and Expression

Trang understood a limited number of words for objects, actions, and relations. He often failed to follow classroom instructions, particularly those that involved words for time (e.g., yesterday, after, week) and space (e.g., beneath, in front of, around). His conversation with other children often broke down because he did not understand fully what they were saying, nor could he express his own ideas clearly. As a result he was not a favored playmate, and most of the children in his class ignored him. His limited interactions further reduced Trang's opportunities for improving and practicing his already weak language skills. Additional assessment, conducted with the assistance of a Vietnamese interpreter, revealed that Trang showed similar receptive and expressive language deficits in Vietnamese. His nonverbal skills, however, were generally appropriate for his age. He readily constructed intricate buildings and vehicles with small, plastic building blocks; he easily completed complex jigsaw puzzles; and he successfully solved numerical, conceptual, or analogical problems, as long as they were presented nonverbally.

Adapted from Johnson & Beitchman, 2000b, p. 2642.

Difficulties in language reception involve comprehending the communication of others. Single words, phrases, sentences, the multiple meanings of a word, word play, and the past tense may all be problematic. The child may fail to respond to speech, seem deaf, respond inappropriately to others' speech, be uninterested in television, or fail to follow instructions.

When considering language disorder, it is helpful to keep in mind the considerable variation across children in the kinds and severity of problems experienced. Imagine, if you will, the difference between a child who has only minor articulation deficits and one whose speech can hardly be understood by others. Life is different too for the child with relatively simple speech impairments and a child unable to comprehend much of what is being communicated by others. It is also helpful to recognize that speech sound, expressive, and reception difficulties often occur together. The description of a

5-year-old boy, Trang, illustrates this point. Trang lived with his parents and siblings, who were proficient in both English and Vietnamese. His development in both languages was much slower than that of his siblings, and kindergarten assessment revealed impairments in both reception and expression.

Epidemiology and Developmental Course

Limited epidemiological studies suggest overall rates of specific language impairments in the range of 3 to 7% (Hulme & Snowling, 2009; Tomblin, 2006). Even so, prevalence varies with age and type of disorder. Boys are widely reported as having higher rates than girls. Although higher prevalence in clinic samples may reflect referral bias, this does not seem to completely account for the gender difference (Viding et al., 2004).

Higher rates also have been noted in children from low socioeconomic groups (Carroll et al., 2005; McDowell, Lonigan, & Goldstein, 2007; Toppelberg & Shapiro, 2000).

What might explain this correlation? If hereditary factors play a role, family language disabilities might result in families attaining low educational and occupational status. It is also possible that poor children who use dialects different from standard English employed in standardized assessment instruments are overidentified.

Language disorders usually appear by age 3 or 4, but mild difficulties may not be identified until later (American Psychiatric Association, 2013). Some impairments may first become apparent with the demands of schoolwork and greater complexity of language. It may be more difficult to ascertain what a child understands than to observe impairments in the expression of speech.

Studies of children and adults of various ages, followed for various periods of time, indicate that improvement can occur over time and that language abilities can reach the normal range (Leonard, 1998). However, a hierarchy of risk based on the type of disorder has been suggested. Children who display only articulation problems are at lowest risk, those with expressive problems are at middle risk, and those with receptive problems are at highest risk for later language impairments (Baker & Cantwell, 1989; Rutter, Mawhood, & Howlin, 1992; Whitehurst & Fischel, 1994).

Speech sound problems, especially when they are mild or occur without other language difficulties, often remit over time, and frequently respond to intervention (American Psychiatric Association, 2013). A substantial number of children with early expressive difficulties continue to exhibit impairment. Some children, often referred to as "late talkers," eventually reach the normal range of language development but still fall somewhat short of most of their peers (Preston et al., 2010; Rescorla, 2009). Regarding receptive difficulties, many children may never develop completely normal language and their problems may increase over time. A study that followed boys with severe receptive–expressive impairments into their early twenties found that 20% had a level of comprehension below that of 10-year-old children and about 25% had equally poor expressive skills (Mawhood, Howlin, & Rutter, 2000). Little change occurred over the next decade for this group (Clegg et al., 2005). In general, when problems do not remit by 5 to 6 years of age, children are at risk for continued language difficulties and later problems in reading (Hulme & Snowling, 2009). It has also been reported that even when remittance occurs, reading difficulties may arise later.

Co-occurring Disorders

One of the burdens of language disorder is its association with poor academic progress. School achievement is affected: more students are retained at grade level and fewer students attend high school. At least in part, this

TABLE 10.4 Risk of Having a Learning Disability* at Age 19 in a Group Identified with Language Impairments at Age 5

Learning Disability	Risk
Reading	4.6
Spelling	4.1
Math	3.7
Reading + spelling	4.7
Reading + math	9.4
Spelling + math	4.4
Reading + spelling + math	7.8

*A learning disability was defined by performance below the 25th percentile on tests of reading, spelling, or math, and an IQ (verbal or performance) of at least 80.
Adapted from Young et al., 2002.

finding is due to the association of language disorders with learning disabilities (Tomblin et al., 2000; Young et al., 2002). For instance, one longitudinal study found that language-impaired children were 4.6 times as likely to have later reading disability compared to typically developing children (Table 10.4). In another study, 51% of children with language disorder had reading disability and 55% of children with reading disability had language impairment (McArthur et al., 2000). The role that language plays in reading problems is suggested by the finding that weaknesses in early language (e.g., knowing names and sounds of letters, vocabulary, grammar) are associated with later reading problems (DeThorne et al., 2006; Lonigan, Burgess, & Anthony, 2000; Raitano et al., 2004). Youth with the combination of language and learning disabilities—in both clinic and community samples—also have a higher than average risk for other disturbances (Beitchman et al., 1996; Conti-Ramsden & Botting, 2004; Rutter, Mawhood, & Howlin, 1992).

Language impairment has been associated with externalizing and internalizing problems in youths of various ages. A study of 5-year-olds showed that 40% displayed withdrawn behavior, bodily symptoms, and aggressive behavior (van Daal, Verhoeven, & van Balkom, 2007). The continuity of behavioral disturbance is suggested by a longitudinal study of a community sample identified with language deficits at age 5 (Beitchman et al., 1996; 2001). Follow-up conducted at about age 19 indicated that the individuals had higher rates of anxiety disorder than a control group, and males were at risk for antisocial personality. Nevertheless, some investigations indicate relatively low risk and the need to consider type and severity of language disabilities (Snowling et al., 2006). Children with only articulation problems appear to show the fewest and least severe psychological difficulties (van Daal et al., 2007).

Cognitive Deficits and Theories

Children with language impairments commonly exhibit nonlinguistic cognitive deficits. Speed of information processing, auditory perception, and memory are among the areas examined (Leonard, 1998; Leonard et al., 2007).

A general limitation in information-processing capacity is hypothesized to play a role in language disorder. The information-processing model assumes, among other things, that rapid handling of information facilitates processing. Limitation in speed of processing is notable in children with language disabilities (Leonard et al., 2007). They appear to respond more slowly across a variety of tasks, which suggests that a processing limitation affects performance across domains. When a particular language operation requires especially rapid processing, detrimental effects would be expected. A difficulty with the hypothesis that processing speed accounts for language disability is that processing speed is deficient in youths with general learning problems, so why would effects show up only in language (Hulme & Snowling, 2009)?

A second hypothesis relates language impairments to various deficits in auditory processing (Corriveau, Pasquini, & Goswami, 2007; Leonard, 1998). Perception of brief, rapid sound is considered important in language, so a child who cannot catch rapidly flowing sound cues might well have language difficulties. Research has shown that children with language impairments do appear to have difficulty identifying very fast sounds embedded in speech (Tallal & Benasich, 2002). Moreover, infants at family risk for language/learning impairments have been shown to exhibit longer processing times for auditory stimuli. Further support for the hypothesis comes from studies indicating that when sound cues in speech syllables are extended in experimental studies, speech discrimination improves. Nevertheless, research findings are inconsistent. In summarizing this work, Hulme and Snowling (2009) speculate on possible reasons for inconsistency. Perhaps the youths examined had different kinds of language impairments, or age mattered, or there is a maturational delay in auditory processing. It is also possible that different tasks employed in the research made different demands on the youths, or that auditory processing contributes to language acquisition in the context of other risk factors. Still, it was concluded that auditory processing at best makes only a weak contribution to language disabilities.

A third proposal implicating cognition in language disability focuses on verbal short-term and working memory (Gathercole & Alloway, 2006). A distinction can be made between these aspects of memory. Verbal short-term memory is specialized for the temporary storage of information pertaining to language. It is thought to be involved with the sound structure, or phonology, of language. Deficits in verbal short-term memory are apparent in a variety of tasks, including the immediate repetition of a string of nonwords (e.g., "mep," "shom") that has been said aloud. Research, including meta-analysis, shows that children with language disabilities have deficits in nonword repetition and phonological memory (Bishop, 2002; Conti-Ramsden, 2003; Estes, Evans, & Else-Quest, 2007). However, the question has been raised as to whether this task is simply a pure measure of phonological processing rather than an index of phonological memory (Hulme & Snowling, 2009). It is worth noting, nonetheless, that in typically developing children, phonological memory is related to the acquisition of speech production, vocabulary, comprehension, and the processing of syntax (Marton & Schwartz, 2003).

With regard to verbal working memory, both the storage and the processing of verbal information are involved. Verbal working memory requires holding verbal information in mind while it is being used, for example, in following a sequence of directions. Children with language disorders do poorly on measures of complex verbal memory (Gathercole & Alloway, 2006). Such difficulty may not be an underlying cause of language problems, but it likely contributes to the reading and mathematics problems that are associated with language disabilities.

Although progress is being made in understanding cognitive deficits exhibited by children with language impairments, much is yet to be investigated. Given the heterogeneity of problems, multiple deficits are probably involved.

LEARNING DISABILITIES: READING, WRITING, ARITHMETIC

The terms *learning disabilities* (LD), *specific learning disabilities* (SLI) and *learning disorders* refer to specific developmental problems in reading, writing, and arithmetic—the "three Rs" essential to classroom learning and everyday functioning. Historically, these disorders, respectively, have been known as *dyslexia, dysgraphia,* and *dyscalculia.* Although learning disabilities are often described as if they are "pure," deficits frequently occur in combinations. Most children with learning disorders have reading problems, and many have additional learning difficulties. Specific learning disabilities are recognized by the educational system and by the DSM and ICD.

DSM Classification and Diagnosis

The DSM-5 refers to learning disabilities as Specific Learning Disorders, defined as difficulties in learning and using academic skills that have persisted for at least 6 months regardless of appropriate interventions (American Psychiatric Association, 2013). The impaired skills include difficulties in the following: word reading, understanding what is read, spelling, written expression, understanding number, and mathematical reasoning. These can be specified in three domains—as impairments in reading, written expression, or mathematics, and more than one domain can be specified. Subskills in each affected domain also are to be specified, as described by DSM (e.g., number sense, accurate arithmetic calculation).

The problems must begin during the school-age years, although they may become fully manifest only when demand for the skill exceeds the person's abilities. Diagnosis requires that a person's achievement in at least one domain be substantially lower than expected for age, and the difficulties must interfere with academic or occupational performance or daily living activities that require the skill. Such deficits must be confirmed by individually administered standardized measures and a clinical assessment. Further, the difficulties cannot be accounted for by intellectual disabilities, visual or auditory acuity, other mental or neurological disorders, psychosocial adversity, lack of proficiency in the language of academic instruction, or inadequate educational instruction.

We discuss specific topics for each of these disorders before examining more general issues. Emphasis is placed by far on reading disabilities because of their high prevalence and because they have been most investigated.

Reading Disabilities (RD)

DESCRIPTION   Reading can be defined as "the process of extracting and constructing meaning from written text for some purpose" (Vellutino et al., 2004, p. 5). It requires the ability to readily identify words in running text in order to discern the meaning of the text. Among the many skills involved in this "on-line" process are language abilities, cognitive skills, understanding of the conventions of written text (e.g., reading from left to right on a page), and a store of knowledge about the world.

An enormously complex process, reading virtually always entails instruction. When it is not mastered, children may struggle to recognize single written words or to pronounce them correctly when reading aloud, read excessively slowly or haltingly, have limited vocabulary, lack understanding of what they have read, or not remember what they have read. Given these complexities, extensive efforts have been made to discover whether reading problems fall into subtypes based on reading skills or underlying cognitive

deficits. These efforts have largely failed to generate valid subtypes (Siegel, 2003; Tannock, 2005c). However, an important distinction is made between problems in word-level reading and in the comprehension of written text.

Dyslexia: Word-Level Reading   The term *dyslexia* has been used in different ways and currently most often refers to impairment in word-level reading, or the acquisition of basic reading skills. Historically, various processes have been implicated in dyslexia. Theories of visual system abnormalities were the most influential throughout the twentieth century until the 1970s and 1980s (Vellutino et al., 2004). For example, Samuel Orton, a central figure in early research on reading, erroneously noted that among other difficulties visual–perceptual deficits caused dyslexic children to reverse letters (*d* for *b; saw* for *was*) and even to write in mirror images (Vellutino, 1979). Other theorists have suggested that dyslexia is caused by visual system defects that lead to impairments in scanning, tracking, or processing visual stimuli. Currently, it is believed that perceptual processing deficits, including auditory processing, may be involved in some way in some reading problems (Boden & Giaschi, 2007; Tannock, 2005c).

Nonetheless, the present view of dyslexia emphasizes its fundamental relationship with language impairment. A critical role is given to **phonological processing**, that is, using the sound structure of language to process written material. Before they can learn to read, children must realize that spoken words can be segmented into sounds, an ability referred to as phonological awareness. For instance, they much recognize that the word *sad* contains three sounds, even though *sad* is said as one unit of sound. Also essential to reading is phonological decoding, that is, understanding that letters (graphemes) correspond to sounds (phonemes) and being able to map letters to sounds.

Much evidence supports the importance of phonological processing in learning to read (Lipka & Siegel, 2006). Young children who are aware of the sounds of their language and who can decode letters, syllables, and single words become better readers. In contrast, phonological processing deficits are associated with difficulty in naming single words, reading, and spelling. Moreover, interventions that target phonological processing deficits improve single word identification and reading. Cross-cultural studies confirm the importance of phonological processing in the reading of alphabet-based languages other than English.

Problems of Comprehension   As critical as phonological processing is, some children—perhaps 5 to 10%—who do not exhibit deficient processing nevertheless have difficulties in understanding what they read (Hulme & Snowling, 2009; Lyon et al., 2003). These children can decode

The classroom is often an unhappy place for a child with a learning disability.

and recognize single words; indeed, they may accurately read aloud a passage of text, but fail to understand it. They may often go unidentified by teachers (Nation et al., 2004).

Comprehension of written material is complex and entails many processes (Hulme & Snowling, 2009). Among these is vocabulary, that is, knowledge of word meanings. Competence regarding the grammatical structure of language is necessary. Recall that grammar consists of the formation of words (morphology) and the organization of words into phrases and sentences to give meaning (syntax). Competence in grammar would contribute, for example, to understanding who is happy in "Susan gave Jane an apple and she was happy" (Snowling, 2000). One longitudinal study of children showed that at about ages 6 to 8 years, word-level reading was a powerful predictor of comprehension and beyond that vocabulary and grammatical skills explained much of the children's success in comprehension.

Word-level skill is less important in older children, whose comprehension depends more on other aspects of language and cognition. One of these is the ability to make inferences from the specific information provided by text. Another is metacognitive ability, which might include considering the purpose of the text, evaluating one's understanding of the text, and rereading and revising one's understanding if necessary. There is considerable need for further investigation of these and other processes that underlie deficits in comprehension, possible developmental paths, and interventions (Berninger et al., 2006; Lipka, Lesaux, & Siegel, 2006).

LATE EMERGING PROBLEMS Although problems in the early acquisition of reading have been of great interest, it appears that reading difficulties—both in word-level reading and comprehension—can first emerge around the fourth or

fifth grade (Leach, Scarborough, & Rescorla, 2003). What accounts for this phenomenon? Lipka and colleagues (2006) conducted a study that addressed this issue. They identified a group of fourth graders as reading disabled. The group had been drawn from a large representative sample of children who had been tested annually on several measures of reading, starting in kindergarten. The data showed that the children with reading disability in fourth grade had moved along three paths (Figure 10.2). One path involved consistently poor reading (PR); a second path involved some fluctuation (FR). Of most interest was a path showing a more dramatic drop-off, with scores falling into the disability range only at fourth grade (LE). On the basis of the various measures available

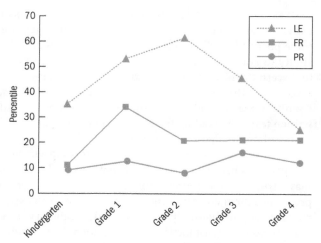

FIGURE 10.2 Developmental paths of fourth-grade students with reading disabilities. (Impairment was identified as reading achievement at or below the 25th percentile on a standardized reading test.) *Adapted from Lipka, Lesaux, & Siegel, 2006.*

over the years, the investigators suggested that children following this late-emerging path actually (1) had not mastered early phonological processing skills, but had masked the deficit by learning to sight read many words, or (2) had only inadequately mastered phonological processing skills, so that the increased demands of fourth-grade reading had taken their toll. Noteworthy is that this late-emerging group represented 36% of the reading-disabled children and that other studies have found somewhat larger rates of children whose reading problems appear to emerge relatively late. The study by Lipka and colleagues suggests that such children may have early subtle deficits that require monitoring. Late-emerging reading problems warrant further investigation.

EPIDEMIOLOGY AND DEVELOPMENTAL COURSE The reported prevalence of RD varies considerably: a conservative estimate is 4 to 10% of the U.S. school-age population (Tannock, 2005c). Lyon and colleagues (2006) noted that estimates historically have fallen between 10 and 15% of the U.S. school-age population. Discrepancies in reported rates may be due in part to sampling differences and definitional inconsistency. For example, rates are higher in inner city samples, and when disabilities are defined by low reading achievement rather than by an IQ-achievement discrepancy (Tannock, 2005c).

Boys have been more often diagnosed with RD than girls, and genetic influence and selection bias have been proposed as explanations (Lipka & Siegel, 2006). The male to female ratio may be about 3 or 4 to 1 in clinic samples, and perhaps smaller in the general child population (Willcutt & Pennington, 2000).

Reading disorders have been identified at varying rates in many countries (Grigorenko, 2001). Further research would be useful in clarifying the degree to which this might be explained by the differing structures of different languages, societal attitudes toward reading disabilities, or methodological factors.

Disorder tends to persist during the school years into adolescence and adulthood (McGee et al., 2002; Snowling, Muter, & Carroll, 2007). Some variation is seen in outcome, however (Shaywitz et al., 2003; Williams & McGee, 1996). Some children with poor reading skills in early childhood have been reported to catch up with their peers by preadolescence or adolescence, and improvement can occur even later. However, reading disability can remain about the same or worsen over time.

The so-called **"Mathew Effect"** refers to the widening over time of the gap between strong and weak readers (McNamara, Scissons, & Gutknecth, 2011). Although not always found, evidence exists for the effect regarding reading and other disabilities. Social class and behavior problems are among the possible predictors (Morgan, Farkas, & Wu, 2011). It is also thought that youths with initially severe

problems are further disadvantaged by not being able to practice reading, because experience and practice with print material are important in improving literacy skills.

CO-OCCURRING DISORDERS We have already noted that RD is associated with language and other learning disabilities. In addition, it has frequently been linked to conduct disturbance, particularly in boys. Several causal connections are possible, and longitudinal research has suggested an indirect path from reading disorder to later conduct problems. Early behavior problems and family factors are thought to play a role (Fergusson & Lynskey, 1997; Prior et al., 1999; Williams & McGee, 1996). A twin study of boys indicated that the association of reading disabilities and antisocial behavior was largely due to shared environmental factors but, importantly, that each problem had an effect on the other (Trzesniewski et al., 2006). That is, not only was genetic influence relatively small, but also reading and antisocial problems were intertwined and as one changed so did the other.

Finally, RD and ADHD are associated with each other (Yoshimasu et al., 2010). Comorbidity is estimated at about 3.5% of the U.S. school-age population (Smith & Adams, 2006). Reading deficits are thought to be linked more to the inattention of ADHD than to hyperactivity-impulsivity, and deficits of the comorbid group appear to be a combination of the deficits shown in each disorder (Gooch, Snowling, & Hulme, 2011; Paloyelis et al., 2010).

Willcutt and colleagues (2001) compared the cognitive deficits of nonreferred twins who displayed reading disorder, ADHD, or both disorders. Reading disability was associated with deficits regarding the sounds and memory of words, ADHD with deficits in inhibition. Children who exhibited both disorders had deficits in both areas that combined to make them the most disabled. Moreover, the co-occurrence of RD and ADHD was associated with heightened risk for still other disorders. Figure 10.3 demonstrates this finding in males; a somewhat different and weaker effect was found for females.

Disabilities of Written Expression

Children with disorders of written expression are the last to hand in classwork and may sit for hours over homework. Their writings may be rife with errors, be difficult to decipher, and contain disorganized content lacking in length and richness. Writing is multidimensional and implicates multiple language processes as well as visual–motor and other cognitive abilities (Lyon et al., 2006; Tannock, 2005a). It has been useful to make a distinction between transcription and text generation—that is, composition.

Transcription involves putting ideas into written form; it is fundamental in the early development of writing (Berninger & Amtmann, 2003). Many deficiencies are observed in poor transcription—in punctuation,

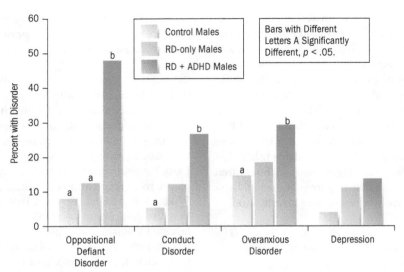

FIGURE 10.3 The influence of co-occurring ADHD on the prevalence of four other disorders among males with RD. *Adapted from Willcutt & Pennington, 2000.*

capitalization, word placement—but problems in handwriting and spelling are central. Disabilities can occur in one or both of these. In typical development, smooth, rapid, and clear handwriting develops gradually and entails effort. A child with transcription problems produces letters and words on paper slowly and laboriously, and sometimes is unsuccessful at writing (Figure 10.4). Good handwriting requires not only motor skill, but also that letters be stored

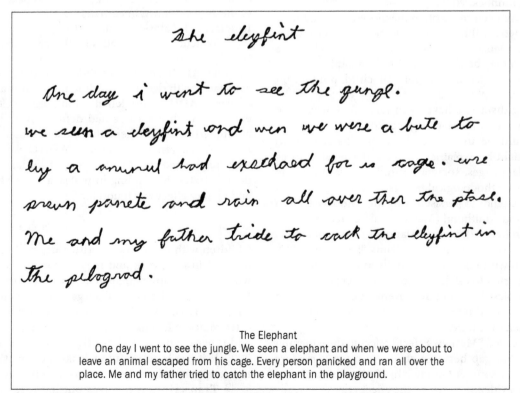

The Elephant
One day I went to see the jungle. We seen a elephant and when we were about to leave an animal escaped from his cage. Every person panicked and ran all over the place. Me and my father tried to catch the elephant in the playground.

FIGURE 10.4 The writing of an 11-year-old boy and the probable translation. The writing shows imagination, a rich vocabulary, and a basic grasp of storytelling. There also are misspellings of common and uncommon words, poorly formed letters, and retracing of letters that suggest difficulty in mechanics of writing. *Adapted from Taylor, 1988.*

in working and long-term memory, planned for, and retrieved from memory. Good spelling depends, among other abilities, on understanding the connections between sounds and conventional spelling, on word recognition, and on knowledge and retrieval of learned letters/words from memory (Berninger & Amtmann, 2003; Lyon et al., 2003). The case description of 11-year-old C.J. demonstrates some of the difficulties of deficient transcription and also the implication it has for text generation.

Text generation (or composition) can be viewed as the creation of meaning in written form. Among other requirements it demands that the child be able to retrieve

C.J.

Writing, Writing, All Day Long

Fifth-grader C.J.'s problems had been increasing; he exhibited deteriorating grades, failure to complete assigned schoolwork, and some inattention and oppositional behaviors. C.J.'s identical twin had an early history of language and reading problems. C.J. participated in class discussions and had no problems with reading or math computation, but his written work was putting him at risk for failing his grade level. C.J. had an increasing dislike for school, sometimes skipped classes, found writing to be extremely tedious, and expressed a desire to talk rather than write about his many ideas. "It's writing, writing all day long—even in math and science." He reported that his teacher thought he was lazy and his writing atrocious. "He slings my work back at me to do over again, gives me detention, and when I try to explain he tells me I've got a bad attitude."

An assessment with the Wide Range Achievement Test-3 revealed average to high-average reading and math performance, but significant problems in spelling. C.J. also did poorly on a standardized test of written expression and an informal text generation task. On the latter, he produced three barely legible short sentences that lacked punctuation and capitalization but contained several spelling and grammar errors. C.J. attained average scores on a standardized oral language test but omitted sounds or syllables on a nonword test. The latter is sensitive to mild residual language impairments and written language impairments. The diagnosis of disorder of written expression was formulated by the assessment team, with no other DSM disorder.

Adapted from Tannock, 2005a, pp. 3126–3127.

from memory words, sentence structure, and stored information about the topic of interest. Also critical are higher-order executive functions and metacognitive skills, the latter involving the person's understanding of how information gets processed (Graham & Harris, 2003; Schumaker & Deshler, 2003; Wong et al., 1997). Disabled writers lack skills in understanding the goal of their writing, developing a plan, organizing the points to be made, linking ideas, monitoring and revising their work, and the like. Many of these components apply to language and thinking more generally and are thus less specific to writing disorders than is transcription (Lyon et al., 2003). This does not mean, of course, that these skills are less important in understanding and ameliorating children's difficulties in writing. Figure 10.5 provides an example of the work of an adolescent assigned to write a compare-and-contrast essay. The essay is comprehensible, but demonstrates weak sentence construction, awkward phrasing, lack of paragraphing, and deficits in organization. This student's writing greatly improved through an intervention program aimed at teaching cognitive and metacognitive skills.

EPIDEMIOLOGY AND DEVELOPMENTAL COURSE The prevalence of writing disorders is not definitively known. Perhaps 6 to 10% of school-age children have some form of writing disability (Lyon et al., 2003; Tannock, 2005a). Standardized tests for writing skill are limited and assessment may require analyses of a child's written work.

Hokey and basketball are two sports they both have comparesions they both sports, they contrast in many ways like in hokey you use a stick and a puck, but in basketball you use one ball and your hands. They also compare in that when you play them the goal is to get the puck or basketball into a goal or net. Another contrast is that hokey is played on ice and basketball is played on courts. When you play hokey or basketball you noticed that the puck and ball both touch the ground that is another way to compare.In hokey the goal.net is placed on the ground and in basketball the net is on a backboard in the air that is another contrast.If you have ever been to a hokey or basketball game there is always quaters or periods in a game so that the players can take a break,in that way they compare. Basketball has four quarters and Hockey has three periods to a game and they are different in that way.But the best comparisions in hokey and basketball is the fans,many people love hockey and basketball that's why they are one of most played and favored sports in the world.

FIGURE 10.5 A compare-and-contrast essay written by an adolescent with learning disabilities. *Adapted from Wong et al. 1997.*

Developmental norms are important, of course, in judging the quality of writing; for example, before age 8 or so, motor skills may not be well developed and only simple narrative can be expected (Lipka & Siegel, 2006). By second grade, though, the disorder is usually apparent (American Psychiatric Association, 2000), and referral for problems sharply increases around the fourth grade, when school curricula demand increased writing (Berninger & Amtmann, 2003; Tannock, 2005b). Longitudinal studies of development are lacking but cross-sectional research suggests that the disorder persists for some youths.

Mathematics Disabilities (MD)

The term *mathematics* encompasses many domains, such as the sciences of algebra, calculus, and set theory (Tannock, 2005b). However, mathematics disorder or disabilities is a diagnostic label that refers to, or emphasizes, problems in basic arithmetic skills or mathematical reasoning. Descriptions of mathematics disorder in children indicate an array of difficulties including performing simple addition and subtraction, understanding arithmetic terms and symbols, memorizing mathematical facts, and understanding spatial organization (Geary, 2003). The defining features of MD are not established, but the core deficits are thought to involve the understanding of number and the learning, representation, and retrieval of basic arithmetic facts (Cirino et al., 2007), which are emphasized in this discussion.

BASIC UNDERSTANDING OF NUMBER

It appears that primitive numerical abilities exist in some animals and in preverbal human infants (Hulme & Snowling, 2009). Chimps, for example, were taught to match a half-filled glass of water with another half-full, rather than three-quarters full, glass of water. When later expected to match the half-full glass with half an apple or three-quarters of an apple, they selected the half apple. This suggests some numerical appreciation or sense of quantity. Human 6-month-olds are able to distinguish between groups of 8 and 16 dots, or 16 and 32 dots, but they do not differentiate between 16 and 24. Such demonstrations indicate that prior to acquiring language, humans have a representation of magnitude upon which to build mathematics abilities.

EARLY PROCEDURAL AND STRATEGY IMPAIRMENTS

Research on problems in mathematics has emphasized basic understanding of children's early counting and arithmetic abilities (Geary, 2003; 2004; Torbeyns, Verschaffel, & Ghesquière, 2004). Even the relatively simple calculations accomplished by very young children require some understanding of number and counting. By age 5, many typically developing children understand basic

principles of counting (e.g., an object in an array of objects can be counted only once), although they may have difficulties with other principles (e.g., objects in an array can be counted in any order). As children take on simple calculations, there is a gradual transition to more advanced procedures. For example, *counting all* (e.g., 2 + 3 is added by counting 1-2-3-4-5) gradually gives way to *counting on* (e.g., the child starts with 2 and then adds on 3-4-5). Counting procedures are soon represented in memory and arithmetic facts can then be called up automatically. The addition of 2 + 3 thus no longer requires counting; rather, 5 is quite effortlessly and rapidly retrieved.

Children with arithmetic disabilities acquire many of these early counting and basic arithmetic procedures and strategies more slowly. They also employ them less frequently and with less speed and accuracy. In addition, deficits or delays exist in memory-based retrieval processes, which persist through the elementary school years. Thus, children in third grade or above may exhibit errors in rapid retrieval of number facts (e.g., $7 \times 9 = 63$). It is possible, then, that the mathematics difficulties of older children hark back to difficulties in the acquisitions of basic procedures not mastered earlier in life (Hulme & Snowling, 2009). Problems occur in addition, subtraction, multiplication, and division for more complex problems; and in employing fractions and decimals (Tannock, 2005b). Youths with co-occurring reading problems are particularly susceptible to errors in arithmetic word problems and complex calculation (Cirino et al., 2007).

In examining these findings, the following are worth noting. *First*, longitudinal investigations are necessary for a more complete understanding of the developmental course of disabilities. *Second*, some investigators have failed to distinguish children with only mathematics disability from children who also have reading disabilities. The co-occurring condition, which may affect about 50% of children with mathematics disorder, is linked to more pronounced difficulties, perhaps especially in areas such as word problems rather than in understanding of number or retrieval of math facts (Speece & Hines, 2007). *Third*, research is needed on underlying cognitive deficits that are likely involved such as working memory, simultaneous processing functions, and visual-spatial skills (Hulme & Snowling, 2009; Iglesias-Sarmiento & Deaño, 2011). *Fourth*, although limited family and twin studies give evidence of genetic influence, the acquisition of arithmetic skills is highly sensitive to the quality of instruction in the classroom (Lyon et al., 2006; Tannock, 2005b).

EPIDEMIOLOGY AND DEVELOPMENTAL COURSE

There are relatively few studies of the prevalence of mathematics disabilities and they vary in how they define and measure deficits. Given this, it appears that 5 to 8% of school-age children display some form of mathematics disabilities (Geary, 2004; Lyon et al., 2003). A smaller figure is likely when cases with co-occurring reading disabilities and ADHD are excluded (American Psychiatric Association, 2000). Gender differences have not been found in most studies.

Similarly lacking are studies of the course and continuity of mathematics disabilities. There is indication of some persistence of disabilities, however. For example, Prior and colleagues (1999) found that 57% of children with arithmetic disorder at age 7 to 8 had arithmetic problems 4 years later. Although further study is required, mathematics disabilities can be identified during the early school years and can persist into adolescence and adulthood (Lyon et al., 2003; Tannock, 2005b). Fortunately, research-based child intervention has appeared, focusing on basic skills (such as fact retrieval and procedures) and higher order skills (such as word problems) (Lyon et al., 2006).

SOCIAL AND MOTIVATIONAL PROBLEMS

Although many children and adolescents with language and learning disabilities do quite well socially, develop a positive sense of self, and maintain interest in learning, others find these areas problematic.

Social Relations and Competence

The social relations of at least some children with disabilities are less than satisfactory. Teachers associate learning disabilities with a variety of problematic behaviors (Mishna, 2003), and peers often rate children with learning disorders as less popular, more rejected, and more neglected than nondisabled youngsters (Nowicki, 2003; Ochoa & Palmer, 1995). Overall, these children may have fewer friends, lower quality of friendship, and higher levels of loneliness (Wiener & Tardif, 2004).

What underlies social difficulties? There is no definitive answer to this question. Behavioral problems associated with learning disabilities, such as ADHD, may adversely affect peers (Vaughn, La Greca & Kuttler, 1999). In addition, children with learning disorders appear to have lower social competence than their nondisabled peers, which might well affect social relationships (Lipka & Siegel, 2006; Nowicki, 2003; Toro et al., 1990). They may have difficulties in identifying the emotional expression of others, understanding social situations, guessing how other youngsters feel in particular situations, and solving social problems.

Whatever the underlying causes, poor social relationships and poor social skills increase risk for school alienation and dropout, loneliness, and withdrawal (Deater-Deckard, 2001; Vaughn et al., 1999). Risk for victimization or bullying by peers may also be increased (Nowicki, 2003). For example, in one study three times as many 11-year-olds with language impairments reported experiencing victimization more than once a week than did typical 11-year-olds (Conti-Ramsden & Botting, 2004).

Academic Self-Concept and Motivation

Research with typically developing youths indicates that beliefs about achievement can influence effort and performance (Molden & Dweck, 2006). In general, the

Social interaction and motivational factors play an important role in the development of language and learning difficulties.

belief that intelligence is malleable and that effort stimulates ability are adaptive. Moreover, responding to failure with a mastery orientation is more adaptive than responding with a helplessness orientation. Mastery is indicated by attributing failure to lack of effort or task difficulty, expecting future improvement, and maintaining problem solving and positive affect. In contrast, a helplessness orientation involves expecting failure, giving up, and demonstrating negative self-cognition and affect. Similarly, beliefs about one's abilities and about competence to carry out a task, is related to outcome on that task (Bandura, 1997).

Meta-analyses indicate that learning disorders are associated with a lowered sense of worth (Elbaum & Vaughn, 2003; Nowicki 2003). Some children with disabilities rate their general sense of self as relatively low and more consistently rate their academic abilities negatively (Lipka & Siegel, 2006). Compared with typical students, those with LD report more helplessness and lower self-efficacy even when their school grades are comparable (Lackaye et al., 2006; Núñez et al., 2005). In adolescence, confidence in the ability to manage learning has been shown to decline and also to be related to success in school (Klassen, 2010).

Given these considerations, it is easy to see that children with disabilities can enter a vicious cycle of academic failure and low motivation that works against them (Licht & Kistner, 1986). As a result of academic failure, they come to doubt their intellectual abilities and believe that their efforts to achieve are futile. Such learned helplessness exacerbates the situation as the children are more likely to give up in the face of difficulty. In turn, further failure is experienced, which reinforces their belief in lack of ability and control (Figure 10.6).

Nevertheless, not all youth with disabilities adopt negative perceptions and behaviors (Núñez et al., 2005). This was demonstrated in a study of the self-perceptions of middle-school students with LD (Meltzer et al.,

2004). Some of the students reported positive academic self-perceptions; others held negative self-perceptions. The former group reported expending greater effort on schoolwork than the latter group and employing learning strategies to bypass the effects of their impairments. Their teachers viewed them similarly, and also saw them as performing at a similar academic level as their peers without LD. This and related research suggest a need for further understanding of resilience factors regarding youths with LD.

BRAIN ABNORMALITIES IN LANGUAGE AND LEARNING DISABILITIES

Language and learning problems are associated with cerebral palsy, epilepsy, nervous system infections, head injury, prenatal alcohol use, very preterm/low birthweight, and neurological delays and soft signs (e.g., Aarnoudse-Moens et al., 2009; Snowling, 1991; Taylor, 1989; Vellutino et al., 2004). Direct study of the brain indicates how it might be implicated in specific disabilities. Many regions of the brain are likely to be involved in some way; for example, the cerebellum and certain visual and auditory pathways could play a role in perceptual processing in language or reading disorders (Heim & Benasich, 2006). A major focus of investigation has been the left hemisphere, long considered crucial to language functions.

Language and Reading: Brain Structure

Structures of the brain have been investigated through postmortem examination and brain scans. Especially implicated is the planum temporale and the surrounding region (Hynd, Marshall, & Gonzalez, 1991; Hynd & Semrud-Clikeman, 1989a; 1989b; Peterson, 1995). This area, which roughly corresponds with Wernicke's area and is used in language, involves the upper surface of the temporal lobe extending to the lower surface of the parietal lobe. In most—but not all—adults in the general population the area is larger in the left hemisphere than the right. In persons with specific language and reading disorders, asymmetry often is absent. The right side has been found to be as large or even larger than the left, and the left temporal lobe to be smaller than normal (Eliez et al., 2000).

In addition, cell abnormalities in the brain have been observed to be more common in individuals with specific disabilities. However, as informative and interesting as these and other structural findings are, caution is needed in drawing conclusions. Differences in the brains of adults with disabilities may not be the same as in children, research samples are often small, and findings are not completely consistent (Vellutino et al., 2004).

FIGURE 10.6 Children with learning disorders may experience a vicious cycle of academic failure and low motivation.

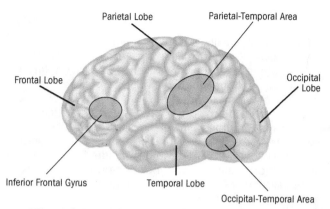

Parietal Lobe   Parietal-Temporal Area

Frontal Lobe

Occipital Lobe

Inferior Frontal Gyrus   Temporal Lobe

Occipital-Temporal Area

FIGURE 10.7 Approximate locations of the left hemisphere regions involved in language and reading. *Adapted from Shaywitz & Shaywitz, 2003.*

Language and Reading: Brain Function

Much attention has been given to evaluating brain activity with a variety of scanning methods as children and adults engage in language and reading tasks. Differences have been shown between impaired and nonimpaired readers in brain regions involved in language and reading (Shaywitz, 2003) (Figure 10.7). An area in the front of the brain (corresponding to Broca's area) aids in word analysis. A second area, the parietal-temporal area (including Wernicke's area) plays a central role in phonological processing, that is, in integrating the visual and sound aspects of language. A third area at the junction of the occipital and temporal lobes is especially involved in rapid word recognition; it becomes increasingly important as readers come to rely more on automatic, almost instantaneous word recognition rather than on basic phonological processes. In general, strong readers rely more on the back areas of the brain when reading, and most processing occurs on the left side.

It has been proposed that reading disorders involve faulty wiring of the system necessary for good language and reading. Several studies show that patterns of brain activation are different in children and adults with or without reading problems when they engage in various phonological and reading tasks (e.g., Cao et al., 2006). In individuals with reading disabilities, the posterior left side appears underactive and the corresponding posterior right side may be overactive (Breier et al., 2003; Shaywitz et al., 1998). There is also some evidence that the front left area of the brain may be relatively overactive, and that as children with reading disabilities get older they may increasingly employ the frontal area of the brain (Shaywitz & Shaywitz, 2003).

In examining these findings, it is helpful to recall that the brain is a dynamic network: abnormalities in one area might affect another, perhaps as an effort to compensate for what is not working properly. Shaywitz and colleagues suggest that the use of alternative routes—greater reliance on the front brain area and the right hemisphere—allows some readers to achieve accurate, although not rapid and fluent, reading (Shaywitz, 2003; Shaywitz et al., 2003).

In an interesting recent study, Preston and colleagues (2010) examined elementary schoolchildren who had been early, on-time, or late talkers. Brain images were recorded while the children listened to and read words or pronounced non-words. Children who had been late talkers showed lower activation in several cortical and sub-cortical areas previously implicated in speech and reading. This group of children also performed less well on the language and literary tasks.

Progress is being made in understanding brain functioning in language and reading disorders. Meanwhile, fascinating results have come from research that shows brain changes associated with interventions for reading and language deficits. (See Accent: "Intervention and Brain Changes.")

ACCENT
Intervention and Brain Changes

Simos and colleagues (2002) worked with 7- to 17-year-olds with average intelligence but severe disabilities in word recognition and phonological skills. Preintervention brain scans indicated an abnormal activation pattern for phonological tasks: little or no activation of the left posterior (parietal-temporal) region and increased activation of the corresponding region of the right brain. The youths received about 80 hours of phonological training over 8 weeks. Not only did measures of word accuracy show improvement into the normal range, but brain scans also indicated

increased activation in the left posterior hemisphere relative to the corresponding right side. No changes over time were shown in activation patterns for the normal control group. Figure 10.8 exemplifies the findings in one of the treated children. Simos and colleagues (2007) subsequently reported similarly positive results in 7- to 9-year-olds who received intervention focusing on phonological processing and reading fluency.

A more extensive investigation of 6- to 9-year-olds with reading disabilities examined the outcome

(continued)

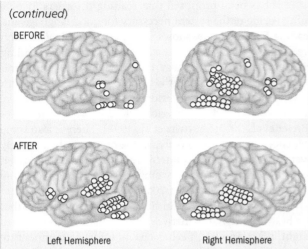

(continued)

BEFORE

AFTER

Left Hemisphere   Right Hemisphere

FIGURE 10.8 Changes in brain activation in a child after intervention. Most notable is increased activation in left posterior regions. *Based on Simos et al., 2002. Courtesy of J. M. Fletcher.*

of a phonologically based intervention delivered at school over 8 months (Shaywitz et al., 2004). Daily 50-minute sessions progressively focused on letter-sound associations, phoneme analysis of words, timed reading of words, oral story reading, and word dictation. After intervention, the treated participants significantly improved in reading and brain activation was more in keeping with that of a nonimpaired control group. Follow-up of some of the children 1 year after intervention indicated continued improvement in the occipital-temporal region, known for its involvement with automatic word processing.

Research that documents both improvement in select language/reading skills and correlated neurobiological change suggests that psychosocial intervention can affect brain development. It holds promise of increased understanding of disabilities and of treatments for children who have difficulty in reading (Coyne et al., 2004; Hatcher et al., 2004).

ETIOLOGY OF LANGUAGE AND LEARNING DISABILITIES

Genetic Influences

Genetic effects on language and learning disabilities have been investigated with a gamut of genetic methods.

LANGUAGE The study of the genetics of speech and language disorders has lagged somewhat compared to that of other developmental disorders but is making enormous gain (Newbury & Monaco, 2010). The identification of the FOXP2 gene in a family exhibiting a specific speech impairment laid the foundation for subsequent research. (See Accent: "The FOXP2 Story.")

Specific language disorders aggregate in families. Children with a family history of language impairments are at increased risk for language and reading deficits (Flax et al., 2009). Although data vary across studies, a median rate of 35% compared to 11% in control families has been reported (Grigorenko, 2009). Twin comparisons show concordance in MZ pairs to be about 75% and about 45% in DZ pairs (Plomin, 2008). High heritability has been documented in twins for articulation problems, expressive language difficulties, and nonword repetition tasks that are considered an index of phonological memory (DeThorne et al., 2006; Grigorenko, 2009).

Targeted and genome-wide linkage and association studies have identified regions on several chromosomes and candidate genes for speech and language deficits. Among the implicated chromosomes are 1, 3, 6, 7, 13, 15,

16, and 19. Two genes on chromosome 16 serve as examples of the investigation of specific language disability. The ATP2C2 and CMIP genes have been associated with performance on a task of phonological short-term memory.

READING Parents of youth with RD have high rates of reading problems and, conversely, about 30 to 50% of youth with a parent with RD will develop the disorder (Peterson & McGrath, 2009a). Twin comparisons give evidence of genetic influence, with concordance in MZ twins being about 85% and in DZ about 50% (Plomin, 2008). Heritability has been estimated at about 60% (Stevenson et al., 2005). Influence on several components of reading has been shown, including on phonological processing and single-word reading. For instance, several gene locations linked to RD have been associated with phonological disorder (Smith et al., 2005). This is a particularly interesting finding given the importance of these processes in language and reading disorders.

Some progress has been made in identifying specific chromosomes that might contribute to RD. Chromosomes 6 and 15 were the first to be identified and subsequent linkage studies have implicated several other chromosomes (Peterson & McGrath, 2009a). Further, several candidate genes have been identified, and some of these are involved in migrations of neurons and axon path finding in brain development.

The involvement of multiple genes in RD is supported by evidence that reading skills in children at family risk, and in the general population, appear to fall on a

ACCENT
The FOXP2 Story

The FOXP2 gene, the first gene implicated in speech and language disorder, was identified through the study of a large family known as the KE family (Newbury & Monaco, 2010). Many family members exhibited symptoms of a distinctive form of speech disorder called verbal dyspraxia. Multiple symptoms of verbal dyspraxia affect both oral and written language (Grigorenko, 2009). Problems exist in speech articulation and in expressive and receptive vocabulary, morphology, and syntax. Cognition is affected, and members of the KE family with the condition exhibit lower nonverbal IQ than family members without the condition.

Transmitted in a dominant pattern, the FOXP2 gene on chromosome 7 appears responsible for the malady. A mutation in the gene has been found in all affected but not unaffected family members. The gene codes for proteins that control the transcription of other genes and thus can have wide influence. FOXP2 is thought to be important in early prenatal development, especially at the time of brain development.

The discovery of FOXP2 stirred considerable interest: perhaps other speech and language disorders could be traced to FOXP2 or to other single genes. Investigators searched for but did not find FOXP2 to be related to other speech and language disorders, nor do single-gene abnormalities appear to play an important role in these problems. Nevertheless, the discovery of FOXP2 is a landmark because it precipitated an explosion of research to find other genes, which has resulted in increased understanding of speech and language disabilities.

continuum (Plomin 2008). Moreover, both general reading *ability* and *disability* are heritable and are genetically linked (Harlaar et al., 2005). The findings suggest that a number of genes work together with other risk factors to produce susceptibility to reading disorders. Some single-gene and chromosome syndromes are associated with reading problems, but they involve rare, severe forms of learning disabilities (Plomin, 2008).

WRITING AND MATHEMATICS Genetic influence on written expression is seen with regard to spelling. Family aggregation of spelling problems has been revealed, as well as heritability in twin studies (Schulte-Körne, 2001; Tannock, 2005a). Chromosome 15 may be linked to spelling disorder.

Shalev and colleagues (2001) found that parents and siblings of probands with mathematics disabilities exhibited rates of impairment about 10 times higher than what would be expected in the general population. In addition, limited twin data indicate higher concordance for mathematics disability in identical than fraternal pairs (Lyon et al., 2003). A recent genome-wide association study of mathematics ability and disability has pointed to several locations of interest (Docherty et al., 2010). The authors note that although this work requires replication, interesting candidate genes are implicated. Further, the findings from this and other research indicate that mathematic ability and disability are influenced by many genes of small effect.

SHARED GENETIC INFLUENCES AND GENERALIST GENES As we saw earlier in this chapter, language and learning disabilities in youths frequently occur together.

Moreover, co-occurrence of these disabilities "runs" in families—thus the question, Do these disorders share a genetic predisposition? Research has made it clear that the answer is "yes." For example, one study showed a genetic correlation of .67 between reading and mathematics disabilities (Kovas et al., 2007).

Important research also indicates that the same set of genes—so-called generalist genes—that influence one disorder also influences another. As noted by Plomin, Kovas, & Haworth (2007), this finding appears counterintuitive because some children have, say, a reading problem without a math problem, or vice versa. Such dissociation of the difficulties can be accounted for by the fact that only *some* genes are shared and that unshared environmental effects also play a role in making children different from one another. In any event, given the existence of generalist genes, the identification of a specific gene for one disability may be critical for understanding another disability.

Psychosocial Influences

Genetic behavior studies point to a role for both genetic and environmental influences on normal and impaired development relevant to specific disabilities. From other types of research, we know that several psychosocial variables are important in typical language development (Chapman, 2000; Weizman & Snow, 2001). Early vocabulary growth is predicted by the number or sophistication of words the child hears from its mother. And more rapid language development is predicted by, for example, the mother's elaborating on the child's speech and commenting on what the child is paying attention to. Although family variables may not be the root of language problems, they may play a role in maintaining deficits (Whitehurst & Fischel, 1994).

Stevenson and Fredman (1990) found that large family size and certain aspects of mother–child interaction were linked to reading problems, and they noted that family involvement in the child's learning may be especially influential on early reading acquisition. However, family factors are not always found (Snowling et al., 2007). On the other hand, there is evidence that children with reading disabilities shun the activity, and that the amount of reading a child does is related to reading skills. Lowered expectations of teachers and children themselves may be especially hazardous for those whose learning requires extraordinary effort.

It is also generally believed that factors such as overcrowded classrooms, math anxiety, and quality of instruction can affect the acquisition of mathematics skills (Shalev et al., 2001). Indeed, quality of teaching, class size, and interactive computer programs can markedly affect

academic skills (Nisbett et al., 2012). Early learning especially may be facilitated by cognitive stimulation across home, preschool, and first-grade settings (Crosnoe et al., 2010).

ASSESSING LANGUAGE AND LEARNING DISABILITIES

Children's language or learning problems are typically first noticed by parents or teachers, whose sensitivity to the difficulties is valuable for early intervention. (See Accent: "Clues for Identifying Reading Disorder.")

When language disorders are suspected in preschoolers, parents seek assessment from a variety of professionals. Family and child history, speech and language evaluation, assessment of verbal and nonverbal intelligence, and screening for hearing, neurological, and medical problems are generally appropriate (Bishop, 2002). Detailed speech and language assessment usually are conducted by specialists who have broad knowledge of the language system, as well as

ACCENT
Clues for Identifying Reading Disorder

Sally Shaywitz (2003), a neuroscientist and physician who has been in the forefront of reading disorder research, notes that parents can play an important role in identifying reading disorder. The identification requires the parents to carefully observe the child, know what to look for, and be willing to spend time listening to the child speak and read. With this in mind, Shaywitz has presented clues for recognizing that a child may need further assessment.

CLUES DURING THE PRESCHOOL YEARS
Delayed language
Difficulty in learning and appreciating common nursery rhymes
Mispronounced words; persistent baby talk
Difficulty in learning (and remembering) names of letters
Failure to know the letters in child's own name

CLUES DURING KINDERGARTEN AND FIRST GRADE
Failure to understand that words can be segmented and sounded out
Inability to learn to associate letters with their appropriate sounds

Reading errors not connected to the sounds of the letters, for example, *big* is read as *goat*
Inability to read common one-syllable words or to sound out even simple words
Complaints about the difficulty of reading, or avoidance of reading
History of reading difficulties in parents or siblings

CLUES FROM SECOND GRADE AND BEYOND
Among the many clues in speaking:

mispronunciation of long, unfamiliar, or complicated words; influent speech (hesitations, pauses, use of "ums"); inability to find the exact word; inability to reply rapidly when questioned; difficulty in remembering bits of verbal information such as dates and lists.

Among the many clues in reading:

slow reading progress; difficulty in reading unfamiliar words, function words such as *that* and *in*, or multisyllable words; omitting parts of words; oral reading that is choppy, labored, or slow; avoidance of reading; reading that improves in accuracy but not in fluency; family history of reading and spelling difficulties.

intervention (Bishop & Norbury, 2008). A multidisciplinary team including language specialists, preschool teachers, psychologists, and physicians, among others, may be formed to plan intervention (Kirk, Gallagher, & Anastasiow, 2000). Later occurring or more subtle language problems and learning handicaps may be assessed in mental health settings, but are often evaluated in the educational system, following procedures recommended by government regulations for the assessment and education of handicapped youth.

Crucial in identifying language and learning disabilities—and understanding a child's particular deficits—are standardized tests to evaluate language, reading, spelling, and mathematics (Lipka & Siegel, 2006). Tests are available to assess specific components of these domains, for example, vocabulary or receptive language (Bishop & Norbury, 2008).

Tests of general intelligence are also valuable, and may be essential to establish an IQ-achievement discrepancy for diagnosis or requirements for special education services. Additional psychological assessment, such as of cognitive processing or motor skills, may or may not be useful, depending on the goals of assessment (Lipka & Siegel, 2006).

When it is relevant, the evaluator should also discuss the child's study habits, motivations, self-esteem, and concerns (e.g., Bryan, 1997). Because language and learning disabilities are defined in terms of achievement and intelligence, there is probably a tendency to bypass the behavioral, social, and motivational contexts in which the child is operating. Yet, psychosocial factors can facilitate or have adverse influences on the child's functioning.

INTERVENTION FOR LANGUAGE AND LEARNING DISABILITIES

Prevention

As general rule, prevention of developmental disorders is linked to early identification and treatment. Regarding language disabilities, with the exception of severe cases, it can be challenging to identify meaningful impairments in toddlers. Children 2 to 3 years old who are late talkers or exhibit other expressive problems can fall into the normal range of language development by early school age or they can continue to have difficulties (Rescorla, 2002). Thus, prevention requires the monitoring of early language problems.

There is considerable interest today in the prevention of learning problems. At the national level, much concern is expressed over the substantial number of youths who are not acquiring necessary academic skills.

Some of these children have specific disabilities while others have more general achievement problems. We also know that untreated disabilities often continue, and that later treatment is not as successful as earlier intervention. Yet, too many reading problems go undetected until the second or third grade (Shaywitz, 2003), and referrals for learning problems too often occur only after several years of academic failure. Research is continuing into early risk factors for RD and early identification (Puolakanaho et al., 2007).

As we saw earlier in this chapter, the Response to Intervention approach is viewed by some as an approach to prevention of reading impairment. Fuchs and colleagues (2007) have referred to the multiple instruction levels of RTI as prevention efforts. The initial exposure of all children to a carefully selected intervention (curriculum) is conceptualized as primary (universal) prevention. Students who do less well than their peers at this level are considered at risk and are provided with more intense educational efforts, or secondary (selective) prevention. Those who respond poorly to this second tier of intervention are viewed as demonstrating unexpected failure and they receive comprehensive evaluation to determine the appropriateness of special education services—that is, tertiary (indicated) prevention. RTI thus merges prevention and treatment. Regardless of how youth are identified with reading disability, early intervention tends to target basic skills, and reading programs predominate. Thus, many efforts focus on phonological processing and word-level reading.

Intervention for Language Disabilities

The history and literature on treatment for language impairments differs somewhat from that for learning disabilities, and our discussion only touches briefly on this area. Reviews and meta-analyses of interventions indicate that language development can be enhanced, although effects depend in part on the type of disability and the measures employed (Law & Garrett, 2004; Leonard, 1998). Articulation and expressive skills (e.g., syntax, vocabulary) are more easily remediated than receptive abilities. There is some evidence that both clinician- and parent-directed therapy can be effective, and a suggestion that longer duration of treatment has the potential for better outcome.

In his discussion of treatment, most of which focused on expressive disorders, Leonard (1998) noted that in many ways, interventions appear similar to the way that parents and other adults teach language to typically developing children. Operant procedures and modeling are widely used in treatment, and it is not unusual for toys and pictures to be a part of the training procedures. For example, the trainer presents language forms (e.g., plural nouns) and the child is encouraged to imitate the trainer, and/or reinforcers are given for the child's communication in natural settings. Leonard reported that treatment can result in some children, on some tasks, closing the gap between themselves and their typically developing peers (e.g., Leonard et al., 2006). There is limited evidence for the generalization of training; for instance, an acquired language form may be used in different sentences in spontaneous speech. In addition, follow-up evaluations showed that the effects of training may endure over time.

Despite these findings, though, the picture is not all positive. Language often improves but does not reach adequate levels, so that many youngsters remain socially and academically disadvantaged. There is little evidence for the success of therapies for receptive deficits. Moreover, different treatments appear to work to about the same degree and may have common elements but these elements have not been established (Peterson & McGrath, 2009b). Thus, both success and the need for empirically supported interventions are evident.

The treatments described above focus, for the most part, on the specific language deficits exhibited by the children. One intervention that has received considerable recent attention aims at improving the speed of auditory processing deficits hypothesized to underlie oral language and reading skills. Fast ForWord consists of computer programs of audiovisual games for youths ages 4 to 14 years that contain acoustically modified speech, as well as language training techniques similar to those used by speech and language therapist (Strong et al., 2011). It is commercially produced, with claims of producing language gains in a short period of time, and widely used in schools and clinics in several countries. However, the claims have been challenged and are not supported by several studies and a recent meta-analysis (Hulme & Snowling, 2009; Stevenson, 2011; Strong et al., 2011).

Intervention for Learning Disabilities

Historically, interventions for learning disorders have reflected the multidisciplinary nature of the field. Psychologists, physicians, educators, optometrists, and communication therapists have all had a hand in treatment. In the late 1960s and 1970s, many different approaches were employed (Hammill, 1993; Lyon & Cutting, 1998). Conceptually they could be classified as medical, psychoeducational, or behavioral (Figure 10.9).

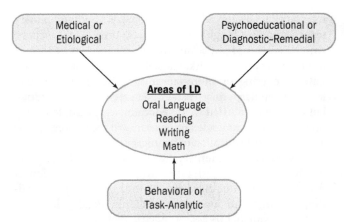

FIGURE 10.9   Historic approaches to the treatment of learning disabilities. *Adapted from Lyon et al., 2006.*

The medical (or etiological) oriented approach viewed LD as stemming from biological pathology (Lyon et al., 2006). Deficits in underlying neurological processes were hypothesized to hinder the development of language, visual and auditory perception, perceptual–motor functioning, and the like. For example, oral language problems might be viewed as the result of brain damage from anoxia, and treatment might entail exercise to stimulate the brain areas relevant to language. Nevertheless, there was little evidence to support the model and treatment methods.

Particularly prevalent was the psychoeducational (or diagnostic–remedial) approach, which targeted various perceptual and cognitive processes assumed to underlie disabilities (Hammill, 1993). Training programs that involved practice in eye–hand coordination, spatial relationships, or language were offered by educational specialists. Unlike the medical approach, the teaching of academic and information processing skills was advocated (Lyon et al., 2006). Student strengths in visual, auditory, language, and motor modalities were taken into account. Despite the popularity of these efforts, many fell by the wayside due to lack of documented success (Dean & Burns, 2002; Hammill, 1993).

In contrast to other approaches, the behavioral (or task-analytic) model made no assumptions about underlying organic pathology or information processing deficits (Lyon et al., 2006). Its aim was to improve academic or social skills through techniques based on learning principles, such as contingency management, feedback, and modeling (Lyon & Cutting, 1998).

As described by Lyon and colleagues (2006), the three historic approaches have contributed to current interventions. Today's neuropsychological models hark back to the early medical approach in their emphasis on underlying brain functioning, and they also incorporate the early psychoeducational approach by linking instruction to student strengths and weaknesses in cognitive processing. Behavioral or task analytic methods are represented in today's direct instruction that pinpoints the acquisition of needed skills and teaches to them.

EFFECTIVENESS OF INTERVENTION   There is a voluminous literature on treatment for reading, mathematics, writing, and spelling disabilities. Direct instruction (task-analytic), along with cognitive and cognitive-behavioral approaches, have generally been shown to be more effective than other approaches to learning disabilities (Hatcher, Hulme, & Snowling, 2004; Lyon et al., 2003; 2006; Torgesen et al., 2001).

In direct instruction if a child has a disability in writing, for example, exercises and practice are provided in writing sentences and paragraphs. Among other things, direct instruction entails selecting and stating goals, presenting new material in small steps and with clear and detailed explanations, incorporating student practice and student feedback, guiding students, and monitoring student progress (Gettinger & Koscik, 2001; Lyon & Cutting, 1998).

The cognitive approach seeks to increase student awareness of the demands of the learning task, the use of learning strategies appropriate to the task (e.g., rehearsal of material), monitoring the success of strategies, and switching strategies when necessary. Organization and strategy use are key elements. The approach has been applied to reading comprehension, mathematics, written expression, memory skills, and study skills (Maccini & Hughes, 1997; Wong et al., 2003).

The cognitive-behavioral approach puts special emphasis on students directing their own learning. Students are taught to record their learning activities, assess their progress, self-reinforce their own behavior, and otherwise manage or regulate learning. The combination of cognitive and cognitive-behavioral techniques is exemplified in intervention for writing skills deficits by, among other things, instructing students how to organize the writing task, employ different strategies, and evaluate their work (Graham & Harris, 2003).

Swanson and Hoskyn have conducted extensive meta-analyses of intervention. One of these contrasted 180 interventions with control comparisons (Swanson & Hoskyn, 1998). A variety of learning disabilities, including language deficits, were targeted with reading disabilities the most frequently treated. Both direct instruction and strategy instruction (emphasizing prompts, explanations,

and modeling of strategies and cognitive approaches) showed positive effects of moderate size and an even larger effect when combined. Another meta-analysis examined the instructional activities embedded in interventions for older children and adolescents (Swanson & Hoskyn, 2001). Particularly effective was the teaching of organizational skills and explicit practice. The latter included repeated practice, reviews, and feedback. It has been suggested that optimal instruction includes both lower order (instruction at the skill level) and higher order instruction (emphasis on the knowledge base and explicit strategies), because reading, mathematics, and other academic areas involve several component processes.

Overall, the possibility of substantial remediation of learning disabilities through thoughtfully designed and implemented interventions is indicated. This is not to say, of course, that the task is of equal challenge across disabilities, nor that equal progress has been made across disabilities. For example, there is significant understanding of dyslexia and evidence for the success of interventions that include training in phonological awareness, letter knowledge, and grapheme–phoneme correspondence within the context of reading and writing tasks (Duff & Clarke, 2011). On the other hand, treatments for difficulties in reading comprehension have been more challenging and have included metacognitive strategies, vocabulary, and spoken narrative. Finally, it is important to note that even when interventions are relatively ameliorative, a proportion of children are not helped. Further efforts are required to address the needs of these non-responders.

SPECIAL EDUCATION SERVICES

In the United States, education services for persons with various kinds of disabilities have evolved dramatically over the last decades. Criticisms of services, legal decisions, and a growing social commitment to the rights of children with disabilities to appropriate education resulted in the Education for All Handicapped Children Act of 1975. Subsequent federal regulations extended opportunities and rights. Public Law 99-457 amended the Education for All Handicapped Children Act, extending provisions to developmentally delayed 3- to- 5-year-olds and creating voluntary intervention for infants. The Education for All Handicapped Children Act was expanded under the title the Individuals with Disabilities Education Act (IDEA) in 1990, and IDEA was reauthorized and amended in 1997 and in 2004.

IDEA encompasses several categories for serving youth with disabilities that include speech or language impairments, learning disabilities, intellectual disability

"A lot of homework?"

(mental retardation), emotional disturbance, autism, and sensory and medical impairments such as blindness, deafness, and orthopedic problems. Increasing numbers of individuals have been served under IDEA. About 6.7 million persons, ages 3 to 21 years, received services in 2005–2006 (U.S. Department of Education, 2007). Forty-one percent of these had specific learning disabilities, and 22% had speech or language impairments.

The four purposes of IDEA have remained essentially unchanged over the years (U.S. Department of Education, 2000):

- To ensure that all students with disabilities obtain an appropriate free public education that emphasizes special education and related services to meet their particular needs
- To ensure that the rights of these students and their parents are protected
- To assist states and localities in providing education to children with disabilities

- To assess and ensure the effectiveness of these educational efforts.

Appropriate education fundamentally means educational experiences tailored to each child's needs. An **individual education plan (IEP)** is constructed by a team of professionals, with parental participation, for each student receiving special education. Among other things, IEPs must consider the child's present functioning; annual educational goals; how and when the child's progress will be measured; special educational and other services to be provided; and, for older students, goals and services for the transition from school to postsecondary life (Building the Legacy: IDEA, 2004). The plans must be systematically reviewed by a committee and the child's parents.

Under IDEA, students with disabilities are to be educated in the **least restrictive environment**, that is, with their nondisabled peers to the maximum extent appropriate. Mainstreaming these students in regular classrooms became a central feature of educational placement. Then, in the late 1980s, through the Regular Education Initiative, a call went out for **inclusion** of students beyond mainstreaming. The premise of inclusion is that public schools should be restructured to be supportive, nurturing communities that meet the needs of all students (Mercer & Mercer, 2001), with the general education teacher assuming primary responsibility for included students (Beirne-Smith et al., 2006).

In practice, consistent with the concept of appropriate education in the least restrictive environment, several options should be available for students in need of special education services. The options range from the general education classroom, with or without supplemental services, to special classes in community schools, to special day and residential schools (Figure 10.10). These settings provide increasing levels of support, and appropriate education means matching the child with the appropriate setting.

By 2008, 95% of students with disabilities, ages 6 to 21, were served in the regular schools, 3% in separate public schools for youth with disabilities, and the small remainder in other various settings (U.S. Department of Education, 2011). Most students with learning disabilities and speech or language disabilities are in general education

classrooms with varying degrees of supplemental services, such as special instruction in the classroom or part-time instruction in resource rooms. About 70% of youth with LD spend less than 21% of their time outside of the general classroom.

Inclusion: Benefits and Concerns

The issue of how best to serve students with special needs has been controversial. This is not an easy matter to settle, because research must address a variety of kinds and severity of disabilities, as well as many alternative programs. Given the complexity of the issue, a considerable amount of early research did not clearly support the once-anticipated academic and social benefits of contained special education classrooms (Detterman & Thompson, 1997; Howlin, 1994).

With the policy of inclusion came both approval and criticism (Beirne-Smith et al., 2006). Advocates have pointed to research showing benefits to academic achievement and social outcomes for the included students (Hobbs & Westling, 1998; Rea, McLaughlin, & Walther-Thomas, 2002; Waldron & McLeskey, 1998). Included students have been found to do better on standardized achievement tests and in relating to others, with no greater

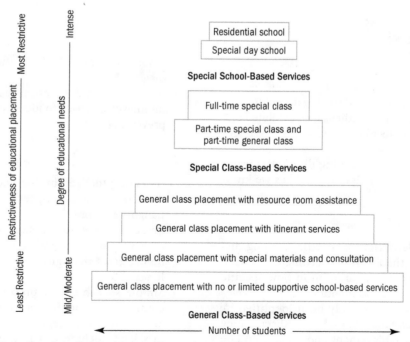

FIGURE 10.10 Alternative educational settings according to degree of restrictiveness and educational needs. *Adapted from Mercer, 1997.*

behavioral difficulties. Outcomes for nondisabled students in these classrooms have also been reported as favorable (Cole, Waldron, & Majd, 2004; Staub & Peck, 1994/1995). Advocates of inclusion believe that concern is best directed not toward *whether* inclusive education should be provided but toward *how* it should be implemented to maximize its effectiveness.

In contrast, critics of inclusion point to data that do not support it, including reports of little academic advantage and lower levels of self-esteem among students with disabilities (Cole et al., 2004). It is also argued that although the inclusion policy has helped reduce discrimination and segregation of students with disabilities, it has strengthened a false belief that no student requires special consideration and that placement in special education settings is a harmful discriminatory approach (Kauffman, McGee, & Brigham, 2004). Moreover, opponents see inclusion as violating both children's rights and federal mandates for appropriate educational placement. It is argued that a continuum of educational settings best serves varying student needs—and is consistent with the desires of many parents and educators.

Overall, research is more supportive than not for students with LD spending most of their time in general classrooms, and teachers are mostly supportive (e.g., McLesky et al., 2004). However, inclusion does require that those in the educational setting effectively work with students who require accommodation in curricula, instructional materials, teaching strategies, testing, and management (Polloway et al., 2010). The demands made on general education teachers can be substantial, and these teachers have expressed concern that they lack specialized knowledge for the task and have inadequate resources and time to implement special curricula and practices (DeSimone & Parmar, 2006). In addition, special education teachers who formerly taught in relatively autonomous special classrooms are called on to work in collaboration with regular teachers in general classrooms (Polloway et al., 2010). Moreover, although parents of children with disabilities desire quality educational experiences for their children, some have concerns about their child's welfare, perhaps especially if the child has severe disabilities (Palmer et al., 2001). The policy of inclusion clearly has brought benefits and has also made demands on the educational system. Both "good" and "poor" programs likely are being implemented (Cole et al., 2004), and schools that conduct successful programs are being recognized (Morocco et al., 2006).

Overview/Looking Back

A BIT OF HISTORY: UNEXPECTED DISABILITIES, UNMET NEEDS

- Today's field of language and learning disabilities can be traced to interest in individuals who exhibited discrepant abilities and to advocacy to improve services to them.
- Kirk's 1963 definition of learning disabilities was a milestone for the interdisciplinary field as we know it today.

DEFINITIONAL CONCERNS

- The influential definition of specific learning disability offered by the federal government has been criticized and has led to variation in how specific disabilities are defined and identified.
- Specific disorders have usually been identified by an IQ-achievement discrepancy or a discrepancy between a youth's achievement and what would be expected based on age or grade level. Criticism of the IQ-achievement discrepancy approach has weakened it somewhat but IQ is still often considered during diagnosis.
- Response to intervention is a newly developing, multilevel approach to identifying disabilities and/or preventing them.

LANGUAGE DISABILITIES

- As conceptualized by the DSM, specific language disabilities include Speech Sound Disorder and Language Disorder.
- Epidemiological studies suggest a rate of 3 to 7%, but rates vary with age and type of disorder. Boys have higher rates than girls, and disability is linked to lower SES.
- Simple speech sound problems often remit; outcome is more variable for early expressive problems and poorest for receptive difficulties. Co-occurring problems include learning disabilities, academic difficulties, and internalizing and externalizing difficulties.

- Among the cognitive deficits proposed as contributing to language disorders are slow general information processing, impaired auditory processing, and memory deficits.

LEARNING DISABILITIES: READING, WRITING, ARITHMETIC

- Specific reading disability (RD) can be viewed in terms of word-level (dyslexia) and comprehension problems. Phonological processing deficits are considered critical in dyslexia. Impaired comprehension entails many language and cognitive processes.
- RD, the most common learning disability, may occur in 4 to 15% of school-age children, and rates are higher in boys. Reading problems can diminish but often tend to persist.
- Specific writing disorder entails deficits that affect transcription and text generation. Prevalence is estimated at about 6 to 10% of school-age children, and many children also display reading problems.
- The study of specific mathematics disabilities has focused on basic arithmetic skills. Basic deficits in understanding number, counting, calculation, and retrieval of arithmetic facts have been documented. Five to 8% of school-age children may be affected. Mathematics disabilities can be identified during the early school years and can persist.

SOCIAL AND MOTIVATIONAL PROBLEMS

- A disproportionate number of students with language and learning problems are at risk for poor social relations, self-concept, academic self-perceptions, self-efficacy, and a helplessness orientation.

BRAIN ABNORMALITIES IN LANGUAGE AND LEARNING DISABILITIES

- Abnormalities of brain structure and brain activation are associated with specific disabilities. Most centrally involved in RD and language are the temporal-parietal, temporal-occipital, and frontal lobes. Limited research suggests that intervention can lead to change in brain activation.

ETIOLOGY OF LANGUAGE AND LEARNING DISABILITIES

- Genetic transmission of various disabilities is documented in behavior genetic and quantitative genetic studies. Progress is slowly being made in identifying specific genes. There is evidence for multiple gene effects, generalist genes, and shared genetic influence on co-occurring difficulties.
- Psychosocial factors, for example, family variables, poor instruction, and lowered expectations, may be implicated in etiology.

ASSESSING LANGUAGE AND LEARNING DISABILITIES

- Parents may call on a variety of professionals to assess early language disorders. Evaluation of later occurring language and learning problems is commonly conducted in educational settings.
- Standardized tests of language, reading, spelling, and arithmetic skills are critical in assessment. Intelligence tests can be helpful or necessary. Evaluation of cognitive and social functioning and the child's family context can provide a fuller assessment.

INTERVENTION FOR LANGUAGE AND LEARNING DISABILITIES

- Early identification and intervention are critical to prevention efforts. Current interest exists in the response to intervention (RTI) approach. Early intervention focuses on basic skills, and most are directed to reading disabilities.
- Intervention for speech and language impairments can be helpful, particularly for articulation and expressive language disorders, but there is a need for more effective and empirically supported treatments.
- Early treatment models of LD can be conceptualized as medical, psychoeducational, and behavioral. Current evidence supports the effectiveness of task-analytic, cognitive, and cognitive-behavioral approaches.
- Well-implemented interventions can be effective, for both language and learning disorders, although there is a continuing need to improve treatments.

SPECIAL EDUCATION SERVICES

- The Individuals with Disabilities Education Act (IDEA) ensures a public education in the least restrictive environment possible to disabled students, and also safeguards the rights of families and ensures assistance in providing effective services.
- Of the children served by IDEA, about 41% are categorized as learning disabled and about 22% as language impaired. Most attend general education classrooms with varying degrees of supplemental supports.
- Some disagreement continues over full inclusion of students with different impairments in regular classrooms.

Key Terms

Education for All Handicapped
   Children Act *249*
Individuals with Disabilities
   Education Act (IDEA) *249*
phonology *251*
phonemes *251*
graphemes *251*

morphology *251*
syntax *251*
grammar *251*
semantics *251*
pragmatics *251*
receptive language *251*
expressive language *252*

phonological processing *257*
Mathew Effect *259*
transcription (written text) *259*
text generation *261*
individual education plan (IEP) *272*
least restrictive environment *272*
inclusion *273*

CHAPTER 11

Intellectual Disability

LOOKING FORWARD

After reading this chapter, you should be able to discuss:

- AAIDD and DSM conceptualizations and classifications of ID
- The nature and measurement of intelligence and adaptive behavior
- Disabilities, characteristics, and co-occurring problems of youths with ID
- The epidemiology and developmental course of ID
- Organic, multigenic, psychosocial, and multifactor etiology
- Down, Fragile X, Williams, and Prader-Willi syndromes
- Family accommodations and experiences
- Assessment of intelligence and adaptive behavior
- Approaches to prevention and intervention

Intellectual disability (ID), previously known as mental retardation, has long been recognized, but until about 1700 it was poorly understood and scarcely viewed as different from other disorders (Reschly, 1992). By the early 1800s, the problem was understood to involve deficient intellectual functioning and handicaps in the daily tasks of living. These two features remain central, although ideas about intellectual disability have evolved and are evolving even today.

Perhaps more strongly than many disturbances, intellectual disability had been seen as a trait of the individual. This perspective has largely being replaced by the view that ID is not "something you have, like blue eyes," nor "something you are, like being short or thin," nor a medical or mental disorder (Luckasson et al., 1992). Rather, it is a state of functioning that is best described as a fit between the abilities of the individual and his or her personal and social environment. Biological causation is fully recognized, but the numerous ways in which the environment plays a role are being given more than passing attention.

The labels applied to intellectual disability have also changed over time. The terms *idiot*, from the Greek meaning "ignorant person," *imbecile*, from the Latin meaning "weakness," and *moron*, meaning "foolish or having deficient judgment," were all once employed in the professional literature (Potter, 1972; Scheerenberger, 1983). These terms had been used as clinical descriptions, but they took on increasingly negative connotations, and changes in terminology were partly an attempt to substitute more positive labels. The term *mental retardation*, employed for decades, was replaced by *intellectual disability* by the influential American Association on Mental Retardation and the organization itself took the name American Association on Intellectual and Developmental Disabilities (AAIDD). In 2010, President Obama signed Rosa's Law (S.2781), which adopted the change in terminology in federal law regarding intellectual disability. Similarly, the fifth edition of the DSM replaced *mental retardation* with *intellectual disability* (American Psychiatric Association, 2013). The new designation is thought to more accurately describe individuals with general cognitive deficits while avoiding negative connotations. (See Accent: "Sticks and Stones and Stigma.") In this chapter, the term *mental retardation* (MR) only is used for the sake of clarity when it appears in the past clinical or research literature.

DEFINITION AND CLASSIFICATION

The AAIDD Approach

The American Association on Intellectual and Developmental Disabilities, founded in 1876, has led efforts to understand and ameliorate intellectual impairment. This organization has long provided conceptualizations of intellectual disability that have often been adopted by other professional groups. In its latest manual, published in 2010, it offered the following definition:

> Intellectual disability is characterized by significant limitations both in intellectual functioning and in adaptive behavior as expressed in conceptual, social, and practical adaptive skills. This disability originates before age 18 (Schalock et al., 2010, p. 5).

Three criteria must be met before a person can be diagnosed with ID. The *age criterion*, before 18, signifies that ID is seen as a disturbance in development. Age 18 is approximately the age at which individuals in our

---

ACCENT
Sticks and Stones and Stigma

A recent study demonstrated how the term *mental retardation* has been corrupted into a common slang term that carries negative connotations (Siperstein, Pociask, & Collins, 2010). The term *retard* appears to communicate a sense of disapproval when it is used in phrases such as "Don't be a retard," or "That is so retarded."

Employing an online survey, the investigators explored the use of the term *retard* in the everyday speech of 8- to 18-year-olds. Seven questions were asked, two of which required only a "yes" or "no" response:

1. Have you ever heard a person call someone a "retard"?
2. Have you ever heard a person call someone with intellectual disabilities (mental retardation) a "retard"?

Ninety-two percent of the participants answered in the affirmative to question 1, and 36% had heard the term "retard" directed toward someone with intellectual disabilities. Most participants had heard the term used by their peers. Only 20% of the participants reported that they had ever used the term in this way.

The investigators were interested in understanding how the participants had responded to hearing the term. The participants were asked to describe their reactions by selecting from a list of items and they could choose multiple items. Reactions depended on whom the term was directed toward. When "retard" was directed toward someone with intellectual disabilities, the participants were more likely to

feel bad or sorry and to tell the person using the term that it was wrong to say the word. In contrast, when "retard" was directed to someone in general, the participants were more likely to laugh, not care, or do nothing.

There were also differences in reactions according to whether a friend or non-friend had used the term. When a friend used it, participants were more likely to laugh or join in; when a non-friend used it, participants were more likely to feel sorry for the person being called a "retard." Gender and age of the participants also mattered. Females and younger participants were more likely to actively oppose the term and feel sorry for the person being picked on; males and older participants were more likely to be apathetic.

Overall, the term was reported more as a general insult rather than being directed toward those with ID. Under certain circumstances, but not others, reactions were sympathetic to those picked on. At the least there was a good deal of apathy. Although the survey involved self-report, the findings were informally confirmed through discussions the investigators had with students actively working toward eliminating the derogatory use of "retard." These discussions revealed that many youths believe it is acceptable to use "retard" if it is not directed toward someone with ID or if the person with ID does not hear it employed. The investigators thus noted that there is lack of understanding of how the term stigmatizes and marginalizing people with intellectual disability.

society assume adult roles and when crucial psychosocial development and brain development have typically occurred. *Limitation in intellectual functioning* refers to functioning defined by performance on general tests of intelligence, that is, to scores that are approximately two or more standard deviations below the mean on tests such as the Stanford–Binet and the Wechsler scales. Scores of 70 or below usually meet this criterion. *Limitation in adaptive skills* is defined as performance at least two standard deviations below the mean on standardized tests of conceptual, social, or practical skills. The requirement of *both* intellectual and adaptive behavior deficits means that individuals who fall into the range of deficiency on intelligence tests but otherwise get along adequately at home, school, or work do not meet the criteria for intellectual disability. Nor do those with deficits in adaptive behavior who perform adequately on intelligence tests warrant the diagnosis. In addition, assessment and judgments of functional limitation must consider the contexts of the individual's life, that is, the community, cultural diversity, and the like.

The AAIDD has presented a framework of human functioning to aid in understanding ID. As indicated in Figure 11.1, the model has two major components: five dimensions and a depiction of the role of supports in individual functioning. The manifestations of ID entail engagement between the five dimensions—intellectual abilities, adaptive behavior, physical and mental health, participation in daily life and social interaction/roles, characteristics of the environment and of the person—and supports the

person receives. Consonant with this multidimensional framework, intellectual disability is not viewed as an absolute trait of the individual, and it is assumed that appropriate supports generally result in improved functioning. Moreover, children or adolescents with mental disability are viewed as complex individuals who have strengths as well as limitations.

LEVELS OF NEEDED SUPPORTS Because great variability exists in the range of abilities of people with ID, it might seem reasonable to use subgroupings based on the severity of intellectual impairment in intervention and research. Following this line of reasoning, the AAIDD once employed four levels of impairment: mild, moderate, severe, and profound. Individuals were assigned to a subgroup according to their intelligence test scores. This approach was widely adopted by other classification systems. Nonetheless, the AAIDD eliminated the approach in 1992. It noted that IQ subgroups might be appropriate for research purposes, but not for making decisions about the care of individuals with ID (Schalock et al., 2010). AAIDD recommended instead that each individual be assessed for levels of needed supports, that is, resources and strategies that will promote development and well-being. This approach recognizes that needs for supports might be different in one area of functioning than another and might change over time. It also highlights the view of ID as dynamically linked to the social environment rather than as a static quality of the individual.

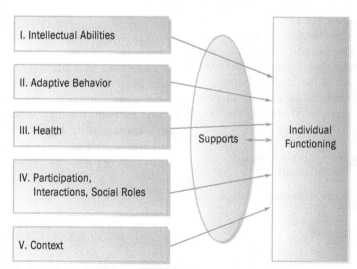

FIGURE 11.1 AAIDD's multidimensional model in which supports provided to the individual play a mediational role in the individual's functioning. *Adapted from Schalock et al., 2010.*

The DSM and Past Approaches

The DSM-5 approach to diagnosis and classification is similar to the current AAIDD approach (American Psychiatric Association, 2013). Although no specific age of onset is noted, onset must occur during the developmental period. Concurrent intellectual and adaptive limitations are required for diagnosis. The DSM notes that intellectual functioning is usually measured by appropriate, individually administered, standardized intelligence tests (e.g., a Wechsler scale), and that scores of 70±5 are usually attained by persons with ID. Adaptive behavior is assessed by clinical judgment and appropriate individually administered instruments; at least one domain of functioning must be impaired.

The DSM specifies severity of ID based on adaptive functioning. Severity levels range from mild to profound. For example, with regard to personal self-care, the person may display age-appropriate skills but need some support for complex tasks (mild), require early extended teaching and time to reach independent self-care in adulthood (moderate), require support for all activities (severe), or rely on others for all aspects of care (profound).

It is worth noting that prior to 2013, the DSM assigned levels of severity of ID based on IQ scores. It was widely felt that the elimination of classification by IQ would leave clinicians and researchers without a reliable and meaningful way to group individuals (Baumeister & Baumeister, 2000). In fact, classification by IQ scores has been customary for most researchers and many practitioners (Hodapp et al., 2006), as is reflected in this chapter.

Table 11.1 shows the four levels of disability often employed (Einfeld & Emerson, 2008). About 85% of all cases are of mild disability. These are viewed as quite different in functioning and in other important ways from persons classified at the other three levels. Thus, in practice, a distinction is commonly made between mild disability and more severe impairment, with the IQ of about 50 marking the boundary.

Also noteworthy is that mild and moderate retardation were once respectively labeled *educable mentally*

retarded and *trainable mentally retarded* by educators in the United States. This classification provided a basis for school placement. Changes in educational policy and practices have made the classification less relevant and today's educators rely less on IQ and more on functional descriptions of the child's needs (Handen & Gilchrist, 2006a).

Changes in the diagnostic criteria for intellectual disability frequently have precipitated criticism. Many professionals criticized the AAIDD in 1992 when it recommended that 75 be considered the ceiling for the IQ criterion for diagnosis. The recommendation took into account the standard error of measurement of intelligence tests, which is about 5 points. However, the ceiling of 75 meant that the number of persons being diagnosed could be doubled (King, Hodapp, & Dykens, 2005), and especially affect persons from certain socially disadvantaged groups. To go back even further in time, there was concern in 1959 when the AAIDD employed a definition that allowed individuals to be diagnosed with ID when they scored one or more standard deviations below the mean on intelligence tests (Figure 11.2). Those who scored in the approximate range of 69 to 85 were labeled as retarded at the borderline level. By this definition, about 16% of the population could be diagnosed as mentally deficient. Critics argued that the criterion was unreasonable and that it disproportionately labeled some disadvantaged groups as retarded. Subsequently, the AAIDD shifted the IQ criterion. Changes in and controversy about the definition of ID demonstrate the degree to which ID is a socially constructed category that has sometimes provoked heated debate.

NATURE OF INTELLIGENCE AND ADAPTIVE BEHAVIOR

Because measures of intelligence and adaptive behavior have been central in defining ID, it is important to look more closely at their development and the concepts that underlie them. Discussion takes a historical perspective and, among other topics, considers test reliability and validity, as well as the relationship between intelligence and adaptive behavior.

Measured Intelligence

As simple as the concept of intelligence seems on the surface, its meaning has raised many questions. We might agree, as have theorists, that it involves the knowledge possessed by a person, the ability to learn or think, or the capacity to adapt to new situations. Beyond these general

TABLE 11.1	Commonly Recognized Levels of Intellectual Disability

Level	Approximate IQ Range
Mild	50–70
Moderate	35–50
Severe	20–35
Profound	below 20

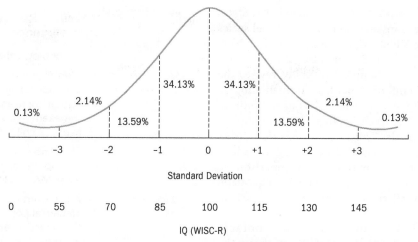

FIGURE 11.2 The distribution of scores on the WISC-R test of general intelligence fitted to the normal distribution. Standard deviation units indicate how far above or below a score is from the mean of 100. The standard deviation for the WISC-R is 15 points. When ID is defined by one or more standard deviations below the mean, approximately 16% of the population is disabled. When ID is defined by two or more standard deviations below the mean, 2 to 3% of the population is disabled.

definitions, we might run into disagreements. Theorists themselves argue, at times passionately, about the precise nature of intelligence, and they hold various perspectives on it. Although we can hardly do justice to this topic, our goal is to address issues that are most relevant to understanding intellectual disabilities.

Modern intelligence testing goes back to the work of Alfred Binet and his colleagues at the beginning of the twentieth century. Their approach—the traditional psychometric approach—focused on individual differences and on the idea that underlying abilities explained differences in intellectual functioning (Beirne-Smith, Ittenbach, & Patton, 1998). Intelligence is often viewed as consisting of a general ability, called *g*, and numerous specific abilities, for example, motor and verbal abilities (Johnson et al., 2004). Intelligence is measured by the presentation of tasks that tap both general and specific abilities. This psychometric approach is sometimes described as examining the products of intellectual, or cognitive, abilities rather than the processes involved in the abilities.

In recent years, information-processing theories have come to the fore, focusing on the processes by which individuals perceive sensory stimuli, store information, manipulate information, and perhaps act on it. Different theorists have somewhat different ways of conceptualizing these processes, but in any case, intelligence is measured according to how well a person performs on processing tasks. For example, the ability to attend to and simultaneously deal with several bits of information might be measured. Information-processing approaches contribute much to the understanding of ID and are increasingly integrated into the measurement of intelligence. However, it was the psychometric approach that largely shaped views of intelligence throughout most of the twentieth century.

EARLY TEST CONSTRUCTION AND ASSUMPTIONS

When Binet and his colleague Simon were asked by school officials in Paris to find a way to identify children who needed special educational experiences, they tested students of different ages on brief tasks relevant to classroom learning. In 1905, their work resulted in the first intelligence scale, consisting of tasks that average students of various ages passed. When children were evaluated on the scale, they were assigned a **mental age** (MA), that is, the age corresponding to the chronological age (CA) of children whose performance they equaled. Thus a 7-year-old who passed the tests that average 7-year-olds passed was assigned a MA of 7; a 7-year-old who only passed the tests that average 5-year-olds passed obtained a MA of 5.

Binet made several assumptions about intelligence (Siegler, 1992). He believed that intelligence encompassed many complex processes, was malleable within limits, and was influenced by the social environment. Binet argued that carefully constructed standardized tests were necessary to minimize inaccurate evaluations of children. Moreover, he and his colleagues devised methods to improve intellectual functioning, and they recommended that educational programs be fitted to each child's special needs.

Intelligence testing was brought to the United States when Henry Goddard translated and used the Binet scales with residents of the Vineland Training School in New Jersey. Then, in 1916, about 5 years after Binet's death, Lewis Terman, working at Stanford University, revised the early scales into the Stanford–Binet test. Terman adopted the idea of the **intelligence quotient** (IQ) as the ratio of an individual's mental age to chronological age, multiplied by 100 to avoid decimals. The ratio IQ enabled direct comparison between children of different ages. Today's major intelligence tests employ statistical comparison, so that what is often referred to as IQ is no longer a quotient, but a score that nevertheless denotes age comparison (Table 11.2).

Goddard and Terman made some notably different assumptions from those of Binet about the nature of intelligence. They assumed that the tests measured inherited intelligence that would remain stable over the life of the individual (e.g., Cravens, 1992). They also saw the need for eugenics, the improvement of the human species by control of inheritance. These beliefs had social implications that were to generate heated debate about the assumptions and uses of intelligence tests, as well as the treatment of persons with

TABLE 11.2	Measures Relevant to Tests of Intelligence
CA	Chronological age.
MA	Mental age. The age score corresponding to the chronological age of children whose performance the examinee equals. For the average child, MA = CA.
IQ (ratio)	The ratio of mental age to chronological age multiplied by 100. IQ = MA/CA × 100.
IQ (deviation)	A standard score derived from statistical procedures that reflects the direction and degree to which an individual's performance deviates from the average score of the age group.

ID. (See Accent: "Measured Intelligence: A History of Abusive Ideas.")

STABILITY AND VALIDITY OF INTELLIGENCE TESTS Intrinsic to the debates about intelligence is the issue

ACCENT
Measured Intelligence: A History of Abusive Ideas

Not long after their introduction, intelligence tests became entwined with social and political issues in the United States and Europe (Dennis et al., 2009). In the United States, IQ tests played a role in establishing immigration quotas for people of southern European background and in introducing laws for the sterilization of people considered mentally deficient (Strickland, 2000). In fact, "unsexing" the "unfit," which had already begun, increased during the early 1900s (Wehmeyer, 2003). Many states passed sterilization laws, and such a law was upheld in 1927 by the Supreme Court in a Virginia case, *Buck v. Bell*. California law called for the sterilization of state hospital inmates and "feeble-minded" children residing in state-run homes. Forced sterilization affected over 50,000 persons before scientists and others overtly criticized the controversial practice.

Although not as overtly egregious, the use of intelligence tests in the schools has been controversial. After compulsory education laws were passed, the public schools employed intelligence tests to assess children's capacity for school learning (MacMillan & Reschly, 1997). Children of poor and some minority families generally performed relatively poorly on the tests. In more recent times, this group included children of African American, Hispanic, and Native American background, although the confounding of social class and racial/ethnic background should be

recognized. Concern was—and still is—raised about test results disproportionately identifying minority and poor children as intellectually deficient—and their placement in special education classrooms (e.g., Schalock et al., 2010). Critics charged that standard English tests were used with bilingual students, the content of tests did not relate well to the students' subcultures, and the tests were not of good quality. Confrontations with the educational system ensued, some of which reached the courts (MacMillan, Keogh, & Jones, 1986). Legal outcomes often, but not always, favored plaintiffs for minority groups. The influential *Larry P. v. Riles* case, brought by black plaintiffs, resulted in restrictions on the use of intelligence tests for identifying and placing black children into special education programs in California. Overall, the educational system was required to stringently monitor the use and administration of intelligence tests.

Inherent in the early uses and abuses of tests was the assumption that measured intelligence is a stable, biologically programmed characteristic of individuals. The currently more accepted view is that intelligence tests assess important aspects of functioning that result from the interaction of heredity and environment and that at least to some degree are modifiable by environmental factors (Fagan & Holland, 2002).

of whether measured intelligence is stable over time. Stability can be examined by studying a group of people longitudinally and correlating earlier IQ scores with later IQ scores. When such test–retest measurements are made after preschool age, a median correlation of 0.77 has been found (King et al., 2005). Further, the IQ scores of persons with intellectual disability appear more stable than the IQ scores of persons with average or above scores, and the lower the score, the greater the stability. It is important to note, however, that such analyses examine groups of people and that individual scores can change, often in response to changing family situations or educational opportunities.

Another central issue about intelligence is what an IQ score tells us about a person. This is a question about the validity of intelligence tests—whether the test tells us what it is designed to tell us. Intelligence tests are reasonably good predictors of school grades (Nisbett et al., 2012). Measured intelligence is also related to later school completion, employment, and income (Fergusson, Horwood, & Ridder, 2005). On the other hand, IQ tests tell us less about a variety of social behaviors (e.g., social adjustment). Nevertheless, it is relevant to note that IQ scores that fall below the average range are generally better predictors of academic and non-academic performance than those in the normal range.

Overall, then, intelligence tests are an important tool, but caution is necessary in interpreting them. IQ scores are relatively stable, but they are not cast in stone. They provide important information about individual functioning but cannot tell us everything. Serious questions have been raised about the cultural bias of the tests, and about their limitations as well; for example, IQ tests may not well reflect problem solving in the real world (Sternberg et al., 1995). Consider also the uncertainty of intelligence tests due to the **Flynn effect**, the finding that IQ scores in populations systematically improve over time. Periodic updating of the tests—that is, construction of new norms—results in resetting the mean score and the test becomes more difficult (Kanaya & Ceci, 2007). Performance then drops several points on average for both typical children and those scoring in the disability range. Thus, as Kanaya, Scullin, and Ceci (2003) noted, the diagnosis of ID can be affected by how old the test norms are when the child is assessed. In considering whether a child meets the IQ criterion for disability, "it may not be sufficient to simply look to see whether the IQ score is below some cutoff point" (p. 790).

Adaptive Functioning

Historically, the failure to socially adapt to one's environment was at the heart of the concept of intellectual disability, even though intelligence testing became dominant in assessment (Schalock et al., 2007). Several decades ago, working at the Vineland Training School, Edgar Doll focused on

The ability to engage in routine activities and tasks substantially heightens the well-being of youth with intellectual disabilities.

the importance of social and personal competence in the everyday lives of persons with ID (King et al., 2005). He published a scale to measure what today is the concept of adaptive behavior. In 1959, the AAIDD first included deficits in adaptive functioning as a criterion for intellectual disability.

Adaptive behavior has generally been thought of as "what people do to take care of themselves and to relate to others in daily living...." (Grossman, 1983, p. 42). Based on research as to what constitutes adaptive behavior, some consensus has emerged that it is multidimensional and includes the following (Schalock et al., 2010):

- Conceptual skills: language, reading and writing, time, and number concepts
- Social skills: interpersonal skills, social responsibility, self-esteem, gullibility, rule following, avoidance of being victimized, social problem solving
- Practical skills: activities and personal care of daily living, use of money, safety, health care, travel, routines, use of telephone, occupational skills.

When considering adaptive skills, developmental level obviously must be taken into account. Behaviors associated with sensorimotor, communication, self-help, and primary socialization skills are emphasized in early life, whereas during later childhood and adolescence, reasoning and judgments about the environment and social relationships increase in importance. When judgments of adaptation are made, consideration also should be given to expectations of the community and the sociocultural context in which the person is functioning. For example, a child may have social skill deficits in a school setting and yet meet the expectations of the neighborhood.

Adaptive behavior is viewed as overlapping with but not identical to intelligence. Research shows a positive correlation in the range of 0.3 to 0.6 between scores on adaptive behavior tests and intelligence tests (Kanaya et al., 2003; McGrath & Peterson, 2009c). Thus, as measured intelligence decreases, individuals are more likely to have difficulties in everyday functioning, and this appears especially true for individuals with lower levels of intelligence (King et al., 2005).

Not all professionals have been in favor of adaptive behavior being as heavily weighed as intelligence in the definition of ID (Baumeister & Baumeister, 2000; Einfeld & Emerson, 2008). Some view adaptive behavior as the result or correlate of intellectual impairment rather than an independent ability. Concern has also been expressed about measuring adaptive behavior. In fact, the development of adaptive behavior scales lagged behind that for intelligence, and judgments of adaptive behavior vary with the person evaluating it. Nevertheless, adaptive behavior scales have improved, and it is widely agreed that daily living skills are critical to the adjustment and satisfaction of youth with intellectual disability.

DESCRIPTION

ID is associated with many identified syndromes as well as less understood conditions. In some cases, the deficits are mild but in others there are severe impairments in cognitive, sensory, motor, language, socioemotional, or behavioral systems. For our purposes, differences in functioning can be illustrated in several ways. It is important to recognize the importance of measures of tested intelligence in descriptions of ID—and in many other topics relevant to the disorder. Although IQ is receiving less emphasis, it has been a prominent criterion for ID, and it has been inextricably woven into the concept of mental deficiency (Baumeister & Baumeister, 2000).

Thus, one way in which variation in functioning can be seen is by examining descriptions based on levels of intelligence. Table 11.3 provides a brief depiction of mild, moderate, severe, and profound disability with a focus on expectations for communication skills, academic learning, and need for supervisory living arrangements. Such a presentation provides a sense of the enormous differences in abilities. The case description of Annalise provides a brief account of some problems experienced by a child diagnosed with profound intellectual disability.

In looking at variation in functioning, it is also informative to compare the developmental profiles of individual cases of children with ID. As an example, Figure 11.3 shows the profiles for Bob and Carol, both 10 years of age (Kirk, Gallagher, & Anastasiow, 2000). Bob's functioning has been judged as mildly retarded, Carol's as severely retarded. Bob's physical characteristics (height, weight, motor coordination) do not vary much from those of his

TABLE 11.3 Brief Description of Functioning According to Levels of ID

Mild
Usually develops social and communication skills in preschool years

Has minimal sensorimotor deficits

Can acquire about sixth-grade academic skills by late teens

Usually achieves adult vocational and social skills for self-support

May need guidance, assistance, supervised living, but often lives successfully in the community

Moderate
Usually develops communication skills in early childhood

Can attend to personal care, with support

Is unlikely to progress beyond second-grade academic skills

Can benefit from social and occupational skills training and perform unskilled or semiskilled work

Can adapt to supervised community living

Severe
May learn to talk and minimally care for self at school age

Has limited ability to profit from preacademic training

In adulthood, may perform simple tasks with supervision

In most cases, can adapt to community living with family or in group homes

Profound
In most cases, has a neurological condition

Has sensorimotor impairments in childhood

With training, may show improvement in motor, self-care, and communication skills

May do simple supervised tasks

Requires structure and constant supervision with individual caregiver for optimal development

Based on American Psychiatric Association, 2000; Singh, Oswald, & Ellis, 1998.

typically developing peers, but his abilities in the language, academic, and social areas lag by approximately 3 years (or grade levels). In contrast, Carol is somewhat further behind her peers in physical attributes and otherwise is functioning at the 4-year-old level. It was suggested that,

ANNALISE

Profound Intellectual Disability

Annalise was born after an unremarkable pregnancy. Her mother recalled significant feeding difficulties in the first few weeks of life, and Annalise's developmental milestones were delayed. She did not walk, for example, until approximately 4 years of age. Her progress was variable while she was enrolled in an early intervention program. She has essentially never been able to use spoken language.

The family reports that Annalise's medical history is extraordinarily complicated. It includes an episode of congestive heart failure, thyroid problems, diabetes, and an apparent allergy to milk. When she was 4 or 5 years of age, she became preoccupied with food, consuming everything in sight. Genetic testing for Prader–Willi syndrome was negative, but a deletion on chromosome 1 was later revealed.

Annalise has never been very sensitive to the thoughts or feelings of others, and she sometimes literally walked over other children. She has many circumscribed interests, and if allowed would watch small vignettes from Disney videos over and over again. She has been preoccupied with sorting and stacking objects, and at one time she would tantrum if not permitted to organize stones and pebbles as she passed them. Due to her preoccupation with food, the family has had to lock the refrigerator and food cabinets. They are hoping that medication will reduce Annalise's anxiety and obsessions that hinder her from fuller participation in activities.

Adapted from King et al., 2005, pp. 3084–3085.

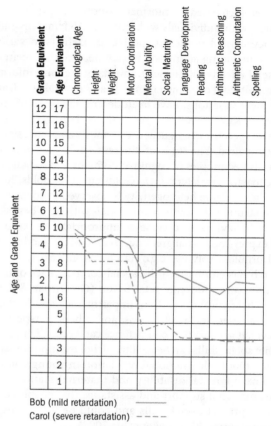

FIGURE 11.3 Developmental profiles of two children with different levels of ID. *From Kirk, Gallagher, & Anastasiow, 2000.*

with appropriate support, Bob might benefit from typical academic experiences, but that Carol would require specialized training to help her develop her potential.

A third way in which the clinical picture can be understood is by further description of the physical/medical, learning/cognitive, and social functioning of children with intellectual disability. Most youth with ID, particularly those with mild impairments, show no unusual physical characteristics and blend into the general population. But a sizable number do show atypical appearance that ranges from minor to more obvious abnormalities. Disturbances in physical functions also occur. The problems include seizure disorder, motor difficulties, impaired vision, and deafness. Abnormalities of physical appearance and function are especially associated with the more severe levels of ID, as are many medical conditions, such as cerebral palsy, epilepsy, cardiac problems, and kidney disease. The lifespan of those with ID is below the average lifespan, although it has noticeably increased. In the United States, it rose from a mean of 25 years to 49 years between 1983 and 1997 (Lenhard et al., 2007).

Investigators have described learning and cognition from various perspectives. Children with ID can learn, but there is immense variability with level of disability and etiology. Early investigations of classical and operant conditioning showed that basic learning is possible at all levels of ID, although accommodations are often required, particularly in severe cases. Over the years, operant learning has been of specific interest regarding treatment. New behaviors can be shaped by successive approximations; desirable behaviors can be maintained and undesirable behaviors weakened by consistent application of appropriate contingencies.

Research based on information-processing approaches, primarily with individuals with mild or moderate disability, has documented numerous problems. Deficits in various abilities, including attention, perception, working memory, the use of effective strategies to mentally organize information, monitoring one's own thinking, and generalizing learning to new situations, have been described (Beirne-Smith, Patton, & Kim, 2006; Tomporowski & Tinsley, 1997). In addition, speech and language are variously and often significantly impaired. The study of different syndromes of ID has demonstrated profiles of cognitive strengths and weaknesses, a topic to which we later return (Goldstein & Reynolds, 2011).

Finally, large heterogeneity is observed in social skills and social understanding in individuals with ID. These skills include behaviors as diverse as appropriate eye contact, facial expression, social greeting, reciprocal interaction, and social problem solving (e.g., Handen & Gilchrist, 2006a). Research has emphasized the social competencies of those with mild and moderate retardation (Greenspan & Love, 1997). These youths do exhibit impairments in understanding social cues, social situations, and others' perspectives. However, it appears that competence can gradually improve and that social skills can be facilitated. For example, research suggests that both emotional regulation in young children with developmental disability and maternal scaffolding— that is, maternal support and assistance that enables child success—predict social skills and could be important for increasing social skills (Baker et al., 2007).

It is reasonable to assume that some of the social problems of children with ID are attributable to the intellectual impairments, language deficits, and physical/medical problems characteristic of ID. It would be a mistake, however, not to recognize the influence of social experience. Youth with ID tend to experience greater social isolation despite today's heightened commitment to include them in social and educational activities. It is also likely that other people, perhaps due to discomfort, behave somewhat atypically during social interactions with these youths. Thus, individuals with ID likely have insufficient opportunity to practice social interaction and observe appropriate models and social relations.

CO-OCCURRING DISORDERS

The well-being and adaptation of individuals with ID are hindered by various psychological problems, some of which are sufficiently severe to meet the criteria for clinical diagnoses. Prevalence of diagnosed or significant problems for children and adolescents is in the range of 30 to 50%, with most research suggesting two to four times the rates found in the general population (Baker et al., 2010; Einfeld & Emerson, 2008).

The kinds of disturbances exhibited are similar to those shown in the general population. Among the most common are attention-deficit hyperactivity disorder and oppositional/conduct problems (Handen & Gilchrist, 2006a; Hodapp et al., 2006). Anxiety, depression, aggression, obsessive-compulsive behavior, schizophrenia, autism, stereotypes, and self-injury have all been reported. The developmental trajectories for many problems appear similar to those found for typical children (de Ruiter et al., 2007). Co-occurring problems are present in toddlers, tend to decline gradually into young adulthood, but still remain higher than in the general population (Einfeld & Emerson, 2008).

However, the kinds of problems may differ with level of disability. Individuals with mild ID display depressive feelings, anxiety, and antisocial problems observed in others of the same mental age. In addition to these kinds of problems, individuals with moderate or severe ID also may exhibit problems that are less common in the general population, such as autism, psychosis, and self-injurious behavior. Finally, particular problems are associated with specific syndromes of ID. For example, Lesch–Nyhan syndrome is associated with self-injury and Prader–Willi syndrome with insatiable eating.

It can be difficult to accurately identify or diagnose co-occurring problems. One reason is that professionals tend to view such difficulties as an intricate part of ID and thus fail to recognize them (Hodapp et al., 2006; Jopp & Keys, 2001). **Overshadowing**, as it is called, has been documented among different professionals working in different settings. A second reason is that the cognitive and communication impairments of ID can make it difficult to identify problems. Symptoms involving emotions and internal states are especially difficult to assess, particularly in individuals with severe ID (Adams & Oliver, 2011). The task of describing emotions may be complicated even for youths with mild disability. We would expect, for example, that depressive symptoms might be challenging to assess because the youth must be able to identify and label sadness, hopelessness, and the like. Still another factor can hinder diagnosis of co-occurring problems. Although standard diagnostic criteria apply quite well when IQ is about 50 or higher, they do not apply well at lower levels of disability (Einfeld & Emerson, 2008).

What accounts for high rates of problems or disorders in ID? Neurological factors no doubt explain some disturbances and probably play a stronger role in more severe disability. Indeed, biological causation is suggested by the association of specific genetic syndromes with specific problems (Hodapp, Thornton-Wells, & Dykens, 2009). But social-psychological variables enter into the picture as well. A recent study reporting high prevalence of behavior problems in developmentally delayed 5-year-olds showed that mothers'

TABLE 11.4	Factors That May Contribute to Psychological Problems in ID

Underlying neurobiological processes

Side effects of medication

Communication deficits

Inadequate problem-solving and coping skills

Reduced opportunity for development of social skills

Reduced opportunity for development of supportive social relationships

Stigma leading to low self-concept

Family stress

Vulnerability to exploitation and abuse

Based in part on King, Hodapp, & Dykens, 2000; 2005.

less sensitive teaching and family stress predicted the continuance of externalizing problems (Baker et al., 2010). The stigma of ID, low quality of living arrangements, and lack of developmental opportunities are among the factors that may underlie behavioral disturbances (Table 11.4). Some of these factors clearly can be modified. For example, social contacts can be broadened to facilitate learning the give-and-take of social interaction. Such efforts are worthwhile as co-occurring problems lower the quality of life and can affect family functioning, school placement, and community adjustment.

EPIDEMIOLOGY

Prevalence of ID often is cited as between 1 and 3% (Handen, 2007). A recent meta-analysis of population studies conducted in developed countries and published between 1980 and 2009 showed a prevalence at about 1% (Maulik et al., 2011). Rates varied across the studies, and were higher in research conducted with youth and in low- and middle-income countries.

The prevalence of ID is interesting in several aspects. If we assume a normal distribution of intelligence test scores and an IQ of about 70 as the criterion for ID, a rate of over 2% would be expected (Figure 11.2). In fact, a greater number of cases than predicted by the normal distribution is found at the low end of the distribution, which suggests a somewhat higher rate. However, the definition of ID addresses both intelligence and adaptive behavior, and we might expect higher prevalence when both are taken into account. Nevertheless, adaptive behavior seems to be neglected in many studies of prevalence, and its inclusion has not always resulted in higher rates (Obi et al., 2011).

Prevalence is especially interesting when age and severity of ID are inspected. Rates are lower prior to school age, and the children identified tend to have moderate or lower IQ scores. It appears that the more severe cases attract more immediate attention, and also that professionals hesitate to diagnose so early, preferring to consider young children as developmentally delayed (Handen, 2007). A dramatic shift then occurs when children enter school. Prevalence increases as more mild cases are diagnosed, probably at least in part due to new demands and increased evaluations. Rates then fall in adolescence and decline further in adulthood. The latter may in part be due to the capacity of some adults to successfully work in unskilled jobs and otherwise function adequately, or perhaps adults become less available for evaluation. At the lower levels of ID, rates may drop because of the relatively short lifespan of these individuals.

Other variables are important when prevalence is examined (Einfeld & Emerson, 2008). ID appears more in males than females—perhaps due to reporting bias, other environmental factors, and male vulnerability to biological influences. In fact, males are at greater risk for genetic syndromes associated with ID. In addition, children and adolescents from families of low socioeconomic circumstances account for a disproportionate number of cases, especially mild cases—an important finding revisited later in the chapter. Interestingly, it has been noted that societal changes could impact future rates. In high-income countries, increased parental age, survival of very low birthweight infants, and assisted conception may increase incidence of the disorder. On the other hand, availability of prenatal screening for disorders associated with ID, as well as improved care of at risk-infants, could decrease incidence.

DEVELOPMENTAL COURSE AND CONSIDERATIONS

Very different life trajectories can be anticipated for children with ID. Stability of diagnosis is not inevitable and individuals with mild disability can, with appropriate training and opportunity, develop adequate intellectual or adaptive skills so that criteria for the disorder are no longer met (American Psychiatric Association, 2000). For most youths, though, ID is lifelong. Severity and cause of the disorder make a difference in course and outcome, as do factors such as associated medical problems, associated psychopathology, and family variables (Volkmar & Dykens, 2002).

Theorists and practitioners have been interested in developmental issues pertaining to cognition in children with ID relative to typical growth. Earlier research tended to focus on milder retardation for which there was no identified cause; later efforts included more severe retardation with known organic etiologies.

The *rate* of intellectual development has been of interest. Typical development is seen as occurring gradually over time throughout childhood and adolescence, with some spurts and regressions. Development is slower than usual in children with ID, but for many youths the rate of growth is fairly steady (King et al., 2005). Nonetheless, different patterns have been observed for specific syndromes, for example, a slowing after a few years of steady growth.

Another developmental consideration has to do with the *sequence* of intellectual growth. Intelligence normally develops in some orderly way. Does this course hold in children with ID? Early research focused on whether youngsters with ID followed the four stages of cognitive growth that, according to Jean Piaget, all typically developing youngsters display as they come to think in more complex ways. Research confirmed that children with ID generally do progress through the same Piagetian stages—and other cognitive sequences—as do non-ID children, but do so more slowly and ultimately do not progress as far (Hodapp & Dykens, 2003; Hodapp & Zigler, 1997). (The participants in early research were children with ID for which there was no clear organic cause, and subsequent research included children with Down syndrome.)

These findings have practical implications for working with youth with ID. For example, the fact that the sequence of development in mild disability is often similar to that of typical development provides a guideline for teaching these children.

ETIOLOGY

Although intellectual disabilities are associated with hundreds of specific medical and genetic conditions, as well as with environmental circumstances, causation is not clearly identified in a substantial number of cases. For example, surveys of the more severe cases of ID indicated unknown cause for 45 to 50% (Einfeld & Emerson, 2008). Similarly, etiology is not understood in large numbers of cases of mild ID, as noted in the case of Johnny.

JOHNNY

Unknown Cause of MR

Johnny is a 10-year-old boy with mild mental retardation. Although from birth his parents considered him somewhat "slow," Johnny was not diagnosed...until his early grade-school years. To this day, no clear [cause] has been provided for Johnny's mild mental retardation. As measured by the Stanford–Binet IV, his IQ is 67, with no significant difference between his verbal and perceptual processing scores. Johnny does, however, show impulsivity and problems in attending.... Johnny's mental retardation first became apparent at the end of the first grade. At that time, a student study team at his school worked with Johnny's classroom teacher and the resource room teacher to help Johnny improve his basic work organizational skills and increase his attention span. At his parents' request, Johnny was also evaluated for attention-deficit hyperactivity disorder by the local psychiatrist, who prescribed stimulant medication that seemed to help.

Adapted from King, Hodapp, & Dykens, 2000, p. 2599.

Historically the **two-group approach** to the etiology of ID has been influential in both theory and research (Volkmar & Dykens, 2002). Accordingly, individuals with intellectual disabilities are viewed as falling into two categories that differ in several ways. The groups, as indicated in Table 11.5 are referred to as the organic group and the cultural–familial group. Biological etiology is clear for the organic group, and in the 1960s and 1970s causation for the cultural–familial group was attributed primarily to

TABLE 11.5 The Two-Group Approach to ID	
Organic	**Cultural–Familial**
Individual shows a clear organic cause of mental retardation	Individual shows no obvious cause of retardation; sometimes another family member is also retarded
More prevalent at moderate, severe, and profound levels of retardation	More prevalent in mild mental retardation
Equal or near-equal rates across all ethnic and SES levels	Higher rates within minority groups and low-SES groups
More often associated with other physical disabilities	Few associated physical or medical disabilities

Adapted from Hodapp, & Dykens, 2003.

environmental deprivation. Current knowledge and theory indicates the wisdom of viewing causation as more complex and interactive. A multicausal model underlies our discussion, but it is informative to distinguish pathological organic, multigenic, and psychosocial etiology or risks.

Pathological Organic Influences

Attributing ID to pathological organic factors implies that some biological condition is crucial in accounting for disordered brain function and intellectual disability. There is considerable evidence for biological risk and causation. As already noted, IQ scores of persons with ID are normally distributed except for a "bump" at the low end (Burack, 1990; Zigler, Balla, & Hodapp, 1984). This excess of low scores, it is suggested, is accounted for by individuals who have suffered major biological impairment (McGrath & Peterson, 2009c; Simonoff, Bolton, & Rutter, 1996). In fact, evidence exists for a group of individuals with more severe disability that comes from all social classes and shows an excess of genetic abnormalities, multiple congenital anomalies, brain dysfunction such as in cerebral palsy, and reduced life expectancy. Underlying such cases may be genetic processes, prenatal or birth adversities, postnatal circumstances such as brain injury and disease, or some combination of these factors.

Multigenic Influences

Heredity has long been linked to intellectual disability. In early times, the link between inherited biological "defect" and ID was often based on flimsy or flawed "proof." For example, in his influential study of the Kallikak family, Goddard (1912) traced the quite distinct genealogical lines of Martin Kallikak. One line originated from Kallikak's liaison with a barmaid, the second from later marriage to a woman of "better stock." From information on several hundred of Kallikak's descendants, Goddard found a pronounced difference in the two families, namely, that the first liaison had resulted in more mental deficiency, criminality, alcoholism, and immorality. Obvious weaknesses existed in this study, most notably the questionable accuracy of the data. But the results were taken as evidence that ID was an inherited biological trait—although family environment could just as well have played a role.

Current understanding of hereditary influences on intelligence in the general population has a basis in behavior genetic research (Plomin, DeFries, & McClearn, 1990). Intelligence test performance of identical twins is more similar than that of fraternal twins; when identical twins are reared apart, similarity decreases but is still high. Studies of families and adopted children lend support to the twin findings. It is estimated that about 50% of the variation in tested intelligence in the general population is due to genetic transmission of multiple genes, and the same

appears to hold true for individuals with mild ID (McGrath & Peterson, 2009c).

Heritability is lower for those with moderate and severe ID. Moreover, pathological organic factors are more strongly associated with the more severe levels of disability, whereas the opposite appears to hold for multigenic influences. One family study, for example, revealed that the IQs of siblings of children with severe retardation averaged 103, hinting that severe ID did not "run in families" and that some specific organic factor had caused retardation in the affected child. In contrast, the IQs of siblings of children with mild retardation averaged 85, suggesting general family influence—perhaps multigenic inheritance, shared environmental effects, or a combination of these (Broman et al., 1987; Scott, 1994).

This is not to say, of course, that pathological organic factors never cause mild ID. Indeed, we might anticipate that biological advances will reveal now-undetected organic abnormalities that contribute to mild impairments. Nevertheless, multiple factors are likely involved in the etiology of mild cases and these may include multiple genes as well as psychosocial influences (Hodapp et al., 2006).

Psychosocial Influences

Interest in psychosocial causation of intellectual disabilities was historically tied to the conceptualization of **cultural-familial retardation**. The terms *garden variety* and *undifferentiated* also were used, reflecting the large number of cases that were not readily distinguished from one another (Crnic, 1988). These children appeared quite normal, possessed relatively good adaptive skills, were often first identified on entering school, and as adults often blended into the general population. Their family members were frequently described in similar ways.

It has been observed for many years that mild ID occurs disproportionately in lower socioeconomic classes and in some minority groups, and could be caused by psychosocial disadvantage. Many psychosocial variables associated with lower SES put children at risk—such as low parental education, particular parental attitudes, lack of social support, and stressful life events (Sameroff, 1990). The adverse effects of psychosocial variables may operate through more than one pathway. Inadequate intellectual stimulation might hinder early brain development, especially the growth of synaptic pathways. Or there may be insufficient support of behavior and motivation conducive to success in the classroom or other learning environments.

Associations have been demonstrated among social class, home environment, and children's intellectual development. For instance, child ability at age 3 has been related to social class and parental practices, for example, parents interacting with and talking to their children

(Hart & Risley, 1992). In general, parenting is a strong predictor of children's cognitive and academic performance (Burchinal et al., 2006; Pungello et al., 2010). As a group, educational and economically deprived parents may lack the skills or otherwise be unable to stimulate children's language and cognitive growth. One team of investigators, which over many years engaged in an intervention and research program for disadvantaged preschool children, proposed a model for the development of ID that reaches across generations (Greenwood et al., 1992; 1994). In this model, due to limited parental interactions, young children begin to fall behind intellectually. When they reach school, the children's home situation combines with school practices that lead to low motivation, education exposure, and achievement, resulting in high rates of school dropout. In turn, when these children become parents, they are unable to contribute to the cognitive growth of their offspring.

It is nevertheless difficult to pinpoint any one cause of intellectual disability in disadvantaged children. These youths are also at risk for major inherited abnormalities, prenatal and birth adversities, postnatal malnutrition and disease, and unfavorable schools and neighborhoods. Variation due to multiple-gene inheritance is not ruled out. Given what is known about the

intricacies of development, multifactor explanations might frequently apply.

Multifactor Causation

Although it is still easy to fall back on the historical tendency to view intellectual disability as a result of *either* biological *or* psychosocial factors, more complex explanations are now clearly recognized. The AAIDD suggests that multifactor explanations are not necessarily inconsistent with the two-group approach (Schalock et al., 2010). In some cases, biomedical factors may predominate, whereas in other cases, social, behavioral, or educational factors may predominate. But even when a known genetic syndrome is strongly associated with ID, the level of disability may be determined, within limits, by some mix of other biological and psychosocial factors. For example, intelligence, adaptive behavior, language development, and behavioral problems are influenced by the home and school environment in children with fragile X syndrome (Reiss & Dant, 2003; Warren et al., 2010). The AAIDD views the development of disabilities within a multiple risk model that encompasses biomedical, social, behavioral, and educational factors that can operate at different times in life (Table 11.6).

TABLE 11.6 The Four AAIDD Categories of Risk and Etiology Pertaining to Intellectual Disability

Timing	Biomedical	Social	Behavioral	Educational
Prenatal	1. Chromosomal disorders 2. Single-gene disorders 3. Syndromes 4. Metabolic disorders 5. Cerebral dysgenesis 6. Maternal illnesses 7. Parental age	1. Poverty 2. Maternal malnutrition 3. Domestic violence 4. Lack of access to prenatal care	1. Parental drug use 2. Parental alcohol use 3. Parental smoking 4. Parental immaturity	1. Parental cognitive disability without supports 2. Lack of preparation for parenthood
Perinatal	1. Prematurity 2. Birth injury 3. Neonatal disorders	1. Lack of access to birth care	1. Parental rejection of caretaking 2. Parental abandonment of child	1. Lack of medical referral for intervention services at discharge
Postnatal	1. Traumatic brain injury 2. Malnutrition 3. Meningoencephalitis 4. Seizure disorders 5. Degenerative disorders	1. Impaired child-caregiver interaction 2. Lack of adequate stimulation 3. Family poverty 4. Chronic illness in the family 5. Institutionalization	1. Child abuse and neglect 2. Domestic violence 3. Inadequate safety measures 4. Social deprivation 5. Difficult child behaviors	1. Impaired parenting 2. Delayed diagnosis 3. Inadequate early intervention services 4. Inadequate special-educational services 5. Inadequate family support

Adapted from Schalock et al., 2010.

GENETIC SYNDROMES AND BEHAVIORAL PHENOTYPES

A major trend in the research on ID is the investigation of genetic syndromes. This approach has two particularly interesting aspects. *First*, it is consistent with the view that psychopathology is best understood in terms of categories. And yet, diagnosis of ID considers performance on intelligence and adaptive behavior tests that assume a continuum of functioning. Thus, the diagnosis of ID may argue for the usefulness of both the category and dimensional views of disorder (McGrath & Peterson, 2009c). *Second*, research on genetic syndromes allows comparison of groups with known organic etiology, and holds promise for shedding light on the links among genes, brain functioning, cognition, and behavior (Hodapp & Dykens, 2009; Simon, 2010).

In this discussion, we highlight four syndromes—Down, fragile X, Williams, Prader–Willi—noting the different genetic mechanism underlying each and describing some of the cognitive features. As well, Table 11.7 briefly describes the physical appearance and behavior often reported for these syndromes. The association of specific syndromes and behavior has led to the notion of **behavioral phenotypes**, meaning that a specific disorder predisposes individuals to certain behaviors. Whereas this is clear in some instances (e.g., excessive eating in Prader-Willi syndrome), overlap of behavioral difficulties also is observed.

Down Syndrome (DS)

Down syndrome, the most common single disorder of ID, occurs in 1 in 800 to 1,200 live births (Capone, 2001; Hazlett et al., 2011). The condition was described in 1866 by John Langdon Down, who attributed it to maternal tuberculosis. In 1959, only 3 years after human chromosomes were first described, trisomy 21 was discovered in persons with DS. As shown in Figure 11.4, chromosome 21 appears in a triplet instead of a pair. About 95% of all cases are attributed to this abnormality, which is caused by failure of the chromosome pair to divide in meiosis, the process in which ova and sperm are formed. (The remaining cases involve other anomalies of chromosome 21.) Trisomy 21 seems to occur almost randomly, is not inherited, and is mostly traced to the mother. It is progressively related to advancing maternal age: the risk for DS is 1 in 2400 for 15- to 19-year-old mothers and 1 in 40 in 45- to 49-year-old mothers (McGrath & Peterson, 2009c).

Several parts of the brain are affected, with abnormalities that include reduced brain size, reduced number and density of neurons, and abnormal dendrites. Brain pathology very similar to the abnormal plaques and tangles found in the brains of Alzheimer's disease patients is observed in many persons with ID by age 40, and dementia is seen in three-quarters by the time they reach 70. There is substantial risk of other health problems, such as heart defects, respiratory anomalies, gastrointestinal problems, and visual difficulties (Hazlett et al., 2011). However, life expectancy has climbed considerably in recent decades, and is about 60 years.

TABLE 11.7 Some Physical and Behavioral Attributes Associated with Four Syndromes of Intellectual Disability

	Physical	Behavioral
Down	Upward slant and folds at corner of eyes, flat facial features, fissured tongue, broad hands and feet, poor muscle tone, short stature	Relatively mild, socially engaging behaviors. Relatively few behavior problems but a wide array (e.g., noncompliance, stubbornness, augumentativeness, inattention, social withdrawal, depression in adolescence)
Fragile X	Long faces, large ears, soft skin, high arched palate, double-jointed thumbs, oversized testicles in boys. These features less likely in females	Inattention, hyperactivity, stereotyped movements, anxiety, tantrums, social avoidance, poor peer interaction. Co-occurring autism that is associated with greater developmental delay
Williams	"Elfinlike" face (e.g., small lower jaw, prominent cheeks), growth deficiency, often an aged appearance in late adolescence or early adulthood	Anxiety, fears and phobias, inattention, hyperactivity, indiscriminate and overly friendly social interaction, poor social judgment
Prader–Willi	Almond-shaped eyes, downturned mouth, short stature, small hands and feet, poor muscletone, underdeveloped gonads, obesity	Excessive eating and food hoarding, obsessions and compulsions, stubbornness, tantrums, aggression, disobedience, anxiety, impulsivity

Based on Corrice & Glidden, 2009; DiNuovo & Buono, 2009; Dykens et al., 2011; Hagerman, 2011; Hazlett et al., 2011; Hodapp et al., 2009.

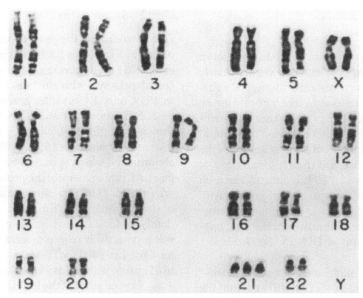

FIGURE 11.4 The chromosome complement of a female with trisomy 21. *Courtesy of the March of Times Birth Defects Foundation.*

Although children with DS show substantial intellectual growth during the first few years of life, disability is usually evident and the rate of development slows throughout childhood and adolescence (Hazlett et al., 2011). Disability typically ranges from moderate to severe, but learning can continue beyond adolescence. Evidence exists for deficits in verbal short-term memory and auditory processing (Laws & Gunn, 2004). Visual–spatial abilities are relatively good. Most children acquire speech but it is delayed, with expressive language more affected than comprehension. Unusually large declines in cognitive and adaptive functioning have inconsistently been reported in adults; these are perhaps related to the development of dementia (Hawkins et al., 2003).

Interestingly, although children with DS display a variety of social and emotional problems, they are thought to experience fewer psychiatric difficulties than found in other groups with ID (Hazlett et al., 2011). For this and other reasons, they may be relatively easy to rear. (See Accent: "The Down Syndrome Advantage.")

Fragile X Syndrome (FXS)

First described in 1969, fragile X syndrome (FXS) is second to Down syndrome as a cause of ID and is the most common inherited form of ID. It affects an estimated 1 in 4,000 males and 1 in 6,000 females (From Discovery to Cure, 2010), and has been found in different countries and ethnicity/race (Hagerman, 2011).

Much investigative work was necessary to track down the complex X-linked mutation and mechanism underlying

FXS (Simonoff et al., 1996; Thapar et al., 1994). The disorder involves mutation in the FMR1 gene such that there are repeats of a triplet of DNA nucleotides (cytosine, guanine, guanine). Normal persons carry less than 50 repeats, but this number can increase in gamete production and be transmitted to offspring (McGrath & Peterson, 2009c). Individuals with 55 to 200 repeats are carriers of the "premutation," which increases the risk of a still larger number of repeats in the next generation. When the number of repeats exceeds 200, the FMR1 gene is not expressed and the full-blown fragile X syndrome is manifest. The disorder involves excessive protein production at the synapse and weakened brain circuitry (Hagerman, 2011). Structural abnormalities have been found in several brain areas, and the brain may be affected prenatally and after birth (Hoeft et al., 2010).

The pattern of inheritance is complex (Hagerman, 2011). A male with an affected X chromosome will pass it to all daughters, but not to sons as they receive only the Y chromosome from fathers. A woman with an affected chromosome has a 50% chance of transmitting it to either sons or daughters. However, daughters are somewhat protected by the second X chromosome that they carry. Moreover, the premutation expands to the full syndrome when females but not males transmit it. Thus a variety of symptoms, or none at all, are seen in families with an affected X chromosome. The case of Sammie tells of a boy diagnosed with FXS by DNA testing.

Several brain anomalies have been reported implicating, among other regions, the cerebellum and the frontal and parietal lobes (McGrath & Peterson, 2009c). The large head

ACCENT
The Down Syndrome Advantage

A popular notion exists that individuals with Down syndrome are easier to rear compared to children with other developmental disabilities (Corrice & Glidden, 2009). Two major questions have been raised about this "Down syndrome advantage." Is it true? and if so, What explains it? Several investigations have addressed the questions.

If rearing children with Down syndrome is actually relatively easy, it is reasonable to expect that their families would be comparably well adjusted and/or satisfied, optimistic, and so forth. Although not all results support this expectation, the weight of the evidence favors it (Esbensen & Seltzer, 2011). Mothers of young children with Down syndrome experience less stress, have more satisfying social support, and are less pessimistic about their children. The families are more cohesive and harmonious. Mothers of adolescents with the syndrome display better psychological adjustment, are less pessimistic, and report a reciprocated, closer relationship with their child. Further, there is similar evidence for mothers of adult children with the syndrome. In attempts to explain these findings, researchers have looked to both the (1) attributes of the individuals with the syndrome and (2) factors peripherally related to the syndrome.

Regarding the syndrome itself, temperament, social behavior, and functional behavior have garnered considerable research interest. Evidence exists that individuals with DS, relative to those with other syndromes, are perceived by their parents as displaying more socially engaging behaviors, higher levels of adaptive behavior, and fewer behavioral problems (Corrice & Glidden, 2009). Moreover, these behaviors are associated with well-being in caretakers (Blacher & McIntyre, 2006; Esbensen & Seltzer, 2011).

Additional factors also seem to be involved. One of these is maternal age. Mothers of Down syndrome children often are older than mothers in comparison groups, and older age when the child is born correlates with some measures of well-being (e.g., less burden, greater satisfaction). Perhaps the greater maturity of mothers, and the financial stability that often comes with age, play a role. In addition, Down syndrome mothers may be less biologically vulnerable to poor functioning than mothers of some comparison groups—such as fragile X syndrome and autism.

Thus, although there is something about the syndrome itself underlying the "Down syndrome advantage," the picture is complex. Increased understanding of this issue is worthwhile because it has implications for informing and supporting families with a child with ID.

SAMMIE
An Example of Fragile X Syndrome

As a newborn, 51-month-old [Sammie] showed only minor problems. Developmental norms were slightly delayed: he sat at 10 months and walked at 15 months. In his first year, Sammie began to flap and bite his hands. He chews excessively on things, has poor eye contact, and displays tantrums. He is easily stimulated and exhibits high activity level, impulsivity, and distractibility. Among other physical features, Sammie has prominent ears, a high-arched palate, and double-jointed thumbs. On the Bayley Scale of Infant Development, he performs as a child 23 to 25 months of age. On the Vineland Adaptive Behavior Scales, Sammie's performance is similar to that of a child 21 to 22 months.

Adapted from Hagerman, 2011, pp. 280–281.

circumference found in children with FXS indicates enlarged brain structures, which in turn suggests insufficient pruning of cells early in development.

Nearly all males with FXS have intellectual disability, usually moderate to severe (Bailey et al., 2009). There is a predictable slowing of cognitive growth as early as age 5, with development reaching a plateau by late childhood or early adolescence (Reiss & Dant, 2003). Weaknesses are notable in visual–spatial cognition, sequential information processing, motor coordination, arithmetic, and executive functions. Verbal long-term memory and acquired information appear to be relative strengths (Volkmar & Dykens, 2002). Nowhere near as many females with FXS display ID and when they do, it tends to be mild. Learning disabilities, behavior problems, and social impairments are common in females with an affected X chromosome. Autism spectrum disorder occurs in a high percentage of boys with FXS (Hagerman, 2011).

Some research has been conducted on the functional, or adaptive, skills of individuals with FSX. In a recent study, Bailey and colleagues (2009) asked a large group of parents to rate specific functional skills of their affected offspring,

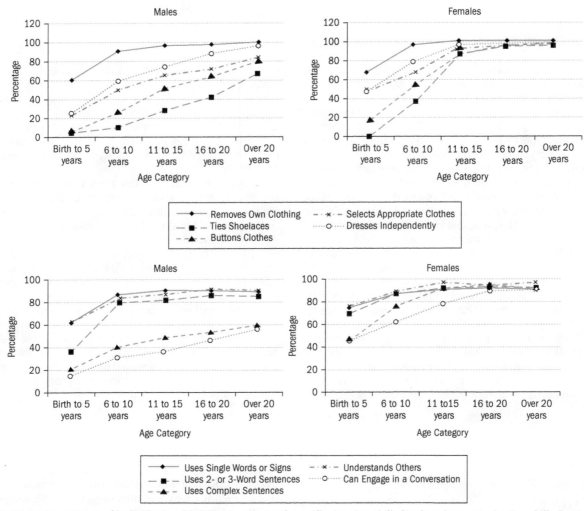

FIGURE 11.5 Percentage of individuals with FXS who attained specific dressing skills (top) and communication skills (bottom), according to gender and age. *From Bailey et al., 2009.*

both male and female, across a wide age range. The results indicated that by early adulthood, the majority of offspring had mastered many basic skills in the seven areas examined (eating, dressing, toileting, bathing and hygiene, communication, speech articulation, reading), but distinct deficiencies remained. Figure 11.5 depicts some of the findings for both genders. The researchers noted that the overall results are consonant with previous reports of relative strength in daily living skills and relative weakness in communication skills. In addition, females outperformed male in all seven areas.

Williams Syndrome (WS)

This rare syndrome, occurring in an estimated 1 case in 7,000 to 20,000, results from a random mutation involving small deletions of several genes on chromosome

7 (Dodd, Schniering, & Porter, 2009; Karmiloff-Smith & Thomas, 2003). Cardiac and kidney problems are among the reported medical difficulties. The syndrome is typically associated with mild to moderate mental retardation, with IQs mostly in the range of 50 to 70. Both reduced and enlarged volumes are reported for several brain regions, as well as abnormal brain activation during tasks involving response inhibition, visual processing, and auditory processing of music and noise (Kesler et al., 2011).

Children and adults with WS are described as having relative strengths in auditory processing and music. Perhaps most striking is the difference between visual–spatial abilities and linguistic functioning. Short-term visual–spatial memory is deficient, and visual–spatial skills are far below what would be expected in keeping with mental age. Even at adolescence, there is an inability to perceive gross differences in spatial orientation and to copy simple stick figures. In contrast, short-term verbal memory is stronger and verbal IQ is typically significantly higher than performance IQ. Despite some weaknesses in aspects of language such as syntax and reading, individuals with the syndrome display strength in grammar and can employ a sophisticated vocabulary (Karmiloff-Smith & Thomas, 2003; Laing et al., 2001).

Also notable, from an early age individuals with Williams syndrome are excessively outgoing and friendly (Santos, Rosset, & Deruelle, 2009). They may show increased sensitivity to social cues, including the human face. It has also been suggested that low social anxiety underlies the excess sociability, but this has not been supported and individuals with WS experience generalized anxiety and specific phobias. Many of the characteristic behaviors and abilities of the syndrome are evident in the case description of Robert.

Prader–Willi Syndrome (P-WS)

This syndrome occurs in an estimated 1 in 10,000 to 15,000 births (Dykens, Cassidy, & DeVries, 2011; King et al., 2005). It was first described in 1956 and is the first syndrome found to be caused by a microdeletion of chromosome material and also the first human disorder to demonstrate genomic imprinting. The latter term refers to genes being expressed depending on whether they are inherited from the mother or father. Prader–Willi syndrome involves genes on the long arm of chromosome 15 that are normally expressed solely by the chromosome inherited from the father (Milner et al., 2005). In approximately 70% of cases, there is a deletion of these genes. In most remaining cases, both chromosomes 15 are inherited from the mother so that the relevant paternal genes are absent. Abnormal functioning of the hypothalamus and of the neurotransmitter serotonin are implicated (Dykens et al., 2011).

Intellectual functioning ranges widely, but IQ is often about 70 (Dykens, Cassidy, & DeVries, 2011). Some cases exhibit relative strength in spatial-perceptual organization and visual processing. Relative weakness may exist in short-tem motor, auditory, and visual memory.

Professionals have been particularly interested in the hyperphagia (excessive eating) and food hoarding that develops between ages 2 and 6, is lifelong, and is a leading cause of death. Research also has recently focused on the

ROBERT

An Example of Williams Syndrome

Robert's mother was a music teacher, his father a science teacher. Born after an unremarkable pregnancy, Robert was extremely fussy as a newborn and later he was a picky eater. His parents thought him high-strung, and he often cried or cringed when his sisters played too loudly. Robert's milestones were slightly delayed, but a pediatrician reassured his parents that boys often showed slight delay and that Robert was a lively, social child who would catch up.

When Robert was 3 years of age, his parents insisted on an assessment. Modest delays were found in motor, linguistic, and cognitive functioning. He was described as friendly and engaging, a charming child with a cute, appealing face. Robert was enrolled in a special kindergarten and the remainder of his school years was spent in a combination of special and regular classrooms.

At age 7, Robert was assessed as having an IQ of 66, with near-normal short-term memory and expressive language and notable deficits in visual–spatial skills. He had difficulty with writing and arithmetic, loved science and music, and was amazingly conversant when he had the chance to talk with others. Indeed, his parents felt he was overly friendly and active.

During early adolescence, Robert became increasingly anxious. He developed fears of storm clouds and dogs, refused to ride on elevators, and worried about his sister. Despite having nightmares, occasionally pacing with worry, and complaining of stomachaches, Robert attended school, had a small group of friends from Special Olympics, sang in the high school choir, and was often selected to play the piano at school concerts. When Robert was 17 years of age, his parents happened to see a television program on Williams syndrome and were "jolted" to see the similarly between their son and the people being portrayed. Genetic testing confirmed the diagnosis. This led to Robert's meeting and engaging in activities with other youth with WS and feeling less alone. His parents found a social community with which to share their feelings and concerns.

Adapted from King et al., 2005, p. 3082.

high rates of nonfood obsessions and compulsions exhibited in Prader–Willi syndrome, which appear during the preschool years. These include skin picking and concerns with exactness, order, cleanliness, and sameness in the environment.

Interestingly, some evidence suggests that the features of P-WS may be different for genetic subtypes (Dykens et al., 2011; King et al., 2005; Milner et al., 2005). Cases of paternal gene deletion may show lower intelligence, especially verbal, and more frequent or severe behavioral difficulties. At the same time, the ability to solve jigsaw puzzles is high. Cases involving two maternal number 15 chromosomes may show decreased performance on visual–spatial tasks, fewer facial characteristics, and a tendency for severe depressive symptoms and impairments in social interaction. Further investigation of these differences is needed and holds promise—as does research of other syndromes—of advancing our understanding of intellectual disabilities.

FAMILY ACCOMMODATIONS AND EXPERIENCES

The birth of a child with a disability is likely to be a traumatic and sad event for a family. Parents worry about the child, realize that expectations will never be fulfilled, and in some instances experience a stressful and frustrating diagnostic process (Bailey, Skinner, & Sparkman, 2003). An unusual amount of attention must be given to the intellectual and psychological needs of the youth, and often to physical needs as well. In addition, parents often experience stigmatization—directed at both their child and themselves (Mukolo, Heflinger, & Wallston, 2010). They often also must face decisions that are unique or uncommon in typical families concerning, for example, living and school arrangements, health, and future planning for lifetime care and supervision. At times, these decisions have involved especially difficult practical and ethical issues. (See Accent: "Deciding What's Best for Children with ID.")

How should we think about families who have a child with ID or other developmental disorders? Early investigations emphasized adverse effects on family members and proposed, for example, that mothers experienced denial, anger, depression, and other negative reactions (Hodapp et al., 2009). However, it was obvious that some families did not experience difficulties and a shift of perspective occurred. Today, families are viewed in a more normative way—as coping with stress. Overall, these families show only slightly negative outcomes, and joy and satisfaction are recognized as part and parcel of their experience.

Numerous factors can affect parent coping and satisfaction, including child behavior problems, marital

ACCENT
Deciding What's Best for Children with ID

Particularly difficult decisions can arise concerning the care and management of children with ID. Two quite different examples demonstrate this point.

Since the 1970s, an unknown, probably small, number of parents opted for reconstructive facial surgery for their children with Down syndrome (Goeke et al., 2003). The surgery most often involved multiple procedures that included tongue reduction and implants in the nose, chin, and other facial areas. The stated goals were improved physical functioning (e.g., speech, breathing) and appearance. The distinctive and commonly recognized facial features of DS presumably act to stigmatize the child, which entails the devaluation, prejudice, and discrimination that has long occurred with mental disorders (Hinshaw, 2005; Major & O'Brien, 2005). Thus, reconstructive surgery for DS can in part be an attempt to lessen stigmatization. Nevertheless, questions have been raised about whether this goal is met, particularly in light of the pain surgery causes and possible negative psychological effects. It has also been suggested that reconstructive surgery may actually decrease the acceptance of Down syndrome.

In a quite different instance, controversy arose in the wake of a medical intervention to cause growth attenuation in a 6-year-old girl through high doses of estrogen and removal of the uterus and breast buds (Gunther & Diekema, 2006). The child, who was severely disabled, was cared for at home by loving parents who feared that, as she grew, they would no longer be able to provide care for her. Improved quality of life for the child was the main consideration, and the intervention was approved by a review committee. However, strong criticism of the decision was voiced, including by the AAIDD (AAIDD Position Paper, 2007). The drastic treatment was criticized as having unknown medical risk with no guarantee of avoiding eventual out-of-home care. The AAIDD also argued that growth attenuation devalues a child, has the potential for future medical abuse, and should be rejected as a treatment option. The organization advocated instead for support and services to parents who care for youths with extraordinary needs.

interaction, parental intellectual functioning, daily hassles, siblings' perceptions, social class variables, professional services, and social support (e.g., Atkinson et al., 1995; Stoneman & Gavidia-Payne, 2006; Wolf et al., 1998). The effects of having a child with disabilities also may vary with family ethnic/racial background (Neely-Barnes & Marchenko, 2004). Differences have been reported across ethnic/racial groups in perceptions about disability and about participation in the systems that provide services. These numerous factors—child characteristics, family characteristics, and social variables—create a complex picture.

Family members likely are affected in different ways to varying degrees. The child's behavioral problems are correlated with parental reports of stress, depression, and anxiety, and mothers may be more affected than fathers (Hastings et al., 2005). When mothers are employed, they face greater than usual work-related stress, for example, in finding child care and services for a youngster with unique needs (Parish, 2006; Warfield, 2001). Moreover, marital partners affect each other, and mothers' distress and children's behavior problems have a bidirectional relationship (Hastings et al., 2006).

Siblings also are undoubtedly challenged by the need to accommodate the child with ID. There is evidence that siblings provide more than usual custodial care and emotional support to the child with disabilities (Hannah & Midlarsky, 2005). Siblings may have difficulties in knowing how to talk to others about their sister or brother with disabilities, and they are often socialized to anticipate caring for the child with ID in the future (Orsmond & Seltzer, 2000; Turnbull, 2004). The overall research findings are mixed regarding outcomes for siblings. There are no differences from other youths in self-concept and self-efficacy, but findings are mixed for behavior problems, depression, and loneliness (Meadan, Stoner, & Angell, 2010). As is true for child-parent relationships, numerous variables may influence sibling relationships.

Rewards and Satisfactions

Despite the challenges of rearing a youth with developmental disabilities, many families do well and report positive aspects of their experiences. Scorgie and Sobsey (2000) investigated transformations in the lives of parents of children with disabilities. Transformations were defined as significant positive changes set into motion by a traumatic or challenging event. The parents reported learning to speak out, becoming stronger, seeing life from a new perspective, and having greater compassion. These parents recognized negative aspects of rearing a child with special needs—for example, career limitations and reduced social

Youngsters with mental retardation or other developmental disabilities require and benefit from extraordinary care and nurturing from their families. The extent to which these families experience stress, adjust to high demands, and are fulfilled depends on many factors.

participation—and they emphasized the importance of balancing the challenging and positive aspects.

Some siblings have reported positive consequences of their experiences—such as increased empathy, patience, acceptance of differences, ability to help others, and appreciation for health and family (Eisenberg, Baker, & Blacher, 1998; Flaton, 2006). One woman, looking back on her extraordinary commitment to her brother with intellectual disability noted:

> I don't know who I would be if Danny wasn't born. He gave me from a very early age, a direction. He has taught me in his own somewhat unorthodox way about prioritizing and about what's important.... And he's taught me compassion and a lot about diversity.... Certainly, I have learned patience because he has his own time frame...the only thing Danny does quickly is eat.... I like to think that being Danny's sister has made me more empathetic.... (Flaton, 2006, p. 140–141)

Fortunately, considerable recognition is now given to more complete portraits of family interaction and functioning. Family systems perspectives focus on understanding numerous family needs and facilitating family quality of life (Turnbull, 2004). In addition, federal mandates for services for very young children have led to early interventions that are sensitive to family resources and priorities (Hodapp et al., 2009). Research indicates that helping families identify and obtain community resources can be especially advantageous (Handen & Gilchrist, 2006a). Among others things, these resources can provide child and family therapy, child care, economic assistance, medical and dental care, and adult education.

ASSESSMENT

Assessment for intellectual disability may be conducted for several purposes. An initial diagnosis can guide parents and teachers, and allow the family to obtain school and community services. Beyond this, more specific information about the child's cognitive strengths and weaknesses can contribute to educational planning. Assessment of the youth's behavioral tendencies and problems, as well as family dynamics, may be necessary for insuring psychological well-being. Medical evaluation can shed light on current or potential health problems, and the diagnosis of a specific syndrome can be valuable in understanding health, intellectual, and behavioral issues. A large number of psychological instruments can be helpful to comprehensively assess individuals for ID (for extended discussion, see Handen, 2007). Our discussion only briefly describes some

of the widely used tests to assess intelligence and adaptive behavior; later in the chapter we look at functional assessment as part of an approach to treatment.

Developmental and Intelligence Tests

Standardized, individually given intelligence tests are central to diagnosing ID. For infants, toddlers, or children with severe deficiency, developmental tests substitute for intelligence tests.

INFANT AND TODDLER TESTS   Several standardized, individually given scales exist to assess infants and preschoolers. Among the most popular is the Bayley scales. The newest version, the Bayley Scales of Infant and Toddler Development-Third Edition, which covers age 1 month to 42 months, includes scales for cognition, language, and motor development (Bayley, 2005). These domains are tested by presenting the child with situations or tasks designed to elicit observable behavioral responses. In addition, the parent or caregiver completes a social-emotional and an adaptive behavior scale.

Performance on tests for young children is referred to as a developmental quotient (DQ), because somewhat different abilities are evaluated than for IQ of older children. These scales give greater emphasis to sensorimotor functioning and less emphasis to language and abstraction. This feature may partly explain why performance on early tests is not highly correlated with later IQ in the general population. Nevertheless, developmental tests may be better predictors of ID, especially of severe disability, than of average or above intelligence (Hodapp et al., 2009).

STANFORD–BINET INTELLIGENCE SCALES   This test (SB5) is now in its fifth edition (Roid & Barram, 2004). Five areas are assessed: Fluid Reasoning, Knowledge, Quantitative Reasoning, Visual–Spatial Processing, and Working Memory. The SB5 includes toys and objects helpful in assessing young children, and nonverbal evaluation is possible in each cognitive area. Scores can be obtained for each of the cognitive areas; in addition, a Nonverbal, Verbal, and Full-Scale IQ can be obtained. The standardization group for the SB5 is a representative U.S. sample, ages 2 to 85 years.

WECHSLER TESTS   Like the Stanford-Binet scales, these tests are immensely popular for assessing ID. The Wechsler Preschool and Primary Scale of Intelligence-III (WPPSI-III) is designed for ages 2.5 to 7.3 years (Wechsler, 2002). It contains subscales that assess verbal, performance, or processing speed functioning. For children 4 years and older, the test provides a comprehensive cognitive measure, whereas for the younger children it serves as a screening tool.

The Wechsler Intelligence Scale for Children–Fourth Edition (WISC-IV) is based more on cognitive models than earlier versions of this test (Wechsler, 2003). Examples of subtests are vocabulary, block design, digit span, and coding. Instead of earning a verbal and performance IQ, the child obtains four index scores: Verbal Comprehension, Perceptual Reasoning, Working Memory, and Processing Speed. A Full-Scale IQ is derived from ten core subtests included in these four indices. The WISC-IV was standardized on a sample of U.S. children ages 6 to 16.

KAUFMAN BATTERY   The Kaufman Assessment Battery for Children–Second Edition (KABC-II), designed for ages 3 to 18 years, 11 months, emphasizes cognitive processing (Kaufman & Kaufman, 2004). Five scales are offered: sequential processing, simultaneous processing, planning, learning, knowledge. For example, the sequential processing/short-term memory scale requires step-by-step processing of content, whereas the simultaneous processing scale requires integrating several pieces of visual–spatial information at the same time. The KABC-II permits the evaluator to employ specific scales based on two different models relevant to the reason for referral or the child's background. One of the models is more applicable to the child from a mainstream language and cultural background, whereas the other may be more suitable for a child of different background. Both models result in a global intelligence score.

Assessing Adaptive Behavior

Adaptive behavior can be assessed through interviews with families or caretakers, direct observation, and self-report in some cases. Several standardized scales have been constructed, and attention has been given to reliability and validity.

VINELAND ADAPTIVE BEHAVIOR SCALES   These scales, originated by Doll at the Vineland Training School and now in their second edition, are widely employed (Sparrow, Cicchetti, & Balla, 2005). Information can be collected for individuals from birth to age 90 through semistructured interviews or rating scales with parents or caregivers. Also available is a questionnaire for teachers to assess individuals ages 3 through 21 years. The scales cover communication, daily living skills, socialization, and motor skills. In addition, the optional domain of maladaptive behavior can be used (Table 11.8). Scores from the separate domains and an overall score can be compared with scores from a normal standard group and special groups with disabilities.

TABLE 11.8	Domains Evaluated by the Vineland Adaptive Behavior Scales (Vineland-II)
Communication	Receptive Expressive Written
Daily Living Skills	Personal Domestic Community
Socialization	Interpersonal Relationships Play and Leisure Time Coping Skills
Motor Skills	Fine Gross
Maladaptive Behavior (optional)	Internalizing Externalizing Other

ADAPTIVE BEHAVIOR SCALES   For several years, the AAIDD has published adaptive behavior scales to be employed in the schools and community (Luckasson et al., 2002). The Adaptive Behavior Scales–School Edition (ABS-S:2) examines a wide range of behaviors that includes language development, physical development, personal and community self-sufficiency, social responsibility, and adjustment. The comparison norm groups consist of public school children with or without disabilities. This instrument applies to youths 3 to 18 years of age and is designed to guide school personnel. The Adaptive Behavior Scales–Residential and Community (ABS-RC:2), which taps many of the same factors as the school scale, is based on performance of persons ages 18 and over with developmental disabilities. In addition, AAIDD is releasing a new Diagnostic Adaptive Behavior Scale (DABS). Designed for persons age 4 to 21 years, it focuses on information relevant to determining significant limitations in adaptive behavior, thereby aiding diagnosis (AAIDD, 2011).

AAIDD'S ASSESSMENT FOR SUPPORTS   The AAIDD has developed guidelines for assessing each person's needs for supports (Schalock et al., 2010). Although this is not assessment for adaptive behavior, the idea of needed supports is aligned with facilitating adaptive behavior. Consistent with the AAIDD's philosophy, the aim is to provide services to improve the functional capabilities of those with ID. The process involves identifying areas in which support is needed, appropriate support activities, and the level of support needed in each activity. For example, an adolescent may require aid in interacting with community members or in personal hygiene. Support could be provided through simple monitoring, teaching activities, or physical supports. The level of support judged necessary could range from minimal to substantial. The AAIDD also has published the Supports Intensity Scale, based on an interview that evaluates practical support needs in 87 daily living, medical, and behavioral areas (Thompson et al., 2004). Based on norms for adults with developmental disabilities, it is appropriate for persons 16 years and over and thus has limited application to youth. A scale is reportedly being developed for youth of about 5 to 15 years of age.

INTERVENTION

Changing Views; Greater Opportunity

Attitudes toward intellectual disability have reflected the general beliefs of the times and have influenced how those with ID were treated by the societies in which they lived (Cytryn & Lourie, 1980). Modern attitudes can be traced to the late 1700s and the case of the "Wild Boy of Aveyron," otherwise known as Victor. The boy, first seen running naked through the woods, was captured and assigned to a medical officer, Jean M. Itard, at the National Institute for the Deaf and Dumb in Paris. Victor's senses were underdeveloped; his memory, attention, and reasoning were deficient; and his ability to communicate was almost nil (Itard, as cited in Harrison & McDermott, 1972). Itard attributed the boy's deficits to lack of contact with civilized people, but the treatment he designed failed and Victor remained in custodial care until his death. Despite the disappointing outcome, Itard's effort stimulated interest in the "feebleminded" or "retarded" (Rie, 1971).

The middle to late 1800s saw a favorable climate spread across the United States. Residential schools opened to educate children with ID and then return them to the community (Szymanski & Crocker, 1985). Unfortunately, optimism waned. Increased interest in biological causation, the rise of psychoanalysis, and the misuse or misunderstanding of IQ tests strengthened the belief that persons with ID could hardly be helped and were a detriment, if not a danger, to society. Widespread institutionalization and custodial care ensued, with institutions growing in number and size throughout the first half of the twentieth century.

The last several decades have again witnessed more favorable attitudes, conditions, and interventions. In addition to increased knowledge and scientific advances, the 1960s brought commitment to the rights of poor, handicapped, and minority populations. Extensively adopted was the philosophy of **normalization**, which contends that each individual has the right to life experiences that are as normal and as least restrictive as possible. Normalization has influenced many aspects of life for people with ID, including living arrangements, educational services, work life, and treatments.

Regarding living arrangements, at one time families were encouraged to place their children with disability in out-of-home care (Llewellyn et al., 1999). Substantial numbers resided in large institutions that provided questionable care. Although some individual circumstances may still warrant out-of-home arrangements, attitudes have shifted dramatically. The proportion of youth with intellectual or developmental disabilities, age 21 or younger, residing in out-of-home placements dropped from an estimated 37% in 1979 to 8% in 1999, with estimates leveling off since then (Larson et al., 2010). Many large institutions have been closed or downsized (Coucouvanis et al., 2003; Lakin et al., 2003). In place are small out-of-home community settings, which generally have improved the quality of life for residents (Felce, 2006; Kozma, Mansell, & Beadle-Brown, 2009). Moreover, most youths with intellectual disability live at home and to varying degrees are integrated into their neighborhoods. Because ID usually persists at some level, concern for these young people underscores the need for social and work opportunities in their adult years.

When applied to intervention for ID, the goal of normalization is to produce behaviors that are as normal as possible by employing methods that are as culturally normal as possible (Mesibov, 1992; Thompson & McEvoy, 1992; Wolfensberger, 1980). This applies to prevention, educational efforts, and treatment.

Prevention

In keeping with the multiple risks and causes of ID, prevention efforts vary substantially. Universal prevention includes prenatal care and diet, as well the avoidance of alcohol and other teratogens during pregnancy. Efforts continue to identify and reduce environmental chemicals that adversely affect prenatal and postnatal cognitive development. Advances in genetics have contributed to prevention through prenatal screening or early postnatal detection. For example, Down syndrome can be recognized prenatally, and early postnatal identification of PKU enables immediate dietary adjustments to reduce intellectual disability.

The provision of early intervention programs that focus on at-risk infants and preschoolers is an important selective prevention effort for cognitive and other deficits. Federal policies have encouraged intervention during the first 5 years of life (McGrath & Peterson, 2009c). Many of the programs emphasize child and family needs, include several elements, and entail an educational component. (See Accent: "Examples of Early Intervention Programs.")

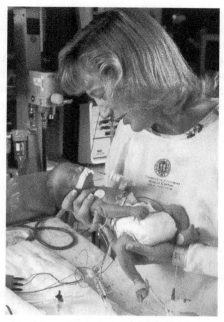

Medical advances have lowered the death rate of premature or low birthweight infants and investigations are under way in how best to optimize development and prevent problems.

As we turn to school services and treatments, it is important to recognize the multiple needs of youths with ID. Intervention can be as varied as academic classes in reading or arithmetic, programs to teach self-help or social skills, interventions for communication problems, physical therapy, efforts to reduce maladaptive behaviors, medication to reduce seizures or hyperactivity, and psychotherapy. The following discussion examines, to varying degrees, educational services, behavioral intervention, pharmacological treatment, and psychotherapy.

Educational Services

Special education was historically closely aligned to the needs of children with intellectual disability, especially mild disability (Polloway et al., 2010). These youths were central in much of the initial research and development of the field, as well as to the early criticism of educational practices that isolated them from other children. In the 1960s and 1970s, most children with ID were in self-contained classrooms, either for educable (mild) disability or trainable (moderate or lower) disability. As previously noted (p. 271), the adoption of IDEA and subsequent federal policies gradually changed the face of education for exceptional students.

ACCENT
Examples of Early Intervention Programs

The goal of one type of early intervention for children at risk for ID is to prevent or reduce adverse outcomes of low birthweight or prematurity. Some programs are delivered in hospital neonatal care units. In one type of intervention, newborns receive systematic bodily massage or exercise (Field, Diego, & Hernandez-Reif, 2010). Stroking and/or flexion and extension of the upper and lower limbs are applied daily. A recent review concluded that treated infants achieved significantly greater weight gain—an important goal for these infants—and earlier hospital discharge. In the "PremieStart" hospital program, parents received several weeks of training aimed at buffering the effects of infant stress and enhancing brain development (Milgrom et al., 2010). The multiple components included training to recognized stress reactions in the newborns; to provide vocal and visual stimulation; and to engage in touch and movement interactions. Training has been associated with maturation and connectivity of white matter of the brain.

Other programs for low birthweight children provide support after hospital discharge. An example is the multisite Infant Health and Development Program, a comprehensive 3-year randomized clinical trial that consisted of home visits, family education and support, and educational day care for the children (Bradley et al., 1994). Evaluation of the at-risk children at age 3 showed several positive effects, including benefits to cognitive development. At age 8, children of relatively high birthweight (2,100–2,500 grams), but not those weighing less, showed some cognitive and academic benefits (McCarton et al., 1997). At age 18, this group had better language skills and mathematics achievement, although there was no difference from controls in grade retention and special education placement (Olds, Sadlar, & Kitzman, 2007).

Among the most significant early intervention efforts are multipurpose programs for preschoolers designed to reduce the risks of economic disadvantage. It is assumed that early experience is vital for cognitive and social growth. A major effort is Head Start, which was initiated by the federal government in 1965 (Ripple & Zigler, 2003). In addition to a child educational component, Head Start included child health care, parent education and involvement, and social services. It now serves children from birth to age 5, including those with disabilities. Over a 30-year period, the effectiveness of many preschool interventions, including that of Head Start, has been studied (Guralnick, 1998; Ramey, 1999; Ramey & Ramey, 1998; St. Pierre & Layzer, 1998; U. S. Department of Health and Human Services, 2010). Among the conclusions is that (1) children in these programs receive cognitive and social benefits and (2) it is crucial to continue educational and other supports into childhood.

For persons with ID, this meant increased individualized programming, parent participation in the education of their offspring, and opportunity for alternative educational settings. Despite variation that exists across school districts and regions, more children with ID are attending local schools and joining their peers in general classrooms. Overall, students with ID can be integrated into community schools, and outcome is influenced more by instructional and other variables than by placement itself.

Effective inclusion does, however, require considerable investment of resources, time, effort, and commitment (Beirne-Smith et al., 2006; Hocutt, 1996). And several issues remain. Many of the children with ID in general classrooms actually spend substantial time outside of this setting; close to half spend more than 60% of their time segregated from their peers without disability (U. S. Department of Education, 2011). And the benefits of inclusion are still sometimes questioned. Inclusion

JIM

Life in the Mainstream

At birth, Jim was identified as being developmental at risk. He was diagnosed with a cleft palate, failure to thrive, microcephaly, and possible cortical blindness. At 4 months, he began to receive at-home intervention services that focused on language and physical development. He was fed with a gastrointestinal tube until his cleft palate was repaired at age 2. Jim then attended preschool from age 3 to 5, spending part of the time in a general preschool and part in a self-contained special education program. Evaluations at ages 3 and 5 indicated an overall IQ score of 40.

Jim's mother's request that he be enrolled in a general kindergarten class was denied by the school district on the basis that he would not benefit from inclusion and that communication needs would not be met. Jim's parents refused to sign his Individualized Education Plan (IEP), and invoked due process complaints. Meanwhile, the school district moved Jim to a half-day, general kindergarten setting with supports. His parents' due process claim was decided in their favor, and Jim spent a second year in all-day, general kindergarten class, with various services somewhat more coordinated. He made notable progress in language development and reduction of anxiety.

Jim's subsequent school years were spent in general education. His disability label changed from "multiple disabilities" to "cognitive disability." Beginning in the third grade, his IEPs focused on academic content. Curricula for science, social studies, math, and reading were modified and emphasis was put on Jim's participation to the fullest extent possible. He continued to receive language, occupational, and physical therapies,

with many of these services delivered in the general classroom.

This pattern generally was maintained in middle school. IEPs focused on functional academic skills, including keyboarding and the development of first grade skills in reading, writing, and math. Progress was demonstrated, and no particular academic or behavioral concerns were reported. In the fifth grade, with parental encouragement, Jim began to participate in regularly scheduled extracurricular activities with special supports. He developed positive relationships with other students, although no close friendships beyond the school context.

During the 3 years of high school for which data were kept, Jim was in general classes with modified curricula, materials, instruction, and assessment. An exception occurred in his junior year, when he spent 1.5 hours a day in a special education classroom. Although this was discrepant with his IEP, the special education teacher who provided the instruction noted that she did not favor inclusive education. Jim performed academically at a K-2nd grade level, and his IQ was reported as 46. He continued to participate in marching band, track, and student clubs, including Students Against Driving Drunk. His experiences in high school focused on participating with age peers without disabilities. He "hung out" until the school bell rang for class; used his locker appropriately; prepared for and participated in class activities as others did; and exchanged smiles, brief verbal greetings, and "high-fives" with other students. In many ways, Jim blended into the social context of the school.

Adapted from Ryndak et al., 2010, pp. 43–49.

of students with severe disability—many of whom have physical problems and special health needs—is particularly challenging. Indeed, parents of these children have not always been supportive of inclusion. For example, in a study that asked parents whether full inclusion would be a "good idea," 45% answered in the negative regarding their child (Palmer et al., 2001). The most cited reason was belief that the child's impairments precluded any benefit. Concern also was voiced that their child's needs for a curriculum that emphasizes basic living skills or functional skills would not be met and that their child might be neglected, harmed, or ridiculed. These parents also believed that full inclusion would place undue burden on teachers and be detrimental to typically developing students. Nevertheless, some parents do strongly support inclusion at all levels of ID, as indicated in the description of Jim, which also provides a glimpse of general education for a child with severe disability.

In addition to how best to deliver educational services to students with ID are the issues of the relatively low rate of high school graduation and of planning for transition to life after school. IDEA specifies that all children should have transitional services, which should be reflected in their IEPs (AAIDD Fact Sheet, 2007). Transitional services are activities to facilitate movement into postsecondary education, vocational education, employment, independent living, or community participation (Building the Legacy: IDEA 2004). Although increased progress is required in this area, it is promising that community integration across the lifespan is now an aspect of educational planning for youths with ID (Polloway et al., 2010).

Behavioral Intervention and Support

In the 1960s, advocates of behavior modification began to work in institutions that provided custodial care but little training or education (Whitman, Hantula, & Spence, 1990). Behavior modification gradually became dominant and was the subject of an enormous amount of research. A wide range of behaviors at all levels of handicap was targeted. Operant procedures were used to enhance adaptive skills and reduce maladaptive behavior.

Over the years, behavioral techniques have progressed. Guidelines have been established for various methods, and precision in teaching and generalization of learned skills have been advanced (Handen, 1998). An important distinction has been made between **discrete trial learning** and **naturalistic, or incidental, learning**. In discrete trial learning, the clinician selects the task to be learned and provides clear directives, prompts, and consequences for appropriate behavior. Teaching is

Increased numbers of children with mental handicaps now are attending community schools in which they are fully or partially integrated into general education classrooms.

usually conducted in a quiet place, away from distractions. In naturalistic learning the teaching situation is informal and less structured. It is more likely to be initiated by the child, amid everyday contexts; for example, the child's request for a toy is used as an opportunity for teaching. Both discrete trial learning and naturalistic learning have been shown to be effective, and naturalistic learning is believed to be especially effective for generalization of learning.

Efforts have also been made to train those who work with youngsters with ID—in the home, school, community programs, or residential placements. Courses and curricula have been developed to disseminate information to caregivers. Parent training has been shown to be effective, and parents can profit from ongoing contact with professionals (Handen, 1998). Overall, behavioral intervention has had considerable success in serving young people with ID.

ENHANCING ADAPTIVE BEHAVIOR Operant techniques have been employed to enhance a variety of adaptive behaviors. These include self-help skills, imitation, language, social behavior, academic skills, and work behaviors. Here, we comment on two of these areas.

The acquisition of daily living skills is an important goal of intervention. For youths with more severe levels of retardation, it may be a central component (Beirne-Smith et al., 2006). Children and adolescents who cannot dress and feed themselves or otherwise cannot take care of their basic needs are often limited from participating in educational and social activities. Those who are unable to shop, order food in restaurants, wash their clothes, or catch a bus can hardly enjoy independence in community living. Thus self-help programs target a gamut of everyday living skills.

Considerable attention also has been given to facilitate social skills, mostly but not exclusively for mild and moderate disability (e.g., Matson, LeBlanc, & Weinheimer, 1999). Training has been provided in various settings and has included behavioral and cognitive-behavioral techniques such as instruction, self-instruction, modeling, role playing, and reinforcement (Hughes, 1999; Marchetti & Campbell, 1990). The presence of normally developing peers has been shown to facilitate social interaction, as have teacher encouragement and prompts (Handen & Gilchrist, 2006a). In addition to these treatments, it is recognized that everyday activities can enhance social development. For example, participation in sports and Special Olympics by children and adults with ID has been linked with psychosocial benefits such as social competence and self-esteem (Dykens & Cohen, 1996; Glidden et al., 2011).

Special Olympics is an example of community programs that attempt to normalize the lives of youth with disability and to provide opportunities to develop social skills as well as a sense of accomplishment and self-worth.

REDUCING CHALLENGING BEHAVIOR   Self-stimulation, bizarre speech, tantrums, aggression, and self-injury are among the behaviors that interfere with social relationships, learning, and community living—and sometimes directly harm individuals with ID. A variety of techniques have been employed to reduce these challenging behaviors, and success has been documented with single-subject research designs.

In this discussion, we emphasize self-injury because intervention for this behavior has been especially problematic. An estimated 5 to 16% of individuals with ID exhibit **self-injurious behavior** (SIB), and it may be more common at the lower levels of intellectual disability (Handen & Gilchrist, 2006a; Mahatmya, Zobel, & Valdovinos, 2008). Self-injurious behaviors differ in form—head banging, biting, hitting the self, and such—and intensity ranges from minor to life-threatening damage. Biological or environmental factors, or their combination, may underlie the behavior. The association of SIB with Lesch–Nyhan and other genetic syndromes suggests an abnormal organic need for sensory stimulation that self-injurious behavior might provide. Even so, SIB is clearly influenced by environmental variables.

The history of treating SIB shows that it can be relatively difficult to change (Bregman & Gerdtz, 1997). Medications are only somewhat successful, and early behavioral interventions often failed. When self-injury threatened the child and interventions were ineffective, punishments such as squirting lemon juice into the mouth and contingent electric shock were sometimes employed. Although aversive consequences were somewhat effective, they raised serious ethical questions and are dissonant with a respectful approach to treatment. They are not recommended or recommended only in brief interventions for severe cases after review and consent (AAIDD/ARC Position Papers, 2007; Bregman & Gerdtz, 1997). Effective and more acceptable procedures have evolved.

Positive Behavioral Support (PBS)   This approach is among the most effective ways to ameliorate a variety of problem behaviors (Erbas, 2010). **Positive behavioral support** (PBS) has been adapted to various settings and employed with youths diagnosed with ID, autism, and other developmental disabilities. With origins in applied behavior analysis, PBS relies on behavioral principles and **functional assessment**, or analysis (Handen & Gilchrist, 2006a). Central to the approach are modification of the environment and behavioral consequences, with the teaching of new responses to substitute for maladaptive behaviors often incorporated.

The rationale for functional assessment is the assumption that understanding the variables that influence

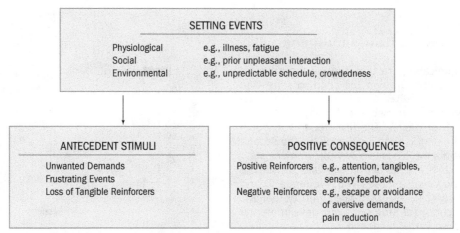

FIGURE 11.6 A schema of variables that can influence maladaptive behaviors. *Adapted from Newsom, 1998.*

challenging behaviors can be helpful in preventing or alleviating them. Figure 11.6 presents a schema that conceptualizes such influences and can be applied to SIB (Newsom, 1998). It considers the environmental context in which the behavior occurs and the consequences that accrue to the behavior. *Setting events* are background variables that can affect the probability that the behavior will occur. For example, fatigue can make it more likely that the child will respond with SIB. *Antecedent stimuli* occur just prior to self-injury and precipitate the behavior. *Positive consequences* are contingencies that likely strengthen or maintain SIB.

Numerous studies have shown that SIB (and other challenging behaviors) is reinforced by consequences that commonly fall into four categories: attention seeking, tangible-item seeking, escape or avoidance, and nonsocial contingencies (Mahatmya et al., 2008; Matson et al., 2011; Petursdottir et al., 2010). As Figure 11.6 indicates, self-injury can be positively reinforced by attention from caretakers as they try to deter a child from the behavior and by tangibles such as food and activities. Self-injury also can be negatively reinforced. For example, when unwanted demands are made, the child may engage in self-injury, with the result that caregivers may cease to make the demands—thereby allowing the child to escape the demands. In other cases, reinforcement appears nonsocial, and is often attributed to some unknown sensory consequence experienced by the child. Figure 11.6 also points to how challenging behaviors can be modified. Altering the setting events and antecedent stimuli—for example, by minimizing them—can prevent SIB from occurring at all. Altering reinforcement contingencies can reduce or eliminate self-injury.

Functional assessment examines how the child is behaving in what situations, with what consequences, and perhaps with what motivation (Handen, 2007; Handen

& Gilchrist, 2006a). It can be conducted by acquiring information from detailed interviews with adults interacting with the child or observation of the child in the natural setting. Rating scales have been developed to aid in such assessment, such as the Questions About Behavioral Function scale. Assessment can also be accomplished by an analogue (or experimental) **functional analysis**, which entails a manipulation of variables to determine their influence on the behavior. Based on functional assessment, an individual treatment plan is constructed which might include modification of the environment, and/or the behavioral consequences operating, as well as the teaching of new responses. A recent review found that intervention most often employed reinforcement, reinforcement with extinction, or functional communication training with or without reinforcement (Matson et al., 2011). For a demonstration of the latter approach, see Accent: "Functional Communication Training."

Research findings support the effectiveness of positive behavioral support. Further, although extensive planning and training are important, there is continued sensitivity to maximizing the usefulness of PBS (Lang et al., 2010). More generally, the American Psychological Association considers behavioral interventions to be empirically validated treatment for developmental disabilities (Handen & Gilchrist, 2006a).

Psychopharmacology and Psychotherapy

PHARMACOLOGICAL TREATMENT Medications are not known to strengthen intellectual functioning in cases of ID, but are aimed at alleviating medical and psychological symptoms. Although data are lacking with regard to the number of children or adolescents taking medication, it is likely to be substantial. Given the prevalence and

ACCENT
Functional Communication Training

Functional Communication Training aims to reduce challenging behavior by encouraging the child to substitute in its place an adaptive behavior. It is assumed that maladaptive behaviors are often used intentionally as a way to communicate needs or desires. The first step in Functional Communication Training is functional analysis; the second is to select and train a more positive way to communicate.

The approach is exemplified in the case of Matt, a 5-year-old boy who was diagnosed with moderate ID and cerebral palsy (Durand, 1999). Matt lived with his parents and attended a school for students with developmental disabilities. He lacked verbal language, but he was able to point to express his desires. Matt frequently bit his hand and screamed—behaviors that had not succumbed to prior interventions. The treatment strategy had several components:

- Matt's teacher was trained to conduct the intervention in the classroom.
- The teacher determined the circumstances in which Matt most frequently engaged in self-biting and screaming. She assessed Matt's behavior by using a rating scale and also by systematically observing his behavior under four conditions: low teacher attention during a task, low access to a preferred tangible object during a task, a more difficult task, and a control condition. This analysis showed that Matt's maladaptive behavior occurred when he was faced with a difficult task.
- Matt was trained to ask for help on difficult tasks by pressing a pad on a device, which activated a voice saying "I need help."
- The effectiveness of the training was evaluated.

The entire intervention required several weeks. The results of the functional analysis (A) and the final evaluation of Matt's behavior (B) are shown in Figure 11.7. The positive outcome is consistent with similar studies showing the effectiveness of Functional Communication Training in which youngsters are taught to communicate their desires

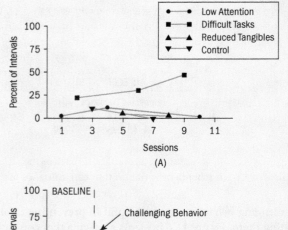

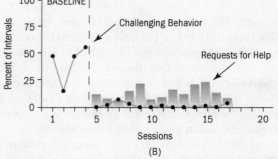

FIGURE 11.7 (A) Functional analysis showed that Matt's challenging behaviors occurred mostly during difficult tasks. (B) The training sessions indicated a drop in Matt's challenging behaviors and Matt's requests for help. *From Durand, 1999.*

through adaptive spoken language or with mechanical devices when needed. Of particular interest in the present study is that it included trips to a community store in which Matt had experienced difficulty and frustration handling money as he purchased candy. After intervention, Matt used the mechanical device to ask the shopkeeper for help in managing his money.

variation of psychological problems associated with ID, all major categories of psychotropic medications have been prescribed. Nevertheless, limited evidence exists for the effectiveness of pharmacological treatment.

We comment here only on two classes of medications. The symptoms of ADHD, which affect perhaps 9 to 16% of children with ID, lessen with stimulant medication. However, response rates are lower than for typical cases of ADHD, perhaps particularly for those with moderate and severe ID, and negative side effects may be greater (Handen & Gilchrist, 2006b; Pearson et al., 2004). The use of typical antipsychotic medications

has been most investigated in treating ID (Einfeld & Emerson, 2008). These medications have been employed to treat aggressiveness, antisocial behavior, and stereotypies. More recently, the atypical antipsychotic medications became the treatment of choice, because they may have fewer side effects. Nevertheless, evidence for the efficacy of antipsychotics is limited. Furthermore, possible side effects—for example, weight gain, sedation, movement disorder—require serious consideration.

Overall, it appears that medication response is similar to that shown by other populations, but that fewer persons with ID benefit from medications and that negative side effects are more frequent (Handen & Gilchrist, 2006b; King et al., 2005). Moreover, research on the efficacy of medications is inadequate both for youths and adults. Indeed, there is general concern over inappropriate practices, including inadequate evaluation of effects and side effects and questionable choice of medication and prescription dosage (Einfeld & Emerson, 2008). It is clear, however, that the management of medication for youths with ID requires special consideration. The difficulty of diagnosing comorbid psychopathology raises the issue of the appropriateness of any prescribed medication. Added to this, determining the effectiveness and side effects of drugs is especially challenging due to the limited ability of those with ID to describe what they are experiencing. Possible drug interactions also require a watchful eye, particularly in cases involving medical conditions (King et al., 2000).

PSYCHOTHERAPY APPROACHES   Research into the use and effectiveness of psychotherapy for individuals with ID is scant (Beail, 2003; Handen & Gilchrist, 2006a). There is some indication that professionals recommend behavioral interventions over more traditional counseling or "talking" approaches. In addition, the literature indicates disagreement on the effectiveness and usefulness of psychotherapy. Some professionals argue that it has little or no place in treating youth with intellectual disabilities (Sturmey, 2005). Others argue that it should not be precluded in the presence of mild and moderate intellectual deficits (Hurley, 2005).

It is agreed that psychotherapy techniques must be adapted to the developmental level of the child or adolescent (King et al., 2000). In addition, therapists should probably be directive and set specific goals. Language should be concrete and clear, and nonverbal techniques (e.g., play or other activities) are necessary when communication deficits exist. Short, frequent sessions also may be required.

Substantial agreement also exists that the research on psychotherapy is methodologically weak (Handen & Gilchrist, 2006a; Prout & Nowak-Drabik, 2003). There is an interest in encouraging high-quality investigation into what psychotherapy methods are effective for what kinds of problems and at what level of retardation.

Overview/Looking Back

- Perspectives on intellectual disability have changed over the decades, as have the labels applied to the disorder.

DEFINITION AND CLASSIFICATION

- ID is defined by subaverage intellectual functioning with concurrent deficits in adaptive skills manifested before age 18 or during the developmental period.
- The AAIDD views ID as multidimensional, with environmental supports mediating outcome.
- The severity of intellectual disability historically has been recognized as mild, moderate, severe, and profound, based on IQ performance. More recently, severity is specified by levels of needed supports (AAIDD) or adaptive behavior (DSM).

NATURE OF INTELLIGENCE AND ADAPTIVE BEHAVIOR

- Binet and colleagues viewed intelligence as somewhat malleable and influenced by the social environment. The subsequent assumption of fixed inheritance and the misuse of intelligence tests resulted in controversies and legal battles.
- Measured intelligence is relatively reliable for most people and correlates reasonably well with academic-related achievements. IQ scores must be interpreted with care, however.
- Adaptive behavior refers to domains of everyday behavior, and includes conceptual, social, and practical skills.

DESCRIPTION

- The abilities of young people with ID show immense variation. Difficulties are manifest in intellectual and adaptive functioning, physical and medical attributes, learning and cognitive ability, communication, and social functioning.

CO-OCCURRING DISORDERS

- Rates of psychological problems and disorders are high in youths with ID. The kinds of problems appear similar to those in the general population, but can be difficult to identify and diagnose.

EPIDEMIOLOGY

- The prevalence of ID in the general population is 1 to 3%. Rates are disproportionately high in school-age children, males, and individuals of lower social class.

DEVELOPMENTAL COURSE AND CONSIDERATIONS

- The developmental course and outcome of ID varies widely but most youths will require some degree of support throughout life.
- Compared with typically developing intelligence, the intellectual abilities of youth with ID tend to develop in the same sequences but at slower rates.

ETIOLOGY

- The historic two-group approach to etiology conceptualized ID as falling into an organic or a cultural–familial group.
- Pathological organic influences, which are associated with more severe ID, can originate in genetic, prenatal, birth, or postnatal adversities.
- Multiple-gene effects are considered especially important in mild MR of unknown etiology.
- Psychosocial influence, which may operate across generations of socially disadvantaged families, is also viewed as particularly relevant to milder levels of retardation.
- AAIDD's multiple risk model reflects the current perspective of etiology as complex and interactive.

GENETIC SYNDROMES AND BEHAVIORAL PHENOTYPES

- Genetic syndromes—such as Down, fragile X, Williams, and Prader–Willi—are currently receiving much research attention. Each syndrome tends to be associated with a particular physical, cognitive, and behavioral phenotype.

FAMILY ACCOMMODATIONS AND EXPERIENCES

- Family adjustment to having a child with ID is influenced by child characteristics, family characteristics, and social variables.
- Family members likely are affected differently and experience both unique stress and rewards.

ASSESSMENT

- Comprehensive assessment for ID is best guided by its goals. Diagnosis requires assessment of intelligence and adaptive behavior with standardized tests.

INTERVENTION

- Treatment for ID historically has varied in approach and quality. In recent decades, the philosophy of normalization has taken center stage.
- Universal and selective prevention for ID targets prenatal care, diet, genetic conditions, environmental risks, and the risks of low birthweight and economic disadvantage.
- IDEA and related policies have brought increased educational integration to students with ID, although complex issues remain about school inclusion.
- A range of behavioral techniques are effective in strengthening appropriate skills and weakening maladaptive behaviors. Positive behavioral support and functional assessment are effective approaches.
- Pharmacological treatment and psychotherapy are both in need of controlled outcome studies. The former is relatively common, but several concerns exist regarding medication use. Psychotherapy, with adaptations, arguably may be useful in mild or moderate ID.

Key Terms

mental age *281*
intelligence quotient *282*
Flynn effect *283*
overshadowing *286*
two-group approach *288*

cultural-familial retardation *289*
behavioral phenotype *291*
normalization *300*
discrete trial learning *303*
naturalistic (incidental) learning *303*

self-injurious behavior *304*
positive behavioral support *304*
functional assessment *304*
functional analysis *305*

CHAPTER 12

Autism Spectrum Disorder and Schizophrenia

LOOKING FORWARD

After reading this chapter, you should be able to discuss:

- The historical association of schizophrenia and autism spectrum disorder
- The DSM approach to autism spectrum disorder
- Description, etiology, assessment, treatment, and other aspects of autism
- Asperger's disorder, PDD-NOS, and CDD
- Assessment and intervention for autism spectrum disorder
- Classification, diagnosis, description, and other aspects of schizophrenia
- Etiology of schizophrenia
- Assessment and intervention for schizophrenia

The disorders discussed in this chapter are characterized by pervasive problems in social, emotional, and cognitive functioning that have a basis in neurobiological abnormality. Development may be qualitatively different from typical development in ways that have compelled an enormous amount of interest and investigation. Autism spectrum disorder and schizophrenia in youth are now considered distinct from each other, but they share a rich history.

A BIT OF HISTORY

Although the disorders we are about to discuss have long been recognized, confusion and debate have surrounded them. Historically, these disorders were associated with adult psychoses—that is, severely disruptive disturbances implying abnormal perceptions of reality. Psychotic disturbances were noted in early twentieth-century classifications of mental disorders based on Kraepelin's work. Bleuler applied the term "schizophrenias" to these disorders, which involve disturbances in reality, such as hearing voices and seeing images that do not exist. Investigators noted a small percentage of cases that had begun in childhood (Marenco & Weinberger, 2000).

Ideas about psychoses and other severe disturbances developed gradually over many years. Some investigators described groups of children with early onset of schizophrenia, and others pointed to syndromes that appeared similar, but not identical, to schizophrenia. Various diagnostic terms were applied, including *disintegrative psychoses* and *childhood psychoses*. Beginning around 1930 and for several years afterward, *childhood schizophrenia* served as a general label for many severe early occurring disturbances (Asarnow & Kernan, 2008).

In a landmark report in 1943, Leo Kanner described what he called "early infantile autism," arguing that it was different from other cases of severe disturbance, which generally had later onset. Shortly afterward, Hans Asperger, working in a different country, described a group of children whose symptoms overlapped with Kanner's cases. These men did not know each other—and apparently believed they were writing about different types of disturbances (Frith, 2004).

By the early 1970s, data from several countries showed that severe disturbances in youth were age related. A relatively large number of cases appeared before age 3, remarkably few appeared during childhood, and prevalence increased in adolescence (Kolvin, 1971). This pattern suggested that different syndromes might underlie the earlier-occurring and later-occurring disturbances. Gradually, on the basis of symptoms and several other features, a distinction was made between schizophrenia and a group of nonpsychotic disturbances of youth. Schizophrenia affects a small number of children, rises in frequency in adolescence, and increases still more in early adulthood. The syndromes described by Kanner and Asperger, along with other similar disturbances, appear early in life and children displaying manifestations of these disorders are now widely diagnosed with autism spectrum disorder. This perspective is reflected in the DSM.

DSM: AUTISM SPECTRUM DISORDER

To understand the current approach to autism and related disturbances, it is helpful to take a historical perspective of DSM classification and diagnoses. The DSM-IV included, among disorders first evident in youth, the category of Pervasive Developmental Disorders. Specifically described were Autistic Disorder, Asperger's Disorder, Childhood Disintegrative Disorder (CDD), and Pervasive Developmental Disorder Not Otherwise Specified (PDD-NOS). (Also included was Rett's Disorder, which is now seen as different and is not discussed here.) To varying degrees, these disorders displayed similar characteristics, but several issues were raised about their relationship to

each other. For example, some investigators questioned whether Autistic Disorder and Asperger's Disorder were two distinct disturbances rather than a single disorder.

In DSM-5, the disorders named above are no longer recognized as distinct. Rather, Autism Spectrum Disorder (ASD) serves as the diagnosis for individuals who display an array or continuum of symptoms previously encompassed by the DSM-IV disorders.

According to the DSM-5, the primary symptoms of ASD fall into two domains.

- Persistent deficits in social communication and interaction across multiple contexts. These are shown in social-emotional reciprocity, nonverbal communicative behaviors, and social relationships.
- Restrictive, repetitive patterns of behaviors, interests, and activities. These must be displayed by two or more of the following:

    Stereotyped or repetitive motor movements, use of objects, or speech insistence on sameness, inflexible adherence to routines, or ritualized behavior restricted, fixated interests of abnormal intensity or focus over- or undersensitivity to sensory input or unusual interest in sensory aspects of the environment.

Symptoms must occur during the early developmental period and significantly impair social, occupational, and other aspects of functioning. Moreover, the disorder cannot better be attributed to intellectual disability or global developmental delay.

It is noteworthy that when the DSM-5 adopted the category of ASD, this conceptualization already had been used by many workers in the field. However, some professionals in the field still question the wisdom of collapsing the previously recognized disorders into one broad category.

In the following sections, we discuss many aspects of autism and briefly look at Asperger's disorder, childhood disintegrative disorder, and pervasive developmental disorder not otherwise specified. By far, emphasis is placed on autism. This strategy is consistent with the literature on which discussion is based. It reflects the transition from distinct disorders to an emphasis on a spectrum of autism and the changes in terminology that went with it.

AUTISTIC DISORDER (AUTISM)

Kanner's early descriptions of autism noted communication deficits, good but atypical cognitive potential, and behavioral problems such as obsessiveness, repetitious actions, and unimaginative play. He emphasized, however, that the fundamental disturbance was an inability to relate to people and situations from the beginning of

PAUL

Autistic Aloneness

Paul was a slender, well built, attractive child, whose face looked intelligent and animated....He rarely responded to any form of address, even to the calling of his name....He was obviously so remote that the remarks did not reach him. He was always vivaciously occupied with something and seemed to be highly satisfied....There was, on his side, no affective tie to people. He behaved as if people as such did not matter or even exist. It made no difference if one spoke to him in a friendly or harsh way. He never looked up at people's faces. When he had any dealings with persons at all, he treated them, or rather parts of them, as if they were objects.

Adapted from Kanner, 1943, reprinted, 1973, pp. 14–15.

life. He quoted parents who referred to their disturbed children as "self-sufficient," "like in a shell," "happiest when left alone," and "acting as if people weren't there" (Kanner, 1973, p. 33). To this extreme disturbance in socioemotional contact with others, Kanner applied the term "autistic." The case description of Paul is a brief depiction of one of the cases presented by Kanner in his classic paper.

Although not all of Kanner's observations proved accurate, most of the characteristics described were subsequently noted by others. An enormous amount of research has increased our understanding of autism and related disorders.

Description: Primary Features

In examining the features of autism, it is necessary to recognize that all children with the disorder do not necessarily display all features, nor are they identical in the severity of their symptoms.

SOCIAL INTERACTION AND COMMUNICATION

Children with autism show few symptoms at 6 months, but many show subtle differences from typically developing infants before 12 months (Dawson & Faja, 2008). Very young children with autism are less likely to be visually responsive, less likely to respond to their names, and more likely to show aversion to being touched by another person (Baranek, 1999; Werner et al., 2000). They fail to track people visually, avoid eye contact, exhibit an "empty" gaze, fail to respond to others with emotional expression and positive affect, and show little interest in being held (e.g., Adrien et al., 1993; Stone, 1997).

Quite striking in autism are deficits in **joint attention** interactions, which usually develop after 6 months. These interactions involve gestures, such as pointing and eye contact that center the child's and caregiver's attention on an object or situation, in order to share an experience. In addition, young children with autism imitate the actions of others less than typical youngsters (Rogers et al., 2004). They appear to miss out on the mutual connection between two people and the potential it holds for learning about themselves and others.

Because such behaviors interfere with social interaction, we might expect a lack of attachment to parents. A meta-analysis showed that slightly over half of the children with autism showed secure attachment in the Strange Situation (Rutgers et al., 2004). A study using a different measure found that 2-year-olds with autism spectrum disorder were rated as less secure than other clinical (ID or language delay) or non-clinical comparison groups (Rutgers et al., 2007). However, secure, insecure, and disorganized attachment have all been demonstrated in children with autism (van IJzendoorn et al., 2007; Willemsen-Swinkels et al., 2000). Given the enormous variability of these children—and the stress that parents can experience in caring for an infant with autistic symptoms—further understanding of attachment in these children could be helpful in facilitating and supporting parenting practices.

Abnormal processing of social stimuli, notably of the face, is another component of atypical social interaction. Facial processing is considered crucial to development (Dawson & Toth, 2006). Typically developing infants are attracted to the human face and rapidly recognize the faces of their mothers. Children with autism often show impairment in recognizing faces, matching emotional faces, and memorizing faces. They may also visually process faces in unusual ways, for example, by focusing on the mouth or eyes in ways different from what typically developing children do (Chawarska & Shic, 2009).

Overall, delayed or atypical social behaviors occur early in at least 5 domains of social behavior: orienting to social stimuli, joint attention, emotion, imitation, and face processing (Dawson & Faja, 2008). Although there is some symptom change over time, many social abnormalities persist. During childhood, a variety of social deficits, such as lack of understanding of social cues and inappropriate social actions, are evident. There is a certain aloofness, disinterest, and lack of social reciprocity and empathy. The child may ignore others, fail to engage in cooperative play, or seem overly content to be alone (Volkmar et al., 1997). Even higher functioning adolescents and adults may seem "odd," have difficulty with the subtleties of social interaction, and have problems forming friendships as they move through life.

Disturbed communication—both nonverbal and verbal—is a widely observed aspect of autism. Nonverbal communication involving gestures, visual gaze, and facial expression of emotion is atypical or deficient. In addition, perhaps 30% of children with autism never develop spoken language (Dawson & Toth, 2006). In those who acquire language, development is delayed and often abnormal. Babbling and verbalizations may be abnormal in tone, pitch, and rhythm (Sheinkopf et al., 2000; Tager-Flüsberg, 1993). Echolalia and pronoun reversal are commonly observed. In **echolalia** the person echoes back what another has said, a behavior also seen in dysfunctions such as language disorders, schizophrenia, and blindness. **Pronoun reversal** is more common in autism than in other disorders or normal development and may persist into adulthood. The child may refer to others as *I* or *me*, and to the self as *he, she, them,* or *you.*

Difficulties in syntax, comprehension, and other structural forms of language also exist; these may resemble, but are not identical to, specific language impairments (Williams, Botting, & Boucher, 2008). Notable is impairment in pragmatics, that is, the communicative and social use of language (Klinger, Dawson, & Renner, 2003). Conversation may be marked by irrelevant details, inappropriate shifts in topic, or disregard of normal give-and-take of conversation—or there may be an overall failure to develop conversation.

It is worth noting, however, that within the wide range of symptoms of autism, some children do function at a higher level. They may be able to communicate better when given prompts, tell stories, (Loveland & Tunali-Kotoski, 1997), and read. Some exhibit hyperlexia, a little-understood feature in which single-word reading is extraordinary but comprehension of what is read is problematic (Grigorenko, Klin, & Volkmar, 2003).

RESTRICTED, REPETITIVE, STEREOTYPED BEHAVIOR AND INTERESTS (RRSBS) Some repetitious behaviors—such as kicking and rocking in infancy and later preference for sameness—are features of typical development that mostly subside by school age (Honey et al., 2008). In contrast, both younger and older youths with autism display odd behaviors, interests, and activities that are described as restricted, repetitive, and stereotyped.

This somewhat-neglected core feature of autism has recently garnered more research attention, including efforts to understand possible subtypes of these heterogeneous behaviors. Although various subtypes have been found in factor analysis, two categories are widely recognized (Mirenda et al., 2010).

One of these is characterized as lower-level "repetitive sensorimotor behaviors" such as hand flapping, rocking, twirling, and toe walking, repetitive use of objects, and some self-injurious behaviors. Although such peculiarities are seen in typically developing young children and in children with other disorders, they occur in autism more frequently and with greater severity (Bodfish et al., 2000; Turner, 1999). They appear to be especially common in younger children with autism and those with lower intelligence.

The second category of RRSBs is characterized as higher-level "insistence on sameness" (Mirenda et al., 2010; Turner, 1999). Here, children appear preoccupied with aspects of the environment. Children may seem obsessed with numbers, compulsively collect articles, or be overly absorbed in hobbies. They may adopt motor routines, such as rearranging objects, and insist on following rituals for eating and going to bed. Minor changes in the environment, such as rearrangement of furniture or schedules, can upset

Stereotyped movements commonly occur in youth with autism.

them. These obsessive behaviors may be more common in older children with ASD.

Why RRSBs occur or how they are maintained is not understood (Honey et al., 2008). Perhaps excessive arousal or anxiety plays a role, or perhaps some of the behaviors serve as self-stimulation that results from the child's inability to engage the world in other ways. For whatever reasons, a study that examined RRSBs from age 2 to 9 years in children with ASD found sizeable heterogeneity in patterns of change over time (Richler et al., 2010).

Description: Secondary Features

Although not necessary for diagnosis, several additional features are often associated with autism and related disorders and are meaningful in understanding the disturbances.

SENSORY/PERCEPTUAL IMPAIRMENTS The sensory organs are intact but abnormal responses to stimuli make sensation and perception suspect. Both oversensitivity and undersensitivity occur significantly more than in typical development (Ben-Sasson et al., 2009; Dawson & Toth, 2006). These features, frequently described in autism, have been given increased importance in the DSM-5. Youths who are oversensitive to stimuli may be disturbed by the sound of a vacuum cleaner, seams on their clothing, or a light embrace. Sensory input may thus be disliked, feared, or avoided. One adult with autism described her earlier experiences as "horrible oversensitivity" to sound and touch and as "an overwhelming, drowning wave of stimulation" in response to being touched by another person (Grandin, 1997). In contrast, undersensitivity, which may be the more common problem, is exemplified by children's failing to respond to voices or other sounds or walking into things. The clinical picture may be puzzling; for example, a child may seem unaware of a loud noise but fascinated by the quiet ticking of a watch (Volkmar & Klin, 2000). In some cases, a child's failure to respond to sound leads parents to think their child is deaf.

Overselectivity is also common in autism. Here, the individual focuses on a select portion of a stimulus array while neglecting other components (Ploog, 2010). Overselectivity occurs in many populations, including typically developing children and those with specific and general learning problems. It has been variously conceptualized (e.g., as sensory overload or a deficit in attention), and is recognized as interfering with normal development and functioning. Neglecting specific aspects of a learning task obviously can hinder performance on the task. Social interaction can also be affected and have social consequences. The child with ASD, for example,

may pay attention to a toy held by another child but not to the accompanying verbalization (e.g., "Let's play with the truck" versus "Go away, this is my truck").

INTELLECTUAL PERFORMANCE Although there is a wide range of intelligence in autism, including above average, intellectual deficiency is common and includes severe and profound deficits. In past years, the prevalence of intellectual disability was often estimated at about 70% but it is currently estimated as between 40 and 55% (Corbett & Gunther, 2011). The lower estimates may take into account the fact that autistic symptoms affect measurement of intelligence. Lower estimates may also be due to the diagnosis of the disorder in children who once would not have met diagnostic criteria, or it may reflect improved functioning due to early intervention (CDC, 2009).

A distinction based on intelligence is made between individuals functioning at a higher or lower level, with an IQ of about 70 being the defining score. This distinction is an important way in which persons with autism differ. Higher IQ is associated with less severe autistic symptoms, different educational needs, and greater chance of normal functioning in later life (Howlin et al., 2004; Stevens et al., 2000; Wing, 1997).

The test profiles of persons with autism generally indicate uneven cognitive development. Deficits exist in abstract and conceptual thinking, language, and social understanding. Relative strengths appear in rote learning, rote memory, and visual–spatial skills (Happé, 1994; Volkmar & Klin, 2000). Non-verbal IQ scores are usually higher than verbal scores. This discrepancy can lessen from preschool age to adolescence in higher functioning autism, perhaps due to the development of language skills (Joseph, Tager-Flüsberg, & Lord, 2002). Efforts are being made to better understand how discrepancies between verbal and non-verbal IQ are related to autistic symptoms and adaptive behavior (Black et al., 2009).

That autistic symptoms occur amid such wide variability in general intelligence is puzzling. To make matters more perplexing, a small minority of youth exhibits so-called **splinter skills**—abilities much higher than expected on the basis of their general intelligence—and **savant abilities**, which are skills that are strikingly better than those seen in normally developing youth. Savant abilities are not unique to autism, but they occur at high rates (Volkmar, Klin, & Schultz, 2005). Spectacular feats are displayed—usually in memory, mathematics, calendar calculations, word recognition, drawing, and music (Heaton & Wallace, 2004; Miller, 1999). Although often associated with higher IQ levels, savant abilities have been reported in individuals with IQs as low as 55 and in children whose deficits preclude testing.

ADAPTIVE BEHAVIOR Autism is characterized by difficulties in dealing with the comings and goings of everyday life. Even at high-functioning levels, youths with ASD do less well on the Vineland Adaptive Behavior Scales (VABS) compared to typical developing peers matched on IQ, and less well than would be expected based on IQ scores (Mazefsky, Williams, & Minshew, 2008).

Self-help and daily living skills are roughly what is expected on the basis of mental ability, communication skills fall somewhat short of this, and social skills are most notably deficient (Carter et al., 1998; Kenworthy et al., 2010; Kraijer, 2000). Impairments tend to increase with age and, in general, the mismatch with intelligence is greater in high-functioning autism (Kanne et al., 2010). In addition, family factors may help explain the enormous variability shown in adaptive behavior; for example, in one study a history of family depression and shyness was related to VABS scores, especially in the social domain (Mazefsky et al., 2008).

SOCIAL COGNITION: THEORY OF MIND Evidence exists that children with ASD have an impairment in **theory of mind** (ToM), a deficit in the ability to infer mental states in others and in one's self. Having a theory of mind means that we understand that mental states exist—that humans have desires, intentions, beliefs, feelings, and so forth—and that these mental states are connected to action. Theory of mind can be thought of as the ability to read others' minds, which guides our interaction with others. In typical development, by age 3 to 4 years children have first-order abilities, that is, some understanding of people's private mental states (Wellman, 1993). At about age 6, children acquire second-order abilities: They can think about another person's thinking about a third person's thoughts.

Aspects of ToM have been evaluated with various tasks. The Sally–Anne test determines whether a child understands that another person can hold a false belief (Baron-Cohen, 1989). The child is told that after Sally placed a marble in a basket and left the room, Anne transferred the marble to another container and also exited. The child is asked where Sally will look for the marble when she returns. To demonstrate ToM, the child must understand that Sally falsely believes the marble is in the basket where she placed it. This first-order task can be modified to evaluate second-order ability. In this case, when Sally leaves the room, she peeks back and sees Anne transfer the marble. The child being tested is asked, "Where does Anne think Sally will look for the marble?" The child must "read" what Anne is thinking about Sally's thoughts. There is compelling evidence that the majority of children with autism fails first-order tests and that a greater number fails second-order tests (Baron-Cohen & Swettenham, 1997). Exactly what

accounts for these failures is not completely understood. Language ability and executive functions do correlate with ToM (Miller, 2009), but false belief impairment in young toddlers has been demonstrated in a task not requiring verbal ability (Senju et al., 2010).

Many measures of ToM have been developed. For example, the ToM Storybooks presents several tasks so as to gain a comprehensive understanding of ToM development in preschool children (Blijd-Hoogewys et al., 2008). It taps various aspects of ToM, such as emotions, desires, and beliefs. Figure 12.1 shows one of the tests, which evaluates the child's emotional understanding and recognition.

More challenging tasks have been developed for older children or children who are able to pass second-order tests. In the faux pas test the child is told stories in which character A commits a faux pas—that is, unintentionally says something that might negatively impact character B. The child being evaluated is asked to identify the faux pas. In order to succeed on this task, the child must understand that (1) the two characters in the stories have different knowledge and that (2) the statement of character A emotionally affects character B. On this test, children with autism or a related disorder who were able to pass second-order ToM tests did less well than typically developing children (Baron-Cohen et al., 1999).

Overall, the research evidence shows that ToM deficits in autism exist across different ages and can be present in higher functioning autism. Since ToM is considered critical in understanding the social world, it is hypothesized that such deficits—sometimes referred to as "mind blindness"—may underlie many of the social and communication deficits of autism.

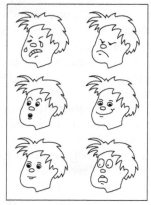

FIGURE 12.1 An example of an emotion recognition task from the Theory of Mind Storybooks. The child is told, "Sam has won shooting marbles. He has won the most beautiful marble." The child is asked to choose the appropriate face and provide the correct emotion label. Additional situations are depicted. *From Blijd-Hoogewys et al., 2008.*

COGNITION: CENTRAL COHERENCE AND EXECUTIVE FUNCTION

Central Coherence In normal cognition, individuals have a tendency to use context to weave together bits of information to make a whole, to give global meaning. This penchant, which is referred to as **central coherence**, is viewed as varying from strong to weak in the general population (Happé, Briskman, & Frith, 2001). On the basis of performance on specific visual–perceptual tasks, Frith and Happé proposed that individuals with autism are weak in central coherence; that is, they tend to focus on parts of stimuli rather than on integrating information into wholes. Simply put, they see the trees rather than the forest. _et

Performance on perceptual tasks illustrates deficits in central coherence. For example, children with autism generally perform better than controls on embedded figure tasks, which call for recognizing a stimulus figure that is embedded within a larger picture. In an important study, Shah and Frith (1993) investigated the quite striking superior performance that persons with autism show on the block design task of the Wechsler intelligence test. They not only perform well compared with their achievement on other IQ tasks, but also outperform typically developing children and control children with intellectual disability. Ability to break the block design into segments helps on this task (Figure 12.2).

Such findings suggest that youths with autism have a bias to process information in a more analytic, less global and integrative way than do normal youths—which can lead to exceptional performance on some tasks and poor performance on others. Further understanding of weak central coherence has been sought; for example,

its relationship with ToM and executive functions has been examined (Happé & Frith, 2006). It also has been suggested that weak central coherence on some tasks may be accounted for by impaired communication across the brain's hemispheres (David et al., 2010).

Executive Function Children, adolescents, and adults with autism perform more poorly than control groups on tests of executive functions (Corbett et al., 2009; McEvoy, Rogers, & Pennington, 1993; Ozonoff, 1997). It has been proposed that executive dysfunction may underlie and account for autistic symptoms. However, data have been accumulating that executive dysfunction does not exist in late preschool-age children, and a study of toddlers (mean age 2.9 years) showed almost no differences from the performance of age-matched typical children (Yerys et al., 2007). It thus seems that executive dysfunction is not a primary deficit but develops secondarily in autism.

At one time, the notion that a single deficit might explain the symptoms of autism was applied to several cognitive or perceptual deficits of autism, including impairments in ToM and central coherence. However, no single impairment accounts for all ASD symptoms, all persons with autism do not display all deficits, nor are all deficits specific to autism. Although these impairments are still of importance, researchers are extensively exploring early-occurring behaviors such as face perception, joint visual attention, and imitation (Berger, 2006; Kylliäinen & Hietanen, 2004; Volkmar et al., 2004). Many of these are thought to be involved in the development of affective social development that is so deviant in autism. To some extent, this interest harks back to a perspective that has persisted since Kanner's time—that is, to **intersubjectivity**, a special awareness that persons have of each other that motivates them, from the moment of birth, to communicate with the emotions and interests of others (McGrath & Peterson, 2009b; Trevarthen & Aitken, 2001).

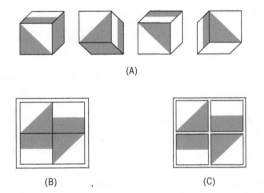

(A)

(B)　.　(C)

FIGURE 12.2 A block design task. Participants are asked to use four patterned blocks (A) to make a design (B). In some instances, they are first shown the design as segmented (C). Control groups benefit from observing (C); participants with autism perform as well with or without observing (C). This finding suggests that persons with autism have greater ability to "see" the parts of the design. *From Happé, Briskman, & Frith, 2001.*

PHYSICAL AND OTHER FEATURES Young children with autism are often described as physically attractive, but higher than normal physical abnormalities, including minor physical anomalies (MPAs), are associated with ASD (Ozgen et al., 2010; Ozgen et al., 2011) (Figure 12.3). Examples of MPAs are a prominent forehead, a high narrow palate, and low-set ears. MPAs are not medically or cosmetically of consequence, but they implicate genetic processes and disturbed prenatal development. The head/face, limbs, and brain develop from the same prenatal cell layers in early gestation, and MPAs in these bodily areas may point to abnormal neuron migration affecting brain development (Mittal & Walker, 2011).

Some individuals with autism possess a certain gracefulness and bodily agility, but others exhibit poor

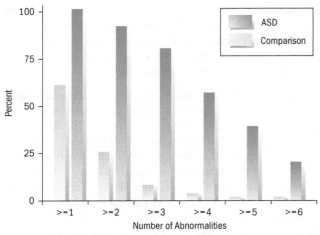

FIGURE 12.3 Percent of children with ASD and a matched group of typically developing children with minor physical abnormalities. Children with ASD did not have intellectual disability nor any known syndrome. *From Ozgen et al., 2011.*

balance, uncoordinated gait, impaired gross motor skills, and motor awkwardness from infancy into adulthood (Fournier et al., 2010; Pan, Tsai, & Chu, 2009). In addition, unusual eating preferences are observed, and rates of sleep problems, between 40 and 80%, are higher than for typical youth and youth with ID without autism (Giannotti et al., 2008; Mattila et al., 2010). Behaviorally, youths with ASD exhibit a variety of maladaptive behaviors, such as aggression, uncooperativeness, withdrawal, and self-injurious behaviors (Oliver & Richards, 2010).

Co-occurring Disorders

We have already seen that the coexistence of intellectual disability with autism spectrum disorder creates a varied clinical presentation of autism. Co-occurring emotional and behavioral problems engender even greater heterogeneity (Gjevik et al., 2011). Determining comorbidity can be especially challenging because language and cognitive problems hinder communication. In addition, some primary features of ASD and psychiatric disorders may be difficult to distinguish. For example, the abnormal social interactions observed in youths with ASD may be difficult to differentiate from social phobia, and the repetitive/ritualistic behaviors of ASD may be hard to tell from obsessive-compulsive disorder. Due in part to such hindrances, as well as to differences in samples and methodology, the extent of co-occurrence is unclear—although it is thought to be high, especially in clinic samples. For example, one community/clinic study of 9- to 16-year-olds found 74% comorbidity, and many youths had multiple co-occurring disorders (Mattila et al., 2010). Among the symptoms and disorders that

co-occur with ASD are anxiety, depression, hyperactivity, and oppositional-defiant behaviors.

As an example, we look briefly at comorbidity with anxiety, which includes simple phobias, social phobias, and generalized anxiety (White et al., 2009). An array of unknown factors might underlie the association of ASD and anxiety. Excessive sensitivity to stimuli is found in about half of the children with ASD, raising the possibility that oversensitivity might lead to some forms of anxiety, such as fear of loud noises (Green & Ben-Sasson, 2010). Or consider that older children and adolescents with ASD appear to experience greater levels of anxiety, as do those functioning at higher cognitive levels. This suggests that awareness of the social deficits of ASD generates anxiety, which leads to worsening social interactions and social isolation and, in turn, increased anxiety. Thus, bi-directional effects may operate for ASD and anxiety.

Level of intellectual functioning may be related to the co-occurrence of other symptoms as well (Totsika et al., 2011). For example, lower functioning may be especially associated with irritability and hyperactivity, whereas higher functioning may be especially related to depression. More generally, although many youths with ASD have intellectual impairments, the effects of ID are often not separated from those of ASD. To address this issue, Totsika and colleagues drew on research that surveyed emotional and behavioral problems in representative samples of youths with ASD, age 5 to 16 years. They compared four groups: ASD only, ASD with ID, ID only, and a group with neither condition. Although both ASD and ID were associated with problems, difficulties were more likely with ASD, with or without ID (Figure 12.4). In conjunction with other research, these results point to the need to address comorbidity, which impairs functioning in youths with ASD.

Epidemiology

Many epidemiological studies of autism or autism spectrum disorders have been conducted over the years. An extensive report examined 43 studies from several countries that included a wide age range but mostly school-age children (Fombonne, 2009). The studies were published between 1996 and 2008, with over half since 2000. The rates of disorder varied a good deal across the studies, which differed in diagnostic criteria, method, size and age of the population, and the like. The best estimate of prevalence was about 20/10,000 for autistic disorder, and 37/10,000 for pervasive developmental disorder not otherwise specified. Asperger's disorder, usually reported as less prevalent than autistic disorder, was estimated as 6/10,000. The figure for childhood disintegrative disorder was 2/10,000. From the studies that examined all four

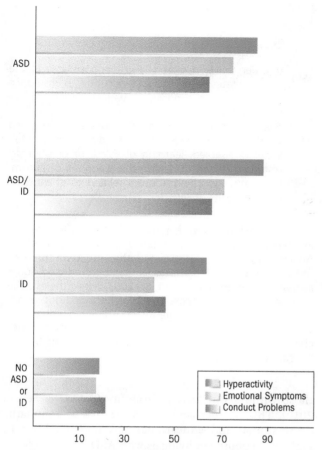

FIGURE 12.4 Percent of behavioral and emotional problems by child group. *Data from Totsika et al., 2011.*

Legend:
- Hyperactivity
- Emotional Symptoms
- Conduct Problems

severe symptoms are more likely in girls, so that the gender ratio is perhaps 2 to 1 in lower functioning ASD. It is worth noting that boys are at greater risk for several genetic disorders associated with autism, which could, at least in part, explain differences in gender prevalence. More generally, it has been hypothesized that underlying autism is the tendency to systematize the world—to detail or analyze in terms of underlying rules—a tendency more characteristic of the male brain (Baron-Cohen, Knickmeyer, & Belmonte, 2005). The importance of this suggestion has been questioned, however (van Engeland & Buitelaar, 2008).

Epidemiological research has largely failed to support the once-held belief that autism and social class are related. Early reports of high prevalence in the upper social classes probably resulted from nonrepresentative samples (Fombonne, 2003). There is evidence, however, that ASD is diagnosed more in Caucasian children in the United States, and rates are more rapidly rising for African American and Hispanic children (CDC, 2012).

Developmental Course

Understanding the onset and early development of ASD is provided by retrospective parental reports, videotapes of infants taken prior to diagnosis, and more recent prospective study of the at-risk siblings of children with ASD. Although most parents of children with autism become concerned about symptoms by the time their infants are 2 years of age, diagnosis usually occurs a few years later, with parents often citing language delays and social abnormalities (Kalb et al., 2010).

Three patterns of onset have been described (Kalb et al., 2010). The *first* pattern occurs in most children and indicates that abnormalities become obvious in the first year of life or soon afterward. The *second* pattern is manifest by mild delays until about age 2 and then a gradual or abrupt developmental arrest and plateau. The *third* pattern involves regression, in which typical or near typical development is followed by arrested skill acquisition and loss of previously acquired language, social, and/or motor skills.

Regression occurs in 15 to 40% of children with autism, frequently in the second year of life (Pickles et al., 2009). Among other behaviors, children stop using meaningful words, orienting to their names, or spontaneously imitating others (Goldberg et al., 2003; Lord, Shulman, & DiLavore, 2004). There is evidence that regressed children, despite relatively good early development, show more severe autism symptoms and poorer outcome than children with other types of onset (Baird et al., 2008; Kalb et al., 2010).

Research has pointed to heterogeneous developmental pathways. Six common trajectories, from diagnosis

conditions, the combined prevalence was consistently estimated as 60–70 youths per 10,000.

These data can be compared to investigations of children in the United States. Diagnosis of ASD in 3- to 17-year-olds, as reported by their parents, put prevalence at 110 per 10,000 youths (Kogan et al., 2009). The Centers for Disease Control and Prevention (2009), based on population surveillance of 8-year-olds conducted through health departments in 11 U.S. states, concluded that one child in 110 was classified as having an ASD. More recently, the CDC (2012) put this figure at one child in 88. The most striking aspect of the overall epidemiologic research is the increase in prevalence over time. As might be expected, there is considerable concern about this phenomenon. (See Accent: "An Epidemic of Autism?")

One aspect of autism that has remained constant over time is gender difference. In both epidemiological and clinic studies, boys display autism more often than girls, generally cited in the range of 3–4.5 boys to 1 girl (CDC, 2009; Dawson & Faja, 2008; Volkmar et al., 2005). Intellectual disability and

ACCENT
An Epidemic of Autism?

What accounts for the escalating rates of autism or ASD? Is there a true increase of disorder or are other factors at work? Many investigators have addressed this issue and they emphasize the influence of several changes in the conceptualization, understanding, and management of the disorders (CDC, 2009; Fombonne, 2009; Newsom & Hovanitz, 2006; Wazana, Bresnahan, & Kline, 2007). Consider the following.

- The criteria for autism, or ASD, have broadened over several years. It appears that children at both higher and lower levels of functioning are more likely to be diagnosed.
- Children are being diagnosed at younger ages. In part, this is attributable to better understanding of pervasive developmental disorders and the availability of early screening and diagnostic tests.
- Increased awareness has resulted in more cases being identified. Parents are more familiar with the symptoms of the disorders and physicians are receiving better training about developmental disorders.
- Diagnosis of autism or ASD has been encouraged by expansion of services. Medical clinics for developmental disorders have increased, and diagnosis rose in the United States after changes occurred in insurance benefits and in the Individuals with Disabilities Education Act (IDEA).
- There is evidence of "diagnostic switching," in which youth who were once likely to be diagnosed as intellectually disabled, learning disabled, or emotionally disturbed began to receive the diagnosis of autism. Diagnostic switching appears related to changes in the availability of services.

The extent to which these factors influence the incidence of autism and related disorders is unclear. An investigation that estimated the effect of three of the factors concluded that each factor predicted some increase in autism (Wazana et al., 2007). Nevertheless, the possibility of a true increase in ASD is not ruled out, and it is an important issue. A true increase in incidence would pose critical questions about etiology, especially whether changing environmental variables are putting children at increased risk.

---

to age 14, were described in a study of a large community population (Fountain, Winter, & Bearman, 2012). Regarding social and communication behaviors, most children improved over time. But some trajectories showed slower change and little improvement. Children whose symptoms were least severe at diagnosis tended to improve more rapidly. Interestingly, though, one group—identified as "bloomers"—began at low functioning and improved so rapidly that at adolescence it resembled a group whose functioning had been consistently high. In general, children of white, well-educated mothers showed higher functioning at outcome.

Other investigations indicate that from childhood onward, modest improvement occurs in social, communication, and self-help skills (Piven et al., 1996; Sigman, 1998; Taylor & Seltzer, 2010). These findings were demonstrated in longitudinal research examining change from early childhood into adulthood (Shattuck et al., 2007). Many individuals showed decreases in the core symptoms of ASD and in associated maladaptive behaviors as well. Still, considerable variation occurred across individuals. Overall, individuals with intellectual disability improved less and lower family income also was related to less improvement, suggesting less availability of quality services. Interestingly, yet another study showed that improvement slowed after adolescents and young adults exited the secondary school system, especially for those without intellectual disability (Taylor & Seltzer, 2010). This was perhaps due to the lack of stimulating occupational and educational activities available for higher functioning individuals with ASD.

Despite modest improvement over time, symptoms generally persist into adulthood for most persons with ASD. Perhaps 15% achieve independence, with successful work placement and some social life (Volkmar et al., 2005). Research consistently shows that long-term outcome is relatively poor when early general intelligence and communicative language are impaired (Howlin et al., 2004; Shattuck et al., 2007; Volkmar & Klin, 2000). A follow-up of study found that those with childhood IQs 70 or above did notably better, suggesting that this IQ level is a good predictor of adult independent living (Seltzer et al., 2003). For these individuals, although some difficulties may persist, life may include typical achievements and rewards. Temple Grandin, who has extensively written about her experiences as a person diagnosed with autism and whose personal and career achievements were depicted in an award winning television film, wrote of the motivations and balances in her life in this way:

Many people with autism become disillusioned and upset because they do not fit in socially and they do not have a girlfriend or boyfriend. I have just accepted that such a relationship will not be part of my life. . . . I want to be appreciated for the work I do. I am happiest when I am doing something for fun, like designing an engineering project, or making something that makes a contribution to society. (Grandin, 1997)

On an optimistic note, as we see later in the chapter, progress in early intervention could be lessening the impact of ASD, particularly for higher functioning youths.

Neurobiological Abnormalities

Diverse evidence exists for neurobiological anomalies in autism, including neurological soft signs, abnormal EEGs and epilepsy, high rates of MPAs, and co-occurring ID (Akshoomoff et al., 2007; Minshew, Sweeney, & Bauman, 1997; Volkmar & Klin, 2000). More directly, various brain structures and regions have been examined with postmortem examination, brain imaging, and other types of research. Most studied and implicated are the temporal lobe–limbic system, the frontal lobes, and the cerebellum (Corbett & Gunther, 2011; Schultz & Klin, 2002). These connected regions are part of what is sometimes referred to as the "social brain" (Frith, 2004).

A consistent finding is altered brain growth. Unusually large brain size—perhaps by 5 to 10%—is found in toddlers (van Engeland & Buitelaar, 2008; Volkmar et al., 2004). At birth, brain size is small to normal, but an atypical growth spurt occurs soon afterward—perhaps as early as 6 months—and soon levels off (Dawson & Faja, 2008). One study found brain enlargement of the cortex at age 2, with white matter of the temporal lobe disproportionately large (Hazlett et al., 2011).

Numerous other investigations of youths and adults with ASD indicate brain volume anomalies. Excessive volume of gray and white tissue has been found in the cerebrum and excessive white matter in the cerebellum. Also demonstrated are compromises in many white matter tracts that connect different regions of the brain to each other and connect the hemispheres (Pardo & Eberhart, 2007; Shukla, Keehn, & Müller, 2011).

Microscopic studies of the temporal lobe–limbic system, frontal lobes, and cerebellum indicate abnormalities in cell structure and organization (Filipek, 1999; Tanguay, 2000; van Engeland & Buitelaar, 2008). These include decreased number and size of cells, high cell density, less dendritic branching, and abnormal cell migration. Some of the microscopic cell studies suggest that brain anomalies may develop prenatally.

With regard to brain functioning, reduced activity has been shown in several regions, most notably the frontal lobes and limbic system, particularly the amygdala (Newsom & Hovanitz, 2006). Many studies of brain function during visual or auditory tasks suggest the use of brain regions not typically employed to process information and otherwise abnormal responses (van Engeland & Buitelaar, 2008). For example, studies of the electrical activity of the brain showed slowed face processing.

Although interest exists in the biochemical systems, consistent findings are lacking. The most dependable, although not understood, biochemical finding is high levels of serotonin in blood platelets in 25 to 50% of cases. Very early in development, serotonin plays a role in the development of neurons, and brain serotonin and its synthesis are implicated in the expression of autism symptoms (van Engeland & Buitelaar, 2008). Among other neurotransmitters examined are dopamine, glutamate (important in excitation), and GABA (important in inhibition). In general, there are conflicting findings about their roles. Several additional biochemicals have been examined. Findings related to oxytocin and vasopressin, which are implicated in social behavior, have not provided a clear picture, whereas studies of secretin and melatonin give no support to their involvement. At times, the importance of some of these substances has received media attention that appeared to go beyond research results (Azar, 2011).

Understanding of the neurobiology of autism is progressing, although a definitive portrait has not yet emerged. Important in this work are efforts to connect brain structure and functioning to the clinical picture of ASD. For example, enlargement of the amygdala in toddlers has been associated with more severe course of development during the preschool period (Dawson & Faja, 2008), and, as just noted, abnormal brain activity may occur during tasks such as face processing. Research findings and the mix of symptoms of the disorder point to abnormalities of multiple brain regions and networks. Overall, ASD may result from early brain overgrowth and neuron anomalies leading to a cascade of biological aberrations, including atypical or decreased connections between brain regions (Corbett & Gunther, 2011).

Etiology

Dominant among early etiological proposals was that parenting played a critical role in autism. Kanner described the typical parents of a child with autism as highly intelligent, professionally accomplished people who were preoccupied with scientific, literary, and artistic concerns, and who treated their offspring in a coldly mechanical way (Kanner, 1943; Kanner & Eisenberg, 1956). Inadequate, "refrigerator" parenting became implicated in causing autism, even though Kanner hypothesized an innate social deficit. Bettelheim's (1967a; 1967b) psychoanalytic theory was an especially influential psychosocial explanation (Mesibov & Van Bourgondien, 1992). Accordingly, autism was caused by parental rejection or pathology that resulted in the young child's retreating into an autistic "empty fortress." Due to lack of evidence, this approach eventually went by the wayside, and the explanation currently is viewed as regrettable. Today's parents play important roles in advocacy and treatment for their children. Current interest in etiology emphasizes variables that might account for neurobiological abnormalities.

GENETIC INFLUENCE

Twin and Family Studies   Major twin studies of autism document much higher concordance in monozygotic twins than in dizygotic twins (Bailey et al., 1995; Steffenburg et al., 1989). Monozygotic twins of probands have about a 60% chance of having autism, and an even greater probability (90%) when autism-like disorder is included (Corbett & Gunthrer, 2011; Veenstra-vanderweele & Cook, 2003). The comparative figure for dizygotic cotwins is about 4.5%.

Family studies of autism point to genetic influence. The rate of autism in siblings of autistic children varies from 2 to 7%, and about 8% of extended families have an additional autistic member (Bailey, Phillips, & Rutter, 1996; Newsom, 1998; Rutter et al., 1999). Yet other interesting findings have emerged. *First,* a higher than expected rate of autism-like developmental disorders is found in families. *Second,* 20 to 30% of family members exhibit impairments in social, communicative, and repetitive behaviors that are similar to autism but not severe enough for diagnosis (Piven & Palmer, 1997; Szatmari et al., 2000; Wallace et al., 2010). *Third,* some siblings of youth with ASD can show very early differences, for example, atypical pre-speech vocalizations in their first year of life (Paul et al., 2011). Some siblings with early manifestations (e.g., low rates of joint attention) go on to be diagnosed with ASD (Rozga et al., 2011). *Fourth,* family members show characteristics that, although not diagnosable symptoms of ASD, are observed in those with autism, such as macrocephaly, elevated serotonin, and neuroanatomical abnormalities (Mosconi et al., 2010).

Some of the problems found in families have been shown to increase as the genetic relationship becomes closer (Pickles et al., 2000). Moreover, genetic influence was suggested in a study that found greater social, communication, and repetitive behavior impairments in biological than adoptive families (Szatmari et al., 2000). The combined research supports the view that genetic predisposition leads to autism, autism-like disorders, or milder related problems. Because what is transmitted in families is broader than the specific symptoms of the diagnostic category of autism, a dimensional conceptualization of autism is suggested rather than a category of disorder (McGrath & Peterson, 2009b). Support for dimensionality also comes from studies indicating that autistic traits—such as social reciprocity and language skills—are continuously distributed in the general population (Robinson et al., 2011).

Chromosomes and Genes   What do we know more specifically about genetic influence? The picture is complex. Single gene syndromes and chromosomal abnormalities appear in less than 10 to 20% of cases, with intellectual disability often present in these (Corbett & Gunther, 2011; McGrath & Peterson, 2009b). Two genetic conditions notably associated with autism are fragile X syndrome (p. 292) and tuberose sclerosis, the latter caused by inherited or new gene mutations resulting in tumors of the brain and other organs. A duplication of genes in a particular region of chromosome 15 also has been observed in an estimated 1 to 3% of cases of autism (Sutcliffe & Nurmi, 2003), and this region is linked to other developmental disorders. In addition, genome-wide association studies have revealed copy number variations, for example, involving 30 genes on chromosome 16 (Corbett & Gunther, 2011).

The research on ASD reflects the usual strategies for identifying susceptibility chromosomes and genes. Many chromosomes have been implicated, including 2, 6, 7, 13, 15, 16, 17, 19, and 22 (McGrath & Peterson, 2009b; Newsom & Hovanitz, 2006). Progress has made in identifying several susceptibility genes and their implications for brain functioning. For example, the RELN, MECP2, NLGN3, and NLGN4 susceptibility genes affect early brain development.

Some investigators favor the idea that many interacting genes best explain most cases of ASD. This possibility is suggested by the continuum of disorder, the varied clinical picture, and research findings. The fact that concordance in less than 100% in MZ twins with autism also suggests that gene-environment interactions and epigenetic processes may play some role in the development of autism, and there is evidence for both (James et al., 2008).

PRENATAL AND PREGNANCY RISK   Numerous pregnancy and birth variables have been inconsistently associated with autism and related disorders (Newsom & Hovanitz, 2006). A recent meta-analysis that included over 50 prenatal factors found 6 of them to be risk factors for autism: advanced paternal and maternal age, maternal medication, maternal bleeding, gestational diabetes, birth order (being born first versus third or later), and having a mother born abroad (Gardener, Spiegelman, & Buka, 2009). Many of these factors were also indicated in a study conducted in China of prenatal and perinatal risk (Zhang et al., 2010). There is also some evidence implicating uterine inflammation or abnormal maternal immune responses (Corbett & Gunther, 2011).

MEDICAL CONDITIONS AND VACCINES   In addition to the already-mentioned genetic syndromes, numerous medical conditions are associated with autism—cerebral palsy, infections such as meningitis, hearing impairment, and seizure disorders. About 25% of those with autism have seizure disorders (Schultz & Klin, 2002), with onset disproportionate in early childhood and adolescence (Volkmar et al., 2005).

Related to medical conditions is the controversial issue of an association between autistic spectrum disorder and vaccines given to prevent diseases otherwise unassociated with ASD. The issue arose when parents in England associated their children's onset of pervasive developmental disorders with the measles, mumps, and rubella vaccine (MMR) they had received to prevent these diseases. The parents had sought advice from gastrointestinal experts after the children had developed intestinal problems. From this consultation, Wakefield and colleagues (1998) hypothesized that, through a complex route involving immune responses, measles virus in the vaccine was responsible for both the intestinal illness and developmental disorder. Subsequently, another group of researchers proposed that an atypical autoimmune response to the vaccination affected the brain and caused autism (Newsom & Hovanitz, 2006). However, several investigations in different countries have failed to find a connection between MMR and autism (Honda, Shimizu, & Rutter, 2005; Institute of Medicine, 2004; Taylor et al., 1999).

Concern also has been expressed that vaccines with thimerosal, a mercury-containing preservative, put children at risk for pervasive developmental disorders. The potential negative effects of mercury are well known, and among the arguments is that (1) some children may be especially susceptible, and (2) the amount of thimerosal received by children has increased due to an increase in recommended vaccinations. As with the MMR studies, the weight of the evidence does not appear to support a relationship between pervasive developmental disorders and thimerosal-containing vaccines (Costello, Foley, & Angold, 2006; Newsom & Hovanitz, 2006). In any event, mercury in vaccines has been eliminated or reduced in many countries (Kirby, 2005).

The debate over vaccines and autism continues to be contentious (Deer, 2011; Godlee, 2011). The original article by Wakefield and his colleagues was retracted by the journal in which it had been published and Wakefield, who lost his British professional credentials, has become a controversial figure, as depicted in the *New York Times Magazine* (Dominus, 2011). Reviews by major government and professional groups in the United States have not supported the role of vaccines as causative, although some investigators recognize that a small number of children could be unusually susceptible to MMR (Honda et al., 2005). Meanwhile, parents tell of the plight of their damaged children in court, advocacy groups call for more research, and some parents refuse vaccines that protect children from hazardous diseases.

ENVIRONMENT AND SOCIAL INTERACTION The search for etiology clearly has focused on possible causes of early brain abnormalities to the relative neglect of possible later-occurring environmental and psychosocial influences. Noting the importance of a developmental model for autism, Dawson and Faja (2008) presented a three-component formulation with a more comprehensive perspective. As shown in Figure 12.5, genetic and/or early environmental susceptibility factors lead to brain abnormalities that influence interactions between the child and his or her environment. In turn, these altered interactions are hypothesized to disrupt input critical for further brain development, leading to additional brain anomalies and autism. The model proposes that individual pathways of altered interactions mediate the connection between initial brain abnormalities and later outcome. These developmental pathways, which involve the context of the child's environment, can vary and change to a limited extent, but the longer the child travels a maladaptive pathway, the less probable is normal development. The Dawson and Faja model contributes to our thinking about ASD by focusing on child-environment interactions and the advisability of early intervention, topics to which we return later in the chapter.

Autism and Related Disorders

So far in this chapter we have emphasized autism. We now turn to briefly discuss Asperger's disorder, PDD-NOS, and CDD, as they have been considered as distinct disturbances. Although the overlap of symptoms in these disorders is obvious, some differences from each other and from autistic disorder can be seen. This discussion allows us to better understand the kinds of problems that currently are seen as characterizing autism spectrum disorder.

ASPERGER'S DISORDER (AS) Although Asperger first wrote of this syndrome in 1944, many years passed before English-speaking professionals took notice and the

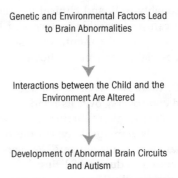

Genetic and Environmental Factors Lead
to Brain Abnormalities

Interactions between the Child and the
Environment Are Altered

Development of Abnormal Brain Circuits
and Autism

FIGURE 12.5 A developmental model of autism. *Adapted from Dawson & Faja, 2008.*

diagnosis was not recognized by the DSM and ICD until the early 1990s (Klin & Volkmar, 1997). Asperger's disorder, or Asperger syndrome, is marked by qualitative deficits in social interaction and by restrictive, repetitive, stereotyped interests and behaviors. In these ways, it resembles autism. However, youths with Asperger's disorder display no significant delay in language, cognitive development, adaptive behavior (except in the social domain), or curiosity about the environment.

Individuals with AS have difficulties in establishing friendships and other positive social bonds. They have deficits in the use of nonverbal social gestures, emotional expression, and early sharing behaviors. Social awkwardness, inappropriateness, lack of empathy, and insensitivity are apparent. They seem to have some interest in other people, but their lives are often marked by loneliness. Although research indicates impairment in ToM skills and the perception of complex emotions, the exact nature of their social deficits is not fully understood (Frith, 2004).

Particularly striking are obsessive and restricted interests, the focus of which seems to know few bounds; astronomy, kitchen appliances, historical events, and geographical locales are a few examples. The child may collect an inordinate number of facts and recite them in a pedantic, egocentric, long-winded style. Indeed, Asperger referred to his patients as "little professors." Adults with AS are known for their meticulous work—whether in art or science (Frith, 2004), and youths and adults often exhibit imagination, for example, in art.

Other difficulties, considered secondary, have been observed. A variety of motor problems may exist, as well as behavioral problems such as noncompliance, negativism, and aggression (Miller & Ozonoff, 2000; Volkmar & Klin, 2000).

The rate of AS is not established, although prevalence is less than for autism (Fombonne, 2009). Boys are identified more often than girls, and diagnosis occurs on average much later than for autism (Dawson & Toth, 2006). Outcome appears fair to good (Volkmar et al., 2005). Asperger himself thought that many of his patients could do reasonably well, and clinical impressions agree that outcome can be favorable in terms of living independently, finding employment, and having a family (Frith, 2004). Social impairments, however, may persist over time.

Currently there is considerable interest in Asperger's syndrome and controversy over its relationship to autistic disorder, especially to higher functioning autism. Of debate is the question, "Is Asperger's syndrome distinct from autism or a manifestation of autism?" Perhaps some of the difference of opinion is due to AS being defined somewhat differently by various clinicians and investigators (Mattila et al., 2007). Nevertheless, one position argues that autistic disorder and AS are hardly distinguishable. Indeed several studies found little consistent evidence of significant differences between AS and high functioning autism (Sanders, 2009; Witwer & Lecavalier, 2008). Accordingly, AS may be viewed as a variant of autism diagnosed on the basis of verbal and/or cognitive higher functioning, not a *qualitatively* separate disorder. This is consistent with AS being conceptualized as an autistic spectrum disorder, and may suggest that the diagnosis of AS is unnecessary (Ghaziuddin, 2010).

The counter argument calls attention to how AS is qualitatively different from autism, such as later onset, verbal IQ greater than performance IQ rather than the reverse, more complex or different language, more noticeable restricted interests, and fewer motor mannerisms (Miller & Ozonoff, 2000; Volkmar & Klin, 2000). Notably different is the manner of communication observed in Asperger's disorder, which is portrayed as one-sided or pedantic and with stilted expressions and excessive details (Ghaziuddin, 2010). Or to take another example, social behavior in AS is often described as active and odd whereas in autism it is described as aloof and passive. Accordingly, Asperger's disorder is viewed as a distinct disorder. There are, of course, implications for how AS is conceptualized: distinct disorders lead to the search for different developmental course and outcome, neurobiology, etiology, prognosis, intervention, and the like.

PDD-NOS This DSM-IV category applied when symptoms appeared related to, but failed to meet, the diagnostic criteria for autism and other pervasive developmental disorders. The diagnostic criteria were only generally described, with no specific items. Youths with PDD-NOS had to display impaired reciprocal social interaction and *either* impaired communication or stereotyped behavior and interests (American Psychiatric Association, 2000). Cases of so-called atypical autism fell into the PDD-NOS category, that is, cases in which the criteria for autistic disorder were not met due to late onset, atypical symptoms, milder symptoms, or all of these. Among the disorders currently viewed as falling within autism spectrum disorder, PDD-NOS is most common but its diagnosis is also the least stable over time, whether due to the vagueness of the diagnostic criteria, a tendency for diagnosticians to use the diagnosis in the face of uncertainty, or other reasons (Daniels et al., 2011). The case of Leslie briefly describes a child who had been diagnosed with PDD-NOS.

CHILDHOOD DISINTEGRATIVE DISORDER (CDD) In 1908, Heller first described what is referred to as childhood disintegrative disorder. He termed it *dementia infantilis*, and it also has been called *Heller's syndrome* and *disintegrative psychosis* (Volkmar & Klin,

LESLIE

PDD-NOS

Leslie was a difficult baby, although her motor and communicative development seemed appropriate. She related socially and sometimes enjoyed social interaction. However, she was easily overstimulated, and appeared unusually sensitive to aspects of the environment. She sometimes flapped her hands out of excitement. When she was 4 years of age, Leslie's parents sought an evaluation because in nursery school she exhibited peer interaction problems and a preoccupation with adverse events. At this time, her communication and cognitive skills were in the normal range. However, she had difficulties in social interaction and a tendency to impose routines on social interaction.

Leslie attended a therapeutic nursery school and her social skills improved. She did well academically in a special kindergarten, but peer interaction problems and unusual affective response continued. As an adolescent, Leslie viewed herself as a loner who tended to enjoy solitary activities.

Adapted from Volkmar et al., 2005, p. 3181.

2000). According to the DSM-IV criteria, development must be normal for at least 2 years and symptoms must be present before age 10. By this time, many acquired skills are lost. As we have seen, some children with autistic disorder manifest regression after mostly typical development, but loss of skills in CDD occurs later than in regressed autism (Palomo et al., 2008). Diagnosis of CDD calls for significant loss in at least two areas of the following: language, social skills, bowel or bladder control, play, or motor skills. In addition, impairment must be present in two areas that characterize autism, that is, in social interaction, social communication, or RRSBs.

This rare disorder appears more often in males than females, with onset—either gradual or abrupt—usually between 3 and 4 years of age. Impairment remains fairly constant over time, and after regression the disorder appears similar to severe autism (Palomo et al., 2008). More children with CDD than with autism are mute, display loss of self-help skills, and have IQ scores less than 40 (Volkmar & Klin, 2000). The case of Nicholas illustrates the striking loss of function that can occur in childhood disintegrative disorder.

Assessment of ASD

Although assessment has focused disproportionately on autistic disorder, much of the following discussion can be applied to ASD. Because ASD encompasses many areas of functioning and implicates neurobiological deficits, it requires broad-based assessment (American Academy of Child and Adolescent Psychiatry, 1999; Charman & Baird, 2002). The clinician must involve the parents in order to obtain a unique picture of the child's functioning and also to lay the groundwork for possible treatment. It is also important to take a history of prenatal, birth, developmental, familial, and medical factors, as well as of any past intervention. Medical examination may be valuable in helping to identify ASD, investigate its causes, and treat associated conditions such as seizures.

Psychological and behavioral evaluations typically include interviews, direct observation of the child, and psychological tests. Tests of intelligence, adaptive behavior, and language are among the useful instruments, depending on the individual case. Several instruments exist to specifically assess autistic behaviors or Asperger's disorder. These tools are based on observation of the child and/or reports of past or present behavior. Of these, the following briefly described instruments serve somewhat different purposes or employ somewhat different approaches.

EVALUATING AUTISTIC BEHAVIORS The goal of early screening is to identify very young children who may or may not be showing blatant manifestations of disorder. Early identification is crucial due to the importance of early intervention. Pediatricians are among the professionals who come into contact with very young children, and The Academy of Pediatrics has published guidelines for screening young children at risk for ASD (Johnson & Myers, 2007). Discussion with parents, direct observation of the child, and the use of screening tools are suggested. An example of an early screening instrument is the M-CHAT, the Modified Checklist for Autism in Toddlers (Robins, 2008; Robins et al., 2001). A brief set of questions is asked of parents or caregivers about the child's behavior, such as whether the child takes an interest in other children, seems oversensitive to noise, or responds to his/her name being called. It is recommended that a child suspected of developmental delay or risk immediately be referred for more extensive evaluation or for attendance in an early intervention program. A "wait and see" posture is to be avoided.

The Childhood Autism Rating Scale (CARS2) is widely employed for screening children and older persons (Schopler et al. 2010). Two forms are available: (1) the

NICHOLAS

Childhood Disintegrative Disorder

Nicholas's medical history, parental reports, and home videos indicated nothing of concern up to 47 months. At this time, he exhibited eye contact and smiles toward others, joint attention behaviors, fluent communication in full sentences, and complex social behaviors like showing off. The family had experienced specific stress when Nicholas was 38 to 42 months of age, and during this time Nicholas had displayed behaviors unusual for him (e.g., he had slept less, was very active, and was slower to follow directions). However, home video showed him to be social and communicative, and with lessened family stress Nicholas's behavior returned to normalcy. A baby brother was born when Nicholas was 44 months of age; Nicholas was shown on video affectionately cuddling the infant, responding to questions, gesturing, and smiling.

Just prior to his fourth birthday, Nicholas's preschool recommended an evaluation of behavior problems, including aggression and social withdrawal. His parents had noticed anxiety and agitation. He would scream into the mirror, "Bad Nicholas! You are stupid, I hate you," run around, pinch himself, and bang his head on walls and mirrors. Within 2 months, among other losses, Nicholas's parents reported the loss of most language, motor skills, and imaginative play. He did not want to be touched, and was no longer toilet trained. Home video revealed changes in his fifth year of life, corroborating his parents' description of dramatic regression around his fourth birthday (Figure 12.6).

Adapted from Palomo et al., 2008, pp. 1853–1858.

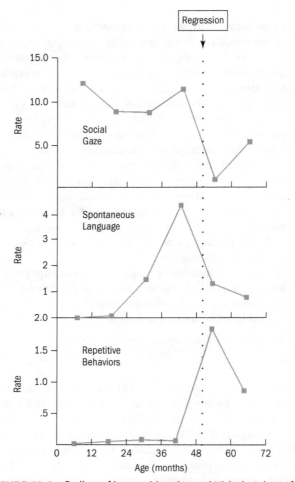

FIGURE 12.6 Coding of home video showed Nicholas's loss of social and language skills, and increased repetitive behaviors, around 48 months of age. *Adapted from Paloma et al., 2008.*

standard form for children under age 6 or individuals with communication problems or below-average estimated IQ, and (2) a newer form for verbally fluent persons 6 years or older with IQ above 80. There is also a questionnaire to gather information from parents or caregivers. Both assessment forms consist of 15 items rated by a professional after observation of the individual. The items cover many areas of functioning, including emotional response, imitation, social relations, communication, and perception. The CARS2 distinguishes autism from other severe cognitive deficits and also indicates the severity of autism.

The Autism Diagnostic Interview–Revised (ADI-R) is a widely used 93-item semistructured interview conducted with parents and caregivers (Rutter, LeCouteur, & Lord, 2006). It provides comprehensive assessment of individuals suspected of autism or ASD. It assesses communication, social interaction, and restricted, repetitive behavior and interests in youths and adults with a mental age above 2 years. The ADI-R is useful for diagnosis and treatment/educational planning, and it discriminates autism from other developmental disorders. It is considered a goal standard for assessment for ASD.

The Autism Diagnostic Observation Schedule (ADOS), also a gold standard instrument, was developed out of the need to assess children in direct interaction with a clinician (Lord, 2010). It consists of several modules of standardized activities that create the opportunity for the person to display behaviors relevant to autism, for example, while engaging in standardized play activity or a construction task. One of the modules is selected as relevant to the age and language abilities of the person being evaluated. Modules are available (or in process) to assess toddlers 12 to 30 months of age, children, adolescents, and verbal adults. During the session, observations are recorded and later coded for a diagnosis. This instrument is sensitive to the differences between autism and PDD-NOS (Chawarska et al., 2007). In addition, severity of symptoms can be compared to severity shown in a large sample of persons of similar age and expressive language.

Prevention of ASD

As with other early-onset developmental disorders with an apparent genetic and neurobiological etiology, universal prevention includes prenatal care and improvement in environmental quality. However, early identification and intervention are at the heart of prevention, an approach that merges with treatment.

Common settings for early intervention programs for young children are the home, public schools, preschool settings in universities, and classrooms originating from private educational organizations (Charman, 2011; Newsom & Hovanitz, 2006). Behavioral approaches are frequently employed. The curriculum often focuses on social skills such as joint attention and social engagement with others, imitation, and language. Research indicates that these programs can improve intelligence, language, and the rate of overall development, as well as decrease autistic symptoms in some children (Charman, 2011; Harris & Handleman, 2000). However, many questions remain, including why only some children profit from the programs.

Outcome research on early programs—which vary in duration and intensity—has improved, and efforts continue to better establish efficacy as well as the programs themselves. A major effort is the development and evaluation of the Early Start Denver Model, which recently was evaluated in a randomized controlled study of toddlers (See Accent: "The Early Start Denver Model"). Committed to the belief that this program could be effective with even younger children, attempts are being made to identify and treat such children. Infants at high risk, due to having a sibling with ASD, are observed and videotaped in social interaction in hopes of determining and modifying behaviors that lead to ASD.

Intervention for ASD

The mainstay approaches to treatment for ASD are behavioral and educational. Pharmacological intervention has an ancillary role.

PHARMACOLOGICAL TREATMENT Medication mostly targets problem behaviors such as aggression, self-injury, agitation, and stereotypic behaviors. The typical antipsychotic medications antagonistic to dopamine can help some youth by reducing problematic behaviors, but adverse side effects occur over time in a minority of cases (American Psychological Association, 2006). Of particular concern are side effects such as motor problems, including tremors and tardive dyskinesia (involuntary repetitive movements of the tongue, mouth, and jaw). Typical antipsychotic medications have thus been largely replaced by second-generation, or atypical, antipsychotic medications that are antagonistic both to dopamine and serotonin. Risperidone is an example: it is considered effective for irritability, aggression, self-injury, and temper tantrums (Corbett & Gunther, 2011).

Stimulant medication has been shown to lessen disruptive behavior in children and adolescents with ASD (American Psychological Association, 2006). However, methylphenidate appears to have negative side effects (agitation, irritability, insomnia) for many of these children. In one study it had to be discontinued in 18% of children.

Many other classes of medications are employed, but evidence for efficacy is weak or not established. Side effects may be relatively high. Although a substantial number of children with autism spectrum disorders receive medication, much is still unknown about the effects, including long-term effects.

BEHAVIORAL INTERVENTION Behavioral treatments can be viewed as falling into two approaches (American Psychological Association, 2006). One approach focuses on specific targets. These may involve deficits, such as in language or social skills, or specific maladaptive behaviors, such as stereotyped behaviors or self-injury. The second approach is intensive, comprehensive treatment over a relatively long period of time that aims to improve numerous primary and secondary problems of autism.

Early behavioral intervention consisted of simple demonstrations of behavior change in children with autism (Koegel, Koegel, & McNerney, 2001; Schreibman, 2000). Subsequent efforts were made to teach a variety of adaptive behaviors and to discourage undesirable behaviors. An

ACCENT
The Early Start Denver Model (ESDM)

The ESDM is based on a broad developmental approach combined with the principles of applied behavior analysis. The efficacy of the ESDM was evaluated in a randomized, controlled trial (Dawson et al., 2010). The participants, 22 months of age on average, mostly had been diagnosed with autistic disorder, a few with PDD-NOS. Seventy-two percent were Caucasian; the remainder were Asian, Latino, and multiracial. The male–female ratio was 3.5:1.

The toddlers were assigned to either the ESDM or a comparison group (A/M) that was referred for intervention commonly provided in the community. ESDM intervention was conducted in the home and followed a detailed manual. Trained therapists worked with each child for 20 hours weekly for 2 years. Verbal and nonverbal communication was emphasized with developmentally appropriate strategies involving positive affect, real-life activities, and sensitivity to the child's cues. Teaching techniques included operant conditioning, shaping, and the like. An individualized plan was followed for each child. In addition, parents were taught the principles and techniques of the ESDM and were asked to use the ESMD strategies with the child.

The intervention was evaluated by comparing measures taken prior to the program with outcome at 1 and 2 years later. The primary outcome measures were scores on the Vineland Adaptive Behavior Scales and on the Mullen Scales of Early Learning, a developmental test for children from birth to 68 months of age that evaluates motor, visual reception, and language performance. The ESDM toddlers improved in cognition at both year 1 and 2, as shown on the Mullen scales (Figure 12.7). At year 2, they had gained 17.6 points compared to 7.0 for the comparison

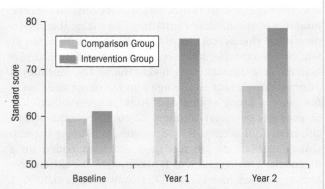

FIGURE 12.7 Mean scores on the Mullen Scales of Early Learning for children in the ESDM and the comparison groups at baseline, and 1 and 2 years after entering the program. *Adapted from Dawson et al., 2010.*

groups, mostly due to increases in language performance. Adaptive behavior scores differed only on year 2 measures, with ESDM performance showing a steady rate of development and the control group children showing decline. Two years after the beginning of the intervention, the ESDM children were significantly more likely than the comparison children to have an improved diagnosis, moving from autistic disorder to PDD-NOS. Two secondary measures indicated no group difference for autistic symptoms. This randomized, controlled demonstration of significant improvement in Mullen scales scores, language, adaptive behavior, and diagnosis holds promise for early efforts to modify or prevent the maladaptive and damaging pathways to ASD.

outstanding example of this early work was the approach taken by Lovaas and his colleagues at the University of California at Los Angeles, who were among the first to teach verbal communication to children with autism (Lovaas, Young, & Newsom, 1978; Newsom, 1998). In highly structured sessions, they used the tools of operant intervention, such as contingent reinforcement, prompts, shaping, modeling, and procedures to facilitate the generalization of learning.

Early behavioral efforts enjoyed success but were also challenged by failures. For instance, youngsters receiving language training often failed to initiate speech or to use speech in everyday activities (Koegel, 2000). Children who acquired responses often did not generalize the responses to different situations. Some maladaptive behaviors could only be modified by punishment, and other behaviors were hardly modifiable at all (Schreibman, 1997).

Improved behavioral procedures have brought increased success and substantial efforts to improve behaviors such as social skills, joint attention, and emotion regulation. Functional analysis of maladaptive behavior and Functional Communication Training (p. 305) have been successfully used with children with autism, including those with intellectual disability. These children can acquire adaptive behaviors through both discrete trial and naturalistic learning that is more likely to generalize to other settings. In addition, the acquisition of some skills may facilitate other positive behaviors; for example, teaching children to initiate social and academic interactions may help them learn language and social skills. These various behavioral approaches have been incorporated into strategies known as incidental teaching, milieu teaching, pivotal response treatment, and the like (Schreibman, 2000).

Pivotal Response Treatment Building on the techniques of applied behavior analysis, Pivotal Response Treatment (PRT) assumes that strengthening pivotal behaviors will improve other behaviors (Koegel et al., 2010; Koegel, Koegel, & Brookman, 2003). The overall goal is to provide comprehensive treatment in areas that will facilitate the child's independence. Intervention occurs in naturalistic settings with parents, teachers, and other service providers. Because impairments in autism tend to be extensive, and because targeting each problem is extremely time consuming and expensive, pivotal response training holds promise for time-efficient and cost-effective intervention.

Table 12.1 shows some of the strategies employed in PRT. Motivation is seen as a key component: it is pivotal to almost all areas of functioning. Motivation may be particularly problematic in ASD because the child has experienced repeated failures, as well as noncontingent assistance and reinforcement from caretakers. Specific strategies are employed to mitigate this unfortunate history—strategies that include child selection of activities, liberal and contingent reinforcement, and opportunity for the practice of acquired responses. Areas of function that have been targeted for improvement include expressive language, social interaction, and motivation to self-initiate (e.g., to seek information, initiate joint attention). It is presumed that improved motivation and behaviors tend to spill over to other areas and strengthen independence and learning.

PRT has been evaluated with different research designs in varied research settings with manualized procedures (Koegel et al., 2010). These studies indicate treatment gains in both targeted behaviors and untargeted spill-over behaviors. Preliminary evidence exists for the effectiveness of PRT group training for parents (Minjarez et al., 2011) and for the sustainability of PRT in a community setting (Smith et al., 2010).

The Young Autism Project A key assumption of the Young Autism Project is that intensive comprehensive programs are necessary to bring about substantial improvement in the lives of children with autism. In 1970, a groundbreaking intervention was developed by Lovaas and his colleagues that aimed at multiple positive outcomes (Lovaas, 1987; Lovaas & Smith, 1988). This work had enormous influence. It encouraged specialized interventions and research that continues to this day, and affected the schools and other agencies involved in providing services to children with autism (Rogers & Vismara, 2008).

Intervention employs discrete trial learning throughout, incidental learning after the first few months, and small group teaching in preschool during the final years (Table 12.2). Initially, it is usually necessary to reduce maladaptive behaviors that interfere with learning, such as tantrums; to teach imitation and compliance with verbal commands; and to train basic behaviors such as dressing and playing with toys. Considerable effort is then given to language and communication skills, as well as to peer interaction and interactive play. During the last year or so, emphasis is placed on advanced communication and school adjustment. Parents are an integral part of the intervention. They attend all meetings regarding their child, work with therapists for the first 3 to 4 months implementing discrete trial learning, and subsequently use incidental learning to encourage appropriate behaviors in everyday settings.

Participants in the original outcome study of the Young Autism Project were children under age 4 who were free of major medical problems (Lovaas & Smith, 2003). Most received 40 hours per week of one-to-one intervention with experienced behavioral therapists, with sessions tapering off near the end of the program. An initial evaluation compared three groups. Group I had received behavioral treatment for more than 40 hours each week, Group II had received almost the same treatment but for fewer than 10 hours weekly, and Group III had received no training in the project. The groups were similar in characteristics and intervention lasted for 2 or more years. Group I children, who now averaged 7 years of age, had an increase of 30 points in IQ, and significantly higher educational placement than the other two groups, which did not differ from each other. A second evaluation when Group I children averaged 13 years of age showed

---

TABLE 12.1	Procedures Used in Pivotal Response Training to Strengthen the Child's Motivation to Initiate and Respond to Environmental Stimuli

To Increase Motivation to Respond

   Child is permitted to select activities and objects.

   Tasks are varied.

   Reinforcement is given liberally to the child's attempts to respond.

   Natural reinforcers are employed.

   Opportunity is given to the child to use acquired responses as new ones are learned.

Child Is Taught to Respond to Multiple Cues in the Environment

Child Is Taught Self-Regulation

Child Is Taught to Initiate Behavior

Based on Koegel, Koegel, & McNerney, 2001.

TABLE 12.2	Treatment Stages in the Young Autism Project		
Stage	Length	Teaching Methods	Goals (Examples)
1. Establishing a teaching relationship	~2–4 weeks	Primarily discrete trial training (DTT)	Following directions such as "sit" or "come here," reducing interfering behaviors such as tantrums
2. Teaching foundational skills	~1–4 months	Primarily DTT	Imitating gross motor actions, identifying objects, dressing, beginning play with toys
3. Beginning communication	~6+ months	DTT, incidental teaching	Imitating speech sounds, expressively labeling objects, receptively identifying actions and pictures, expanding self-help and play skills
4. Expanding communication, beginning peer interaction	~12 months	DTT, incidental teaching, dyads with typical peers	Labeling colors and shapes, beginning language concepts such as big/little and yes/no, beginning sentences such as "I see —," beginning pretend play and peer interaction
5. Advanced communication, adjusting to school	~12 months	DTT, incidental teaching, small group, regular education preschool	Conversing with others, describing objects and events, comprehending stories, understanding perspective of others, working independently, helping with chores

Adapted from Lovaas & Smith, 2003.

that they had maintained improvements over Group II youngsters (McEachin, Smith, & Lovaas, 1993). Eight of the nine Group I children who had done well at the first evaluation were holding their own in regular classrooms and approached normal functioning.

Although this outcome study had a stronger scientific design than most treatment studies at that time (Rogers, 1998), it received some criticism (Mundy, 1993; Rogers, 1998; Schopler, Short, & Mesibov, 1989). Since then, additional evaluations of behavioral programs similar to the Lovaas approach have described several benefits (Newsom & Hovanitz, 2006; Reichow & Wolery, 2009; Rogers & Vismara, 2008; Virués-Ortega, 2010). Some children "recovered" in that they attained IQs in the normal range and placement in typical age-level classrooms. Improved language skills, social behavior, and adaptive functioning have also been found. Not all children benefited from treatment, however, suggesting that the approach does not fit all children (Smith, 2010).

Indeed, limitations and evaluations of applied behavior interventions have been variously noted. Some investigators cite a need for better controlled studies that compare behavioral programs with specified other interventions (rather than "eclectic" programs). Nevertheless, the overall findings have made the behavioral approach a leading option for treatment. Drawing on evaluations of behavioral approaches—and also of psychoeducational interventions such as TEACCH, which is discussed in the next section—Schreibman's (2000) summary of the following well-established facts is informative.

- Intensive treatments—that is, treatments given for many hours a day and/or in many of the child's daily environments—can be extremely effective.
- Intervention when children are very young has the potential for significant gains.
- Effective treatments are associated with carefully controlled learning situations.
- Effective interventions must use techniques to promote generalization and maintenance of acquired learning (e.g., naturalistic teaching).
- When parents are trained to be major treatment providers, children are more likely to generalize and maintain their learning.
- Variation exists in outcome and different children may benefit from different approaches.

TEACCH: PSYCHOEDUCATIONAL TREATMENT AND SERVICES TEACCH, which stands for Treatment and Education of Autistic and related Communication handicapped Children, is a university-based statewide program in North Carolina mandated by law to provide services, research, and training for autism and related disorders (Schopler, 1997). The approach has evolved over several decades as an alternative to a psychoanalytic-based approach used in the 1960s at the University of North Carolina. From the beginning, families played a critical role in developing TEACCH, and priority was given to three areas: home adjustment, education, and community adaptation. A clear philosophy and set of values emerged over the years, which included formal assessment for individualized treatment, teaching new skills through cognitive and behavior theory, parent-professional collaboration, and a holistic orientation to deal with the whole situation.

The TEACCH Autism Program operates regional centers that provide individual assessment, training for parents to serve as cotherapists for their children, family support, employment support for older persons with autism, consultation, professional training, and collaboration with other relevant agencies. TEACCH affiliates with hundreds of North Carolina classrooms, and offers training for teachers. Students are enrolled in the classrooms after they are assessed by TEACCH and receive an individualized educational plan. Parents and professionals also collaborate on educating the wider community about autism and on developing additional community services. In recent years, the program has collaborated with other university programs and investigators examining such areas as the genetics, neurology, and epidemiology of ASD (TEACCH Autism Program, 2011).

TEACCH has been evaluated in various ways (Ozonoff & Cathcart, 1998; Schopler, 1994; 1997). Although there are weaknesses in the outcome studies, including lack of control groups (Smith, 1999), as a broad psychoeducational approach TEACCH has been recognized for excellence and implemented across the United States and in Europe.

EDUCATIONAL OPPORTUNITIES ASD is among the disabilities included in the Individuals with Disabilities Education Act (IDEA). School districts are obliged to identify children with ASD, provide services from birth, include families in evaluation and intervention, and deliver appropriate educational programs. Commitment

The successful teaching of children with autism usually requires special strategies and intensive interaction.

to the least restrictive placements and school inclusion has diminished institutionalization and has increased educational opportunities for children with autism.

Perhaps unsurprising, full school inclusion is an issue regarding the education of children with ASD (Rogers & Vismara, 2008). It is argued that the marked differences in abilities in persons with autism require alternative educational settings, including special classrooms with special services. Concern also is expressed that inclusion in regular classrooms puts children with ASD at risk for peer rejection and unfavorable social and emotional outcomes (Jones & Fredrickson, 2010). There is evidence that many mainstreamed children with high functioning ASD have relatively fewer reciprocal friendships and poorer quality friendships (Kasari et al., 2011). On the other hand, it is argued that typically developing peers can be active participants in intervention and otherwise model socially appropriate behavior. It does appear that some children with autism can benefit from inclusion (Rogers & Vismara, 2008; White et al., 2007). However, critical questions require further examination: What factors predict successful integration into mainstream classrooms? and Do some children benefit from alternative school settings and, if so, which settings best advantage which students?

In the broader schemes of things, support to families is essential as they experience many challenges making their way through the complexities of acquiring the best educational services for their child and otherwise rearing a child with disabilities (Schieve et al., 2007). Also important are postschool services that promote independent functioning and quality of life for youth with ASD. A recent study revealed that almost 40% of young adults with autism received no services during the first few years after high school (Shattuck et al., 2011). Much progress has been made in improving the lives of youth with ASD, due to both rigorous research and the commitment and advocacy of families and professionals alike, but sustained efforts are crucial.

SCHIZOPHRENIA

As we noted at the beginning of this chapter, for many years the term *childhood schizophrenia* was applied to heterogeneous groups of children with certain severe impairments. Even after diagnostic confusion was reduced—for example, by defining autism as a distinct disorder—a fundamental question remained: Did schizophrenia appearing in children differ from adult schizophrenia or was it the same basic disorder with different manifestations at different times of life? By 1980, some consensus was reached that the essential features of schizophrenia hold across age, and the same basic diagnostic criteria were applied to individuals of all ages.

Thus, although our primary interest in this chapter is schizophrenia of young people, we consider adult-onset schizophrenia when it bears on this topic. In keeping with the clinical and research literature, our discussion often distinguishes between childhood-onset schizophrenia (COS), with onset usually defined as before age 13, and adolescent schizophrenia, which is viewed as more similar to adult-onset schizophrenia.

DSM Classification and Diagnosis

The DSM-5 places schizophrenia in the broad category of Schizophrenia Spectrum and Other Psychotic Disorders (American Psychiatric Association, 2013). The essential features of schizophrenia are:

hallucinations

delusions

disorganized speech

disorganized or catatonic behavior

negative symptoms.

For diagnosis, at least two of these features are required for a significant part of time during a 1-month period, with the presence of at least one of the first three symptoms above. Continuous signs of disorder must persist for at least 6 months. When onset occurs in childhood or adolescence, there must be failure to reach expected levels of interpersonal, academic, or occupational achievement.

The first four of these features, referred to as **positive symptoms**, indicate distortion or excess in normal functioning. **Hallucinations**, or erroneous perceptions, and **delusions**, or erroneous beliefs, are viewed as hallmarks of the psychosis of schizophrenia. **Disorganized speech**, which reflects thought disorder, is another critical feature. **Disorganized behavior** is manifested in many ways: inappropriate silliness, unexpected agitation or aggression, lack of self-care, and the like. **Catatonic behaviors** are motor disturbances, such as decreased or excessive motor reactivity, and rigid and strange bodily postures.

Individuals with schizophrenia also may display **negative symptoms**, that is, a diminution or lack of normally occurring behaviors. Thus they may exhibit little emotion (flat affect), their speech may consist of brief replies that do not seem to convey much information (alogia), or they may neither initiate nor maintain goal-directed actions (avolition).

The diagnosis of youth with schizophrenia is reasonably reliable (Hollis, 2008), but the strong emphasis on positive symptoms, such as hallucinations and delusions, has implication for very young children. Early

developmental level may not lend itself to these psychotic manifestations, nor to such symptoms being reported by the child or being reliably assessed. In fact, few cases are diagnosed before age 10.

Description: Primary and Secondary Features

HALLUCINATIONS   Hallucinations are false perceptions that occur in the absence of identifiable stimuli. Individuals experiencing hallucinations report hearing, seeing, or smelling things that others do not hear, see, or smell. Such perceptual abnormalities can vary in content and in complexity. For example, simple hallucinations are indistinct shapes or sounds, whereas complex hallucinations are more organized, such as identifiable figures or voices (Volkmar et al., 1995).

Table 12.3 shows some of the symptoms of four samples of children diagnosed with schizophrenia, including the hallucinations they reported. Auditory hallucinations were the most common; visual hallucinations were reported fairly often. These findings are in keeping with studies of adolescents and adults with schizophrenia. The following examples of hallucinations were drawn from the accounts of a study with 9-year-olds (Russell, Bott, & Sammons, 1989).

Auditory: The kitchen light said to do things and "shut up."

Visual: A ghost with a red, burned, scarred face was seen several times in different places.

Command: A man's voice said "murder your stepfather" and "go play outside."

Persecutory: Monsters said that the child is "stupid" and that they will hurt him.

DELUSIONS   Delusions are false beliefs that are maintained even in the face of realistic contradiction. They vary in content. For example, delusions of persecution involve beliefs of impending harm from someone, whereas delusions of reference involve inaccurate beliefs that certain events or objects have particular significance. Delusions can also be simple or complex, and fragmented or organized. As shown in Table 12.3, delusions occurred quite consistently in the majority of the children diagnosed with schizophrenia. The following are examples (Russell et al., 1989).

Persecutory: A child believed his father had escaped jail and was coming to kill him.

Somatic: A child believed that a boy and a girl spirit lived inside his head.

| TABLE 12.3 | Some Features of Childhood Schizophrenia in Four Studies |

				Percent of Cases Showing Symptoms			
	Mean Age	Male: Female	Mean IQ	Hallucinations		Delusions	Thought Disorder
				Auditory	Visual		
Kolvin et al., 1971 N = 33	≈11.1	2.66:1	86	82	30	58	60
Green et al., 1992 N = 38	9.58	2.17:1	86	84	47	55	100
Russell et al., 1989 N = 35	9.54	2.2:1	94	80	37	63	40
Volkmar et al., 1988 N = 14	≈7.86	2.5:1	82	79	28	86	93

Adapted from Green et al., 1992; Russell et al., 1989; and Volkmar, 1991.

Bizarre: A boy was convinced he was a dog and growing fur. One time he refused to leave a veterinarian's office unless he got a shot.

Grandiose: A boy had the firm belief that he was different and able to kill people. He believed that when God zoomed through him, he became strong.

THOUGHT DISORDER   Delusions are a disturbance in the content of thought, but the form of thinking is also distorted in schizophrenia. Thought disorder involves difficulties in organizing thoughts and is reflected in disorganized speech. There are several indications of thought disorder. The person may display loose associations, that is, jump from topic to topic with no obvious connection between topics. Speech may be illogical, incoherent, and incomprehensible to others. It may also convey little information because it is vague, too abstract or concrete, or repetitive. It may include neologisms, made-up words that are meaningless to others. Thought disorder is suggested in this excerpt from an interview with a 7-year-old boy:

> I used to have a Mexican dream. I was watching TV in the family room. I disappeared outside of this world and then I was in a closet. Sounds like a vacuum dream. It's a Mexican dream. When I was close to that dream earth I was turning upside down. I don't like to turn upside down. Sometimes I have Mexican dreams and vacuum dreams. It's real hard to scream in dreams. (Russell et al., 1989, p. 404)

Thought disorder has been reported in high percentages of cases of COS but with varying rates (Table 12.3). Perhaps these differences are real, but they may also be due to difficulty in identifying disorganized speech and thinking (Asarnow & Kernan, 2008).

SECONDARY FEATURES   Among the secondary features associated with COS are motor abnormalities that include awkwardness, delayed milestones, poor coordination, and peculiar posture (Eggers, 1978; Nicolson & Rapoport, 2000; Watkins, Asarnow, & Tanguay, 1988). In addition, minor physical abnormalities (MPAs)—irregularities of the face, head, hand, and feet—occur at elevated rates in schizophrenia (Weinberg et al., 2007).

Impaired communication is common (McClellan et al., 2001). For example, when asked a question, children with schizophrenia may be less likely to give any reply, and when they do reply, they may be less likely to give information to supplement their simple answers (Abu-Akel et al., 2000). These children also use fewer conjunctions and other speech forms to connect ideas (Caplan et al., 2000). Atypical features such as echolalia and neologisms may be present.

A general cognitive deficit is reflected in intelligence test scores. Many children with schizophrenia score in the low average or borderline range on IQ tests; perhaps 10 to 20% of cases show significant impairment (McClellan, 2005). A pattern of deterioration around the time of onset of psychosis, followed by stability, has been observed. One study found that test scores declined from about 2 years before onset of psychotic symptoms to about 1.7 years after onset of psychotic symptoms, with no further deterioration found up to the 13 years examined (Gochman et al., 2005).

Consonant with general cognitive impairments, neuropsychological and other evaluations indicate specific deficits in COS and adolescent schizophrenia, for example, on tasks of attention, memory, abstraction, and executive functions (Cervellione et al., 2007; Kumra et al., 2000; Ross et al., 2005). Many deficits are generally similar to those of adult schizophrenia (Reichenberg & Harvey, 2007), but are reported to be more severe (Frazier et al., 2007).

Emotional and social impairments also are evident in COS. Some reflect the flat affect and lack of social interest—the negative symptoms—that reportedly are more common in early-onset than adulthood-onset schizophrenia (Hollis, 2002). Social problems include shyness, withdrawal, isolation, and ineptness (Bettes & Walker, 1987; Eggers, Bunk, & Krause, 2000; Watkins et al., 1988). In addition, inappropriate emotion, moodiness, anxiety, and depression have been reported (e.g., Green et al., 1992; Prior & Werry, 1986).

Epidemiology

The prevalence of schizophrenia in children is not established, but the disorder is considered rare. Schizophrenia appears in 1% or less of the general population. It is estimated that no more than 1% of all these cases occurs before 10 years of age, and 4% before the age of 15 (McClellan, 2005). Onset climbs during adolescence into early adulthood, and generally peaks from about age 15 to 30. Childhood schizophrenia appears more common in boys, with the sex ratio becoming nearly equal in adolescence (Asarnow & Kernan, 2008).

COS may occur at higher rates in less educated and less professionally successful families; however, the data are mixed and may be biased by reliance on hospital samples (McClellan et al., 2001). In adulthood, schizophrenia is more prevalent in the lower socioeconomic classes and in urban settings (Brown, Bresnahan, & Susser, 2005). It also is observed in cultures all over the world, with similar symptom profiles.

Developmental Course

The onset of schizophrenia in childhood is likely to be gradual, or **insidious**, with only 5% of cases being acute (Asarnow & Kernan, 2008). Nonpsychotic symptoms occur prior to psychotic symptoms and diagnosis. Early premorbid characteristics include delays and aberrations in language, motor, sensory, and cognitive functions—as well as social withdrawal, peer difficulties, school problems, and "odd" personality (Asarnow, Tompson, & McGrath, 2004; Brennan & Walker, 2010; McClellan et al., 2003; Nicolson & Rapoport, 2000).

As we might expect, developmental level makes its way into children's symptoms, including psychotic experiences

(Eggers, 1978; Russell et al., 1989). Early hallucinations are likely to include animals, toys, and monsters, and to be simple. Similarly, when delusions first appear, they are quite simple (e.g., a monster wants to kill me), and then they gradually become more elaborate, complex, abstract, and systematized. These changes are in keeping with cognitive and socioemotional development (Volkmar, 1996b).

Adolescent onset of schizophrenia seems not to be as insidious as child onset. Many diagnosed adolescents nonetheless have histories of attention, motor-perceptual, and other neurodevelopmental problems as well as worry, shyness, moodiness, and aggression. This picture is more similar to adulthood-onset schizophrenia, in which there is considerable variation in the timing, severity, and nature of early features (Rossi et al., 2000). The psychotic symptoms exhibited by adolescents also are more similar to those seen in adults. For instance, persecutory and grandiose delusions are more common than in child cases, and delusions are more complex and systematized (Volkmar et al., 1995).

In general, variation has been reported in the course of schizophrenia, that is, some persons have a chronic condition, some experience episodes of difficulties that come and go, and still others partially or fully recover. Poor adjustment before onset, insidious onset, an extended initial psychotic episode, negative symptoms, and a longer time lapse before treatment predict poor outcome of schizophrenia (Hollis, 2002). From studies of children and adolescents, it appears that about one-fifth has good outcome with mild impairments, and one-third remains severely impaired (Hollis, 2008). Early age of onset is associated with severe symptoms and cognitive impairments (Frazier et al., 2007), as well as poor outcome. Figure 12.8 shows the severity of symptoms in youths compared to adults with the disorder.

Child and adolescent schizophrenia carries a higher than usual risk for premature death, as does adulthood-onset schizophrenia (Hollis, 2008; Meltzer et al., 2003). This outcome appears to be due to a mix of causes, such as undetected medical conditions, suicide, and other violent events. The case description of Mary depicts childhood-onset schizophrenia that terminated in tragedy.

Neurobiological Abnormalities

Nervous system abnormalities have been revealed for schizophrenia and linked with several brain regions. Many findings come from adult cases and from children at high risk who were diagnosed in adolescence or adulthood, but important studies also have been conducted with children diagnosed with the disorder. The findings are notably similar across age groups. Neurobiological dysfunction is suggested by general symptoms of children with schizophrenia, such as motor delay, coordination problems, and

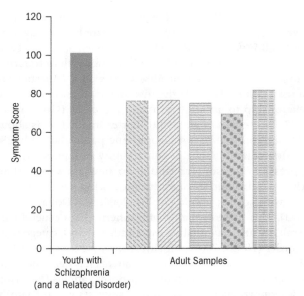

FIGURE 12.8 Comparison of the severity of symptoms in youth with schizophrenia (and a related disorder) and samples of adults with schizophrenia. *From Frazier et al., 2007.*

minor physical abnormalities. More direct evidence comes from brain imaging and postmortem studies.

Regarding the structure of the brain, neurons sometimes appear abnormal and in abnormal locations. Neurons appear densely packed and with fewer synaptic processes and connections. A common finding is enlargement of the brain's fluid-filled lateral ventricles, which has been found across age groups, including children (Brennan & Walker, 2010). In contrast, small volume of brain tissue often has been found, particularly in the frontal and temporal-limbic areas (Lawrie et al., 2008; Via et al., 2011). Brain abnormalities have been reported early in the course of the disorder (Price et al., 2010). Moreover, reduced brain volume and enlarged ventricles generally have been associated with negative symptoms, poor adjustment before diagnosis, and neuropsychological deficits (Buchanan & Carpenter, 2000; Davis et al., 2003; Gur et al., 1998).

Of special interest to our discussion are brain imaging studies with youths enrolled in a comprehensive ongoing National Institute of Mental Health investigation of COS. Gray matter loss was shown to occur early in the parietal lobe and later in adolescence in the frontal and temporal lobes (Gogtay, 2007). Interestingly, the progression of loss mirrors the back-to-front pattern of brain development in healthy youth.

In a study of white matter, comparison was made between 14-year-olds with childhood onset schizophrenia and matched healthy youths. MRI images were obtained annually for 4.5 years (Gogtay et al., 2008). For those with

MARY

A Tragic Course of Childhood Schizophrenia

Mary had always been a very shy child. She would become mute at times, had severe difficulties making friends, was frequently oppositional, and had occasional enuresis. By the time she reached roughly 10 years of age, Mary showed academic difficulties in addition to continuing social isolation. She became depressed, felt that the devil was trying to make her do bad things, believed that her teacher was trying to hurt her, and was preoccupied with germs. Her behavior became increasingly disorganized. She talked of killing herself, appeared disheveled, and ran in front of a moving car in an apparent suicide attempt.

This episode precipitated an inpatient psychiatric evaluation, during which Mary continued to show bizarre behavior.... Although Mary's functioning improved during hospitalization and she returned to her family, throughout her childhood and adolescent years she was tormented by fears, hallucinations, the belief that others were out to get her, and occasional bouts of depression often accompanied by suicide attempts. She continued to be socially isolated and withdrawn, and to perform poorly in school. At age 17 (after several brief inpatient hospitalizations), Mary was admitted to a state hospital, where she remained until the age of 19. During this period her affect was increasingly flat, and her psychotic symptoms persisted. One week after discharge from the hospital, Mary went into her room, locked the door, and overdosed on her medications. She was found dead the next morning.

Adapted from Asarnow & Asarnow, 2003, p. 455.

COS, significantly slower growth was seen each year in the frontal, parietal, and occipital lobes, especially in the right hemisphere. This occured in the same pattern as white tissue growth in typically developing youth—that is, front-to-back. This disturbance in maturation implicated myelination of fibers and connectivity of brain regions. Important in this and other studies was the finding that brain growth was correlated with measures of clinical functioning (Figure 12.9).

Brain anomalies have been demonstrated in other ways. Brain activity has been examined with various types

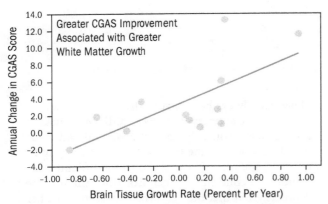

FIGURE 12.9 The relationship between a measure of clinical functioning (CGAS) and brain tissue growth. *From Gogtag et al., 2008.*

of scans. The findings indicate a complex picture of under- and overactivity in different brain regions and on different tasks (Lawrie et al., 2008).

Research conducted over many years indicates that dopamine dysregulation plays a role in schizophrenia (Howes & Kapur, 2009). Dopamine is important in several cerebral pathways, including the frontal and temporal–limbic areas. This neurotransmitter is blocked by medications that relieve psychosis, and substances that increase dopamine worsen symptoms of schizophrenia. Nevertheless, other neurotransmitters are implicated. Second-generation antipsychotic medications strongly impede serotonin. The possible roles of glutamate and GABA, which are important in cerebral functioning, are being investigated. It appears that numerous complex transmitter dysfunctions might exist.

What is to be made of the various findings about the brain? Taken together, the evidence suggests that several brain areas and neurotransmitters, functioning in complex ways, are central in schizophrenia. Structural, functional, and biochemical studies suggest that the disorder involves abnormalities in the connections among parts of a distributed network, predominately of frontal and temporal–limbic circuits (Asarnow & Kernan, 2008).

Etiology

Given the evidence for brain abnormalities, etiological hypotheses and investigations have sought to explain both their origins and how they might account for schizophrenia. Again, there is a disproportionate amount of research for adulthood-onset, but increased study of youth with schizophrenia.

GENETIC FACTORS Extensive research conducted in several countries on adult-onset schizophrenia suggests heritability as high as 80% (Wray & Visscher, 2010). Twin data show greater concordance in identical than fraternal pairs—on average, about 59% versus 14% (Asarnow & Kernan, 2008). Risk for the disorder increases as genetic relationship to an adult proband increases (Gottesman, 1993; Mortensen et al., 1999). For example, risk is about 12% for children of a schizophrenic parent but only 2% for first cousins. Genetic vulnerability in families is also expressed in disorders similar to but less severe than schizophrenia and in cognitive processing deficits associated with schizophrenia (Hollis, 2008; MacDonald et al., 2003). This suggests that what is inherited is a general vulnerability and quantitative traits rather than a category of disorder (Hollis, 2008). Finally, risk for schizophrenia-like disorders in the parents of COS patients has been found to be higher than for parents of adult-onset patients (Nicolson & Rapoport, 2000). This finding suggests greater family vulnerability in COS.

No single gene with substantial effect has been found, and it is generally believed that multiple genes with small to moderate effects are involved. Research of COS has replicated the presence of a few of the susceptibility genes found in adult-onset schizophrenia (Addington & Rapoport, 2009). The identified susceptibility genes, located on several chromosomes, are associated with brain structure and function consistent with what is known about schizophrenia (Brennan & Walker, 2010). For example, the COMT gene (chromosome 22) is implicated in dopamine regulation, the DISC gene (chromosome 1) in reduced brain matter, and the NRD1 gene (chromosome 8) in neuron migration and connectivity.

In addition, genome-wide studies have revealed rare copy number variations—that is, deletions and duplications of genes sequences—at rates much higher than in a comparison group. Finally, there is evidence for epigenetic processes (James et al., 2008). Roth and Sweatt (2011) reported as many as 100 relevant gene locations showing epigenetic change, that is, altered methylation. As they speculate, epigenetic changes initiated in early prenatal or postnatal life could predispose the development of schizophrenia.

The involvement of several genes and several processes creates a complex etiological picture, but genetic influences may not tell the entire story. The fact that so many identical cotwins of adults with schizophrenia do not have schizophrenia suggests that non-genetic influences likely play some role. Twin studies indicate small but significant shared environmental influences, which could include early exposure to toxins, infections, and prenatal influences

(Sullivan, Kendler, & Neale, 2003; Wray & Visscher, 2010). Some environmental effects may operate independently of genetic influence; for example, perhaps some prenatal factors directly affect the brain (Brennan & Walker, 2010). Other environmental effects likely act in conjunction with genes, such as in epigenetic effects and gene-environment interactions.

PRENATAL FACTORS AND PREGNANCY COMPLICATIONS Prenatal adversities are sometimes linked to child and adult schizophrenia. Among these are malnutrition and infectious agents. Famines in Holland and China increased the risk of schizophrenia in individuals conceived or in early gestation during the times of famine (Xu et al., 2009). Regarding prenatal infection, interesting results came from a study of Finnish women who had been exposed in pregnancy to influenza virus during an epidemic (Mednick et al., 1988). Children whose mothers had been exposed during the second trimester of pregnancy had a greater risk for eventually developing schizophrenia. Some additional studies have replicated risk from influenza, whereas others have not (Brown et al., 2005; Marenco & Weinberger, 2000; Selten et al., 2010). Additional research has implicated the exposure of the fetus to bacterial infections (Sørensen et al., 2009).

Numerous complications of pregnancy and birth have been associated with schizophrenia, for example, bleeding during pregnancy and emergency cesarean birth (Asarnow & Kernan, 2008; Brown et al., 2005). In fact, birth complications, particularly those in which the infant is deprived of oxygen, have shown a stronger association with schizophrenia relative to other environmental factors (Cannon & Rosso, 2002). Birth complications have been associated with enlarged brain ventricles (Brennan & Walker, 2010). Nonetheless, it is difficult to draw firm conclusions from these findings. Obstetrical complications may cause schizophrenia, but could also result from fetuses already abnormal due to genetic or prenatal factors. The interaction of genetic and obstetric factors must also be considered. Indeed, evidence exists that serious obstetric complications interact with specific genes to affect the risk of schizophrenia (Nicodemus et al., 2008).

PSYCHOSOCIAL INFLUENCES There is reason to believe that psychosocial stress could contribute to schizophrenia in youths. For adult-onset schizophrenia, adverse life events (stress) have been found to increase in the weeks prior to symptom occurrence (Fowles, 1992), and increased stress hormones have been related to subclinical manifestations of schizophrenia (Evans et al., 2005).

Psychosocial stress also has been linked to worsening of symptoms (Docherty et al., 2008). Moreover, stress during the prenatal period has been associated with increased psychopathology, including schizophrenia, in offspring. In addition, in a study of at-risk adolescents, those who went on to develop schizophrenia had a more dramatic increase in cortisol compared to those who did not develop the disorder (Brennan & Walker, 2010).

Family characteristics have long been suspected of causing schizophrenia. Indeed, the phrase "schizophrenogenic mothering" was once used to capture the idea that pathological parenting was the basic cause of the condition. Although that hypothesis currently is given no credence, there has been vacillating interest in the role of family interaction.

Limited research with adoptees has implicated family processes. The possible influence of family climate was shown in the Finnish Adoption Study, which examined adopted children of mothers with schizophrenia or related disorders and a comparison adopted group whose mothers had no such diagnoses (Tienari, Wynne, & Wahlberg, 2006; Tienari et al., 1990). Ratings of the functioning of the adoptive families permitted analysis of the rearing environment. The findings indicated that the genetically at-risk adoptees who later developed schizophrenia and related disorders had been reared in families with disturbed relationships. Also suggested was that low genetic risk served as protection against negative family climate, thereby implicating gene-environment interaction.

NEURODEVELOPMENTAL MODEL Present knowledge about schizophrenia has led to the proposal that etiology involves multiple factors. A vulnerability-stress model is often invoked as a general framework. It assumes that an organismic vulnerability, probably genetic but possibly prenatal, interacts with environmental stress to produce somewhat different developmental paths and outcomes. Some individuals reach a threshold to exhibit diagnosable schizophrenic symptoms or similar but less severe symptoms, whereas others do not.

The last few decades have seen growing interest in and support for the neurodevelopmental model of schizophrenia (Bearden et al., 2006; Brennan & Walker, 2010; Weinberger & McClure, 2002). Indeed, much of the research we examined supports such a perspective. According to this model, early development of the brain goes awry, affecting critical brain circuits (Figure 12.10). Early development is marked by premorbid difficulties, such as motor and language problems, and increased difficulties occur in cognitive, social, and psychological function. In most cases

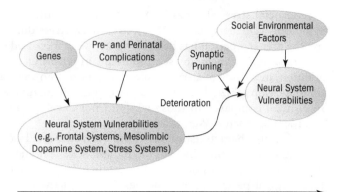

FIGURE 12.10 A neurodevelopmental model of schizophrenia. *From Bearden et al., 2006.*

of schizophrenia, the core psychotic symptoms are manifested when the brain further matures in adolescence or early adulthood. Investigators have pointed to numerous changes occurring in the hormonal and brain systems during adolescence that could "enable" expression of the disorder (Marenco & Weinberger, 2000). Of particular interest is that late adolescence is an important time for selective pruning of the synapses in the frontal lobes and association areas. It is hypothesized that excessive pruning at this time is related to the appearance of symptoms. Although brain changes are viewed as biological, it is well established that social environmental influences interact with biological factors to produce development.

The exact way or extent to which the neurodevelopmental model applies to childhood schizophrenia is unclear. As we have seen, numerous similarities between early-onset and late-onset schizophrenia strongly suggest that they are not different disorders. However, there is evidence that COS involves more severe symptoms, less favorable outcome, and greater family vulnerability. This suggests that greater genetic liability or greater biological vulnerability, perhaps combined with greater environmental adversity, may produce the disorder so early in life.

Assessment

The following categories can serve as a guide for comprehensive assessment for suspected child or adolescent schizophrenia (Hollis, 2008; McClellan et al., 2001; Volkmar, 1996b):

- Historical information, including data on pregnancy complications, early development, age of onset, course of symptoms, and medical and family history.

- Assessment for the positive and negative symptoms of schizophrenia and associated features.
- Psychological assessment that includes evaluation of intelligence, communication, and adaptive skills.
- Physical examination, as well as EEGs, brain scans, and laboratory tests, as needed in some cases.
- Consultation with the school and social services as necessary.

Although early identification can facilitate appropriate treatment, it presents particular challenges. The early-occurring nonpsychotic behavioral maladjustments of schizophrenia are observed in other disorders as well. In addition, children with other disorders—such as bipolar disorder and major depression—relatively often report hallucinations (Shaw & Rapoport, 2006). Indeed, children with schizophrenia may initially receive diagnoses of PDD, ADHD, mood disorders, and anxiety disorders, among others (Schaeffer & Ross, 2002).

As previously noted, it may be difficult to identify the positive symptoms of schizophrenia in children. Standardized rating scales and semi-structured interviews can be helpful. Nevertheless, children in nonclinic and clinic populations report seeing ghosts or shapes, hearing voices, and the like—and such hallucinations often do not indicate psychosis (McGee, Williams, & Poulton, 2000; Mertin & Hartwig, 2004; Vickers & Garralda, 2000). Similarly, it can be difficult to tell whether bizarre ideas, obsessions, and preoccupations reported by the young should be considered psychotic delusions. This is especially true in children younger than 5 or 6, who are still limited in thinking logically and in distinguishing reality from fantasy (Volkmar et al., 1995). In addition, assessment of thought disorder has been especially difficult. It can be affected by a child's language skills, which are crucial in evaluating thinking processes. Moreover, what is considered abnormal thinking varies with developmental level (Caplan, 1994; Caplan et al., 2000).

Assessment of adolescents, especially older adolescents, is less problematic than that of children. Psychotic symptoms appear more similar to those of adult-onset schizophrenia, although they do not always indicate full-blown schizophrenia (Altman, Collins, & Mundy, 1997; Mertin & Hartwig, 2004). Psychotic symptoms at this time of life can be associated with several disorders, including substance abuse, epilepsy, and mood disorders (Calderoni et al., 2001; McClellan et al., 2003; Ulloa et al., 2000). Thus, manifestations of psychosis must be interpreted within the broader clinical presentation.

Prevention

Although considerable interest exists in prevention, limited knowledge about etiology hinders progress. The association of schizophrenia with prenatal and birth complications suggests the advisability of special care during pregnancy, especially in high-risk families. Similarly, increased sensitivity to early cognitive deficits, poor social functioning (Tarbox & Pogue-Geile, 2008), and behavior problems with the approach of adolescence may be helpful in early identification (Rajji, Ismail, & Mulsant, 2009).

Early identification and treatment generally are associated with improved outcome for schizophrenia, and the insidious onset that occurs in many youths presents a window of opportunity for preventive efforts. Currently, there is considerable interest in recognizing a "risk syndrome" for individuals who appear to be at very high risk and are displaying attenuated symptoms (Nelson & Yung, 2011). Persons so identified have been shown to develop the onset of psychosis at higher rates than the general population. Nonetheless, identifying young people, especially very young children, who are at risk for transition into psychosis is problematic. Many of the early problems of youths who eventually are diagnosed with schizophrenia are evident in other young people. Further, even adolescents and adults whose symptoms put them at very high risk often show remission and/or do not eventually progress to full-blown schizophrenia (McGorry, Killackey, & Yung, 2008; Ziermans et al., 2011). Despite this dilemma—and the peril of stigmatizing or medicating youths who are falsely identified—some investigations are committed to early intervention. In the words of McGorry and colleagues, "Withholding treatment until severe and less reversible symptomatic and functional impairment have become entrenched represents a failure of care" (McGorry et al., 2008, p. 148). Early intervention aims to delay, attenuate, or even prevent schizophrenia.

Intervention

As with other aspects of early-occurring schizophrenia, we must generalize from what is known about treatment of adults. Treatment can vary substantially, depending on the severity of the case, whether the case is in an acute or a chronic phase, available opportunities for intervention, and community/family support. Many children and adolescents with the disorder may live at home and attend local schools (Frazier et al., 2007). Among those with severe disturbance, some remain at home and may attend special schools; others are placed in hospitals and other residential settings for periods of time. It is believed that the best treatment strategy employs multiple methods to alleviate the multiple problems frequently encountered.

PHARMACOLOGICAL TREATMENT Traditional antipsychotic and second-generation antipsychotic agents are central in treating schizophrenia. In adults and youths, they can alleviate hallucinations, delusions, thought disturbance, and other symptoms—although not all individuals respond to antipsychotic medications. Second-generation antipsychotic medications (e.g., risperidone, clozapine, olanzapine) are widely used as they have fewer side effects. But these medications do have some adverse side effects, which may impact youths more than adults (Correll et al., 2009). Among these are weight gain, sedation, and elevated cholesterol and triglyceride levels. Clozapine, which appears especially effective for children and adolescents, carries greater risk for serious adverse side effects and thus warrants cautious use (Kreyenbuhl et al., 2010). In addition to some medications being somewhat risky in themselves, adverse side effects may lead young people to discontinue treatment, which is associated with relapse of symptoms (Finding et al., 2010).

PSYCHOSOCIAL INTERVENTION Medications largely aim at reducing psychotic symptoms, whereas psychosocial treatment encompasses broader objectives. Among the approaches that are ameliorative or most promising are skills training, behavioral-cognitive therapy, and family approaches (Kern et al., 2009; Kreyenbuhl et al., 2010).

The goal of skills training is to increase social and daily living skills through instruction, modeling, positive reinforcement, and other behavioral techniques. Behavioral-cognitive therapy recognizes that the symptoms of schizophrenia—particularly hallucinations and delusions—interfere with social functioning and aims to temper these symptoms or facilitate coping with them. Family therapy is an accepted strategy for adults that is likely to be critical for youth. Today's family interventions are fueled by a collaborative philosophy in which blame is not placed on families, as it sometimes was in the past (Asarnow et al., 2004). Table 12.4 indicates some of the major components of family therapy.

Over the last two decades there has been an increase in approaches to treating cognitive deficits that commonly occur in schizophrenia, such as deficits in memory, attention, speed of processing, and problem solving (Kern et al., 2009). Computer-based programs are frequently employed to enhance cognition and are encouraging. An additional newer approach is social cognition training, which seeks

TABLE 12.4	Major Components of Family Interventions for Schizophrenia

Education about schizophrenia (e.g., causal hypotheses, course, treatments)

Enhancing strategies for coping with schizophrenia

Training in family communication emphasizing clarity and feedback tactics

Training in problem solving; managing everyday situations and stress

Crisis intervention during severe stress and/or signs of relapse of the disorder

Adapted from Asarnow, Tompson, & McGrath, 2004.

to improve the perception and understanding of the social world (e.g., of emotion and theory of mind).

A comprehensive approach and a supportive environment are recommended for treating schizophrenia (American Psychological Association, 2006). For young people, disruption of normal development must be addressed (McClellan et al., 2001). Thus treatment must include not only the reduction of specific symptoms but also the facilitation of psychological, social, educational, and occupational development. Since youths with schizophrenia may require relatively intensive home and community services that include the schools (Schiffman & Daleiden, 2006), systematic case management and coordination is beneficial (Asarnow et al., 2004).

And as with other aspects of early-onset schizophrenia, the importance of research in advancing knowledge about the effectiveness of intervention can hardly be overstated. Fortunately, a more optimistic approach to treatment and prevention has been evident since the 1990s (McGorry et al., 2008). Schizophrenia is now viewed as more malleable, and evidence-based care has been promoted (Kreyenbuhl et al., 2010). The previous pessimistic focus on long-term disability has shifted to a more hopeful emphasis on recovery.

Overview/Looking Back

A BIT OF HISTORY

- Today autism spectrum disorder and schizophrenia of youth are viewed as distinct categories of disturbance but were historically associated with each other.

DSM: AUTISM SPECTRUM DISORDER

- Autism, Asperger's disorder, childhood disintegrative disorder, and pervasive developmental disorder not otherwise specified, once considered as distinct, are now widely viewed together as autism spectrum disorder.

AUTISTIC DISORDER (AUTISM)

- The core manifestations of autistic disorder are impaired social communication and interaction and restricted, repetitive behaviors and interests. Secondary features involve perception, intelligence, adaptive behavior, cognition, MPAs, and motor skills.
- Considerable research has been devoted to theory of mind, central coherence, and executive functions.
- Co-occurrence of autism or ASD, with or without intellectual disabilities, and other disorders is high and includes anxiety, depression, hyperactivity, and oppositional-defiant behaviors.

- The prevalence of autism or ASD has greatly increased in recent years. Methodological and social factors may at least partly account for increases. Prevalence is higher in boys and is unrelated to social class.
- Autistic symptoms are often recognized by age 2. Different patterns of onset and developmental pathways have been reported. From childhood onward, symptoms can lessen, but perhaps only 15% of youths with autism achieve independent living.
- Neurobiological research suggests that autism involves impairment in multiple brain areas or networks. Altered brain growth often is observed, and most implicated are the frontal lobe, temporal lobe–limbic system, and the cerebellum.
- The evidence for genetic influence is substantial and prenatal/birth complications may play some causal role. Dawson and Faja's developmental perspective gives importance to child-environment interactions. Research does not support a causal role for vaccines or thimerosal.
- Asperger's disorder, PDD-NOS, and childhood disintegrative disorders, once viewed as distinct disorders, are both similar and dissimilar to autism and each other.
- Assessment for autism and ASD must be broad based. Several valid instruments exist for the assessment of autistic symptoms.

- Early identification/intervention is critical in preventing maladaptive pathways to ASD. Behavioral and educational interventions are the mainstay of treatment and prevention, with medication as an adjunct. Autism falls under the mandates of the Individuals with Disabilities Education Act.

SCHIZOPHRENIA

- The hallmarks of schizophrenia are hallucinations, delusions, thought disorder, disorganized behavior, and negative symptoms. Secondary features include MPAs, impaired communication and cognition, motor abnormalities, and social dysfunction.
- The prevalence of schizophrenia is low in childhood and escalates in adolescence. Rates appear higher in males during childhood but the gender difference may flatten in adolescence.
- The onset of child schizophrenia often is insidious, with nonpsychotic symptoms appearing prior to psychotic symptoms. The course of schizophrenia can vary, but good outcome occurs only in 20% of cases of child- and adolescent-onset schizophrenia. Childhood schizophrenia is viewed as a severe form of the disorder.
- Neurobiological abnormalities in schizophrenia are evidenced in several ways. Frontal and temporal–limbic circuits and dopamine are especially implicated, and the disorder likely involves several regions, several neurotransmitters, and brain connectivity.
- Complex genetic influences, prenatal/birth variables, and psychosocial factors are causally implicated in schizophrenia. These multiple susceptibility factors are incorporated into neurodevelopmental models of the disorder.
- Comprehensive assessment is required for schizophrenia. It can be problematic to identify psychotic symptoms in children.
- Prevention is challenging and emphasis is on early intervention. A multimethod, supportive treatment approach is recommended, which includes antipsychotic medications and psychosocial treatments such as behavioral-cognitive therapy, social skills training, and family therapy.

Key Terms

joint attention *311*
echolalia *312*
pronoun reversal *312*
overselectivity *313*
splinter skills/savant abilities *313*
theory of mind *314*

central coherence *315*
intersubjectivity *315*
positive symptoms *330*
hallucinations *330*
delusions *330*
disorganized speech *330*

disorganized behavior *330*
catatonic behavior *330*
negative symptoms *330*
insidious onset *332*

CHAPTER 13

Disorders of Basic Physical Functions

LOOKING FORWARD

After reading this chapter, you should be able to discuss:

- Classification of the elimination disorders of enuresis and encopresis
- Etiology of elimination disorders and their treatment
- Common sleep problems and the description and classification of sleep disorders
- Treatment of sleep problems
- Early feeding and eating problems and disorders
- Influences on the development of and interventions for obesity
- The definition and classification of eating disorders
- The epidemiology and developmental course of anorexia nervosa and bulimia nervosa
- Biological, psychosocial, and cultural influences on the development of eating disorders
- Treatment and prevention of eating disordered behavior

In this chapter and the next we discuss problems of physical functioning and health. Because in many ways these problems represent the interface between psychology and pediatrics, the term *pediatric psychology* is often applied to this field of research and practice. For many of the problems discussed (e.g., toilet training, sleep difficulties), parents first turn to their pediatrician for help. Some problems may require collaboration between psychologists and physicians. The life-threatening starvation of adolescents with anorexia nervosa and the problem of enlarged colons in children with encopresis are two examples.

It is common for children to exhibit some difficulty in acquiring appropriate habits of elimination, sleep, and eating. Both the child's ability to master these relevant tasks and the parents' ability to assist the child in developing skills are important to the immediate well-being of both. Parents may be judged by themselves and others by how they manage these early child-rearing tasks. Also, how these tasks are handled can set the foundation for later interactions. Although parents solve many early difficulties themselves, they also frequently seek professional assistance. This chapter examines some commonly encountered difficulties that are part of normal development. The principal focus, however, is on problems that are serious enough to be of clinical concern.

PROBLEMS OF ELIMINATION

Typical Elimination Training

Toilet training is an important concern for parents of young children (Schroeder & Gordon, 2002). Parents may view control of elimination as a developmental milestone for the child. Furthermore, entry into day care or another program may depend on achievement of appropriate toileting. For the child, pleasing the parent, a sense of mastery, and the feeling of no longer being a "baby" may all contribute to the importance of achieving toileting control.

The usual sequence of acquisition of control over elimination is nighttime bowel control, daytime bowel control, daytime bladder control, and finally, nighttime bladder control. Although there is considerable variation as to when children are developmentally ready to achieve control over elimination, bowel and daytime bladder training usually are completed between the ages of 18 and 36 months.

Parents differ on when they feel it is appropriate to begin daytime training. Much of this decision is related to cultural values, attitudes, and real-life pressures on the parent (e.g., day care requirements, other siblings). An example of how day-to-day considerations probably affect this decision is illustrated by the advent of the disposable diaper. Ready availability of disposable diapers reduced many parents' inclinations to start training early.

There are probably several factors that contribute to successful training. Being able to determine that the child is developmentally ready to begin training is certainly important. Also, correctly judging when the child has to go to the toilet can lead to important early success experiences. Adequate preparation, such as using training pants rather than a diaper, having the child in clothes that are easy to remove, and having a child-size potty seat available are also helpful. Finally, the common practice of providing praise and concrete positive reinforcers (e.g., stickers, raisins) for appropriate toileting behavior, and doing so in a relaxed manner, has been demonstrated to be effective (Schroeder & Gordon, 2002).

Enuresis

DESCRIPTION AND CLASSIFICATION
The term **enuresis** comes from the Greek word meaning "I make water." It refers to the repeated voiding of urine during the day or night into the bed or clothes when such voiding is not due to a physical disorder (e.g., diabetes, urinary tract infection). A certain frequency of lack of control is required before the diagnosis of enuresis would be made, and the frequency employed typically varies with the age of the child. The DSM definition requires that wetting occur at least twice weekly for at

JAY

Enuresis and Its Consequences

Jay, a 7-year-old, had never achieved nighttime continence but had been continent during daytime for several years. He wets his bed an average of 4 days per week. No other significant behavior problems are present except for mild academic difficulties, and Jay's developmental history is unremarkable except for mild oxygen deprivation at birth and a delay in acquiring speech. Jay's biological father wet the bed until age nine.

Jay's mother and stepfather disagree on how they view his bedwetting. His mother feels he will grow out of it. His stepfather views Jay's bedwetting as laziness and removes privileges following episodes of enuresis. Both parents change the sheets when they are wet and attempt to restrict Jay's fluids prior to bedtime. They see the enuresis as a significant source of distress for the family and the conflict over how to handle it as exacerbating the problem.

Adapted from Ondersma & Walker, 1998, pp. 364–365.

least three consecutive months. The diagnosis of enuresis may also be made when wetting is less frequent if wetting is associated with clinically significant distress or impairment in important areas of functioning. A lack of urinary control is not usually diagnosed as enuresis prior to age 5 (or the equivalent developmental level). The age/developmental level of 5 is selected, as this is when continence might be expected (American Psychiatric Association [APA], 2013).

A distinction is typically made between the more common nighttime bedwetting and daytime wetting. Enuresis is also referred to as **primary** if the child has never demonstrated bladder control and as **secondary** when the problem is preceded by a period of urinary continence. About 85% of all cases of enuresis are of the nighttime wetting alone/primary type (Houts, 2010).

EPIDEMIOLOGY
Estimates of prevalence indicate that about 10% of school-age children exhibit enuresis. Prevalence declines steadily with age, and by age 18 prevalence decreases to 1% for males and less than 1% for females. The problem is at least twice as common among boys compared to girls (Campbell, Cox, & Borowitz, 2009; Houts, 2010).

ETIOLOGY
A number of factors have been proposed as causes of enuresis. At one time, enuresis was widely

believed to be the result of emotional disturbance (Gerard, 1939). However, evidence does not support the view that enuresis is primarily a psychopathological disorder. When emotional difficulties are present in a child with enuresis, they most commonly are a consequence of enuresis rather than a cause (Campbell et al., 2009). Parents of children with combined nighttime and daytime wetting may be particularly likely to report psychological problems in their children (Van Hoecke et al., 2006). Enuretic children, especially as they become older, are very likely to experience difficulties with peers and other family members. Also, enuresis and emotional problems may occur together because similar factors (e.g., a chaotic home environment) contribute to the development of both.

A maturational delay in the ability to recognize the sensation of a full bladder while asleep is the most common explanation for the development of enuresis. Other explanations are also sometimes offered.

It is sometimes suggested that sleep abnormalities contribute to the development of enuresis. Many adults, for example, assume that nocturnal enuresis occurs because the child is an unusually deep sleeper. Indeed, parents often spontaneously report difficulty in arousing their enuretic children during the night. However, research regarding the role of sleep and arousal is inconsistent (Mikkelsen, 2001). Wetting can occur in any of the stages of sleep, not just in deep sleep. This and other evidence raises doubts about viewing all or most cases of enuresis as a disorder of sleep arousal (Campbell et al., 2009). However, in some subgroups of youths, enuresis may, at least in part, be due to sleep arousal patterns.

Another biological pathway that has been suggested is reduced bladder capacity or higher production of urine due to a lack of normal nocturnal increases in antidiuretic hormone (ADH). Among evidence for this hypothesis is the fact that some enuretic children respond well to an antidiuretic medication (desmopressin acetate, a hormone analog). However, evidence is not consistent and does not support low levels of ADH as the only or the primary cause of enuresis, although it may be a factor in some cases (Mikkelsen, 2001).

Family histories of youths with enuresis frequently reveal a number of relatives with the same problem. Higher rates of concordance for enuresis also have been reported among monozygotic than dizygotic twins, and multigenerational studies further support the notion of a significant genetic contribution to the disorder. Specific gene loci are yet to be identified and it is likely that complex genetic and environmental interactions are involved (Butler, 2008; von Gontard et al., 2011).

Overall, information regarding biological influences strongly suggests that at least some number of enuretic children have an organic predisposition toward enuresis (Sethi, Bhargava, & Phil, 2005). This predisposition may or may not result in the development of enuresis, depending on various experiential factors, such as parental attitude and training procedures.

The central tenet of behavioral theories of enuresis is that wetting results from a failure to learn control over reflexive wetting. Failure can result from either faulty training or other environmental influences that interfere with learning (e.g., a chaotic or stressful home environment). Most behavioral theories incorporate some maturational delay/physical difficulty, such as bladder capacity or arousal deficit, into their explanation.

TREATMENT Prior to beginning any treatment, the child should be evaluated by a physician to rule out any medical cause for the urinary difficulties. If a parent seeks treatment for a very young child, a discussion of developmental norms may be helpful. Finally, if treatment for enuresis is to be initiated, careful preparation and parental cooperation are necessary.

A variety of pharmacological agents have been used in the treatment of enuresis. Desmopressin acetate (DDAVP) has become the primary pharmacological treatment for enuresis, in part because it may have a lower risk of side effects than other pharmacological agents. Desmopressin was suggested as a treatment on the basis of its ability to control high urine output during sleep. Research findings suggest that DDAVP may reduce bedwetting even in cases that are difficult to treat. However, relapse occurs; that is, wetting resumes if the drug is discontinued (Butler, 2008; Mikkelsen, 2001; Reiner, 2008).

Behavioral treatments for nocturnal enuresis have received considerable research attention (Houts, 2010). The most well-known method is the urine-alarm system. This procedure was originally introduced by the German pediatrician Pflaunder in 1904 and was adapted and systematically applied by Mowrer and Mowrer (1938). Since then, the device and the procedures have been refined by a number of investigators. The basic device consists of an absorbent sheet between two foil pads. When urine is absorbed by the sheet, an electric circuit is completed which activates an alarm that sounds until it is manually turned off (see Figure 13.1). The parents are instructed to awaken the child when the alarm sounds. The child is taught to turn off the alarm and to go to the bathroom to finish voiding. The bedding is then changed, and the child returns to sleep. Usually the family keeps records of dry and wet nights, and after 14 consecutive nights of dryness, the device is removed.

Research conducted on treatments using the urine-alarm system indicates that it is successful in a clear majority of cases and that it is the treatment of choice

FIGURE 13.1 A urine alarm for treatment of enuresis. The child wears a urine sensor in the underclothes attached to an alarm worn on the nightclothes or wrist.

for enuresis (APA, 2006). It is also more cost-effective than medications such as DDAVP (Houts, 2010). Relapse has been reported in about 40% of cases, but reinstituting training most often results in a complete cure (Christophersen & Mortweet, 2001; Houts, 2010).

Modifications of the standard urine-alarm procedures have been introduced to reduce relapses. Full Spectrum Home Training was designed to build on initial treatment success, to reduce relapse, and to decrease the rate at which families dropped out of treatment (Houts, 2010). The procedure, which is cost-effective, is a treatment manual–guided package that includes a urine-alarm system; cleanliness training (having the child change his or her own bed and night clothes); a procedure to increase bladder capacity, which is known as retention control training; and overlearning, a process of training children to a higher criterion of successive dry nights than is usually thought to be necessary. The training program is delivered in a single 90-minute group or individual session or two 1-hour sessions. The parents and children then contract to complete the training at home with regular calls from the treatment staff. Thirty-minute follow-up sessions are scheduled, as needed, and typically treatment is completed in a 16–20-week period.

A study by Houts, Peterson, and Whelan (1986) illustrated the program's success and examined the contribution of the components to reducing relapse. Participating families received one of three treatment combinations: Group 1 received the urine-alarm system plus cleanliness training (BP), Group 2 received these two components plus retention control training (BP-RCT), and Group 3 received these three components plus overlearning (BP-RCT-OL)—the full package. A control group of children was followed over an 8-week period. No spontaneous remission of wetting occurred in control children, and they were then randomly assigned to one of the three treatment conditions. The findings of this study indicate that the three conditions were equally effective in treating enuresis. However, at a 3-month follow-up, relapse was significantly less in the BP-RCT-OL group than in the other two groups. These results suggest the importance of overlearning in preventing relapse.

Encopresis

DESCRIPTION AND CLASSIFICATION Functional **encopresis** refers to the passage of feces into the clothing or other unacceptable area when this is not due to physical disorder. The diagnosis is given when this event occurs at least once a month, for at least 3 months, in a child of at least 4 years of age or the equivalent developmental level (APA, 2013). Two subtypes of encopresis are recognized on the basis of the presence or absence of constipation.

SUSAN

Encopresis and Its Consequences

Susan, a 6-year-old, had been soiling at least once per day since birth. The frequency of soiling had not decreased despite nearly constant attempts to convince her to use the toilet. Following careful medical examination, Susan's physician was certain that all medical causes for her condition had been ruled out. Tests, however, did reveal a considerable amount of fecal matter in her colon. During the course of the assessment, Susan's mother indicated that both she and her daughter were becoming very frustrated. It was also revealed that Susan was experiencing significant anxiety and pain with toileting. It appeared that Susan had learned to retain feces and to fear toileting following early experiences with large and painful bowel movements. The toileting problems had begun to affect Susan's social functioning and self-esteem.

Adapted from Ondersma & Walker, 1998, pp. 371–372.

The vast majority of encopretic children are chronically constipated and are classified as having constipation with overflow incontinence (or retentive encopresis).

EPIDEMIOLOGY   Estimates of the prevalence of encopresis range between 1.5 and 7.5% of children. Percentages appear to decrease with age, and the condition is very rare by adolescence. The problem occurs more frequently in males (Campbell et al., 2009; Walker, 2003).

Pediatricians, who are likely to see a broad population of children, argue that the majority of children with encopresis have no associated psychopathology, a position supported by other professionals (Campbell et al., 2009). However, because encopresis occurs during the day more often than at night, it is more socially evident than enuresis and also is more likely to carry a social stigma. Consequently, encopresis is likely to be a source of considerable distress to both parents and children, and may therefore be associated with more behavior problems. For example, children with encopresis who had been referred to a pediatric gastroenterology clinic were reported to have more behavior problems and lower social competence scores than children without toileting problems (Young et al., 1996). Following treatment, these children had fewer problems and improved social skills. To the extent that associated psychological difficulties do exist, they may be a consequence, rather than an antecedent, of encopresis, or both may be related to common environmental factors (e.g., stressful family circumstances).

ETIOLOGY   Most theories acknowledge that encopresis may result from a variety of causative mechanisms (Butler, 2008; Campbell et al., 2009; Reiner, 2008). Initial constipation and soiling may be influenced by factors such as diet, fluid intake, medications, environmental stresses, or inappropriate toilet training. The rectum and colon may become distended by the hard feces. The bowel then becomes incapable of responding with a normal defecation reflex to normal amounts of fecal matter.

Medical perspectives on the problem tend to stress a neurodevelopmental approach (Butler, 2008; Mikkelsen, 2001; Reiner, 2008). Encopresis is viewed as more likely to occur in the presence of developmental inadequacies in the structure and functioning of the physiological and anatomical mechanisms required for bowel control. These organic inadequacies are viewed as temporary.

A behavioral perspective on encopresis stresses faulty toilet training procedures. Poor dietary choices may combine with the failure to apply appropriate training methods consistently. Some cases of encopresis may also

be accounted for by avoidance conditioning principles. Avoidance of pain or fear reinforces retention. Positive consequences may also maintain soiling, and inadequate reinforcement may be given for appropriate toileting (Doleys, 1989). These various learning explanations are not incompatible with physiological explanations. For example, poor toilet training may compound insufficient physiological–neurological mechanisms.

TREATMENT   Most treatments for encopresis combine medical and behavioral management (Campbell et al., 2009; McGrath, Mellon, & Murphy, 2000; Reiner, 2008). After the parent and the child have been educated about encopresis, the first step usually consists of an initial cleanout phase using enemas or high fiber intake to eliminate fecal impactions. Next, parents are asked to schedule regular toilet times and to use suppositories if defecation does not occur. Modifications in fluid intake, diet, laxatives, and stool softeners are employed to facilitate defecation. Positive consequences, such as a shared activity chosen by the child, are used to reward unassisted (no suppository) bowel movements in the toilet, as well as clean pants. If soiling occurs, children may be instructed to clean themselves and their clothes. Later in the course of training, laxatives and suppositories are withdrawn. While interventions are not as well established as for enuresis, research suggests that such treatment is effective and that relapse rates are low (APA, 2006; Kuhl et al., 2010; Mikkelsen, 2001). In cases where soiling is being used to manipulate the environment (e.g., being allowed to leave school, getting the mother's time and attention) additional family therapy may be indicated (Walker, 2003).

SLEEP PROBLEMS

Parents commonly complain of difficulties in getting their young children to go to sleep and to sleep through the night. Nightmares are another concern that parents often report. To understand these problems, as well as more serious sleep disorders, it is necessary to understand the variations in normal sleep for children.

Sleep Development

At all ages, there is considerable individual variability in a normal sleep pattern. Furthermore, patterns of sleep change with development (Meltzer & Mindell, 2009; Owens & Burnham, 2009). For example, the average newborn sleeps between 10 and 18 hours per day. By the time children are 1 year old, the average amount of sleep has fallen to 12 hours.

The typical 6- to 12-year-old sleeps 10 to 11 hours each day. In addition to the number of hours of sleep, other aspects change as well. For example, newborns distribute their sleeping equally between day and night. Fortunately for parents, by about 3 months of age, infants have adopted the day–night pattern typical in adults, and by 18 months, sleep patterns are usually quite stable.

Within sleep periods there are two broad phases: **rapid eye movement (REM)** sleep and **nonrapid eye movement (NREM)** sleep. NREM sleep is divided into four stages. Stages 3 and 4, the deepest part of sleep, are characterized by very slow waves in the EEG and are thus sometimes referred to as slow wave sleep. Throughout the night, the brain cycles through these stages of sleep. The time spent in different stages of sleep varies and changes with development. In the first year of life, for example, active (REM) sleep changes from about 8 hours to about half this amount, thus also reducing the proportion of time spent in REM relative to other phases of sleep. The sequencing, or pattern in which the various stages of sleep occur, also changes. The phases of sleep are intermixed in an irregular pattern in infants. However, as the child develops, regular patterns of light NREM, deep NREM, and REM sleep are gradually established.

Common Sleep Problems

During the first year of life, parents' most frequent complaint is that the child does not sleep through the night. A reluctance to go to sleep and nightmares often occur during the second year, and 3- to 5-year-old children may present a variety of problems, including difficulty in going to sleep, nighttime awakenings, and nightmares. Surveys suggest that up to one-quarter of infants and younger children experience some form of sleep problem that is disturbing to the family (Owens & Burnham, 2009). Differences in parent's expectations and tolerance levels may, in part, determine whether a "sleep problem" exists. Coulombe & Reid, 2012.

School-age children also experience a variety of sleep problems, including bedtime resistance, delayed sleep onset, and night waking (Blader et al., 1997; Sadeh, Raviv, & Gruber, 2000). Indeed, sleep problems in older children may be underestimated, because older children are less likely to alert their parents to their difficulties (Gregory, Rijsdijk, & Eley, 2006; Owens et al., 2000). Even in adolescence, complaints regarding sleep are common, particularly the need for more sleep and difficulty in falling asleep (Dahl & Harvey, 2008). At this age, youths often experience decreasing amounts of sleep due to later bedtimes combined with earlier school start times. Indeed, Snell, Adam, & Duncan (2007) report that, on the basis of a nationally representative sample of U.S. children 3–18 years of age, total sleep time declined, particularly on weekdays, as children aged. On weekdays, older children go to bed later and wake up earlier. The greatest decrease in sleep duration appears to occur at the time of transition from middle to high school, and there is actually an increase in sleep time as adolescents transition out of high school. Insufficient sleep may contribute to problems such as poor academic performance, anxiety, depression, and health difficulties (Buckhalt, El-Sheikh, & Keller, 2007; Fredriksen et al., 2004; Meijer et al., 2010; Moore et al., 2009; Snell et al., 2007).

FIGURE 13.2   Insufficient sleep may contribute to poor academic performance and other problems.

*"I'm worried about a monster under my bed
and I'm worried about college."*

Whether early sleep difficulties continue and/or develop into more serious sleep disorders is probably a function of a complex interplay of individual and environmental influences (Dauvilliers, Maret, & Tafti, 2005; El-Sheikh et al., 2006; Warren et al., 2006). Indeed, clear discrimination between common sleep difficulties and some sleep disorders is difficult. However, sleep problems that are frequent, persistent, and associated with other problems for the young person are considered sleep disorders. Sleep problems that do not cause the youth significant distress or do not result in impairment in important areas of functioning would not be considered a diagnosable disorder (APA, 2000).

Sleep Disorders

There are many types of sleep disorders that are of concern to clinicians working with infants, children, and adolescents (Dahl & Harvey, 2008; Meltzer & Mindell, 2009; Owens & Burnham, 2009). The sleep disorders of primary concern are sometimes classified into two major categories: difficulties in initiating and maintaining sleep or of excessive sleepiness and disorders of arousal, partial arousal, or sleep-stage transitions (**parasomnias**).

DIFFICULTIES INITIATING OR MAINTAINING SLEEP
Problems of getting to sleep and sleeping through the night are common. If they are severe and chronic enough, they may fall into the category of behavioral insomnia of childhood (American Academy of Sleep Medicine, 2005). These sleep and waking problems are frequently viewed as manifestations of the child's neurophysiological development and therefore are expected eventually to resolve. However, child, parental, and environmental factors do play a role in a substantial number of cases. For example, when a parent rocks and soothes a young child to assist the child in falling asleep at night, the child may not learn to soothe herself or himself or learn to return to sleep during a normal night waking. A comparison of poor sleepers and good sleepers between 12 and 36 months of age revealed some surprising findings (Minde et al., 1993). Mothers' sleep diaries indicated more night wakings for the poor sleepers. However, filmed recordings indicated no differences in the actual number of wakings for the two groups. The poor sleepers were unable or unwilling to go back to sleep and woke their parent. In contrast, good sleepers were able to return to sleep on their own either by looking around and falling asleep or by quieting themselves, for example, by hugging

a toy animal or sucking their thumbs. Also, parental failure to provide bedtime routines and set limits may help maintain difficulties in falling asleep. Whatever the cause, these problems may persist over many years, and they can result in considerable distress to the children and families involved (Dahl & Harvey, 2008; Owens & Burnham, 2009).

The presence of this type of sleep problem may be underestimated. Young children's reports of difficulty in getting to sleep or staying asleep may be mistaken for attention seeking or the young child's level of cognitive development may not allow them to recognize a sleep problem. Alternatively, a child may present with a variety of difficulties, and objective recording of sleep may reveal sleep problems that were not recognized by either the child or the parent (Sadeh et al., 2000). Sleep problems may result in impairment in social, educational, or other areas of functioning. Yet the family may not be aware that sleep difficulties are contributing to these other problems.

Sleep problems may be related to other problems in a number of ways. On the one hand, for example, children's fear or worries may contribute to the development of problems in falling and staying asleep. In older children, sleep problems may stem from worrisome cognitions—concerns about school or peers, ruminations about past or anticipated experiences, or fears. Also, sleep difficulties are often described as part of the presentation of other disorders such as ADHD, autism, depression, and anxiety (Meltzer & Mindell, 2009; Owens & Burnham, 2009). Another reason that sleep difficulties and other problems may occur together is that they may be manifestations of a common set of etiological mechanisms such as difficult temperament, family discord, or parenting practices.

SLEEP AROUSAL DISORDERS   Several of the childhood sleep disorders that cause concern for parents fall into the category of disorders of sleep arousal or parasomnias. This spectrum of related disorders includes sleepwalking and sleep terrors.

Sleepwalking   An episode of **sleepwalking** (somnambulism) begins with the child's sitting upright in bed. The eyes are open but appear "unseeing." Usually the child leaves the bed and walks around, but the episode may end before the walking stage is reached. During the episode the child may be non-responsive. For example, not answering or responding when her or

his name is called. An episode may last for a few seconds or 30 minutes or longer. The child usually has no later memory of the episode. This failure to remember the sleepwalking episode may result in confusion or distress. The child may, for example, wake up in a different room of the house after going to sleep in his or her own room. Thus, children who are sleepwalkers may experience distress and concern about their sleep problem but be otherwise well adjusted—functioning well at school and with family and peers. It was once believed that the sleepwalking child was exceptionally well coordinated and safe. This belief has proven to be a myth, and physical injury is a danger of the disorder.

Approximately 15% of children between the ages of 5 and 12 have isolated experiences of walking in their sleep. Sleepwalking disorder, that is, persistent sleepwalking, is estimated to occur in 1 to 6% of the population. The problem may continue for a number of years but is likely to diminish in frequency with increasing age (APA, 2013).

The vast majority of sleepwalking episodes occur in the first 1 to 3 hours following sleep onset. The fact that sleepwalking occurs during the later stages of NREM sleep (deep sleep) appears to invalidate the idea that sleepwalking is the acting out of a dream, because dreams occur in REM sleep. A characteristic EEG pattern has been found to precede each episode of sleepwalking. This EEG pattern exists in 85% of all children during the first year of life but is present in only 3% of 7- to 9-year-olds. Thus, it has been suggested that central nervous system immaturity is of significance in sleepwalking disorder, and knowledge that the disorder is usually outgrown is consistent with that conceptualization. This view does not, however, rule out psychological or environmental factors. Thus, frequency of sleepwalking has been reported to be influenced by insufficient sleep, changes in sleep routines, the specific setting, and by stress and physical illness (Dahl & Harvey, 2008; Meltzer & Mindell, 2009). There appears to be a strong genetic component. Greater concordance rates for sleepwalking among monozygotic twins than among dizygotic twins and family patterns of sleepwalking have also been reported, with 80–90% of patients having an identifiable first-degree relative with a history of parasomnias (Meltzer & Mindell, 2009).

Sleep Terrors   **Sleep terrors**, also known as **night terrors**, are experienced by approximately 3% of children. Sleep terrors typically occur between the ages of 4 and 12 and most individuals outgrow the problem by adolescence (Meltzer & Mindell, 2009).

Sleep terrors occur during deep, slow-wave sleep and at a fairly constant time, usually about 2 hours into sleep. The event is quite striking in that the still-sleeping child suddenly sits upright in bed and screams. The face shows obvious distress, and there are signs of autonomic arousal, such as rapid breathing and dilated pupils. In addition, repetitive motor movements may occur, and the child appears disoriented and confused. Attempts to comfort the child are largely unsuccessful. The child usually returns to sleep without fully awakening and has little or no memory of this event the next morning. The conceptualization of the causes of sleep terrors is similar to that previously described for sleepwalking, and, indeed, they occur in the same part of the sleep cycle.

Nightmares Both sleep terrors and **nightmares** are fright reactions that occur during sleep. Nightmares and sleep terrors are often confused, but they differ in a number of ways (see Table 13.1).

Nightmares are common in children between the ages of 3 and 6 years (Mindell & Owens, 2003). These dreams occur during REM sleep. Parents may underestimate their children's nighttime fears. The findings

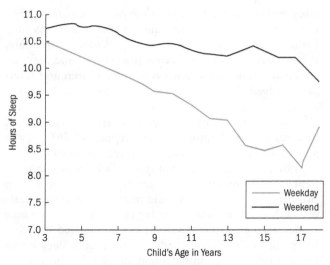

FIGURE 13.3 Percentage of children and their parents reporting that the children experience nighttime fears. *Adapted from Muris et al., 2001.*

illustrated in Figure 13.3 suggests that this may be particularly true for older children (Muris et al., 2001). It is frequently thought that the dreams are a direct manifestation of anxieties that the child faces. It has been suggested that children typically extinguish their fears by gradually exposing themselves during daytime hours to the feared stimulus (Kellerman, 1980). Factors such as parental protectiveness or lack of awareness of their children's fears, however, might limit the child's ability to engage in such daytime exposure or coping. In the absence of exposure and coping, anxieties and associated nightmares may continue or be exacerbated.

No single theoretical framework has proven successful in explaining the development of nightmares, and explanations allowing for multiple causes (e.g., developmental, physiological, and environmental factors) are likely to have the greatest utility.

Treating Sleep Problems

INITIATING AND MAINTAINING SLEEP A number of different interventions have been demonstrated to be effective in dealing with the problems of bedtime refusal, difficulty in falling asleep, and nighttime wakings (Mindell et al., 2006; Sadeh, 2005).

Parents are taught to put the child to bed at a designated, consistent time and also are taught to develop a consistent bedtime routine at the regularly scheduled bedtime. The routine involves calm activities that the child

TABLE 13.1	Characteristics Differentiating Nightmares and Sleep Terrors
Nightmares	**Sleep Terrors**
Occur during REM sleep	Occur during NREM sleep
During middle and latter portions of the night	During first third of night
Verbalizations, if any, are subdued	Child wakes with cry or scream, and verbalizations usually present
Only moderate physiological arousal	Intense physiological arousal (increased heart rate, profuse sweating, pupils dilated)
Slight or no movements	Motor activity, agitation
Easy to arouse and responsive to environment	Difficult to arouse and unresponsive to environment
Episodes frequently remembered	Very limited or no memory of the episode
Quite common	Somewhat rare (1 to 6%)

Adapted from Wilson & Haynes, 1985.

enjoys. Once the routine is completed and the child is in bed, the parents are told to ignore the child until a set time the next morning. Extinction (ignoring) procedures are based on the assumption that attention to nighttime fussing maintains children's sleep problems. Some parents find it very stressful to ignore long periods of bedtime crying, so they may use a variant of the extinction procedure, graduated extinction, that has proven to be successful. First, parents ignore bedtime crying for an agreed-upon time for which they feel comfortable, and then over several nights, they increase the period before they check on the child.

There also is research to support the value of parent education in preventing the development and worsening of these kinds of sleep problems. Parents are provided information about sleep, the importance of routine, and the importance of putting the child to bed while partially awake so that the child can learn to go to sleep without an adult being present.

Pharmacological agents have been among the most widely used treatments. However, good support for their effectiveness is lacking, and there is concern regarding negative side effects and recurrences of sleep disturbances with discontinuation of treatment.

MATTHEW

Recurrent Nightmares

The recurrent nightmares that 11-year-old Matthew experienced led his parents to seek help. Matthew was doing well in school, was involved in many activities, and had friends. His parents described him as sensitive and serious, but quite happy. A sleep diary indicated that nightmares had occurred on 11 of 14 nights. Matthew went to sleep in his own bed, but after the nightmare slept in his parents' or older brother's bedroom. Although his parents and brother did not mind, Matthew felt it was immature to have to sleep in their rooms. Recently, Matthew had been taking longer to fall asleep at night. Matthew complained of being tired during the day and upset about having another nightmare.

The parents indicated that Matthew had experienced occasional night terrors between the ages of 4 and 6. These had begun at the time of his maternal grandfather's death and after a difficult bout with the flu and high fever. During his preschool years Matthew had at least one nightmare a week, but since then only occasional nightmares until the past month. There were no health or other problems in the family except that the paternal grandfather had experienced a heart attack 2 months earlier, but he was home and recovering.

Matthew described his life as enjoyable and stimulating, but reported a number of situations that made him very sad or angry. Several bullies on the school bus repeatedly teased and pushed younger children including his younger brother. Matthew was also having

difficulty completing a particular Scout badge and he described his older brother as being particularly irritating to the entire family.

The parents of Matthew were reassured and told that he was a child with many strengths and also sensitivity to injustices and others being hurt. It was suggested that his nightmares were related to these stresses at home and at school. A brief intervention was recommended. The treatment consisted of Matthew discussing the content of his nightmares with his parents and keeping a diary of the content. Matthew was also taught relaxation techniques. The clinician and Matthew reviewed the content of the nightmares and role played responses that resulted in a victory over the scary events. There was also a focus on the events that were creating stress. Matthew and the clinician took a problem-solving approach to the bullies on the bus and the parents had the school principal investigate and intervene in the bullying incidents. The family discussed sibling squabbles and the older brother was encouraged to spend more time with his own friends.

Matthew's nightmares decreased over the next month. This coincided with Matthew's having greater control over daily events and the resolution of the bullying problem. Matthew realized that he might have occasional nightmares and that if they became recurrent he would identify and cope with stressors in his environment.

Adapted from Schroeder & Gordon, 2002, pp. 214–216.

Establishing a predictable bedtime routine is helpful in reducing children's sleep problems.

Given such concerns, behavioral interventions are recommended for most problems prior to the use of pharmacological treatments (Dahl & Harvey, 2008; Owens & Burnham, 2009).

PARASOMNIAS   In many cases of sleep terrors and sleepwalking, intensive treatment may not be indicated, because the episodes usually disappear spontaneously. Education and support along with procedures to ensure the child's safety may be sufficient. However, a number of treatments have been suggested. These include increasing sleep time, instructional procedures, and anxiety-reduction procedures (Dahl & Harvey, 2008; Meltzer & Mindell, 2009).

NIGHTMARES   Consistent with the view of anxiety as the basis for nightmares, the majority of treatments for nighttime fears have involved cognitive-behavioral anxiety-reduction techniques (Gordon et al., 2007). These treatments have typically been effective, but the active components of the various treatments need to be clarified.

ACCENT
Sleep Apnea

Young people may experience disrupted or inadequate sleep for a number of reasons. One of these is **obstructive sleep apnea** (OSA), a respiratory sleep disorder characterized by repeated brief episodes of upper airway obstruction and resulting multiple transient arousals from sleep. These events result in fragmented and insufficient sleep and daytime fatigue and inattention. Mindell and Owens (2003) provide some basic information about the disorder.

Common nighttime symptoms of sleep apnea include loud snoring, pauses and difficulty in breathing, restless sleep, sweating during sleep, and bedwetting. Episodes may occur primarily during REM sleep in the later part of the night. In addition to fatigue, daytime symptoms may include mouth breathing, chronic nasal congestion or infection, and morning headaches.

Parents may be unaware of the symptoms that occur during sleep or otherwise fail to report them to their pediatricians. Instead, parents often initially complain of difficulties such as excessive sleepiness, behavior problems, hyperactivity, inattentiveness and academic problems. OSA symptoms may become evident only after the parents are directly questioned about their child's sleep. Information from interview and physical examination is important, but

the only way to reliably diagnose OSA is by a sleep study, in which the youth sleeps overnight in a laboratory. EEG and other physiological measurements are taken and the youth's sleep is observed (Meltzer & Mindell, 2009; Mulvaney et al., 2006).

OSA is a common sleep disorder with peaks of prevalence among children between the ages of 2 and 6 years and in adolescence. In young children enlarged tonsils and adenoids are the most common risk factors. In adults the disorder is most commonly associated with obesity. Increasing prevalence of obesity suggests that this may become more of a risk for children and adolescents.

Removal of the tonsils and adenoids is the most common treatment in children, and symptom relief typically follows. Not all youths are candidates for such surgery, however. The use of a CPAP (continuous positive airway pressure) device can relieve apnea symptoms, but does not cure the problem. The youth wears a nasal/face mask during sleep and the device delivers pressure to keep the airways open. Many children have difficulties tolerating this device and adherence is a problem (Olsen, Smith, & Oei, 2008). For young people who are obese, weight loss is recommended.

PROBLEMS OF FEEDING, EATING, AND NUTRITION

Establishing eating habits and food preferences is one of the primary aspects of early socialization. Mealtimes are often an occasion for family interactions and rituals, and other social interactions frequently revolve around food and eating. These and other considerations suggest the importance of food and eating-related behaviors.

Common Eating and Feeding Problems

A wide range of problems having to do with eating and feeding are commonly reported in young children (Budd & Chugh, 1998). These include undereating, finicky eating, overeating, problems in chewing and swallowing, bizarre eating habits, annoying mealtime behaviors, and delays in self-feeding. Many of these problems can cause considerable concern for parents and appreciable disruption of family life. For example, Crist and Napier-Phillips (2001) indicated that over 50% of parents report one problem feeding behavior and more than 20% report multiple problems. Also, O'Brien (1996) found that approximately 30% of a sample of parents of infants and toddlers reported that their children refuse to eat the foods presented to them. Adequate nutrition and growth are clearly a concern, but eating and feeding difficulties are also often accompanied by behavioral problems such as tantrums, spitting, and gagging. Severe cases of such difficulties may be associated with even more difficult social and psychological problems, and may result in medical complaints and malnourishment. Indeed, some cases of **failure to thrive** (life-threatening weight loss or failure to gain weight) can be conceptualized as a special case of eating and feeding difficulties (Benoit, 2009; Kelly & Heffer, 1990; Kerwin & Berkowitz, 1996). Thus some feeding and eating problems may actually endanger the physical health of the child. The problems discussed in the following sections are disorders that appear in the DSM chapter Feeding and Eating Disorders or are problems that have attracted attention from researchers and clinicians.

Early Feeding and Eating Disorders

RUMINATION DISORDER **Rumination disorder** is characterized by the voluntary and repeated regurgitation of food or liquid in the absence of an organic cause. When infants ruminate, they appear deliberately to initiate regurgitation. The child throws his or her head back and makes chewing and swallowing movements until food is brought up. In many instances, the child initiates rumination by placing his or her fingers down the throat or by chewing on objects. The child exhibits little distress; rather, pleasure appears to result from the activity. If rumination continues, serious medical complications can result, with death being the outcome in extreme cases (APA, 2013).

Rumination is most often observed in two groups, in infants and in persons with intellectual

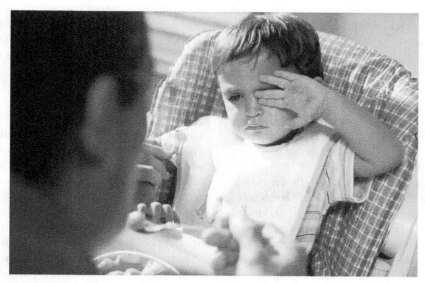

Young children often exhibit feeding and eating problems. This difficulty may result in disruption and cause their parents considerable distress.

disabilities. Among children who are developmentally normal, rumination usually appears during the first year of life and is thought to be a form of self-stimulation. Sensory and/or emotional deprivation are both associated with rumination. In individuals with intellectual disabilities, later onset is often observed, and the incidence of the disorder seems to increase with greater degrees of intellectual disability. In both groups, rumination appears to be more prevalent in males (Kerwin & Berkowitz, 1996; Mayes, 1992; Silverman & Tarbell, 2009).

Management of the problem will probably involve a multidisciplinary team. Treatments emphasizing the use of social attention contingent on appropriate behavior have been successful, and there is some suggestion that with infant ruminators, improving mothers' ability to provide a nurturing and responsive environment is effective (Mayes, 1992; Nicholls, 2004). These procedures have the advantage of being easily implemented by the parents in the home and of being acceptable to them. However, controlled evaluations of interventions are needed.

PICA   Pica is the Latin term for magpie, a bird known for the diversity of objects that it eats. **Pica** is characterized by the habitual eating of substances usually considered inedible, such as paint, dirt, paper, fabric, hair, and bugs.

During the first year of life, most infants put a variety of objects into their mouths, partly as a way of exploring the environment. Within the next year, they typically learn to explore in other ways and come to discriminate between edible and inedible materials. The diagnosis of pica is therefore usually made when there is persistent consumption of inedibles beyond this age, and pica is most common in 2- and 3-year-olds.

Information regarding prevalence is limited, but pica is reported to be particularly high among individuals with intellectual disabilities (APA, 2013; McAlpine & Singh, 1986; Nicholls, 2004). Pica can lead to a variety of damage, including parasitic infection and intestinal obstruction due to the accumulation of hair and other materials. The disorder also appears to be related to accidental lead poisoning (APA, 2013; Halmi, 1985).

A number of causes for pica have been postulated including parental inattention, lack of supervision, and lack of adequate stimulation (Kerwin & Berkowitz, 1996). Cultural influences such as superstitions regarding eating certain substances should also be considered (Millican & Lourie, 1970; Paniagua, 2000). The diagnosis of pica should be made only when the eating behavior is not part of a culturally supported or normative practice (APA, 2013).

Educational approaches aimed at informing parents of the dangers of pica and at encouraging them to deter the behavior may be somewhat successful. However, it is necessary to supplement such interventions with more intensive therapeutic endeavors in some cases. Behavioral interventions that address antecedents and consequences of pica behavior have been suggested (Bell & Stein, 1992; Linscheid & Rasnake, 2001).

AVOIDANT/RESTRICTIVE FOOD INTAKE DISORDER   The essential feature of this disorder is a persistent failure to eat adequately. This may result in a number of serious difficulties. The child may fail to gain weight (or experience a significant weight loss), experience nutritional deficiency, experience appreciable interference with psychosocial functioning, and/or may become dependent on methods of directly supplying nutrition to the stomach or intestinal tract (e.g., tube feeding) or to the use of oral nutritional supplements. The DSM-5 diagnosis of **Avoidant/Restrictive Food Intake Disorder** replaces the earlier term Feeding Disorder of Infancy or Early Childhood (APA, 2013). The DC: 0-3 system has a comparable Feeding Behavior Disorder category (Zero to Three, 2005). Restrictive and avoidant types of eating problems that occur during infancy and early childhood are often discussed as one aspect of "failure to thrive," and conceptualization of these feeding problems and their treatment often are discussed as part of this larger construct.

Approximately 1 to 5% of pediatric hospital admissions are due to failure to thrive, and about one-half of these may be due to feeding disturbances. The prevalence of failure to thrive based on community samples is estimated to be about 3–10%. Avoidant/restrictive food intake disorder appears to be equally common in males and females and is more prevalent in infants and children with low birthweight and those with developmental disabilities or medical illness (Benoit, 2009).

That an infant or a young child would cease to eat adequately is puzzling and clearly troublesome. This problem and associated malnutrition can result in disruption in multiple areas of physical, cognitive, and social-emotional development at this critical time. The young child may be irritable and difficult to console or may appear apathetic and withdrawn—characteristics that may further contribute to feeding difficulties.

Multiple causes, including, physiological, behavioral, and environmental factors, most likely contribute to the development of food intake disorders (Benoit, 2009). The particular influences that contribute are difficult to determine, in part because it is difficult to observe the child and family prior to the development of the problem. Drotar and Robinson's (2000) review and discussion of failure to thrive suggests that one might conceptualize the development of a food intake disorder in terms of the parent's competence—defined as sensitivity to the child's developing repertoire and as communication and involvement with the child. In this conceptualization, the parent's competence is influenced by three sets of factors.

The first set is the parent's personal resources. Identification with the parental role, knowledge of effective parenting skills, and attachment and relationships with their children may be disrupted in these parents. This problem may, in part, be due to traumatic experiences in the parent's own childhood that disrupted the development of these parenting processes. Parental psychopathology may also contribute to diminished parental resources. Maternal eating disorders, for example, may lead to the mother experiencing anxiety and depression surrounding feeding and thereby increase the risk for food intake difficulties in her offspring (Micali et al., 2011).

The second set of factors is characteristics of the infant or child that may contribute to the problem by increasing the complexity of child-rearing for parents with limited personal resources. Thus factors such as low birthweight, acute physical illnesses, various disabilities, and temperamental characteristics may contribute to the development of a problem.

Finally, the family's social context is likely to interact with personal parental resources and child characteristics to affect parenting competence. Poverty or economic stress, serious parental or family conflict, the family's social networks and resources, and availability of community resources are among the contextual factors that may be implicated.

The focus of intervention has been on treating the physical/nutritional symptoms to improve growth and developmental outcome. Multidisciplinary treatments that include behavioral, medical, nutritional, educational, and psychological components are typical. There is considerable evidence supporting the use of behavioral interventions as a central part of these treatments of problematic eating and feeding behaviors (Linscheid, 2006; Sharp et al., 2010; Silverman & Tarbell, 2009; Woods et al., 2010). Several behavioral procedures are typically included in interventions, but most include an escape/extinction component with a less intrusive level of prompting (e.g., food refusal behaviors are placed on extinction—the spoon with food is not removed for some set period of time, disruptive behaviors are ignored).

Obesity

Although childhood obesity is not a feeding or eating disorder, it is a problem for which psychology has made an important contribution. **Obesity** is typically defined in terms of **body mass index (BMI,** weight in kilograms divided by square of height in meters). A BMI at or above the 85th percentile for age and gender is often defined as overweight and at or above the 95th percentile as obese. However, sometimes the terms overweight and obese are used interchangeably.

Obesity is an important health problem and is among the most prevalent nutritional diseases in children and adolescents. An estimated 10% or infants and toddlers and 17% of U.S. children and adolescents ages 2–19 are overweight. Certain ethnic/racial groups appear to be at particular risk (Olvera & Power, 2010). For example, Mexican-American male adolescents and non-Hispanic black female adolescents are more likely to be obese. In addition, reports indicate that rates of child and adolescent obesity have been increasing for all age groups, for both boys and girls, and among all ethnic/racial groups (Center for Disease Control, 2010; Ogden et al., 2010). Data from the National Health and Nutrition Examination Survey (NHANES) illustrate this increasing trend (Figure 13.4). Findings such as these lead the U.S. Surgeon General, the American Academy of Pediatrics, the White House, and others to call for a plan to reduce obesity (American Academy of Pediatrics, 2003; Levi, Segal, & Gadola, 2007; White House Task Force on Childhood Obesity, 2011).

Obesity in childhood is associated with numerous physical, psychological, interpersonal, and educational difficulties (Jelalian & Hart, 2009). Physical health problems associated with obesity include diabetes, heart disease, asthma, and sleep apnea (Daniels, 2006; Morrison, Friedman, & Gray-McGuire, 2007). In addition, there are associations with educational, social, and psychological difficulties (Loth et al., 2011; Puhl & Latner, 2007; Zametkin et al., 2004). For example, Geier and colleagues (2007) found that among a sample of inner city fourth to sixth graders, overweight children were absent significantly more than normal weight children even when controlling for age, gender, and race/ethnicity. Also, in a study by Israel and Shapiro (1985), the behavior problem scores of children who were enrolled in a weight-loss program were significantly higher than the norms for the general population, but significantly lower than the norms for children referred to clinics for psychological services. This is consistent with other findings that suggest that overweight youth are not necessarily at risk for significant psychological difficulties,

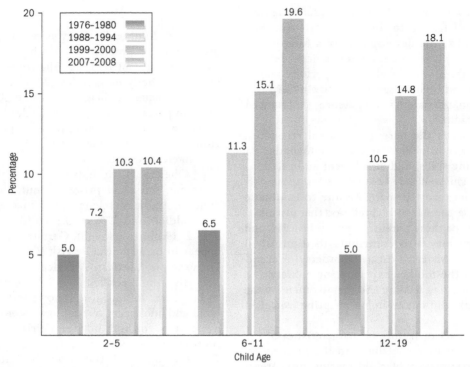

FIGURE 13.4   Percent of obese children and adolescents.   *Adapted from Centers for Disease Control and Prevention 2010.*

but that identifying the factors that help predict which youth are at risk is of potential importance (Jelalian & Hart, 2009).

The obese child's social interactions may be adversely affected by negative evaluations (Puhl & Latner, 2007). Because children hold negative views of obesity, children who are perceived as overweight are ranked as less liked (Latner & Stunkard, 2003). Negative attitudes toward overweight peers have been found in children as young as age 3. Overweight youths may experience social isolation, teasing, rejection, and bullying (Griffiths et al., 2006; Jensen & Steele, 2012). In contrast, having a close friend may protect them from social consequences (Reiter-Purtill et al., 2010). Effects of being overweight appear to continue throughout development. College acceptance rates are lower for obese adolescent girls than for nonobese girls with comparable academic credentials, and discrimination and lowered expectations may continue into college (Puhl & Latner, 2007). The obese youth's self-esteem may be adversely affected by such experiences (Nelson, Jensen, & Steele, 2011; Stern et al., 2007). For example, overweight adolescent girls have reported greater body dissatisfaction and made more negative attributions regarding their appearance than did their normal-weight peers (Thompson et al., 2007). However, many obese youths do not have adjustment difficulties and they may maintain their general self-esteem despite reactions to their physical appearance (Israel & Ivanova, 2002).

ETIOLOGY   The causes of obesity are certainly multiple and complex. Any explanation must include biological, psychological, and social/cultural influences (Cawley, 2006; Cope, Fernández, & Allison, 2004; Jelalian & Hart, 2009; Sallis & Glanz, 2006).

Biological influences include the metabolic effects of diet and exercise and genetic factors. Twin and adoption studies suggest a heritable component of body size and composition and for aspects of food intake. In addition, ongoing research suggests promise in locating specific genes that may be associated with obesity. Multiple genes are likely to be involved and genetic contributions are likely to be complex rather than simple. Of course, biological influences are not independent of environmental influences; rather, these influences interact (Jelalian & Hart, 2009; Kral & Faith, 2009).

Psychosocial factors are also important in the development of obesity. Both logic and research suggest that the food intake and activity level of obese children are in need of change (Anderson & Butcher, 2006). Problematic food intake and inactivity are likely to be affected by family, peer, and other environmental influences and to be learned in the same manner as any other behavior (Laessle, Uhl, & Lindel, 2001; Olvera & Power, 2010; Salvy et al., 2012; Storch et al., 2007). For example,

SEAN

Obesity and Family Environment

Sean, a 10-year-old who was 50% overweight for his height and age, enrolled in a treatment program for obese children and their families. Sean's pediatrician described a history of steady, greater than expected weight gains with extreme increases in the last 3 years. Sean's father was normal weight, but his mother was about 40% overweight and had made numerous unsuccessful weight-loss attempts. Neither of Sean's two siblings was overweight. Sean snacked frequently on large amounts of high-calorie food, with most of his calories consumed after school while his parents were at work. His mother often found candy wrappers in Sean's room and pockets. Sean's parents reported that as Sean gained weight, his physical activity decreased and most of his leisure time was spent watching television. They were concerned with his frequent shortness of breath. Sean had no close friends and was something of a loner. He was teased about his weight at school and by his siblings. Although the parents indicated that they were committed to Sean's losing weight, there were indications of some family "sabotage." Much of the family's activities revolved around food, and food was used as a reward. Sean's father described himself as a gourmet cook, and his high-calorie, high-fat meals were "family times." Sean spent considerable time visiting his grandmother, who took pleasure in providing him with food and snacks.

Adapted from Israel & Solotar, 1988.

Interventions that target obesity address both problematic food intake and inactivity.

Larger cultural influences are also germane. Television provides a striking example of how the larger society might contribute to the development of weight problems. American children and adolescents have easy access to high-caloric foods, watch a great deal of television, frequently play video games, and in general lead a sedentary lifestyle. In addition to the negative effects of inactivity associated with television watching, the negative impact is probably due to the influence of television viewing on food intake. The vast majority of food product advertisements viewed by children and adolescents are high in sugar and fat (Powell et al., 2007). There is similar concern about the marketing of unhealthy food choices to children via computer games and other electronic media (Jelalian & Hart, 2009; White House Task Force on Childhood Obesity, 2011).

INTERVENTIONS Multifaceted programs that emphasize behavioral interventions and education are the most effective treatments for childhood obesity (Cooperberg & Faith, 2004; Wilfley, Kolko, & Kass, 2011; Young et al., 2007). The work of Israel and his colleagues (Israel et al., 1994; Israel & Solotar, 1988) illustrates the general approach. Children and parents attend meetings during which the following four areas are regularly addressed: *intake*, which includes nutritional information, caloric restriction, and changes in actual eating and food preparation behaviors; *activity*, which includes both specific exercise programs and increasing the energy expended in daily activities—for example, walking to a friend's house rather than being driven; *cues*, which identify the external and internal stimuli associated with excessive eating or inactivity; and *rewards*, which provide positive consequences for progress by both the child and the parent. Homework assignments are employed to encourage the families to

parents influence and support weight-related behaviors (Moens, Braet, & Soetens, 2007; Sato et al., 2011; van den Berg et al., 2010). And children also observe and imitate the eating behavior of their parents and others around them, and are reinforced for engaging in that style of eating (Klesges & Hanson, 1988). Eating and inactivity may also become strongly associated with physical and social stimuli, so that they become almost automatic in some circumstances. Moreover, people may learn to use food to overcome stress and negative mood states, such as boredom and anxiety. The treatment of obesity that has been developed from a social learning perspective seeks to break these learned patterns and to develop more adaptive ones.

change their environments and to practice more appropriate behavior.

The role of parental involvement has been noted as an important element (Kitzman-Ulrich et al., 2010). Israel, Stolmaker, and Andrian (1985), for example, provided parents with a brief course in the general principles of child management. The parents then participated with their children in a behavioral weight-reduction program that emphasized the application of the general parenting skills to weight reduction. Another group of parents and children received only the behavioral weight-reduction program. At the end of treatment, both groups achieved a significantly greater weight loss than the control children who were not receiving treatment. One year following treatment, children whose parents had received separate child-management training had maintained their weight losses better than other treated children.

These results and others suggest the importance of changing family lifestyles and of providing parents with the skills necessary to maintain appropriate behavior once the treatment program has ended (Israel, 1988; Kitzman-Ulrich et al., 2010; Young et al., 2007). This is a particularly important issue in light of repeated evidence that individuals frequently regain the weight they have lost. In addition to parental involvement, the importance of increased activity, particularly when it is part of the family's lifestyle, and various other family factors have been shown to be related to treatment outcome (Epstein et al., 1995; Israel, Silverman, & Solotar, 1986).

In addition to improving parental involvement, enhancing the child's self-regulatory skills may be valuable (Israel et al., 1994). Children receiving a multidimensional treatment program, comparable to the four-area program described before, were compared with children receiving a similar intervention plus enhanced training in comprehensive self-management skills. The results of this study are presented in Figure 13.5. In the 3 years prior to treatment, children in the two conditions had shown similar patterns of increasing percentage of overweight. Both treatment conditions resulted in comparable reductions in the percentage of overweight during treatment. However, whereas children in the standard condition appeared to return to pretreatment trends in the 3 years following intervention, children in the enhanced self-regulation condition did not.

Although research supports the effectiveness of the multifaceted/behavioral approach to children's weight reduction (Cooperberg & Faith, 2004; Israel, 1990; Israel & Zimand, 1989; Young et al., 2007), there is a need for improved interventions that produce greater, more consistent, and more long-lasting weight loss and for attention to issues of setting appropriate treatment goals and tailoring interventions to particular populations (Braet & Beyers, 2009; Israel, 1999; Jelalian et al., 2007).

With increases in the prevalence of childhood obesity there have been calls for interventions that impact larger numbers of youth. Thus, broader societal interventions

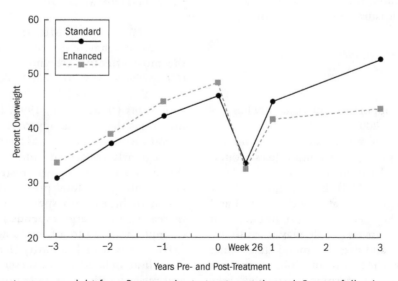

FIGURE 13.5 Mean percentage overweight from 3 years prior to treatment through 3 years following treatment. *Adapted from Israel et al., 1994.*

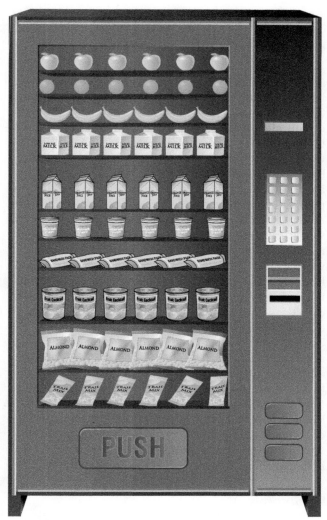

FIGURE 13.6 Providing healthy food options in the school setting may help prevent childhood obesity.

and prevention efforts are also needed (Stice, Shaw, & Marti, 2006). Programs targeting the general population that can be implemented on a national or statewide level are one approach. Targeting the nutritional content of diet and increasing physical activity also can be implemented at the school district level. School interventions may include improved availability of healthy food options and restricted accessibility of unhealthy food options along with increased time in physical education classes and increased physical activities during breaks and before and after school (Brown & Summerbell, 2009; De Bourdeaudhuij et al., 2011; Hoffman et al., 2010). These programs should seek, through the media and schools, to educate youths and

their families and to actively change harmful nutritional and activity lifestyles.

EATING DISORDERS: ANOREXIA AND BULIMIA NERVOSA

Anorexia nervosa and bulimia nervosa are eating disorders that involve maladaptive attempts to control body weight, significant disturbances in eating behavior, and abnormal attitudes about body shape and weight. These disorders typically begin during adolescence. However, the weight-control behaviors and attitudes toward body shape and weight that are characteristic of these disorders have also been noted in younger children.

Definition and Classification: An Overview

How might one best define and classify eating disorders (Walsh & Sysko, 2009; Wonderlich et al., 2007)? Several dimensions are involved in making distinctions between eating disorders or attempting to subcategorize a particular disorder. An individual's weight status is one such consideration. A person with an eating disorder may be underweight, within the normal weight range, or overweight.

A second consideration is whether the individual engages in binge eating. **Binge eating** is defined by the DSM as (1) eating a larger amount of food during a discrete period of time (e.g., a 2-hour period) than most people would be expected to eat during that time and (2) feeling a lack of control of eating during this episode. However, there is some question as to whether the amount of food consumed is important in defining the episode as a binge (Anderson & Paulosky, 2004; Wolfe et al., 2009). Some suggest that the feeling of loss of control and the violation of dietary standards are the central characteristics of a binge.

A third consideration is the method that the person uses to control her or his weight. A distinction is often made between restricting and purging strategies. The first strategy refers to severely **restricting** food intake and/or engaging in highly vigorous exercise. The second strategy involves **purging** oneself of unwanted calories through methods such as vomiting or the misuse of laxatives, diuretics, or enemas.

Weight status, the presence or absence of binge eating, and the method employed to control one's weight, therefore are important considerations in thinking about eating disorders. We turn now to how these dimensions are involved in describing eating disorders.

ALMA

Like a Walking Skeleton

When she came for consultation she looked like a walking skeleton, scantily dressed in shorts and a halter, with her legs sticking out like broomsticks, every rib showing, and her shoulder blades standing up like little wings. Her mother mentioned, "When I put my arms around her I feel nothing but bones, like a frightened little bird." Alma's arms and legs were covered with soft hair, her complexion had a yellowish tint, and her dry hair hung down in strings. Most striking was the face-hollow like that of a shriveled-up old woman with a wasting disease, sunken eyes, a sharply pointed nose on which the juncture between bone and cartilage was visible.

From Bruch, 1979, p. 2.

Classification and Description: DSM Approach

The DSM describes two primary eating disorder diagnoses: Anorexia Nervosa and Bulimia Nervosa. The DSM also includes a category of Eating Disorder Not Otherwise Specified (EDNOS). This diagnosis may be applied to eating disorders that would not meet the criteria for either anorexia nervosa or bulimia nervosa. One such disorder is Binge-Eating Disorder (BED). BED is characterized by recurrent binge eating; however, the individual does not engage in the inappropriate weight-control behaviors that are part of bulimia nervosa (described below).

ANOREXIA NERVOSA Individuals with eating disorders whose body weight is well below minimally normal or expected levels are likely to be given the diagnosis of **anorexia nervosa** (AN). The diagnosis of AN has three essential features. The first is a persistent restriction of energy intake that results in lower than expected body weight. In addition, the diagnosis of AN requires a fear of gaining weight or persistent behavior to avoid gaining weight. Finally, a disturbance in how the individual perceives their weight or shape is part of the criteria. These individuals may "feel fat" despite their low body weight, self-esteem may be unduly influenced by body weight and shape considerations, or there may be lack of adequate recognition of the seriousness of the medical implications of current low body weight. The DSM distinguishes between two subtypes of AN—restricting type and binge-eating/purging type—on the basis of whether or not the person binges.

The seriousness of the extreme weight loss associated with anorexia nervosa is illustrated by Bruch's (1979) classic description of one of her clients, Alma.

BULIMIA NERVOSA In contrast to anorexia nervosa, individuals with eating disorders whose body weight is not below expected levels are likely to be given the diagnosis of **bulimia nervosa** (BN). The diagnosis of BN requires the presence of three central features. First, individuals with a diagnosis of BN engage in recurrent episodes of binge eating. Again, **binge eating** is defined as consuming a larger than expected quantity of food in a discrete period of time and there is a feeling of a lack of control of eating during these episodes. Second, in order to prevent weight gain, the individual employs some inappropriate method of compensating for binge eating. Self-induced vomiting is probably the most common method employed; however, some individuals use multiple methods including both "purging"—vomiting and the use of laxatives or diuretics—and "restricting"—excessive exercise, or fasting—strategies. The third diagnostic criterion is that body shape and weight unduly influence the individual's self-evaluation.

To receive the diagnosis of bulimia nervosa, the binge eating and inappropriate compensatory behaviors must both occur at least once a week for 3 months. Also, the symptoms must not occur exclusively during episodes of anorexia nervosa—that is, a person who displays the symptoms as part of anorexia nervosa would not receive both diagnoses.

Epidemiology

Eating disorders occur predominantly in young women. The rate of occurrence in males is about one-tenth of that in females (APA, 2013; Eddy et al., 2008; Thompson & Smolak, 2001). Thus, females represent over 90% of all cases. The lifetime prevalence of AN in females is reported to be between 1.4 and 2%. BN is more commonly diagnosed, with a lifetime prevalence of between 1.1 and 4.6% of females (Stice & Bulik, 2008).

These numbers may actually underestimate the prevalence of eating disorders, because individuals with these disorders may be overrepresented among those who do not cooperate with prevalence studies (Wilson, Becker, & Heffernan, 2003). Perhaps more importantly, the stated prevalence rates are based on individuals' meeting full diagnostic criteria for AN or BN. But many other individuals exhibit various aspects of disordered eating and disturbances of body image (Ackard, Fulkerson, & Neumark-Sztainer, 2007). Of these individuals, many may meet the criteria for Other (Specified or Unspecified)

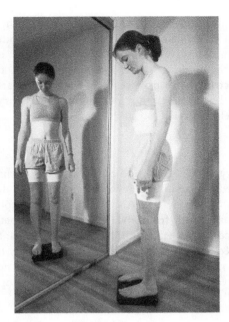

Extreme concern with weight and body shape has become common among girls and young women.

Eating Disorders (OED; formerly Eating Disorder Not Otherwise Specified—EDNOS), and this type of diagnosis seems to be more common than AN or BN in young people (Eddy et al., 2008; Walsh et al., 2005a; Wonderlich et al., 2007). These cases are also sometimes described as a "partial syndrome" or as "subclinical." Prevalence of subthreshold anorexia nervosa has been estimated at 1.1 to 3% of adolescent girls and subthreshold bulimia nervosa at 1.1 to 4.6% (Stice & Bulik, 2008). Youths with a partial syndrome may experience substantial social and educational impairment. And adolescents who do not fully meet diagnostic criteria for AN or BN may in many ways resemble those who do and may be at considerable risk for the development of other disorders, especially depression (Eddy et al., 2008; Lewinsohn, Striegel-Moore, & Seeley, 2000).

Of particular interest is the finding that subclinical concerns with weight and shape and unusual eating behaviors are increasingly common among younger adolescents and even preadolescent girls. Thus, although eating disorders that meet full diagnostic criteria typically occur in late adolescence, dieting and disordered eating behaviors and attitudes appear in younger children (Stinton & Birch, 2005; Thompson & Smolak, 2001). These problems may be precursors of more serious eating disorders.

We have known for some time that by the fourth and fifth grade, many girls are worried about being or becoming overweight and desire to become thinner. Among middle-school children, concerns about weight remain prevalent, and more extreme weight control behaviors seem to be employed (Childress et al., 1993). Evidence suggests that extreme weight concern in these young girls is predictive of the emergence of later eating disorder symptoms and of depression, lowered self-esteem, and feelings of inadequacy and personal worthlessness (Killen et al., 1994a,b; Lewinsohn et al., 1993a; Stice & Bearman, 2001). Such feelings may, in turn, lead to increased concern with weight and shape among girls who already place great personal value on these physical attributes (Cohen-Tovee, 1993). Even at this young age concerns with weight and shape have been reported to be more prevalent among girls than boys (Shapiro, Newcomb, & Loeb, 1997; Thelen et al., 1992). There, however, has been increasing concern regarding disordered eating and body dissatisfaction among young males (McCabe & Ricciardelli, 2004).

ETHNIC AND CULTURAL DIFFERENCES Eating disorders are usually reported to occur predominantly in young women, particularly young white women from middle to upper class backgrounds. However, information regarding ethnic/racial differences among adolescents is somewhat limited. Several studies have found no racial or ethnic differences in the prevalence of eating disorder symptoms or risk factors for eating disorders. However, one consistent finding is of lesser body dissatisfaction among young African American females than among their white counterparts (Stice & Bulik, 2008).

It is suggested that eating disorders are a culturally related phenomena, particularly bulimia nervosa (Eddy, Keel, & Leon, 2010; Keel & Klump, 2003). This would suggest that the more "Westernized" young women from other cultures become, the more likely they are to develop eating disorders. Within Western culture certain groups may be at particular risk. These include individuals involved in activities such as gymnastics, wrestling, ballet, and cheerleading in which weight-control behaviors and abnormal eating are used to enhance performance or appearance (Eddy et al., 2010; Jacobi et al., 2004; Smolak, Murnen, & Ruble, 2000; Thomas, Keel, & Heatherton, 2006).

CO-OCCURRING DISORDERS Eating disorders commonly co-occur with a number of other disorders (O'Brien & Vincent, 2003; Stice & Bulik, 2008). Lewinsohn, Striegel-Moore, and Seeley (2000) report that in a community sample of adolescent girls, 90% of those with full syndrome eating disorders experienced one or more co-occurring disorders. Depression, anxiety disorders, and substance use disorders, in particular, are commonly reported as co-occurring with eating- and weight-related difficulties and with anorexia and bulimia nervosa (Fischer & Le Grange, 2007; Lock et al., 2005; Rawana et al., 2010).

Developmental Course and Prognosis

ANOREXIA NERVOSA   The age of onset of AN is typically during adolescence, with peaks at ages 14 and 18 (Eddy et al., 2010; Halmi et al., 1979). Cases of earlier onset are rare but do exist (Gowers & Bryant-Waugh, 2004; Lask & Bryant-Waugh, 1992). Some individuals may experience a single episode; others fluctuate between periods of restoration of normal weight and relapse (perhaps to dangerously low levels of weight that require hospitalization). Other individuals may gain weight and no longer meet the diagnostic criteria for AN, but they continue to engage in eating disordered behaviors and may meet the criteria for BN or Other (Specified or Unspecified) Eating Disorders (OED) (APA, 2013; Walsh et al., 2005a).

Anorexia nervosa is a serious disorder, and a substantial proportion of young women with the disorder have poor outcomes although prognosis appears better for adolescents than adult women (Doyle & Le Grange, 2009; Fairburn & Gowers, 2008; Katzman, 2005; Steinhausen, 1997). Extreme weight loss can lead to significant medical complications (e.g., anemia, hormonal changes, cardiovascular problems, dental problems, loss of bone density), and the disorder may be life-threatening (Doyle & LeGrange, 2009). It has been reported that women with AN are 11–12% more likely to die than other women of a similar age, many of the deaths resulting from suicide (Birmingham et al., 2005; Stice & Bulik, 2008).

BULIMIA NERVOSA   The onset of BN extends from adolescence into early adulthood with a peak period of onset between 14 and 19 years of age in females (Stice & Bulik, 2008). Binge eating often begins during or after a period of restrictive dieting driven by extreme dissatisfaction with body shape and weight. The DSM describes the course of the disorder as either chronic or intermittent, with periods of remission alternating with recurrences of binge eating. However, over the long term, symptoms of BN diminish in many individuals (APA, 2013). Although some individuals may no longer meet the diagnostic criteria for BN, problems may persist. They may, for example, continue to binge but no longer engage in inappropriate compensatory behaviors. Some of these individuals may meet the criteria for binge eating disorder or OED, and many meet the criteria for major depressive disorder (Fairburn et al., 2000; Lewinsohn et al., 2000; Stice & Bulik, 2008).

The recurrent vomiting associated with BN can result in dental problems such as the loss of tooth enamel and gum disease. Other medical problems such as irritation of the esophagus, alterations of the colon, and fluid and electrolyte disturbances may also occur, particularly among those who employ purging compensatory behaviors (Mehler, 2011).

Etiology

A variety of risk factors and causal mechanisms have been proposed to explain the development of eating disorders. Indeed, it is likely that AN and BN are multiply determined and result from a variety of different patterns of influences (Eddy et al., 2010; Jacobi et al., 2004; Striegel-Moore & Bulik, 2007). Being female is probably the most reliable risk factor. Other factors, however, are needed to help explain the gender difference and the development of eating disorders.

BIOLOGICAL INFLUENCES   Eating and the biological mechanisms behind it are complex; thus, numerous biological mechanisms have been studied. There is some suggestion that prenatal sex hormone exposure (lower testosterone and higher estrogen) may be associated with eating-disordered behavior. Also, the onset of anorexia nervosa is most often around puberty. While there is no definitive explanation of why puberty may increase risk, it is hypothesized that hormonal changes during puberty may moderate genetic influences on eating-disordered behavior (Eddy et al., 2010; Klump et al., 2007).

Research on biological influences has also focused on neurobiological and genetic influences. Eating behavior can both be influenced by and effect changes in neurobiological and neuroendocrine systems, so determining causal relationships is not easy. It has been difficult to determine whether a particular biological difference found in young women with eating disorders placed them at initial risk for the disorder or has resulted from changes in the biological system due to disordered eating.

Research suggests differences in neurotransmitter (e.g., serotonin, norepinephrine) activity are associated with eating disorders (Eddy et al., 2010; Halmi, 2009; Jacobi et al., 2004; Kaye et al., 2008; Klump & Gobrogge, 2005). For example, serotonin plays a major role in the inhibition of feeding, and decreased serotonin activity has been observed in individuals with anorexia and bulimia nervosa—both during the illness and after recovery.

A genetic contribution to eating disorders has also been suggested (Eddy et al., 2010; Halmi, 2009; Jacobi et al., 2004; Klump & Gobrogge, 2005; Striegel-Moore & Bulik, 2007). There are higher than expected rates of eating

RILEY

A Combination of Factors Leading to an Eating Disorder

Riley, a 17-year-old who had begun to talk about "feeling suicidal," began treatment at an eating disorders clinic. Riley's mother reported that Riley had always been healthy and performed well in school and in a variety of extracurricular activities. Indeed, during the past summer she had been selected for and attended an 8-week enrichment program for gifted and talented students. Riley had attended summer camps since the age of 10, but this was her longest period away from home, family, and friends. Riley had difficulty with this transition and reported that early in the summer program she had a hard time meeting people and making friends. She felt particularly insecure about interactions with boys and perceived that everyone, including her roommate, was pairing up into couples. To avoid feeling awkward, Riley used her free time to begin an intensive exercise program and reasoned that this would ensure that she was in particularly good shape for her school's fall soccer season. Initially, Riley was happy with this rigorous exercise program, but one day she overheard some boys making derogatory comments about her body. She entered the locker room, looked in the mirror, and thought that her thighs looked "pale and lumpy like cottage cheese" and reported realizing at that moment that she was "too fat." She began restricting her diet to small amounts of "healthy foods." Riley indicated that she developed her diet based on articles she had read in her mother's magazines on how

to "lose 10 pounds in a week!" She reported that she and her mother had gone on a diet together when she was 12 years old (around the age of puberty) and that she and her friends had previously gone on short-lived diets together. The summer experience was her first rigid program of diet and exercise. She reported that it made her feel "great" "strong" and "in control" and that she was frequently complimented by her roommate for how "good" she was.

When Riley returned home after the summer her mother was concerned with how much weight her daughter had lost. Riley refused to eat anything with her family, but her mother noticed that certain food items would disappear overnight. Riley reported that after 4 months of rigid adherence to her summer program she "lost control" and ate entire package of cookies. She was distraught by her binge and ate nothing the next time and doubled her exercise routine. This was the beginning of a pattern of binges that became more frequent and increased during times of stress. Despite frantic efforts to fast and exercise, Riley regained all of the weight she had lost. By late fall she felt that she had lost control and was becoming increasingly anxious and depressed. Her mother was concerned about Riley's mood and also about the impact that Riley's eating disorder was having on the family. Riley's 10-year-old sister had begun to talk about "feeling fat" and "needing to lose weight."

Adapted from Eddy, Keel, & Leon, 2010, pg. 440–441.

disorders among family members of individuals with AN and BN. Twin studies also suggest a genetic component to eating disorders. It seems likely that multiple genetic influences contribute to the development of AN and BN and interact with environmental influences in complex ways. Klump and colleagues (2010), for example, examined genetic influences on weight/shape concerns in a large female twin sample (10–41 years of age). They found that genetic influences were modest in preadolescents, but significant from early adolescent through middle adulthood. An opposite pattern emerged for shared environmental factors—the largest contribution of shared environment was in the youngest age group. Nonshared environmental influences were relatively constant across age.

Research regarding the identity of particular genes and the manner in which genes contribute to eating disorders is underway (Kaye et al., 2004; 2008). For example, the serotonin transporter gene (5-HTTLPR) has been implicated in eating disorders as well as in other disorders such as depression and, indeed, may moderate the co-occurrence of these disorders (Calati et al., 2011; Mata & Gotlib, 2011).

EARLY FEEDING DIFFICULTIES There may be continuities from early childhood feeding difficulties to later eating problems and disorders. Clinical reports mention early feeding difficulties in individuals with eating disorders, and there is some research support for this position.

For example, Marchi and Cohen (1990) longitudinally traced maladaptive eating patterns in a group of children. Their findings suggested that early childhood pica was a risk factor and that picky eating was a protective factor for bulimic symptoms in adolescence. On the other hand, picky eating and digestive problems in early childhood were risk factors for elevated symptoms of AN in adolescence. Kotler and colleagues (2001) found that maternal reports during early childhood of eating conflicts, struggles with food, and unpleasant meals were predictive of later AN in adolescence or young adulthood, whereas eating too little during childhood was somewhat protective regarding a future diagnosis of BN. It may be that experiences that begin early in childhood, such as differentiating internal cues of hunger from other emotional reactions, food acceptance patterns, and the balance between external and self-control of eating, are among potential factors shaping later eating problems (Eddy et al., 2010; Fisher & Birch, 2001).

WEIGHT HISTORY   Family weight history and the individual's previous weight history are frequently considered as possible risk factors. For example, there is debate about the idea that the self-starvation that is characteristic of AN begins as an attempt to control genuine overweight. It has been suggested that comments that the young girl is "getting plump" may stimulate normal dieting, which evolves into anorexic refusal to eat. Similar considerations have been discussed regarding BN, and there does seem to be evidence that supports personal and family history of overweight as a risk factor (Wilson et al., 2003). Some young women with such a history may become bulimic. Their problematic behaviors may begin as more typical attempts to reduce weight that could not meet the thin cultural ideal. However, the frequency of dieting among adolescent girls raises the question of why some girls who begin this common social ritual persist well beyond the point of socially desired slimness. Research regarding the mechanisms that might link early dieting and weight concerns to eating disorders for some girls is ongoing (Eddy et al., 2010).

TEMPERAMENT/PERSONALITY TRAITS   The temperament quality of negative affectivity has been associated with eating disordered behaviors and attitudes. But negative affectivity is also associated with other disorders such as anxiety and depression that frequently co-occur with eating disorders. Thus, this temperament quality may be a non-specific risk factor for eating disorders (Eddy et al., 2010). The relationship between certain personality traits and eating disorders also has received considerable attention. For example,

perfectionism (striving for unreasonably high standards and defining one's worth based on accomplishments) has been reported to be associated with eating disorders (Bardone-Cone et al., 2007). However, research does not support viewing perfectionism and other personality traits such as obsessionality, impulsivity, restraint, and conformity as preexisting risk factors for specific eating disorders. At best, the relationship between personality traits and eating disorders remains unclear. Alternatively, personality traits may be factors that affect the course of an eating disorder, or they may be consequences of an eating disorder (Walsh et al., 2005b; Wonderlich et al., 2005).

SEXUAL ABUSE   Reports based on clinical cases have suggested early sexual abuse as a cause of eating disorders. Reviews suggest a small but significant association between childhood sexual abuse and eating-disordered behavior (Smolak & Murnen, 2002). The nature of this relationship remains unclear. However, sexual abuse would appear to be a risk factor for psychopathology in general, rather than a specific risk for the development of eating disorders (Eddy et al., 2010; Jacobi et al., 2004; Walsh et al., 2005b). This, of course, does not mean that clinicians working with young people should not consider the occurrence of sexual abuse, which may be part of a pathway to eating disturbance for some individuals (Feldman & Meyer, 2007; Wonderlich et al., 2001).

CULTURAL INFLUENCES AND BODY DISSATISFACTION
Any discussion of the development of eating disorders is likely to address cultural influences and gender roles for women and the problem of body dissatisfaction (Eddy et al., 2010; Smolak & Murnen, 2004; Striegel-Moore & Bulik, 2007). Our society's emphasis on and valuing of slim and young bodies, particularly for women, likely contributes to body dissatisfaction and the development of eating disorders (Mirkin, 1990; Striegel-Moore & Bulik, 2007). For example, Dittmar, Halliwell & Ive (2006) asked the question, "Does Barbie make girls want to be thin?" Many young girls own at least one Barbie doll. Barbie is exceptionally thin and her body proportions are unattainable and unhealthy. In the study, girls ages 5 to 8 were exposed to picture-book images of either Barbie dolls, Emme dolls (body proportions of a dress size 16), or neutral stimuli without any descriptions of bodies. Girls exposed to Barbie reported lower body esteem and greater desire for a thinner body than girls in the other conditions. This was particularly true for younger girls. Girls exposed to Emme did not differ from those who viewed neutral images. Such findings raise concerns that at a very young age girls may internalize a thin ideal.

Media, peers, and families transmit these cultural messages of thinness (Dohnt & Tiggeman, 2006; Wertheim, Paxton, & Blaney, 2004). Clark & Tiggeman (2007), for example, found that, among girls in grades 4 to 7, greater exposure to television shows and magazines that emphasized appearance, along with involvement in appearance conversations with peers, were related to greater body dissatisfaction. The relationship of these cultural influences to body dissatisfaction was mediated by appearance schemas—acceptance of the importance placed on appearance. Additional research also points to the influence of the media and suggests that young women may unfavorably compare themselves to persons depicted in the media (Levine & Harrison, 2004; Wiseman, Sunday, & Becker, 2005). Similar concerns are increasing with regard to young men. (See Accent: "Being Buff: Weight and Shape Concerns in Young Men.") Beyond possible direct influences, body dissatisfaction also can contribute to lowered self-esteem and depressed mood (Paxton et al., 2006) which, in turn, may contribute to the development of eating disorders (Measelle, Stice, & Hogansen, 2006).

Thus, one perspective on the development of eating disorders emphasizes contemporary social influences that place too great an emphasis on physical appearance, and may transmit a message that personal, social, and economic opportunity are associated with appearance and a particular body shape (Anderson-Fye & Becker, 2004; Eddy et al., 2010; Smith et al., 2007). It is important to understand both this exposure and the social pressure to internalize this message in order to counteract their contribution to the development of eating-disordered behavior.

Dissatisfaction with weight and body shape has come to be viewed as defining characteristic of eating disorders and as one of the early aspects of the development of such problems. Pictorial instruments that graphically assess body dissatisfaction in young children have been developed as part of a comprehensive assessment of eating disorders (Collins, 1991; Gardner, 2001; Stewart & Williamson, 2004). Use of such instruments (see Figure 13.7) has contributed to the view that body dissatisfaction and other problematic beliefs and behaviors are common and are present even in very young children.

ACCENT
Being Buff: Weight and Shape Concerns in Young Men

Much of the literature has focused on eating-disordered behavior and weight and body image concerns in young women. This is, at least in part, due to the high rates of such difficulties among females. More recently, attention has begun to turn to young men, and whether eating, weight, and body shape concerns are underestimated in the male population. Part of what we should recognize here is a possible gender bias in how a disorder is defined. So, for example, drawing from the literature on young women, interest has largely focused on issues such as the desire for a smaller and thinner body and losing weight. Although losing weight may be a concern for some young men who are overweight, most young men do not desire a small, thin body. The ideal for many young men may be a larger or at least more muscular body. Perhaps defining body dissatisfaction and weight concerns in a different way would paint a different picture regarding body image concerns and disordered eating in young men.

Indeed, it has become accepted among researchers and others that weight and shape concerns and body dissatisfaction have become more common among males. McCabe and Ricciardelli (2004) highlighted some of the reasons for this trend. Male bodies featured in popular magazines have become more muscular. Popular athletes, film stars, and many other male icons also have become increasingly muscular. Action figures, such as G.I. Joe, have followed the same trend and are likely to have physiques equal to or exceeding those of advanced body builders. Also, weight training has become more prevalent among young men and may be viewed as normative. Thus, similar to what young women have experienced, cultural pressures may be increasingly affecting young men.

What are the consequences of these trends? Appearance and weight have, for a long time, been considered overly important influences on young women's self-esteem. Similar concerns may be emerging as central to men's feelings of self-worth and mood (Paxton et al., 2006). Problematic eating styles may be increasing. In addition, excessive exercise and muscle-building strategies may be escalating among young males, including the use of steroids to achieve results.

The literature is not extensive regarding disordered eating and body dissatisfaction in young men. Nonetheless, there is information that suggests the presence of eating-disordered behavior in young men. In addition, both disordered eating and the pursuit of muscularity in adolescent males seem to be influenced by similar factors. Furthermore, several factors consistently associated with disordered eating in young women (e.g., importance of appearance, body mass index, negative affect, self-esteem, perfectionism, and pressure from others to lose weight) also appear to be associated with problematic eating behaviors in young men (Ricciardelli & McCabe, 2004).

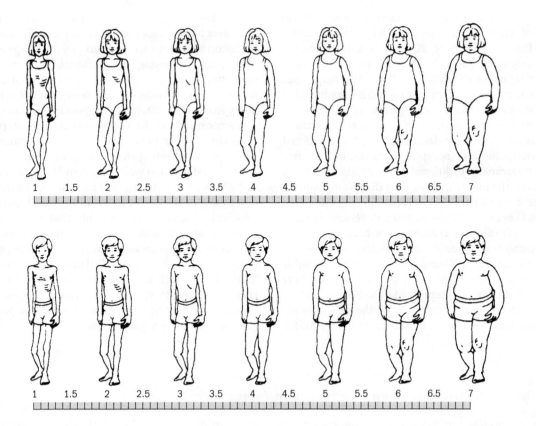

FIGURE 13.7 Pictures like these are employed to assess children's body perception. *Adapted from Collins, 1991.*

Some authors remind us that unusual eating styles are not recent phenomena, and that historical accounts can assist us in examining our conceptualization of eating disorders (Attie & Brooks-Gunn, 1995). There was, for example, a group of women living in the High Middle Ages (thirteenth through sixteenth centuries) who maintained extreme eating restrictions and what might be viewed as bizarre and pervasive behaviors and images regarding eating and food (Bell, 1985; Brumberg, 1986). Descriptions of the behavior of these women bear a remarkable similarity to contemporary eating disorders. The most interesting twist to this tale, however, is that these women were later canonized as saints. Bell (1985) chose the term "holy anorexia" to describe the condition of these women and to call attention to the cultural dimension in diagnostic efforts.

FAMILY INFLUENCES Historically, many explanations regarding the development of eating disorders emphasized family variables. Bruch's (1979) description of Ida is a classic example of family influences. The girl is described as the object of much family attention and control, and as trapped by a need to please. Anorexia nervosa, according to Bruch, is a desperate attempt by the child to express an individual identity.

Families are often described as having a high incidence of weight problems, affective disorder, and alcoholism or drug abuse. Parental attitudes and beliefs concerning eating, weight, and body shape may be particularly important. Also, aspects of the family environment, such as periods of low parental contact and high parental expectations, have been suggested as risk factors (Fairburn et al., 1997). Families of young women with eating disorders have variously been described as exhibiting parental discord and as controlling, indifferent, rejecting, and overprotective (Jacobi et al., 2004). While some research does suggest that family patterns are associated with eating disorders, there is no clear support for any pattern of relationships nor any "typical eating-disordered family" (Doyle & le Grange, 2009; Eisler, Lock, & le Grange, 2010; Steinberg & Phares, 2001; Walsh et al., 2005b).

IDA

A Sparrow in a Golden Cage

Even as a child Ida had considered herself not worthy of all the privileges and benefits that her family offered her, because she felt she was not brilliant enough. An image came to her, that she was like a sparrow in a golden cage, too plain and simple for the luxuries of her home, but also deprived of the freedom of doing what she truly wanted to do. Until then she had spoken only about the superior features of her background; now she began to speak about the ordeal, the restrictions, and obligations of growing up in a wealthy home.

From Bruch, 1979, pp. 22–23.

Furthermore, it is difficult to determine whether any pattern observed in a family subsequent to the onset of a disturbance is a cause or an effect. This is especially the case in AN, in which family observations have frequently followed the young person's life-threatening refusal to eat. In addition, it is important to realize that family influences are not either the exclusive or perhaps primary influences contributing to risk (Eisler et al., 2010; Le Grange et al., 2010). "Family blaming" may not only be inaccurate, but also may hinder the important role family may play in facilitating treatment of individuals with eating disorders.

Intervention

As we have seen, eating disorders likely develop from and are maintained by a variety of influences, and there is considerable heterogeneity among individuals with eating disorders. Thus, interventions that address multiple influences are needed and we briefly highlight some approaches.

In general, there is more research supporting interventions for BN than for AN. However, interventions specifically targeting adolescents with BN are limited and, thus, recommendations regarding BN are based largely on controlled studies with adults (APA, 2006; Keel & Haedt, 2008; Wilson, Grilo, & Vitousek, 2007). With regard to adolescents with AN, there is evidence supporting family-based approaches.

FAMILY APPROACHES Family therapy for eating disorders derives from the observation by clinicians of

varying persuasions that families are intimately involved in the maintenance of this behavior. Family therapy is widespread in clinical practice, but research support is more limited.

There is support for the effectiveness of family interventions for adolescents with AN (Keel & Haedt, 2008; Robin & le Grange, 2010; Wilfley et al., 2012) and the evidence is strongest for the Maudsley family-based treatment for AN (FBT-AN; Eisler et al., 2010; Lock & le Grange, 2005). This approach avoids viewing families as pathological and blaming them for the development of AN. The position taken is that the causes of the disorder are unknown and the family is considered the most important resource for the adolescent's recovery. Thus, the goal is to remobilize family resources to work with the professionals rather than seeking to "treat the family." Treatment, which initially involves intense support of the family that is gradually faded over time, is broadly divided into three phases. The first phase is highly focused on the eating disorder, refeeding, and weight gain and also seeks to reinvigorate the parents in their role as agents of change. Families are encouraged, with therapist consultation, to work out for themselves the best way to refeed their anorexic child. Once the adolescent is gaining weight and eating takes place with minimal struggle, the second phase begins. Eating disorder symptoms are the main subject of sessions, but the goal is to assist the family in finding ways to return control back to the adolescent. As this occurs other family issues can begin to be reviewed. Once the adolescent achieves a healthy weight the final phase is undertaken. General issues of adolescent development and the ways they have been affected by AN are addressed. The goal is to assure that the adolescent is back on a normal developmental trajectory and that the family is prepared to manage typical developmental concerns (Eisler et al., 2010).

Two modes of family involvement in FBT-AN have been compared: conjoint family therapy (CFT), in which the whole family is seen together, and separated family therapy (SFT), in which the same therapist sees the adolescent individually and the parents in separate sessions. Overall, CFT and SFT produced significant and comparable weight gain, improved menstrual functioning, and improved psychological functioning by the end of treatment and at a 5-year follow-up (Eisler et al., 2000; 2007). For a subset of families in which mothers were highly critical, adolescents who received SFT achieved greater weight gain during follow-up than did those who received CFT. Family involvement may have to be tailored to the family and/or adjusted over the course of treatment.

A family-based therapy for adolescents with BN, adapted from FBT-AN, has been developed (le Grange & Locke, 2010). Although initial findings are promising (Le Grange et al., 2007), there is still only limited research regarding its effectiveness.

COGNITIVE-BEHAVIORAL TREATMENTS Cognitive-behavioral treatment (CBT) of BN has appreciable research support and is viewed by many as a treatment of choice for this disorder (Mitchell, Agras, & Wonderlich, 2007; Wilfley et al., 2012; Wilson, 2010). Controlled research has shown the cognitive behavioral approach to the treatment of BN to be superior to no treatment and to alternative treatments, including pharmacotherapy and a variety of other psychotherapies. However, treatment evidence is based largely on adult samples that include some older adolescents (APA, 2006; Keel & Haedt, 2008).

Treatment involves a multifaceted program that is largely based on the rationale that a dysfunctional schema for self-evaluation—one that overvalues shape and weight and their control—is what maintains eating disorder pathology (Cooper & Fairburn, 2010; Fairburn, 1997). According to this view, these cognitions regarding shape and weight are the primary features of the disorder and other features—such as dieting and self-induced vomiting—are secondary expressions of these concerns. The "dietary slips" and binges that are part of the pattern of behavior among individuals with BN are most likely to occur in response to negative moods or adverse events.

In the initial stage of treatment, the patient is educated regarding BN, and the cognitive view of the disorder is made clear. During this early stage, behavioral techniques are also employed to reduce bingeing and compensatory behaviors (e.g., vomiting) and to establish control over eating patterns. These techniques are supplemented with cognitive restructuring techniques, and as treatment progresses, there is an increasing focus on targeting inappropriate weight-gain concerns and on training self-control strategies for resisting binge eating. Next, additional cognitively oriented interventions address inappropriate beliefs concerning food, eating, weight, and body image. Finally, a maintenance strategy to sustain improvements and to prevent relapses is also included.

As discussed earlier, most adolescents do not meet the diagnostic criteria for AN or BN. Their problems may be diagnosed in the general OED category. Thus, adolescents seeking treatment may present with a wide range of eating-disorder problems. Fairburn and colleagues (Cooper & Fairburn, 2010; Fairburn, Cooper, & Shafran, 2003) have developed a cognitive-behavioral individualized treatment program based on a "transdiagnostic" model of eating disorders. This intervention is an "enhanced" version of CBT for Bulimia (CBT-E). The program matches specific therapeutic interventions to the particular eating-disorder features of the individual, rather than providing treatment based on diagnosis. Fairburn and colleagues (2009) have evaluated CBT-E with a population of adults either meeting diagnostic criteria for BN or for those with symptoms that do not meet full BN diagnostic criteria (e.g., OED). The treatment was comparably effective for both groups—about half of the treated individuals reached a level on eating disorder measures that was close to the mean of a community sample. The success of CBT-E for individuals who do not meet full diagnostic criteria for BN further suggests that a cognitive-behavioral approach may also be appropriate for adolescents.

INTERPERSONAL PSYCHOTHERAPY Interpersonal psychotherapy (IPT) focuses on interpersonal problems involved in the development and maintenance of a disorder. Research suggests that IPT also may be an effective treatment for BN in adults (Tanofsky-Kraff & Wilfley, 2010). This therapeutic approach does not directly target eating symptoms, but seeks to enhance interpersonal functioning and communication skills. The rationale for such an approach is based, in part, on research indicating poor interpersonal functioning in individuals with BN and the role of interpersonal influences (e.g., actions of peers, friends, family; comparison with others) on the development of body image and self-esteem (Tanofsky-Kraff & Wilfley, 2010). An assessment of the individual's interpersonal history is obtained. One or more of four interpersonal problem areas are the focus of the intervention: interpersonal deficits, interpersonal role disputes, role transitions, and grief.

PHARMACOLOGICAL TREATMENT Although case reports suggest that different pharmacological treatments can be successful with eating-disordered patients, controlled research, particularly regarding adolescents, is either lacking or presents a somewhat more cautious picture. There seems to be little support for the effectiveness of any pharmacological approach in the treatment of AN; however, the use of medications continues to be explored (APA, 2006; Crow et al., 2009; Kaplan & Howlett, 2010). In controlled studies with adults, SSRIs, such as fluoxetine, or other antidepressant medications have been reported to be effective in treating BN (Broft, Berner, & Walsh, 2010). Effectiveness may be limited to only some patients, and medication would not appear to be the primary treatment of choice. The role of medication in treating BN in adolescents remains unclear and research is limited (Broft et al., 2010). Moreover, caution is indicated regarding side effects with individuals who are already psychologically and physiologically at risk.

PREVENTION There is a considerable prevalence among adolescents of eating-disordered behavior that does not meet the criteria for anorexia or bulimia nervosa or is considered "subclinical." In addition, signs of eating-disordered behavior and attitudes in younger children are frequent. Thus, there is reason to think in terms of prevention (Wilfley et al., 2011). However, empirical studies on the prevention of eating disorders are relatively limited.

Evaluations of universal prevention programs have largely focused on programs that target older youths (Walsh et al., 2005b). Some programs address issues related to healthy weight regulation (HWR) and focus on issues such as restrictive dieting, body image, and social and cultural influences. Other programs focus on broader issues such as self esteem and social competence (SESC) as a way to prevent the onset of eating-disordered behavior and attitudes. Evidence is limited, but does offer some suggestion regarding interventions (Walsh et al., 2005b). There are some promising findings for SESC approaches among middle-school students. For example, Steiner-Adair and colleagues (2002) employed a curriculum that taught recognition and critical evaluation of cultural messages and prejudices regarding appearance, weight, and eating, and was designed to help seventh-grade girls become more assertive and supportive of each other. Eating disorder knowledge and weight-related body esteem were significantly higher by the end of the curriculum, and remained high at a 6-month follow-up. It seems less clear whether programs using the HWR approach are of benefit for middle-school children, and universal prevention programs targeting high school students have found no significant effects on attitudes or behavior. Given these findings and limited studies it is unclear whether universal interventions are effective in preventing eating disorders.

Targeted prevention studies have primarily focused on interventions for self-selected samples of older adolescents and college students. Research suggests that these interventions may reduce risk factors for high-risk individuals, at least in the short term, but care should be taken in generalizing these findings to adolescents or younger children (Walsh et al., 2005b).

Overview/Looking Back

- It is common for children to exhibit some difficulty in acquiring habits of elimination, sleep, and eating. For some children, these problems are serious enough to be of clinical concern.

PROBLEMS OF ELIMINATION

- Toilet training is an important concern for parents of young children. Knowledge of the typical sequence of control over elimination and of appropriate parenting practices can contribute to successful training.
- Enuresis and encopresis are disorders of elimination that seem best explained by a combination of biological predisposition and failure to train and/or learn bodily control.
- Desmopressin is the best-supported medically oriented procedure for treating enuresis. Behavioral interventions that include a urine-alarm procedure have high success rates and low rates of remission, and they are the treatments of choice at present.
- Encopresis is probably best dealt with through a combination of medical and behavioral procedures.

SLEEP PROBLEMS

- Sleep problems are common in infants, children, and adolescents. Sleep disorders are persistent sleep difficulties that cause the child distress or interfere with other functioning.
- Difficulties in initiating and maintaining sleep may be related to neurophysiological development, but are probably also affected by environmental influences such as bedtime routines and the appropriate cues for sleep. Sleep disorders such as sleepwalking and sleep terrors (parasomnias) are probably best conceptualized as resulting from a combination of nervous system immaturity and environmental factors.

PROBLEMS OF FEEDING, EATING, AND NUTRITION

- A wide range of problems having to do with eating and feeding are commonly reported in young children. Many of these problems cause considerable concern for parents and appreciable disruption of family life.
- Some eating and feeding problems are more serious and persistent, and may actually endanger the physical health of the young person.
- The DSM describes a number of early feeding and eating disorders including rumination disorder, pica, and avoidant/restrictive food intake disorder (also often discussed as failure to thrive).
- Childhood obesity is quite prevalent. It is an important health problem that may be associated with a variety of physical, social, and psychological difficulties. The development of obesity is influenced by a complex interaction of biological, psychological, and socio-cultural influences.
- The learning of adaptive eating and activity patterns is the basis of behavioral treatment programs for obesity. This approach to treatment is probably the most successful. However, greater weight loss and better maintenance still need to be achieved, and priority needs to be given to prevention and early intervention.

EATING DISORDERS: ANOREXIA AND BULIMIA NERVOSA

- Weight status, the presence or absence of binge eating, and the method employed to control one's weight are important considerations in thinking about eating disorders.
- The DSM describes two primary eating disorders: anorexia nervosa and bulimia nervosa. Binge-eating disorder and other (specified and unspecified) eating disorders are also described.
- Anorexia nervosa (AN) is a serious disorder characterized by extreme weight loss, an intense fear of gaining weight, persistent behaviors meant to avoid weight gain, and disturbance in the perception of body weight and shape. A number of other physical and psychological problems are present as well. A distinction is made between restricting and binge-eating/purging anorexia.
- Bulimia nervosa (BN) refers to a repeated pattern of binge eating followed by some inappropriate compensatory behaviors. An undue influence of body shape and weight on self-esteem also is part of the criteria for a diagnosis of BN.

- Females represent about 90% of all cases of eating disorders (AN and BN). A diagnosis of Other (Specified or Unspecified) Eating Disorder may be more common than AN or BN among youths. Increasing prevalence of eating-disordered behavior and attitudes among young girls has been noted. There is also increased concern regarding disordered eating and body dissatisfaction in young males.
- Ethnic and cultural differences deserve further consideration and certain groups, such as some athletes and dancers, may be at particular risk.
- Depression, anxiety disorders, and substance abuse commonly co-occur with eating disorders.
- Age of onset for AN is typically during adolescence. For many individuals the disorder, or other eating problems, persists over a considerable period of time. Significant medical complications may occur and for some, the disorder may be life threatening.
- The onset of BN extends from adolescence into early adulthood. Although symptoms diminish for many individuals, there is concern regarding persistent eating difficulties and depression. Also, various medical problems may occur particularly among those who purge.
- Explanations that incorporate multiple influences are needed to understand the development and maintenance of eating disorders. Genetic and other biological influences, early feeding difficulties, weight history, cultural influences, and family influences are among the influences to consider.
- Treatments for BN specific to adolescents have received limited attention, and current treatment recommendations are therefore based largely on downward extensions of studies with adults.
- The use of family therapy or family involvement in treatment is widespread in clinical practice, but empirical support is more limited. The Maudsley approach to treating AN is the best-studied family therapy.
- Cognitive-behavioral treatment is the intervention for BN for which there is the best research support. A similar program for individuals who may fall in the subclinical or Other Eating Disorders category has been developed. Interpersonal psychotherapy has also proven to be effective with young adults.
- Controlled studies regarding the effectiveness of pharmacological treatments for eating disorders in adolescents is limited and findings unclear.
- Empirical studies of prevention of eating disorders are relatively limited.

Key Terms

enuresis *341*
primary enuresis *341*
secondary enuresis *341*
encopresis *343*
rapid eye movement (REM)
   sleep *345*
nonrapid eye movement (NREM)
   sleep *345*
parasomnias *346*
sleepwalking *347*

sleep terrors (night
   terrors) *347*
nightmares *348*
obstructive sleep
   apnea *350*
failure to thrive *351*
rumination disorder *351*
pica *352*
avoidant/restrictive food intake
   disorder *352*

obesity *353*
body mass index (BMI) *353*
binge eating *357*
restricting *357*
purging *357*
anorexia nervosa *358*
bulimia nervosa *358*

CHAPTER 14

Psychological Factors Affecting Medical Conditions

In this chapter we examine how psychological factors contribute to our understanding of youths with chronic medical conditions. We also examine how psychological influences contribute to the delivery of effective medical treatment. In addressing these topics, we touch on issues such as the role of the family, youths' adaptation and adjustment to chronic conditions, and the adherence of youths and families to regimens recommended by health care practitioners. In order to illustrate the interfaces between psychology and medicine, we describe the application of psychology to various medical conditions such as asthma, cancer, diabetes, and HIV/AIDS. To understand the evolution of current thinking and practice, it is helpful to have some appreciation of the history of such endeavors.

HISTORICAL CONTEXT

The topics discussed in this chapter would in the past have come under the heading of **psychosomatic disorders**. The focus of interest was on physical conditions, such as asthma, headaches, and ulcers, that were presumed to be affected by psychological factors. Terminology has undergone a number of changes in the last few decades. The term *Psychosomatic Disorders* was replaced in previous versions of the DSM by the terms *Psychophysiological Disorders*, *Psychological Factors Affecting Physical Condition*, and *Psychological Factors Affecting Medical Condition*. In DSM-5 a new chapter—Somatic Symptoms and Related Disorders—includes the category *Psychological Factors Affecting Other Medical Conditions*.

The uncertainty over terminology reflects a long-standing controversy over the nature of the relationship between mind and body, the psyche and the soma. During the twentieth century, interest in the effects of psychological processes on the body resulted in the development of the field of **psychosomatic medicine**. Early investigators began to accumulate evidence and to develop theories of how psychological factors played a causative role in specific physical disorders (Alexander, 1950; Grace & Graham, 1952; Selye, 1956). As this field developed, several trends emerged. An increasing number of physical disorders were seen to be related to psychological factors. Even the common cold was thought to be affected by emotional factors. The question therefore arose as to whether it was fruitful to identify a specific group of psychosomatic disorders or whether psychological factors were operating in all physical conditions. In addition, the focus began to shift from psychogenesis, that is, psychological cause, to multicausality, the idea that biological, social, and psychological factors all contribute to both health and illness at multiple points. The latter view is holistic, assuming a continuous transaction among influences.

With this shift in thinking, the field began to expand considerably. The ongoing role of social and psychological factors in the development, consequences, and treatment of medical conditions and the role of those same factors in prevention and health maintenance all began to receive increased attention. When the focus of such interest is on children and adolescents, the field is typically referred to as **pediatric psychology**. The redefinition and expansion of the field is also reflected in the formation of professional societies and journals with a pediatric psychology focus (Aylward et al., 2009).

In this chapter, we will examine some of the specific medical problems that have received the attention of psychologists and look at some other selected topics of interest. Our examination will allow us to illustrate the changes that have occurred and the current status and diversity of this field.

PSYCHOLOGICAL AND FAMILY INFLUENCES ON MEDICAL CONDITIONS

In this section, we will look at information on asthma to illustrate how psychological and family variables may influence the symptoms of pediatric medical problems. This examination of asthma will allow us to see how thinking about the role of psychological variables in physical illness has changed and expanded.

Asthma

DESCRIPTION AND PREVALENCE   Defining and describing asthma is complex (McQuaid & Abramson, 2009; National Institutes of Health, 2007). Asthma is a disorder of the respiratory system that is characterized by hyperresponsiveness of the airways to a potentially wide range of stimuli. Hyperresponsiveness results in chronic inflammation and narrowing of air passages, and air exchange is impaired, particularly during expiration. Intermittent episodes of wheezing and shortness of breath result. Severe attacks, known as status asthmaticus, which are life threatening may occur and require emergency medical treatment. The fear of not being able to breathe and the danger of severe attacks are likely to create appreciable anxiety in the young person and in family members.

Asthma is a common chronic illness in young people. Approximately 10% of youths are affected by asthma, and urban, minority, and poor children are overrepresented (Koinis-Mitchell et al., 2007; McQuaid & Abramson, 2009;

LOREN

Managing Asthma

Loren is a 12-year-old boy with moderate to severe asthma. For the fourth time in a year, he was hospitalized because of asthma. At hospital rounds, Loren's physician pointed out that his asthma could be controlled if he avoided triggers of his asthma, including exercise-induced attacks, and if he complied with his medication regimen. It was also pointed out that Loren did not use his nebulizer properly. Instead of alleviating his respiratory distress, most of the medication was wasted because of inappropriate inhaler use. Lack of quick relief frustrated Loren. As a result he tended to become angry, a behavior that only exacerbated his asthma. It was decided to (1) teach Loren to identify and avoid triggers of his asthma, (2) review his medication and adjust the regimen if possible, (3) improve his compliance to his medical treatment regimen, (4) teach him how to use his nebulizer correctly, and (5) teach him skills to control his frustration.

Adapted from Creer, 1998, p. 411.

Miller, 2000). Asthma is a potentially reversible disorder, but the impact of the disease on the young person is considerable. It can include hospitalization, emergency room use, and many lost school days (Weiss, Gergen, & Hodgson, 1992; Yeatts & Shy, 2001).

Clearly, the greatest threat is loss of life, and all measures used to treat the physical symptoms of asthma—daily medication to prevent wheezing, environmental control of potential irritants, desensitization to allergens, avoidance of infection, and emergency treatment to stop wheezing—are geared to prevent death. Although much has been done to improve treatment, high prevalence rates, as well as increases in medical costs, hospitalization, and mortality rates, are reasons for continuing concern and, again, urban poor youth are at particular risk (Bray et al., 2006; Inkelas et al., 2008; Koinis-Mitchell et al., 2007; McQuaid & Abramson, 2009).

ETIOLOGY The causes of asthma are complex, and there is a considerable history of controversy concerning etiology. However, it is broadly acknowledged that genetic or other factors place some youths at risk for developing asthma (National Institutes of Health [NIH], 2007). Some cause or a number of causes produce a hypersensitivity of the air passages. Once established, this hypersensitivity results in the young person's responding to various irritants more easily than would a nonasthmatic individual.

Individuals with highly sensitive and labile respiratory tracts are potentially exposed to a set of factors that influence whether asthmatic attacks occur. These influences have come to be thought of as *trigger* mechanisms or *irritants*, rather than direct causes of asthma. Every child or adolescent has different triggers and triggers can differ over time for the same youth (McQuaid & Abramson, 2009).

Repeated respiratory infection may play a role in the development of asthma, and respiratory viral infections can set off or worsen the severity of an attack. Allergies may also be related to the development and occurrence of asthmatic attacks. A young person may have allergies to inhaled substances (such as dust, the dander of a pet, or pollen) or to ingested substances (such as milk, wheat, or chocolate). Physical factors such as cold temperatures, tobacco smoke, pungent odors, and exercise and rapid breathing may also contribute to wheezing. Furthermore, psychological stimuli and emotional upset are often considered important triggers of asthma attacks (McQuaid & Abramson, 2009; Wood et al., 2007a).

PSYCHOLOGICAL AND FAMILY INFLUENCES Although we have come to view the causes of asthma differently, in much of the early literature asthma was viewed primarily as a disease with psychological causes and, indeed, was at one time referred to as "asthma nervosa" (Alexander, 1950).

However, over time it became clear that there is little, if any, convincing evidence that psychological or family factors play a significant role as an original cause of the reduced respiratory capacity characteristic of asthma. There is, however, evidence that these factors may play an important role in precipitating or triggering asthmatic attacks in at-risk youths.

For example, like many other investigators, Purcell and his colleagues (1969)—working at the Children's Asthma Research Institute and Hospital (CARIH) in Denver—observed that some children became free of symptoms fairly soon after being sent away from their parents for treatment. Indeed, in the 1950s, "parentectomy" was suggested as the treatment of choice for some children (Peshkin, 1959). Was asthma caused by excessive emotional involvement with the parent? Were the observed effects of separation due to changes in the emotional environment or in the physical environment?

An interesting study on separation suggested some answers to these questions (Purcell et al., 1969). Prior to the beginning of the study, parents of asthmatic children were interviewed and asked about the degree to which emotions precipitated asthmatic attacks. Children for whom emotions were important precipitants were expected to respond positively to separation from their parents (predicted positive), whereas children for whom emotions played less of a role were not expected to show improvement. For the predicted positive group, all measures of asthma improved during the separation period. The children who were not predicted to respond to separation exhibited no differences across phases on any measure.

The findings of this research study, and of others like it, led investigators to view changes in the psychological atmosphere as a basis for improvement in asthmatic symptoms. However, over time both the investigators at CARIH and other investigators came to view such findings somewhat differently. Although the magnitude of changes reported might be statistically significant, they were not clinically significant. And changes might have been due to increased compliance with prescribed medical regimens when the substitute parents moved in and the children's parents lived in a hotel. Indeed, current treatments to improve asthmatic functioning do focus on improving management and adherence (NIH, 2007).

This does not mean that psychological factors and family functioning play no role in asthma. There seems little doubt that these factors, in general, do play a role (Berz et al., 2007; Kaugars, Klinnert, & Bender, 2004; Koinis-Mitchell et al., 2012; McQuaid & Abramson, 2009). Home environment (e.g., dust, animal dander), activities

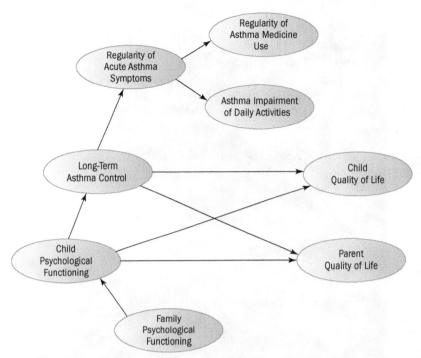

FIGURE 14.1 The relationship among asthma, child and parent functioning, and quality of live. *Adapted from Annett et al., 2010.*

of family members (e.g., smoking, outdoor activities), and stress (e.g., family fights, divorce) may act as triggers for asthmatic attacks. For example, Wood and colleagues (2007b) found, in a sample of young people aged 7 to 17 with asthma, that negative family emotional climate was associated with disease severity. These findings suggest that negative emotional climate was associated with the young person's depressive symptoms, which were associated both directly and indirectly (through emotional triggers) with the severity of the youth's asthma. The young person's asthma also may affect the family in many ways. Parents may experience increased anxiety, lose work days because of their child's illness, and suffer high medical costs. Siblings may experience loss of attention and restrictions in choice of family activities. Annett and colleagues (2010) investigated the relationships among the aspects of the child's asthmatic condition, child and family psychological functioning, and child and parent quality of life. Their findings support the idea that family functioning affects the child's functioning and that the child's functioning and the control of the child's asthmatic condition affect both the child's and parent's quality of life (see Figure 14.1).

Family members likely have to assist in the management of the disease, especially for younger children. It is therefore not surprising that interventions have included basic medical management, pharmacological management, and psychological components that have focused on educating families about the triggers of asthma attacks, on the consequences of asthma, and on helping young people and their families manage the disease (Canino et al., 2008; McQuaid & Abrams on, 2009; Seid et al., 2010).

Thus, the focus on psychological and family factors has shifted from the cause of a chronic illness such as asthma to an interest in how children, parents, family, and health care professionals may influence the frequency and severity of symptoms and the management of the disorder (Kaugars et al., 2004; McQuaid & Abramson, 2009; McQuaid et al., 2007; Wood et al., 2007b).

CONSEQUENCES OF CHRONIC CONDITIONS

What are the consequences of chronic medical conditions for young people and their families? This is another interest that has become part of the interface between psychology and medicine. The effects of any chronic illness are likely to be pervasive, particularly if the illness is life threatening. The young person is likely to experience substantial stress and anxiety. In addition, limitations due to illness often place obstacles in the way of normal development. For example, contact with peers may be limited or school attendance may be disrupted.

Parental concern over precipitating a symptomatic attack may lead children with chronic illnesses, such as asthma, to spend appreciable time isolated from their peers.

Of course, the family, too, needs to cope with the illness, its treatment, and its effects over long periods of time. Such long-term demands are bound to be difficult to handle, and the consistency required by treatment regimens is stressful in its own right. Thus the entire family may experience considerable anxiety and have appreciable stress placed on its daily routines.

Adjustment and Chronic Illness

Research on chronic illness has become a priority for pediatric psychologists (Phelps, 2006; Roberts & Steele, 2009). One frequent question is whether chronic illness leads to poor adjustment. The answer would appear to be not necessarily, but these illnesses and related life experiences probably place the young person at increased risk for adjustment problems (Greenley et al., 2010; Hysing et al., 2007; LeBovidge et al., 2003; Pinquart & Shen, 2011; Rodenburg et al., 2005; Schwartz & Drotar, 2006). Research findings suggest that there is considerable variation in adjustment among chronically ill youths. Although the

majority of young people with a chronic illness do not experience serious adjustment problems, subsets of more vulnerable patients do exist (Patenaude & Kupst, 2005; Pinquart & Shen, 2011; Schwartz & Drotar, 2006; Vannatta, Salley, & Gerhardt, 2009).

However, measuring adjustment at any one time is unlikely to provide a complete picture. Adjustment for the young person and family members is likely to be an ongoing process, beginning at diagnosis and continuing through treatment, treatment completion, perhaps relapse, and the long-term course that is inherent in a chronic illness (Jurbergs et al., 2009; Quittner et al., 2009; Wakefield et al., 2010). This has led some professionals to consider a traumatic stress framework to understand the initial reaction to diagnosis and treatment and to adjustment over time (Bruce, 2006; Kazak et al., 2006; Schwartz & Drotar, 2006; Stuber & Shemesh, 2006).

Adjustment to chronic illness is best thought of as a complex function of a number of variables (Vanatta et al., 2009). Characteristics of the young person and family members probably contribute to the adjustment of both

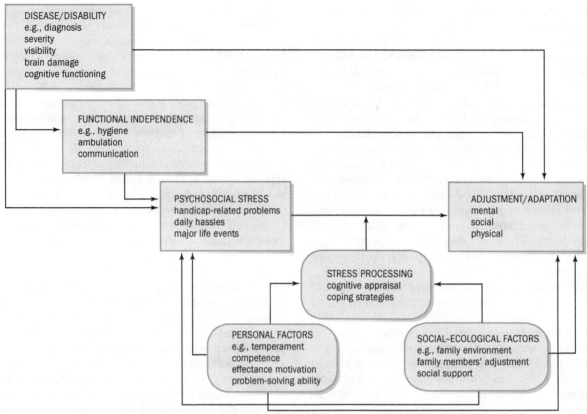

FIGURE 14.2   A conceptual model of child adjustment to chronic illness or disorder. Square-corner boxes indicate risk factors; round-corner boxes indicate resistance (protective) factors.   *From Wallander & Varni, 1998.*

the young person and the family; for example, the youth's existing competencies and the types and variety of coping skills that the young person possesses are likely to be important in this process. A second category of variables is disease factors, such as severity, degree of impairment, and the functional independence of the young person. In addition, the youth's environment (e.g., family, school, health care) is likely to be a factor in variations in adjustment. An appreciation of the complexity of the problem is illustrated in the model offered by Wallander, Varni, and their colleagues (Wallander & Varni, 1998; see Figure 14.2).

In the following sections, we examine two of the categories of influences on adjustment to chronic illness: illness parameters and family functioning.

ILLNESS PARAMETERS AND ADJUSTMENT   In seeking to understand the adjustment among young people with chronic illnesses, it is reasonable to ask whether aspects of the illness itself contribute to differences in adjustment. In attempting to answer this question, the severity of the illness, predictability of the illness, stress related to the illness, perceptions regarding the illness, and the degree of

functional impairment produced by the illness are among the variables that have been examined. Of course, analyzing these dimensions separately is not always possible. For example, a more severe illness is likely to be related to greater restrictions in normal functioning. However, each of these variables seems important.

Certain conditions are more severe than others, but severity of illness also can vary among young people with the same condition. What, then, might be the impact of severity of the medical problem? Findings are conflicting (Miceli, Rowland, & Whitman, 1999); however, some research does suggest a relationship between illness severity and adjustment (Blackman & Gurka, 2007; McQuaid, Kopel, & Nassau, 2001). For example, a longitudinal examination of youths with juvenile rheumatoid arthritis (JRA) found that although there were no significant overall differences in social functioning between children with JRA and control youths, severity of disease was a risk factor. Peers' ratings of liking declined over the 2-year period for children with more severe disease compared with those with mild disease. Also, children with active disease were chosen fewer times as a best friend than children in remission (Reiter-Purtill et al., 2003). However, more severe forms of a disorder are not always associated with poorer adjustment, and relationships are likely to be complex and may rely on the youth's and family's perceptions of the severity of the condition (Barakat, Alderfer, & Kazak, 2006; Klinnert et al., 2000; Wallander & Varni, 1998).

The young person's attitude toward the illness and the degree of stress experienced by the youth and family also may impact adjustment. For example, LeBovidge, Lavigne, & Miller (2005) examined the adjustment of young people aged 8 to 18 with chronic arthritis. Greater illness-related and nonillness-related stresses were both associated with higher levels of anxiety and depressive symptomatology and parent reports of adjustment problems. A more positive attitude toward illness, in contrast, was associated with lower levels of anxiety and depressive symptomatology. Figure 14.3 illustrates the relationship of arthritis-related stress and illness attitude to depressive symptomatolgy.

Adjustment also may be associated with the degree of **functional limitation** (how restricted the youth is) due to the chronic condition (Bleil et al., 2000; Meijer et al., 2000). Functional limitations may affect the number of absences from school, relationships with friends or other aspects of the youth's functioning. For example, inflammatory bowel disease (IBD) is a condition characterized by chronic inflammation of the gastrointestinal tract. Children with IBD experience frequent diarrhea, abdominal pain, weight loss, growth delay, delayed puberty, fatigue, and other symptoms. IBD is an unpredictable and potentially embarrassing disease. Youth may be embarrassed about their symptoms and frequent bathroom visits and this may lead to their limiting social activities. Also, social activities may be canceled due to disease flare-ups. The youth's short

stature and delayed puberty also can contribute to feeling different from one's peers (Greenley et al., 2010).

Ethically, we cannot manipulate emotional conditions or illness severity, nor can we randomly assign young people to diseases. Thus, interpreting the impact of aspects of illness is inevitably difficult. Furthermore, although illness factors may help predict adjustment, predictive ability is not very strong. Integrating illness factors into a more normative approach—one that combines these factors with the stress, risk, and resilience factors included in etiological models for young people without chronic medical disorder—is a useful approach (Soliday, Kool, & Lande, 2000). Such an approach would allow for identification of factors relatively unique to chronic illness, as well as those common to other young people and families. Among the variables that might be the focus of such a normative approach is family functioning.

FAMILY FUNCTIONING AND ADJUSTMENT The majority of research suggests no mean differences in family functioning between families of children with a chronic illness and normative data or control groups. However, it is not surprising that family functioning is related to the psychological adjustment of chronically ill children and adolescents (Kaugars et al., 2004; Long & Marsland, 2011; Power, 2006). Without denying the particular risks and stressors associated with chronic conditions, it is reasonable as a starting point to assume that some of the family influences that are related to adjustment of other children and adolescents, such as parenting behaviors, parental depression, disruptions in family life, and marital conflict, are also related to the adjustment of young people with chronic illness. Indeed, this seems to be the case (Lavigne & Faier-Routman, 1993; Otsuki et al., 2010; Wood et al., 2007b).

A variety of family influences known to be related to child and adolescent adjustment in general have also been investigated in populations of young people with a chronic condition (Long & Marsland, 2011; Quittner et al., 2009; Wallander et al., 2003). Timko and her colleagues (1993), working with youths with juvenile rheumatoid arthritis, examined how parental risk and resilience factors predicted disease-related **functional disabilities** (e.g., ability to grip things, ability to do routine household chores), pain, and psychosocial adjustment. After the age of the youths and initial levels of their functioning were controlled for, parents' personal strain and depressed mood and fathers' drinking were associated with poorer adjustment in the young people 4 years after initial contact. Better parental social functioning, the mothers' involvement in social activities, and the fathers' number of close relationships, on the other hand, seemed to facilitate the youths' adjustment. Given that attention has often concentrated on the contribution of maternal factors, it is interesting that the fathers'

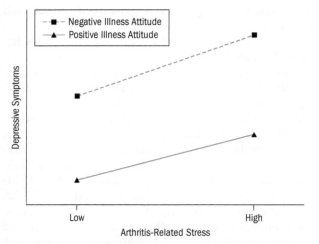

FIGURE 14.3 Arthritis-related stress, illness attitude, and depressive symptomatology. *Adapted from LeBovidge, Lavigne, & Miller, 2005.*

LISA

Diabetes Management and Family Context

Lisa is a 14-year-old with a history of insulin-dependent diabetes mellitus and a variety of behavior and health status problems. Her mother reports difficulties with Lisa's diabetes management, which have gotten worse recently, resulting in 10 hospitalizations in the past 12 months.

Lisa is the only adopted child in a family of four youths. She has three brothers, ages 20 years, 2 years, and 1 month. The 2-year-old was born seriously ill and required several operations, although he is now in good health. During the assessment process, Mrs. L openly expressed her hostility toward Lisa. In contrast, the oldest son is seen as perfect. Mrs. L is also exceptionally nurturing toward her two younger sons.

The births of the two younger brothers clearly changed Lisa's role in the family from youngest child and the focus of Mrs. L's nurturance to sibling caretaker. Mrs. L is feeling increasingly stressed and recently left work to care for the two boys. She is angry at her husband for his passive stance, but this remains largely unexpressed. The oldest son's decision to leave home for college leaves her without any male support. Mrs. L directs much of her anger toward Lisa. Lisa is angry also, and this is directed primarily toward her father. It is possible that she may be receiving subtle encouragement from her mother for this. At the same time, Lisa's difficulties draw her parents together. Lisa's behavior and hospitalizations also shift the family focus of attention away from her brothers and toward her.

Adapted from Johnson, 1998, pp. 428–429.

risk and resilience factors contributed to the youths' functioning and adjustment beyond what was already accounted for by maternal factors and other influences.

Illness-related parameters and family factors do not operate independently of each other. Illness-related and family factors may moderate or mediate each other's relationship to adjustment. Findings by Wagner and her colleagues (2003), for example, suggest that parental distress may interact with illness-related factors to affect child adjustment. Among youths with juvenile rheumatoid arthritis, the impact of parental distress was evident for those young people who perceived their illness to be more

intrusive—that is, interfering with their ability to engage in activities. These young people were more depressed. In contrast, parental distress was unrelated to the depression of youths with low levels of perceived illness intrusiveness.

Berg and colleagues (2011) examined the role of parental involvement in young adolescents with diabetes. Better quality of both the mothers' and fathers' relationships with their child (acceptance, independence and encouragement, and communication) was associated with better diabetes outcomes (metabolic control and adherence). In addition, mothers' and fathers' monitoring of the youths' general daily activities and of the youths' diabetes care behaviors was associated with better diabetes outcomes. Many of the relationships between parental involvement and diabetes outcomes were mediated by the adolescents' perceptions of self-efficacy. That is, better parental involvement was associated with the adolescents' greater confidence in their ability to manage diabetes situations and this, in turn, was associated with better diabetes outcomes.

Family variables such as conflict, control, and organization also appear to be associated with adjustment. In their comparison of diabetic youths and matched controls with acute illness, Wertlieb, Hauser, and Jacobson (1986) found that overt expression of family conflict was related to greater problem behavior in both groups. However, other factors differentiated the groups. One particularly interesting finding involved differences in attempts to control and maintain the family system. Among the acutely ill youths, a greater control orientation in the family was strongly related to a greater probability of behavior problems. In contrast, among the diabetic youth, low levels of family organization were associated with high levels of behavior problems. Families with a diabetic child have appreciable demands placed on them to organize daily routines involved in the management of the illness. Successful management of the diabetes probably requires appreciable organization and structure, as well as overtly dealing with issues of control. Structured and controlling family environments may be associated with better metabolic control of the diabetic condition. The relationship of family environment to adjustment among youths with chronic illness, however, is likely to be complex (Seiffge-Krenke, 1998; Wallander et al., 2003; Weist et al., 1993).

For example, cohesion is another family variable that seems to be important with regard to adjustment. It is often suggested that a life-threatening illness draws family members closer together. Increased cohesion, although not a universal reaction to illness, has been observed in families coping with a variety of illnesses (Long & Marsland, 2011; Wood et al., 1989). Level of cohesion also is frequently associated with management of the chronic condition and the adjustment of the young person and other family members (Helgeson et al., 2003; Lavigne & Faier-Routman, 1993; Stepansky et al., 2010).

A study of adolescent cancer survivors illustrates the importance of cohesion; however, it too suggests that relationships are likely to be complex (Rait et al., 1992). Adolescents who had previously been treated for leukemia, Hodgkin's disease, or non-Hodgkin's lymphoma, and who were currently in remission, participated in the study. The participants were 12 to 19 years old at the time of the assessment. The authors hypothesized that the experience of cancer would result in greater family cohesion and that cohesion would be associated with the psychosocial adjustment of these cancer survivors.

The adolescents completed a standard measure of family adaptability and cohesion. The cancer survivors' scores did differ from a normative community group, but not in the predicted direction. The adolescents who had survived cancer described their families as less cohesive than the community sample. There was, though, the expected relationship between cohesion and adjustment. Greater cohesion was associated with better posttreatment psychological adjustment. However, an interesting complexity was suggested. Among "recent" survivors (treatment completed a year or less ago) and "long-term" survivors (treatment completed more than 5 years ago), there was a strong relationship between family cohesiveness and adjustment. For "intermediate" survivors (treatment completed between 1 and 5 years ago), however, the association between family cohesiveness and adjustment was dramatically decreased.

These findings illustrate the importance of studying adjustment as a process over time and attending to critical developmental transitions such as transition to school and to early adolescence. The young person's condition may change, and the effect of the illness on the family may not be static. Furthermore, changes in the young person and in the illness may require changing styles of family involvement. Because young people with chronic illnesses have a greater chance of survival than ever before, these findings suggest the need for continued exploration of how time since treatment, current developmental level, age at diagnosis, and other variables may be related to the association of family environment and the young person's psychological adjustment (Helgeson et al., 2007; Holmbeck, Bruno, & Jandasek, 2006; Quittner et al., 2009; Vannatta et al., 2009).

As more children and adolescents survive chronic illnesses, the complexities of studying long-term adjustment become clear. Rather than asking about better disease adjustment, it may be more reasonable to ask how the experience of chronic illness affects individual development.

Cancer: Adapting to Chronic Illness

Cancer has long been viewed as a fatal and little-understood disease. Although this frightening image still remains, it is not as accurate as was once the case. With increasing survival rates, the emphasis has shifted from "dying from" to "living with" cancer (Eiser, 1998). It may now, for many youths, be more appropriate to view cancer as a chronic condition rather than a fatal disease (Cruce & Stinnett, 2006). For example, in 1960, acute lymphocytic leukemia, the most common form of childhood cancer, had a survival rate of 1% 5 years after diagnosis. By the mid-1970s, the survival rate had increased to about 49%, and by the early twenty-first century, to about 88%. Advances in treatment have improved the overall 5-year survival rate for childhood cancers to about 80% (Howlander et al., 2011).

Families may require continuing assistance to help them in supporting their child with cancer.

However, treatments are often lengthy, highly invasive, stressful, and accompanied by considerable pain. Working with this population thus presents multiple and complex challenges. In addition to the initial task of helping the young person and family understand and come to accept the illness, it is important to assist them in coping with a long and stressful treatment regimen and the additional stressors that the illness and its treatment place on them. For example, advice regarding the young person's school, teacher, and peer group is likely to be important during treatment and afterward (Cruce & Stinnett, 2006). Also, concerns regarding the longer-term psychosocial impact of the disease and its treatment are considerable (Vannatta et al., 2009). Potential effects are probably related to developmental period. For adolescents the disease may interfere with the development of autonomy as a result of increased dependence on family and medical staff, and it may impose restrictions on social life and the development of close interpersonal relationships.

Adolescence also is a developmental period during which some high-risk behaviors (substance use) may be somewhat normative. Even brief involvement in such behaviors can have significant consequences for young people with cancer. Problematic outcomes, however, are not inevitable. The provision of ongoing psychosocial services to families throughout this process may buffer the impact of the cancer experience and allow these young people to develop and function much like their peers. Such support and services may also assist siblings and other family members who are affected (Alderfer et al., 2010; Dolgin et al., 2007; Kazak, 2005; Lobato & Kao, 2005).

One must also be aware that the very treatments that have resulted in longer survival may contribute to other long-term challenges. Advances in treatments such as chemotherapy and radiation have contributed to increased life expectancy. However, young people who have completed these treatments are at increased risk for

ACCENT
The Impact of HIV/AIDS in Children and Adolescents

An appreciable number of those infected with HIV and AIDS are women of childbearing age. The HIV-positive children born to these women are some of the saddest images of the AIDS story. These babies are often very sick and frequently are given away or taken from their mothers. Many of them are taken in by foster parents who are willing to take on the challenge of caring for such a child. Fortunately, with medical advances, the number of HIV babies born to HIV-positive women in the United States has dropped dramatically over time. However, this problem remains a considerable international concern (Culver, Gardener, & Operario, 2007; Fang et al., 2009).

Although many young people become infected through vertical transmission from their mothers, some, such as those with hemophilia, become infected through the blood supply. For older children and adolescents, there is also risk for transmission by drug use or sexual contact (Donenberg, Paikoff, & Pequegnat, 2006; Lescano et al., 2009).

With medical advances producing greater survival rates, attention has shifted from terminal care for affected youths to management of the condition and improving quality of life (Armstrong, Willen, & Sorgen, 2003; Benton, 2010; MacDonnell et al., 2010; Outlaw et al., 2010).

We have known for some time that children born infected with HIV are likely to have developmental and neurocognitive problems. Improved antiretroviral therapy, however, has improved the situation by slowing down the progression of central nervous system disease (Benton, 2010). However, by school age if these neurological problems exist, they may result in significant learning, language, and attention difficulties, and emotional and social difficulties may also be evident.

The impact may be greater for young people with greater compromise of their immune system (Bordeaux et al., 2003). Young people with HIV/AIDS are thus likely to have to continue to adapt to extraordinary circumstances and are also likely to present their caregivers with exceptional challenges.

It is important to remember that not all HIV-infected youths have clinically significant cognitive, emotional, and behavioral problems. However, among those who do, a complex set of influences is likely contributing to the difficulties. Clearly, some of the problems are direct outcomes of their disease. The medical treatments and the stress of adhering to a long-term medical regimen and a chronic illness are probably factors as well (Bachanas et al., 2001; Benton, 2010; Fang et al., 2009; Malee et al., 2009; New et al., 2007; Steele, Nelson, & Cole, 2007; Wachsler-Felder & Golden, 2002).

Families also face difficult decisions regarding disclosure of the illness both to the child and others. In addition, many of these young people were born to mothers whose prenatal care was not optimal, who abused drugs when they were pregnant, or who had serious psychopathology themselves. Those youths who contract the disease from drug use or sexual contact are also likely to have been exposed to other risk factors (Outlaw et al., 2010). All of these powerful influences, as well as family and environmental risks that the young people may have faced after their births, make current problematic outcomes understandable. The adaptation challenges are considerable and call for a coordinated and intensive program of assistance for these young people and their families (Lescano et al., 2009).

physical health difficulties such as growth and reproductive difficulties, cardiological, pulmonary, renal/urological, orthopedic, sensorymotor, and neurological impairments, and secondary malignancies. Cosmetic impairments and functional limitations (e.g., diminished stamina) have also been frequently noted. Some of these effects may not be apparent immediately after treatment, but may occur later among survivors, and their impact may evolve over time (Moore, 2005; Ness & Gurney, 2007; Vannatta et al., 2009). Interventions designed to help promote healthy behaviors and decrease high risk behaviors can help prevent and control negative physical outcomes (Butler et al., 2008; Tercyak et al., 2006).

Challenges in psychological and cognitive domains may also be associated with medical treatments. For example, the immediate and long-term impacts on the central nervous system (CNS) of treatments such as craniospinal irradiation (CSI) and chemotherapy to prevent central nervous system occurrence of leukemia are of concern. Impairment does appear to occur in cognitive and academic functioning from such treatments and, thus, CSI may be reserved for children who relapse or who are at high risk for CNS involvement. Nonetheless, continued concern and attention to long-term neurocognitive impacts remain and require monitoring and intervention (Butler et al., 2008; Carey et al., 2007; Moore, 2005; Vannatta et al., 2009).

The shift to coping, adjusting, and adapting to cancer is clearly a more optimistic approach than in years past when survival rates were very low. However, while we continue to attempt to understand this process and assist young people and families, we must also monitor long-term outcomes and side effects of treatment. In addition, relapse remains possible, and these individuals are at increased risk for secondary cancers. Maintaining vigilance without creating additional and undue anxiety, and at the same time promoting an optimistic and adaptive attitude, presents a considerable challenge.

A similar perspective on adaptation applies to other chronic illnesses such as sickle cell disease and HIV/AIDS (see Accent: "The Impact of HIV/AIDS in Children and Adolescents"). The consequences of the illness or condition itself as well as the impact of intensive, demanding, and long-term treatments need to be addressed in understanding adaptation to these chronic conditions over time (Brown et al., 2006; Kucera & Sullivan, 2011; Lemanek & Ranalli, 2009; New, Lee, & Elliott, 2007).

FACILITATING MEDICAL TREATMENT

Attempts to provide psychological treatment that would improve a patient's medical condition have long been an aspect of the interface between psychology/psychiatry and medicine. The vast majority of early attempts sought to provide the patient with psychotherapy as a means of reducing physical symptoms or curing illness. Such direct assaults on illness through psychotherapy proved to be largely ineffective (Werry, 1986). More recent efforts are likely to take a somewhat different approach to integrating a psychological perspective into the clinically relevant, empirically supported treatment of medical problems (Beale, 2006; Nelson & Steele, 2009). Although a comprehensive review of these multiple efforts and strategies is beyond the scope of the present chapter, a few important illustrations follow.

Adherence to Medical Regimens

The terms **adherence** and **compliance** describe how well a young person or family follows recommended medical treatments such as taking medications, following diets, or implementing lifestyle changes. Diabetes provides an excellent illustration of the way psychologists have increasingly attempted to understand the complex tasks encountered by families managing chronic childhood disorders (La Greca & Mackay, 2009; Wysocki, Buckloh, & Greco, 2009).

A DESCRIPTION OF DIABETES   Diabetes is one of the most common chronic diseases in young people, affecting approximately 1.8 youths per 1,000. Type 1 diabetes (T1D), also known as insulin-dependent diabetes mellitus, is a lifelong disorder that results when the pancreas produces insufficient insulin. Daily replacement of insulin by injection is required. Because the onset of T1D typically occurs in childhood, this form of diabetes is often referred to as a childhood or juvenile diabetes. In Type 2 diabetes rather than insulin deficiency, insulin resistance occurs, impairing cellular uptake of insulin. Type 2 diabetes was previously viewed as an adult-onset disorder. However, along with increases in childhood obesity, there has been an increase in type 2 diabetes such that 10 to 20% of new cases of diabetes in youth are of this type. Type 2 diabetes is disproportionately high among African American, American Indian, and Latino/Hispanic populations. Type 2 diabetes may be managed by weight reduction, exercise, and careful diet. However, many young people with this form of diabetes need insulin injections (National Diabetes Information Clearinghouse, 2008; Sandberg & Zurenda, 2006; Wysocki, 2006).

Onset of T1D occurs most often around puberty, but can occur at any time from infancy to early adulthood. Genetic factors appear to be involved in the etiology of T1D. Both forms of diabetes increase the long-term risk for damage to the heart, kidneys, eyes, and nervous system.

If the disorder is not controlled, a condition known as ketosis, or ketoacidosis, may occur. This is a very serious condition that can lead to coma and death.

The young person and family face a treatment regimen that includes dietary restrictions, daily injections of insulin, monitoring of urine, and testing of blood glucose levels (see Table 14.1). On the basis of the daily tests for level of sugar—and factors such as timing of meals, diet, exercise, physical health, and emotional state—the daily dosages of insulin must be adjusted. Even under the best of circumstances, "insulin reactions" occur often. Thus the youngster must be sensitive to the signs and symptoms of both hyperglycemia (excessively high levels of blood glucose) and hypoglycemia (excessively low blood glucose). Adverse reactions involve irritability, headache, tremor/shaking, weakness and—if not detected early enough—unconsciousness and seizures. The fact that symptoms are different for different individuals and are subjectively experienced

makes the task of identifying them complicated. Parents and youths are therefore faced with a difficult, often unpredictable, and emotion-laden therapeutic program that requires careful integration into daily life and into their functioning in school and other settings (Kucera & Sullivan, 2011; Wysocki et al., 2009).

MANAGEMENT OF THE DIABETIC CONDITION The first task in treatment is for the team of professionals to gain and maintain control of the diabetic condition. As this task is achieved, insulin requirements often decrease, and the initial fears and concerns of the youth and family are often reduced. This has come to be known as the "honeymoon period." This period of partial remission may terminate gradually and often ends about 1 to 2 years after initial diagnosis. In any case, beginning a diabetes self-management program with families during the first few months after diagnosis may avoid any deterioration in metabolic function, and early intervention with young children may help to reduce adherence problems and problems in diabetic control during later periods (Davis et al., 2001; Delamater et al., 1990). Transferring control for management of the disease from the professional to the family and child or adolescent, as well as requiring maintenance of such control over long periods of time, is one of the challenges of working with chronic illness (Berg et al., 2011; La Greca & Mackey, 2009).

ADHERENCE TO THE DIABETIC REGIMEN The concept of adherence is multifaceted (La Greca & Mackey, 2009). Appreciation of this complexity has led to the development of intervention programs that combine strategies such as education, training in self-management skills, and facilitating family involvement and communication. Such programs appear to be promising (Graves et al., 2010; La Greca & Mackey, 2009; Wysocki et al., 2009). The initial step in most programs is to educate the youth and family about the disease. Although such efforts are regularly made, it cannot be assumed that, following these efforts, the family's knowledge will be adequate. Therefore, it is helpful to regularly assess knowledge. Behavioral observation methods have been employed to assess whether the young person knows how to execute necessary skills such as urine and blood glucose testing. Questionnaires are frequently used to measure knowledge of the disease and the application of that knowledge to different situations (e.g., the role of insulin and adjusting diet based on blood sugar readings). However, adherence is not just a matter of accurate information and knowledge; it requires that the prescribed tasks be accurately and consistently carried out.

TABLE 14.1 Some Activities Required of Diabetic Children and Families

Inject insulin regularly
Test blood regularly
Exercise regularly
Avoid sugar
Check for symptoms—low
Check for symptoms—high
Be careful when sick
Shower regularly
Wear diabetes ID
Watch weight
Eat meals regularly
Adjust diet to exercise
Carry sugar
Test blood as directed
Change injection site
Inject insulin as directed
Watch dietary fat
Take care of injuries
Eat regular snacks
Control emotions
Inspect feet

Adapted from Karoly & Bay, 1990.

We will highlight several important variables that are involved in adherence. Developmental level is one important variable (Iannotti & Bush, 1993; La Greca & Mackey, 2009; Palmer et al., 2004). For example, children under 9 years may have difficulty accurately measuring and injecting insulin. In general, knowledge and skills seem to increase with age (Heidgerken et al., 2007).

Adolescence is a period during which management of diabetes often deteriorates (Helgeson et al., 2009; Johnson, 1995). The adolescent's knowledge of the disease and its management may be overestimated. Adolescents may, for instance, make errors in estimating their blood glucose levels, particularly when blood glucose levels are quite variable (Meltzer et al., 2003). Whereas increasing cognitive development potentially allows the adolescent to better understand the illness and the complex routine, there are other aspects of cognition that may affect management of the disease. For example, Berg and colleagues (2011) found that greater adolescent perceived diabetes self-efficacy—confidence in the ability to manage difficult diabetes situations—was related to better adherence and a better level of metabolic control.

During adolescence control is often gradually transferred to the youth, and parental participation often ceases, but total withdrawal of adult involvement may not be advisable (Helgeson et al., 2008; Holmes et al., 2006). It may be important, for example, for the parent to continue to monitor the adolescent's diabetic care behaviors (Berg et al., 2011; Ellis et al., 2007; Palmer et al., 2011). Also, individual judgments of a young person's developmental readiness, psychological functioning, and the balance of child and parent involvement must be made (Hanna, DiMeglio, & Fortenberry, 2007; Helgeson et al., 2009; Palmer et al., 2009; Wiebe et al., 2005).

For example, Palmer and colleagues (2004) studied young people between the ages of 10 and 15 who had a diagnosis of T1D for at least 1 year. Mothers' and children's perceptions of who was responsible for various aspects of diabetes management were assessed. Measures of the youth's developmental maturity were also obtained. The youths also completed a measure of their level of self-reliance/autonomy, and their pubertal status was assessed through mothers' reports of the extent to which their child displayed specific signs of puberty. Metabolic control of the diabetes was assessed through medical records of Hba_{1c} (glycosylated hemoglobin test—reflecting average blood glucose levels). Among individuals with low levels of self-reliance/autonomy and low pubertal status, transfer of diabetes responsibility from mother to child was associated with higher Hba_{1c} values (poorer control). The effects on metabolic control of self-reliance, pubertal status, and maternal responsibility for diabetes are illustrated in Figure 14.4.

Social and emotional concerns, such as peer acceptance and greater participation in activities, also are associated with decreased adherence (Helgeson et al., 2010; Thomas, Peterson, & Goldstein, 1997; Wysocki et al., 2009). Young people with diabetes may wish to avoid appearing different. The unusual behaviors required for control of their condition (e.g., injections, glucose testing), the dietary demands of eating frequently (when others are not), and the need to avoid high-fat foods and sweets (when others are eating junk food), make conformity difficult. Some of these social challenges are illustrated in Table 14.2. These vignettes are used to assess social problem solving among diabetic youth. In addition, conflicts with parents over issues of independence are likely to be present. Such social and interpersonal issues most likely combine with actual physical changes, like those

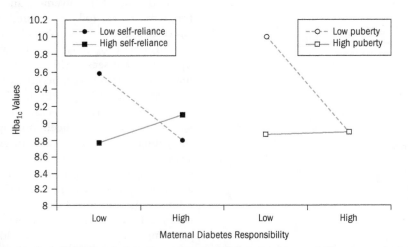

FIGURE 14.4 Metabolic control of diabetes as a function of maternal diabetes responsibility, youngster's level of self-reliance, and youngster's pubertal status. *Adapted from Palmer et al., 2004.*

TABLE 14.2 Examples of Vignettes to Evaluate Social Problem-Solving in Diabetic Youth

Glucose Testing

Your friends ask you to go to a video arcade, and it's almost time for you to test your glucose. You don't have your test materials with you, and your friends are impatient to leave. If you stop and test, they will leave without you.

Diet—Sweets

You are invited to your best friend's birthday party, where they are going to serve cake and ice cream at a time when you are supposed to have a snack. But cake and ice cream would not fit into your diet plan at all, since you are supposed to have a snack that is low in sugar and fat.

Diet—Time of Eating

Your friends invite you out for dinner at your favorite restaurant, but they want to go really late, a lot later than you would normally eat.

Alcohol

Your friends invite you to a big party. You go there, and you find out that almost everyone is drinking beer. Your friends offer you some beer and seem to expect that you will drink it just as everyone else did.

Adapted from Thomas, Peterson, & Goldstein, 1997.

associated with delayed puberty, to increase management and compliance difficulties for adolescents. Interventions should maintain parental involvement yet minimize parent–adolescent and peer conflict and improve communication and problem-solving skills (La Greca & Mackey, 2009; Wysocki et al., 2009).

Many other problems regarding adherence are worthy of continued attention. For example, anticipating environmental obstacles to compliance is important. Creating interventions that help adolescents deal with peers concerning their diabetes and that facilitate appropriate peer support, for instance, are likely to facilitate compliance with recommendations (Greco et al., 2001; Wagner et al., 2006; Wysocki et al., 2009). The realization that the immediate consequences of diabetes management are often negative, and therefore may reduce the individual's commitment to adherence, may also help to anticipate difficulties. For example, the immediate consequence of injections is discomfort, whereas the adverse effect of skipping injections is not immediate. Thus, interventions that reduce the immediate negative effects of compliance may be of value.

Caregivers also may be impacted by the illness and the disease management process (Driscoll et al., 2010). Attention to the needs of caregivers is likely to improve adherence. Attention to the role of the health care system and primary care providers (pediatrician, nurse) is another important aspect of the adherence process (Dunbar-Jacob, 1993; La Greca & Mackey, 2009). The behavior of health care providers is important. Information provided must be sufficient and presented in a manner that allows the family to carry out complex regimens (DiMatteo, 2000; Ievers et al., 1999). Health care providers, too, must be sufficiently aware of the youth's level of cognitive development so as to not overestimate or underestimate the youth's understanding of the illness and treatment regimen. Providers also must assist the youth and family in achieving a developmentally appropriate balance of responsibilities for diabetes care (Lewin et al., 2006). These issues suggest the importance of training health care providers to be sensitive to the needs of individual families and youths and to improve professional–patient communication (DiMatteo, 2000; Power, 2006).

Psychological Modification of Chronic Pain

The Eastern mystic who walks on hot coals, voluntarily slows the heart, and by the power of the mind closes a wound has always fascinated inhabitants of the Western world. Fascinating, too, are the shaman's cures by removal of evil spirits, the miracles performed by faith healers, and cures of medical ailments by inert placebos (Ullmann & Krasner, 1975). These phenomena highlight in a dramatic fashion the possible role of psychological interventions in the treatment of medical disorders. Each phenomenon suggests that psychological procedures can directly affect physical functioning. The systematic and scientific study of how psychology can be used to directly treat physical symptoms such as pain has become part of the shifting emphasis in understanding mind–body relationships.

The use of relaxation and biofeedback to treat young people's headaches is one example of attempts to directly modify physical functioning through psychological interventions. Headaches are usually classified as tension, migraine, or a combination of the two. The pain and suffering that can accompany intense headaches, and the desire to avoid potential negative aspects of drug treatment led to the exploration of nonpharmacological approaches (Andrasik, Blake, & McCarran, 1986; Dahlquist & Nagel, 2009).

Biofeedback refers to a procedure in which some device gives immediate feedback to the person about a particular biological function. Feedback is usually provided by a signal such as a light or tone or by some graphic display. Such feedback, some form of relaxation training or a combination of the two, seem effective in producing clinically meaningful levels of improvement in children's headaches (Burke & Andrasik, 1989; Holden, Deichmann, & Levy, 1999; Larsson et al., 2005; Powers, Jones, & Jones, 2005).

Relaxation procedures also have been employed as part of cognitive-behavioral packages for the treatment of chronic pain associated with headache and other conditions such as arthritis, sickle-cell disease, and recurrent abdominal pain. These cognitive-behavioral treatments often include imagery training to reduce or control pain and teaching youth to replace negative and catastrophizing thoughts with positive and encouraging self-statements (Dahlquist & Nagel, 2009).

CINDY

Chronic Headache Pain

Cindy, 14 years old, attended a demanding private school. She reported that she had been experiencing daily headaches for 18 months. She described constant pain that varied in intensity but she never experienced total relief from the pain. She had carefully followed the medication and other recommendations of her neurologist, but experienced only minimal improvement. Cindy did not feel well enough to participate in social activities and had become isolated from her friends. She could not concentrate when the pain intensified and her grades had begun to suffer. Cindy also stopped participating in sports to avoid exacerbating the pain. She described experiencing fatigue and frustration and believed that she would never get rid of her headaches. Cindy received biofeedback-assisted relaxation training that incorporated guided imagery, breathing exercises, and progressive muscle relaxation. Within three sessions Cindy was able to produce dramatic changes in the physiological indices targeted by the biofeedback and reported decreased pain and anxiety while practicing the cognitive-behavioral techniques. Cindy was encouraged to use these skills at school. After six sessions, Cindy reported marked decreases in the intensity of her headaches and feelings of efficacy in coping with pain. Her headaches rarely decreased to the level of being undetectable, but the pain levels dropped to the point where she was able to resume her previous activities, and her grades improved.

Adapted from Powers, Jones, & Jones, 2005, p. 72.

Innovations to increase accessibility of treatments have also been explored. Connelly and colleagues (2006), for example, developed a minimal therapist contact cognitive-behavioral treatment for recurrent pediatric headache. As an adjunct to the recommendations of their neurologist, participants received CD-ROMs containing the "Headstrong" program. Participants completed 4 week-long modules (education, relaxation, thought-changing, and pain behavior modification) and received weekly phone contact to answer questions. Children who received the CD-ROM program had significant improvements in their headaches beyond that of the control group who continued following their neurologists' prescriptions.

Reducing Procedure-Related Pain and Distress

Developing psychologically based procedures for enhancing the effectiveness of medical treatment is another important and growing area of interest. Procedures for dealing with pain and discomfort associated with medical treatment illustrate this potentially important contribution.

PAIN AND DISTRESS   Despite its seeming simplicity, pain is a complex phenomenon that is difficult to assess. It is difficult, for example, to separate the pain or discomfort that the person is suffering from the anxiety that the person is experiencing while undergoing a painful medical procedure. This difficulty has led some to use the term *distress* to encompass pain, anxiety, and other negative affect (Jay, 1988; Varni, Katz, & Waldron, 1993). Whatever term is chosen, multiple assessment methods have been employed and three different response systems might be assessed: cognitive-affective, behavioral, and physiological (Blount, Piira, & Cohen, 2003; Cohen et al., 2008; McCulloch & Collins, 2006).

Self-report measures of the cognitive-affective component of pain are the measures most frequently employed. Because pain is a subjective experience, assessing the youth's experience of pain is important. In addition, the greater accessibility of this component and the relative ease of measurement are certainly factors. However, measurement is not without its difficulties. For example, the young person's developmental level plays a large role in selecting a self-report measure. Because older children may be able to describe pain in semantic terms, they can be assessed by means of interviews and questionnaires. For younger children, professionals rely on concrete and visual methods. In very young children faces with expressions ranging from neutral or smiles to severe frowns may be useful (see Figure 14.5). If photographs are employed, use of ethnically appropriate images may be important (Beyer & Knott, 1998; Hicks et al., 2001).

FIGURE 14.5   Drawings of faces have been used to assess pain distress in young children. Illustrated are drawings that may suggest two ends of a range of choices—neutral (left) through very painful (right).

The behavioral component of children's distress (e.g., behaviors that require the child to be physically restrained) can often interfere with effective medical treatment. Observational methods are often used to assess children's distress behaviors. Structured behavioral observations employing a system of defined behaviors and trained observers have been employed in a variety of contexts (Blount et al., 2009). Such procedures can be expensive and time consuming; an alternative is to use global ratings of the young person's distress behaviors by parents or nurses.

Assessment of the physiological aspect of pain is far less common. Melamed and Siegel's (1975) measurement of palmar sweat before and after youths underwent elective surgery and Jay and colleagues' (1987) monitoring of pulse rate prior to bone marrow aspiration are examples of use of physiological measures. However, the equipment necessary and the difficulty involved in reliably obtaining measures such as heart rate, blood pressure, and skin conductance make such measures less likely to be employed.

HELPING THE CHILD COPE   Procedures have been developed to assist young people in coping with the pain associated with their disease or disorder, or with the treatments they receive (Blount et al., 2009; Dahlquist & Nagel, 2009; Powers et al., 2005). Many of the medical procedures used to assess and treat children with chronic disorders are aversive. Well-timed preparation of the young person that contains appropriate information that he or she can understand and remember is the first step in reducing distress and in helping the young person cope. The basic rationale for preparation is that unexpected stress is worse than predictable stress. From the simple statement that preparation is good follows the complex question of how this is best achieved for varying situations and for different young people. Research provides some guidelines and suggests

certain procedures (Blount et al., 2009; Jaaniste, Hayes, & von Baeyer, 2007; Peterson & Mori, 1988).

Children's distress and experiences of pain during medical procedures are related to the behavior of their parents (Blount et al., 2009). When parents use strategies to distract the child or to direct the child to use coping techniques, the child exhibits less distress. Parental focus on symptoms and parental anxiety may increase distress and reduce the effectiveness of distraction techniques (Dahlquist & Pendley, 2005; Williams, Blount, & Walker, 2011). Also, when parents attempt to comfort the child by reassuring statements or apologies, distress may be greater (Manimala et al., 2000; Salmon & Pereira, 2002).

The behavior of the medical practitioner is also likely to affect the young person. For example, Dahlquist,

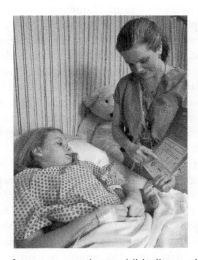

It is common for young people to exhibit distress during medical procedures. Techniques that reduce or help control distress can facilitate good medical care.

Power, & Carlson (1995) found that information presented by a professional in a reassuring manner may reduce child distress. It may be that young people respond differently to parents and to staff and that an appropriate combination of distraction/direction and reassurance may be beneficial to the young person (Friedman et al., 1998; Mahoney, Ayers, & Seddon, 2010).

Young people themselves have made some recommendations regarding coping strategies (Ross, 1988). Many of these suggestions cluster around the perception of being in control (Carpenter, 1992), and many involve the young person's controlling the environment during the aversive treatment procedure. The following comment by a 10-year-old boy undergoing emergency room burn treatment illustrates this phenomenon:

> I said, "How about a hurting break?" and he (intern) said, "Hey, man, are you serious?" And I said, "Sure. Even when ladies are having babies they get a little rest between the bad pains." And they (the pediatric emergency room personnel) all laughed and he said, "OK, you get a 60-second break whenever you need it," and then it was much, much better, like you wouldn't believe it. (Ross, 1988, p. 5)

Although young people may be capable of generating their own strategies for coping with pain and distress, procedures for teaching effective stress management/coping skills are also needed. Most interventions consist of a variety of coping strategies derived from behavioral and cognitive-behavioral perspectives and these seem to be effective procedures (Blount et al., 2009; Powers, 1999).

The work of Jay and her colleagues on reducing the distress of youths undergoing bone marrow aspirations is a good example of such efforts (Jay et al., 1987; 1991; 1995). Bone marrow aspirations (BMAs) are often conducted for children and adolescents with leukemia in order to examine the marrow for evidence of cancer cells. The procedure, in which a large needle is inserted into the hip bone and the marrow is suctioned out, is very painful. The use of general anesthesia and intramuscular injections of sedatives are avoided because there is concern regarding substantial medical risks and side effects.

The intervention package developed by Jay and her colleagues consists of five major components: filmed modeling, breathing exercises, emotive imagery/distraction, positive incentive, and behavioral rehearsal. The intervention package is administered on the day of the scheduled BMA, about 30 to 45 minutes prior to the procedure.

In the first step, the young person is shown an 11-minute film of a same-age model undergoing BMA. The model, on a voice overlay, narrates the steps involved in the procedure, as well as his or her thoughts and feelings at crucial points. The model also exhibits positive coping behaviors and self statements. The child in the film exhibits a realistic amount of anxiety but copes with it rather than exhibiting no anxiety and distress at all. After observing the film, the patients are taught simple breathing exercises, which are intended as active attention distracters but may also promote some relaxation.

The patients are then taught imagery/distraction techniques. Emotive imagery (Lazarus & Abramavitz, 1962) is a technique in which images are used to inhibit anxiety. A child's hero images are ascertained in a discussion with the child. They are then woven into a story that elicits positive affect that is presumed to be incompatible with anxiety, that transforms the meaning of the pain, and that encourages mastery rather than avoidance of pain. One girl's emotive imagery resembled the following story:

> She pretended that Wonderwoman had come to her house and asked her to be the newest member of her Superpower Team. Wonderwoman had given her special powers. These special powers made her very strong and tough so that she could stand almost anything. Wonderwoman asked her to take some tests to try out these superpowers. The tests were called bone marrow aspirations and spinal taps. These tests hurt, but with her new superpowers, she could take deep breaths and lie very still. Wonderwoman was very proud when she found out that her superpowers worked, and she made the Superpower team. (Jay et al., 1985, p. 516)

Another imagery distraction technique involves teaching the young person to form a pleasant image that is incompatible with the experience of pain (e.g., a day at the beach). The young person chooses either the emotive or the incompatible strategy and is given guidance during the bone marrow procedure to help in forming the images.

A positive incentive component of the intervention includes a trophy presented as a symbol of mastery and courage. The young person is told she can win the trophy if she does "the best that she can possibly do." The situation is structured so that every patient can be successful in getting the trophy.

There is also a behavioral rehearsal phase during which younger children "play doctor" with a doll, whereas older children are guided in conducting a "demonstration." The young people are instructed step-by-step in the administration of the BMA. As the young person goes through the procedure, the doll is instructed to lie still and do the breathing exercises and imagery.

ACCENT
Preventing Childhood Injury

Prevention and health maintenance is another aspect of current pediatric psychology. Prevention of injury is one example of such efforts. Many efforts to prevent injury to children are inspired by the work of Lizette Peterson (DiLillo & Tremblay, 2005).

Each year millions of children are injured. Indeed, injuries are the leading cause of death and medical visits for youths over the age of 1 in the United States (Kochanek et al., 2011). Clearly, the loss of life and function is tragic, and the medical costs and psychological consequences can be considerable (Brosbe, Hoefling, & Faust, 2011; Niska, Bhuiya, & Xu, 2010; Schwebel & Gaines, 2007).

There are a number of challenges to injury prevention (Brown Kirschman, Mayes, & Perciful, 2009; Tremblay & Peterson, 1999). One obstacle is that serious injuries are often mistakenly assumed to occur infrequently and to be chance events and, thus, unavoidable. Such assumptions do not encourage an active prevention effort. Professionals therefore suggest abandoning the common term *accident* in favor of **unintentional injury**, a term that acknowledges that the event, though not deliberate, might have been avoided.

Another challenge to injury prevention described by Tremblay and Peterson (1999) is the variety of modes of injury and thus potential interventions: "A toddler mastering the operation of the gate blocking access to the swimming pool, a 7-year-old riding a bicycle without a helmet, and a 16-year-old driving with peers who ridicule him when he stays within the speed limit are all candidates for a variety of potential interventions ...."

A basic contribution of psychology is the perspective that there are important behavioral antecedents to injury prevention. Behaviors of young people (e.g., impulsivity, risk taking), parents (e.g., supervision, protectiveness), and peers (persuasion, modeling), and environment-based variables (e.g., chaos, hazards), can contribute to child injury and likely interact with each other (Brown Kirschman et al., 2009; Morrongiello, Kane, & Zdzieborski, 2011; Schwebel & Brezausek, 2010). The risk, for example, of a child's ingesting household poisons is increased when the child is old enough to explore his or her environment but still young enough to impulsively ingest a substance, and by a setting in which poisons are accessible and constant supervision is lacking.

Prevention efforts can involve tactics directed at the entire population (e.g., legislative action, consumer product safety, multimedia campaigns), particular subsets of the population (bicycle safety programs for families with young children), or at certain milestones (counseling at yearly visits to the pediatrician). Providing education about vulnerability and the seriousness and extent of childhood injuries as well as information regarding safety behaviors can be part of the effort (Mc Laughlin & Glang, 2010; Morrongiello & Matheis, 2007a). Information may not be sufficient, however. Parents should not be lulled into a false sense of security. For example, parents whose children use safety equipment such as bicycle helmets may allow their children to take greater risks and young people themselves may feel less vulnerable (Morrongiello & Matheis, 2007b). This may offset some of the benefits of safety instruction and equipment (De Lillo & Tremblay, 2001).

Multiple-component prevention programs aimed at modifying risk behaviors and that include modeling, and rewards and incentives for appropriate injury-prevention behavior are needed to supplement information (Barton, Schwebel, & Morrongiello, 2007; Brown Kirschman et al., 2009; Peterson, Reach, & Grabe, 2003; Schwebel et al., 2006).

Jay and her colleagues (1987) compared this cognitive-behavioral package with a low-risk pharmacological intervention (oral Valium) and a minimal treatment-attention control condition. Each young person experienced each of these interventions during three different BMAs. It was randomly determined which of the six possible orders of these interventions was received. When in the cognitive-behavioral intervention condition, young people had significantly lower behavioral distress, lower pain ratings, and lower pulse rates than when they were in the control condition. When young people were in the Valium condition, they showed no significant differences from the control condition except that they had lower blood pressure scores.

The findings of this study represent one example of interventions that can help young people and families cope with the distress associated with certain medical procedures. The incorporation of parents or other family members into such programs can improve the maintenance of child coping, reduce parent/family distress, and improve the cost-effectiveness of interventions that otherwise might require a great deal of professional time. Such interventions hold the promise of making delivery of effective medical treatment more likely (Blount et al., 2009).

Preparation for Hospitalization

Young people suffering from chronic illness often require periodic hospitalization to stabilize their functioning. Other young people, too, may need to enter the hospital for scheduled surgery, for some other procedure, or in an emergency. Indeed, about one-third of all young people are hospitalized at least once. Siegel and Conte (2001), writing on the history and status of hospitalization for medical care, indicated that in the mid-1950s the importance of the child's psychological reaction to early hospitalization and surgery began to be recognized. Two films by James Robertson at the Tavistock Clinic are suggested to have been instrumental in changing attitudes and practices. One film portrayed a young child's intense distress at being separated from his parents for a week while undergoing minor surgery. The other film demonstrated the positive adjustment of a young person whose mother remained with him while he was hospitalized for surgery. Also, a substantial research literature documented the stressful effects of hospitalization (Siegel & Conte, 2001). Improvements have occurred since the 1950s and 1960s, when much of this research was conducted. For example, in 1954 most New York hospitals allowed parental contact only during 2 visiting hours per week. In contrast, Roberts and Wallander (1992), describing a 1988 survey of 286 hospitals in the United States and Canada, found that 98% of the hospitals had unrestricted visiting for parents and that 94% allowed parent rooming-in.

Prehospital preparation for both the child and the parents when admissions are planned is now common (O'Byrne, Peterson, & Saldana, 1997; Wright et al., 2007). One well-supported method involves models who, although apprehensive, cope with the hospitalization stresses. Melamed and Siegel's (1975) film, *Ethan Has an Operation*, showed a 7-year-old boy prior to, during, and after surgery. The child narrated the story and showed realistic but adaptive reactions to the procedures. The film has been shown to be an effective means of preparation for hospitalization and surgery (Melamed & Siegel, 1980; Peterson et al., 1984). Interventions often combine modeling with explicit training of coping techniques and programs targeting preparation for surgery include these and other educational and anxiety reduction procedures (Blount et al., 2009). Current efforts are directed at preparation procedures that are well timed; are matched to individual characteristics of the child, parent, and family; and are cost-effective.

Hospital-related anxiety and stressors require attention, because improvements in these areas appear to improve medical aspects of treatment and are associated with earlier discharge (Blount et al., 2009). Interventions also appear to enhance the mood state and adjustment of young people and this seems particularly important to those youths who are chronically ill and may require frequent hospitalizations.

THE DYING CHILD

Clearly, one of the most distressing aspects of working with severely ill children and adolescents is the prospect of death. Even though much progress has been made at increasing survival rates, the numbers still fall appreciably short of 100% (Howlander et al., 2011). Increased survival rates may make the death of a child even harder to bear when it does occur (Eiser, 1994). Several important and difficult questions are raised by the prospect of a dying child:

- What is the child's understanding of death?
- How can we best prepare the young person and the family?
- How do we prepare people for death while sustaining their motivation for treatment?
- Can we help the family begin to accept the child's impending death but prevent the family from prematurely distancing from the child?
- What do we do after the young person dies?
- How is the helper affected by working with the dying child?

Children's ideas about death change during development and are influenced by experiences, family attitude, and cultural factors. Cognitive development plays a role in the evolving conceptualization of death (Candy-Gibbs, Sharp, & Petrun, 1985; Gerhardt et al., 2009; Oltjenbruns, 2001). Young children may think of death as being less alive and assume it to be reversible. At about 5 years of age, an appreciation of the finality of death may be present, but death still does not seem inevitable. An understanding of death as final and inevitable and of personal mortality emerges at about age 9 or 10. Nevertheless, children may be aware of death and be worried about their fatal illness even if they do not have a fully developed concept of death. Although adolescents' understanding of death may be similar to that of adults, attention to the particular aspects of this stage of development is needed (Balk & Corr, 2001; Freyer et al., 2006).

Family members, too, must certainly be made aware of the seriousness of the young person's illness (Duncan, Joselow, & Hilden, 2006; Gerhardt et al., 2009; Wolfe et al., 2000b). However, an appropriate balance between acceptance of death and hope for life is probably adaptive. It is a genuine challenge to prepare parents for the death of their child, while also enabling them to help the child emotionally and to assist with the treatment regimen. This undertaking requires knowledgeable and sensitive mental health staff. As our ability to lengthen survival—and perhaps to raise hopes of some future cure—increases, the problem becomes even more difficult. Integration of support services into the total treatment program and immediate availability and access are important in delivering needed help. Once a point is reached where the child's death is likely, the focus of intervention must shift. Information and support are still needed, but the focus must change to helping the child and family to be most comfortable and to make the best use of the remaining time. Moreover, the family should not be abandoned after the young person's death. Continued assistance is needed and such support should be a part of the total treatment (Duncan et al., 2006; Gerhardt et al., 2009; Wolfe et al., 2000a).

Caregivers, too, are not immune to the effects of observing a dying child or adolescent. Efforts must be made to educate caregivers and to reduce the high cost of helping: the inevitable stress, the feelings of helplessness, and the likelihood of burnout (Koocher, 1980; Sahler et al., 2000). These are not trivial matters. The helpers' adjustment, their efficiency, and the potential impact of their behavior on the family and youngster are of concern (Hilden et al., 2001). In *Who's Afraid of Death on a Leukemia Ward?* (1965), Vernick and Karon offered poignant anecdotes to this effect. One anecdote describes the impact of helpers' behavior on a 9-year-old patient who, after taking a turn for the worse, received some medical treatment and began to show improvement:

> One day while she was having breakfast I commented that she seemed to have gotten her old appetite back. She smiled and agreed . . . . I mentioned that it looked as if she had been through the worst of this particular siege. She nodded in agreement. I went on to say that it must have been very discouraging to feel so sick that all she could do was worry—worry about dying. She nodded affirmatively. I recognized that the whole episode must have been very frightening and that I knew it was a load off her mind to be feeling better. She let out a loud, "Whew," and went on to say that except for me, nobody really talked with her. "It was like they were getting ready for me to die." (p. 395)

Certainly, one of the most difficult decisions is what to tell the dying youth. A protective approach or "benign lying" was once advocated. The young person was not to be burdened, and a sense of normalcy and optimism was to be maintained. Most professionals now feel that this approach is not helpful and probably is doomed to failure anyway. The stress on the family of maintaining this deception is great, and the likelihood that the young person will believe the deception is questionable. In this decision, and in other aspects of working with the child and family, some balance must be struck that takes into consideration the child's developmental level, past experiences, timing, and an understanding of the family's culture and belief system (Dolgin & Jay, 1989; Gerhardt et al., 2009; Oltjenbruns, 2001). An example of such a balance is illustrated in the following excerpt:

> A child with a life-threatening illness should be told the name of the condition, given an accurate explanation of the nature of the illness (up to the limit of his ability to comprehend), and told that it is a serious illness of which people sometimes die. At the same time, however, the child and family can be told about treatment options and enlisted as allies to fight the disease. An atmosphere must be established in which all concerned have the opportunity to ask questions, relate fantasies, and express concerns, no matter how scary or far fetched they may seem. When the patient is feeling sick, weak, and dying, there is no need to [be reminded] of the prognosis. If a family and patient know a prognosis is poor but persist in clinging to hope, one has no right to wrest that from them. The truth, humanely tempered, is important, but we must be mindful of the patient and how [the patient's] needs are served. To tell the "whole truth" or a "white lie" for the benefit of the teller serves no one in the end. (Koocher & Sallan, 1978, p. 300)

Overview/Looking Back

HISTORICAL CONTEXT

- The current view that psychological factors are relevant to physical disorders in a number of different ways represents a shift from the earlier, more limited view of psychosomatic diseases caused by emotional factors.

PSYCHOLOGICAL AND FAMILY INFLUENCES ON MEDICAL CONDITIONS

- Current conceptualizations of the role of psychological and family factors in chronic illness are illustrated through the example of asthma. Psychological and family influences are among a variety of possible trigger mechanisms that can bring on an asthmatic episode. The child's asthma may impact other family members, and family assistance is needed in managing the medical condition.

CONSEQUENCES OF CHRONIC CONDITIONS

- There is likely to be considerable individual variability in the adjustment of youths with chronic illnesses and in how youths and families cope with chronic conditions. Adjustment is likely to be an ongoing process and is influenced by a number of variables.
- Researchers have sought to determine the impact of characteristics of the youth, parameters of the illness, such as severity, and of aspects of family functioning, such as control, organization, and parental distress, on the chronically ill youth's adjustment.
- With increasing survival rates for young people with chronic conditions, the adaptation over time of the young person and family to the illness and its treatment are of great interest. Adaptation to cancer and HIV/AIDS are two examples.

FACILITATING MEDICAL TREATMENT

- Psychology can contribute to effective treatment of medical conditions in a number of ways.
- Medical treatment may be rendered ineffective because of difficulties that the patient and family experience in trying to adhere to prescribed treatment regimens. Attempts to improve adherence require attention to multiple dimensions such as the young person's developmental level, peer and social influences, family patterns of interaction, and the role of the health care professional.
- Psychological treatments (e.g., relaxation and biofeedback) may modify physical functioning and the pain associated with chronic conditions. Treatment of headaches is an example of this kind of application.
- Psychologically based procedures may also facilitate the delivery of medical interventions. Treatment programs to reduce the pain and distress felt by young people who are undergoing medical procedures and preparation for hospitalization are examples of psychological influences enhancing medical interventions.
- Understanding the antecedents of unintentional injury and developing interventions to prevent such injuries is another example of ongoing efforts at the interface of psychology and medicine.

THE DYING CHILD

- Despite increasingly high survival rates, the prospect of death is one of the most distressing aspects of working with some chronically ill youth. Psychological contributions to helping these children, their families, and the professionals who work with them can be an aid in effective and caring treatment.

Key Terms

psychosomatic disorders *370*
psychosomatic medicine *371*
pediatric psychology *371*
functional limitation *376*
functional disabilities *376*
adherence to (compliance with) medical regimens *380*
biofeedback *383*
unintentional injury *387*

CHAPTER 15

Evolving Concerns for Youth

LOOKING FORWARD

After reading this chapter, you should be able to discuss:

- Effects of nonparental care and self-care on children
- Facts and issues regarding adoption and foster care
- Specific needs for better mental health services for youth
- Efforts to provide mental health services for youth
- Specific adversities experienced by children in developing countries

his final chapter addresses select current concerns for children and adolescents. It is a truism that the future of every society depends on its youth, and that the welfare of children and adolescents is tied to many factors. The lives of youth are affected by what is happening in the lives of their parents and in their communities, the value assigned to the young, the priorities given to health care and education, and a host of other factors. The economic resources of nations make a difference, so that even basic care and opportunity are problematic in developing countries. Nevertheless, because the implementation of programs devoted to youth also depends on social attitudes, care can vary enormously even when resources are adequate. Sensitive and attentive adults are looking at such influences with an eye toward better care for youth.

Progress in understanding human development also is stimulating efforts toward optimizing the potential of the young. Although knowledge about development is incomplete, we have come far from viewing children and adolescents simply as incomplete adults. Their unique needs are better known; the general course of physical, intellectual, and social growth is well on the way to being mapped; and developmental influences, including risk and protective factors, are increasingly understood. There is enthusiasm for using this knowledge to enhance development, even as we seek to better understand the experiences of young people.

In this chapter, we discuss three areas of current concerns regarding youth. Reflecting the importance of family influence woven throughout the text, we first look at family issues regarding the care of children. Next, mental health services for youth are discussed. Finally, the well-being of children and adolescents living in nations other than the United States is briefly examined.

WHO CARES FOR CHILDREN: FAMILY ISSUES

U.S. families have changed dramatically in the last several decades, perhaps most obviously through increased rates of divorced, single-parenting, and step-parent households (for a discussion of divorce, see p. 54). Concerns are voiced by many people about the well-being of the family. Nevertheless, scholars who have studied its history have challenged the idea that the family has decayed from some past idyllic form. They point out that there have always been various family forms and that family well-being relies less on family structure than on family attributes such as warmth, communication, and support. Recent studies indicate that such attributes benefit various family forms, which continue to evolve due to changed attitudes and technologies such as in vitro fertilization (Golombok, 2006).

It is nonetheless appropriate to ask questions about the impact of social change on the family and, more specifically, on who is caring for children, under what circumstances, and with what consequences. Although the scope of discussion is necessarily limited, it is our purpose to draw attention to the issue by examining maternal employment and day care for children. In addition, we look at two other areas—adoption and foster care—that directly influence the care and experiences of a large number of children.

Maternal Employment and Child Care

The increase of women in the labor force has transformed family life. In 1950, 12% of married women with a preschool child worked outside the home. In 2003, that figure was 60%—and 77% for married women with a child age 6 to 17 (U.S. Bureau of the Census, 2004). Data for 2009, although collected in a somewhat different way, were nearly identical (U.S. Census Bureau, 2011). A major concern has been whether maternal employment adversely affects children's development. Overall, having a mother work outside of the home appears not to harm children, can have small positive effects on child achievement and behavior, and is moderated by factors such as child gender, family structure, and socioeconomic variables (Goldberg et al., 2008; Lucas-Thompson, Goldberg, & Prause, 2010). The public largely is accepting of working mothers and believes that employed women can be good mothers. However, particular concern exists about the influence on infants and toddlers being cared for by adults other than their parents.

The effects of day care on children depend, in part, on the quality of the programs, the amount of time spent in day care, and the family background of the child.

EFFECTS OF NONPARENTAL CARE ON YOUNG CHILDREN

Infants and young children of employed mothers experience many different **nonparental care** arrangements. Care is provided by relatives or nonfamily, in or out of the family home, or by nonfamily in center-based settings. In general, parents prefer less formal arrangements for infants under 2 years, and more formal settings, such as center-based care, as children get older (McCartney, 2006). In 2010, center-based care was the primary setting for 24% of children ages 0–4 years and other nonrelative care for 14% (Federal Interagency Forum on Child and Family Statistics, 2011). In general, economic resources play a role in the selection of child care settings, with greater social advantage being associated with higher quality care, more hours per week in care, and the child remaining in center care for a longer period (NICHD Early Child Care Research Network, 2006). Family ethnicity is somewhat related to care as well; for example, Latino families prefer informal arrangements.

What is known about the impact of nonparental care on young children's well-being? Decades of research on this topic have been marked by debate—sometimes rancorous—among professionals and in the public press. Investigators have examined cognitive and social outcomes for children and have especially considered the *quality* of care, the *amount* of care, and some *family characteristics*. Interpretations of the findings have been made difficult by the correlation between family characteristics and the choice of settings and quality of care. For example, if highly competent parents are more likely to select high-quality day care, the cause of positive child outcomes of day care may be unclear. For this reason, the more recent research has tended to control for the possible effects of family selection of care, as well as other factors.

Many studies indicate that the effects of early child care depend in part on the quality of day care, which is defined by several indices, such as staff training, developmentally appropriate curricula, and the like. High-quality care is positively related to the development of cognition and language for youngsters who day care early in life (Belsky, 2001; NICHD Early Child Care Research Network, 2006). These benefits have been observed as long as 10 years after day care for youths of various socioeconomic levels (Vandell et al., 2010). Benefits also apply to social behavior, such as prosocial skills, albeit to a smaller extent.

The effects of the amount of day care that children receive—that is, the hours of care per week and/or the age at which children begin nonparental care—are more complex. Debate has centered on psychosocial outcomes, and some studies claim that more time in care is associated with child troublesome behavior while other studies do not show this link (Loeb et al., 2004; NICHD

Early Child Care Research Network, 2003). Overall, there may be some negative effect, with children who spent more time in center-based care exhibiting relatively more externalizing problems. Findings from a major study that evaluated children from 4.5 years of age through age 15 found an association in the early years that no longer held by third grade but appeared at age 15 (Belsky et al., 2007; Vandell et al., 2010).

The interface of child care effects with family characteristics has received attention. Interest in economically disadvantaged families heightened after 1996 federal regulations put higher employment demands on women on welfare, resulting in greater employment of these women. Loeb and colleagues (2004) found positive cognitive outcomes for children of low-income families who attended day care centers and whose mothers entered the workforce when the children were 12–42 months of age. Quality of care had some influence in the expected direction. The children cared for by family members showed no cognitive effects but more behavioral problems. In another study, as shown in Figure 15.1, children from low SES families who had full-time nonmaternal care during the first year of life performed better on a receptive language task at age 4–5 years than children from low SES families who were in maternal care or part-time nonmaternal care (Geoffroy et al., 2007). Still another study of low-income families found that both high-quality care and more extensive time in care were linked to beneficial effects on cognitive and behavioral development (Votruba-Drzal, Coley, & Chase-Lansdale, 2004).

From a somewhat different perspective, Watamura and colleagues (2011) examined children who experienced a "double jeopardy" of low-quality care. Children from disadvantaged families who experienced low-quality care

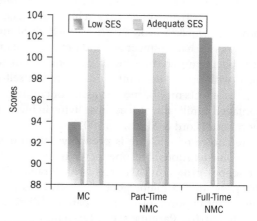

FIGURE 15.1 Receptive language scores according to SES and child care arrangements in the first year of life. MC = maternal care; NMC = nonmaternal care. *From Geoffroy et al., 2007.*

both at home and in other settings showed high levels of problem behavior and low levels of prosocial behavior compared to other children. However, there was evidence that children from these disadvantaged homes could benefit from high-quality child care. As the researchers noted, the findings were consistent with other investigations suggesting that the characteristics of child care may be especially important for children from disadvantaged background.

The larger lesson to be learned from the research on child care for young children is that the effects of different arrangements vary depending on the broad context of children's lives. More generally, the issue of nonparental care has implications for social policy. It is noteworthy that child care effects tend to be small to moderate in size (NICHD Early Child Care Research Network, 2006; Vandell et al., 2010). Nevertheless, even small child care effects can be important when they involve large numbers of children and provide special benefit to disadvantaged children. In a nation that depends heavily on nonmaternal care, the availability of quality day care is far from incidental to children's welfare.

CARE OF SCHOOL-AGE CHILDREN   Although professional debate over child care has focused on early care, concern exists for after-school care for older children. These youths are less likely to be in center-based care and more likely to be in the care of relatives or in self-care. Perhaps unsurprising, self-care rises with age, notably from 9 to 12 years, and is of particular concern (Federal Interagency Forum on Child and Family Statistics, 2011).

The effects of self-care are linked to many variables: the amount of time in self-care, the child's developmental level, family influences, neighborhood characteristics, and available social supports. Studies of the impact of self-care suggest either problematic outcomes for some children or no differences from other after-school arrangements (Shumow, Smith, & Smith, 2009; Vandell & Shumow, 1999). Factors such as younger age and time spent hanging out with peers rather than being at home seem to be associated with poorer outcomes for children in self-care. The negative effects may be more evident for children from disadvantaged families, as well as those living in high-crime neighborhoods (Lord & Mahoney, 2007).

The choice of self-care is probably determined by multiple considerations, but one factor is the availability of after-school programs. There is considerable interest in these programs, a major goal of which is to provide supervision for children of working parents (Pierce, Bolt, & Vandell, 2010). Parents see after-school programs as not only keeping children safe but also providing opportunities for facilitating social skills, physical activity,

Many children return to empty homes after school. The impact of such self-care requires further study.

and school success (America After 3PM, 2009). Many current after-school programs include services to low-income youths to improve academic functioning. Evidence supports the benefit of sustained participation in high-quality after-school programming both to academic and social behaviors (Durlak & Weissberg, 2007; Little, Wimer, & Weiss, 2008). Among the positive outcomes are academic achievement, on-time promotion, better attitudes toward school, improved feelings of self-confidence, positive social behavior, and reduced behavioral problems. Not all programs are successful in producing positive results, of course, and among the features of effective programs are good staff–child relationships, availability of diverse activities, intentional focusing on learning goals, and strong partnerships with schools, families, and community.

Adoptive Families

Our discussion so far has focused on youths living with at least one biological parent, but millions of children live in other kinds of arrangements, including adoptive families. In 2007, approximately 1.8 million children lived with adoptive parents (Federal Interagency Forum on Child and Family Statistics, 2011). **Adoption** is arranged through foster care agencies, private groups, or international organizations, with most children being younger than age 6 (Figure 15.2). Adopted children in the United States are more likely to be African American and Asian than

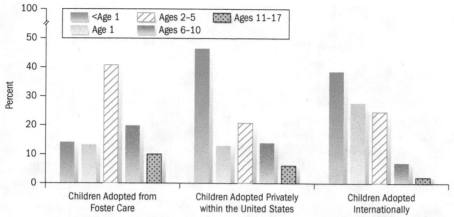

FIGURE 15.2 Percent of adopted children ages 0–17 by adoption type and age at adoption, 2007. *Federal Interagency Forum on Child and Family Statistics, 2011.*

Caucasian or Hispanic. International adoptions have increased, with children coming to their new families from countries as diverse as China, Korea, Romania, Russia, Guatemala, and the Philippines. About one-fifth of children adopted in 2008 were of different race than their adoptive parents.

Adoption is frequently seen as a constructive way to meet the needs of both child and parents. In the United States and similar countries, adoption most often involves middle-class couples choosing to enlarge their families and children who come from less advantaged situations. Nevertheless, there has been concern over the development of adopted children. Research has shown that adoptees are seen in disproportionate numbers at mental health clinics, and learning disabilities, ADHD, and conduct problems are noted (Federal Interagency Forum on Child and Family Statistics, 2011). Questions have been raised about whether adopted children from disadvantaged backgrounds can overcome their earlier negative experiences in adoptive homes (van IJzendoorn & Juffer, 2006). Unfortunate preadoptive situations exist and children not adopted immediately can experience various kinds of hardships. Some of these youths may be affected by poor prenatal care; poor diet; living with birth families made dysfunctional by poverty, drug addiction, or psychological problems; or living in transitional settings such as orphanages or foster care settings.

What then does research tell us about the development of adopted children? In broaching this issue, it is appropriate to keep in mind that the various circumstances of adoptions can make it difficult to sort out the findings, and not all issues have been examined. Nevertheless, numerous investigations allow for some reasonably supported general conclusions.

A major outcome study consisted of a series of meta-analyses of more than 270 studies of adoptions within countries and across countries (van IJzendoorn & Juffer, 2006; van IJzendoorn, Juffer, & Poelhuis, 2005). Depending on the data available in the studies, the adopted youth were compared with (1) "past peers"—the peers or siblings they left behind in institutions or their family of origin—and (2) "current peers"—unadopted peers or siblings in their current adoptive environments. More data were available for current peers than past peers. Most relevant to our discussion are the following findings:

- Adoptees surpassed their past peers on IQ and school achievement and performed only negligibly lower than their current peers. However, more learning problems and special education referrals were reported for adoptees.
- On measures of attachment to caregivers, adoptees were more secure than past peers but less secure than current peers.
- On measures of self-esteem, adopted children showed no differences from their current peers.
- Adoptees exhibited more psychological problems than their current peers, although the differences were small. Adoptees were more often referred to mental health settings.

This large body of research indicates that adoption generally benefits children in that they surpass the peers they left behind. Moreover, most adoptees function within the normal range in intellectual and psychosocial domains, although there is a small to moderate chance of early attachment and behavioral difficulties.

International and interracial adoption can bring unique enrichment and challenge.

Meta-analyses of research also indicate three commonly found risk factors. More likely to be associated with poor outcome are late age of adoption, male gender, and preadoption factors such as neglect/abuse, prenatal drug exposure, behavioral problems, and foster or institutional care (e.g., Gunnar et al., 2007; Hawk & McCall, 2010; Rutter et al., 2007). Despite these risks, many researchers note the resilience of adoptive children, particularly those who move from disadvantaged or abusive preadoptive circumstances. We do not mean to oversimplify issues relevant to adoption, such as the need to encourage adoption for older children and questions regarding the identity of children who may struggle with adoption into families of culture and race different from their own. In the final analysis, of course, these issues do not detract from the positive aspects of adoption (Miller et al., 2000). Rather, they suggest the need for research and for specific policies (e.g., early adoption) and support for adoptive families.

Foster Care

Foster care settings include nonrelative and relative family homes, group homes, emergency shelters, residential facilities, and homes preparing for adoption (Child Welfare Information Gateway, 2011). Although it is ordinarily preferable for children and adolescents to remain with their birth families, substitute care is not always avoidable. Substitute placement occurs involuntarily or voluntarily when families are unable to care for their offspring. In earlier times in the United States and other countries, these youths were placed in institutions and had few connections to their families. Concerns about harmful effects of institutionalization led to family foster care, with a major goal of returning the children to their biological families (Benoit, M. B., 2000). However, many youths remained in foster care for long periods of time, some until they reached the legal age to be independent. Further, although foster care certainly can have positive influences, it also can be inadequate and the rate of disruption is high, with children being moved from placement to placement (Barber, Delfabbro, & Cooper, 2001; Minty, 1999). In an effort to improve this situation, the federal government enacted the **Adoption and Safe Families Act** (ASFA) in 1997 (Figure 15.3). ASFA has brought substantial change in foster care. Here, we discuss two aspects of efforts to improve the foster care system.

TREATMENT FOSTER CARE Because youth in foster care are at risk for psychological problems, **treatment foster care** programs have been created (Benoit, M. B., 2000; Dore & Mullin, 2006; Rosenfeld et al., 1997). Prior to the child's being placed in their care, foster parents understand that the child requires mental health services and that they will serve as agents of change. An example was described in Chapter 8 (p. 212), in which multidimensional treatment foster care was designed specifically for delinquent youths (Smith & Chamberlain, 2010). In such programs, special training and help is given to foster parents; links may be forged with community mental health services; and foster parents may work with the child's family to facilitate reunion with the child.

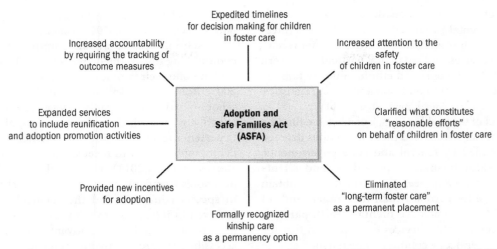

FIGURE 15.3   Changes in foster care due to the Adoption and Safe Families Act of 1997.   *From Allen & Bissell, 2004.*

Linares and colleagues (2006) offered an example of the potential benefits of parent and coparent training. Intervention was provided to biological and foster parent *pairs* of maltreated (primarily neglected) 3- to 10-year-olds who had been placed in foster care. It was reasoned that training in pairs would facilitate cooperation and communication between families and avoid fragmented services. The Incredible Years (IY) parent training program (p. 210) was employed, based on evidence of its effectiveness in teaching parenting skills and in reducing externalizing problems, a common difficulty of children in foster care. A separate coparenting component addressed communication, conflict resolution, and cooperative parenting of the child. There were significant differences between intervention families and control families at the end of treatment and at a 3-month follow-up. Both sets of intervention families exhibited significant gains and at the follow-up reported a trend for fewer child externalizing problems.

EXITING FOSTER CARE   Among other priorities of the ASFA is the provision of a permanent home for every youth in foster care. Within a specified time each child must either be returned to the biological family, or be adopted, or be permanently placed with a foster family, which can include relatives or legal guardians. The ASFA provides the states with a financial incentive for the adoption of children in temporary foster care. In some circumstances, it may be difficult to attain this goal (Becker, Jordan, & Larsen, 2007). Administrative agencies, including the courts, can be so overloaded that they are unable to operate in a competent and timely fashion. And the task is substantial; for example, in 2009, there were almost 224,000 children in foster care (Child Welfare Information Gateway, 2011). Such youths are disproportionately of minority background, and many experience chaotic or traumatized lives and require special behavioral, educational, or medical care.

Nevertheless, the goal of finding a permanent family for youths in foster care has met with some success. Of those exiting foster care in 2009, 51% were reunited with parents or primary caretakers, 20% were adopted, 8% went to live with other relatives, 7% went to live with a guardian, and the remainder were emancipated or had other outcomes (Child Welfare Information Gateway, 2011).

One positive turn of events is that the frequency of adoption from foster care has increased. This is attributable in part to substantial increase in kin adoptions (Howard & Berzin, 2011). Disagreement has existed over the benefits and disadvantages of adoption by relatives. Kin, compared to nonfamily adoptive parents, tend to be older, are often single, and have less income. On the other hand, disruptions in the child–family relationship occur less frequently, the children have more contact with siblings, and kin report greater levels of satisfaction and better child outcomes than outcomes for other adoptees. Overall, attitudes and practices concerning kin adoptions are more favorable than in the past, with relatives being viewed as a valuable resource.

It is noteworthy, however, that finding families for older children is particularly difficult. Moreover, those who leave foster care because they reach the age of emancipation are too often left without sufficient social, educational, and financial support (Howard & Berzin, 2011).

MENTAL HEALTH SERVICES FOR YOUTH

We now turn to a brief discussion of mental health services for youth. Over the years, many studies of mental health services have been conducted. It is widely agreed that children and adolescents are underserved (Hoagwood,

2005; Kazak et al., 2010; President's New Freedom Commission on Mental Health, 2003). Two-thirds to three-fourths of youth with diagnosable disorders do not receive mental health services and this is of particular concern for youths from low-income and ethnic minority families (Federal Interagency Forum on Child and Family Statistics, 2011; Kazak et al., 2010; Merikangas et al., 2011).

One aspect of the problem is lack of adequate funding for services to persons who need them. To various degrees, funding is provided by federal and state governments, third-party (health insurance) providers, and clients themselves. It has usually been more difficult to obtain financial coverage for mental health than other kinds of health needs. Efforts to achieve **mental health parity**—funding for mental health services equivalent to that for other health care services—continue to be pursued at state and federal levels (DeLeon et al., 2011; Gould, Roberts, & Beals, 2009). Relevant is the passage of the Mental Health Parity and Addiction Equity Act of 2008 (P.L. 110–343).

However, the issue of providing services goes beyond funding and includes stigma, attitudes toward mental health care, integration of services into primary health care and other community settings (e.g., shelters, community centers), the need for preventive care and early intervention, and attention to cultural context. In addition, many families—particularly those residing in rural settings and those of ethnic minority background—find it difficult to access services (DeLeon et al., 2011; Gerwitz & August, 2008; Haas, 2011; Huey & Polo, 2010; Kazak et al., 2010; Polaha, Dalton, & Allen, 2011; Tolan & Dodge, 2005).

Early mental health services for youth emphasized a community approach (Pumariega & Glover, 1998). Child guidance clinics provided interdisciplinary and low-cost services to children and adolescents and their families. Services subsequently became more hospital-based, and guidance and mental health clinics experienced lack of funding and support. Hospital and residential care increased during the 1970s and 1980s, partly because of increased third-party payment. Meanwhile there was a dramatic increase in the population of poor minority children who needed but could not obtain mental health services. Many of these children went into the child welfare system when their parents were unable to care for them, and many were placed in residential and detention facilities. This dire situation and growing medical costs resulted in a call for publicly funded community-based services. Today's services are delivered in various settings, including mental health clinics, psychiatric or full service hospitals, residential centers, private professional practices, child welfare and juvenile agencies, and schools (Weisz et al., 2005). It has been suggested that an emphasis should be placed on providing services in community-based settings that are frequently utilized by youngsters and their families (DeLeon et al., 2011; Tolan & Dodge, 2005).

Schools can play an important and perhaps coordinating role in the delivery of services to millions of students and their families (Huang et al., 2005; Kratochwill, 2007; Romer & McIntosh, 2005; Weist, 1997). Indeed, school-based mental health services may be an especially effective way in which underserved populations, families experiencing challenging circumstances, or those at demographic risk can receive care (Kataoka et al., 2007; Stormshak et al., 2011). Traditional mental health services in schools frequently may be limited to children enrolled in special education and the relatively small number involved in interventions with school psychologists. Yet, the school setting has clear advantages in that it is readily accessible, can provide frequent contact, and can avoid the stigma of mental health consultation. In making this point, Kestenbaum (2000) quotes a colleague who said,

> I decided to adopt what I have come to refer to as the Willie Sutton Theory of Children's Mental Health. When reporters asked Willie Sutton, the notorious bank robber of the 1930s, why he robbed banks, he answered "that's where the money is." If you wanted to provide mental health services to children, I reasoned, you had to go where the children were: in the schools. (p. 6)

Efforts to expand school services include the entire range from prevention to treatment to posttreatment monitoring. Increases in the kinds of programs offered and improved coordination are commonly recommended (Huang et al., 2005). For example, one idea is to set up partnerships between schools and community mental health agencies. Some schools now have general health centers, and mental health services could be readily embedded in these.

More generally, call has gone out to incorporate a public health perspective into mental health settings, with an emphasis on serving broad populations, early detection and prevention of problems, strengthening positive behaviors, ongoing evaluations, family involvement and empowerment, and coordinated services (Kazak et al., 2010; Strein, Hoagwood, & Cohn, 2003; Weist & Christodulu, 2000). "Full-service schools" can be the primary neighborhood institution for promoting child and family development, which includes educational, health, and mental health goals within a framework of community-based participation.

Fragmentation, Utilization, Evaluation

Concerns have generally been expressed about the fragmentation of mental health services (Gould et al., 2009; Sterling et al., 2010). A single family may have contact with and receive services from a variety of uncoordinated mental health, educational, social service, juvenile justice, substance abuse, and other agencies. In addition, transition into adult services, if eventually needed, is made challenging by the separateness of youth and adult services (Singh, 2009).

In recognition of the need for better coordinated services, a number of efforts have been made to ensure that multiple systems interact in ways that facilitate delivery of services. There have been efforts to develop community-based, interagency systems of care that "wrap around" individual youths and families (Mental Health: A Report of the Surgeon General, 2001; Suter & Bruns, 2009). This might be achieved, for example, by having a "single point of entry" into the various services/programs or by having a group of representatives from the various programs coordinate services. Coordination of services has also been addressed by having a primary therapist responsible for ensuring the use of effective interventions and for coordinating and integrating services for the youth and family—an approach taken by Multisystemic Therapy (Henggeler & Schaeffer, 2010; see p. 213). Training "family or parent partners"—parents experienced with mental health, child welfare, and other agencies who help families to understand their options and navigate "the system"—is another way to facilitate access to, and coordination of, services (Kazak et al., 2010). These efforts have been aided by federal initiatives. For example, the Comprehensive Community Mental Health Services for Children and Their Families Program provides financial support to the states, territories, and Indian tribal organizations to care for millions of children through a coordinated, comprehensive network of mental health and other services (Foster et al., 2007; Mental Health: A Report of the Surgeon General, 2001). Evaluations of such systems of care indicate benefits such as reduced use of residential and out-of-state treatments, parental satisfaction with care, and improved functional behavior of the children.

Whereas fragmentation of services certainly can be problematic, so can low utilization of available services. Help-seeking behavior is likely to be complex and to vary with demographic, personal, and other variables (Logan & King, 2001; Reeb & Conger, 2011; Sears, 2004; Yeh et al., 2004). Several demographic variables predict service use. Caucasian families, those of higher social class and those living in urban areas, are more likely to use professional services. Ethnic minority families may be more likely to seek help from family and community contacts rather than professionals, and premature termination of services is higher for Hispanic and African American youngsters and their families (Mental Health: A Report of the Surgeon General, 2001). Beliefs about causes of problems in children may, in part, be responsible for differences in service utilization (Yeh et al., 2005). If programs are to successfully serve diverse ethnic/racial populations, they must incorporate cultural traditions, beliefs, and ways of interpersonal interactions (Huey & Polo, 2010).

Technological advances are becoming part of the provision of mental health services and may aid in increasing access to and utilization of services (Dimeff et al., 2011). Web- or computer-based technology, mobile communication technology, virtual reality (immersing the client in a 3-dimensional computer simulation), and social networking are examples of promising arenas. Videos and videoconferencing, for example, have been employed to train and assist professionals in the use of evidence-based treatments (Grus, 2011). These technologies have also been used to provide education and services to rural and remote areas where professional services may be limited (Pignatiello et al., 2011). Similarly, technology creates options for the delivery of psychological services. For example, materials to directly assist youths and their families can be made available through DVDs or the Internet. E-mail or text messaging can be employed to report on homework assignments or to communicate achievement of treatment goals. Educational material and aspects of evidence-based practice can be used by youths and families as part of a self-help approach or in coordination with professional assistance.

An example of the use of technology in the treatment of children is provided by the work of Spence, March and colleagues' treatment program for Australian children with anxiety disorders. Spence and colleagues (2006) randomly assigned children (ages 7–14) to one of two treatment conditions or a waiting-list control. Youths received either a standard clinic-based cognitive-behavioral therapy or the same treatment protocol with half of the sessions delivered via the Internet. At posttreatment, 60% of children in the treatment groups compared to 13% of control children no longer met the criteria for their primary anxiety disorder. There was no significant difference between the treatment conditions, and treatment effects were comparable to those found in other studies with anxious children. By the 12-month follow-up the 2 treatments still did not differ significantly, and the percentage of children who no longer met diagnostic criteria had increased to 89.5 and 73.9% for the clinic and clinic–Internet treatments, respectively. An extension of this research examined the same treatment delivered by Internet alone (March, Spence, & Donovan, 2009). The Internet-alone treatment was effective compared to a waiting-list control. However, the percentage of children undergoing treatment who no longer met diagnostic criteria (30%) was lower than that achieved by the clinic or clinic–Internet treatment strategies employed in the earlier study.

The use of technology is potentially valuable in disseminating and implementing evidence-based interventions and ensuring broader access to services. However, like other interventions, the effectiveness of technology-based efforts should be supported by research findings (Cushing & Steele, 2010; Dimeff et al., 2011).

Indeed, there is continuing need to evaluate services and disseminate information about effective services. It is clear that evidence-based treatments for young people have the potential to ameliorate a variety of disorders (Hibbs & Jensen, 2005; Weisz & Kazdin, 2010). Equally clear, research efforts need to address transporting these treatments into general clinical practice. It is essential that the public and families have information about children's mental health, effective treatments, and the availability and costs of care. Similarly, agencies and institutions providing services would profit from greater dissemination of information about evidence-based prevention and treatment programs (Chorpita, Miranda, & Bernstein, 2011; Hoagwood, 2005; Kazak et al., 2010; Tolan & Dodge, 2005).

Although mental health services are improving, and government agencies have created mechanisms to facilitate the provision of evidence-based interventions, continuing needs are recognized. The Subcommittee on Children and Families of the President's New Freedom Commission on Mental Health articulated 10 challenges to be addressed in order to achieve a stronger system of mental health care for youth and families (Huang et al., 2005). The aspects of this vision are listed in Table 15.1. The goal of all such efforts is effective coordinated services that can be accessed by all who need them.

TABLE 15.1	Vision for Children's Mental Health Services

Comprehensive home- and community-based services and supports

Family partnership and support

Culturally competent care

Individualized care

Evidence-based practice

Coordination of services, responsibility, and funding

Prevention, early identification, and early intervention

Early childhood intervention

Mental health services in schools

Accountability

Adapted from Huang et al., 2005.

YOUTH IN THE GLOBAL SOCIETY

As we turn our attention to the international scene, we note that mass transportation and communication, including the Internet, are making the functional world smaller day by day. The lives of youth are already being strongly influenced by this phenomenon, and the impact will become even more pervasive throughout the twenty-first century.

Third World Poverty and Health

Although poverty in the United States is rightly of concern, the effects of being poor are dramatically worse in developing countries. The link between poverty and developmental well-being is observed in various measures—nutrition, disease, lack of opportunity, disability, and death. For example, malnutrition and specific mineral deficiencies (e.g., iron) are associated with cognitive and behavioral risk (Baker, Greer, & Committee on Nutrition 2010; Gottlieb et al., 2009).

Youth in developing countries can benefit from public health programs that include improved nutrition, prenatal care, immunization, screening for medical conditions, treatment of disease, child safety, family planning, and the like (Rahman et al., 2000). Progress has been made on several fronts. For instance, disease has been reduced, fewer children are underweight, and more families are consuming iodine in their diets. Figure 15.4 shows the reduction that occurred from 1990 to 2009 in the mortality of children under the age of 5 years, a measure viewed as an overall indication of how well children are doing.

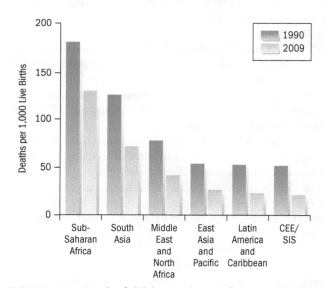

FIGURE 15.4 Death of children under age five per 1,000 live births, 1990 and 2009. *CEE/CIS = Central and Eastern Europe/ Commonwealth of Independent States. Adapted from UN Inter-agency Group in Child Mortality Estimation, Levels and Trends in Child Mortality Report, 2010.*

TABLE 15.2	Mortality of Children under the Age of Five: Facts and Figures

Globally, the rate of mortality fell by one-third from 1990 to 2009.

The rate of decline accelerated over 2000–2009 compared to the 1990s.

Most progress was made in Northern Africa and Eastern Asia.

In sub-Saharan Africa, which has the highest rate, 1 in 8 children dies before age 5.

About half of the deaths were concentrated in five countries: India, Nigeria, Democratic Republic of the Congo, Pakistan, and China.

About 40% of deaths occur within the first month of life; about 70% within the first year.

The largest killers are pneumonia, diarrhea, malaria, and HIV/AIDS, which accounted for 43% of deaths in 2008.

Adapted from UN Inter-agency Group in Child Mortality Estimation, Levels and Trends in Child Mortality Report, 2010.

Despite progress, however, continued effort is much needed (Table 15.2). For example, in 2009, AIDS-related death in youth under age 15 had decreased 19% from the previous 5 years (UNAIDS, 2010). The reduction was due in part to treatment of infected children and to antiviral medication to reduce the transmission of the virus from pregnant women to the fetus. Nonetheless, 2.5 million children were living with AIDS in 2009, and overall the disease had orphaned more than 16 million children.

Some international attention has been paid to psychological and behavioral problems of youth (Rahman et al., 2000). Epidemiological reports attest to a substantial rate and range of disabilities (e.g., internalizing, externalizing, intellectual disability, pervasive developmental disorders). However, mental health professionals are in short, even dire, supply in some regions of the world (Omigbodun et al., 2007). In addition, a relative neglect of mental health needs may be due, at least in part, to an understandable focus on diseases and conditions causing high mortality, the lack of perceived need for treatment, and the stigma associated with mental disorders (Sorsdahl & Stein, 2010). Ultimately, if interventions are to be successful, local community involvement as well as standards and values are important considerations.

Exposure to Armed or Sociopolitical Conflict

Exposure to armed conflict or to threatening sociopolitical environments affects the development of a significant minority of young people throughout the world. Youth have experienced the horrors of "ethnic cleansing," have lived in areas in which the threat of war was chronic, and have been abducted into or otherwise became part of the military. Moreover, thousands have fled their homelands to live in refugee camps or to relocate to foreign countries. In addition to direct traumatic experiences and bodily threats to the self and loved ones, these situations are often characterized by uncertainty, temporary or permanent separation from family, loss of community, inadequate nutrition, lack of shelter, and the like.

Thousands of children have been affected by armed conflict in a particular abhorrent way: they served in the military. In Sierra Leone, for example, boys and girls as young as 7 were in combat or served in support roles as cooks, messengers, human shields, and the like (Betancourt et al., 2010). Many were brutalized, drugged, and forced into these activities. And many witnessed, experienced, or actively engaged in torture, killings, or rape. These youths likely suffer increased rates of mental problems.

It is worth noting that research on the effects of war itself is not easy to accomplish. It is difficult to collect data immediately or soon after armed conflict, and longer-term outcome is confounded by less-than-optimal experiences following war. Investigations often have been conducted with immigrant groups and especially refugee groups, who may be living in camps and still experiencing trauma, loss, and poor living conditions.

Given this circumstance, rates of psychopathology vary tremendously across studies. Different problems are evident, including posttraumatic stress disorder (PTSD), depression, anxiety, somatic complaints, sleep problems, and behavior problems (American Psychological Association, 2010). Of these, PTSD, depression, and anxiety have been especially noted.

Psychological upset can be enduring. Young adults who as children had experienced trauma during the Pol Pot regime in Cambodia had a lifetime rate of PTSD of 59% (Hubbard et al., 1995). Although their experiences were probably especially horrific and threatening, other studies indicate both persistence and reduction of disorder over time. A variety of risk factors operate regarding the development of disorder (Ehntholt & Yule, 2006). In general, higher rates of disturbance go hand in hand with higher rates and accumulation of exposure to trauma. Other risk factors include lack of information about missing family members, inability to respond to new situations, separation from family, poor family cohesion or mental health, low levels of social support, and postmigration stress. Findings are mixed with regard to the developmental timing of exposure to war-related events (American Psychological Association, 2010). A complex of variables might explain this. For example, older children and adolescents have

Significant numbers of youth throughout the world are exposed to the risks of sociopolitical conflict and life in refugee camps. *(Jose Cendon/APWorld Wide Photos)*

higher rates of exposure, which could adversely affect the developmental tasks of forming trusting social relationships and a secure identity. On the other hand, older youths may be protected by greater cognitive understanding and the ability to engage in coping mechanisms.

Research does suggest gender differences in war-related experiences, with girls more at risk for sexual trauma, including rape, sexually transmitted disease, and cultural stigmatization. Boys may have greater exposure to nonsexual violence and be involved as perpetuators of violence. When families resettle in foreign countries, gender differences may also operate. For instance, girls may be more pressured by their families regarding the social expectations of their new environments, whereas boys may be pressured to engage in the outside world at the expense of their cultural identity. More generally, the demands to adjust to a foreign culture can be made more difficult in the presence of ethnic/racial prejudice and discrimination.

Despite the multiple challenges of war-related experiences, young people may exhibit remarkable resilience (Lustig et al., 2004). Even some of those who served as child soldiers may avoid significant behavioral and emotional problems; in one study this held for about 28% of the youths (Klasen et al., 2010). Numerous factors are thought to contribute to the resilience of these youths (Betancourt & Kahn, 2008):

- child characteristics such as coping skills, intelligence, and sense of agency
- religious beliefs and practices
- attachment relationships

- parental or caregiver mental health
- characteristics of child care institutions and schools
- cultural beliefs about the meanings of war-related experiences
- cultural beliefs and practices regarding mental health.

Efforts are underway to prevent or treat the negative effects of war-related disorders. These vary, of course, depending on the problems and situation—that is, whether young people remain in war-threatened countries, live in refugee camps, or are adjusting to resettlement in unknown communities and countries. Three principles of intervention with refugee families are widely recognized (American Psychological Association, 2010). *First*, it is important that practitioners be culturally competent. *Second*, evidence-based practices should be employed when possible. However, because there are few studies of the effectiveness of interventions with war-affected youth, the efforts of those working in the field need to be integrated. *Third*, interventions should be comprehensive since families may have economic, social, and psychological difficulties.

Treatment of mental health problems can take many approaches, such as group therapy, family or individual intervention, and school-based services. As a general approach to intervention involving specific war-related symptoms, a three-phase model is recommended by Ehntholt & Yule (2006) (Figure 15.5). Initially, it is often necessary to establish a sense of safety and trust in the youths, which can be a particularly difficult task with persons who have experienced serious threats or witnessed horrifying events. The second phase of intervention targets

FIGURE 15.5 A phased model approach to intervention. *From Ehntholt & Yule, 2006.*

specific problems, for example, PTSD or depression. The third phase focuses on building for the future, and includes discussion of both practical plans and future aspirations. The model recognizes that moving back and forth between the phases is often necessary.

The more we understand about treating the victims of war and conflict—including the mediators and moderators of stress reactions and resilience—the better our chance of alleviating and preventing emotional adversity. Nevertheless, few would dispute the opinion that war "must be regarded with abhorrence in terms of its terrible human toll in human suffering, especially on its most innocent bystanders—children and adolescents" (Jensen & Shaw, 1993, p. 697).

Diversity and International Cooperation

An obvious implication of the shrinking world is the increased challenge to get along well with others of different facial appearance, color, dress, custom, behavior, and belief. The task of adapting to diversity, although not new by any means, is substantial and is heightened by the current massive relocations of people across the globe into foreign countries and cultures.

In the United States, the challenge of diversity has a long history. Prejudice and fears often have had adverse effects on peoples of various groups—Native Americans, African Americans, Irish, Poles, Asians, Arabs, Latinos, Jews, and Catholics, to name a few. Being of minority status remains a risk factor for quality of life, health, and opportunity, even as the United States becomes increasingly multicultural (Hawkins, Cummins, & Marlatt, 2004; Lurie & Dubowitz, 2007; Nyborg & Curry, 2003).

As a discipline, psychology has participated in the study of issues related to diversity, although efforts have perhaps not always been as timely as could be hoped. A historic example is the work of Kenneth Clark and his colleagues that played a role in the 1954 Supreme Court decision *Brown v. Board of Education*, which overthrew the "separate but equal" doctrine that had permitted racial segregation in the public schools (Clark, Chein, & Cook, 2004). Clark, an African American, became president of the American Psychological Association in the late 1960s (Pickren & Tomes, 2002). At about that time, the American Psychological Association became more committed to addressing problems of race and related matters. Today, concerns exist about the problems and progress of diverse cultural and racial groups living in the United States.

The need also exists for increased study across cultures and the processes of international cooperation. In fact, an important outgrowth of closer communication among the peoples of the world is greater international effort to solve problems and to optimize living conditions. Over several decades, the United Nations has drawn world attention to promoting the healthy development of children and protecting, among other rights, basic rights to a family environment, an adequate standard of living, education, and freedom from harms such as abuse and exploitation. Recently, the United Nations declared 2010–2011 as the International Year of Youth with a commitment to enhance the well-being of older youth. The United Nations has sponsored world summits and conferences, numerous programs to benefit children, and the collection of data on youth to monitor progress and make recommendations. Countless other concerned organizations—both private and public—are addressing global issues such as poverty, education, infant mortality, medical and mental health needs, violence, and environmental pollution. Because such efforts can have a crucial influence on the development of children and adolescents, international cooperation holds the promise of optimizing the lives of young people.

Overview/Looking Back

WHO CARES FOR CHILDREN: FAMILY ISSUES

- Maternal employment appears not to harm children and can have positive effects.
- The effects of nonmaternal day care on young children depend on many factors. High-quality care can benefit cognitive and behavioral development, especially in children from disadvantaged homes. Relatively high amounts of care may be associated with externalizing problems.

- The effects of self-care by older children are variable. High-quality after-school programs are advantageous, perhaps especially for disadvantaged families.
- Most adopted youths function in the normal range, and benefit from adoption. There is some risk for behavioral and learning problems, with late age at adoption, male gender, and adverse preadoption experiences associated with less favorable outcome.

- Current policy regarding foster care assumes that the child either will return to the birth family or will join a permanent adoptive or foster care family. Concerns about foster care are being addressed.

MENTAL HEALTH SERVICES FOR YOUTH

- Most youths do not receive needed mental health services due to factors such as underfunding, fragmented services, poor access, and underutilization by certain groups.
- Services are best offered in community-based settings, including schools. The use of technology is becoming a part of the delivery of services. Federally sponsored efforts encourage comprehensive, coordinated, accessible services.

YOUTH IN THE GLOBAL SOCIETY

- Many challenges to the development of young people are evident worldwide, such as poverty, disease, poor nutrition, and lack of mental care services.
- Millions of children and adolescents suffer loss and physical and psychological damage from armed and sociopolitical conflicts. Although resilience is compelling, there is a need for interventions to alleviate and prevent war-related disorders.
- A functionally smaller world has heightened the need for people to adapt to and be enriched by diversity. International cooperation holds promise for improving the lives of needy children and adolescents.

Key Terms

nonparental care *393*

adoption *394*

foster care *396*

Adoption and Safe Families Act *396*

treatment foster care *396*

mental health parity *398*

GLOSSARY

ABA (reversal) research design Single-case experimental design in which the behavior being examined is measured during a baseline period (A), a period of manipulation (B), and a period in which the manipulation is removed (A). The manipulation (B) is reintroduced when treatment is the goal.

Accelerated longitudinal research designs Various designs that combine the longitudinal and cross-sectional research strategies to maximize the strengths of those methods.

Acute onset The sudden (rather than gradual) onset of a disorder.

Adaptive behavior scales Psychological instruments that measure an individual's ability to perform in the everyday environment—for example, to wash one's hair, interact socially, and communicate.

Adoption studies In genetic research, the comparison of adopted children with their biological and their adoptive families to determine hereditary and environmental influences on characteristics.

Affect Emotion or mood. By extension, an affective disorder is a mood disorder such as depression or mania.

Agoraphobia Excessive anxiety about being in a situation in which escape might be difficult or embarrassing.

Anoxia Lack of oxygen.

Antisocial behavior A pattern of behavior that violates widely held social norms and brings harm to others (e.g., stealing, lying).

Aphasia Loss or impairment of language, caused by brain anomalies.

Attachment A strong socioemotional bond between individuals. Usually discussed in terms of the child–parent or child–caretaker relationship, attachment is generally viewed as having a strong influence on a child's development.

Attention The focusing or concentration of mental energy on an object or event. Attention has many components, which are linked to different brain regions. Attention deficits are manifested in problems such as distractibility and difficulty in sustaining effort.

Attribution (attributional style) The way an individual thinks about or explains actions and outcomes; for example, a child's attributing his or her school failure to lack of innate intelligence.

Authoritative parenting Style of parenting in which parents set rules and expectations for their children, follow through with consequences, and simultaneously are warm, accepting, and considerate of their children's needs. This style is thought to be associated with positive development in children.

Autoimmune disorder A condition in which the body's immune system attacks its own healthy tissue.

Autonomic nervous system A part of the nervous system that regulates functions usually considered involuntary, such as the operation of smooth muscles and glands. The system controls physiological changes associated with emotion. (*See* central nervous system.)

Baseline The measured rate of a behavior before an intervention is introduced. Baseline rates of a behavior being examined can then be compared with rates measured during and following an intervention.

Behavior therapy/behavior modification An approach to treatment that is based primarily on learning principles.

Behaviorally inhibited temperament A temperamental tendency in which the individual is highly reactive to and stressed by unfamiliar stimuli.

Binge A relatively brief episode of excessive consumption (e.g., of food) over which the individual feels no control.

Biofeedback Procedures by which an individual is provided immediate information (feedback) about his or her physiological functioning (e.g., muscle tension, skin temperature). It is assumed that the individual can come to control bodily functioning through such feedback.

Brain imaging Methods of studying the brain that depict brain structure or functioning. Examples are PET (positive emission tomography), MRI (magnetic resonance), and fMRI (functional magnetic resonance) scans.

Case study Method of research in which an individual case is described. The case study can be informative, but cannot be generalized with confidence to other persons or situations.

Categorical approach Conceptualizing behavior into qualitatively different groupings. When applied to behavior disorder, persons are viewed as either displaying or not displaying the behavior, for example, as either displaying or not displaying anxiety. *See* dimensional approach.

Central coherence The tendency of individuals to weave bits of information together so as to create a whole, or global, meaning. Central coherence is contrasted with the (analytic) tendency to focus on parts of stimuli, rather than the whole.

Central nervous system In humans, the brain and spinal cord. (*See* autonomic nervous system.)

Child guidance movement An early to mid-20th-century effort in the United States to treat and prevent childhood mental disorders. Importance was given to the influence of family and wider social systems on the child.

Chromosome A threadlike structure in the cell nucleus that contains the genetic code. Human cells possess 23 pairs of chromosomes, except for the ovum and sperm, which possess 23 single chromosomes.

Chromosome abnormalities Abnormalities in the number and/or structure of the chromosomes, which can lead to fetal death or anomalies in development.

Classical conditioning A form of learning, also referred to as Pavlovian conditioning. In classical conditioning, an individual comes to respond to a stimulus (conditioned stimulus or CS) that did not previously elicit a response. Classical conditioning occurs when a CS is paired with another stimulus (the unconditioned stimulus, or UCS) that does elicit the desired response (unconditioned response, or UCR). When this response is elicited by the conditioned stimulus alone, it is called a conditioned response (CR).

Clinical significance The degree to which research findings are meaningful regarding real-life applications.

Clinical utility The adequacy of a classification system, diagnosis, or assessment instrument; judged on the basis of how fully the observed phenomena are described and how useful the descriptions are.

Coercion A process in which a noxious or aversive behavior of one person (e.g., aggression by a child) is rewarded by another person (e.g., a parent). Often applied to the development of conduct-disordered behavior.

Cognitive-behavioral therapy An approach to treatment that is based on a theoretical perspective that considers behavioral events, cognitive processes, and their interactions.

Cognitive distortion Inaccurate thought processes that are dysfunctional. An example is a depressed person's believing that he or she is incompetent even though others do not hold this view.

Cognitive strategies Strategies related to information processing, memory, and the like; for example, rehearsing and categorizing information or addressing the interpretation of an experience or event.

Cohort A particular age group of individuals. A cohort may differ in life experiences and values from an age group born and raised during a different era.

Comorbidity A term used when an individual meets the criteria for more than one disorder (e.g., Attention-Deficit Hyperactivity Disorder and Oppositional Defiance Disorder). (*See* co-occurrence.)

Compulsions Behaviors the individual feels compelled to repeat over and over again, even though they appear to have no rational basis.

Computerized tomography (CT) scan A procedure that assesses the density of brain tissue and produces a photographic image of the brain. A CT scan allows investigators to directly assess abnormalities of brain structures. Also sometimes referred to as a computerized axial tomography (CAT) scan.

Concordant In genetic research, refers to individuals who are similar in particular attributes; for example, individuals may be concordant in activity level or in meeting the diagnostic criteria for a disorder.

Conditioned stimulus (CS) A neutral stimulus, which through repeated pairings with a stimulus (unconditioned stimulus) that already elicits a particular response, comes to elicit a similar response (conditioned response).

Contingency management Use of procedures that seek to modify behavior by altering the causal relationship between stimulus and response events, for example, modifying a particular outcome or consequence of a behavior.

Control group In an experiment, a group of participants treated differently from the group of participants who receive the experimental manipulation. The two groups are later compared. The purpose of a control group is to ensure that the results of the experiment can be attributed to the manipulation rather than to other variables.

Co-occurrence A term used when individuals experience the problems (symptoms) associated with more than one disorder (e.g., anxiety and depression). (*See* comorbidity.)

Correlation coefficient A number, obtained through statistical analysis, that reflects the presence or absence of a correlation and the strength and direction (positive or negative) of a correlation. Pearson r is a commonly used coefficient. (*See* positive correlation; negative correlation.)

Correlational research A research method aimed at establishing whether two or more variables covary, or are associated. (*See* positive correlation; negative correlation.) The establishment of a correlation permits the prediction of one variable from the other, but does not automatically establish a causal relationship.

Cortisol A stress hormone produced by the adrenal gland.

Covert behaviors Behaviors that are not readily observable. When describing antisocial behaviors this term refers to behaviors that are concealed, such as lying, stealing, and truancy. (*See* overt behaviors.)

Cross-sectional research A research strategy aimed at observing and comparing different groups of participants at one point in time. Cross-sectional research is a highly practical way to gather certain kinds of information.

Cultural familial retardation A term, less popular now, referring to the majority of cases of milder mental retardation (intellectual disability) "running in families" and for which biological causation is not established.

Defense mechanisms In psychoanalytic theory, psychological processes that distort or deny reality so as to control anxiety. Examples are repression, projection, and reaction formation.

Deinstitutionalization The movement to place or treat people with disorders at home or in various community settings rather than in institutions.

Delinquency A legal term that refers to an illegal behavior by a person under 18. Such behavior may be illegal for an adult as well (e.g., theft) or may be illegal only when committed by a juvenile (e.g., truancy).

Delusion An idea or belief that is contrary to reality and is not widely accepted in one's culture (e.g., delusions of grandeur or of persecution).

Dependent variable In the experimental method of research, the measure of behavior that may be influenced by the manipulation (the independent variable).

Development Change in structure and function that occurs over time in living organisms. Typically viewed as change from the simple to the complex, development is the result of transactions among several variables.

Developmental level The level at which an individual is functioning with regard to physical, intellectual, or socioemotional characteristics.

Developmental psychopathology The study of behavioral disorders within the context of developmental influences.

Developmental quotient (DQ) A measure of performance on infant tests of development, paralleling the intelligence quotient (IQ) derived from intelligence tests for older children.

Diathesis Vulnerability to a disease or disorder.

Differential reinforcement of other behaviors (DRO) In behavior modification, application of relatively more reinforcement to desirable behaviors that are incompatible with specific undesirable behaviors.

Difficult temperament Tendency of an individual to display negative mood, intense reactions to stimuli, irritability, and the like. A difficult temperament is a risk factor for behavior problems.

Dimensional approach Conceptualizing behavior as varying along a quantitative continuum, such as anxiety being manifested from very low, through moderate, to very high. When applied to behavior disorder, persons are evaluated along a continuum rather than being viewed as either displaying or not displaying anxiety. *See* categorical approach.

Discordant In genetic research, refers to individuals who are dissimilar in particular attributes; for example, two individuals may be discordant in activity level or clinical diagnosis.

Discrete trial learning Method of modifying behavior or teaching in which the clinician or teacher presents specific tasks or materials in small steps, provides clear directives or prompts, and applies consequences. The setting is structured for learning. (*See* incidental learning.)

Dizygotic (fraternal) twins Twins resulting from two independent unions of ova and sperm that occur at approximately the same time. Dizygotic twins are genetically no more alike than are nontwin siblings.

DNA Deoxyribonucleic acid. The chemical carrier of the genetic code, found in the chromosomes and composed of sugar, phosphates, and nucleotides. The nucleotides carry the hereditary information.

Dyslexia General term referring to reading disorder not due to general intellectual deficiency.

Echolalia The repetition of the speech of others, either immediately or delayed in time. A pathological speech pattern found in autism and other disorders.

Education for All Handicapped Children Act of 1975 Public Law 94–142, which set influential federal guidelines for the rights of handicapped children to an appropriate public education. Reauthorized and expanded, the law is now titled the Individuals with Disabilities Education Act (IDEA).

Electroencephalograph (EEG) A recording of the electrical activity of the brain.

Empirical The process of verification or proof by accumulating information or data through observation or experiment (in contrast to reliance on impression or theory).

Empirically supported assessments and treatments *See* Evidence-based assessments and treatments.

Epidemiology The study of the occurrence and distribution of a disorder within a population. Epidemiology seeks to understand the development and etiology of disorder.

Epigenetic Modification of the genome that helps regulate gene function without changing the genetic code. Such modification can occur in response to the environment, implicating environmental influence on gene expression. The term "epigenetics" often is used to refer to the study of epigenetic processes.

Equifinality The concept that different factors or paths can result in the same or similar developmental outcomes. For example, somewhat different paths can lead to conduct-disordered behavior.

Etiology The cause or origin of a disease or behavior disorder.

Eugenics Efforts to improve human characteristics through the systematic control of reproduction and thus genetics.

Evidence-based assessments and treatments Assessments and interventions for which there is empirical support for their effectiveness; procedures that have been deemed worthy through scientific evaluation.

Executive functions Higher order mental abilities involved in goal-directed behavior. Included among executive function are planning and organizing behavior, using short-term or working memory, inhibiting responses, and evaluating and switching strategies.

Experimental research A research method that can establish causal relationships among variables. Participants are exposed to the independent variable in order to determine possible effects on the dependent variable. Comparison groups are included and procedures are carefully controlled to help rule out effects of extraneous factors.

External validity In research, the degree to which findings of an investigation can be generalized to other populations and situations.

Externalizing disorders Behavioral disorders in which the problems exhibited seem directed at others (e.g., aggression and lying).

Extinction A weakening of a learned response, produced when reinforcement that followed the response no longer occurs.

Factor analysis A statistical procedure that suggests which behaviors or characteristics tend to occur together by correlating each item with every other item and then grouping correlated items into factors.

Flynn effect Refers to the finding that scores on general tests of intelligence tend to increase over time as the tests become older.

Fraternal twins *See* dizygotic twins.

Functional analysis Behavior analysis; that is, the assessment of variables that might be influencing the occurrence and maintenance of a behavior. Determining such antecedent variables and consequences for behavior can be crucial in modifying the behavior.

Functional magnetic resonance imaging (fMRI) A noninvasive magnetic radiowave technology which produces images that indicate areas of brain activity by tracking subtle changes in oxygen in different parts of the brain. (*See* magnetic resonance imaging.)

Gene The unit of the chromosome that carries the genetic code.

Gene–environment correlation Correlation indicating the presence of genetic differences in exposure to environments. That is, genetic influences play a role in determining the experiences a person has. For example, a child who is genetically predisposed to be shy may be treated in certain ways by others or may elect to avoid highly social activities.

Gene–environment interaction Differential sensitivity to experience due to differences in genotype. For example, children with recessive genes for PKU (phenylketonuria), but not other children, develop intellectual disabilities when they ingest certain kinds of foods.

Generalization of learning The process by which a response is made to a new stimulus that is different from, but similar to, the stimulus present during learning.

Genome All the biological information needed to construct and maintain life. In humans, the term often refers to genes and noncoding sequences of DNA in the cell nucleus. It may also include information not carried in the nucleus, such as in DNA found in the cell's mitochrondria of females that is transmitted to offspring.

Genome-wide association studies A promising method to help identify genes associated with a disorder or trait. The genome is searched for small variations in DNA (single nucleotide polymorphisms, SNPs) that occur more often in persons with a disorder than in those without the disorder. Large number of genomes must be searched, and the method is especially appropriate for complex disorders.

Genome-wide linkage studies A method to help identify genes associated with a disorder or trait that is found in families. The genomes of family members are searched for variations in DNA and comparison is made between members displaying or not displaying the disorder.

Genotype The complement of genes that a person carries; the genetic endowment.

Goodness-of-fit Degree to which an individual's attributes or behaviors match or fit the attributes or demands of the individual's environment.

Grapheme A unit of a writing system—a letter or a combination of letters—that represents the sounds of a language (the phonemes).

Hallucination A false perception (e.g., hearing a noise, seeing an object) that occurs in the absence of any apparent environmental stimulation.

Heritability The degree to which genetic influences account for variations in an attribute among individuals in a population.

Heterotypic continuity The continuity of a disorder over time in which the form of the problem behaviors changes over time. Contrasts with homotypic continuity, in which the form does not change.

High-risk prevention strategies (also called selective prevention strategies) Prevention strategies targeted at individuals who are at higher than average risk for disorder.

Hypothesis In science, a proposition or "educated guess" put forth for evaluation by some scientific method.

Identical twins See monozygotic twins.

Impulsivity Acting without thinking; a failure to inhibit behavior. Some children with attention-deficit hyperactvity disorder exhibit impulsivity.

Incidence Number or proportion of persons in a population newly diagnosed with a disorder during a specific time period.

Incidental learning Method of modifying behavior or teaching in informal, natural settings. Incidental learning takes advantage of the everyday context—for example, by teaching tasks relevant to what a child is engaging in at the moment. Learning procedures, such as contingency management, are typically employed.

Inclusion The idea that all children with disabilities can best be educated, and should be included, in regular classrooms.

Independent variable In the experimental method of research, the variable manipulated by the researcher.

Indicated prevention strategies Prevention strategies that are targeted at high-risk individuals who show minimal symptoms or early signs of a disorder, or who have biological markers for a disorder, but do not meet the criteria for the disorder.

Individual Education Plan (IEP) Detailed educational plan legally mandated for each person being served by the Individuals with Disabilities Education Act.

Individuals with Disabilities Education Act (IDEA) Current federal law ensuring the rights of handicapped persons from birth to age 21 to appropriate public education.

Information processing Complex mental processes by which the organism attends to, perceives, interprets, and stores information. (*See* attention, working memory, executive functions, cognitive strategies.)

Informed consent In research or treatment, the ethical and legal guideline that potential participants be reasonably informed about the research or treatment as a basis for their consent or willingness to participate.

Insidious onset Gradual, rather than sudden (acute), onset of a disorder.

Intelligence quotient (IQ), deviation A standard score, derived from statistical procedures, that reflects the direction and degree to which an individual's performance on an intelligence test deviates from the average score of the individual's age group.

Intelligence quotient (IQ), ratio The ratio of mental age (MA), derived from performance on tests of intelligence, to chronological age (CA), multiplied by 100. (IQ = MA/CA × 100).

Interactional model of development The view that development is the result of the interplay of organismic and environmental variables. (*See* transactional model of development.)

Internal validity The degree to which research findings can be attributed to certain factors. Internal validity frequently concerns the degree to which the result of an experiment can be attributed to the experimental manipulation (the independent variable) rather than to extraneous factors.

Internalizing disorders The large category of disorders—many of which were traditionally referred to as neuroses—in which the problems exhibited seem directed more at the self than at others, (e.g., fears, depression, and withdrawal).

Interrater reliability The extent to which different raters agree on a particular diagnosis or measurement.

In vivo A term referring to the natural context in which behavior occurs. For example, in vivo treatment is delivered in the setting in which the behavior problem occurs (e.g., the home rather than the clinic).

Joint attention interactions Behaviors, such as pointing and eye contact, that simultaneously focus the attention of two or more people on the same object or situation, presumably for sharing an experience.

Learned helplessness Passivity and a sense of lack of control over one's environment that is learned through experiences in which one's behavior was ineffective in controlling events.

Least restrictive environment Regarding education, refers to the idea that individuals with disabilities have the right to be educated with their typically developing peers to the extent that such education is maximally feasible.

Lifetime prevalence Number or proportion of persons in a population diagnosed with a disorder at any time during life.

Longitudinal research A research strategy in which the same participants are observed over a relatively long period of time, with their behavior measured at certain points in time. Longitudinal research is particularly helpful in tracing developmental change.

Magnetic resonance imaging (MRI) A noninvasive procedure that creates a magnetic field around the brain. Cells in the brain respond to the radio waves, and a three-dimensional image of the structures of the brain is created. (*See* functional magnetic resonance imaging.)

Mainstreaming The educational practice of placing individuals with disabilities into community schools and into the least restrictive settings appropriate to their needs. Most of the children who are mainstreamed spend the majority of their school time in classrooms with typically developing peers, with various degrees of special support.

Maturation Changes that occur in individuals relatively independently of the environment, provided that basic conditions are satisfied. For example, most humans develop the ability to walk, given normal physical health and opportunity for movement.

Mediating influence The effect that a variable has to bring about or cause an outcome. For example, when variable *A* affects variable *M*, which, in turn, affects variable *B*, the impact of *A* on *B* is said to be mediated by *M*.

Mental age (MA) The score corresponding to the chronological age (CA) of persons whose intellectual test performance the examinee equals. For the average child, MA = CA.

Mental hygiene movement An effort organized in the United States early in the 20th century to bring effective, humane treatment to the mentally ill and to prevent mental disorders. The mental hygiene movement was closely associated with the child guidance movement.

Metacognition The understanding of one's own information-processing system.

Metamemory The understanding of the working of one's memory or the strategies used to facilitate memory.

Minimal brain dysfunction (MBD) The assumption that the central nervous system or brain is functioning in a pathological way to a degree that is not clearly detectable.

Moderating influence The effect that a variable has to reduce or strengthen an outcome. For example, when the relationship of variable *A* to variable *B* depends on the level of variable *M*, *M* is said to be the moderator of the relationship of *A* to *B*.

Monozygotic (identical) twins Twins resulting from one union of an ovum and a sperm. The single zygote divides early into two, with the new zygotes having identical genes (and thus being of the same sex).

Morphology Regarding language, refers to the forms of words or the study of word formation.

Multifinality The concept that a factor may lead to different developmental outcomes. For example, child abuse may result in different kinds of behavior problems.

Multigenic influence The influences of multiple genes that combine in some way to affect an attribute or behavior. Also referred to as multiple-gene or polygenic influence.

Multiple baseline research designs Single-case experimental designs in which a manipulation is made and multiple behaviors or multiple participants are measured over time.

Mutation Spontaneous change in the genes that can be transmitted to the next generation. One of the genetic mechanisms that accounts for variation in species and individuals.

Nature vs. nurture controversy The debate about the relative influence of innate and experiential factors on the shaping of the individual. Also known as the hereditary vs. environmental debate.

Negative (inverse) correlation Correlation in which two (or more) variables covary such that high scores on one variable are associated with low scores on the other and vice versa.

Negative reinforcement The process whereby the probability or strength of a response increases because the response was followed by the removal of an aversive stimulus.

Neuropsychological assessment The use of psychological tests and behavioral measures to indirectly evaluate the functioning of the nervous system. Performance on these measures is known or presumed to reflect specific aspects of the functioning of the brain.

Neurotransmitter A chemical that carries the nerve impulse from one neuron, across the synaptic space, to another neuron. Examples of neurotransmitters are serotonin, dopamine, and norepinephrine.

Nonnormative developmental influences The effects on development which stem from events that are not necessarily unusual in themselves, but that occur only to some individuals, perhaps at unpredictable times. Examples are serious injury in childhood and the premature death of a parent. (*See* normative developmental influences.)

Nonshared environmental influences Environmental influences on an attribute that are experienced by one family member, but not other members. (*See* shared environmental influences.)

Normal distribution (curve) The bell-shaped theoretical distribution or probability curve that describes the way in which many attributes (e.g., height, intelligence) occur or are assumed to occur in the population.

Normalization The philosophy that persons with disabilities have the right to experiences that are as normal as possible for the individual. (*See* mainstreaming; least restrictive environment.)

Normative developmental influences The effects on development which stem from events that happen to most individuals in some more or less predictable way. An example is puberty. (*See* nonnormative developmental influences.)

Norms Data based on information gathered from a segment of the population that represents the entire population. Norms serve as standards for evaluating individual development or functioning.

Nuclear family A family unit consisting of the father, mother, and children.

Observational learning Learning that occurs through viewing the behavior of others. Modeled behavior can be presented in live or symbolic form.

Obsessions Recurring and intrusive irrational thoughts over which the individual feels no control.

Operant learning Learning in which responses are acquired, maintained, or eliminated as the result of consequences (e.g., reinforcement, punishment) and other learning processes.

Operational criteria (definition) A specified set of observable operations that are measurable and that allow one to define some concept. For example, maternal deprivation might be defined by the amount of time the child is separated from its mother.

Overlearning The procedure whereby learning trials are continued beyond the point at which the child has satisfied the stated criteria. Overlearning is intended to increase the likelihood that the new behavior will be maintained.

Overt behaviors Behaviors that are readily observable. When describing antisocial behaviors, this term refers to behaviors that are confrontational such as physical aggression, temper tantrums, and defiance. (*See* covert behaviors.)

Panic attack A discrete period of intense apprehension, fear, or terror that has a sudden onset and reaches a peak quickly.

Paradigm A shared perspective or framework consisting of a set of assumptions and conceptions that guide the work of a group of scientists.

Partial correlation statistical procedure A statistical procedure that aids in the interpretation of a demonstrated correlation by removing the effects of one or more specific variables.

Perinatal The period at or around the time of birth.

Phenotype Observable attributes of an individual that result from the individual's genetic endowment, developmental processes, and the transactions of these.

Phobia Anxiety about, and avoidance of, some object or situation. This reaction is judged to be excessive, overly persistent, unadaptive, or inappropriate.

Phonological awareness The understanding that spoken words can be segmented into sounds (e.g., that "cat" has three sounds) and that sounds are represented by letters or combinations of letters of the alphabet.

Phonological decoding In alphabet-based languages, mapping letters to sounds.

Phonological processing Using the sound structure of a language to process written material. Deficits in such processing are central in reading disorders.

Phonology The sounds of a language or the study of speech sounds.

Placebo A treatment that alters a person's behavior because he or she expects that change will occur. Placebos are often employed as control conditions to evaluate whether a treatment being tested is effective for reasons other than the person's belief in it.

Positive (direct) correlation Correlation in which two (or more) variables covary with each other such that high scores on one variable are associated with high scores on the other variable and low scores on the one variable are associated with low scores on the other.

Positive reinforcement The process whereby the probability or strength of a response increases because the response is followed by a positive stimulus.

Positron emission tomography (PET scan) A procedure for directly assessing activity in different parts of the brain by assessing the use of oxygen and glucose that fuel brain activity.

Pragmatics (of language) The use of speech and gestures in a communicative way, considering the social context. Pragmatic skills include using appropriate gestures and language style.

Predictive validity The extent to which predictions about future behavior can be made (e.g., by knowing the individual's diagnosis or performance on some test).

Premorbid adjustment The psychological, social, or academic/vocational adjustment of a person prior to the onset of the symptoms of a disorder or its diagnosis.

Prenatal Having to do with the period of development that occurs during pregnancy or gestation.

Prevalence Number or proportion of persons in a population with a disorder at a given time.

Proband The designated individual whose relatives are assessed to determine whethar an attribute occurs in other members of the individual's family. Also called an index case.

Prognosis A forecast or prediction of the probable course or outcome of a disorder.

Projective tests Psychological tests that present ambiguous stimuli to the person. The person's response is presumed to reflect unconscious thoughts and feelings that are unacceptable to the ego and therefore cannot be expressed directly.

Pronoun reversal Deviant speech pattern in which speakers refer to themselves as "you," "she," or "he" and refer to others as "I" or "me." Often found in autism.

Prospective research designs Designs that identify participants and then follow them over time. (*See* retrospective research designs.)

Psychoactive (psychotropic) drugs Chemical substances that influence psychological processes (e.g., behavior, thinking, emotions) by their effects on nervous system functioning. Examples are stimulants and antidepressants.

Psychopharmacological treatment An approach to treatment through the use of psychoactive medications that affect behavior, thinking, or the emotions. Examples are the use of stimulant medications for attention-deficit hyperactivity disorder and selective serotonin reuptake inhibitors for depression.

Psychosis A general term for severe mental disorder that affects thinking, the emotions, and other psychological systems. The hallmark of a psychosis is disturbed contact with reality.

Punishment A process whereby a response is followed by either an unpleasant stimulus or the removal of a pleasant stimulus, thereby decreasing the frequency of the response.

Qualitative research A research approach which assumes that events are best understood when they are observed in context and from a personal frame of reference. The methods employed include in-depth interviews and intensive case studies. (*See* quantitative research.)

Quantitative research A research approach that places a high value on objective quantitative measurement in a highly controlled situation, as characterized by the experiment. (*See* qualitative research.)

Random assignment In research, the assignment of individuals to different groups so that each individual has an equal chance of being assigned to any group. Such chance assignment helps make the groups comparable on factors that might influence the findings.

Recidivism The return to a previous undesirable pattern. The juvenile delinquent who again commits a crime after completing a treatment program illustrates recidivism.

Reinforcement A process whereby a stimulus that occurs contingent on a particular behavior results in an increase in the likelihood of that behavior. (*See* positive reinforcement; negative reinforcement.)

Relapse The reoccurrence of a problem after it has been successfully treated.

Reliability The degree to which an observation is consistently made. The term can be applied to a test or other measurement or to a system of classification. (*See* test–retest reliability; interrater reliability.)

Remission As applied to disorder or disease, disappearance or reduced manifestation of symptoms.

Resilience The ability to overcome adversities or risk factors and function adaptively despite negative circumstances.

Response prevention A behavioral treatment procedure in which the person is not allowed to engage in, or is discouraged from engaging in, a compulsive ritual or avoidant behavior.

Retrospective research designs Designs that utilize information about past events; follow-back designs. (*See* prospective research designs.)

Risk The degree to which variables (risk factors) operate to increase the chance of behavior problems.

Savant abilities Specific and remarkable cognitive abilities (e.g., in memory or arithmetic) of individuals who otherwise exhibit intellectual disability.

Scientific method An empirical approach to understanding phenomena. The scientific approach involves systematic formulation, observation and measurement, and interpretation of findings.

Selective prevention strategies (*See* high-risk prevention strategies)

Self-injurious behavior Repetitious action that damages the self physically, such as head banging or pulling one's own hair. Self-injurious behavior is observed especially in autism and intellectual disability.

Self-monitoring A procedure in which the individual observes and records his or her own behaviors or thoughts and the circumstances under which they occur.

Self-stimulatory behavior Sensorimotor behavior that serves as stimulation for the person. Often refers to a pathological process, such as when an autistic child repetitiously flaps his or her hands.

Semantics The study of meanings in language.

Separation anxiety Childhood anxiety regarding separation from the mother or other major attachment figures.

Shared environmental influences Environmental influences on an attribute that are experienced by two or more family members. (*See* nonshared environmental influences.)

Single-case experiments Experimental research designs employed with a single participant (or a few participants) in which a manipulation is made and measurements are taken across periods of time. (*See* ABA; multiple baseline designs.)

Socioeconomic status (SES) Social class. Indices of SES include income, amount of education, and occupational level.

Spectrum of disorder This term is applied to disorders that are thought to share certain psychological, behavioral, or biological characteristics. The disorders are viewed not as separate but as a part of a larger spectrum. An example is autism spectrum disorder, which is applied to autism, Asperger's syndrome, childhood disintegrative disorder, and pervasive developmental disorders not otherwise specified.

Stage theories of development   Theories of development which postulate that growth occurs in a recognizable order of noncontinuous stages or steps that are qualitatively different from each other. Examples are Piaget's cognitive theory and Freud's psychosexual theory.

Statistical significance   In research, the probability equal to or below which the findings are due merely to chance. By tradition, a finding is statistically significant when there is a 5-percent-or-less probability that it occurred by chance.

Stereotypy   A repetitive action or movement, such as hand flapping.

Stigmatization   Refers to stereotyping, prejudice, discrimination, or self-degradation associated with membership in a socially devalued group.

Stop-signal task   A method for evaluating behavioral inhibition. The individual must press a button when a target stimulus comes on a screen but must withhold this response when a special signal also comes on.

Stress   A situation or event that brings strain to the individual. Stress is considered a risk factor for behavioral and physical illness.

Sympathetic nervous system   A part of the autonomic nervous system that, among other things, accelerates the heart rate, increases blood glucose, inhibits intestinal activity, and, in general, seems to prepare the organism for stress or activity.

Syndrome   A group of behaviors or symptoms likely to occur together.

Syntax   The aspect of grammar that deals with the way words are put together to form phrases, clauses, and sentences.

Systematic desensitization   A behavioral treatment for anxiety. In systematic desensitization, the client visualizes a hierarchy of scenes, each of which elicits more anxiety than the previous scene. The visualizations are paired with relaxation until they no longer produce anxiety.

Systematic direct observation   Observation of specific behaviors of an individual or group of individuals in a particular setting, with the use of a specific observational code or instrument.

Temperament   Individual differences in emotionality, social responsiveness, activity level, and self-control. One's temperament is a biologically based disposition that can be transformed by experience.

Teratogens   Conditions or agents that are potentially harmful to the prenatal organism.

Test–retest reliability   The degree to which a test or diagnostic system yields the same result when applied to the same individual(s) at different times.

Theory   An integrated set of propositions that explains phenomena and guides research.

Theory of mind   The ability to infer mental states (e.g., beliefs, knowledge) in others or the self.

Time-out   Behavior modification technique in which an individual displaying an undesirable behavior is removed from the immediate environment, usually by placement in an isolated room. Time-out is viewed conceptually as the elimination of positive reinforcement or as punishment.

Token economy   A behavioral treatment procedure developed from operant conditioning principles. A set of behaviors is established that earns or costs reward points, given in the form of some scrip, such as poker chips. These tokens can then be exchanged for prizes, activities, or privileges.

Transactional model of development   The view that development is the result of the continuous interplay of organismic and environmental variables. The transactional model of development is conceptually similar to the interactional model of development, but emphasizes the ongoing, mutual influences of factors.

Translational research   A term that in general refers to efforts to apply research findings to the "real world" of clinical practice and community programs.

Trauma   An event outside of everyday experience that would be distressing to almost anyone.

Treatment foster care   An effort to alleviate behavioral problems of children in foster care by working with foster parents and linking the child to the community mental health system.

Twin study   In genetic research, the comparison of monozygotic twin pairs with dizygotic twin pairs to determine whether the former are more like each other than the latter. A type of research investigation frequently employed to examine the effects of hereditary and environmental variables.

Unconditioned stimulus (UCS)   A stimulus that elicits a particular response prior to any conditioning trials. The loud noise that causes an infant to startle is an example of an unconditioned stimulus.

Universal prevention strategies   Prevention strategies that are targeted at entire populations for which greater-than-average risk has not been identified.

Validity   A term used in several different ways, all of which address issues of correctness, meaningfulness, and relevancy. (*See* internal validity; external validity; predictive validity.)

Wait-list (waiting-list) control group   Group of participants in a research study who do not receive the treatment being investigated. A wait-list control group allows the investigators to compare changes in a group of individuals who received treatment with changes in a group of similar individuals who did not receive treatment. The term *wait list* is derived from the fact that those in the control group are offered treatment once the comparison is completed.

Working memory   Part of the memory system that briefly holds and actively manipulates, or works on, information that it receives from the sensory systems or calls up from long-term memory. Working memory is sometimes referred to as short-term memory.

Zygote   The cell mass formed by the joining of an ovum and sperm; the fertilized egg.

REFERENCES

AAIDD Diagnostic Adaptive Behavior Scale. (2012). Retrieved October 2011 from http://www.aamr.org/content_106.cfm?navID=23

AAIDD Fact Sheet. (2007). Transition. Retrieved July 20, 2007 from http://www.aamr.org/Policies/faq-transition.shtml

AAIDD Position Paper. (2007). Board position statement: Growth attenuation. Retrieved July 20, 2007 from http://www.aamr.org/Policies/growth.shtml

AAIDD/ARC Position Papers. (2007). Behavioral supports. Retrieved July 23, 2007 from http://www.aaidd.org/Policies/pos-beh-sppts.shtml

Aarnoudse-Moens, C. S. H., Weisglas-Kuperus, N., van Goudoever, J. B., & Oosterlaan, J. (2009). Meta-analysis of neurobiological outcomes in very preterm and/or very low birth weight children. *Pediatrics, 124,* 717–728.

Abela, J. R. Z., & Hankin, B. L. (2008). Cognitive vulnerability to depression in children and adolescents: A developmental perspective. In J. R. Z. Abela & B. L. Hankin (Eds.), *Handbook of depression in children and adolescents.* New York: The Guilford Press.

Abela, J. R. Z., Hankin, B. L., Sheshko, D. M., Fishman, M. B., & Stolow, D. (2012). Multi-wave prospective examination of the stress-reactivity extension of response styles theory of depression in high-risk children and early adolescents. *Journal of Abnormal Child Psychology, 40,* 277–287.

Abidin, R. R. (1995). *Parenting stress index: Professional manual* (3rd ed.). Odessa, FL: Psychological Assessment Resources.

Abikoff, H., Hechtman, L., Klein, R. G., Gallagher, R., Fleiss, K., Etcovitch, J. et al. (2004a). Social functioning in children with ADHD treated with long-term methylphenidate and multimodal treatment. *Journal of the American Academy of Child and Adolescent Psychiatry, 43,* 820–829.

Abikoff, H., Hechtman, L., Klein, R. G., Weiss, G., Fleiss, K., Etcovitch, J. et al. (2004b). Symptomatic improvement in children with ADHD treated with long-term methylphenidate and multimodal psychosocial treatment. *Journal of the American Academy of Child and Adolescent Psychiatry, 43,* 802–811.

Ablon, S. L. (1996). The therapeutic action of play. *Journal of the American Academy of Child and Adolescent Psychiatry, 35,* 545–547.

Abramowitz, J. S., Whiteside, S. P., & Deacon, B. J. (2005). The effectiveness of treatment for pediatric obsessive-compulsive disorder: A meta-analysis. *Behavior Therapy, 36,* 55–63.

Abramson, L. Y., Metalsky, G. I., & Alloy, L. B. (1989). Hopelessness depression: A theory-based subtype of depression. *Psychological Bulletin, 96,* 358–372.

Abu-Akel, A., Caplan, R., Guthrie, D., & Komo, S. (2000). Childhood schizophrenia: Responsiveness to questions during conversation. *Journal of the American Academy of Child and Adolescent Psychiatry, 39,* 779–786.

Achenbach, T. M. (1982). *Developmental psychopathology.* New York: Wiley.

Achenbach, T. M. (1990). Conceptualizations of developmental psychopathology. In M. Lewis & S. M. Miller (Eds.), *Handbook of developmental psychopathology.* New York: Plenum.

Achenbach, T. M. (1998). Diagnosis, assessment, taxonomy and case formulations. In T. H. Ollendick & M. Hersen (Eds.), *Handbook of child psychopathology* (3rd ed.). New York: Plenum Press.

Achenbach, T. M. (2000). Assessment of psychopathology. In A. J. Sameroff, M. Lewis, & S. M. Miller (Eds.), *Handbook of developmental psychopathology* (2nd ed.). New York: Kluwer Academic/Plenum Publishers.

Achenbach, T. M. (2011). Definitely more than measurement error: But how should we understand and deal with informant discrepancies? *Journal of Clinical Child and Adolescent Psychology, 40,* 80–86.

Achenbach, T. M., Dumenci, L., & Rescorla, L. A. (2003). DSM-oriented and empirically based approaches to constructing scales from the same item pools. *Journal of Clinical Child and Adolescent Psychology, 32,* 328–340.

Achenbach, T. M., Howell, C. T., McConaughy, S. H., & Stanger, C. (1995). Six-year predictors of problems in a national sample of children and youth: II. Signs of disturbance. *Journal of the American Academy of Child and Adolescent Psychiatry, 34,* 488–498.

Achenbach, T. M., McConaughy, S. H., & Howell, C. T. (1987). Child/adolescent behavioral and emotional problems: Implications of cross-informant correlations for situational specificity. *Psychological Bulletin, 101,* 213–232.

Achenbach, T. M., & Rescorla, L. A. (2000). *Manual for the ASEBA preschool forms & profiles.* Burlington, VT: University of Vermont Research Center for Children, Youth, and Families.

Achenbach, T. M., & Rescorla, L. A. (2001). *Manual for the ASEBA school-age forms & profiles.* Burlington, VT: University of Vermont, Research Center for Children, Youth, & Families.

Achenbach, T. M., & Rescorla, L. A. (2007). *Multicultural supplement to the manual for the ASEBA school-age forms & profiles.* Burlington, VT: University of Vermont, Research Center for Children, Youth and Families.

Achenbach, T. M., Rescorla, L. A., & Ivanova, M. Y. (2005). Crosscultural consistencies and variations in child and adolescent psychopathology. In K. F. Frisbay & C. Reynolds (Eds.), *Handbook of multicultural school psychology.* New York: John Wiley.

Ackard, D. M., Fulkerson, J. A., & Neumark-Sztainer, D. (2007). Prevalence and utility of DSM-IV eating disorder diagnostic criteria among youth. *International Journal of Eating Disorders, 40,* 409–417.

Adams, D., & Oliver, C. (2011). The expression and assessment of emotions and internal states in individuals with severe or profound intellectual disabilities. *Clinical Psychology Review, 31,* 293–306.

Addington, A. M., & Rapoport, J. L. (2009). The genetics of childhood-onset schizophrenia: When madness strikes the prepubescent. *Current Psychiatric Reports, 11,* 156–161.

Adelman, H. S. (1996). Appreciating the classification dilemma. In W. Stainback & S. Stainback (Eds.), *Controversial issues confronting special education: Divergent perspectives* (2nd ed.). Boston, MA: Allyn and Bacon.

Adrian, M., Zeman, J., Erdley, C., Lisa, L., & Sim, L. (2011). Emotional dysregulation and emotional difficulties as risk factors for nonsuicidal self-injury in adolescent girls. *Journal of Abnormal Child Psychology, 39,* 389–400.

Adrien, J. L., Lenoir, P., Martineau, J., Perrot, A., Hameury, L., Larmande, C., & Sauvage, D. (1993). Blind ratings of early symptoms of autism based upon home movies. *Journal of the American Academy of Child and Adolescent Psychiatry, 32,* 617–626.

Aguiar, A., Eubig, P. A., & Schantz, S. L. (2010). Attention deficit/hyperactivity disorder: A focused overview for children's environmental health researchers. *Environmental Health Perspectives, 118,* 1646–1653.

Ainbinder, J. G., Blanchard, L.W., Singer, G. H. S., Sullivan, M. E., Powers, L. K., Marquis, J. G., & Santelli, B. (1998). A qualitative study of parent to parent support for parents of children with special needs. *Journal of Pediatric Psychology, 23,* 99–109.

Akinbami, L. J., Liu, X., Pastor, P. N., & Reuben, C. A. (2011). Attention deficit hyperactivity disorder among children age 5–17 years in the United States, 1998–2009. NCHS data brief, no. 70. Hyattsville, MD: National Center for Health Statistics.

Akshoomoff, N., Farid, N., Courchesne, E., & Haas, R. (2007). Abnormalities on the neurological examination and EEG in young children with pervasive developmental disorders. *Journal of Autism and Developmental Disorders, 37,* 887–893.

Alarcón, R. D., Bell, C. C., Kirmayer, L. J., Lin, K. M., Üstün, B., & Wisner, K. L. (2002). Beyond the funhouse mirrors. Research agenda on culture and psychiatric diagnosis. In D. J. Kupfer, M. B. First, & D. A. Regier (Eds.), *A research agenda for DSM-V.* Washington, DC: American Psychiatric Association.

Albano, A. M., Chorpita, B. F., & Barlow, D. H. (2003). Childhood anxiety disorders. In E. J. Mash & R. A. Barkley (Eds.), *Child psychopathology* (2nd ed.). New York: Guilford Press.

Albano, A. M., & DiBartolo, P. M. (1997). Cognitive-behavioral treatment of obsessive-compulsive disorder and social phobia in children and adolescents. In L. VandeCreek (Ed.), *Innovations in clinical practice* (Vol. 15). Sarasota, FL: Professional Resource Exchange.

Albee, G.W. (1986). Toward a just society. Lessons from observations on the primary prevention of psychopathology. *American Psychologist, 41,* 891–898.

Albee, G.W. (1996). Revolutions and counterrevolutions in prevention. *American Psychologist, 51,* 1130–1133.

Albers, E. M., Riksen-Walraven, J. M., Sweep, F. C. G. J., & de Weerth, C. (2008). Maternal behavior predicts infant cortisol recovery from a mild everyday stressor. *Journal of Child Psychology and Psychiatry, 49,* 97–103.

Alderfer, M. A., Long, K. A., Lown, A., Marsland, A. L., Ostrowski, N. L., Hock, J. M. et al. (2010). Psychosocial adjustment of siblings of children with cancer: A systematic review. *Psycho-Oncology, 19,* 789–805.

Alexander, F. (1950). *Psychosomatic medicine: Its principles and applications.* New York: W. W. Norton and Co.

Algozzine, B. (1977). The emotionally disturbed child: Disturbed or disturbing? *Journal of Abnormal Child Psychology, 5,* 205–211.

Alloy, L. B., Abramson, L. Y., Walshaw, P. D., Keyser, J., & Gerstein, R. K. (2010). Adolescent onset bipolar spectrum disorders: A cognitive vulnerability-stress perspective. In D. J. Miklowitz & D. Cicchetti (Eds.), *Understanding bipolar disorder: A developmental psychopathology perspective.* New York: The Guilford Press.

Altman, H., Collins, M., & Mundy, P. (1997). Subclinical hallucinations and delusions in nonpsychotic adolescents. *Journal of Child Psychology and Psychiatry, 38,* 413–420.

Amato, P. R. (2000). The consequences of divorce for adults and children. *Journal of Marriage and the Family, 62,* 1269–1287.

Amato, P. R., & Irving, S. (2006). Historical trends in divorce in the United States. In M. A. Fine & J. H. Harvey (Eds.), *Handbook of divorce and relationship dissolution.* Mahwah, NJ: Lawrence Erlbaum Associates.

Amato, P. R., & Keith, B. (1991). Parental divorce and the well-being of children: A metaanalysis. *Psychological Bulletin, 110,* 26–46.

Ambrosini, P. J. (2000). Historical development and present status of the Schedule for Affective Disorders and Schizophrenia for School-Age Children (K-SADS). *Journal of the American Academy of Child and Adolescent Psychiatry, 39,* 48–58.

America After 3pm (2009). Washington, DC: Afterschool Alliance.

American Academy of Child and Adolescent Psychiatry. (1999). Practice parameters for the assessment and treatment of children, adolescents, and adults with autism and other pervasive developmental disorders. *Journal of the American Academy of Child and Adolescent Psychiatry, 38* (suppl.), 32s–54s.

American Academy of Child and Adolescent Psychiatry. (2001). Practice parameters for the assessment and treatment of children and adolescents with suicidal behavior. *Journal of the American Academy of Child and Adolescent Psychiatry, 40,* 24S–51S.

American Academy of Child and Adolescent Psychiatry. (2007a). Practice parameter for the assessment and treatment of children and adolescents with attention-deficit/hyperactivity disorder. *Journal of the American Academy of Child and Adolescent Psychiatry, 46,* 894–921.

American Academy of Child and Adolescent Psychiatry. (2007b). Practice parameter for the assessment and treatment of children and adolescents with oppositional defiant disorder. *Journal of the American Academy of Child and Adolescent Psychiatry, 46,* 126–141.

American Academy of Child and Adolescent Psychiatry. (2007c). Practice parameters for the assessment and treatment of children and adolescents with anxiety disorders. *Journal of the American Academy of Child and Adolescent Psychiatry, 46,* 267–283.

American Academy of Child and Adolescent Psychiatry. (2007d). Practice parameters for the assessment and treatment of children and adolescents with bipolar disorder. *Journal of the American Academy of Child and Adolescent Psychiatry, 46,* 107–125.

American Academy of Child and Adolescent Psychiatry. (2012). Practice parameter for the assessment and treatment of children and adolescents with obsessive-compulsive disorder. *Journal of the American Academy of Child and Adolescent Psychiatry, 51,* 98–113.

American Academy of Pediatrics. (2000). Fetal alcohol syndrome and alcohol-related neurodevelopmental disorders. *Pediatrics, 106,* 358–361.

American Academy of Pediatrics. (2003). Prevention of pediatric overweight and obesity. *Pediatrics, 112,* 424–430.

American Academy of Pediatrics. (2009). Policy statement—media violence. *Pediatrics, 124,* 1495–1503.

American Academy of Sleep Medicine. (2005). *International classification of sleep disorders: Diagnostic and coding manual* (2nd ed.). Westchester, IL: American Academy of Sleep Medicine.

American Psychiatric Association. (1952, 1968, 1980, 1987, 1994, 2000). *Diagnostic and statistical manual of mental disorders.* Washington, DC: American Psychiatric Association.

American Psychiatric Association. (2013). *Diagnostic and statistical manual of mental disorders* (5th ed.). Washington, DC: American Psychiatric Association.

American Psychiatric Association. (2011). *DSM-5 development* Retrieved July 2011 from http://www.dsm5.org

American Psychological Association. (2002). *Ethical principles of psychologists and code of conduct.* Washington, DC: Author.

American Psychological Association. (2003). Guidelines on multicultural education, training, research, practice, and organizational change for psychologists. *American Psychologist, 58,* 377–402.

American Psychological Association. (2006). *APA working group on psychoactive medications for children and adolescents.* Washington, DC: Author.

American Psychological Association. (2007). Increasing access and coordination of quality mental health services for children and adolescents. Retrieved May 27, 2007 from http://www.apa.org/ppo/issues/tfpacoord.html

American Psychological Association. (2010). *Resilience and recovery after war: Refugee children and families in the United States.* Washington, DC: Author.

Anastasi, A., & Urbina, S. (1997). *Psychological testing.* Upper Saddle River, NJ: Prentice Hall.

Anastopoulos, A. D., & Farley, S. E. (2003). A cognitive-behavioral training program for parents of children with attention-deficit/hyperactivity disorder. In A. E. Kazdin & J. R. Weisz (Eds.), *Evidence-based psychotherapies for children and adolescents.* New York: Guilford Press.

Anastopoulos, A. D., Rhoads, L. H., & Farley, S. E. (2006). Counseling and training parents. In R. A. Barkley (Ed.), *Attention-deficit hyperactivity disorder. A handbook for diagnosis and treatment.* New York: The Guilford Press.

Anastopoulos, A. D., Smith, J. M., & Wien, E. E. (1998). Counseling and training parents. In R. A. Barkley, *Attention-deficit hyperactivity disorder.* New York: Guilford Press.

Anderson, C. A., Berkowitz, L., Donnerstein, E., Huesmann, R., Johnson, J. D., Linz, D. et al. (2003). The influence of media violence on youth. *Psychological Science in the Public Interest, 4,* 81–110.

Anderson, C. A., Shibuya, A., Ihori, N., Swing, B. L., Bushman, B. J., Sakamto, A. et al. (2010). Violent video game effects on aggression, empathy, and prosocial behavior in Eastern and Western countries: A meta-analytic review. *Psychological Bulletin, 136,* 151–173.

Anderson, D. A., & Paulosky, C. A. (2004). Psychological assessment of eating disorders and related features. In J. K. Thompson (Ed.), *Handbook of eating disorders and obesity.* Hoboken, NJ: John Wiley.

Anderson, E. R., & Hope, D. A. (2008). A review of the tripartite model for understanding the link between anxiety and depression in youth. *Clinical Psychology Review, 28,* 275–287.

Anderson, E. R., & Mayes, L. C. (2010). Race/ethnicity and internalizing disorders in youth: A review. *Clinical Psychology Review, 30,* 338–348.

Anderson, J. C., Williams, S., McGee, R., & Silva, P. A. (1987). DSM-III disorders in preadolescent children: Prevalence in a large sample from the general population. *Archives of General Psychiatry, 44,* 69–76.

Anderson, P. M., & Butcher, K. F. (2006). Childhood obesity trends and potential causes. *The Future of Children, 16,* 19–45.

Anderson, V., Northam, E., Hendy, J., & Wrennall, J. (2001). *Developmental neuropsychology. A clinical approach.* Philadelphia: Taylor & Francis.

Anderson-Fye, E. P., & Becker, A. E. (2004). Sociocultural aspects of eating disorders. In J. K. Thompson (Ed.), *Handbook of eating disorders and obesity.* Hoboken, NJ: John Wiley.

Andrasik, F., Blake, D. D., & McCarran, M. S. (1986). A biobehavioral analysis of pediatric headache. In N. A. Krasnegor, J. D. Arasteh, & M. F. Cataldo (Eds.), *Child health behavior: A behavioral pediatrics perspective*. New York: Wiley.

Angold, A., & Costello, E. J. (2009). Nosology and measurement in child and adolescent psychiatry. *Journal of Child Psychology and Psychiatry, 50*, 9–15.

Angold, A., Costello, E. J., & Erkanli, A. (1999). Comorbidity. *Journal of Child Psychology and Psychiatry, 40*, 57–87.

Angold, A., & Rutter, M. (1992). Effects of age and pubertal stratus on depression in a large clinical sample. *Development and Psychopathology, 4*, 5–28.

Annett, R. D., Turner, C., Brody, J. L., Sedillo, D., & Dalen, J. (2010). Using structural equation modeling to understand child and parent perceptions of asthma quality of life. *Journal of Pediatric Psychology, 35*, 870–882.

Anthony, E. J. (1970). Behavior disorders. In P. H. Mussen (Ed.), *Carmichael's manual of child psychology* (Vol. II). New York: John Wiley.

Anthony, E. J. (1981). The psychiatric evaluation of the anxious child: Case record summarized from the clinic records. In E. J. Anthony & D. C. Gilpin (Eds.), *Three further clinical faces of childhood*. New York: S P Medical & Scientific Books.

Antrop, I., Roeyers, H., Van Oost, P., & Buysse, A. (2000). Stimulation seeking and hyperactivity in children with ADHD. *Journal of Child Psychology and Psychiatry, 41*, 225–231.

Antshel, K. M., Faraone, S. V., Stallone, K., Nave, A., Kaufman, F. A., Doyle, A. et al. (2007). Is attention deficit hyperactivity disorder a valid diagnosis in the presence of high IQ? Results from the MGH Longitudinal Family Studies of ADHD. *Journal of Child Psychology and Psychiatry, 48*, 687–694.

Anway, M. D., & Skinner, M. K. (2006). Epigenetic transgenerational actions of endocrine disrupters. *Endocrinology, 147*, s43–s49.

Aos, S., Miller, M., & Drake, E. (2006). *Evidence-based public policy options to reduce future prison construction, criminal justice costs and crime rates*. Retrieved August 2007 from http://www.wsipp.wa.gov/rptfiles/06-10-1201.pdf

APA Working Group on Psychoactive Medications for Children and Adolescents. (2006). *Report of the working group on psychoactive medications for children and adolescents. Psychopharmacological, psychosocial, and combined interventions for childhood disorders: Evidence base, contextual factors, and future directions*. Washington, DC: American Psychological Association.

Ariés, P. (1962). *Centuries of childhood*. New York: Vintage Books.

Armstrong, F. D., Willen, E. J., & Sorgen, K. (2003). HIV and AIDS in children and adolescents. In M. C. Roberts (Eds.), *Handbook of pediatric psychology* (3rd ed.). New York: Guilford Press.

Armstrong, T. D., & Costello, E. J. (2002). Community studies of adolescent substance use, abuse, or dependence and psychiatric comorbidity. *Journal of Consulting and Clinical Psychology, 70*, 1224–1239.

Arnold, P. D., Hanna, G. L., & Rosenberg, D. R. (2010). Imaging the amygdala: Changing the face of gene discovery in child psychiatry. *Journal of the American Academy of Child and Adolescent Psychiatry, 49*, 7–10.

Arsenio, W. F., & Lemerise, E. A. (2004). Aggression and moral development: Integrating social information processing and moral domain models. *Child Development, 75*, 987–1002.

Asarnow, J. R., & Asarnow, R. F. (2003). Childhood-onset schizophrenia. In E. J. Mash & R. A. Barkley (Eds.), *Child psychopathology*. New York: Guilford Press.

Asarnow, J. R., Emslie, G. J., Clarke, G., Wagner, K. D., Spirito, A. Vitiello, B. et al. (2009). Treatment of SSRI-resistant depression in adolescents (TORDIA): Predictors and moderators of treatment response. *Journal of the American Academy of Child and Adolescent Psychiatry, 48*, 330–339.

Asarnow, J. R., Tompsom, M. C., & McGrath, E. P. (2004). Annotation: Childhood-onset schizophrenia: Clinical and treatment issues. *Journal of Child Psychology and Psychiatry, 45*, 180–194.

Asarnow, R. F., & Kernan, C. L. (2008). Childhood schizophrenia. In T. P. Beauchine & S. P. Hinshaw (Eds.), *Child and adolescent psychopathology*. New York: John Wiley & Sons.

Askew, C., & Field, A. P. (2008). The vicarious learning pathway to fear 40 years on. *Clinical Psychology Review, 28*, 1249–1265.

Astley, S. J., Aylward, E. H., Olson, H. C., Kerns, K., Brooks, A., Coggins, T. E. et al. (2009). Magnetic resonance imaging outcomes from a comprehensive magnetic resonance study of children with fetal alcohol spectrum disorders. *Alcoholism: Clinical and Experimental Research, 33*, 1–19.

Atkinson, L., Scott, B., Chrisholm, V., Blackwell, J., Dickens, S., Tam, F., & Goldberg, S. (1995). Cognitive coping, affective distress, and maternal sensitivity: Mothers of children with down syndrome. *Developmental Psychology, 31*, 668–676.

Attie, I., & Brooks-Gunn, J. (1995). The development of eating regulation across the life span. In D. Cicchetti & D. J. Cohen (Eds.), *Developmental psychopathology, Vol. 2: Risk, disorder, and adaptation*. New York: John Wiley.

Austin, A. A., & Chorpita, B. F. (2004). Temperament, anxiety, and depression: Comparisons across five ethnic groups of children. *Journal of Clinical Child and Adolescent Psychology, 33*, 216–226.

Auyeung, A., Wheelwright, S., Allison, C., Atkinson, M., Samarawickrema, N., & Baron-Cohen, S. (2009). The Children's Empathy Quotient and Systemizing Quotient: Sex differences in typical development and in autism spectrum conditions. *Journal of Autism and Developmental Disorders, 39*, 1509–1521.

Axelson, D., Birmaher, B. J., Brent, D., Wassick, S., Hoover, C., Bridge, J., & Ryan, N. (2003). A preliminary study of the Kiddie Schedule for Affective Disorders and Schizophrenia for

School-Age Children mania rating scale for children and adolescents. *Journal of Child and Adolescent Psychopharmacology, 13,* 463–470.

Axline, V. M. (1947). *Play therapy.* Boston, MA: Houghton Mifflin.

Aylward, B. S., Bender, J. A., Graves, M. M., & Roberts, M. C. (2009). Historical developments and trends in pediatric psychology. In M. C. Roberts & R. G. Steele (Eds.), *Handbook of pediatric psychology* (4th ed.). New York: The Guilford Press.

Azar, B. (2011). Oxytocin's other side. *Monitor on Psychology, 42(3),* 40–42.

Azar, S. T., & Bober, S. L. (1999). Children of abusive parents. In W. K. Silverman & T. H. Ollendick (Eds.), *Development issues in the clinical treatment of children.* Boston, MA: Allyn & Bacon.

Azar, S. T., Ferraro, M. H., & Breton, S. J. (1998). Intra-familial child maltreatment. In T. H. Ollendick & M. Hersen (Eds.), *Handbook of child psychopathology* (3rd ed.). New York: Plenum Press.

Azar, S. T., & Wolfe, D. A. (2006). Child physical abuse and neglect. In E. J. Mash & R. A. Barkley (Eds.), *Treatment of childhood disorders* (3rd ed.). New York: The Guilford Press.

Babinski, L. M., Hartsough, C. S., & Lambert, N. M. (1999). Childhood conduct problems, hyperactivity-impulsivity, and inattention as predictors of adult criminal activity. *Journal of Child Psychology and Psychiatry, 40,* 347–355.

Bachanas, P. J., Kullgren, K. A., Schwartz, K. S., Lanier, B., Mc-Daniel, J. S., Smith, J., & Nesheim, S. (2001). Predictors of psychological adjustment in school-age children infected with HIV: Stress, coping, and family factors. *Journal of Pediatric Psychology, 26,* 343–352.

Bachman, J. G., O'Malley, P. M., Schulenberg, J. E., Johnston, L. D., Bryant, A. L., & Merline, A. C. (2002). *The decline of substance use in young adulthood: Changes in social activities, roles, and beliefs.* Mahwah, NJ: Erlbaum.

Bailey, A., Le Couteur, A., Gottesman, I., Bolton, P., Simonoff, E., Yuzda, E., & Rutter, M. (1995). Autism as a strongly genetic disorder: Evidence from a British twin study. *Psychological Medicine, 25,* 63–78.

Bailey, A., Phillips, W., & Rutter, M. (1996). Autism: Towards an integration of clinical, genetic, neuropsychological, and neurobiological perspectives. *Journal of Child Psychology and Psychiatry, 37,* 89–126.

Bailey, D. B., Raspa, M., Holiday, M., Bishop, E., & Olmsted, M. (2009). Functional skills of individuals with fragile X syndrome: A lifespan cross-sectional analysis. *American Journal on Intellectual and Developmental Disabilities, 114,* 289–303.

Bailey, D. B., Skinner, D., & Sparkman, K. L. (2003). Discovering fragile X syndrome: Family experiences and perceptions. *Pediatrics, 111,* 407–416.

Baird, G., Charman, T., Pickles, A., Chandler, S., Loucas, T., Meldrum D. et al. (2008). Regression, developmental trajectory and associated problems in disorders in the autism spectrum: The SNAP study. *Journal of Autism and Developmental Disorders, 38,* 1827–1836.

Baker, B. L., Neece, C. L., Fenning, R. M., Crnic, K. A., Blacher, J. (2010). Mental disorders in five year old children with or without developmental delay: Focus on ADHD. *Journal of Clinical Child and Adolescent Psychology, 39,* 492–505.

Baker, J. K., Fenning, R. M., Crnic, K. A., Baker, B. L., & Blacher, J. (2007). Prediction of social skills in 6–year-old children with and without developmental delays: Contributions of early regulation and maternal scaffolding. *American Journal on Mental Retardation, 112,* 375–391.

Baker, L., & Cantwell, D. P. (1989). Specific language and learning disorders. In T. H. Ollendick & M. Hersen (Eds.), *Handbook of child psychopathology.* New York: Plenum.

Baker, R. D., Greer, F. R., & the Committee on Nutrition. (2010). *Pediatrics, 126,* 1040–1050.

Balk, D. E., & Corr, C. A. (2001). Bereavement during adolescence: A review of research. In M. S. Stroebe, R. O. Hansson, W. Stroebe, & H. Schut (Eds.), *Handbook of bereavement research: Consequences, coping, and care.* Washington, DC: American Psychological Association.

Ball, H. A., Arseneault, L., Taylor, A., Maughan, B. Caspi, A., & Moffitt, T. E. (2008). Genetic and environmental influences victims, bullies, and bully-victims in childhood. *Journal of Child Psychology and Psychiatry, 49,* 104–112.

Banaschewski, T., & Brandeis, D. (2007). What electrical brain activity tells us about brain function that other techniques cannot tell us-a child psychiatric perspective. *Journal of Child Psychology and Psychiatry, 48,* 415–435.

Bandura, A. (1977). *Social learning theory.* Englewood Cliffs, NJ: Prentice Hall.

Bandura, A. (1997). *Self-efficacy: The exercise of control.* New York: Freeman.

Bandura, A., & Menlove, F. L. (1968). Factors determining vicarious extinction of avoidance behavior through symbolic modeling. *Journal of Personality and Social Psychology, 8,* 99–108.

Barakat, L. P., Alderfer, M. A., & Kazak, A. E. (2006). Posttraumatic growth in adolescent survivors of cancer and their mothers and fathers. *Journal of Pediatric Psychology, 31,* 413–419.

Baranek, G. T. (1999). Autism during infancy: A retrospective video analysis of sensory-motor and social behaviors at 9–12 months of age. *Journal of Autism and Developmental Disorders, 29,* 213–224.

Barber, B. L., & Demo, D. H. (2006). The kids are alright (at least most of them): Links between divorce and dissolution and child well-being. In M. A. Fine & J. H. Harvey (Eds.), *Handbook of divorce and relationship dissolution.* Mahwah, NJ: Lawrence Erlbaum Associates.

Barber, J. G., Delfabbro, P. H., & Cooper, L. L. (2001). The predictors of unsuccessful transition to foster care. *Journal of Child Psychology and Psychiatry, 42,* 785–790.

Bardone-Cone, A. M., Wonderlich, S. A., Frost, R. O., Bulik, C. M., Mitchell, J. E., Uppala, S., & Simonich, H. (2007). Perfectionism and eating disorders: Current status and future directions. *Clinical Psychology Review, 27,* 384–405.

Barkley, R. A. (1990). *Attention-deficit hyperactivity disorder.* New York: Guilford.

Barkley, R. A. (1997). Attention-deficit/hyperactivity disorder. In E. J. Mash & L. G. Terdal (Eds.), *Assessment of childhood disorders.* New York: Guilford Press.

Barkley, R. A. (1998). *Attention-deficit/hyperactivity disorder.* New York: Guilford Press.

Barkley, R. A. (2003). Attention-deficit/hyperactivity disorder. In E. J. Mash & R. A. Barkley (Eds.), *Child psychopathology.* New York: Guilford Press.

Barkley, R. A. (2006a). Associated cognitive, developmental, and health problems. In R. A. Barkley (Ed.), *Attention-deficit hyperactivity disorder. A handbook for diagnosis and treatment.* New York: The Guilford Press.

Barkley, R. A. (2006b). A theory of ADHD. In R. A. Barkley (Ed.), *Attention-deficit hyperactivity disorder. A handbook for diagnosis and treatment.* New York: The Guilford Press.

Barkley, R. A. (2006c). Comorbid disorders, social and family adjustment, and subtyping. In R. A. Barkley (Ed.), *Attentiondeficit hyperactivity disorder. A handbook for diagnosis and treatment.* New York: The Guilford Press.

Barkley, R. A. (2006d). Etiologies. In R. A. Barkley (Ed.), *Attention-deficit hyperactivity disorder. A handbook for diagnosis and treatment.* New York: The Guilford Press.

Barkley, R. A. (2006e). Primary symptoms, diagnostic criteria, prevalence, and gender differences. In R. A. Barkley (Ed.), *Attention-deficit hyperactivity disorder. A handbook for diagnosis and treatment.* New York: The Guilford Press.

Barkley, R. A. (2010). Against the status quo: Revising the diagnostic criteria for ADHD. *Journal of the American Academy of Child and Adolescent Psychiatry, 49,* 205–207.

Barkley, R. A., & Edwards, G. (2006). Diagnostic interview, behavior rating scales, and the medical examination. In R. A. Barkley (Ed.), *Behavioral and emotional disorders in adolescents. Nature, assessment, and treatment.* New York: The Guilford Press.

Barkley, R. A., Shelton, T. L., Crosswait, C., Moorehouse, M., Fletcher, K., Barrett, S., Jenkins, L., & Metevia, L. (2002). Preschool children with disruptive behavior: Three-year outcome as a function of adaptive disability. *Development and Psychopathology, 14,* 45–67.

Barlow, D. H. (2002). *Anxiety and its disorders: The nature and treatment of anxiety and panic* (2nd ed.). New York: Guilford Press.

Baron-Cohen, S. (1989). The autistic child's theory of mind: A case of specific developmental delay. *Journal of Child Psychology and Psychiatry, 30,* 285–297.

Baron-Cohen, S., Knickmeyer, R. C., & Belmonte, M. K. (2005). Sex differences in the brain: Implications for explaining autism. *Science, 310,* 819–823.

Baron-Cohen, S., O'Riordan, M., Stone, V., Jones, R., & Plaisted, K. (1999). Recognition of faux pas by normally developing children and children with Asperger syndrome or high-functioning autism. *Journal of Autism and Developmental Disabilities, 29,* 407–418.

Baron-Cohen, S., & Swettenham, J. (1997). Theory of mind in autism: Its relationship to executive functions and central coherence. In D. J. Cohen & F. R. Volkmar (Eds.), *Handbook of autism and pervasive developmental disorders.* New York: John Wiley.

Barrett, P. M., Dadds, M. R., & Rapee, R. M. (1996). Family treatment of childhood anxiety: A controlled trial. *Journal of Consulting and Clinical Psychology, 64,* 333–342.

Barrett, P. M., Farrell, L., Pina, A. A., Peris, T. S., & Piacentini, J. (2008). Evidence-based psychosocial treatments for child and adolescent obsessive-compulsive disorder. *Journal of Clinical Child and Adolescent Psychology, 37,* 131–155.

Barrett, P. M., Farrell, L. J., Ollendick, T. H., & Dadds, M. (2006). Long-term outcomes of an Australian universal prevention trial of anxiety and depression symptoms in children and youth: An evaluation of the Friends Program. *Journal of Clinical Child and Adolescent Psychology, 35,* 403–411.

Barrios, B. A., & O'Dell, S. L. (1998). Fears and anxieties. In E. J. Mash & R. A. Barkley (Eds.), *Treatment of childhood disorders* (2nd ed.). New York: Guilford Press.

Barton, B. K., Schwebel, D. C., & Morrongiello, B. A. (2007). Increasing children's safe pedestrian behaviors through simple skills training. *Journal of Pediatric Psychology, 32,* 475–480.

Bauermeister, J. J., Canino, G., Polanczyk, G., & Rohde, L. A. (2010). ADHD across cultures: Is there evidence for a bidimensional organization of symptoms? *Journal of Clinical Child and Adolescent Psychology, 39,* 362–372.

Bauermeister, J. J., Matos, M., Reina, G., Salas, C. C., Martinez, J. V., Cumba, E. et al. (2005). Comparison of the DSM-IV combined and inattentive types of ADHD in a school-based sample of Latino/Hispanic children. *Journal of Child Psychology and Psychiatry, 46,* 166–179.

Baumeister, A. A., & Baumeister, A. A. (2000). Mental retardation: Causes and effects. In M. Hersen & R. T. Ammerman (Eds.), *Advanced abnormal child psychology.* Mahwah, NJ: Lawrence Erlbaum.

Bayley, N. (2005). *Bayley Scales of Infant and Toddler Development, Third Edition (Bayley-III).* San Antonio, TX: Harcourt Assessment.

Beail, N. (2003). What works for people with mental retardation? Critical commentary on cognitive-behavioral and psychodynamic psychotherapy research. *Mental Retardation, 41,* 468–472.

Beale, I. L. (2006). Efficacy of psychological interventions for pediatric chronic illnesses. *Journal of Pediatric Psychology, 31,* 437–451.

Bear, M. F., Connars, B. W., Paradiso, M. A. (2001). *Exploring the Brain.* (2nd ed.). Baltimore, MD: Lippincott Williams & Wilkins.

Bearden, C. E., Meyer, S. E., Loewy, R. L., Niendam, T. A., & Cannon, T. D. (2006). The neurodevelopmental model of schizophrenia: Updated. In D. Cicchetti & D. J. Cohen (Eds.), *Developmental psychopathology* (Vol. 3). Hoboken, NJ: John Wiley & Sons.

Beardslee, W. R., Keller, M. B., Seifer, R., Lavorie, P. W., Staley, J., Podorefsky, D., & Shera, D. (1996). Prediction of adolescent affective disorder: Effects of prior parental affective disorders and child psychopathology. *Journal of the American Academy of Child and Adolescent Psychiatry, 35*, 279–288.

Beardslee, W. R., Versage, E. M., & Gladstone, T. R. G. (1998). Children of affectively ill parents: A review of the past 10 years. *Journal of the American Academy of Child and Adolescent Psychiatry, 37*, 1134–1141.

Beauchaine, T. P. (2001). Vagal tone, development, and Gray's motivational theory: Toward an integrated model of autonomic nervous system functioning in psychopathology. *Development and Psychopathology, 13*, 183–214.

Beauchaine, T. P., Hong, J., & Marsh, P. (2008). Sex differences in autonomic correlates of conduct problems and aggression. *Journal of the American Academy of Child and Adolescent Psychiatry, 47*, 788–796.

Beauchaine, T. P., Katkin, E. S., Strassberg, Z., & Snarr, J. (2001). Disinhibitory psychopathology in male adolescents: Discriminating conduct disorder from attention-deficit/hyperactivity disorder through concurrent assessment of multiple autonomic states. *Journal of Abnormal Psychology, 110*, 610–624.

Beauchaine, T. P., & Neuhaus, E. (2008). Impulsivity and vulnerability to psychopathology. In T. P. Beauchaine & S. P. Hinshaw (Eds.), *Child and adolescent psychopathology*. Hoboken, NJ: John Wiley & Sons.

Beck, A. T. (1967). *Depression: Clinical, experimental, and theoretical aspects*. New York: Harper & Row.

Beck, A. T. (1976). *Cognitive theory and emotional disorders*. New York: International Universities Press.

Beck, H. P., Levinson, S., & Irons, G. (2009). Finding Little Albert. A journey to John B. Watson's infant laboratory. *American Psychologist, 64*, 605–614.

Becker, K. D., Stuewig, J., Herrera, V. M., & McCloskey, L. A. (2004). A study of firesetting and animal cruelty in children: Family influences and adolescent outcomes. *Journal of the American Academy of Child and Adolescent Psychiatry, 43*, 905–912.

Becker, M. A., Jordan, N., & Larsen, R. (2007). Predictors of successful permanency planning and length of stay in foster care: The role of race, diagnosis and place of residence. *Children and Youth Services Review, 29*, 1102–1113.

Beidel, D. C., Silverman, W. K., & Hammond-Laurence, K. (1996). Overanxious disorder: Subsyndromal state or specific disorder? A comparison of clinic and community samples. *Journal of Clinical Child Psychology, 25*, 25–32.

Beidel, D. C., & Turner, S. M. (1997). At risk for anxiety: I. Psychopathology in the offspring of anxious parents. *Journal of the American Academy of Child and Adolescent Psychiatry, 36*, 918–924.

Beidel, D. C., Turner, S. M., & Morris, T. L. (1995). A new inventory to assess childhood social anxiety and phobia: The social phobia and anxiety inventory for children. *Psychological Assessment, 7*, 73–79.

Beidel, D. C., Turner, S. M., & Morris, T. L. (1999). Psychopathology of childhood social phobia. *Journal of the American Academy of Child and Adolescent Psychiatry, 38*, 630–646.

Beirne-Smith, M., Ittenbach, R. F., & Patton, J. R. (1998). *Mental retardation*. Upper Saddle River, NJ: Prentice Hall.

Beirne-Smith, M., Patton, J. R., & Kim, S. H. (2006). *Mental retardation*. Upper Saddle River, NJ: Pearson.

Beitchman, J. H., Wilson, B., Brownlie, E. B., Walters, H., Inglis, A., & Lancee, W. (1996). Long-term consistency in speech/language profiles: II. behavioral, emotional, and social outcomes. *Journal of the American Academy of Child and Adolescent Psychiatry, 35*, 815–825.

Beitchman, J. H., Wilson, B., Johnson, C. J., Atkinson, L., Young, A., Adlaf, E. et al. (2001). Fourteen-year follow-up of speech/language-impaired and control children: Psychiatric outcome. *Journal of the American Academy of Child and Adolescent Psychiatry, 40*, 75–82.

Bell, K. E., & Stein, D. M. (1992). Behavioral treatments for pica: A review of empirical studies. *International Journal of Eating Disorders, 11*, 377–389.

Bell, R. (1985). *Holy anorexia*. Chicago: University of Chicago Press.

Bellak, L., & Abrams, D. M. (1997). *The T.A.T., C.A.T., and S.A.T. in clinical use* (6th ed.). Needham Heights, MA: Allyn and Bacon.

Bellak, L., & Bellak, S. (1982). *Children's Apperception Test (CAT)*. Lutz, FL: Psychological Assessment Resources, Inc.

Belsky, J. (1993). Etiology of child maltreatment: A developmental-ecological analysis. *Psychological Bulletin, 114*, 413–434.

Belsky, J. (2001). Developmental risks (still) associated with early child care. *Journal of Child Psychology and Psychiatry, 42*, 845–859.

Belsky, J., & Pluess, M. (2009). The nature (and nurture?) of plasticity in early human development. *Perspectives on Psychological Science, 4*, 345–351.

Belsky, J., Vandell, D. L., Burchinal, M., Clarke-Stewart, A., McCartney, K., & Owen, M. T. (2007). Are there long-term effects of early child care? *Child Development, 78*, 681–701.

Benoit, D. (2009). Feeding disorders, failure to thrive, and obesity. In C. H. Zeanah, Jr. (Ed.), *Handbook of infant mental health* (3rd ed.). New York: The Guilford Press.

Benoit, M. B. (2000). Foster care. In B. J. Sadock and V. A. Sadock (Eds.), *Comprehensive textbook of psychiatry* (Vol. II). Philadelphia: Lippincott Williams & Wilkins.

Ben-Sasson, A., Hen, L., Fluss, R., Cermak, S. A., Engel-Yeger, B., & Gal, E. (2009). A meta-analysis of sensory modulation symptoms in individuals with autism spectrum disorders. *Journal of Autism and developmental Disorders, 39*, 1–11.

Bental, B., & Tirosh, E. (2007). The relationship between attention, executive functions, and reading domain abilities in attention deficit hyperactivity disorder and reading disorder: A comparative study. *Journal of Child Psychology and Psychiatry, 48*, 455–463.

Benton, T. D. (2010). Psychiatric considerations in children and adolescents with HIV/AIDS. *Child and Adolescent Psychiatric Clinics of North America, 19,* 387–400.

Berg, C. A., King, P. S., Butler, J. M., Pham, P., Palmer, D., & Wiebe, D. J. (2011). Parental involvement and adolescents' diabetes management: The mediating role of self-efficacy and externalizing and internalizing behavior. *Journal of Pediatric Psychology, 36,* 329–339.

Berger, M. (2006). A model of preverbal social development and its application to social dysfunctions in autism. *Journal of Child Psychology and Psychiatry, 47,* 338–391.

Berninger, V. W., Abbott, R. D., Vermeulen, K., & Fulton, C. M. (2006). Paths to reading comprehension in at-risk second-grade readers. *Journal of Reading Disabilities, 39,* 334–351.

Berninger, V. W., & Amtmann, D. (2003). Preventing written expression disabilities through early and continuing assessment and intervention for handwriting and/or spelling problems: Research into practice. In H. L. Swanson, K. R. Harris, & S. Graham (Eds.), *Handbook of learning disabilities.* New York: Guilford Press.

Bernstein, D. M. (1996). The discovery of the child: A historical perspective on child and adolescent psychiatry. In M. Lewis (Ed.), *Child and adolescent psychiatry: A comprehensive textbook.* Baltimore: Williams & Wilkins.

Bernstein, G. A., Bernat, D. H., Davis, A. A., & Layne, A. E. (2008). Symptom presentation and classroom functioning in a nonclinical sample of children with social phobia. *Depression and Anxiety, 25,* 752–760.

Bernstein, G. A., Hektner, J. M., Borchardt, C. M., & McMillan, M. H. (2001). Treatment of school refusal: One-year followup. *Journal of the American Academy of Child and Adolescent Psychiatry, 40,* 206–213.

Berz, J. B., Carter, A. S., Wagmiller, R. L., Horwitz, S. M., Murdock, K. K., & Briggs-Gowan, M. (2007). Prevalence and correlates of early onset asthma and wheezing in a healthy birth cohort of 2- to 3-year olds. *Journal of Pediatric Psychology, 32,* 154–166.

Betancourt, T. S., Borisova, I. I. Williams, T. P., Brennan, R. T., Whitfield, T. H., De La Soudiere, M. et al. (2010). Sierra Leone's former child soldiers: A follow-up study of psychological adjustment and community reintegration. *Child Development, 81,* 1077–1095.

Betancourt, T. S., & Khan, K. T. (2008). The mental health of children affected by armed conflict: Protective processes and pathways to resilience. *International Review of Psychiatry, 20,* 317–328.

Bettelheim, B. (1967a). *The empty fortress.* New York: Free Press.

Bettelheim, B. (1967b, Feb. 12). *Where self begins.* New York Times.

Bettes, B. A., & Walker, E. (1987). Positive and negative symptoms in psychotic and other psychiatrically disturbed children. *Journal of Child Psychology and Psychiatry, 28,* 555–568.

Beyer, J. E., & Knott, C. (1998). Construct validity estimation for the African-American and Hispanic Oucher Scale. *Journal of Pediatric Nursing, 13,* 20–31.

Biederman, J., Faraone, S., Mick, E., Moore, P., & Lelon, E. (1996). Child behavior checklist findings further support comorbidity between ADHD and major depression in a referred sample. *Journal of the American Academy of Child and Adolescent Psychiatry, 35,* 734–742.

Biederman, J., Faraone, S. V., Marrs, A., Moore, P., Garcia, J., Ablon, S. et al. (1997). Panic disorder and agoraphobia in consecutively referred children and adolescents. *Journal of the American Academy of Child and Adolescent Psychiatry, 36,* 214–223.

Biederman, J., Faraone, S. V., Mick, E., Williamson, S., Wilens, T. E., Spencer, T. J. et al. (1999). Clinical correlates of ADHD in females: Findings from a large group of girls ascertained from pediatric and psychiatric referral sources. *Journal of the American Academy of Child and Adolescent Psychiatry, 38,* 966–975.

Biederman, J., Monuteaux, M. C., Mick, E., Spencer, T., Wilens, T. E., Silva, J. M. et al., (2006). Young adult outcome of attention deficit hyperactivity disorder: A controlled 10-year follow-up study. *Psychological Medicine, 32,* 167–179.

Biederman, J., Petty, C. R., Monuteaux, M. C., Fried, R., Byrne, D., Mirto, T. et al. (2010). Adult psychiatric outcomes of girls with attention deficit hyperactivity disorder: 11-year follow-up in a longitudinal case-control study. *American Journal of Psychiatry, 167,* 409–417.

Biederman, J., Rosenbaum, J. F., Bolduc-Murphy, E. A., Faraone, S. V., Chaloff, J., Hirshfeld, D. R., & Kagan, J. (1993). A 3-year follow-up of children with and without behavioral inhibition. *Journal of the American Academy of Child and Adolescent Psychiatry, 32,* 814–821.

Bierman, K. L. (2004). *Peer rejection: Developmental processes and intervention strategies.* New York: Guilford Press.

Bierman, K. L., & Schwartz, L. A. (1986). Clinical child interviews: Approaches and developmental considerations. *Journal of Child and Adolescent Psychotherapy, 3,* 267–278.

Bifulco, A., Harris, T., & Brown, G. (1992). Mourning or early inadequate care? Reexamining the relationship of maternal loss in childhood with adult depression and anxiety. *Development and Psychopathology, 4,* 433–449.

Bijou, S. W., Peterson, R. F., Harris, F. R., Allen, K. E., & Johnston, M. S. (1969). Methodology for experimental studies of young children in natural settings. *The Psychological Record, 19,* 177–210.

Binggeli, N. J., Hart, S. N., & Brassard, M. R. (2001). *Psychological maltreatment of children.* Thousand Oaks, CA: Sage Publications.

Birmaher, B., & Axelson, D. (2005). Bipolar disorder in children and adolescents. In A. Marneros & F. Goodwin (Eds.), *Bipolar disorders: Mixed states, rapid cycling, and atypical forms.* Cambridge, UK: Cambridge University Press.

Birmaher, B., Brent, D., Chiapetta, L., Bridge, J., Monga, S., & Bauger, M. (1999). Psychometric properties for the Screen for Child Anxiety Related Emotional Disorders (SCARED): A replication study. *Journal of the American Academy of Child and Adolescent Psychiatry, 38,* 1230–1236.

Birmaher, B., Khetarpal, S., Brent, D., Cully, M., Balach, L., Kaufman, J., & McKenzie Neer, S. (1997). The Screen for Child Anxiety Related Emotional Disorders (SCARED): Scale construction and psychometric characteristics. *Journal of the American Academy of Child and Adolescent Psychiatry, 36*, 545–553.

Birmaher, B., Ryan, N. D., Williamson, D. E., Brent, D. A., Kaufman, J., Dahl, R. E., Perel, J., & Nelson, B. (1996). Childhood and adolescent depression: A review of the past 10 years. Part I. *Journal of the American Academy of Child and Adolescent Psychiatry, 35*, 1427–1439.

Birmingham, C. L., Su, J., Hlynsky, J. A., Goldner, E. M., & Gao, M. (2005). The mortality rate from anorexia nervosa. *International Journal of Eating Disorders, 38*, 143–146.

Bishop, D. V. M. (2002). Speech and language difficulties. In M. Rutter & E. Taylor (Eds.), *Child and adolescent psychiatry*, Oxford, UK: Blackwell Publishing.

Bishop, D. V. M., & Norbury, C. F. (2008). Speech and language disorders. In M. Rutter, D. V. M. Bishop, D. S. Pine, S. Scott., J. Stevenson, E. Taylor., & A. Thapar (Eds.), *Rutter's child and adolescent psychiatry* (5th ed.). Malden, MA: Blackwell Publishing.

Blacher, J., & McIntyre, L. L. (2006). Syndrome specificity and behavioural disorders in young adults with intellectual disability: Cultural differences in family impact. *Journal of Intellectual Disabilities Research, 50*, 184–198.

Black, B., & Uhde, T. W. (1995). Psychiatric characteristics of children with selective mutism: A pilot study. *Journal of the American Academy of Child and Adolescent Psychiatry, 34*, 847–856.

Black, D. O., Wallace, G. L., Sokoloff, J. L., & Kenworthy, L. (2009). Brief report: IQ split predicts social symptoms and communication abilities in high-functioning children with autism spectrum disorders. *Journal of Autism and Developmental Disorders, 39*, 1613–1619.

Blackman, J. A., & Gurka, M. J. (2007). Developmental and behavioral comorbidities of asthma in children. *Journal of Developmental & Behavioral Pediatrics, 28*, 92–99.

Blader, J. C., & Carlson, G. A. (2007). Increased rates of bipolar disorder diagnoses among U.S. child, adolescent, and adult inpatients, 1996–2004. *Biological Psychiatry, 62*, 107–114.

Blader, J. C., Koplewicz, H. C., Abikoff, H., & Foley, C. (1997). Sleep problems of elementary school children: A community survey. *Archives of Pediatrics and Adolescent Medicine, 151*, 473–480.

Blagg, N., & Yule, W. (1994). School refusal. In T. H. Ollendick, N. J. King, & W. Yule (Eds.), *International handbook of phobic and anxiety disorders in children and adolescents*. New York: Plenum Press.

Bleil, M. E., Ramesh, S., Miller, B. D., & Wood, B. L. (2000). The influence of parent-child relatedness on depressive symptoms in children with asthma: Tests of moderator and mediator models. *Journal of Pediatric Psychology, 25*, 481–491.

Blijd-Hoogewys, E. M. A., van Geert, P. L. C., Serra, M., & Minderaa, R. B. (2008). Measuring theory of mind in children. Psychometric properties for the ToM Storybooks. *Journal of Autism and Developmental Disorders, 38*, 1907–1930.

Blount, R. L., Piira, T., & Cohen, L. L. (2003). Management of pediatric pain and distress due to medical procedures. In M. C. Roberts (Eds.), *Handbook of pediatric psychology* (3rd ed.). New York: Guilford Press.

Blount, R. L., Zempsky, W. T., Jaaniste, T., Evans, S., Cohen, L. L., Devine, K. A., & Zeltzer, L. K. (2009). Management of pediatric pain and distress due to medical procedures. In M. C. Roberts & R. G. Steele (Eds.), *Handbook of pediatric psychology* (4th ed.). New York: The Guilford Press.

Boden, C., & Giaschi, D. (2007). M-stream deficits and readingrelated visual processes in developmental dyslexia. *Psychological Bulletin, 133*, 346–366.

Bodfish, J. W., Symons, F. J., Parker, D. E., & Lewis, M. H. (2000). Varieties of repetitive behavior in autism: Comparisons to mental retardation. *Journal of Autism and Developmental Disorders, 30*, 237–243.

Bogels, S. M., & Brechman-Toussaint, M. L. (2006). Family issues in child anxiety: Attachment, family functioning, parental rearing and beliefs. *Clinical Psychology Review, 26*, 834–856.

Bolger, K. E., & Patterson, C. J. (2001). Developmental pathways from child maltreatment to peer rejection. *Child Development, 72*, 549–568.

Bolton, D., Eley, T. C., O'Connor, T. G., Perrin, S., Rabe-Hesketh, S., Fijsdilk, F., & Smith, P. (2006). Prevalence and genetic and environmental influences on anxiety disorders in 6-year-old twins. *Psychological Medicine, 36*, 335–344.

Bonner, B. L., Kaufman, K. L., Harbeck, C., & Brassard, M. R. (1992). Child maltreatment. In C. E. Walker & M. C. Roberts (Eds.), *Handbook of clinical child psychology*. New York: Wiley.

Boomsma, D. I., van Beijsterveldt, C. E. M., & Hudziak, J. J. (2005). Genetic and environmental influences on anxious/depression during childhood: A study from the Netherlands twin register. *Genes, Brain, and Behavior, 48*, 466–481.

Bordeaux, J. D., Loveland, K. A., Lachar, D., Stehbens, J., Bell, T. S., Nichols, S. et al. (2003). Hemophilia growth and development study: Caregiver report of youth and family adjustment to HIV disease and immunologic compromise. *Journal of Pediatric Psychology, 28*, 175–183.

Boris, N. W. (2009). Parental substance abuse. In C. H. Zeanah, Jr. (Ed.), *Handbook of infant mental health*. New York: Guilford Press.

Bosquet, M., & Egeland, B. (2006). The development and maintenance of anxiety symptoms from infancy through adolescence in a longitudinal sample. *Development and Psychopathology, 18*, 517–550.

Bowlby, J. (1960). Grief and mourning in infancy and early childhood. *Psychoanalytic Study of the Child, 15,* 9–52.

Bowlby, J. (1969). *Attachment and loss* (Vol. 1). New York: Basic Books.

Bradley, R. B., & Corwyn, R. F. (2008). Infant temperament, parenting, and externalizing behavior in first grade: A test of the differential susceptibility hypothesis. *Journal of Child Psychology and Psychiatry, 49,* 124–131.

Bradley, R. H., Whiteside, L., Mundfrom, D. J., Casey, P. H., Kelleher, K. J., & Pope, S. K. (1994). Contributions of early interventions and early caregiving experiences to resilience in low-birthweight, premature children living in poverty. *Journal of Clinical Child Psychology, 23,* 425–434.

Braet, C., & Beyers, W. (2009). Subtyping children and adolescents who are overweight: Different symptomatology and treatment outcomes. *Journal of Consulting and Clinical Psychology, 77,* 814–824.

Brassard, M. R., Hart, S. N., & Hardy, D. B. (2000). Psychological and emotional abuse of children. In R. T. Ammerman & M. Hersen (Eds.), *Case studies in family violence* (2nd ed.). New York: Kluwer Academic/Plenum Publishers.

Braver, S. L., Ellman, I. M., & Fabricius, W. V. (2003). Relocation of children after divorce and children's best interests: New evidence and legal considerations. *Journal of Family Psychology, 17,* 206–219.

Bray, M. A., Kehle, T. J., Theodore, L. A., & Peck, H. L. (2006). Respiratory impairments. In L. Phelps (Ed.), *Chronic healthrelated disorders in children: Collaborative medical and psychoeducational interventions.* Washington, DC: American Psychological Association.

Bregman, J. D., & Gerdtz, J. (1997). Behavioral interventions. In D. J. Cohen & F. R. Volkmar (Eds.), *Handbook of autism and pervasive developmental disorders.* New York: John Wiley.

Breier, J. I., Simos, P. G., Fletcher, J. M., Castillo, E. M., Zhang, W., & Papanicolaou, A. C. (2003). Abnormal activation of temporoparietal language areas during phonetic analysis in children with dyslexia. *Neuropsychology, 17,* 610–621.

Bremner, J. D. (2006). Traumatic stress from a multiple-levels-of analysis perspective. In D. Cicchetti & D. J. Cohen (Eds.), *Developmental psychopathology. Vol. 2. Developmental neuroscience.* (2nd ed.). Hoboken, NJ: John Wiley & Sons.

Brendgen, M., Vitaro, F., Tremblay, R. E., & Lavoie, F. (2001). Reactive and proactive aggression: Predictions to physical violence in different contexts and moderating effects of parental monitoring and caregiving behavior. *Journal of Abnormal Child Psychology, 29,* 293–304.

Brennan, P. A., Le Brocque, R., & Hammen, C. (2003). Maternal depression, parent-child relationships, and resilient outcomes in adolescence. *Journal of the American Academy of Child and Adolescent Psychiatry, 42,* 1469–1477.

Brennan, P. A. & Walker, E. F. (2010). Vulnerability to schizophrenia in childhood and adolescence. In R. E. Ingram & J. M. Price (Eds.), *Vulnerability to psychopathology across the lifespan.* New York: Guilford Press.

Brent, D., Holder, D., Kolko, D., Birmaher, B., Baugher, M., Roth, C., Iyenagar, S., Johnson, B. (1997). A clinical psychotherapy trial for adolescent depression comparing cognitive, family, and supportive therapy. *Archives of General Psychiatry, 54,* 877–885.

Brent, D. A. (2006). Commentary: Glad for what TADS adds, but many TADS grads still sad. *Journal of the American Academy of Child and Adolescent Psychiatry, 45,* 1461–1464.

Brestan, E. V., & Eyberg, S. M. (1998). Effective psychosocial treatments of conduct-disordered children and adolescents: 29 years, 82 studies, and 5,272 kids. *Journal of Clinical Child Psychology, 27,* 180–189.

Bridge, J. A., Goldstein, T. R., & Brent, D. A. (2006). Adolescent suicide and suicidal behavior. *Journal of Child Psychology and Psychiatry, 47,* 372–394.

Briggs, K., Hubbs-Tait, L., Culp, R. E., & Morse, A. S. (1994). Sexual abuse label: Adults' expectations for children. *The American Journal of Family Therapy, 22,* 304–314.

Brinkmeyer, M. Y., & Eyberg, S. M. (2003). Parent-child interaction therapy for oppositional children. In A. E. Kazdin & J. R. Weisz (Eds.), *Evidence-based psychotherapies for children and adolescents.* New York: Guilford Press.

Brodeur, D. A., & Pond, M. (2001). The development of selective attention in children with attention deficit hyperactivity disorder. *Journal of Abnormal Child Psychology, 29,* 229–239.

Brody, G. H., Chen, Y. F., Murry, V. M., Ge, X., Simons, R. L., Gibbons, F. X. et al. (2006). Perceived discrimination and the adjustment of African American youths: A five-year longitudinal analysis with contextual moderation effects. *Child Development, 77,* 1170–1189.

Brody, G. H., Ge, X., Conger, R., Gibbons, F. X., Murry, V. M., Gerrard, M., & Simons, R. L. (2001). The influence of neighborhood disadvantage, collective socialization, and parenting on African-American children's affiliation with deviant peers. *Child Development, 72,* 1231–1246.

Broft, A., Berner, L. A., & Walsh, T. (2010). Pharmacotherapy for bulimia nervosa. In C. M. Grilo & J. E. Mitchell (Eds.), *The treatment of eating disorders: A clinical handbook.* New York: The Guilford Press.

Broman, S., Nichols, P. L., Shaughnessy, P., & Kennedy, W. (1987). *Retardation in young children: A developmental study of cognitive deficit.* Hillsdale, NJ: Erlbaum.

Bronfenbrenner, U. (1977). Toward an experimental ecology of human development. *American Psychologist, 32,* 320–335.

Brook, D. W., Brook, J. S., Zhang, C., & Koppel, J. (2010). Association between attention-deficit/hyperactivity disorder in adolescence and substance use disorders in adulthood. *Archives of Pediatrics and Adolescent Medicine, 164,* 930–934.

Brookes, K-J., Mill, J., Guindalini, C., Curran, S., Xu, X., Knight, J. et al. (2006). A common haplotype of the dopamine transporter gene associated with attention-deficit/hyperactivity disorder and interacting with maternal use of alcohol during pregnancy. *Archives of General Psychiatry, 63,* 74–81.

Brooks-Gunn, J., Auth, J. J., Peterson, A. C., & Compas, B. E. (2001). Physiological processes and the development of childhood and adolescent depression. In I. M. Goodyer (Ed.), *The depressed child and adolescent* (2nd ed.). Cambridge, UK: Cambridge University Press.

Brosbe, M. S., Hoefling, K., & Faust, J. (2011). Predicting posttraumatic stress following pediatric injury: A systematic review. *Journal of Pediatric Psychology, 36*, 718–729.

Brotman, M. A., Schmajuk, M., Rich, B. A., Dickstein, D. P., Guyer, A. E., Costello, E. J. et al. (2006). Prevalence, clinical correlates, and longitudinal course of severe mood dysregulation in children. *Biological Psychiatry, 60*, 991–997.

Brown, A. S., Bresnahan, M., & Susser, E. S. (2005). Schizophrenia: Environmental epidemiology. In B. J. Sadock & V. A. Sadock (Eds.), *Comprehensive textbook of psychiatry* (Vol. 1). Philadelphia: Lippincott Williams & Wilkins.

Brown, J. V., Bakeman, R., Coles, C. D., Platzman, K. A., & Lynch, M. E. (2004). Prenatal cocaine exposure: A comparison of 2-year-old children in parental and nonparental care. *Child Development, 75*, 1282–1295.

Brown, R. T., Connelly, M., Rittle, C., & Clouse, B. (2006). A longitudinal examination predicting emergency room use in children with sickle cell disease and their caregivers. *Journal of Pediatric Psychology, 31*, 163–173.

Brown, R. T., Daly, B. P., Carpenter, J. L., & Cohen, J. S. (2009). Pediatric pharmacology and psychopharmacology. In M. C. Roberts & R. G. Steele (Eds.), *Handbook of Pediatric Psychology* (4th ed.). New York: The Guilford Press.

Brown, R. T., & McMillan, K. K. (2011). Rett syndrome: A truly pervasive developmental disorder. In S. Goldstein & C. R. Reynolds (Eds.), *Handbook of neurodevelopmental and genetic disorders*. New York: Guilford Press.

Brown, T., & Summerbell, C. (2009). Systematic review of school-based interventions that focus on changing dietary intake and physical activity levels to prevent childhood obesity: An update to the obesity guidance produced by the National Institute for Health and Clinical Excellence. *Obesity Reviews, 10*, 110–141.

Brown Kirschman, K. J., Mayes, S., & Perciful, M. S. (2009). Prevention of unintentional injury in children and adolescents. In M. C. Roberts & R. G. Steele (Eds.), *Handbook of pediatric psychology* (4th ed.). New York: The Guilford Press.

Bruce, M. (2006). A systematic and conceptual review of posttraumatic stress in childhood cancer survivors and their parents. *Clinical Psychology Review, 26*, 233–256.

Bruch, H. (1979). *The golden cage: The enigma of anorexia nervosa*. New York: Vintage Books.

Brumariu, L. E., & Kerns, K. A. (2010). Parent-child attachment and internalizing symptoms in childhood and adolescence: A review of empirical findings and future directions. *Development and Psychopathology, 22*, 177–203.

Brumberg, J. J. (1986). "Fasting girls": Reflections on writing the history of anorexia nervosa. In A. B. Smuts & J. W. Hagen (Eds.), *History and research in child development. Monographs of the Society for Research in Child Development, 50* (4–5, Serial No. 211).

Bryan, T. (1997). Assessing the personal and social status of students with learning disabilities. *Learning Disabilities Research & Practice, 12*, 63–76.

Buchanan, R. W., & Carpenter, W. T. (2000). Schizophrenia: Introduction and overview. In B. J. Sadock & V. A. Sadock (Eds.), *Comprehensive textbook of psychiatry* (Vol. II). Philadelphia: Lippincott Williams & Wilkins.

Buck, J. N. (1992). *House-Tree-Person projective drawing technique (H-T-P): Manual and interpretive guide* (Revised by W. L. Warren). Los Angeles, CA: Western Psychological Services.

Buckhalt, J. A., El-Sheikh, M., & Keller, P. (2007). Children's sleep and cognitive functioning: Race and socioeconomic status as moderators of effects. *Child Development, 78*, 213–231.

Buckner, J. C., Mezzacappa, E., & Beardslee, W. R. (2003). Characteristics of resilient youth living in poverty: The role of selfregulatory processes. *Development and Psychopathology, 15*, 139–162.

Budd, K. S., & Chugh, C. S. (1998). Common feeding problems in young children. In T. H. Ollendick & R. J. Prinz (Eds.), *Advances in clinical child psychology* (Vol. 20). New York: Plenum Press.

Building the Legacy: IDEA. (2004). Secondary transition. U.S. Department of Education. Downloaded October 10, 2011. http://idea.ed.gov/explore/view/p/%2Croot%2Cdynamic%2CTopicalBrief%2C17%2C

Bukowski, W. M., & Adams, R. (2005). Peer relationships and psychopathology: Markers, moderators, mediators, mechanisms, and meanings. *Journal of Clinical Child and Adolescent Psychology, 34*, 3–10.

Bukowski, W. M., Laursen, B., & Hoza, B. (2010). The snowball effect: Friendship moderates escalations in depressed affect among avoidant and excluded children. *Development and Psychopathology, 22*, 749–757.

Burack, J. A. (1990). Differentiating mental retardation: The two-group approach and beyond. In R. M. Hodapp, J. A. Burack, & E. Zigler (Eds.), *Issues in the developmental approach to mental retardation*. New York: Cambridge University Press.

Burchinal, M., Roberts. J. E., Zeisel, S. A., Hennon, E. A., & Hooper, S. (2006). Social risk and protective child, parenting, and child care factors in early elementary school years. *Parenting: Science and Practice, 6*, 79–113.

Burke, E. J., & Andrasik, F. (1989). Home vs. clinic-based biofeedback treatment for pediatric migraine: Results of treatment through one-year follow-up. *Headache, 29*, 434–440.

Burke, J. D., Loeber, R., Lahey, B. B., & Rathouz, P. J. (2005). Developmental transitions among affective and behavioral disorders in adolescent boys. *Journal of Child Psychology and Psychiatry, 46*, 1200–1210.

Burke, J. D., Pardini, D. A., & Loeber, R. (2008). Reciprocal relationships between parenting behavior and disruptive psychopathology from childhood through adolescence. *Journal of Abnormal Child Psychology, 36*, 679–692.

Burns, R. C. (1987). *Kinetic House-Tree-Person Drawings: K-H-T-P: An interpretive manual*. London: Routledge.

Burt, S. A. (2009). Rethinking environmental contributions to child and adolescent psychopathology: A meta-analysis of shared environmental influences. *Psychological Bulletin, 135*, 608–637.

Burt, S. A., Klahr, A. M., Rueter, M. A., McGue, M., & Iacono, W. G. (2011). Confirming the etiology of adolescent acting-out behaviors: An examination of observer-ratings in a sample of adoptive and biological siblings. *Journal of Child Psychology and Psychiatry, 52*, 519–526.

Burt, S. A., Krueger, R. F., McGue, M., & Iacono, W. G. (2001). Sources of covariation among attention-deficit/hyperactivity disorder, oppositional defiant disorder, and conduct disorder: The importance of shared environment. *Journal of Abnormal Psychology, 110*, 516–525.

Bushman, B. J., & Anderson, C. A. (2001). Media violence and the American public: Scientific facts versus media misinformation. *American Psychologist, 56*, 477–489.

Butler, R. J. (2008). Wetting and soiling. In M. Rutter et al. (Eds.), *Rutter's child and adolescent psychiatry* (5th ed.). Malden, MA: Blackwell Publishing.

Butler, R. W., Copeland, D. R., Fairclough, D. L., Mulhern, R. K., Katz, E. R., Kazak, A. E. et al. (2008). A multicenter, randomized clinical trial of a cognitive remediation program for childhood survivors of pediatric malignancy. *Journal of Consulting and Clinical Psychology, 76*, 367–378.

Byrd, A. L., Loeber, R., & Pardini, D. A. (2012). Understanding desisting and persisting forms of delinquency: The unique contributions of disruptive behavior disorders and interpersonal callousness. *Journal of Child Psychology and Psychiatry, 53*, 371–380.

Cadesky, E. B., Mota, V. L., & Schachar, R. J. (2000). Beyond words: How do children with ADHD and/or conduct problems process nonverbal information about affect? *Journal of the American Academy of Child and Adolescent Psychiatry, 39*, 1160–1167.

Calati, R., De Ronchi, D., Bellini, M., & Serretti, A. (2011). The 5-HTTLPR polymorphism and eating disorders: A meta-analysis. *International Journal of Eating Disorders, 44*, 191–199.

Calderoni, D., Wudarsky, M., Bhangoo, R., Dell, M. L., Nicolson, R., Hamburger, S. D. et al. (2001). Differentiating childhoodonset schizophrenia from psychotic mood disorders. *Journal of the American Academy of Child and Adolescent Psychiatry, 40*, 1190–1196.

Callender, K. A., Olson, S. L., Choe, D. E., & Sameroff, A. J. (2012). The effects of parental depressive symptoms, appraisals, and physical punishment on later child externalizing behavior. *Journal of Abnormal Child Psychology, 40*, 471–483.

Campbell., F. A., & Ramey, C. T. (1994). Effects of early intervention on intellectual and academic achievement: A follow-up study of children from low-income families. *Child Development, 65*, 684–698.

Campbell, F. A., Ramey, C. T., Pungello, E. P., Miller-Johnson, S., & Burchinal, M. (2001). The development of cognitive and academic abilities: Growth curves from an early childhood educational experiment. *Developmental Psychology, 37*, 231–242.

Campbell, L. K., Cox, D. J., & Borowitz, S. M. (2009). Elimination disorders: Enuresis and encopresis. In M. C. Roberts & R. G. Steele (Eds.), *Handbook of pediatric psychology* (4th ed.). New York: The Guilford Press.

Campbell, S. B. (1995). Behavior problems in preschool children: A review of recent research. *Journal of Child Psychology and Psychiatry, 36*, 113–149.

Campbell, S. B. (2000). Attention-deficit/hyperactivity disorder. In A. J. Sameroff, M. Lewis, & S. M. Miller (Eds.), *Handbook of developmental psychopathology*. New York: Kluwer Academic/Plenum.

Campbell, S. B. (2002). *Behavior problems in preschool children*. New York: The Guilford Press.

Candy-Gibbs, S. E., Sharp, K. C., & Petrun, C. J. (1985). The effects of age, object, and cultural/religious background on children's concepts of death. *Omega Journal of Death and Dying, 15*, 329–346.

Canino, G., & Alegria, M. (2008). Psychiatric diagnosis: Is it universal or relative to culture? *Journal of Child Psychology and Psychiatry, 49*, 237–250.

Canino, G., Shrout, P. E., Rugio-Stipic, M., Bird, H. R., Bravo, M., Ramirez, R. et al. (2004). The DSM-IV rates of child and adolescent disorders in Puerto Rico. *Archives of General Psychiatry, 61*, 85–93.

Canino, G., Vila, D., Normand, S. L. T., Acosta-Perez, E., Ramirez, R., Garcia, P., & Rand, C. (2008). Reducing asthma health disparities in poor Puerto Rican children: The effectiveness of a culturally tailored family intervention. *Journal of Allergy and Clinical Immunology, 121*, 665–670.

Cannon, T. D., & Rosso, I. M. (2002). Levels of analysis in etiological research on schizophrenia. *Development and Psychopathology, 14*, 653–666.

Cantor, S., & Kestenbaum, C. (1986). Psychotherapy with schizophrenic children. *Journal of the American Academy of Child Psychiatry, 25*, 623–630.

Cantwell, D. P. (1980). The diagnostic process and diagnostic classification in child psychiatry: DSM-III. *Journal of the American Academy of Child Psychiatry, 19*, 345–355.

Cao, F., Bitan, T., Chou, T-L., Burman, D. D., & Booth, J. R. (2006). Deficient orthographic and phonological representations in children with dyslexia revealed by brain activation patterns. *Journal of Child Psychology and Psychiatry, 47*, 1041–1050.

Capaldi, D., DeGarmo, D., Patterson, G. R., & Forgatch, M. (2002). Contextual risk across the early life span and association with antisocial behavior. In J. B. Reid, G. R. Patterson, & J. Snyder (Eds.), *Antisocial behavior in children and adolescents: A developmental analysis and model for intervention*. Washington, DC: American Psychological Association.

Caplan, G. (1964). *The principles of preventive psychiatry.* New York: Basic Books.

Caplan, R. (1994). Thought disorder in childhood. *Journal of the American Academy of Child and Adolescent Psychiatry, 33,* 605–615.

Caplan, R., Guthrie, D., Tang, B., Komo, S., & Asarnow, R. F. (2000). Thought disorder in childhood schizophrenia: Replication and update of concept. *Journal of the American Academy of Child and Adolescent Psychiatry, 39,* 771–778.

Capone, G. T. (2001). Down syndrome: Advances in molecular biology and the neurosciences. *Developmental and behavioral pediatrics, 22,* 40–59.

Cappadocia, M. C., Desrocher, M., Pepler, D., & Schroeder, J. H. (2009). Conceptualizing the neurobiology of conduct disorder in an emotion dysregulation framework. *Clinical Psychology Review, 29,* 506–518.

Carey, M. E., Hockenberry, J. J., Moore, I. M., Hutter, J. J., Krull, K. R., Pasvogel, A., & Kaemingk, K. L. (2007). Effect of intravenous methotrexate dose and infusion rate on neuropsychological function one year after diagnosis of acute lymphoblastic leukemia. *Journal of Pediatric Psychology, 32,* 189–193.

Carlson, G. A., & Cantwell, D. P. (1980). Unmasking masked depression in children and adolescents. *American Journal of Psychiatry, 137,* 445–449.

Carpenter, P. J. (1992). Perceived control as a predictor of distress in children undergoing invasive medical procedures. *Journal of Pediatric Psychology, 17,* 757–773.

Carr, L., Henderson, J., & Nigg, J. T. (2010). Cognitive control and attentional selection in adolescents with ADHD versus ADD. *Journal of Clinical Child and Adolescent Psychology, 39,* 726–740.

Carrey, N., & Ungar, M. (2007). Resilience theory and the diagnostic and statistical manual: Incompatible bed fellows? *Child and Adolescent Psychiatric Clinics of North America, 16,* 497–513.

Carroll, J. M., Maughan, B., Goodman, R., & Meltzer, H. (2005). Literacy difficulties and psychiatric disorders: Evidence for comorbidity. *Journal of Child Psychology and Psychiatry, 46,* 524–532.

Carson, C., & Rutter, M. (1991). Comorbidity in child psychopathology: Concepts, issues and research strategies. *Journal of Child Psychology and Psychiatry, 32,* 1063–1080.

Carter, A. S., Volkmar, F. R., Sparrow, S. S., Wang, J-J., Lord, C., Dawson, G. et al. (1998). The Vineland adaptive behavior scales: Supplementary norms for individuals with autism. *Journal of Autism and Developmental Disorders, 28,* 287–302.

Casey, B. J., Castellanos, F. X., Giedd, J. N., Marsh, W. L., Hamburger, S. D., Schubert, A. B., Vauss, Y. C., Vaituzis, A. C., Dickstein, D. P., Sarfatti, S. E., & Rapoport, J. L. (1997). Implication of right frontostriatal circuity in response inhibition and attention-deficit/hyperactivity disorder. *Journal of the American Academy of Child and Adolescent Psychiatry, 36,* 374–383.

Caspi, A., Elder, G. H., Jr., & Bem, D. J. (1987). Moving against the world: Life-course patterns of explosive children. *Developmental Psychology, 23,* 308–313.

Caspi, A., Sudgen, K., Moffitt, T. E., Taylor, A., Craig. I. W., Harrington, H. et al. (2003). Influence of life stress on depression: Moderation by a polymorphism in the 5–HTT gene. *Science, 301,* 386–389.

Castellanos-Ryan, N., & Conrod, P. J. (2011). Personality correlates of the common and unique variance across conduct disorder and substance misuse symptoms. *Journal of Abnormal Child Psychology, 39,* 563–576.

Catalan, J. (2000). Sexuality, reproductive cycle and suicidal behaviour. In K. Hawton & K. van Heeringen (Eds.), *The international handbook of suicide and attempted suicide.* Chichester, UK: John Wiley & Sons, Ltd.

CATS Consortium. (2007). Implementing CBT for traumatized children and adolscents after September 11: Lessons learned from the Child and Adolescent Trauma Treatments and Services (CATS) Project. *Journal of Clinical Child Psychology, 36,* 581–592.

Caughty, M. O., O'Campo, P. J., Randolph, S. M., & Nickerson, K. (2002). The influence of racial socialization practices on the cognitive and behavioral competence of African American preschoolers. *Child Development, 73,* 1611–1625.

Cavell, T. A., Ennett, S. T., & Meehan, B. T. (2001). Preventing alcohol and substance abuse. In J. N. Hughes, A. M. La Greca, & J. C. Conoley (Eds.), *Handbook of psychological services for children and adolescents.* New York: Oxford University Press.

Cawley, J. (2006). Markets and childhood obesity policy. *The Future of Children, 16,* 69–88.

CDC. (2010). Attention-deficit/hyperactivity disorder. Data and statistics in the United States. Centers for Disease Control and Prevention. http://www.cdc.gov/ncbddd/adhd/data.html

Centers for Disease Control and Prevention. (2007). *WISQARSTM Web-based Inquiry Statistics Query and Reporting System.* Retrieved September 30, 2007 from: http://www.cdc.gov/ncipc/wisqars/

Centers for Disease Control and Prevention. (2009). *Prevalence of autism-autism and developmental disabilities monitoring network, United States, 2006* (Surveillance Summaries, December 18, 2009. MMWR 2006: 58, No. 5510:1–20).

Centers for Disease Control and Prevention (2012). Autism spectrum disorders (ASDs). Data and statistics. Retrieved from http://www.cdc.gov/ncbddd/autism/data.html

Centers for Disease Control and Prevention: National Center for Health Statistics. (2010). *Prevalence of obesity among children and adolescents: United States, trends 1963–1965 through 2007–2008.* Retrieved July 2011 from http://www/cdc.gov/nchs/hestat/obesity_child_07_08/obesity_child_07_08.htm

Centers for Disease Control and Prevention. Youth Risk Behavior Surveillance-United States. (2009). Surveillance Summaries, June 2010. MMWR 2010: 59(No. SS-5).

Cervellione, K. L., Burdick, K. E., Cottone, J. G., Rhinewine, J. P., & Kurma, S. (2007). Neurocognitive deficits in adolescents with schizophrenia: Longitudinal stability and predictive utility for short-term functional outcome. *Journal of the American Academy of Child and Adolescent Psychiatry, 46,* 867–878.

Chamberlain, P., & Smith, D. K. (2003). Antisocial behavior in children and adolescents: The Oregon multidimensional treatment foster care model. In A. E. Kazdin & J. R. Weisz (Eds.), *Evidence-based psychotherapies for children and adolescents.* New York: Guilford Press.

Chambers, R. A., Taylor, J. R., & Potenza, M. N. (2003). Developmental neurocircuitry of motivation in adolescence: A critical period of addiction vulnerability. *American Journal of Psychiatry, 160,* 1041–1052.

Chambless, D. L., & Hollon, S. D. (1998). Defining empirically supported therapies. *Journal of Consulting and Clinical Psychology, 66,* 7–18.

Chandler, L. A. (2003). The projective hypothesis and the development of projective techniques for children. In C. R. Reynolds & R. W. Kamphaus (Eds.), *Handbook of psychological & educational assessment of children: Personality, behavior, and context* (2nd ed.). New York: Guilford Press.

Chapman, R. S. (2000). Children's language learning: An interactionist perspective. *Journal of Child Psychology and Psychiatry, 4,* 33–54.

Charach, A., Yeung, E., Climans, T., & Lillie, E. (2011). Childhood attention-deficit/hyperactivity disorder and future substance use disorders: Comparative meta-analysis. *Journal of the American Academy of Child and Adolescent Psychiatry, 50,* 9–21.

Charman, T. (2011). Commentary: Glass half full or half empty? Testing social communication interventions for young children with autism-reflections on Landa, Holman, O'Neill, and Stuart (2011). *Journal of Child Psychology and Psychiatry, 52,* 22–23.

Charmon, T., & Baird, G. (2002). Practitioner review: Diagnosis of autism spectrum disorder in 2- and 3-year-old children. *Journal of Child Psychology and Psychiatry, 43,* 289–305.

Chasnoff, I. J., Wells, A. M., Telford, E., Schmidt, C., & Messer, G. (2010). Neurodevelopmental functioning in children with FAS, pFAS, and ARND. *Journal of Developmental and Behavioral Pediatrics, 31,* 192–201.

Chassin, L., Beltran, I., Lee, M., Haller, M., & Villalta, I. (2010). Vulnerability to substance use disorders in childhood and adolescence. In R. E. Ingram & J. M. Price (Eds.), *Vulnerability to psychopathology: Risk across the lifespan* (2nd ed.). New York: The Guilford Press.

Chassin, L., Hussong, A. M., & Beltran, I. (2009). Adolescent substance use. In R. M. Lerner & L. Steinberg (Eds.), *Handbook of adolescent psychology* (3rd ed.). Hoboken, NJ: Wiley.

Chassin, L., Presson, C. C., Todd, M., Rose, J., & Sherman, S. J.(1998). Maternal socialization of adolescent smoking: The intergenerational transmission of parenting and smoking. *Developmental Psychology, 34,* 1189–1201.

Chavira, D. A., Shipon-Blum, E., Hitchcock, C., Cohan, S., & Stein, M. B. (2007). Selective mutism and social anxiety disorder: All in the family? *Journal of the American Academy of Child and Adolescent Psychiatry, 46,* 1464–1472.

Chavira, D. A., & Stein, M. B. (2005). Childhood social anxiety disorder: From understanding to treatment. *Child and Adolescent Psychiatric Clinics of North America, 14,* 797–818.

Chawarska, K., Klin, A., Paul, R., & Volkmar, F. (2007). Autism spectrum disorder in the second year: Stability and change in syndrome expression. *Journal of Child Psychology and Psychiatry, 48,* 128–138.

Chawarska, K., & Shic, F. (2009). Looking but not seeing: A typical visual scanning and recognition of faces in 2- and 4-year-old children with autism spectrum disorder. *Journal of Autism and Developmental Disorders, 39,* 1663–1672.

Chess, S., & Thomas, A. (1972). Differences in outcome with early intervention in children with behavior disorders. In M. Roff, L. Robins, & M. Pollack (Eds.), *Life history research in psychopathology* (Vol. 2). Minneapolis: University of Minnesota Press.

Chess, S., & Thomas, A. (1977). Temperamental individuality from childhood to adolescence. *Journal of the American Academy of Child Psychiatry, 16,* 218–226.

Child Welfare Information Gateway. (2011). *Foster care statistics 2009.* Washington, DC: U.S. Department of Health and Human Services, Children's Bureau.

Childress, A. C., Brewerton, T. D., Hodges, E. L., & Jarrell, M. P. (1993). The Kids' Eating Disorders Survey (KEDS): A study of middle school students. *Journal of the American Academy of Child and Adolescent Psychiatry, 32,* 843–850.

Chorpita, B. F. (2001). Control and the development of negative emotions. In M. W. Vasey & M. R. Dadds (Eds.), *The developmental psychopathology of anxiety.* New York: Oxford University Press.

Chorpita, B. F. (2002). The tripartite model and dimensions of anxiety and depression: An examination of structure in a large school sample. *Journal of Abnormal Child Psychology, 30,* 177–190.

Chorpita, B. F., & Barlow, D. H. (1998). The development of anxiety: The role of control in the early environment. *Psychological Bulletin, 124,* 3–21.

Chorpita, B. F., & Daleiden, E. L. (2010). Building evidence-based systems in children's mental health. In J. R. Weisz & A. E. Kazdin (Eds.), *Evidence-based psychotherapies for children and adolescents* (2nd ed.). New York: The Guilford Press.

Chorpita, B. F., Miranda, J., & Bernstein, A. (2011). Creating public health policy: The dissemination of evidence-base psychological interventions. In D. H. Barlow (Ed.), *The Oxford handbook of clinical psychology.* New York: Oxford University Press.

Chorpita, B. F., & Southam-Gerow, M. A. (2006). Fears and anxieties. In E. J. Mash & R. A. Barkley (Eds.), *Treatment of childhood disorders* (3rd ed.). New York: The Guilford Press.

Christophersen, E. R., & Mortweet, S. L. (2001). *Treatments that work with children: Empirically supported strategies for managing childhood problems.* Washington, DC: American Psychological Association.

Chronis, A. M., Pelham, W. E., Gnagy, E. M., Roberts, J. E., & Aronoff, H. R. (2003). The impact of late-afternoon stimulant dosing for children with ADHD on parent and parent-child domains. *Journal of Clinical Child and Adolescent Psychology, 32,* 118–126.

Chronis-Tuscano, A., Degnan, K. A., Pine, D. S., Perez-Edgar, K., Henderson, H. A., & Diaz, Y. et al. (2009). Stable early maternal report of behavioral inhibition predicts lifetime social anxiety disorder in adolescence. *Journal of the American Academy of Child and Adolescent Psychiaty, 48,* 928–935.

Chung, H. L., & Steinberg, L. (2006). Relations between neighborhood factors, parenting behaviors, peer deviance, and delinquency among serious juvenile offenders. *Developmental Psychology, 42,* 319–331.

Cicchetti, D. (1984). The emergence of developmental psychopathology. *Child Development, 55,* 1–7.

Cicchetti, D. (1989). Developmental psychology: Some thoughts on its evolution. *Development and Psychopathology, 1,* 1–3.

Cicchetti, D. (2006). Development and psychopathology. In D. Cicchetti & D. J. Cohen (Eds.), *Developmental psychopathology, Vol. 1: Theory and method.* Hoboken, NJ: John Wiley & Sons.

Cicchetti, D. (2010a). A developmental psychopathology perspective on bipolar disorder. In D. J. Miklowitz & D. Cicchetti (Eds.), *Understanding bipolar disorder: A developmental psychopathology perspective.* New York: Guilford Press.

Cicchetti, D. (2010b). Resilience under conditions of extreme stress: A multilevel perspective. *World Psychiatry, 9,* 145–154.

Cicchetti, D., & Hinshaw, S. P. (2002). Editorial: Prevention and intervention science: Contributions to developmental theory. *Development and Psychopathology, 14,* 667–671.

Cicchetti, D., & Lynch, M. (1995). Failures in the expectable environment and their impact on individual development: The case of child maltreatment. In D. Cicchetti & D. J. Cohen (Eds.), *Developmental psychopathology: Risk, disorder, and adaptation* (Vol. 2). New York: John Wiley & Sons.

Cicchetti, D., & Manly, J. T. (2001). Operationalizing child maltreatment: Developmental processes and outcomes. *Development and Psychopathology, 13,* 755–757.

Cicchetti, D., & Olsen, K. (1990). The developmental psychopathology of child maltreatment. In M. Lewis & S. M. Miller (Eds.), *Handbook of developmental psychopathology.* New York: Plenum Press.

Cicchetti, D., & Rogosch, F. A. (2002). A developmental psychopathology perspective on adolescence. *Journal of Consulting and Clinical Psychology, 70,* 6–20.

Cicchetti, D., & Sroufe, L. A. (2000). Editorial: The past as prologue to the future: The times, they've been a-changin'. *Development and Psychopathology, 12,* 255–264.

Cicchetti, D., Toth, S., & Bush, M. (1988). Developmental psychopathology and incompetence in childhood: Suggestions for intervention. In B. B. Lahey & A. E. Kazdin (Eds.), *Advances in clinical child psychology* (Vol. 11). New York: Plenum.

Cicchetti, D., & Toth, S. L. (1998). The development of depression in children and adolescents. *American Psychologist, 53,* 221–241.

Cicchetti, D., & Toth, S. L. (2009). The past achievements and future promises of developmental psychopathology: The coming of age of a discipline. *Journal of Child Psychology and Psychiatry, 50,* 16–25.

Cicchetti, D., Toth, S. L., & Maughan, A. (2000). An ecological-transactional model of child maltreatment. In A. J. Sameroff, M. Lewis, & S. M. Miller (Eds.), *Handbook of developmental psychopathology* (2nd ed.). New York: Kluwer Academic/ Plenum Publishers.

Cirino, P. T., Fletcher, J. M., Ewing-Cobbs, L., Barnes, M. A., & Fuchs, L. S. (2007). Cognitive arithmetic differences in learning difficulty groups and the role of behavioral inattention. *Learning Disabilities Research & Practice, 22,* 25–35.

Clarizio, H. F. (1994). Assessment of depression in children and adolescents by parents, teachers, and peers. In W. M. Reynolds and H. F. Johnston (Eds.), *Handbook of depression in children and adolescents.* New York: Plenum Press.

Clark, D. B., Smith, M. G., Neighbors, B. D., Skerlec, L. M., & Randall, J. (1994). Anxiety disorders in adolescence: Characteristics, prevalence, and comorbidities. *Clinical Psychology Review, 14,* 113–137.

Clark, K. B., Chein, I., & Cook, S. W. (2004). The effects of segregation and the consequences of desegregation: A (September 1952) Social Science Statement in the *Brown v. Board of Education of Topeka* Supreme Court Case. *American Psychologist, 59,* 495–501.

Clark, L., & Tiggemann, M. (2007). Sociocultural influences and body image in 9- to 12-year-old girls: The role of appearance schemas. *Journal of Clinical Child and Adolescent Psychology, 36,* 76–86.

Clark, L. A., & Watson, D. (1991). Tripartite model of anxiety and depression: Psychometric evidence and taxonomic implications. *Journal of Abnormal Psychology, 100,* 316–336.

Clarke, G. N., & DeBar, L. L. (2010). Group cognitive-behavioral treatment for adolescent depression. In J. R. Weisz & A. E. Kazdin (Eds.), *Evidence-based psychotherapies for children and adolescents* (2nd ed.). New York: The Guilford Press.

Clarke, G. N., Hornbrook, M., Lynch, F., Polen, M., Gale, J., Beardslee, W. et al. (2001). A randomized trial of a group cognitive intervention for preventing depression in adolescent offspring of depressed parents. *Archives of General Psychiatry, 58,* 1127–1134.

Clarke, G. N., Rhode, P., Lewinsohn, P. M., Hops, H., & Seeley, J. R. (1999). Cognitive-behavioral treatment for adolescent depression: Efficacy of acute group treatment and booster sessions. *Journal of the American Academy of Child and Adolescent Psychiatry, 38,* 272–279.

Clegg, J., Hollis, C., Mawhood, L., & Rutter, M. (2005). Developmental language disorders—a follow-up in later adult life: Cognitive, language, and psychosocial outcomes. *Journal of Child Psychology and Psychiatry, 46,* 128–149.

Cohan, S. L., Chavira, D. A., Shipon-Blum, E., Hitchock, C., Roesch, S. C., & Stein, M. (2008). Refining the classification of children with selective mutism: A latent profile analysis. *Journal of Clinical Child and Adolescent Psychology, 37,* 770–784.

Cohen, G. L., Garcia, J., Purdie-Vaughns, V., Apfel, N., & Brzustoski, P. (2009). Recursive processes in self-affirmation: Intervening to close the minority gap. *Science, 324,* 400–403.

Cohen, L. L., Lemanek, K., Blount, R. L., Dahlquist, L. M., Lim, C. S., Palermo, T. M. et al. (2008). Evidence-based assessment of pediatric pain. *Journal of Pediatric Psychology, 33,* 939–955.

Cohen, P., Cohen, J., & Brook, J. (1993a). An epidemiological study of disorders in late childhood and adolescence-II. Persistence of disorders. *Journal of Child Psychology and Psychiatry, 34,* 869–877.

Cohen, P., Cohen, J., Kasen, S., Velez, C. N., Hartmark, C., Johnson, J., Rojas, M., Brook, J., & Streuning, E. L. (1993b). An epidemiological study of disorders in late childhood and adolescence-I. Age- and gender-specific prevalence. *Journal of Child Psychology and Psychiatry, 34,* 851–867.

Cohen-Tovee, E. M. (1993). Depressed mood and concern with weight and shape in normal young women. *International Journal of Eating Disorders, 14,* 223–227.

Coie, J. D., Belding, M., & Underwood, M. (1988). Aggression and peer rejection in childhood. In B. B. Lahey & A. E.Kazdin (Eds.), *Advances in clinical child psychology* (Vol. 11). New York: Plenum.

Coie, J. D., & Dodge, K. A. (1998). Aggression and antisocial behavior. In W. Damon (Series Ed.) & N. Eisenberg (Vol. Ed.), *Handbook of child psychology: Vol. 3. Social, emotional, and personality development* (5th ed.). New York: John Wiley.

Coie, J. D., Miller-Johnson, S., & Bagwell, C. (2000). Prevention science. In A. J. Sameroff, M. Lewis, & S. M. Miller (Eds.), *Handbook of developmental psychopathology.* New York: Kluwer Academic/Plenum.

Colder, C., Chassin, L., Villalta, I., & Lee, M. (2009). Affect regulation and substance use: A developmental perspective. In J. Kassel (Ed.), *Substance use and emotion.* Washington, DC: American Psychological Association.

Cole, C. M.,Waldron, N., & Majd, M. (2004). Academic progress of students across inclusive and traditional settings. *Mental Retardation, 42,* 136–144.

Cole, W. R., Mostofsky, S. H., Gidley Larson, J. C., Denckla, M. B., Mahone, E. M. (2008). Age-related changes in motor subtle signs among girls and boys with ADHD. *Neurology, 71,* 1514–1520.

Collett, B. R., Ohan, J., & Myers, K. M. (2003). Ten-year review of rating scales. V: Scales assessing attention-deficit/hyperactivity disorder. *Journal of the American Academy of Child and Adolescent Psychiatry, 42,* 1015–1037.

Collins, E. (1991). Body figure perceptions and preferences among preadolescent children. *International Journal of Eating Disorders, 10,* 199–208.

Collishaw, S., Maughan, B., Goodman, R., & Pickles, A. (2004). Time trends in adolescent health. *Journal of Child Psychology and Psychiatry, 45,* 1350–1362.

Collishaw, S., Maughan, B., Natarajan, L., & Pickles, A. (2010). Trends in adolescent emotional problems in England: A comparison of two national cohorts twenty years apart. *Journal of Child Psychology and Psychiatry, 51,* 885–894.

Colonnesi, C., Draijer, E. M., Stams, G. J. J. M., Van der Bruggen, C. O., & Bögels, S. M. (2011). The relation between insecure attachment and child anxiety: A meta-analytic review. *Journal of Clinical Child and Adolescent Psychology, 40,* 630–645.

Comer, J. S., Fan, B., Duarte, C. S., Wu, P., Musa, G. J., Mandell, D. J. et al. (2010). Attack-related life disruptions and child psychopathology in New York City public schoolchildren 6-months post-9/11. *Journal of Clinical Child and Adolescent Psychology, 39,* 460–469.

Compas, B. E. (1997). Depression in children and adolescents. In E. J. Mash & L. G. Terdal (Eds.), *Assessment of childhood disorders* (3rd ed.). New York: Guilford Press.

Compas, B. E., Connor-Smith, J., & Jaser, S. S. (2004). Temperament, stress reactivity, and coping: Implications for depression in childhood and adolescence. *Journal of Clinical Child and Adolescent Psychology, 33,* 21–31.

Compas, B. E., Ey, S., & Grant, K. E. (1993). Taxonomy, assessment, and diagnosis of depression during adolescence. *Psychological Bulletin, 14,* 323–344.

Compas, B. E., Hinden, B. R., & Gerhardt, C. (1995). Adolescent development: Pathways and processes of risk and resilience. *Annual Review of Psychology, 46,* 265–293.

Compas, B. E., Oppedisano, G., Connor, J. K., Gerhardt, C. A., Hinden, B. R., Achenbach, T. M., & Hammen, C. (1997). Gender differences in depressive symptoms in adolescence: Comparison of national samples of clinically referred and nonreferred youths. *Journal of Consulting and Clinical Psychology, 65,* 617–626.

Conduct Problems Prevention Research Group. (1992). A developmental and clinical model for the prevention of conduct disorder: The fast track program. *Development and Psychopathology, 4,* 509–527.

Conduct Problems Prevention Research Group. (1999). Initial impact of the fast track prevention trial for conduct problems: I. The high-risk sample. *Journal of Consulting and Clinical Psychology, 67,* 631–647.

Conduct Problems Prevention Research Group. (2002a). Evaluation of the first 3 years of the fast track prevention trial with children at high risk for adolescent conduct problems. *Journal of Abnormal Child Psychology, 30,* 19–36.

Conduct Problems Prevention Research Group. (2002b). The implementation of the fast track program: An example of large-scale prevention science efficacy trial. *Journal of Abnormal Child Psychology, 30,* 1–18.

Conduct Problems Prevention Research Group. (2004). The effects of the fast track program on serious problem outcomes at the end of elementary school. *Journal of Clinical Child and Adolescent Psychology, 33,* 650–661.

Conley, C. S., Haines, B. A., Hilt, L. M., & Metalsky, G. I. (2001). The children's attributional style interview: Developmental tests of cognitive diathesis-stress theories of depression. *Journal of Abnormal Child Psychology, 29,* 445–463.

Connell, A. M., Dishion, T. J., Yasui, M., & Kavanagh, K. (2007). An adaptive approach to family intervention: Linking engagement in family-centered intervention to reductions in adolescent problem behavior. *Journal of Consulting and Clinical Psychology, 75,* 568–579.

Connell, J. P. (1985). A new multidimensional measure of children's perceptions of control. *Child Development, 56,* 1018–1041.

Connelly, C. D., & Straus, M. A. (1992). Mother's age and risk for physical abuse. *Child Abuse & Neglect, 16,* 709–718.

Connelly, M., Rapoff, M. A., Thompson, N., & Connelly, W. (2006). Headstrong: A pilot study of a CD-ROM intervention for recurrent pediatric headache. *Journal of Pediatric Psychology, 31,* 737–747.

Conners, C. K. (2008). *Conners' Rating Scales-3rd Edition: Conners 3 manual.* North Tonawanda, NY: Multi-Health Systems, Inc.

Connor, D. K. (2006). Stimulants. In R. A. Barkley (Ed.), *Attention-deficit hyperactivity disorder. A handbook for diagnosis and treatment.* New York: The Guilford Press.

Conti-Ramsden, G. (2003). Processing and linguistic markers in young children with specific language impairment (SLI). *Journal of Speech, Language, and Hearing Research, 46,* 1029–1037.

Conti-Ramsden, G., & Botting, N. (2004). Social difficulties and victimization in children with SLI at 11 years of age. *Journal of Speech, Language, and Hearing Research, 47,* 145–161.

Cooley, M. R., & Boyce, C. A. (2004). An introduction to assessing anxiety in child and adolescent multiethnic populations: Challenges and opportunities for enhancing knowledge and practice. *Journal of Clinical Child and Adolescent Psychology, 33,* 210–215.

Cooper, Z., & Fairburn, C. G. (2010). Cognitive behavior therapy for bulimia nervosa. In C. M. Grilo & J. E. Mitchell (Eds.), *The treatment of eating disorders: A clinical handbook.* New York: The Guilford Press.

Cooperberg, J., & Faith, M. S. (2004). Treatment of obesity II: Childhood and adolescent obesity. In J. K. Thompson (Ed.), *Handbook of eating disorders and obesity.* Hoboken, NJ: John Wiley.

Cope, M. B., Fernández, J. R., & Allison, D. B. (2004). Genetic and biological risk factors. In J. K. Thompson (Ed.), *Handbook of eating disorders and obesity.* Hoboken, NJ: John Wiley.

Copeland, W., Shanahan, L., Costello, E. J., & Angold, A. (2011). Cumulative prevalence of psychiatric disorders by young adulthood: A prospective cohort analysis from the great smoky mountains study. *Journal of the American Academy of Child and Adolescent Psychiatry, 50,* 252–261.

Copeland, W. E., Shanahan, L., Costello, E. J., & Angold, A. (2009). Childhood and adolescent psychiatric disorders as predictors of young adult disorders. *Archives of General Psychiatry, 66,* 764–772.

Corbett, B., & Gunther, J. (2011). Autism spectrum disorders. In S. Goldstein & C. R. Reynolds (Eds.), *Handbook of neurodevelopmental and genetic disorders in children.* New York: Guilford Press.

Corbett, B. A., Constantine, L. J., Hendren, R., Rocke, D., & Ozonoff, S. (2009). Examining executive functioning in children with autism spectrum disorder, attention deficit hyperactivity disorder and typical development. *Psychiatry Research, 166,* 210–222.

Correl, C. U. (2008). Antipsychotic use in children and adolescents: Minimizing adverse effect to maximize outcomes. *Journal of the American Academy of Child and Adolescent Psychiatry, 47,* 9–20.

Correll, C. U., Manu, P., Olshanskiy, V., Napolitano, B., Kane, J. M., Malhotra, A. K. (2009). Cardiometabolic risk of second-generation antipsychotic medications during first-time use in children and adolescents. *Journal of the American Medical Association, 302,* 1765–1773.

Corrice, A. M., & Glidden, L. M. (2009). The down syndrome advantage: Fact or fiction? *American Journal on Intellectual and Developmental Disabilities, 114,* 254–268.

Corriveau, K., Pasquini, E., & Goswami, U. (2007). Basic auditory processing skills and specific language impairment: A new look at an old hypothesis. *Journal of Speech, Language, and Hearing Research, 50,* 647–666.

Costello, E. J. (1989). Developments in child psychiatric epidemiology. *Journal of the American Academy of Child and Adolescent Psychiatry, 28,* 836–841.

Costello, E. J., & Angold, A. (1995). Developmental epidemiology. In D. Cicchetti & D. J. Cohen (Eds.), *Developmental psychopathology.* New York: John Wiley.

Costello, E. J., & Angold, A. C. (2000). Developmental epidemiology: A framework for developmental psychopathology. In A. J. Sameroff, M. Lewis, & S. M. Miller (Eds.), *Handbook of developmental psychopathology.* New York: Kluwer Academic/Plenum Publishers.

Costello, E. J., & Angold, A. (2001). Bad behaviour: An historic perspective on disorders of conduct. In J. Hill & B. Maughan (Eds.), *Conduct disorders in childhood and adolescence.* New York: Cambridge University Press.

Costello, E. J., & Angold., A. (2006). Developmental epidemiology. In D. Cicchetti & D. J. Cohen (Eds.), *Developmental psychopathology. Vol. 1. Theory and method.* Hoboken, NJ: John Wiley & Sons.

Costello, E. J., Compton, S. N., Keeler, G., & Angold, A. (2003). Relationships between poverty and psychopathology. *Journal of the American Medical Association, 290,* 2023–2029.

Costello, E. J., Egger, H., & Angold, A. (2005a). 10-Year research update review: The epidemiology of child and adolescent psychiatric disorders: I. Methods and public health burden. *Journal of the American Academy of Child and Adolescent Psychiatry, 44,* 972–986.

Costello, E. J., Egger, H. L., & Angold, A. (2005b). The developmental epidemiology of anxiety disorders: Phenomenology, prevalence, and comorbidity. *Child and Adolescent Psychiatric Clinics of North America, 14,* 631–648.

Costello, E. J., Erkanli, A., & Angold, A. (2006). Is there an epidemic of child or adolescent depression? *Journal of Child Psychology and Psychiatry, 47,* 1263–1271.

Costello, E. J., Erkanli, A., Fairbank, J. A., & Angold, A. (2002). The prevalence of potentially traumatic events in childhood and adolescence. *Journal of Traumatic Stress, 15,* 99–112.

Costello, E. J., Foley, D. L., & Angold, A. (2006). 10-year research update review: The epidemiology of child and adolescent psychiatric disorders: II. Developmental epidemiology. *Journal of the American Academy of Child and Adolescent Psychiatry, 45,* 8–25.

Costin, J., Vance, A., Barnett, R., O'Shea, M., & Luk, E. S. (2002). Attention deficit hyperactivity disorder and comorbid anxiety: Practitioner problems in treatment planning. *Child and Adolescent Mental Health, 7,* 16–24.

Coucouvanis, K., Polister, B., Prouty, R., & Lakin, K. C. (2003). Continuing reduction in populations of large state residential facilities for persons with intellectual and developmental disabilities. *Mental Retardation, 41,* 67–70.

Coulombe, J. A., & Reid, G. J. (2012). Agreement with night-waking strategies among community mothers of preschool-aged children. *Journal of Pediatric Psychology, 37,* 319–328.

Cowen, E. L. (1991). In pursuit of wellness. *American Psychologist, 46,* 404–408.

Cowen, E. L. (1994). The enhancement of psychological wellness: Challenges and opportunities. *American Journal of Community Psychology, 22,* 149–179.

Coy, K., Speltz, M. L., DeKlyen, M., & Jones, K. (2001). Socialcognitive processes in preschool boys with and without oppositional defiant disorder. *Journal of Abnormal Child Psychology, 29,* 107–119.

Coyne, M. D., Kame'enui, E. J., Simmons, D. C., & Harn, B. A. (2004). Beginning reading intervention as inoculation or insulin: First-grade reading performance of strong responders to kindergarten intervention. *Journal of Learning Disabilities, 37,* 90–104.

Craig, W., Harel-Fisch, Y., Fogel-Grinvald, H., Dostaler. S., Hetland, J., Simons-Morton, B. et al. (2009). A cross-national profile of bullying and victimization among adolescents in 40 countries. *International Journal of Public Health, 54,* S216–S224.

Craske, M. G. (2012). The R-DOC initiative: Science and practice. *Depression and Anxiety, 29,* 253–256.

Cravens, H. (1992). A scientific project locked in time: The Terman genetic studies of genius, 1920s–1950s. *American Psychologist, 47,* 183–189.

Cravens, H. (1993). *Before head start: The iowa station and America's children.* Chapel Hill, NC: University of North Carolina Press.

Creer, T. L. (1998). Childhood asthma. In T. H. Ollendick & M. Hersen (Eds.), *Handbook of child psychopathology* (3rd ed.). New York: Plenum Press.

Crick, N. R., Casas, J. F., & Ku, H. C. (1999). Relational and physical forms of peer victimization in preschool. *Developmental Psychology, 35,* 376–385.

Crick, N. R., Casas, J. F., & Mosher, M. (1997). Relational and overt aggression in preschool. *Developmental Psychology, 33,* 579–588.

Crick, N. R., & Dodge, K. A. (1994). A review and reformulation of social information-processing mechanisms in children's social adjustment. *Psychological Bulletin, 115,* 74–101.

Crick, N. R., & Grotpeter, J. K. (1995). Relational aggression, gender, and social-psychological adjustment. *Child Development, 66,* 710–722.

Crick, N. R., & Grotpeter, J. K. (1996). Children's treatment by peers: Victims of relational and overt aggression. *Development and Psychopathology, 8,* 367–380.

Crick, N. R., & Nelson, D. A. (2002). Victimization within peer relationships and friendships: Nobody told me there'd be friends like these. *Journal of Abnormal Child Psychology, 30,* 599–607.

Crick, N. R., & Zahn-Waxler, C. (2003). The development of psychopathology in females and males: Current progress and future challenges. *Development and Psychopathology, 15,* 719–742.

Criss, M. M., Petit, G. S., Bates, J. E., Dodge, K. A., & Lapp, A. L. (2002). Family adversity, positive peer relationships, and children's externalizing behavior: A longitudinal perspective on risk and resilience. *Child Development, 73,* 1220–1237.

Crist, W., & Napier-Phillips, A. (2001). Mealtime behaviors of young children: A comparison of normative and clinical data. *Journal of Developmental and Behavioral Pediatrics, 22,* 279–286.

Crnic, K. A. (1988). Mental retardation. In E. J. Mash & L. G. Terdal (Eds.), *Behavioral assessment of childhood disorders: Selected core problems.* New York: Guilford.

Crockett, L. J., Randall, B. A., Shen, Y. L., Russell, S. T., & Driscoll, A. K. (2005). Measurement equivalence of the center for epidemiological studies depression scale for Latino and Anglo adolescents: A national study. *Journal of Consulting and Clinical Psychology, 73,* 47–58.

Crosnoe, R., Leventhal, T., Wirth, R. J., Pierce, K. M., & Pianta, R. (2010). Family socioeconomic status and consistent environmental stimulation in early childhood. *Child Development, 81,* 972–987.

Crosnoe, R., Morrison, F., Burchinal, M., Pianta, R., Keating, D., Friedman, S. L. et al. (2010). Instruction, teacher-student relations, and math achievement trajectories in elementary school. *Journal of Educational Psychology, 102,* 407–417.

Crow, S. J., Mitchell, J. E., Roerig, J. D., & Steffen, K. (2009). What potential role is there for medication treatment in anorexia nervosa? *International Journal of Eating Disorders, 42,* 1–8.

Crowell, S. E., Beauchaine, T. P., & Lenzenweger, M. F. (2008). The development of borderline personality disorder and self-injurious behavior. In T. P. Beauchaine & S. P. Hinshaw (Eds.), *Child and adolescent psychopathology.* Hoboken, NJ: John Wiley & Sons.

Crowell, S. E., Beauchaine, T. P., & Linehan, M. M. (2009). A biosocial developmental model of borderline personality: Elaborating and extending Linehan's theory. *Psychology Bulletin, 135,* 495–510.

Cruce, M. K., & Stinnett, T. A. (2006). Children with cancer. In L. Phelps (Ed.), *Chronic health-related disorders in children: Collaborative medical and psychoeducational interventions.* Washington, DC: American Psychological Association.

Cullen, D. (2009). *Columbine.* New York: Twelve. Hachette Book Group.

Cullerton-Sen, C., Cassidy, A. R., Murray-Close, D., Cicchetti, D., Crick, N. R., & Rogosch, F. A. (2008). Childhood maltreatment and the development of relational and physical aggression: The importance of a gender-informed approach. *Child Development, 79,* 1736–1751.

Culver, L., Gardener, F., & Operario, D. (2007). Psychological distress amongst AIDS-orphaned children in urban South Africa. *Journal of Child Psychology and Psychiatry, 48,* 755–763.

Cummings, E. M., Davies, P. T., & Campbell, S. B. (2000). *Developmental psychopathology and family process: Theory, research, and clinical implications.* New York: The Guilford Press.

Cummings, E. M., El-Sheikh, M., Kouros, C. D., & Buckhalt, J. A. (2009). Children and violence: The role of children's regulation in the marital aggression-child adjustment link. *Clinical Child and Family Psychology Review, 12,* 3–15.

Cummings, E. M., Goeke-Morey, M. C., & Papp, L. M. (2004). Everyday marital conflict and child aggression. *Journal of Abnormal Child Psychology, 32,* 191–202.

Curtis, N. M., Ronan, K. R., & Borduin, C. M. (2004). Multisystemic treatment: A meta-analysis of outcome studies. *Journal of Family Psychology, 18,* 411–419.

Cushing, C. C., & Steele, R. G. (2010). A meta-analytic review of eHealth interventions for pediatric health promoting and maintaining behaviors. *Journal of Pediatric Psychology, 35,* 937–949.

Cyranowski, J. M., Frank, E., Young, E., & Shear, M. K. (2000). Adolescent onset of the gender difference in lifetime rates of major depression: A theoretical model. *Archives of General Psychiatry, 57,* 21–27.

Cytryn, L., & Lourie, R. S. (1980). Mental retardation. In H. I. Kaplan, A. M. Freedman, & B. J. Sadock (Eds.), *Comprehensive textbook of psychiatry/III* (Vol. 3). Baltimore: Williams & Wilkins.

Cytryn, L., & McKnew, D. (1974). Factors influencing the changing clinical expression of the depressive process in children. *American Journal of Psychiatry, 131,* 879–881.

Dadds, M. R., Barrett, P. M., Rapee, R. M., & Ryan, S. (1996). Family process and child anxiety and aggression: An observational analysis. *Journal of Abnormal Child Psychology, 24,* 715–734.

Dadds, M. R., Holland, D. E., Laurens, K. R., Mullins, M., Barrett, P. M., & Spence, S. H. (1999). Early intervention and prevention of anxiety disorders in children: Results at 2-year follow-up. *Journal of Consulting and Clinical Psychology, 67,* 145–150.

Dadds, M. R., Rapee, R. M., & Barrett, P. M. (1994). Behavioral observation. In T. H. Ollendick, N. J. King, & W. Yule (Eds.), *International handbook of phobic and anxiety disorders in children and adolescents* (pp. 349–364). New York: Plenum Press.

Dadds, M. R., Sanders, M. R., Morrison, M., & Rebgetz, M. (1992). Childhood depression and conduct disorder: II. An analysis of family interaction patterns in the home. *Journal of Abnormal Psychology, 101,* 505–513.

Dahl, R. E., & Harvey, A. G. (2008). Sleep disorders. In M. Rutter et al. (Eds.), *Rutter's child and adolescent psychiatry* (5th ed.). Malden, MA: Blackwell Publishing.

Dahlquist, L., Power, T., & Carlson, L. (1995). Physician and parent behavior during invasive cancer procedures: A multidimensional assessment. *Journal of Pediatric Psychology, 20,* 477–490.

Dahlquist, L. M., & Nagel, M. S. (2009). Chronic and recurrent pain. In M. C. Roberts & R. G. Steele (Eds.), *Handbook of pediatric psychology* (4th ed.). New York: The Guilford Press.

Dahlquist, L. M., & Pendley, J. S. (2005). When distraction fails: Parental anxiety and children's responses to distraction during cancer procedures. *Journal of Pediatric Psychology, 30,* 623–628.

Daniels, A. M., Rosenberg, R. E., Law, J. K., Lord, C., Kaufmann, W. E., & Law, P. A. (2011). Stability of initial autism spectrum disorder diagnoses in community settings. *Journal of Autism and Developmental Disorders, 41,* 110–121.

Daniels, S. R. (2006). The consequences of childhood overweight and obesity. *The Future of Children, 16,* 47–67.

Danielson, C. K., Youngstrom, E. A., Findling, R. L., & Calabrese, J. R. (2003). Discriminative validity of the General Behavior Inventory using youth report. *Journal of Abnormal Child Psychology, 31,* 29–39.

Danner, S., Fristad, M. A., Arnold, L. E., Youngstrom, E. A., Birhamer, B., Horwitz, S. M. et al. The LAMS Group (2009). Early-onset bipolar spectrum disorders: Diagnostic issues. *Clinical Child and Family Psychology Review, 12,* 271–293.

Dauvilliers, Y., Maret, S., & Tafti, M. (2005). Genetics of normal and pathological sleep in humans. *Sleep Medicine Review, 9,* 91–100.

David, N., Rose, M., Schneider, T. R., Vogeley, K., & Engel, A. K. (2010). Brief report: Altered horizontal binding of single dots to coherent motion in autism. *Journal of Autism and Developmental Disorders, 40,* 1549–1551.

David-Ferdon, C., & Hertz, M. F. (2007). Electronic media, violence, and adolescents: An emerging public health problem. *Journal of Adolescent Health, 41,* S1–S5.

David-Ferdon, C., & Kaslow, N. J. (2008). Evidence-based psychosocial treatments for child and adolescent depression. *Journal of Clinical Child and Adolescent Psychology, 37,* 62–104.

Davies, P. T., & Cummings, E. M. (2006). Interparental discord, family process, and developmental psychopathology. In D. Cicchetti & D. J. Cohen (Eds.), *Developmental psychopathology, Vol. 3: Risk, disorder, and adaptation* (2nd ed.). Hoboken, NJ: John Wiley & Sons, Inc.

Davis, C. L., Delamater, A. M., Shaw, K. H., La Greca, A. M., Edison, M. S., Perez-Rodriguez, J. E., & Nemery, R. (2001). Parenting styles, regimen adherence, and glycemic control in 4- to 10-year-old children with diabetes. *Journal of Pediatric Psychology, 26,* 123–129.

Davis, K. L., Stewart, D. G., Friedman, J. I., Buchsman, M., Harvey, P. D., Hof, P. R. et al. (2003). White matter changes in schizophrenia. *Archives of General Psychiatry, 60,* 443–456.

Dawson, G., & Faja, S. (2008). Autism spectrum disorders: A developmental perspective. In T. P. Beauchine & S. P. Hinshaw (Eds.), *Child and adolescent psychopathology.* New York: John Wiley & Sons.

Dawson, G., Rogers, S., Munson, J., Smith, M., Winter, J., Greenson, J. et al. (2010). Randomized, controlled trial of an intervention for toddlers with autism: The Early Start Denver Model. *Pediatrics, 125,* e17–e23.

Dawson, G., & Toth, K. (2006). Autism spectrum disorders. In D. Cicchetti & D. J. Cohen (Eds.), *Developmental psychopathology* (Vol. 3). Hoboken, NJ: John Wiley & Sons.

Dean, V. J., & Burns, M. K. (2002). Inclusion of intrinsic processing difficulties in LD diagnostic models: A critical review. *Learning Disability Quarterly, 25,* 170–176.

Deater-Deckard, K. (2001). Recent research examining the role of peer relationships in the development of psychopathology. *Journal of Child Psychology and Psychiatry, 42,* 565–579.

Deater-Deckard, K., Dodge, K. A., & Sorbring, E. (2005). Cultural differences in the effects of physical punishment. In M. Rutter & M. Tienda (Eds.), *Ethnicity and causal mechanisms.* New York: Cambridge University Press.

De Bellis, M. D. (2001). Developmental traumatology: The psychobiological development of maltreated children and its implications for research, treatment, and policy. *Development and Psychopathology, 13,* 539–564.

De Bellis, M. D., & Van Dillen, T. (2005). Childhood posttraumatic stress disorder: An overview. *Child and Adolescent Psychiatric Clinics of North America, 14,* 745–772.

de Boo, G. M., & Prins, P. J. M. (2007). Social incompetence in children with ADHD: Possible moderators and mediators in social-skills training. *Clinical Psychology Review, 27,* 78–97.

De Bourdeaudhuij, I., Van Cauwenberghe, E., Spittaels, H., Oppert, J. M., Rostami, C., Brug, J. et al. (2011). School-based interventions promoting both physical activity and healthy eating in Europe: A systematic review within the HOPE project. *Obesity Reviews, 12,* 205–216.

de Castro, B., Slot, N. W., Bosch, J. D., Koops, W., & Weerman, J. W. (2003). Negative feelings exacerbate hostile attributions of intent in highly aggressive boys. *Journal of Clinical Child and Adolescent Psychology, 32,* 56–65.

Deer, B. (2011). Secrets of the MMR scare. How the case against the MMR vaccine was fixed. British *Medical Journal, 342,* c5347.

Degnan, K. A., Almas, A. N., & Fox, N. A. (2010). Temperament and the environment in the etiology of childhood anxiety. *Journal of Child Psychology and Psychiatry, 51,* 497–517.

Dekker, M. C., Ferdinand, R. F., van Lang, N. D. J., Bongers, I. L., van der Ende, J., & Verhulst, F. C. (2007). Developmental trajectories of depressive symptoms from early childhood to late adolescence: Gender differences and adult outcome. *Journal of Child Psychology and Psychiatry, 48,* 657–666.

Dekovic, M., & Janssens, A. M. (1992). Parents' child-rearing style and child's sociometric status. *Developmental Psychology, 28,* 925–932.

Delamater, A. M., Bubb, J., Davis, S. G., Smith, J. A., Schmidt, L., White, N. H., & Santiago, J. V. (1990). Randomized prospective study of self-management training with newly diagnosed diabetic children. *Diabetes Care, 13,* 492–498.

DeLeon, P. H., Kenkel, M. B., Oliveira Gray, J. M., & Sammons, M. T. (2011). Emerging policy issues for psychology: A key to the future of the profession. In D. H. Barlow (Ed.), *The Oxford handbook of clinical psychology.* New York: Oxford University Press.

De Los Reyes, A., & Kazdin, A. E. (2005). Informant discrepancies in the assessment of childhood psychopathology: A critical review, theoretical framework, and recommendations for further study. *Psychological Bulletin, 131,* 483–509.

Demos, J., & Demos, V. (1972). Adolescence in historical perspective. In D. Rogers (Ed.), *Issues in adolescent psychology.* Englewood Cliffs, NJ: Prentice-Hall.

DeNavas-Walt, C., Procter, B. D., & Lee, C. H. (2006). Current Population Reports, P60–231, *Income, Poverty, and Health Insurance Coverage in the United States: 2005.* U.S. Government Printing Office, Washington, DC.

Denham, S. A., Caverly, S., Schmidt, M., Blair, K., DeMulder, E., Caal, S. et al. (2002). Preschool understanding of emotions: Contributions to classroom anger and aggression. *Journal of Child Psychology and Psychiatry, 43,* 901–916.

Dennis, M., Francis, D. J., Cirino, P. T., Schachar, R., Barnes, M. A., & Fletcher, J. M. (2009). Why IQ is not a covariate in cognitive studies of neurodevelopmental disorders. *Journal of International Neuropsychology Society, 15,* 331–343.

de Ruiter, K. P., Dekker, M. C., Verhulse, F. C., & Koot, H. M. (2007). Developmental course of psychopathology in youths with and without intellectual disabilities. *Journal of Child Psychology and Psychiatry, 48,* 498–507.

DeSimone, J. R., & Parmar, R. S. (2006). Middle school mathematics teachers' beliefs about inclusion of students with learning disabilities. *Learning Disabilities Research & Practice, 21*, 98–110.

DeThorne, L. S., Hart, S. A., Deater-Deckard, K., Thompson, L. A., Schatschneider, C., & Davison, M. D. (2006). Children's history of speech-language difficulties: Genetic influences and associations with reading-related measures. *Journal of Speech, Language, and Hearing Research, 49*, 1280–1293.

Detterman, D. K., & Thompson, L. A. (1997). What is so special about special education? *American Psychologist, 52*, 1082–1090.

De Wilde, E. J., Kienhorst, C. W. M., & Diekstra, R. R. W. (2001). Suicidal behaviour in adolescents. In I. M. Goodyer (Ed.), *The depressed child and adolescent* (2nd ed.). Cambridge, UK: Cambridge University Press.

De Young, A. C., Kenardy, J. A., & Cobham, V. E. (2011). Diagnosis of posttraumatic stress disorder in preschool children. *Journal of Clinical Child and Adolescent Psychology, 40*, 375–384.

DiBartolo, P. M., Albano, A. M., Barlow, D. H., & Heimberg, R. G. (1998). Cross-informant agreement in the assessment of social phobia in youth. *Journal of Abnormal Child Psychology, 26*, 213–220.

Dickstein, S. G., Bannon, K., Castellanos, F. X., & Milham, M. P. (2006). The neural correlates of attention deficit hyperactivity disorder: An ALE meta-analysis. *Journal of Child Psychology and Psychiatry, 47*, 1051–1062.

Diler, R. S., Birmaher, B., & Miklowitz, D. J. (2010). Clinical presentation and longitudinal course of bipolar spectrum disorders in children and adolescents. In D. J. Miklowitz & D. Cicchetti (Eds.), *Understanding bipolar disorder: A developmental psychopathology perspective.* New York: The Guilford Press.

DiLillo, D., & Tremblay, G. (2001). Maternal and child reports of behavioral compensation in response to equipment usage. *Journal of Pediatric Psychology, 26*, 175–184.

DiLillo, D., & Tremblay, G. C. (2005). Lizette Peterson: A collaboration of passion and science. *Journal of Pediatric Psychology, 30*, 533–535.

DiMatteo, M. R. (2000). Practitioner-family-patient communication in pediatric adherence: Implications for research and clinical practice. In D. Drotar (Ed.), *Promoting adherence to medical treatment in chronic childhood illness: Concepts, methods, and interventions.* Mahwah, NJ: Lawrence Erlbaum Associates.

Dimeff, L. A., Paves, A. P., Skutch, J. M., & Woodcock, E. A. (2011). Shifting paradigms in clinical psychology: How innovative technologies are shaping treatment delivery. In D. H. Barlow (Ed.), *The Oxford handbook of clinical psychology.* New York: Oxford University Press.

Di Nuovo, S., & Buono, S. (2009). Cognitive profiles of genetic syndromes with intellectual disability. *Life Span and Disability, XII*, 29–40.

Dishion, T. J. (1990). The family ecology of boys' relations in middle childhood. *Child Development, 61*, 874–892.

Dishion, T. J., & Dodge, K. A. (2005). Peer contagion in interventions for children and adolescents: Moving towards an understanding of the ecology and dynamics of change. *Journal of Abnormal Child Psychology, 33*, 395–400.

Dishion, T. J., French, D. C., & Patterson, G. R. (1995). The development and ecology of antisocial behavior. In D. Cicchetti & D. J. Cohen (Eds.), *Developmental psychopathology, Vol. 2: Risk, disorder and adaptation.* New York: John Wiley & Sons.

Dishion, T. J., & Kavanagh, K. A. (2002). The adolescent transitions program: A family-centered prevention strategy for schools. In J. B. Reid, G. R. Patterson, & J. Snyder (Eds.), *Antisocial behavior in children and adolescents: A developmental analysis and model for intervention.* Washington, DC: American Psychological Association.

Dishion, T. J., & Owen, L. D. (2002). A longitudinal analysis of friendships and substance use: Bidirectional influence from adolescence into adulthood. *Developmental Psychology, 28*, 480–491.

Dishion, T. J., & Patterson, G. R. (2006). The development and ecology of antisocial behavior in children and adolescents. In D. Cicchetti & D. J. Cohen (Eds.), *Developmental psychopathology, Vol. 3: Risk, disorder, and adaptation* (2nd ed.). Hoboken, NJ: John Wiley & sons.

Dishion, T. J., & Stormshak, E. A. (2007). *Intervening in children's lives: An ecological, family-centered approach to mental health care.* Washington, DC: American Psychological Association.

Dittmar, H., Halliwell, E., & Ive, S. (2006). Does Barbie make girls want to be thin? The effect of experimental exposure to images of dolls on the body image of 5- to 8-year-old girls. *Developmental Psychology, 42*, 283–292.

Dix, T., Stewart, A. D., Gershoff, E. T., & Day, W. H. (2007). Autonomy and children's reactions to being controlled: Evidence that both compliance and defiance may be positive markers in early development. *Child Development, 78*, 1204–1221.

Dixon, L., Hamilton-Giachritsis, C., & Browne, K. (2005). Attributions and behaviours of parents abused as children: A mediational analysis of the intergenerational continuity of child maltreatment (Part II). *Journal of Child Psychology and Psychiatry, 46*, 58–68.

Docherty, N. M., St-Hilaire, A., Aakre, J. M., & Seghers, J. P. (2008). Life events and high-trait reactivity together predict psychotic symptom increase in schizophrenia. *Schizophrenia Bulletin, 35*, 638–645.

Docherty, S. J., Davis, O. S. P., Kovas, Y., Meaburn, E. L., Dale, P. S., Petrill, S. A. et al. (2010). Genes, Brain and Behavior, 9, 234–247.

Dodd, H. F., Schniering, C. A., & Porter, M. A. (2009). Beyond behavior: Is social anxiety low in Williams syndrome? *Journal of Autism and Developmental Disorders, 39*, 1673–1681.

Dodge, K. A. (1991). The structure and function of reactive and proactive aggression. In D. Pepler & K. Rubin (Eds.),

The development and treatment of childhood aggression. Hillsdale, NJ: Erlbaum.

Dodge, K. A. (2000). Conduct disorder. In A. J. Sameroff, M. Lewis, & S. M. Miller (Eds.), *Handbook of developmental psychopathology* (2nd ed.). New York: Kluwer Academic/Plenum Publishers.

Dodge, K. A. (2003). Do social information-processing patterns mediate aggressive behavior? In B. B. Lahey, T. E. Moffitt, & A. Caspi (Eds.), *Causes of conduct disorder and juvenile delinquency.* New York: Guilford Press.

Dodge, K. A., & Rabiner, D. L. (2004). Returning to roots: On social information processing and moral development. *Child Development, 75,* 1003–1008.

Dogra, N., Parkin, A., Gale, F., & Frake, C. (2009). *A multi-disciplinary handbook of child and adolescent mental health for front-line professionals.* Philadelphia, PA: Jessica Kingsley Publishers.

Dohnt, H., & Tiggermann, M. (2006). The contribution of peer and media influences on the development of body satisfaction and self-esteem in young girls: A prospective study. *Developmental Psychology, 42,* 929–936.

Doleys, D. M. (1989). Enuresis and encopresis. In T. H. Ollendick & M. Hersen (Eds.), *Handbook of child psychopathology* (2nd ed.). New York: Plenum.

Dolgin, M. J., & Jay, S. M. (1989). Childhood cancer. In T. H. Ollendick & M. Hersen (Eds.), *Handbook of child psychopathology* (2nd ed.). New York: Plenum.

Dolgin, M. J., Phipps, S., Fairclough, D. L., Sahler, O. J. Z., Askins, M., Noll, R.B. et al. (2007). Trajectories of adjustment in mothers of children with newly diagnosed cancer: A natural history investigation. *Journal of Pediatric Psychology, 32,* 771–782.

Dominus, S. (2011). The denunciation of Dr. Wakefield. *New York Times Magazine,* April 24, pp. 36–39, 50–52.

Donenberg, G. R., Paikoff, R., & Pequegnat, W. (2006). Introduction to the special section on families, youth, and HIV: Family-based intervention studies. *Journal of Pediatric Psychology, 31,* 869–873.

D'Onofrio, B. M., Slutske, W. S., Turkheimer, E., Emery, R. E., Harden, P., Heath, A. C. et al. (2007). Intergenerational transmission of childhood conduct problems: A children of twins study. *Archives of General Psychiatry, 64,* 820–829.

Donovan, C. L., & Spence, S. H. (2000). Prevention of childhood anxiety disorders. *Clinical Psychology Review, 20,* 509–531.

Dore, M. M., & Mullin, D. (2006). Treatment foster care: Its history and current role in the foster care continuum. *Families in Society, 87,* 475–482.

Dowdney, L. (2000). Childhood bereavement following parental death. *Journal of Child Psychology and Psychiatry, 41,* 819–830.

Dowell, K. A., & Ogles, B. M. (2010). The effects of parent participation on child psychotherapy outcomes: A meta-analytic review. *Journal of Child and Adolescent Psychology, 39,* 151–162.

Doyle, A. C., & le Grange, D. (2009). Eating disorders. In M. C. Roberts & R. G. Steele (Eds.), *Handbook of pediatric psychology* (4th ed.). New York: The Guilford Press.

Doyle, K. W., Wolchik, S. A., Dawson-McClure, S. R., & Sandler, I. N. (2003). Positive events as a stress buffer for children and adolescents in families in transition. *Journal of Clinical Child and Adolescent Psychology, 32,* 536–545.

Driscoll, K. A., Johnson, S. B., Barker, D., Quittner, A. L., Deeb, L. C., Geller, D. E. et al. (2010). Risk factors associated with depressive symptoms in caregivers of children with type 1 diabetes or cystic fibrosis. *Journal of Pediatric Psychology, 35,* 814–822.

Drotar, D., & Robinson, J. (2000). Developmental psychopathology of failure to thrive. In A. J. Sameroff, M. Lewis, & S. M. Miller (Eds.), *Handbook of developmental psychopathology* (2nd ed.). New York: Kluwer Academic/Plenum Publishers.

Drummond, K., Gandhi, A., & Elledge, A. (2011). *What is response to intervention? The Complex Ecology of Response to Intervention.* National Center on Response to Intervention. http://www.rti4success.org

DuBois, D. L., Burk-Braxton, C., Swenson, L. P., Tevendale, H.D., & Hardesty, J. L. (2002). Race and gender influences on adjustment in early adolescence: Investigation of an integrative model. *Child Development, 73,* 1573–1592.

Duff, F. J., & Clarke, P. J. (2011). Practitioner review: Reading disorders: What are the effective interventions and how should they be implemented and evaluated? *Journal of Child Psychology and Psychiatry, 52,* 3–12.

Dumas, J. E., & Lechowicz, J. G. (1989). When do noncompliant children comply? Implications for family behavior therapy. *Child and Family Behavior Therapy, 11,* 21–38.

Dunbar-Jacob, J. (1993). Contributions to patient adherence: Is it time to share the blame? *Health Psychology, 12,* 91–92.

Duncan, G. J., & Brooks-Gunn, J. (2000). Family poverty, welfare reform, and child development. *Child Development, 71,* 188–196.

Duncan, J., Joselow, M., & Hilden, J. M. (2006). Program interventions for children at the end of life and their siblings. *Child and Adolescent Psychiatric Clinics of North America, 15,* 739–758.

Dunn, J. (1996). Children's relationships: Bridging the divide between cognitive and social development. *Journal of Child Psychology and Psychiatry, 37,* 507–518.

DuPaul, G. J., McGoey, K. E., Eckert, T. L., & VanBrakle, J. (2001). Preschool children with attention-deficit/hyperactivity disorder: Impairments in behavioral, social, and school functioning. *Journal of the American Academy of Child and Adolescent Psychiatry, 40,* 508–509.

DuPaul, G. J., Pérez, V. H., Kuo. A., & Stein, M. (2010). Juan: A 9-year-old Latino boy with ADHD. *Journal of Developmental and Behavioral Pediatrics, 31,* s55–s59.

Durand, V. M. (1999). Functional communication training using assistive devices: Recruiting natural communities of reinforcement. *Journal of Applied Behavior Analysis, 32,* 247–267.

Durlak, J. A., & Weissberg, R. P. (2007). *The impact of after-school programs that promote personal and social skills.* Chicago, IL: Collaborative for Academic, Social, and Emotional Learning.

Durlak, J. A., Weissberg, R. P., Dymnicki, A. B., Taylor, R. D., & Schellinger, K. B. (2011). The impact of enhancing students' social and emotional learning: A meta-analysis of school-based universal intervention. *Child Development, 821,* 405–432.

Durlak, J. A., & Wells, A. M. (1997). Primary prevention mental health programs for children and adolescents: A meta-analytic review. *American Journal of Community Psychology, 25,* 115–152.

Durston, S., Pol, H. E. H., Schnack, H. G., Buitelaar, J. K., Steenhuis, M. P., Minderaa, R. B. et al. (2004). Magnetic resonance imaging of boys with attention-deficit/hyperactivity disorder. *Journal of the American Academy of Child and Adolescent Psychiatry, 43,* 332–340.

Dyck, M. K., Hay, D., Anderson, M., Smith, L. M., Piek, J., & Hallmayer, J. (2004). Is the discrepancy criteria for defining developmental disorders valid? *Journal of Child Psychology and Psychiatry, 45,* 979–995.

Dykens, E. M., Cassidy, S. B., & DeVries, M. L. (2011). Prader Willi syndrome. In S. Goldstein & C. R. Reynolds (Eds.), *Handbook of neurodevelopmental and genetic disorders in children* (2nd ed.). New York: Guildford Press.

Dykens, E. M., & Cohen, D. J. (1996). Effects of Special Olympics International on social competence in persons with mental retardation. *Journal of the American Academy of Child and Adolescent Psychiatry, 35,* 223–229.

Dykens, E. M., Roof, E., Bittel, D., & Butler, M. G. (2011). TPH2 G/T polymorphism is associated with hyperphagia, IQ, and internalizing problems in Prader-Willi syndrome. *Journal of Child Psychology and Psychiatry, 52,* 580–587.

Eaves, L., Silberg, J., & Erkanli, A. (2003). Resolving multiple epigenetic pathways to adolescent depression. *Journal of Child Psychology and Psychiatry, 44,* 1006–1014.

Eaves, L. J., Silberg, J. L., Meyer, J. M., Maes, H. H., Simonoff, E., Pickles, A., Rutter, M., Neale, M. C., Reynolds, C. A., Erickson, M. T., Heath, A. C., Loeber, R., Truett K. R., & Hewitt, J. K. (1997). Genetics and developmental psychopathology: 2. The main effects of genes and environment on behavioral problems in the Virginia Twin Study of Adolescent Behavioral Development. *Journal of Child Psychology and Psychiatry, 38,* 965–980.

Eddy, K. T., Doyle, A. C., Hoste, R. R., Herzog, D. B., & Grange, D. (2008). Eating disorder not otherwise specified in adolescents. *Journal of the American Academy of Child and Adolescent Psychiatry, 47,* 156–164.

Eddy, K. T., Keel, P. K., & Leon, G. R. (2010). Vulnerability to eating disorders in childhood and adolescence. In R. E. Ingram & J. M. Price (Eds.), *Vulnerability to psychopathology: Risk across the lifespan* (2nd ed.). New York: The Guilford Press.

Edelbrock, C., Rende, R., Plomin, R., & Thompson, L. A. (1995). A twin study of competence and problem behavior in childhood and early adolescence. *Journal of Child Psychology and Psychiatry, 36,* 775–785.

Edwards, G., Barkley, R. A., Laneri, M., Fletcher, K., & Metevia, L.(2001). Parent-adolescent conflict in teenagers with ADHD and ODD. *Journal of Abnormal Child Psychology, 29,* 557–573.

Egeland, J. A., Hostetter, A. M., Pauls, D. L., & Sussex, J. N. (2000). Prodromal symptoms before onset of manic-depressive disorder suggested by first hospital admission histories. *Journal of the American Academy of Child and Adolescent Psychiatry, 39,* 1245–1252.

Egger, H. L., & Angold, A. (2006). Common emotional and behavioral disorders in preschool children: Presentation, nosology, and epidemiology. *Journal of Child Psychology and Psychiatry, 47,* 313–337.

Egger, H. L., & Emde, R. N. (2011). Developmentally sensitive diagnostic criteria for mental health disorders in early childhood: The diagnostic and statistical manual of mental disorders-IV, the research diagnostic criteria—preschool age, and the Diagnostic Classification of Mental Health and Mental Disorders of Infancy and Early Childhood-Revised. *American Psychologist, 66,* 95–106.

Eggers, C. (1978). Course and prognosis of childhood schizophrenia. *Journal of Autism and Childhood Schizophrenia, 8,* 21–36.

Eggers, C., Bunk, D., & Krause, D. (2000). Schizophrenia with onset before the age of eleven: Clinical characteristics of onset and course. *Journal of Autism and Developmental Disorders, 30,* 29–38.

Ehntholt, K. A., & Yule, W. (2006). Practitioner review: Assessment and treatment of refugee children and adolescents who have experienced war-related trauma. *Journal of Child Psychology and Psychiatry, 47,* 1197–1210.

Eichelsheim, V. I., Buist, K. L., Dekovic, M., Wissink, I. B., Frijns, T., van Lier, P. A. C. et al. (2010). Associations among the parent-adolescent relationship, aggression and delinquency in different ethnic groups: A replication across two Dutch samples. *Social Psychiatry and Psychiatric Epidemiology, 45,* 293–300.

Einfeld, S., & Emerson, E. (2008). Intellectual disability. In M. Rutter, D. Bishop, D. Pine, S. Scott, J. Stevenson, E. Taylor, & A Thapar (Eds.), *Rutter's child and adolescent psychiatry* (5th ed.). Malden, MA: Blackwell Publishing.

Eisenberg, L. (2001). The past 50 years of child and adolescent psychiatry: A personal memoir. *Journal of the American Academy of Child and Adolescent Psychiatry, 40,* 743–748.

Eisenberg, L., Baker, B. L., & Blacher, J. (1998). Siblings with children with mental retardation living at home or in residential placement. *Journal of Child Psychology and Psychiatry, 39,* 355–363.

Eisenberg, N. (2006). Emotion-related regulation. In H. E. Fitzgerald, B. M. Lester, & B. Zukerman (Eds.), *The crisis in mental health. Critical issues and effective programs* (Vol. 1). Westport, CT: Praeger.

Eisenberg, N., Cumberland, A., Spinrad, T. L., Fabes, R. A., Shepard, S. A., Reiser, M., Murphy, B. C., Losoya, S. H., & Guthrie, I. K. (2001). The relations of regulation and emotionality to children's externalizing and internalizing problem behavior. *Child Development, 72,* 1112–1134.

Eisenberg, N., Fabes, R. A., Shepard, S. A., Murphy, B. C., Guthrie, I. K., Jones, S., Friedman, J., Poulin, R., & Maszk, P. (1997). Contemporaneous and longitudinal prediction of children's social functioning from regulation and emotionality. *Child Development, 68,* 642–664.

Eisenberg, N., & Silver, R. C. (2011). Growing up in the shadow of terrorism: Youth in America after 9/11. *American Psychologist, 66,* 468–481.

Eisenberg, N., Spinard, T. L., & Eggum, N. D. (2010). Emotion-related self-regulation and its relation to children's maladjustment. *Annual Review of Clinical Psychology, 6,* 495–525.

Eisenberg, N., Vidmar, M., Spinrad, T. L., Eggum, N. D., Edwards, A., Gaertner, B. et al. (2010). Mothers' teaching strategies and children's effortful control: A longitudinal study. Developmental Psychology, 46, 1294–1308.

Eiser, C. (1994). The eleventh Jack Tizard Memorial Lecture. Making sense of chronic disease. *Journal of Child Psychology and Psychiatry, 35,* 1373–1389.

Eiser, C. (1998). Long-term consequences of childhood cancer. *Journal of Child Psychology and Psychiatry, 39,* 621–633.

Eiser, C., Eiser, J. R., Mayhew, A. G., & Gibson, A. T. (2005). Parenting the premature infant: Balancing vulnerability and quality of life. *Journal of Child Psychology and Psychiatry, 46,* 1169–1177.

Eisler, I., Dare, C., Hodes, M., Russell, G., Dodge, E., & le Grange, D. (2000). Family therapy for adolescent anorexia nervosa: The results of a controlled comparison of two family interventions. *Journal of Child Psychology and Psychiatry, 41,* 727–736.

Eisler, I., Lock, J., & le Grange, D. (2010). Family-based treatments for adolescents with anorexia nervosa: Single-family and multifamily approaches. In C. M. Grilo & J. E. Mitchell (Eds.), *The treatment of eating disorders: A clinical handbook.* New York: The Guilford Press.

Eisler, I., Simic, M., Russell, G. F. M., & Dare, C. (2007). A randomised controlled treatment trial of two forms of family therapy in adolescent anorexia nervosa: A five-year follow-up. *Journal of Child Psychology and Psychiatry, 48,* 552–560.

Eisner, E. W. (2003). On the art and science of qualitative research in psychology. In P. M. Camic, J. E. Rhodes, & L. Yardley (Eds.), *Qualitative research in psychology.* Washington, DC: American Psychological Association.

Elbaum, B., & Vaughn, S. (2003). Self-concept and students with learning disabilities. In H. L. Swanson, K. R. Harris, & S. Graham (Eds.), *Handbook of learning disabilities.* New York: Guilford Press.

Eley, T. C. (1997). General genes: A new theme in developmental psychology. *Current Directions in Psychological Science, 6,* 90–95.

Eley, T. C., Bolton, D., O'Connor, T. G., Perrin, S., Smith, P., & Plomin, R. (2003). A twin study of anxiety-related behaviours in pre-school children. *Journal of Child Psychology and Psychiatry, 44,* 945–960.

Eley, T. C., Lichtenstein, P., & Moffitt, T. E. (2003). A longitudinal behavioral genetic analysis of the etiology of aggressive and nonaggressive antisocial behavior. *Development and Psychopathology, 15,* 383–402.

Eley, T. C., & Rijsdijk, F. (2005). Introductory guide to the statistics of molecular genetics. *Journal of Child Psychology and Psychiatry, 46,* 1042–1044.

Elgar, F. J., McGrath, P. J., Waschbusch, D. A., Stewart, S. H., & Curtis, L. J. (2004). Mutual influences on maternal depression and child adjustment problems. *Clinical Psychology Review, 24,* 441–459.

Elia, J., Gai, X., Xie, H. M., Perin, J. C., Geiger, E., Glessner, J. T. et al. (2010). Rare structural variants found in attention-deficit hyperactivity disorder are preferentially associated with neurodevelopmental genes. *Molecular Psychiatry, 15,* 637–646.

Eliez, S., Rumsey, J. M., Giedd, J. N., Schmitt, E: J., Padwardhan, A. J., & Reiss, A. L. (2000). Morphological alteration of temporal lobe gray matter in dyslexia: An MRI study. *Journal of Child Psychology and Psychiatry, 41,* 637–644.

Elliot, D. S., Huizinga, D., & Ageton, S. S. (1985). *Explaining delinquency and drug use.* Beverly Hills, CA: Sage.

Ellis, B. J. (2004). Timing of pubertal maturation in girls: An integrated life history approach. *Psychological Bulletin, 130,* 920–958.

Ellis, B. J., Boyce, W. T., Belsky, J., Bakermans-Kranenburg, M. J., & van IJzendoorn, M. H. (2011). Differential susceptibility to the environment: An evolutionary-developmental theory. *Development and Psychopathology, 23,* 7–28.

Ellis, D. A., Podolski, C. L., Frey, M., Naar-King, S., Wang, B., & Moltz, K. (2007). The role of parental monitoring in adolescent health outcomes: Impact on regimen adherence in youth with Type 1 diabetes. *Journal of Pediatric Psychology, 32,* 907–917.

Ellis, D. M., & Hudson, J. L. (2010). The metacognitive model of generalized anxiety disorder in children and adolescents. *Clinical Psychology Review, 13,* 151–163.

El-Sheikh, M., Buckhalt, J. A., Acebo, C., & Mize, J. (2006). Marital conflict and disruption of children's sleep. *Child Development, 77,* 31–43.

El-Sheikh, M., & Flanagan, E. (2001). Parental problem drinking and children's adjustment: Family conflict and parental depression as mediators and moderators of risk. *Journal of Abnormal Child Psychology, 29,* 417–432.

Emery, R. E., & Kitzmann, K. M. (1995). The child in the family: Disruptions in family functions. In D. Cicchetti & D. J. Cohen (Eds.), *Developmental psychopathology: Risk, disorder, and adaptation* (Vol. 2). New York: John Wiley & Sons.

Emslie, G., Kratochvil, C., Vitiello, B., Silva, S., Mayes, T., McNutty, S. et al., & the TADS Team. (2006). Treatment for Adolescents With Depression Study (TADS): Safety results.

Journal of the American Academy of Child and Adolescent Psychiatry, 45, 1440–1455.

Emslie, G. J., Armitage, R., Weinberg, W. A., Rush, A. J., Mayes, T. L., & Hoffmann, R. F. (2001). Sleep polysomnography as a predictor of recurrence in children and adolescents with major depressive disorder. International Journal of Neuropsychopharmacology, 4, 159–168.

English, D. J. (1998). The extent and consequences of child maltreatment. The Future of Children, 8, 39–53.

Enzer, N. B., & Heard, S. L. (2000). Psychiatric prevention in children and adolescents. In B. J. Sadock & V. A. Sadock (Eds.), Comprehensive textbook of psychiatry (Vol. II). Philadelphia: Lippincott Williams & Wilkins.

Epstein, L. H., Valoski, A. M., Vara, L. S., McCurley, J., Wisniewski, L., Kalarchian, M. A., Klein, K. R., & Schrager, L. R. (1995). Effects of decreasing sedentary behavior and increasing activity on weight change in obese children. Health Psychology, 14, 109–115.

Erath, S. A., Bierman, K. L., & the Conduct Problems Prevention Research Group. (2006). Aggressive marital conflict, maternal harsh punishment, and child aggressive-disruptive behavior: Evidence for direct and indirect relations. Journal of Family Psychology, 20, 217–226.

Erbas, D. (2010). A collaborative approach to implement positive behavior support plans for children with problem behaviors: A comparison of consultation versus consultation and feedback approach. Education and Training in Autism and Developmental Disabilities, 45, 94–106.

Erickson, S. K., Lilienfeld, S. O., & Vitacco, M. J. (2007). A critical examination of the suitability and limitations of psychological tests in family court. Family Court Review, 45, 157–174.

Esbensen, A. J., & Seltzer, M. M. (2011). Accounting for the "Down syndrome advantage." American Journal on Intellectual and Developmental Disabilities, 116, 3–15.

Essau, C., Conradt, J., & Petermann, F. (1999). Frequency and comorbidity of social phobia and social fears in adolescents. Behaviour Research and Therapy, 37, 831–843.

Essau, C. A. (2003). Epidemiology and comorbidity. In C. A. Essau (Ed.), Conduct and oppositional defiant disorders: Epidemiology, risk factors, and treatment. Mahwah, NJ: Erlbaum.

Essau, C. A., Conradt, J., & Petermann, F. (1999). Frequency of panic attacks and panic disorder in adolescents. Depression and Anxiety, 9, 19–26.

Essau, C. A., Conradt, J., & Petermann, F. (2000). Frequency, comorbidity, and psychosocial impairment of specific phobia in adolescents. Journal of Clinical Child Psychology, 29, 221–231.

Essex, M. J., Armstrong, J. M., Burk, L. R., Goldsmith, H. H., & Boyce, W. T. (2011). Biological sensitivity to context moderates the effects of the early teacher-child relationship on the development of mental health by adolescence. Development and Psychopathology, 23, 149–161.

Estes, K. G., Evans, J. L., & Else-Quest, N. M. (2007). Differences in the nonword repetition performance of children with and without specific language impairment: A meta-analysis. Journal of Speech, Language, and Hearing Research, 50, 177–195.

Eubig, P. A., Aguiar, A., & Schantz, S. L. (2010). Lead and PBCs as risk factors for attention deficit/hyperactivity disorder. Environmental Health Perspective, 118, 1654–1667.

Evans, D. L. & the Commission on Adolescent Depression and Bipolar Disorder. (2005a). Defining depression and bipolar disorder. In D. L. Evans, E. B. Foa, R. E. Gur, H. Hendin, C. P. O'Brien, M. E. P. Seligman, & B. T. Walsh (Eds.), Treating and preventing adolescent mental health disorders. What we know and what we don't know: A research agenda for improving mental health of our youth. New York: Oxford University Press.

Evans, D. L. & the Commission on Adolescent Depression and Bipolar Disorder. (2005b). Prevention of depression and bipolar disorder. In D. L. Evans, E. B. Foa, R. E. Gur, H. Hendin, C. P. O'Brien, M. E. P. Seligman, & B. T. Walsh (Eds.), Treating and preventing adolescent mental health disorders. What we know and what we don't know: A research agenda for improving mental health of our youth. New York: Oxford University Press.

Evans, D. L., Foa, E. B., Gur, R. E., Hendin, H., O'Brien, C. P., Seligman, M. E. P., & Walsh, B. T. (Eds.) (2005). Treating and preventing adolescent mental health disorders. What we know and what we don't know: A research agenda for the mental health of our youth. New York: Oxford University Press.

Evans, D. W., & Leckman, J. F. (2006). Origins of obsessivecompulsive disorder: Developmental and evolutionary perspectives. In D. Cicchetti & D. J. Cohen (Eds.), Developmental psychopathology (Vol. 1, 2nd ed.). Hoboken, NJ: John Wiley & Sons.

Evans, G. W. (2004). The environment of childhood poverty. American Psychologist, 59, 77–92.

Evans, R. B., & Koelsch, W. A. (1985). Psychoanalysis arrives in America. American Psychologist, 40, 942–948.

Exner, J. E., Jr., & Weiner, I. B. (1995). The Rorschach: A comprehensive system, Vol. 3: Assessment of children and adolescents (2nd ed.). New York: Wiley.

Eyberg, S., & Pincus, D. (1999). Eyberg Child Behavior Inventory & Sutter–Eyberg Student Behavior Inventory–Revised. Lutz, FL: Psychological Assessment Resources.

Eyberg, S. M., Nelson, M. M., Duke, M., & Boggs, S. R. (2005). Manual for the Dyadic Parent–child Interaction Coding System (3rd ed.). Gainesville, FL: University of Florida.

Fabiano, G. A., Pelham, W. E., Gnagy, E. M., Burrows-MacLean, L., Coles, E. K., Chacko, A. et al. (2007). The single and combined effects of multiple intensities of behavior modification and methylphenidate for children with attention deficit hyperactivity disorder in a classroom settings. School Psychology Review, 36, 195–216.

Fabiano, G. A., Pelham, W. E., Jr., Coles, E. K., Gnagy, E. M., Chronis-Tuscano, A., & O'Connor, B. C. (2009). A meta-analysis of behavioral treatments for attention-deficit/hyperactivity disorder. Clinical Psychology Review, 29, 129–140.

Fagan, A. A., & Najman, J. M. (2003). Association between early childhood aggression and internalizing behavior for sibling pairs. *Journal of the American Academy of Child and Adolescent Psychiatry, 42,* 1093–1100.

Fagan, J. F., & Holland, C. R. (2002). Equal opportunity and racial differences in IQ. *Intelligence, 30,* 361–387.

Fairburn, C. G. (1997). Eating disorders. In D. M. Clark & C. G. Fairburn (Eds.), *Science and practice of cognitive behaviour therapy.* Oxford: Oxford University Press.

Fairburn, C. G., Cooper, Z., Doll, H. A., Norman, P., & O'Connor, M. (2000). The natural course of bulimia nervosa and binge eating disorder in young women. *Archives of General Psychiatry, 57,* 659–665.

Fairburn, C. G., Cooper, Z., Doll, H. A., O'Connor, M. E., Bohn, K., Hawker, D. M. et al. (2009). Transdiagnostic cognitive behavior therapy for patients with eating disorders: A two-site trial with 60-week follow-up. *American Journal of Psychiatry, 166,* 311–319.

Fairburn, C. G., Cooper, Z., & Shafran, R. (2003). Cognitive behaviour therapy for eating disorders: A "transdiagnostic" theory and treatment. *Behaviour Research and Therapy, 43,* 509–529.

Fairburn, C. G., & Gowers, S. G. (2008). Eating disorders. In M. Rutter et al. (Eds.), *Rutter's child and adolescent psychiatry* (5th ed.). Malden, MA: Blackwell Publishing.

Fairburn, C. G., Welch, S. L., Doll, H. A., Davies, B. A., & O'Connor, M. E. (1997). Risk factors for bulimia nervosa: A community-based case-control study. *Archives of General Psychiatry, 54,* 509–517.

Fang, X., Li, X., Stanton, B., Hong, Y., Zhang, L., Zhao, G. et al. (2009). Parental HIV/AIDS and psychosocial adjustment among rural Chinese children. *Journal of Pediatric Psychology, 34,* 1053–1062.

Faraone, S., Biederman, J., Mennin, D., Russell, R., & Tsuang, M. T. (1998). Familial subtypes of attention deficit hyperactivity disorder: A follow-up study of children from antisocial-ADHD families. *Journal of Child Psychology and Psychiatry, 39,* 1045–1053.

Faraone, S. V., & Antshel, K. M. (2008). Diagnosing and treating attention-deficit/hyperactivity disorder in adults. *World Psychiatry, 7,* 131–136.

Faraone, S. V., Biederman, J., Morley, C. P., & Spencer, T. J. (2008). Effects of stimulants on height and weight : A review of the literature. *Journal of the American Academy of Child and Adolescent Psychiatry, 47,* 994–1009.

Farrington, D. P. (1986). Stepping stones to adult criminal careers. In D. Olweus, J. Block, & M. R. Yarrow (Eds.), *Development of antisocial behavior and prosocial behavior.* New York: Academic Press.

Farrington, D. P. (1995). The development of offending and antisocial behaviour from childhood: Key findings from the Cambridge Study in Delinquent Development. *Journal of Child Psychology and Psychiatry, 36,* 929–964.

Farrington, D. P., Jolliffe, D., Loeber, R, Stouthamer-Loeber, M. & Kalb, L. M. (2001). The concentration of offenders in families, and family criminality in the prediction of boys' delinquency. *Journal of Adolescence, 24,* 579–596.

Farrington, D. P., Ullrich, S., & Salekin, R. T. (2010). Environmental influences on child and adolescent psychopathy. In R. T. Salekin & D. R. Lyman (Eds.), *Handbook of child and adolescent psychopathy.* New York: The Guilford Press.

Feder, A., Nestler, E. J., & Charney, D. S. (2009). Psychobiology and molecular genetics of resilience. Nature Reviews Neuroscience, *10,* 446–457.

Federal Interagency Forum on Child and Family Statistics. (2011). *America's children: Key national indicators of well-being, 2011.* Washington, DC: U.S. Government Printing Office.

Felce, D. (2006). Both accurate interpretation of deinstitutionalization and a post institutional research agenda are needed. *Mental Retardation, 44,* 375–382.

Feldman, M. B., & Meyer, I. H. (2007). Childhood abuse and eating disorders in gay and bisexual men. *International Journal of Eating Disorders, 40,* 418–423.

Fergusson, D., Swain-Campbell, N., & Horwood, J. (2004). How does childhood economic disadvantage lead to crime? *Journal of Child Psychology and Psychiatry, 45,* 956–966.

Fergusson, D. M., & Horwood, L. J. (1998). Early conduct problems and later life opportunities. *Journal of Child Psychology and Psychiatry, 39,* 1097–1108.

Fergusson, D. M., & Horwood, L. J. (1999). Prospective childhood predictors of deviant peer affiliations in adolescence. *Journal of Child Psychology and Psychiatry, 40,* 581–592.

Fergusson, D. M., Horwood, L. J., & Ridder, E. M. (2005a). Show me the child at seven: The consequences of conduct problems in childhood for psychosocial functioning in adulthood. *Journal of Child Psychology and Psychiatry, 46,* 837–849.

Fergusson, D. M., Horwood, L. J., & Ridder, E. M. (2005b). Show me the child at seven II: Childhood intelligence and later outcomes in adolescence and young adulthood. *Journal of Child Psychology and Psychiatry, 46,* 850–858.

Fergusson, D. M., Horwood, L. J., & Ridder, E. M. (2007). Conduct and attentional problems in childhood and adolescence substance use, abuse and dependence: Results of a 25-year longitudinal study. *Drug and Alcohol Dependence, 88,* S14–S26.

Fergusson, D. M., & Lynskey, M. T. (1997). Early reading difficulties and later conduct problems. *Journal of Child Psychology and Psychiatry, 38,* 899–907.

Fergusson, D. M., Lynskey, M. T., & Horwood, L. J. (1997). Attentional difficulties in middle childhood and psychosocial outcomes in young adulthood. *Journal of Child Psychology and Psychiatry, 38,* 633–644.

Fergusson, D. M., & Woodward, L. J. (2000). Educational, psychological, and sexual outcomes of girls with conduct problems in early adolescence. *Journal of Child Psychology and Psychiatry, 41,* 779–792.

Ferster, C. B. (1974). Behavioral approaches to depression. In R. J. Friedman & M. M. Katz (Eds.), *The psychology of depression: Contemporary theory and research.* Washington, DC: Winston.

Fetal Alcohol Syndrome. (2003). Retrieved March 2004 from http://www.cdc.gov/ncbdd/fas/fasask.htm

Field, A. P. (2006). Is conditioning a useful framework for understanding the development and treatment of phobias? *Clinical Psychology Review, 26,* 857–875.

Field, A. P., & Lester, K. J. (2010). Is there room for 'development' in the developmental models of information processing biases to threat in children and adolescents? *Clinical Child and Family Psychology Review, 13,* 315–332.

Field, A. P., & Schorah, H. (2007). The verbal information pathway to fear and heart rate changes in children. *Journal of Child Psychology and Psychiatry, 48,* 1088–1093.

Field, T., Diego, M., & Hernandez-Reif, M. (2010). Preterm infant massage therapy research: A review. *Infant Behavior and Development, 33,* 115–124.

Fiese, B. H., & Bickman, N. L. (1998). Qualitative inquiry: An overview for pediatric psychology. *Journal of Pediatric Psychology, 23,* 79–86.

Filipek, P. A. (1999). Neuroimaging in the developmental disorders: The state of the science. *Journal of Child Psychology and Psychiatry, 40,* 113–128.

Finding, R., Johnson, J. L., McClellan, J., Frazier, J. A., Vitiello, B., Hamer, R. M. et al. (2010). Double-blind maintenance safety and effectiveness findings from the TEOSS. *Journal of the American Academy of Child and Adolescent Psychiatry, 49,* 583–594.

Fine, M. A., & Harvey, J. H. (2006). Divorce and relationship dissolution in the 21st century. In M. A. Fine & J. H. Harvey (Eds.), *Handbook of divorce and relationship dissolution.* Mahwah, NJ: Lawrence Erlbaum Associates.

Fine, S. E., Izard, C. E., Mostow, A. J., Trentacosta, C. J., & Ackerman, B. P. (2003). First grade emotion knowledge as a predictor of fifth grade self-reported internalizing behaviors in children from economically disadvantaged families. *Development and Psychopathology, 15,* 331–342.

Finkelhor, D. (1994). The international epidemiology of child sexual abuse. *Child Abuse & Neglect, 18,* 409–417.

Finkelhor, D., Ormrod, R. K., & Turner, H. A. (2007). Re-victimization patterns in a national longitudinal sample of children and youth. *Child Abuse & Neglect, 31,* 479–502.

Finkelstein, H. (1988). The long term effects of early parent death: A review. *Journal of Clinical Psychology, 44,* 3–9.

Fischer, M., Barkley, R. A., Fletcher, K. E., & Smallish, L. (1993). The adolescent outcome of hyperactive children: Predictors of psychiatric, academic, social, and emotional adjustment. *Journal of the American Academy of Child and Adolescent Psychiatry, 32,* 324–332.

Fischer, S., & Le Grange, D. (2007). Co-morbidity and high-risk behaviors in treatment seeking adolescents with bulimia nervosa. *International Journal of Eating Disorders, 40,* 751–753.

Fisher, J. O., & Birch, L. L. (2001). Body image in children. In J. K. Thompson & L. Smolak (Eds.), *Body image, eating disorders,* *and obesity in youth: Assessment, prevention, and treatment.* Washington, DC: American Psychological Association.

Fixsen, D. L., Blasé, K. A., Duda, M. A., Naoom, S. F., & Van Dyke, M. (2010). Implementations of evidence-based treatments for children and adolescents. In J. R. Weisz & A. K. Kazdin (Eds.), *Evidence-based psychotherapies for children and adolescents* (2nd ed.). New York: Guilford Press.

Fixsen, D. L., Wolf, M. M., & Phillips, E. L. (1973). Achievement place: A teaching-family model of community-based group homes for youth in trouble. In L. Hammerlynck, L. Handy, and E. Mash (Eds.), *Behavior change: Methodology, concepts and practice.* Champaign, IL: Research Press.

Flament, M. F., Whitaker, A., Rapoport, J. L., Davies, M., Berg, C. Z., Kalikow, K., Sceery, W., & Shafer, D. (1988). Obsessive compulsive disorder in adolescence: An epidemiological study. *Journal of the American Academy of Child and Adolescent Psychiatry, 27,* 764–771.

Flannery-Schroeder, E. C. (2004). Generalized anxiety disorder. In T. L. Morris & J. S. March (Eds.), *Anxiety disorders in children and adolescents.* New York: Guilford Press.

Flaton, R. A. (2006). "Who would I be without Danny?" Phenomenological case study of an adult sibling. *Mental Retardation, 44,* 135–144.

Flax, J. F., Realpe-Bonilla, T., Roesler, C., Choudhury, N., & Benasich, A. (2009). Using early standardized language measures to predict later language and early reading outcomes in children at high risk for language-learning impairments. *Journal of Learning Disabilities, 42,* 61–75.

Flay, B. R., Biglan, A., Boruch, R. F., Castro, F. G., Gottfredson, D., Kellam, S. G. et al. (2005). Standards of evidence: Criteria for efficacy, effectiveness and dissemination. *Prevention Science, 6,* 151–175.

Fleck, D. E., Cerullo, M. A., Nandagopal, J., Adler, C. M., Patel, N.C., Strakowski, S. M., & DelBello, M. P. (2010). Neurodevelopment in bipolar disorder: A neuroimaging perspective. In D. J. Miklowitz & D. Cicchetti (Eds), *Understanding bipolar disorder: A developmental psychopathology perspective.* New York: The Guilford Press.

Fleitlich-Bilyk, B., & Goodman, R. (2004). Prevalence of child and adolescent psychiatric disorders in southeast Brazil. *Journal of the American Academy of Child and Adolescent Psychiatry, 43,* 727–734.

Fleming, J. E., Offord, D. R., & Boyle, M. H. (1989). Prevalence of childhood and adolescent depression in the community: Ontario Child Health Study. *British Journal of Psychiatry, 155,* 647–654.

Fletcher, K. E. (2003). Childhood posttraumatic stress disorder. In E. J. Mash & R. A. Barkley (Eds.), *Child psychopathology* (2nd ed.). New York: Guilford Press.

Flisher, A. J. (1999). Mood disorder in suicidal children and adolescents: Recent developments. *Journal of Child Psychology and Psychiatry, 40,* 315–324.

Flory, K., Lynam, D., Milich, R., Leukefeld, C., & Clayton, R. (2004). Early adolescent through young adult alcohol and marijuana use trajectories: Early predictors, young adult outcomes, and predictive utility. *Development and Psychopathology, 16,* 193–213.

Flouri, E. (2010). Fathers' behaviors and children's psychopathology. *Clinical Psychology Review, 30,* 363–369.

Foa, E. B., & Commission on Adolescent Anxiety Disorders. (2005a). Defining anxiety disorders. In D. L. Evans, E. B. Foa, R. E. Gur, H. Hendin, C. P. O'Brien, M. E. P. Seligman, & B. T. Walsh (Eds.), *Treating and preventing adolescent mental health disorders. What we know and what we don't know: A research agenda for improving mental health of our youth.* New York: Oxford University Press.

Foa, E. B., & Commission on Adolescent Anxiety Disorders. (2005b). Prevention of anxiety disorders. In D. L. Evans, E. B. Foa, R. E. Gur, H. Hendin, C. P. O'Brien, M. E. P. Seligman, & B. T. Walsh (Eds.), *Treating and preventing adolescent mental health disorders. What we know and what we don't know: A research agenda for improving mental health of our youth.* New York: Oxford University Press.

Follette, W. C., & Houts, A. C. (1996). Models of scientific progress and the role of theory in taxonomy development: A case study of DSM. *Journal of Consulting and Clinical Psychology, 64,* 1120–1132.

Fombonne, E. (2002). Case identification in an epidemiological context. In M. Rutter & E. Taylor (Eds.), *Child and adolescent psychiatry.* Oxford, UK: Blackwell Publishing.

Fombonne, E. (2003). Epidemiological surveys of autism and pervasive developmental disorders: An update. *Journal of Autism and Developmental Disorders, 33,* 365–382.

Fombonne, E. (2009). Epidemiology of pervasive developmental disorders. *Pediatric Research, 65,* 591–598.

Fonagy, P., & Target. (2003). *Psychoanalytic theories. Perspectives from developmental psychopathology.* New York: Brunner- Routledge.

Fonesca, A. C., Yule, W., & Erol, N. (1994). Cross-cultural issues. In T. H. Ollendick, N. J. King, & W. Yule (Eds.), *International handbook of phobic and anxiety disorders in children and adolescents.* New York: Plenum Press.

Fontaine, R. G., Burks, V. S., & Dodge, K. A. (2002). Response decision processes and externalizing behavior problems in adolescents. *Development and Psychopathology, 14,* 107–122.

Ford, M. A., Sladeczek, I. E., Carlson, J., & Kratochwill, T. R. (1998). Selective mutism: Phenomenological characteristics. *School Psychology Quarterly, 13,* 192–227.

Ford, T., Goodman, R., & Meltzer, H. (2003). The British child and adolescent mental health survey 1999: The prevalence of DSM-IV disorders. *Journal of the American Academy of Child and Adolescent Psychiatry, 42,* 1203–1211.

Forehand, R., King, H. E., Peed, S., & Yoder, P. (1975). Mother-child interactions: Comparisons of a noncompliant clinic group and a non-clinic group. *Behaviour Research and Therapy, 13,* 79–84.

Forehand, R., & McMahon, R. J. (1981). *Helping the noncompliant child: A clinician's guide to parent training.* New York: Guilford.

Forgatch, M. S., & Patterson, G. R. (2010). Parent management training-Oregon Model: An intervention for antisocial behavior in children and adolescents. In J. R. Weisz & A. E. Kazdin (Eds.), *Evidence-based psychotherapies for children and adolescents* (2nd ed.). New York: The Guilford Press.

Foster, E. M., Stephens, R., Krivelyova, A., & Gamfi, P. (2007). Can system integration improve mental health outcome for children and youth? *Children and Youth Services Review, 29,* 1301–1319.

Foster, S. L., & Robin, A. L. (1997). Family conflict and communication in adolescence. In E. J. Mash & L. G. Terdal (Eds.), *Assessment of childhood disorders* (3rd ed.). New York: Guilford Press.

Fountain, C., Winter, A. S., & Bearman, P. S. (2012). Six developmental trajectories characterize children with autism. *Pediatrics, 129,* e1112–e1120.

Fournier, K. A., Hass, C. J., Naik, S. K., Lodha, N., & Cauraugh, J. H. (2010). Motor coordination in autism spectrum disorders: A synthesis and meta-analysis. *Journal of Autism and Developmental Disorders, 40,* 1227–1240.

Fowers, B. J., & Davidow, B. J. (2006). The virtue of multiculturism. *American Psychologist, 61,* 581–594.

Fowles, D. C. (1992). Schizophrenia: Diathesis-stress revisited. *Annual Review of Psychology, 43,* 303–336.

Fox, N. A. (2010). Factors contributing to the emergence of anxiety among behaviorally inhibited children: The role of attention. In H. Gazelle & K. H. Rubin (Eds.), *Social anxiety in childhood: Bridging developmental and clinical perspectives. New Directions for Child and Adolescent* (Vol. 127, pp.33–49). San Francisco, CA: Jossey-Bass.

Fox, N. A., Hane, A. A., & Pine, D. S. (2007). Plasticity for human neurocircuitry: How the environment affects gene expression. *Current Directions in Psychological Science, 16,* 1–5.

Fox, N. A., Henderson, H. A., Marshall, P. J., Nichols, K. E., & Ghera, M. M. (2005). Behavioral inhibition: Linking biology and behavior within a developmental framework. *Annual Review of Psychology, 56,* 235–262.

Fox, N. A., & Pine, D. S. (2012). Temperament and the emergence of anxiety disorders. *Journal of the American Academy of Child and Adolescent Psychiatry, 51,* 125–128.

Frances, A., & Ross, R. (2001). *DSM-IV-TR case studies: A clinical guide to differential diagnosis.* Washington, DC: American Psychiatric Association.

Franić, S., Middeldorp, C. M., Dolan, C. V., Ligthart, L., & Boomsma, D. I. (2010). Childhood and adolescent anxiety and depression: Beyond heritability. *Journal of the American Academy of Child and Adolescent Psychiatry, 49,* 820–829.

Franklin, M. E., Freeman, J., & March, J. S. (2010). Treating pediatric obsessive-compulsive disorder using exposure-based cognitive-behavioral therapy. In J. R. Weisz & A. E.

Kazdin (Eds.), *Evidence-based psychotherapies for children and adolescents* (2nd ed.). New York: The Guilford Press.

Frazier, J. A., McClellan, J., Findling, R. L., Vitiello, B., Anderson, R., Zablotsky, B. et al. (2007). Treatment of early-onset schizophrenia spectrum disorders (TEOSS): Demographic and clinical characteristics. *Journal of the American Academy of Child and Adolescent Psychiatry, 46,* 979–988.

Frazier, T. W., Youngstrom, E. A., Glutting, J. J., & Watkins, M. W. (2007). ADHD and achievement: Meta-analysis of the child, adolescent, and adult literature and a concomitant study with college students. *Journal of Learning Disabilities, 40,* 49–65.

Fredriksen, K., Rhodes, J., Reddy, R., & Way, N. (2004). Sleepless in Chicago: Tracking the effects of adolescent sleep loss during the middle school years. *Child Development, 75,* 84–95.

Freeman, J. B., Choate-Summers, M. L., Garcia, A. M., Moore, P. S., Sapyta, J., Khanna, M. et al. (2009). The Pediatric Obsessive-Compulsive Disorder Treatment Study II: Rationale, design and methods. *Child and Adolescent Psychiatry and Mental Health, 3,* 4.

Fremont, W. P. (2004). Childhood reactions to terrorism-induced trauma: A review of the past 10 years. *Journal of the American Academy of Child and Adolescent Psychiatry, 43,* 381–392.

Freud, A. (1946). *The psycho-analytical treatment of children.* London: Imago.

Freud, S. (1953). *Analysis of a phobia in a five-year-old boy (1909).* Standard Edition. Vol. 10. Ed. and trans. James Strachey London: The Hogarth Press.

Freyer, D. R., Kuperberg, A., Sterken, D. J., Pastyrnak, S. L., Hudson, D., & Richards, T. (2006). Multidisciplinary care of the dying adolescent. *Child and Adolescent Psychiatric Clinics of North America, 15,* 693–715.

Frick, P. J. (1998). Conduct disorders. In T. H. Ollendick & M. Hersen (Eds.), *Handbook of child psychopathology* (3rd ed.). New York: Plenum Press.

Frick, P. J., & Kamphaus, R. W. (2001). Standardized rating scales in the assessment of children's behavioral and emotional problems. In C. E. Walker & M. C. Roberts (Eds.), *Handbook of clinical child psychology* (3rd ed.). New York: John Wiley & Sons.

Frick, P. J., & Morris, A. S. (2004). Temperament and developmental pathways to conduct problems. *Journal of Clinical Child and Adolescent Psychology, 33,* 54–68.

Frick, P. J., & White, S. F. (2008). The importance of callous-unemotional traits for developmental models of aggressive and antisocial behavior. *Journal of Child Psychology and Psychiatry, 49,* 359–375.

Friedman, A. G., Latham, S. A., & Dahlquist, L. M. (1998). Childhood cancer. In T. H. Ollendick & M. Hersen (Eds.), *Handbook of child psychopathology* (3rd ed.). New York: Plenum Press.

Fristad, M. A., & Goldberg-Arnold, J. S. (2003). Family interventions for early-onset bipolar disorder. In B. Geller & M. P. DelBello (Eds.), *Bipolar disorder in childhood and early adolescence.* New York: Guilford Press.

Frith, U. (2004). Emmanuel Miller lecture: Confusions and controversies about Asperger syndrome. *Journal of Child Psychology and Psychiatry, 45,* 672–686.

From Discovery to Cure. Accelerating the Development of New and Personalized Interventions for Mental Illness. (2010). Report of the National Advisory Mental Health Council's Workgroup. www.nimh.nih.gov/.../namhc/reports

Fryer, S. L., McGee, C. L., Matt, G. E., Riley, E. P., & Mattson, S. N. (2007). Evaluation of psychopathological conditions in children with heavy prenatal alcohol exposure. *Pediatrics, 119,* e733–e741.

Fuchs, D., Fuchs, L. S., & Stecker, P. M. (2010). The "blurring" of special education in a new continuum of general education placements and services. *Exceptional Children, 76,* 301–323.

Fuchs, L. S., Fuchs, D., & Hollenbeck, K. N. (2007). Extending responsiveness to intervention to mathematics at first and third grades. *Learning Disabilities Research & Practice, 22,* 13–23.

Gabbard, G. O. (2000). Psychoanalysis and psychoanalytic psychotherapy. In B. J. Sadock & V. A. Sadock (Eds.), *Kaplan & Sadock's comprehensive textbook of psychiatry* (Vol. II). Philadelphia: Lippincott Williams & Wilkins.

Gadow, K. D., & Nolan, E. E. (2002). Differences between preschool children with ODD, ADHD, and ODD+ADHD symptoms. *Journal of Child Psychology and Psychiatry, 43,* 191–201.

Gadow, K. D., Nolan, E. E., Litcher, L., Carlson, G. A., Panina, N., Golovakha, E. et al. (2000). Comparison of attentiondeficit/ hyperactivity disorder symptom subtypes in Ukrainian schoolchildren. *Journal of the American Academy of Child and Adolescent Psychiatry, 39,* 1520–1527.

Gadow, K. D., Sverd, J., Nolan, E. E., Sprafkin, J., & Schneider, J. (2007). Immediate-release methylphenidate for ADHD in children with comorbid chronic multiple tic disorder. *Journal of the American Academy of Child and Adolescent Psychiatry, 46,* 840–847.

Galéra, C., Melchior, M., Chastang, J. F., Bouvard, M. P., & Fombonne, E. (2009). Childhood and adolescent hyperactivity-inattention symptoms and academic achievement 8 years later: The GAZEL Youth study. *Psychological Medicine, 39,* 1895–1906.

Garber, J. (2010). Vulnerability to depression in childhood and adolescence. In R. E. Ingram & J. M. Price (Eds.), *Vulnerability to psychopathology: Risk across the lifespan* (2nd ed.). New York: The Guilford Press.

Garber, J., & Flynn, C. (2001). Predictors of depressive cognitions in young adolescents. *Cognitive Therapy and Research, 25,* 353–376.

Garber, J., & Kaminski, K. M. (2000). Laboratory and performance-based measures of depression in children and adolescents. *Journal of Clinical Child Psychology, 29,* 509–525.

Garcia Coll, C., Crnic, K., Lamberty, G., Wasik, B. H., Jenkins, R., Garcia, H. V. et al. (1966). An integrative model for the study of developmental competencies in minority children. *Child Development, 67,* 1891–1914.

Gardener, H., Spiegelman, D., & Buka, S. L. (2009). Prenatal risk factors for autism: Comprehensive meta-analysis. *British Journal of Psychiatry, 195,* 7–14.

Gardner, F., Burton, J., & Klimes, I. (2006). Randomised controlled trial of a parenting intervention in the voluntary sector for reducing conduct problems in children: Outcomes and mechanisms of change. *Journal of Child Psychology and Psychiatry, 47,* 1123–1132.

Gardner, R. M. (2001). Assessment of body image disturbance in children and adolescents. In J. K. Thompson & L. Smolak (Eds.), *Body image, eating disorders, and obesity in youth: Assessment, prevention, and treatment.* Washington, DC: American Psychological Association.

Garner, A. A., Marceaux, J., Mrug, S., Patterson, C., & Hodgens, B. (2010). Dimensions and correlates of attention deficit/hyperactivity disorder and sluggish cognitive tempo. *Journal of Abnormal Child Psychology, 38,* 1097–1107.

Gathercole, S. E., & Alloway, T. P. (2006). Practitioner review: Short-term and working memory impairments in neurodevelopmental disorders: Diagnosis and remedial support. *Journal of Child Psychology and Psychiatry, 47,* 4–15.

Gaub, M., & Carlson, C. L. (1997). Gender difference in ADHD: A meta-analysis and critical review. *Journal of the American Academy of Child and Adolescent Psychiatry, 36,* 1035–1045.

Gaylord-Harden, N. K., Elmore, C. A., Campbell, C. L., & Wethington, A. (2011). An examination of the tripartite mode of depressive and anxiety symptoms in African American youth: Stressors and coping strategies as common and specific correlates. *Journal of Clinical Child and Adolescent Psychology, 40,* 360–374.

Gazelle, H. (2010). Anxious solitude/withdrawal and anxiety disorders: Conceputalization, co-occurrence, and peer processes leading toward and away from disorder in childhood. In H. Gazelle & K. H. Rubin (Eds.), *Social anxiety in childhood: Bridging developmental and clinical perspectives. New Directions for Child and Adolescent* (Vol. 127, pp. 67–78). San Francisco, CA: Jossey-Bass.

Ge, X., Conger, R. D., Lorenz, F. O., Shanahan, M., & Elder, G. H. (1995). Mutual influences in parent and adolescent psychological distress. *Developmental Psychology, 31,* 406–419.

Geary, D. C. (2003). Learning disabilities in arithmetic: Problemsolving differences and cognitive deficits. In H. L. Swanson, K. R. Harris, & S. Graham (Eds.), *Handbook of learning disabilities.* New York: Guilford Press.

Geary, D. C. (2004). Mathematics and learning disabilities. *Journal of Learning Disabilities, 37,* 4–15.

Geier, A. B., Foster, G. D., Womble, L. G., McLaughlin, J., Borradaile, K. E., Nachmani, J. et al. (2007). The relationship between relative weight and school attendance among elementary schoolchildren. *Obesity, 15,* 2157–2161.

Geller, B., Craney, J. L., Bolhofner, K., DelBello, M. P., Axelson, D., Luby, J.,Williams, M., Zimerman, B., Nickelsburg, M. J., Frazier, J., & Beringer, L. (2003). Phenomenology and longitudinal course of children with prepubertal and early adolescent bipolar disorder phenotype. In B. Geller & M. P. DelBello (Eds.), *Bipolar disorder in childhood and early adolescence.* New York: Guilford Press.

Geller, B., Tillman, R., & Bolhofner, K. (2007). Proposed definitions of bipolar I disorder episodes and daily rapid cycling phenomena in preschoolers, school-aged children, adolescents, and adults. *Journal of Child and Adolescent Psychopharmacology, 17,* 217–222.

Geller, B., Zimerman, B., Williams, M., Bolhofner, K., Craney, J. L., DeBello, M. P., & Soutullo, C. A. (2000). Diagnostic characteristics of 93 cases of prepubertal and early adolescent bipolar disorder phenotype by gender, puberty and comorbid attention deficit hyperactivity disorder. *Journal of Child and Adolescent Psychopharmacology, 10,* 157–164.

Geller, B., Zimerman, B.,Williams, M., Bulhofner, K., Craney, J. L., DelBello, M. P., & Soutullo, C. (2001). Reliability of the Washington University in St. Louis Kiddie Schedule for Affective Disorders and Schizophrenia (WASH-U-KSADS) mania and rapid cycling sections. *Journal of the American Academy of Child and Adolescent Psychiatry, 40,* 450–455.

Geller, D. A., Biederman, J., Stewart, E., Mullin, B., Farrell, C., Wagner, K. D., Emslie, G., & Carpenter, D. (2003a). Impact of comorbidity on treatment response to paroxetine in pediatric obsessive-compulsive disorder: Is the use of exclusion criteria empirically supported in randomized clinical trials? *Journal of Child and Adolescent Psychopharmacology, 13,* S19–S29.

Gencöz, T., Voelz, A. R., Gencöz, F., Pettit, J. W., & Joiner, T. E. (2001). Specificity of information processing styles to depressive symptoms in youth psychiatric inpatients. *Journal of Abnormal Child Psychology, 29,* 255–262.

Geoffroy, M.-C., Côté, S. M., Borge, A. I. H., Larouche, F., Séguin, J. R., & Rutter, M. (2007). Association between nonmaternal care in the first year of life and children's receptive language skills prior to school entry: The moderating role of socioeconomic status. *Journal of Child Psychology and Psychiatry, 48,* 490–497.

Georgiades, K., & Boyle, M. H. (2007). Adolescent tobacco and cannabis use: Young adult outcomes from the Ontario Child Health Study. *Journal of Child Psychology and Psychiatry, 48,* 724–731.

Georgiades, K., Lewinsohn, P. M., Monroe, S. M., & Seeley, J. R. (2006). Major depressive disorder in adolescence: The role of subthreshold symptoms. *Journal of the American Academy of Child and Adolescent Psychiatry, 45,* 936–944.

Gerard, M. W. (1939). Enuresis: A study in etiology. *American Journal of Orthopsychiatry, 9,* 48–58.

Gerber, A. J., & Peterson, B. S. (2008). What is an image? *Journal of the American Academy of Child and Adolescent Psychiatry, 47,* 245–248.

Gerhardt, C.A.,Baughcum,A.E.,Young-Saleme,T.,&Vannatta,K. (2009). Palliative care, end of life, and bereavement. In M. C. Roberts & R. G. Steele (Eds.), *Handbook of pediatric psychology* (4th ed.). New York: The Guilford Press.

Gerull, F. C., & Rapee, R. M. (2002). Mother knows best: The effects of maternal modeling on the acquisition of fear and avoidance behaviour in toddlers. *Behaviour Research and Therapy, 40,* 279–287.

Gerwitz, A. H., & August, G. J. (2008). Incorporating multifaceted mental health prevention services in community sectors-of-care. *Clinical Child and Family Psychology Review, 11,* 1–11.

Gettinger, M., & Koscik, R. (2001). Psychological services for children with learning disabilities. In J. N. Huges, A. M. La Greca, & J. C. Conoley (Eds.), *Handbook of psychological services for children and adolescents.* New York: Oxford University Press.

Ghaziuddin, M. (2010). Brief report: Should the DSM drop Asperger syndrome? *Journal of Autism and Developmental Disorders, 40,* 1146–1148.

Giannotti, F., Cortesi, F., Cerquiglini, A., Miraglia, D., Vagnoni, C., Sebastiani, T., & Bernabei, P. (2008). An investigation of sleep characteristics, EEG abnormalities and epilepsy in developmentally regressed and non-regressed children with autism. *Journal of Autism and Developmental Disorders, 38,* 1888–1897.

Gibbs, J. T. (2003). African American children and adolescents. In J. T. Gibbs, L. N. Huang, and Associates (Eds.), *Children of color: Psychological interventions with culturally diverse youth.* San Francisco: Jossey-Bass.

Gil, A. G., Wagner, E. F., & Vega, W. A. (2000). Acculturation, familism, and alcohol use among Latino adolescent males: Longitudinal relations. *Journal of Community Psychology, 28,* 443–458.

Gill, A. M., Hyde, L. W., Shaw, D. S., Dishion, T. J., & Wilson, M. N. (2008). The family check-up in early childhood: A case study of intervention process and change. *Journal of Clinical Child and Adolescent Psychology, 37,* 893–904.

Gilmour, J., Hill, B., Place, M., Skuse, D. H. (2004). Social communication deficits in conduct disorder: A clinical and community survey. *Journal of Child Psychology and Psychiatry, 45,* 967–978.

Ginsburg, G. S., LaGreca, A. M., & Silverman, W. K. (1998). Social anxiety in children with anxiety disorders: Relation with social and emotional functioning. *Journal of Abnormal Psychology, 26,* 175–185.

Ginsburg, G. S., Riddle, M. A., & Davies, M. (2006). Somatic symptoms in children and adolescents with anxiety disorders. *Journal of the American Academy of Child and Adolescent Psychiatry, 45,* 1179–1187.

Ginsburg, G. S., & Silverman, W. K. (1996). Phobic and anxiety disorders in Hispanic and Caucasian youth. *Journal of Anxiety Disorders, 10,* 517–528.

Ginsburg, G. S., & Silverman, W. K. (2000). Gender role orientation and fearfulness in children with anxiety disorders. *Journal of Anxiety Disorders, 14,* 57–67.

Gjevik, E., Eldevik, S., Fjaeran-Granum, T., & Sponheim, E. (2011). Kiddie-SADS reveals high rates of DSM-IV disorders in children and adolescents with autism spectrum disorder. *Journal of Autism and Developmental Disorders, 41,* 761–769.

Glantz, L. H. (1996). Conducting research with children: Legal and ethical issues. *Journal of the American Academy of Child and Adolescent Psychiatry, 35,* 1283–1291.

Gleason, M. M. (2009). Psychopharmacology in early childhood: Does it have a role? In C. H. Zeanah, Jr. (Ed.), *Handbook of infant mental health* (3rd ed.). New York: Guilford Press.

Gleason, M. M., Egger, H. L., Emsile, G. J., Greenhill, L. L., Kowatch, R. A., Lieberaman, A. F. et al. (2007). Pharmacological treatment for very young children: Contexts and guidelines. *Journal of the American Academy of Child and Adolescent Psychiatry, 46,* 1532–1572.

Glidden, L. M., Bamberger, K. T., Draheim, A. R., & Kersh, J. (2011). Parent and athlete perceptions of Special Olympics participation: Utility and danger of proxy responding. *Intellectual and Developmental Disabilities, 49,* 37–45.

Gliner, J. A., Morgan, G. A., & Harmon, R. J. (2000). Single-subject designs. *Journal of the American Academy of Child and Adolescent Psychiatry, 39,* 1327–1329.

Glowinski, A. L., Madden, P. A. F., Bucholz, K. K., Lynskey, M. T., & Heath, A. C. (2003). Genetic epidemiology of self-reported lifetime DSM-IV major depressive disorder in a populationbased twin sample of female adolescents. *Journal of Child Psychology and Psychiatry, 44,* 988–996.

Glueck, S., & Glueck, E. T. (1968). *Delinquents and nondelinquents in perspective.* Cambridge, MA: Harvard University Press.

Gochman, P. A., Greenstein, D., Sporn, A. Gogtay, N., Keller, B., Shaw, P., & Rapoport, J. L. (2005). IQ stabilization in childhood-onset schizophrenia. *Schizophrenia Research, 77,* 271–277.

Goddard, H. H. (1912). *The Kallikak family.* New York: Macmillan.

Godlee, F. (2011). Wakefield's article linking MMR vaccine and autism was fraudulent. *British Medical Journal, 342,* c7452.

Goeke, J., Kassow, D., May, D., & Kundert, D. (2003). Parental opinions about plastic surgery for individuals with down syndrome. *Mental Retardation, 41,* 29–34.

Gogtay, N. (2007). Cortical brain development in schizophrenia: Insights from neuroimaging studies in childhood-onset schizophrenia. *Schizophrenia Bulletin, 34,* 30–36.

Gogtay, N., Lu, A., Leow, A. D., Klunder, A. D., Lee, A. D., Chavez, A. et al. (2008). Three-dimensional brain growth abnormalities in childhood-onset schizophrenia visualized by using tensor-based morphometry. *Proceedings of the National Academy of Science, 105,* 15979–15984.

Goldberg, W. A., Osann, K., Filipek, P. A., Laulhere, T., Jarvis, K., Modahl, C. et al. (2003). Language and other regression: Assessment and timing. *Journal of Autism and Developmental Disorders, 33,* 607–616.

Goldberg, W. A., Prause, J. A., Lucas-Thompson, R., & Himsel, A. (2008). Maternal employment and children's achievement in context: A meta-analysis of four decades of research. *Psychological Bulletin, 134,* 77–108.

Golden, C. J. (1997). The Nebraska neuropsychological children's battery. In C. R. Reynolds & E. Fletcher-Janzen (Eds.),

Handbook of clinical child neuropsychology (2nd ed.). New York: Plenum Press.

Goldstein, S. (2011). Attention-deficit/hyperactivity disorder. In S. Goldstein & C. R. Reynolds (Eds.), *Handbook of neurodevelopmental and genetic disorders in children.* New York: Guilford Press.

Goldstein, S., & Reynolds, C. R. (Eds.) (2011). *Handbook of neurodevelopmental and genetic disorders in children.* New York: Guilford Press.

Goldston, D. B., & Compton, J. S. (2007). Adolescent suicidal and nonsuicidal self-harm behaviors and risk. In E. J. Mash & R. A. Barkley (Eds.), *Assessment of childhood disorders* (4th ed.). New York: The Guilford Press.

Golombok, S. (2006). New family forms. In A. Clarke-Stewart & J. Dunn (Eds.), *Families count. Effects on child and adolescent development.* New York: Cambridge University Press.

Gomez, R., Gomez, A., DeMello, L., & Tallent, R. (2001). Perceived maternal control and support: Effects on hostile biased social information processing and aggression among clinic-referred children with high aggression. *Journal of Child Psychology and Psychiatry, 42,* 513–522.

Gomez, R., Harvey, J., Quick, C., Scharer, I., & Harris, G. (1999). DSM-IV AD/HD: Confirmatory factor models, prevalence, and gender and age differences based on parent and teacher ratings of Australian primary school children. *Journal of Child Psychology and Psychiatry, 40,* 265–274.

Gooch, D., Snowling, M., & Hulme, C. (2011). Time perception, phonological skills and executive function in children with dyslexia and/or ADHD symptoms. *Journal of Child Psychology and Psychiatry, 52,* 195–203.

Goodman, R., & Stevenson, J. (1989). A twin study of hyperactivity- II. The aetiological role of genes, family relationships and perinatal adversity. *Journal of Child Psychology and Psychiatry, 30,* 691–709.

Goodman, S. H., & Brand, S. R. (2009). Infants of depressed mothers. In C. H. Zeanah, Jr. (Ed.), *Handbook of infant mental health* (3rd ed.). New York: The Guilford Press.

Goodman, S. H., Rouse, M. H., Connell, A. M., Broth, M. R., Hall, C. M., & Heyward, D. (2011). Maternal depression and child psychopathology: A meta-analytic review. *Clinical Child and Family Psychology Review, 14,* 1–27.

Goodyer, I. M., & Cooper, P. (1993). A community study of depression in adolescent girls: II. The clinical features of identified disorder. *British Journal of Psychiatry, 163,* 374–380.

Goodyer, I. M., Park, R. J., & Herbert, J. (2001). Psychosocial and endocrine features of chronic first-episode major depression in 8–16 year olds. *Biological Psychiatry, 50,* 351–357.

Gordis, E. B., Feres, N., Olezeski, C. L., Rabkin, A. N., & Trickett, P. K. (2010). Skin conductance reactivity and respiratory sinus arrhythmia among maltreated and comparison youth: Relations with aggressive behavior. *Journal of Pediatric Psychology, 35,* 547–558.

Gordis, E. B., Granger, D. A., Susman, E. J., & Trickett, P. K. (2006). Asymmetry between salivary cortisol and α-amylase reactivity to stress: Relation to aggressive behavior in adolescents. *Psychoneuroendocrinology, 31,* 976–987.

Gordis, E. B., Margolin, G., & John, R. S. (2001). Parents' hostility in dyadic marital and triadic family settings and children's behavior problems. *Journal of Consulting and Clinical Psychology, 69,* 727–734.

Gordon, J., King, N. J., Bullone, E., Muris, P., & Ollendick, T. H. (2007). Treatment of children's nighttime fears: The need for a modern randomized controlled trial. *Clinical Psychology Review, 27,* 98–113.

Gordon, M., Barkley, R. A., & Lovett, B. J. (2006). Tests and observational measures. In R. A. Barkley (Ed.), *Attention-deficit hyperactivity disorder. A handbook for diagnosis and treatment.* New York: The Guilford Press.

Gottesman, I. I. (1993). Origins of schizophrenia: Past as prologue. In R. Plomin & G. E. McClearn (Eds.), *Nature and nurture & psychology.* Washington, DC: American Psychological Association.

Gottlieb, C. A., Maenner, M. J., Cappa, C., & Durkin, M. S. (2009). Child disability screening, nutrition, and early learning in 18 countries with low and middle incomes: Data from the third round of UNICEF's Multiple Indicator Cluster Survey (2005–2006). *The Lancet, 374,* 1831–1839.

Gould, M. S., Greenberg, T., Velting, D. M., & Shaffer, D. (2003). Youth suicide risk and preventive interventions: A review of the past 10 years. *Journal of the American Academy of Child and Adolescent Psychiatry, 42,* 386–405.

Gould, S. R., Roberts, M. C., & Beals, S. E. (2009). Do state mental health plans address the New Freedom Commission's goals for children's mental health? *Clinical Child and Family Psychology Review, 12,* 295–309.

Gowers, S., & Bryant-Waugh, R. (2004). Management of child and adolescent eating disorders: The current evidence base and future directions. *Journal of Child Psychology and Psychiatry, 45,* 63–83.

Graber, J., & Sontag, L. M. (2009). Internalizing problems during adolescence. In R. M. Lerner & L. Steinberg (Eds.), *Handbook of adolescent psychology, Vol. 2: Contextual influences on adolescent development* (3rd ed.). Hoboken, NJ: John Wiley & Sons.

Graber, J. A., Seeley, J. R., Brooks-Gunn, J., & Lewinsohn, P. M. (2004). Is pubertal timing associated with psychopathology in young adulthood? *Journal of the American Academy of Child and Adolescent Psychiatry, 43,* 718–726.

Grace, W. J., & Graham, D. T. (1952). Relationship of specific attitudes and emotions to certain bodily diseases. *Psychosomatic Medicine, 14,* 243–251.

Grados, M. A. (2010). The genetics of obsessive-compulsive disorder and Tourette Syndrome: An epidemiological and pathway-based approach to gene discovery. *Journal of the American Academy of Child and Adolescent Psychiatry, 49,* 810–819.

Graetz, B. W., Sawyer, M. G., Hazell, P. L., Arney, F., & Baghurst, P. (2001). Validity of DSM-IV ADHD subtypes in a nationally representative sample of Australian children and adolescents. *Journal of the American Academy of Child and Adolescent Psychiatry, 40,* 410–417.

Graham, S., & Harris, K. R. (2003). Students with learning disabilities and the process of writing: A meta-analysis of SRSD studies. In H. L. Swanson, K. R. Harris, & S. Graham (Eds.), *Handbook of learning disabilities.* New York: Guilford Press.

Grandin, T. (1997). A personal perspective on autism. In D. J. Cohen & F. R. Volkmar (Eds.), *Handbook of autism and pervasive developmental disorders.* New York: John Wiley.

Grant, K. E., Compas, B. E., Stuhlmacher, A. F., Thurm, A. E., McMahon, S. D., & Halpert, J. A. (2003). Stressors and child and adolescent psychopathology: Moving from markers to mechanisms of risk. *Psychological Bulletin, 129,* 447–466.

Graves, M. M., Roberts, M. C., Rapoff, M., & Boyer, A. (2010). The efficacy of adherence interventions for chronically ill children: A meta-analytic review. *Journal of Pediatric Psychology, 35,* 368–382.

Gray, J. A. (1987). *The psychology of fear and stress.* New York: Cambridge University Press.

Greco, L. A., & Morris, T. L. (2004). Assessment. In T. L. Morris & J. S. March (Eds.), *Anxiety disorders in children and adolescents.* New York: Guilford Press.

Greco, P., Pendley, J. S., McDonell, K., & Reeves, G. (2001). A peer group intervention for adolescents with type 1 diabetes and their best friends. *Journal of Pediatric Psychology, 26,* 485–490.

Green, J. (2006). Annotation: The therapeutic alliance—a significant but neglected variable in child mental health treatment studies. *Journal of Child Psychology and Psychiatry, 47,* 425–435.

Green, J., & Goldwyn, R. (2002). Annotation: Attachment disorganization and psychopathology: New findings in attachment research and their potential implications for developmental psychopathology in childhood. *Journal of Child Psychology and Psychiatry, 43,* 835–846.

Green, S. A., & Ben-Sasson, A. (2010). Anxiety disorders and sensory over-responsivity in children with autism spectrum disorders: Is there a causal relationship? *Journal of Autsim and Developmental Disorders, 40,* 1495–1504.

Green, W. H., Padron-Gayol, M., Hardesty, A. S., & Bassiri, M. (1992). Schizophrenia with childhood onset: A phenomenological study of 38 cases. *Journal of the American Academy of Child and Adolescent Psychiatry, 31,* 968–976.

Greene, R. W. (1995). Students with ADHD in school classrooms: Teacher factors related to compatibility, assessment, and intervention. *School Psychology Review, 24,* 81–93.

Greenhill, L., Kollins, S., Abikoff, H., McCracken, J., Riddle, M., Swanson, J. et al. (2006). Efficacy and safety of immediaterelease methylphenidate treatment for preschoolers with ADHD. *Journal of the American Academy of Child and Adolescent Psychiatry, 45,* 1284–1293.

Greenhill, L. L., Jensen, P. S., Abikoff, H., Blumer, J. L., De-Veaugh-Geiss, J., Fisher, C. (2003). Developing strategies for psychopharmacological studies in preschool children. *Journal of the American Academy of Child and Adolescent Psychiatry, 42,* 406–414.

Greenley, R. N., Hommel, K. A., Nebel, J., Raboin, T., Li, S. H., Simpson, P., & Mackner, L. (2010). A meta-analytic review of the psychosocial adjustment of youth with inflammatory bowel disease. *Journal of Pediatric Psychology, 35,* 857–869.

Greenspan, S., & Love, P. F. (1997). Social intelligence and developmental disorder: Mental retardation, learning disabilities, and autism. In W. E. MacLean (Ed.), *Ellis' handbook of mental deficiency, psychological theory and research.* Mahwah, NJ: Lawrence Erlbaum.

Greenwood, C. R., Carta, J. J., Hart, B., Kamps, D., Terry, B., Arreaga-Mayer, C., Atwater, J., Walker, D., Risley, T., & Delquadri, J. C. (1992). Out of the laboratory and into the community: 26 years of applied behavior analysis at the Juniper Gardens Children's Project. *American Psychologist, 47,* 1464–1474.

Greenwood, C. R., Hart, B., Walker, D., & Risley, T. (1994). The opportunity to respond and academic performance revisited: A behavioral theory of developmental retardation and its prevention. In R. Gardner et al. (Eds.), *Behavior analysis in education: Focus on measurably superior instruction.* Pacific Grove, CA: Brooks/Cole.

Gregory, A. M., & Eley, T. C. (2007). Genetic influences on anxiety in children: What we've learned and where we're heading. *Clinical Child and Family Psychology Review, 10,* 199–212.

Gregory, A. M., Eley, T. C., & Plomin, R. (2004). Exploring the association between anxiety and conduct problems in a large sample of twins aged 2–4. *Journal of Abnormal Child Psychology, 32,* 111–122.

Gregory, A. M., Rijsdijk, F. V., & Eley, T. C. (2006). A twin-study of sleep difficulties in school-aged children. *Child Development, 77,* 1668–1679.

Greven, C. U., Asherson, P., Rijsdijk, F. V., & Plomin, R. (2011). A longitudinal twin study on the association between inattentive and hyperactive-impulsive ADHD symptoms. *Journal of Abnormal Child Psychology, 39,* 623–632.

Greven, C. U., Rijsdijk, F. V., Asherson, P., & Plomin, R. (2011). A longitudinal twin study on the association between ADHD symptoms and reading. *Journal of Child Psychology and Psychiatry, 53,* 234–242.

Griffiths, L. J., Wolke, D., Page, A. S., & Horwood, J. P. (2006). Obesity and bullying: Different effects for boys and girls. *Archives of Disease in Childhood, 91,* 121–125.

Grigorenko, E. L. (2001). Developmental dyslexia: An update on genes, brains, and environments. *Journal of Child Psychology and Psychiatry, 42,* 91–125.

Grigorenko, E. L. (2009). Speaking genes or genes for speaking? Deciphering the genetics of speech and language. *Journal of Child Psychology and Psychiatry, 50,* 116–125.

Grigorenko, E. L., Klin, A., & Volkmar, R. (2003). Annotation: Hyperlexia: Disability or superability? *Journal of Child Psychology and Psychiatry, 44,* 1079–1091.

Gross, D., Fogg, L., Webster-Stratton, C., Garvey, C. W., & Grady, J. (2003). Parent training with parents of toddlers in day care in low-income urban communities. *Journal of Consulting and Clinical Psychology, 71,* 261–278.

Grossman, A. W., Churchill, J. D., McKinney, B. C., Kodish, I. M., Otte, S. L., & Greenough, W. T. (2003). Experience effects on brain development: Possible contributions to psychopathology. *Journal of Child Psychology and Psychiatry, 44,* 33–63.

Grossman, H. J. (1983). *Classification in mental retardation.* Washington, DC: American Association on Mental Deficiency.

Grus, C. L. (2011). Training, credentialing, and new roles in clinical psychology: Emerging trends. In D. H. Barlow (Ed.), *The Oxford handbook of clinical psychology.* New York: Oxford University Press.

Grusec, J. E. (1992). Social learning theory and developmental psychology: The legacies of Robert Sears and Albert Bandura. *Developmental Psychology, 28,* 776–786.

Grych, J. H., & Fincham, F. D. (1999). Children of single parents and divorce. In W. K. Silverman & T. H. Ollendick (Eds.), *Developmental issues in the clinical treatment of children.* Boston, MA: Allyn and Bacon.

Guerra, N. G., Graham, S., & Tolan, P. H. (2011). Raising healthy children: Translating child development research into practice. *Child Development, 82,* 7–16.

Gullone, E. (2000). The development of normal fear: A century of research. *Clinical Psychology Review, 20,* 429–451.

Gunnar, M. R., Van Dulmen, M. H. M., and The International Adoption Project Team. (2007). Behavior problems in postinstitutionalized internationally adopted children. *Development and Psychopathology, 19,* 129–148.

Gunther, D., & Diekema, D. (2006). Attenuating growth in children with developmental disability: A new approach to an old dilemma. *Archives of Pediatric and Adolescent Medicine, 160,* 1013–1017.

Gur, R. E., Cowell, P., Turetsky, B. I., Gallacher, F., Cannon, T., Bilker, W., & Gur, R. C. (1998). A follow-up magnetic resonance imaging study of schizophrenia. *Archives of General Psychiatry, 55,* 145–152.

Guralnick, M. J. (1998). Effectiveness of early intervention for vulnerable children: A developmental perspective. *American Journal on Mental Retardation, 102,* 319–345.

Gurwitch, R. H., Kees, M., & Becker, S. M. (2002). In the face of tragedy: Placing children's reactions to trauma in a new context. *Cognitive & Behavioral Practice, 9,* 286–295.

Haas, L. J. (2011). Clinical psychology interventions in primary care. In D. H. Barlow (Ed.), *The Oxford handbook of clinical psychology.* New York: Oxford University Press.

Hagen, K. A., Ogden, T., & Bjornebekk, G. (2011). Treatment outcomes and mediators of parent management training:

A one-year follow-up of children with conduct problems. *Journal of Clinical Child and Adolescent Psychology, 40,* 165–178.

Hagerman, R. J. (2011). Fragile X syndrome and fragile X-associated disorders. In S. Goldstein & C. R. Reynolds (Eds.), *Handbook of neurodevelopmental disorders in children.* New York: Guilford Press.

Hakvoort, E. M., Bos, H. M. W., Van Balen, F., & Hermanns, J. M. A. (2011). Postdivorce relationships in families and children's psychosocial adjustment. *Journal of Divorce and Remarriage, 52,* 125–146.

Hallahan, D. P., & Kauffman, J. M. (1978). *Exceptional children: Introduction to special education.* Englewood Cliffs, NJ: Prentice Hall.

Hallahan, D. P., & Mock, D. R. (2003). A brief history of the field of learning disabilities. In H. L. Swanson, K. R. Harris, & S. Graham (Eds.), *Handbook of learning disabilities.* New York: Guilford Press.

Halmi, K. A. (1985). Eating disorders. In H. I. Kaplan & B. J. Sadock (Eds.), *Comprehensive textbook of psychiatry* (4th ed.). Baltimore: Williams & Wilkins.

Halmi, K. A. (2009). Perplexities and provocations of eating disorders. *Journal of Child Psychology and Psychiatry, 50,* 163–169.

Halmi, K. A., Casper, R. C., Eckert, E. D., Goldberg, S. C., & Davis, J. M. (1979). Unique features associated with age of onset of anorexia nervosa. *Psychiatry Research, 1,* 209–215.

Hammad, T. A., Laughren, T., & Racoosin, J. (2006). Suicidality in pediatric patients treated with antidepressant drugs. *Archives of General Psychiatry, 63,* 332–339.

Hammen, C. (1992). Cognitive, life stress, and interpersonal approaches to a developmental psychopathology model of depression. *Development and Psychopathology, 4,* 189–206.

Hammen, C., Burge, D., Burney, E., & Adrian, C. (1990). Longitudinal study of diagnosis in children of women with unipolar and bipolar affective disorders. *Archives of General Psychiatry, 47,* 1112–1117.

Hammen, C., & Rudolph, K. D. (2003). Childhood mood disorders. In E. J. Mash & R. A. Barkley (Eds.), *Child psychopathology* (2nd ed.). New York: Guilford Press.

Hammill, D. D. (1993). A brief look at the learning disabilities movement in the United States. *Journal of Learning Disabilities, 26,* 295–310.

Handen, B. L. (1998). Mental retardation. In E. J. Mash & L. G. Terdal (Eds.), *Treatment of childhood disorders.* New York: Guilford Press.

Handen, B. L. (2007). Intellectual disability (mental retardation). In E. J. Mash & R. A. Barkley (Eds.), *Assessment of childhood disorders* (4th ed.). New York: Guilford Press.

Handen, B. L., & Gilchrist, R. (2006a). Mental retardation. In E. J. Mash & R. A. Barkley (Eds.), *Treatment of childhood disorders.* New York: The Guilford Press.

Handen, B. L., & Gilchrist, R. (2006b). Practitioner review: Psychopharmacology in children and adolescents with mental retardation. *Journal of Child Psychology and Psychiatry, 47,* 871–882.

Hane, A. A., & Fox, N. A. (2006). Ordinary variations in maternal caregiving influence human infants' stress reactivity. *Psychological Science, 17,* 550–556.

Hanish, L. D., & Guerra, N. G. (2002). A longitudinal analysis of patterns of adjustment following peer victimization. *Development and Psychopathology, 14,* 69–89.

Hankin, B. L., Abramson, L. Y., Moffitt, T. E., Silva, P. A., McGee, R., & Angell, K. E. (1998). Development of depression from preadolescence to young adulthood: Emerging gender differences in a 10-year longitudinal study. *Journal of Abnormal Psychology, 107,* 128–140.

Hankin, B. L., Fraley, R. C., Lahey, B. B., & Waldman, I. D. (2005). Is depression best viewed as a continuum or discrete category? A taxometric analysis of childhood and adolescent depression in a population-based sample. *Journal of Abnormal Psychology, 114,* 96–110.

Hanna, K. M., DiMeglio, L. A., & Fortenberry, J. D. (2007). Initial testing of scales measuring parent and adolescent perceptions of adolescents' assumption of diabetes management. *Journal of Pediatric Psychology, 32,* 245–249.

Hannah, M. E., & Midlarsky, E. (2005). Helping in siblings of children with mental retardation. *American Journal on Mental Retardation, 110,* 87–99.

Hansen, C., Weiss, D., & Last, C. G. (1999). ADHD boys in young adulthood: Psychosocial adjustment. *Journal of the American Academy of Child and Adolescent Psychiatry, 38,* 165–171.

Hanson, J. L., Chandra, A., Wolfe, B. L., & Pollak, S. D. (2011). Association between income and the hippocampus. *PloS ONE, 6,* e18712.

Happé, F., Briskman, J., & Frith, U. (2001). Exploring the cognitive phenotype of autism: Weak "central coherence" in parents and siblings of children with autism: I. Experimental tests. *Journal of Child Psychology and Psychiatry, 42,* 299–307.

Happé, F., & Frith, U. (2006). The weak coherence account: Detail-focused cognitive style in autism spectrum disorders. *Journal of Autism and Developmental Disorders, 36,* 5–25.

Happé, F. G. E. (1994). Wechsler IQ profile and theory of mind in autism: A research note. *Journal of Child Psychology and Psychiatry, 35,* 1461–1471.

Harcourt Assessment. (2003). *The Stanford Achievement Test,* Tenth Edition. San Antonio, TX: Harcourt Assessment.

Harkness, S., & Super, C. M. (2000). Culture and psychopathology. In A. J. Sameroff, M. Lewis, & S. M. Miller (Eds.), *Handbook of developmental psychopathology.* New York: Kluwer/Plenum Publishers.

Harlaar, N., Spinath, F. M., Dale, P. S., & Plomin, R. (2005). Genetic influences on early word recognition abilities and disabilities: A study of 7-year-old twins. *Journal of Child Psychology and Psychiatry, 46,* 373–384.

Harley, J. P., & Matthews, C. G. (1980). Food additives and hyperactivity in children: Experimental investigations. In R. M. Knights and D. J. Bakker (Eds.), *Treatment of hyperactive and learning disordered children.* Baltimore: University Park Press.

Harrington, R., Rutter, M., Weissman, M., Fudge, H., Groothues, C., Bredenkamp, D., Pickles, A., Rende, R., & Wickramaratne, P. (1997). Psychiatric disorders in the relatives of depressed probands: I. Comparison of prepubertal, adolescent and early adult onset cases. *Journal of Affective Disorders, 42,* 9–22.

Harris, S. L., & Handelman, J. S. (2000). Age and IQ at intake as predictors of placement for young children with autism: A four-to-six-year follow-up. *Journal of Autism and Developmental Disorders, 30,* 137–142.

Harrison, S. I., & McDermott, J. K. (1972). *Childhood psychopathology.* New York: International University Press.

Hart, B., & Risley, T. R. (1992). American parenting of languagelearning children: Persisting differences in family-child interactions observed in natural home environment. *Developmental Psychology, 28,* 1096–1105.

Harter, S. (1985). *Manual for the self-perception profile for children.* Denver, CO: University of Denver.

Hartman, C. A., Gelhorn, H., Crowley, T. J., Sakai, J. T., Stallings, M., Young, S. E. et al. (2008). Item response theory analysis of DSM-IV cannabis abuse and dependence criteria in adolescents. *Journal of the American Academy of Child and Adolescent Psychiatry, 47,* 165–173.

Hartman, C. A., Willcutt, E. G., Rhee, S. H., & Pennington, B. F. (2004). The relation between sluggish cognitive tempo and DSM-IV ADHD. *Journal of Abnormal Child Psychology, 32,* 491–503.

Hartung, C. M., & Widiger, T. A. (1998). Gender differences in the diagnosis of mental disorders: Conclusions and controversies of the DSM-IV. *Psychological Bulletin, 123,* 260–278.

Haskett, M. E., Nears, K., Ward, C. S., & McPherson, A. V. (2006). Diversity in adjustment of maltreated children: Factors associated with resilient functioning. *Clinical Psychology Review, 26,* 796–812.

Hastings, R. P., Daley, D., Burns, C., & Beck, A. (2006). Maternal distress and expressed emotion: Cross-sectional and longitudinal relationships with behavior problems of children with intellectual disabilities. *American Journal on Mental Retardation, 111,* 48–61.

Hastings, R. P., Kovshoff, H., Ward, N. J., degli Espinosa, F., Brown, T., & Remington, B. (2005). Systems analysis of stress and positive perceptions in mothers and fathers of preschool children with autism. *Journal of Autism and Developmental Disorders, 35,* 635–644.

Hatcher, P. J., Hulme, C., & Snowling, M. J. (2004). Explicit phoneme training combined with phonic reading instruction helps young children at risk of reading failure. *Journal of Child Psychology and Psychiatry, 45,* 338–359.

Hathaway, W. L., Dooling-Litfin, J. K., & Edwards, G. (2006). Integrating the results of an evaluation. In R. A. Barkley (Ed.), *Attention-deficit hyperactivity disorder. A handbook for diagnosis and treatment.* New York: The Guilford Press.

Hawes, D. J., Dadds, M. R., Frost, A. D. J., & Hasking, P. A. (2011). Do childhood callous-unemotional traits drive changes in parenting practices? *Journal of Clinical Child and Adolescent Psychology, 40,* 507–518.

Hawk, B., & McCall, R. B. (2010). CBCL behavior problems of post-institutional international adoptees. *Clinical Child and Family Psychological Review, 13,* 199–211.

Hawker, D. S. J., & Boulton, M. J. (2000). Twenty years' research on peer victimization and psychosocial maladjustment: A meta-analytic review of cross-sectional studies. *Journal of Child Psychology and Psychiatry, 41,* 441–455.

Hawkins, B. A., Eklund, S. J., James, D. R., & Foose, A. K. (2003). Adaptive behavior and cognitive function of adults with down syndrome: Modeling change with age. *Mental Retardation, 41,* 7–28.

Hawkins, E. H., Cummins, L. H., & Marlatt, G. A. (2004). Preventing substance abuse in American Indians and Alaska Native youths: Promising strategies for healthier communities. *Psychological Bulletin, 130,* 304–323.

Hawton, K., & Fortune, S. (2008). Suicidal behavior and deliberate self-harm. In M. Rutter et al. (Eds.), *Rutter's child and adolescent psychiatry* (5th ed.). Malden, MA: Blackwell Publishing.

Hay, D. F., Pawlby, S., Sharp, D., Schmucker, G., Mills, A., Allen, H., & Kumar, R. (1999). Parents' judgements about young children's problems: Why mothers and fathers might disagree yet still predict later outcomes. *Journal of Child Psychology and Psychiatry, 40,* 1249–1258.

Hay, D. F., Payne, A., & Chadwick, A. (2004). Peer relations in childhood. *Journal of Child Psychology and Psychiatry, 45,* 84–108.

Hayes, G. J. (2003). Institutional review boards: Balancing conflicting values in research. In W. O'Donohue & K. Ferguson (Eds.), *Handbook of professional ethics for psychologists.* Thousand Oaks, CA: Sage Publications.

Hayward, C., Wilson, K. A., Lagle, K., Killen, J. D., & Taylor, C. B. (2004). Parent-reported predictors of adolescent panic attacks. *Journal of the American Academy of Child and Adolescent Psychiatry, 43,* 613–620.

Hayward, C., Wilson, K. A., Lagle, K., Kraemer, H. C., Killen, J. D., & Barr Taylor, C. (2008). The developmental psychopathology of social anxiety in adolescents. *Depression and Anxiety, 25,* 200–206.

Hazlett, H. C., Hammer, J., Hooper, S. R., & Kamphaus, R. W. (2011). Down syndrome. In S. Goldstein & C. R. Reynolds (Eds.), *Handbook of neurodevelopmental and genetic disorders in children.* New York: Guilford Press.

Hazlett, H. C., Poe, M. D., Gerig, G., Styner, M., Chappell, C., Smith, R. G. et al. (2011). Early brain overgrowth in autism associated with an increase in cortical surface area before age 2 years. *Archives of General Psychiatry, 68,* 467–476.

Heaton, P., & Wallace, G. L. (2004). Annotation: The savant syndrome. *Journal of Child Psychology and Psychiatry, 45,* 899–911.

Hechtman, L. (1991). Developmental, neurobiological, and psychosocial aspects of hyperactivity, impulsivity, and inattention. In M. Lewis (Ed.), *Child and adolescent psychiatry: A comprehensive textbook.* Baltimore: Williams & Wilkins.

Hechtman, L. (2005). Attention-deficit disorders. In B. J. Sadock & V. A. Sadock (Eds.), *Comprehensive textbook of psychiatry.* Philadelphia: Lippincott Williams and Wilkens.

Hechtman, L. (2011). Prospective follow-up studies of ADHD: Helping establish a valid diagnosis in adults. *Journal of the American Academy of Child and Adolescent Psychiatry, 50,* 533–535.

Heidgerken, A. D., Merlo, L., Williams, L. B., Lewin, A. B., Gelfand, K., Malasanos, T. et al. (2007). Diabetes responsibility and awareness test: A preliminary analysis of development and psychometrics. *Children's Health Care, 36,* 117–136.

Heilborn, N., & Prinstein, M. J. (2010). Adolescent peer victimization, peer status, suicidal ideation, and nonsuicidal self-injury. *Merrill-Palmer Quarterly, 56,* 388–419.

Heim, S., & Benasich, A. A. (2006). Developmental disorders of language. In D. Cicchetti & D. J. Cohen (Eds.), *Developmental psychopathology: Vol. III. Risk, disorder, and adaptation.* Hoboken, NJ: John Wiley & Sons.

Heinonen, K., Räikkönen, K., Pesonen, A. K., Andersson, S., Kajantie, E., Eriksson, J. G. et al. (2010). Behavioural symptoms of attention deficit/hyperactivity disorder in preterm and term children born small and appropriate for gestational age: A longitudinal study. *BMC Pediatrics, 10,* 91.

Helgeson, V. S., Janicki, D., Lerner, J., & Barbarin, O. (2003). Adjustment to juvenile rheumatoid arthritis: A family systems perspective. *Journal of Pediatric Psychology, 28,* 347–353.

Helgeson, V. S., Reynolds, K. A., Siminerio, L., Escobar, O., & Becker, D. (2008). Parent and adolescent distribution of responsibility for diabetes self care: Links to health outcomes. *Journal of Pediatric Psychology, 33,* 497–508.

Helgeson, V. S., Siminerio, L., Escobar, O., & Becker, D. (2009). Predictors of metabolic control among adolescents with diabetes: A 4-year longitudinal study. *Journal of Pediatric Psychology, 34,* 254–270.

Helgeson, V. S., Snyde, P. R., Seltman, H., Escobar, O., Becker, D., & Siminerio, L. (2010). Trajectories of glycemic control over early to middle adolescence. *Journal of Pediatric Psychology, 35,* 1161–1167.

Helgeson, V. S., Snyder, P. R., Escobar, O., Siminerio, L., & Becker, D. (2007). Comparison of adolescents with and without diabetes on indices of psychosocial functioning for three years. *Journal of Pediatric Psychology, 32,* 794–806.

Hellander, M., Sisson, D. P., & Fristad, M. A. (2003). Internet support for parents of children with early-onset bipolar disorder. In B. Geller & M. P. DelBello (Eds.), *Bipolar disorder in childhood and early adolescence.* New York: Guilford Press.

Heller, K. (1996). Coming of age of prevention science: Comments on the 1994 National Institute of Mental Health–Institute of medicine prevention reports. *American Psychologist, 51,* 1123–1127.

Hendin, H., & Commission on Adolescent Suicide Prevention. (2005a). Defining youth suicide. In D. L. Evans, E. B. Foa, R. E. Gur, H. Hendin, C. P. O'Brien, M. E. P. Seligman, & B. T. Walsh (Eds.), *Treating and preventing adolescent mental health disorders. What we know and what we don't know: A research agenda for improving mental health of our youth.* New York: Oxford University Press.

Hendin, H., & Commission on Adolescent Suicide Prevention. (2005b). Targeted youth suicide prevention programs. In D. L. Evans, E. B. Foa, R. E. Gur, H. Hendin, C. P. O'Brien, M. E. P. Seligman, & B. T. Walsh (Eds.), *Treating and preventing adolescent mental health disorders. What we know and what we don't know: A research agenda for improving mental health of our youth.* New York: Oxford University Press.

Hendin, H., & Commission on Adolescent Suicide Prevention. (2005c). Universal approaches to youth suicide prevention. In D. L. Evans, E. B. Foa, R. E. Gur, H. Hendin, C. P. O'Brien, M. E. P. Seligman, & B. T. Walsh (Eds.), *Treating and preventing adolescent mental health disorders. What we know and what we don't know: A research agenda for improving mental health of our youth.* New York: Oxford University Press.

Henggeler, S. W., Melton, G. B., & Smith, L. A. (1992). Family preservation using multisystemic therapy: An effective alternative to incarcerating serious juvenile offenders. *Journal of Consulting and Clinical Psychology, 60,* 953–961.

Henggeler, S. W., & Schaeffer, C. (2010). Treating serious antisocial behavior using multisystemic therapy. In J. R. Weisz & A. E. Kazdin (Eds.), *Evidence-based psychotherapies for children and adolescents* (2nd ed.). New York: The Guilford Press.

Henggeler, S. W., Schoenwald, S. K., Borduin, C. M., Rowland, M. D., & Cunningham, P. B. (1998). *Multisystemic treatment of antisocial behavior in children and adolescents.* New York: Guilford Press.

Henin, A., & Kendall, P. C. (1997). Obsessive-compulsive disorder in childhood and adolescence. In T. H. Ollendick & R. J. Prinz (Eds.), *Advances in clinical child psychology* (Vol. 19). New York: Plenum Press.

Hetherington, E. M., Bridges, M., Insabella, G. (1998). What matters? What does not? Five perspectives on the association between marital transitions and children's adjustment. *American Psychologist, 53,* 167–184.

Hetherington, E. M., & Kelly, J. (2002). *For better or worse: Divorce reconsidered.* New York: W. W. Norton & Company.

Hetherington, E. M., & Stanley-Hagan, M. (1999). The adjustment of children with divorced parents: A risk and resiliency perspective. *Journal of Child Psychology and Psychiatry, 40,* 129–140.

Hiatt, K. D., & Dishion, T. J. (2008). Antisocial personality development. In T. P. Beauchaine & S. P. Hinshaw (Eds.), *Child and adolescent psychopathology.* Hoboken, NJ: John Wiley & Sons.

Hibbs, E. D., & Jensen, P. S. (2005a). Analyzing the research: What this book is all about. In E. D. Hibbs & P. S. Jensen (Eds.), *Psychosocial treatments for child and adolescent disorders.* Washington, DC: American Psychological Association.

Hibbs, E. D., & Jensen, P. S. (2005b). *Psychosocial treatments for child and adolescent disorders: Empirically based strategies for clinical practice* (2nd ed.). Washington, DC: American Psychological Association.

Hicks, C. L., von Baeyer, C. L., Spafford, P. A., van Korlaar, I., & Goodenough, B. (2001). The Faces Pain Scale-Revised: Toward a common metric in pediatric pain measurement. *Pain, 93,* 173–183.

Higgins, E. L., Raskind, M. H., Goldberg, R. J., & Herman, K. L. (2002). Stages of acceptance of a learning disability: The impact of labeling. *Learning Disability Quarterly, 25,* 3–17.

Hilden, J. M., Emanuel, E. J., Fairclough, D. L., Link, M. P., Foley, K. M., Clarridge, B. C. et al. (2001). Attitudes and practices among pediatric oncologists regarding end-of-life care: Results of the 1998 American Society of Clinical Oncology survey. *Journal of Clinical Oncology, 19,* 205–212.

Hill, C. (2011). Effective treatment of behavioural insomnia in children. *Journal of Child Psychology and Psychiatry, 52,* 731–740.

Hinshaw, S. P. (1998). Is ADHD an impairing condition in childhood and adolescence? Chapter prepared for NIH Consensus Development Conference on Attention-Deficit Hyperactivity Disorder (ADHD): Diagnosis and Treatment. Bethesda, MD.

Hinshaw, S. P. (2001, Winter). Is the inattentive type of ADHD a separate disorder? *Clinical Psychology: Science and Practice, 8,* 498–501.

Hinshaw, S. P. (2002a). Prevention/intervention trials and developmental theory: Commentary on the fast track special section. *Journal of Abnormal Child Psychology, 30,* 53–60.

Hinshaw, S. P. (2002b). Preadolescent girls with attentiondeficit/hyperactivity disorder: I. Background characteristics, comorbidity, cognitive and social functioning, and parenting practices. *Journal of Consulting and Clinical Psychology, 70,* 1086–1098.

Hinshaw, S. P. (2005). The stigmatization of mental illness in children and parents: Developmental issues, family concerns, and research needs. *Journal of Child Psychology and Psychiatry, 46,* 714–734.

Hinshaw, S. P. (2008). Developmental psychopathology as a scientific discipline: Relevance to behavioral and emotional disorders of childhood and adolescence. In T. P. Beauchaine & S. P. Hinshaw (Eds.), *Child and adolescent psychopathology.* Hoboken, NJ: John Wiley & Sons.

Hinshaw, S. P. (2010). Growing up in a family with bipolar disorder: Personal experience, developmental lessons, and overcoming stigma. In D. J. Miklowitz & D. Cicchetti (Eds.), *Understanding bipolar disorder: A developmental psychopathology perspective.* New York: The Guilford Press.

Hinshaw, S. P., Carte, E. T., Sami, N., Treuting, J. J., & Zupan, B. A. (2002). Preadolescent girls with attention-deficit/hyperactivity disorder: II. Neuropsychological performance in relation to subtypes and individual classification. *Journal of Consulting and Clinical Psychology, 70,* 1099–1111.

Hinshaw, S. P., & Erhardt, D. (1993). Behavioral treatment. In V. B. Van Hasselt & M. Hersen (Ed.), *Handbook of behavior therapy and pharmacotherapy for children: A comparative analysis.* Boston, MA: Allyn and Bacon.

Hinshaw, S. P., Lahey, B. B., & Hart, E. L. (1993). Issues of taxonomy and comorbidity in the development of conduct disorder. *Development and Psychopathology, 5,* 31–49.

Hinshaw, S. P., & Lee, S. S. (2003). Conduct and oppositional defiant disorders. In E. J. Mash & R. A. Barkley (Eds.), *Child psychopathology* (2nd ed.). New York: Guilford Press.

Hinshaw, S. P., Owens, E. B., Sami, N., & Fargeon, S. (2006). Prospective follow-up of girls with attention-deficit/hyperactivity disorder into adolescence: Evidence for continuing cross-domain impairment. *Journal of Consulting and Clinical Psychology, 74,* 489–499.

Hinshelwood, J. (1917). *Congenital word-blindness.* London: H. K. Lewis.

Hirshfeld-Becker, D. R. (2010). Familial and temperamental risk factors for social anxiety disorder. In H. Gazelle & K. H. Rubin (Eds.), *Social anxiety in childhood: Bridging developmental and clinical perspectives. New directions for child and adolescent, 127,* 51–65. San Francisco, CA: Jossey-Bass.

Hoagwood, K. E. (2005a). Family-based services in children's mental health: A research review and synthesis. *Journal of Child Psychology and Psychiatry, 46,* 690–713.

Hoagwood, K. E. (2005b). The research, policy, and practice context for delivery of evidence-based mental health treatments for adolescents: A systems perspective. In D. L. Evans, E. B. Foa, R. E. Gur, H. Hendin, C. P. O'Brien, M. E. P. Seligman, & B. T. Walsh (Eds.), *Treating and preventing adolescent mental health disorders. What we know and what we don't know: A research agenda for improving mental health of our youth.* New York: Oxford University Press.

Hoagwood, K. E., & Cavaleri, M. A. (2010). Ethical issues in child and adolescent psychosocial treatment research. In J. R. Weisz & A. E. Kazdin (Eds.), *Evidence-based psychotherapies for children and adolescents.* New York: Guilford Press.

Hoagwood, K. E., Vogel, J. M., Levitt, J. M., D'Amico, P. J., Paisner, W. I., & Kaplan, S. J. (2007). Implementing an evidence-based trauma treatment in a state system after September 11: The CATS Project. *Journal of the American Academy of Child and Adolescent Psychiatry, 46,* 773–779.

Hobbs, T., & Westling, D. L. (1998). Promoting successful inclusion through collaborative problem-solving. *Teaching Exceptional Children, 31,* 12–19.

Hocutt, A. M. (1996). Effectiveness of special education: Is placement the critical factor? *The Future of Children, 6,* 77–102.

Hodapp, R. M., & Dykens, E. M. (2003). Mental retardation (Intellectual disabilities). In E. J. Mash & R. A. Barkley (Eds.), *Child psychopathology.* New York: Guilford Press.

Hodapp, R. M., & Dykens, E. M. (2009). Intellectual disabilities and child psychiatry: Looking to the future. *Journal of Child Psychology and Psychiatry, 50,* 99–107.

Hodapp, R. M., Kazemi, E., Rosner, B. A., & Dykens, E. M. (2006). Mental retardation. In D. A. Wolfe & E. J. Mash (Eds.), *Behavioral and emotional disorders in adolescents.* New York: The Guilford Press.

Hodapp, R. M., Thornton-Wells, T. A., & Dykens, E. M. (2009). Intellectual disabilities. In C. H. Zeanah, Jr. (Ed.), *Handbook of infant mental health.* New York: Guilford Press.

Hodapp, R. M., & Zigler, E. (1997). New issues in the developmental approach to mental retardation. In W. E. MacLean (Ed.), *Ellis' handbook of mental deficiency, psychological theory and research.* Mahwah, NJ: Lawrence Erlbaum.

Hoeft, F., Carter, J. C., Lightbody, A. A., Hazlett, H. C., Piven, J., & Reiss, A. L. (2010). Region-specific alterations in brain development in one-to-three-year-old boys with fragile X syndrome. *Proceedings of the National Academy of Science, 107,* 9335–9339.

Hoffman, J. A., Franko, D. L., Thompson, D. R., Power, D. J., & Stallings, V. A. (2010). Longitudinal behavioral effects of a school-based fruit and vegetable promotion program. *Journal of Pediatric Psychology, 35,* 61–71.

Hogan, D. M. (1998). The psychological development and welfare of children of opiate and cocaine users: Review and research needs. *Journal of Child Psychology and Psychiatry, 39,* 609–620.

Hoge, C. W., & Pavlin, J. A. (2002). Psychological sequelae of September 11. *New England Journal of Medicine, 347,* 443.

Holden, E. W., Deichmann, M. M., & Levy, J. D. (1999). Empirically supported treatment in pediatric psychology: Recurrent pediatric headache. *Journal of Pediatric Psychology, 24,* 91–109.

Hollenbeck, A. M. (2007). From IDEA to implementation: A discussion of foundational and future responsiveness-to-intervention research. *Learning Disabilities Research & Practice, 22,* 137–146.

Hollis, C. (2002). Schizophrenia and allied disorders. In M. Rutter & E. Taylor (Eds.), *Child and adolescent psychiatry.* Oxford, UK: Blackwell Publishing.

Hollis, C. (2008). Schizophrenia and allied disorders. In M. Rutter, D. V. M. Bishop, D. S. Pine, S. Scott, J. Stevenson, E. Taylor et al. (Eds.), *Rutter's child and adolescent psychiatry.* Malden, MA: Blackwell Publishing.

Holmbeck, G. N., Bruno, E. F., & Jandasek, B. (2006). Longitudinal research in pediatric psychology: An introduction to the special issue. *Journal of Pediatric Psychology, 31,* 995–1001.

Holmbeck, G. N., Devine, K. A., & Bruno, E. F. (2010). Developmental issues and considerations in research and practice. In J. R. Weisz & A. E. Kazdin (Eds.), *Evidence-based psychotherapies for children and adolescents.* New York: Guilford Press.

Holmes, C. S., Chen, R., Streisand, R., Marschall, D. E., Souter, S., Swift, E. E., & Peterson, C. C. (2006). Predictors of youth diabetes care behaviors and metabolic control: A structural equation modeling approach. *Journal of Pediatric Psychology, 31,* 770–784.

Honda, H., Shimizu, Y., & Rutter, M. (2005). No effect of MMR withdrawal on the incidence of autism: A total population study. *Journal of Child Psychology and Psychiatry, 46,* 572–579.

Honey, E., McConachie, H., Randle, V., Shearer, H., & Le Couteur, A. S. (2008). One-year change in repetitive behaviours in young children with communication disorders including autism. *Journal of Autism and Developmental Disorders, 38,* 1439–1450.

Hoover, H. D., Dunbar, S. B., & Frisbie, D. A. (2001). *The Iowa tests of basic skills, Form A.* Itasca, IL: Riverside Publishing.

Hops, H., Andrews, J. A., Duncan, S. C., Duncan, T. E., & Tildesley, E. (2000). Adolescent drug use development: A social interactional and contextual perspective. In A. J. Sameroff, M. Lewis, & S. M. Miller (Eds.), *Handbook of developmental psychopathology* (2nd ed.). New York: Kluwer Academic/Plenum Publishers.

Hops, H., Biglan, A., Sherman, L., Arthur, J., Friedman, L., & Osteen, V. (1987). Home observations of family interactions of depressed women. *Journal of Consulting and Clinical Psychology, 55,* 341–346.

Hops, H., Davis, B., & Longoria, N. (1995). Methodological issues in direct observation: Illustrations with the Living in Familial Environments (LIFE) coding system. *Journal of Clinical Child Psychology, 24,* 193–203.

Horowitz, F. D. (1992). John B. Watson's legacy: Learning and environment. *Developmental Psychology, 28,* 360–367.

Horsley, T. A., de Castro, B. O., & Van der Schoot, M. (2010). In the eye of the beholder: Eye-tracking assessment of social information processing in aggressive behavior. *Journal of Abnormal Child Psychology, 38,* 587–599.

Houts, A. C. (2002). Discovery, invention, and the expansion of the modern diagnostic and statistical manual of mental disorders. In L. E. Beutler & M. L. Malik (Eds.), *Rethinking the DSM.* Washington, DC: American Psychological Association.

Houts, A. C. (2010). Behavioral treatment for enuresis. In J. R. Weisz & A. E. Kazdin (Eds.), *Evidence-based psychotherapies for children and adolescents* (2nd ed.). New York: The Guilford Press.

Houts, A. C., Peterson, J. K., & Whelan, J. P. (1986). Prevention of relapse in full-spectrum home training for primary enuresis: A component analysis. *Behavior Therapy, 17,* 462–469.

Hoven, C. W., Duarte, C. S., Wu, P., Doan, T., Singh, N., Mandell, D. J. et al. (2009). Parental exposure to mass violence and child mental health: The first responder and WTC evacuee study. *Clinical Child and Family Psychology Review, 12,* 95–112.

Howard, J., & Berzin, S. (2011). *Never too late: Achieving permanency and sustaining connections for older youth in foster care.* New York: Evan B. Donaldson Adoption Institute.

Howes, O. D., & Kapur, S. (2009). The dopamine hypothesis of schizophrenia: Version II-the final common pathway. *Schizophrenia Bulletin, 35,* 549–562.

Howlander, N., Noone, A. M., Krapcho, M., Neyman, N., Aminou, R., Waldron, W. et al. (Eds.) (2011). *SEER cancer statistics review, 1975–2008.* National Cancer Institute. Bethesda, MD. http://seer.cancer.gov/csr/1975-2008/ based on November 2010 SEER data submission, posted by the SEER web site, 2011.

Howlin, P. (1994). Special education treatment. In M. Rutter, E. Taylor, & L. Hersov (Eds.), *Child and adolescent psychiatry: Modern approaches.* Cambridge, MA: Blackwell Scientific.

Howlin, P., Goode, S., Hutton, J., & Rutter, M. (2004). Adult outcome for children with autism. *Journal of Child Psychology and Psychiatry, 45,* 212–229.

Hoza, B., Murray-Close, D., Arnold, L. E., Hinshaw, S. P., Hechtman, L., & the MTA Cooperative Group. (2010). Time-dependent changes in positively biased self-perceptions of children with attention-deficit/hyperactivity disorder: A developmental psychopathology perspective. *Development and Psychopathology, 22,* 375–390.

Huang, L., Stroul, B., Friedman, R., Mrazek, P., Friesen, B., Pires, S., & Mayberg, S. (2005). Transforming mental health care for children and their families. *American Psychologist, 60,* 615–627.

Huang-Pollock, C. L., Nigg, J. T., & Carr, T. H. (2005). Deficient attention is hard to find: Applying the perceptual load model of selective attention to attention deficit hyperactivity disorder. *Journal of Child Psychology and Psychiatry, 46,* 1211–1218.

Hubbard, J., Realmuto, G. M., Northwood, A. K., & Masten, A. S. (1995). Comorbidity of psychiatric diagnosis with posttraumatic stress disorder in survivors of childhood trauma. *Journal of the American Academy of Child and Adolescent Psychiatry, 34,* 1167–1173.

Hudson, J. L., Comer, J. S., & Kendall, P. C. (2008). Parental responses to positive and negative emotions in anxious and non anxious children. *Journal of Clinical Child and Adolescent Psychology, 37,* 303–313.

Hudson, J. L., Doyle, A. M., & Gar, N. (2009). Child and maternal influence on parenting behavior in clinically anxious children. *Journal of Clinical Child and Adolescent Psychology, 38,* 256–262.

Hudson, J. L., & Rapee, M. (2002). Parent-child interactions in clinically anxious children and their siblings. *Journal of Clinical Child and Adolescent Psychology, 31,* 548–555.

Hudziak, J. J., Achenbach. T. M., Althoff, R. R., & Pine, D. (2007). A dimensional approach to developmental psychopathology. *International Journal of Methods in Psychiatric Research, 16(S1),* S16–S23.

Hudziak, J. J., Derks, E. M., Althoff, R. R., Rettew, D. C., & Boomsma, D. I. (2005). The genetic and environmental contributions to attention deficit-hyperactivity disorder as measured by the Conners' Rating Scales—Revised. *American Journal of Psychiatry, 162,* 1614–1620.

Hudziak, J. J., Heath, A. C., Madden, P. F., Reich, W., Bucholz, K. K., Slutske, W., Bierut, L. J., Neuman, R. J., & Todd, R. D. (1998). Latent class and factor analysis of DSM-IV ADHD: A twin study of female adolescents. *Journal of the American Academy of Child and Adolescent Psychiatry, 37,* 848–857.

Huesmann, L. R., Eron, L. D., Lefkowitz, M. M., & Walder, L. O. (1984). Stability of aggression over time and generations. *Developmental Psychology, 20,* 1120–1134.

Huey, S. J., & Polio, A. J. (2010). Assessing the effects of evidence-based psychotherapies on ethnic minority youths. In J. R. Weiss & A. E. Kazdin (Eds.), *Evidence-based psychotherapies for children and adolescents* (2nd ed.). New York: The Guilford Press.

Hughes, C. (1999). Identifying critical social interaction behaviors among high school students with and without disabilities. *Behavior Modification, 23,* 41–60.

Hulme, C., & Snowling, M. J. (2009). *Developmental disorders of language learning and cognition.* Malden, MA: Wiley-Blackwell.

Humphreys, L., Forehand, R., McMahon, R., & Roberts, M. (1978). Parent behavioral training to modify child noncompliance: Effects on untreated siblings. *Journal of Behavior Therapy and Experimental Psychiatry, 9,* 235–238.

Hunsley, J., & Mash, E. J. (2011). Evidence-based assessment. In D. H. Barlow (Ed.), *The Oxford handbook of clinical psychology.* New York: Oxford University Press.

Hurley, A. D. (2005). Psychotherapy is an essential tool in the treatment of psychiatric disorders for people with mental retardation. *Mental Retardation, 43,* 445–448.

Hussong, A. M., Bauer, D. J., & Chassin, L. (2008). Telescoped trajectories from alcohol initiation to disorder in children of alcoholic parents. *Journal of Abnormal Psychology, 117,* 63–78.

Hutchings, J., Gardner, F., Bywater, T., Daley, D., Whitaker, C., Jones, K. et al. (2007). Parenting intervention in Sure Start services for children at risk of developing conduct disorder: Pragmatic randomized control trial. *British Medical Journal, 334,* 1–7.

Hynd, G. W., Marshall, R., & Gonzalez, J. (1991). Learning disabilities and presumed central nervous system dysfunction. *Learning Disability Quarterly, 14,* 283–296.

Hynd, G. W., & Semrud-Clikeman, M. (1989a). Dyslexia and brain morphology. *Psychological Bulletin, 106,* 447–482.

Hynd, G. W., & Semrud-Clikeman, M. (1989b). Dyslexia and neurodevelopmental pathology: Relationships to cognition, intelligence, and reading skill acquisition. *Journal of Learning Disabilities, 22,* 205–218.

Hysing, M., Elgen, I., Gillbert, C., Lie, S. A., & Lundervold, A. J. (2007). Chronic physical illness and mental health in children. Results from a large-scale population study. *Journal of Child Psychology and Psychiatry, 48,* 785–792.

Iannotti, R. J., & Bush, P. J. (1993). Toward a developmental theory of compliance. In N. A. Krasnegor, L. Epstein, S. B. Johnson, & S. Yaffe (Eds.), *Developmental aspects of health compliance behavior.* Hillsdale, NJ: Lawrence Erlbaum Associates.

Ievers, C. E., Brown, R. T., Drotar, D., Caplan, D., Pishevar, B. S., & Lambert, R. G. (1999). Knowledge of physician prescriptions and adherence to treatment among children with cystic fibrosis and their mothers. *Journal of Developmental and Behavioral Pediatrics, 20,* 335–343.

Iglesias-Sarmiento, V., & Deaño, M. (2011). Cognitive processing and mathematical achievement. A study with schoolchildren between fourth and sixth grade of primary education. *Journal of Learning Disabilities, 44,* 570–583.

Ingoldsby, E., & Shaw, D. S. (2002). Neighborhood contextual factors and the onset and progression of early-starting antisocial pathways. *Clinical Child and Family Psychology Review, 5,* 21–55.

Ingram, R. E., & Price, J. M. (2010). Understanding psychopathology. The role of vulnerability. In R. E. Ingram & J. M. Price (Eds.), *Vulnerability to psychopathology. Risk across the lifespan.* New York: Guilford Press.

Inkelas, M., Garro, N., McQuaid, E. L., & Ortega, A. N. (2008). Race/ethnicity, language, and asthma care: Findings from a 4-state survey. *Annals of Allergy and Immunology, 100,* 120–127.

Institute of Medicine. 2004. *Immunization Safety Review: Vaccines and Autism (2004). A report of the Institute of Medicine.* Washington, DC: National Academies Press.

Israel, A. C. (1988). Parental and family influences in the etiology and treatment of childhood obesity. In N. A. Krasnegor, G. D. Grave, & N. Kretchmer (Eds.), *Childhood obesity: A biobehavioral perspective.* Caldwell, NJ: The Telford Press.

Israel, A. C. (1990). Childhood obesity. In A. S. Bellack, M. Hersen, & A. E. Kazdin (Eds.), *International handbook of behavior modification and therapy.* New York: Plenum.

Israel, A. C. (1999). Commentary: Empirically supported treatments for pediatric obesity: Goals, outcome criteria, and the societal context. *Journal of Pediatric Psychology, 24,* 249–250.

Israel, A. C., Guile, C. A., Baker, J. E., & Silverman, W. K. (1994). An evaluation of enhanced self-regulation training in the treatment of childhood obesity. *Journal of Pediatric Psychology, 19,* 737–749.

Israel, A. C., & Ivanova, M.Y. (2002). Global and dimensional selfesteem in preadolescent and early adolescent children who are overweight: Age and gender differences. *International Journal of Eating Disorders, 31,* 424–429.

Israel, A. C., Pravder, M. D., & Knights, S. (1980). A peeradministered program for changing the classroom behavior of disruptive children. *Behavioural Analysis and Modification, 4,* 224–238.

Israel, A. C., Roderick, H. A., & Ivanova, M.Y. (2002). A measure of the stability of family activities in a family environment. *Journal of Psychopathology and Behavioral Assessment, 24,* 85–95.

Israel, A. C., & Shapiro, L. S. (1985). Behavior problems of obese children enrolling in a weight reduction program. *Journal of Pediatric Psychology, 10*, 449–460.

Israel, A. C., Silverman, W. K., & Solotar, L. C. (1986). An investigation of family influences on initial weight status, attrition, and treatment outcome in a childhood obesity program. *Behavior Therapy, 17*, 131–143.

Israel, A. C., & Solotar, L. C. (1988). Obesity. In M. Hersen & C. G. Last (Eds.), *Child behavior therapy casebook*. New York: Plenum.

Israel, A. C., Stolmaker, L., & Andrian, C. A. G. (1985). The effects of training parents in general child management skills in a behavioral weight loss program for children. *Behavior Therapy, 16*, 169–180.

Israel, A. C., & Zimand, E. (1989). Obesity. In M. Hersen (Ed.), *Innovations in child behavior therapy*. New York: Springer.

Ivanova, M. Y., Achenbach, T. M., Dumenci, L., Rescorla, L. A., Almqvist, F., Weintraub, S. et al. (2007a). Testing the 8-syndrome structure of the CBCL in 30 societies. *Journal of Clinical Child and Adolescent Psychology, 36*, 405–417.

Ivanova, M. Y., Achenbach, T. M., Rescorla, L. A., Dumenci, L., Almqvist, F., Bathiche, M. et al. (2007b). The generalizability of teacher's report form syndromes in 20 cultures. *School Psychology Review 36*, 468–483.

Ivanova, M. Y., Achenbach, T. M., Rescorla, L. A., Harder, V. S., Ang, R. P., Bilenbert, N. et al. (2010). Preschool psychopathology reported by parents in 23 societies: Testing the seven-syndrome model of the child behavior checklist for ages 1.5–5. *Journal of the American Academy of Child and Adolescent Psychiatry, 49*, 1215–1224.

Ivanova, M. Y., & Israel, A. C. (2006). Family stability as a protective factor against psychopathology for urban children receiving psychological services. *Journal of Clinical Child and Adolescent Psychology, 35*, 564–570.

Izard, C. E., Fine, S., Mostow, A., Trentacosta, C., & Campbell, J. (2002). Emotion processes in normal and abnormal development and prevention intervention. *Development and Psychopathology, 14*, 761–787.

Izard, C. E., Youngstrom, E. A., Fine, S. E., & Mostow, A. (2006). Emotions and developmental psychopathology. In D. Cicchetti & D. J. Cohen (Eds.), *Developmental psychopathology, Vol. 1. Theory and method*. Hoboken, NJ: John Wiley & Sons.

Jaaniste, T., Hayes, B., & von Baeyer, C. L. (2007). Providing children with information about forthcoming medical procedures: A review and synthesis. *Clinical Psychology: Science and Practice, 14*, 124–143.

Jacob, R. G., & Pelham, W. H. (2000). Behavior therapy. In B. J. Sadock & V. A. Sadock (Eds.), *Kaplan & Sadock's Comprehensive textbook of psychiatry* (Vol. II). Philadelphia: Lippincott Williams & Wilkins.

Jacobi, C., Hayward, C., de Zwaan, M., Kraemer, H. C., & Agras, W. S. (2004). Coming to terms with risk factors for eating disorders: Application of risk terminology and suggestions for a general taxonomy. *Psychological Bulletin, 130*, 19–65.

Jacobson, C. M., Muehlenkamp, J. J., Miller, A. L., & Turner, E. B. (2008). Psychiatric impairment among adolescents engaging in different types of deliberate self-harm. *Journal of Clinical Child and Adolescent Psychology, 37*, 363–375.

Jacobson, C. M., & Mufson, L. (2010). Treating adolescent depression using interpersonal psychotherapy. In J. R. Weisz & A. E. Kazdin (Eds.), *Evidence-based psychotherapies for children and adolescents* (2nd ed.). New York: The Guilford Press.

Jaffee, P. G., Poisson, S. E., & Cunningham, A. (2001). Domestic violence and high-conflict divorce: Developing a new generation of research for children. In S. A. Graham-Bermann & J. L. Edleson (Eds.), *Domestic violence in the lives of children: The future of research, intervention, and social policy*. Washington, DC: American Psychological Association.

Jaffee, S. R., Caspi, A., Moffitt, T. E., Dodge, K., Rutter, M., Taylor, A. et al. (2005). Nature x nurture: Genetic vulnerabilities interact with physical maltreatment to promote conduct problems. *Development and Psychopathology, 17*, 67–84.

Jaffee, S. R., Caspi, A., Moffitt, T. E., Polo-Tomás, M., & Taylor, A. (2007). Individual, family, and neighborhood factors distinguish resilient from non-resilient maltreated children: A cumulative stressors model. *Child Abuse & Neglect, 31*, 231–253.

Jaffee, S. R., Caspi, A., Moffitt, T. E., & Taylor, A. (2004). Physical maltreatment victim to antisocial child: Evidence of an environmentally mediated process. *Journal of Abnormal Psychology, 113*, 44–55.

Jaffee, S. R., Moffitt, T. E., Caspi, A., & Taylor, A. (2003). Life with (or without) father: The benefits of living with two biological parents depend on the father's antisocial behavior. *Child Development, 74*, 109–126.

James, S. J., Melnyk, S., Jernigan, S., Hubanks, A., Rose, S., & Gaylor, D. W. (2008). Abnormal transmethylation/transsulfuration metabolism and DNA hypomethylation among parents of children with autism. *Journal of Autism and Developmental Disorders, 38*, 1966–1975.

Jarrett, M. A., & Ollendick, T. H. (2008). A conceptual review of the comorbidity of attention-deficit/hyperactivity disorder and anxiety: Implications for future research and practice. *Clinical Psychology Review, 28*, 1266–1280.

Javdani, S., Sadeh, N., & Verona, E. (2011). Expanding our lens: Female pathways to antisocial behavior in adolescence and adulthood. *Clinical Psychology Review, 31*, 1324–1348.

Jay, S. M. (1988). Invasive medical procedures: Psychological intervention and assessment. In D. K. Routh (Ed.), *Handbook of pediatric psychology*. New York: Guilford.

Jay, S. M., Elliott, C. H., Fitzgibbons, I., Woody, P., & Siegel, S. (1995). A comparative study of cognitive behavioral therapy versus general anesthesia for painful medical procedures in children. *Pain, 62*, 3–9.

Jay, S. M., Elliot, C. H., Katz, E., & Siegel, S. E. (1987). Cognitive behavioral and pharmacologic intervention for children's distress during painful medical procedures. *Journal of Consulting and Clinical Psychology, 55,* 860–865.

Jay, S. M., Elliot, C. H., Ozolins, M., Olson, R., & Pruitt, S. (1985). Behavioral management of children's distress during painful medical procedures. *Behavior Research and Therapy, 23,* 513–520.

Jay, S. M., Elliot, C. H., Woody, P. D., & Siegel, S. (1991). An investigation of cognitive-behavioral therapy combined with oral valium for children undergoing painful medical procedures. *Health Psychology, 10,* 317–322.

Jelalian, E., & Hart, C. N. (2009). Pediatric obesity. In M. C. Roberts & R. G. Steele (Eds.), *Handbook of pediatric psychology* (4th ed.). New York: The Guilford Press.

Jelalian, E., Wember, Y. M., Bungeroth, H., & Birmaher, V. (2007). Bridging the gap between research and clinical practice in pediatric obesity. *Journal of Child Psychology and Psychiatry, 48,* 115–127.

Jensen, C. D., & Steele, R. G. (2012). Longitudinal associations between teasing and health-related quality of life among treatment-seeking overweight and obese youth. *Journal of Pediatric Psychology, 37,* 438–447.

Jensen, P. S., Arnold, L. E., Swanson, J. M., Vitiello, B., Abikoff, H. B., Greenhill, L. L. et al. (2007). 3-year follow-up of the NIMH MTA study. *Journal of the American Academy of Child and Adolescent Psychiatry, 46,* 989–1002.

Jensen, P. S., Martin, B. A., & Cantwell, D. P. (1997). Co-morbidity in ADHD: Implications for research, practice, and DSM-IV. *Journal of the Academy of Child and Adolescent Psychiatry, 36,* 1065–1075.

Jensen, P. S., & Mrazek, D. A. (2006). Research and clinical perspectives in defining and assessing mental disorders in children and adolescents. In P. S. Jensen, P. Knapp, & D. A. Mrazek (Eds.), *Toward a new diagnostic system for child psychopathology.* Moving beyond the DSM. New York: The Guilford Press.

Jensen, P. S., & Shaw, J. (1993). Children as victims of war: Current knowledge and future research needs. *Journal of the American Academy of Child and Adolescent Psychiatry, 32,* 697–708.

Jersild, A. T., & Holmes, F. B. (1935). Children's fears. Child Development Monograph, No. 20.

Jessor, R., & Jessor, S. L. (1977). *Problem behavior and psychosocial development.* New York: Academic Press.

Jockin, V., McGue, M., & Lykken, D. T. (1996). Personality and divorce: A genetic analysis. *Journal of Personality and Social Psychology, 71,* 288–299.

Johnson, C. J., & Beitchman, J. H. (2005a). Expressive language disorder. In B. J. Sadock & V. A. Sadock (Eds.), *Comprehensive textbook of psychiatry.* Philadelphia: Lippincott Williams and Wilkens.

Johnson, C. J., & Beitchman, J. H. (2005b). Mixed receptiveexpressive disorder. In B. J. Sadock & V. A. Sadock (Eds.), *Comprehensive textbook of psychiatry* (Vol. II). Philadelphia: Lippincott Williams and Wilkens.

Johnson, C. J., & Beitchman, J. H. (2005c). Phonological disorder. In B. J. Sadock & V. A. Sadock (Eds.), *Comprehensive textbook of psychiatry.* Philadelphia: Lippincott Williams and Wilkens.

Johnson, C. P., Myers, S. M., & the Council on Children with Disabilities. (2007). Identification and evaluation of children with autism spectrum disorders. Retrieved October 29, 2007 from http://www.aap.org

Johnson, J. H., Rasbury, W. C., & Siegel, L. J. (1997). *Approaches to child treatment: Introduction to theory, research, and practice* (2nd ed.). Boston, MA: Allyn and Bacon.

Johnson, S., Hollis, C., Kochhar, P., Hennessy, E., Wolke, D., & Marlow, N. (2011). Psychiatric disorders in extremely preterm infants: Longitudinal finding at age 11 years in the EPICure Study. *Journal of the American Academy of Child and Adolescent Psychiatry, 49,* 453–463.

Johnson, S. B. (1995). Managing insulin-dependent diabetes mellitus in adolescence: A developmental perspective. In J. Wallander & L. Siegel (Eds.), *Adolescent health problems: Behavioral perspectives.* New York: Guilford Press.

Johnson, S. B. (1998). Juvenile diabetes. In T. H. Ollendick & M. Hersen (Eds.), *Handbook of child psychopathology* (3rd ed.). New York: Plenum Press.

Johnson, W., Bouchard, T. J., Krueger, R. F., McGue, M., & Gottesman, I. I. (2004). Just one *g*: Consistent results from three test batteries. *Intelligence, 32,* 95–107.

Johnston, C., & Mash, E. J. (2001). Families of children with attention deficit/hyperactivity disorder: Review and recommendations for future research. *Clinical Child and Family Psychology Review, 4,* 183–207.

Johnston, C., & Ohan, J. L. (1999). Externalizing disorders. In W. K. Silverman & T. H. Ollendick (Eds.), *Developmental issues in the clinical treatment of children.* Boston, MA: Allyn and Bacon.

Johnston, L. D., O'Malley, P. M., Bachman, J. G., Schulenberg, J. E. (2011). *Monitoring the future: National results on adolescent drug use: Overview of key findings, 2010.* Ann Arbor, MI: Institute for Social Research, The University of Michigan.

Joiner, T. E. (2000). A test of hopelessness theory of depression in youth psychiatric inpatients. *Journal of Clinical Child Psychology, 29,* 167–176.

Joinson, C., Heron, J., Emond, A., & Butler, R. (2007). Psychological problems in children with bedwetting and combined (day and night) wetting: A UK population-based study. *Journal of Pediatric Psychology, 32,* 605–616.

Jones, A. P., & Frederickson, N. (2010). Multi-informant predictors of social inclusion for students with autism spectrum disorders attending mainstream school. *Journal of Autism and Developmental Disorders, 40,* 1094–1103.

Jones, M. C. (1924). A laboratory study of fear: The case of Peter. *Pedagogical Seminary, 31,* 308–315.

Jopp, D. A., & Keys, C. B. (2001). Diagnostic overshadowing reviewed and reconsidered. *American Journal on Mental Retardation, 106,* 416–433.

Joseph, R. M., Tager-Flüsberg, H., & Lord, C. (2002). Cognitive profiles and social-communicative functioning in children with autism spectrum disorder. *Journal of Child Psychology and Psychiatry, 43*, 807–821.

Jouriles, E. N., Murphy, C. M., & O'Leary, K. D. (1989). Interspousal aggression, marital discord, and child problems. *Journal of Consulting and Clinical Psychology, 57*, 453–455.

Juffer, F., Bakermans-Kranenburg, M. J., & van IJzendoorn, M. H. (2005). The importance of parenting in the development of disorganized attachment: Evidence from a preventive intervention study in adoptive families. *Journal of Child and Adolescent Psychology, 46*, 263–274.

Jurbergs, N., Long, A., Ticona, L., & Phipps, S. (2009). Symptoms of posttraumatic stress in parents of children with cancer: Are they elevated relative to parents of healthy children? *Journal of Pediatric Psychology, 34*, 4–13.

Kagan, J. (1997). Temperament and the reactions to unfamiliarity. *Child Development, 68*, 139–143.

Kagan, J., Reznick, J. S., & Snidman, N. (1990). The temperamental qualities of inhibition and lack of inhibition. In M. Lewis & S. M. Miller (Eds.), *Handbook of developmental psychopathology*. New York: Plenum Press.

Kahn, R. E., Frick, P. J., Youngstrom, E., Findling, R. L., & Youngstrom, J. K. (2012). The effects of including a callous-unemotional specifier for the diagnosis of conduct disorder. *Journal of Child Psychology and Psychiatry, 53*, 271–282.

Kalb, L. G., Law, J. K., Landa, R., & Law, P. A. (2010). Onset patterns prior to 36 months in autism spectrum disorders. *Journal of Autism and Developmental Disorders, 40*, 1389–1402.

Kalff, A. C., de Sonneville, L. M. J., Hurks. P. P. M., Hendriksen, J. G. M., Kroes, M., Feron, F. J. M. et al. (2003). Low- and highlevel controlled processing in executive motor control tasks in 5–6-year-old children at risk for ADHD. *Journal of Child Psychology and Psychiatry, 44*, 1049–1057.

Kamin, L. J. (1974). *The science and politics of IQ*. Potomac, MD: Erlbaum.

Kamon, J., Tolan, P. H., & Gorman-Smith, D. (2006). Interventions for adolescent psychopathology. In D. A. Wolfe & E. J. Mash (Eds.), *Behavioral and emotional disorders in adolescents*. New York: The Guilford Press.

Kamphaus, R. W. (1993). *Clinical assessment of children's intelligence*. Boston, MA: Allyn & Bacon.

Kamphaus, R.W., & Frick, P. J. (1996). *Clinical assessment of child and adolescent personality and behavior*. Boston, MA: Allyn and Bacon.

Kanaya, T., & Ceci, S. J. (2007). Are all IQ scores created equal? The differential costs of IQ cutoff scores for at-risk children. *Child Development Perspectives, 1*, 52–56.

Kanaya, T., Scullin, M. H., & Ceci, S. J. (2003). The Flynn effect and U.S. policies. *American Psychologist, 58*, 778–790.

Kanne, S. M., Gerber, A. J., Qirmbach, L. M., Sparrow, S. S., Cicchetti, D. V., & Saulnier, C. A. (2010). The role of adaptive behavior in autism spectrum disorders: Implications for functional outcome. *Journal of Autism and Developmental Disorders*, November 2. DOI: 10.1007/s10803-010-1126-4.

Kanner, L. (1943). Autistic disturbances of affective contact. *Nervous Child, 2*, 217–250.

Kanner, L. (1973). *Childhood psychoses: Initial studies and new insights*. Washington, DC: V. H. Winston & Sons.

Kanner, L., & Eisenberg, L. (1956). Early infantile autism, 1943–1955. *American Journal of Orthopsychiatry, 26*, 55–65.

Kaplan, A. S., & Hewlett, A. (2010). Pharmacotherapy for anorexia nervosa. In C. M. Grilo & J. E. Mitchell (Eds.), *The treatment of eating disorders: A clinical handbook*. New York: The Guilford Press.

Kaplan, R. M. (1985). The controversy related to the use of psychological tests. In B. Wolman (Ed.), *Handbook of intelligence*. New York: Wiley.

Karmiloff-Smith, A., & Thomas, M. (2003). What can developmental disorders tell us about the neurocomputational constraints that shape development? The case of Williams syndrome. *Development and Psychopathology, 15*, 969–990.

Kasari, C., Locke, J., Gulsrud, A., & Rotheram-Fuller, E. (2011). Social networks and friendships at school: Comparing children with and without ASD. *Journal of Autism and Developmental Disorders, 41*, 533–544.

Kashani, J. H., Daniel, A. E., Dandoy, A. C., & Holcomb, W. R. (1992). Family violence: Impact on children. *Journal of the American Academy of Child and Adolescent Psychiatry, 31*, 181–189.

Kashani, J. H., & Orvaschel, H. (1990). A community study of anxiety in children and adolescents. *American Journal of Psychiatry, 147*, 313–318.

Kaslow, N. J., Adamson, L. B., & Collins, M. H. (2000). A developmental psychopathology perspective on the cognitive components of child and adolescent depression. In A. J. Sameroff, M. Lewis, & S. M. Miller (Eds.), *Handbook of developmental psychopathology* (2nd ed.). New York: Kluwer Academic/Plenum Publishers.

Kaslow, N. J., & Racusin, G. R. (1990). Childhood depression: Current status and future directions. In A. S. Bellack, M. Hersen, & A. E. Kazdin (Eds.), *International handbook of behavior modification and therapy* (2nd ed.). New York: Plenum.

Kataoka, S., Stein, B. D., Nadeem, E., & Wong, M. (2007). Who gets care? Mental health service use following a school-based suicide prevention program. *Journal of the American Academy of Child and Adolescent Psychiatry, 46*, 1341–1348.

Katz, L. J., & Slomka, G. T. (1990). Achievement testing. In G. Goldstein & M. Hersen (Eds.), *Handbook of psychological assessment* (2nd ed.). New York: Pergamon.

Katzman, D. K. (2005). Medical complications in adolescents with anorexia nervosa: A review of the literature. *International Journal of Eating Disorders, 37 (Suppl.)*, 52–59.

Kauffman, J. M., McGee, K., & Brigham, M. (2004). Enabling or disabling? Observations on changes in special education. *Phi Delta Kappan, 85,* 613–620.

Kaufman, A. S., & Kaufman, N. L. (2004). *Administration and scoring material for the Kaufman assessment battery for children, Second Edition (KABC-II).* Circle Pines, MN: American Guidance Service.

Kaufman, J., Blumberg, H., & Young, C. S. (2004). The neurobiology of early-onset mood disorders. In D. S. Charney & E. J. Nestler (Eds.), *Neurobiology of mental illness* (2nd ed.). New York: Oxford University Press.

Kaufman, J., & Zigler, E. (1987). Do abused children become abusive parents? *American Journal of Orthopsychiatry, 57,* 186–192.

Kaugars, A. S., Klinnert, M. D., & Bender, B. G. (2004). Family influences on pediatric asthma. *Journal of Pediatric Psychology, 29,* 475–491.

Kaye, W. H., Bulik, C. M., Plotnicov, K., Thorton, L., Devlin, B., Fichter, M. M. et al. (2008). The genetics of anorexia nervosa collaborative study: Methods and sample description. *International Journal of Eating Disorders, 41,* 289–300.

Kaye, W. H., Devlin, B., Barbarich, N., Bulik, C. M., Thornton, L., Bacanu, S. A. et al. (2004). Genetic analysis of bulimia nervosa: Methods and sample description. *International Journal of Eating Disorders, 35,* 556–570.

Kazak, A. E. (2005). Evidence-based interventions for survivors of childhood cancer and their families. *Journal of Pediatric Psychology, 30,* 29–39.

Kazak, A. E., Hoagwood, K., Weisz, J. R., Hood, K., Kratochwill, T. R., Vargas, L. A. et al. (2010). A meta-systems approach to evidence-based practice for children and adolescents. *American Psychologist, 65,* 85–97.

Kazak, A. E., Kassam-Adams, N., Schneider, S., Zelikovsky, N., Alderfer, M. A., & Rourke, M. (2006). An integrative model for pediatric medical traumatic stress. *Journal of Pediatric Psychology, 31,* 343–355.

Kazdin, A. E. (1985). *Treatment of antisocial behavior in children and adolescents.* Homewood, IL: Dorsey.

Kazdin, A. E. (1989). Identifying depression in children: A comparison of alternative selection criteria. *Journal of Abnormal Child Psychology, 17,* 437–454.

Kazdin, A. E. (1994). Informant variability in the assessment of childhood depression. In W. M. Reynolds and H. F. Johnston (Eds.), *Handbook of depression in children and adolescents.* New York: Plenum Press.

Kazdin, A. E. (1997). Practitioner review: Psychosocial treatments for conduct disorder in children. *Journal of Child Psychology and Psychiatry, 38,* 161–178.

Kazdin, A. E. (1998). Drawing valid inferences from case studies. In A. E. Kazdin (Ed.), *Methodological issues and strategies in clinical research.* Washington, DC: American Psychological Association.

Kazdin, A. E. (2005a). Child, parent, and family-based treatment of aggressive and antisocial child behavior. In E. D. Hibbs & P. S. Jensen (Eds.), *Psychosocial treatments for child and adolescent disorders: Empirically based strategies for clinical practice* (2nd ed.). Washington, DC: American Psychological Association.

Kazdin, A. E. (2005b). Evidence-based assessment for children and adolescents: Issues in measurement development and clinical application. *Journal of Clinical Child and Adolescent Psychology, 34,* 548–558.

Kazdin, A. E. (2010). Problem-solving skills training and parent management training for oppositional defiant disorder and conduct disorder. In J. R. Weisz & A. E. Kazdin (Eds.), *Evidence-based psychotherapies for children and adolescents* (2nd ed.). New York: The Guilford Press.

Kazdin, A. E. (2011a). *Single-case research designs methods for clinical and applied settings.* New York: Oxford University Press.

Kazdin, A. E. (2011b). Evidence-based treatment research: Advances, limitations, and next steps. *American Psychologist, 66,* 685–698.

Kazdin, A. E., & Kolko, D. J. (1986). Parent psychopathology and family functioning among childhood firesetters. *Journal of Abnormal Child Psychology, 14,* 315–329.

Kazdin, A. E., Rodgers, A., & Colbus, D. (1986). The hopelessness scale for children: Psychometric characteristics and concurrent validity. *Journal of Consulting and Clinical Psychology, 54,* 241–245.

Kazdin, A. E., Whitley, M., & Marciano, P. L. (2006). Child–therapist and parent–therapist alliance and therapeutic change in the treatment of children referred for oppositional, aggressive, and antisocial behavior. *Journal of Child Psychology and Psychiatry, 47,* 436–445.

Kearney, C. A. (2008). School absenteeism and school refusal behavior in youth: A contemporary review. *Clinical Psychology Review, 28,* 451–471.

Kearney, C. A., Albano, A. M., Eisen, A. R., Allan, W. D., & Barlow, D. H. (1997). The phenomenology of panic disorder in youngsters: An empirical study of a clinical sample. *Journal of Anxiety Disorders, 11,* 49–62.

Kearney, C. A., Eisen, A., & Silverman, W. K. (1995). The legend and myth of school phobia. *School Psychology Quarterly, 10,* 65–85.

Kearney, C. A., & Silverman, W. K. (1992). Let's not push the "panic button": A critical analysis of panic and panic disorder in adolescents. *Clinical Psychology Review, 12,* 293–305.

Kearney, C. A., Sims, K. E., Prusell, C. R., & Tillotson, C. A. (2003). Separation anxiety disorder in young children: A longitudinal and family analysis. *Journal of Clinical Child and Adolescent Psychology, 32,* 593–598.

Kearney, C. A., Wechsler, A., Kaur, H., & Lemos-Miller, A. (2010). Posttraumatic stress disorder in maltreated youth: A review of contemporary research and thought. *Clinical Child and Family Psychology Review, 13,* 46–76.

Keel, P. K., & Haedt, A. (2008). Evidence-based psychosocial treatments for eating problems and eating disorders. *Journal of Clinical Child and Adolescent Psychology, 37,* 39–61.

Keel, P. K., & Klump, K. (2003). Are eating disorders culturebound syndromes? Implications for conceptualizing their etiology. *Psychological Bulletin, 129,* 747–769.

Keller, M. B., Lavori, P. W., Wunder, J., Beardslee, W. R., Schwartz, C. E., & Roth, J. (1992). Chronic course of anxiety disorders in children and adolescents. *Journal of the American Academy of Child and Adolescent Psychiatry, 31,* 595–599.

Keller, P. S., Cummings, E. M., & Davies, P. T. (2005). The role of marital discord and parenting in relations between parental problem drinking and child adjustment. *Journal of Child Psychology and Psychiatry, 46,* 943–951.

Kellerman, J. (1980). Rapid treatment of nocturnal anxiety in children. *Journal of Behavior Therapy and Experimental Psychiatry, 11,* 9–11.

Kelly, J. B. (2000). Children's adjustment in conflicted marriage and divorce: A decade review of research. *Journal of the American Academy of Child and Adolescent Psychiatry, 39,* 963–973.

Kelly, M. L., & Heffer, R. W. (1990). Eating disorders: Food refusal and failure to thrive. In A. M. Gross & R. S. Drabman (Eds.), *Handbook of clinical behavioral pediatrics.* New York: Plenum.

Kempe, C. H., Silverman, F. N., Steele, B. B., Droegemueller, W., & Silver, H. K. (1962). The battered child syndrome. *Journal of the American Medical Association, 181,* 17–24.

Kendall, P. C. (1992). *Coping cat workbook.* Ardmore, PA: Workbook Publishing.

Kendall, P. C. (2006). Guiding theory for therapy with children and adolescents. In P. C. Kendall (Ed.), *Child and adolescent therapy: Cognitive-behavioral procedures.* New York: The Guilford Press.

Kendall, P. C., Choudbury, M. S., Hudson, J. L., & Webb, A. (2002). *The C.A.T. Project.* Ardmore, PA: Workbook.

Kendall, P. C., Chu, B. C., Pimentel, S. S., & Choudhury, M. (2000). Treating anxiety disorders in youth. In P. C. Kendall (Ed.), *Child and adolescent therapy: Cognitive-behavioral procedures.* New York: Guilford.

Kendall, P. C., Flannery-Schroeder, E., Panichelli-Mindel, S., Southam-Gerow, M., Henin, A., & Warman, M. (1997a). Therapy for youth with anxiety disorders: A second randomized clinical trial. *Journal of Consulting and Clinical Psychology, 65,* 366–380.

Kendall, P. C., Furr, J. M., & Podell, J. L. (2010). Child-focused treatment for anxiety. In J. R. Weisz & A. E. Kazdin (Eds.), *Evidence-based psychotherapies for children and adolescents* (2nd ed.). New York: The Guilford Press.

Kendall, P. C., & Hedtke, K. (2006). *Coping cat workbook* (2nd ed.). Ardmore, PA: Workbook Publishing.

Kendall, P. C., Hedtke, K. A., & Aschenbrand, S. G. (2006). Anxiety disorders. In D. A. Wolfe & E. J. Mash (Eds.), *Behavioral and emotional disorders in adolescents: Nature, assessment, and treatment.* New York: The Guilford Press.

Kendall, P. C., Hudson, J., Gosch, E., Flannery-Schroeder, E., & Suveg, C. (2008). Cognitive-behavioral therapy for anxiety disordered youth: A randomized clinical trial evaluating child and family modalities. *Journal of Consulting and Clinical Psychology, 76,* 282–297.

Kendall, P. C., Khanna, M. S., Edson, A., Cummings, C., & Harris, M.S. (2011). Computers and psychosocial treatments for child anxiety: Recent advances and ongoing efforts. *Depression and Anxiety, 28,* 58–66.

Kendall, P. C., Panichelli-Mindel, S. M., Sugarman, A., & Callahan, S. A. (1997b). Exposure to child anxiety: Theory, research, and practice. *Clinical Psychology: Science and Practice, 4,* 29–39.

Kendall, P. C., Safford, S., Flannery-Schroeder, E., & Webb, A. (2004). Child anxiety treatment: Outcomes in adolescence and impact on substance use and depression at 7.4-year follow-up. *Journal of Consulting and Clinical Psychology, 72,* 276–287.

Kendall, P. C., & Suveg, C. (2006). Treating anxiety disorders in youth. In P. C. Kendall (Ed.), *Child and adolescent therapy: Cognitive-behavioral procedures* (3rd ed.). New York: The Guilford Press.

Kendler, K. S., Neale, M. C., Kessler, R. C., Heath, A. C., & Eaves, L. J. (1992a). A population-based twin study of major depression in women: The impact of varying definitions of illness. *Archives of General Psychiatry, 49,* 257–266.

Kendler, K. S., Neale, M. C., Kessler, R. C., Heath, A. C., & Eaves, L. J. (1992b). The genetic epidemiology of phobias in women: The interrelationship of agoraphobia, social phobia, situational phobia, and simple phobia. *Archives of General Psychiatry, 49,* 273–281.

Kennard, B., Silva, S., Vitiello, B., Curry, J., Kratochvil, C., Simons, A. et al. and the TADS Team. (2006). Remission and residual symptoms after short-term treatment in the Treatment of Adolescents With Depression Study (TADS). *Journal of the American Academy of Child and Adolescent Psychiatry, 45,* 1404–1411.

Kent, K. M., Pelham, W. E., Molina, B. S. G., Sibley, M. H., Waschbusch, D. A., Yu, J. et al. (2011). The academic experience of male high school students with ADHD. *Journal of Abnormal Child Psychology, 39,* 451–462.

Kenworthy, L., Case, L., Harms, M. B., Martin, A., & Wallace, G. L. (2010). Adaptive behavior ratings correlate with symptomatology and IQ among individuals with high-functioning autism spectrum disorders. *Journal of Autism and Developmental Disorders, 40,* 416–423.

Kern, R. S., Glynn, S. M., Horan, W. P., & Marder, S. R. (2009). Psychosocial treatments to promote functional recovery in schizophrenia. *Schizophrenia Bulletin, 35,* 347–361.

Kerwin, M. E., & Berkowitz, R. I. (1996). Feeding and eating disorders: Ingestive problems of infancy, childhood, and adolescence. *School Psychology Review, 25,* 316–328.

Kesler, S. R., Wilde, E., Bruno, J. L., & Bigler, E. D. (2011). Neuroimaging and genetic disorders. In S. Goldstein & C. R.

Reynolds (Eds.), *Handbook of neurodevelopmental and genetic disorders in children* (2nd ed.). New York: The Guilford Press.

Kessler, J. W. (1966, 1988). *Psychopathology of childhood.* Englewood Cliffs, NJ: Prentice Hall.

Kessler, R. C., Avenevoli, S., Green, J., Gruber, M. J., Guyer, M., He, Y. et al. (2009). National comorbidity survey replication adolescent supplement (NCS-A): III. Concordance of DSM-IV/CIDI diagnoses with clinical reassessments. *Journal of the American Academy of Child and Adolescent Psychiatry, 48,* 386–399.

Kessler, R. C., Avenevoli, S., & Merikangas, K. R. (2001). Mood disorders in children and adolescents: An epidemiologic perspective. *Biological Psychiatry, 49,* 1002–1014.

Kestenbaum, C. J. (2000). How shall we treat children in the 21st century? *Journal of the American Academy of Child and Adolescent Psychiatry, 39,* 1–10.

Killen, J. D., Hayward, C., Wilson, D. M., Taylor, C. B., Hammer, L. D., Litt, I., Simmonds, B., & Haydel, F. (1994a). Factors associated with eating disorder symptoms in a community sample of 6th and 7th grade girls. *International Journal of Eating Disorders, 15,* 357–367.

Killen, J. D., Taylor, C. B., Hayward, C., Wilson, D. M., Haydel, K. F., Hammer, L. D., Simmonds, B., Robinson, T. N., Litt, I., Varady, A., & Kraemer, H. (1994b). Pursuit of thinness and onset of eating disorder symptoms in a community sample of adolescent girls: A three-year prospective analysis. *International Journal of Eating Disorders, 16,* 227–238.

King, B. H., Hodapp, R. M., & Dykens, E. M. (2000). Mental retardation. In B. J. Sadock & V. A. Sadock (Eds.), *Comprehensive textbook of psychiatry* (Vol. II). Philadelphia: Lippincott Williams & Wilkins.

King, B. H., Hodapp, R. M., & Dykens, E. M. (2005). Mental retardation. In B. J. Sadock & V. A. Sadock (Eds.), *Kaplan and Sadock's comprehensive textbook of psychiatry.* New York: Lippincott Williams & Wilkins.

King, N., Tonge, B. J., Heyne, D., & Ollendick, T. H. (2000). Research on the cognitive-behavioral treatment of school refusal: A review and recommendations. *Clinical Psychology Review, 20,* 495–507.

King, N. J., & Bernstein, G. A. (2001). School refusal in children and adolescents: A review of the past 10 years. *Journal of the American Academy of Child and Adolescent Psychiatry, 40,* 197–205.

King, N. J., Ollendick, T. H., & Gullone, E. (1990). School-related fears of children and adolescents. *Australian Journal of Education, 34,* 99–112.

King, N. J., Ollendick, T. H., Mattis, S. G., Yang, B., & Tonge, B. (1997). Nonclinical panic attacks in adolescents: Prevalence, symptomatology, and associated features. *Behaviour Change, 13,* 171–183.

King, R. A., Pfeffer, C., Gammon, G. D., & Cohen, D. J. (1992). Suicidality of childhood and adolescence: Review of the literature and proposal for establishment of a DSM-IV category. In B. B. Lahey & A. E. Kazdin (Eds.), *Advances in clinical child psychology* (Vol. 14). New York: Plenum.

Kirby, D. (2005). *Evidence of harm.* New York: St Martin's Press.

Kirigin, K. A. (1996). Teaching-family model of group home treatment of children with severe behavior problems. In M. C. Roberts (Ed.), *Model programs in child and family mental health.* Mahwah, NJ: Erlbaum.

Kirk, S. A., Gallagher, J. J., & Anastasiow, N. J. (2000). *Educating exceptional children.* Boston, MA: Houghton Mifflin Company.

Kirov, R., Kinkelbur, J., Banaschewski, T., & Rothenberger, A. (2007). Sleep patterns in children with attention-deficit/hyperactivity disorder, tic disorder, and comorbidity. *Journal of Child Psychology and Psychiatry, 48,* 561–570.

Kistner, J. A., David-Ferdon, C. F., Lopez, C. M., & Dunkel, S. B. (2007). Ethnic and sex differences in children's depressive symptoms. *Journal of Clinical Child and Adolescent Psychology, 36,* 171–181.

Kitzman-Ulrich, H., Wilson, D. K., St. George, S. M., Lawman, H., Segal, M., & Fairchild, A. (2010). The integration of a family systems approach for understanding youth obesity, physical activity, and dietary programs. *Clinical Child and Family Review, 13,* 231–253.

Klahr, A. M., Rueter, M. A., McGue, M., Iacono, W. G., & Burt, S. A. (2011). The relationship between parent-child conflict and adolescent antisocial behavior: Confirming shared environment mediation. *Journal of Abnormal Child Psychology, 39,* 683–694.

Klasen, F., Oettinger, G., Daniels, J., Post, M., Hoyer, C., Adam, H. (2010). Posttraumatic resilience in former Ugandan child solders. *Child Development, 81,* 1096–1113.

Klassen, R. (2010). Confidence to manage learning: The self-efficacy for self-regulated learning of early adolescents with learning disabilities. *Learning Disability Quarterly,* January 1.

Kleiger, J. H. (2001). Projective testing with children and adolescents. In C. E. Walker & M. C. Roberts (Eds.), *Handbook of clinical child psychology* (3rd ed.). New York: John Wiley & Sons.

Klein, D. F., Mannuzza, S., Chapman, T., & Fyer, A. (1992). Child panic revised. *Journal of the American Academy of Child and Adolescent Psychiatry, 31,* 112–113.

Klein, D. N., Dougherty, L. R., & Olino, T. M. (2005). Toward guidelines for evidence-based assessment of depression in children and adolescents. *Journal of Clinical Child and Adolescent Psychology, 34,* 412–432.

Klein, D. N., Lewinsohn, P. M., Seeley, J. R., & Rohde, P. (2001). A family study of major depressive disorder in a community sample of adolescents. *Archives of General Psychiatry, 58,* 13–20.

Klein, D. N., Torpey, D. C., & Bufferd, S. J. (2008). Depressive disorders. In T. P. Beauchaine & S. P. Hinshaw (Eds.), *Child and adolescent psychopathology.* Hoboken, NJ: John Wiley & Sons.

Klein, M. (1932). *The psycho-analysis of children.* London: Hogarth Press.

Klein, R. G. (2011). Thinning of the cerebral cortex during development: A dimension of ADHD. *American Journal of Psychiatry, 168,* 111–113.

Klesges, R. C., & Hanson, C. L. (1988). Determining the environmental causes and correlates of childhood obesity: Methodological issues and future research directions. In N. A. Krasnegor, G. D. Grave, & N. Kretchmer (Eds.), *Childhood obesity: A biobehavioral perspective.* Caldwell, NJ: The Telford Press.

Klima, T., & Repetti, R. L. (2008). Children's peer relations and their psychological adjustment: Differences between close friendships and the larger peer group. *Merrill-Palmer Quarterly, 54,* 151–178.

Klin, A., & Volkmar, F. R. (1997). Asperger's Syndrome. In D. J. Cohen & F. R. Volkmar (Eds.), *Handbook of autism and pervasive development disorders.* New York: John Wiley.

Klinger, L. G., Dawson, G., & Renner, P. (2003). Autistic disorder. In E. J. Mash & R. A. Barkley (Eds.), *Child psychopathology.* New York: Guilford Press.

Klinnert, M. D., McQuaid, E. L., McCormich, D., Adinoff, A. D., & Bryant, N. E. (2000). A multimethod assessment of behavioral and emotional adjustment in children with asthma. *Journal of Pediatric Psychology, 25,* 35–46.

Klump, K. L., Burt, S. A., Spanos, A., McGue, M., Iacono, W. G., & Wade, T. D. (2010). Age differences in genetic and environmental influences on weight and shape concerns. *International Journal of Eating Disorders, 43,* 679–688.

Klump, K. L., & Gobrogge, K. L. (2005). A review and primer of molecular genetic studies of anorexia nervosa. *International Journal of Eating Disorders, 37 (Suppl.),* 43–48.

Klump, K. L., Perkins, P. S., Burt, S. A., McGue, M., Iacono, W. G. (2007). Puberty moderates genetic influences on disordered eating. *Psychological Medicine, 37,* 627–634.

Knapp, P., & Jensen, P. S. (2006). Recommendations for DSM-V. In P. S. Jensen, P. Knapp, & D. A. Mrazek (Eds.), *Toward a new diagnostic system for child psychopathology. Moving beyond the DSM.* New York: The Guilford Press.

Knoff, H. M. (1998). Review of the Children's Apperception Test (1991 Revision). In J. C. Impara & B. S. Plake (Eds.), *The thirteenth mental measurement yearbook.* Lincoln: The University of Nebraska-Lincoln.

Kobak, R., Cassidy, J., Lyons-Ruth, K., & Ziv, Y. (2006). Attachment, stress, and psychopathology. In D. Cicchetti & D. J. Cohen (Eds.), *Developmental psychopathology. Vol. 1. Theory and method.* Hoboken, NJ: John Wiley & Sons.

Kochanska, G., Philibert, R. A., & Barry, R. A. (2009). Interplay of genes and early mother-infant relationship in the development of self-regulation from toddler to preschool age. *Journal of Child Psychology and Psychiatry, 50,* 1331–1338.

Kochanek, K. D., Xu, J. Q., Murphy, S. L., Miniño, A. M., & Kung, H. C. (2011). *Deaths: Preliminary Data for 2009.* National Vital Statistics Reports; Vol 59, no 4. Hyattsville, MD: National Center for Health Statistics.

Koegel, L. K. (2000). Interventions to facilitate communication in autism. *Journal of Autism and Developmental Disorders, 30,* 383–391.

Koegel, R. L., Koegel, L. K., & Brookman, L. I. (2003). Empirically supported pivotal response interventions for children with autism. In A. E. Kazdin & J. R. Weisz (Eds.), *Evidence-based psychotherapies for children and adolescents.* New York: Guilford Press.

Koegel, R. L., Koegel, L. K., & McNerney, E. K. (2001). Pivotal areas in intervention for autism. *Journal of Clinical Child Psychology, 30,* 19–32.

Koegel, R. L., Koegel, L. K., Vernon, T. W., & Brookman-Frazee, L. I. (2010). Empirically supported pivotal response treatment for children with autism spectrum disorders. In R. J. Weisz & A. E. Kazdin (Eds.), *Evidence-based psychotherapies for children and adolescents.* New York: Guilford Press.

Koelch, M., Schnoor, K., & Fegert, J. M. (2008). Ethical issues in psychopharmacology of children and adolescents. *Current Opinion in Psychiatry, 21,* 598–605.

Kofler, M. J., Rapport, M. D., & Alderson, R. M. (2008). Quantifying ADHD classroom inattentiveness, its moderators, and variability: A meta-analytic review. *Journal of Child Psychology and Psychiatry, 49,* 59–69.

Kogan, M. D., Blumberg, S. J., Schieve, L. A., Boyle, C. A., Perrin, J. M., Ghandour, R. M. et al. (2009). Prevalence of parent-reported diagnosis of autism spectrum disorder among children in the US, 2007. *Pediatrics, 124,* 1395–1403.

Koger, S. M., Schettler, T., & Weiss, B. (2005). Environmental toxicants and development disabilities. *American Psychologist, 60,* 243–255.

Koinis-Mitchell, D., McQuaid, E. L., Seifer, R., Kopel, S. J., Esteban, C., Canino, G. et al. (2007). Multiple urban and asthma-related risks and their association with asthma morbidity in children. *Journal of Pediatric Psychology, 32,* 582–595.

Koinis-Mitchell, S. J., McQuaid, E. L., Jandasek, B., Kopel, S. J., Seifer, R., Klein, R. B. et al. (2012). Identifying individual, cultural and asthma-related risk and protective factors associated with resilient asthma outcomes in urban children and families. *Journal of Pediatric Psychology, 37,* 424–437.

Kolko, D. (1987). Simplified inpatient treatment of nocturnal enuresis in psychiatrically disturbed children. *Behavior Therapy, 18,* 99–112.

Kolko, D. J. (Ed.). (2002). *Handbook of firesetting in children and youth.* San Diego, CA: Academic Press.

Kolko, D. J. (2005). Treatment and education for childhood firesetting: Description, outcomes, and implications. In E. D. Hibbs & P. S. Jensen (Eds.), *Psychosocial treatments for child and adolescent disorders: Empirically based strategies for clinical practice* (2nd ed.). Washington, DC: American Psychological Association.

Kolko, D. J., Day, B. T., Bridge, J. A., & Kazdin, A. E. (2001). Twoyear prediction of children's firesetting in clinically referred and nonreferred samples. *Journal of Child Psychology and Psychiatry, 42,* 371–380.

Kolvin, I. (1971). Psychoses in childhood—a comparative study. In M. Rutter (Ed.), *Infantile autism: Concepts, characteristics, and treatments.* London: Churchill-Livingstone.

Koocher, G. P. (1980). Pediatric cancer: Psychosocial problems and the high costs of helping. *Journal of Clinical Child Psychology, 9,* 2–5.

Koocher, G. P., & Sallan, S. E. (1978). Pediatric oncology. In P. R. Magrab (Ed.), *Psychological management of pediatric problems* (Vol. 1). Baltimore: University Park Press.

Kopp, C. B. (1994). Trends and directions in studies of developmental risk. In C. A. Nelson (Ed.), *Threats to optimal development: Integrating biological, psychological, and social risk factors: The Minnesota symposium on child psychology* (Vol. 27). Hillsdale, NJ: Erlbaum.

Koppitz, E. M. (1984). *Psychological evaluation of human figure drawings by middle school pupils.* Orlando, FL: Grune & Stratton.

Korbin, J. E., Coulton, C. J., Chard, S., Platt-Houston, C., & Su, M. (1998). Impoverishment and child maltreatment in African American and European American neighborhoods. *Development and Psychopathology, 10,* 215–233.

Kotimaa, A. J., Moilanen, I., Taanila, A., Ebeling, H., Smalley, S. L., McGough, J. J. et al. (2003). Maternal smoking and hyperactivity in 8-year-old children. *Journal of the American Academy of Child and Adolescent Psychiatry, 42,* 826–833.

Kotler, L. A., Cohen, P., Daview, M., Pine, D. S., & Walsh, B. T. (2001). Longitudinal relationships between childhood, adolescent, and adult eating disorders. *Journal of the American Academy of Child and Adolescent Psychiatry, 40,* 1434–1440.

Kovacs, M. (1992, 2003). *Children's Depression Inventory (CDI): Technical manual update.* North Tonawanda, NY: Multi-Health Systems, Inc.

Kovacs, M. (1996). Presentation and course of major depressive disorder during childhood and later years of the life span. *Journal of the American Academy of Child and Adolescent Psychiatry, 35,* 705–715.

Kovacs, M. (1997). Depressive disorders in childhood: An impressionistic landscape. *Journal of Child Psychology and Psychiatry, 38,* 287–298.

Kovacs, M., Goldston, D., & Gatsonis, C. (1993). Suicidal behaviors and childhood-onset depressive disorders: A longitudinal investigation. *Journal of the American Academy of Child and Adolescent Psychiatry, 32,* 8–20.

Kovas, Y., Haworth, C. M. A., Harlaar, N., Petrill, S. A., Dale, P. S., & Plomin, R. (2007). Overlap and specificity of genetic and environmental influences on mathematics and reading disability in 10-year-old twins. *Journal of Child Psychology and Psychiatry, 48,* 914–922.

Kowatch, R. A., & DelBello, M. P. (2006). Pediatric bipolar disorder: Emerging diagnostic and treatment approaches. *Child and Adolescent Psychiatric Clinics of North America, 15,* 73–108.

Kowatch, R. A., Fristad, M., Birmaher, B., Wagner, K. D., Findling, R. L., & Hellander, M. (2005). Treatment guidelines for children and adolescents with bipolar disorder. *Journal of the American Academy of Child and Adolescent Psychiatry, 44,* 213–235.

Kowatch, R. A., Strawn, J. R., & DelBello, M. P. (2010). Developmental considerations in the pharmacological treatment of youth with bipolar disorder. In D. J. Miklowitz & D. Cicchetti (Eds.), *Understanding bipolar disorder: A developmental psychopathology perspective.* New York: The Guilford Press.

Kozma, A., Mansell, J., & Beadle-Brown, J. (2009). Outcomes in different residential settings for people with intellectual disability: A systematic review. *American Journal on Intellectual and Developmental Disabilities, 114,* 193–222.

Krahn, G. L., Hohn, M. F., & Kime, C. (1995). Incorporating qualitative approaches into clinical child psychology research. *Journal of Clinical Child Psychology, 24,* 204–213.

Kraijer, D. (2000). Review of adaptive behavior studies in mentally retarded persons with autism/pervasive developmental disorder. *Journal of Autism and Developmental Disorders, 30,* 39–47.

Kral, T. V., & Faith, M. S. (2009). Influences on child eating and weight development from a behavioral genetics perspective. *Journal of Pediatric Psychology, 34,* 596–605.

Kratochwill, T. R. (2007). Preparing psychologists for evidence-based school practice: Lessons learned and challenges ahead. *American Psychologist, 62,* 826–843.

Kratochwill, T. R., & Levin, J. R. (1992). *Single-case research design and analysis.* Hillsdale, NJ: Lawrence Erlbaum.

Kreyenbuhl, J., Buchanan, R. W., Dickerson, F. B., & Dixon, L. B. (2010). The Schizophrenic Patient Outcomes Research Team (PORT): Updated treatment recommendations 2009. *Schzophrenia Bulletin, 36,* 94–103.

Kucera, M., & Sullivan, A. L. (2011). The educational implications of Type 1 diabetes mellitus: A review of research and recommendations for school psychological practice. *Psychology in the Schools, 48,* 587–603.

Kuczynski, L., & Kochanska, G. (1995). Function and contexts of maternal demands: Developmental significance of early demands for competent action. *Child Development, 66,* 616–628.

Kuhl, E. S., Hoodin, F., Rice, J., Felt, B. T., Rausch, J. R., & Patton, S. R. (2010). Increasing daily water intake and fluid adherence in children receiving treatment for retentive encopresis. *Journal of Pediatric Psychology, 35,* 1144–1151.

Kuhn, T. S. (1962). *The structure of scientific revolutions.* Chicago: University of Chicago Press.

Kumpulainen, K., Räsänen, E., & Henttonen, I. (1999). Children involved in bullying: Psychological disturbance and the persistence of the involvement. *Child Abuse and Neglect, 23,* 1253–1262.

Kumra, S., Bedwell, J., Smith, A. K., Arling, E., Albus, K. et al. (2000). Neuropsychological deficits in pediatric patients with childhood-onset schizophrenia and psychotic disorder not otherwise specified. *Schizophrenia Research, 42,* 135–144.

Kupersmidt, J. B., & Patterson, C. J. (1991). Childhood peer rejection, aggression, withdrawal, and perceived competence as predictors of self-reported behavior problems in preadolescence. *Journal of Abnormal Child Psychology, 19,* 427–449.

Kupfer, D. J., First, M. B., & Regier, D. A. (2002). Introduction. In D. J. Kupfer, M. B. First, & D. A. Regier (Eds.), *A research agenda for DSM-V*. Washington, DC: American Psychiatric Association.

Kupfer, D. J., & Reynolds, C. F. (1992). Sleep and affective disorders. In E. S. Paykel (Ed.), *Handbook of affective disorders* (2nd ed.). New York: Guilford Press.

Kylliäinen, A., & Hietanen, J. K. (2004). Attention orienting by another's gaze direction in children with autism. *Journal of Child Psychology and Psychiatry, 45*, 435–444.

Lachar, D., & Gruber, C. P. (2001). *Personality inventory for children-second edition*. Los Angeles: Western Psychological Services.

Lackaye, T., Margalit, M., Ziv, O., & Ziman, T. (2006). Comparisons of self-efficacy, mood, effort, and hope between students with learning disabilities and their non-LD-matched peers. *Learning Disability Research & Practice, 21*, 111–121.

Laessle, R. G., Uhl, H., & Lindel, B. (2001). Parental influences on eating behavior in obese and nonobese preadolescents. *International Journal of Eating Disorders, 30*, 447–453.

La Greca, A. M. (1999). *Manual and instructions for the SASC, SASC-R, SAS-A (Adolescents) and parent versions of the scales*. Miami, FL: University of Miami.

La Greca, A. M., & Harrison, H. M. (2005). Adolescent peer relations, friendships, and romantic relationships: Do they predict social anxiety and depression? *Journal of Clinical Child and Adolescent Psychology, 34*, 49–61.

La Greca, A. M., & Mackey, E. R. (2009). Adherence to pediatric treatment regimens. In M. C. Roberts & R. G. Steele (Eds.), *Handbook of pediatric psychology* (4th ed.). New York: The Guilford Press.

La Greca, A. M., Silverman, W. K., Vernberg, E. M., & Prinstein, M. J. (1996). Symptoms of posttraumatic stress in children after Hurricane Andrew: A prospective study. *Journal of Consulting and Clinical Psychology, 64*, 712–723.

La Greca, A. M., Silverman, W. K., & Wasserstein, S. B. (1998). Children's predisaster functioning as a predictor of post-traumatic stress following Hurricane Andrew. *Journal of Consulting and Clinical Psychology, 66*, 883–892.

Lahey, B. B. (2001, Winter). Should the combined and predominantly inattentive types of ADHD be considered distinct and unrelated disorders? *Clinical Psychology: Science and Practice, 8*, 494–497.

Lahey, B. B. (2008). Oppositional defiant disorder, conduct disorder, and juvenile delinquency. In T. P. Beauchaine & S. P. Hinshaw (Eds.), *Child and adolescent psychopathology*. Hoboken, NJ: John Wiley & Sons.

Lahey, B. B., Applegate, B., McBurnett, K., Biederman, J., Greenhill, L., Hynd, G. W., Barkley, R. A., Newcorn, J., Jensen, P., Richters, J., Garfinkel, B., Kerdyk, L., Frick, P. J., Ollendick, T., Perez, D., Hart, E. L., Waldman, I., & Shaffer, D. (1994). DSM-IV field trials for attention deficit hyperactivity disorder in children and adolescents. *American Journal of Psychiatry, 151*, 1673–1685.

Lahey, B. B., D'Onofrio, B. M., & Waldman, I. D. (2009). Using epidemiological methods to test hypotheses regarding causal influences on child and adolescent mental disorders. *Journal of Child Psychology and Psychiatry, 50*, 53–62.

Lahey, B. B., Pelham, W. E., Stein, M. A., Loney, J., Trapani, C., Nugent, K., Kipp, H., Schmidt, E., Lee, S., Cale, M., Gold, E., Hartung, C. M., Willcutt, E., & Baumann, B. (1998). Validity of DSM-IV attention-deficit/hyperactivity disorder for younger children. *Journal of the American Academy of Child and Adolescent Psychiatry, 37*, 695–702.

Lahey, B. B., Van Hulle, C. A., Keenan, K, Rathouz, P. J., D'Onofrio, B. M., Rodgers, J. L. et al. (2008). Temperament and parenting during the first year of life predict future child conduct problems. *Journal of Abnormal Child Psychology, 36*, 1139–1158.

Lahey, B. B., Van Hulle, C. A., Singh, A. L., Waldman, I. D., & Rathouz, P. J. (2011). Higher-order genetic and environmental structure of prevalent forms of child and adolescent psychopathology. *Archives of General Psychiatry, 68*, 181–189.

Lahey, B. B., Waldman, I. D., & McBurnett, K. (1999). The development of antisocial behavior: An integrative causal model. *Journal of Child Psychology and Psychiatry, 40*, 669–682.

Lahey, B. B., & Willcutt, E. G. (2010). Predictive validity of a continuous alternative to nominal subtypes of attention-deficit/hyperactivity disorder for DSM-V. *Journal of Clinical Child and Adolescent Psychology, 39*, 761–775.

Lahti, J., Räikkönen, K., Kajantie, E., Heinonen, K., Pesonen, A-K., Järvenpää A-L., & Stranberg, T. (2006). Small body size at birth and behavioural symptoms of ADHD in children aged five to six years. *Journal of Child Psychology and Psychiatry, 47*, 1167–1174.

Laing, E., Hulme, C., Grant, J., & Karmiloff-Smith, A. (2001). Learning to read in Williams syndrome: Looking beneath the surface of atypical reading development. *Journal of Child Psychology and Psychiatry, 42*, 729–739.

Laird, R. D., Jordan, K. Y., Dodge, K. A., Petit, G. S., & Bates, J. E. (2001). Peer rejection in childhood, involvement with antisocial peers in early adolescence and the development of externalizing behavior problems. *Development and Psychopathology, 13*, 337–354.

Lakin, K. C., Prouty, R., Polister, B., & Coucouvanis, K. (2003). Selected changes in residential service systems over a quarter century, 1977–2002. *Mental Retardation, 41*, 303–306.

Lamb, M. E. (2010). *The role of the father in child development* (5th ed.). New York: John Wiley.

Lambert, N. M. (1988). Adolescent outcomes for hyperactive children: Perspectives on general and specific patterns of childhood risk for adolescent educational, social, and mental health problems. *American Psychologist, 43*, 786–799.

Lambie, I., & Randell, I., (2011). Creating a firestorm: A review of children who deliberately light fires. *Clinical Psychology Review, 31*, 307–327.

Lang, P. J. (1984). Cognition in emotion: Concept and action. In C. E. Izard, J. Kagan, R. B. Zajonc (Eds.), *Emotions, cognition, and behavior*. New York: Cambridge University Press.

Lang, R., Sigafoos, J., Lancioni, G., Didden, R., & Rispoli, M. (2010). Influence of assessment settings on the results of functional analyses of problem behavior. *Journal of Applied Behavior Analysis, 43*, 565–567.

Lansford, J. E., Chang, L., Dodge, K. A., Malone, P. S., Oburu, P., Palmérus, K. et al. (2005). Physical discipline and children's adjustment: Cultural normativeness as a moderator. *Child Development, 76*, 1234–1246.

Lansford, J. E., Deater-Deckard, K., Dodge, K. A., Bates, J. E., & Pettit, G. S. (2004). Ethnic differences in the link between physical discipline and later adolescent externalizing behaviors. *Journal of Child Psychology and Psychiatry, 45*, 801–812.

Lansford, J. E., Dodge, K. A., Pettit, G. S., Bates, J. E., Crozier, J., & Kaplow, J. (2002). A 12-year prospective study of the longterm effects of early childhood physical maltreatment on psychological, behavioral, and academic problems in adolescence. *Archives of Pediatrics and Adolescent Medicine, 156*, 824–830.

Lapouse, R., & Monk, M. A. (1959). Fears and worries in a representative sample of children. *American Journal of Orthopsychiatry, 29*, 803–818.

Larkin, R. W. (2007). *Comprehending Columbine.* Philadelphia, PA: Temple University Press.

Larson, S. A., Lakin, K. C., Salmi, P., Scott, N., & Webster, A. (2010). Children and youth with intellectual or developmental disabilities living in congregate care settings (1977–2009): Healthy People 2010 Objective 6.7b outcomes. *Intellectual and Developmental Disabilities, 48*, 396–400.

Larsson, B., Carlsson, J., Fichtel, A., & Melin, L. (2005). Relaxation treatment of adolescent headache sufferers: Results from a school-based replication series. *Headache, 45*, 692–704.

Lask, B., & Bryant-Waugh, R. (1992). Early-onset anorexia nervosa and related eating disorders. *Journal of Child Psychology and Psychiatry, 33*, 281–300.

Last, C. G. (1988). Separation anxiety. In M. Hersen & C. G. Last (Eds.), *Child behavior therapy casebook.* New York: Plenum Press.

Last, C. G., Hersen, M., Kazdin, A. E., Orvaschel, H., & Perrin, S. (1991). Anxiety disorders in children and their families. *Archives of General Psychiatry, 48*, 928–934.

Last, C. G., & Perrin, S. (1993). Anxiety disorders in African-American and white children. *Journal of Abnormal Child Psychology, 21*, 153–164.

Last, C. G., Perrin, S., Hersen, M., & Kazdin, A. E. (1992). DSMIII- R anxiety disorders in children: Sociodemographic and clinical characteristics. *Journal of the American Academy of Child and Adolescent Psychiatry, 31*, 1070–1076.

Last, C. G., Perrin, S., Hersen, M., & Kazdin, A. E. (1996). A prospective study of childhood anxiety disorders. *Journal of the American Academy of Child and Adolescent Psychiatry, 35*, 1502–1510.

Last, C. G., & Strauss, C. C. (1989). Panic disorder in children and adolescents. *Journal of Anxiety Disorders, 3*, 87–95.

Last, C. G., & Strauss, C. C. (1990). School refusal in anxiety-disordered children and adolescents. *Journal of the American Academy of Child and Adolescent Psychiatry, 29*, 31–35.

Last, C. G., Strauss, C. C., & Francis, G. (1987). Comorbidity among childhood anxiety disorders. *Journal of Nervous and Mental Disease, 175*, 726–730.

Latner, J. D., & Stunkard, A. J. (2003). Getting worse: The stigmatization of obese children. *Obesity Research, 11*, 452–456.

Lau, A. S., & Weisz, J. R. (2003). Reported maltreatment among clinic-referred children: Implications for presenting problems, treatment attrition, and long-term outcomes. *Journal of the American Academy of Child and Adolescent Psychiatry, 42*, 1327–1334.

Lavigne, J. V., & Faier-Routman, J. (1993). Correlates of psychological adjustment to pediatric physical disorders: A meta-analytic review and comparison with existing models. *Developmental and Behavioral Pediatrics, 14*, 117–123.

Lavigne, J. V., Hopkins, J., Gouze, K. R., Bryant, F. B., LeBailley, S. A., Binns, H. J., et al. (2010). Is smoking during pregnancy a risk factor for psychopathology in young children? A methodological caveat and report on preschoolers. *Journal of Pediatric Psychology, 36*, 10–24.

Lavigne, J. V., LeBailly, S. A., Hopkins, J., Gouze, K. R., & Binns, H. J. (2009). The prevalence of ADHD, ODD, depression, and anxiety in a community sample of 4-year-olds. *Journal of Clinical Child and Adolescent Psychology, 38*, 315–328.

Law, J., & Garrett, Z. (2004). Speech and language therapy: Its potential role in CAMHS. *Child and Adolescent Mental Health, 9*, 50–55.

Law, J., Garrett, Z., & Nye, C. (2004). The efficacy of treatment for children with developmental speech and language delay/disorder: A meta-analysis. *Journal of Speech, Language, and Hearing Research, 47*, 924–943.

Lawrie, S. M., McIntosh, A. M., Hall, J., Owens, D. G. C., & Johnstone, E. C. (2008). Brain structure and function changes during the development of schizophrenia: The evidence from studies of subjects at increased genetic risk. *Schizophrenia Bulletin, 34*, 330–340.

Laws, G., & Gunn, D. (2004). Phonological memory as a predictor of language comprehension in down syndrome: A five-year follow-up study. *Journal of Child Psychology and Psychiatry, 45*, 326–327.

Lazarus, A., & Abramavitz, A. (1962). The use of emotive imagery in the treatment of children's phobia. *Journal of Mental Science, 108*, 191–192.

Leach, J. M., Scarborough, H. S., & Rescorla, L. (2003). Lateemerging reading disabilities. *Journal of Educational Psychology, 95*, 211–224.

Lebel, C., Roussotte, F., & Sowell, E. R. (2011). Imaging the impact of prenatal alcohol exposure on the structure of the developing brain. *Neuropsychology Review, 21*, 102–118.

LeBovidge, J. S., Lavigne, J. V., Donenberg, G. R., & Miller, M. L. (2003). Psychological adjustment of children and adolescents with chronic arthritis: A meta-analytic review. *Journal of Pediatric Psychology, 28,* 29–39.

LeBovidge, J. S., Lavigne, J. V., & Miller, M. L. (2005). Adjustment to chronic arthritis of childhood: The roles of illness-related stress and attitude toward illness. *Journal of Pediatric Psychology, 30,* 273–286.

Le Couteur, A., & Gardner, F. (2008). Use of structured interviews and observational methods in clinical settings. In M. Rutter et al. (Eds.), *Rutter's child and adolescent psychiatry* (5th ed.). Malden, MA: Blackwell Publishing.

Leckman, J. F., King, R. A., Gilbert, D. L., Coffey, B. J., Singer, H. S., Dure, L. S. et al. (2011). Streptococcal upper respiratory tract infections and exacerbations of tic and obsessive-compulsive symptoms: A prospective longitudinal study. *Journal of the American Academy of Child and Adolescent Psychiatry, 50,* 108–118.

Lee, S. S. (2011). Deviant peer affiliation and antisocial behavior: Interaction with monoamine oxidase A (MAOA) genotype. *Journal of Abnormal Child Psychology, 39,* 321–332.

Lee, S. S., Humphreys, K. L., Flory, K., Liu, R., & Glass, K. (2011). Prospective association of childhood attention-deficit/hyperactivity disorder (ADHD) and substance use and abuse/dependence: A meta-analytic review. *Clinical Psychology Review, 31,* 328–341.

Lefkowitz, M., & Burton, N. (1978). Childhood depression: A critique of the concept. *Psychological Bulletin, 85,* 716–726.

Leflot, G., van Lier, P. A., Onghena, P., & Colpin, H. (2010). The role of teacher behavior management in the development of disruptive behaviors: An intervention study with the good behavior game. *Journal of Abnormal Child Psychology, 38,* 869–882.

le Grange, D., Crosby, R., Rathouz, P., & Leventhal, B. (2007). A controlled comparison of family-based treatment and supportive psychotherapy for adolescent bulimia nervosa. *Archives of General Psychiatry, 64,* 1049–1056.

le Grange, D., & Lock, J. (2010). Family-based treatment for adolescents with bulimia nervosa. In C. M. Grilo & J. E. Mitchell (Eds.), *The treatment of eating disorders: A clinical handbook.* New York: The Guilford Press.

Le Grange, D., Lock, J., Loeb, K., & Nicholls, D. (2010). The role of the family in eating disorders. *International Journal of Eating Disorders, 43,* 1–5.

Leibenluft, E., & Rich, B. A. (2008). Pediatric bipolar disorder. *Annual Review of Clinical Psychology, 4,* 163–187.

Leinonen, J. A., Solantaus, T. S., & Punamäki, R-L. (2003). Parental mental health and children's adjustment: The quality of marital interaction and parenting as mediating factors. *Journal of Child Psychology and Psychiatry, 44,* 227–241.

Leitenberg, H., Yost, L. W., & Carroll-Wilson, M. (1986). Negative cognitive errors in children: Questionnaire development, normative data, and comparisons between children with and without self-reported symptoms of depression, low selfesteem, and evaluation anxiety. *Journal of Consulting and Clinical Psychology, 54,* 528–536.

Lemanek, K. L., & Ranalli, M. (2009). Sickle cell disease. In M. C. Roberts & R. G. Steele (Eds.), *Handbook of pediatric psychology* (4th ed.). New York: The Guilford Press.

Lemerise, E. A., & Arsenio, W. F. (2000). An integrated model of emotion processes and cognition in social information processing. *Child Development, 71,* 107–118.

Lenhard, W., Breitenbach, E., Ebert, H., Schindelhauer-Deutscher, H. J., Zang, K. D., & Henn, W. (2007). Attitudes of mothers towards their child with Down syndrome before and after the introduction of prenatal diagnosis. *Intellectual and Developmental Disabilities, 45,* 98–102.

Leonard, H. L., Ale, C. M., Freeman, J. B., Garcia, A. M., & Ng, J. S. (2005). Obsessive-compulsive disorder. *Child and Adolescent Psychiatric Clinics of North America, 14,* 727–743.

Leonard, L. B. (1998). *Children with specific language impairment.* Cambridge, MA: The MIT Press.

Leonard, L. B., Camarata, S. M., Pawlowska, M., Brown, B., & Camarata, M. N. (2006). Tense and agreement morphemes in the speech of children with specific language impairment during intervention: Phase 2. *Journal of Speech, Language, and Hearing Research, 49,* 749–770.

Leonard, L. B., Weismer, S. E., Miller, C. A., Francis, D. J., Tomblin, J. B., & Kail, R. V. (2007). Speed of processing, working memory, and language impairment in children. *Journal of Speech, Language, and Hearing Research, 50,* 408–428.

Lescano, C. M., Brown, L. K., Raffaelli, M., & Lima, L. (2009). Cultural factors and family-based HIV prevention intervention for Latino youth. *Journal of Pediatric Psychology, 34,* 1041–1052.

Leslie, L. K., Plemmons, D., Monn, A. R., & Palinkas, L. A. (2007). Investigating ADHD treatment trajectories: Listening to families' stories about medication use. *Journal of Developmental and Behavioral Pediatrics, 28,* 179–188.

Leslie, L. K., Weckerly, J., Landsverk, J., Hough, R. L., Hurlbut, M. S., & Wood, P. A. (2003). Racial/ethnic differences in the use of psychotropic medication in high-risk children and adolescents. *Journal of the American Academy of Child and Adolescent Psychiatry, 42,* 1433–1442.

Lester, B. M., Andreozzi, L., & Appiah, L. (2006). Substance use during pregnancy: Research and social policy. In H. E. Fitzgerald, B. M. Lester, & B. Zuckerman (Eds.), *The crisis in youth mental health* (Vol. 1). Westport, CT: Praeger.

Leventhal, T., & Brooks-Gunn, J. (2000). The neighborhoods they live in: The effects of neighborhood residence on child and adolescent outcomes. *Psychological Bulletin, 126,* 309–337.

Levi, J., Segal, L. M., & Gadola, E. (2007). *F as in fat: How obesity policies are failing America.* Washington, DC: Trust for America's Health.

Levine, M. P., & Harrison, K. (2004). Media's role in the perpetuation and prevention of negative body image and disordered eating. In J. K. Thompson (Ed.), *Handbook of eating disorders and obesity.* Hoboken, NJ: John Wiley.

Lewin, A. B., Heidgerken, A. D., Geffken, G. R., Williams, L. B., Storch, E. A., Gelfand, K. M., & Silverstein, J. H. (2006). The relationship between family factors and metabolic control: The role of diabetes adherence. *Journal of Pediatric Psychology, 31,* 174–183.

Lewinsohn, P. (1974). A behavioral approach to depression. In R. J. Friedman & M. M. Katz (Eds.), *The psychology of depression: Contemporary theory and research.* Washington, DC: Winston.

Lewinsohn, P. M., Clarke, G. N., Hops, H., & Andrews, J. (1990). Cognitive behavioral treatment for depressed adolescents. *Behavior Therapy, 21,* 385–402.

Lewinsohn, P. M., Clarke, G. N., Seeley, J. R., & Rohde, P. (1994). Major depression in community adolescents: Age at onset, episode duration, and time to recurrence. *Journal of the American Academy of Child and Adolescent Psychiatry, 33,* 809–818.

Lewinsohn, P. M., Hops, H., Roberts, R. E., Seeley, J. R., & Andrews, J. A. (1993a). Adolescent psychopathology: I. Prevalence and incidence of depression and other DSM-III-R disorders in high school students. *Journal of Abnormal Psychology, 102,* 133–144.

Lewinsohn, P. M., Klein, D. N., & Seeley, J. R. (1995a). Bipolar disorders in a community sample of older adolescents: Prevalence, phenomenology, comorbidity, and course. *Journal of the American Academy of Child and Adolescent Psychiatry, 34,* 454–463.

Lewinsohn, P. M., Rohde, P., Klein, D. N., & Seeley, J. R. (1999). Natural course of adolescent Major Depressive Disorder: I. Continuity into young adulthood. *Journal of the American Academy of Child and Adolescent Psychiatry, 38,* 56–63.

Lewinsohn, P. M., Rohde, P., & Seeley, J. R. (1995b). Adolescent psychopathology: III. The clinical consequences of comorbidity. *Journal of the American Academy of Child and Adolescent Psychiatry, 34,* 510–519.

Lewinsohn, P. M., Rohde, P., & Seeley, J. R. (1996). Adolescent suicidal ideation and attempts: Prevalence, risk factors, and clinical implications. *Clinical Psychology: Science and Practice, 3,* 25–46.

Lewinsohn, P. M., Rohde, P., & Seeley, J. R. (1998). Major depressive disorder in older adolescents: Prevalence, risk factors, and clinical implications. *Clinical Psychology Review, 18,* 765–794.

Lewinsohn, P. M., Rohde, P., Seeley, J. R., & Fischer, S. A. (1993b). Age-cohort changes in the lifetime occurrence of depression and other mental disorders. *Journal of Abnormal Psychology, 102,* 110–120.

Lewinsohn, P. M., Seeley, J. R., & Klein, D. N. (2003). Bipolar disorder in adolescents: Epidemiology and suicidal behavior. In B. Geller & M. P. DelBello (Eds.), *Bipolar disorder in childhood and early adolescence.* New York: Guilford Press.

Lewinsohn, P. M., Solomon, A., Seeley, J. R., & Zeiss, A. (2000). Clinical implications of "subthreshold" depressive symptoms. *Journal of Abnormal Psychology, 109,* 345–351.

Lewinsohn, P. M., Striegel-Moore, R. H., & Seeley, J. R. (2000). Epidemiology and natural course of eating disorders in young women from adolescence to young adulthood. *Journal of the American Academy of Child and Adolescent Psychiatry, 39,* 1284–1292.

Lewis, K. (2010). Treatment options for attention-deficit/hyperactivity disorder. *U. S. Pharmacist, 35,* 33–38.

Lewis-Fernández, R., Hinton, D. E., Laria, A. J., Patterson, E. H., Hofmann, S. G., Craske, M. G., et al. (2010). Culture and the anxiety disorders: Recommendations for DSM-V. *Depression and Anxiety, 27,* 212-229.

Leyfer, O., & Brown, T. A. (2011). The anxiety-depression spectrum. In D. H. Barlow (Ed.), *The Oxford handbook of clinical psychology.* New York: Oxford University Press.

Liaw, F., & Brooks-Gunn, J. (1994). Cumulative familial risk and low-birthweight children's cognitive and behavioral development. *Journal of Clinical Child Psychology, 23,* 360–372.

Liber, J. M., Van Widenfelt, B. M., Utens, E. M., Ferdinand, R. F., Van der Leeden, A. J., Van Gastel, W., et al. (2008). No differences between group and individual treatment of childhood anxiety disorders in a randomized clinical trial. *Journal of Child Psychology and Psychiatry, 49,* 886–893.

Licht, B. G., & Kistner, J. A. (1986). Motivational problems of learning-disabled children: Individual differences and their implications for treatment. In J. K. Torgesen & B. Y. L. Wong (Eds.), *Psychological and educational perspectives on learning disabilities.* New York: Academic Press.

Lichtenstein, P., & Annas, P. (2000). Heritability and prevalence of specific fears and phobias in childhood. *Journal of Child Psychology and Psychiatry, 41,* 927–937.

Lilienfeld, S. O. (2003). Comorbidity between and within childhood externalizing and internalizing disorders: Reflections and directions. *Journal of Abnormal Child Psychology, 31,* 285–291.

Lilienfeld, S. O., Lynn, S. J., & Lohr, J. M. (2003). *Science and pseudoscience in clinical psychology.* New York: Guilford Press.

Lilienfeld, S. O., Waldman, I. D., & Israel, A. C. (1994). A critical examination of the use of the term and concept of comorbidity in psychopathology research. *Clinical Psychology: Science and Practice, 1,* 71–83.

Lilienfeld, S. O., Wood, J. M., & Garb, H. N. (2000). The scientific status of projective techniques. *Psychological Science in the Public Interest, 1,* 27–66.

Lilly, M. S. (1979). Special education. Emerging issues. In M. S. Lilly (Ed.), *Children with exceptional needs.* New York: Holt, Rinehart and Winston.

Limond, J., & Leeke, R. (2005). Practitioner review: Cognitive rehabilitation for children with acquired brain injury. *Journal of Child and Adolescent Psychology, 46,* 339–352.

Lin, K. K., Sandler, I. N., Ayers, T. S., Wolchik, S. A., & Luecken, L. J. (2004). Resilience in parentally bereaved children and adolescents seeking preventive services. *Journal of Clinical Child and Adolescent Psychology, 33,* 673–683.

Linares, L. O., Montalto, D., Li, M. M., & Oza, V. S. (2006). A promising parenting intervention in foster care. *Journal of Consulting and Clinical Psychology, 74*, 32–41.

Lindström, K., Lindblad, F., & Hjern, A. (2011). Preterm birth and attention-deficit/hyperactivity disorder. *Pediatrics, 127*, 858–865.

Linnet, K. M., Dalsgaard, S., Obel, C., et al. (2003). Maternal lifestyle factors in pregnancy risk of attention deficit hyperactivity disorder and associated behaviors: Review of the current literature. *American Journal of Psychiatry, 160*, 1028–1040.

Linscheid, T. J. (2006). Behavioral treatments for pediatric feeding disorders. *Behavior Modification, 30*, 6–23.

Linscheid, T. R., & Rasnake, L. K. (2001). Eating problems in children. In C. E. Walker & M. C. Roberts (Eds.), *Handbook of clinical child psychology* (3rd ed.). New York: John Wiley & Sons.

Lipka, O., Lesaux, N. K., & Siegel, L. S. (2006). Retrospective analyses of the reading development of grade 4 students with reading disabilities. *Journal of Learning Disabilities, 39*, 364–378.

Lipka, O., & Siegel. L. S. (2006). Learning disabilities. In D. A. Wolfe & E. J. Mash (Eds.), *Behavioral and emotional disorders in adolescents. Nature, assessment, and treatment.* New York: The Guilford Press.

Lipschitz, D. S., Rasmusson, A. M., Yehuda, R., Wang, S., Anyan, W., Gueoguieva, R., et al. (2003). Salivary cortisol responses to dexamethasone in adolescents with posttraumatic stress disorder. *Journal of the American Academy of Child and Adolescent Psychiatry, 42*, 1310–1317.

Little, P. M. D., Wimer, C., & Weiss, H. B. (2008). *After school programs in the 21st century. Their potential and what it takes to achieve it.* Cambridge, MA: Harvard Family Research Project.

Liu, H. Y., Potter, M. P., Woodworth, K. Y., Yorks, D. M., Petty, C. R., Wozniak, J. R., et al. (2011). Pharmacologic treatments for pediatric bipolar disorder: A review and meta-analysis. *Journal of the American Academy of Child and Adolescent Psychiatry, 50*, 749–762.

Liu, X., Akula, N., Skup, M., Brotman, M. A., Leibenluft, E., & McMahon, F. J. (2010). Amygdala activation in youth with and without bipolar disorder. *Journal of the American Academy of Child and Adolescent Psychiatry, 49*, 33–41.

Livingston, G., & Parker, K. (2011). A tale of two fathers. More are active, but more are absent. *Pew Social & Demographic Trends.* Retrieved October 2011 from http://www.pewsocialtrends.org/2011/06/15/a-tale-of-two-fathers/2/

Llewellyn, G., Dunn, P., Fante, M., Turnbull, L., & Grace, R. (1999). Family factors influencing out-of-home placement decisions. *Journal of Intellectual Disability Research, 43*, 219–233.

Lobato, D. J., & Kao, B. T. (2005). Family-based group intervention for young siblings of children with chronic illness and developmental disability. *Journal of Pediatric Psychology, 30*, 678–682.

Lochman, J. E., Boxmeyer, C. L., Powell, N. P., Barry, T. D., & Pardini, D. A. (2010). Anger control training for aggressive youths. In J. R. Weisz & A. E. Kazdin (Eds.), *Evidence-based psychotherapies for children and adolescents* (2nd ed.). New York: The Guilford Press.

Lochman, J. E., Whidby, J. M., & FitzGerald, D. P. (2000). Cognitive-behavioral assessment and treatment with aggressive children. In P. C. Kendall (Ed.), *Child and adolescent therapy: Cognitive-behavioral procedures* (2nd ed.). New York: Guilford.

Lock, J., Agras, W. S., Bryson, S., & Kraemer, H. (2005). A comparison of short- and long-term family therapy for adolescent anorexia nervosa. *Journal of the American Academy of Child and Adolescent Psychiatry, 44*, 632–639.

Lock, J., & le Grange, D. (2005). Family-based treatment of eating disorders. *International Journal of Eating Disorders, 37 (Suppl.)*, 64–67.

Loeb, S., Fuller, B., Kagan, S. L., & Carrol, B. (2004). Child care in poor communities: Early learning effects of type, quality, and stability. *Child Development, 75*, 47–65.

Loeber, R. (1988). Natural histories of conduct problems, delinquency, and associated substance use: Evidence for developmental progressions. In B. B. Lahey & A. E. Kazdin (Eds.), *Advances in clinical child psychology* (Vol. 11). New York: Plenum.

Loeber, R., Burke, J. D., Lahey, B. B., Winters, A., & Zera, M. (2000). Oppositional defiant and conduct disorder: A review of the past 10 years, Part I. *Journal of the American Academy of Child and Adolescent Psychiatry, 39*, 1468–1484.

Loeber, R., Burke, J. D., & Pardini, D. A. (2009a). Development and etiology of disruptive and delinquent behavior. *Annual Review of Clinical Psychology, 5*, 291–310.

Loeber, R., Burke, J. D., & Pardini, D. A. (2009b). Perspective on oppositional defiant disorder, conduct disorder, and psychopathic features. *Journal of Child Psychology & Psychiatry, 50*, 133–142.

Loeber, R., & Farrington, D. P. (2000). Young children who commit crime: Epidemiology, developmental origins, risk factors, early interventions, and policy implications. *Development and Psychopathology, 12*, 737–762.

Loeber, R., & Hay, D. F. (1994). Developmental approaches to aggression and conduct problems. In M. Rutter & D. F. Hay (Eds.), *Development through life: A handbook for clinicians.* Malden, MA: Blackwell Scientific.

Loeber, R., & Keenan, K. (1994). Interaction between conduct disorder and its comorbid conditions: Effects of age and gender. *Clinical Psychology Review, 14*, 497–523.

Loeber, R., & Schmaling, K. B. (1985) Empirical evidence for overt and covert patterns of antisocial conduct problems: A meta-analysis. *Journal of Abnormal Child Psychology, 13*, 337–354.

Loeber, R., & Stouthamer-Loeber, M. (1998). Development of juvenile aggression and violence: Some common misconceptions and controversies. *American Psychologist, 53*, 242–259.

Loeber, R., Wung, P., Keenan, K., Giroux, B., Stouthamer-Loeber, M., Van Kammen, W. B., & Maughan, B. (1993).

Developmental pathways in disruptive child behavior. *Development and Psychopathology, 5,* 103–133.

Logan, D. E., & King, C. A. (2001). Parental facilitation of adolescent mental health service utilization: A conceptual and empirical review. *Clinical Psychology: Science and Practice, 8,* 319–333.

Long, K. A., & Marsland, A. L. (2011). Family adjustment to childhood cancer: A systematic review. *Clinical Child and Family Psychology Review, 14,* 57–88.

Long, P., Forehand, R., Wierson, M., & Morgan, A. (1994). Does parent training with young noncompliant children have long term effects? *Behaviour Research and Therapy, 32,* 101–107.

Lonigan, C. J., Burgess, S. R., & Anthony, J. L. (2000). Development of emergent literacy and early reading skills in preschool children: Evidence from a latent-variable longitudinal study. *Developmental Psychology, 36,* 596–613.

Lonigan, C. J., Vasey, M. W., Phillips, B. M., & Hazen, R. A. (2004). Temperament, anxiety, and the processing of threat-relevant stimuli. *Journal of Clinical Child and Adolescent Psychology, 33,* 8–20.

Lorch, E. P., Milich, R., Sanchez, R. P., van den Broek, P., Baer, S., Hooks, K., et al. (2000). Comprehension of televised stories in boys with attention deficit/hyperactivity disorder and nonreferred boys. *Journal of Abnormal Psychology, 109,* 321–330.

Lord, C., Shulman, C., & DiLavore, P. (2004). Regression and word loss in autistic spectrum disorders. *Journal of Child Psychology and Psychiatry, 45,* 936–955.

Lord, C. E. (2010). Autism: From research to practice. *American Psychologist, 65,* 815–826.

Lord, H., & Mahoney, J. L. (2007). Neighborhood crime and self-care: Risks for aggression and lower academic performance. *Developmental Psychology, 43,* 1321–1333.

Lorian, R. P. (2000). Community, prevention, and wellness. In M. Hersen & R. T. Ammerman (Eds.), *Advanced abnormal child psychology.* Mahwah, NJ: Lawrence Erlbaum Associates.

Loth, K. A., Mond, J., Wall, M., & Neumark-Sztainer, D. (2011). Weight status and emotional well-being: Longitudinal findings from Project EAT. *Journal of Pediatric Psychology, 36,* 216–225.

Lovaas, O. I. (1987). Behavioral treatment and normal educational and intellectual functioning in young autistic children. *Journal of Consulting and Clinical Psychology, 55,* 3–9.

Lovaas, O. I., & Smith, T. (1988). Intensive behavioral treatment for young autistic children. In B. B. Lahey & A. E. Kazdin (Eds.), *Advances in clinical child psychology,* (Vol. 2). New York: Plenum.

Lovaas, O. I., & Smith, T. (2003). Early and intensive behavioral intervention in autism. In A. E. Kazdin & J. R. Weisz (Eds.), *Evidence-based psychotherapies for children and adolescents.* New York: Guilford Press.

Lovaas, O. I., Young, D. B., & Newsom, C. D. (1978). Childhood psychosis: Behavioral treatment. In B. B. Wolman (Ed.), *Handbook of treatment of mental disorders in childhood and adolescence.* Englewood Cliffs, NJ: Prentice Hall.

Lovejoy, M. C., Graczyk, P. A., O'Hare, E., & Newman, G. (2000). Maternal depression and parenting behavior: A meta-analytic review. *Clinical Psychology Review, 20,* 561–592.

Loveland, K. A., & Tunali-Kotoski, B. (1997). The school-age child with autism. In D. J. Cohen & F. R. Volkmar (Eds.), *Handbook of pervasive and developmental disorders.* New York: John Wiley.

Luby, J. L. (2009). Depression. In C. H. Zeanah, Jr. (Ed.), *Handbook of infant mental health* (3rd ed.). New York: The Guilford Press.

Luby, J. L., Belden, A. C., & Tandon, M. (2010). Bipolar disorder in the preschool period. In D. J. Miklowitz & D. Cicchetti (Eds.), *Understanding bipolar disorder: A developmental psychopathology perspective.* New York: The Guilford Press.

Lucas-Thompson, R. G., Goldberg, W. A., & Prause, J. (2010). Maternal work early in the lives of children and its distal associations with achievement and behavior problems: A meta-analysis. *Psychological Bulletin, 136,* 915–942.

Luckasson, R. et al. (1992). *Mental retardation: Definition, classification, and systems of supports.* Washington, DC: American Association on Mental Retardation.

Luckasson, R. et al. (2002). *Mental retardation: Definition, classification, and systems of support.* Washington, DC: American Association on Mental Retardation.

Ludwig, J., & Mayer, S. (2006). "Culture" and the intergenerational transmission of poverty: The prevention paradox. *Opportunity in America. Future of Children, 16,* 176–196.

Luman, M., Oosterlaan, J., Hyde, C., van Meel, C. S., Sergeast, J. A., (2007). Heart rate and reinforcement sensitivity in ADHD. *Journal of Child Psychology and Psychiatry, 48,* 890–898.

Luman, M., van Noesel, S. J. P., Papanikolau, A., van Oostenbruggen-Scheffer, J., Veugelers, D., Sergeant, J. A., et al. (2009). Inhibition, reinforcement sensitivity and temporal information processing in ADHD ann ADHD+ODD: Evidence of a separate entity? *Journal of Abnormal Child Psychology, 37,* 1123–1135.

Lurie, N., & Dubowitz, T. (2007). Health disparities and access to health. *Journal of the American Medical Association, 297,* 1118–1121.

Lustig, S. L., Kia-Keating, M., Knight, W. G., Geltman, P., Ellis, H., Kinzie, J. D., et al. (2004). Review of child and adolescent mental health. *Journal of the American Academy of Child and Adolescent Psychiatry, 43,* 24–36.

Luthar, S. S. (2006). Resilience in development: A synthesis of research across five decades. In D. Cicchetti & D. J. Cohen (Eds.), *Developmental psychopathology. Vol. 3. Risk, disorder, and adaptation.* Hoboken, NJ: John Wiley & Sons.

Luthar, S. S., & Goldstein, A. (2004). Children's exposure to community violence: Implications for understanding risk and resilience. *Journal of Clinical Child and Adolescent Psychology, 33,* 499–505.

Ly, T. M. (2008). Asian American parents' attributions of children with Down syndrome: Connections with child characteristics and culture. *Intellectual and Developmental Disabilities, 46,* 129–140.

Lynch, M., & Cicchetti, D. (1998). An ecological–interactional analysis of children and contexts: The longitudinal interplay among child treatment, community violence, and children's symptomatology. *Development and Psychopathology, 10,* 235–257.

Lyon, G. R., & Cutting, L. E. (1998). Learning disabilities. In E. J. Mash & R. A. Barkley (Eds.), *Treatment of childhood disorders.* New York: Guilford Press.

Lyon, G. R., Fletcher, J. M., & Barnes, M. C. (2003). Learning disabilities. In E. J. Mash & R. A. Barkley (Eds.), *Child psychopathology.* New York: Guilford Press.

Lyon, G. R., Fletcher, J. M., Fuchs, L. S., & Chhabra, V. (2006). Learning disabilities. In E. J. Mash & R. A. Barkley (Eds.), *Treatment of childhood disorders.* New York: The Guilford Press.

Lyons-Ruth, K., Zeanah, C. H., & Benoit, D. (2003). Disorder and risk for disorder during infancy and toddlerhood. In E. J. Mash & R. A. Barkley (Eds.), *Child psychopathology.* New York: Guilford Press.

Maccini, P., & Hughes, C. A. (1997). Mathematics interventions for adolescents with learning disabilities. *Learning Disabilities Research and Practice, 12,* 168–176.

Maccoby, E. E. (1992). The role of parents in the socialization of children: An historic overview. *Developmental Psychology, 28,* 1006–1017.

Maccoby, E. E., & Martin, J. A. (1983). Socialization in the context of the family: Parent-child interaction. In P. H. Mussen (Ed.), *Handbook of child psychology* (Vol. IV). New York: John Wiley.

MacDonald, A. W., Pogue-Geile, M. F., Johnson, M. K., & Carter, C. S. (2003). A specific deficit in context processing in the unaffected siblings of patients with schizophrenia. *Archives of General Psychiatry, 60,* 57–63.

MacDonnell, K. E., Naar-King, S., Murphy, D. A., Parsons, J. T., & Harper, G. W. (2010). Predictors of medication adherence in high risk youth of color living with HIV. *Journal of Pediatric Psychology, 35,* 593–601.

MacFarlane, J. W., Allen, L., & Honzik, M. P. (1954). *A developmental study of the behavior problems of normal children between 21 months and 14 years.* Berkeley: University of California Press.

Machover, K. (1949). *Personality projection in the drawing of the human figure.* Springfield, IL: Chas. C. Thomas.

MacKay, S., Henderson, J., Del Bove, G., Marton, P., Warling, D., & Root, C. (2006). Fire interest and antisociality as fisk factors in the severity and persistence of juvenile firesetting. *Journal of the American Academy of Child and Adolescent Psychiatry, 45,* 1077–1084.

MacLean, K. (2003). The impact of institutionalization on child development. *Development and Psychopathology, 15,* 853–884.

MacMillan, D. L., Keogh, B. K., & Jones, R. L. (1986). Special educational research on mildly handicapped learners. In M. C. Wittrock (Ed.), *Handbook of research on teaching.* New York: Macmillan.

MacMillan, D. L., & Reschly, D. J. (1997). Issues of definition and classification. In W. E. MacLean, Jr. (Ed.), *Ellis' handbook of mental deficiency, psychological theory and research.* Mahwah, NJ: Lawrence Erlbaum.

MacMillan, R., McMorris, B. J., Kruttschnitt, C. (2004). Linked lives: Stability and change in maternal circumstances and trajectories of antisocial behavior in children. *Child Development, 75,* 205–220.

Madsen, K. M., Lauritsen, M. B., Pedersen, C. B., Thorsen, P., Plesner, A-M., Andersen, P. H., & Mortensen, P. B. (2003). Thimerosal and the occurrence of autism: Negative ecological evidence from Danish population-based data. *Pediatrics, 112,* 604–606.

Maguin, E., & Loeber, R. (1996). Academic performance and delinquency. In M. Tonry (Ed.), *Crime and justice* (Vol. 20). Chicago: University of Chicago Press.

Mahatmya, D., Zobel, A., & Valdovinos, M. G. (2008). Treatment approaches for self-injurious behavior in individuals with autism: Behavioral and pharmacological methods. *Journal of Early and Intensive Behavioral Intervention, 5,* 106–118.

Mahoney, L., Ayers, S., & Seddon, P. (2010). The association between parent's and healthcare professional's behavior and children's coping and distress during venepuncture. *Journal of Pediatric Psychology, 35,* 985–995.

Main, M. (1996). Introduction to the special section on attachment and psychopathology: 2. Overview of the field of attachment. *Journal of Consulting and Clinical Psychology, 64,* 237–243.

Major, B., & O'Brien, L. T. (2005). The social psychology of stigma. *Annual Review of Psychology, 56,* 393–421.

Malee, K., Williams, P. L., Montepiedra, G., Nichols, S., Sirois, P. A., Storm, D., et al. (2009). The role of cognitive functioning in medication adherence of children and adolescents with HIV infection. *Journal of Pediatric Psychology, 34,* 164–175.

Malmquist, C. P. (1977). Childhood depression: A clinical and behavioral perspective. In J. G. Schulterbrandt & A. Raskin (Eds.), *Depression in childhood: Diagnosis, treatment, and conceptual models.* New York: Raven Press.

Manassis, K., Fung, D., Tannock, R., Sloman, L., Fiksenbaum, L. & McInnes, A. (2003). Characterizing selective mutism: Is it more than social anxiety? *Depression and Anxiety, 18,* 153–161.

Manassis, K., Tannock, R., & Barbosa, J. (2000). Dichotic listening and response inhibition in children with comorbid anxiety disorders and ADHD. *Journal of the American Academy of Child and Adolescent Psychiatry, 39,* 1152–1159.

Manimala, R., Blount, R. L., & Cohen, L. L. (2000). The effects of parental reassurance versus distraction on child distress and coping during immunizations. *Child Health Care, 29,* 161–177.

Manly, J. T., Kim, J. E., Rogosch, F. A., & Cicchetti, D. (2001). Dimensions of child maltreatment and children's adjustment: Contributions of developmental timing and subtype. *Development and Psychopathology, 13,* 759–782.

Mannuzza, S., Klein, R. G., Bessler, A., Malloy, P., & LaPadula, M. (1993). Adult outcome of hyperactive boys. *Archives of General Psychiatry, 50,* 565–576.

Mannuzza, S., Klein, R. G., Bessler, A., Malloy, P., & LaPadula, M. (1998). Adult psychiatric status of hyperactive boys grown up. *American Journal of Psychiatry, 155,* 493–498.

March, J. S., & Albano, A. M. (1998). New developments in assessing pediatric anxiety disorders. In T. H. Ollendick & R. J. Prinz (Eds.), *Advances in clinical child psychology* (Vol. 20). New York: Plenum Press.

March, J. S., Franklin, M. E., Leonard, H. L., & Foa, E. B. (2004). Obsessive-compulsive disorder. In T. L. Morris & J. S. March (Eds.), *Anxiety disorders in children and adolescents.* New York: Guilford Press.

March, J. S., & Mulle, K. (1998). *OCD in children and adolescents: A cognitive-behavioral treatment manual.* New York: Guilford Press.

March, J. S., Parker, J. D. A., Sullivan, K., Stallings, P., & Conners, C. K. (1997). The multidimensional anxiety scale for children (MASC): Factor structure, reliability and validity. *Journal of the American Academy of Child and Adolescent Psychiatry 36,* 554–565.

March, S., Spence, S. H., & Donovan, C. L. (2009). The efficacy of an internet-based cognitive-behavioral therapy intervention for child anxiety disorders. *Journal of Pediatric Psychology, 34,* 474–487.

Marchetti, A. G., & Campbell, V. A. (1990). Social skills. In J. L. Matson (Ed.), *Handbook of behavior modification with the mentally retarded.* New York: Plenum.

Marchi, M., & Cohen, P. (1990). Early childhood eating behaviors and adolescent eating disorders. *Journal of the American Academy of Child and Adolescent Psychiatry, 29,* 112–117.

Marcus, D. K., Fulton, J. J., & Clarke, E. J. (2010). Lead and conduct problems: A meta-analysis. *Journal of Clinical Child and Adolescent Psychology, 39,* 234–241.

Marcus, S. C., & Durkin, M. (2011). Stimulant adherence and academic performance in urban youth with attention-deficit/hyperactivity disorder. *Journal of the American Academy of Child and Adolescent Psychiatry, 50,* 480–489.

Marenco, S., & Weinberger, D. R. (2000). The neurodevelopmental hypothesis of schizophrenia: Following a trail of evidence from cradle to grave. *Development and Psychopathology, 12,* 501–527.

Margolin, G. (1998). Effects of domestic violence on children. In P. K. Trickett & C. J. Schellenbach (Eds.), *Violence against children in the family and the community.* Washington, DC: American Psychological Association.

Margolin, G., & Gordis, E. B. (2000). The effects of family and community violence on children. *Annual Review of Psychology, 51,* 445–479.

Margolin, G., & Gordis, E. B. (2004). Children's exposure to violence in the family and community. *Current Directions in Psychological Science, 13,* 152–155.

Margolin, G., Vickerman, K. A., Ramos, M. C., Serrano, S. D., Gordis, E. B., Iturralde, E., et al. (2009). Youth exposed to violence: Stability, co-occurrence, and context. *Clinical Child and Family Psychology Review, 12,* 39–54.

Martell, M., Nikolas, M., & Nigg, J. T. (2007). Executive function in adolescents with ADHD. *Journal of the American Academy of Child and Adolescent Psychiatry, 46,* 1437–1444.

Martinez, C. R., Jr., & Eddy, J. M. (2005). Effects of culturally adapted parent management training on Latino youth behavioral health outcomes. *Journal of Consulting and Clinical Psychology, 73,* 841–851.

Marton, K., & Schwartz, R. G. (2003). Working memory capacity and language processes in children with specific language impairment. *Journal of Speech, Language, and Hearing Research, 46,* 1138–1153.

Masi, G., Favilla, L., Mucci, M., & Millepiedi, S. (2000). Panic disorder in clinically referred children and adolescents. *Child Psychiatry and Human Development, 31,* 139–151.

Masi, G., Millepiedi, S., Mucci, M., Poli, P., Bertini, N., & Milantoni, L. (2004). Generalized anxiety disorder in referred children and adolescents. *Journal of the American Academy of Child and Adolescent Psychiatry, 43,* 752–760.

Masten, A. S. (2001). Ordinary magic: Resilience processes in development. *American Psychologist, 56,* 227–238.

Masten, A. S., & Coatsworth, J. D. (1998). The development of competence in favorable and unfavorable environments: Lessons from research on successful children. *American Psychologist, 53,* 205–220.

Masten, A. S., & Shaffer, A. (2006). How families matter in child development: Reflections from research on risk and resilience. In A. Clarke-Stewart & J. Dunn (Eds.), *Families count. Effects on child and adolescent development.* New York: Cambridge University Press.

Mata, J., & Gotlib, I. H. (2011). 5-HTTLPR moderates the relation between changes in depressive and bulimic symptoms in adolescent girls: A longitudinal study. *International Journal of Eating Disorders, 44,* 383–388.

Matson, J. L., Kozlowski, A. M., Worley, J. A., Shoemaker, M. E., Sipes, M., & Horovitz, M. (2011). What is the evidence for causes of challenging behaviors in persons with intellectual disabilities and autism spectrum disorders? *Research in Developmental Disabilities, 32,* 693–698.

Matson, J. L., LeBlanc, L. A., & Weinheimer, B. (1999). Reliability of the Matson Evaluation of Social Skills with Severe Retardation (MESSIER). *Behavior Modification, 23,* 647–661.

Matson, J. L., Shoemaker, M. E., Sipes, M., Horovitz, M., Worley, J. A., & Kozlowski, A. M. (2010). Replacement behaviors for identified functions of challenging behaviors. *Research in Developmental Disabilities, 32,* 681–684.

Matthews, C. A., & Grados, M. A. (2011). Familiarity of Tourette syndrome, obsessive-compulsive disorder, and attention-deficit/hyperactivity disorder: Heritability analysis in a large sib-pair sample. *Journal of the American Academy of Child and Adolescent Psychiatry, 50,* 46–54.

Mattila, M-L., Hurtig, T., Haapsamo, H., Jussila, K., Kuusikko-Gauffin, S., Kielinen, M., et al. (2010). Comorbid psychiatric disorders associated with Asperger syndrome/high-functioning autism: A community and clinic-based study. *Journal of Autism and Developmental Disorders, 40,* 1080–1093.

Mattila, M-L., Kielinen, M., Jussila, K., Linna, S. L., Bloigu, R.,Ebeling, H., et al. (2007). An epidemiological and diagnostic study of Asperger syndrome according to four sets of diagnostic criteria. *Journal of the American Academy of Child and Adolescent Psychiatry, 46,* 636–446.

Mattison, R. E. (2000). School consultation: A review of research on issues unique to the school environment. *Journal of the American Academy of Child and Adolescent Psychiatry, 39,* 402–413.

Maughan, B., Rowe, R., Messer, J., Goodman, R., & Meltzer, H. (2004). Conduct disorder and oppositional defiant disorder in a national sample: Developmental epidemiology. *Journal of Child Psychology and Psychiatry, 45,* 609–621.

Maughan, B., & Rutter, M. (1998). Continuities and discontinuities in antisocial behavior from childhood to adult life. In T. H. Ollendick & R. J. Prinz (Eds.), *Advances in clinical child psychology* (Vol. 20). New York: Plenum Press.

Maughan, D. R., Christiansen, E., Jenson, W. R., Olympia, D., & Clark, E. (2005). Behavioral parent training as a treatment for externalizing behaviors and disruptive behavior disorders: A meta-analysis. *School Psychology Review, 34,* 267–286.

Maulik, P. K., Mascarenhas, M. N., Mathers, C. D., Dua, T., & Saxena, S. (2011). Prevalence of intellectual disability: A meta-analysis of population-based studies. *Research in Developmental Disabilities, 32,* 419–436.

Mawhood, L., Howlin, P., & Rutter, M. (2000). Autism and developmental receptive language disorder—a comparative followup in early adult life I: Cognitive and language outcomes. *Journal of Child Psychology and Psychiatry, 41,* 547–559.

Mayes, L. C., & Suchman, N. E. (2006). Developmental pathways to substance abuse. In D. Cicchetti & D. J. Cohen (Eds.), *Developmental psychopathology, Vol. 3: Risk, disorder, and adaptation* (2nd ed.). Hoboken, NJ: John Wiley & Sons.

Mayes, S. D. (1992). Rumination disorder: Diagnosis, complications, mediating variables, and treatment. In B. B. Lahey & A. E. Kazdin (Eds.), *Advances in clinical child psychology* (Vol. 14). New York: Plenum.

Mazefsky, C. A., Williams, D. L., & Minshew, N. J. (2008). Variability in adaptive behavior in autism: Evidence for the importance of family history. *Journal of Abnormal Child Psychology, 36,* 591–599.

McAlonan, G. M., Cheung, V., Chua, S. E., Oosterlaan, J., Hung, S., Tang, C., et al. (2009). Age-related grey matter volume correlates of response inhibition and shifting in attention-deficit hyperactivity disorder. *British Journal of Psychiatry, 194,* 123–129.

McAlpine, C., & Singh, N. N. (1986). Pica in institutionalized mentally retarded persons. *Journal of Mental Deficiency Research, 30,* 171–178.

McArthur, G. M., Hogben, J. H., Edwards, V. T., Heath, S. M., & Mengler, E. D. (2000). On the "specifics" of specific reading disability and specific language impairment. *Journal of Child Psychology and Psychiatry, 41,* 869–874.

McCabe, M. P., & Ricciardelli, L. A. (2004).Weight and shape concerns of boys and men. In J. K. Thompson (Ed.), *Handbook of eating disorders and obesity.* Hoboken, NJ: John Wiley.

McCaffrey, R. J., Lynch, J. K., & Westervelt, H. J. (2011). Clinical neuropsychology. In D. H. Barlow (Ed.), *The Oxford handbook of clinical psychology.* New York: Oxford University Press.

McCartney, K. (2006). The family-child-care mesosystem. In A. Clarke-Stewart & J. Dunn (Eds.), *Families count. Effects on child and adolescent development.* NewYork: Cambridge University Press.

McCarton, C. M., Brooks-Gunn, J., Wallace, I. F., & Bauer, C. R. (1997). Results at age 8 years of early intervention for lowbirth-weight premature infants: The infant health and development program. *Journal of the American Medical Association, 277,* 126–132.

McCarty, C. A., McMahon, R. J., & Conduct Problems Prevention Research Group. (2005). Domains of risk to the developmental continuity of firesetting. *Behavior Therapy, 36,* 185–195.

McCauley, E., Pavlidis, K., & Kendall, K. (2001). Developmental precursors of depression: The child and the social environment. In I. M. Goodyer (Ed.), *The depressed child and adolescent* (2nd ed.). Cambridge, UK: Cambridge University Press.

McClellan, J., Breiger, D., McCurry, C., & Hlastala, S. A. (2003). Premorbid functioning in early-onset psychotic disorders. *Journal of the American Academy of Child and Adolescent Psychiatry, 42,* 666–672.

McClellan, J. M. (2005). Early-onset schizophrenia. In B. J. Sadock & V. A. Sadock (Eds.), *Comprehensive textbook of psychiatry* (Vol. 2). Philadelphia: Lippincott Williams & Wilkins.

McClellan, J. M.,Werry, J., et al. (2001). Practice parameter for the assessment and treatment of children and adolescents with schizophrenia. *Journal of the American Academy of Child and Adolescent Psychiatry, 40:7* Supplement, 4S–23S.

McClellan, J. M., & Werry, J. S. (2000). Research psychiatric diagnostic interviews for children and adolescents. Introduction. *Journal of the American Academy of Child and Adolescent Psychiatry, 39,* 19–27.

McClure, E. B., Connell, A. M., Zucker, M., Griffith, J. R., & Kaslow, N. J. (2005). The Adolescent Depression Empowerment Project (ADEPT): A culturally sensitive family treatment for depressed African American girls. In E. D. Hibbs & P. S. Jensen (Eds.), *Psychosocial treatments for child and adolescent disorders:*

Empirically based strategies for clinical practice (2nd ed.). Washington, DC: American Psychological Association.

McClure-Tone, E. B. (2010). Social cognition and cognitive flexibility in bipolar disorder. In D. J. Miklowitz & D. Cicchetti (Eds.), *Understanding bipolar disorder: A developmental psychopathology perspective*. New York: The Guilford Press.

McConaughy, S. H. (2005). *Clinical interviews for children and adolescents: Assessment to intervention*. New York: The Guilford Press.

McCrory, E., De Brito, S. A., & Viding, E. (2010). The neurobiology and genetics of maltreatment and adversity. *Journal of Child Psychology and Psychiatry, 51,* 1079–1095.

McCulloch, R., & Collins, J. J. (2006). Pain in children who have life-limiting conditions. *Child and Adolescent Psychiatric Clinics of North America, 15,* 657–682.

McDowell, K. D., Lonigan, C. J., & Goldstein, H. (2007). Relations among SES, age, and predictors of phonological awareness. *Journal of Speech, Language, and Hearing Research, 50,* 1079–1092.

McEachin, J. J., Smith, T., & Lovaas, O. I. (1993). Long-term outcome for children with autism who received early intensive behavioral treatment. *American Journal on Mental Retardation, 97,* 359–372.

McEvoy, R. E., Rogers, S. J., & Pennington, B. F. (1993). Executive functions and social communication deficits in young autistic children. *Journal of Child Psychology and Psychiatry, 34,* 563–578.

McGee, R., Feehan, M., Williams, S., & Anderson, J. (1992). DSMIII disorders from age 11 to age 15 years. *Journal of the American Academy of Child and Adolescent Psychiatry, 31,* 50–59.

McGee, R., Feehan, M., Williams, S., Partridge, F., Silva, P. A., & Kelly, J. (1990). DSM-III disorders in a large sample of adolescents. *Journal of the American Academy of Child and Adolescent Psychiatry, 29,* 611–619.

McGee, R., Prior, M., Williams, S., Smart, D., & Sanson, A. (2002). The long-term significance of teacher-rated hyperactivity and reading ability in childhood: Findings from two longitudinal studies. *Journal of Child Psychology and Psychiatry, 43,* 1004–1017.

McGee, R., Williams, S., & Poulton, R. (2000). Hallucinations in nonpsychotic children. *Journal of the American Academy of Child and Adolescent Psychiatry, 39,* 12–13.

McGee, R. A., & Wolfe, D. A. (1991). Psychological maltreatment: Toward an operational definition. *Development and Psychopathology, 3,* 3–18.

McGorry, P. D., Killackey, E., & Yung, A. (2008). Early intervention in psychosis: Concepts, evidence and future directions. *World Psychiatry, 7,* 148–156.

McGorry, P. D., Purcell, R., Goldstone, S., & Amminger, G. P. (2010). Age of onset and timing of treatment for mental and substance use disorders; implications for preventive intervention strategies and models of care. *Current Opinion in Psychiatry, 24,* 301–306.

McGrath, L. M., & Peterson, R. L. (2009a). Attention-deficit/hyperactivity disorder. In B. F. Pennington (Ed.), *Diagnosing learning disorders*. New York: Guilford Press.

McGrath, L. M., & Peterson, R. L. (2009b). Autism spectrum disorder. In B. F. Pennington (Ed.), *Diagnosing learning disorders*. (2nd ed.). New York: Guilford Press.

McGrath, L. M., & Peterson, R. L. (2009c). Intellectual disability. In B. F. Pennington (Ed.), *Diagnosing learning disorders*. New York: Guilford Press.

McGrath, M. L., Mellon, M. M., & Murphy, L. (2000). Empirically supported treatments in pediatric psychology: Constipation and encopresis. *Journal of Pediatric Psychology, 25,* 225–254.

McGue, M., & Lykken, D. T. (1992). Genetic influence on risk of divorce. *Psychological Science, 6,* 368–373.

McHugh, R. K., & Barlow, D. H. (2010). The dissemination and implementation of evidence-based psychological treatments. *American Psychologist, 65,* 73–84.

McKinney, C., & Renk, K. (2011). Atypical antipsychotic medications in the management of disruptive behaviors in children: Safety guidelines and recommendations. *Clinical Psychology Review, 31,* 465–471.

McLanahan, S., & Sandefur, G. (1994). *Growing up with a single parent: What hurts, what helps?* Cambridge, MA: Harvard University Press.

McLaughlin, K. A., Hilt, L. M., & Nolen-Hoeksema, S. (2007). Racial/ethnic differences in internalizing and externalizing symptoms in adolescence. *Journal of Abnormal Child Psychology, 35,* 801–816.

McLaughlin, K. A., & Glang, A. (2010). The effectiveness of a bicycle safety program for improving safety-related knowledge and behavior in young elementary students. *Journal of Pediatric Psychology, 35,* 343–353.

McLeskey, J., Hoppey, D., Williamson, P., & Rentz, T. (2004). Is inclusion an illusion? An examination of national and state trends toward the education of students with learning disabilities in general education classrooms. *Learning Disabilities Research and Practice, 19,* 109–115.

McMahon, R. J., & Forehand, R. L. (2003). *Helping the noncompliant child: Family-based treatment for oppositional behavior* (2nd ed.). New York: The Guilford Press.

McMahon, R. J., & Frick, P. J. (2007). Conduct and oppositional disorders. In E. J. Mash & R. A. Barkley (Eds.), *Assessment of childhood disorders*. (4th ed.). New York: The Guilford Press.

McMahon, R. J., Wells, K. C., & Kotler, J. S. (2006). Conduct problems. In E. J. Mash & R. A. Barkeley (Eds.), *Treatment of childhood disorders* (3rd ed.). New York: The Guilford Press.

McMaster, F. P., O'Neill, J., & Rosenberg, D. R. (2008). Brain imaging in pediatric obsessive-compulsive disorder. *Journal of the American Academy of Child and Adolescent Psychiatry, 47,* 1262–1272.

McNamara, J. K., Scissons, M., & Gutknecth, N. B. (2011). A longitudinal study of kindergarten children at risk for reading disabilities. The poor really are getting poorer. *Journal of Learning Disabilities, 44*, 421–430.

McNulty, M. A. (2003). Dyslexia and the life course. *Journal of Learning Disabilities, 36*, 363–381.

McQuaid, E. L., & Abramson, N. W. (2009). Pediatric asthma. In M. C. Roberts & R. G. Steele (Eds.), *Handbook of pediatric psychology.* (4th ed.). New York: The Guilford Press.

McQuaid, E. L., Kopel, S. J., & Nassau, J. H. (2001). Behavioral adjustment in children with asthma: A meta-analysis. *Journal of Developmental and Behavioral Pediatrics, 22*, 430–439.

McQuaid, E. L., Mitchell, D. K., Walders, N., Nassau, J. H., Kopel, S. J., Klein, R. B., et al. (2007). Pediatric asthma morbidity: The importance of symptom perception and family response to symptoms. *Journal of Pediatric Psychology, 32*, 167–177.

McReynolds, P. (1987). Lightner Witmer: Little-known founder of clinical psychology. *American Psychologist, 42*, 849–858.

Meadan, H., Stoner, J. B., & Angell, M. E. (2010). Review of literature related to the social, emotional, and behavioral adjustment of siblings with autism spectrum disorder. *Journal of Developmental and Physical Disabilities, 22*, 83–100.

Measelle, J. R., Stice, E., & Hogansen, J. M. (2006). Developmental trajectories of co-occurring depressive, eating, antisocial, and substance abuse problems in female adolescents. *Journal of Abnormal Psychology, 115*, 524–538.

Mednick, S. A., Machon, R. A., Huttunen, M. O., & Bonnett, D. (1988). Fetal viral infection and adult schizophrenia. *Archives of General Psychiatry, 45*, 189–192.

Mehler, P. S. (2011). Medical complications of bulimia nervosa and their treatments. *International Journal of Eating Disorders, 44*, 95–104.

Meijer, A. M., Reitz, E., Dekovic, M., van den Wittenboer, G. l. H., & Stoel, R. D. (2010). Longitudinal relations between sleep quality, time in bed and adolescent problem behaviour. *Journal of Child Psychology and Psychiatry, 51*, 1278–1286.

Meijer, S. A., Sinnema, G., Bijstra, J. O., Mellenbergh, G. J., & Wolters, W. H. G. (2000). Social functioning in children with a chronic illness. *Journal of Child Psychology and Psychiatry, 41*, 309–317.

Meins, E., Fernyhough, C., Fradley, E., & Tuckey, M. (2001). Rethinking maternal sensitivity: Mothers' comments on infants' mental processes predict security of attachment at 12 months. *Journal of Child Psychology and Psychiatry, 42*, 637–648.

Melamed, B. G., & Siegel, L. J. (1975). Reduction of anxiety in children facing hospitalization and surgery by use of filmed modeling. *Journal of Consulting and Clinical Psychology, 43*, 511–521.

Melamed, B. G., & Siegel, L. J. (1980). *Behavioral medicine: Practical applications in health care.* New York: Springer.

Melnick, S. M., & Hinshaw, S. P. (1996). What they want and what they get: The social goals of boys with ADHD and comparison boys. *Journal of Abnormal Child Psychology, 24*, 169–185.

Meltzer, H. Y., Alphs, L., Green, A. I., Altamura, C., Anand, R., Bertoldi, A., et al. (2003). Clozapine treatment for suicidality in schizophrenia. *Archives of General Psychiatry, 60*, 82–91.

Meltzer, L., Reddy, R., Pollica, L. S., Roditi, B., Sayer, J., & Theokas, C. (2004). Positive and negative selfperceptions: Is there a cyclical relationship between teachers' and students' perceptions of effort, strategy use, and academic performance? *Learning Disabilities Research & Practice, 19*, 33–44.

Meltzer, L. J., Johnson, S. B., Pappachan, S., & Silverstein, J. (2003). Blood glucose estimation in adolescence with type 1 diabetes: Predictors of accuracy and error. *Journal of Pediatric Psychology, 28*, 203–211.

Meltzer, L. J., & Mindell, J. A. (2009). Pediatric sleep. In M. C. Roberts & R. G. Steele (Eds.), *Handbook of pediatric psychology* (4th ed.). New York: The Guilford Press.

Mendenhall, A. N., & Fristad, M. A. (2010). Psychoeducational psychotherapy for children with bipolar disorder. In D. J. Miklowitz & D. Cicchetti (Eds.), *Understanding bipolar disorder: A developmental psychopathology perspective.* New York: The Guilford Press.

Menning, C. L. (2002). Absent parents are more than money: The joint effect of activities and financial support on youth's educational attainment. *Journal of Family Issues, 23*, 648–671.

Mental Health: A Report of the Surgeon General. (2001). Surgeongeneral. gov/library/mentalhealth/index.html. Washington, DC: Office of the Surgeon General, Department of Health and Human Services.

Mercer, C. D., & Mercer, A. R. (2001). *Teaching students with learning problems.* Upper Saddle River, NJ: Merrill/Prentice Hall.

Merikangas, K. R. (2005). Vulnerability factors for anxiety disorders in children and adolescents. *Child and Adolescent Psychiatric Clinics of North America, 14*, 649–679.

Merikangas, K. R., He, J-P., Brody, D., Fisher, P. W., Bourdon, K., & Koretz, S. S. (2010a). Prevalence and treatment of mental disorders among US children in the 2001–2004 NHANES. *Pediatrics, 125*, 75–81.

Merikangas, K. R., He, J-P., Burstein, M., Swanson, S. A., Avenevoli, S., Cui, L., Benjet, C., Georgiades, K., & Swendsen, J. (2010b). Lifetime prevalence of mental disorders in U.S. adolescents: Results from the National Comorbidity Survey Replication-Adolescent Supplement (NCS-A). *Journal of the American Academy of Child and Adolescent Psychiatry, 49*, 980–989.

Merikangas, K. R., He, J-P., Burstein, M., Swendsen, J., Avenevoli, S., Case, B., et al. (2011). Service utilization for lifetime mental disorders in U.S. adolescents: Results of the National Comorbidity Survey-Adolescent Supplement (NCS-A). *Journal of the American Academy of Child and Adolescent Psychiatry, 50*, 32–45.

Merikangas, K. R., Nakamura, E. F., & Kessler, R. C. (2009). Epidemiology of mental disorders in children and adolescents. *Dialogues in Clinical Neuroscience, 11*, 7–20.

Mertin, P., & Hartwig, S. (2004). Auditory hallucinations in nonpsychotic children: Diagnostic considerations. *Child and Adolescent Mental Health, 9*, 9–14.

Merz, E. C., & McCall, R. B. (2011). Parent ratings of executive functioning in children adopted from psychosocially depriving institutions. *Journal of Child Psychology and Psychiatry 52*, 537–546.

Mesibov, G. B. (1992). Letters to the editors. Response to Thompson and McEvoy. *Journal of Autism and Developmental Disorders, 22*, 672–673.

Mesibov, G. B. & Van Bourgondien, M. E. (1992). Autism. In S. R. Hooper, G. W. Hynd, & R. E. Mattison (Eds.), *Developmental disorders. Diagnostic criteria and clinical assessment*. Hillsdale, NJ: Erlbaum.

Meyer, S. E., & Carlson, G. A. (2010). Development, age of onset, and phenomenology in bipolar disorder. In D. J. Miklowitz & D. Cicchetti (Eds.), *Understanding bipolar disorder: A developmental psychopathology perspective*. New York: The Guilford Press.

Meyers, J. L., & Dick, D. M. (2010). Genetic and environmental risk factors for adolescent-onset substance use disorders. *Child and Adolescent Psychiatric Clinics of North America, 19*, 465–477.

Micali, N., Simonoff, E., Stahl, D., & Treasure, J. (2011). Maternal eating disorders and infant feeding difficulties: Maternal and child mediators in a longitudinal general population study. *Journal of Child Psychology and Psychiatry, 52*, 800–807.

Miceli, P. J., Rowland, J. F., & Whitman, T. L. (1999). Chronic illnesses in childhood. In T. L. Whitman, T. V. Merluzzi, & R. D. White (Eds.), *Life-span perspectives on health and illness*. Mahwah, NJ: Lawrence Erlbaum Associates.

Mick, E., Biederman, J., Faraone, S. V., Sayer, J., & Kleinman, S. (2002). Case-control study of attention-deficit hyperactivity disorder and maternal smoking, alcohol use, and drug use during pregnancy. *Journal of the American Academy of Child and Adolescent Psychiatry, 41*, 378–385.

Mijanovich, T., & Weitzman, B. C. (2010). Disaster in context: The effects of 9/11 on youth distant from the attacks. *Community Mental Health Journal, 46*, 601–611.

Mikami, A., Jack, A., Emeh, C., & Stephens, H. (2010). Parental influence on children with attention-deficit/hyperactivity disorder: I. Relationships between parent behaviors and child peer status. *Journal of Abnormal Child Psychology, 38*, 721–736.

Mikami, A. Y. (2010). The importance of friendship for youth with attention-deficit/hyperactivity disorder. *Clinical Child and Family Psychology Review, 13*, 181–198.

Mikami, A. Y., Calhoun, C. D., & Abikoff, H. B. (2010). Positive illusory bias and response to behavioral treatment among children with attention-deficit/hyperactivity disorder. *Journal of Clinical Child and Adolescent Psychology, 39*, 373–385.

Mikkelsen, E. J. (2001). Enuresis and encopresis: Ten years of progress. *Journal of the American Academy of Child and Adolescent Psychiatry, 40*, 1146–1158.

Miklowitz, D. J., & Goldstein, T. R. (2010). Family-based approaches to treating bipolar disorder in adolescents: Family-Focused therapy and dialectical behavior therapy. In D. J. Miklowitz & D. Cicchetti (Eds.), *Understanding bipolar disorder: A developmental psychopathology perspective*. New York: The Guilford Press.

Milan, S., Pinderhughes, E. E., & The Conduct Problems Prevention Research Group. (2006). Family instability and child maladjustment trajectories during elementary school. *Journal of Abnormal Child Psychology, 34*, 43–56.

Milgrom, J., Newnhan, C., Anderson, P. J., Doyle, L. W., Gemmill, A. W., Lee. K., et al. (2010). Early sensitivity training for parents of preterm infants: Impact on the developing brain. *Pediatric Research, 67*, 330–335.

Milich, R., Balentine, A. C., & Lynam, D. R. (2001, Winter). ADHD combined type and ADHD predominantly inattentive type are distinct and unrelated disorders. *Clinical Psychology: Science and Practice, 8*, 463–488.

Miller, B. C., Fan, X., Christensen, M., Grotevant, H. D., & van Dulmen, M. (2000). Comparisons of adopted and nonadopted adolescents in a large, nationally representative sample. *Child Development, 71*, 1458–1473.

Miller, J. E. (2000). The effects of race/ethnicity and income on early childhood asthma prevalence and health care use. *American Journal of Public Health, 90*, 428–430.

Miller, J. N., & Ozonoff, S. (2000). The external validity of Asperger's disorder: Lack of evidence from the domain of neuropsychology. *Journal of Abnormal Psychology, 109*, 227–238.

Miller, L. C., Barrett, C. L., & Hampe, E. (1974). Phobias of childhood in a prescientific era. In A. Davids (Ed.), *Child personality and psychopathology: Current topics* (Vol. 1). New York: John Wiley.

Miller, L. D., Laye-Gindhi, A., Bennett, J. L., Liu, Y., Gold, S., March, J. S., et al. (2011). An effectiveness study of a culturally enriched school-based CBT anxiety prevention program. *Journal of Clinical Child and Adolescent Psychology, 40*, 618–629.

Miller, L. K. (1999). The savant syndrome: Intellectual impairment and exceptional skill. *Psychological Bulletin, 125*, 31–46.

Miller, M., & Hinshaw, S. P. (2010). Does childhood executive function predict adolescent functional outcome in girls with ADHD? *Journal of Abnormal Child Psychology, 38*, 315–326.

Miller, S. A. (1998). *Developmental research methods*. Upper Saddle River, NJ: Prentice-Hall.

Miller, S. A. (2009). Children's understanding of second-order mental states. *Psychological Bulletin, 135*, 749–773.

Miller, T. W., Nigg, J. T., & Miller, R. L. (2009). Attention deficit hyperactivity disorder in African American children: What can be concluded from the past ten years. *Clinical Psychology Review, 29*, 77–86.

Millican, F. K., & Lourie, R. S. (1970). The child with pica and his family. In E. J. Anthony & C. Koupernik (Eds.), *The child in his family* (Vol. 1). New York: Wiley-Interscience.

Milner, K. A., Craig, E. E., Thompson, R. J., Veltman, M. W. M., Thomas, N. S., Roberts, S., et al. (2005). Prader-Willi syndrome: Intellectual abilities and behavioural features by genetic subtype. *Journal of Child Psychology and Psychiatry, 46,* 1089–1096.

Minde, K., Popiel, K., Leos, N., Falkner, S., Parker, K., & Handley-Derry, M. (1993). The evaluation and treatment of sleep disturbances in young children. *Journal of Child Psychology and Psychiatry, 34,* 521–533.

Mindell, J. A., Kuhn, B. R., Lewin, D. S., Meltzer, L. J., Sadeh, A., & Owens, J. A. (2006). Behavioral treatment of bedtime problems and nighttime wakings in infants and young children. *Sleep, 29,* 1263–1276.

Mindell, J. A., & Owens, J. A. (2003). *A clinical guide to pediatric sleep: Diagnosis and management of sleep problems.* Philadelphia: Lippincott Williams & Wilkins.

Mineka, S., & Zinbarg, R. (2006). A contemporary learning theory perspective on the etiology of anxiety disorders: It's not what you thought it was. *American Psychologist, 61,* 10–26.

Minjarez, M. B., Williams, S. E., Mercier, E. M., & Hardan, A. Y. (2011). Pivotal response group treatment program for parents of children with autism. *Journal of Autism and Developmental Disabilities, 41,* 92–101.

Minshew, N. J., Sweeney, J. A., & Bauman, M. L. (1997). Neurological aspects of autism. In D. J. Cohen & F. R. Volkmar (Eds.), *Handbook of autism and pervasive developmental disorders.* New York: John Wiley.

Minty, B. (1999). Annotation: Outcomes in long-term foster family care. *Journal of Child Psychology and Psychiatry, 40,* 991–999.

Mirenda, P., Smith, I. M., Vaillancourt, T., Georgiades, S., Duku, E., Szatmari, P., et al. (2010). Validating the Repetitive Behavior Scale-R in young children with autism spectrum behavior. *Journal of Autism and Developmental Disorders, 40,* 1521–1530.

Mirkin, M. P. (1990). Eating disorders: A feminist family therapy perspective. In M. P. Mirkin (Ed.), *The social and political contexts of family therapy.* Boston, MA: Allyn & Bacon.

Mishna, F. (2003). Learning disabilities and bullying: Double jeopardy. *Journal of Learning Disabilities, 36,* 336–347.

Mitchell, J., Trent, R., & McArthur, R. (1993). *Human Figure Drawing Test (HFDT): An illustrated handbook for clinical interpretation and standardized assessment of cognitive impairment.* Los Angeles, CA: Western Psychological Services.

Mitchell, J. E., Agras, S., & Wonderlich, S. (2007). Treatment of bulimia nervosa: Where are we and where are we going? *International Journal of Eating Disorders, 40,* 95–101.

Mitsis, E. M., McKay, K. E., Schulz, K. P., Newcorn, J. H., & Halperin, J. M. (2000). Parent-teacher concordance for DSM-IV Attention-Deficit/Hyperactivity Disorder in a clinicreferred sample. *Journal of the American Academy of Child and Adolescent Psychiatry, 39,* 308–313.

Mittal, V. A., & Walker, E. F (2011). Minor physical anomalies and vulnerability in prodromal youth. *Schizophrenia Research, 129,* 116–121.

MMWR Morbidity and Mortality Weekly Report (MMWR). Increasing prevalence of parent-reported Attention-Deficit/Hyperactivity Disorder among children—United States, 2003 and 2007. November 12, 2010/ 59(44): 1439–1443.

MMWR Morbidity and Mortality Weekly Report, Centers for Disease Control and Prevention. January 14, 2011/ Supplement/60, http://www.cdc.gov/mmwr/pdf/other/su6001.pdf

Moens, E., Braet, C., & Soetens, B. (2007). Observation of family functioning at mealtime: A comparison between families of children with and without overweight. *Journal of Pediatric Psychology, 32,* 52–63.

Moffitt, T. E. (1993). Adolescence-limited and life-courseper-sistent antisocial behavior: A developmental taxonomy. *Psychological Review, 100,* 674–701.

Moffitt, T. E. (2006). Life-course-persistent versus adolescence limited antisocial behavior. In D. Cicchetti & D. J. Cohen (Eds.), *Developmental psychopathology, Vol. 3: Risk, disorder, and adaptation* (2nd ed.). Hoboken, NJ: John Wiley & Sons.

Moffitt, T. E., Arseneault, L., Belsky, D., Dickson, N., Hancox, R. J., Harrington, H., et al. (2011). A gradient of childhood self-control predicts health, wealth, and public safety. *Proceedings of the National Academy of Science, 108,* 2693–2698.

Moffitt, T. E., Arseneault, L., Jaffee, S. R., Kim-Cohen, J., Koenen, K. C., Odgers, C. L., Slutske, W. S., & Viding, E. (2008). DSM-V conduct disorder: Research needs for an evidence base. *Journal of Child Psychology and Psychiatry, 49,* 3–33.

Moffitt, T. E., Caspi, A., Harrington, H., & Milne, B. J. (2002). Males on the life-course-persistent and adolescence-limited antisocial pathways: Follow-up at age 26 years. *Development and Psychopathology, 14,* 179–207.

Moffitt, T. E., Caspi, A., Rutter, M., & Silva, P. (2001). *Sex differences in antisocial behaviour: Conduct disorder, delinquency, and violence in the Dunedin longitudinal study.* Cambridge, UK: Cambridge University Press.

Molden, D. C., & Dweck, C. S. (2006). Finding "meaning" in psychology. *American Psychologist, 61,* 192–203.

Molina, B. S. G., Hinshaw, S. P., Swanson, J. M., Arnold, L. E., Vitiello, B., Jensen, P. S. et al. (2009). The MTA at 8 years: Prospective follow-up of children treated for combined-type ADHD in a multisite study. *Journal of the American Academy of Child and Adolescent Psychiatry, 48,* 484–500.

Moore, B. D. (2005). Neurocognitive outcomes in survivors of childhood cancer. *Journal of Pediatric Psychology, 30,* 51–63.

Moore, M., Kirchner, H. L., Drotar, D., Johnson, N., Rosen, C., Ancoli-Israel, S., & Redline, S. (2009). Relationships among sleepiness, sleep time, and psychological functioning in adolescents. *Journal of Pediatric Psychology, 34,* 1175–1183.

Moos, B. S., & Moos, R. H. (1994). *Family Environment Scale* (3rd ed.). Menlo, CA: Mind Garden, Inc.

Moreno, C., Laje, G., Blanco, C., Jiang, H., Schmidt, A. B., & Olfson, M. (2007). National trends in the outpatient diagnosis and treatment of bipolar disorder in youth. *Archives of General Psychiatry, 64,* 1032–1039.

Moreno, C., Roche, A. M., & Greenhill, L. L. (2006). Pharmacotherapy of child and adolescent depression. *Child and Adolescent Psychiatric Clinics of North America, 15,* 977–998.

Morgan, D. L., & Morgan, R. K. (2001). Single-participant research design. *American Psychologist, 56,* 119–127.

Morgan, P. L., Farkas, G., & Wu, Q. (2011). Kindergarten children's growth trajectories in reading and mathematics. Who falls increasingly behind? *Journal of Learning Disabilities, 44,* 472–488.

Morgan, R. K. (1999). *Case studies in child and adolescent psychopathology.* Upper Saddle River, NJ: Prentice-Hall.

Morrison, J., & Anders, T. F. (1999). *Interviewing children and adolescents: Skills and strategies for effective DSM-diagnosis.* New York: The Guilford Press.

Morrison, J. A., Friedman, L. A., & Gray-McGuire, C. (2007). Metabolic syndrome in childhood predicts adult cardiovascular disease 25 years later: The Princeton Lipid Research Clinics follow-up study. *Pediatrics, 120,* 340–345.

Morroco, C. C., Aguilar, C. M., Clay, K., Brigham, N., & Zigmond, N. (2006). Good high schools for students with disabilities. Introduction to the special issue. *Learning Disabilities Research & Practice, 21,* 135–145.

Morrongiello, B. A., Kane, A., & Zdzieborski, D. (2011). "I think he is in his room playing a video game": Parental supervision of young elementary school children at home. *Journal of Pediatric Psychology, 36,* 708–717.

Morrongiello, B. A., & Matheis, S. (2007a). Assessing the issue of falls off playground equipment: An empirically-based intervention to reduce fall-risk behaviors on playgrounds. *Journal of Pediatric Psychology, 32,* 819–830.

Morrongiello, B. A., & Matheis, S. (2007b). Understanding children's injury-risk behaviors: The independent contributions of cognitions and emotions. *Journal of Pediatric Psychology, 32,* 926–937.

Mortensen, P. B. et al. (1999). Effects of family history and place and season of birth on the risk of schizophrenia. *New England Journal of Medicine, 340,* 603–608.

Mosconi, M. W., Kay, M., D'Cruz, A-M., Guter, S., Kapur, K., Macmillan, C., et al. (2010). Neurobehavioral abnormalities in first-degree relatives of individuals with autism. *Archives of General Psychiatry, 67,* 830–840.

Mowrer, O. H., & Mowrer, W. M. (1938). Enuresis: A method for its study and treatment. *American Journal of Orthopsychiatry, 8,* 436–459.

MTA Cooperative Group. (1999a). A 14-month randomized clinical trial of treatment strategies for attention-deficit/hyperactivity disorder. *Archives of General Psychiatry, 56,* 1073–1086.

MTA Cooperative Group. (1999b). Moderators and mediators of treatment response for children with attention-deficit/hyperactivity disorder. *Archives of Psychiatry, 56,* 1088–1096.

MTA Cooperative Group. (2004a). National Institute of Mental Health Multimodal Treatment Study of ADHD follow-up: Changes in effectiveness and growth after the end treatment. *Pediatrics, 113,* 762–769.

MTA Cooperative Group. (2004b). National Institute of Mental Health Multimodal Treatment Study of ADHD follow-up: 24-month outcomes of treatment strategies for attention-deficit/hyperactivity disorder. *Pediatrics, 113,* 754–761.

Mufson, L., Dorta, K. P., Wickramaratne, P., Nomuar, Y., Olfson, M. & Weissman, M. M. (2004). A randomized effectiveness trial of interpersonal psychotherapy for depressed adolescents. *Archives of General Psychiatry, 61,* 577–584.

Mufson, L., Pollack Dorta, K., Wickramaratne, P., Nomura, Y., Olfson, M., & Weissman, M. M. (2004). The effectiveness of interpersonal psychotherapy for depressed adolescents. *Archives of General Psychiatry, 45,* 742–747.

Mufson, L., Weissman, M. M., Moreau, D., & Garfindel, R. (1999). Efficacy of interpersonal therapy for depressed adolescents. *Archives of General Psychiatry, 56,* 573–579.

Mukolo, A., Heflinger, C. A., & Wallston, K. A. (2010). The stigma of childhood mental disorders: A conceptual framework. *Journal of the American Academy of Child and Adolescent Psychiatry, 49,* 92–103.

Mulvaney, S. A., Goodwin, J. L., Morgan, W. J., Rosen, G. R., Quan, S. F., & Kaemingk, K. L. (2006). Behavior problems associated with sleep disordered breathing in school-aged children—The Tucson Children's Assessment of Sleep Study. *Journal of Pediatric Psychology, 31,* 322–330.

Mundy, P. (1993). Normal versus high functioning status in children with autism. *American Journal on Mental Retardation, 97,* 381–384.

Munoz, R. F., Mrazek, P. J., & Haggerty, R. J. (1996). Institute of Medicine report on prevention of mental disorders: Summary and commentary. *American Psychologist 51,* 1116–1122.

Muris, P. (2006). The pathogenesis of childhood anxiety disorders: Considerations from a developmental psychopathology perspective. *International Journal of Behavioral Development, 30,* 5–11.

Muris, P., & Field, A. P. (2010). The role of verbal threat information in the development of childhood fear. "Beware the Jabberwock!" *Clinical Child and Family Psychology Review, 13,* 129–150.

Muris, P., Merckelbach, H., Ollendick, T. H., King, N. J., & Bogie, N. (2001). Children's nighttime fears: Parent-child ratings of frequency, content, origins, coping behaviors and severity. *Behaviour Research and Therapy, 39,* 13–28.

Murphy, A. (2001). Front-Runner. *Sports Illustrated*, 95(21), 62–66.

Murray, H. A. (1943). *Thematic apperception test*. Bloomington, MN: Pearson Assessments.

Murray, L., de Rosnay, M., Pearson, J., Bergeron, C., Schofield, E. Royal-Lawson, M., & Cooper, P. J. (2008). Intergenerational transmission of social anxiety: The role of social referencing processes in infancy. *Child Development, 79*, 1049–1064.

Nadder, T. S., Silberg, J. L., Rutter, M., Maes, H. H., & Eaves, L. J. (2001). Comparison of multiple measures of ADHD symptomatology: A multivariate genetic analysis. *Journal of Child Psychology and Psychiatry, 42*, 475–486.

Nader, K., Pynoos, R. S., Fairbanks, L., & Frederick, C. (1991). Childhood PTSD reactions one year after a sniper attack. *American Journal of Psychiatry, 147*, 1526–1530.

Nagy, Z., Lagercrantz, H., & Hutton, C. (2011). Effects of preterm birth on cortical thickness measured in adolescence. *Cerebral Cortex, 21*, 300–306.

Nansel, T. R., Craig, W., Overpeck, M. D., Saluja, G., & Ruan, W. J. (2004). Cross-national consistency in the relationship between bullying behaviors and psychosocial adjustment. *Archives of Pediatric & Adolescent Medicine, 158*, 730–736.

Nansel, T. R., Overpeck, M., Pilla, R. S., Ruan, W. J., Simons-Morton, B., & Scheidt, P. (2001). Bullying behaviors among US youth: Prevalence and association with psychosocial adjustment. *Journal of the American Medical Association, 285*, 2094–2100.

Nathan, P. E., & Langenbucher, J. W. (1999). Psychopathology: Description and classification. *Annual Review of Psychology, 50*, 79–107.

Nation, K., Clarke, P., Marshall, K. M., & Durand, M. (2004). Hidden language impairments in children: Parallels between poor reading comprehension and specific language impairment? *Journal of Speech, Language, and Hearing Research, 47*, 199–211.

National Center for Health Statistics. Health, United States, 2010: With special feature on death and dying. Hyattsville, MD. 2011.

National Center for Health Statistics/Centers for Disease Control (2011). National marriage and divorce rate trends. Retrieved July 2011 from http://www.cdc.cov/nchs/marriage_divorce_tables.htm

National Commission for the Protection of Human Subjects of Biomedical and Behavioral Research. (1979). *The Belmont Report: Ethical principles and guidelines for the protection of human subjects of research*. Washington, DC: U.S. Government Printing Office.

National Diabetes Information Clearinghouse. (2008). Diabetes. Retrieved July, 2011. From http://diabetes.niddk.nih.gov/

National Institute of Mental Health. (1977). *Child abuse and neglect programs: Practice and theory*. Washington, DC: U.S. Government Printing Office.

National Institute on Drug Abuse. (2006). *NIDA InfoFacts*. Retrieved August 2007 from http://www.drugabuse.gov

National Institutes of Health (NIH). (2007). *Expert panel report 3: Guidelines for the diagnosis and management of asthma-full report 2007*. Bethesda, MD: Author.

Neal, J. A., & Edelmann, R. J. (2003). The etiology of social phobia: Toward a developmental profile. *Clinical Psychology Review, 23*, 761–786.

Neale B. M., Medland. S., Ripke, S., Armey, R. J. L., Asherson, P., Buitelaar, J., et al. (2010). Case-control genome-wide association study of attention-deficit/hyperactivity disorder. *Journal of the American Academy of Child and Adolescent Psychiatry, 49*, 906–920.

Neely-Barnes, S., & Marchenko, M. (2004). Predicting impact of childhood disability on families: Results from the 1995 National Health Interview Survey Disability Supplement. *Mental Retardation, 42*, 284–293.

Nelson, B., & Yung, A. R. (2011). Should a risk syndrome for first episode psychosis be included in the DSM-5? *Current Opinions in Psychiatry, 24*, 128–133.

Nelson, F., & Mann, T. (2010). Opportunities in public policy to support infant and early childhood mental health. *American Psychologist, 66*, 129–139.

Nelson, T. D., Jensen, C. D., & Steele, R. G. (2011). Weight-related criticism and self-perceptions among preadolescents. *Journal of Pediatric Psychology, 36*, 106–115.

Nelson, T. D., & Steele, R. G. (2009). Evidence-based practice in pediatric psychology. In M. C. Roberts & R. G. Steele (Eds.), *Handbook of pediatric psychology* (4th ed.). New York: The Guilford Press.

Ness, K. K., & Gurney, J. G. (2007). Adverse late effects of childhood cancer and its treatment on health and performance. *Annual Review of Public Health, 28*, 279–302.

New, M. J., Lee, S. S., & Elliott, B. M. (2007). Psychological adjustment in children and families living with HIV. *Journal of Pediatric Psychology, 32*, 123–131.

Newbury, D. F., & Monaco, A. P. (2010). Genetic advances in the study of speech and language disorders. *Neuron, 68*, 309–320.

Newsom, C. (1998). Autistic disorder. In E. J. Mash & R. A. Barkley (Eds.), *Treatment of childhood disorders*. New York: Guilford Press.

Newsom, C., & Hovanitz, C. A. (2006). Autistic spectrum disorders. In E. J. Mash & R. A. Barkley (Eds.), *Treatment of childhood disorders*. New York: The Guilford Press.

NICHD Early Child Care Research Network. (2003). Does amount of time spent in child care predict socioeconomic adjustment during the transition to kindergarten? *Child Development, 74*, 976–1005.

NICHD Early Child Care Research Network. (2004). Trajectories of physical aggression from toddlerhood to middle childhood: Predictors, correlates, and outcomes. *Monographs of the Society for Research in Child Development, 69* (4, serial no. 278).

NICHD Early Child Care Research Network. (2006). Child-care effect sizes for the NICHD Study of Child Care and Youth Development. *American Psychologist, 61,* 99–116.

Nicholls, D. (2004). Eating problems in childhood. In J. K. Thompson (Ed.), *Handbook of eating disorders and obesity.* Hoboken, NJ: John Wiley.

Nicodemus, K. K., Marenco. S., Batten, A. J., Vakkalanka, R., Egan, M. F., Straub, R. E., et al. (2008). Serious obstetric complications interact with hypoxia-regulated/vascular expression genes to influence schizophrenia risk. *Molecular Biology, 13,* 873–877.

Nicolson, R., & Rapoport, J. L. (2000). Childhood-onset schizophrenia: What can it teach us? In J. L. Rapoport (Ed.), *Childhood onset of "adult" psychopathology.* Washington, DC: American Psychiatric Press.

Nigg, J., & Nikolas, M. (2008). Attention-deficit/hyperactivity disorder. In T. P. Beauchaine & S. P. Hinshaw (Eds.), *Child and adolescent psychopathology.* New York: John Wiley & Sons.

Nigg, J. T. (2001). Is ADHD a disinhibitory disorder? *Psychological Bulletin, 127,* 571–598.

Nigg, J. T. (2006a). Attention deficits and hyperactivity-impulsivity in children: A multilevel overview and causes and mechanism. In H. E. Fitzgerald, B. M. Lester, & B. Zuckerman (Eds.), *The crisis in youth mental health. Critical issues and effective programs* (Vol. 1).Westport, CT: Praeger Publishers.

Nigg, J. T. (2006b). Temperament and developmental psychopathology. *Journal of Child Psychology and Psychiatry, 47,* 395–422.

Nigg, J. T., Blaskey, L. G., Huang-Pollock, C. L., & Rappley, M. D. (2002). Neuropsychological executive functions and DSM-IV ADHD subtypes. *Journal of the American Academy of Child and Adolescent Psychiatry, 41,* 59–66.

Nigg, J. T., & Hinshaw, S. P. (1998). Parent personality traits and psychopathology associated with antisocial behaviors in childhood attention-deficit hyperactive disorder. *Journal of Child Psychology and Psychiatry, 39,* 145–159.

Nigg, J. T., Hinshaw, S. P., & Huang-Pollock, C. (2006). Disorders of attention and impulse regulation. In D. Cicchetti & D. J. Cohen (Eds.), *Developmental psychopathology. Vol. III. Risk, disorder, and adaptation.* Hoboken, NJ: John Wiley & Sons.

Nigg, J. T., Knotterus, G. M., Martel, M. M., Nikolas, M., Cavanagh, K., Karmaus, W. et al. (2008). Low blood lead levels associated with clinically diagnosed attention-deficit/hyperactivity disorder and mediated by weak cognitive control. *Biological Psychiatry, 63,* 325–331.

Nigg, J. T., Lewis, K., Edinger, T., & Falk, M. (2012). Meta-analysis of attention-deficit/hyperactivity disorder or attention-deficit/hyperactivity disorder symptoms, restriction diet, and synthetic food color additives. *Journal of the American Academy of Child and Adolescent Psychiatry, 51,* 86–97.

Nijmeijer, J. S., Mindera, R. B., Buitelaar, J. K., Mulligan, A., Hartman, C. A., & Hoekstra, P. J. (2008). Attention-deficit/hyperactivity disorder and social dysfunctioning. *Clinical Psychology Review, 28,* 692–708.

Nisbett, R. E., Aronson, J., Blair, C., Dickens, W., Flynn, J., Halpern, D. F., et al. (2010). Intelligence: New findings and theoretical developments. *American Psychologist, 67,* 130–159.

Nisbett, R. E., Aronson, J., Blair, C., Dickens, W., Flynn, J., Halpern, D. F., et al. (2012). Intelligence. New findings and theoretical developments. *American Psychologist, 67,* 130–159.

Niska, R., Bhuiya, F., & Xu, J. (2010). National hospital ambulatory medical care survey: 2007 emergency department summary. *National Health Statistics Reports, 26,* 1–32.

Nock, M., Joiner, T. E., Gordon, K. H., Lloyd-Richardson, E., & Prinstein, M. J. (2006). Non-suicidal self-injury among adolescents: Diagnostic correlates and relation to suicidal attempts. *Psychiatric Research, 144,* 65–72.

Nock, M. K., Kazdin, A. E., Hiripi, E., & Kessler, R. C. (2007). Lifetime prevalence, correlates, and persistence of oppositional defiant disorder: Results from the National Comorbidity Survey Replication. *Journal of Child Psychology and Psychiatry, 48,* 703–713.

Nolan, E. E., Gadow, K. D., & Sprafkin, J. (2001). Teacher reports of DSM-IV ADHD, ODD, and CD symptoms in schoolchildren. *Journal of the American Academy of Child and Adolescent Psychiatry, 40,* 241–248.

Nolen-Hoeksema, S. N., & Girgus, J. S. (1994). The emergence of gender differences in depression during adolescence. *Psychological Bulletin, 115,* 424–443.

Noppe, I. C., Noppe, L. D., & Bartell, D. (2006). Terrorism and resilience: Adolescents' and teachers' responses to September 11, 2001. *Death Studies, 30,* 41–60.

Novins, D. K., Beals, J., & Mitchell, C. M. (2001). Sequences of substance abuse among American Indian adolescents. *Journal of the American Academy of Child and Adolescent Psychiatry, 40,* 1168–1174.

Novins, D. K., Duclos, C.W., Martin, C., Jewett, C. S., & Manson, S. M. (1999). Utilization of alcohol, drug, and mental health treatment services among American Indian adolescent detainees. *Journal of the American Academy of Child and Adolescent Psychiatry, 38,* 1102–1108.

Nowicki, E. A. (2003). A meta-analysis of the social competence of children with learning disabilities compared to classmates of low and average to high achievement. *Learning Disability Quarterly, 26,* 171–188.

Núñez, J. C., González-Pienda, J. A., González-Pumariega, S., Roces, G., Alvarez, L., & González, P. (2005). Subgroups of attributional profiles in students with learning disabilities and their relation to self-concept and academic goal. *Learning Disabilities Research & Practice, 20,* 86–97.

Nyborg, V. M., & Curry, J. F. (2003). The impact of perceived racism: Psychological symptoms among African American boys. *Journal of Clinical Child and Adolescent Psychology, 32,* 258–266.

Obi, O., Van Narrden Braun, K., Baoi, J., Drews-Botsch, C., Devine, O., & Yeargin-Allsopp, M., (2011). Effect of incorporating adaptive function scores on the prevalence of intellectual disability. *American Journal on Intellectual and Developmental Disabilities, 116,* 360–370.

Obradovic, J., Bush, N. R., Stamperdahl, J., Adler, N. E., & Boyce, W. T. (2010). Biological sensitivity to context: The interactive effects of stress reactivity and family adversity on socioemotional behavior and school readiness. *Child Development, 81,* 270–289.

O'Brien, K. M., & Vincent, N. K. (2003). Psychiatric comorbidity in anorexia and bulimia nervosa: Nature, prevalence, and causal relationships. *Clinical Psychology Review, 23,* 57–74.

O'Brien, M. (1996). Child-rearing difficulties reported by parents of infants and toddlers. *Journal of Pediatric Psychology, 21,* 433–446.

O'Byrne, K. K., Peterson, L., & Saldana, L. (1997). Survey of pediatric hospitals' preparation programs: Evidence of the impact of health psychology research. *Health Psychology, 16,* 147–154.

Ochoa, S. H., & Palmer, D. J. (1995). A meta-analysis of peer rating of sociometric studies with learning disabled students. *Journal of Special Education, 29,* 1–19.

O'Connor, E. E., Dearing, E., & Collins, B. A. (2011). Teacher-child relationship and behavior problem trajectories in elementary school. *American Educational Research Journal, 48,* 120–162.

O'Connor, T. G. (2003). Natural experiments to study the effects of early experience: Progress and limitations. *Development and Psychopathology, 15,* 837–852.

O'Connor, T. G., Dunn, J., Jenkins, J. M., & Rasbash, J. (2006). Predictors of between-family and within-family variation in parent-child relationships. *Journal of Child Psychology and Psychiatry, 47,* 498–510.

O'Connor, T. G., & Parfitt, D. B. (2009). Applying research findings on early experience to infant mental health. In C. H. Zeanah, Jr. (Ed.), *Handbook of infant mental health.* New York: Guilford Press.

Ogden, C. L., Carroll, M. D., Curtin, L. R., Lamb, M. M., & Fiegal, K. M. (2010). Prevalence of high body mass index in US children and adolescents, 2007–2008. *Journal of the American Medical Association, 303,* 242–249.

Olds, D. L., Sadler, D., & Kitzman, H. (2007). Programs for parents of infants and toddlers: Recent evidence from randomized trials. *Journal of Child Psychology and Psychiatry, 48,* 355–391.

O'Leary, K. D., & Emery, R. E. (1985). Marital discord and child behavior problems. In M.D. Levine & P. Satz (Eds.), *Developmental variation and dysfunction.* New York: Academic Press.

Olfson, M., Crystal, S., Huang, C., & Gerhardt, T. (2010). Trends in antipsychotic drug use by very young, privately insured children. *Journal of the American Academy of Child and Adolescent Psychiatry, 49,* 13–23.

Oliver, C., & Richards, C. (2010). Self-injurious behaviour in people with intellectual disability. *Current Opinion in Psychiatry, 23,* 412–416.

Ollendick, T. H. (1983). Reliability and validity of the Revised Fear Survey Schedule for Children (FSSC-R). *Behaviour Research and Therapy, 21,* 685–692.

Ollendick, T. H., Birmaher, B., & Mattis, S. G. (2004a). Panic disorder. In T. L. Morris & J. S. March (Eds.), *Anxiety disorders in children and adolescents.* New York: Guilford Press.

Ollendick, T. H., Davis, T. E., & Muris, P. (2004b). Treatment of specific phobia in children and adolescents. In P. M. Barrett & T. H. Ollendick (Eds.), *Handbook of interventions that work with children and adolescents: Prevention and treatment.* Hoboken, NJ: John Wiley & Sons.

Ollendick, T. H., & King, N. J. (1998). Empirically supported treatments for children with phobic and anxiety disorders: Current status. *Journal of Clinical Child Psychology, 27,* 156–167.

Ollendick, T. H., King, N. J., & Chorpita, B. F. (2006). Empirically supported treatments for children and adolescents. In P. C. Kendall (Ed.), *Child and adolescent therapy: Cognitive-behavioral procedures.* New York: The Guilford Press.

Olsen, S., Smith, S., & Oei, T. P. S. (2008). Adherence to continuous positive airway pressure therapy in obstructive sleep apnea sufferers: A theoretical approach to treatment adherence and intervention. *Clinical Psychology Review, 28,* 1355–1371.

Oltjenbruns, K. A. (2001). Developmental context of childhood grief and regrief phenomena. In M. S. Stroebe, R. O. Hansson, W. Stroebe, & H. Schut (Eds.), *Handbook of bereavement research: Consequences, coping, and care.* Washington, DC: American Psychological Association.

Oltmanns, T. F., & Emery, R. E. (2007). *Abnormal psychology.* Upper Saddle River, NJ: Pearson Education, Inc.

Olvera, N., & Power, T. G. (2010). Parenting styles and obesity in Mexican American children: A longitudinal study. *Journal of Pediatric Psychology, 35,* 243–249.

Olweus, D. (1993). *Bullying at school: What we know and what we can do.* Cambridge, MA: Blackwell.

Olweus, D. (1994). Bullying at school: Basic facts and effects of a school based intervention program. *Journal of Child Psychology and Psychiatry, 35,* 1171–1190.

Omigbodun, O., Bella, T., Dogra, N., & Simovan, O. (2007). Training health professionals for child and adolescent mental health care in Nigeria: A qualitative analysis. *Child and Adolescent Mental Health, 12,* 132–137.

Ondersma, S. J., & Walker, E. (1998). Elimination disorders. In T. H. Ollendick & M. Hersen (Eds.), *Handbook of child psychopathology* (3rd ed.). New York: Plenum Press.

Oosterlaan, J., Logan, G. D., & Sergeant, J. A. (1998). Response inhibition in AD/HD, CD, comorbid AD/HD+CD, anxious, and control children: A meta-analysis of studies with the Stop task. *Journal of Child Psychology and Psychiatry, 39,* 411–425.

Organista, K. C. (2003). Mexican American children and adolescents. In J. T. Gibbs, L. N. Huang, & Associates (Eds.), *Children of color: Psychological interventions with culturally diverse youth*. San Francisco: Jossey-Bass.

Orsmond, G. I., & Seltzer, M. M. (2000). Brothers and sisters of adults with mental retardation: Gendered nature of the sibling relationship. *American Journal on Mental Retardation, 105,* 486–508.

Öst, L. (1987). Age of onset in different phobias. *Journal of Abnormal Psychology, 96,* 123–145.

Otsuki, M., Eakin, M. N., Arceneaux, L. L., Rand, C. S., Butz, A. M., & Riekert, K. A. (2010). Prospective relationship between maternal depressive symptoms and asthma morbidity among inner-city African American children. *Journal of Pediatric Psychology, 35,* 758–767.

Otto, M., Henin, A., Hirshfeld-Becker, D. R., Pollack, M. H., Biederman, J., & Rosenbaum, J. (2007). Posttraumatic stress disorder symptoms following media exposure to tragic events: Impact of 9/11 on children at risk for anxiety disorders. *Journal of Anxiety Disorders, 21,* 888–902.

Outlaw, A., Naar-King, S., Green-Jones, M., Wright, K., Condon, K., Sherry, L., & Janisse, H. (2010). Predictors of optimal HIV appointment adherence in minority youth: A prospective study. *Journal of Pediatric Psychology, 35,* 1011–1015.

Owens, E. B., Hinshaw, S. P., Lee, S. S., & Lahey, B. B. (2009). Few girls with childhood attention-deficit/hyperactivity disorder show positive adjustment during adolescence. *Journal of Clinical Child & Adolescent Psychology, 38,* 132–143.

Owens, J., & Burnham, M. M. (2009). Sleep disorders. In C. H. Zeanah, Jr., (Ed.), *Handbook of infant mental health* (3rd ed.). New York: The Guilford Press.

Owens, J. A., Spirito, A., McGuinn, M., & Nobile, C. (2000). Sleep habits and sleep disturbance in elementary school-aged children. *Developmental and Behavioral Pediatrics, 21,* 27–36.

Owens, J. S., Goldfine, M. E., Evangelista. N. M., Hoza, B., & Kaiser, N. M. (2007). A critical review of self-perceptions and the positive illusory bias in children with ADHD. *Clinical Child and Family Psychology Review, 10,* 335–351.

Ozgen, H., Hellemann, G. S., Stellato, R. K., Lahuis, B., van Daalen, E., Staal, W. G., et al. (2011). Morphological features in children with autism spectrum disorders: A matched case-control study. *Journal of Autism and Developmental Disorders, 41,* 23–31.

Ozgen, H. M., Hop, J. W., Hox, J. J., Beemer, F. A., & van Engeland, H. (2010). Minor physical anomalies in autism: A meta-analysis. *Molecular Psychiatry, 15,* 300–307.

Ozonoff, S. (1997). Casual mechanisms of autism: Unifying perspectives from an information-processing framework. In D. J. Cohen & F. R. Volkmar (Eds.), *Handbook of autism and pervasive developmental disorders*. New York: John Wiley.

Ozonoff, S., & Cathcart, K. (1998). Effectiveness of a home program intervention for young children with autism. *Journal of Autism and Developmental Disorder, 28,* 25–32.

Pahl, K. M., & Barrett, P. M. (2010). Interventions for anxiety disorders in children using group cognitive-behavioral therapy with family involvement. In J. R. Weisz & A. E. Kazdin (Eds.), *Evidence-based psychotherapies for children and adolescents.* (2nd ed.). New York: The Guilford Press.

Palmer, D. L., Berg, C. A., Butler, J., Fortenberry, K., Murray, M., Lindsay, R., et al. (2009). Mothers', fathers', and children's perceptions of parental diabetes responsibility in adolescence: Examining the roles of age, pubertal status, and efficacy. *Journal of Pediatric Psychology, 34,* 195–204.

Palmer, D. L., Berg, C. A., Wiebe, D. J., Beveridge, R. M., Korbel, C. D., Upchurch, R., et al. (2004). The role of autonomy and pubertal status in understanding age differences in maternal involvement in diabetes responsibility across adolescence. *Journal of Pediatric Psychology, 29,* 35–46.

Palmer, D. L., Osborn, P., King, P. S., Berg, C. A., Butler, J., Butner, J., et al. (2011). The structure of parental involvement and relations to disease management for youth with type 1 diabetes. *Journal of Pediatric Psychology, 36,* 596–605.

Palmer, D. S., Fuller, K., Arora, T., & Nelson, M. (2001). Taking sides: Parent views on inclusion for their children with severe disabilities. *Exceptional Children, 67,* 467–484.

Palomo, R., Thompson, M., Colombi, C., Cook, I., Goldring, S. Young, G. S., et al. (2008). A case study of childhood disintegrative disorder using systematic analysis of family home movies. *Journal of Autism and Developmental Disorders, 38,* 1853–1858.

Paloyelis, Y., Rijsdiik, F., Wood, A. C., Asherson, P., & Kuntsi, J. (2010). The genetic association between ADHD symptoms and reading difficulties: The role of inattentiveness and IQ. *Journal of Abnormal Child Psychology, 38,* 1083–1095.

Pan, C-Y., Tsai, C-L., & Chu, C-H. (2009). Fundamental movement skills in children diagnosed with autism spectrum disorders and attention deficit disorder. *Journal of Autism and Developmental Disorders, 39,* 1694–1705.

Paniagua, F. A. (2000). Culture-bound syndromes, cultural variations, and psychopathology. In I. Cuéllar & F. A. Paniagua (Eds.), *Handbook of multicultural mental health*. San Diego: Academic Press.

Papolos, D. F. (2003). Bipolar disorder and comorbid disorders: The case for a dimensional nosology. In B. Geller & M. P. Del-Bello (Eds.), *Bipolar disorder in childhood and early adolescence*. New York: Guilford Press.

Pappadopulos, E., Jensen, P. S., Chait, A. R., Arnold, L. E., Swanson, J. M., Greenhill. L. L., et al. (2009). Medication adherence in the MTA: Saliva methylphenidate samples versus parent report and mediating effect of concomitant behavioral treatment. *Journal of the Academy of Child and Adolescent Psychiatry, 48,* 501–510.

Pardini, D., Stepp, S., Hipwell, A., Stouthamer-Loeber, M., & Loeber, R. (2012). The clinical utility of the proposed DSM-5 callous-unemotional subtype of conduct disorder in young girls. *Journal of the American Academy of Child and Adolescent Psychiatry, 51*, 62–73.

Pardo, C. A., & Eberhart, C. G. (2007). The neurobiology of autism. *Brain Pathology, 17*, 434–447.

Parish, S. L. (2006). Juggling and struggling: A preliminary worklife study of mothers with adolescents who have developmental disabilities. *Mental Retardation, 44*, 393–404.

Parker, J. G., Rubin, K. H., Erath, S. A., Wojslawowicz, J. C., & Buskirk, A. A. (2006). Peer relationships, child development, and adjustment: A developmental psychopathology perspective. In D. Cicchetti & D. J. Cohen (Eds.), *Developmental psychopathology. Vol. 1. Theory and method.* Hoboken, NJ: John Wiley & Sons.

Patenaude, A. F., & Kupst, M. J. (2005). Psychosocial functioning in pediatric cancer. *Journal of Pediatric Psychology, 30*, 9–27.

Patterson, G. R. (1976). The aggressive child: Victim and architect of a coercive system. In L. A. Hamerlynck, L. C. Handy, & E. J. Mash (Eds.), *Behavior modification and families.* New York: Brunner/Mazel.

Patterson, G. R., DeBaryshe, B. D., & Ramsey, E. (1989). A developmental perspective on antisocial behavior. *American Psychologist, 44*, 329–335.

Patterson, G. R., DeGarmo, D. S., & Knutson, N. (2000). Hyperactive and antisocial behaviors: Comorbid or two points in the same process? *Development and Psychopathology, 12*, 91–106.

Patterson, G. R., Reid, J. B., & Dishion, T. J. (1992). *Antisocial boys.* Eugene, OR: Castalia Publishing Company.

Patterson, G. R., Reid, J. B., & Eddy, J. M. (2002). A brief history of the Oregon Model. In J. B. Reid, G. R. Patterson, & J. Snyder (Eds.), *Antisocial behavior in children and adolescents: A developmental analysis and model for intervention.* Washington, DC: American Psychological Association.

Patterson, G. R., Reid, J. B., Jones, R. R., & Conger, R. E. (1975). *A social learning approach to family intervention* (Vol. 1) Eugene, OR: Castalia.

Paul, R., Fuerst, Y., Ramsey, G., Chawarska, K., & Klin, A. (2011). Out of the mouth of babes: Vocal production in infant siblings of children with ASD. *Journal of Child Psychology and Psychiatry, 52*, 588–598.

Pavuluri, M. N., Birmaher, B., & Naylor, M.W. (2005). Pediatric bipolar disorder: A review of the past 10 years. *Journal of the American Academy of Child and Adolescent Psychiatry, 44*, 846–871.

Pavuluri, M. N., & Sweeney, J. A. (2008). Integrating functional brain neuroimaging and developmental cognitive neuroscience in child psychiatry research. *Journal of the American Academy of Child and Adolescent Psychiatry, 47*, 1273–1288.

Pavuluri, M. N., West, A., Hill, S. K., Jindal, K., & Sweeney, J. A. (2009). Neurocognitive function in pediatric bipolar disorder: 3-year follow-up shows cognitive development lagging behind healthy youths. *Journal of the American Academy of Child and Adolescent Psychiatry, 48*, 299–307.

Paxton, S. J., Neumark-Sztainer, D., Hannan, P. J., & Eisenberg, M. E. (2006). Body dissatisfaction prospectively predicts depressive mood and low self-esteem in adolescent girls and boys. *Journal of Clinical Child and Adolescent Psychology, 35*, 539–549.

Pearson, D. A., Lane, D. M., Santos, C. W., Casat, C. D., Jerger, S. W., Loveland, K. A., et al. (2004). Effects of methylphenidate treatment in children with mental retardation and ADHD: Individual variation in medication response. *Journal of the American Academy of Child and Adolescent Psychiatry, 43*, 686–698.

Pedersen, P. B., & Pope, M. (2010). Inclusive cultural empathy for successful global leadership. *American Psychologist, 65*, 841–854.

Pederson, S., Vitaro, F., Barker, E.D., & Borge, A. I. H. (2007). The timing of middle-childhood peer rejection and friendship: Linking early behavior to early-adolescent adjustment. *Child Development, 78*, 1037–1051.

Pediatric OCD Treatment Study (POTS) Team. (2004). Cognitive- behavior therapy, sertraline, and their combination for children and adolescents with obsessive-compulsive disorder: The Pediatric OCD Treatment Study (POTS) randomized controlled trial. *Journal of the American Medical Association, 292*, 1969–1976.

Pelham, W. E. (2001, Winter). Are ADHD/I and ADHD/C the same or different? Does it matter? *Clinical Psychology: Science and Practice, 8*, 502–506.

Pelham, W. E., Fabiano, G. A., Gnagy, E. M., Greiner, A. R., & Hoza, B. (2005). The role of summer treatment programs in the context of comprehensive treatment for attentiondeficit/hyperactivity disorder. In E. D. Hibbs & P. S. Jensen (Eds.), *Psychosocial treatments for child and adolescent disorders.* Washington, DC: American Psychological Association.

Pelham, W. E., Gnagy, E. M., Greiner, A. R., Waschbusch, D. A., Fibiano, G. A. & Burrows-MacLean, L. (2010). Summer treatment programs for attention-deficit/hyperactivity disorder. In J. R. Weisz & A. E. Kazdin (Eds.), *Evidence-based psychotherapies for children and adolescents.* New York: Guilford Press.

Pelkonen, M., Marttunen, M., Laippala, P., & Lönnqvist, J. (2000). Factors associated with early dropout from adolescent psychiatry outpatient treatment. *Journal of the American Academy of Child and Adolescent Psychiatry, 39*, 329–336.

Pelsser, L. M., Frankena, K., Toorman, J., Savelkoul, H. F., Dubois, A. E., Pereira, R. R. et al. (2011). Effects of a restricted elimination diet on the behaviour of children with attention-deficit hyperactivity disorder (INCA study): A randomized controlled trial. *The Lancet, 377*, 494–503.

Penn, D. L., Judge, A., Jamieson, P., Garczynski, J., Hennessy, M., & Romer, D. (2005). Stigma. In D. L. Evans, E. B. Foa, R. E. Gur, H. Hendin, C. P. O'Brien, M. E. P. Seligman, & B. T. Walsh (Eds.), *Treating and preventing adolescent mental health* disorders. *What we know and what we don't know: A research agenda for improving mental health of our youth.* New York: Oxford University Press.

Pennington, B. F. (2009). How neuropsychology informs our understanding of developmental disorders. *Journal of Child Psychology and Psychiatry, 50,* 72–78.

Perera, F. P., Wang, S., Vishnevetsky, J., Zhang, B., Cole. K. J., Tang, D. et al. (2011). Polycyclic aromatic hydrocarbons-aromatic DNA adducts in cord blood and behavior scores in New York City children. *Environmental Health Perspective, 119,* 1176–1181.

Pérez-Edgar, K., & Fox, N. A. (2005). Temperament and anxiety disorders. *Child and Adolescent Psychiatric Clinics of North America, 14,* 681–706.

Perez-Edgar, K., Roberson-Nay, R., Hardin, M. G., Poeth, K., Guyer. A. E., Nelson, E. E., et al. (2007). Attention alters neural responses to evocative faces in behaviorally inhibited adolescents. *Neuroimage, 35,* 1538–1546.

Perlman, M.D., & Kaufman, A. S. (1990). Assessment of Child Intelligence. In G. Goldstein & M. Hersen (Eds.), *Handbook of psychological assessment* (2nd ed.). New York: Pergamon.

Perren, S., & Alsaker, F. D. (2006). Social behavior and peer relationships of victims, bully-victims, and bullies in kindergarten. *Journal of Child Psychology and Psychiatry, 47,* 45–57.

Perrin, S., Smith, P., & Yule, W. (2000). The assessment and treatment of post-traumatic stress disorder in children and adolescents. *Journal of Child Psychology and Psychiatry, 41,* 277–289.

Pescosolido, B. A., Jensen, P. S., Martin, J. K., Perry, B. L., Olafsdottir, S., & Fettes, D. (2008). Public knowledge and assessment of child mental health problems: Findings from the National Stigma Study-Children. *Journal of the American Academy of Child and Adolescent Psychiatry, 47,* 339–349.

Peshkin, M. M. (1959). Intractable asthma of childhood: Rehabilitation at the institutional level with a follow-up of 150 cases. *International Archives of Allergy, 15,* 91–101.

Peters, R., Petrunka, K., & Arnold, R. (2003). The Better Beginnings, Better Futures Project: A universal, comprehensive, community-based prevention approach for primary school children and their families. *Journal of Child and Adolescent Psychology, 32,* 215–227.

Peterson, B. S. (1995). Neuroimaging in child and adolescent neuropsychiatric disorders. *Journal of the American Academy of Child and Adolescent Psychiatry, 34,* 1560–1576.

Peterson, L., Reach, K., & Grabe, S. (2003). Health-related disorders. In M. C. Roberts (Ed.), *Handbook of pediatric psychology* (3rd ed.). New York: Guilford Press.

Peterson, L., Schultheis, K., Ridley-Johnson, R., Miller, D. J., & Tracy, K. (1984). Comparison of three modeling procedures on the presurgical and postsurgical reactions of children. *Behavior Therapy, 15,* 197–203.

Peterson, L. J., & Mori, L. (1988). Preparation for hospitalization. In D. K. Routh (Ed.), *Handbook of pediatric psychology.* New York: Guilford.

Peterson, R. L., & McGrath, L. M. (2009a). Dyslexia. In B. F. Pennington (Ed.), *Diagnosing learning disorders.* New York: Guilford Press.

Peterson, R. L., & McGrath, L. M. (2009b). Speech and language disorders. In B. F. Pennington (Ed.), *Diagnosing learning disorders.* New York: Guilford Press.

Petursdottir, A. I., Esch, J. W., Sautter, R. A., & Stewart, K. K. (2010). Characteristics and hypothesized functions of challenging behavior in a community-based sample. *Education and Training in Autism and Developmental Disabilities, 45,* 81–93.

Pfeffer, C. R. (2000). Suicidal behaviour in children: An emphasis on developmental influences. In K. Hawton & K. van Heeringen (Eds.), *The international handbook of suicide and attempted suicide.* Chichester, UK: John Wiley & Sons, Ltd.

Pfefferbaum, B. (1997). Posttraumatic stress disorder in children: A review of the past 10 years. *Journal of the American Academy of Child and Adolescent Psychiatry, 36,* 1503–1511.

Pfefferbaum, B., Nixon, S., Tivis, R., Doughty, D. E., Pynoos, R. S., Gurwitch, R. H., & Foy, D. W. (2001). Television exposure in children after a terrorist incident. *Psychiatry, 64,* 202–211.

Pfefferbaum, B., Nixon, S. J., Krug, R. S., Tivis, R. D., Moore, V. L., Brown, J. M., Pynoos, R. S., Foy, D., & Gurwitch, R. H. (1999a). Clinical needs assessment of middle and high school students following the 1995 Oklahoma City bombing. *American Journal of Psychiatry, 156,* 1069–1074.

Pfefferbaum, B., Nixon, S. J., Tuckerm, P. M., Tivis, R. D., Moore, V. L., Gurwitch, R. H., Pynoos, R. S., & Geis, H. K. (1999b). Posttraumatic stress responses in bereaved children after the Oklahoma City bombing. *Journal of the American Academy of Child and Adolescent Psychiatry, 38,* 1372–1379.

Pfefferbaum, B., Seale, T., & McDonald, N. (2000). Posttraumatic stress two years after the Oklahoma City bombing in youths geographically distant from the explosion. *Psychiatry, 63,* 358–370.

Pfiffner, L. J., Barkley, R. A., & DuPaul, G. J. (2006). Treatment of ADHD in school settings. In R. A. Barkley (Ed.), *Attentiondeficit hyperactivity disorder. A handbook for diagnosis and treatment.* New York: The Guilford Press.

Phelps, L. (2006). *Chronic health-related disorders in children: Collaborative medical and psychoeducational interventions.* Washington, DC: American Psychological Association.

Phillips, E. L. (1968). Achievement place: Token reinforcement procedures in a home-style rehabilitation setting for 'pre-delinquent' boys. *Journal of Applied Behavior Analysis, 1,* 213–223.

Piacentini, J., Bergman, L., Keller, M., & McCracken, J. (2003). Functional impairment in children and adolescents with obsessive-compulsive disorder. *Journal of Child and Adolescent Psychopharmacology, 13,* S61–S69.

Pianta, R. C. (2006). School, schooling, and developmental psychopathology. In D. Cicchetti & D. J. Cohen (Eds.), *Developmental psychopathology. Vol. 1. Theory and method.* Hoboken, NJ: John Wiley & Sons.

Pickles, A., Simonoff, E., Conti-Ramsden, G., Falcaro, M., Simkin, Z., Charman, T., et al. (2009). Loss of language in early development of autism and specific language impairment. *Journal of Child Psychology and Psychiatry, 50,* 843–852.

Pickles, A., Starr, E., Kazak, S., Bolton, P., Papanikolaou, K., Bailey, A. et al., (2000). Variable expression of the autism broader phenotype: Findings from extended pedigrees. *Journal of Child Psychology and Psychiatry, 41,* 491–502.

Pickren, W. E., & Tomes, H. (2002). The legacy of Kenneth B. Clark to APA. *American Psychologist, 57,* 51–59.

Pierce, K. M., Bolt, D. M., & Vandell, D. L. (2010). Specific features of after-school program quality: Associations with children's functioning in middle childhood. *American Journal of Community Psychology, 45,* 381–393.

Pignatiello, A., Teshima, J., Boydell, K. M., Minden, D., Volpe, T., & Braunberger, P. G. (2011). Child and youth telepsychiatry in rural and remote primary care. *Child and Adolescent Psychiatric Climes of North America, 20,* 13–28.

Pina, A. A., & Silverman, W. K. (2004). Clinical phenomenology, somatic symptoms, and distress in Hispanic/Latino and European American youths with anxiety disorders. *Journal of Clinical Child and Adolescent Psychology, 33,* 227–236.

Pine, D. S., Costello, J., Dahl, R., James, R., Leckman, J., Leibenluft, E., et al. (2011). Increasing the developmental focus in DSM-V: Broad issues and specific potential applications in anxiety. In D. A. Regier, W. E. Narrow, E. A. Kuhl, & D. J. Kupfer (Eds.), *The conceptual evolution of DSM-5.* Arlington, VA: American Psychiatric Publishing.

Pine, D. S., Guyer, A. E., & Leibenluft, E. (2008). Functional magnetic resonance imaging and pediatric anxiety. *Journal of the American Academy of Child and Adolescent Psychiatry, 47,* 1217–1221.

Pinquart, M., & Shen, Y. (2011). Depressive symptoms in children and adolescents with chronic physical illness: An updated meta analysis. *Journal of Pediatric Psychology, 36,* 375–384.

Pisecco, S., Huzinec, C., & Curtis, D. (2001). The effect of child characteristics on teachers' acceptability of classroom-based behavioral strategies and psychostimulant medication for the treatment of ADHD. *Journal of Clinical Child Psychology, 30,* 413–421.

Piven, J., Harper, J., Palmer, P., & Arndt, S. (1996). Course of behavioral change in autism: A retrospective study of high-IQ adolescents and adults. *Journal of the American Academy of Child and Adolescent Psychiatry, 35,* 523–529.

Piven, J., & Palmer, P. (1997). Cognitive deficits in parents from multiple-incidence autism families. *Journal of Child Psychology and Psychiatry, 38,* 1011–1022.

Pliszka, S. and the AACAP Work Group on Quality Issues. (2007). Practice parameter for the assessment of children and adolescents with attention-deficit/hyperactivity disorder. *Journal of the Academy of Child and Adolescent Psychiatry, 46,* 894–921.

Pliszka, S. R. (2011). Anxiety disorders. In S. Goldstein & C. R. Reynolds (Eds.), *Handbook of neurodevelopmental and genetic disorders in children.* (2nd ed.). New York: The Guilford Press.

Plomin, R. (1994a). Genetic research and identification of environmental influences. *Journal of Child Psychology and Psychiatry, 35,* 817–834.

Plomin, R. (1994b). *Genetics and experience. The interplay between nature and nurture.* Thousand Oaks, CA: Sage Publications.

Plomin, R. (2005). Finding genes in child psychology and psychiatry: When we are going to be there? *Journal of Child Psychology and Psychiatry, 46,* 1030–1038.

Plomin, R. (2008). Genetics and the future diagnosis of learning disabilities. *Mental Capital and Wellbeing: Making the most of ourselves in the 21st century.* www.foresight.gov.uk

Plomin, R., & Crabbe, J. (2000). DNA. *Psychological Bulletin, 126,* 806–828.

Plomin, R., & Davis, O. S. P. (2009). The future of genetics in psychology and psychiatry: Microarrays, genome-wide association, and non-coding RNA. *Journal of Child Psychology and Psychiatry, 50,* 63–71.

Plomin, R., DeFries, J. C., & McClearn, G. E. (1990). *Behavioral genetics: A primer* (2nd ed.). New York: W. H. Freeman and Company.

Plomin, R., Kovacs, Y., & Haworth, C. M. A. (2007). Generalist genes: Genetic links between brain, mind, and education. *Mind, Brain, and Education, 1,* 11–19.

Plomin, R., & McGuffin, P. (2003). Psychopathology in the post-genomic era. *Annual Review of Psychology, 54,* 205–225.

Ploog, B. O. (2010). Stimulus overselectivity four decades later: A review of the literature and its implications for current research in autism spectrum disorder. *Journal of Autism and Developmental Disorders, 40,* 1332–1349.

Pluess, M., & Belsky, J. (2011). Prenatal programming of postnatal plasticity? *Development and Psychopathology, 23,* 29–38.

Polaha, J., Dalton, W. T., & Allen, S. (2011). The prevalence of emotional and behavioral problems in pediatric primary care serving rural children. *Journal of Pediatric Psychology, 36,* 652–660.

Pollock, L. A. (2001). Parent-child relations. In D. I. Kertzer & M. Barbagoli (Eds.), *The history of the European family. Vol. One. Family life in early modern times, 1500–1789.* New Haven, CT: Yale University Press.

Polloway, E. A., Lubin, J., Smith, J. D., & Patton, J. R. (2010). Mild intellectual disabilities: Legacies and trends in concepts and educational practices. *Education and Training in Autism and Developmental Disabilities, 45,* 54–68.

Popkin, S. J., Leventhal, T., & Weismann, G. (2008). Girls in the hood: The importance of feeling safe. Three-City Study of Moving to Opportunity, Brief No. 1. Retrieved October 2011, www.urban.org/Uploaded PDF/411636_girls_in_the_hood.pdf.

Porrino, L., Rapoport, J. L., Behar, D., Sceery, W., Ismond, D. R., & Bunney, W. E. (1983). A naturalistic assessment of the motor activity of hyperactive boys: I. Comparison with normal controls. *Archives of General Psychiatry, 40,* 681–687.

Porter, S., & Woodworth, M. (2006). Psychopathy and aggression. In C. J. Patrick (Ed.), *Handbook of Psychopathy.* New York: The Guilford Press.

Posthumus, J. A., Raaijmakers, M A. J., Maassen, G. H., van Engeland, H., & Matthys, W. (2012). Sustained effects of Incredible Years as a preventive intervention in preschool children with conduct problems. *Journal of Abnormal Child Psychology, 40,* 487–500.

Potter, D. (2010). Psychosocial well-being and the relationship between divorce and children's academic achievement. *Journal of Marriage and Family, 72,* 933–946.

Potter, H.W. (1972). Mental retardation in historical perspective. In S. I. Harrison & J. F. McDermott (Eds.), *Childhood psychopathology.* New York: International Universities Press.

Pottick, K. J., Kirk, S. A., Hsieh, D. K., & Tian, X. (2007). Judging mental disorder in youths: Effects of client, clinician, and contextual differences. *Journal of Consulting and Clinical Psychology, 75,* 1–8.

Powell, L. M., Szczypka, G., Chaloupka, F. J., & Braunschweig, C. L. (2007). Nutritional content of television food advertisements seen by children and adolescents in the United States. *Pediatrics, 120,* 576–583.

Power, T. J. (2006). Collaborative practices for managing children's chronic health needs. In L. Phelps (Ed.), *Chronic healthrelated disorders in children: Collaborative medical and psychoeducational interventions.* Washington, DC: American Psychological Association.

Powers, S. W. (1999). Empirically supported treatments in pediatric psychology: Procedure-related pain. *Journal of Pediatric Psychology, 24,* 131–145.

Powers, S. W., Jones, J. S., & Jones, B. A. (2005). Behavioral and cognitive-behavioral interventions with pediatric populations. *Clinical Child Psychology and Psychiatry, 10,* 65–77.

President's New Freedom Commission on Mental Health. (2003). *Achieving the promise: Transforming mental health care in America. Final report* (U.S. DHHS Pub. No. SMA-03-3832). Rockville, MD: U.S. Department of Health and Human Services.

Preston, J. L., Frost, S. J., Mencl, W. E., Fulbright, R. K., Landi, N., Grigorenko, E., et al. (2010). Early and late talkers: School-age language, literacy, and neurolinguistic differences. *Brain, 133,* 2185–2195.

Price, G., Cercignani, M., Chu, E. M., Barnes. T. R. E., Barker, G. J., Joyce, E., M., et al. (2010). Brain pathology in first-episode psychosis: Magnetization transfer imaging provides additional information to MRI measurements of volume loss. *Neuroimage, 49,* 185–192.

Price, J. M., & Zwolinski, J. (2010). The nature of child and adolescent vulnerability. In R. E. Ingram & J. M. Price (Eds.), *Vulnerability to psychopathology. Risk across the lifespan.* New York: Guilford Press.

Prinstein, M. J., Boergers, J., & Vernberg, E. M. (2001). Overt and relational aggression in adolescents: Social-psychological adjustment of aggressors and victims. *Journal of Clinical Child Psychology, 30,* 479–491.

Prior, M., Smart, D., Sanson, A., & Oberklaid, F. (1999). Relationship between learning difficulties and psychological problems in preadolescent children from a longitudinal sample. *Journal of the American Academy of Child and Adolescent Psychiatry, 38,* 429–436.

Prior, M., & Werry, J. S. (1986). Autism, schizophrenia, and allied disorders. In H. C. Quay and J. S. Werry (Eds.), *Psychopathological disorders of childhood.* New York: Wiley.

Prout, H. T., & Nowak-Drabik, K. M. (2003). Psychotherapy with persons who have mental retardation: An evaluation of effectiveness. *American Journal on Mental Retardation, 108,* 82–93.

Puhl, R. M., & Latner, J. D. (2007). Stigma, obesity, and the health of the nation's children. *Psychological Bulletin, 133,* 557–580.

Pumariega, A. J., & Glover, S. (1998). New developments in service delivery research for children, adolescents, and their families. In T. H. Ollendick & R. J. Prinz (Eds.), *Advances in clinical child psychology* (Vol. 20). New York: Plenum Press.

Pungello, E. P., Kainz, K., Burchinal, M., Wasik, B. H., Sparling, J. J., Ramey, C. T., et al. (2010). Early educational intervention, early cumulative risk, and the early home environment as predictors of young adult outcomes within a high-risk sample. *Child Development, 81,* 410–426.

Puolakanaho, A., Ahonen, T., Aro, M., Eklund, K., Leppänen, P. H. T., Poikkeus, A-M., et al. (2007). Very early phonological and language skills: Estimating individual risk of reading disability. *Journal of Child Psychology and Psychiatry, 48,* 923–931.

Purcell, K., Brady, K., Chai, H., Muser, J., Molk, L., Gordon, N., & Means, J. (1969). The effect on asthma in children of experimental separation from the family. *Psychosomatic Medicine, 31,* 144–164.

Pynoos, R. S., Frederick, C., Nader, K., Arroyo, W., Steinberg, A., Eth, S., Nunez, F., & Fairbanks, L. (1987). Life threat and posttraumatic stress in school-age children. *Archives of General Psychiatry, 44,* 1057–1063.

Quay, H. C. (1993). The psychobiology of undersocialized aggressive conduct disorder: A theoretical perspective. *Development and Psychopathology, 5,* 165–180.

Querido, J. G., Bearss, K., & Eyberg, S. M. (2002). Theory, research, and practice of parent-child interaction therapy. In F.W. Kaslow & T. Patterson (Eds.), *Comprehensive handbook of psychotherapy: Vol. 2. Cognitive/behavioral/ functional approaches.* New York: John Wiley.

Querido, J. G., & Eyberg, S. M. (2005). Parent-child interaction therapy: Maintaining treatment gains of preschoolers with disruptive behavior disorders. In E. D. Hibbs & P. S. Jensen (Eds.), *Psychosocial treatments for child and adolescent* disorders: Empirically based strategies for clinical practice (2nd ed.). Washington, DC: American Psychological Association.

Quittner, A. L., Barker, D. H., Marciel, K. K., & Grimley, M. E. (2009). Cystic fibrosis: A model for drug discovery and patient care. In M. C. Roberts & R. G. Steele (Eds.), Handbook of pediatric psychology (4th ed.). New York: The Guilford Press.

Rachman, S. J. (1977). The conditioning theory of fear acquisition: A critical examination. Behaviour Research and Therapy, 15, 372–387.

Rachman, S. J. (1991). Neo-conditioning and the classic theory of fear acquisition. Clinical Psychology Review, 11, 155–173.

Rahman, A., Mubbashar, M., Harrington, R., & Gater, R. (2000). Annotation: Developing child mental health services in developing countries. Journal of Child Psychology and Psychiatry, 41, 539–546.

Raine, A. (2005). The interaction of biological and social measures in the explanation of antisocial and violent behavior. In D. M. Stoff & E. J. Sussman (Eds.), Developmental psychobiology of aggression. New York: Cambridge University Press.

Raine, A., Moffitt, T. E., Caspi, A., Loeber, R., Stouthamer-Loeber, M., & Lynam, D. (2005). Neurocognitive impairments in boys on the life-course persistent antisocial path. Journal of Abnormal Psychology, 114, 38–49.

Rait, D. S., Ostroff, J. S., Smith, K., Cella, D. F., Tan, C., & Lesko, L. M. (1992). Lives in a balance—perceived family functioning and the psychosocial adjustment of adolescent cancer survivors. Family Process, 31, 383–397.

Raitano, N. A., Pennington, B. F., Tunick, R. A., Boada, R., & Shriberg, L. D. (2004). Pre-literacy skills of subgroups of children with speech sound disorders. Journal of Child Psychology and Psychiatry, 45, 821–835.

Rajji, T. K., Ismail, Z., & Mulsant, B. H. (2009). Age at onset and cognition in schizophrenia: Meta-analysis. British Journal of Psychiatry, 195, 286–293.

Ramey, C. T., & Campbell, F. A. (1984). Preventive education for high-risk children: Cognitive consequences of the Carolina Abecedarian Project. American Journal of Mental Deficiency, 88, 515–523.

Ramey, C. T., & Ramey, S. L. (1998). Early intervention and early experience. American Psychologist, 53, 109–120.

Ramsey, M. (2010). Genetic and epigenetic insights into fetal alcohol spectrum disorders. Genome Medicine, 2:27. Available at http://genomemedicine.com/content/2/4/27

Ramey, S. L. (1999). Head Start and preschool education: Toward continued improvement. American Psychologist, 54, 344–346.

Rapee, R. M., & Coplan, R. J. (2010). Conceptual relations between anxiety disorder and fearful temperament. In H. Gazelle & K. H. Rubin (Eds.), Social anxiety in childhood: Bridging developmental and clinical perspectives. New Directions for Child and Adolescent, 127, 17–31. San Francisco, CA: Jossey-Bass.

Rapee, R. M., Kennedy, S., Ingram, M., Edwards, S., & Sweeney, L. (2005). Prevention and early intervention of anxiety disorders in inhibited preschool children. Journal of Consulting and Clinical Psychology, 73, 488–497.

Rapee, R. M., Schniering, C. A., & Hudson, J. L. (2009). Anxiety disorders during childhood and adolescence: Origins and treatment. Annual Review of Clinical Psychology, 5, 311–341.

Rapoport, J. L. (1989). The biology of obsessions and compulsions. Scientific American, 260, 83–89.

Rapoport, J. L. & Gogtay, N. (2008). Brain neuroplasticity in healthy, hyperactive, and psychotic children: Insights from neuroimaging. Neuropsychopharmacology, 33, 181–197.

Rapoport, J. L., & Inhoff-Germain, G. (2000). Treatment of obsessive-compulsive disorder in children and adolescents. Journal of Child Psychology and Psychiatry, 41, 419–431.

Rapoport, J. L., Inhoff-Germain, G., Weissman, M. M., Greenwald, S., Narrow, W. E., Jensen, P. S., Lahey, B. B., & Canino, G. (2000). Childhood obsessive-compulsive disorder in the NIMH MECA study: Parent versus child identification of cases. Journal of Anxiety Disorders, 14, 535–548.

Rapoport, J. L., & Ismond, D. R. (1996). DSM-IV training guide for diagnosis of childhood disorders. New York: Brunner/Mazel.

Rauch, S. L., & Britton, J. C. (2010). Developmental neuroimaging studies of OCD: The maturation of a field. Journal of the American Academy of Child and Adolescent Psychiatry, 49, 1186–1188.

Rawana, J. S., Morgan, A. S., Nguyen, H., & Craig, S. G. (2010). The relation between eating- and weight-related disturbances and depression in adolescence: A review. Clinical Child and Family Psychology Review, 13, 213–230.

Ray, D. C. (2007). Two counseling interventions to reduce teacher-child relationship stress. Professional School Counseling, 10, 428–440.

Rea, P. J., McLaughlin, V. L., & Walther-Thomas, C. (2002). Outcome for students with learning disabilities in inclusive and pullout programs. Exceptional Children, 68, 203–222.

Reddy, R., Rhodes, J. E., & Mulhall, P. (2003). The influence of teacher support on student adjustment in the middle school years: A latent growth curve. Development and Psychopathology, 15, 119–138.

Reeb, B. T., & Conger, K. J. (2011). Mental health service utilization in a community sample of rural adolescents: The role of father-offspring relations. Journal of Pediatric Psychology, 36, 661–668.

Regier, D. A., & Burke, J. D. (2000). Epidemiology. In B. J. Sadock & V. A. Sadock (Eds.), Kaplan & Sadock's comprehensive textbook of psychiatry (Vol. I). Philadelphia: Lippincott Williams & Wilkins.

Regier, D. A., Narrow, W. E., Kuhl, E. A., & Kupfer, D. J. (2009). The conceptual development of DSM-V. American Journal of Psychiatry, 166, 645–650.

Reich, W. (2000). Diagnostic Interview for Children and Adolescents (DICA). Journal of the American Academy of Child and Adolescent Psychiatry, 39, 59–66.

Reich, W., Huang, H., & Todd, R. D. (2006). ADHD medication use in a population-based sample of twins. *Journal of the Academy of Child and Adolescent Psychiatry, 45,* 801–807.

Reichenberg, A., & Harvey, P. D. (2007). Neuropsychological impairments in schizophrenia: Integration of performance-based and brain imaging findings. *Psychological Bulletin, 133,* 833–858.

Reichow, B., & Wolery, M. (2009). Comprehensive synthesis of early intensive behavioral intervention for young children with autism based on the UCLA Young Autism Project Model. *Journal of Autism and Developmental Disorders, 39,* 23–41.

Reid, J.B.(Ed.) (1978). *A social learning approach to family intervention* (Vol. 2: *Observations in home settings*). Eugene, OR: Castalia.

Reid, J. B., Patterson, G. R., & Snyder, J. (Eds.) (2002). *Antisocial behavior in children and adolescents: A developmental analysis and model for intervention.* Washington, DC: American Psychological Association.

Reid, M. J., Webster-Stratton, C., & Baydar, N. (2004). Halting the development of conduct problems in Head Start children: The effects of parent training. *Journal of Clinical Child and Adolescent Psychology, 33,* 279–291.

Reifman, A., Villa, L. C., Amans, J. A., Rethinam, V., & Telesca, T.Y. (2001). Children of divorce in the 1990s: A meta-analysis. *Journal of Divorce and Remarriage, 36,* 27–36.

Reiner, W. G. (2008). Pharmacotherapy in the management of voiding and storage disorders, including enuresis and encopresis. *Journal of the American Academy of Child and Adolescent Psychiatry, 47,* 491–498.

Reiss, A. L., & Dant, C. C. (2003). The behavioral neurogenetics of fragile X syndrome: Analyzing gene-brain-behavior relationships in child developmental psychopathologies. *Development and Psychopathology, 15,* 927–968.

Reitan, R. M., & Wolfson, D. (1993). *The Halstead-Reitan Neuropsychological Test Battery: Theory and clinical interpretation* (2nd ed.). Tucson: Neuropsychology Press.

Reiter-Purtill, J., Gerhardt, C. A., Vannatta, K., Passo, M. H., & Noll, R. B. (2003). A controlled longitudinal study of the social functioning of children with juvenile rheumatoid arthritis. *Journal of Pediatric Psychology, 28,* 17–28.

Reiter-Purtill, J., Ridel, S., Jordan, R., & Zeller, M. H. (2010). The benefits of reciprocal friendships for treatment-seeking obese youth. *Journal of Pediatric Psychology, 35,* 905–914.

Rende, R. D., Plomin, R., Reiss, D., & Hetherington, E. M. (1993). Genetic and environmental influences on depressive symptomatology in adolescence: Individual differences and extreme scores. *Journal of Child Psychology and Psychiatry, 34,* 1387–1398.

Renouf, A. G., & Kovacs, M. (1994). Concordance between mothers' reports and children's self-reports of depressive symptoms: A longitudinal study. *Journal of the American Academy of Child & Adolescent Psychiatry, 33,* 208–216.

Reppucci, N. D., Woolard, J. L., & Fried, C. S. (1999). Social, community, and preventive interventions. *Annual Review of Psychology, 50,* 387–418.

Reschly, D. J. (1992). Mental retardation: Conceptual foundations, definitional criteria, and diagnostic operations. In S. R. Hooper, G. W. Hynd, & R. W. Mattison (Eds.), *Assessment and diagnosis of child and adolescent psychiatric disorders, Vol. II. Developmental disorders.* Hillsdale, NJ: Erlbaum.

Rescorla, L. (2002). Language and reading outcomes to age 9 in late-talking toddlers. *Journal of Speech, Language, and Hearing Research, 45,* 360–371.

Rescorla, L. (2009). Age 17 language and reading outcomes in late-talking toddlers: Support for a dimensional perspective on language delay. *Journal of Speech, Language, and Hearing Research, 52,* 16–30.

Rescorla, L., Achenbach, T., Ivanova, M.Y., Dumenci, L., Almqvist, F., Bilenberg, N., et al. (2007). Behavioral and emotional problems reported by parents of children ages 6 to 16 in 31 societies. *Journal of Emotional and Behavioral Disorders, 15,* 130–142.

Rescorla, L. A., Achenbach, T. M., Ivanova, M. Y., Harder,V. S., Otten, L., Bilenberg, N., et al. (2011). International comparisons of behavioral and emotional problems in preschool children: Parents' reports from 24 societies. *Journal of Clinical Child and Adolescent Psychology, 40,* 456–467.

Rettew, D. C., Swedo, S. E., Leonard, H. L., Lenane, M. C., & Rapoport, J. L. (1992). Obsessions and compulsions across time in 79 children and adolescents with obsessive compulsive disorder. *Journal of the American Academy of Child and Adolescent Psychology, 31,* 1050–1056.

Reuther, E. T., Davis, T. E., Moree, B. N., & Matson, J. L. (2011). Treating selective mutism using modular CBT for child anxiety: A case study. *Journal of Clinical Child and Adolescent Psychology, 40,* 156–163.

Reyes, M. M., Panza, K. E., Martin, A., & Bloch, M. H. (2011). Time-lag bias in trials of pediatric antidepressants: A systematic review and meta-analysis. *Journal of the American Academy of Child and Adolescent Psychiatry, 50,* 63–72.

Reynolds, C. R., & Kamphaus, R.W. (2004). *Behavioral Assessment System for Children, Second Edition (BASC-2).* Bloomington, MN: Pearson Assessments.

Reynolds, C. R., & Mayfield, J. W. (2011). Neuropsychological assessment in genetically linked neurodevelopmental disorders. In S. Goldstein & C. R. Reynolds (Eds.), *Handbook of neurodevelopmental and genetic disorders in children* (2nd ed.).New York: The Guilford Press.

Reynolds, C. R., & Richmond, B. O. (2008). *Revised Children's Manifest Anxiety Scale: Second Edition (RCMAS-2).* Los Angeles, CA: Western Psychological Services.

Reynolds, W. M. (1987, 2002). *RADS-2, Reynolds Adolescent Depression Scale: Professional manual.* Lutz, FL: Psychological Resources, Inc.

Reynolds, W. M. (1989). *Reynolds child depression scale.* Lutz, FL: Psychological Assessment Resources, Inc.

Reynolds, W. M. (1994). Assessment of depression in children and adolescents by self-report questionnaires. In W. M. Reynolds and H. F. Johnston (Eds.), *Handbook of depression in children and adolescents.* New York: Plenum Press.

Rhee, S. H., & Waldman, I. D. (2003). Testing alternative hypotheses regarding the role of development on genetic and environmental influences underlying antisocial behavior. In B. B. Lahey, T. E. Moffitt, & A. Caspi (Eds.), *Causes of conduct disorder and juvenile delinquency.* New York: Guilford Press.

Ricciardelli, L. A., & McCabe, M. P. (2004). A biopsychosocial model of disordered eating and the pursuit of muscularity in adolescent boys. *Psychological Bulletin, 130,* 179–205.

Rice, F., Harold, G., & Thapar, A. (2002). The genetic aetiology of childhood depression: A review. *Journal of Child Psychology and Psychiatry, 43,* 65–79.

Richards, D. F. (2003). The central role of informed consent in ethical treatment and research with children. In W. O'Donohue & K. Ferguson (Eds.), *Handbook of professional ethics for psychologists.* Thousand Oaks, CA: Sage Publications.

Richards, M. H., Larson, R., Miller, B. V., Luo, Z., Sims, B., Parrella, D. P., & McCauley, C. (2004). Risky and protective contexts and exposure to violence in urban African American young adolescents. *Journal of Clinical Child and Adolescent Psychology, 33,* 138–148.

Richler, J., Huerta, M., Bishop, S. L., & Lord, C. (2010). Developmental trajectories of restricted and repetitive behaviors and interests in children with autism spectrum disorders. *Development and Psychopathology, 22,* 55–69.

Richters, J. E., & Cicchetti, D. (1993). Mark Twain meets DSMIIIR: Conduct disorder, development, and the concept of harmful dysfunction. *Development and Psychopathology, 5,* 5–29.

Rie, H. E. (1971). Historical perspectives of concepts of child psychopathology. In H. E. Rie (Ed.), *Perspectives in child psychopathology.* New York: Aldine-Atherton.

Rieppi, R., et al. (2002). Socioeconomic status as a moderator of ADHD treatment outcomes. *Journal of the American Academy of Child and Adolescent Psychiatry, 41,* 269–277.

Ripple, C. H., & Zigler, E. (2003). Research, policy, and the federal role in prevention initiatives for children. *American Psychologist, 58,* 482–490.

Roberts, G. E. (2005). *Roberts Apperception Test for Children 2.* Los Angeles, CA: Western Psychological Services.

Roberts, M. C., & Steele, R. G. (Eds.) (2009). *Handbook of pediatric psychology* (4th ed.). New York: The Guilford Press.

Roberts, M. C., & Wallander, J. L. (1992). Family issues in pediatric psychology: An overview. In M. C. Roberts & J. L Wallander (Eds.), *Family issues in pediatric psychology.* Hillsdale, NJ: Erlbaum.

Roberts, R. E., Ramsay Roberts, C., & Xing, Y. (2006). Prevalence of youth-reported DSM-IV psychiatric disorders among African, European, and Mexican American adolescents. *Journal of the American Academy of Child and Adolescent Psychiatry, 45,* 1329–1337.

Roberts, R. E., Roberts, C. R., & Xing, Y. (2007). Comorbidity of substance use disorders and other psychiatric disorders among adolescents: Evidence from an epidemiological survey. *Drug and Alcohol Dependence, 88S,* S4–S13.

Robin, A. L. (2006). Training families with adolescents with ADHD. In R. A. Barkley (Ed.), *Attention-deficit hyperactivity disorder. A handbook for diagnosis and treatment.* New York: The Guilford Press.

Robin, A. L., Koepke, T., & Moye, A. (1990). Multidimensional assessment of parent-adolescent relations. *Psychological Assessment, 2,* 451–459.

Robin, A. L., & le Grange, D. (2010). Family therapy for adolescents with anorexia nervosa. In J. R. Weisz & A. E. Kazdin (Eds.), *Evidence-based psychotherapies for children and adolescents* (2nd ed.). New York: The Guilford Press.

Robins, D., Fein, D., Barton, M., & Green, J. (2001). The modified checklist for autism in toddlers: An initial study investigating the early detection of autism and pervasive developmental disorders. *Journal of Autism and Developmental Disorders, 31,* 131–144.

Robins, D. L. (2008). Screening for autism spectrum disorders in primary care settings. *Autism, 12,* 537–556.

Robinson, E. B., Munir, K., Munafò, M. R., Hughes, M., McCormick, M. C., & Koenen, K. C. (2011). Stability of autistic traits in the general population: Further evidence for a continuum of impairment. *Journal of the Academy of Child and Adolescent Psychology, 50,* 376–384.

Roblek, T., & Piacentini, J. (2005). Cognitive-behavior therapy for childhood anxiety disorders. *Child and Adolescent Psychiatric Clinics of North America, 14,* 863–876.

Rodenburg, R., Stams, G. J., Meijer, A. M., Aldenkamp, A. P., & Dekovic, M. (2005). Psychopathology in children with epilepsy: A meta-analysis. *Journal of Pediatric Psychology, 30,* 453–468.

Rodriguez, A., & Bohlin, G. (2005). Are maternal smoking and stress during pregnancy related to ADHD symptoms in children? *Journal of Child Psychology and Psychiatry, 46,* 246–254.

Rogers, A. G. (2000). When methods matter: Qualitative research issues in psychology. *Harvard Educational Review, 70,* 75–85.

Rogers, S. (1998). Empirically supported comprehensive treatments for young children with autism. *Journal of Clinical Child Psychology, 27,* 168–179.

Rogers, S. J., Hepburn, S. L., Stackhouse, T., & Wehner, E. (2004). Imitation performance in toddlers with autism and those with other developmental disorders. *Journal of Child Psychology and Psychiatry, 44,* 763–781.

Rogers, S. J., & Virmara, L. A. (2008). Evidence-based comprehensive treatments for early autism. *Journal of Clinical Child and Adolescent Psychology, 37,* 8–38.

Rohde, P., Lewinsohn, P. M., Clarke, G. N., Hops, H., & Seeley, J. R. (2005). The adolescent coping with depression course: A cognitive-behavioral approach to the treatment of adolescent depression. In E. D. Hibbs & P. S. Jensen (Eds.), *Psychosocial* treatments for child and adolescent disorders: Empirically based strategies for clinical practice (2nd ed.). Washington, DC: American Psychological Association.

Roid, G. H., & Barram, R. A. (2004). Essentials of Stanford-Binet Intelligence Scales (SB5). Hoboken, N.J.: John Wiley & Sons.

Romer, D., & McIntosh, M. (2005). The roles and perspectives of school mental health professionals in promoting adolescent mental health. In D. L. Evans, E. B. Foa, R. E. Gur, H. Hendin, C. P. O'Brien, M. E. P. Seligman, & B. T. Walsh (Eds.), Treating and preventing adolescent mental health disorders. What we know and what we don't know: A research agenda for improving mental health of our youth. New York: Oxford University Press.

Ronan, K., Kendall, P. C., & Rowe, M. (1994). Negative affectivity in children: Development and validation of a self-statement questionnaire. Cognitive Therapy and Research, 18, 509–528.

Rosenblum, K. L., Dayton, C. J., & Muzik, M. (2009). Infant social and emotional development. In C. H. Zeanah, Jr. (Ed.), Handbook of infant mental health. New York: Guilford Press.

Rosenfeld, A. A., Pilowsky, D. J., Fine, P., Thorpe, M., Fein, E., Simms, M. D., Halfon, N., Irwin, M., Alfaro, J., Saletsky, R., & Nickman, S. (1997). Foster care: An update. Journal of the American Academy of Child and Adolescent Psychiatry, 36, 448–458.

Ross, A. O. (1972). The clinical child psychologist. In B. J. Wolman (Ed.), Manual of child psychopathology. New York: McGraw-Hill.

Ross, D. M. (1988). Aversive treatment procedures: The school-age child's view.Newsletter of the Society of Pediatric Psychology, 12, 3–6.

Ross, R. G., Heinlein, S., Zerbe, G. O., & Radant, A. (2005). Saccadic eye movement task identifies cognitive deficits in children with schizophrenia, but not in unaffected child relatives. Journal of Child Psychology and Psychiatry, 46, 1354–1362.

Rosselló, J., & Bernal, G. (1999). The efficacy of cognitive-behavioral and interpersonal treatments for depression in Puerto Rican adolescents. Journal of Consulting and Clinical Psychology, 67, 734–745.

Rosselló, J., & Bernal, G. (2005). New developments in cognitivebehavioral and interpersonal treatments for depressed Puerto Rican adolescents. In E. D. Hibbs & P. S. Jensen (Eds.), Psychosocial treatments for child and adolescent disorders: Empirically based strategies for clinical practice (2nd ed.). Washington, DC: American Psychological Association.

Rossi, A., Pollice, R., Daneluzzo, E., Marinangeli, M. G., & Stratta, P. (2000). Behavioral neurodevelopment abnormalities and schizophrenic disorder: A retrospective evaluation with the Childhood Behavior Checklist (CBCL). Schizophrenia Research, 44, 121–128.

Roth, T. L., & Sweatt, J. D. (2011). Annual research review: Epigenetic mechanisms and environmental shaping of the brain during sensitive periods of development. Journal of Child Psychology and Psychiatry, 52, 398–408.

Rothbart, M. K., & Posner, M. I. (2006). Temperament, attention, and developmental psychopathology. In D. Cicchetti & D. J. Cohen (Eds.), Developmental psychopathology. Vol. 2. Developmental neuroscience. Hoboken, NJ: John Wiley & Sons.

Rothenberger, A. (2009). Brain oscillations forever—neurophysiology in future research of child psychiatric problems. Journal of Child Psychology and Psychiatry, 50, 79–86.

Rowe, R., Simonoff, E., & Silberg, J. L. (2007). Psychopathology, temperament, and unintentional injury: Cross-sectional and longitudinal relationships. Journal of Child Psychology and Psychiatry, 48, 71–79.

Rozga, A., Hutman, T., Young, G. S., Rogers, S. J., Ozonoff, S., Dapretto, M., et al. (2011). Behavioral profiles of affected and unaffected siblings of children with autism: Contribution of measures of mother-infant interaction and nonverbal communication. Journal of Autism and Developmental Disorders, 41, 287–301.

Rubia, K., Halari, R., Smith, A. B., Mohammed, M., Scott, S., Giampietro, V., et al. (2008). Dissociated functional brain abnormalities of inhibition in boys with pure conduct disorder and in boys with pure attention deficit hyperactivity disorder. American Journal of Psychiatry, 165, 889–897.

Rubia, K., Smith, A. B., Halari, R., Matsukura, F., Mohammad, M., Taylor, E., et al. (2009). Disorder-specific dissociation of orbitofrontal dysfunction in boys with pure conduct disorder during reward and ventrolateral prefrontal dysfunction in boys with pure ADHD during sustained attention. American Journal of Psychiatry, 166, 83–94.

Rubin, K., Bukowski, W., & Parker, J. (2006). Peer interaction and social competence. In W. Damon & R. L. Lerner (Eds.), Handbook of child psychology. Vol. 3 (6th ed.). New York: John Wiley & Sons.

Rubin, K. H., Burgess, K. B., Kennedy, A. E., & Stewart, S. L. (2003). Social withdrawal in childhood. In E. J. Mash & R. A. Barkley (Eds.), Child psychopathology (2nd ed.). New York: Guilford Press.

Rubin, K. H., Wojslawowicz, J. C., Rose-Krasnor, L., Booth-LaForce, C., & Burgess, K.B. (2006). The best friendships of shy/withdrawn children: Prevalence, stability, and relationship quality. Journal of Abnormal Child Psychology, 34, 143–157.

Rucklidge, J. J., & Tannock, R. (2002).Neuropsychological profiles of adolescents with ADHD: Effects of reading difficulties and gender. Journal of Child Psychology and Psychiatry, 43, 988–1003.

Rudolph, K. D., & Asher, S. R. (2000). Adaptation and maladaptation in the peer system: Developmental processes and outcomes. In A. J. Sameroff, M. Lewis, & S. M. Miller (Eds.), Handbook of developmental psychopathology (2nd ed.). New York: Kluwer Academic/ Plenum Publishers.

Rudolph, K. D., Hammen, C., & Daley, S. E. (2006). Mood disorders. In D. A. Wolfe & E. J. Mash (Eds.), Behavioral and emotional disorders in adolescents: Nature, assessment, and treatment. New York: The Guilford Press.

Rudolph, K. D., & Lambert, S. F. (2007). Child and adolescent depression. In E. J. Mash & R. A. Barkley (Eds.), *Assessment of childhood disorders* (4th ed.). New York: The Guilford Press.

Rueger, S. Y., & Malecki, C. K. (2011). Effects of stress, attributional style and perceived parental support on depressive symptoms in early adolescence: A prospective analysis. *Journal of Clinical Child and Adolescent Psychology, 40,* 347–359.

Rusby, J. C., Estes, A., & Dishion, T. (1991). *The Interpersonal Process Code (IPC).* Unpublished manuscript. Oregon Social Learning Center, Eugene.

Russ, S.W. (1995). Play psychotherapy research: State of the science. In T. H. Ollendick & R. J. Prinz (Eds.), *Advances in clinical child psychology* (Vol. 17). New York: Plenum.

Russell, A. T., Bott, L., & Sammons, C. (1989). The phenomenology of schizophrenia occurring in childhood. *Journal of the American Academy of Child and Adolescent Psychiatry, 28,* 399–407.

Russell, S. T., & Joyner, K. (2001). Adolescent sexual orientation and suicide risk: Evidence from a national study. *American Journal of Public Health, 91,* 1276–1281.

Rutgers, A. H., Bakersman-Kranenburg, M. J., van Ijzendoorn, M. H., & van Berckelaer-Onnes, I. A. (2004). Autism and attachment: A meta-analytic review. *Journal of Child Psychology and Psychiatry, 45,* 1123–1134.

Rutgers, A. H., van IJzendoorn, M. H., Bakerman-Kranenburg, M. J., Swinkels, S. H. N., van Daalen, E., Dietz, C., et al. (2007). Autism, attachment and parenting: A comparison of children with autism spectrum disorder, mental retardation, language disorder, and non-clinical children. *Journal of Abnormal Child Psychology, 35,* 859–870.

Rutherford, H. J. V., Mayes, L. C., & Potenza, M. N. (2010). Neurobiology of adolescent substance use disorders: Implications for prevention and treatment. *Child and Adolescent Psychiatric Clinics of North America, 19,* 479–492.

Rutten, B. P. F., & Mill, J. (2009). Epigenetic mediation of environmental influences in major psychotic disorders. *Schizophrenia Bulletin, 35,* 1045–1056.

Rutter, M. (1989). Pathways from childhood to adult life. *Journal of Child Psychology and Psychiatry, 30,* 23–51.

Rutter, M. (2005). Natural experiments, causal influences, and policy development. In M. Rutter & M. Tienda (Eds.), *Ethnicity and causal mechanisms.* New York: Cambridge University Press.

Rutter, M. (2006). The promotion of resilience in the face of adversity. In A. Clarke-Stewart & J. Dunn (Eds.), *Families count: Effects on child and adolescent development.* New York: Cambridge University Press.

Rutter, M. (2011). Research review: Child psychiatric diagnosis and classification: Concept, findings, challenges, and potential. *Journal of Child Psychology and Psychiatry, 52,* 647–660.

Rutter, M., Caspi, A., & Moffitt, T. E. (2003). Using sex differences in psychopathology to study causal mechanisms: Unifying issues and research strategies. *Journal of Child Psychology and Psychiatry, 44,* 1092–1115.

Rutter, M., Colvert, E., Kreppner, J., Beckett, C., Castle, J., Grootheus, C., et al. (2007). Early adolescent outcomes for institutionally deprived adoptees. I: Disinhibited attachment. *Journal of Child Psychology and Psychiatry, 48,* 17–30.

Rutter, M., Kreppner, J., & Sonuga-Barke, E. (2009). Attachment insecurity, disinhibited attachment, and attachment disorders: Where do research findings leave the concept? *Journal of Child Psychology and Psychiatry, 50,* 529–543.

Rutter, M., LeCouteur, A., & Lord, C. (2006). Autism Diagnostic Interview, R (ADI-R). Torrance, CA: Western Psychological Services.

Rutter, M., Mawhood, L., & Howlin, P. (1992). Language delay and social development. In P. Fletcher & D.Hall (Eds.), *Specific speech and language disorders in children.* San Diego, CA: Singular Publishing Group.

Rutter, M., Moffitt, T. E., & Caspi, A. (2006). Gene-environment interplay and psychopathology: Multiple varieties but real effects. *Journal of Child Psychology and Psychiatry, 47,* 226–261.

Rutter, M., & Silberg, J. (2002). Gene-environment interplay in relation to emotional and behavioral disturbance. *Annual Review of Psychology, 54,* 463–490.

Rutter, M., Silberg, J., O'Connor, T., & Simonoff, E. (1999). Genetics and child psychiatry: II Empirical research findings. *Journal of Child Psychology and Psychiatry, 40,* 19–55.

Rutter, M., & Sroufe, L. A. (2000). Developmental psychopathology: Concepts and challenges. *Development and Psychopathology, 12,* 265–296.

Ryan, N. D., Puig-Antich, J., Ambrosini, P., Ravinovich, H., Robinson, D., Neilson, B., Iyenhar, S., & Toomey, J. (1987). The clinical picture of major depression in children and adolescents. *Archives of General Psychiatry, 44,* 854–861.

Ryndak, D., Ward, T., Alper, S., Storch, J. F., & Montgomery, J. W. (2010). Long-term outcomes in inclusive and self-contained settings for siblings with comparable significant disabilities. *Education and Training in Autism and Developmental Disabilities, 45,* 38–53.

Rynn, M., Puliafico, A., Heleniak, C., Rikhi, P., Ghalib, K., & Vidair, H. (2011). Advances in pharmacotherapy for pediatric anxiety disorders. *Depression and Anxiety, 28,* 76–87.

Sadeh, A. (2005). Cognitive-behavioral treatment for childhood sleep disorders. *Clinical Psychology Review, 25,* 612–628.

Sadeh, A., Raviv, A., & Gruber, R. (2000). Sleep patterns and sleep disruptions in school-age children. *Developmental Psychology, 36,* 291–301.

Sahler, O. J., Frager, G., Levetown, M., Cohn, F. G., & Lipson, M. A. (2000). Medical education about end-of-life care in the pediatric setting: Principles, challenges, and opportunities. *Pediatrics, 105,* 575–584.

Salekin, R. T. (2006). Psychopathy in children and adolescents: Key issues in conceptualization and assessment. In C. J. Patrick (Ed.), *Handbook of Psychopathy*. New York: The Guilford Press.

Saler, L., & Skolnick, N. (1992). Childhood parental death and depression in adulthood: Roles of surviving parent and family environment. *American Journal of Orthopsychiatry, 62*, 504–516.

Sallis, J. F., & Glanz, K. (2006). The role of built environments in physical activity, eating, and obesity in childhood. *The Future of Children, 16*, 89–108.

Salmon, K., & Bryant, R. A. (2002). Posttraumatic stress disorder in children: The influence of developmental factors. *Clinical Psychology Review, 22*, 163–188.

Salmon, K., & Pereira, J. K. (2002). Predicting children's response to an invasive medical investigation: The influence of effortful control and parent behavior. *Journal of Pediatric Psychology, 27*, 227–233.

Salvy, S. J., Bowker, J. C., Nitecki, L. A., Kluczynski, M. A., Germeroth, L. J., & Roemmich, J. N. (2012). Effects of ostracism and social connection-related activities on adolescents' motivation to eat and energy intake. *Journal of Pediatric Psychology, 37*, 25–32.

Salzinger, S., Feldman, R. S., Ng-Mak, D. S., Mojica, E., & Stockhammer, T. F. (2001). The effect of physical abuse on children's social and affective status: A model of cognitive and behavioral processes explaining the association. *Development and Psychopathology, 13*, 805–825.

Sameroff, A. (2006). Identifying risk and protective factors for healthy child development. In A. Clarke-Stewart & J. Dunn (Eds.), *Families count: Effects on child and adolescent development*. New York: Cambridge University Press.

Sameroff, A. J. (1990). Neo-environmental perspectives on developmental theory. In R. M. Hodapp, J. A. Burack, & E. Zigler (Eds.), *Issues in the developmental approach to mental retardation*. New York: Cambridge University Press.

Sandberg, D. E., & Zurenda, L. (2006). Endocrine disorders. In L. Phelps (Ed.), *Chronic health-related disorders in children: Collaborative medical and psychoeducational interventions*. Washington, DC: American Psychological Association.

Sanders, J. L. (2009). Qualitative or quantitative differences between Asperger's disorder and autism? *Journal of Autism and Developmental Disorders, 39*, 1560–1567.

Sandler, I. N., Ma, Y., Tein, J. Y., Ayers, T. S., Wolchik, S., Kennedy, C., & Milsap, R. (2010). Long-term effects of the Family Bereavement Program on multiple indicators of grief in parentally bereaved children and adolescents. *Journal of Consulting and Clinical Psychology, 78*, 131–143.

Sanson, A., Letcher, P., Smart, D., Prior, M., Toumbourou, J. W., & Oberklaid, F. (2009). Associations between early childhood temperament clusters and later psychosocial adjustment. *Merrill-Palmer Quarterly, 55*, 26–54.

Sanson, A., Smart, D., Prior, M., & Oberklaid, F. (1993). Precursors of hyperactivity and aggression. *Journal of the American Academy of Child and Adolescent Psychiatry, 32*, 1207–1216.

Santos, A., Rosset, D., & Deruelle, C., (2009). Human versus non-human face processing: Evidence from Williams syndrome. *Journal of Autism and Developmental Disorders, 39*, 1552–1559.

Santostefano, S. (1978). A biodevelopmental approach to clinical child psychology. New York: Wiley-Interscience.

Sapienza, J. K., & Masten, A. S. (2011). Understanding and promotion resilience in children and youth. *Current Opinion in Psychiatry, 24*, 267–273.

Sato, A. F., Jelalian, E., Hart, C. N., Lloyd-Richardson, E. E., Mehlenbeck, R. S., Neill, M., & Wing, R. R. (2011). Associations between parent behavior and adolescent weight control. *Journal of Pediatric Psychology, 36*, 451–460.

Sattler, J. M. (1992). *Assessment of children.* (Revised and updated 3rd ed.). San Diego: Jerome M. Sattler, Publisher.

Sattler, J. M. (1998). *Clinical and forensic interviewing of children and families: Guidelines for the mental health, education, pediatric, and child maltreatment fields.* San Diego: Jerome M. Sattler, Publisher, Inc.

Savin-Williams, R. C., & Ream, G. L. (2003). Suicide attempts among sexual-minority male youth. *Journal of Clinical Child and Adolescent Psychology, 32*, 509–522.

Saylor, C. F., Cowart, B. L., Lipovsky, J. A., Jackson, C., & Finch, A.J., Jr. (2003). Media exposure to September 11: Elementary school students' experiences and posttraumatic symptoms. *American Behavioral Scientist, 46*, 1622–1642.

Saylor, C. F., Powell, P., & Swenson, C. (1992). Hurricane Hugo blows down the broccoli: Preschoolers' post-disaster play and adjustment. *Child Psychiatry and Human Development, 22*, 139–149.

Schachar, R., & Tannock, R. (2002). Syndromes of hyperactivity and attention deficit. In M. Rutter & E. Taylor (Eds.), *Child and adolescent psychiatry.* Oxford, UK: Blackwell Publishing.

Schaeffer, J. L., & Ross, R. G. (2002). Childhood-onset schizophrenia: Premorbid and prodromal diagnostic and treatment histories. *Journal of the American Academy of Child and Adolescent Psychiatry, 41*, 538–545.

Schalock, R. L., Luckasson, R. A., Shogren, K. A., et al. (2007). The renaming of mental retardation: Understanding the change to the term intellectual disability. *Intellectual and Developmental Disabilities, 45*, 116–124.

Schalock, R. L., et al. (2010). *Intellectual disability: Definition, classification, and systems of support.* Washington, DC: American Association on Intellectual and Developmental Disabilities.

Scharf, J. M., Miller, L. L., Mathews, C. A., & Ben-Shlomo, Y. (2012). Prevalence of Tourette syndrome and chronic tics in the population-based Avon Longitudinal Study of Parents and Children cohort. *Journal of the American Academy of Child and Adolescent Psychiatry, 51*, 192–201.

Scharfstein, L. A., Beidel, D. C., Finnell, L. R., Distier, A., & Carter, N. T. (2011). Do pharmacological and behavioral interventions differentially affect treatment outcome for children with social phobia? *Behavior Modification, 35,* 451–467.

Scheerenberger, R. C. (1983, 1987). *A history of mental retardation.* Baltimore: Brookes Publishing Co.

Scheeringa, M. S. (2009). Posttraumatic stress disorder. In C. H. Zenah, Jr. (Ed.), *Handbook of Infant Mental Health* (3rd ed.). New York: The Guilford Press.

Scheffler, R. M., Brown, T. T., Fulton, B. D., Hinshaw, S. P., Levine, P., & Stone, S. (2009). Positive association between attention-deficit/hyperactivity disorder medication use and academic achievement during elementary school. *Pediatrics, 123,* 1272–1279.

Schepman, K., Collishaw, S., Gardner, F., Maughan, B., Scott., J., & Pickles, A. (2011). Do changes in parent mental health explain trends in youth emotional problems? *Social Science and Medicine, 73,* 293–300.

Schetky, D. H. (2000). Ethical issues in child and adolescent psychiatry. In B. J. Sadock & V. A. Sadock (Eds.), *Comprehensive textbook of psychiatry* (Vol. II). Philadelphia: Lippincott Williams & Wilkins.

Schieve, L. A., Blumberg, S. J., Rice, C., Visser, S. N., & Boyle, C. (2007). The relationship between autism and parenting stress. *Pediatrics, 119 Suppl.* S114–121.

Schiffman, J., & Daleiden, E. L. (2006). Population and service characteristics of youth with schizophrenia-spectrum diagnoses in the Hawaii system of care. *Journal of Child Psychology and Psychiatry, 47,* 58–62.

Schippell, P. L., Vasey, M. W., Cravens-Brown, L. M., & Bretveld, R. A. (2003). Suppressed attention to rejection, ridicule, and failure cues: A unique correlate of reactive but not proactive aggression. *Journal of Clinical Child and Adolescent Psychology, 32,* 40–55.

Schmitz, M., Ludwig, H., & Rohde, L. A. (2010). Do hyperactive symptoms matter in ADHD-I restricted phenotype? *Journal of Clinical Child and Adolescent Psychology, 39,* 741–748.

Schniering, C. A., & Rapee, R. M. (2002). Development and validation of a measure of children's automatic thoughts: The Children's Automatic Thoughts Scale. *Behaviour Research and Therapy, 40,* 1091–1109.

Schopler, E. (1994). Behavioral priorities for autism and related developmental disorders. In E. Schopler & G. B. Mesibov (Eds.), *Behavioral issues in autism.* New York: Plenum.

Schopler, E. (1997). Implementation of TEACCH philosophy. In D. J. Cohen & F. R. Volkmar (Eds.), *Handbook of autism and pervasive developmental disorders.* New York: John Wiley.

Schopler, E., Short, A., & Mesibov, G. (1989). Relation of behavioral treatment to "normal functioning": Comment on Lovaas. *Journal of Consulting and Clinical Psychology, 57,* 162–164.

Schopler, E., Van Bourgondien, M., Wellman, G. J., & Love, S. R. (2010). *Childhood Autism Rating Scale, Second Edition (CARS).* Los Angeles, CA: Western Psychological Services.

Schreibman, L. (1997). Theoretical perspectives on behavioral intervention for individuals with autism. In D. J. Cohen & F. R. Volkmar (Eds.), *Handbook of autism and pervasive developmental disorders.* New York: John Wiley.

Schreibman, L. (2000). Intensive behavioral/psychoeducational treatments for autism: Research needs and future directions. *Journal of Autism and Developmental Disorders, 30,* 373–378.

Schroeder, C. S., & Gordon, B. N. (2002). *Assessment and treatment of childhood problems: A clinician's guide* (2nd ed.). New York: Guilford Press.

Schulte-Körne, G. (2001). Annotation: Genetics of reading and spelling disorder. *Journal of Child Psychology and Psychiatry, 42,* 985–997.

Schultz, D., Izard, C. E., Ackerman, B. P., & Youngstrom, E. A. (2001). Emotion knowledge in economically disadvantaged children: Self-regulatory antecedents and relations to social difficulties and withdrawal. *Development and Psychopathology, 13,* 53–67.

Schultz, R. T., & Klin, A. (2002). Genetics of childhood disorders: XLIII. Autism, Part 2: Neural foundations. *Journal of the American Academy of Child and Adolescent Psychiatry, 41,* 1259–1262.

Schumaker, J. B., & Deshler, D. D. (2003). Can students with LD become competent writers? *Learning Disability Quarterly, 26,* 129–141.

Schuster, M. A., Stein, B. D., Jaycox, L. H., Collins, R. L., Marshall, G. N., Elliott, M. N., et al. (2001). A national survey of stress reactions after the September 11, 2001 terrorist attacks. *New England Journal of Medicine, 345,* 1507–1512.

Schwab-Stone, M., Chen, C., Greenberger, E., Silver, D., Lichtman, J., & Voyce, C. (1999). No safe haven II: The effects of violence exposure on urban youth. *Journal of the American Academy of Child and Adolescent Psychiatry, 38,* 359–367.

Schwartz, C. E., Kunwar, P. S., Greve, D. N., Moran. L. R., Viner, J. C., Coviner, J. M., et al. (2010). Structural differences in adult orbital and ventromedial prefrontal cortex predicted by infant temperament at 4 months of age. *Archives of General Psychiatry, 67,* 78–84.

Schwartz, D., Dodge, K. A., & Coie, J. D. (1993). The emergence of chronic peer victimization in boys' play groups. *Child Development, 64,* 1755–1772.

Schwartz, D., Dodge, K. A., Coie, J. D., Hubbard, J. A., Cillessen, A. H. N., Lemerise, E. A., & Bateman, H. (1998). Socialcognitive and behavioral correlates of aggression and victimization in boys' play groups. *Journal of Abnormal Child Psychology, 26,* 431–440.

Schwartz, D., Dodge, K. A., Pettit, G. S., & Bates, J. E. (1997). The early socialization of aggressive victims of bullying. *Child Development, 68,* 665–675.

Schwartz, J. A. J., Gladstone, T. R. G., & Kaslow, N. J. (1998). Depressive disorders. In T. H. Ollendick & M. Hersen (Eds.), *Handbook of child psychopathology* (3rd ed.). New York: Plenum Press.

Schwartz, J. A. J., Kaslow, N. J., Seeley, J., & Lewinsohn, P. (2000). Psychological, cognitive, and interpersonal correlates of attributional changes in adolescents. *Journal of Clinical Child Psychology, 29,* 188–198.

Schwartz, L., & Drotar, D. (2006). Posttraumatic stress and related impairment in survivors of childhood cancer in early adulthood compared to healthy peers. *Journal of Pediatric Psychology, 31,* 356–366.

Schwebel, D. C., & Brezausek, M. S. (2010). How do mothers and fathers influence pediatric injury risk in middle childhood? *Journal of Pediatric Psychology, 35,* 806–813.

Schwebel, D. C., & Gaines, J. (2007). Pediatric unintentional injury: Behavioral risk factors and implications for prevention. *Journal of Developmental & Behavioral Pediatrics, 28,* 245–254.

Schwebel, D. C., Summerlin, A. L., Bounds, M. L., & Morrongiello, B. A. (2006). The Stamp-in-Safety Program: A behavioral intervention to reduce behaviors that can lead to unintentional playground injury in a preschool setting. *Journal of Pediatric Psychology, 31,* 152–162.

Scorgie, K., & Sobsey, D. (2000). Transformational outcomes associated with parenting children who have disabilities. *Mental Retardation, 38,* 195–206.

Scott, S. (1994). Mental retardation. In M. Rutter, E. Taylor, & L. Hersov (Eds.), *Child and adolescent psychiatry. Modern approaches.* Cambridge, MA: Blackwell.

Scourfield, J., Rice, F., Thapar, A., Harold, G. T., Martin, N., & McGuffin, P. (2003). Depressive symptoms in children and adolescents: Changing aetiological influences with development. *Journal of Child Psychology and Psychiatry, 44,* 968–976.

Scruggs, T. E., & Mastropieri, M. A. (2002). On babies and bathwater: Addressing the problems of identification of learning disabilities. *Learning Disability Quarterly, 25,* 155–168.

Sears, H. A. (2004). Adolescents in rural communities seeking help: Who reports problems and who sees professionals? *Journal of Child Psychology and Psychiatry, 45,* 396–404.

Sears, R. R. (1975). *Your ancients revisited: A history of child development.* Chicago: University of Chicago Press.

Seedat, S., Scott, K. M., Angermeyer, M. C., Berglund, P., Bromet, E. J., Brugha, T. S., et al. (2009). Cross-national associations between gender and mental disorders in the World Health Organization World Health Surveys. *Archives of General Psychiatry, 66,* 785–795.

Seid, M., Varni, J. W., Gidwani, P., Gelhard, L. R., & Slymen, D. J. (2010). Problem-solving skills training for vulnerable families of children with persistent asthma: Report of a randomized trial on health-related quality of life outcomes. *Journal of Pediatric Psychology, 35,* 1133–1143.

Seiffge-Krenke, I. (1998). The highly structured climate in families of adolescents with diabetes: Functional or dysfunctional for metabolic control? *Journal of Pediatric Psychology, 23,* 313–322.

Seligman, M. P., & Peterson, C. (1986). A learned helplessness perspective on childhood depression: Theory and research. In M. Rutter, C. E. Izard, & P. B. Read (Eds.), *Depression in young people: Developmental and clinical perspectives.* New York: Guilford.

Selten, J-P., Frissen, A., Lensvelt-Mulders, G., & Morgan, V. A. (2010). Schizophrenia and the 1957 pandemic of influenza: Meta-analysis. *Schizophrenia Bulletin, 36,* 219–228.

Seltzer, M. M., Krauss, M. W., Shattuck, P. T., Orsmond, G., Swe, A., & Lord, C. (2003). The symptoms of autism spectrum disorders in adolescence and adulthood. *Journal of Autism and Developmental Disorders, 33,* 565–581.

Selye, H. (1956). *The stress of life.* New York: McGraw-Hill.

Semrud-Clikeman, M., Steingard, R. J., Filipek, P., Biederman, J., Bekken, K., & Renshaw, P. F. (2000). Using MRI to examine brain-behavior relationships in males with attention deficit disorder with hyperactivity. *Journal of the American Academy of Child and Adolescent Psychiatry, 39,* 477–484.

Senju, A., Southgate, V., Miura, Y., Matsui, T., Hasegawa, T., Tojo, Y., et al. (2010). Absence of spontaneous action anticipation by false belief attribution in children with autism spectrum disorder. *Development and Psychopathology, 22,* 353–360.

Serafica, F. C., & Vargas, L. A. (2006). Cultural diversity in the development of child psychopathology. In D. Cicchetti & D. J. Cohen (Eds.), *Developmental psychopathology. Vol. I. Theory and method.* Hoboken, NJ: John Wiley & Sons.

Sethi, S., Bhargava, S., & Phil, S. M. (2005). Nocturnal enuresis: A review. *Journal of Pediatric Neurology, 31,* 11–18.

Shadish, W. R., Cook, T. D., & Campbell, D. T. (2002). *Experimental and quasi-experimental designs for generalized causal inference.* Boston, MA: Houghton Mifflin.

Shaffer, A., Yates, T. M., & Egeland, B. R. (2009). The relation of emotional maltreatment to early adolescent competence: Developmental processes in a prospective study. *Child Abuse and Neglect, 33,* 36–44.

Shaffer, D., & Jacobson, C. (2009). *Proposal to the DSM-V Childhood Disorder and Mood Disorder Work Groups to include non-suicidal self-injury (NSSI) as a DSM-V disorder.* Retrieved June 2011 from http://www.dsm5.org

Shah, A., & Frith, U. (1993). Why do autistic individuals show superior performance on the block design task? *Journal of Child Psychology and Psychiatry, 34,* 1351–1364.

Shakoor, S., Jaffee, S. R., Andreou, P., Bowes, L., Amber, A. P., Caspi, A., et al. (2011). Mothers and children as informants of bullying victimization: Results from an epidemiological cohort of children. *Journal of Abnormal Child Psychology, 39,* 379–387.

Shalev, R. S., Manor, O., Kerem, B., Ayali, M., Badichi, N., Friedlander, Y., et al. (2001). Developmental dyscalculia is a familial learning disability. *Journal of Learning Disabilities, 34,* 59–65.

Shanahan, L., Copeland, W., Costello, E. J., & Angold, A. (2008). Specificity of putative psychosocial risk factors for psychiatric disorders in children and adolescents. *Journal of Child Psychology and Psychiatry, 49*, 34–42.

Shapiro, S., Newcomb, M., & Loeb, T. B. (1997). Fear of fat, disregulated-restrained eating, and body-esteem: Prevalence and gender differences among eight- to ten-year-old children. *Journal of Clinical Psychology, 26*, 358–365.

Sharp, W. G., Jaquess, D. L., Morton, J. F., & Herzinger, C. V. (2010). Pediatric feeding disorders: A quantitative synthesis of treatment outcomes. *Clinical Child and Family Review, 13*, 348–365.

Shattuck, P. T., Seltzer, M. M., Greenberg, J. S., Orsmond, G. I., Bolt, D., Kring, S., et al. (2007). Change in autism symptoms and maladaptive behaviors in adolescents and adults with an autism spectrum disorder. *Journal of Autism and Developmental Disorders , 37*, 1735–1747

Shattuck, P. T., Wagner, M., Narendorf, S., Sterzing, P., & Hensley, M. (2011). Post-high school service use among young adults with autism spectrum disorder. *Archives of Pediatrics & Adolescent Medicine, 165*, 141–146.

Shaw, D. S., Lacourse, E., & Nagin, D. S. (2005). Developmental trajectories of conduct problems and hyperactivity from ages 2 to 10. *Journal of Child Psychology and Psychiatry, 46*, 932–942.

Shaw, P., Eckstrand, K., Sharp, W., Blumenthal, J., Lerch, J. P., Greenstein, D., et al. (2007). Attention-deficit/hyperactivity disorder is characterized by a delay in cortical maturation. *Proceedings of the National Academy of Sciences, 104*, 19649–19654.

Shaw, P., Gilliam, M., Liverpool, M., Weddle, C., Malek, M., Sharp, W., et al. (2011). Cortical development in typically developing children with symptoms of hyperactivity and impulsivity: Support for a dimensional view of attention deficit hyperactivity disorder. *American Journal of Psychiatry, 168*, 143–151.

Shaw, P., & Rapoport, J. L. (2006). Decision making about children with psychotic symptoms: Using the best evidence in choosing a treatment. *Journal of the American Academy of Child and Adolescent Psychiatry, 45*, 1381–1386.

Shaw, P., Sharp, W. S., Morrison, M., Eckstrand, K., Greenstein, D. K., Clasen, L. S., et al. (2009). Poststimulant treatment and the developing cortex in attention deficit hyperactivity disorder. *American Journal of Psychiatry, 166*, 58–63.

Shaywitz, B. A., Shaywitz, S. E., Blachman, B. A., Pugh, K. R., Fulbright, R. K., Skudlarski, P., et al. (2004). Development of left occipitotemporal systems for skilled reading in children after a phonologically-based intervention. *Biological Psychiatry, 55*, 926–933.

Shaywitz, S. (2003). *Overcoming dyslexia.* New York: Knopf.

Shaywitz, S. E., Fletcher, J. M., & Shaywitz, B. A. (1996). A conceptual model and definition of dyslexia: Findings emerging from the Connecticut Longitudinal Study. In J. H. Beitchman, N. J. Cohen, M. M. Konstantareas, & R. Tannock (Eds.), *Language, learning, and behavior disorders.* New York: Cambridge University Press.

Shaywitz, S. E., & Shaywitz, B. A. (2003). Neurobiological indices of dyslexia. In H. L. Swanson, K. R.Harris, & S. Graham (Eds.), *Handbook of learning disabilities.* New York: The Guilford Press.

Shaywitz, S. E., Shaywitz, B. A., Fulbright, R. K., Skudlarski, P., Mencl, W. E., Constable, R. T., et al. (2003). Neural systems for compensation and persistence: Young adult outcome of childhood reading disability. *Biological Psychiatry, 54*, 25–33.

Shaywitz, S. E., Shaywitz, B. A., Pugh, K. R., Fulbright, R. K., Constable, R. T., Mencl, W. E., Shankweiler, D. P., Liberman, A. M., Skudlarski, P., Fletcher, J. M., Katz, L., Marchione, K. E., Lacadie, C., Gatenby, C., & Gore, J. C. (1998). Functional disruption in the organization of the brain for reading in dyslexia. *Proceedings of the National Academy of Sciences, 95*, 2636–2641.

Shedler, J. (2010). The efficacy of psychodynamic psychotherapy. *American Psychologist, 65*, 98–109.

Sheffield, J. K., Spence, S. H., Rapee, R. M., Kowalenko, N., Wignall, A., Davis, A., et al. (2006). Evaluation of universal, indicated, and combined cognitive-behavioral approaches to the prevention of depression among adolescents. *Journal of Consulting and Clinical Psychology, 74*, 66–79.

Sheinkopf, S. J., Munday, P., Oller, D. K., & Steffens, M. (2000). Vocal atypicalities of preverbal autistic children. *Journal of Autism & Developmental Disorders, 30*, 345–354.

Sheppard, S. C., Malatras, J. W., & Israel, A. C. (2010). The impact of deployment on U.S. military families. *American Psychologist, 65*, 599–609.

Shukla, D. K., Keehn, B., & Müeller, R-A. (2011). Tract-specific analyses of diffusion tensor imaging show widespread white matter compromise in autism spectrum disorder. *Journal of Child Psychology and Psychiatry, 52*, 286–295.

Shumaker, D. M., Deutsch, R. M., & Brenninkmeyer, L. (2009). How do I connect? Attachment issues in adolescence. *Journal of Child Custody, 6*, 91–112.

Shumow, L., Smith, T. J., & Smith, M. C. (2009). Academic and behavioral characteristics of young adolescents in self-care. *Journal of Early Adolescence, 29*, 233–257.

Siegel, L. J., & Conte, P. (2001). Hospitalization and medical care of children. In C. E. Walker & M. C. Roberts (Eds.), *Handbook of clinical child psychology* (3rd ed.). New York: John Wiley & Sons, Inc.

Siegel, L. S. (2003). Basic cognitive processes and reading disabilities. In H. L. Swanson, K. R. Harris, & S. Graham (Eds.), *Handbook of learning disabilities.* New York: Guilford Press.

Siegler, R. S. (1992). The other Alfred Binet. *Developmental Psychology, 28*, 179–190.

Sigman, M. (1998). Change and continuity in the development of children with autism. *Journal of Child Psychology and Psychiatry, 39*, 817–828.

Silenzio, V. M., Pena, J. B., Duberstein, P. R., Cerel, J., & Know, K. L. (2007). Sexual orientation and risk factors for suicidal ideation and suicide attempts among adolescents and young adults. *American Journal of Public Health, 97*, 2017–2019.

Silk, J. S., Nath, S. R., Siegel, L. R., & Kendall, P. (2000). Conceptualizing mental disorders in children: Where have we been going and where are we going? *Development and Psychopathology, 12*, 713–735.

Silverman, A. H., & Tarbell, S. (2009). Feeding and vomiting problems in pediatric populations. In M. C. Roberts & R. G. Steele (Eds.), *Handbook of pediatric psychology* (4th ed.). New York: The Guilford Press.

Silverman, W. K., & Albano, A. M. (1996). *The Anxiety Disorders Interview Schedule for Children for DSM-IV: Clinical Manual (Child and Parent Versions)*. San Antonio, TX: Psychological Corporation.

Silverman, W. K., & Dick-Niederhauser, A. (2004). Separation anxiety disorder. In T. L. Morris & J. S. March (Eds.), *Anxiety disorders in children and adolescents*. New York: Guilford Press.

Silverman, W. K., & Ginsburg, G. S. (1998). Anxiety disorders. In T. H. Ollendick & M. Hersen (Eds.), *Handbook of child psychopathology* (3rd ed.). New York: Plenum.

Silverman, W. K., & Kurtines, W. M. (2005). Progress in developing an exposure-based transfer-of-control approach to treating internalizing disorders in youth. In E. D. Hibbs & P. S. Jensen (Eds.), *Psychosocial treatments for child and adolescent disorders: Empirically based strategies for clinical practice* (2nd ed.). Washington, DC: American Psychological Association.

Silverman, W. K., La Greca, A. M., & Wasserstein, S. (1995). What do children worry about? Worries and their relation to anxiety. *Child Development, 66*, 671–686.

Silverman, W. K., & Moreno, J. (2005). Specific phobia. *Child and Adolescent Psychiatric Clinics of North America, 14*, 819–843.

Silverman, W. K., & Ollendick, T. H. (2005). Evidence-based assessment of anxiety and its disorders in children and adolescents. *Journal of Clinical Child and Adolescent Psychology, 34*, 380–411.

Silverman, W. K., Pina, A. A., & Viswesvaran, C. (2008). Evidence-based psychosocial treatments for phobic and anxiety disorders in children and adolescents. *Journal of Clinical Child and Adolescent Psychology, 37*, 105–130.

Simon, T. J. (2010). Rewards and challenges of cognitive neuroscience studies of persons with intellectual and developmental disabilities. *American Journal on Intellectual and Developmental Disabilities, 115*, 79–82.

Simonoff, E., Bolton, P., & Rutter, M. (1996). Mental retardation: Genetic findings, clinical implications and research agenda. *Journal of Child Psychology and Psychiatry, 37*, 259–280.

Simons, L. E., & Blount, R. L. (2007). Identifying barriers to medication adherence in adolescent transplant recipients. *Journal of Pediatric Psychology, 32*, 831–844.

Simonton, D. K. (2003). Qualitative and quantitative analysis of historical data. *Annual Review of Psychology, 54*, 617–640.

Simos, P. G., Fletcher, J. M., Bergman, E., Breier, J. I., Foorman, B. R., & Castillo, E. M., et al. (2002). Dyslexia-specific brain activation profile becomes normal following successful remedial training. *Neurology, 58*, 1203–1213.

Simos, P. G., Fletcher, J. M., Sarkari, S., Billingsley-Marshall, R., Denton, C. A., & Papanicolaou, A. C. (2007). Intensive instruction affects brain magnetic activity associated with oral word reading in children with reading disabilities. *Journal of Learning Disabilities, 40*, 37–48.

Singer, L., Arendt, R., Farkas, K., Minnes, S., Huang, J., & Yamashita, T. (1997). Relationship of prenatal cocaine exposure and maternal postpartum psychological distress to child development outcome. *Development and Psychopathology, 9*, 473–489.

Singh, S. P. (2009). Transition of care from child to adult mental health services: The great divide. *Current Opinion in Psychiatry, 22*, 386–390.

Sinzig, J., Walter, D., & Doepfner, M. (2009). Attention deficit/hyperactivity disorder in children and adolescents with autism spectrum disorder. Symptom or syndrome? *Journal of Attention Disorders, 13*, 117–126.

Siperstein, G. N., Pociask, S. E., & Collins, M. A. (2010). Sticks, stones, and stigma: A study of students' use of the derogatory term "retard." *Intellectual and Developmental Disabilities, 48*, 126–134.

Skinner, B. F. (1948). *Walden two*. London: Macmillan.

Skinner, B. F. (1953). *Science and human behavior*. New York: Macmillan.

Skinner, B. F. (1968). *The technology of teaching*. New York: Appleton-Century-Crofts.

Skovgaard, A. M., Houmann, T., Christiansen, E., Landorph, S., Jørgensen, T., & Copenhagen Child Cohort 2000 Study Team. (2007). The prevalence of mental health problems in children 11/2 years of age—The Copenhagen Child Cohort 2000. *Journal of Child Psychology and Psychiatry, 48*, 62–70.

Slomkowski, C., Klein, R., & Mannuzza, S. (1995). Is self-esteem an important outcome in hyperactive children? *Journal of Abnormal Child Psychology, 23*, 303–315.

Slusarek, M., Velling, S., Bunk, D., & Eggers, C. (2001). Motivational effects on inhibitory control in children with ADHD. *Journal of the American Academy of Child and Adolescent Psychiatry, 40*, 355–363.

Smith, B. H., Barkley, R. A., & Shapiro, C. J. (2006). Attentiondeficit/hyperactivity disorder. In E. J. Mash & R. A. Barkley (Eds.), *Treatment of childhood disorders*. New York: The Guilford Press.

Smith, D. K., & Chamberlain, P. (2010). Multidimensional treatment foster care for adolescents: Processes and outcomes. In J. R. Weisz & A. E. Kazdin (Eds.), *Evidence-based psychotherapies for children and adolescents* (2nd ed.). New York: The Guilford Press.

Smith, G. T., & Goldman, M. S. (1994). Alcohol expectancy theory and the identification of high risk adolescents. *Journal of Research on Adolescence, 4*, 229–248.

Smith, G. T., Goldman, M. S., Greenbaum, P. E., & Christiansen, B. A. (1995). Expectancy for social facilitation from drinking: The divergent paths of high-expectancy and low-expectancy adolescents. *Journal of Abnormal Psychology, 104*, 32–40.

Smith, G. T., Simmons, J. R., Flory, K., Annus, A. M., & Hill, K. K. (2007). Thinness and eating expectancies predict subsequent binge-eating and purging behavior among adolescent girls. *Journal of Abnormal Psychology, 116,* 188–197.

Smith, I. M., Koegel, R. L., Koegel, L. K., Openden, D. A., Fossum, K. L., & Bryson, S, E., (2010). Effectiveness of a novel community-based intervention model for children with autistic spectrum disorder. *American Journal on Intellectual and Developmental Disabilities, 115,* 504–523.

Smith, S. D., Pennington, B. F., Boada, R., & Shriberg, L. D. (2005). Linkage of speech sound to reading disability loci. *Journal of Child Psychology and Psychiatry, 46,* 1057–1066.

Smith, T. (1999, Spring). Outcome of early intervention for children with autism. *Clinical Psychology: Science and Practice, 6,* 33–49.

Smith, T. (2010). Early and intensive behavioral intervention in autism. In R. J. Weisz & A. E. Kazdin (Eds.), *Evidencebased psychotherapies for children and adolescents.* New York: Guildford Press.

Smith, T. J., & Adams, G. (2006). The effect of comorbid AD/HD and learning disabilities on parent-reported behavioral and academic outcomes of children. *Learning Disabilities Quarterly, 29,* 101–112.

Smolak, L., & Murnen, S. K. (2002). A meta-analytic examination of the relationship between child sexual abuse and eating disorders. *International Journal of Eating Disorders, 31,* 136–150.

Smolak, L., & Murnen, S. K. (2004). A feminist approach to eating disorders. In J. K. Thompson (Ed.), *Handbook of eating disorders and obesity.* Hoboken, NJ: John Wiley.

Smolak, L., Murnen, S. K., & Ruble, A. E. (2000). Female athletes and eating problems: A meta-analysis. *International Journal of Eating Disorders, 27,* 371–380.

Smoller, J. W., Gardner-Schuster, E., & Misiaszek, M. (2008). Genetics of anxiety: Would the genome recognize the DSM? *Depression and Anxiety, 25,* 368–377.

Smuts, A. B. (2006). *Science in the service of children.* 1893–1935. New Haven, CT: Yale University Press.

Smyke, A. T., Koga, S. F., Johnson, D. E., Fox, N. A., Marshall, P. J., Nelson, C. A., et al. (2007). The caregiving context in institution-reared and family-reared infants and toddlers in Romania. *Journal of Child Psychology and Psychiatry, 48,* 210–218.

Snell, E. K., Adam, E. K., & Duncan, G. J. (2007). Sleep and the body mass index and overweight status of children and adolescents. *Child Development, 78,* 309–323.

Snowling, M. J. (1991). Developmental reading disorders. *Journal of Child Psychology and Psychiatry, 32,* 49–77.

Snowling, M. J. (2000). Language and literacy skills:Who is at risk and why? In D.V. M. Bishop & L. B. Leonard (Eds.), *Speech and language impairments in children: Causes, characteristics, intervention and outcome.* Philadelphia: Taylor & Francis.

Snowling, M. J., Bishop, D. V. M., Stothard, S. E., Chipchase, B., & Kaplan, C. (2006). Psychosocial outcomes at 15 years of children with a preschool history of speech-language impairment. *Journal of Child Psychology and Psychiatry, 47,* 759–765.

Snowling, M. J., Muter, V., & Carroll, J. (2007). Children at family risk of dyslexia: A follow-up in early adolescence. *Journal of Child Psychology and Psychiatry, 48,* 609–618.

Snyder, H. N., & Sickmund, M. (2006). *Juvenile offenders and victims: 2006 national report.* Washington, DC: U.S. Department of Justice, Office of Justice Programs, Office of Juvenile Justice and Delinquency Prevention.

Snyder, J. (2002). Reinforcement and coercion mechanisms in the development of antisocial behavior: Peer relationships. In J. B. Reid, G. R. Patterson, & J. Snyder (Eds.), *Antisocial behavior in children and adolescents: A developmental analysis and model for intervention.* Washington, DC: American Psychological Association.

Sokolowski, K. L., & Israel, A. C. (2008). Perceived anxiety control as a mediator of the relationship between family stability and adjustment. *Journal of Anxiety Disorders, 22,* 1454–1461.

Soliday, E., Kool, E., & Lande, M. B. (2000). Psychosocial adjustment in children with kidney disease. *Journal of Pediatric Psychology, 25,* 93–103.

Sonuga-Barke, E., Bitsakou, P., & Thompson. M. (2010). Beyond the dual pathway model: Evidence for the dissociation of timing, inhibitory, and delay-related impairments in attention-deficit/hyperactivity disorder. *American Journal of the Academy of Child and Adolescent Psychiatry, 49,* 345–355.

Sonuga-Barke, E. J. S. (1994). On dysfunction and function in psychological theories of childhood disorder. *Journal of Child Psychology and Psychiatry, 35,* 801–815.

Sonuga-Barke, E. J. S. (1998). Categorical models of childhood disorder: A conceptual and empirical analysis. *Journal of Child Psychology and Psychiatry, 39,* 115–133.

Sonuga-Barke, E. J. S., Dalen, L., & Remington, B. (2003). Do executive deficits and delay aversion make independent contributions to preschool attention-deficit/hyperactivity disorder? *Journal of the American Academy of Child and Adolescent Psychiatry, 42,* 1335–1342.

Sonuga-Barke, E. J. S., De Houwer, J., De Ruiter, K., Ajzenstzen, M., & Hollands, S. (2004). AD/HD and the capture of attention by briefly exposed delay-related cues: Evidence from a conditioning paradigm. *Journal of Child Psychology and Psychiatry, 45,* 274–283.

Sørensen, H. J., Mortensen, E. L., Reinisch, J. M., & Mednick, S. A. (2009). Association between prenatal exposure to bacterial infection and risk of schizophrenia. *Schizophrenia Bulletin, 35,* 631–637.

Sorsdahl, K. R., & Stein, D. J. (2010). Knowledge of and stigma associated with mental disorders in a South African community sample. *Journal of Nervous and Mental Disease, 198,* 742–747.

Sourander, A., Jensen, P., Davies, M., Niemelä, S., Elonheimo, H., Ristkari, T., et al. (2007). Who is at greatest risk of adverse long-term outcomes? The Finnish from a boy to a man study. *Journal of the American Academy of Child and Adolescent Psychiatry, 46*, 1148–1161.

Southam-Gerow, M. A., & Chorpita, B. F. (2007). Anxiety in children and adolescents. In E. J. Mash & R. A. Barkley (Eds.), Assessment of childhood disorders (4th ed.). New York: The Guilford Press.

Sowell, E. R., Thompson, P. M., Welcome, S. E., Henkenius, A. L., Toga, A. W., & Peterson, B. S. (2003). Cortical abnormalities in children and adolescents with attention-deficit hyperactivity disorder. *The Lancet, 362*, 1699–1707.

Sparrow, S. S., Cicchetti, D. V., & Balla, D. A. (2005). *Vineland adaptive behavior scales-second edition (Vineland-II).* Bloomington, MN: American Guidance Service.

Speece, D. L., & Hines, S. J. (2007). Learning disabilities. In E. J. Mash & R. A. Barkley (Eds.), *Assessment of childhood disorders* (4th ed.). New York: Guilford Press.

Spence, S. H., Holmes, J. M., March, S., & Lipp, O. V. (2006). The feasibility and outcome of clinic plus internet delivery of cognitive-behavior therapy for childhood anxiety. *Journal of Consulting and Clinical Psychology, 74*, 614–621.

Spence, S. H., Sheffield, J., & Donovan, C. L. (2003). Preventing adolescent depression: An evaluation of the problem solving for life program. *Journal of Consulting and Clinical Psychology, 71*, 3–13.

Spence, S. H., Sheffield, J., & Donovan, C. L. (2005). Long-term outcome of a school-based universal approach to prevention of depression in adolescents. *Journal of Consulting and Clinical Psychology, 73*, 160–167.

Spence, S. H., & Shortt, A. L. (2007). Research review: Can we justify the widespread dissemination of universal, school-based interventions for the prevention of depression among children and adolescents? *Journal of Child Psychology and Psychiatry, 48*, 526–542.

Spencer, M. B., Harpalani, V., Cassidy, E., Jacobs, C. Y., Donde, S., Goss, T. N., et al. (2006). Understanding vulnerability and resilience from a normative developmental perspective: Implications for racially and ethnically diverse youth. In D. Cicchetti & D. J. Cohen (Eds.), *Developmental Psychopathology. Vol. 1. Theory and method.* Hoboken, New York: John Wiley & Sons.

Spessot, A. L., & Peterson, B. S. (2006). Tourette's syndrome: A multifactorial, developmental psychopathology. In D. Cicchetti & D. J. Cohen (Eds.), *Developmental psychopathology. Vol. 3. Risk, disorder, and adaptation* (2nd ed.). Hoboken, NJ: John Wiley & Sons.

Spicer, P., & Sarche, M. C. (2006). Responding to the crisis in American Indian and Alaska Native children's mental health. In H. E. Fitzgerald, B. M. Lester, & B. Zuckerman (Eds.), *The crisis in youth mental health. Childhood disorders (Vol. 1).* Westport, CT: Praeger Publishers.

Spielberger, C. D. (1973). *Manual for the state-trait anxiety inventory for children.* Lutz, FL: Psychological Assessment Resources, Inc.

Spitz, R. A. (1946). Anaclitic depression. In *The psychoanalytic study of the child* (Vol. 2). New York: International Universities Press.

Spitzer, R. L., Gibbon, M., Skodol, A. E., Williams, J. B. W., & First, M. B. (2000). *DSM-IV-TR case book.* Washington, DC: American Psychiatric Publishing.

Spock, B. M., & Rothenberg, M. (1992). *Dr. Spock's baby and child care.* New York: Pocket Books.

Spring, B., Chiodo, J., & Bowen, D. J. (1987). Carbohydrates, tryptophan, and behavior: A methodological review. *Psychological Bulletin, 102*, 234–256.

Springer, K. W., Sheridan, J., Kuo, D., & Carnes, M. (2007). Longterm physical and mental health consequences of childhood physical abuse: Results from a large population-based sample of men and women. *Child Abuse & Neglect, 31*, 517–530.

Sroufe, L. A. (1997). Psychopathology as an outcome of development. *Development and Psychopathology, 9*, 251–268.

Sroufe, L. A. (2009). The concept of development in developmental psyehopathology. *Child Development Perspectives, 3*, 178–183.

Sroufe, L. A., Cofilno, B., & Carlson, E. A. (2010). Conceptualizing the role of early experience: Lessons from the Minnesota Longitudinal Study. *Developmental Review, 30*, 36–51.

Sroufe, L. A., Duggal, S., Weinfeld, N., & Carlson, E. (2000). Relationships, development, and psychopathology. In A. J. Sameroff, M. Lewis, & S. M. Miller (Eds.), *Handbook of developmental psychopathology* (2nd ed.). New York: Kluwer Academic/Plenum Publishers.

Sroufe, L. A., Egeland, B., Carlson, E. A., & Collins, W. A. (2005). *The development of the person.* New York: The Guilford Press.

Stahl, A. (1991). Beliefs of Jewish-Oriental mothers regarding children who are mentally retarded. *Education and Training in Mental Retardation, 26*, 361–369.

Standart, S., & Le Couteur, A. (2003). The quiet child: A literature review of selective mutism. *Child and Adolescent Mental Health, 8*, 154–160.

Stanger, C., Achenbach, T. M., & Verhulst, F. C. (1997). Accelerated longitudinal comparisons of aggressive versus delinquent syndromes. *Development and Psychopathology, 9*, 43–58.

Stanger, C., MacDonald, V. V., McConaughy, S. H., & Achenbach, T. M. (1996). Predictors of cross-informant syndromes among children and youths referred for mental health services. *Journal of Abnormal Child Psychology. 24*, 597–614.

Stanovich, K. E. (1989). Learning disabilities in broader context. *Journal of Learning Disabilities, 22*, 287–291, 297.

Stark, K. D., Reynolds, W. M., & Kaslow, N. J. (1987). A comparison of the relative efficacy of self-control therapy and a behavioral problem-solving therapy for depression in children. *Journal of Abnormal Child Psychology, 15*, 91–113.

Stark, K. D., Rouse, L., & Livingston, R. (1991). Treatment of depression during childhood and adolescence: Cognitive behavioral procedures for the individual and family. In P. Kendall (Ed.), *Child and adolescent therapy.* New York: The Guilford Press.

Stark, K.D., Schmidt, K. L., & Joiner, T. E. (1996). Cognitive triad: Relationship to depressive symptoms, parents' cognitive triad, and perceived parental messages. *Journal of Abnormal Child Psychology, 24,* 615–631.

Stark, K. D., Streusand, W., Krumholz, L. S., & Patel, P. (2010). Cognitivie-behavioral therapy for depression. The ACTION Treatment Program for Girls. In J. R. Weisz & A. E. Kazdin (Eds.), *Evidence-based psychotherapies for children and adolescents* (2nd ed.). New York: The Guilford Press.

Staub, D., & Peck, C. A. (January 1994/December 1995). What are the outcomes for nondisabled students? *Educational Leadership, 52,* 36–40.

Steele, C. M. (1997). A threat in the air: How stereotypes shape intellectual identity and performance. *American Psychologist, 52,* 613–629.

Steele, R. G., Nelson, T. D., & Cole, B. P. (2007). Psychosocial functioning of children with AIDS and HIV infection: Review of the literature from a sociological framework. *Journal of Developmental & Behavioral Pediatrics, 28,* 58–69.

Steffenburg, S., Gillberg, C., Hellgren, L., Andersson, L., Gillberg, I. C., Jakobsson, G., & Bohman, M. (1989). A twin study of autism in Denmark, Finland, Iceland, Norway and Sweden. *Journal of Child Psychology and Psychiatry, 30,* 405–416.

Stein, D. J., Fineberg, N. A., Bienvenu, J., Denys, D., Lochner, C., Nestadt, G., et al. (2010). Should OCD be classified as an anxiety disorder in DSM-V? *Depression and Anxiety, 27,* 495–506.

Steinberg, A. B., & Phares, V. (2001). Family functioning, body image, and eating disturbances. In J. K. Thompson & L. Smolak (Eds.), *Body image, eating disorders, and obesity in youth: Assessment, prevention, and treatment.* Washington, DC: American Psychological Association.

Steinberg, L. (2007). Risk taking in adolescence. *Current Directions in Psychological Science, 16,* 55–59.

Steinberg, L. (2009). Should the science of adolescent brain development inform public policy? *American Psychologist, 64,* 739–750.

Steinberg, L. (2009). Adolescent development and juvenile justice. *Annual Review of Clinical Psychology, 5,* 459–485.

Steinberg, L., Lamborn, S. D., Darling, N., Mounts, N. S., & Dornbusch, S. M. (1994). Over-time changes in adjustment and competence among adolescents from authoritative, authoritarian, indulgent, and neglectful families. *Child Development, 65,* 754–770.

Steiner-Adair, C., Sjostrom, L., Franko, D. L., Pai, S., Tucker, R., Becker, A.E., et al. (2002). Primary prevention of eating disorders in adolescent girls: Learning from practice. *International Journal of Eating Disorders, 32,* 401–411.

Steinhausen, H. C. (1997). Outcome of anorexia nervosa in the younger patient. *Journal of Child Psychology and Psychiatry, 38,* 271–276.

Stepansky, M. A., Roache, C. R., Holmbeck, G. N., & Schultz, K. (2010). Medical adherence in young adolescents with spina bifida: Longitudinal associations with family functioning. *Journal of Pediatric Psychology, 35,* 167–176.

Sterba, S. K., Prinstein, M. J., & Cox, M. J. (2007). Trajectories of internalizing problems across childhood: Heterogeneity, external validity, and gender differences. *Development and Psychopathology, 19,* 345–366.

Sterling, S., Weisner, C., Hinman, A., & Parthasarathy, S. (2010). Access to treatment for adolescents with substance use and co-occurring disorders: Challenges and opportunities. *Journal of the American Academy of Child and Adolescent Psychiatry, 49,* 637–646.

Stern, M., Mazzeo, S. E., Gerke, C. K., Porter, J. S., Bean, M. K., & Laver, J. H. (2007). Gender, ethnicity, psychological factors, and quality of life among severely overweight, treatmentseeking adolescents. *Journal of Pediatric Psychology, 32,* 90–94.

Sternberg, R. J., Wagner, R. K., Williams, W. M., & Horvath, J. A. (1995). Testing common sense. *American Psychologist, 50,* 912–927.

Stetson, E. G., & Stetson, R. (2001). Educational assessment. In C. E. Walker & M. C. Roberts (Eds.), *Handbook of clinical child psychology* (3rd ed.). New York: John Wiley & Sons.

Stevens, M. C., Fein, D. A., Dunn, M., Allen, D., Waterhouse, L. H., Feinstein, C., & Rapin, I. (2000). Subgroups of children with autism by cluster analysis: A longitudinal examination. *Journal of the American Academy of Child & Adolescent Psychiatry, 39,* 346–352.

Stevenson, J. (2011). Commentary: A contribution to evidence-informed policy-reflections on Strong, Torgerson, Torgeson, and Hulme (2011). *Journal of Child Psychology and Psychiatry, 52,* 236–237.

Stevenson, J., & Fredman, G. (1990). The social environmental correlates of reading ability. *Journal of Child Psychology and Psychiatry, 31,* 681–698.

Stevenson, J., Langley, K., Pay, H., Payton, A., Worthington, J., Ollier, W., et al. (2005). Attention-deficit hyperactivity disorder with reading disabilities: Preliminary genetic findings on the involvement of the ADRA2A gene. *Journal of Child Psychology and Psychiatry, 46,* 1081–1088.

Stewart, A. J., Steiman, M., Cauce, A. M., Cochran, B. N., Whitbeck, L. B., & Hoyt, D. R. (2004). Victimization and posttraumatic stress disorder among homeless adolescents. *Journal of the American Academy of Child and Adolescent Psychiatry, 43,* 325–331.

Stewart, T. M., & Williamson, D. A. (2004). Assessment of body image disturbances. In J. K. Thompson (Ed.), *Handbook of eating disorders and obesity.* Hoboken, NJ: John Wiley.

Stice, E., & Bearman, S. K. (2001). Body image and eating disturbances prospectively predict increases in depressive symptoms in adolescent girls: A growth curve analysis. *Developmental Psychology, 37*, 1–11.

Stice, E., & Bulik, C. M. (2008). Eating disorders. In T. P. Beauchaine & S. P. Hinshaw (Eds.), *Child and adolescent psychopathology*. Hoboken, NJ: John Wiley & Sons.

Stice, E., Shaw, H., & Marti, C. N. (2006). A meta-analytic review of obesity prevention programs for children and adolescents: The skinny on interventions that work. *Psychological Bulletin, 132*, 667–691.

Stiffman, A. R., Alexander-Eitzman, B., Silmere, H., Osborne, V., & Brown, E. (2007). From early to late adolescence: American Indian youths' behavioral trajectories and their major influences. *Journal of the American Academy of Child and Adolescent Psychiatry, 46*, 849–859.

Stinton, M. M., & Birch, L. L. (2005). Weight status and psychosocial factors predict the emergence of dieting in preadolescent girls. *International Journal of Eating Disorders, 38*, 346–354.

Stone, W. L. (1997). Autism in infancy and early childhood. In D. J. Cohen & F. R. Volkmar (Eds.), *Handbook of autism and pervasive developmental disorders*. New York: John Wiley.

Stoneman, Z., & Gavidia-Payne, S. (2006). Marital adjustment in families of young children with disabilities: Associations with daily hassles and problem-focused coping. *American Journal on Mental Retardation, 111*, 1–14.

Storch, E. A., Milsom, V. A., DeBraganza, N., Lewin, A. B., Geffken, G. R., & Silverstein, J. H. (2007). Peer victimization, psychosocial adjustment, and physical activity in overweight and at-risk-for-overweight youth. *Journal of Pediatric Psychology, 32*, 80–89.

Storch, E. A., Stigge-Kaufman, D., Marien, W. E., Sajid, M., Jacob, M. L., Geffken, G. R., et al. (2008). Obsessive-compulsive disorder in youth with and without a chronic tic disorder. *Depression and Anxiety, 25*, 761–767.

Storck, M., Beal, T., Bacon, J. G., & Olsen. P. (2009). Behavioral and mental challenges for indigenous youth: Research and clinical perspectives. In A. B. Chang & R. Singleton (Eds.), *Pediatric Clinics of North America, 56*. Philadelphia, PA: W. B. Saunders.

Stormshak, E. A., Connell, A. M., Veronneau, M. H., Meyers, M. W., Dishion, T. J., Kavanagh, K., & Caruthers, A. S. (2011). An ecological approach to promoting early adolescent mental health and social adaptation: Family-centered intervention in public middle schools. *Child Development, 82*, 209–225.

St. Pierre, R. G., & Layzer, J. I. (1998). Improving the life chances of children in poverty: Assumptions and what we have learned. Social Policy Report. *Society for Research in Child Development*. Vol. XII (4).

Strauss, C. C. (1994). Overanxious disorder. In T. H. Ollendick, N. J. King, & W. Yule (Eds.), *International handbook of phobic and anxiety disorders in children and adolescents*. New York: Plenum Press.

Strauss, C. C., & Last, C. G. (1993). Social and simple phobias in children. *Journal of Anxiety Disorders, 7*, 141–152.

Strauss, C. C., Lease, C. A., Last, C. G., & Francis, G. (1988). Overanxious disorder: An examination of developmental differences. *Journal of Abnormal Child Psychology, 16*, 433–443.

Strein, W., Hoagwood, K., & Cohn, A. (2003). School psychology: A public health perspective I. Prevention, populations, and systems change. *School Psychology, 41*, 23–38.

Streissguth, A. P., Bookstein, F. L., Sampson, P. D., & Barr, H. M. (1995). Attention: Prenatal alcohol and continuities of vigilance and attentional problems from 4 through 14 years. *Development and Psychopathology, 7*, 419–446.

Strickland, B. R. (2000). Misassumptions, misadventures, and the misuse of psychology. *American Psychologist, 55*, 331–338.

Striegel-Moore, R. H., & Bulik, C. M. (2007). Risk factors for eating disorders. *American Psychologist, 62*, 181–198.

Stringaris, A., & Goodman, R. (2009). Longitudinal outcome of youth oppositionality: Irritable, headstrong, and hurtful behaviors have distinctive predictions. *Journal of the American Academy of Child and Adolescent Psychiatry, 48*, 404–412.

Strong, G. K., Torgerson, C. J., Torgerson, D., & Hulme, C. (2011). A systematic meta-analytic review of evidence for the effectiveness of the "Fast Forword" language intervention program. *Journal of Child Psychology and Psychiatry, 52*, 224–235.

Stuber, J., Fairbrother, G., Galea, S., Pfefferbaum, B., Wilson-Genderson, M., & Vlahov, D. (2002). Determinants of counseling for children in Manhattan after the September 11 attacks. *Psychiatric Services, 53*, 815–822.

Stuber, M. L., & Shemesh, E. (2006). Post-traumatic stress response to life-threatening illness in children and their parents. *Child and Adolescent Psychiatric Clinics of North America, 15*, 597–609.

Sturmey, P. (2005). Against psychotherapy with people who have mental retardation. *Mental Retardation, 43*, 55–57.

Sue, S. (2003). In defense of cultural competency in psychotherapy and treatment. *American Psychologist, 58*, 964–970.

Sugden, K., Arseneault, L., Harrington, H., Moffitt, T. E., Williams, B., & Caspi, A. (2010). Serotonin transporter gene moderates the development of emotional problems among children following bullying victimization. *Journal of the American Academy of Child and Adolescent Psychiatry, 49*, 830–840.

Suglia, S. F., Gryparis, A., Wright, R. O., Schwartz, J., & Wright, R. J. (2008). Association of black carbon with cognition among children in a prospective birth cohort study *American Journal of Epidemiology, 167*, 280–286.

Sullivan, P. F., Kendler, K. S., & Neale, M. C. (2003). Schizophrenia as a complex trait. *Archives of General Psychiatry, 60*, 1187–1192.

Sun, Y., & Li, Y. (2011). Effects of family structure type and stability on children's academic performance trajectories. *Journal of Marriage and Family, 73*, 541–556.

Sutcliffe, J. S., & Nurmi, E. L. (2003). Genetics of childhood disorders: XLVII. Autism, Part 6: Duplication and inherited susceptibility of chromosome 15q11–q13 genes in autism.

Journal of the American Academy of Child and Adolescent Psychiatry, 42, 253–256.

Suter, J. C., & Bruns, E. J. (2009). Effectiveness of the wraparound process for children with emotional and behavioral disorders: A meta-analysis. *Clinical Child and Family Psychology Review, 12,* 336–351.

Sutton, P. D. (2003). Births, marriages, divorces, and deaths: Provisional data for October–December 2002. *National Vital Statistics Reports* (Vol. 51). Hyattsville, MD: National Center for Health Statistics.

Suveg, C., Aschenbrand, S. G., & Kendall, P. C. (2005). Separation anxiety disorder, panic disorder, and school refusal. *Child and Adolescent Psychiatric Clinics of North America, 14,* 773–795.

Swain, J. E., Scahill, L., Lombroso, P. J., King, R. A., & Leckman, J. F. (2007). Tourette disorder and tic disorders: A decade of progress. *Journal of the American Academy of Child and Adolescent Psychiatry, 46,* 947–968.

Swanson, H. L., & Hoskyn, M. (1998). Experimental intervention research on students with learning disabilities: A meta-analysis of treatment outcomes. *Review of Educational Research, 68,* 277–321.

Swanson, H. L. & Hoskyn, M. (2001). Instructing adolescents with learning disabilities: A component and composite analysis. *Learning Disabilities Research & Practice, 16,* 109–119.

Swanson, J. M., McBurnett, K., Christian, D. L., & Wigal, T. (1995). Stimulant medications and the treatment of children with ADHD. In T. H. Ollendick & R. J. Prinz (Eds.), *Advances in clinical child psychology.* New York: Plenum Press.

Swanson, J. M., & Volkow, N. D. (2009). Psychopharmacology: Concepts and opinions about the use of stimulant medications. *Journal of Child Psychology and Psychiatry, 50,* 180–193.

Swearer, S. M., Wang, C., Givens, J., Berry, B., & Reinemann, D. (2011). Mood disorders. In S. Goldstein & C. R. Reynolds (Eds.), *Handbook of neurodevelopmental and genetic disorders in children* (2nd ed.). New York: The Guilford Press.

Swedo, S. E., Rapoport, J. L., Leonard, H., Lenane, M., & Cheslow, D. (1989). Obsessive-compulsive disorder in children and adolescents: Clinical phenomenology of 70 consecutive cases. *Archives of General Psychiatry, 46,* 335–341.

Sweeting, H., West, P., Young, R., & Der, G. (2010). Can we explain increases in young people's psychological distress over time? *Social Science & Medicine, 71,* 1819–1830.

Sweeting, H., Young, R., & West, P. (2009). GHQ increases among Scottish 15 year olds 1987–2006. *Social Psychiatry and Psychiatric Epidemiology, 44,* 579–586.

Szatmari, P., MacLean, J. E., Jones, M. B., Bryson, S. E., Zwaigenbaum, L., Bartolucci, G., et al. (2000). The familial aggregation of the lesser variant in biological and nonbiological relatives of PDD probands: A family history study. *Journal of Child Psychology and Psychiatry, 41,* 579–586.

Szymanski, L. S., & Crocker, A. C. (1985). Mental retardation. In H. I. Kaplan & B. J. Sadock (Eds.), *Comprehensive textbook of psychiatry/IV.* Baltimore: Williams and Wilkins.

Tager-Flüsberg, H. (1993). What language reveals about the understanding of minds in children with autism. In S. Baron-Cohen, H. Tager-Flüsberg, & D. J. Cohen (Eds.), *Understanding other minds.* New York: Oxford.

Talge, N. M., Neal, C., Glover, V. (2007). Antenatal maternal stress and long-term effects on child neurodevelopment: How and why? *Journal of Child Psychology and Psychiatry, 48,* 245–261.

Tallal, P., & Benasich, A. A. (2002). Developmental language learning impairments. *Development and Psychopathology, 14,* 559–579.

Tanguay, P. E. (2000). Pervasive developmental disorders: A 10-year review. *Journal of the American Academy of Child and Adolescent Psychiatry, 39,* 1079–1095.

Tannock, R. (1998). Attention deficit hyperactivity disorder: Advances in cognitive, neurobiological, and genetic research. *Journal of Child Psychology and Psychiatry, 39,* 65–99.

Tannock, R. (2005a). Disorders of written expression and learning disorders not otherwise specified. In B. J. Sadock & V. A. Sadock (Eds.), *Comprehensive textbook of psychiatry.* Philadelphia: Lippincott Williams and Wilkens.

Tannock, R. (2005b). Mathematics disorder. In B. J. Sadock & V. A. Sadock (Eds.), *Comprehensive textbook of psychiatry.* Philadelphia: Lippincott Williams and Wilkens.

Tannock, R. (2005c). Reading disorder. In B. J. Sadock & V. A. Sadock (Eds.), *Comprehensive textbook of psychiatry.* Philadelphia: Lippincott Williams and Wilkens.

Tanofsky-Kraff, M., & Wilfley, D. E. (2010). Interpersonal psychotherapy for bulimia nervosa and binge-eating disorder. In C. M. Grilo & J. E. Mitchell (Eds.), *The treatment of eating disorders: A clinical handbook.* New York: The Guilford Press.

Tantleff-Dunn, S., Gokee-LaRose, J., & Peterson, R. D. (2004). Interpersonal psychotherapy for the treatment of anorexia nervosa, bulimia nervosa, and binge eating disorder. In J. K. Thompson (Ed.), *Handbook of eating disorders and obesity.* Hoboken, NJ: John Wiley.

Tarbox, S. I., & Pogue-Geile, M. F. (2008). Development of social functioning in preschizophrenia children and adolescents: A systematic review. *Psychological Bulletin, 134,* 561–583.

Taylor, B., Miller, E., Farrington, C. P., Petropoulos, M-C., Favot- Mayaud, I., Li, J., & Waight, P. A. (1999). Autism and measles, mumps and rubella vaccine: No epidemiological evidence for a causal association. *Lancet, 353,* 2026–2029.

Taylor, E. (1994). Syndromes of attention deficit and hyperactivity. In M. Rutter, E. Taylor, & L. Hersov (Eds.), *Child and adolescent psychiatry: Modern approaches.* New York: Blackwell Scientific.

Taylor, E. (2009). Developing ADHD. *Journal of Child Psychology and Psychiatry, 50,* 126–132.

Taylor, E., & Rogers, J. W. (2005). Practitioner review: Early adversity and developmental disorders. *Journal of Child Psychology and Psychiatry, 46,* 451–467.

Taylor, E., & Sonuga-Barke, E. (2008). Disorders of attention and activity. In M. Rutter et al. (Eds.), *Rutter's child and adolescent psychiatry* (5th ed.). Malden. MA: Blackwell Publishing.

Taylor, H. G. (1988). Learning disabilities. In E. J. Mash & L. G. Terdal (Eds.), *Behavioral assessment of childhood disorders* (2nd ed.). New York: Guilford.

Taylor, H. G. (1989). Learning disabilities. In E. J. Mash & R. A. Barkley (Eds.), *Treatment of childhood disorders*. New York: Guilford.

Taylor, J. L., & Seltzer, M. M. (2010). Changes in the autism behavioral phenotype during the transition to adulthood. *Journal of Autism and Developmental Disorders, 40,* 1431–1446.

TEACCH Autism Program (2011). Available at TEACCH.com.

Tennant, C. (1988). Parental loss in childhood: Its effects in adult life. *Archives of General Psychiatry, 45,* 1045–1050.

Tercyak, K. P., Donze, J. R., Prahlad, S., Mosher, R. B., & Shad, A. T. (2006). Identifying, recruiting, and enrolling adolescent survivors of childhood cancer into a randomized controlled trial of health promotion: Preliminary experiences in the Survivor Health and Resilience Education (SHARE) Program. *Journal of Pediatric Psychology, 31,* 252–261.

Terr, L. (1979). Children of Chowchilla. *The Psychoanalytic Study of the Child, 34,* 522–563.

Terr, L. (1983). Chowchilla revisited: The effects of psychic trauma four years after a school-bus kidnapping. *American Journal of Psychiatry, 140,* 1543–1550.

Thapar, A., Gottesman, I. I., Owen, M. J., O'Donovan, M., & McGuffin, P. (1994). The genetics of mental retardation. *British Journal of Psychiatry, 164,* 747–758.

Thase, M. (2009). Neurobiological aspects of depression. In I. H. Gotlib & C. L. Hammen (Eds.), *Handbook of depression.* New York: The Guilford Press.

Thase, M. E., Jindal, R., & Howland, R. H. (2002). Biological aspects of depression. In I. H. Gotlib & C. L. Hammen (Eds.), *Handbook of depression.* New York: The Guilford Press.

The Carolina Abecedarian Project—FPG Child Development (2008). www.fpg.unc.edu/-abc.

Thelen, E., & Adolph, K. E. (1992). Arnold L. Gessell: The paradox of nature and nuture. *Developmental Psychology, 28,* 368–380.

Thelen, M. H., Powell, A. L., Lawrence, C., & Kuhnert, M. E. (1992). Eating and body image concerns among children. *Journal of Consulting and Clinical Psychology, 21,* 41–46.

Them, M. A., Israel, A. C., Ivanova, M. Y., & Chalmers, S. M. (2003). *An investigation of the assessment and of and relationships between various aspects of family stability.* Boston, MA: Association for the Advancement of Behavior Therapy.

Thomas, A. M., Peterson, L., & Goldstein, D. (1997). Problem solving and diabetes regimen adherence by children and adolescents with IDDM in social pressure situations: A reflection on normal development. *Journal of Pediatric Psychology, 22,* 541–561.

Thomas, J. J., Keel, P. K., & Heatherton, T. F. (2006). Disordered eating attitudes and behaviors in ballet students: Examination of environmental and individual risk factors. *International Journal of Eating Disorders, 38,* 263–258.

Thompson, J. K., Shroff, H., Herbozo, S., Cafri, G., Rodriguez, J., & Rodriguez, M. (2007). Relations among multiple peer influences, body dissatisfaction, eating disturbance, and self-esteem: A comparison of average weight, at risk of overweight, and overweight adolescent girls. Journal of Pediatric Psychology, 32, 24–29.

Thompson, J. K., & Smolak, L. (2001). Body image, eating disorders, and obesity in youth—The future is now. In J. K. Thompson & L. Smolak (Eds.), *Body image, eating disorders, and obesity in youth: Assessment, prevention, and treatment.* Washington, DC: American Psychological Association.

Thompson, J. R., Bryant, B. R., Campbell, E. M., Craig, E. M., Hughes, C., Rotholz, D. R., et al. (2004). *Supports intensity scale.* Washington, DC: AAIDD.

Thompson, J. R., & McEvoy, M. A. (1992). Letters to the editor. Normalization—still relevant today. *Journal of Autism and Developmental Disorders, 22,* 666–671.

Thompson, R. A. (2000). The legacy of early attachments. *Child Development, 71,* 145–152.

Thompson-Schill, S. L., Ramscar, M., & Chrysikou, E. G. (2009). Cognition without control. *Current Directions in Psychological Science, 18,* 259–263.

Thorell, L. B. (2007). Do delay aversion and executive function deficits make distinct contributions to the functional impact of ADHD symptoms? A study of early academic skill deficits. *Journal of Child Psychology and Psychiatry, 48,* 1061–1070.

Thorndike, E. L. (1905). *The elements of psychology.* New York: Seiler.

Thurber, C. A., & Sigman, M. D. (1998). Preliminary models of risk and protective factors for childhood homesickness: Review and empirical synthesis. *Child Development, 69,* 903–934.

Tick, N. T., van der Ende, J., & Verhulst, F. C. (2008). Ten-year trends in self-reported emotional and behavioral problems of Dutch adolescents. *Social Psychiatry and Psychiatric Epidemiology, 43,* 349–355.

Tienari, P., Lahti, I., Sorri, A., Naarala, M., Moring, J., Kaleva, M., Wahlberg, K-E., & Wynne, L. C. (1990). Adopted-away offspring of schizophrenics and controls: The Finnish adoptive family study of schizophrenia. In L. N. Robins & M. Rutter (Eds.), *Straight and devious pathways from childhood to adulthood.* New York: Cambridge University Press.

Tienari, P., Wynne, L. C., & Wahlberg, K. E. (2006). Genetics and family relationships in schizophrenia and the schizophrenia spectrum disorders. In S. M. Miller, S. H. McDaniel, J. S. Rolland, & S. L. Feetham (Eds.), *Individuals, families, and the new era of genetics.* New York: W. W. Norton & Co.

Tienda, M., & Haskins, R. (2011, Spring). Immigrant children: Introducing the issues. *The Future of Children, 21,* 3–18.

Timko, C., Baumgartner, M., Moos, R. H., & Miller, J. III (1993). Parental risk and resistance factors among children with juvenile rheumatic disease: A four-year predictive study. *Journal of Behavioral Medicine, 16,* 571–588.

Todd, R. D., Huang, H., Smalley, S. L., Nelson, S. F., Willcutt, E. G., Pennington, B. F., et al. (2005). Collaborative analysis of DRD4 and DAT genotypes in population-defined ADHD subtypes. *Journal of Child Psychology and Psychiatry, 46,* 1067–1073.

Tolan, P. H., & Dodge, K. A. (2005). Children's mental health as a primary care and concern: A system for comprehensive support and service. *American Psychologist, 60,* 602–614.

Tolan, P. H., & Thomas, P. (1995). The implications of age of onset for delinquency risk II: Longitudinal data. *Journal of Abnormal Child Psychology, 23,* 157–181.

Tolani, N., & Brooks-Gunn, J. (2006). Are there socioeconomic disparities in children's mental health? In H. E. Fitzgerald, B. M. Lester, & B. Zuckerman (Eds.), *The crisis in youth mental health* (Vol. 1). Westport, CT: Praeger.

Tomblin, J. B. (2006). A normativist account of language-based learning disability. *Learning Disabilities Research & Practice, 21,* 8–18.

Tomblin, J. B., Zhang, X., Buckwalter, P., & Catts, H. (2000). The association of reading disability, behavioral disorders, and language impairment among second-grade children. *Journal of Child Psychology and Psychiatry, 41,* 473–482.

Tomporowski, P. D., & Tinsley, V. (1997). Attention in mentally retarded persons. In W. E. MacLean (Ed.), *Ellis' handbook of mental deficiency, psychological theory and research.* Mahwah, NJ: Lawrence Erlbaum.

Tompson, M. C., Pierre, C. B., Bogar, K. D., McKowen, J. W., Chan, P. T., & Freed, R. D. (2010). Maternal depression, maternal expressed emotion, and youth psychopathology. *Journal of Abnormal Child Psychology, 38,* 105–117.

Tonge, B. (1994). Separation anxiety disorder. In T. H. Ollendick, N. J. King, & W. Yule (Eds.), *International handbook of phobic and anxiety disorders in children and adolescents.* New York: Plenum Press.

Toplak, M. E., Connors, L., Shuster, J., Knezevic, B., & Parks, S. (2008). Review of cognitive, cognitive-behavioral, and neural-based interventions for Attention-Deficit/Hyperactivity Disorder (ADHD). *Clinical Psychology Review, 28,* 801–823.

Toppelberg, C. O., & Shapiro, T. (2000). Language disorders: A 10-year research update review. *Journal of the American Academy of Child and Adolescent Psychiatry, 39,* 143–152.

Torbeyns, J., Verschaffel, L., & Ghesquière, P. (2004). Strategy development in children with mathematical disabilities: Insights from the choice/no-choice method and the chronologicalage/ability-level-match design. *Journal of Learning Disabilities, 37,* 119–131.

Torgesen, J. K., Alexander, A. W., Wagner, R. K., Rashotte, C. A., Voeller, K. K. S., & Conway, T. (2001). Intensive remedial instruction for children with severe reading disabilities: Immediate and long-term outcomes from two instructional approaches. *Journal of Learning Disabilities, 34,* 33–58, 78.

Torney-Purta, J. V. (2009). International research that matters for policy and practice. *American Psychologist, 64,* 825–837.

Toro, P. A., Weissberg, R. P., Guare, J., & Liebenstein, N. L. (1990). A comparison of children with and without learning disabilities on social problem-solving skill, school behavior, and family background. *Journal of Learning Disabilities, 23,* 115–120.

Toth, S. L., Stronach, E. P., Rogosch, F. A., Caplan, R., & Cicchetti, D. (2011). Illogical thinking and thought disorder in maltreated children. *Journal of the American Academy of Child and Adolescent Psychiatry, 50,* 659–668.

Totsika, V., Hastings, R. P., Emerson, E., Lancaster, G. A., & Berridge, D. M. (2011). A population-based investigation of behavioural and emotional problems and maternal mental health: Associations with autism spectrum disorder and intellectual disability. *Journal of Child Psychology and Psychiatry, 52,* 91–99.

Treatment for Adolescents with Depression Study. (TADS) Team. (2004). Fluoxetine, cognitive-behavioral therapy, and their combination for adolescents with depression: Treatment for Adolescents with Depression Study (TADS) randomized controlled trial. *Journal of the American Medical Association, 292,* 807–820.

Treatment for Adolescents with Depression Study. (TADS) Team. (2005). The Treatment for Adolescents with Depression Study (TADS): Demographic and clinical characteristics. *Journal of the American Academy of Child & Adolescent Psychiatry, 44,* 28–40.

Treatment for Adolescents with Depression Study Team. (2007). The Treatment for Adolescents with Depression Study (TADS): Long-term effectiveness and safety outcomes. *Archives of General Psychiatry, 64,* 1132–1143.

Treatment for Adolescents with Depression Study Team. (2009). The Treatment for Adolescents with Depression Study (TADS): Outcome over one year of naturalistic follow-up. *American Journal of Psychiatry, 166,* 1141–1149.

Tremblay, G. C., & Israel, A. C. (1998). Children's adjustment to parental death. *Clinical Psychology: Science and Practice, 5,* 424–438.

Tremblay, G. C., & Peterson, L. (1999). Prevention of childhood injury: Clinical and public policy issues. *Clinical Psychology Review, 19,* 415–434.

Tremblay, R. E. (2010). Developmental origins of disruptive behaviour problems: The 'original sin' hypothesis, epigenetics and their consequences for prevention. *Journal of Child Psychology and Psychiatry, 51,* 341–367.

Trevarthen, C., & Aitken, K. J. (2001). Infant intersubjectivity: Research, theory, and clinical applications. *Journal of Child Psychology and Psychiatry, 42,* 3–48.

Trickett, P. K., Allen, L., Schellenbach, C. J., & Zigler, E. F. (1998). Integrating and advancing the knowledge base about violence against children: Implications for intervention and prevention. In P. K. Trickett & C. J. Schellenbach (Eds.), *Violence against children in the family and the community.* Washington, DC: American Psychological Association.

Trickey, D., Siddaway, A. P., Meiser-Stedman, R., Serpell, L., & Field, A. P. (2012). A meta-analysis of risk factors for post-traumatic stress disorder in children and adolescents. *Clinical Psychology Review, 32*, 122–138.

Tronick, E., & Beeghly, M. (2011). Infants' meaning-making and the development of mental health problems. *American Psychologist, 66*, 107–119.

Trosper, S. E., Whitton, S. W., Brown, T. A., & Pincus, D. B. (2012). Understanding the latent structure of the emotional disorders in children and adolescents. *Journal of Abnormal Child Psychology, 40*, 621–632.

Trzesniewski, K. H., Moffitt, T. E., Caspi, A., Taylor, A., & Maughan, B. (2006). Revisiting the association between reading achievement and antisocial behavior: New evidence of an environmental explanation from a twin study. *Child Development, 77*, 72–88.

Tsai, A. C., Rosenlicht. N. Z., Jureidini, J. N., Parry, P. I., Spielmans, G. I., & Healy, D. (2011). Aripiprazole in the maintenance treatment of bipolar disorder: A critical review of the evidence and its dissemination into the scientific literature. *PLOS Medicine, 8(5)*: e1000434. doi10.1371/journal.pmed.1000434.

Tully, L. A., Arseneault, L., Caspi, A., Moffit, T. E., & Morgan, J. (2004). Does maternal warmth moderate the effects of birth-weight on twins' Attention-Deficit/Hyperactivity Disorder (ADHD) symptoms and low IQ? *Journal of Consulting and Clinical Psychology, 72*, 218–226.

Turnbull, A. P. (2004). President's address 2004: "Wearing two hats": Morphed perspectives on family quality of life. *Mental Retardation, 42*, 383–399.

Turner, M. (1999). Annotation: Repetitive behaviour in autism: A review of psychological research. *Journal of Child Psychology and Psychiatry, 40*, 839–849.

Twenge, J. M., Gentile, B., DeWall, C. N., Ma, D., Lacefield, K., Schurtz, D. R. (2010). Birth cohort increases in psychopathology among Americans, 1938–2007: A cross-temporal meta-analysis of the MMPI. *Clinical Child Review, 30*, 145–154.

Udwin, O., Boyle, S., Yule, W., Bolton, D., & O'Ryan, D. (2000). Risk factors for long-term psychological effects of a disaster experienced in adolescence: Predictors of Post Traumatic Stress Disorder. *Journal of Child Psychology and Psychiatry, 41*, 969–979.

Ullmann, L. P., & Krasner, L. (1975). *A psychological approach to abnormal behavior* (2nd ed.). Englewood Cliffs, NJ: Prentice Hall.

Ulloa, R. L. et al. (2000). Psychosis in a pediatric mood and anxiety disorders clinic: Phenomenology and correlates. *Journal of the American Academy of Child and Adolescent Psychiatry, 39*, 337–345.

UNAIDS (2010). *UNAIDS Report on the Global AIDS epidemic, 2010.* http://www.unaids.org/globalreport/Global_report.htm

U.S. Bureau of the Census. (1998). *Statistical Abstract of the United States: 1998* (118th ed.). Washington, DC: U.S. Government Printing Office.

U.S. Bureau of the Census. (2004). *Statistical Abstract of the United States, 2004. The National Data Book* (124th ed.). Washington, DC: U.S. Government Printing Office.

U.S. Bureau of the Census (2011). Income, Poverty, and Health Insurance Coverage in the United States: 2010. Report P60, n. 238, Table B-2, pp. 68–73.

U.S. Census Bureau. (2003). *Adopted children and stepchildren: 2000.* Retrieved May 2007 from http://www.census.gov

U.S. Census Bureau. (2010). Statistical Abstract of the United States. *Population.* Retrieved July 2011 from http://www.census.gov/prod/www/abs/statab2006_2010.html

U. S. Census Bureau. (2011). Statistical Abstract of the United States, 2011. *Labor Force, Employment, and Earnings. Employment Status of Women by Presence and Age of Children: 1970–2009.*

U.S. Department of Education. (2000). *Summary—Twenty-second Annual Report to Congress on the Implementation of the Individuals with Disabilities Education Act.* Retrieved August 16, 2004, from http://www.ed.gov

U. S. Department of Education. (2007). National Center for Educational Statistics. Digest of Education Statistics. Retrieved November 20, 2007, from http://nces.ed.gov/programs/digest/d06/tables/dt06_048.asp

U.S. Department of Education, National Center for Education Statistics, 2011. Downloaded October 10, 2011. http://nces.ed.gov/fastfacts/display.asp?id=59

U.S. Department of Health and Human Services. (2005). *Code of Federal Regulations, Title 45, Public Welfare.* Revised June 23, 2005.

U.S. Department of Health and Human Services, Administration for Children and Families, Administration on Children, Youth, and Families, Children's Bureau. (2010). *Child Maltreatment 2009.* Available from http://www.acf.hhs.gov/programs/cb/stats_research/index.htm#can

U. S. Department of Health and Human Services, Administration for Children and Families. (2010). Head Start Impact Study. Final Report. Washington, DC.

U.S. Department of Health and Human Services, Children's Bureau. Child Welfare Information Gateway. (2011). *Child Maltreatment 2009: Summary of key findings.* Washington, DC: U.S. DHHS.

U.S. Department of Justice. (2010). *Crime in the United States, 2009.* Washington, DC: Federal Bureau of Investigation. Retrieved May 2011 from http;//www2.fbi.gov

U.S. Food and Drug Administration. (2007). *Revisions to product labeling.* Retrieved July 11, 2007, from http://www.fda.gov/cder/drug/antidepressants/antidepressants_label_change_2007.pdf

U.S. Implementation of the Individuals with Disabilities Education Act. Retrieved August 16, 2004, from http://www.ed.gov

U.S. Office of Education. (1977). Definition and criteria for defining students as learning disabled. Federal Register, 42:250, p. 65083. Washington, DC: U.S. Government Printing Office.

Vaidyanathan, U., Patrick, C. J., & Cuthbert, B. N. (2009). Linking dimensional models of internalizing psychopathology to neurobiological systems: Affect-modulated startle as an indicator of fear and distress disorders and affiliated traits. *Psychological Bulletin, 135*, 909–942.

Valo, S., & Tannock, R. (2010). Diagnostic instability of DSM-IV ADHD subtypes: Effects of informant source, instrumentation, and methods for combining symptom reports. *Journal of Clinical Child and Adolescent Psychology, 39*, S749–S760.

van Daal, J., Verhoeven, L., & van Balkom, H. (2007). Behaviour problems in children with language impairment. *Journal of Child Psychology and Psychiatry, 48*, 1139–1147.

Vandell, D. L., Belsky, J., Burchinal, M., Steinberg, L., Vandergrift, N., and the NICHD Early Child Care Research Network. (2010). Do effects of early child care extend to age 15 years? Results from the NICHD Study of early child care and youth development. *Child Development, 81*, 737–756.

Vandell, D. L., & Shumow, L. (1999). After-school child care programs. *The Future of Children, 9(2)*, 64–80.

van den Akker, A. L., Dekovic, M., Prinzie, P., & Asscher, J. J. (2010). Toddlers' temperament profile: Stability and relations to negative and positive parenting. *Journal of Abnormal Child Psychology, 38*, 485–495.

van den Berg, P. A., Keery, H., Eisenberg, M., Neumark-Sztainer, D. (2010). Maternal and adolescent report of mothers' weight-related concerns and behaviors: Longitudinal associations with adolescent body dissatisfaction and weigh control practices. *Journal of Pediatric Psychology, 35*, 1093–1102.

van der Bruggen, C. O., Stams, G. J. J. M., & Bögels, S. M. (2008). The relation between child and parent anxiety and parental control: A meta-analytic review. *Journal of Child Psychology and Psychiatry, 49*, 1257–1269.

Van der Oord, S., Prins, P. J. M., Oosterlaan, J., & Emmelkamp, P. M. G. (2008). Efficacy of methylphenidate, psychosocial treatments and their combination in school-aged children with ADHD: A meta-analysis. *Clinical Psychology Review, 28*, 783–800.

van Engeland, H., & Buitelaar, J. K. (2008). Autism spectrum disorder. In M. Rutter et al. (Eds.), *Rutter's child and adolescent psychiatry*. Malden, MA: Blackwell Publishing.

van Goozen, S. H. M., Fairchild, G., Snoek, H., & Harold, G. T. (2007). The evidence for a neurobiological model of childhood antisocial behavior. *Psychological Bulletin, 133*, 149–182.

Van Hoecke, E., De Fruyt, F., De Clercq, B., Hoebeke, P., & Vande Walle, J. (2006). Internalizing and externalizing problem behavior in children with nocturnal and diurnal enuresis: A fivefactor model perspective. *Journal of Pediatric Psychology, 31*, 460–468.

van IJzendoorn, M., & Juffer, F. (2006). The Emanuel Miller Memorial Lecture 2006: Adoption as intervention. Metaanalytic evidence for massive catch-up and plasticity in physical, socio-emotional, and cognitive development. *Journal of Child Psychology and Psychiatry, 47*, 1228–1245.

van IJzendoorn, M. H., Juffer, F., & Poelhuis, C. W. K. (2005). Adoption and cognitive development: A meta-analytic comparison of adopted and nonadopted children's IQ and school performance. *Psychological Bulletin, 131*, 301–316.

van IJzendoorn, M. H., Rutgers, A. H., Bakersman-Kranenburg, M. J., Swinkels, S. H. N., van Daalen, E., Dietz, C., et al. (2007). Parental sensitivity and attachment in children with autism spectrum disorder: Comparison with children with mental retardation, with language delays, and with typical development. *Child Development, 78*, 597–608.

van Lier, P., Boivin M., Dionne, G., Vitaro, F., Brendgen, M., Koot, H., et al. (2007a). Kindergarten children's genetic vulnerabilities interact with friends' aggression to promote children's own aggression. *Journal of the American Academy of Child and Adolescent Psychiatry, 46*, 1080–1087.

van Lier, P. A. C., van der Ende, J., Koot, H. M., & Verhulst, F. C. (2007b). Which better predicts conduct problems? The relationship of trajectories of conduct problems with ODD and ADHD symptoms from childhood into adolescence. *Journal of Child Psychology and Psychiatry, 48*, 601–608.

van Lier, P. A., & Koot, H. M. (2010). Developmental cascades of peer relations and symptoms of externalizing and internalizing problems from kindergarten to fourth-grade elementary school. *Development and Psychopathology, 22*, 569–582.

Vannatta, K., Salley, C. G., & Gerhardt, C. A. (2009). Pediatric oncology. In M. C. Roberts & R. G. Steele (Eds.), *Handbook of pediatric psychology* (4th ed.). New York: The Guilford Press.

van Oort, F. V. A., van der Ende, J., Wadsworth, M. E., Verhulst, F. C., & Achenbach, T. M. (2011). Cross-national comparison of the link between socioeconomic status and emotional and behavioral problems in youths. *Social Psychiatry and Psychiatric Epidemiology, 46*, 167–172.

Varela, R. E., Vernberg, E. M., Sanchez-Sosa, J. J., Riveros, A., Mitchell, M., & Mashunkashey, J. (2004). Anxiety reporting and culturally associated interpretation biases and cognitive schema: A comparison of Mexican, Mexican American, and European American families. *Journal of Clinical Child and Adolescent Psychology, 33*, 237–247.

Varni, J. W., Katz, E. R., & Waldron, S. A. (1993). Cognitivebehavioral treatment interventions in childhood cancer. *The Clinical Psychologist, 46*, 192–197.

Vasey, M. W., & Daleiden, E. L. (1994). Worry in children. In G. C. L. Davey & F. Tallis (Eds.), *Worrying: Perspectives on theory, assessment and treatment*. Chichester, England: Wiley.

Vaughn, S., La Greca, A. M., & Kuttler, A. (1999). The why, who, and how of social skills. In W. N. Bender (Ed.), *Professional issues in learning disabilities*. Austin, TX: PRO-ED.

Veenstra-vanderweele, J., & Cook, E. H. (2003). Genetics of childhood disorders: XLVI. Autism, Part 5: Genetics of autism. *Journal of the American Academy of Child and Adolescent Psychiatry, 42*, 116–118.

Velez, C. E., Wolchik, S. A., Tein, J. Y., & Sandler, I. (2011). Protecting children from the consequences of divorce: A longitudinal study of the effects of parenting on children's coping processes. *Child Development, 82*, 244–257.

Vellutino, F. R. (1979). *Dyslexia. Theory and research.* Cambridge MA: MIT Press.

Vellutino, F. R., Fletcher, J. M., Snowling M. J., & Scanlon, D. M. (2004). Specific reading disability (dyslexia): What have we learned in the past four decades? *Journal of Child Psychology and Psychiatry, 45*, 2–40.

Velting, O. N., & Albano, A. M. (2001). Current trends in the understanding and treatment of social phobia in youth. *Journal of Child Psychology and Psychiatry, 42*, 127–140.

Verduin, T. L., & Kendall, P. C. (2003). Differential occurrence of comorbidity within childhood anxiety disorders. *Journal of Clinical Child and Adolescent Psychology, 32*, 290–295.

Verhulst, F. C., & van der Ende, J. (1997). Factors associated with mental health service use in the community. *Journal of the American Academy of Child and Adolescent Psychiatry, 36*, 901–909.

Vernick, J., & Karon, M. (1965). Who's afraid of death on a leukemia ward? *American Journal of Diseases of Children, 109*, 393–397.

Via, E., Radua, J., Cardoner, N., Happé. F., & Mataix-Cols, D. (2011). Meta-analysis of gray matter abnormalities in autism spectrum disorder. Archives of General Psychiatry, 68, 409–418.

Viana, G. A., Beidel, D. C., & Rabian, B. (2009). Selective mutism: A review and integration of the last 15 years. *Clinical Psychology Review, 29*, 57–67.

Vickers, B., & Garralda, E. (2000). Hallucinations in nonpsychotic children. *Journal of the Academy of Child and Adolescent Psychiatry, 39*, 1073.

Viding, E., Blair, R. J. R., Moffitt, T. E., & Plomin, R. (2005). Evidence for substantial genetic risk for psychopathy in 7-year-olds. *Journal of Child Psychology and Psychiatry, 46*, 592–597.

Viding, E., Jones, A. P., Frick, P. J., Moffitt, T. E., & Plomin, R. (2008). Heritability of antisocial behaviour at 9: Do callous-unemotional traits matter? *Developmental Science, 11*, 17–22.

Viding, E., & Larsson, H. (2010). Genetics and child and adolescent psychopathy. In R. T. Salekin & D. R. Lyman (Eds.), *Handbook of child and adolescent psychopathy.* New York: The Guilford Press.

Viding, E., Spinath, F. M., Price, T. S., Bishop, D.V. M., Dale, P. S., & Plomin, R. (2004). Genetic and environmental influences on language impairment in 4-year-old same-sex and oppositesex twins. *Journal of Child Psychology and Psychiatry, 45*, 315–325.

Virués-Ortega, J. (2010). Applied behavior analytic intervention for autism in early childhood: Meta-analysis, meta-regression and dose-response meta-analysis of multiple outcomes. *Clinical Psychology Review, 30*, 387–399.

Vitiello, B. (2006). An update on publicly funded multisite trials in pediatric psychopharmacology. *Child and Adolescent Psychiatric Clinics of North America, 15*, 1–12.

Vitiello, B., Severe, J. B., Greenhill, L. L., Arnold, L. E., Abikoff, H. B., Bukstein, O. G., et al. (2001). Methylphenidate dosage for children with ADHD over time under controlled conditions: Lessons from the MTA. *Journal of the American Academy of Child and Adolescent Psychiatry, 40*, 188–196.

Vitiello, B., Silva, S., Rohde, P., Kratochvil, C., Kennard, B., Reinecke, M., et al. (2009). Suicidal events in the Treatment for Adolescents with Depression Study (TADS). *Journal of Clinical Psychiatry, 70*, 741–747.

Vitiello, B., & Swedo, S. (2004). Antidepressant medications in children. *New England Journal of Medicine, 350*, 1489–1491.

Vitiello, B., Zuvekas, S. H., & Norquist, G. S. (2006). National estimates of antidepressant medication use among U.S. children, 1997–2002. *Journal of the American Academy of Child and Adolescent Psychiatry, 45*, 271–279.

Volkmar, F. R. (1996). Childhood and adolescent psychosis: A review of the past 10 years. *Journal of the American Academy of Child and Adolescent Psychiatry, 35*, 843–851.

Volkmar, F. R., Becker, D. F., King, R. A., & McGlashan, T. H. (1995). Psychotic processes. In D. Cicchetti & D. J. Cohen (Eds.), *Developmental psychopathology.* New York: John Wiley.

Volkmar, F. R., Carter, A., Grossman, J., & Klin, A. (1997). Social development in autism. In D. J. Cohen & F. R. Volkmar (Eds.), *Handbook of autism and pervasive developmental disorders.* New York: John Wiley.

Volkmar, F. R., & Dykens, E. (2002). Mental retardation. In M. Rutter & E. Taylor (Eds.), *Child and adolescent psychiatry.* Oxford, UK: Blackwell Publishing.

Volkmar, F. R., & Klin, A. (2000). Pervasive developmental disorders. In B. J. Sadock & V. A. Sadock (Eds.), *Comprehensive textbook of psychiatry* (Vol. II). Philadelphia: Lippincott Williams & Wilkins.

Volkmar, F. R., Klin, A., & Schultz, R. T. (2005). Pervasive developmental disorders. In B. J. Sadock & V. A. Sadock (Eds.), *Comprehensive textbook of psychiatry (Vol. 2).* Philadelphia: Lippincott Williams & Wilkins.

Volkmar, F. R., Klin, A., Schultz, R. T., Rubin, E., & Bronen, R. (2000). Asperger's disorder. *American Journal of Psychiatry, 157*, 262–267.

Volkmar, F. R., Lord, C., Bailey, A., Schultz, R. T., & Klin, A. (2004). Autism and developmental pervasive disorders. *Journal of Child Psychology and Psychiatry, 45*, 135–170.

Volkow, N. D., Wang, G-J., Kollins, S. H., Wigal, T. L., Newcorn, J. H., Telang, R., et al. (2009). Evaluating dopamine reward pathway in ADHD: Clinical implications. *Journal of the American Medical Association, 302*, 1084–1091.

von Gontard, A., Schaumburg, H., Hollmann, E., & Rittig, S. (2011). The genetics of enuresis: A review. *The Journal of Urology, 166,* 2438–2443.

Votruba-Drzal, E., Coley, R. L., & Chase-Lansdale, P. L. (2004). Child care and low-income children's development: Direct and moderated effects. *Child Development, 75,* 296–312.

Vuijk, P., van Lier, P. A. C., Huizink, A. C., Verhulst, F. C., & Crijnen, A. A. M. (2006). Prenatal smoking predicts nonresponsiveness to an intervention targeting attention-deficit/hyperactivity symptoms in elementary schoolchildren. *Journal of Child Psychology and Psychiatry, 47,* 891–901.

Vujeva. H. M., & Furman, W. (2011). Depressive symptoms and romantic relationship qualities from adolescence through emerging adulthood: A longitudinal examination of influences. *Journal of Clinical Child and Adolescent Psychology, 40,* 123–135.

Wachsler-Felder, J. L., & Golden, C. J. (2002). Neuropsychological consequences of HIV in children: A review of current literature. *Clinical Psychology Review, 22,* 441–462.

Wade, T. J., Cairney, J., & Pevalin, D. J. (2002). Emergence of gender differences in depression during adolescence: National panel results from three countries. *Journal of the American Academy of Child and Adolescent Psychiatry, 2002, 41,* 190–198.

Wagner, B. M., Silverman, M. A., & Martin, C. E. (2003). Family factors in youth suicidal behaviors. *American Behavioral Scientist, 46,* 1171–1191.

Wagner, J., Heapy, A., James, A., & Abbott, G. (2006). Glycemic control, quality of life, and school experiences among students with diabetes. *Journal of Pediatric Psychology, 31,* 764–769.

Wagner, J. L., Chaney, J. M., Hommel, K. A., Page, M. C., Mullins, L. L., White, M. M., & Jarvis, J. N. (2003). The influence of parental distress on child depressive symptoms in juvenile rheumatic diseases: The moderating effect of illness intrusiveness. *Journal of Pediatric Psychology, 28,* 453–462.

Wahler, R. G., & Dumas, J. E. (1989). Attentional problems in dysfunctional mother-child interactions: An interbehavioral model. *Psychological Bulletin, 105,* 116–130.

Wakefield, A. J. et al. (1998). Ileal-lymphoid-nodular hypoplasia, non-specific colitis, and pervasive developmental disorder in children. *Lancet, 351,* 637–641.

Wakefield, C. E., McLoone, J., Goodenough, B., Lenthen, K., Cairns, D. R., & Cohn, R. J. (2010). The psychological impact of completing childhood cancer treatment: A systematic review of the literature. *Journal of Pediatric Psychology, 35,* 262–274.

Wakschlag, L. S., & Danis, B. (2009). Characterizing early childhood disruptive behavior: Enhancing developmental sensitivity. In C. H. Zeanah, Jr. (Ed.), *Handbook of infant mental health.* (3rd ed.). New York: The Guilford Press.

Waldron, H. B., & Brody, J. L. (2010). Functional family therapy for adolescent substance use disorders. In J. R. Weisz & A. E. Kazdin (Eds.), *Evidence-based psychotherapies for children and adolescents.* (2nd ed.). New York: The Guilford Press.

Waldron, N. L., & McLeskey, J. (1998). The effects of an inclusive school program on students with mild and severe learning disabilities. *Exceptional Children, 64,* 395–405.

Walker, C. E. (2003). Elimination disorders: Enuresis and encopresis. In M. C. Roberts (Ed.), *Handbook of pediatric psychology* (3rd ed.). New York: Guilford Press.

Walker, J. S., Coleman, D., Lee, J., Squire, P. N., & Friesen, B. J. (2008). Children's stigmatization of childhood depression and ADHD: Magnitude and demographic variation in a national sample. *Journal of the American Academy of Child and Adolescent Psychiatry, 47,* 912–920.

Walkup, J. T., Albano, A. M., Piacentini, J., Birmaher, B., Compton, S. N., Sherrill, J. T., et al. (2008). Cognitive behavioral therapy, sertraline, or a combination in childhood anxiety. *The New England Journal of Medicine, 359,* 2753–2766.

Wallace, S., Sebastian, C., Pellicano, E., Parr, J., & Bailey, A. (2010). Face processing abilities in relatives of individuals with ASD. *Autism Research, 3,* 345–349.

Wallander, J. L., Thompson, R. J., Jr., & Alriksson-Schmidt, A. (2003). Psychosocial adjustment of children with chronic physical conditions. In M. C. Roberts (Ed.), *Handbook of pediatric psychology* (3rd ed.). New York: Guilford Press.

Wallander, J. L., & Varni, J. W. (1998). Effects of pediatric chronic physical disorders on child and family adjustment. *Journal of Child Psychology and Psychiatry, 39,* 29–46.

Waller, M. R. (2010) Viewing low-income fathers' ties to families through a cultural lens: Insights for research and policy. *Annals of the American Academy of Political and Social Science, 629,* 102–124.

Wallerstein, J. S. (1991). The long-term effects of divorce on children: A review. *Journal of the American Academy of Child and Adolescent Psychiatry, 30,* 349–360.

Walsh, B. T. and the Commission on Adolescent Eating Disorders. (2005a). Defining eating disorders. In D. L. Evans, E. B. Foa, R. E. Gur, H. Hendin, C. P. O'Brien, M. E. P. Seligman, & B. T. Walsh (Eds.), *Treating and preventing adolescent mental health disorders. What we know and what we don't know: A research agenda for improving mental health of our youth.* New York: Oxford University Press.

Walsh, B. T. and the Commission on Adolescent Eating Disorders. (2005b). Prevention of eating disorders. In D. L. Evans, E. B. Foa, R. E. Gur, H. Hendin, C. P. O'Brien, M. E. P. Seligman, & B. T. Walsh (Eds.), *Treating and preventing adolescent mental health disorders. What we know and what we don't know: A research agenda for improving mental health of our youth.* New York: Oxford University Press.

Walsh, B. T., & Sysko, R. (2009). Broad categories for the diagnosis of eating disorders (BCD-ED): An alternative system for classification. *International Journal of Eating Disorders, 42,* 754–764.

Walton, K. E., Ormel, J., & Krueger, R. F. (2011). The dimensional nature of externalizing behaviors in adolescence: Evidence from a direct comparison of categorical, dimensional, and hybrid models. *Journal of Abnormal Child Psychology, 39,* 553–561.

Warfield, M. E. (2001). Employment, parenting, and well-being among mothers of children with disabilities. *Mental Retardation, 39,* 297–309.

Warren, S. F., Brady, N., Sterling, A., Fleming, K., & Marquis, J. (2010). Maternal responsivity predicts language development in young children with fragile X syndrome. *American Journal on Intellectual and Developmental Disabilities, 115,* 54–75.

Warren, S. L., Gunnar, M. R., Kagan, J., Anders, T. F., Simmens, S. J., Rones, M., Wease, S., Aron, E., Dahl, R. E., & Sroufe, L. A. (2003). Maternal panic disorder: Infant temperament, neurophysiology, and parenting behaviors. *Journal of the American Academy of Child and Adolescent Psychiatry, 42,* 814–825.

Warren, S. L., Howe, G., Simmens, S. J., & Dahl, R. E. (2006). Maternal depressive symptoms and child sleep: Models of mutual influence over time. *Development and Psychopathology, 18,* 1–16.

Waschbusch, D. A. (2002). A meta-analytic examination of comorbid hyperactive-impulsive-attention problems and conduct problems. *Psychological Bulletin, 128,* 118–150.

Waschbusch, D. A., & King, S. (2006). Should sex-specific norms be used to assess attention-deficit/hyperactivity disorder or oppositional defiant disorder? *Journal of Consulting and Clinical Psychology, 74,* 179–185.

Waslick, B. (2006). Psychopharmacology interventions for pediatric anxiety disorders: A research update. *Child and Adolescent Psychiatric Clinics of North America, 15,* 51–71.

Watamura, S., Phillips, D. A., Morrissey, T. W., McCartney, K., & Bub, K. (2011). Double jeopardy: Poorer social-emotional outcomes for children in the NICHD SECCYD experiencing home and child-care environments that confer risk. *Child Development, 82,* 48–65.

Watkins, C. E., Campbell, V. L., Nieberding, R., & Hallmark, R. (1995). Contemporary practice of psychological assessment by clinical psychologists. *Professional Psychology: Research and Practice, 26,* 54–60.

Watkins, J. M., Asarnow, R. F., & Tanguay, P. E. (1988). Symptom development in childhood onset schizophrenia. *Journal of Child Psychology and Psychiatry, 29,* 865–878.

Watson, D., O'Hara, M. W., & Stuart, S. (2008). Hierarchical structures of affect and psychopathology and their implications for the classification of emotional disorders. *Depression and Anxiety, 25,* 282–288.

Watson, H. J., & Rees, C. S. (2008). Meta-analysis of randomized, controlled treatment trials for pediatric obsessive-compulsive disorder. *Journal of Child Psychology and Psychiatry, 49,* 489–498.

Watson, J. B. (1930). *Behaviorism.* New York: Norton.

Watson, J. B., & Rayner, R. (1920). Conditioned emotional reactions. *Journal of Experimental Psychology, 3,* 1–14.

Wazana, A., Bresnahan, M., & Kline, J. (2007). The autism epidemic: Fact or artifact? *Journal of the American Academy of Child and Adolescent Psychiatry, 46,* 721–730.

Webster-Stratton, C. (2005). The incredible years: A training series for the prevention and treatment of conduct problems in young children. In E. D. Hibbs & P. S. Jensen (Eds.), *Psychosocial treatments for child and adolescent disorders: Empirically based strategies for clinical practice* (2nd ed.). Washington, DC: American Psychological Association.

Webster-Stratton, C., & Hancock, L. (1998). Parent training: Content, methods, and process. In E. Schaefer (Ed.), *Handbook of parent training* (2nd ed.). New York:Wiley.

Webster-Stratton, C., & Reid, M. J. (2010). The Incredible Years parents, teachers, and children training series: A multifaceted treatment approach for young children. In J. R. Weisz & A. E. Kazdin (Eds.), *Evidence-based psychotherapies for children and adolescents.* (2nd ed.). New York: The Guilford Press.

Wechsler, D. (2002). *Wechsler Preschool and Primary Scale of Intelligence—Third Edition (WPPSI-III).* San Antonio, TX: Harcourt Assessment.

Wechsler, D. (2003). *Wechsler Intelligence Scale for Children—Fourth Edition (WISC-IV).* San Antonio, TX: Harcourt Assessment.

Weersing, V. R., & Brent, D. A. (2010). Treating depression in adolescents using individual cognitive-behavioral therapy. In J. R. Weisz & A. E. Kazdin (Eds.), *Evidence-based psychotherapies for children and adolescents* (2nd ed.). New York: The Guilford Press.

Wehmeyer, M. L. (2003). Eugenics and sterilization in the heartland. *Mental Retardation, 41,* 57–60.

Weinberg, S. M., Jenkins, E. A., Marazita, M. L., & Maher, B. S. (2007). Minor physical anomalies in schizophrenia: A metaanalysis. *Schizophrenia Research, 89,* 72–85.

Weinberger, D. R., & McClure, R. K. (2002). Neurotoxicity, neuroplasticity, and magnetic resonance imaging morphometry. *Archives of General Psychiatry, 59,* 553–558.

Weinrott, M. R., Jones, R. R., & Howard, J. R. (1982). Costeffectiveness of teaching family programs for delinquents: Results of a national evaluation. *Evaluation Review, 6,* 173–201.

Weiss, B., & Garber, J. (2003). Developmental differences in the phenomenology of depression. *Development and Psychopathology, 15,* 403–430.

Weiss, G., & Hechtman, L. T. (1986). *Hyperactive children grown up.* New York: Guilford.

Weiss, K. B., Gergen, P. J., & Hodgson, T. A. (1992). An economic evaluation of asthma in the United States. *New England Journal of Medicine, 326,* 862–866.

Weissberg, R. P., Kumpfer, K. L., & Seligman, M. E. P. (2003). Prevention that works for children: An introduction. *American Psychologist, 58,* 425–432.

Weissman, M. M., Kidd, K. K., & Prusoff, B. A. (1982). Variability in rates of affective disorders in relatives of depressed and normal probands. *Archives of General Psychiatry, 39,* 1397–1403.

Weissman, M. M., Warner, V., Wickramarante, P., Moreau, D., & Olfson, M. (1997). Offspring of depressed parents: 10 years later. *Archives of General Psychiatry, 54,* 932–940.

Weissman, M. M., Wickramaratne, P., Nomura, Y., Warner, V., Verdeli, H., Pilowsky, D. J., Grillon, C., & Bruder, G. (2005). Families at high and low risk for depression: A 3-generation study. *Archives of General Psychiatry, 62,* 29–36.

Weist, M. D. (1997). Expanded school mental health services: A national movement in progress. In T. H. Ollendick & R. J. Prinz (Eds.), *Advances in clinical child psychology* (Vol. 19). New York: Plenum Press.

Weist, M.D., & Christodulu, K.V. (2000). Expanded school mental health programs: Advancing reform and closing the gap between research and practice. *Journal of School Health, 70,* 195–200.

Weist, M. D., Finney, J. W., Barnard, M. U., Davis, C. D., & Ollendick, T. H. (1993). Empirical selection of psychosocial treatment targets for children and adolescents with diabetes. *Journal of Pediatric Psychology, 18,* 11–28.

Weisz, J. R., Chaiyasit, W., Weiss, B., Eastman, K. L., & Jackson, E. W. (1995). A multimethod study of problem behavior among Thai and American children in school: Teacher reports versus direct observations. *Child Development, 66,* 402–415.

Weisz, J. R., & Kazdin, A. E. (Eds.) (2010a). *Evidence-based psychotherapies for children and adolescents* (2nd ed.). New York: The Guilford Press.

Weisz, J. R., & Kazdin, A. E. (2010b). The present and future of evidence-based psychotherapies for children and adolescents. In J. R. Weisz & A. E. Kazdin (Eds.), *Evidence-based psychotherapies for children and adolescents* (2nd ed.). New York: The Guilford Press.

Weisz, J. R., McCarty, C. A., & Valeri, S. M. (2006). Effects of psychotherapy for depression in children and adolescents: A meta-analysis. *Psychological Bulletin, 132,* 132–149.

Weisz, J. R., Sandler, I. N., Durlak, J. A., & Anton, B. S. (2005). Promoting and protecting youth mental health through evidence- based prevention and treatment. *American Psychologist, 60,* 628–648.

Weisz, J. R., Sweeney, L., Proffitt, V., & Carr, T. (1993). Controlrelated beliefs and self-reported depressive symptoms in late childhood. *Journal of Abnormal Psychology, 102,* 411–418.

Weisz, J. R., Weiss, B., Suwanlert, S., & Chaiyasit, W. (2006). Culture and youth psychopathology: Testing the syndromal sensitivity model in Thai and American adolescents. *Journal of Consulting and Clinical Psychology, 74,* 1098–1107.

Weizman, Z. O., & Snow, C. E. (2001). Lexical input as related to children's vocabulary acquisition: Effects of sophisticated exposure and support for meaning. *Developmental Psychology, 37,* 265–279.

Wekerle, C., Wall, A. M., Leung, E., & Trocmé, N. (2007). Cumulative stress and substantiated maltreatment: The importance of caregiver vulnerability and adult partner violence. *Child Abuse & Neglect, 31,* 427–443.

Wekerle, C., & Wolfe, D. A. (2003). Child maltreatment. In E. J. Mash & R. A. Barkley (Eds.), *Child psychopathology* (2nd ed.). New York: Guilford Press.

Wellman, H. M. (1993). Early understanding of mind: The normal case. In S. Baron-Cohen, H. Tager-Flüsberg, & D. J. Cohen (Eds.), *Understanding other minds.* New York: Oxford Press.

Wells, K. C., Forehand, R., & Griest, D. L. (1980). Generality of treatment effects from treated to untreated behaviors resulting from a parent training program. *Journal of Clinical Child Psychology, 9,* 217–219.

Wender, P. H., Kety, S. S., Rosenthal, D., Schulsinger, F., Ortmann, J., & Lunde, I. (1986). Psychiatric disorders in the biological and adoptive families of adopted individuals with affective disorders. *Archives of General Psychiatry, 43,* 923–929.

Werner, E., Dawson, G., Osterling, J., & Dinno, N. (2000). Brief report: Recognition of autism spectrum disorder before one year of age: A retrospective study based on home videotapes. *Journal of Autism and Developmental Disorders, 30,* 157–162.

Werner, E. E., & Smith, R. S. (1982). *Vulnerable but invincible.* New York: McGraw-Hill.

Werner, E. E., & Smith, R. S. (2001). *Journeys from childhood to midlife.* Ithaca, NY: Cornell University Press.

Werry, J. S. (1986). Physical illness, symptoms and allied disorders. In H. C. Quay & J. S.Werry (Eds.), *Psychopathological disorders of childhood* (3rd ed.). New York:Wiley.

Wertheim, E. H., Paxton, S. J., & Blaney, S. (2004). Risks factors for the development of body image disturbances. In J. K. Thompson (Ed.), *Handbook of eating disorders and obesity.* Hoboken, NJ: John Wiley.

Wertlieb, D., Hauser, S. T., & Jacobson, A. M. (1986). Adaptation to diabetes: Behavior symptoms and family context. *Journal of Pediatric Psychology, 11,* 463–479.

West, M. O., & Prinz, R. J. (1987). Parental alcoholism and childhood psychopathology. *Psychological Bulletin, 102,* 204–218.

West, S. G., Sandler, I., Pillow, D. R., Baca, L., & Gersten, J. C. (1991). The use of structural equation modeling in generative research: Toward the design of a preventative intervention for bereaved children. *American Journal of Community Psychology, 19,* 459–480.

Westenberg, P. M., Drewes, M. J., Goedhart, A. W., Siebelink, B. M., & Treffers, P. D. A. (2004). A developmental analysis of self-reported fears in late childhood through mid-adolescence: Social-evaluative fears on the rise? *Journal of Child Psychology and Psychiatry, 45,* 481–495.

Weyandt, L. L., Verdi, G., & Swentosky, A. (2011). Oppositional, conduct, and aggressive disorders. In S. Goldstein & C. R. Reynolds (Eds.), *Handbook of neurodevelopmental and genetic disorders in children* (2nd ed.). New York: The Guilford Press.

Whalen, C. K., Henker, B., King, P. S., Jamner, L. D., & Levine, L. (2004). Adolescents react to the events of September 11, 2001: Focused versus ambient impact. *Journal of Abnormal Child Psychology, 32,* 1–11.

Whitaker, A., Johnson, J., Shaffer, D., Rappoport, J., Kalikow, K., Walsh, B. T., Davies, M., Braiman, S., & Dolinsky, A. (1990). Uncommon troubles in young people: Prevalence estimates of selected psychiatric disorders in a nonreferred adolescent population. *Archives of General Psychiatry, 47,* 487–496.

White, H. R., Bates, M. E., & Buyske, S. (2001). Adolescencelimited delinquency: Extending Moffitt's hypothesis into adulthood. *Journal of Abnormal Psychology, 110,* 600–609.

White, K. J., & Kistner, J. (1992). The influence of teacher feedback on young children's peer preferences and perceptions. *Developmental Psychology, 28,* 933–940.

White, S. F., & Frick, P. J. (2010). Callous-unemotional traits and their importance to causal models of severe antisocial behavior in youth. In R. T. Salekin & D. R. Lyman (Eds.), *Handbook of child and adolescent psychopathy.* New York: The Guilford Press.

White, S. H. (1992). G. Stanley Hall: From philosophy to developmental psychology. *Developmental Psychology, 28,* 25–34.

White, S. W., Oswald, D., Ollendick, T., & Scahill, L. (2009). Anxiety in children and adolescents with autism spectrum disorders. *Clinical Psychology Review, 29,* 216–229.

White, S. W., Scahill, L., Klin, A., Koenig, K., & Volkmar, F. R. (2007). Educational placements and service use patterns of individuals with autism spectrum disorders. *Journal of Autism and Developmental Disorders, 37,* 1403–1412.

White House Task Force on Childhood Obesity. (2011). *One year progress report.* Retrieved July 2011, from http://www.letsmove.gov/white-house-task-force-childhood-obesity-report-president

Whitehurst, G. J., & Fischel, J. E. (1994). Early developmental language delay: What, if anything, should the clinician do about it? *Journal of Child Psychology and Psychiatry, 35,* 613–648.

Whitman, T. L., Hantula, D. A., & Spence, B. H. (1990). Current issues in behavior modification with mentally retarded persons. In J. L. Matson (Ed.), *Handbook of behavior modification with the mentally retarded.* New York: Plenum.

Widiger, T. A., & Clark, L. A. (2000). Toward DSM-V and the classification of psychopathology. *Psychological Bulletin, 126,* 946–961.

Widiger, T. A., Frances, A. J., Pincus, H. A., Davis, W. W., & First, M. B. (1991). Toward an empirical classification for DSM-IV. *Journal of Abnormal Psychology, 100,* 280–288.

Wiebe, D. J., Berg, C. A., Korbel, C., Palmer, D. L., Beveridge, R. M., Upchurch, R., et al. (2005). Children's appraisals of maternal involvement in coping with diabetes: Enhancing our understanding of adherence, metabolic control, and quality of life across adolescence. *Journal of Pediatric Psychology, 30,* 167–178.

Wiener, J., & Tardif, C. Y. (2004). Social and emotional functioning of children with learning disabilities: Does special education placement make a difference? *Learning Disabilities Research & Practice, 19,* 20–32.

Wigal, T., Greenhill, L., Chuang, S., McGough, J., Vitiello, B., Skrobala, A., et al. (2006). Safety and tolerability of methylphenidate in preschool children with ADHD. *Journal of the American Academy of Child and Adolescent Psychiatry, 45,* 1294–1303.

Wight, R. G., Sepúlveda, J. E., & Aneshensel, C. S. (2004). Depressive symptoms: How do adolescents compare with adults? *Journal of Adolescent Health, 34,* 314–323.

Wilens, T. E. (2011). A sobering fact: ADHD leads to substance abuse. *Journal of the American Academy of Child and Adolescent Psychiatry, 50,* 6–8.

Wilfley, D. E., Kass, A. E., Kolko, R. P., & Slein, R. I. (2012). Eating disorders and obesity. In P. C. Kendall (Ed.), *Child and adolescent therapy: Cognitive-behavioral procedures* (4th ed.). New York: The Guilford Press.

Wilfley, D. E., Kolko, R. P., & Kass, A. E. (2011). Cognitive-behavioral therapy for weight management and eating disorders in children and adolescents. *Child and Adolescent Psychiatric Clinics of North America, 20,* 271–285.

Wilkinson, G. S., & Robertson, G. J. (2006). *Wide Range Achievement Test 4 (WRAT-4).* Lutz, FL: Psychological Assessment Resources, Inc.

Willcutt, E., & McQueen, M. (2010). Genetic and environmental vulnerability to bipolar spectrum disorders. In D. J. Miklowitz & D. Cicchetti (Eds.), *Understanding bipolar disorder: A developmental psychopathology perspective.* New York: The Guilford Press.

Willcutt, E. G., & Pennington, B. F. (2000). Psychiatric comorbidity in children and adolescents with reading disability. *Journal of Child Psychology and Psychiatry, 41,* 1039–1048.

Willcutt, E. G., Pennington, B. F., Brada, R., Ogline, J. S., Tunick, R. A., Chhabildas, N. A., & Olson, R. K. (2001). A comparison of the cognitive deficits in reading disability and attention deficit/hyperactivity disorder. *Journal of Abnormal Psychology, 110,* 157–172.

Willemsen-Swinkels, S. H. N., Bakermans-Franenburg, M. J., Buitelaar, J. K., van IJzendoorn, M. H., & van Engeland, H. (2000). Insecure and disorganized attachment in children with a pervasive developmental disorder: Relationship with social interaction and heart rate. *Journal of Child Psychology and Psychiatry, 41,* 759–767.

Williams, B., & Pow, J. (2007). Gender differences and mental health: An exploratory study of knowledge and attitudes to mental health among Scottish teenagers. *Child and Adolescent Mental Health, 12,* 6–12.

Williams, D., Botting, N., & Boucher, J. (2008). Language in autism and specific language impairment: Where are the links? *Psychological Bulletin, 134,* 944–963.

Williams, N. M., Zaharieva, I., Martin, A., Langley, K., Mantripragada, K., Fossdal, R., et al. (2010). Rare chromosomal deletions and duplications in attention-deficit hyperactivity disorder: A genome-wide analysis. *The Lancet, 376,* 1401–1408.

Williams, S., & McGee, R. (1996). Reading in childhood and mental health in early adulthood. In J. H. Beitchman, N. J. Cohen, M. M. Konstantareas, & R. Tannock (Eds.), *Language learning, and behavior disorders*. New York: Cambridge University Press.

Williams, S. E., Blount, R. L., & Walker, L. S. (2011). Children's pain threat appraisal and catastrophizing moderate the impact of parent verbal behavior on children's symptom complaints. *Journal of Pediatric Psychology, 36*, 55–63.

Williamson, D. E., Forbes, E. E., Dahl, R. E., & Ryan, N. D. (2005). A genetic epidemiologic perspective on comorbidity of depression and anxiety. *Child and Adolescent Psychiatric Clinics of North America, 14*, 707–726.

Willoughby, M.T. (2003). Developmental course of ADHD symptomatology during the transition from childhood to adolescence: A review with recommendations. *Journal of Child Psychology and Psychiatry, 44*, 88–106.

Wills, T. A., & Dishion, T. J. (2004). Temperament and adolescent substance abuse: A transactional analysis of emerging selfcontrol. *Journal of Clinical and Child and Adolescent Psychology, 33*, 69–81.

Wilson, A. C., Lengua, L. J., Metzoff, A. N., & Smith, K. A. (2010). Parenting and temperament prior to September 11, 2001, and parenting specific to 9/11 as predictors of children's posttraumatic stress symptoms following 9/11. *Journal of Clinical Child and Adolescent Psychology, 39*, 445–459.

Wilson, G. T. (2010). What treatment research is needed for bulimia nervosa? In C. M. Grilo & J. E. Mitchell (Eds.), *The treatment of eating disorders: A clinical handbook*. New York: The Guilford Press.

Wilson, G. T., Becker, C. B., & Heffernan, K. (2003). Eating disorders. In E. J. Mash & R. A. Barkley (Eds.), *Child psychopathology* (2nd ed.). New York: Guilford Press.

Wilson, G. T., Grilo, C. M., & Vitousek, K. M. (2007). Psychological treatment of eating disorders. *American Psychologist, 62*, 199–216. Winerman, L. (2011). Closing the achievement gap. *Monitor on Psychology, 42*, 36–40.

Winerman, L. (2011). Closing the achievement gap. *Monitor on Psychology, 42*, 36–40.

Wing, L. (1997). Syndromes of autism and atypical development. In D. J. Cohen & F. R. Volkmar (Eds.), *Handbook of autism and pervasive developmental disorders*. New York: John Wiley.

Winsper, C., Lereya, T., Zanarini, M., & Wolke, D. (2012). Involvement in bullying and suicide-related behavior at 11 years: A prospective birth cohort study. *Journal of the American Academy of Child and Adolescent Psychiatry, 51*, 271–282.

Wiseman, C. V., Sunday, S. R., & Becker, A. E. (2005). Impact of the media on adolescent body image. *Child and Adolescent Psychiatric Clinics of North America, 14*, 453–471.

Witwer, A. N., & Lecavalier, L. (2008). Examining the validity of autism spectrum disorder subtypes. *Journal of Autism and Developmental Disorders, 38*, 1611–1624.

Wolf, L., Fisman, S., Ellison, D., & Freeman, T. (1998). Effect of sibling perception of differential parental treatment in sibling dyads with one disabled child. *Journal of the American Academy of Child and Adolescent Psychiatry, 37*, 1317–1325.

Wolf, M. M., Braukmann, C. J., & Ramp, K. A. (1987). Serious delinquent behavior as part of a significantly handicapping condition: Cures and supportive environments. *Journal of Applied Behavior Analysis, 20*, 347–359.

Wolfe, B. E., Baker, C. W., Smith, A. T., & Kelly-Weeder, S. (2009). Validity and utility of the current definition of binge eating. *International Journal of Eating Disorders, 42*, 674–686.

Wolfe, D. A., Rawana, J. S., & Chiodo, D. (2006). Abuse and trauma. In D. A. Wolfe & E. J. Mash (Eds.), *Behavioral and emotional disorder in adolescents: Nature, assessment, and treatment*. New York: The Guilford Press.

Wolfe, J., Grier, H. E., Klar, N., Levin, S. B., Ellenbogen, J. M., Salem-Schatz, S., et al. (2000a). Symptoms and suffering at the end of life in children with cancer. *New England Journal of Medicine, 342*, 326–333.

Wolfe, J., Klar, N., Grier, H. E., Duncan, J., Salem-Schatz, S., Emanuel, E. J., & Weeks, J. C. (2000b). Understanding of prognosis among parents of children who died of cancer: Impact on treatment goals and integration of palliative care. *Journal of the American Medical Association, 284*, 2469–2475.

Wolfe, V. V. (2006). Child sexual abuse. In E. J. Mash & R. A. Barkley (Eds.), *Treatment of childhood disorders* (3rd ed.). New York: The Guilford Press.

Wolfensberger, W. (1980). *The principle of normalization in human services*. Toronto: National Institute on Mental Retardation.

Wolke, D., Woods, S., Bloomfield, L., & Karstadt, L. (2000). The association between direct and relational bullying and behaviour problems among primary school children. *Journal of Child Psychology and Psychiatry, 41*, 989–1002.

Wolraich, M., Wilson, D. B., & White, J. W. (1995). The effect of sugar on behavior or cognition in children. *Journal of the American Medical Association, 274*, 1617–1621.

Wonderlich, S., Crosby, R., Mitchell, J., Thompson, K., Redlin, J., Demuth, G., & Smyth, J. (2001). Pathways mediating sexual abuse and eating disturbance in children. *Journal of Eating Disorders, 13*, 25–34.

Wonderlich, S. A., Joiner, T. E., Keel, P. K., Williamson, D. A., & Crosby, R.D. (2007). Eating disorder diagnoses. *American Psychologist, 62*, 167–180.

Wonderlich, S. A., Lilenfeld, L. R., Riso, L.P., Engel, S., & Mitchell, J. E. (2005). Personality and anorexia nervosa. *International Journal of Eating Disorders, 37*, S68–S71.

Wong, B. Y. L., Butler, D. L., Ficzere, S. A., & Kuperis, S. (1997). Teaching adolescents with learning disabilities and low achievers to plan, write, and revise compare-and-contrast essays. *Learning Disabilities Research & Practice, 12*, 2–15.

Wong, B. Y. L., Harris, K. R., Graham, S., & Butler, D. L. (2003). Cognitive strategies instruction research in learning disabilities. In H. L. Swanson, K. R. Harris & S. Graham (Eds.), *Handbook of learning disabilities*. New York: Guilford Press.

Wood, A. C., Buitelaar, J., Rijsdijk, F., Asherson, P., & Kuntsi, J. (2010). Rethinking shared environment as a source of variance underlying attention-deficit/hyperactivity disorder symptoms: Comment on Burt (2009). *Psychological Bulletin, 136*, 331–340.

Wood, B., Watkins, J. B., Boyle, J. T., Noguiera, J., Aimand, E., & Carrol, L. (1989). The "psychosomatic family" model: An empirical analysis. *Family Process, 28*, 399–417.

Wood, B. L, Cheah, P. A., Lim, J. H., Ritz, T., Miller, B. D., Stern, T., & Ballow, M. (2007a). Reliability and validity of the Asthma Trigger Inventory applied to a pediatric population. *Journal of Pediatric Psychology, 32*, 552–560.

Wood, B. L., Lim, J. H., Miller, B. D., Cheah, P. A., Simmons, S., Stern, T., et al. (2007b). Family emotional climate, depression, emotional triggering of asthma, and disease severity in pediatric asthma: Examination of pathways of effect. *Journal of Pediatric Psychology, 32*, 542–551.

Wood, J. J., McLeod, B. D., Sigman, M., Hwang, W. C., & Chu, B. C. (2003). Parenting and childhood anxiety: Theory, empirical findings, and future directions. *Journal of Child Psychology and Psychiatry, 44*, 134–151.

Wood, J. J., Piacentini, J. C., Southam-Gerow, M., Chu, B. C., & Sigman, M. (2006). Family cognitive behavioral therapy for child anxiety disorders. *Journal of American Academy of Child and Adolescent Psychiatry, 45*, 314–321.

Wood, M., & Valdez-Menchaca, M. C. (1996). The effect of a diagnostic label of language delay on adults' perceptions of preschool children. *Journal of Learning Disabilities, 29*, 582–588.

Woodcock, R. W. (2011). *Woodcock Reading Mastery Tests* (3rd ed.). San Antonio, TX: Pearson.

Woods, J. N., Borrero, J. C., Laud, R. B., & Borrero, S. W. (2010). Descriptive analyses of pediatric food refusal: The structure of parental attention. *Behavior Modification, 34*, 35–56.

Woodward, L. J., Fergusson, D. M., & Horwood, L. J. (2000). Driving outcomes of young people with attentional difficulties in adolescence. *Journal of the American Academy of Child and Adolescent Psychiatry, 39*, 627–634.

World Health Organization. (1992). *International classification of diseases: Tenth revision*. Chapter V. Mental and behavioural disorders. Diagnostic criteria for research. Geneva: Author.

Wray, N. R., & Visscher, P. M. (2010). Narrowing the boundaries of the genetic architecture of schizophrenia. *Schizophrenia Bulletin, 36*, 14–23.

Wren, F. J., Berg, E. A., Heiden, L. A., Kinnamon, C. J., Ohlson, L. A., Bridge, J. A., et al. (2007). Childhood anxiety in a diverse primary care population: Parent-child reports, ethnicity, and SCARED factor structure. *Journal of the American Academy of Child and Adolescent Psychiatry, 46*, 332–340.

Wright, H. F. (1960). Observational child study. In P. H. Mussen (Ed.), *Handbook of research methods in child development*. New York: John Wiley.

Wright, K. D., Stewart, S. H., Finley, G. A., & Buffert-Jerrott, S. E. (2007). Prevention and intervention strategies to alleviate preoperative anxiety in children: A critical review. *Behavior Modification, 31*, 52–79.

Wysocki, T. (2006). Behavioral assessment and intervention in pediatric diabetes. *Behaviour Modification, 30*, 1–21.

Wysocki, T., Buckloh, L. M., Greco, P. (2009). The psychological context of diabetes mellitus in youths. In M. C. Roberts & R. G. Steele (Eds.), *Handbook of pediatric psychology* (4th ed.). New York: The Guilford Press.

Xu, M-Q, Sun, W-S., Liu, B.-X., Feng, G.-Y., Yu, L., Yang, L., He, L. (2009). Prenatal malnutrition and adult schizophrenia: Further evidence from the 1959–1961 Chinese famine. *Schizophrenia Bulletin, 35*, 568–576.

Yang, T. T., Simmons, A. N., Matthews, S. C., Tapert, S. F., Frank, G. K., Max, J. E., et al. (2010). Adolescents with major depression demonstrate increased amygdala activation. *Journal of the American Academy of Child and Adolescent Psychiatry, 49*, 42–51.

Yeates, K. O., Bigler, E. D., Dennis, M., Gerhardt, C. A., Rubin, K. H., Stancin, T., et al. (2007). Social outcomes in childhood brain disorder: A heuristic integration of social neuroscience and developmental psychology. *Psychological Bulletin, 133*, 535–556.

Yeatts, K. B., & Shy, C. M. (2001). Prevalence and consequences of asthma and wheezing in African-American and White adolescents. *Journal of Adolescent Health, 29*, 314–319.

Yeganeh, R., Beidel, D. C., Turner, S. M., Pina, A. A., & Silverman, W. K. (2003). Clinical distinctions between selective mutism and social phobia: An investigation of childhood psychopathology. *Journal of the American Academy of Child and Adolescent Psychiatry, 42*, 1069–1075.

Yeh, M., Hough, R. L., McCabe, K., Lau, A., & Garland, A. (2004). Parental beliefs about the cause of child problems: Exploring racial/ethnic patterns. *Journal of the American Academy of Child and Adolescent Psychiatry, 43*, 605–612.

Yeo, R. A., Hill, D. E., Campbell, R. A., Vigil, J., Petropoulos, H., Hart, B., et al. (2003). Proton magnetic resonance spectroscopy investigation of the right frontal lobe in children with attention- deficit/hyperactivity disorder. *Journal of the American Academy of Child and Adolescent Psychiatry, 42*, 303–310.

Yerys, B. E., Hepburn, S. L., Pennington, B. F., & Rogers, S. J. (2007). Executive function in preschoolers with autism: Evidence consistent with a secondary deficit. *Journal of Autism and Developmental Disorders, 37*, 1068–1079.

Yoshikawa, H., Weisner, T. S., Kalil, A., & Way, N. (2008). Mixing qualitative and quantitative research in developmental science: Uses and methodological choices. *Developmental Psychology, 44*, 344–354.

Yoshimasu, K., Barbaresi, W. J., Colligan, R. C., Killiam, J. C., Voight, R. G., Weaver, A., L., et al. (2010). Gender, attention-deficit/hyperactivity disorder, and reading disability in a population-based birth cohort. *Pediatrics, 126*, e788–e795.

Young, A. R., Beitchman, J. H., Johnson, C., Douglas, L., Atkinson, L., Escobar, M., & Wilson, B. (2002). Young adult academic outcomes in a longitudinal sample of early identified language impaired and control children. *Journal of Child Psychology and Psychiatry, 43*, 635–645.

Young, K. M., Northern, J. J., Lister, K. M., Drummond, J. A., & O'Brien, W. H. (2007). A meta-analysis of family-behavioral weight-loss treatments for children. *Clinical Psychology Review, 27*, 240–249.

Young, M. H., Brennan, L. C., Baker, R. D., & Baker, S. S. (1996). Functional encopresis. In R. S. Feldman (Ed.), *The psychology of adversity*. Amherst: University of Massachusetts Press.

Young, R. C., Biggs, J. T., Ziegler, V. E., & Meyer, D. A. (1978). A rating scale for mania: Reliability, validity, and sensitivity. *British Journal of Psychiatry, 133*, 429–435.

Young, S. E., Friedman, N. P., Miyake, A., Willcutt, E. G., Corley, R. P., Haberstick, B. C., et al. (2009). Behavioral disinhibition: Liability for externalizing spectrum disorders and its genetic and environmental relation to response inhibition across adolescence. *Journal of Abnormal Psychology, 118*, 117–130.

Youngstrom, E. A. (2010). A developmental psychopathology perspective on the assessment and diagnosis of bipolar disorder. In D. J. Miklowitz & D. Cicchetti (Eds.), *Understanding bipolar disorder: A developmental psychopathology perspective*. New York: The Guilford Press.

Youngstrom, E. A., Findling, R. L., Danielson, C. K., & Calabrese, J. R. (2001). Discriminative validity of parent report of hypomanic and depressive symptoms in the General Behavior Inventory. *Psychological Assessment, 13*, 267–276.

Youngstrom, E. A., Findling, R. L., & Feeny, N. (2004). Assessment of bipolar spectrum disorders in children and adolescents. In S. L. Johnson & R. L. Leahy (Eds.), *Psychological treatment of bipolar disorder*. New York: Guilford Press.

Yow, V. R. (2005). *Recording oral history*. Walnut Creek, CA: AltaMira Press.

Yule, W., Udwin, O., & Murdoch, K. (1990). The "Jupiter" sinking: Effects on children's fears, depression and anxiety. *Journal of Child Psychology and Psychiatry, 31*, 1051–1061.

Zahn-Waxler, C., Crick, N. R., Shirtcliffe, E. A., & Woods, K. E. (2006). The origins and development of psychopathology in females and males. In D. Cicchetti & D. J. Cohen (Eds.), *Developmental psychopathology. Vol. 1. Theory and method*. Hoboken, NJ: John Wiley & Sons.

Zahn-Waxler, C., Shirtcliff, E. A., & Marceau, K. (2008). Disorders of childhood and adolescence: Gender and psychopathology. *Annual Review of Clinical Psychology, 4*, 275–303.

Zalecki, C. A., & Hinshaw, S. P. (2004). Overt and relational aggression in girls with attention deficit hyperactivity disorder. *Journal of Clinical Child and Adolescent Psychology, 33*, 125–137.

Zalsman, G., Brent, D. A., & Weersing, V. R. (2006a). Depressive disorders in childhood and adolescence: An overview: Epidemiology, clinical manifestation and risk factors. *Child and Adolescent Clinics of North America, 15*, 827–841.

Zalsman, G., Oquendo, M. A., Greenhill, L., Goldberg, P. H., Kamali, M., Martin, A., & Mann, J. J. (2006b). Neurobiology of depression in children and adolescents. *Child and Adolescent Psychiatric Clinics of North America, 15*, 843–868.

Zametkin, A. J., & Rapoport, J. L. (1986). The pathophysiology of attention deficit disorder with hyperactivity: A review. In B. B. Lahey & A. E. Kazdin (Eds.), *Advance in clinical child psychology* (Vol. 9). New York: Plenum.

Zametkin, A. J., Zoon, C. K., Klein, H. W., & Munson, S. (2004). Psychiatric aspects of child and adolescent obesity: A review of the past 10 years. *Journal of the American Academy of Child and Adolescent Psychiatry, 43*, 134–150.

Zeanah, C. H., & Smyke, A. T. (2009). Attachment disorders. In C. H. Zeanah (Ed.), *Handbook of infant mental health*. (3rd ed.). New York: Guilford Press.

Zeanah, C. H., Jr., & Zeanah, P. D. (2009). The scope of infant mental health. In C. H. Zeanah, Jr. (Ed.), *Handbook of infant mental health*. New York: Guilford Press.

Zeanah, P. D., & Gleason, M. M. (2009). Infant mental health in primary health care. In C. H. Zeanah, Jr. (Ed.), *Handbook of infant mental health*. New York: Guilford Press.

Zero to Three/National Center for Infants, Toddlers and Families. (2005). *Diagnostic classification of mental health and developmental disorders of infancy and early childhood, Revised*. Washington, D.C.: Author.

Zhang, X., Lv, C-C., Tain, J., Miao, R-J., Xi, W., Hertz-Picciotto, I., & Qi, L. (2010). Prenatal and perinatal risk factors for autism in China. *Journal of Autism and Developmental Disorders, 40*, 1311–1321.

Ziermans, T. B., Schothorst, P. F., Sprong. M., & van Engeland, H. (2011). Transition and remission in adolescents at ultra-high risk for psychosis. *Schizophrenia Research, 126*, 58–64.

Zigler, E., Balla, D., & Hodapp, R. (1984). On the definition and classification of mental retardation. *American Journal of Mental Deficiency, 89*, 215–230.

Zima, B. T., Bussing, R., Tang, L., Zhang, L., Ettner, S., Belin, T. R. et al. (2010). Quality of care for childhood attention-deficit/hyperactivity disorder in a managed care medical program. *Journal of the American Academy of Child and Adolescent Psychiatry, 49*, 1225–1237.

Zisser, A., & Eyberg, S. M. (2010). Parent-child interaction therapy and the treatment of disruptive behavior disorders. In J. R. Weisz & A. E. Kazdin (Eds.), *Evidence-based psychotherapies for children and adolescents* (2nd ed.). New York: The Guilford Press.

Zito, J. M., Safer, D. J., dos Reis, S., Gardner, J. F., Boles, M., & Lynch, F. (2000). Trends in the prescribing of psychotropic medications to preschoolers. *Journal of the American Medical Association, 283*, 1025–1031.

Zito, J. M., Safer, D. J., de Jong-van den Berg, L. T. W., Janhsen, K., Fegert, J. M., Gardner, J. F., et al. (2008). A three-country comparison of psychotropic medication prevalence in youth. *Child and Adolescent Psychiatry and Mental Health*, 2:26. Retrieved from http://www.capmh.com/content/2/1/26/abstract/

Zucker, R. A. (2006). Alcohol use and the alcohol use disorders: A developmental-biopsychosocial systems formulation covering the life course. In D. Cicchetti & D. J. Cohen (Eds.), *Developmental psychopathology, Vol. 3: Risk, disorder, and adaptation* (2nd ed.). Hoboken, NJ: John Wiley & Sons.

Zuvekas, S. H., Vitiello, B., & Norquist, G. S. (2006). Recent trends in stimulant medication use among U.S. children. *American Journal of Psychiatry, 163*, 579–585.

CREDITS

"Adolescent development: Pathways and processes of risk and resilience" by Compas, Hinden, and Gerhardt. *Annual Review of Psychology*, 46, pp. 265–293. © 1995 by Annual Reviews. Reprinted with permission; p. 27 Source: "The development of competence in favorable and unfavorable environments: Lessons from research on successful children" by Masten and Coatsworth. *The American Psychologist*, 53 (1998), pp. 205–220; p. 27 Adapted from *Developmental Psychopathology and Family Process: Theory, Research, and Clinical Implications* by Cummings, Davies, and Campbell. © 2000 by Guilford Press. Reprinted with permission; p. 28 Graph from "Understanding psychopathology. The role of vulnerability" R. E. Ingram and J. M. Price. *Vulnerability to Psychopathology. Risk Across the Lifespan*, edited by R. E. Ingram and J.M. Price. © 2010 by Guilford Press. Reprinted with permission; p. 31 Adapted from "Disorder and risk for disorder during infancy and toddlerhood" by Lyons-Ruth, Zeanah, and Benoit. *Child Psychopathology*, edited by E. J. Mash and R. A. Barkley. © 2003 by Guilford Press. Reprinted with permission; p. 32 Adapted from "Temperamental individuality from childhood to adolescence" by Chess and Thomas. *Journal of the American Academy of Child Psychiatry*, 16, pp. 220–221. © 1977 by Elsevier. Reprinted with permission; p. 33 Adapted from "Infant temperament, parenting, and externalizing behavior in first grade: A test of the differential susceptibility hypothesis" by R. B. Bradley and R. F. Corwyn. *Journal of Child Psychology and Psychiatry*, 49, pp. 124–131. © 2008 by John Wiley & Sons. Reprinted with permission.

Chapter 3: p. 45 Adapted from *Genetics and Experience. The Interplay between Nature and Nurture* by Robert Plomin. © 1994 by Sage. Reprinted with permission; p. 50 Based in part on "Socialization in the context of the family: Parent-child interaction" by Macoby and Martin. *Handbook of Child Psychology*, Vol. IV, edited by p. H. Mussen. © 1993 by John Wiley & Sons. Reprinted with permission; p. 51 Table from *The Future of Children*, a publication of the David and Lucile Packard Foundation from 1991 to 2004. Reprinted with permission; p. 54 Figure from "Developmental traumatology: The psychobiological development of maltreated children and its implications for research, treatment, and policy," by Michael De Bellis. *Development and Psychopathology*, September 2001, Volume 31(3). © 2001 by Cambridge University Press. Reprinted with permission.

Chapter 5: p. 90 Table adapted from "Manual for the ASEBA School-Age Forms & Profiles" by T. M. Achenbach and L. Rescorla. © 2001 by University of Vermont, Research Center for Children, Youth & Families. Reprinted with permission; p. 93 Adapted from *Assessment and Treatment of Childhood Problems: A Clinician's Guide* by Carolyn S. Schroeder and Betty N. Gordon. © 2002 by Guilford Press. Reprinted with permission.

Chapter 6: p. 112 Table from "Manual for the ASEBA School-Age Forms & Profiles" by T. M. Achenbach and L. Rescorla.

© 2001 by T. M. Achenbach. Reprinted by permission; p. 114 Adapted from "Specific phobia," by Silverman and Moreno. *Child and Adolescent Psychiatric Clinics of North America*, 14(4), pp. 819–843. © 2005, with permission from Elsevier; p. 115 Adapted from "Anxiety disorders" by Silverman and Ginsburg. *Handbook of Child Psychopathology* (3rd ed.), edited by Ollendick and Hersen. © 1998 by Plenum. Reprinted with permission; p. 116 Adapted from "Treating selective mutism using modular CBT for child anxiety: A case study" by E. T. Reuther et al. *Journal of Clinical Child and Adolescent Psychology*, 40, pp. 156–163. © 2011 by Taylor & Francis. Reprinted with permission; p. 118 Separation anxiety." *Child Behavior Therapy Casebook*, edited by M. Hersen and C. G. Last. © 1988 by Plenum. Reprinted with permission; p. 127 Adapted from "Childhood posttraumatic stress disorder" by Fletcher. *Child Psychopathology*, edited by E. J. Mash and R. A. Barkley. © 2003 by Guilford Press. Reprinted with permission.

Chapter 7: p. 145 Table adapted from "Identifying depression in children: A comparison of alternative selection criteria" by A. E. Kazdin. *Journal of Abnormal Child Psychology*, 17, pp. 437–454. © 1989 by Springer. Reprinted with permission; p. 147 Adapted from "Depression in children and adolescents" by Compas. *Assessment of Childhood Disorders* by E. J. Mash and L. G. Terdal. © 1997 by Guilford Press. Reprinted with permission; p. 149 Figure adapted from "Ethnic and sex differences in children's depressive symptoms" by Kistner et al. *Journal of Clinical Child and Adolescent Psychology*, 36, pp. 171–181. © 2007 by Taylor & Francis. Reprinted with permission; p. 157 Adapted from *Developmental Psychopathology and Family Process: Theory, Research, and Clinical Implications* by Cummings, Davies, and Campbell. © 2000 by Guilford Press. Reprinted with permission; p. 158 Adapted from *Developmental Psychopathology and Family Process: Theory, Research, and Clinical Implications* by Cummings, Davies, and Campbell. © 2000 by Guilford Press. Reprinted with permission; p. 162 From "Cognitive-behavioral therapy for depression. The ACTION Treatment Program for Girls" by Stark et al. *Evidence-Based Psychotherapies for Children and Adolescents*, edited by Weisz and Kazdin. © 2010 by Guilford Press. Reprinted with permission; p. 162 Table from "Cognitive-behavioral therapy for depression. The ACTION Treatment Program for Girls" by Stark et al. *Evidence-Based Psychotherapies for Children and Adolescents*, edited by J. R. Weisz and A. E. Kazdin. © 2010 by Guilford Press. Reprinted with permission; p. 166 Adapted from "Bipolar disorder in the preschool period" by J. L. Luby et al. *Understanding Bipolar Disorder: A Developmental Psychopathology Perspective*, edited by D. J. Miklowitz and D. Cichetti. © 2010 by Guilford Press. Reprinted with permission; p. 167 Table adapted from "Phenomenology and longitudinal course of children with prepubertal and early adolescent bipolar disorder phenotype" by Geller et al. *Bipolar Disorder in Childhood and Early Adolescence*, edited by B. Geller and M. p. DelBello. © 2003 by Guilford Press. Reprinted with permission; p. 167 Table adapted from "Pediatric bipolar disorder:

Emerging diagnostic and treatment approaches" by Kowatch and DelBello. *Child and Adolescent Psychiatric Clinics of North America*, 15, pp. 73–108. © 2006, with permission from Elsevier; p. 168 Adapted from "Internet support for parents of children with early-onset bipolar disorder" by Hellander et al. *Bipolar Disorder in Childhood and Early Adolescence*, edited by B. Geller and M. p. DelBello. © 2003 by Guilford Press. Reprinted with permission; p. 169 Adapted from "Prodromal symptoms before onset of manic-depressive disorder suggested by first hospital admission histories" Egeland, Hostetter, Pauls, and Sussex. *Journal of the American Academy of Child and Adolescent Psychiatry*, 39, pp. 1245–1252. © 2000, with permission from Elsevier.

Chapter 8: p. 180 Adapted from *Assessment and Treatment of Childhood Problems: A Clinician's Guide* by Schroeder and Gordon. © 2002 by Guilford Press. Reprinted with permission; p. 184 *Diagnostic and Statistical Manual of Mental Disorders* (4th ed.). Text Revision. © 2000 by the American Psychiatric Association. Reprinted with permission; p. 000 Table adapted from "Manual for the ASEBA School-Age Forms & Profiles" by T. M. Achenbach and L. Rescorla. © 2001 by T. M. Achenbach. Reprinted by permission; p. 185 Figure from "Accelerated longitudinal comparisons of aggressive versus delinquent syndromes," by Catherine Stanger, Thomas M. Achenbach, and Frank C. Verhulst. *Development and Psychopathology*, March 1997, Volume 9(1). © 1997 by Cambridge University Press. Reprinted with permission; pp. 193–194 From "Issues of taxonomy and comorbidity in the development of conduct disorder" by Stephen p. Hinshaw, Benjamin B. Lahey, and Elizabeth L. Hart. *Development and Psychopathology*, January 1993, Volume 5(1). © 1993 by Cambridge University Press. Reprinted with permission; p. 194 "Developmental approaches to aggression and conduct problems" by Loeber and Hay. *Development Through Life: A Handbook for Clinicians*, edited by Rutter and Hay. © 1994 by John Wiley & Sons. Reprinted with permission; p. 195 Table adapted from "Young children who commit crime: Epidemiology, developmental origins, risk factors, early interventions, and policy implications" by Rolf Loeber and David p. Farrington. *Development and Psychopathology*, December 2000, Volume 12(4). © 2000 by Cambridge University Press. Reprinted with permission; p. 209 Table adapted from "Practitioner review: Psychosocial treatments for conduct disorder in children" by Alan Kazdin. *Journal of Child Psychology and Psychiatry*, 38, pp. 161–178. © 1997 by John Wiley & Sons. Reprinted with permission; p. 211 Table adapted from "Anger control training for aggressive youths" by Lochman et al. *Evidence-Based Psychotherapies for Children and Adolescents*, edited by J. R. Weisz and A. E. Kazdin. © 2010 by Guilford Press. Reprinted with permission; p. 213 Adapted from *Multisystemic Treatment of Antisocial Behavior in Children and Adolescents* by Hengeller et al. © 1998 by Guilford Press. Reprinted with permission.

Chapter 9: p. 217 From "Attention-deficit/hyperactivity disorder" by L. M. McGrath and R. L. Peterson. *Diagnosing Learning Disorders*, edited by B. F. Pennington. © 2009 by Guilford Press. Reprinted with permission; p. 222 Adapted from *Case Studies in Child and Adolescent Psychopathology* by Robin K. Morgan. Reprinted and electronically reproduced by permission of Pearson Education, Inc., Upper Saddle River, New Jersey; p. 219 Figure adapted from "Does actigraphy differentiate ADHD subtypes in a clinical research setting" by Andrew V. Dane, Russell J. Schachar, and Rosemary Tannock. *Journal of American Academy of Child and Adolescent Psychiatry*, 39(6), pp. 752–760. © 2000, with permission from Elsevier; p. 224 Adapted from "Integrating the results of an evaluation" by Hathaway, Dooling-Litfin, and Edwards. *Attention-Deficit Hyperactivity Disorder. A Handbook for Diagnosis and Treatment*, edited by R. A. Barkley. © 2006 by Guilford Press. Reprinted with permission; p. 225 Adapted from "Integrating the results of an evaluation" by Hathaway, Dooling-Litfin, and Edwards. *Attention-Deficit Hyperactivity Disorder. A Handbook for Diagnosis and Treatment*, edited by R. A. Barkley. © 2006 by Guilford Press. Reprinted with permission; p. 227 Figure adapted from "Developmental transitions among affective and behavioral disorders in adolescent boys" by Burke et al. *Journal of Child Psychology and Psychiatry*, 46, pp. 1200–1210. © by John Wiley & Sons. Reprinted with permission; p. 229 Figure adapted from "Developmental trajectories of conduct problems and hyperactivity from ages 2 to 10" by Shaw et al. *Journal of Child Psychology and Psychiatry*, 46, pp. 932–942. © 2005 by John Wiley & Sons. Reprinted with permission; p. 230 Graph from "Adult psychiatric outcomes of girls with attention deficit hyperactivity disorder: 11-year follow-up in a longitudinal case-control study" by Biederman et al. *American Journal of Psychiatry*, 167, pp. 409–417. © 2010 by the American Psychiatric Association. Reprinted with permission; p. 236 Graph based on "Disorders of attention and activity" by E. Taylor and E. Sonuga-Barke. *Rutter's Child and Adolescent Psychiatry*, edited by M. Rutter et al. © 2008 by John Wiley & Sons. Reprinted with permission; p. 237 Table adapted from "Diagnostic interview, behavior rating scales, and medical examination" by Barkley and Edwards. *Behavior and Mental Disorders in Adolescents: Nature, Assessment, and Treatment*, edited by Barkley. © 2006 by Guilford Press. Reprinted with permission; p. 245 Reprinted from "The MTA at 8 years: Prospective follow-up of children treated for combined-type ADHD in a multisite study" by Brooke S. G. Molina, Stephen p. Hinshaw, James M. Swanson, L. Eugene Arnold, et al. *Journal of the American Academy of Child and Adolescent Psychiatry*, 48, © 2009, with permission from Elsevier; p. 253 Adapted from "Phonological disorder" by Johnson and Beitchman. *Comprehensive Textbook of Psychiatry*, edited by Sadock and Sadock. © 2005 by Lippincott, Williams, and Wilkins. Reprinted by permission.

Chapter 10: p. 248 Table based on "A brief history of the field of learning disabilities" by Hallahan and Mock. *Handbook of Learning Disabilities*, edited by Swanson, Harris, and Graham. © by Guilford Press. Reprinted with permission; p. 250 "What

© 2000 by John Wiley and Sons. Reprinted with permission; p. 323 Adapted from "Pervasive developmental disorders" by Volkmar et al. *Comprehensive Textbook of Psychiatry (Vol. II)*, edited by Sadock and Sadock. © 2005 by Lippincott, Williams, and Wilkins. Reprinted with permission; p. 324 Adapted from "Case study of childhood disintegrative disorder using systematic analysis of family home movies" by R. Palomo et al. *Journal of Autism and Developmental Disorders*, 38, pp. 1853–1858. © 2008 by Springer. Reprinted with permission; p. 324 "A case study of childhood disintegrative disorder using systematic analysis of family home movies" by Palomo et al. *Journal of Autism and Developmental Disorders*, 38, pp. 1853–1858. © 2008 by Springer. Reprinted with permission; p. 328 Table adapted from "Early and intensive behavioral intervention in autism" by Lovaas and Smith. *Evidence-Based Psychotherapies for Children and Adolescents*, edited by Kazdin and Weisz. © 2003 by Guilford Press. Reprinted with permission; p. 334 Figure from "Three-dimensional brain growth abnormalities in childhood-onset schizophrenia visualized by using tensor-based morphometry" by Gognay et al. *Proceedings of the National Academy of Sciences*, 105, pp. 15979–15984. © 2008 by The National Academy of Sciences, U.S.A. Reprinted with permission. p. 338 Table adapted from "Annotation: Childhood-onset schizophrenia: Clinical and treatment issues" by Asarnow et al. *Journal of Child Psychology and Psychiatry*, 45, pp. 180–194. © 2004 by John Wiley & Sons. Reprinted with permission; p. 333 Adapted from "Childhood-onset schizophrenia" by Asarnow and Asarnow. *Child Psychopathology*, edited by Mash and Barkley. © 2003 by Guilford Press. Reprinted with permission; p. 333 Figure from "ADHD and achievement: Meta-analysis of the child, adolescent, and adult literature and a concomitant study with college students" by Frazier et al. *Journal of Learning Disabilities*, 40, pp. 49–65. © 2007 by Sage. Reprinted with permission; p. 336 Figure from "The neurodevelopmental model of schizophrenia: Updated" by Bearden et al. *Developmental Psychopathology (Vol III)*, edited by Cichetti and Cohen. © 2006 by John Wiley & Sons. Reprinted with permission.

Chapter 13: p. 341 Adapted from "Elimination disorders" by Ondersma and Walker. *Handbook of Child Psychopathology*, edited by Ollendick and Hersen. © 1998 by Plenum. Reprinted with permission; p. 343 Adapted from "Elimination disorders" by Ondersma and Walker. *Handbook of Child Psychopathology*, edited by Ollendick and Hersen. © 1998 by Plenum. Reprinted with permission; p. 348 Reprinted from "Children's nighttime fears: Parent–child ratings of frequency, content, origins, coping behaviors and severity" by Peter Muris, Harald Merckelbach, Thomas H Ollendick, Neville J King, and Nicole Bogie. *Behaviour Research and Therapy*, 39(1), pp. 13–28. © 2001, with permission from Elsevier; p. 349 Adapted from *Assessment and Treatment of Childhood Problems: A Clinician's Guide, by Schroeder and Gordon*. © 2002 by Guilford Press. Reprinted with permission; p. 355 Adapted from "Obesity" by

Israel and Solotar. *Child Behavior Therapy Casebook*, edited by Hersen and Last. © 1988 by Plenum. Reprinted with permission; p. 356 Figure from "An evaluation of enhanced self-regulation training in the treatment of childhood obesity" by Israel et al. *Journal of Pediatric Psychology*, 19, pp. 737–749. © 1994 by the Oxford University Press. Reprinted with permission; p. 361 Adapted from "Vulnerability to eating disorders in childhood and adolescence" by K. T. Eddy, p. K. Keel, and G. R. Leon. *Vulnerability to Psychopathology: Risk Across the Lifespan*. © 2010 by Guilford Press. Reprinted with permission; p. 364 Figure adapted from "Body figure perceptions and preferences among preadolescent children" by Collins. *International Journal of Eating Disorders*, 10, pp. 199–208. © 1991 by John Wiley & Sons. Reprinted with permission.

Chapter 14: p. 371 Adapted from "Childhood asthma" by Creer. *Handbook of Child Psychopathology* (3rd ed.), edited by Ollendick and Hersen. © 1998 by Plenum. Reprinted with permission; p. 375 Figure from *Effects of the Pediatric Chronic Physical Disorders on Child and Family Adjustment* by Jan L. Wallander and James W. Varni. © 1998 by John Wiley & Sons. Reprinted with permission; p. 373 Figure adapted from "Using structural equation modeling to understand child and parent perceptions of asthma quality of life" by Robert D. Annett et. al. *Journal of Pediatric Psychology*, 35.8, pp. 870–882. © 2010 by the Oxford University Press. Reprinted with permission; p. 376 Figure adapted from "Adjustment to chronic arthritis of childhood: The roles of illness-related stress and attitude toward illness" by Jennifer Soriano LeBovidge, John V. Lavigne, and Michael L. Miller. *Journal of Pediatric Psychology*, 30.3, pp. 273–286. © 2005 by the Oxford University Press. Reprinted with permission; p. 377 Adapted from "Juvenile diabetes" by Johnson. *Handbook of Child Psychopathology* (3rd ed.), edited by Ollendick and Hesen. © 1998 by Plenum. Reprinted with permission; p. 381 Tables adapted from "Diabetes self-care goals and their relation to children's metabolic control" by Paul Karoly and R. Curtis Bay. *Journal of Pediatric Psychology*, 15.1, pp. 83–95. © 1990 by the Oxford University Press. Reprinted with permission; p. 382 Figure adapted from "Mothers', fathers', and children's perceptions of parental diabetes responsibility in adolescence: Examining the role of age, pubertal status and efficacy" by Debra L. Palmer, et. al. *Journal of Pediatric Psychology*, 34.2, pp. 195204. © 2009 by the Oxford University Press. Reprinted with permission; p. 383 Table adapted from "Problem solving and diabetes regimen adherence by children and adolescents with IDDM in social pressure situations: A reflection of normal development" by Ann Muir Thomas, Lizette Peterson, and David Goldstein. *Journal of Pediatric Psychology*, 22.4, pp. 541–561. © 1997 by permission the Oxford University Press. Reprinted with permission; p. 384 Adapted from "Behavioral and cognitive- behavioral interventions with pediatric populations" by Powers, Jones, and Jones. *Clinical Child Psychology and Psychiatry*, 10, pp. 65–77. © 2005 by Sage. Reprinted with permission.

NAME INDEX

Molden, D. C., 263
Monk, M. A., 111
Moore, B. D., 380
Moore, M., 345
Moos, B. S., 96
Moos, R. H., 96
Moreno, C., 114, 160, 168
Morgan, D. L., 75
Morgan, G. A., 75
Morgan, P. L., 259
Morgan, R. K., 2, 20, 75, 222
Mori, L., 385
Morocco, C. C., 274
Morris, A. S., 135, 193
Morris, T. L., 115, 135
Morrison, J., 205
Morrison, J. A., 353
Morrongiello, B. A., 387
Mortensen, P. B., 334
Mortweet, S. L., 343
Mosconi, M. W., 320
Mosher, M., 184
Mota, V. L., 222
Mowrer, O. H., 342
Mowrer, W. M., 342
Moye, A., 96
Mrazek, D. A., 86
Mrazek, P. J., 102
MTA Cooperative Group, 244
Mufson, L., 163
Mukolo, A., 92, 296
Mulhall, P., 59
Mulle, K., 129
Mullin, D., 396
Mulvaney, S. A., 350
Mundy, P., 328, 337
Munoz, R. F., 102
Murdoch, K., 125
Muris, P., 131, 133, 136, 348
Murnen, S. K., 359, 362
Murphy, A., 189
Murphy, C. M., 198
Murphy, L., 344
Murray, H. A., 97
Murray, L., 133
Muter, V., 259
Myers, K. M., 237
Myers, S. M., 324

N

Nadder, T. S., 226
Nader, K., 127
Nagin, D. S., 229
Najman, J. M., 105
Nansel, T. R., 187
Napier-Phillips, A., 351
Nassau, J. H., 375
Nathan, P. E., 87
Nation, K., 258
National Center for Health Statistics, 54, 171
National Diabetes Information
  Clearinghouse, 380

National Institute of Mental Health, 51, 333
National Institute on Drug Abuse, 204
National Institutes of Health, 73, 371, 372
Naylor, M. W., 166
Neal, C., 40
Neal, J. A., 117
Neale, B. M., 234
Neale, M. C., 335
Neely-Barnes, S., 297
Nelson, B., 337
Nelson, D. A., 184
Nelson, F., 7
Nelson, T. D., 354, 379
Ness, K. K., 380
New, M. J., 379, 380
Newcomb, M., 359
Newsom, C., 305, 318, 319, 320, 321, 325, 326, 328
NICHD Early Child Care Research Network, 191, 393, 394
Nicholls, D., 352
Nicodemus, K. K., 335
Nicolson, R. I., 331, 332, 334
Nigg, J. T., 31, 32, 132, 219, 220, 224, 225, 227, 228, 229, 231, 232
Nikolas, M., 219, 227, 228, 231
Nisbett, R. E., 268, 283
Niska, R., 387
Nock, M. K., 174, 189
Nolan, E. E., 226, 227
Nolen-Hoeksema, S. N., 88, 149
Noppe, I. C., 128
Noppe, L. D., 128
Norquist, G. S., 160, 240
Novins, D. K., 63
Nowak-Drabik, K. M., 307
Nowicki, E. A., 263, 264
Nuñez, J. C., 264
Nurmi, E. L., 320
Nyborg, V. M., 63, 403

O

Obi, O., 287
Obradovic, J., 33
O'Brien, K. M., 359
O'Brien, L. T., 296
O'Brien, M., 351
O'Byrne, K. K., 388
Ochoa, S. H., 263
O'Connor, T. G., 25, 26, 50, 55, 59
O'Dell, S. L., 110
Offord, M. H., 148
Ogden, C. L., 209, 353
Ohan, J. L., 181, 190, 237
Olds, D. L., 301
O'Leary, K. D., 198
Olfson, M., 240
Oliver, C., 286, 316
Ollendick, T. H., 47, 106, 111, 120, 122, 123, 134, 135, 136, 225
Olsen, K., 50
Olsen, S., 350

Oltjenbruns, K. A., 388, 389
Oltmanns, T. F., 17
Olvera, N., 353, 354
Olweus, D., 187, 188, 189
Omigbodun, O., 401
Ondersma, S. J., 341, 343
Oosterlaan, J., 220
Organista, K. C., 149
Ormrod, R., 54
Orsmond, G., 297
Orton, S., 257
Orvaschel, H., 121
Öst, L., 114
Oswald, D. P., 284
Otsuki, M., 376
Otto, M., 128
Outlaw, A., 379
Owen, M. J., 206
Owens, J., 344, 345, 346, 347, 350
Owens, J. A., 222, 230, 345, 347, 350
Ozgen, H., 315, 316
Ozgen, H. M., 315
Ozonoff, S., 315, 322, 329

P

Pahl, K. M., 138, 139
Paikoff, R., 379
Palmer, D., 382
Palmer, D. J., 263
Palmer, D. S., 274, 303
Palmer, P., 320
Palomo, R., 323, 324
Paloyelis, Y., 226, 259
Pan, C.-Y., 316
Paniagua, F. A., 352
Papolos, D. F., 168
Papp, L. M., 198
Pardo, C. A., 319
Pardini, D. A., 181, 191, 194
Parish, S. L., 297
Parker, J. G., 49, 58, 59, 104, 115, 117, 134, 154, 159, 190, 200
Parmar, R. S., 274
Pasquini, E., 256
Patenaude, A. F., 374
Patterson, C. J., 158, 199
Patterson, D. J., 179, 183, 184
Patterson, G. R., 190, 193, 194, 195, 196, 197, 198, 206, 208
Patton, J. R., 281, 286
Paul, R., 320
Paulosky, C. A., 358
Pauls, D. L., 169
Pavlidis, K., 158
Pavlin, A. J., 128
Pavuluri, M. N., 100, 166, 168
Paxton, S. J., 363
Payne, A., 58, 187
Pearson, D. A., 306
Peck, C. A., 274
Pederson, S., 159
Pelham, W. E., 224, 238, 243

SUBJECT INDEX

Mixed syndromes, 90
Modeling, anxiety disorders and, 136
Models, 20–21
Moderate retardation, 286
Moderators, 22
Molecular genetics, 44
Monitoring the Future (MTF) study, 205
Monozygotic (MZ) twins, 43, 320
Mood disorders
  attention-deficit hyperactivity disorder
    and, 228
  DSM approach to, 144
  historical perspective on, 144
Mood stabilizer medications, bipolar disorders
  and, 170
Morphology, 251
Motivation, academic self-concept and,
  263–264
Motor skills, attention-deficit hyperactivity
  disorder and, 220
Multiaxial classification systems, 85
Multicultural diversity, 403
Multidimensional Anxiety Scale for Children
  (MASC), 135
Multidimensional treatment foster care
  (MTFC), 212
Multifinality, 24
Multigenic influences, intellectual disabilities
  and, 289
Multimodal Treatment Assessment Study
  (MTA), 242–244
Multiple baseline designs, 74
Multiple-gene inheritance, 43
Multisystemic therapy, conduct problems and,
  212–213
Mutual responsibilities, research, 80

N

Narrowband syndromes, 90
National Health and Nutrition Examination
  Survey (NHANES), 353
Naturalistic observations, 67, 78
Necessary cause, 22
Negative Affect Self-Statement
  Questionnaire, 135
Negative affectivity, 132
Negative correlation, 71
Negative reinforcement, 46, 197
Negative symptoms, schizophrenia, 330
Neglect, 51–52
Neglectful parenting, 50
Neighborhood/community influences, 61–62
Neologisms, schizophrenia and, 331
Nervous system
  development of, 37–38
  disordered functioning and, 40–41
  neurotransmission, 39–40
  perinatal damages and, 41
  postnatal damages and, 41
  prenatal influences and, 41
  structure of, 38–39
Nervous system functioning assessment, 99–100

Neurobiological abnormalities
  autism and, 319
  schizophrenia and, 333–334
Neurobiological outcomes, maltreatment and,
  53–54
Neurochemistry, depression and, 151–153
Neurodevelopmental model, schizophrenia
  and, 335–337
Neuroendocrine system, depression and, 151
Neurological assessment, 99–100
Neurophysiological influences, conduct
  problems and, 203–204
Neuropsychological deficits, conduct problems
  and, 203–204
Neuropsychological evaluations, 100
Neurotransmission, 39–40
Neurotransmitters
  anxiety disorders and, 131
  attention-deficit hyperactivity disorder
    and, 233
  depression and, 151
Nicotine use, 205
Night terrors, 349
Nightmares, 349
Nighttime awakenings, 345
Nocturnal enuresis, 342
Nondestructive behaviors, 183
Nonexperimental research methods, 68
Nonharmful procedures, 80
Nonmaleficence, 81
Nonnormative experience, 25
Nonparental child care, 393–394
Nonrapid eye movement (NREM) sleep, 345
Nonshared environmental influences, 43
Non-suicidal self-injury, 174
Normalization philosophy, 300
Normative experience, 25
Normative samples, 90
Nucleotide sequence in DNA, 42

O

Obesity, 353–357
  etiology of, 354
  family environment and, 355
  interventions, 355–357
  physical health problems and, 353
  percent of, 354
  social interactions and, 354
Observational assessment, 14, 47, 67–68, 96
  anxiety disorders and, 135
  conduct problems and, 208–209
  depression and, 159
Observer "blindness," 68
Observer drift, 96
Obsessions, 129. See also Obsessive-compulsive
  disorder (OCD)
Obsessive-compulsive disorder (OCD),
  128–130
  biological influences on, 131
  common obsessions and compulsions, 129
  description of, 129–130
  developmental course and prognosis, 130

  diagnostic criteria and, 128–129
  epidemiology of, 130
  treatment for, 138–139
Obstructive sleep apnea (OSA), 356
Oklahoma City bombing, 128
Operant learning, 14, 45–47
Oppositional defiant disorder (ODD), 179–181.
  See also Conduct problems
  age and, 190
  co-occurence patterns and, 190–191
  ethnicity and, 190
  gender and, 190
  pharmacological intervention and, 213
  socioeconomic differences and, 190
Ordinary magic of resilience, 27
Oregon Adolescent Depression Project
  (OADP), 148
Oregon Model, 196–197
Organic influences, intellectual disabilities
  and, 289
Overselectivity, autism and, 313
Overshadowing, 286
Overt behaviors, 183

P

Pain
  cognitive-behavioral treatment and, 384–388
  coping strategies and, 385–387
  procedure-related, 384–388
  psychological modification of, 383–384
PANDAS, 132
Panic attacks, 121–123
  description of, 123
  developmental pattern of, 123
  diagnostic criteria and, 121
  epidemiology of, 122–123
Panic disorder, 121–123
  description of, 123
  developmental pattern of, 123
  diagnostic criteria and, 121
  epidemiology of, 122–123
  separation anxiety disorder and, 123
Parasomnias, 346, 350
Parent-child interaction therapy (PCIT), 209
Parent training programs
  attention-deficit hyperactivity disorder and,
    240–241
  conduct problems and, 104–105, 197–198,
    209–210
Parents. See also Families
  abusive, 52
  behavioral patterns of, 50
  child conduct problems and, 196–198
  consent of, 80
  depression and, 155–156
  parenting styles/roles, 16–17, 49–51, 133–134
  psychopathology and, 198
  separation and, 372
Participant selection, research, 66–67
Pathways of development, 22–24
Pearson r, 70
Pediatric neuropsychology, 100